HOLT

CALIFORNIA EDITION

American Anthem

Modern American History

Edward L. Ayers
Robert D. Schulzinger
Jesús F. de la Teja
Deborah Gray White

Senior Program Consultant
Sam Wineburg
Professor of Education, Stanford University

HOLT, RINEHART AND WINSTON
A Harcourt Education Company
Orlando • **Austin** • New York • San Diego • London

Authors

Edward L. Ayers

Edward L. Ayers is Dean of the College and Graduate School of Arts & Sciences at the University of Virginia. He was named National Professor of the Year in 2003 and his book *In the Presence of Mine Enemies: The Civil War in the Heart of America, 1859–1863* won the Bancroft Prize and the Beveridge Prize in 2004. *The Promise of the New South: Life After Reconstruction* was a finalist for the Pulitzer Prize and the National Book Award. Ayers is also the creator of the acclaimed Web project, "Valley of the Shadow: Two Communities in the American Civil War," a comprehensive examination of everyday life before and during the Civil War in two small communities on either side of the Mason-Dixon Line.

Jesús F. de la Teja

Jesús F. de la Teja is chair of the history department at Texas State University at San Marcos, Texas. Prof. de la Teja has a number of books either in progress or recently published on colonial history of Mexico and Spanish borderlands including *Texas: Crossroads of North America* and *San Antonio de Béxar: A Community on New Spain's Northern Frontier*, which was the 1996 winner of the Presidio La Bahia Award. A Fellow of the Texas State Historical Association, Prof. de la Teja has received Texas State's Excellence Award for teaching. He earned undergraduate and Master's degrees from Seton Hall and a Ph.D. from the University of Texas, Austin. Prof. de la Teja has received a MacArthur Foundation grant for scholarly work on Texas colonization and independence.

Copyright © 2007 by Holt, Rinehart and Winston

All rights reserved. No part of this publication may be reproduced or transmitted in any form or by any means, electronic or mechanical, including photocopy, recording, or information storage and retrieval system, without permission in writing from the publisher.

Requests for permission to make copies of any part of the work should be mailed to the following address: Permissions Department, Holt, Rinehart and Winston, 10801 N. MoPac Expressway, Building 3, Austin, Texas 78759.

For Acknowledgments, see page R143, which is an extension of the copyright page.

HOLT and the **"Owl Design"** are trademarks licensed to Holt, Rinehart and Winston, registered in the United States of America and/or other jurisdictions.

 WORLD ALMANAC® is a trademark of World Almanac Education Group, Inc., registered in the United States of America and/or other jurisdictions.

Printed in the United States of America

> If you have received these materials as examination copies free of charge, Holt, Rinehart and Winston retains title to the materials and they may not be resold. Resale of examination copies is strictly prohibited.

> Possession of this publication in print format does not entitle users to convert this publication, or any portion of it, into electronic format.

ISBN 0-03-043299-5

6 7 8 032 10 09 08

Deborah Gray White

Deborah Gray White is Distinguished Professor of History at Rutgers University. She received her undergraduate degree from SUNY Binghamton, her Master's from Columbia University, and a Ph.D. from the University of Illinois at Chicago. A specialist in American history and the history of African Americans, she is the author of several books including: *Ar'n't I a Woman?: Female Slaves in the Antebellum South*; *Too Heavy A Load: Black Women in Defense of Themselves, 1894–1994*; and *Let My People Go: African Americans 1804–1860*. From 1997–1999 she was the co-director of the Rutgers Center for Historical Analysis, which sponsored the very successful "Black Atlantic: Race, Nation and Gender" project.

Robert Schulzinger

Robert Schulzinger is Director of the International Affairs Program and Professor of History at the University of Colorado, Boulder. Dr. Schulzinger, a member of the U.S. State Department's Historical Advisory Committee, received his undergraduate degree from Columbia University, and a Master's and Ph.D. from Yale. He has written extensively on post-World War II history; his books include *A Time for War: The United States & Vietnam, 1941–1975*.

Senior Program Consultant

Sam Wineburg

Sam Wineburg is Professor of Education at Stanford University, where he directs the only Ph.D. program in History Education in the nation. Educated at Brown and Berkeley, he has spent several years teaching history at the middle and high school level before completing a doctorate in Psychological Studies in Education at Stanford. His book *Historical Thinking and Other Unnatural Acts: Charting the Future of Teaching the Past* won the Frederic W. Ness Award from the Association of American Colleges and Universities. His work with the teacher community won the 2002 "Exemplary Research on Teaching and Teacher Education Award" from the American Educational Research Association. He was a member of the blue-ribbon commission of National Research Council that wrote the widely circulated report, *How People Learn: Brain, Mind, Experience, and School*.

Consultants

Program Consultant

Kylene Beers, Ed.D
Senior Reading Researcher
School Development Program
Yale University
New Haven, Connecticut

Academic Consultants

John Ferguson
Senior Religion Consultant
Assistant Professor
Political Science/Criminal Justice
Howard Payne University
Brownwood, Texas

Gregory Massing
Constitutional Law Consultant; author, Holt's Civics in Practice
Adjunct Professor
Boston College Law School
Chestnut Hill, Massachusetts

Walter Schroeder
Geography Consultant
Assistant Professor Emeritus
Department of Geography
University of Missouri
Columbia, Missouri

Program Advisors

Academic Reviewers

Raymond Hyser, Ph. D.
James Madison University
Harrisonburg, Virginia

Michael S. Mayer, Ph.D.
Department of History
University of Montana
Missoula, Montana

Silvana Siddali, Ph.D
Department of History
St. Louis University
St. Louis, Missouri

Rebecca Tannenbaum, Ph.D
Department of History
Yale University
New Haven, Connecticut

Senior Consulting Writer

Peter Lacey
Sunderland, Massachusetts

Educational Reviewers

Brent Duggins
Glenwood High School
Chatham, Illinois

Conrad Graf
Wayne High School
Fort Wayne, Indiana

Traci S. Lipscomb
Rustburg High School
Rustburg, Virginia

Nancy A. Llombart
Lakeview High School
St. Clair Shores, Michigan

Dean Melson
Niagara Falls High School
Niagara Falls, New York

Robert M. Rodrigues
Chartiers Valley High School
Bridgeville, Pennsylvania

Avon Ruffin
Winston-Salem Forsyth County Schools
Winston-Salem, North Carolina

California Educational Reviewers

Tony Bellotti
Mission San Jose High School
Fremont, California

Gina Capelli
Liberty High School
Brentwood, California

Michael Kim
Schurr High School
Montebello, California

Rich Larsen
Mission San Jose High School
Fremont, California

Romano Luchini
Encina High School
Sacramento, California

Kris Oliveira
Clovis West High School
Fresno, California

Michael Rumley
Clovis West High School
Fresno, California

Scott Schiller
Buchanan High School
Clovis, California

Steven Steinberg, Ed.D
History/Social Sciences Specialist
Los Angeles Unified School District, Local District 7
Los Angeles, California

Paul Theodore
San Pasqual High School
Escondido, California

Glenda Watanabe
Banning High School
Wilmington, California

Field Test Teachers

Melanie Adamek
Niagara Wheatfield Senior High School
Sandborn, New York

David Breen
Fels High School
Philadelphia, Pennsylvania

Jackie Burris
Asheville High School
Asheville, North Carolina

Patrick Eviston
Colonel White High School
Dayton, Ohio

Dena Grevis
Libbey High School
Toledo, Ohio

Ernesto Quiroz
Fillmore High School
Fillmore, California

Judith L. Spurlock
Meadowdale High School
Dayton, Ohio

James Toby
Everett High School
Lansing, Michigan

Robyn Webb
Elsik High School
Houston, Texas

Contents

Reading Like a Historian, by Sam Wineburg xxvi
How to Use Your Textbook xxx
Scavenger Hunt xxxii
The California History–Social Science Standards ST1
Standards Practice and Plan ST9
Skills Handbook H1
Test-Taking Strategies and Practice TT2

UNIT 1

Beginnings – A.D. 1898
The United States Before 1898 1

Prepare to Read 2

 CHAPTER 1 **Beginnings of America** 4

California Standards
History–Social Sciences

8.2 Students analyze the political principles underlying the U.S. Constitution and compare the enumerated and implied powers of the federal government.

11.1 Students analyze the significant events in the founding of the nation and its attempts to realize the philosophy of government described in the Declaration of Independence.

11.3 Students analyze the role religion played in the founding of America, its lasting moral, social, and political impacts, and issues regarding religious liberty.

History's Impact Video Series
Beginnings of America

SECTION 1 The World before 1600 6
SECTION 2 European Colonies in America 13
SECTION 3 Colonial Life 20
Chapter Review 27

 CHAPTER 2 **Forming a New Nation** 28

California Standards
History–Social Sciences

11.1 Students analyze the significant events in the founding of the nation and its attempts to realize the philosophy of government described in the Declaration of Independence.

History's Impact Video Series
Forming a New Nation

SECTION 1 The Revolutionary Era 30
Historic Document: *The Declaration of Independence* 38
SECTION 2 Creating a New Government 42
SECTION 3 Forging the New Republic 50
Chapter Review 57
Historic Document: *Constitution of the United States* 58

CHAPTER 3 · Developing a National Identity 90

California Standards
History–Social Sciences

8.8 Students analyze the divergent paths of the American people in the West from the 1800s to the mid-1800s and the challenges they faced.

11.1 Students analyze the significant events in the founding of the nation and its attempts to realize the philosophy of government described in the Declaration of Independence.

11.3 Students analyze the role religion played in the founding of America, its lasting moral, social, and political impacts, and issues regarding religious liberty.

History's Impact Video Series
Developing a National Identity

- SECTION 1 From Nationalism to Sectionalism 92
- SECTION 2 A Push for Reform 99
- SECTION 3 Expansion Leads to Conflict 106
- Chapter Review 113

CHAPTER 4 · The Union in Crisis 114

California Standards
History–Social Sciences

11.1 Students analyze the significant events in the founding of the nation and its attempts to realize the philosophy of government described in the Declaration of Independence.

11.3 Students analyze the role religion played in the founding of America, its lasting moral, social, and political impacts, and issues regarding religious liberty.

History's Impact Video Series
The Union in Crisis

- SECTION 1 The Nation Splits Apart 116
- SECTION 2 The Civil War 123
- SECTION 3 Reconstruction 132
- Chapter Review 139

CHAPTER 5 · An Industrial Nation 140

California Standards
History–Social Sciences

11.2 Students analyze the relationship among the rise of industrialization, large-scale rural-to-urban migration, and massive immigration from Southern and Eastern Europe.

11.3 Students analyze the role religion played in the founding of America, its lasting moral, social, and political impacts, and issues regarding religious liberty.

History's Impact Video Series
An Industrial Nation

- SECTION 1 The American West 142
- SECTION 2 The Second Industrial Revolution 149
- SECTION 3 Life at the Turn of the 20th Century 156
- Chapter Review 163

UNIT 1 · UNIT IN BRIEF 164

UNIT 2 1898–1920
Becoming a World Power ... 165
Prepare to Read ... 166

CHAPTER 6   The Progressives ... 168

California Standards
History–Social Sciences

11.2 Students analyze the relationship among the rise of industrialization, large-scale rural-to-urban migration, and massive immigration from Southern and Eastern Europe.

11.5 Students analyze the major political, social, economic, technological, and cultural developments of the 1920s.

11.10 Students analyze the development of federal civil rights and voting rights.

History's Impact Video Series
The Progressives

SECTION 1 **Progressivism** ... 170
American Literature: Excerpt from *The Jungle*, by Upton Sinclair ... 176
SECTION 2 **Women and Public Life** ... 177
SECTION 3 **Theodore Roosevelt's Square Deal** ... 183
SECTION 4 **Taft and Wilson** ... 189
Document-Based Investigation: *Impact of Progressivism* ... 194
Chapter Review ... 196

CHAPTER 7   Entering the World Stage ... 198

California Standards
History–Social Sciences

11.1 Students analyze the significant events in the founding of the nation and its attempts to realize the philosophy of government described in the Declaration of Independence.

11.4 Students trace the rise of the United States to its role as a world power in the twentieth century.

History's Impact Video Series
Entering the World Stage

SECTION 1 **The Lure of Imperialism** ... 200
SECTION 2 **The Spanish-American War** ... 206
SECTION 3 **Roosevelt and Latin America** ... 213
History and Geography: Building the Panama Canal ... 218
SECTION 4 **Wilson and the Mexican Revolution** ... 220
Document-Based Investigation: *Views on American Expansionism* ... 224
Chapter Review ... 226

CHAPTER 8 **The First World War** 228

California Standards
History–Social Sciences
11.4 Students trace the rise of the United States to its role as a world power in the twentieth century.

History's Impact Video Series
The First World War

SECTION 1 A World Crisis 230
SECTION 2 The United States in World War I 238
American Literature: Excerpt from *A Farewell to Arms*,
    by Ernest Hemingway 245
SECTION 3 The Home Front 246
Landmark Supreme Court Cases: *Schenck v. United States* (1919) 253
SECTION 4 Peace without Victory 254
Document-Based Investigation: *Perspectives on Trench Warfare* 260
Chapter Review 262

UNIT 2 UNIT IN BRIEF 264

UNIT 3
1919–1940
A Modern Nation 265
Prepare to Read 266

CHAPTER 9 **From War to Peace** 268

California Standards
History–Social Sciences
11.5 Students analyze the major political, social, economic, technological, and cultural developments of the 1920s.

History's Impact Video Series
From War to Peace

SECTION 1 Postwar Havoc 270
SECTION 2 A New Economic Era 276
SECTION 3 The Harding and Coolidge Presidencies 282
Document-Based Investigation: *Tactics of the Red Scare* 288
Chapter Review 290

Museum of the City of New York

CHAPTER 10 — The Roaring Twenties 292

California Standards
History–Social Sciences

11.5 Students analyze the major political, social, economic, technological, and cultural developments of the 1920s.

11.8 Students analyze the economic boom and social transformation of post-World War II America.

11.10 Students analyze the development of federal civil rights and voting rights.

History's Impact Video Series
The Roaring Twenties

SECTION 1 American Life Changes 294
SECTION 2 The Harlem Renaissance 302
SECTION 3 A New Popular Culture is Born 308
Document-Based Investigation: *The 1920s Flapper* ... 314
Chapter Review 316

CHAPTER 11 — The Great Depression Begins 318

California Standards
History–Social Sciences

11.5 Students analyze the major political, social, economic, technological, and cultural developments of the 1920s.

11.6 Students analyze the different explanations for the Great Depression and how the New Deal fundamentally changed the role of the federal government.

History's Impact Video Series
The Great Depression Begins

SECTION 1 The Great Crash 320
SECTION 2 Americans Face Hard Times 328
American Literature: Excerpt from *The Grapes of Wrath*, by John Steinbeck ... 334
SECTION 3 Hoover as President 335
Document-Based Investigation: *Life During the Great Depression* ... 340
Chapter Review 342

| CHAPTER 12 | **The New Deal** | 344 |

California Standards
History–Social Sciences

11.6 Students analyze the different explanations for the Great Depression and how the New Deal fundamentally changed the role of the federal government.
11.8 Students analyze the economic boom and social transformation of post-World War II America.
11.10 Students analyze the development of federal civil rights and voting rights.

History's Impact Video Series
The New Deal

SECTION 1 Launching the New Deal ... 346
History and Geography: Tennessee Valley Authority ... 354
Landmark Supreme Court Cases Schechter Poultry Corporation v. United States (1935) ... 356
SECTION 2 The Second New Deal ... 357
SECTION 3 Life During the New Deal ... 365
SECTION 4 Analyzing the New Deal ... 371
Document-Based Investigation: Perceptions of Roosevelt ... 376
Chapter Review ... 378

UNIT 3 UNIT IN BRIEF ... 380

UNIT 4
1939–1960
A Champion of Democracy ... 381
Prepare to Read ... 382

| CHAPTER 13 | **World War II Erupts** | 384 |

California Standards
History–Social Sciences

11.7 Students analyze America's participation in World War II.
11.10 Students analyze the development of federal civil rights and voting rights.

History's Impact Video Series
World War II Erupts

SECTION 1 The Rise of Dictators ... 386
SECTION 2 Europe Erupts in War ... 394
SECTION 3 The United States Enters the War ... 399
SECTION 4 Mobilizing for War ... 406
Document-Based Investigation: Reactions to Pearl Harbor ... 412
Chapter Review ... 414

CHAPTER 14   The United States in World War II 416

 California Standards
History–Social Sciences
11.7 Students analyze America's participation in World War II.

History's Impact Video Series
The United States in World War II

SECTION 1 The War in Europe and North Africa 418
SECTION 2 The Holocaust 426
American Literature: Excerpt from *Night,* by Elie Wiesel 432
SECTION 3 The War in the Pacific 433
SECTION 4 The Home Front 441
Landmark Supreme Court Cases: *Korematsu v. United States* (1944) 448
SECTION 5 World War II Ends 449
History and Geography: *Island Hopping: The Route to Japan* 456
Document-Based Investigation: *Perspectives on Life in Uniform* 458
Chapter Review 460

CHAPTER 15   The Cold War Begins 462

 California Standards
History–Social Sciences
11.4 Students trace the rise of the United States to its role as a world power in the twentieth century.
11.7 Students analyze America's participation in World War II.
11.8 Students analyze the economic boom and social transformation of post-World War II America.
11.9 Students analyze U.S. foreign policy since World War II.

History's Impact Video Series
The Cold War Begins

SECTION 1 The Iron Curtain Falls on Europe 464
SECTION 2 Healing the Wounds of War 471
SECTION 3 The Second Red Scare 477
SECTION 4 The Korean War 483
Document-Based Investigation: *The Cold War at Home* 490
Chapter Review 492

CHAPTER 16 Postwar America 494

California Standards
History–Social Sciences

11.8 Students analyze the economic boom and social transformation of post-World War II America.

11.9 Students analyze U.S. foreign policy since World War II.

11.11 Students analyze the major social problems and domestic policy issues in contemporary American society.

History's Impact Video Series
Postwar America

SECTION 1 The Eisenhower Era 496
SECTION 2 Atomic Anxiety 502
SECTION 3 The Television Age 509
Document-Based Investigation: *Perspectives on Interstate Highways* 516
Chapter Review 518

UNIT 4 UNIT IN BRIEF 520

UNIT 5
1954–1975
A Nation Facing Challenges 521
Prepare to Read 522

CHAPTER 17 The New Frontier and the Great Society 524

California Standards
History–Social Sciences

11.8 Students analyze the economic boom and social transformation of post-World War II America.

11.9 Students analyze U.S. foreign policy since World War II.

11.11 Students analyze the major social problems and domestic policy issues in contemporary American society.

History's Impact Video Series
The New Frontier and the Great Society

SECTION 1 Kennedy and the Cold War 526
SECTION 2 Kennedy's Thousand Days 535
SECTION 3 The Great Society 541
Landmark Supreme Court Cases: *Miranda v. Arizona (1966)* 549
Document-Based Investigation: *The New Frontier and Great Society* 550
Chapter Review 552

xii CONTENTS

CHAPTER 18 **The Civil Rights Movement** 554

California Standards
History–Social Sciences
11.10 Students analyze the development of federal civil rights and voting rights.

History's Impact Video Series
The Civil Rights Movement

SECTION 1 Fighting Segregation 556
Landmark Supreme Court Cases: *Brown v. Board of Education* (1954) 561
SECTION 2 Freedom Now! 564
American Literature: "Letter from a Birmingham Jail,"
 by Martin Luther King, Jr. 572
SECTION 3 Voting Rights 573
Landmark Supreme Court Cases: *Reynolds v. Sims* (1964) 579
SECTION 4 Changes and Challenges 580
SECTION 5 The Movement Continues 586
Document-Based Investigation: *The Government and Equal Rights* 590
Chapter Review 592

CHAPTER 19 **The Vietnam War** 594

California Standards
History–Social Sciences
11.9 Students analyze U.S. foreign policy since World War II

History's Impact Video Series
The Vietnam War

SECTION 1 The War Develops 596
SECTION 2 U.S. Support of the War at Home and Abroad 604
SECTION 3 1968: A Turning Point 612
SECTION 4 The War Ends 620
Document-Based Investigation: *The Tet Offensive* 628
Chapter Review 630

CONTENTS **xiii**

CHAPTER 20 — A Time of Social Change 632

California Standards
History–Social Sciences

11.8 Students analyze the economic boom and social transformation of post-World War II America.

11.10 Students analyze the development of federal civil rights and voting rights.

11.11 Students analyze the major social problems and domestic policy issues in contemporary American society.

History's Impact Video Series
A Time of Social Change

SECTION 1 Women and Native Americans Fight for Change	634
SECTION 2 Latinos Fight for Rights	642
SECTION 3 Culture and Counterculture	650
Document-Based Investigation: *The Women's Movement*	656
Chapter Review	658

UNIT 5 UNIT IN BRIEF 660

UNIT 6
1968–Present
Looking Toward the Future 661

Prepare to Read 662

CHAPTER 21 — A Search for Order 664

 California Standards
History–Social Sciences

11.9 Students analyze U.S. foreign policy since World War II.

11.10 Students analyze the development of federal civil rights and voting rights.

11.11 Students analyze the major social problems and domestic policy issues in contemporary American society.

 History's Impact Video Series
A Search for Order

SECTION 1 The Nixon Years	666
Landmark Supreme Court Cases: *New York Times Co. v. United States* (1971)	674
SECTION 2 From Watergate to Ford	675
SECTION 3 Carter's Presidency	681
Landmark Supreme Court Cases: *Regents of the University of California v. Bakke* (1978)	687
Document-Based Investigation: *The Watergate Crisis*	688
Chapter Review	690

CHAPTER 22 — A Conservative Era 692

California Standards
History–Social Sciences

11.8 Students analyze the economic boom and social transformation of post-World War II America.

11.9 Students analyze U.S. foreign policy since World War II.

11.11 Students analyze the major social problems and domestic policy issues in contemporary American society.

History's Impact Video Series
A Conservative Era

SECTION 1 Reagan's First Term 694
Landmark Supreme Court Cases: *New Jersey v. T.L.O.* (1985) 700
SECTION 2 Reagan's Foreign Policy 701
SECTION 3 A New World Order 707
SECTION 4 Life in the 1980s 714
Document-Based Investigation: *Wealth in the 1980s* 720
Chapter Review 722

CHAPTER 23 — Into the Twenty-First Century 724

California Standards
History–Social Sciences

11.8 Students analyze the economic boom and social transformation of post-World War II America.

11.9 Students analyze U.S. foreign policy since World War II.

11.11 Students analyze the major social problems and domestic policy issues in contemporary American society.

History's Impact Video Series
Into the Twenty-First Century

SECTION 1 The Clinton Years 726
Landmark Supreme Court Cases: *Vernonia School District v. Acton* (1995) 732
SECTION 2 George W. Bush's Presidency 733
SECTION 3 How September 11, 2001, Changed America 739
SECTION 4 Looking Ahead 747
American Literature: Excerpt from *The Joy Luck Club,* by Amy Tan 753
History and Geography: Hispanic Growth and Influence 754
Document-Based Investigation: *The Global Economy and Society* 756
Chapter Review 758

UNIT 6 UNIT IN BRIEF 760

UNIT 7 Issues in Contemporary American Society: Document-Based Investigation 761
Prepare to Read 762

California Standards
History–Social Sciences

11.8 Students analyze the economic boom and social transformation of post-World War II America.

11.11 Students analyze the major social problems and domestic policy issues in contemporary American society.

ISSUE 1:	Immigration Policy	766
ISSUE 2:	Women in the Military	772
ISSUE 3:	Environmental Conservation	780
ISSUE 4:	Poverty in the United States	788
ISSUE 5:	Crime and Public Safety	794
ISSUE 6:	Regulation and the Internet	800
ISSUE 7:	Outsourcing and Trade	806

Reference Section R1

THE WORLD ALMANAC KEY EVENTS IN AMERICAN HISTORY	R3
Presidents of the United States	R17
Supreme Court Decisions	R22
Facts about the States	R30
American Flag Etiquette	R32
Biographical Dictionary	R33
Atlas	R46
California Governors and Government	R60
California Facts	R61
Geography Handbook	R62
Primary Source Library	R74
Correlation to Holt's Social Studies Library	R94
English and Spanish Glossary	R96
Index	R126
Credits and Acknowledgments	R151

Features

DOCUMENT-BASED INVESTIGATION

Analyze topics in American history by using a variety of primary and secondary source documents.

Impact of Progressivism	**194**
Views on American Expansionism	**224**
Perspectives on Trench Warfare	**260**
Tactics of the Red Scare	**288**
The 1920s Flapper	**314**
Life during the Great Depression	**340**
Perceptions of Roosevelt	**376**
Reactions to Pearl Harbor	**412**
Perspectives on Life in Uniform	**458**
The Cold War at Home	**490**
Perspectives on Interstate Highways	**516**
The New Frontier and Great Society	**550**
The Government and Equal Rights	**590**
The Tet Offensive	**628**
The Women's Movement	**656**
The Watergate Crisis	**688**
Wealth in the 1980s	**720**
The Global Economy and Society	**756**

PRIMARY SOURCES

Examine key documents, speeches, and other primary sources that have shaped American history.

Pamphlet: *Common Sense*	**33**
Washington's Farewell Address	**52**
Political Cartoon: Tensions over slavery	**118**
Political Cartoon: New Immigrants	**157**
Magazine article: Ida Tarbell	**171**
Political Cartoon: Women's Suffrage	**181**
Editorial: *USS Maine*	**208**
Political Cartoon: U.S. territories after the Spanish-American War	**214**
Propaganda Poster: World War I	**251**
Political Cartoon: The Red Scare	**272**
Political Cartoon: Teapot Dome Scandal	**283**
Novel: *The Great Gatsby*	**313**
Political Cartoon: The Great Depression	**337**
Political Cartoon: The New Deal	**352**
Political Cartoon: FDR and the Supreme Court	**363**
Political Cartoon: Contemplating War	**402**
Propaganda Poster: World War II recruitment	**407**
Memoir: Concentration Camp Liberation	**430**
Propaganda Poster: World War II	**444**
Speech: Nixon's Checkers Speech	**497**
Political Cartoon: The Great Society	**547**
Autobiography: John McCain	**625**
Mural: Chicano Art	**648**
Political Cartoon: The Counterculture	**654**
Political Cartoon: Watergate	**678**
Speech: Reagan's "Boys of Pointe de Hoc" speech	**703**

POLITICAL CARTOONS

Interpret and analyze political cartoons to learn about American history.

Tensions over Slavery	**118**
New Immigrants	**157**
Women's Suffrage	**181**
Roosevelt's "No Molly-Coddling Here"	**185**
Roosevelt and Taft	**189**
Theodore Roosevelt and the meat-packing plants	**194**
Imperialism and the United States	**200**
"Speak Softly and Carry a Big Stick"	**213**
U.S. territories after the Spanish-American War	**214**
Annexation of Hawaii	**225**
The Red Scare	**272**
Teapot Dome Scandal	**283**
Deportation of alien radicals	**289**
Scopes Trial	**298**
The Great Depression	**337**
The New Deal	**352**
FDR and the Supreme Court	**363**
FDR and the poor	**377**
FDR and the wealthy	**377**
The Spanish Civil War	**391**
Contemplating War	**402**
U.S. Army in World War II	**458**
House on Un-American Activities Committee	**490**
Cold War Arms Race	**505**
Kennedy and Cuba	**529**
The Great Society	**547**
Civil Rights	**590**
The War in Vietnam	**629**
The Counterculture	**654**
The Women's Movement	**656**
Watergate	**678**
Nixon and Watergate	**689**
Reagan's Deregulation	**696**
Defense Budget	**702**
Corporate Raiders	**720**
Migrant Workers	**771**
Conservation in National Forests	**786**
Social Security	**791**
Youth Violence	**798**
Copyrighted Material and the Internet	**804**
SPAM	**805**
Outsourcing	**809**

American Literature

Learn about the beliefs and experiences of people who lived in other times and places through excerpts from literature.

The Jungle, by Upton Sinclair	176
A Farewell to Arms, by Ernest Hemingway	245
The Grapes of Wrath, by John Steinbeck	334
Night, by Elie Wiesel	432
"Letter from Birmingham Jail," by Martin Luther King Jr.	572
The Joy Luck Club, by Amy Tan	753

Landmark Supreme Court Cases

Study the impact of Supreme Court decisions on American history.

Schenck v. *United States* (1919)	253
Schechter Poultry Corporation v. *United States* (1935)	356
Korematsu v. *United States* (1944)	448
Miranda v. *Arizona* (1966)	549
Brown v. *Board of Education* (1954)	561
Reynolds v. *Sims* (1964)	579
New York Times Co. v. *United States* (1971)	674
Regents of the University of California v. *Bakke* (1978)	687
New Jersey v. *T.L.O.* (1985)	700
Vernonia School District v. *Acton* (1995)	732

Counterpoints

Examine the different viewpoints of people in American history.

Federalist vs. Antifederalist	47
Lincoln-Douglas Debate	120
Views on Reconstruction	134
Social Darwinism	152
How to Win the Vote	192
Annexation of the Philippines	211
The League of Nations	257
For and Against Prohibition	300
Role of Government in Everyday Life	373
Appeasement	392
Dropping the Atomic Bomb	454
The Arms Race	506
Government's Role in Shaping Society	545
The Tactics of Change	583
Views on the Vietnam War	610
The ERA	637
Resolving the Hostage Crisis	685
The Savings and Loan Crisis	717
Views on Free Trade	730

American Liberty

Learn about important civil and religious liberties established by the Constitution.

Voting Rights	135
Native Americans and Citizenship	285
Women and Minorities in the Military	452
Integration and the Military	474
Ending Legal Segregation	559
Twenty-fourth Amendment	576
Smaller Government	696
Churches and Politics	718
Immigration and Religion	749

Tracing History

Study historical themes through key dates and moments in American history.

Women's Rights	178
Isolationism	400
Exploration	536
Civil Rights	574
Native American Policy and Activism	638

History & Geography

Explore the relationships between history and geography.

Building the Panama Canal	218
Tennessee Valley Authority	354
Island Hopping: The Route to Japan	456
Hispanic Growth and Influence	754

FACES OF HISTORY

Meet the people who have influenced history and learn about their lives.

Christopher Columbus	12
George Washington	34
Thomas Jefferson	51
Elizabeth Cady Stanton	103
Frederick Douglass	105
Abraham Lincoln	124
Thomas Edison	155
Theodore Roosevelt	186
Queen Liliouokalani	203
William R. Hearst	207
Woodrow Wilson	239
Henry Ford	277
Calvin and Grace Coolidge	284
Langston Hughes	305
Herbert Hoover	338
Franklin Delano Roosevelt	348
Eleanor Roosevelt	349
Mary McLeod Bethune	366
Dwight Eisenhower	423
James Doolittle	435
Harry S. Truman	473
Douglas MacArthur	488
Jonas Salk	513
John and Jacqueline Kennedy	538
Lyndon B. Johnson	542
Rosa Parks	563
James Farmer	565
Martin Luther King Jr.	568
Ho Chi Minh	598
Robert S. McNamara	615
Betty Friedan	636
Clyde Bellecourt	640
César Chávez	644
Richard Nixon	667
Ronald Reagan	697
Bill Clinton	729
George W. Bush	746

HISTORY CLOSE-UP

Explore key developments and events in history through in-depth and close-up illustrations and photo essays.

Plymouth Colony	16
Oklahoma Land Rush	146
Early Skyscrapers	158
The Triangle Shirtwaist Fire	173
Fighting in the Trenches	234
Autos Drive the Modern Age	278
The Harlem Renaissance	306
Life in a Hooverville	330
Going to the Movies	368
Blitzkrieg	394
Attack on Pearl Harbor	404
The Allied Convoy System	419
D-Day, June 6, 1944	424
Assault on Inchon	487
Milestones in Television History	511
Building Levittown	514
The Berlin Wall	531
Viet Cong Tunnels	607
The Chicano Movement	646
The First Moon Landing	672
The Attacks of September 11, 2001	740

Linking to Today

Link people and events from the past to the world you live in today.

National Park System	187
Epidemics	250
Terrorism in the United States	271
Totalitarian Dictators	390
Return to Iwo Jima	439
The Computer Revolution	512
The Job Corps	543
Integrating Central High School	560
Battlefield Reporting	614
Oil Consumption	682
No Child Left Behind	737

Maps

Interpret maps to see where important events happened and analyze how geography has influenced history.

Native American Culture Areas	8
Columbian Exchange	11
Thirteen Colonies, 1750	22
European Claims in North America, Before 1754	25
European Claims in North America, In 1763	25
Missouri Compromise, 1820	93
Indian Removal, 1830s–1840s	94
Western Trails	107
The Mexican-American War, 1846–1848	111
Major Battles and Native American Territory in the West, 1890	143
Cattle Trails and the Railroads, 1890s	145
Railroads Built by 1910	150
Federal Conservation Lands in the West, 1908	188
The Election of 1912	190
The Spanish-American War, 1898, War in the Caribbean	209
The Spanish-American War, 1898, War in the Philippines	209
Imperialism, c. 1900	216
Alliances, 1914	231
Europe and the Middle East, 1915	258
Europe and the Middle East, 1921	258
African American Migration, 1910–1920	303
The Election of 1928	322
The Dust Bowl	332
The Election of 1932	347
German Aggression, 1938–1941	397
The Holocaust, 1939–1945	429
The Iron Curtain, 1948	466
Korea	484
Cold War Conflict Areas, 1950s	500
U.S. Highways, 1950	517
U.S. Highways, 2000	517
Berlin	531
Nuclear Threat From Cuba	532
Cuba	533
School Segregation, 1952	557
Freedom Rides, 1961	566
Indochina, 1950	599
The Vietnam Conflict, 1964–1975	613
The Election of 1968	619
OPEC Member Nations in the Middle East and Africa	671
The Election of 1980	695
An Empire Falls	710
The Attacks of September 11, 2001	740
Afghanistan	743
Iraq	745
Foreign-Born Population by State, 2000	770
Federal Lands in the United States	784
Poverty in the United States	792
The United States of America: Political	R46
The United States of America: Physical	R48
World: Political	R50
North America: Political	R52
South America: Political	R53
Europe: Political	R54
Asia: Political	R55
Africa: Political	R56
Australia and New Zealand: Political	R57
California: Physical	R58
California: Political	R59
Lines of Latitude	R62
Lines of Longitude	R62
Northern Hemisphere	R63
Southern Hemisphere	R63
Western Hemisphere	R63
Eastern Hemisphere	R63
Mapmaking: Cylindrical Projections	R64
Mapmaking: Conic Projections	R65
Mapmaking: Flat-plane Projections	R65
Battles of the American Revolution, 1775 to 1778	R66
Boundary Changes, 1803–1819	R68
The Louisiana Purchase and Western Expeditions	R69

Interactive Maps

Go online to extend your learning with interactive maps.

European Exploration of the Americas, 1492–1682	14
Triangular Trade	23
Battles of the American Revolution, 1778–1781	36
The Louisiana Purchase and Western Expeditions	54
The Compromise of 1850	117
Kansas-Nebraska Act	117
The War in the West, 1861–1863	125
The War in the East, 1861–1863	126
World War I, 1914–1917	233
World War I, 1917–1918	243
Pearl Harbor	404
World War II in Europe and North Africa, 1941–1944	421
Allied Invasion	425
World War II in the Pacific, 1942–1945	438
Divided Germany, 1949	469
The Spread of Communism, 1945–1949	478
The Korean War, June 1950–January, 1951	487
The Vietnam Conflict, 1964–1975	613
The Persian Gulf War, 1990–1991	712
The Election of 2000	734

Charts and Graphs

Charts, Graphs, and Time Lines

Analyze information presented visually to learn more about history. To examine key facts and concepts, look for this special logo:

CHARTS

The World Before 1600	10
European Colonies in the Americas	18
Tensions between Britain and America, 1765–1775	31
Strengths and Weaknesses of the Continental and British Armies	35
The Revolutionary Era	37
Weaknesses of the Articles of Confederation	43
The Great Compromise	45
Checks and Balances	46
Creating a New Government	48
Causes and Effects of The War of 1812	56
Nationalism and Sectionalism	98
Causes and Effects of the Mexican-American War	112
Causes and Effects of Secession	121
The Generals	128
Causes and Effects of The Civil War	130
Financial Cost of the Civil War	132
Sharecropping and Poverty	136
Causes and Effects of Reconstruction	138
Causes and Effect of Western Migration	148
Populist Movement	160
Progressive Election Reforms	175
Chapter 6 Visual Summary	196
Causes of U.S. Expansionism	201
Chapter 7 Visual Summary	226
Major Battles	232
Somme Statistics	236
Major Provisions of the Treaty of Versailles	256
The Fourteen Points	256
Chapter 8 Visual Summary	262
Effects of World War I	286
Chapter 9 Visual Summary	290
Chapter 10 Visual Summary	316
Causes of the 1929 Stock Market Crash	325
Chapter 11 Visual Summary	342
Major New Deal Programs	360
Chapter 12 Visual Summary	378
Tales of German Hyperinflation	387
Chapter 13 Visual Summary	414
Jewish Losses in the Holocaust	429
Causes and Effects of World War II	455
Chapter 14 Visual Summary	460
Causes of the Cold War	465
The Marshall Plan	468
Programs for a Safer World	475
Population, 1950	479
Chapter 15 Visual Summary	492
The First Hydrogren Bomb Test	503
Chapter 16 Visual Summary	518
Major Great Society Programs	546
Chapter 17 Visual Summary	552
Early Civil Rights Victories	558
Major Civil Rights Reforms	570
African American Gains in the Civil Rights Movement	588
Chapter 18 Visual Summary	592
Causes of the Vietnam War	602
Tet Offensive Casualties	628
Chapter 19 Visual Summary	630
Major Native American Legislation	641
DBI Table	657
Chapter 20 Visual Summary	658
Causes and Effects of the Yom Kippur War	670
The Camp David Accords	684
Chapter 21 Visual Summary	690
Reagan's Foreign Policy	706
Chapter 22 Visual Summary	722
Bush's Foreign Policy Team	738
Chapter 23 Visual Summary	758
Women's Roles in the Military	776
Percentage of Air Force Rank that are Women	778
Commercial Activities Summary	786
Major Types of Federal Lands and Their Uses	787
Top Ten States Receiving Food Stamps in 2003	793
Reported Internet Fraud	803
Plans for Future Outsourcing of Jobs by Industry	811

CONTENTS **xxi**

GRAPHS

U.S. Immigration, 1830–1860	101
The Growth of Unions, 1880–1910	153
European Immigration, 1890–1930	274
Urban and Rural Population, 1890–1930	296
Distribution of Wealth, 1929	323
Average Income and Spending, 1929–1933	329
Farm Bankruptcies, 1928–1933	329
Unemployment Rates, 1928–1933	329
Growth of Union Membership, 1933–1940	361
Gross National Product (GNP), 1933–1938	364
Unemployment, 1933–1940	372
Deficit Spending, 1933–1940	372
U.S. Automobile and Airplane Production During World War II	409
The National Debt, 1930–1946	447
Government Spending, 1930–1946	447
Transportation Mileage, 1950–2000	516
Economic Conditions in Selected Cities, 1960	581
U.S. Forces in Vietnam, 1965–1972	609
Women in the Labor Force, 1950–2000	635
College Graduates, 1950 and 2000	635
American Voters, 1964 and 2000	635
Hispanic Immigrants to the United States, 1960 and 2000	643
Hispanic American Population, 1950–2000	643
Presidential Approval Ratings and the Watergate Crisis	688
Deficit Spending, 1970–1990	699
Defense Spending, 1980–1988	702
Average Family Income in the 1980s	721
Federal Deficits and Surpluses, 1980–2000	728
Stock Market, 1980–2000	728
U.S. Population by Race and Hispanic Origin	748
Poll Results: Should Women Serve in Combat?	776
Total Women in the U.S. Armed Forces	779
Selected Hardships Among U.S. Households with Children	792
Reported Robberies and Aggravated Assaults in the United States, 1960–2002	799
Growth of Insourced and Outsourced Jobs Over the Past 15 Years	811

TIME LINES

Beginnings of America, Beginnings–1763	4
Forming a New Nation, 1763–1815	28
Developing a National Identity, 1815–1860	90
Industrial Revolution	96
The Union in Crisis, 1850–1877	114
An Industrial Nation, 1860–1920	140
The Progressives, 1898–1920	168
Women's Rights	178
Entering the World Stage, 1898–1917	198
The First World War, 1914–1920	228
From War to Peace, 1919–1928	268
The Roaring Twenties, 1920–1929	292
The Great Depression Begins, 1929–1933	318
The New Deal, 1933–1940	344
World War II Erupts, 1939–1941	384
Isolationism	400
The United States in World War II, 1941–1945	416
The Cold War Begins, 1945–1953	462
Postwar America, 1945–1960	494
Height of the Cold War	498
The Cold War Arms Race	505
The New Frontier and the Great Society, 1961–1969	524
Exploration	536
The Civil Rights Movement, 1954–1975	554
Civil Rights	574
The Vietnam War, 1954–1975	594
A Time of Social Change, 1963–1975	632
Native American Policy and Activism	638
A Search for Order, 1968–1980	664
Watergate	676
A Conservative Era, 1980–1992	692
Into the Twenty-First Century, 1992–Present	724
Immigration Policy	766
Women in the Military	772
Environmental Conservation	780
Poverty in the United States	788
Crime and Public Safety	794
Regulation and the Internet	800
Outsourcing and Trade	806

Primary Sources

Relive history through eyewitness accounts, literature, and documents.

UNIT 1

Thomas Paine, *Common Sense,* 1776 33
James Madison, *Federalist No. 45,* 1787 47
Patrick Henry, speech, 1788 47
George Washington, Farewell Address, 1796 52
Stephen A. Douglas, Fourth Joint Debate at Charleston, September 18, 1858 120
Abraham Lincoln, Seventh Joint Debate at Alton, October 15, 1858 120
Abraham Lincoln, speech, June 16, 1858 120
Thaddeus Stevens, speech, 1865 134
Andrew Johnson, speech, 1865 134
William Graham Sumner, essay, c. 1885 152
Walter Rauschenbusch, *Christianity and the Social Crisis,* 1908 152

UNIT 2

Ida Tarbell, *McClure's* magazine, 1903 171
Rose Schneiderman, speech, April 2, 1911 174
Susan B. Anthony, speech, 1872 181
Theodore Roosevelt, letter to Sir Edwin Gray, November 15, 1913 185
Upton Sinclair, *The Jungle,* 1906 186
Theodore Roosevelt, "Arbor day-A message to the School Children of the United States, April 15, 1907 187
Alice Paul, Alice Paul to Elizabeth Marot, 1917 192
Carrie Chapman Catt, "Report of Survey Committee to National Board of NAWSA," 1916 192
Theodore Roosevelt, letter to Charleston citizen, 1902 193
Lincoln Steffens, *The Shame of the Cities,* 1904 195
Florence Kelley, "Wage Earning Children" in *From Jane Addams, Hull House Maps and Papers,* 1895 195
Josiah Strong, "Our Country," 1885 201
King Kalakaua, "Proclamation," 1872 202
The *New York Journal,* editorial on USS Maine, February 17, 1898 208
Theodore Roosevelt, *The Rough Riders,* 1902 210
John Hay, letter to Theodore Roosevelt, 1898 210
Henry Cabot Lodge, speech, 1900 211
George F. Hoar, speech, 1899 211
Theodore Roosevelt, *Roosevelt Corollary,* 1904 217
Princess Kaiulani, speech, 1893 224
John L. Stevens, "The Hawaiian Situation. II. A Plea for Annexation", 1893 225
Woodrow Wilson, speech to Congress, April 2, 1917 240
John Buchan, memoir, in *The King's Grace,* November 11, 1918, ... 244
Woodrow Wilson, Fourteen Points speech, 1918 250
Woodrow Wilson, speech, January, 1918 255
Georges Clemenceau, speech, June, 1919 256

Woodrow Wilson, Appeal for Support of the League of Nations, 1919 257
Henry Cabot Lodge, speech, 1919 257
Woodrow Wilson, speech, 1919 258
Erich Maria Remarque, *All Quiet on the Western Front,* 1929 260
Stull Holt, letter, September 1, 1917 260

UNIT 3

Illinois governor Frank Lowden, quoted in *The Harding Era: Warren G. Harding and His Administration* by Robert K. Murray, 1969 271
Bartolomeo Vanzetti, trial transcript, 1927 275
Henry Ford, announcing plans for his Model T, 1908 277
Carl Sandburg, The *Boll Weevil Song,* 1920 281
Kellogg–Briand Pact, Article I, 1928 287
Attorney General A. Mitchell Palmer, "The Case Against the Reds," *The Forum,* February, 1920 288
Georgia Senator Thomas W. Hardwick, speech, 1918 288
Bruce Bilven, *The New Republic,* September 9, 1925 296
William Allen White, letter to Gabriel Wells, 1927 300
Pauline Sabine, quoted in *The Long Thirst: Prohibition in America, 1920–1933,* by Thomas M. Coffey, 1975 300
Albert Einstein, "My First Impression of the U.S.A.," 1921 301
Claude McKay, "If We Must Die," 1919 305
L. Wolfe Gilber and Abel Baer, "Lucky Lindy," 1927 311
Sinclair Lewis, *Babbitt,* 1922 312
F. Scott Fitzgerald, *The Great Gatsby,* 1925 313
Dorothy Parker, "The Flapper," c.1927 314
The *New York World,* 1923 314
The *New Republic,* 1925 315
John J. Rasko, "Everyone Ought to Be Rich," *Ladies Home Journal,* August, 1929 322
Seattle Post-Intelligencer, October 25, 1929 325
The *New York Times,* October 30, 1929 325
Ed Paulson, quoted in *Hard Times: An Oral History of the Great Depression,* by Studs Terkel, 2000 330
Yip and Gorney Harburg, "Brother Can You Spare a Dime," 1931 332
Woody Guthrie, "Pastures of Plenty," c. 1947 333
Herbert Hoover, speech, October, 1928 336
Nell Blackshear, interview in *Living Atlanta: An Oral History of the City, 1914–1928,* 1990 340
Kitty McCulloch, quoted in *Hard Times,* 2000 341
Franklin D. Roosevelt, Campaign Speech, October 13, 1932 348
Franklin D. Roosevelt, First Inaugural Address, March 4, 1933 349
Franklin Delano Roosevelt, State of the Union Address, 1935 358
Bob Stinson, sit down striker, quoted in *Hard Times,* by Studs Terkel, 2000 361

Senator Lester Dickinson, *The American Mercury*, February, 1936 .... **362**
Merlo J. Pusey, *American Heritage*, April, 1958 ..... **363**
Molly Dewson, quoted in *Beyond Suffrage: Women in the New Deal*, by Susan Ware, 1981 .... **366**
Saturday Evening Post, November 6, 1936 .... **373**
Senator Charles McNary, Congressional Record, 1935 ...... **373**
Representative Daniel Reed, Congressional Record, 1935 .. **373**
Tom Vinciguerra, letter to the *Washington Post*, 1997 ...... **376**
The Nation, editorial, 1936 .... **376**

UNIT 4

Benito Mussolini and Giovanni Gentile, *The Doctrine of Facsism*, 1932 .... **388**
Adolf Hitler, *Mein Kamf*, 1924 .... **389**
Halle Selassie, speech to the League of Nations, June, 1936 . **391**
Neville Chamberlain, address to the House of Commons, 1938 .... **392**
Winston Churchill, address to the House of Commons, 1938 .... **392**
Winston Churchill, speech before the House of Commons, June 4, 1940 .... **397**
Minnie Vautrin, recorded in her diary, 1937 .... **398**
Neutrality Act, 1935 .... **400**
Franklin D. Roosevelt, speech, October 5, 1937 ...... **401**
Franklin Roosevelt, address to Congress, December 8, 1941 .... **405**
Roger Tuttrup, quoted in *The Good War: An Oral History of World War Two*, by Studs Terkel, 1985 .... **407**
Letter from Youth Committee for the Defense of Mexican American youth to Vice President Henry Wallace, 1943 .... **411**
Franklin Roosevelt, address to Congress, December 8, 1941 .... **412**
Duane T. Brigstock, "Pearl Harbor Memories," *Michigan History*, 2005 .... **413**
Frank Walk, quoted in *War Stories: Remembering World War II*, by Elizabeth Mullener, 2002 .... **423**
Tuvia Borzykowski, quoted in *The Second World War: A Complete History*, by Martin Gilbert, 1970 ...... **428**
Gerda Weissman, memoir, c. 1945 .... **430**
Reid Draffen, quoted in War Stories: *Remembering World War II*, by Elizabeth Mullener, 2002 .... **431**
Japanese admiral Isoroku Yamamoto, quoted in *The Second World War: Asia and the Pacific*, Thomas E. Griess, Ed, 1989 .... **434**
Mitsuo Fuchido, quoted in *The Pacific War*, by John Costello, 1981 .... **436**
Franklin D. Roosevelt, radio address, April 28, 1942 ..... **442**
Jean Lechnir, quoted in *Women Remember the War, 1941–1945*, Michael E. Stevens, Ed 1993 .... **443**
Yoshiko Uchlyana, letter reprinted in the *University of Washington Daily*, January, 1943 .... **446**

Franklin D. Roosevelt, report to Congress, March 1, 1945 .... **451**
Takeharu Terao, memoir, 2003 .... **453**
Henry Stimson, in *Harper's Magazine*, 1947 .... **454**
Leo Szliard, the Szilard Petition to the President, 1945 ...... **454**
June Wandrey, letter, January 1944 .... **458**
Paul Curtis, letter, May 1944 .... **458**
Corporal Rupert Trimmingham, letter to *Yank*, April 28, 1944 .... **459**
Bob Hope, *I Never Left Home*, 1944 .... **459**
Winston Churchill, speech at Westminster College, March 5, 1946 .... **467**
Harry S Truman, speech to joint session of Congress, March 12, 1947 .... **467**
George C. Marshall, commencement address, Harvard University, June 5, 1947 .... **468**
Harry S Truman, Executive Order 9981, July 26, 1948 ...... **473**
Harry S Truman to reporters, April 13, 1945 .... **473**
Harry S Truman, message to Congress, July 1950 .... **485**
General Douglas MacArthur, speech, April 19, 1951 .... **488**
Harry S Truman, Executive Order 9835, 1947 .... **490**
Richard Nixon, speech, 1952 .... **497**
Dwight D. Eisenhower, press conference, April 7, 1954 .... **500**
Report of the General Advisory Committee of the Atomic Energy Commission, October, 1949 .... **503**
John Foster Dulles, address before the Associated Press in New York, 1957 .... **506**
Albert Einstein and others, Russell-Einstein Manifesto, 1955 .... **506**
The *New York Times*, June 16, 1955 .... **508**
John Kenneth Galbraith, *The Affluent Society*, 1958 ..... **513**
Dwight D. Eisenhower, message to Congress, 1955 ...... **516**

UNIT 5

John F. Kennedy, inaugural address, January 20, 1961 ...... **527**
John F. Kennedy, Berliner speech, June 26, 1963 ..... **530**
John F. Kennedy, Commencement Address at American University, June 10, 1963 .... **534**
John F. Kennedy, message to Congress, May 25, 1961 ...... **537**
Donna Shalala, quoted in *Ordinary Americans: U.S. History Through the Eyes of Everyday People*, Linda R. Monk, Ed.,1994 .... **540**
Lyndon B. Johnson, speech to Congress, November 27, 1963 .... **543**
Michael Harrington, *The Other America*, 1962 .... **543**
Hubert Humphrey, speech, 1964 .... **545**
Barry Goldwater, announcement of Presidential Candidacy, 1964 .... **545**
Lyndon Johnson, speech, May 22, 1964 .... **545**
John F. Kennedy, inaugural address, January 20, 1961 ...... **550**
Ronald Reagan, speech, 1964 .... **551**
Lyndon Johnson, speech, 1964 .... **551**
Chief Justice Earl Warren, *Brown* v. *Board of Education, of Topeka Kansas*, May 17, 1954 .... **559**

Diane Nash, quoted in *Voices of Freedom: An Oral History of the Civil Rights Movement from the 1950s Through the 1980s,* by Henry Hampton, et al., 1990 565
John Kennedy, speech, June 11, 1963 570
Martin Luther King Jr., *I Have a Dream* speech, August 28, 1963 571
Peter Orris, quoted in *Voices of Freedom: An Oral History of the Civil Rights Movement from the 1950s Through the 1980s,* by Henry Hampton, et al., 1990 575
Fannie Lou Hamer, testimony before the Credentials Committee of the Democratic National Convention of 1964, August 22, 1964 577
Martin Luther King Jr., Nobel lecture, 1964 583
Malcolm X, speech, 1964 583
Stokley Carmichael, appeal to protesters, June 17, 1966 583
Robert Kennedy, speech, April 4, 1968 585
Henrietta Franklin, quoted in the *Washington Post,* May 24, 1968 587
Robert Patterson, interview, c. 1965 590
Fannie Lou Hamer, interview, c. 1963 591
Malcolm X, speech, 1964 591
Ho Chi Minh, speech, September 2, 1945 598
Ho Chi Minh, c. 1954, in *America Inside Out* 598
Henry Cabot Lodge Jr., cable, August 29, 1963 602
Lyndon B. Johnson, speech, August 4, 1964 603
Captain Myron Harrington, quoted in *Vietnam: A History,* by Stanley Karnow, 1983 606
Lieutenant Philip Caputo, interview on CNN, June, 1996 ... 606
Nurse Edie Meeks, quoted in *Newsweek,* March 8, 1999 609
Walt R. Rostow, Sir Montague Burton Lecture, 1967 610
George McGovern, speech, 1967 610
Martin Luther King Jr., sermon, 1967 610
Tran Van Duong, quoted in *Nam: The Vietnam Experience 1965–75,* 1995 614
Walter Cronkite, on CBS television, February 27, 1968 615
Lyndon Johnson, speech, March 31, 1968 615
Robert S. McNamara, letter to President Johnson, May 1967 616
Robert F. Kennedy, announcement of Presidential Candidacy, March 16, 1968 616
John McCain, autobiography, 1967 625
Le Ly Hayslip, *When Heaven and Earth Changed Places,* 1989 625
Frederick Downs Jr., *Aftermath: A Soldier's Return from Vietnam,* 1984, ... 626
General William Westmoreland, *A Soldier Reports,* 1976 628
Walter Cronkite, CBS news broadcast, February 27, 1968 628
NOW's Statement of Purpose, 1966 636
Gloria Steinem, Testimony before Senate Hearings on Equal Rights Amendment, 1970 637

Phyllis Schlafly, interview, 1975 637
Declaration of Indian Purpose, June 1961 639
Russell Means, quoted in *Alcatraz is Not an Island,* PBS documentary, 2002 640
Dolores Huerta, "Proclamation of the Delano Grape Workers for International Boycott Day," 1969 644
Rodolfo Gonzales, "I am Joaquin," 1967 645
Carol Brightman, Interview with David Gans, 1999 652
J. Edgar Hoover, in *The Review of the News,* September 11, 1968 654
Chicago Women's Liberation Union, statement, 1969 656

UNIT 6
Richard Nixon, Acceptance Speech, August 8, 1968 667
Edwin "Buzz" Aldrin, news conference, August 12, 1969 ... 673
Archibald Cox, statement to the press, October 20, 1973 679
Gerald R. Ford, remarks on taking the Oath of Office as President, August 9, 1974 679
Jimmy Carter, televised speech, April 18, 1977 682
Zbigniew Brzezinski, foreign policy meeting, 1979 685
Cyrus Vance, foreign policy meeting, 1979 685
Jimmy Carter, speech, July 15, 1979 686
Richard Nixon, address to the nation, April 29, 1974 688
Richard Nixon, transcript of White House tapes, June 23, 1972 689
Ronald Reagan, "Evil Empire" speech, March 8, 1983 702
Ronald Reagan, speech, June 6, 1984 703
Tim Weber, BBC report, November 9, 1989 709
"A Visionary Who Put an Era Out of Its Misery," *The New York Times,* January 7, 1997 710
Nelson Mandela, Nobel lecture, December 10, 1993 713
Representative Joseph Kennedy II (D., MA), the *New York Times,* 1990 717
Representative James McDermott (D., WA), speech to the House of Representatives, 1989 717
"Gordon Gekko," *Wall Street,* 1987 720
Bill Clinton, the President's radio address, 1993 730
H. Ross Perot, speech, 1992 730
George W. Bush, address to the nation, December 13, 2000 735
George W. Bush, address to the Joint Session of Congress, February 27, 2001 736
Joel Meyerowitz, artist's statement to the exhibit, "Images from Ground Zero," 2004 742
George W. Bush, address to the nation, October 7, 2001 ... 744
Bill Gates, speech, June 25, 2003 749
Tyler Cowen, interview with *Reason,* 2004 756
Newsweek, 2001 757
Mark Rice-Oxley, *The Christian Science Monitor,* 2004 757

Reading like a Historian

When I asked Kevin, a 16-year-old high school junior, what he needed most to do well in history class, he had little doubt: "A good memory."

"Anything else?"

"Nope. Just memorize facts and stuff, know 'em cold, and when you get the test, give it all back to the teacher."

"What about thinking—does thinking have anything to do with history?"

"Not really. It's all pretty simple. Random stuff happened a long time ago. People wrote it down. Others copied it and put it in a book. Poof—history."

I was saddened but not surprised by Kevin's answers. I've spent nearly twenty years studying how high school kids learn history. Over the years I've met many Kevins, students who knew history as nothing but a grim list of names and dates—one random fact after another.

In *American Anthem: Modern American History, California Edition* we have created a textbook that I hope will change the way students such as Kevin learn history. To explore the past and feel its excitement, you must learn to read like a historian.

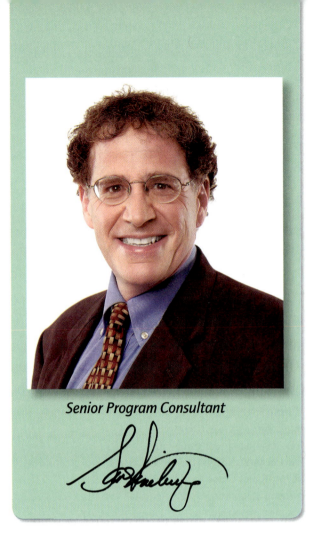

Senior Program Consultant

Be a History Detective

Names, facts, and dates: this is what history has become for a lot of you. But the funny thing is that when you ask historians what they do, an entirely different picture emerges. They see themselves as detectives searching for clues to a puzzle that can never be entirely solved.

Asking questions Traced back to its earliest meaning, the word *history* (in Greek, *istor*) is about *inquiry*. To engage in inquiry means trying to figure things out, asking questions open to debate. Inquiry is about as far from mindless memorization as you can get.

Even when historians are able to piece together the basic story of what happened in the past, rarely do they all line up in agreement about what an event means or what caused it. Historians argue amongst themselves about the past's meaning and what it has to tell us in the present. The past may be over, but history is a moving target.

Gilbert Stuart painted this portrait of George Washington in 1796, while Washington was president. Historians consider this painting a primary source because it was created during Washington's lifetime.

Facts and Their Meaning

Where do facts fit into this picture? Facts are important but hardly the whole story. To historians, history is an argument about what facts *mean*.

If history already happened, you might ask, what's there to argue about? It turns out, a lot. Was the American Revolution a fight against tyranny or an attempt by the well bred to preserve their social position? Was the Civil War fought over the issue of slavery or was it a conflict over states' rights? Was the "Progressive Era" really so progressive? Could the Vietnam War have been prevented?

Reviewing sources Take, for example, a story you probably know—or think you do. Pocahontas, a beautiful Native American woman, falls in love with the handsome English captain John Smith, and later saves his life just as her dad, Powhatan, is ready to club him to death.

Do you believe it?

The facts are these: John Smith wrote two different accounts of his time in Jamestown, one in 1608, the other in 1624. In his first book, he talks about meeting Chief Powhatan, but there is no mention of any threat. In fact he says the opposite: Powhatan "kindly welcomed me with such good wordes, and great Platters...assuring me his friendship." Nor is there any mention of being saved by a young Indian girl—anyway, Pocahontas was only 11 or 12, hardly the gorgeous teenager of cartoon fame—and no hint of any love affair anywhere. Only when Smith published a second book in 1624, well after Pocahontas had already married another colonist, John Rolfe, had a son, became ill, and died in 1617, do we hear of Smith's dramatic rescue by the Indian princess. So which account should we believe, the one Smith wrote in 1608 or 1624?

Weighing opinions Different opinions swirl around this question, and there are actually good reasons for believing a number of them. But while everyone is entitled to an opinion, not every opinion is entitled to being believed. In history, a persuasive opinion is backed up by evidence. It is evidence that distinguishes a solid interpretation from a wild guess. *American Anthem* offers you numerous opportunities to develop the critical reading skills you'll need to analyze evidence like a historian.

Document-Based Investigations give you opportunities to inquire like a historian. You will study a series of documents and then draw your own conclusions about what they mean.

READING LIKE A HISTORIAN

Evidence in History

To find evidence in history we can't talk to the dead. What we can do is examine what they left behind—their diaries, letters, telegrams, secret memos, and in the modern era, their tape recordings and computer records. This is what historians mean when they talk about reading *primary* sources. These sources are considered to be primary—*most important, appearing in the first position, essential*—because they are written by the people we are trying to understand. Their words come to us directly, without being filtered by someone else.

How Historians Read

Learning to read like a historian is different from the other kind of reading you do, like reading your driver's ed manual or your math book. In practically every country, a red road sign means stop. In math 2 + 2 = 4 no matter where you live—in Dallas, San Francisco, or Paris. But because history is always written from a particular perspective, its meanings change from place to place and from one era to the next. Even the book you're holding, while trying to balance different perspectives, makes choices that reflect its perspective: where to begin its story, where to end it, which events to narrate and which to leave out.

Points of view In our chapter covering the Revolutionary War, the rebellious American colonists are referred to as "patriots." Would you expect them to be so described in a British textbook? When you come to the chapters on World War II, D-Day is a large part of the story on the war in Europe. In Russian textbooks, D-Day—referred to as the "opening of the second front"—barely gets mentioned. There, the big story is the siege of Stalingrad, in which the Red Army held off the Nazis for six months, and in the process lost a million of its own citizens—but not before causing the collapse of Hitler's Sixth Army.

It is only natural that historians today have different points of view. The people at the time

---

PRIMARY SOURCES

Speech

In what became known as the Checkers speech, Richard M. Nixon admitted having a secret political fund but denied using it improperly. He detailed his personal finances—and admitted to having accepted one special gift in 1952. The speech was well received, and it saved his political career.

"We did get something, a gift, after the election. A man down in Texas heard [my wife] Pat on the radio mention the fact that our two youngsters would like to have a dog, and ... the day before we left on this campaign trip we got a message from Union Station down in Baltimore, saying they had a package for us. We went down to get it. You know what it was? It was a little cocker spaniel dog, in a crate that he had sent all the way from Texas, black and white, spotted, and our little girl, Tricia, the six-year-old, named it Checkers. And, you know, the kids, like all kids, loved the dog, and I just want to say this, right now, that regardless of what they say about it, we're going to keep it."

Nixon used the image of his daughter and her puppy to build sympathy.

Skills Focus: READING LIKE A HISTORIAN
1. **Analyzing Primary Sources** What was the gift that Nixon admitted to having received?
2. **Drawing Conclusions** speech was effective at en

See **Skills Handbook**, pp. H12

Primary sources are important pieces of historical evidence—and must be read with a historian's critical eye.

COUNTERPOINTS

Tactics of Change

Martin Luther King's commitment to nonviolence never wavered.

"[V]iolence ... seeks to annihilate rather than convert ... Nonviolence is a powerful and just weapon ... which cuts without wounding and ennobles the man who wields it."

Martin Luther King Jr., 1964

Malcolm X was blunt and uncompromising. He inspired hatred from some and respect from others.

"[N]ow you're facing a situation where the young Negro's coming up. They don't want to hear that 'turn-the-other-cheek' stuff, no.... There's new thinking coming in. There's new strategy coming in ... It'll be ballots, or it'll be bullets. It'll be liberty, or it will be death."

Malcolm X, 1964

Skills Focus: READING LIKE A HISTORIAN
Identifying Points of View What does King mean when he says that nonviolence "cuts without wounding"? To what is Malcolm X referring when he speaks of "ballots" or "bullets"?

See **Skills Handbook**, pp. H28–H29

Counterpoints features ask you to analyze different points of view about key historical issues.

did too. The Counterpoints features found in this book show that as history was being made, people disagreed about what was happening and what to do.

Reading for perspective Perspective means a place to stand, and each one of us has to stand somewhere. Where the authors of this book stand is revealed in the words they choose—just think about the difference between calling this book "American Anthem," versus, say, "American Dilemma" or "American Crisis." But determining perspective means paying more attention to words than you're probably used to.

Attention to detail Consider two facts: first, Harry Truman became the 32nd president; and second, he never went to college. The moment we try to combine them, we no longer have two neutral bits of information. We have a historical interpretation. Think about the sentence, "Harry Truman became the 32nd president *but* he never went to college." Change one little word—substitute *because* for *but*—and see what happens. The first sentence suggests that the lack of a college education was something Truman had to overcome. The second seems to say that Truman's humble education *caused*, or at least partially caused, his success. Two completely different ideas rest on one word. Without paying attention, you'd miss it.

The Role of Thinking

The book you are holding offers an interpretation of history, but not the final word. It does its best to combine perspectives, but like any book, it can never escape the fact that it was written by human beings living in a particular time and place. As such, it records the unrecognized assumptions, biases, and blind spots of our time. In reading like a historian, one of your goals is to treat this book like any other account of the past. You should analyze it, evaluate the evidence it offers for its assertions, and read it carefully—more carefully than you've ever read a history textbook before. The thread connecting all of these goals is the very thing that escaped Kevin: the role of thinking.

Kevin's right. Without thinking, history *is* meaningless. But when you add thinking—an ingredient only you can provide—the past springs to life. That is what reading like a historian is all about.

A historian looks at all evidence critically. Valuable information comes not only from text-based documents, but also from paintings, photographs, political cartoons, and other visual media.

How to Use Your Textbook

American Anthem: Modern American History, California Edition was created to make your study of U.S. history an enjoyable, meaningful experience. Take a few minutes to become familiar with the book's easy-to-use structure and special features.

Unit

Each unit of study focuses on a particular time period. Unit openers list the chapter titles and the years the chapters cover. They also provide an overview of the main themes covered in the unit. A historic photograph or illustration previews the material you are about to explore.

Prepare to Read

Each unit begins with an opportunity to reinforce important skills first taught in the Skills Handbook. Taking the time to review these skills will help you as you read the unit.

Reading Skills Call-outs give practical how-to instruction about the skill. Test-taking tips show you how reading skills can help you when taking exams.

Reading Like a Historian This book provides strategies to help you think like a historian. Each call-out applies one of the strategies to the passage or visual being analyzed. California Analysis Skills are listed.

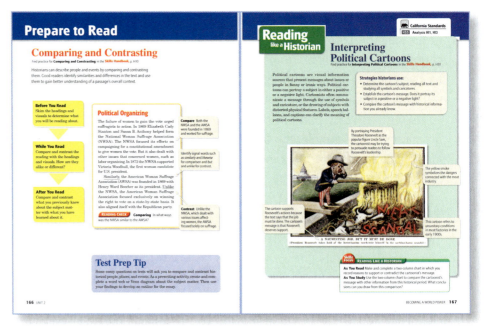

Chapter

Chapter Openers include an introduction called The Big Picture, a timeline for the years covered in the chapter, and photos and illustrations.

Chapter Review pages provide a full array of assessments.

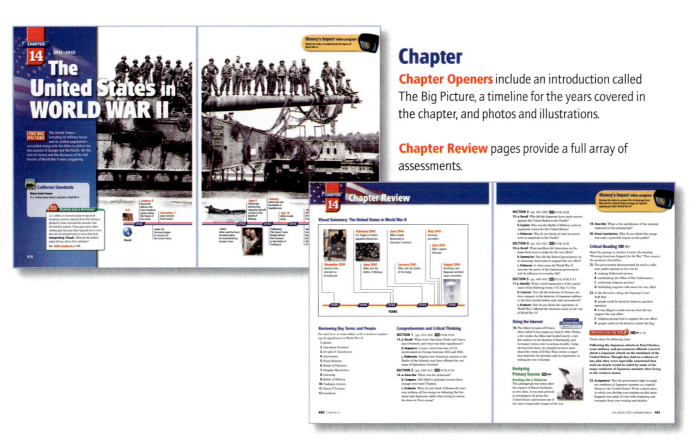

Section

Section opener pages include a Main Idea statement, Focus Questions, and Key Terms and People. In addition, each section includes the following special features:

The Inside Story introduces each section with a compelling story from history.

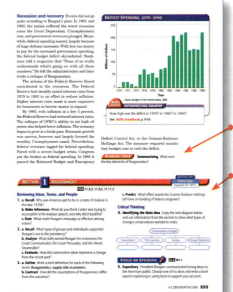

The California History-Social Sciences Standards for 11th Grade covered in the section appear on the section opener.

Reading Check Questions provide opportunities to review and assess your understanding.

Section Assessment boxes offer a quick way to check your understanding of a section's main ideas. There is also assessment practice online.

xxxi

Scavenger Hunt

American Anthem: Modern American History, California Edition contains a great deal of information about U.S. history. Before you begin your journey into the past, take a minute to familiarize yourself with this book and its contents. This will help make your journey easier.

1. How many units and chapters are in the book? How do you know?

2. Where in *American Anthem: Modern American History, California Edition* do you find the atlas?

3. The Reading Like a Historian Skills section in the front of the book offers students exposure to and practice in various skills, such as analyzing primary sources. Where in the book do you find additional Reading Like a Historian skill practice?

4. Where and how do you find key terms and people for Chapter 11, Section 2?

5. Where in *American Anthem: Modern American History, California Edition* do you find a discussion of contemporary issues?

6. *American Anthem: Modern American History, California Edition* was created to help you meet all of the California History–Social Sciences Standards. Where do you find a description of these standards?

7. Where do you find review questions to help you study?

8. Where do you look to find information about interactive maps and other map essentials?

9. Where do you look to find a list of all of the primary sources used?

10. Where can you find reading support for each unit?

The California History–Social Science Standards

Grade Eleven: United States History and Geography: Continuity and Change in the Twentieth and Twenty-First Centuries

Welcome to Holt, Rinehart and Winston's *American Anthem: Modern American History, California Edition.* Throughout this course, you will study the people and events that helped shape our country from prehistory to the present, with an emphasis on the development of the modern United States. To ensure successful study, you will follow the California Grade Eleven Content Standards for United States History and Geography: Continuity and Change in the Twentieth and Twenty-First Centuries. The standards are listed on pages ST2–ST6 of this book.

The California State Board of Education approved the History–Social Science Standards as a guide for what students should achieve throughout the year. The Content Standards list the subject matter that you should learn, and the Historical and Social Science Analysis Skills detail critical thinking skills that you should possess.

Teachers use both the Content Standards and the Historical and Social Science Analysis Skills in tests to assess understanding. Becoming familiar with the Content Standards and the Historical and Social Science Analysis Skills will contribute to your continued success during the school year.

Big Sur Coast

Grade 11 United States History and Geography: Continuity and Change in the Twentieth and Twenty-First Centuries

History–Social Science Standards

CALIFORNIA STANDARDS

11.1 Students analyze the significant events in the founding of the nation and its attempts to realize the philosophy of government described in the Declaration of Independence.

1. Describe the Enlightenment and the rise of democratic ideas as the context in which the nation was founded.
2. Analyze the ideological origins of the American Revolution, the Founding Fathers' philosophy of divinely bestowed unalienable natural rights, the debates on the drafting and ratification of the Constitution, and the addition of the Bill of Rights.
3. Understand the history of the Constitution after 1787 with emphasis on federal versus state authority and growing democratization.
4. Examine the effects of the Civil War and Reconstruction and of the industrial revolution, including demographic shifts and the emergence in the late nineteenth century of the United States as a world power.

11.2 Students analyze the relationship among the rise of industrialization, large-scale rural-to-urban migration, and massive immigration from Southern and Eastern Europe.

1. Know the effects of industrialization on living and working conditions, including the portrayal of working conditions and food safety in Upton Sinclair's *The Jungle*.
2. Describe the changing landscape, including the growth of cities linked by industry and trade, and the development of cities divided according to race, ethnicity, and class.
3. Trace the effect of the Americanization movement.
4. Analyze the effect of urban political machines and responses to them by immigrants and middle-class reformers.
5. Discuss corporate mergers that produced trusts and cartels and the economic and political policies of industrial leaders.
6. Trace the economic development of the United States and its emergence as a major industrial power, including its gains from trade and the advantages of its physical geography.
7. Analyze the similarities and differences between the ideologies of Social Darwinism and Social Gospel (e.g., using biographies of William Graham Sumner, Billy Sunday, Dwight L. Moody).
8. Examine the effect of political programs and activities of Populists.
9. Understand the effect of political programs and activities of the Progressives (e.g., federal regulation of railroad transport, Children's Bureau, the Sixteenth Amendment, Theodore Roosevelt, Hiram Johnson).

11.3 Students analyze the role religion played in the founding of America, its lasting moral, social, and political impacts, and issues regarding religious liberty.

1. Describe the contributions of various religious groups to American civic principles and social reform movements (e.g., civil and human rights, individual responsibility and the work ethic, antimonarchy and self-rule, worker protection, family-centered communities).
2. Analyze the great religious revivals and the leaders involved in them, including the First Great Awakening, the Second Great Awakening, the Civil War revivals, the Social Gospel Movement, the rise of Christian liberal theology in the nineteenth century, the impact of the Second Vatican Council, and the rise of Christian fundamentalism in current times.

ST2 CALIFORNIA STANDARDS

3 Cite incidences of religious intolerance in the United States (e.g., persecution of Mormons, anti-Catholic sentiment, anti-Semitism).

4 Discuss the expanding religious pluralism in the United States and California that resulted from large-scale immigration in the twentieth century.

5 Describe the principles of religious liberty found in the Establishment and Free Exercise clauses of the First Amendment, including the debate on the issue of separation of church and state.

11.4 Students trace the rise of the United States to its role as a world power in the twentieth century.

1 List the purpose and the effects of the Open Door policy.

2 Describe the Spanish-American War and U.S. expansion in the South Pacific.

3 Discuss America's role in the Panama Revolution and the building of the Panama Canal.

4 Explain Theodore Roosevelt's Big Stick diplomacy, William Taft's Dollar Diplomacy, and Woodrow Wilson's Moral Diplomacy, drawing on relevant speeches.

5 Analyze the political, economic, and social ramifications of World War I on the home front.

6 Trace the declining role of Great Britain and the expanding role of the United States in world affairs after World War II.

11.5 Students analyze the major political, social, economic, technological, and cultural developments of the 1920s.

1 Discuss the policies of Presidents Warren Harding, Calvin Coolidge, and Herbert Hoover.

2 Analyze the international and domestic events, interests, and philosophies that prompted attacks on civil liberties, including the Palmer Raids, Marcus Garvey's "back-to-Africa" movement, the Ku Klux Klan, and immigration quotas and the responses of organizations such as the American Civil Liberties Union, the National Association for the Advancement of Colored People, and the Anti-Defamation League to those attacks.

3 Examine the passage of the Eighteenth Amendment to the Constitution and the Volstead Act (Prohibition).

4 Analyze the passage of the Nineteenth Amendment and the changing role of women in society.

5 Describe the Harlem Renaissance and new trends in literature, music, and art, with special attention to the work of writers (e.g., Zora Neale Hurston, Langston Hughes).

6 Trace the growth and effects of radio and movies and their role in the worldwide diffusion of popular culture.

7 Discuss the rise of mass production techniques, the growth of cities, the impact of new technologies (e.g., the automobile, electricity), and the resulting prosperity and effect on the American landscape.

Golden Gate Bridge in San Francisco

11.6 Students analyze the different explanations for the Great Depression and how the New Deal fundamentally changed the role of the federal government.

1. Describe the monetary issues of the late nineteenth and early twentieth centuries that gave rise to the establishment of the Federal Reserve and the weaknesses in key sectors of the economy in the late 1920s.
2. Understand the explanations of the principal causes of the Great Depression and the steps taken by the Federal Reserve, Congress, and Presidents Herbert Hoover and Franklin Delano Roosevelt to combat the economic crisis.
3. Discuss the human toll of the Depression, natural disasters, and unwise agricultural practices and their effects on the depopulation of rural regions and on political movements of the left and right, with particular attention to the Dust Bowl refugees and their social and economic impacts in California.
4. Analyze the effects of and the controversies arising from New Deal economic policies and the expanded role of the federal government in society and the economy since the 1930s (e.g., Works Progress Administration, Social Security, National Labor Relations Board, farm programs, regional development policies, and energy development projects such as the Tennessee Valley Authority, California Central Valley Project, and Bonneville Dam).
5. Trace the advances and retreats of organized labor, from the creation of the American Federation of Labor and the Congress of Industrial Organizations to current issues of a postindustrial, multinational economy, including the United Farm Workers in California.

11.7 Students analyze America's participation in World War II.

1. Examine the origins of American involvement in the war, with an emphasis on the events that precipitated the attack on Pearl Harbor.
2. Explain U.S. and Allied wartime strategy, including the major battles of Midway, Normandy, Iwo Jima, Okinawa, and the Battle of the Bulge.
3. Identify the roles and sacrifices of individual American soldiers, as well as the unique contributions of the special fighting forces (e.g., the Tuskegee Airmen, the 442nd Regimental Combat team, the Navajo Code Talkers).
4. Analyze Roosevelt's foreign policy during World War II (e.g., Four Freedoms speech).
5. Discuss the constitutional issues and impact of events on the U.S. home front, including the internment of Japanese Americans (e.g., *Fred Korematsu* v. *United States of America*) and the restrictions on German and Italian resident aliens; the response of the administration to Hitler's atrocities against Jews and other groups; the roles of women in military production; and the roles and growing political demands of African Americans.
6. Describe major developments in aviation, weaponry, communication, and medicine and the war's impact on the location of American industry and use of resources.
7. Discuss the decision to drop atomic bombs and the consequences of the decision (Hiroshima and Nagasaki).
8. Analyze the effect of massive aid given to Western Europe under the Marshall Plan to rebuild itself after the war and the importance of a rebuilt Europe to the U.S. economy.

11.8 Students analyze the economic boom and social transformation of post-World War II America.

1. Trace the growth of service sector, white collar, and professional sector jobs in business and government.
2. Describe the significance of Mexican immigration and its relationship to the agricultural economy, especially in California.
3. Examine Truman's labor policy and congressional reaction to it.
4. Analyze new federal government spending on defense, welfare, interest on the national debt, and federal and state spending on education, including the California Master Plan.
5. Describe the increased powers of the presidency in response to the Great Depression, World War II, and the Cold War.
6. Discuss the diverse environmental regions of North America, their relationship to local economies, and the origins and prospects of environmental problems in those regions.
7. Describe the effects on society and the economy of technological developments since 1945, including the computer revolution, changes in communication, advances in medicine, and improvements in agricultural technology.
8. Discuss forms of popular culture, with emphasis on their origins and geographic diffusion (e.g., jazz and other forms of popular music, professional sports, architectural and artistic styles).

11.9 Students analyze U.S. foreign policy since World War II.

1. Discuss the establishment of the United Nations and International Declaration of Human Rights, International Monetary Fund, World Bank, and General Agreement on Tariffs and Trade (GATT) and their importance in shaping modern Europe and maintaining peace and international order.
2. Understand the role of military alliances, including NATO and SEATO, in deterring communist aggression and maintaining security during the Cold War.
3. Trace the origins and geopolitical consequences (foreign and domestic) of the Cold War and containment policy, including the following:
   - The era of McCarthyism, instances of domestic Communism (e.g., Alger Hiss) and blacklisting
   - The Truman Doctrine
   - The Berlin Blockade
   - The Korean War
   - The Bay of Pigs invasion and the Cuban Missile Crisis
   - Atomic testing in the American West, the "mutual assured destruction" doctrine, and disarmament policies
   - The Vietnam War
   - Latin American policy
4. List the effects of foreign policy on domestic policies and vice versa (e.g., protests during the war in Vietnam, the "nuclear freeze" movement).
5. Analyze the role of the Reagan administration and other factors in the victory of the West in the Cold War.
6. Describe U.S. Middle East policy and its strategic, political, and economic interests, including those related to the Gulf War.
7. Examine relations between the United States and Mexico in the twentieth century, including key economic, political, immigration, and environmental issues.

Eastern Sierra Nevada

11.10 Students analyze the development of federal civil rights and voting rights.

1. Explain how demands of African Americans helped produce a stimulus for civil rights, including President Roosevelt's ban on racial discrimination in defense industries in 1941, and how African Americans' service in World War II produced a stimulus for President Truman's decision to end segregation in the armed forces in 1948.

2. Examine and analyze the key events, policies, and court cases in the evolution of civil rights, including *Dred Scott* v. *Sandford, Plessy* v. *Ferguson, Brown* v. *Board of Education, Regents of the University of California* v. *Bakke,* and California Proposition 209.

3. Describe the collaboration on legal strategy between African American and white civil rights lawyers to end racial segregation in higher education.

4. Examine the roles of civil rights advocates (e.g., A. Philip Randolph, Martin Luther King, Jr., Malcom X, Thurgood Marshall, James Farmer, Rosa Parks), including the significance of Martin Luther King, Jr.'s "Letter from Birmingham Jail" and "I Have a Dream" speech.

5. Discuss the diffusion of the civil rights movement of African Americans from the churches of the rural South and the urban North, including the resistance to racial desegregation in Little Rock and Birmingham, and how the advances influenced the agendas, strategies, and effectiveness of the quests of American Indians, Asian Americans, and Hispanic Americans for civil rights and equal opportunities.

6. Analyze the passage and effects of civil rights and voting rights legislation (e.g., 1964 Civil Rights Act, Voting Rights Act of 1965) and the Twenty-Fourth Amendment, with an emphasis on equality of access to education and to the political process.

7. Analyze the women's rights movement from the era of Elizabeth Stanton and Susan Anthony and the passage of the Nineteenth Amendment to the movement launched in the 1960s, including differing perspectives on the roles of women.

11.11 Students analyze the major social problems and domestic policy issues in contemporary American society.

1. Discuss the reasons for the nation's changing immigration policy, with emphasis on how the Immigration Act of 1965 and successor acts have transformed American society.

2. Discuss the significant domestic policy speeches of Truman, Eisenhower, Kennedy, Johnson, Nixon, Carter, Reagan, Bush, and Clinton (e.g., with regard to education, civil rights, economic policy, environmental policy).

3. Describe the changing roles of women in society as reflected in the entry of more women into the labor force and the changing family structure.

4. Explain the constitutional crisis originating from the Watergate scandal.

5. Trace the impact of, need for, and controversies associated with environmental conservation, expansion of the national park system, and the development of environmental protection laws, with particular attention to the interaction between environmental protection advocates and property rights advocates.

6. Analyze the persistence of poverty and how different analyses of this issue influence welfare reform, health insurance reform, and other social policies.

7. Explain how the federal, state, and local governments have responded to demographic and social changes such as population shifts to the suburbs, racial concentrations in the cities, Frostbelt-to-Sunbelt migration, international migration, decline of family farms, increases in out-of-wedlock births, and drug abuse.

Geisel Library at the University of California at San Diego

**Grade 11 United States History and Geography:
Continuity and Change in the Twentieth and Twenty-First Centuries**

Historical and Social Sciences Analysis Skills

The intellectual skills noted below are to be learned through, and applied to, the content standards for grades nine through twelve. They are to be assessed *only in conjunction with* the content standards in grades nine through twelve.

In addition to the standards for grades nine through twelve, students demonstrate the following intellectual, reasoning, reflection, and research skills:

Chronological and Spatial Thinking

1. Students compare the present with the past, evaluating the consequences of past events and decisions and determining the lessons that were learned.
2. Students analyze how change happens at different rates at different times; understand that some aspects can change while others remain the same; and understand that change is complicated and affects not only technology and politics but also values and beliefs.
3. Students use a variety of maps and documents to interpret human movement, including major patterns of domestic and international migration, changing environmental preferences and settlement patterns, the frictions that develop between population groups, and the diffusion of ideas, technological innovations, and goods.
4. Students relate current events to the physical and human characteristics of places and regions.

Historical Research, Evidence, and Point of View

1. Students distinguish valid arguments from fallacious arguments in historical interpretations.
2. Students identify bias and prejudice in historical interpretations.
3. Students evaluate major debates among historians concerning alternative interpretations of the past, including an analysis of authors' use of evidence and the distinctions between sound generalizations and misleading oversimplifications.
4. Students construct and test hypotheses; collect, evaluate, and employ information from multiple primary and secondary sources; and apply it in oral and written presentations.

Historical Interpretation

1. Students show the connections, causal and otherwise, between particular historical events and larger social, economic, and political trends and developments.
2. Students recognize the complexity of historical causes and effects, including the limitations on determining cause and effect.
3. Students interpret past events and issues within the context in which an event unfolded rather than solely in terms of present-day norms and values.
4. Students understand the meaning, implication, and impact of historical events and recognize that events could have taken other directions.
5. Students analyze human modifications of landscapes and examine the resulting environmental policy issues.
6. Students conduct cost-benefit analyses and apply basic economic indicators to analyze the aggregate economic behavior of the U.S. economy.

What Do the Standards Mean to Me?

Think of the California History–Social Science Standards as a roadmap of learning. They tell you what you need to know and when you need to know it. The California History–Social Science Standards are specific for each grade and subject, and they cover material that you should learn and master as you take this course.

Holt, Rinehart and Winston's *American Anthem: Modern American History, California Edition* provides all of the information you need to master material listed in the California History–Social Science Standards. *American Anthem: Modern American History, California Edition* has been organized to ensure that its content, including text, features, maps, other visuals, and activities, offers complete coverage of all California History–Social Science Standards for Grade Eleven.

How Does *American Anthem* Help Me Meet the Standards?

Before you can master the standards, you must first know how to interpret them. Each History-Social Science Standard begins with a general statement that helps you identify the broader concept and subject matter being discussed.

11.4 **Students trace the rise of the United States to its role as a world power in the twentieth century.**

Standards are further organized into subcategories, or sub-standards, that support the main standard. These subcategories identify more specific information that you need to know. Standard 11.4 has six subcategories. Two are shown below.

11.4.1 List the purpose and the effects of the Open Door policy.

11.4.2 Describe the Spanish-American War and U.S. expansion in the South Pacific.

Since these are subcategories of the main standard about the rise of the Unites States as a world power, you can infer that the Open Door policy and the Spanish-American War were important factors in that rise.

How to Meet the History–Social Science Standards

- Preview the chapter. The main standards covered in the chapter always appear on the chapter opener page.
- Preview the sections. The sub-standards covered in each section always appear on the section opener page.
- As you read, recall the standards and take notes on relevant information.
- Check the standards following your study of the chapter to ensure that you have learned from the reading what you need to know.

Joshua Tree National Park

CALIFORNIA

Standards Practice and Plan

What events in American history have led to the events of today? What effect have resources, environment, and technology had on the course of American history? What can we learn from historical documents about the actions and intentions of the American people?

The California State Board of Education adopted the History–Social Science Standards to help answer these questions. The eleven standards adopted for Grade 11 highlight the outstanding people and events and the fundamental concepts of American history. You are expected to understand and meet these standards.

Standards Practice and Plan is your guide. This assessment workbook introduces you to the standards you are required to master. Use this resource to help you learn and analyze the information presented in your American history course.

Standards Practice and Plan helps you by

- **Breaking down the learning.** This workbook examines a different standard every two weeks. A practice question is presented for each day of the week. Each question allows you to explore one part of the section's standard. This format ensures that you will meet all requirements of each standard.
- **Connecting the standards to your American history textbook.** References at the end of each question direct you to relevant material in your textbook. You can use these references to find answers and review important information.
- **Using different information sources.** Each section includes questions derived from maps, charts, graphic organizers, images, and primary sources. These questions expose you to different forms of historical documentation and require you to think about historical information in a variety of ways.
- **Giving you answers.** *Standards Practice and Plan* includes an Answer Key against which you can check your mastery of American history.

WEEK 1

STANDARD 11.1 Students analyze the significant events in the founding of the nation and its attempts to realize the philosophy of government described in the Declaration of Independence.

MONDAY
HSS 11.1.1, 11.1.2

1 From which of the following Enlightenment thinkers did the Declaration of Independence adopt many of its principles? *(Chapter 2.1)*
- **A** John Locke
- **B** Jonathan Edwards
- **C** Sir Isaac Newton
- **D** Jean-Jacques Rousseau

> "We hold these truths to be self-evident, that all men are created equal, that they are endowed by their Creator with certain unalienable Rights, that among these are Life, Liberty, and the pursuit of Happiness. That to secure these rights, Governments are instituted among Men, deriving their just powers from the consent of the governed ..."
> —The Declaration of Independence, 1776

TUESDAY
HSS 11.1.1, 11.1.2

2 Social contract theory *(Chapter 2.1)*
- **A** sought to guarantee liberty by dividing the powers of government.
- **B** led to the growth of new Protestant denominations in the mid-1700s.
- **C** questioned the authority of any church to persecute those who did not accept its teachings.
- **D** held that if a government did not protect the citizens and their rights, then citizens were justified in rebelling.

WEDNESDAY
HSS 11.1.2

3 Colonists objected to the Stamp Act, the Townshend Acts, the Tea Act, and the Intolerable Acts because these policies *(Chapter 2.1)*
- **A** led to a boycott of American goods.
- **B** resulted in less government involvement from Britain.
- **C** threatened the colonies' power of self-government.
- **D** jeopardized the colonists' security and ability to settle western lands.

THURSDAY
HSS 11.1.2

4 After the Revolution, a republican form of government under the Articles of Confederation was established, but many were concerned that the Articles *(Chapter 2.2)*
- **A** divided power among too many branches.
- **B** established a weak central government with no power to impose or collect taxes.
- **C** formed a powerful central government that was too much like Britain's monarchy.
- **D** concentrated power in the national government and deprived states of the power to collect taxes and regulate trade.

FRIDAY
HSS 11.1.2

5 Both the Great Compromise and the three-fifths compromise *(Chapter 2.2)*
- **A** increased the power of the states.
- **B** balanced the needs of different states.
- **C** led to the need for another constitutional convention.
- **D** provided checks and balances on different branches of the government.

WEEK 2

 STANDARD 11.1 Students analyze the significant events in the founding of the nation and its attempts to realize the philosophy of government described in the Declaration of Independence.

MONDAY HSS 11.1.2, 11.1.3

1 Several states ratified the Constitution because of *(Chapter 2.2)*

A the promise of a Bill of Rights.

B extensive and organized lobbying by Antifederalist supporters.

C pressures exerted by delegates from North Carolina and Rhode Island.

D the promise of a strong central government that would rival that of Britain.

TUESDAY HSS 11.1.3

2 What is the significance of *Marbury* v. *Madison*? *(Chapter 2.3)*

A It upheld the president's power to appoint judges.

B It led to the formation of new positions in the judiciary branch.

C It established the Supreme Court's right to declare a law unconstitutional.

D It established the Supreme Court's right to refuse presidential appointments.

WEDNESDAY HSS 11.1.3, 11.1.4

3 Before being readmitted to the Union, southern states had to ratify the Fourteenth Amendment, which *(Chapter 4.3)*

A abolished slavery.

B emancipated slaves in the South.

C protected the voting rights of African American men.

D granted citizenship and equal protection under the laws to all persons born or naturalized in the United States.

THURSDAY HSS 11.1.4

4 Which of the following was a key feature of Radical Reconstruction under Congress? *(Chapter 4.3)*

A Black Codes

B Reconstruction Acts

C the Ten-Percent Plan

D the Freedmen's Bureau

FRIDAY HSS 11.1.4

5 This map illustrates what two important developments of the late nineteenth and early twentieth centuries? *(Chapter 5.2)*

A the expansion of the railroads and urbanization

B the expansion of trade and the adoption of time zones

C the expansion of the railroads and the adoption of time zones

D the acquisition of western territories and the adoption of time zones

WEEK 3

STANDARD 11.2 Students analyze the relationship among the rise of industrialization, large-scale rural-to-urban migration, and massive immigration from Southern and Eastern Europe.

MONDAY — HSS 11.2.1

1 What effect did industrialization have on working conditions in the United States in the 1800s? *(Chapter 5.2)*

- **A** Workers enjoyed income equality across classes.
- **B** Laborers worked eight-hour days in well-paying jobs.
- **C** Employers provided benefits to workers, such as vacation time and sick leave.
- **D** Workers labored long hours in poor conditions at low-paying jobs.

TUESDAY — HSS 11.2.1

2 What did Upton Sinclair's *The Jungle* expose? *(Chapter 6.1, 6.3)*

- **A** child labor and unsafe working conditions in the textile industry
- **B** child labor and unsafe working conditions in the mining industry
- **C** poor sanitation and unsafe working conditions in the meatpacking industry
- **D** poor sanitation and unsafe working conditions in the iron and steel industry

WEDNESDAY — HSS 11.2.2

3 This photograph of a New York street in the late 1800s shows how immigrants *(Chapter 5.3)*

- **A** migrated from urban to rural areas.
- **B** built cultural enclaves around cities.
- **C** settled in ethnic neighborhoods in cities.
- **D** integrated into existing neighborhoods and adopted local customs.

THURSDAY — HSS 11.2.3

4 Americanization refers to *(Chapter 5.1)*

- **A** programs designed to acculturate Native Americans.
- **B** laws dissolving reservations and evicting Native Americans.
- **C** the policy of concentrating reservations away from American urban centers.
- **D** a plan to forcibly remove Native Americans from all land held by the United States.

FRIDAY — HSS 11.2.4

5 Urban political machines often gained power by *(Chapter 5.3)*

- **A** changing to the gold standard.
- **B** promising to reduce immigration and competition for jobs.
- **C** organizing labor leaders and reformers to combat corruption.
- **D** offering jobs, housing, and other help to people and their families.

WEEK 4

STANDARD 11.2 Students analyze the relationship among the rise of industrialization, large-scale rural-to-urban migration, and massive immigration from Southern and Eastern Europe.

MONDAY — HSS 11.2.5

1. Corporate trusts and monopolies, such as John D. Rockefeller's Standard Oil, were extensions of business practices grounded in *(Chapter 5.2)*
   - A philanthropy.
   - B mass marketing.
   - C laissez-faire capitalism.
   - D governmental regulation.

TUESDAY — HSS 11.2.6

2. The development of which of the following products led to advances in the transportation industry in the late 1800s and early 1900s? *(Chapter 5.2)*
   - A oil and steel
   - B oil and cotton
   - C coal and steel
   - D cotton and steel

WEDNESDAY — HSS 11.2.7

3. Social Darwinists and the Social Gospel movement *(Chapter 5.2, 5.3)*
   - A worked together to address society's problems.
   - B began as responses to the settlement house movement.
   - C held conflicting views on society's obligations to the poor.
   - D required different forms of service in fulfilling religious obligations.

THURSDAY — HSS 11.2.8

4. The Populist Party made an important and lasting impact on American politics by *(Chapter 5.3)*
   - A overturning the gold standard.
   - B establishing an alternative to the two-party system.
   - C successfully backing William McKinley for president.
   - D giving voice to ordinary citizens against the power of special interests.

FRIDAY — HSS 11.2.9

5. This cartoon illustrates Teddy Roosevelt's determination to *(Chapter 6.3)*
   - A become president of the United States.
   - B break up trusts that were not in the public interest.
   - C persuade voters to embrace his Square Deal platform.
   - D discourage competition by promoting de-regulation of business.

NO MOLLY-CODDLING HERE

Week 5

STANDARD 11.3 Students analyze the role religion played in the founding of America, its lasting moral, social and political impacts, and issues regarding religious liberty.

MONDAY

1. Jonathan Edwards and George Whitefield contributed to the widespread religious revival known as *(Chapter 1.3)*
   - A the Enlightenment.
   - B Transcendentalism.
   - C the Great Awakening.
   - D the Social Gospel movement.

TUESDAY

2. The Second Great Awakening encouraged *(Chapter 3.2)*
   - A individual responsibility, a strong work ethic, and social reform.
   - B a return to traditional values and strict adherence to church rules.
   - C the codification of Christian doctrine as law at all levels of government.
   - D the establishment of new churches based on public displays of faith and denial of material wants.

WEDNESDAY

3. In the late 1800s, the settlement house movement grew largely out of *(Chapter 5.3)*
   - A the Social Gospel.
   - B social Darwinism.
   - C political machines.
   - D conspicuous consumption.

THURSDAY

4. In the 1980s Ronald Reagan became a hero of a growing movement known as the *(Chapter 22.1)*
   - A New Right.
   - B Moral Majority.
   - C Neoconservatives.
   - D New Deal Democrats.

FRIDAY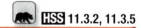

5. This cartoon illustrates one of the most dramatic conflicts between supporters of First Amendment protections and *(Chapter 10.1)*
   - A fundamentalism.
   - B social Darwinism.
   - C transcendentalism.
   - D Protestant revivalism.

GATHERING DATA FOR THE TENNESSEE TRIAL

WEEK 6

STANDARD 11.3 Students analyze the role religion played in the founding of America, its lasting moral, social and political impacts, and issues regarding religious liberty.

MONDAY — HSS 11.3.3

1. Which of the following religious groups was founded by Joseph Smith in the Burned-Over District and forced to flee persecution for its practices in the mid-1800s? *(Chapter 3.2, 3.3)*
   A Shakers
   B Quakers
   C Mormons
   D Seventh-Day Adventists

TUESDAY — HSS 11.3.3

2. The Ku Klux Klan claimed a strong religious base and persecuted not only African Americans but also *(Chapter 10.1)*
   A revivalists.
   B fundamentalists.
   C Catholics and Jews.
   D Protestants and Jews.

WEDNESDAY — HSS 11.3.4

3. Unlike earlier immigrants, most immigrants who came to the United States in the late 1800s and early 1900s *(Chapter 5.1)*
   A did not pass through Ellis Island.
   B came from northern and western Europe.
   C came from southern and eastern Europe.
   D settled in open areas where well-paying jobs were plentiful.

THURSDAY — HSS 11.3.5

4. During the 1960s the Supreme Court under Chief Justice Earl Warren *(Chapter 17.2)*
   A upheld public school segregation.
   B banned formal prayer and Bible readings in public schools.
   C ruled that legislative districts do not need equal populations.
   D denied people the right to lawyers during routine police questioning.

FRIDAY — HSS 11.3.5

5. What is the religious significance of the First Amendment? *(Chapter 2.2)*
   A It establishes an official state religion upon which laws and liberties are based.
   B It grants Congress the power to make laws regarding any religion or religious practice.
   C It grants citizens religious liberty but establishes an official state religion upon which laws are based.
   D It grants citizens religious liberty and prohibits the government from establishing an official state religion.

> "Congress shall make no law respecting an establishment of religion, or prohibiting the free exercise thereof; or abridging the freedom of speech, or of the press; or the right of the people peaceably to assemble, and to petition the Government for a redress of grievances."
> —First Amendment, United States Constitution, 1791

Week 7

 STANDARD 11.4 Students trace the rise of the United States to its role as a world power in the twentieth century.

MONDAY
HSS 11.4.1, 11.4.2, 11.4.3, 11.4.4

1 The interests of the United States in Asia, Latin America, and the Pacific islands in the nineteenth century, as shown on this map, can best be described as *(Chapter 7.1, 7.2, 7.3)*

A diplomatic.
B imperialist.
C democratic.
D commercial.

TUESDAY
HSS 11.4.1

2 Secretary of State John Hay's Open Door Policy was meant to *(Chapter 7.1)*

A isolate China and its products from the rest of the world.
B allow unrestricted Chinese immigration to the United States.
C give the United States exclusive trading privileges with China.
D give all nations, including the United States, equal trading rights in China.

WEDNESDAY
HSS 11.4.2

3 The Spanish-American War ended with the United States in control of *(Chapter 7.2)*

A Mexico.
B the Panama Canal.
C California and Texas.
D Cuba, Guam, Puerto Rico, and the Philippines.

THURSDAY
HSS 11.4.3

4 The United States' role in Panama's revolution against Columbia can best be described as *(Chapter 7.3)*

A neutral.
B protective.
C supportive.
D disapproving.

FRIDAY
HSS 11.4.4

5 Both Theodore Roosevelt's "Big Stick" diplomacy and William Taft's dollar diplomacy were designed to *(Chapter 7.3)*

A help Cuba remain independent.
B protect U.S. interests and influence in Latin America.
C increase European intervention in Latin America.
D establish permanent military bases in countries around the world.

ST16 CALIFORNIA STANDARDS PRACTICE

Week 8

 STANDARD 11.4 Students trace the rise of the United States to its role as a world power in the twentieth century.

MONDAY

1. During World War I the U.S. Supreme court issued a ruling in *Schenk* v. *United States* that *(Chapter 8.3)*
   - A expanded civil liberties.
   - B upheld limits to free speech.
   - C overturned limits to free speech.
   - D made it illegal to refuse military duty.

TUESDAY

2. To conserve food during World War I the U.S. government *(Chapter 8.3)*
   - A introduced daylight saving time.
   - B encouraged Americans to buy war bonds.
   - C created the War Industries Board.
   - D encouraged Americans to plant victory gardens.

WEDNESDAY

3. This poster, used by the Committee on Public Information to build and maintain support for the war effort, is an example of which of the following? *(Chapter 8.3)*
   - A legislation
   - B a war bond
   - C propaganda
   - D an executive order

THURSDAY

4. Which of the following events led to the end of World War II? *(Chapter 14.5)*
   - A Battle of Britain
   - B Battle of the Bulge
   - C attack on Pearl Harbor
   - D dropping of atomic bombs on Hiroshima and Nagasaki

FRIDAY

5. World War II primarily demonstrated U.S. *(Chapter 14.5, 15.1)*
   - A imperialism.
   - B isolationism.
   - C military and economic power.
   - D commitment to moral diplomacy.

WEEK 9

 STANDARD 11.5 Students analyze the major political, social, economic, technological, and cultural developments of the 1920s.

MONDAY

1. Both Warren Harding and Calvin Coolidge would most likely agree with *(Chapter 9.3)*
   - A promoting business and limiting government regulatory power.
   - B limiting big business and funding more public works projects.
   - C increasing government oversight and strictly enforcing business regulations.
   - D supporting the nation's farmers and regulating business only when it conflicts with the public interest.

TUESDAY

2. After World War I, communism and other radical ideas that threatened American norms led to the Red Scare and *(Chapter 9.1)*
   - A renewed confidence in labor unions.
   - B the start of the Bolshevik Revolution.
   - C an attack known as the Palmer Raids.
   - D greater understanding between earlier and more recent immigrants.

WEDNESDAY

3. The revival of the Ku Klux Klan and the establishment of immigration quotas in the 1920s resulted from the *(Chapter 9.1)*
   - A rise of nativism.
   - B growth of labor strife.
   - C unionization of workers.
   - D increase in production demands.

THURSDAY

4. Unlike the National Association for the Advancement of Colored People, Marcus Garvey's Universal Negro Improvement Society attempted to *(Chapter 10.2)*
   - A improve organization among African American groups.
   - B integrate African Americans and whites into one equitable society.
   - C break down barriers between African Americans and whites.
   - D promote the idea that African Americans should protect and advance their own interests without involvement from whites.

FRIDAY

5. Concerns expressed by William Allen White and others led to the passage of which of the following? *(Chapter 10.1)*
   - A Thirteenth Amendment
   - B Fourteenth Amendment
   - C Eighteenth Amendment
   - D Nineteenth Amendment

> "[I]t is the duty of the nine people who do not overdrink, as it seems to me, to give up their liberties so far as drink goes for the good not of the one man who abuses the privilege but for the ten thousands who are his potential victims. That is the whole philosophy of prohibition."
>
> —William Allen White, 1927

WEEK 10

STANDARD 11.5 Students analyze the major political, social, economic, technological, and cultural developments of the 1920s.

MONDAY — HSS 11.5.4

1. The contributions of women during World War I helped win support for the Nineteenth Amendment, which granted *(Chapter 6.4)*

   A full voting rights to women.
   B African American men the right to vote.
   C female workers the right to organize unions.
   D women the right to vote on a state-by-state basis.

TUESDAY — HSS 11.5.5

2. All of the following were renowned figures in the Harlem Renaissance except *(Chapter 10.2)*

   A Marcus Garvey.
   B Langston Hughes.
   C Zora Neale Hurston.
   D James Weldon Johnson.

WEDNESDAY — HSS 11.5.5

3. This map illustrates that the Great Migration was a mass movement of African Americans *(Chapter 10.2)*

   A from east to west.
   B from west to east.
   C from south to north.
   D from north to south.

THURSDAY — HSS 11.5.6, 11.5.7

4. In the 1920s the growth of radio, film, and the automobile helped lead to the *(Chapter 10.3)*

   A Great Depression.
   B end of World War I.
   C suffrage movement.
   D development of a common American culture.

FRIDAY — HSS 11.5.7

5. Henry Ford revolutionized the manufacturing industry by introducing which of the following? *(Chapter 11.2)*

   A the automobile
   B the assembly line
   C welfare capitalism
   D the concept of buying on credit

WEEK 11

 STANDARD 11.6 Students analyze the different explanations for the Great Depression and how the New Deal fundamentally changed the role of the federal government.

MONDAY

1 What cause for concern does this chart illustrate? *(Chapter 11.1)*

A The distribution of wealth and income were well-balanced.

B The boom of the Roaring Twenties hid great economic disparity.

C Only a small percentage of workers invested in the stock market.

D Few workers earned enough income to participate in the new consumer culture.

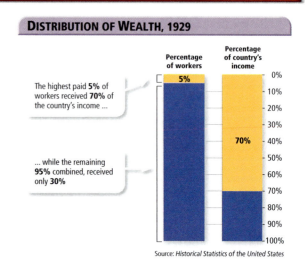

DISTRIBUTION OF WEALTH, 1929

The highest paid **5%** of workers received **70%** of the country's income …

… while the remaining **95%** combined, received only **30%**

Source: *Historical Statistics of the United States*

TUESDAY

2 In the late 1920s the Federal Reserve responded to risky stock market practices by *(Chapter 11.1)*

A making it easier for investors to buy stock on margin.

B making it more difficult for investors to buy stock on margin.

C asking corporations to make loans to investors.

D asking stockbrokers to make loans to investors.

WEDNESDAY

3 Which of the following contributed to the Great Depression? *(Chapter 11.1, 11.2)*

A labor shortages

B stock market expansion

C business and farm foreclosures

D increases in consumer spending

THURSDAY

4 Which of the following compounded the devastation of the Great Depression? *(Chapter 11.2)*

A World War II

B the Red Scare

C an influenza epidemic

D drought and dust storms in the Great Plains

FRIDAY

5 During the 1930s what action did many people who lived in the Dust Bowl states take? *(Chapter 11.2)*

A They migrated west.

B They joined labor unions.

C They went to work on the railroads.

D They withdrew their investments and moved from farms to cities.

WEEK 12

STANDARD 11.6 Students analyze the different explanations for the Great Depression and how the New Deal fundamentally changed the role of the federal government.

MONDAY — HSS 11.6.4

1 Which of the following was an important policy or program under Franklin Roosevelt's New Deal? *(Chapter 12.1)*

- **A** the Federal Reserve
- **B** Smoot-Hawley Tariff Act
- **C** Civilian Conservation Corps
- **D** the National War Labor Board

TUESDAY — HSS 11.6.4

2 One major criticism of the New Deal was that the programs *(Chapter 12.1)*

- **A** failed to alleviate unemployment.
- **B** gave too much power to the executive branch.
- **C** did not include provisions for banking reforms.
- **D** ceded too much federal decision-making to state governments.

WEDNESDAY — HSS 11.6.4

3 Social Security represented a major change in the relationship between the federal government and the citizenry because it *(Chapter 12.2)*

- **A** restructured the federal tax system.
- **B** set up a national pension and healthcare system for all American workers.
- **C** provided immediate economic relief in the form of paid jobs on public works projects.
- **D** promised a government-funded pension and unemployment insurance for many American workers.

THURSDAY — HSS 11.6.5

4 One key difference between the American Federation of Labor and the Committee for Industrial Organization was that the *(Chapter 12.2)*

- **A** CIO represented the interests of unskilled workers.
- **B** AFL represented the interests of unskilled workers.
- **C** AFL represented unions organized across broad industries.
- **D** CIO won every confrontation with American business.

FRIDAY — HSS 11.6.5

5 This graph supports the statement that the 1935 National Labor Relations Act *(Chapter 12.2)*

- **A** increased union membership.
- **B** restricted workers' right to organize.
- **C** encouraged company-sponsored unions.
- **D** discouraged the organizing of unions across industries.

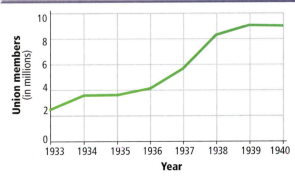

GROWTH OF UNION MEMBERSHIP, 1933–1940

Source: *Historical Statistics of the United States*

WEEK 13

STANDARD 11.7 Students analyze America's participation in World War II.

MONDAY — HSS 11.7.1

1 Which of the following events changed American public opinion in support of U.S. involvement in World War II?
(Chapter 13.3)

- **A** the occupation of France
- **B** Japan's invasion of China
- **C** the attack on Pearl Harbor
- **D** the sinking of the USS *Kearny* and the USS *Reuben James*

TUESDAY — HSS 11.7.2

2 In defeating Nazi Germany, the United States first had to
(Chapter 14.1)

- **A** invade France successfully.
- **B** win control of the Atlantic Ocean.
- **C** concentrate on the war in the Pacific Ocean.
- **D** focus on the war on the European continent.

WEDNESDAY — HSS 11.7.3

3 Who were the WASPs? *(Chapter 13.4)*

- **A** women who joined the military as nurses
- **B** women in the navy who performed clerical jobs
- **C** women who worked in the army, repairing equipment
- **D** women who joined the air force and tested and delivered aircraft

THURSDAY — HSS 11.7.4

4 What did the Atlantic Charter do?
(Chapter 13.3)

- **A** represented an American isolationist policy
- **B** committed the United States to a lend-lease program
- **C** strengthened ties between Britain and the United States
- **D** engaged the United States in a naval war with German U-boats

FRIDAY — HSS 11.7.4

5 What dilemma faced by Franklin Roosevelt does this cartoon illustrate?
(Chapter 13.3)

- **A** whether to institute a military draft
- **B** whether to fight on the side of the Allies or the Axis Powers
- **C** whether to go against public opinion and remain neutral
- **D** whether to go against public opinion and support the Allies

WEEK 14

STANDARD 11.7 Students analyze America's participation in World War II.

MONDAY   HSS 11.7.5

1 Which of the following actions taken during World War II is shown in this image?   *(Chapter 13.4)*

A the Nuremberg trials

B the capture of prisoners of war in Japan

C the use of concentration camps in Nazi Germany

D the internment of Japanese Americans by the United States

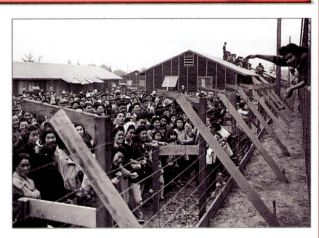

TUESDAY   HSS 11.7.5

2 During World War II, the icon Rosie the Riveter came to represent women   *(Chapter 13.4)*

A working in industry.

B serving in the military.

C volunteering to make uniforms.

D distributing propaganda to keep up support for the war.

WEDNESDAY   HSS 11.7.6

3 During World War II, many factories in the United States   *(Chapter 13.4)*

A shut down production.

B imported war supplies from abroad.

C shifted from production of consumer goods to war supplies.

D increased consumer goods production to distract people at home.

THURSDAY   HSS 11.7.7

4 Who made the decision to drop the atomic bomb on Hiroshima in 1945?   *(Chapter 14.5)*

A Dwight Eisenhower

B Franklin Roosevelt

C Harry Truman

D Woodrow Wilson

FRIDAY   HSS 11.7.8

5 After World War II, the Marshall Plan   *(Chapter 15.1)*

A opened Japan and China to U.S. trade.

B enabled Western European countries to buy goods from American factories.

C established exclusive trading privileges between Britain and the United States.

D set up a system of mutual exchange between the United States and the Soviet Union.

Week 15

STANDARD 11.8 Students analyze the economic boom and social transformation of post–World War II America.

MONDAY — HSS 11.8.1

1. The GI Bill provided which of the following for returning veterans? *(Chapter 15.2)*

A cash bonuses
B employment
C financial assistance to rent apartments
D financial assistance to attend college and get advanced job training.

TUESDAY — HSS 11.8.2

2. In the 1950s migrants helped the population of California *(Chapter 16.3)*

A increase slowly.
B decrease slowly.
C increase rapidly.
D decrease rapidly.

WEDNESDAY — HSS 11.8.3

3. The Taft-Hartley Act, which was passed by Congress over President Truman's veto, gave the president the power to *(Chapter 15.2)*

A regulate union organizing.
B arbitrate disputes between unions and employers.
C disband unions when they conflict with economic growth.
D stop labor strikes when they conflict with national interest.

THURSDAY — HSS 11.8.4

4. In the 1950s, President Eisenhower warned that the arms industry in the United States had *(Chapter 16.2)*

A adjusted slowly to the demands of modern war.
B become a permanent, vast military-industrial complex.
C fallen behind the technological advancements of the Soviet arms industry.
D focused too much on technological development and not enough on maintaining conventional arms.

FRIDAY — HSS 11.8.4

5. Lyndon Johnson's Great Society primarily required more federal funding for *(Chapter 17.3)*

A social programs.
B international aid.
C defense initiatives.
D economic stimulus measures.

Major Great Society Programs

Year Enacted	Legislation	Purpose and Provisions
1964	Economic Opportunity Act	created the Job Corps, VISTA, and eight other programs to fight the "war on poverty"
1964	Tax Reduction Act	cut income tax rates up to 30%, with the greatest cuts going to lower-income Americans
1964	Civil Rights Act	outlawed discrimination in housing, employment, and public accomodations; authorized federal government to enforce desegregation
1964	Wilderness Preservation Act	protected 9.1 million acres of national forest from development
1965	Elementary and Secondary School Act	provided aid to school systems based on number of students from low-income homes
1965	Social Security Amendments	established Medicare and Medicaid
1965	Voting Rights Act	ended the requirement that voters pass literacy tests and allowed federal supervision of voter registration
1965	Omnibus Housing Act	provided housing for low-income Americans
1965	Water Quality Act	required states to clean up rivers and lakes
1965	Clean Air Act Amendments	established exhaust emission standards for new motor vehicles
1965	Higher Education Act	provided scholarships and low-interest loans for college students
1966	National Traffic and Motor Vehicle Safety Act	established safety standards for automobiles and tires
1967	Air Quality Act	set guidelines on air pollution and increased the federal government's power to enforce clean air standards

WEEK 16

STANDARD 11.8 Students analyze the economic boom and social transformation of post-World War II America.

MONDAY — HSS 11.8.5

1 In 1964, in the interest of preventing the spread of Communism in Vietnam, the Tonkin Gulf Resolution expanded presidential powers by *(Chapter 19.1)*

  A stripping Congress of its power to declare war.
  B giving the president the power to declare war even in peacetime.
  C making the president the commander-in-chief of the armed forces.
  D allowing the president to make war in Southeast Asia without a Congressional declaration of war.

TUESDAY — HSS 11.8.6

2 An accident at Three Mile Island in Pennsylvania brought attention to the *(Chapter 21.3)*

  A hazards of toxic waste.
  B need for energy conservation.
  C safety risks of nuclear power.
  D nation's dependence on fossil fuels.

WEDNESDAY — HSS 11.8.7

3 In the mid-1950s a new vaccine developed by Jonas Salk stopped outbreaks of which of the following diseases? *(Chapter 16.3)*

  A influenza
  B polio
  C smallpox
  D tuberculosis

THURSDAY — HSS 11.8.7

4 In the 1980s Steve Jobs and Steve Wozniak of Apple Computer launched the computer revolution by *(Chapter 22.4, Issue 6)*

  A building computer networks.
  B creating the first computer chips.
  C developing user-friendly computer software.
  D making personal computers that were small enough to be used at home.

FRIDAY — HSS 11.8.8

5 This image shows a hit of the new 1950s popular culture introduced by *(Chapter 16.3)*

  A cable.
  B the television.
  C radio broadcasting.
  D Hollywood moviemaking.

WEEK 17

 STANDARD 11.9 Students analyze U.S. foreign policy since World War II.

MONDAY HSS 11.9.1

1. The formation of the World Bank, the International Monetary Fund, and the General Agreement on Tariffs and Trade can *best* be considered responses to
   (Chapter 15.2, Issue 7)

   A economic disparity between world regions.
   B the need to rebuild European nations after World War II.
   C ideological conflicts between communist and capitalist nations.
   D instabilities in the world economy that contributed to worldwide depression and warfare.

TUESDAY HSS 11.9.2

2. In 1949 twelve nations, including the United States, formed the North Atlantic Treaty Organization (NATO) in reaction to the *(Chapter 15.1)*

   A Korean War.
   B Cuban missile crisis.
   C Soviet blockade of Berlin.
   D formation of the Warsaw Pact.

WEDNESDAY HSS 11.9.3

3. Aid given by the United States under the Truman Doctrine and Marshall Plan was part of a broader Cold War policy of *(Chapter 15.1)*

   A détente.
   B containment.
   C brinkmanship.
   D dollar diplomacy.

THE MARSHALL PLAN

Purpose: A U.S. financial aid program to rebuild the economies of European countries in order to create stable conditions for democratic governments.

Total amount of aid: $13.4 billion

Number of countries that received aid: 17

Countries that received the most aid: Great Britain, France, and Italy

THURSDAY HSS 11.9.3

4. McCarthyism was empowered primarily by *(Chapter 15.3)*

   A Ethel and Julius Rosenberg.
   B propaganda films made in Hollywood.
   C public fear of the spread of communism.
   D the conflict surrounding the Vietnam War.

FRIDAY HSS 11.9.3

5. The Bay of Pigs invasion was orchestrated by the CIA to *(Chapter 17.1)*

   A support the French in Vietnam.
   B overthrow Fidel Castro in Cuba.
   C regain control of the Suez Canal.
   D evict the North Koreans from South Korea.

WEEK 18

STANDARD 11.9 Students analyze U.S. foreign policy since World War II.

MONDAY — HSS 11.9.4

1 Which of the following events prompted the formation of the National Aeronautics and Space Administration (NASA)? *(Chapter 16.2)*

A Soviet launching of Sputnik
B Soviet testing of a hydrogen bomb
C development of intercontinental ballistic missiles
D American detonation of a hydrogen bomb in the Marshall Islands

TUESDAY — HSS 11.9.4

2 Reduced oil production after the 1979 Iranian revolution caused which of the following U.S. domestic problems? *(Chapter 21.3)*

A mass protests
B soaring inflation
C the Watergate scandal
D environmental contamination

WEDNESDAY — HSS 11.9.5

3 This quotation about the end of the Cold War refers to the *(Chapter 22.3)*

A velvet revolution.
B fall of the Berlin Wall.
C Soviet withdrawal from Afghanistan.
D meltdown at the Chernobyl nuclear plant.

> "And then I hear the noise. Pick, pick, pick. Chuck, chuck, chuck. Growing louder and louder as hundreds of hammers and chisels attack the wall, taking it down chip by chip. I laugh and laugh? and cry at the same time."
> —BBC reporter Tim Weber, November 9, 1999

THURSDAY — HSS 11.9.6

4 Which of the following statements best describes the United States' interest in Iraq's invasion of Kuwait? *(Chapter 22.3)*

A Kuwait formed a nonmilitary buffer between Iraq and Iran.
B Iraq had rich supplies of petroleum on which the United States depended.
C Iran, Iraq, and Kuwait were allies, making it difficult for the United States to choose sides.
D Kuwait had rich supplies of petroleum on which the United States and its allies depended.

FRIDAY — HSS 11.9.7

5 Critics of the North American Free Trade Agreement (NAFTA) primarily contended that *(Chapter 23.1, Issue 7)*

A trade between Mexico and the United States would decline.
B Mexican immigration into the United States would increase.
C American businesses would not be able to sell more goods in Mexico and Canada.
D lower wages and fewer regulations in Mexican factories would drive American factories out of business.

WEEK 19

STANDARD 11.10 Students analyze the development of federal civil rights and voting rights.

MONDAY — HSS 11.10.1

1 During World War II, African Americans *(Chapter 13.4)*

- **A** did not serve in the military.
- **B** served in the military in segregated units.
- **C** served in the military in noncombat capacities only.
- **D** served in the military without discrimination.

TUESDAY — HSS 11.10.2

2 What was significant about the 1896 Supreme Court decision in *Plessy* v. *Ferguson*? *(Chapter 5.3)*

- **A** It legalized segregation and established the "separate but equal" standard.
- **B** It declared Jim Crow laws unconstitutional and led to voting rights reform.
- **C** It legalized slavery in all United States territories and contributed to sectional conflict.
- **D** It overturned the "separate but equal" standard and made segregation illegal in public schools.

WEDNESDAY — HSS 11.10.3

3 This 1963 photo shows Alabama Governor George Wallace trying to prevent the *(Chapter 18.2)*

- **A** desegregation of public schools.
- **B** registration of African American voters.
- **C** desegregation of the public transportation system.
- **D** desegregation of institutions of higher education.

THURSDAY — HSS 11.10.4

4 The arrest of Rosa Parks in 1955 led to the *(Chapter 18.1)*

- **A** Greensboro sit-ins.
- **B** Albany Movement.
- **C** March on Washington.
- **D** Montgomery bus boycott.

FRIDAY — HSS 11.10.4

5 James Farmer of CORE and Martin Luther King Jr. of SCLC drew on what principle of Mohandas Gandhi when organizing the civil rights movement? *(Chapter 18.2)*

- **A** political action
- **B** massive resistance
- **C** nonviolent resistance
- **D** public accommodations

WEEK 20

 STANDARD 11.10 Students analyze the development of federal civil rights and voting rights.

MONDAY

1 During what event in 1963 did Martin Luther King Jr. give this speech? *(Chapter 18.2)*

A Selma march
B Freedom Rides
C March on Washington
D Birmingham campaign

> "I have a dream that one day this nation will rise up and live out the true meaning of its creed: 'We hold these truths to be self-evident: that all men are created equal.' ... I have a dream that my four little children will one day live in a nation where they will not be judged by the color of their skin, but the content of their character. I have a dream today!"
> —Martin Luther King, Jr., August 28, 1963

TUESDAY
 HSS 11.10.5

2 Which of the following groups played a large role in organizing the actions of the civil rights movement in the 1950s and early 1960s? *(Chapter 18.2)*

A workers and voters
B parents and teachers
C students and ministers
D lawyers and politicians

WEDNESDAY

3 The voter registration efforts of Freedom Summer followed the passage of the *(Chapter 18.3)*

A Civil Rights Act of 1964.
B Voting Rights Act of 1965.
C Equal Rights Amendment.
D Twenty-fourth Amendment.

THURSDAY
 HSS 11.10.6

4 Lyndon Johnson strongly supported the Civil Rights Act of 1964, which *(Chapter 18.2)*

A made harming civil rights workers a federal crime.
B made segregation in institutions of higher education illegal.
C eliminated the use of literacy tests for voting registration.
D banned discrimination in employment and in public accommodations.

FRIDAY

5 When did women in the United States win the right to vote nationwide? *(Chapter 6.2)*

A 1868
B 1896
C 1920
D 1965

Week 21

STANDARD 11.11 Students analyze the major social problems and domestic policy issues in contemporary American society.

MONDAY

1. In the 1980s the United States revised its immigration policy and *(Chapter 22.4, Issue 1)*

A lowered legal immigration limits.

B closed the Mexican-American border to immigration.

C put a hold on granting legal status to immigrants.

D strengthened penalties on employers who knowingly hired illegal workers.

TUESDAY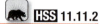

2. In a 1964 speech Lyndon Johnson framed his Great Society as *(Chapter 17.3, Issue 4)*

A a new era of space exploration.

B an end to poverty and racial injustice.

C a foreign policy based on intervention and free trade.

D a return to conservative economics and family values.

WEDNESDAY

3. The Reaganomics of the 1980s emphasized *(Chapter 22.1)*

A supply-side economics.

B corporate tax increases.

C reduced military spending.

D more federal spending on social programs.

THURSDAY

4. Which of the following was an important political gain made by women in the 1980s? *(Chapter 22.4)*

A the proportional increase in women's voting

B the proportional decrease in women's voting

C the rejection by the Senate of Sandra Day O'Connor as a Supreme Court justice

D the swearing-in of Geraldine Ferraro as vice president of the United States

FRIDAY

5. Which of the following U.S. presidents, who invoked executive privilege to protect himself during a scandal, is shown in this image? *(Chapter 21.2)*

A Bill Clinton

B Gerald Ford

C Richard Nixon

D Ronald Reagan

Speaking of sanctuaries...

ST30 CALIFORNIA STANDARDS PRACTICE

WEEK 22

 STANDARD 11.11 Students analyze the major social problems and domestic policy issues in contemporary American society.

MONDAY HSS 11.11.5

1 Who established the Environmental Protection Agency? *(Chapter 21.2)*
- A Jimmy Carter
- B Bill Clinton
- C Richard Nixon
- D Theodore Roosevelt

TUESDAY HSS 11.11.5

2 Which of the following best summarizes the modern land use debate? *(Issue 3)*
- A how to commercialize preservation and conservation efforts
- B how to exploit available resources and reduce government regulation
- C how to reduce greenhouse gases to restore land tracts to a pristine, undeveloped condition
- D how to balance environmental integrity, resource conservation, and commercial and residential development

WEDNESDAY HSS 11.11.6

3 Bill Clinton's 1996 welfare reform plan primarily resulted from *(Chapter 23.1)*
- A economic recession.
- B perceptions about the abuse of the welfare system.
- C the Republican Party's Contract with America.
- D Democratic defeats in the 1994 mid-term elections.

THURSDAY  HSS 11.11.6, 11.11.7

4 Which of the following has George W. Bush cited as an impending crisis resulting from the graying of the American population? *(Chapter 23.1, 23.4, Issue 4)*
- A declining work force
- B failure of the Social Security system
- C inadequate prescription drug coverage
- D collapse of the private healthcare industry

FRIDAY  HSS 11.11.7

5 What does this cartoon imply about the U.S. government's attitude toward international migration? *(Issue 1)*
- A Migrants are not welcome.
- B Migrants searching for opportunity and freedom are welcome.
- C Migrants can come to fill certain jobs but they should not expect to stay and become citizens.
- D Migrants are encouraged to come so long as they are willing to work.

Answer Key

WEEK 1
1. A
2. D
3. C
4. B
5. B

WEEK 2
1. A
2. C
3. D
4. B
5. C

WEEK 3
1. D
2. C
3. C
4. A
5. D

WEEK 4
1. C
2. A
3. C
4. D
5. B

WEEK 5
1. C
2. A
3. A
4. A
5. A

WEEK 6
1. C
2. C
3. C
4. B
5. D

WEEK 7
1. B
2. D
3. D
4. C
5. B

WEEK 8
1. B
2. D
3. C
4. D
5. C

WEEK 9
1. A
2. C
3. A
4. D
5. C

WEEK 10
1. A
2. A
3. C
4. D
5. B

WEEK 11
1. B
2. B
3. C
4. D
5. D

WEEK 12
1. C
2. B
3. D
4. B
5. A

WEEK 13
1. C
2. B
3. D
4. C
5. D

WEEK 14
1. D
2. A
3. C
4. C
5. B

WEEK 15
1. D
2. C
3. D
4. B
5. A

WEEK 16
1. D
2. C
3. B
4. D
5. B

WEEK 17
1. D
2. C
3. B
4. C
5. B

WEEK 18
1. A
2. B
3. B
4. D
5. D

WEEK 19
1. B
2. A
3. D
4. D
5. C

WEEK 20
1. C
2. C
3. D
4. D
5. C

WEEK 21
1. D
2. B
3. A
4. A
5. C

WEEK 22
1. C
2. D
3. B
4. B
5. C

Skills Handbook

To maximize your study and enjoyment of U.S. history, use the Skills Handbook to review and practice a variety of Reading, Social Studies, and Reading Like a Historian skills.

Reading Skills

Becoming an Active Reader by Dr. Kylene Beers	H2
Building Your Vocabulary	H4
Identifying Main Ideas and Details	H5
Summarizing	H6
Making Inferences	H7
Sequencing	H8
Identifying Cause and Effect	H9
Comparing and Contrasting	H10
Identifying Problem and Solution	H11
Drawing Conclusions	H12
Making Generalizations	H13

Social Studies Skills

Interpreting Time Lines	H14
Interpreting Charts	H15
Interpreting Pie and Bar Graphs	H16
Interpreting Line Graphs	H17
Interpreting Infographics	H18
Interpreting Movement Maps	H19
Interpreting Historical Maps	H20
Interpreting Cartograms	H21
Analyzing Costs and Benefits	H22
Evaluating Information on the Internet	H23

Reading Like a Historian

Major Historical Concepts	H24
Themes of History	H26
Analyzing Primary Sources	H28
Interpreting Visuals	H30
Interpreting Political Cartoons	H31
Interpreting Literature as Historical Evidence	H32
Recognizing Bias	H33
Evaluating Sources	H34
Analyzing Secondary Sources	H35
Analyzing Bias in Historical Interpretation	H37
Evaluating Historical Interpretation	H38
Analyzing Alternative Interpretations of the Past	H39
Making Oral Presentations	H40
Making Written Presentations	H41

California Standards

The content in this Skills Handbook correlates to the California Historical Analysis skills standards. The California Standards covered in the Skills Handbook are abbreviated as follows:
Chronological and Spatial Thinking–CS 1, CS 2, CS 3
Historical Research, Evidence, and Point of View–HR 1, HR 2, HR 3, HR 4
Historical Interpretation–HI 1, HI 3, HI 4, HI 6

A mural showing the construction of a dam

Becoming an Active Reader

by Dr. Kylene Beers

Words surround us. In fact, it's unlikely that you can escape written words during a typical day. Each day, you see printed words in books, magazines, and newspapers; on television and the Internet; at home and in shops and restaurants; and along roads and interstates. Just as you are doing now, every day and in almost every place, you are reading. But just as words can be found in different places, so too can words be used for different purposes. Some words are used to educate, others to inform, and still others to entertain. You will read a textbook such as this one differently from how you would read an advertisement for a new video game or a letter from a friend.

Because you read material differently depending on your purpose for reading, it is important to learn and use various skills and strategies to improve your recognition and comprehension of material. In this Handbook, there are opportunities to learn reading skills that you can master and use throughout *American Anthem* to gain greater understanding of your reading.

❶ Key Terms and People At the beginning of each section you will find a list of terms, people, and events that you will need to know. Watch for these words as you read.

❷ Reading Focus and Reading Check The Reading Focus questions act as a type of outline for each section, and the Reading Check questions offer opportunities to assess what you have learned as you go.

❸ Academic Vocabulary When we use a word that is important in all classes, not just in social studies, we define it in the margin under the heading Academic Vocabulary. Because you will see these academic words in other texts, you will benefit by learning what the words mean while reading this book.

Read Like a Skilled Reader

How can you become a more skilled reader? For starters, you first need to *think* about how to become a better reader. You also can use the following ideas and strategies.

Skilled readers . . .
- Preview what they are supposed to read before they begin reading. They look for titles of chapters and sections, listings of main ideas and focus questions, key terms and information in the margin such as Academic Vocabulary, and visuals such as charts, graphs, maps, and photographs.
- Construct tables or K-W-L charts into which they organize ideas from the reading. They write notes in the tables or charts as they read.
- Use clues from the text, such as the signal words shown below, to help determine or cement understanding.
Sequencing words: *first, second, third, before, after, sooner, later, next, then, following that, earlier, finally*
Cause and effect words: *because, so, since, due to, as a result of, the reason for, therefore, brought about, led to, thus, consequently*
Comparison and contrast words: *likewise, similarly, also, as well as, unlike, however, on the other hand*

Read Like an Active Reader

Active readers know that it is up to them to figure out what the text means. Here are some steps you can take to become an active and successful reader.

Predict what will happen next on the basis of what already has happened in the text. When your predictions do not match what happens in the text, reread to clarify meaning.

Question what is happening as you read. Constantly ask yourself why events happen, what certain ideas mean, and what causes events to occur.

Summarize smaller parts of a chapter. Do not try to summarize an entire chapter! Instead, read some of the text and summarize. Then move on.

Connect events in the text to what you already know or have read.

Clarify your understanding by pausing occasionally to ask questions and check for meaning. You may need to reread to clarify or read further to collect more information to gain understanding.

Visualize people, places, and events in the text. Envision events or places by drawing maps, making charts, or taking notes about what you are reading.

Building Your Vocabulary

As you know, skilled readers implement various strategies and use the text itself to answer questions and clarify meaning. Becoming a skilled reader means that you understand not only how ideas relate but also the words that shape the ideas.

Within this textbook, there are two main types of words. The first, academic words, are words that are important in all classes, not just in social studies. Academic words are found in the margin of most sections under the heading Academic Vocabulary. A second type includes words used primarily in social studies. A sampling of both types appears in the chart below.

By understanding the prefixes, suffixes, roots, and **etymologies,** or origins, of words, you can gain greater understanding of words and how they are related to one another. You can see such relationships by grouping previously unfamiliar words in a notebook, on note cards, or on a word wall.

A **word wall** is just what it sounds like it is—a wall of words. Each day, students add words to a wall, grouping them alphabetically or in categories. Over the course of a school year, a word wall becomes like a large dictionary, with words attached to a wall, to a whiteboard, or to a bulletin board.

Academic Word/Definition	Etymology
authority—firm self-assurance	from the Latin *auctoritas,* meaning "opinion, decision, power"
federal—national	from the Latin *foedus,* meaning "compact" or "league"
hypothesis—an idea that is based on facts and is used as a basis for reasoning	from the Greek *hypotithenai,* meaning "to put under, suppose"
interpret—to understand in light of circumstances	from Latin *interpretari* and *interpres,* meaning "agent, negotiator, interpreter"
revolution—a drastic and far-reaching change	from the Latin *revolvere,* meaning "to revolve or roll back"
technique—method	from the Greek *technikos,* meaning "technical"

Social Studies Word/Definition	Prefix/Suffix
civilization—the culture of a particular time or place	Suffix *–ation,* meaning "action" or "resulting state"
century—a period of 100 years	Prefix *cent,* meaning "hundred"
democracy—governmental rule by the people, usually through majority rule	Prefix *demo,* meaning "people"
geography—the study of Earth's physical and cultural features	Prefix *geo,* meaning "Earth"; suffix *graph,* meaning "to write, draw"
independence—the state of being free from rule	Prefix *in,* meaning "not"; root *depend,* meaning "to need"; suffix *–ence,* meaning "action," "state," or "process"
society—a group of people who share common traditions	Prefix *soci,* meaning "to join," "companions"

READING SKILL

Identifying Main Idea and Details

Define the Skill

The **main idea** is the central thought in a passage. It is general and conveys the key concept that the author wants you to know. The main idea can come at the beginning, middle, or end of a passage, though you usually find it near the beginning. The main idea can be one or two sentences and can be implied or directly stated.

Details are facts that support or explain the main idea. Details are specific and provide additional information, such as the *who, what, when, where, why,* and *how.* These include facts, statistics, examples, explanations, and descriptions.

Learn the Skill

Use the following strategies to identify main ideas and details in the reading.

1 Identify the topic by examining the title or other headings.
A section heading usually describes the topic.

2 Find the topic sentence that summarizes the passage's main idea.
Then restate the main idea in your own words.

Life in Colonial America

Early British settlers and newcomers from many countries were creating a new American culture. As Crèvecoeur had noticed, it was not British or European, but something new.

Colonial cities Colonial cities were lively, exciting places. Some had paved streets and sidewalks lit by oil lamps. Ships from foreign ports were anchored in the harbors. People waited eagerly for letters from relatives and the latest British newspapers and magazines, with gossip and drawings of new fashions.

Many colonial cities had libraries, bookshops, and impressive public buildings. City dwellers could go to plays or concerts. They shopped in markets for country produce and luxury goods from Europe. Schools taught music, dancing, drawing, and painting.

3 Look for details that support the main idea.
Supporting details usually follow the main idea and provide more information about it.

Apply the Skill

1. Identify the main idea of the passage and restate it in your own words.
2. What details support the main idea?
3. How do the details add to the main idea?

SKILLS HANDBOOK **H5**

READING SKILL

Summarizing

Define the Skill

Summarizing is the process of condensing what you read into a briefer, easier-to-understand format. A good summary should include only a passage's main ideas and its most important supporting details. When summarizing, remember to use your own words. Knowing how to summarize can help you understand and recall the main ideas of what you read.

Learn the Skill

Use the following strategies to summarize the reading.

1 Identify main ideas in the passage.
Often, a main idea is located at the beginning of a passage or a paragraph.

2 Look for key supporting details.
Include only the most important details in the summary.

> **Different worlds** The economic differences between the primarily industrial North and the primarily agricultural South led to even greater differences between the two regions. Trade and industry encouraged urbanization, and so cities grew in the North much more than in the South. Moreover, the Industrial Revolution and the revolutions in transportation and communication had the greatest impact on the North, where new technology was seized by businesses in pursuit of efficiency and growth.
>
> By contrast, in the South, after the widespread use of the cotton gin, there was relatively little in the way of technological development. Many Southerners saw little use in labor-saving devices, for example, when they had an ample supply of enslaved people to do their bidding.

3 Ask questions and look up unfamiliar words.
Then restate the passage's main idea and most important details in your own words.

Apply the Skill

1. What is the main idea of the second paragraph? How do you know?
2. What details support the main idea in the second paragraph?
3. Write a brief summary of the above passage, including only the main ideas and most important details.

H6 SKILLS HANDBOOK

READING SKILL
Making Inferences

Define the Skill

Inferences are implied, or unstated, ideas drawn from details in the reading. Making inferences means using clues in the text to connect implied ideas with stated facts and your own prior knowledge and common sense. Learning how to make inferences will help you gain greater understanding about particular historical people, places, and events from the reading.

Learn the Skill

Use the following strategies to make inferences about the reading.

1 Identify main ideas and details. Note stated facts and information in the reading.

2 Identify implied ideas in the text. What ideas are suggested but not directly stated in the reading? Statistics and opinionated language can lead to implied understanding.

> The vote in November 1860 was almost completely along sectional lines. Lincoln won every northern state—although he and Douglas split the electoral vote in New Jersey. In the South, Breckinridge and Bell split the vote, with the Lower South going entirely to Breckinridge. What was troubling, however, was that the split in the Democratic Party allowed Lincoln to be elected president with less than 40 percent of the popular vote. Even more worrisome was the fact that of the nearly 2 million votes Lincoln received, only 26,000 came from slave states.
>
> Many Northerners celebrated Lincoln's victory. "The great revolution has finally taken place," one free-soiler wrote. "The country has once and for all thrown off the domination of the slaveholders." Many Southerners looked at the results with concern. "A party founded on the ... hatred of African slavery is now the controlling power," the *New Orleans Delta* warned the slaveholding South.

3 Compare stated and unstated ideas with your prior knowledge. Use facts from the reading, your common sense, and what you already know about a topic or an event to make a valid inference about it.

Apply the Skill

1. From a national perspective, what was troubling about Lincoln's election in 1860?
2. What can you infer about the effect of Lincoln's election on the future of the South?
3. Using the reading and your prior knowledge, explain the effect that multiple candidates can have on a general election.

SKILLS HANDBOOK **H7**

READING SKILL

Sequencing

Define the Skill

By **sequencing** events in chronological, or time order, you can gain greater and more accurate understanding of them. Learning to sequence also can help you understand relationships among events, including how a past event may influence a pending one and eventually lead to a future outcome.

Learn the Skill

Use the following strategies to sequence the reading.

1 Examine all text and visuals for specific dates. Times of the day, seasons of the year, and people's ages are helpful in determining the specific sequence of events, which is known as absolute chronology.

2 Look for words signal. Clue words such as *by, in, after, first, last, before, next, then, soon,* and *finally* help indicate the general sequence of events, which is known as relative chronology.

Carnegie and Steel Andrew Carnegie lived a true rags-to-riches story. Born in 1835 in Scotland to poor parents, Carnegie immigrated to the United States when he was 12. At age 17, he took a job with the Pennsylvania Railroad. He advanced quickly and began investing in the iron, oil, railroad, and telegraph industries. He soon founded his own company and rose to the top of the steel business.

Carnegie held down costs by using vertical integration, buying supplies in bulk, and producing items in large quantities. By 1899 the Carnegie Steel Company dominated the American steel industry. In 1901 Carnegie sold the company to banker J.P. Morgan for $480 million. After retiring, Carnegie began to devote his time to philanthropy, or charity.

3 Identify events that occurred at the same time. Words such as *while, meanwhile,* and *during* signal the occurrence of simultaneous events.

Apply the Skill

1. In what year did Carnegie take a job with the Pennsylvania Railroad? How long after that did he build Carnegie Steel Company into the nation's dominant steel business?
2. To what cause did Carnegie devote himself after his retirement?
3. Use information from the reading to produce a time line of significant events from Carnegie's life.

READING SKILL
Identifying Cause and Effect

Define the Skill

By using **cause and effect,** you can determine why certain events occurred and whether events are related and, if so, how they are related.

A cause is an action that makes another event happen. Often, a cause will be directly stated in the text, but sometimes it will be implied. An effect is something that happens as a result of a cause. One cause may have more than one effect. Similarly, one effect may have more than one cause. Identifying causes and effects can help you better understand what you read.

Learn the Skill

Use the following strategies to identify cause and effect in the reading.

1 Identify the causes of events. Look for a reason or reasons that prompted a given event to occur. Words such as *since, because, so, therefore,* and *due to* can signal a causal relationship among events.

2 Identify the effects of events. Look for phrases and clue words that indicate consequences, such as *thus, brought about, led to, consequently,* and *as a result.*

3 Connect causes and effects. Consider why certain causes led to an event, and why the event turned out as it did. Remember that an event can be both a cause and an effect.

War Breaks Out

Since Russia had promised to protect Serbian Slavs, the Russian army quickly began to mobilize, or prepare for war. Germany viewed Russia's mobilization as an act of aggression against its ally Austria-Hungary and thus declared war on Russia. Then Germany declared war on France, Russia's ally. All-out war was about to begin.

The Germans take Belgium Germany made the first move in the war, following the Schlieffen Plan. On August 14, 1914, German troops crossed the German border into the neutral country of Belgium. Kaiser Wilhelm II believed that he had to catch Belgium and France by surprise. Germany's invasion of Belgium drew a new, powerful nation into the conflict. Because the British had planned to defend Belgium, Great Britain declared war on Germany.

Apply the Skill

1. Why did the Russian army begin to mobilize for war?
2. What was the effect of Russia's mobilization? Explain.
3. List an effect of Germany's decision to invade the neutral nation of Belgium.

READING SKILL

Comparing and Contrasting

Define the Skill

You usually can find the greater meaning of certain time periods, people, places, and events by **comparing and contrasting** information and details from them. Comparing involves looking at both the similarities and differences between two or more people, places, or events. Contrasting means examining only the differences between them. Learning to compare and contrast effectively can give you a deeper contextual understanding of the reading.

Learn the Skill

Use the following strategies in comparing and contrasting parts of the reading.

1 Identify similarities in the reading.
Words such as *also, both, all, like, likewise, similar,* and *as* can signal comparison between people, places, and events.

2 Identify differences in the reading.
Words such as *unlike, different, but, however, not, though, only,* and *while* can indicate differences between people, places, and events.

The Effects of the Crash

In the aftermath of the crash, American business and political leaders rushed to calm the panic and reassure the nation. One business leader wrote optimistically in the days following Black Tuesday, "The recent collapse of stock market prices has no significance as regards the real wealth of the American people as a whole." President Hoover <u>also</u> downplayed the effects of the crash. He and many others firmly believed that the economy would soon recover from the shock and return to prosperity.

The impact on individuals No one denied, <u>however</u>, that the stock market collapse had ruined countless individual investors. Some had lost years of gains. Many saw huge fortunes disappear before their eyes.

Margin buyers were particularly hard hit. When stock prices began to fall, brokers demanded that they pay back the borrowed money. To "make" these margin calls, investors were forced to sell their shares for far less than they had paid for them. Some lost their savings trying to make up the difference.

3 Analyze the information.
Identify relationships between similarities and differences in the text. What do they tell you about a topic in a big-picture sense?

Apply the Skill

1. How did President Hoover's initial reaction to the stock market crash compare to the reactions of other business and political leaders?
2. What did all parties agree was an effect of the stock market collapse?
3. Which group of investors was hit hardest by the stock market collapse? Explain.

READING SKILL

Identifying Problem and Solution

Define the Skill

By **identifying problem and solution,** you can better understand the challenges that people have faced over time and the means by which they have resolved such difficulties. Learning to effectively identify problems and solutions is a valuable skill that you can apply to your understanding of history.

Learn the Skill

Use the following strategies to identify problems and solutions in the reading.

1 Identify the problem. Note the problem to be solved. Some problems are directly stated, while others are not.

2 List all possible solutions to it. Because there is usually more than one way to solve a problem, identify and weigh all of the alternatives. Then consider the advantages and disadvantages of each.

3 Evaluate the chosen solution. Later, use what you know about the topic and your own common sense to evaluate a solution's effectiveness.

> ### Trade and economic development
>
> World War II had raised a number of concerns about the financial relationships between countries. These problems had helped bring about the Great Depression. Now they threatened to limit trade and create conflict between nations. Many leaders hoped that solving these problems would lead to greater prosperity around the world. This, in turn, would promote peace.
>
> Even before the war was over, representatives of many of the world's great powers met at a conference in Bretton Woods, New Hampshire. Out of this conference came an agreement to create two organizations—the **World Bank** and the **International Monetary Fund (IMF)**. Both began operating in 1947.
>
> The World Bank aimed to help poor countries build their economies. It provided grants of money and loans to help with projects that could provide jobs and wealth.
>
> Economic policy was the focus of the IMF. The IMF was designed to encourage economic policies that promoted international trade.

Apply the Skill

1. What problems did world leaders identify after World War II?
2. What solution did world leaders offer to these problems?
3. What did world leaders hope to accomplish by solving the problem?

SKILLS HANDBOOK H11

READING SKILL

Drawing Conclusions

Define the Skill

Historical writing often features cause-and-effect relationships between and among events. In some cases, however, outcomes in the text are implied. In such instances, you can use facts and your own knowledge and experience to **draw conclusions** about the reading. In drawing conclusions, you analyze the reading and form opinions or make judgments about its meaning.

Learn the Skill

Use the following strategies to draw conclusions from the reading.

1 Identify the main idea and supporting details. Read the passage carefully to find clue words and establish meaning.

2 Connect the reading and your prior knowledge. Look for connections between stated facts, implied ideas, and what you already know about the topic.

Creating the Great Society Now that he was an elected president, Johnson pushed even harder for his plans. On inauguration day, he told aides at an inaugural ball, "Don't stay up late. There's work to be done. We're on our way to the Great Society."

Johnson had a personal interest in providing education for the children of the poor. In 1965 Congress passed the Elementary and Secondary School Act, the first large-scale program of government aid to public schools. The Higher Education Act created the first federal scholarships for college students. In February 1965 the Office of Economic Opportunity launched Head Start, an education program for the preschool children of low-income parents.

The president also persuaded Congress to pass the Omnibus Housing Act in 1965. To oversee this and other federal housing programs, Congress created the Department of Housing and Urban Development (HUD). Johnson appointed Robert Weaver to head this new department, making him the first African American to be part of a president's cabinet.

3 Summarize the reading. Summarize the reading in your own words. Then draw a conclusion that states an opinion or makes a judgment about what the reading means to you.

Apply the Skill

1. What can you conclude about Johnson's interest in education?
2. What led Johnson to push even harder for his plans after he became an elected president?
3. What did Johnson mean when he said, "Don't stay up late. There's work to be done. We're on our way to the Great Society"?

READING SKILL
Making Generalizations

Define the Skill

A generalization is made by combining details from a passage with a reader's prior knowledge. People **make generalizations** by looking for people, events, or ideas that share something in common and identifying their connection. As a reader, look for a generalization if an author suggests that a series of facts are connected. Look for clue words, including *all, none, every,* and *never*. Other clue words that sometimes show a generalization are *most, many, few, some, usually,* and *sometimes*.

Learn the Skill

Use the following strategies to make generalizations from the reading.

1 Look for the main idea of the passage. Find similarities between paragraphs that link main ideas together.

John Lewis took part in some of the first sit-ins in 1960. He was also a Freedom Rider in 1961 and participated in the ill-fated Selma march in 1965. The leader of the Student Nonviolent Coordinating Committee in the early 1960s, Lewis was later elected to many terms representing the people of Atlanta, Georgia, in Congress.

As a staff member of Southern Christian Leadership Conference, **Andrew Young** played major roles in the 1963 Birmingham campaign and the Selma march. In 1972, he became Georgia's first black member of Congress since Reconstruction. Young later served as U.S. ambassador to the United Nations and as mayor of Atlanta.

Jesse Jackson was a close adviser to Martin Luther King, Jr. and was with him at the motel in Memphis on the day King was assassinated. Jackson later founded his own civil rights organization, Operation PUSH, and became an international figure for his work on behalf of poor and oppressed peoples around the world. His strong campaigns for the Democratic presidential nomination in the 1980s raised the real possibility that the nation might one day have a black president.

2 Locate supporting details. Listing facts will help you determine what people, places, or events are being grouped together.

3 Identify a common thread and relate it to your prior knowledge. Determine which words (*most, few,* etc.) will be most useful for a generalization. Then compare the generalization against what you already know about the subject.

Apply the Skill

1. What is the main idea of the passage?
2. Make a generalization based on the passage above.
3. What facts support that generalization?

SKILLS HANDBOOK **H13**

SOCIAL STUDIES SKILL
Interpreting Time Lines

Define the Skill

A **time line** chronologically organizes events that occurred during a specific period of time. It has a beginning date and an ending date. The **time span** is the years between the beginning date and the ending date. **Time intervals** mark shorter increments of time within the time span. They appear at regular intervals, such as every 10 or 20 years. Two time lines can be used to list events that happened within a certain time span but at different places. These are called **parallel time lines**.

By organizing events chronologically, time lines can help you see how events are related. Seeing how events are related can help you find cause and effect relationships among the events and remember them. Time lines also allow you to compare, contrast, and draw conclusions about historical events.

Learn the Skill

Use the following strategies to read the time line.

1 Identify the time span of the time line. Look at the beginning date and the ending date to determine the time period.

TIME LINE
The English in North America

- **1607** Captain John Smith and more than 100 colonists settle Jamestown.
- **1619** Virginia's House of Burgesses becomes the first legislature in America.
- **1620** The Pilgrims sign the Mayflower Compact.
- **1639** Connecticut settlers adopt the Fundamental Orders of Connecticut, which allowed men who were not church members to vote.

2 Determine the time intervals of the time line. Check to see whether the years are evenly spaced. Determine whether the time is divided by decades, by centuries, or by another division.

3 Analyze the events on the time line. Recognize the types of events that the time line describes and determine how they are related.

Apply the Skill

1. What is the time span of the time line?
2. What are the time intervals of the time line?
3. How are the events on the time line related?

SOCIAL STUDIES SKILL
Interpreting Charts

Define the Skill
Charts, including simple charts, tables, and diagrams, are visual representations of information, such as facts and statistics. Historians use charts to organize, condense, simplify, and summarize information. **Simple charts** combine or compare information.

Tables classify information by groups. Numbers, percentages, dates, and other data can be classified in the columns and rows of a table for easy reference and comparison. **Diagrams** illustrate processes or steps so that they are easier to understand. Knowing how to read and use charts allows you to interpret, compare, analyze, and evaluate historical information.

Learn the Skill
Use the following strategies to interpret the chart.

1. Identify the type of information presented in the chart.
Read the title and any column headings to understand what the chart is about. The title of this chart is "The English Colonies in America."

2. Look at the way information is organized.
Charts can be organized alphabetically, chronologically, or in other ways.

3. Analyze the information found in the chart.
Interpret, compare, and contrast the information in the chart to draw conclusions and make inferences or predictions.

THE ENGLISH COLONIES IN AMERICA

Joint-stock colonies were established by groups of investors who pooled their money hoping to make a profit.	Virginia* (1607) Massachusetts* (1620)
Royal colonies were under the direct control of the king of England, who appointed a governor.	Delaware (1664)
Proprietary colonies were established by private individuals, or Lord Proprietors, who had power to make and execute laws.	New Hampshire* (1623) New Jersey* (1630) Pennsylvania* (1634) Maryland* (1632) North Carolina* (1655) South Carolina* (1670) Georgia* (1732)
Self-governing colonies were independent of the king or a joint-stock company.	Connecticut (1634) Rhode Island (1636)

* Later became a royal colony

Apply the Skill
1. How is the information in the chart organized?
2. According to the chart, what is one difference and one similarity between the colonies of Virginia and Pennsylvania?

SOCIAL STUDIES SKILL

Interpreting Pie and Bar Graphs

Define the Skill

Graphs are diagrams that present statistical or numeric data. They can display amounts, trends, ratios, and changes over time. A **pie graph** is a circular chart that shows how individual parts relate to the whole. The circle of the pie symbolizes the whole amount. The slices of the pie represent the individual parts of the whole. A **bar graph** compares quantities. A single bar graph compares one set of data. A double bar graph compares two sets of data. Knowing how to interpret graphs will allow you to better understand and evaluate historical data as well as recognize historical trends.

Learn the Skill

Use the following strategies to interpret the pie graph.

1 Identify the subject of the pie graphs.
Read the title and the legend to determine the subject of the pie graphs.

Use the following strategies to interpret the bar graph.

1 Read the title and the legend. This will allow you to determine the subject of the graph.

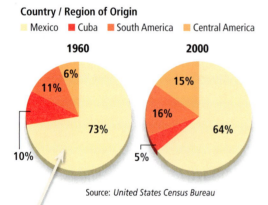

HISPANIC IMMIGRANTS TO THE UNITED STATES

Source: United States Census Bureau

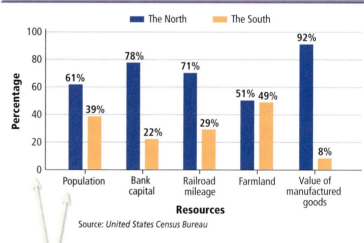

NORTHERN AND SOUTHERN RESOURCES

Source: United States Census Bureau

2 Read the statistics. Compare the sizes of each piece within each graph. Then compare the pieces across the graphs.

3 Draw conclusions Determine what the statistics tell about the subject of the pie graphs.

2 Examine the labels. Read the horizontal and vertical axis labels. These tell what the bar graph measures and the unit of measurement.

3 Analyze the bar graph. Compare the amounts shown on the bar graph. Draw conclusions about what this information tells about the subject.

Apply the Skill

1. What information do the pie graphs compare?
2. What information does the bar graph compare?
3. What conclusions can you draw from the data in the bar graph?

SOCIAL STUDIES SKILL
Interpreting Line Graphs

Define the Skill

A **line graph** is a visual representation of data organized so that you can see the pattern of change over time. On a line graph, usually the **vertical axis** shows quantities and the **horizontal axis** shows time. People may use line graphs to track changes in events such as population growth or the stock market. Line graphs show time in intervals so they are not always exact and may require that you estimate quantities. Knowing how to interpret line graphs can help you recognize historical trends.

Learn the Skill

Use the following strategies to interpret a line graph.

1 Read the title of the graph.
The title tells you the subject or purpose of the graph.

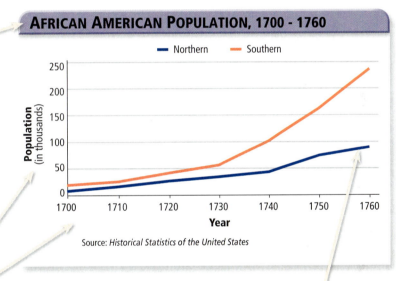

2 Read the horizontal and vertical axis labels.
The labels explain what the line graph measures and what is the unit of measurement.

3 Analyze the statistics on the graph.
Look at the slant of the line. The closer the line is to being parallel to the horizontal axis, the slower the change. The closer the line is to being perpendicular to the horizontal axis, the quicker the change.

Apply the Skill

1. About how big was the African American population in the South in 1740?
2. About how many more African American people lived in the South than in the North in 1760?
3. What conclusion can you draw about the African American population in the North?

SKILLS HANDBOOK **H17**

SOCIAL STUDIES SKILL

Interpreting Infographics

Define the Skill

An **infographic** is a way of presenting a large amount of information in a graphic, or visual, form. Infographics often combine different types of information, such as text, illustrations, maps, charts, tables, graphs, and diagrams. You need to be able to understand what each piece of information is conveying on its own and how each piece works together to convey a larger point. Infographics help readers understand the importance of an event, an object, or a place. An infographic can be a two-dimensional or a three-dimensional model. Some infographics are interactive. Different types of infographics have different uses. For example, tables and charts organize information, whereas pictorial infographics are memorable and bring history to life.

Learn the Skill

Use the following strategies to interpret infographics.

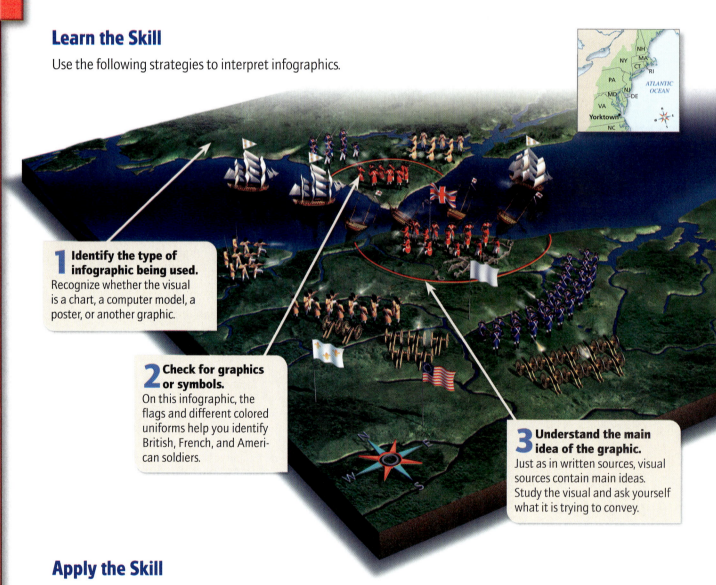

1 Identify the type of infographic being used. Recognize whether the visual is a chart, a computer model, a poster, or another graphic.

2 Check for graphics or symbols. On this infographic, the flags and different colored uniforms help you identify British, French, and American soldiers.

3 Understand the main idea of the graphic. Just as in written sources, visual sources contain main ideas. Study the visual and ask yourself what it is trying to convey.

Apply the Skill

1. What type of infographic is this?
2. What do the ships represent?
3. Why did the British surrender at Yorktown?

Social Studies Skill

Interpreting Movement Maps

Define the Skill

Different types of maps are used for different purposes. **Movement maps** show motion or travel from one point to another. They can track sea voyages, explorations, or migrations. They can span a week, a few months, or thousands of years. Understanding how to read and interpret a movement map can help you learn more about historical events, their chronology, and the geographical locations they affected.

Learn the Skill

Use the following strategies to interpret movement maps.

1 Read the title and legend to learn the subject and purpose of the map. Use that prior knowledge and the map to draw conclusions. What area does the map cover? What time period does the map cover? The legend explains what the symbols and the colors on the map mean.

2 Identify and understand the patterns of movement shown on the map. Trace the path of movement from start to end. What does the map tell you about the explorers' movements?

3 Analyze the information. What do you already know about the subject?

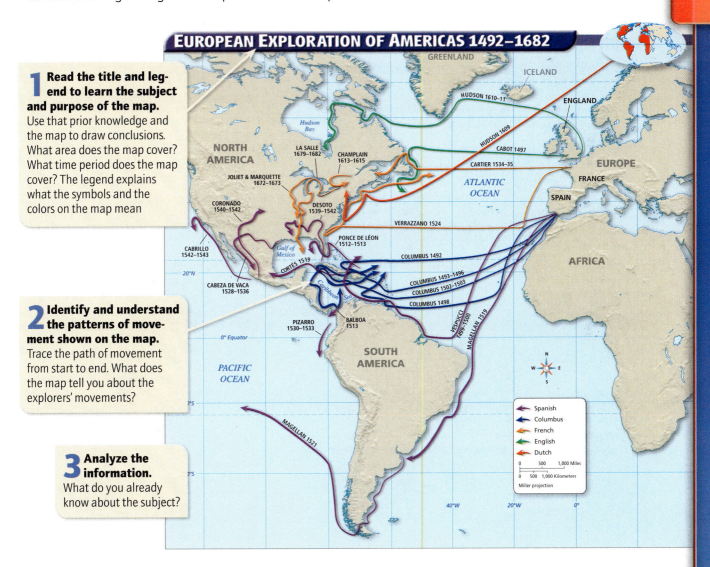

Apply the Skill

1. Describe the path that Magellan took.
2. What patterns can you find?
3. How do the patterns you found relate to the present-day Americas?

H19

SOCIAL STUDIES SKILL

Interpreting Historical Maps

Define the Skill

A map is a representation of features on Earth's surface. Historians use different types of maps to locate historical events, to demonstrate how geography has influenced history, and to illustrate human interaction with the environment.

A **historical map** provides information about a place at a certain time in history. It can illustrate information such as population density, economic activity, political alliances, battles, and movement of people and goods. Knowing how to use historical maps can help you learn how places have changed over time. For example, these historical maps show how the Treaty of Paris changed North America after the French and Indian War.

Learn the Skill

Use the following strategies to interpret historical maps.

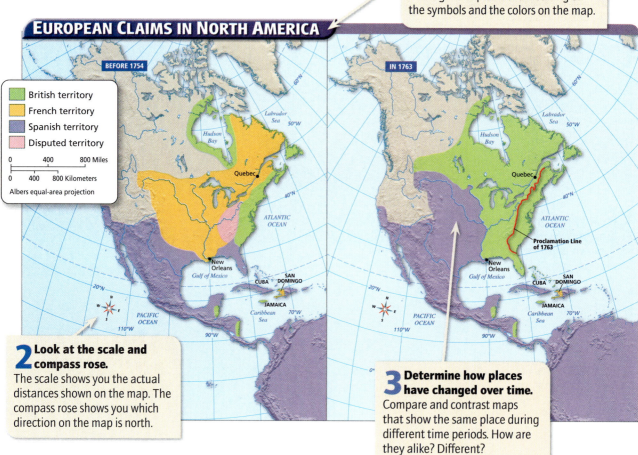

1. **Read the title and legend.** The title will help you identify the subject and the purpose of the map. The legend explains the meaning of the symbols and the colors on the map.

2. **Look at the scale and compass rose.** The scale shows you the actual distances shown on the map. The compass rose shows you which direction on the map is north.

3. **Determine how places have changed over time.** Compare and contrast maps that show the same place during different time periods. How are they alike? Different?

Apply the Skill

1. What is the purpose of these historical maps?
2. Which country claimed Quebec before 1754? Which country claimed Quebec in 1763?

H20 SKILLS HANDBOOK

SOCIAL STUDIES SKILL

Interpreting Cartograms

Define the Skill

A distribution map show how data, such as population, is spread over a certain area. A **cartogram** is a type of distribution map that distorts the sizes and shapes of state, regions, or countries to reflect some value *other* than physical size. For example, a cartogram may display information about the population of a region or the gross national products of several countries. The cartogram is a tool for making visual comparisons. At a glance, you can see how each country, region, or state compares with another in a particular value.

Learn the Skill

Use the following strategies to interpret cartograms.

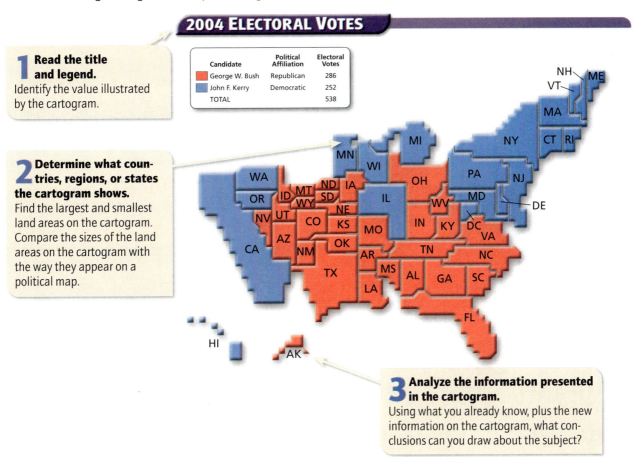

1 **Read the title and legend.** Identify the value illustrated by the cartogram.

2 **Determine what countries, regions, or states the cartogram shows.** Find the largest and smallest land areas on the cartogram. Compare the sizes of the land areas on the cartogram with the way they appear on a political map.

3 **Analyze the information presented in the cartogram.** Using what you already know, plus the new information on the cartogram, what conclusions can you draw about the subject?

Apply the Skill

1. On the cartogram, is Pennsylvania or Missouri more distorted in size when compared with a political map?
2. What does this cartogram tell about the populations of Massachusetts and South Dakota?

SKILLS HANDBOOK **H21**

SOCIAL STUDIES SKILL

Analyzing Costs and Benefits

Define the Skill

Government officials use cost-benefit analyses to help them decide which programs to fund. A **cost-benefit analysis** is a process that measures whether a project or a policy is worthwhile by calculating and comparing its benefits with its costs to society. Basic economic indicators including employment, gross domestic product, and inflation can be used in the analysis. All costs and benefits are expressed in terms of money. Some costs and benefits, however, such as time or safety, cannot be directly measured by how much money is earned or lost. Mathematical formulas are used for these types of costs and benefits to determine how to express their monetary value. One obstacle to cost-benefit analysis is that people may sometimes disagree about the value of the costs and the benefits.

Learn the Skill

Use the following strategies to analyze costs and benefits.

1 Identify and calculate the costs. What are the different costs of the project? Add those together to calculate the total cost.

2 Identify and calculate the benefits. Determine the benefits of the proposed project. Calculate the total amount of money the project will save or earn for society.

3 Analyze the costs and the benefits and draw conclusions. Compare the costs with the benefits. Divide the total benefits by the total costs to determine the benefits-to-cost ratio. If the ratio is more than 1, the project will earn money. If the ratio is less than 1, the project will lose money.

JOB CORPS: COSTS AND BENEFITS TO SOCIETY PER PARTICIPANT

Costs (1995 Dollars)	
Cost of Government-Funded Pay, Food, and Clothing for Participant	$2,361
Program Operating Costs	$14,128

Benefits (1995 Dollars)	
Participant Earns Government-Funded Pay, Food, and Clothing	$2,361
Additional Earnings and Benefits	$27,531
Reduced Crime in Community	$1,240
Reduced Use of Other Job Training Programs	$2,186

Apply the Skill

1. What is the total cost of Job Corps per participant?
2. What is one benefit of Job Corps?
3. How much money will society earn or lose for each dollar the government spends on Job Corps?
4. Will the program earn or lose money?

SOCIAL STUDIES SKILL

Evaluating Information on the Internet

Define the Skill

The **Internet** is an international computer network that connects schools, businesses, government agencies, and individuals. Every Web site on the Internet has its own address, called a **URL**. Each URL has a domain. The **domain** tells you the type of Web site you are reading. Common domains in the United States are .com, .net, .org, .edu, and .gov. A Web site with the domain .edu means that it is sponsored by an educational institution. The collection of web sites throughout the world is called the **World Wide Web**.

The Internet can be a valuable research tool. Unlike the information in books and newspapers, much of the content on the Internet is not checked for accuracy. Anyone can post information on the Web, so it is important to know how to evaluate the content of Internet resources. Evaluating the content found on the Internet will help you determine the accuracy and reliability of the information.

Learn the Skill

Use the following strategies to evaluate information on the Internet.

1 Identify the Web site's domain. Determine who sponsors the Web site. Web sites sponsored by reputable organizations, educational institutions, and government agencies usually provide accurate and reliable information.

2 Understand the purpose of the site. Find out whether the purpose of the site is to inform, to persuade, or to entertain.

3 Identify the author and check for bias. Determine the author's credentials. Is he or she an expert in the field? Decide whether the Web site presents balanced information or is overly biased towards a certain point of view.

4 Check the author's sources. For any research-based information, the author should provide a list of sources he or she used. You can also consult the author's sources for your own research.

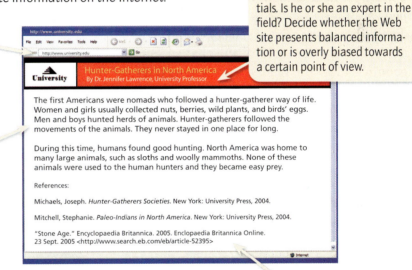

Apply the Skill

1. What is the domain of the Web site? Do you think the information on the Web site will be reliable? Why or why not?
2. Who is the author of the Web site? What are the author's credentials?
3. Do you think this Web site presents a balanced point of view or a biased point of view? Explain your response.

READING LIKE A HISTORIAN

Major Historical Concepts

To think like a historian, you need to be aware of some basic concepts of history—about how history happens and how historians think about the past. Keep these five major historical concepts in mind as you read this textbook.

Continuity and Change in History

Change happens at different rates at different times Historical change doesn't happen at a uniform rate. Some periods see great, sweeping changes that affect the course of history for hundreds of years to come. At other times, the changes are gradual and harder to see.

Some aspects can change while others remain the same Change happens at different rates in different places, too. Just because one part of society changes that doesn't mean all of society will change. For example, after the United States gained its independence, states in the North gradually became more industrialized and outlawed slavery, while states in the South remained largely agricultural and kept slavery.

Change is complicated Historical change affects all areas of life, not just politics or technology. Beliefs and values are also subject to change. Once, women were not permitted to join the armed forces. Today the debate is not over whether women should be allowed to join but what role the hundreds of thousands of military women should have.

Understanding Cause and Effect in History

The limitations of cause and effect One event may have several causes. A proximate, or immediate, cause may seem obvious, such as Germany's invasion of Poland as the proximate cause of World War II. But there also may be deeper causes, such as the war reparations that Germany was forced to pay after the Treaty of Versailles officially ended World War I. It may not always be immediately possible to identify a direct cause for an event or to identify all of the deeper causes.

What causes events? Inflation in Germany after World War I made paper money almost worthless (above left), hastening Adolf Hitler's rise to power.

The Civil Rights Movement involved millions of people and changed American politics, voting patterns, schooling, and entertainment.

The destruction of the USS *Maine* may have been an act of war or it may have been a chance occurrence.

The Role of Chance in History

The impact of historical events An explosion sunk the USS *Maine* in Havana harbor in 1898. The Spanish and the U.S. governments disagreed about the cause of the explosion, which killed all the men aboard. The Spanish-American War ensued, and "Remember the Maine!" became an American battle cry. Chance events can have unexpected and sometimes enormous consequences. Many factors may influence the direction of history, but change just one of those factors and the outcome itself may change. If the USS *Maine* had not exploded there may not have been a Spanish-American War.

Understanding Historical Events in Context

Events as they happened Historians strive to place events in the context of their time, understanding them the way the participants would have. This means understanding the ideas and beliefs of the time and not imposing modern day values on the past. We may still disagree with the actions people took in the past, such as enslaving human beings or denying women the right to vote, but historians need to understand why people acted as they did.

Drawing Lessons from History

Comparing the present with the past Past decisions and the consequences of historical events reverberate through our own time. Decisions made almost 150 years ago—leading up to and during the Civil War—still affect how different regions of the country view one another. Some things have changed; some have stayed the same.

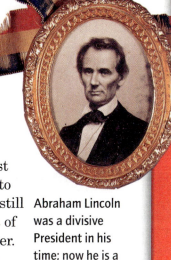

Abraham Lincoln was a divisive President in his time; now he is a beloved figure.

Lessons we have learned We can get a better sense of how to meet the challenges we face today by knowing how people in the past met or failed to meet similar challenges. For example, after the stock market crash of 1929 and the Great Depression that followed, the practice of buying stocks on borrowed money was severely restricted. Today many of the laws that make up the fabric of our nation came from lessons learned in difficult times. Historians are careful not to think the past holds all the answers. No situation is exactly like any other, and we need to be careful not to draw lessons too hastily, or too confidently.

Traders on the New York Stock Exchange are still bound by laws developed in response to the stock market crash of 1929.

READING LIKE A HISTORIAN
Themes of History

Understanding history means understanding the connections between time, places, events, and people. Throughout *American Anthem,* you will find opportunities to make those connections and identify themes that will help you grasp the larger patterns of events across time.

Government and Democracy

The United States was founded on such ideals as human equality, limited government, and democratic representation. Today, as when our nation was founded, the American government is separated into three branches—the executive branch, the legislative branch, and the judicial branch. For over two hundred years, these three branches have worked under a system of checks and balances so that no one branch ever becomes too powerful.

Our Constitution defines the structure of our government.

Individual Rights and Responsibilities

When America was founded, only white men with property could vote in elections or hold office. Over the past two centuries, women and African Americans have fought for and won the right to vote and participate in our democracy. Today, American citizens can register to vote when they are eighteen years old. Voting is one of our most precious individual rights and responsibilities as citizens of the American democracy.

Voting is the most fundamental way citizens exercise both their rights and their responsibilities.

Economic Development

In the United States, the abundance of natural resources, a free-enterprise economic system, and government regulation protecting both private property and the public good all work together to ensure our country's economic success. The offer of social mobility and economic success through hard work has attracted immigrants to the United States from around the world.

Many innovators, such as Thomas Edison, have contributed to America's cultural and economic development.

Immigrants from many nations choose to become citizens of the United States.

Immigration and Migration

People from many nations, representing an extraordinary range of ethnic, racial, national, and religious groups, have come to the United States and become American citizens, making our country the most diverse in the world. At many times in our nation's history, people have also migrated within the country's borders, seeking new opportunities and a better way of life.

Cultural Expressions

A diverse nation has given rise to a diverse culture, drawing on the traditions of many different groups. This blending and remixing of cultural expression among ethnic, racial, and religious groups is the source of tremendous strength and creativity, but it also sometimes causes conflict.

Global Relations

Early American foreign policy reflected the country's origins as a British colony, prompting America to try to remain separate from the affairs of European nations. By the 1900s, however, the United States emerged as a world superpower, with allies and responsibilities around the world.

U.S. leaders can make an important difference in the world.

Science and Technology

A spirit of innovation in science and technology has had an enormous effect on our country's economy and culture. Throughout our history, American inventions have vastly improved quality of life and standards of living not only here but across the globe.

Medical and computer science are important parts of our nation's past and future.

Uniquely American art forms, such as jazz and blues music, have come from cultural diversity.

READING LIKE A HISTORIAN **H27**

READING LIKE A HISTORIAN
Analyzing Primary Sources

Define the Skill

Primary sources are documents or other artifacts created by people present at historical events either as witnesses or participants. You can identify a primary source by reading for first person clues, such as *I, we,* and *our*. Quotation marks signify a speech or writing. These types of sources are valuable to historians because they give information about an event or a time period. All primary sources include a point of view because they were written or created by one person or group. Points of view may differ. For example, a Union soldier writing about a Civil War battle may have a different point of view than a Confederate soldier writing about the same battle. Historians compare primary sources to understand an event from all sides in order to write an accurate historical interpretation.

Primary sources can include:
- Letters
- Photographs
- Diaries
- Newspaper stories
- Pamphlets, books, or other writings
- Court opinions
- Autobiographies
- Pottery, weapons, and other artifacts
- Government data, laws, and statutes
- Speeches

Learn the Skill

Use the following strategies to analyze primary sources.

1 Identify the author or creator of the primary source. There is little information given about Beverly. His role is unclear. A historian should ask more questions about this primary source.

Virginian Robert Beverly on Bacon's Rebellion—

"Four things may be reckoned to have been the main ingredients towards this intestine commotion [violent outbreak]. First, The extreme low price of tobacco, and the ill usage of the planter in the exchange of goods for it, which the country, with all their earnest endeavors, could not remedy. Secondly, The splitting the colony into proprieties, contrary to the original charters; and the extravagant taxes they were [charged]. Thirdly, The heavy restraints and burdens laid upon their trade by act of Parliament in England. Fourthly, The disturbance given by the Indians."

2 Determine the historical event the primary source is describing. Ask yourself whether Beverly's details match what you already know about Bacon's Rebellion.

3 Compare what you already know to details in the primary source. Often a primary source will enhance your knowledge of an event. Which detail in this source tells you something new?

Apply the Skill

1. What is Robert Beverly's point of view?
2. List two details about Bacon's Rebellion provided by this source.
3. How would this source help a historian write a historical interpretation of Bacon's Rebellion?

H28 SKILLS HANDBOOK

Artifacts are also primary sources. This is a twelve shilling note from Pennsylvania, 1777.

Use the following strategies to analyze primary sources.

1 Identify the author or creator of the primary source.
In 1777, the colonies each printed their own money. The monetary system was based on a system of pounds, shillings, and pence.

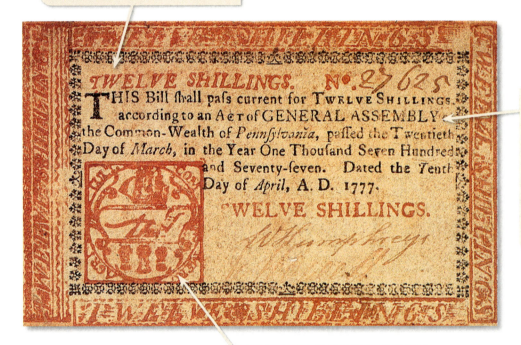

2 Determine the time period that the primary source is describing.
The paragraph printed on the money tells under whose authority it was printed. It also states when the act was passed, dating the note in 1777.

3 Compare what you already know to details in the primary source.
The seal on the note shows a ship, a plow, and bundles of wheat. What can these icons tell you about the colony of Pennsylvania?

Apply the Skill

1. Who is the creator of this primary source?
2. What can you infer about colonial money by viewing this primary source?
3. How would this source be useful to a historian?

READING LIKE A HISTORIAN

Interpreting Visuals

Define the Skill

Visuals can be important historical sources, so interpreting visuals is vital to reading like a historian. Visuals may offer an accurate portrayal of the details of a historical figure or event. Or they may represent an exaggerated or biased point of view. Knowing and understanding an artist or photographer's point of view can sometimes reveal more to a historian than the actual image itself.

To analyze an image, first determine the medium. Is the image a photograph, a piece of fine art, a poster, an advertisement, or a cartoon? What might this tell you about the image's audience? Next, look at the credit line and title, which will tell you who created the image and possibly what the artist intended it to mean. Look for details that could convey meaning. Then study the subject of the visual. Who or what is being portrayed? Are there symbols or familiar landmarks in the image? Why might those elements have been chosen? Finally, compare the image with what you know about the historical time it depicts.

Learn the Skill

Use the following strategies to analyze visuals.

1 Who or what is the subject?
Queen Elizabeth I

2 Examine the details. What is the historical context of this picture? Behind Queen Elizabeth are images of the English fleet defeating the Spanish Armada in 1588.

3 How is the subject depicted? The queen is portrayed in a positive light, as a beautiful, poised woman in rich clothes and luxurious surroundings.

4 Does the image agree or disagree with known historical facts? The right panel behind Elizabeth shows ships sinking in bad weather, which was a historical factor in the Armada's defeat.

Apply the Skill

1. What symbols of power and rule are included in the picture?
2. Elizabeth was 55 years old when the English fleet defeated the Spanish Armada, yet she is portrayed as young and beautiful in this painting. Why might that be so?

READING LIKE A HISTORIAN

Interpreting Political Cartoons

Define the Skill

Political cartoons are another kind of visual found in the historical record. These differ from visuals such as photographs and fine art because political cartoons often exaggerate characteristics of subjects or events in order to convey a specific message, either about politics in particular or society in general. Historians use political cartoons to understand how a particular person or event was perceived at the time. To interpret political cartoons, examine all the elements while considering the social, political, and historical context of the time.

Learn the Skill

Use the following strategies to interpret political cartoons.

1 Identify the cartoon's subject. This cartoon shows Congressman Preston Brooks (D, SC) attacking Senator Charles Sumner (R, MA). The two disagreed about the Kansas-Nebraska compromise over slavery.

4 Compare the message with historical knowledge. Does the cartoon agree or disagree with facts you already know? Preston attacked Sumner in a nearly empty Senate chamber, not in front of a crowd of witnesses as shown in the cartoon.

2 Read any text and study all symbols. Do they provide any clues about point of view? The caption uses the phrase "Southern Chivalry" to describe the beating; this is a use of irony, or meaning the opposite of what is actually stated.

3 Establish the cartoon's message. How is the subject portrayed? Preston Brooks is portrayed in a negative light, attacking a helpless Sumner on the floor of the Senate.

Apply the Skill

1. Does this cartoon look as though it was created by a supporter of slavery or a supporter of abolition?
2. Are there any features in this carton that are exaggerated?
3. Which of the two men is portrayed as the aggressor? Which is portrayed as the victim?

READING LIKE A HISTORIAN

Interpreting Literature as Historical Evidence

Define the Skill

Historians can sometimes use literature written during a particular time period to gain detailed insights into certain people, places, and events. For example, a novel about an upper-class New York City family in the late 1800s can provide historical details about the lifestyle of that social class. Some literature is activist, meaning that its purpose is to inspire an emotional or social response.

Learn the Skill

Use the following strategies to interpret literature.

1 Identify the author's point of view or bias. Does the author have experiences that make the description more reliable? Reflect on what you already know about the book or author before you begin to read.

2 Look for descriptive passages. This sentence gives descriptive details about workers in meatpacking factories. Do these details make the account historically believable?

Excerpt from *The Jungle,* by Upton Sinclair—

The men would tie up their feet in newspapers and old sacks, and these would be soaked in blood and frozen, and then soaked again, and so on until by night time a man would be walking on great lumps the size of feet of an elephant. Now and then, when the bosses were not looking, you would see them plunging their feet and ankles into the steaming hot carcass of the steer, or darting across the room to the hot-water jets.

4 Compare details in the literature with known facts about the event. Sinclair was one of many writers in the early 1900s who investigated businesses and industry. Sinclair's work led to the passage of The Pure Food and Drug Act in 1906, to protect consumers from contaminated beef.

3 Determine whether the literature is meant to describe a certain historical event or to elicit an emotional response. Here, the author wants to elicit an emotional response from the audience. What effect does this strategy have on the usefulness of the literature as an historical interpretation?

Apply the Skill

1. What is the author's point of view or bias?
2. What is the goal of the literature selection?
3. What can historians learn about factory work by reading this selection?

READING LIKE A HISTORIAN
Recognizing Bias

Define the Skill

To ensure an effective analysis of primary sources, historians must learn to recognize bias and the source of bias. Bias is a point of view that is slanted by personal or political beliefs. Every primary source reflects bias, from either the person who created the source or the person viewing the source. Bias appears in primary sources for a variety of reasons and gives clues about an author's intent or background.

For example, the author may be trying to justify an action or sway an opinion. Sometimes an author expresses a personal view without knowing that it is biased. Bias can help historians understand the different attitudes during a certain time in history. To avoid bias, a historian must examine different points of view and primary sources. It is important to look at many sources on the same incident or issue in order to achieve a balanced analysis.

Learn the Skill

Use the following strategies to recognize bias.

1 Identify the document.
This section gives you the context of the statement. Think about how speeches at public celebrations are different from other primary sources, such as private letters.

2 Examine the author's point of view.
What bias does the author express? Identify the author and his occupation. What can this tell you about the author's possible goals?

Dr. H. W. Harkness, Sacramento Newspaper Publisher, at the ceremony to celebrate the first transcontinental railroad—

"The east and west have come together. Never, since history commenced her record of human events, has she been called upon to note the completion of a work so magnificent."

3 Consider the author's goal.
This claim is not a true claim. The speaker is using rhetoric, or the skill of using language effectively and persuasively. Consider whether rhetoric is appropriate for this event.

4 Compare the primary source with historical evidence.
In what ways is the primary source different from other historical accounts? In what ways is it similar?

Apply the Skill

1. What is the author's goal in this statement?
2. Explain how a historian could use this document in preparing a historical account of the celebration marking the completion of the transcontinental railroad.

READING LIKE A HISTORIAN

Evaluating Sources

Define the Skill

Historians must constantly evaluate sources to determine their credibility. Credible sources help historians produce an accurate and reliable historical account. Historians use several criteria for evaluating sources:

- They consider the author or producer of a source.
- They think about where, when, and why a source was created.
- They assess the level of bias in a source.
- They acknowledge that sources are more reliable if the author was close in time and place to a given event.

Learn the Skill

Use the following strategies to evaluate sources.

1 Identify and learn the background of the author of the source. Quotes almost always include the name of the speaker or writer. This title also gives context information.

President Woodrow Wilson, in a speech to Congress, April 2, 1917—

“We shall fight for the things which we have always carried nearest our hearts, for democracy. . . [and to] bring peace and safety to all nations and make the world itself at last free.”

3 Determine whether the source was meant to be public or private. The use of quotation marks and the word "we" help show that this is a primary source. This speech was given to Congress, but who was Wilson really addressing?

2 Examine the context of the source. Consider when, in relation to the event, the source was created. In January, 1917, Germany resumed its submarine warfare. By April, they had sunk five U.S. submarines. Wilson justifies the U.S. entry into World War I by saying that the "peace and safety" of the world is at stake.

Apply the Skill

1. Who is the producer of the source?
2. What is the context of the source? Is the source meant to be public or private?
3. In what way is the source biased? What is the goal of the speaker?
4. How would you evaluate the source, on the basis of its credibility?

READING LIKE A HISTORIAN
Analyzing Secondary Sources

Define the Skill

Secondary sources are accounts produced after a historical event by people who rely on primary sources. Secondary sources often contain summaries and analyses of events and time periods. Your textbook can be considered a secondary source, as can many other history books.

When a historian produces a secondary source, it often contains an interpretation of a historical event, or what the historian thinks actually happened and why. Historians build their interpretations on the basis of available facts and their own analysis. These secondary sources can be analyzed to determine whether they present a complete and accurate accounting of events.

Other kinds of secondary sources include:
- Encyclopedia entries
- Web sites
- Articles and essays by historians
- Biographies

Learn the Skill

Use the following strategies to analyze secondary sources.

1 Identify the source.
This is an encyclopedia article.

"World War I." Encyclopedia Britannica. 2005. Encyclopedia Britannica Online School Edition. 22 Sept. 2005

World War I, *also called* **First World War,** *or* **Great War**—an international conflict that in 1914–18 embroiled most of the nations of Europe along with Russia, the United States, the Middle East, and other regions. The **war** pitted the Central Powers—mainly Germany, Austria-Hungary, and Turkey—against the Allies—mainly France, Great Britain, Russia, Italy, Japan, and, from 1917, the United States. It ended with the defeat of the Central Powers. The **war** was virtually unprecedented in the slaughter, carnage, and destruction it caused.

World War I was one of the great watersheds of 20th-century geopolitical history. It led to the fall of four great imperial dynasties (in Germany, Russia, Austria-Hungary, and Turkey), resulted in the Bolshevik Revolution in Russia, and, in its destabilization of European society, laid the groundwork for **World War II.**

2 Summary
Secondary sources offer summaries of historical facts.

3 Analysis
Secondary sources analyze historical facts and draw conclusions.

4 Consequences
Since they are produced after an event is over, secondary sources can take a longer view of an event's consequences.

Apply the Skill

The first paragraph of the article offers a summary of the subject, World War I. The second paragraph contains an analysis of the importance and effects of the war. Answer these questions based on the excerpt:

1. What important information about World War I can be found in the first paragraph?
2. What are some of the consequences of World War I listed in the article?

READING LIKE A HISTORIAN

Many Web sites are secondary sources, and their use is becoming more common and accepted among historians. Web sites, however, require special care in analysis. Because the World Wide Web uses open architecture, meaning that anyone can post information without any kind of review process, it is harder to determine whether information on these sites is accurate. Pay close attention to the stated source of any historical Web site, as well as the date it was last updated.

Among Web domain extensions, .gov and .edu are considered the most reliable for academic work. Some .org and .com sites are also good resources, but they require careful study to determine their credibility.

> **The domain extensions that appear in a Web address can help. These include the following:**
> - **.gov**—a government site
> - **.org**—usually a nonprofit organization
> - **.edu**—educational entities such as colleges and universities
> - **.com**—for-profit and commercial entities, including book publishers

Learn the Skill

Use the following strategies to analyze secondary sources.

1. What kind of secondary source is it?
This is a biography on a Web site.

2. Determine the author or the publisher of the secondary source.
What do you know about the person's or organization's credibility? The content of this biography is provided by the Smithsonian Institution, a credible source.

3. How does the author or publisher handle primary source material?
Is primary source material drawn from a range of sources for balance? The fine art portrait is identified and sourced. The biography also notes that conflicting opinions exist about General MacArthur and presents generalizations of those opinions.

4. When numbers and statistics are used, examine them carefully.
Are they offering a complete picture or just one part of the story? This biography does not use numbers or statistics, but in other historical writings, visual representations of data would need to be analyzed.

Spotlight: Biography

The Korean War

The Korean War (1950–1953) is often referred to as America's "forgotten war," because it did not capture the nation's attention as had World War II, nor did it arouse controversy as did the war in Vietnam. In fact, although the Korean War was much shorter than the Vietnam War, the casualties were almost as high, with 54,000 Americans killed and 103,000 wounded. Total casualties for the war reached 1.9 million. In 1995, more than forty years after the conflict ended, a memorial honoring the sacrifices and services of Korean War soldiers was dedicated on the Mall in Washington, D.C., directly across from the Vietnam Veterans' Memorial.

Douglas MacArthur (1880–1964)

Howard Chandler Christy (1873–1952)
Oil on canvas, 1952, NPG.78.271
National Portrait Gallery,
Smithsonian Institution, Washington, D.C.
Gift of Henry Ostrow

Though General Douglas MacArthur is perhaps best known for his participation in the Korean War, his military service actually began a half-century earlier. In fact, his was one of the longest and most controversial careers of any American military officer. Douglas MacArthur was the son of another famous soldier, Arthur MacArthur II, who led troops in the Civil War, the Spanish American War, and in the Philippines. Encouraged by his father's military successes as well as an ambitious mother, MacArthur entered the United States Military Academy at West Point...

Apply the Skill

1. What information do you learn about General Douglas MacArthur?
2. This source does not list an author. What information would you look at to help you determine whether this is a credible secondary source?

READING LIKE A HISTORIAN

Analyzing Bias in Historical Interpretation

Define the Skill

When reading works of historical interpretation to determine their credibility and usefulness, it is important to read critically, looking for **bias in historical interpretation.** Most historians try to filter out their own biases when writing history. But they may not succeed, since they may not be aware of their biases. Bias can affect the way a historian tells a story, what facts are included or excluded, which events are highlighted or ignored, and how he or she treats primary sources.

Learn the Skill

Read the excerpt from Theodore Roosevelt's history of the War of 1812 between Great Britain and the United States. Then use the following strategies to analyze bias in historical interpretation.

1 Does the author have a background in the subject matter?
Theodore Roosevelt was a graduate of Harvard and a New York state Assemblyman in 1882. He would later serve as secretary of the Navy, and become President of the United States in 1901.

Theodore Roosevelt, *The Naval War of 1812,* published in 1882—

"But the wrongs done by the Americans were insignificant compared with those they received. Any innocent merchant vessel was liable to seizure at any moment; and when overhauled by a British cruiser short of men was sure to be stripped of most of her crew. . . . If a captain lacked his full complement there was little doubt as to the view he would take of any man's nationality. The wrongs inflicted on our seafaring countrymen by their impressment into foreign ships formed the main cause of the war."

2 Is emotional language used to support a particular point of view?
This emotional language demonstrates Roosevelt's pro-American bias.

3 Are credible primary sources used to support the text?
Are footnotes or cited quotations used? This assertion is not backed up by a primary source or factual citation. The event happened more than 40 years before Roosevelt was born and he cannot have first-hand knowledge of it.

Apply the Skill

1. Who is the author? What important information is found in his background?
2. Are there examples of emotional language in the excerpt? If so, what are they?
3. Is there bias in this passage? Explain your answer.

READING LIKE A HISTORIAN
Evaluating Historical Interpretation

Define the Skill

Historians and others evaluate historical interpretations to determine credibility, the level of bias, and the relevance of the material. A historical interpretation is a way to explain the past. These interpretations can change over time as historians learn more about the people and events of the past. Historians use several criteria for evaluating historical interpretations.

- Consider the age of the interpretation and its current relevance to the material. Some sources, such as encyclopedias, are updated periodically to include new material.
- Assess the level of bias in the interpretation.
- Determine the credibility of the interpretation.

Learn the Skill

Use the following strategies to evaluate historical interpretation.

1 Identify the author or publisher of the source to determine credibility.
The introduction tells you the author's name and his profession. A book by a history professor is almost always a credible source.

2 Consider when the source was created.
This book was published in 2003, so it probably uses current scholarship.

excerpt from *In the Presence of Mine Enemies: War in the Heart of America, 1859–1863,* by Edward L. Ayers, Professor of History, published in 2003—

Together, the stories of Augusta [County, Virginia] and Franklin [County, Pennsylvania] tell of a war both simpler and less straightforward than general accounts reveal. The Civil War was like all wars in that it elevated the worst human emotions and called them virtues. People let themselves be driven by arrogance and revenge as well as by ideology and principle. People watched themselves descend into rage and numbness, knowing themselves unworthy of their feelings. People invoked the Constitution and the Declaration of Independence against enemies invoking the same icons.

3 Examine the level of bias in the interpretation.
Does it detract from the overall credibility? The author's research was based on the people and public records of two counties, one in the North and the other in the South. He is using primary sources and presenting potentially opposing viewpoints. This creates a less-biased source.

Apply the Skill

1. Who is the author of the interpretation?
2. How does bias affect the interpretation?
3. Explain why the source would be valuable to current students.

READING LIKE A HISTORIAN

Analyzing Alternative Interpretations of the Past

Define the Skill

Interpretations of past events can differ in many ways. An interpretation may reflect an extreme bias for one view or another, or it may reflect two different schools of thought. Historians are often faced with alternative interpretations of a time or event in the past. When faced with opposing viewpoints, good historians do additional research to find the accuracies in each account.

Learn the Skill

Use the following strategies to analyze interpretations.

1 Look for information about the author or the source that may give clues to possible bias.
Andrews is a historian while Hacker is an economics professor. How could the different careers affect the authors' point of view?

Charles M. Andrews, historian—

"Primarily, the American Revolution was a political and constitutional movement and only secondarily one that was either financial, commercial or social. At bottom, the fundamental issue was the political independence of the colonies, and in the last analysis the conflict lay between the British Parliament and the colonial assemblies…"

2 Define the main points in each argument.
This will help you compare the interpretations.

Louis M. Hacker, economics professor—

"The struggle was not over high-sounding political and constitutional concepts; over the power of taxation or even, in the final analysis, over natural rights. It was over colonial manufacturing, wild lands and furs, sugar, wine, tea, and currency, all of which meant, simply, the survival or collapse of English mercantile capitalism within the imperial-colonial framework of the mercantilist system."

3 Discount rhetoric or emotional language that is not factual.
Here, Hacker uses rhetoric to demean the "political and constitutional concepts" that Andrews supports.

4 In what ways do the interpretations differ?
Summarize each interpretation to compare them. However, you should read additional information, opinions, or studies before you decide with which interpretation to agree.

Apply the Skill

1. Summarize the two interpretations presented above.
2. What can comparing these interpretations tell you about historical interpretation in general?

READING LIKE A HISTORIAN

Making Oral Presentations

Define the Skill

Historians sometimes make oral presentations. These include speeches, lectures, or interviews. Oral presentations often support a version of or a conclusion about an issue and are given from outlines or note cards. They should be more dynamic than simply reading a written essay aloud. Historians must perform thorough research, make notes, and carefully organize their presentations. As a student of history, an oral presentation allows you to present information on a topic you have researched to an audience.

Learn the Skill

Use the following strategies to make oral presentations.

1 Identify a historical topic you would like to present.
Choose a central idea or theme on which to focus your research. Research the topic to gather relevant facts and vivid details. Include visual aids, such as maps, charts, or pictures, to add to your presentation.

2 Organize your information into an introduction, a body, and a conclusion.
The introduction should clearly state your topic and hypothesis while also generating interest with the listener. The body features the main points of your argument. The conclusion summarizes your main points and draws on those points to formulate a personal opinion about your topic.

3 Proofread your notes to ensure that they are well organized and grammatically correct.
Clearly label your notes. Using the terms introduction, body, and conclusion on your note cards helps you make an organized presentation.

4 Express arguments clearly and persuasively.
Write key words and clues in your notes to use as talking points. It may be helpful to structure this section in outline form. Also, look at how the opening sentence could catch the listeners' attention.

5 Practice reading your presentation aloud.
Make sure that you are comfortable speaking and that your statements are clear. Although you do not want to read directly from your notes while giving an oral presentation, it may be helpful to write sentences in your introduction to get you started.

Topic: Watergate

Introduction: On a summer night in 1972, a bungled break-in would cause the downfall of an American president. My hypothesis is that President Nixon, although a flawed person, was the victim of incompetent subordinates.

Body: Talk about Nixon's top aides
  a. H. R. Haldeman
  b. John Ehrlichman

Apply the Skill

1. Name the three parts of a well-organized oral presentation.
2. What is the topic and hypothesis of this oral presentation?
3. List two visual aids that could be used to add interest and clarity to this presentation.

READING LIKE A HISTORIAN

Making Written Presentations

Define the Skill

Written presentations are one of the ways that historians present their scholarship. Historians must perform careful research and cite all sources in written presentations. They also try to write about a small part of an event. This is called narrowing the focus, and it helps historians make important points and explore new facets of history. For example, a historian might not make a written presentation about World War II, which would take thousands of pages to fully cover. He or she would probably write about one aspect of the war, such as a certain battle. As a student, a written presentation is a way for you to present information on a topic you have researched.

Learn the Skill

Use the following strategies to make written presentations.

1 Identify a historical topic. Be sure to narrow the focus of your idea or theme. Also, clearly state your topic. Make sure that any facts you include relate specifically to this topic.

2 Formulate a hypothesis. This will be the main idea of your presentation. Once you have determined your hypothesis, research will be easier. Find and organize facts, data, and details to support your hypothesis.

3 Keep a bibliography of sources as you research. A bibliography is a list of all sources used or cited in a written presentation. You must cite your sources to retain credibility and avoid plagiarism.

4 Clearly state your hypothesis and the facts that support it in your writing. This will help you organize your presentation. Good historians show both sides of any argument, so be sure to include all relevant facts.

5 Proofread your written presentation to ensure that it is well organized and grammatically correct. Proofreading your notes and your presentation is always important to prevent errors. Read your presentation aloud to make sure that your statements are clear.

Topic: The Camp David Accords, 1978

Hypothesis: The Camp David ~~Accounts~~ Accords were an important first step in establishing peace in the Middle East.

Fact: By signing the agreement, Egypt recognized Israel as a country.

Bibliography: World Book Encyclopedia, 2003 edition; Volume 1, p. 582a

Apply the Skill

1. What is the hypothesis in the written presentation notes above?
2. List an area of history you would like to research.
3. Narrow the focus to a small part of this area, and write a sample hypothesis for your written presentation.

Strategies for Multiple Choice

You can improve your test-taking skills by practicing these strategies for multiple-choice questions. Read the skill-specific tips and samples on the left page. Then practice the skill on the right page. A multiple-choice question usually consists of a single *stem* and four *answer options*. Only one option is the correct answer. The other, incorrect options are *distracters*.

LEARN

1 **Read the stem carefully to determine what it is asking.**

2 **Read carefully when a question is phrased in the negative.**
Some standardized tests phrase questions in the negative. Take care with questions that contain words such as *not* and *except*.

3 **Look for key words and facts within a stem.**

4 **Consider options such as *all of the above* and *none of the above* as you would any other possible response.**
If you choose *all of the above*, ensure that all of the choices are correct.

5 **If two options contradict each other, one of them is likely to be the correct answer.**

6 **Eliminate the answer options that you know are incorrect.**

7 **Watch for modifiers.**
Options that include superlative words such as *always* or *never* are usually incorrect. Superlatives indicate that the correct answer must be an undisputed fact. In social studies, that is rarely the case.

Stem **①**　　　　　　　　　**②**

1. Which of the following was *not* a cause of colonial unrest with Britain?

   Answer Options
   - **A** the Boston Massacre
   - **B** the Olive Branch petition
   - **C** passage of various taxes, such as the Sugar Act, on the colonies
   - **D** the presence of British soldiers in the colonies

2. On April 18, 1775, the <u>first</u> shots of the Revolutionary War were fired at
   - **A** Concord.
   - **B** Lexington.
   - **C** Philadelphia.
   - **D** all of the above ← **④**

   ③ Many shots were fired during the Revolution, but you are looking for those that were fired *first*.

3. During the Revolutionary War, a Loyalist was someone who
   - **A** remained loyal to Britain. ←
   - **B** wanted freedom from Britain. ← **⑤**
   - **C** fought alongside the Continental Army.
   - **D** lived mainly in New England and Virginia.

4. Many changes occurred as a result of the Revolutionary War, including
   - **A** more rights for women.
   - **B** voting rights for <u>all</u> men.
   - **C** Spanish control of the colonies.
   - **D** the formation of the United States.

   ⑥ Absolute words such as *all*, *none*, and *every* often signal an incorrect option.

   ⑦ You can eliminate **C** if you recall that Spain controlled Florida after the Revolutionary War.

TT2 TEST-TAKING STRATEGIES AND PRACTICE

Answers: 1 (B), 2 (B), 3 (A), 4 (D)

PRACTICE

Directions: *Read the following questions and choose the best answer.*

1. Which of the following were considered border states in the Civil War?
   - **A** Kentucky
   - **B** Maryland
   - **C** all of the above
   - **D** none of the above

2. What existing invention was put to use in the Civil War to aid communication?
   - **A** e-mail
   - **B** telephone
   - **C** the telegraph
   - **D** the Pony Express

3. The Emancipation Proclamation freed all
   - **A** enslaved people.
   - **B** debtors from their debts
   - **C** enslaved people in rebelling states.
   - **D** enslaved people who had escaped to the North.

4. Prison camps during the Civil War did not
   - **A** lack food.
   - **B** have disease.
   - **C** have overcrowding.
   - **D** have sanitary conditions.

Strategies for Secondary Sources

You can improve your test-taking skills by practicing these strategies for secondary sources. Read the skill-specific tips and samples on the left page. Then practice the skill on the right page. A secondary source is a written source or a visual created after an event by a person who was not present at the event. The creators of secondary sources research primary sources and other secondary sources to learn about historical events. A biography is an example of a secondary source, as is a history textbook.

LEARN

❶ Identify the type of secondary source.
Is it an encyclopedia entry, a Web site, a scholarly article, or another type of source?

❷ Identify the author of the secondary source.
Note how much time has passed between the event and the time when the author writes about it. Is the author qualified to write about the topic?

❸ Look at the title and topic sentence to preview the content of the passage.

❹ Recognize the historical event or people involved.

❺ Ask yourself whether the author uses any primary sources or other secondary sources for support.

❻ Read the questions before rereading the passage so that you know what information you need to find.

—Paul Johnson, *A History of the American People*, p. 445

Lincoln's object was not merely to put his name and his case before the American people, as well as Illinois voters. It was also to expose the essential pantomime-horse approach of a man who tried to straddle North and South. He succeeded in both. He put to Douglas the key question: 'Can the people of a United States territory, in any lawful way, against the wish of a citizen of the United States, exclude slavery from its limits prior to the formation of a state constitution?' If Douglas said yes, to win Illinois voters, he lost the South. If he said no, to win the South, he lost Illinois. Douglas' answer was: 'It matters not what way the Supreme Court may hereafter decide as to the abstract question whether slavery may or may not go into a territory under the Constitution; the people have the lawful means to introduce it or exclude it as they please, for the reason that slavery cannot exist a day or an hour unless it is supported by the local police regulations.' This answer won Douglas Illinois but lost him the South and hence, two years later, the presidency.

1. Johnson uses primary source quotes to
   A identify the two senatorial candidates.
   B show the similarities between the viewpoints of Lincoln and Douglas.
   C describe the many issues that Lincoln and Douglas debated.
   D show how Lincoln forces Douglas to state his position on slavery.

Answer: 1 (D)

PRACTICE

Directions: *Read the following passage and use your knowledge of U.S. history to answer the questions below.*

> —from *In the Presence of Mine Enemies: War in the Heart of America, 1859–1863*
> By Edward L. Ayers
>
> Michael Hanger, the young carpenter from Augusta in the 5th Virginia Infantry, described the situation he and his comrades faced [in his diary]. "5 O'Clock A.M. we can hear the cannon firing from the hills in front, and a little below us. The Yankees are endeavoring to draw us in that direction. The Junction is strongly fortified . . . in every possible direction." Put into position, Hanger and his comrades lay there for three and a half hours . . .
>
> Things got worse the next day. "It is now raining very hard and has been all night. The wounded on the battlefield must have suffered greatly last night. It is a very muddy and disagreeable day . . ." Hanger gave no fuller evaluation of the battle. He did not say who had won and lost. He only listed the names of the men in his company who had been wounded. He did not give the name the battle was to bear. The Confederates called it Manassas, after the nearby town; the Union called it Bull Run, naming it after the nearby river, as became its custom.

1. What primary source does Ayers use?
   A accounts by Union generals
   B the diary of Michael Hanger
   C Michael Hanger's military record
   D accounts by Confederate generals

2. What historical event is Michael Hanger describing?
   A the Battle of Bull Run
   B the burning of Atlanta
   C the Battle of Yorktown
   D Michael Hanger's death

3. Ayers uses primary sources to
   A analyze the impact of the battle.
   B provide descriptive details of the battle.
   C support political viewpoints of the time.
   D give personal details about fellow soldiers.

4. How did the outcome of this battle affect the Union army?
   A The victory boosted the soldiers' morale.
   B The soldiers realized that it would be a short war.
   C The Union army decreased training for its soldiers.
   D The Union army increased training for its soldiers.

Strategies for Political Cartoons

You can improve your test-taking skills by practicing these strategies for political cartoons. Read the skill-specific tips and samples on the left page. Then practice the skill on the right page. Political cartoons are primary sources. They use comedic images to poke fun at political figures and issues. Cartoons can provide helpful context to the opinions and values of the time.

LEARN

❶ Identify the characters and issues being portrayed.
This figure represents an anarchist.

❷ Read the caption and any other labels to better understand the subject.

❸ Identify any exaggerated images or ideas.
The wild character of the anarchist is a common exaggeration from the time period.

❹ Identify common symbols used to help you recognize the subject of the cartoon.

❺ Identify the cartoonist's point of view.
Recognize whether the subject is portrayed positively or negatively.

❻ Identify the message the cartoonist wanted to send with this cartoon.
Does the cartoonist agree or disagree with the situation?

❷ The figure's hat is labeled "Reds" and the knife says "Bolshevism," a name for Russian communism.

❺ The cartoonist sees anarchy and bolshevism as a threat, and portrays the anarchist in a negative light.

1. Which sentence best summarizes the message of this cartoon?
   A Immigration is anarchy.
   B Anarchy is not welcome in the United States.
   C Immigrants and anarchists are hiding under the U.S. flag.
   D Immigration should be restricted and anarchists should be deported.

2. Which word summarizes the cartoonist opinion regarding immigration practices?
   A positive
   B criminal
   C beneficial
   D dangerous

Answers: 1 (D), 2 (D)

PRACTICE

Directions: *Interpret the following cartoon and answer the questions below.*

1. The symbol the artist uses for the Teapot Dome oil scandal is
   A a steamship.
   B a steamroller.
   C a runaway train.
   D a horse and buggy.

2. Who might the figures running from the scandal represent?
   A ordinary citizens
   B politicians implicated or involved in the scandal
   C people harmed by the illegal oil deals
   D those who brought the scandal to the public's attention

3. What effect does the artist think the scandal will have on President Warren G. Harding?
   A It will help him.
   B It will crush him.
   C It will bypass him.
   D It will not affect him.

4. Which sentence best summarizes the message of this cartoon?
   A President Harding was a criminal.
   B Being involved with an oil company will crush politicians.
   C The Teapot Dome scandal was a minor incident.
   D The Teapot Dome scandal will negatively impact those involved.

STRATEGIES FOR POLITICAL CARTOONS

Strategies for Charts

You can improve your test-taking skills by practicing these strategies for charts. Read the skill-specific tips and samples on the left page. Then practice the skill on the right page. Charts are used to organize and summarize large amounts of information. The table, one of the most common types of charts, organizes data into columns and rows.

LEARN

① Read the title or heading of the chart.
Find out the topic and information covered in the chart.

② Find row and column headings.
Identify the information represented, how it is organized, and how the information is related.

③ Look for similar trends or data patterns between rows and columns.
Also look for data that does not conform to the patterns.

④ Make generalizations and draw conclusions from information in the chart.
One generalization you could make from this chart is that many countries wanted to prevent future conflict.

① PROGRAMS FOR A SAFER WORLD

As World War II came to an end, the countries of the world began seeking ways to prevent the problems and conflicts that helped lead to war. Leaders in the United States and other countries paved the way in establishing the following:

② The first column lists the names of the programs. The second column gives details about each program's purpose.

③ The program in this row is the only one that does not relate directly to economic reconstruction.

Program	Description
World Bank (1944)	• Organization for providing loans and advice to countries for the purpose of reducing poverty
International Monetary Fund (1944)	• System for promoting orderly financial relationships between countries • Designed to prevent economic crises and to encourage trade and economic growth
United Nations (1945)	• Organization in which member nations agree to settle disputes by peaceful means • Replaced the League of Nations
General Agreement on Tariffs and Trade (1946)	• Agreement among member nations on rules and regulations for international trade • Focused on reducing tariffs and other trade barriers

1. Which generalization could you make from the information on this chart?
   A After World War II, many countries believed that financial agreements between countries would help to limit disputes.
   B After World War II, the World Bank primarily dealt with military issues.
   C After World War II, these programs were developed to promote problems and conflicts between countries.
   D After World War II, the wealthy countries around the world would receive loans from poorer countries.

Answer: 1 (A)

PRACTICE

Directions: *Interpret the following chart and answer the questions below.*

JEWISH LOSSES IN THE HOLOCAUST

	c. 1933	c. 1950	Percent Decrease
Europe	9,500,000	3,500,000	63
Selected Countries			
Poland	3,000,000	45,000	98.5
Romania	980,000	28,000	97
Germany	565,000	37,000	93.5
Hungary	445,000	155,000	65
Czechoslovakia	357,000	17,000	95
Austria	250,000	18,000	93
Greece	100,000	7,000	93
Yugoslavia	70,000	3,500	95
Bulgaria	50,000	6,500	87

Source: *United States Holocaust Memorial Museum*

1. Which of the following statements about this chart is true?
   - **A** The data includes every country in Europe.
   - **B** The data shows Jewish population loss in Poland during the Holocaust.
   - **C** The data covers the years 1933 to 1980.
   - **D** The data shows Jewish population losses around the world.

2. Which statement is NOT true about this chart?
   - **A** Poland lost more Jews than any other country on the chart.
   - **B** Bulgaria lost the least number of Jews of any other country on the chart.
   - **C** From 1933 to 1950, Hungary lost more Jews than any other country shown on the chart.
   - **D** Hungary had the smallest percentage drop in Jewish population from 1933 to 1950.

3. What trend is shown in this chart?
   - **A** The Holocaust reduced overall Jewish population in Europe by 75 percent.
   - **B** Jewish population losses during the Holocaust were concentrated in Central and Eastern Europe.
   - **C** Jewish population in Europe increased during the Holocaust.
   - **D** all of the above

4. Which generalization could you make from the data on this chart?
   - **A** The Holocaust dramatically reduced Europe's Jewish population.
   - **B** The Holocaust dramatically increased Europe's Jewish population.
   - **C** The total population of Europe decreased by 65 percent.
   - **D** The total population of Poland decreased by 98.5 percent.

STRATEGIES FOR CHARTS

Strategies for Line and Bar Graphs

You can improve your test-taking skills by practicing these strategies for line and bar graphs. Read the skill-specific tips and samples on the left page. Then practice the skill on the right page. Graphs are used to show the relationship among numerical data. Line graphs illustrate how quantities and trends change over time. Bar graphs compare groups of numbers within categories.

LEARN

1 Read the title of the graph to determine its main idea.

2 Study the label on the vertical axis.
The vertical axis usually indicates the type of information in the graph.

3 Examine the label on the horizontal axis.
The horizontal axis usually tells you the time period the graph covers.

4 If a legend accompanies the graph, study it.
The legend provides additional information. Legends specify what the colors, patterns, or symbols on the graph mean.

5 Identify any trends or patterns that the graph reveals.

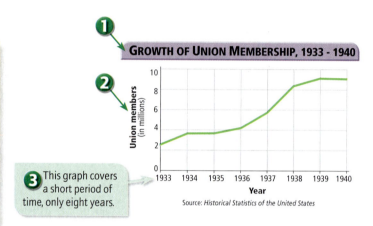

1. Which statement correctly describes the trend in union membership?
   A Union membership grew the most between 1933 and 1935.
   B Union membership grew the most between 1934 and 1936.
   C Union membership grew the most between 1936 and 1938.
   D Union membership grew the most between 1938 and 1940.

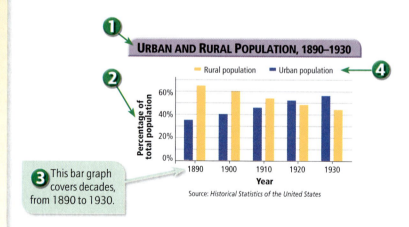

2. Which of these statements describes the rural population between 1890 and 1930?
   A The rural population was lower in 1890 than in 1930.
   B The rural population was higher in 1890 than in 1930.
   C The rural population and the urban population increased at the same rate.
   D The rural population and the urban population declined at the same rate.

Answers: 1 (C), 2 (B)

PRACTICE

Directions: *Use the line graph and the bar graph to answer the questions below.*

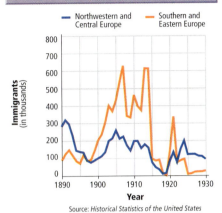

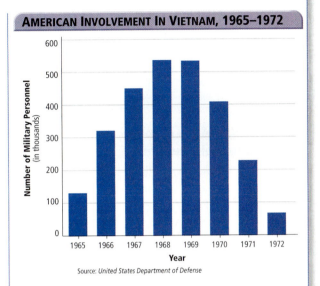

1. Between 1900 and 1910, most European immigrants came from
   A Southern and Eastern Europe.
   B Northern and Central Europe.
   C Southern and Central Europe.
   D Northern and Eastern Europe.

2. Which of the following describes a trend in European immigration to the United States between 1920 and 1930?
   A More European immigrants came from Northern and Eastern Europe.
   B More European immigrants came from Southern and Central Europe.
   C The number of immigrants coming from Southern and Eastern Europe decreased.
   D The number of immigrants coming from Northern and Central Europe remained about the same.

3. How did the number of U.S. military personnel in Vietnam change between 1966 and 1967?
   A It decreased by more than 100,000.
   B It increased by more than 100,000.
   C It increased by more than 200,000.
   D It decreased by more than 200,000.

4. Which of the following statements describes the number of U.S. military personnel in Vietnam from 1969 to 1972?
   A The number of U.S. military personnel in Vietnam did not change.
   B The number of U.S. military personnel in Vietnam increased slightly.
   C The number of U.S. military personnel in Vietnam decreased dramatically.
   D The number of U.S. military personnel in Vietnam increased dramatically.

STRATEGIES FOR LINE AND BAR GRAPHS **TT11**

Strategies for Pie Graphs

You can improve your test-taking skills by practicing these strategies for pie graphs. Read the skill-specific tips and samples on the left page. Then practice the skill on the right page. A pie, or circle, graph shows how parts are related to a whole. Slices of a pie graph should add up to 100% and are proportional to their percentage.

LEARN

❶ Read the title of the graph to learn the topic and time period it covers.
The title explains that the topic is the presidential election of 1800.

❷ Be sure the slices add up to 99–100%.
Compare the slices. Are they similar or do they vary widely? Pie graphs don't always indicate numbers, so you may have to estimate.

❸ Look for the legend or labels to explain what the different slices represent.
The labels indicate the number of electoral votes won by each candidate.

❹ If there are two graphs, compare and contrast them to identify and understand trends.

❺ Draw conclusions about what might cause similarities or differences between slices or graphs.
The narrow margin of victory suggests that the country was evenly divided.

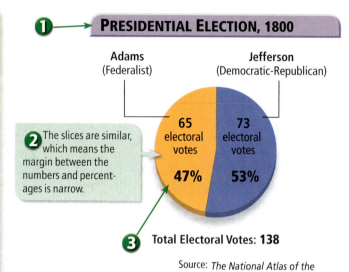

❷ The slices are similar, which means the margin between the numbers and percentages is narrow.

❸ Total Electoral Votes: 138

Source: *The National Atlas of the United States of America*

1. Which sentence best describes the political atmosphere surrounding the election of 1800?
   A The election race was calm, as a clear Republican victory was expected.
   B The election race was vicious, but a clear Federalist victory was expected.
   C U.S. citizens were almost evenly divided between the two candidates
   D The Federalist party had an overwhelming lead in the election race

Answer: 1 (C)

PRACTICE

Directions: *Interpret the following circle graph and answer the questions below.*

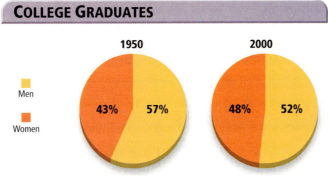

1. What do the different colors of the slices represent?
   A 1950 and 2000
   B men and women
   C the percentages of each slice
   D women who graduated and women who did not graduate

2. What comparison do these two graphs make?
   A the number of male versus female students who graduate from college
   B the number of women who graduate from college versus the number of women who vote
   C the gender of college graduates in 1950 versus 2000
   D the percentage of women who graduate from high school versus the percentage of women who graduate from college

3. From these graphs you can conclude that
   A More women than men graduated from college in 2000.
   B Fewer men than women graduated from college in 1950.
   C Women made up a smaller percentage of all college graduates in 2000 than in 1950.
   D Women made up a larger percentage of all college graduates in 2000 than in 1950.

4. What might explain the trend of women to close the gap on men in college graduations?
   A More men earned college degrees in 2000 than in 1950.
   B More men than women earned college degrees in 1950.
   C Women no longer thought they needed college degrees in 2000.
   D Women found a college degree more important to earn in 2000 than in 1950.

STRATEGIES FOR PIE GRAPHS **TT13**

Strategies for Political and Thematic Maps

You can improve your test-taking skills by practicing these strategies for political and thematic maps. Read the skill-specific tips and samples on the left page. Then practice the skill on the right page. Political maps show countries and the political divisions within them. For example, a political map might show provinces, states, counties, or major cities. They may also highlight physical features, such as mountains or bodies of water.

A thematic map shows patterns of movement, battles, or other special features. Special symbols, such as icons or arrows, are often used on these types of maps.

LEARN

1 Read the title or heading of the map to find the topic and other information that is shown.

2 Find the map legend to find out what different colors or symbols on the map mean.
Also, read any labels on the map. These can give you details about the purpose of the map.

3 Look for any special features on the map.
These may include a locator or an inset map. The arrows on this map show migratory patterns.

4 Use the compass rose to find directions on the map.
If there is no compass rose on the map, you must use your prior knowledge of geography to determine direction and location. The map scale can also help in estimating the distance between two places.

5 Note the lines of longitude and latitude.
These help determine location on a map.

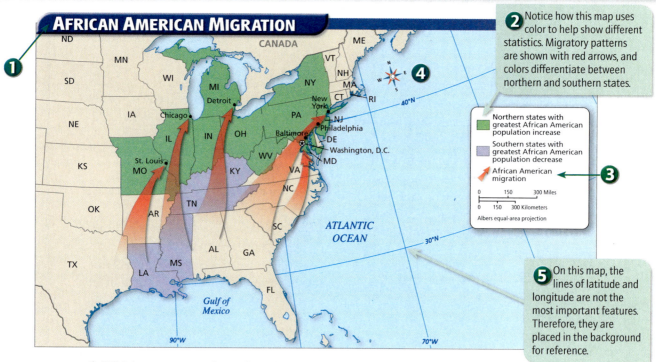

2 Notice how this map uses color to help show different statistics. Migratory patterns are shown with red arrows, and colors differentiate between northern and southern states.

5 On this map, the lines of latitude and longitude are not the most important features. Therefore, they are placed in the background for reference.

1. Which statement about the information on the map is correct?
   A Many African Americans left the East in the early 1900s.
   B Many African Americans left the West in the early 1900s.
   C Many African Americans left the North in the early 1900s.
   D Many African Americans left the South in the early 1900s.

Answer: 1 (D)

PRACTICE

Directions: *Interpret the following thematic map and answer the questions below.*

1. Which statement about the United Kingdom is correct?

   A The United Kingdom was neutral.

   B The United Kingdom was controlled jointly by the Allied and Axis powers.

   C The United Kingdom was controlled by the Axis powers.

   D The United Kingdom was controlled by the Allied powers.

2. In what year did Axis troops advance into the Union of Soviet Socialist Republics?

   A 1938

   B 1939

   C 1940

   D 1941

3. Which of the following accurately shows the order of German occupation?

   A Yugoslavia, France, Poland

   B Poland, France, Yugoslavia

   C France, Poland, Yugoslavia

   D Yugoslavia, Lithuania, France

4. All of the following statements about the map are true except:

   A Neither Bulgaria nor Finland were neutral countries.

   B Both Spain and Turkey were neutral countries.

   C Axis powers controlled most of Europe.

   D Allied powers controlled most of Europe.

STRATEGIES FOR POLITICAL AND THEMATIC MAPS **TT15**

Strategies for Time Lines

You can improve your test-taking skills by practicing these strategies for time lines. Read the skill-specific tips and samples on the left page. Then practice the skill on the right page. A time line is a type of chart which shows events as they occurred in their chronological order. Time lines are a useful visual tool for learning sequence and cause-and-effect.

LEARN

1 **Read the title to learn the subject and time period of the time line.**

2 **Look for the beginning and end dates on the time line.**
Think about what you already know about this time period before you begin reading.

3 **Read the events on the time line in chronological order.**
Try to understand the connections between the events.

4 **Note the intervals between events.**
Are there long or short breaks between events?

5 **Make inferences about the time period from the information on the time line.**

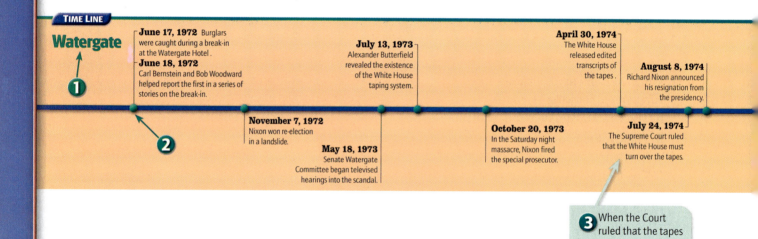

1. What can you infer about the reaction of the American public to Watergate?
   A The public was not affected by the scandal.
   B The public supported President Nixon's policies.
   C The public did not think that the break-in was wrong.
   D The public was disappointed and probably angered by the scandal.

TT16 TEST-TAKING STRATEGIES AND PRACTICE

Answer: 1 (D)

PRACTICE

Directions: *Interpret the following time line and answer the questions below.*

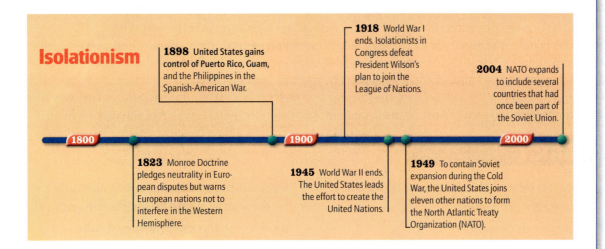

1. What time period does this time line cover?
   A the 1800s
   B the 1900s
   C the 2000s
   D all of the above

2. American foreign policy in the 1800s
   A did not exist.
   B was isolationist.
   C was involved with the politics of other countries.
   D took on a leadership role to the rest of the world.

3. In what way did American foreign policy change as time passed?
   A It became more isolationist.
   B America opened relations with every country immediately.
   C America slowly became more involved with other countries.
   D The United States government thought creating a group of "united nations" would not be helpful and wanted to deal with countries on a one-on-one basis.

4. What can you infer is one reason why the United States wanted to create a group of United Nations?
   A They wanted to return to their isolationist stance.
   B They had just finished a second world war and were looking for a way to keep and encourage peace.
   C They wanted to foster trade relations.
   D They did not want to participate in any international debates.

STRATEGIES FOR TIMELINES **TT17**

Strategies for Constructed Response

You can improve your test-taking skills by practicing these strategies for constructed-response questions. Read the skill-specific tips and samples on the left page. Then practice the skill on the right page. Constructed-response questions are based on different types of documents. These can include excerpts, political cartoons, charts, graphs, maps, time lines, posters, and other visuals.

Each document is investigated through one or more open-ended, short-answer questions, which build from simple to complex and evaluate critical-thinking skills. The first question usually requires an answer that can be found in the document. The second question often asks you to connect the information presented in different parts of the document. The third question often requires an answer that is built on information that is not in the document, but is related to the subject of the document.

LEARN

1 Read the title of the document to identify the subject presented.

2 Study the document.
The callouts give you more information about the subject of the map. Each callout on this map identifies the conflict in the area.

3 Read the questions and then study the document again to locate the answers.

4 Answer the questions carefully.
Complete sentences are not necessary unless the directions say to use them.

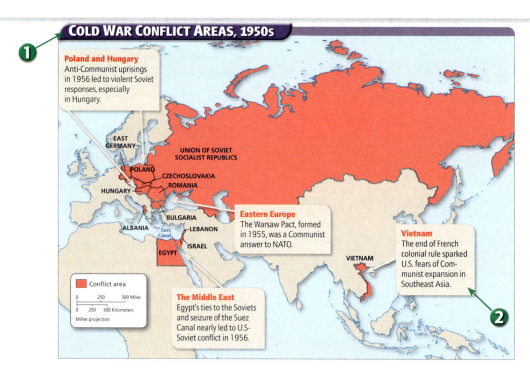

1. What was considered the Communist answer to NATO? _____ the Warsaw Pact _____

2. How was the conflict in the Middle East different than the conflicts in Poland and Hungary?
_____ In the Middle East, Egypt was friendly to the Soviet Union. _____
_____ In Poland and Hungary, there were anti-communist uprisings. _____

3. Which conflict area will the U.S. military be most involved with in the 1960s? _____ Vietnam _____

PRACTICE

Directions: *Look at the following chart and answer the questions below.*

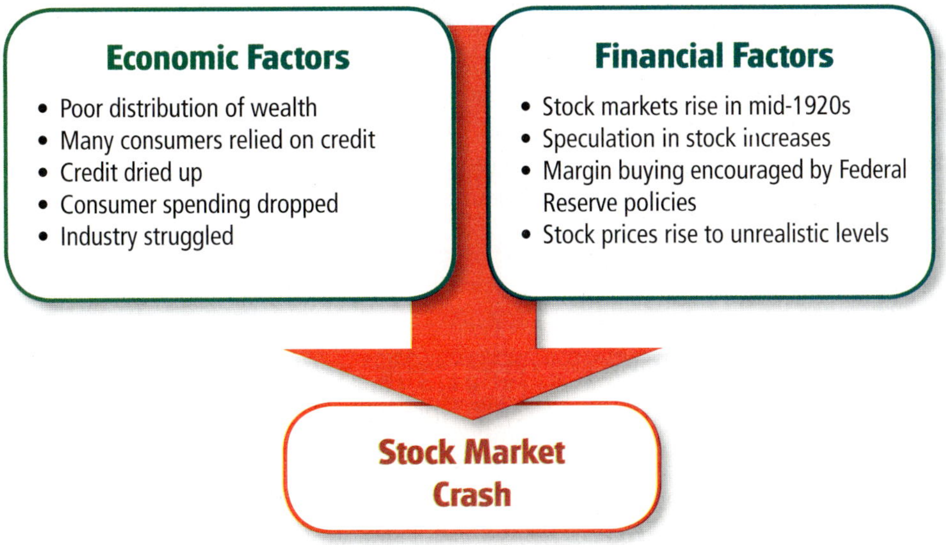

Economic Factors
- Poor distribution of wealth
- Many consumers relied on credit
- Credit dried up
- Consumer spending dropped
- Industry struggled

Financial Factors
- Stock markets rise in mid-1920s
- Speculation in stock increases
- Margin buying encouraged by Federal Reserve policies
- Stock prices rise to unrealistic levels

↓

Stock Market Crash

1. What was one economic factor that led to the crash of the stock market?

2. How was credit spending both an economic and financial factor in the stock market crash?

3. How did the crash of the stock market affect the American economy?

Strategies for Extended Response

You can improve your test-taking skills by practicing these strategies for extended-response questions. Read the skill-specific tips and samples on the left page. Then practice the skill on the right page. Extended-response questions usually focus on a document. Documents can be articles, historical documents, charts, graphs, photographs, political cartoons, and other information sources. Documents can be primary or secondary sources. Some extended-response questions ask you to analyze or summarize the information presented in the document. Others require you to complete a chart, graph, or diagram. In most standardized tests, a document has only one extended-response question.

LEARN

1. **Read the title of the document to learn what the document is about.**
2. **Read the extended-response questions carefully.**
3. **Study and analyze the document.**
   This chart lists important New Deal programs undertaken in response to the stock market crash and the Great Depression.
4. **Analyze any partial or a sample answers provided.**
   Your answers should take the same form as this sample answer.
5. **Take notes and jot down ideas in outline form.**
   Use your notes and outline to prepare for writing an essay or other extended piece of writing.

MAJOR NEW DEAL PROGRAMS

Relief	
Civilian Conservation Corps (CCC), 1933	provided jobs on conservation projects to young men whose families needed relief
Works Progress Administration (WPA), 1935	provided many different types of jobs on public works projects for those needing relief
Social Security Act, 1935	established pensions for retirees, unemployment benefits, and aid for certain groups of low-income or disabled people

Reform	
Securities and Exchange Commission (SEC), 1934	provided increased government regulation of the trading on stock exchanges
National Labor Relations Act, 1935	established the National Labor Relations Board (NLRB) to enforce labor laws

Recovery	
Tennessee Valley Authority (TVA), 1933	promoted development projects in the Tennessee River Valley
Federal Housing Administration (FHA), 1934	provided loans for renovating or building homes

1. In the right-hand column, briefly explain the function of each New Deal program listed in the left-hand column. One entry has been completed for you.

2. This chart explains several important New Deal programs introduced to respond to the stock market crash and the Great Depression. Write a short speech for Franklin D. Roosevelt discussing why these programs are necessary and what he hopes they will accomplish.

PRACTICE

Directions: *Use the time line and your knowledge of American history to answer questions 1 and 2.*

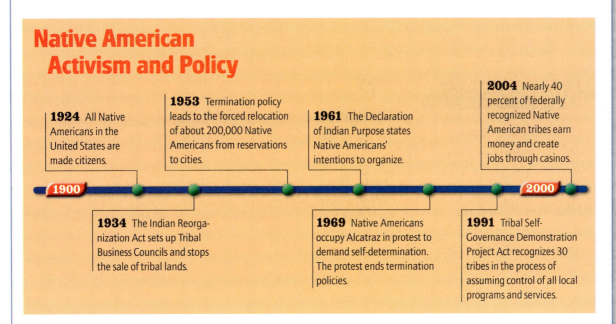

1. Make a chart as shown below on a separate sheet of paper. Complete the chart by listing major events in Native American history since 1800 and explaining each event's significance to the relationship between Native Americans and the United States government.

Year	Event	Significance

2. Identify major changes in United States government policy toward Native Americans as shown on the time line. Write a short essay discussing the difference between Americanization and termination policies, analyzing each policy's effects on the formation of Native American social and political movements.

STRATEGIES FOR EXTENDED RESPONSE **TT21**

Strategies for Document-Based Questions

You can improve your test-taking skills by practicing these strategies for document-based questions. Read the skill-specific tips and samples on the left page. Then practice the skill on the right page. A document-based question consists of the analysis of several written and visual documents. Such documents may include excerpts, quotations, maps, charts, graphs, time lines, political cartoons, and so on. These documents are followed by short-answer questions. Students use their answers to these questions and information from the documents to produce an essay on a certain topic.

LEARN

1. **Read carefully the "Background" to understand the documents that you will be analyzing.**
2. **Read the "Task" portion, which describes in detail the steps you will follow in answering document-based questions and formulating an essay about a given topic.**
3. **"Part A: Short-Answer Questions"** signifies the first part of the document-based question.
4. **Examine and study each document.**
5. **Read and answer each of the document-specific questions.**

Background In the late 1800s and early 1900s women in the United States made many important social and political gains.

Task Using information from the documents and your knowledge of United States history, answer the questions that follow each document in Part A. Your answers to the questions will help you write the Part B essay, in which you will be asked to:

> Describe challenges facing women in the late 1800s and early 1900s.

Part A: Short-Answer Questions

Study each document carefully. Then answer the question or questions that follow each document in the space provided.

DOCUMENT 1

"... The women, dissatisfied as they are with this form of government, that enforces taxation without representation—that compels them to obey laws to which they have never given their consent—that imprisons and hangs them without a trial by a jury of their peers, that robs them, in marriage, of the custody of their own persons, wages and children—are this half of the people left wholly at the mercy of the other half, in direct violation of the spirit and letter of the declarations of the framers of this government, every one of which was based on the immutable [undeniable] principle of equal rights to all."

1. What were Susan B. Anthony's beliefs about women's voting rights?

   She believed that women should have the same voting rights as men.

TT22 TEST-TAKING STRATEGIES AND PRACTICE

DOCUMENT 2

2. What does this political cartoon represent?

It represents tough choices facing women in their home and work lives.

Part B: Essay

Using the documents, your answers to the questions in Part A, and your knowledge of U.S. history, write a well-organized essay about challenges facing women in the late 1800s and early 1900s.

Write your essay.
Include an introductory paragraph that frames your argument, a main body with details that explain it, and a closing paragraph that summarizes your position. Include specific details or documents to support your ideas.

Rubric
The best essays will note challenges such as voting rights (Document 1), and the tough choices relating to women's careers and home life. (Document 2).

PRACTICE

Background In the 1920s, new forms of media emerged that enabled people to share the same information and enjoy the same pastimes.

Task Using information from the documents and your knowledge of U.S. history, answer the questions that follow each document in Part A. Your answers to the questions will help you write the Part B essay, in which you will be asked to:

> Describe the growth of popular American culture in the 1920s.

Document 1

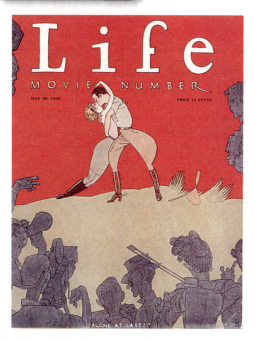

1. What does this magazine cover convey about American culture during the 1920s?

Document 2

2. What can you tell about the popularity of films from this picture?

Part B: Essay

Using the documents, your answers to the questions in Part A, and your knowledge of U.S. history, write a well-organized essay about the growth of popular American culture in the 1920s.

UNIT 1
The United States before 1898

Beginnings–1898

Chapter 1
Beginnings of America
Beginnings–1763

Chapter 2
Forming a New Nation
1763–1815

Chapter 3
Developing a National Identity
1815–1860

Chapter 4
The Union in Crisis
1850–1877

Chapter 5
An Industrial Nation
1860–1920

Themes

Immigration and Migration
People first migrated to America many thousands of years ago and lived throughout the continent before Europeans arrived and began to form colonies.

Government and Democracy
The 13 English colonies declared their independence from Great Britain in 1776, forming the United States of America. Conflicts between the North and the South over the issue of slavery resulted in the outbreak of the Civil War in 1861. The nation reunited during Reconstruction and continued to expand westward and develop into an industrial nation.

The voyage of the *Mayflower* marked a new beginning for not just the settlers on board but for America as well.

THE GRANGER COLLECTION, NEW YORK

Prepare to Read

Identifying Main Idea and Details

Find practice for **Identifying Main Idea and Details** in the **Skills Handbook,** p. H5

The main idea is the most important idea of a passage. Details support, illustrate, or develop main idea.

Before You Read
Look at headings and the Reading Check questions.

While You Read
Look for the topic sentences in each paragraph. These are often the main ideas.

After You Read
Ask yourself questions. What was the main idea? What was the author trying to get across?

War in the South

In 1778 the British shifted their strategy. They had hoped to crush the rebels with an overwhelming military response. Now, instead of sending more troops and supplies from Britain, British officials decided to rely on the many Loyalists in America for support. They hoped the Loyalists would rise up to support them. Because they believed the Loyalist sympathies were strongest in the South, the British planned to campaign there.

The British soon learned that the Patriots were as strong and determined in the South as they were in New England. Small bands of Patriot militiamen frequently struck unsuspecting British troops and then disappeared into the wood. The most famous band was led by Francis Marion, who was nicknamed "the Swamp Fox" for his daring raids from the Carolina swamps.

READING CHECK **Identifying the Main Idea** How did British shift their strategy shift in 1778?

This section heading tells you the topic—Revolutionary War battles in the South.

Main Idea The British chose to shift their battle strategy in 1778.

Detail British officials decided to change their plans and campaign in the South, where British sympathies were believed to be strongest.

Test Prep Tip

Short answer questions on tests often ask you to find details that support a passage's main idea. To find supporting details, form questions using *who, what, when, where, why,* and *how.* You can turn section headings into questions. An example for this passage might be "Why did the Revolutionary War move to the South?"

Reading like a Historian

Analyzing Primary Sources

Find practice for **Analyzing Primary Sources** in the **Skills Handbook**, p. H28

Primary sources are documents created by people who were present at historical events either as witnesses or as participants. These sources can range from letters and diary entries to newspaper stories and photographs.

Strategies historians use:
- Find clues in the text. Look for words that identify a primary source, such as *I*, *we*, and *our*, or note quotation marks indicating that a passage is someone's speech or writing.
- Identify the author. Who is speaking or writing?
- Analyze the source, and weigh its treatment of historical events against your prior knowledge of them.

In January 1776 many colonists were divided about their future relationship with Great Britain. Then Thomas Paine published *Common Sense*, a pamphlet that stated in clear, easy-to-understand terms why the colonies should break free from British rule.

> "[A]ny submission to, or dependence on, Great Britain, tends directly to involve this continent in European wars and quarrels, and set us at variance [odds] with nations who would do otherwise seek our friendship, and against whom we have neither anger nor complaint. As Europe is our market for trade, we ought to form no partial connection with any part of it. 'Tis the true interest of America to steer clear of European contentions, which she can never do while by her dependence on Britain she is made the weight in the scale of British politics."
>
> —*Common Sense* by Thomas Paine, 1776

Quotation marks signal you are reading a primary source.

Arguing that Britain limited American trade appealed to Paine's audience.

Knowing the author and time period helps place the source in historical context.

 READING LIKE A HISTORIAN

As You Read Paraphrase the primary source to make sure you understand any difficult language.

As You Study Try to sort facts from opinions. Use your prior knowledge and information you read in the chapter to assess and reassess the point of view expressed in the primary source.

CHAPTER 1

Beginnings–1763

Beginnings of America

THE BIG PICTURE For thousands of years, people of many cultures have made the Americas home. They came looking for animals to hunt, for gold, for a quicker route to Asia's treasures, or for religious freedom. Some of these communities disappeared while others grew into successful colonies, ruled from afar.

California Standards

History–Social Science

8.2 Students analyze the political principles underlying the U.S. Constitution and compare the enumerated and implied powers of the federal government.

11.1 Students analyze the significant events in the founding of the nation and its attempts to realize the philosophy of government described in the Declaration of Independence.

11.3 Students analyze the role religion played in the founding of America, its lasting moral, social, and political impacts, and issues regarding religious liberty.

Skills Focus: READING LIKE A HISTORIAN

This detail from Portugal's Monument of Discovery shows Prince Henry the Navigator at the forefront of many famous Portuguese explorers. The monument is shaped like the prow of a ship and was built for the 500th anniversary of Prince Henry's death.
Drawing Conclusions Why do you think Portugal built this monument?

See **Skills Handbook**, p. H12

U.S.

38,000–10,000 BC The first people migrate to North America.

World

1500 BC
1200 BC Olmec culture arises along coast of Gulf of Mexico.

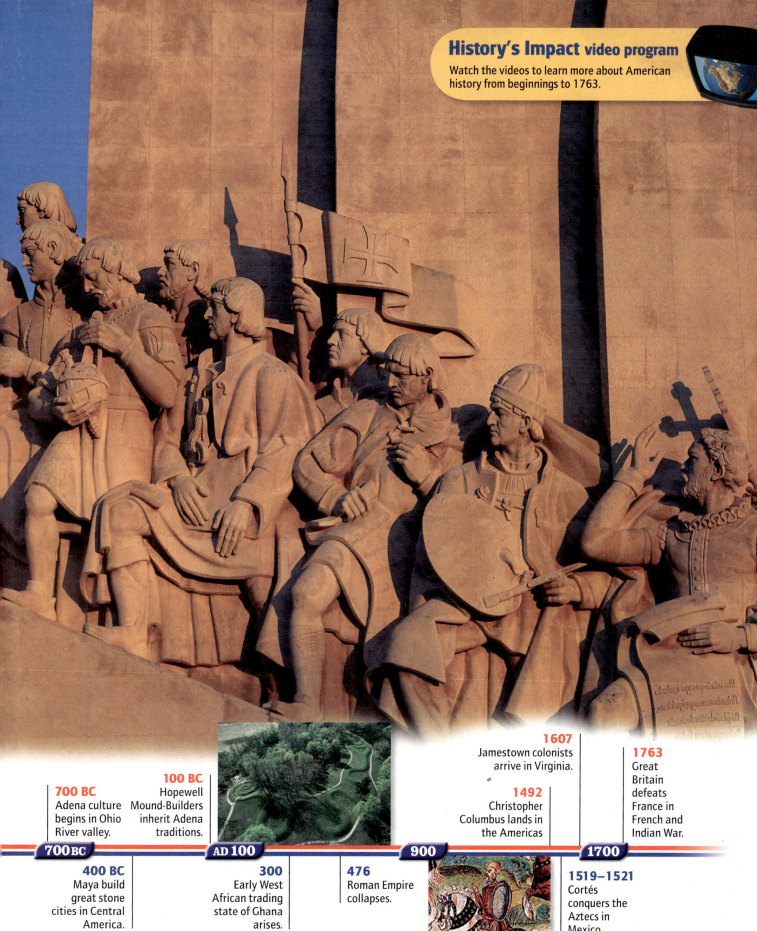

History's Impact video program
Watch the videos to learn more about American history from beginnings to 1763.

700 BC Adena culture begins in Ohio River valley.

100 BC Hopewell Mound-Builders inherit Adena traditions.

1607 Jamestown colonists arrive in Virginia.

1492 Christopher Columbus lands in the Americas

1763 Great Britain defeats France in French and Indian War.

700 BC — **AD 100** — **900** — **1700**

400 BC Maya build great stone cities in Central America.

300 Early West African trading state of Ghana arises.

476 Roman Empire collapses.

1519–1521 Cortés conquers the Aztecs in Mexico.

5

SECTION 1
The World before 1600

BEFORE YOU READ

MAIN IDEA

Diverse cultures existed in the Americas, Europe, and Africa before 1600.

READING FOCUS

1. Who were the first people in the early Americas?
2. In what ways were North American cultures before 1500 different, and in what ways were they similar?
3. What characterized African cultures before 1500?
4. How did European exploration begin?

KEY TERMS AND PEOPLE

Beringia
agricultural revolution
Maya
Aztec
Middle Ages
Magna Carta
Renaissance
Reformation
Christopher Columbus
Columbian Exchange

 HSS 8.2.1 Discuss the significance of the Magna Carta, the English Bill of Rights, and the Mayflower Compact.

The First AMERICANS

◀ Archaeologists discover artifacts, such as this spear straightener, that help reconstruct the past.

THE INSIDE STORY

How do we learn about prehistoric people in the Americas? Prehistory means the time before written records were kept. So with no ancient scrolls or stone tablets to refer to, and certainly no books or newspapers, how do we know about the first people in our part of the world?

Information about early American cultures comes mainly from archaeology. Archaeology is the scientific study of the remains of past human life. Archaeologists carry out digs to unearth ancient towns and campsites. They examine pottery, tools, bones, and other kinds of physical evidence.

One important piece of archaeological evidence is a distinctive stone spear point called the Clovis point. Because these spear points have been found throughout the Americas, scientists have developed theories of early human migration based upon them.

The Early Americas

As recently as 10,000 years ago, during the last Ice Age, thick sheets of ice covered many parts of the world. So much of the earth's water was frozen that sea levels dropped by several hundred feet, exposing land along the coastlines. Today the waters of the Bering Strait divide Alaska from Siberia in northeast Asia. But during the Ice Age a land bridge connected the continents of Asia and North America. Historians call this ancient land area **Beringia**.

Scholars agree that Siberian hunters crossed this land bridge to North America. This migration probably took place between 12,000 and 40,000 years ago, with small groups of hunters crossing the land bridge at different times. These first Americans were nomads, people who moved from place to place with the seasons. They

6 CHAPTER 1

followed a hunter-gatherer way of life, which meant that they hunted animals and gathered plants for food. They did not raise animals or farm crops. When the animals moved, the hunters followed them, never staying in one place for very long.

Approximately 10,000 years ago many of the large North American animals died off, so these early Americans turned to hunting smaller animals and gathering more plants. Then, about 7,000 years ago, some human groups began to plant seeds deliberately. Farming allowed them to settle into villages rather than moving from place to place. This dramatic change in the way people lived is called the agricultural revolution.

Empires of Mesoamerica
Empires rose up in Mesoamerica, a region that is today Mexico and Central America. Olmec culture first began around 1200 BC. The Olmec people had a tremendous influence on later cultures.

The Maya began their rise around 400 BC. They built large pyramids, and they also developed a writing system and a number system that used the number zero. In the 1400s the militaristic Aztec formed a large empire in present-day Mexico. Tenochtitlán, today's Mexico City, was the Aztec capital.

Early cultures of North America
Early Native Americans encountered many different environments in North America—forests, deserts, and fertile land. In each region, different kinds of societies developed. In the Southwest, for example, the Hohokam people farmed in the desert using irrigation systems. Another southwestern group, the Anasazi, built distinctive dwellings made of adobe. Later, these were called pueblos. The Anasazi are the ancestors of today's Pueblo Indians.

Other Native American groups, including the Adena and Hopewell, were known as the Mound Builders because they buried their dead in large earth mounds. Later, the Mississippians were the most advanced farmers north of Mexico. They built towns across the Southeast and southern Midwest, including the great city of Cahokia, which was located near present-day Saint Louis.

READING CHECK Identifying the Main Idea and Details Describe the earliest cultures of North America and Mesoamerica.

North American Cultures before 1500

In each region of North America, Native Americans adapted to differences in climate, geography, and resources. By the 1400s a wide range of cultures existed in North America.

Regional diversity
Native American groups varied by region. The map on the next page shows culture areas and locations of specific Native American groups:

- **Southwest** Here the Pueblo peoples lived in many-roomed adobe dwellings called pueblos. Each pueblo was governed by a council of religious elders.
- **Northwest Coast** Groups in the Northwest Coast region had an abundant supply of natural resources. They held feasts called potlatches, where they showed off their wealth by giving rich gifts to their guests.
- **California** In California many animals and plants were available year-round. Many different hunter-gatherer groups developed.
- **Far North** Groups in the Far North lived in the tundra, land that is partially frozen for most of the year. They hunted seals, seabirds, caribou, beaver, and bear.
- **Great Basin and Plateau** In these two dryland regions behind the mountain ranges of the Pacific Coast, groups remained hunter-gatherers. In the Plateau region, they lived along rivers.
- **Great Plains** The Great Plains region lay west of the Mississippi River. The culture of early Plains Indians depended on the hunting of buffalo.
- **Eastern Woodlands** Thick forests of oak, maple, and other trees covered what is today the eastern United States, from the Atlantic Ocean west to the Mississippi River. Animals, fish, and plants were plentiful in these forests. Groups in the Eastern Woodlands region used forest resources to build their homes. The Iroquois, for example, lived in longhouses, which were rectangular buildings made of logs and bark.
- **Southeast** In the Southeast, most Native Americans had lived in settled farming villages for hundreds of years. Some groups in this region carried on the Mississippian culture into the 1500s and even later.

ACADEMIC VOCABULARY
influence to change, or have an effect on

Shared customs and traditions Native peoples in North America developed a great diversity of social systems and traditions. Still, they shared a number of customs and practices. These included ideas of social and political organization, religion, land use, and trade.

Most villages and nations were organized into clans on the basis of kinship, or blood relations. Sometimes kinship ties were based on the mother's family; other times they were based on the father's. Kinship often determined a person's social status and how property would be inherited.

Native Americans also shared some religious ideas. One was a spiritual connection to the natural world. An Indian of the Wabanaki nation in New England said, "The Great Spirit is our father, but the Earth is our mother." Because of this connection, many Native American groups also did not believe that land should be bought and sold. Some viewed land as a gift from the Great Spirit.

What brought the various Native American cultures together was trade. From their earliest days in North America, bands of hunters exchanged gifts and spear points. Later, people began to travel deliberately to exchange goods. The main trade items were food, raw materials, and luxury goods.

Native Americans usually traded by a barter system, an exchange of goods without using money. In a few places, shells were used as money. By the 1400s thousands of miles of trade networks crisscrossed North America.

READING CHECK Making Generalizations What role did trade play in Native American societies?

African Cultures before 1500

The world's largest desert, the Sahara, divides North Africa from the rest of the continent. This desert has always been a fearsome barrier to travelers. Despite the dangers, trading caravans have crossed the Sahara since ancient times, seeking salt, ivory, and gold.

Desert traders brought something else besides trade goods to West Africa. The religion of Islam had begun in Arabia in the 600s. Not long after, Arab traders brought its teachings into West Africa. Some peoples in West Africa accepted Islam. Others continued to practice traditional African religions.

African trading kingdoms Several important trading kingdoms had developed in West Africa beginning around AD 300:

- **Ghana and Mali** These were the earliest kingdoms, which grew wealthy by taxing traders. Mali's most famous ruler, Mansa Musa, was a Muslim who traveled to Mecca and brought information about the land and peoples of Africa to the outside world.
- **Songhai** Songhai was larger than either Ghana or Mali. Its most famous ruler was Askia Muhammad. He ruled from 1493 until 1528 and made his capital city a center of Islamic learning.
- **Benin and Kongo** Benin and Kongo were two coastal African kingdoms that became powerful in the 1400s and built wealth from the Atlantic trade with Europeans.

Trade changes West Africa Gold and trade were what first attracted European sailors to Africa. Soon, however, the need for workers brought a terrible change. Rather than trading gold or ivory or wood, Europeans began to participate in the slave trade that existed among the African kingdoms.

Sailors from Portugal first explored the west coasts of Africa in the 1400s. They were looking for a sea route to India, but they were also looking for gold. The Portuguese and Spanish built plantations off the African coast. Later, other European nations would build plantations in the Caribbean, Brazil, and North America. Plantation agriculture requires large numbers of workers, and so planters turned to importing Africans as slaves.

The slave trade began in the late 1400s and expanded as planters in the Americas began to demand more workers. It went on for 400 years and devastated societies in West Africa. Although there are no firm figures, historians estimate that almost 20 million enslaved Africans landed in the Americas.

The human cost of the slave trade was tremendous. Parts of Africa suffered great losses in population. In addition, the slave trade weakened Africa and caused divisions among African peoples. The forced labor of millions of Africans enriched other parts of the world—but not Africa itself.

READING CHECK Identifying Cause and Effect How did the demand for slave labor begin?

THE IMPACT TODAY

Government
When the modern African nations of Ghana and Mali became independent, they took the names of ancient West African trading kingdoms. The modern nations do not include the same territories as the earlier states.

BEGINNINGS OF AMERICA **9**

European Exploration

By 1500 the **Middle Ages** were ending in Europe. This period, which had begun in about 500 and lasted for a thousand years, had been a difficult time for Europeans. No governments were strong enough to protect people after the old Roman Empire had collapsed. There was widespread lawlessness. Europeans were often under attack by invaders from distant lands. But two important events of the Middle Ages helped bring dramatic changes in Europe.

First, in 1096, a series of wars began between Christians and Muslims. They were fighting for control of the area of Southwest Asia called Palestine. This area contained Christian shrines and holy places. These wars were known as the Crusades and continued until 1291. Although the lands eventually remained in Muslim control, the Crusades opened European eyes to new lands and peoples.

Another important event of the Middle Ages was the creation of nation-states. Early in the Middle Ages, the lands of Europe were divided among hundreds of nobles. Each noble ruled a piece of land and hoped to rule more. Strong rulers were able to unify nearby lands. By the late 1400s, several countries had begun to consolidate under the authority of monarchs, or rulers. These rulers built nation-states with strong central governments. The most important of these nation-states were England, France, Spain, and Portugal.

In England, however, some barons had acted to curb the king's powers. In 1215 they forced the king to sign the **Magna Carta**. This document showed that limits could be placed on royal power. It established several important principles of government, including no taxation without representation and the right to trial by jury. These became basic principles of English law. After the Revolutionary War, they became part of American law as well.

The Renaissance and the Reformation

As the Middle Ages came to an end, an era of great change began in Europe. Increased trade with the East opened people's minds to new ideas. This wider outlook brought about a revival of ancient knowledge that had been lost during the early Middle Ages. Prosperity brought by trade led to population growth and better education. All these produced a new era of learning and creativity that began in Italy.

This new era, which started in the 1300s, is called the **Renaissance** (REN-uh-sahns), from the French word for "rebirth." Scholars studied the classics of ancient Greece and Rome, and artists created works of lasting beauty. Scientists also made significant advances.

ACADEMIC VOCABULARY
prosperity economic well-being

The World Before 1600

QUICK FACTS

Early Native American Cultures
- Scientists disagree on when and how the first Americans arrived.
- One theory is that the first Americans crossed a land bridge from Asia to America.
- Early Mesoamerican cultures include Olmec, Maya, and Aztec.
- Early North American cultures include Hohokam, Anasazi, Adena, Hopewell, and Mississippian.

North American Cultures in the 1400s
- Native Americans in North America establish diverse cultures based on geography.
- Some North American cultures share characteristics, including social structure, religious beliefs, and technology.
- Trading networks allow North American groups to share goods and ideas.

Africa
- Major kingdoms include Ghana, Mali, Songhai, Benin, and Kongo.
- Portuguese traders arrive in Africa in 1400s.
- European slave trade begins in late 1400s.

Europe
- Magna Carta establishes basic principles of government in 1215.
- The Renaissance begins around 1300.
- The Age of Exploration begins in the late 1400s.
- Christopher Columbus voyages to the Caribbean in 1492.
- The Reformation begins in 1517.

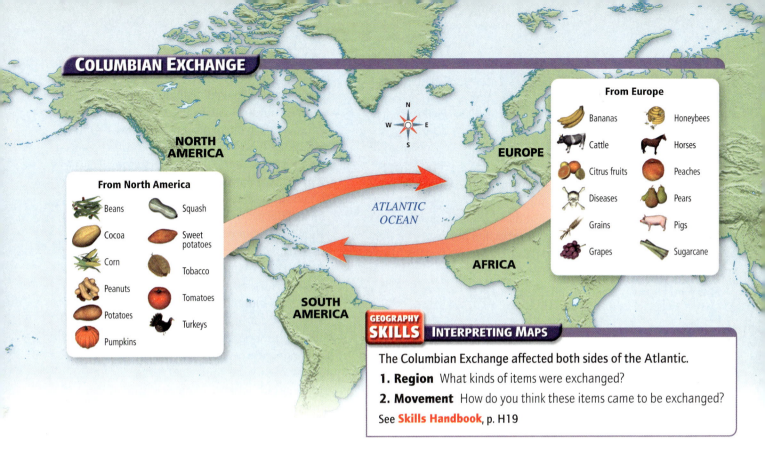

COLUMBIAN EXCHANGE

GEOGRAPHY SKILLS INTERPRETING MAPS

The Columbian Exchange affected both sides of the Atlantic.
1. **Region** What kinds of items were exchanged?
2. **Movement** How do you think these items came to be exchanged?

See **Skills Handbook**, p. H19

Renaissance thinking encouraged people to question long-accepted ideas. That led to challenges to the authority of the Roman Catholic Church. Discontent with the church reached its peak in northern and central Europe. In 1517 a German monk named Martin Luther criticized some church practices and challenged church officials to a public debate. Luther's actions set off a chain of events. Calls for reform spread in a movement known as the **Reformation**. Luther's followers became known as Protestants, for their protests against the church.

The age of exploration The Renaissance changed the way that Europeans saw themselves and the world around them. Advances in science and technology encouraged people to ask questions and think boldly. Rulers of the nation-states of France, England, Spain, and Portugal tried to increase their power by finding new lands and sources of trade.

First, in the 1200s, an Italian explorer named Marco Polo traveled from the trading city of Venice in Italy to China. The accounts of his travels encouraged later explorers.

Two centuries later, Prince Henry of Portugal set up a school and naval observatory to encourage exploration. He sponsored voyages in the Atlantic Ocean and down the coast of Africa. These voyages took advantage of many technological advances in ship construction and navigation.

One of the main goals of Prince Henry's explorers was to find a sea route to Asia to set up trade as the Venetians in Italy had done earlier. In 1498, after Prince Henry's death, the Portuguese explorer Vasco da Gama succeeded, landing on the coast of India.

Columbus reaches the Caribbean The explorer **Christopher Columbus** was born in the Italian trading city of Genoa in 1451. He became a sailor, serving on both merchant ships and warships. While visiting Portugal, Columbus decided that he would attempt to sail west to reach Asia.

It took Columbus many years to convince anyone to back his "Enterprise of the Indies" by providing ships and crews for the voyage. Finally, Columbus won support from Spanish monarchs Ferdinand and Isabella.

On August 3, 1492, Columbus set sail with about 90 men on the caravels *Niña* and *Pinta* and his flagship *Santa Maria*. After three weeks at sea, the crew was frightened and restless. Some were near mutiny. Then they

FACES OF HISTORY

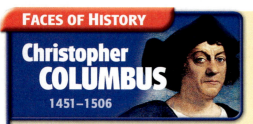

Christopher COLUMBUS
1451–1506

Christopher Columbus's first job was working with his father as a weaver. Wanting to explore the world outside the textile shop, Columbus found work as a sailor on ships in the Mediterranean.

Eventually, Columbus made his way to Portugal where he found a job making maps. During those years, Columbus met many explorers and navigators and began to hear tales of islands that were rich with spices. By sailing west, Columbus was certain he could find the islands and earn wealth and fame.

Make Inferences Why did Columbus sail west?

began to see birds and floating tree branches, which made them believe they were nearing land. At 2:00 in the morning of October 12, a sailor shouted, "Tierra! Tierra!" (Land! Land!) At dawn, they landed on a small island in the Bahamas. Columbus mistakenly believed he was in the Indies in Asia.

The impact of Columbus The voyages of Columbus began the process of European colonization of the Americas. From the very first voyage, European contact had a devastating effect on the native peoples, called Indians by the Spanish. Often, the Indians and Europeans would clash. But the native peoples were no match for the well-armed Europeans.

Columbus's first reaction to meeting the Tainos, a native Caribbean group, was to note "how easy it would be to convert these people [to Christianity] and to make them work for us." At first, the Spaniards recruited the Indians to help mine for gold. But soon they enslaved them. This set a pattern for later Spanish and other European explorers. Columbus also suggested starting a trade in Indian slaves.

Another effect of Columbus's voyages to the Americas was the exchange of plants and animals among Europeans, Native Americans—and later, Africans. Because this began after Columbus, it is known as the **Columbian Exchange.** Many American food products were taken to Europe and vice versa. Europeans also brought horses to America. Horses became a major part of Plains Indians culture.

The Columbian Exchange also had some tragic consequences. Native Americans had no way to resist European diseases, particularly smallpox and measles. Within a few years of the first early contacts with Europeans, disease had wiped out thousands of Native Americans. No one can be sure how many died.

READING CHECK **Making Generalizations** What was Columbus's impact in America?

SECTION 1 ASSESSMENT

go.hrw.com
Online Quiz
Keyword: SE7 HP1

HSS 8.2.1

Reviewing Ideas, Terms, and People

1. **a. Recall** From where did the original settlers in the Americas come?
   b. Explain What changes in the environment led to the agricultural revolution?
2. **a. Identify** What were the differences between the Northwest Coast and Great Basin cultures?
   b. Explain Why did Native American groups trade with one another?
   c. Evaluate Why was trade important to Native American cultures?
3. **a. Recall** Who were the first European explorers on the Atlantic coast of Africa?
   b. Explain What factors motivated the beginning of the Atlantic slave trade?
4. **a. Define** Write a brief definition for each of the following terms: **Renaissance, Reformation**
   b. Compare How did the world view of people in the Renaissance differ from the outlook of the **Middle Ages**?
   c. Rank What do you think were the most valuable products brought to the Americas in the **Columbian Exchange**?

Critical Thinking

5. **Identifying Cause and Effect** Copy the chart below and show the factors that contributed to the enslavement of the native peoples of the Caribbean.

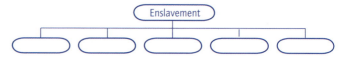

FOCUS ON SPEAKING ELA W1.1

6. **Persuasive** As a member of a Native American group in inland California, write a speech persuading a coastal group to trade shells for your spear points.

12 CHAPTER 1

SECTION 2
European Colonies in America

BEFORE YOU READ

MAIN IDEA
Spain began colonizing America, and later, England built a diverse group of colonies on the Atlantic seaboard.

READING FOCUS
1. Which European nations explored the Americas, and where?
2. Did the English in Virginia succeed in creating settlements?
3. What were the characteristics of the northern colonies?
4. What were the characteristics of the middle and southern colonies?

KEY TERMS AND PEOPLE
viceroyalties
encomienda system
missionaries
Fray Junípero Serra
Roanoke
Jamestown
House of Burgesses
indentured servants
Puritans
Mayflower Compact

 HSS 11.1.1 Describe the Enlightenment and the rise of democratic ideas as the context in which the nation was founded.

SPAIN OR PORTUGAL?

▼ Spanish explorers conquered huge Native American empires in the 1500s.

THE GRANGER COLLECTION, NEW YORK

THE INSIDE STORY *How did two European sea powers carve up the Americas?* In 1493 Queen Isabella of Spain came to the pope with a problem. Columbus had just returned from his successful first voyage, and the queen wanted to move quickly to secure Spain's claim to the Americas. Spain's chief rivals, the skilled navigators of Portugal, were eager to seize land in the New World, as were other European powers. The queen wanted the Roman Catholic Church's stamp of approval on her claims before others rushed in.

Pope Alexander VI, a Spaniard, was happy to help. He drew an imaginary north-south line of demarcation from the North Pole to the South Pole in the Atlantic Ocean. Spain would control of all the lands west of the line that did not have a Christian ruler. Portugal got the lands to the east.

King John II of Portugal protested. The line was so far east that it gave Portuguese navigators little room even to explore Africa. So in 1494, Spanish and Portuguese diplomats met at Tordesillas, Spain, and moved the line more than 800 miles west.

Spain got the best deal from the Treaty of Tordesillas. The treaty did give Portugal a claim to Brazil, but Spain got the rest of the Americas. Not surprisingly, other European nations—including England, France, and Holland—did not accept Pope Alexander's division of the world.

BEGINNINGS OF AMERICA **13**

European Explorers in the Americas

A wave of exploration followed the Treaty of Tordesillas, with Spain leading the way. The Spanish explorers of the 1500s were known as conquistadors, from the Spanish word for "conquerors." Their goals were often described as "God, gold, and glory," which meant they wanted to spread Christianity, find wealth, and become famous for their adventures.

Conquistadors led expeditions into the southern part of present-day United States, from Florida to southern California.

- **Juan Ponce de León** was the first Spanish explorer to reach mainland Florida. He claimed Florida for Spain.
- **Hernán Cortés** and his men conquered the wealthy and powerful Aztec Empire in 1521, including the capital of Tenochtitlán. This conquest inspired later explorers to search for more gold.
- **Hernando de Soto** traveled widely in the Southeast, as far north as the present-day Carolinas and Tennessee. De Soto's expedition also discovered the Mississippi River.
- **Francisco Vásquez de Coronado** led a European expedition that traveled as far as present-day Kansas. Other men in the expedition went into present-day Arizona, New Mexico, Texas, and Oklahoma. They were the first Europeans to see the Grand Canyon.
- **Juan Rodríguez Cabrillo** sailed north from Mexico, exploring the coast of California. He sailed into what is now San Diego Bay and Monterey Bay.

Spain builds an empire While these conquistadors were exploring North America, the government of Spain was beginning to establish colonial governments. A new social hierarchy developed in the Spanish empire. Key political aspects of the Spanish American empire included:

- **Viceroyalties**, or provinces ruled by viceroys, direct representatives of the monarch. The Viceroyalty of New Spain included much of the American Southwest and present-day Mexico, along with Florida, Central America, part of Venezuela, and the Caribbean islands.
- **The encomienda system**, a system under which a landowner had the right to control the people of a certain area.

The new social hierarchy in Spain's American empire depended mainly on a person's ancestry. Peninsulares were people who came from Spain. They considered themselves superior to creoles. Creoles were people born in the Americas of pure European descent. Mestizos were people of mixed Spanish and Native American descent. Lower still on the social scale were people of mixed Spanish and African descent, Africans, and Indians.

Spanish missions in North America

Along with gold, another goal of Spanish exploration in the 1500s was to spread Christianity. To do this, Spain sent **missionaries**. Missionaries are people who convert others to a religion. In North America, their first goal was to teach Christianity to the Native Americans. Many Indians came to live and work at the missions, which were large plantations centered around a church.

Missionary work continued for centuries in the West and Southwest. In 1769 the viceroy of New Spain sent **Fray Junípero Serra** (SE rah), a Franciscan friar, to San Diego, where he founded the first of many California missions. Serra was known for his preaching and for the self-discipline of his strict life. He became head of eight more missions in what is now California. Later, more than 20 missions dotted the California coast.

Other nations explore During the late 1400s and 1500s, explorers from England, France, and the Netherlands also began to explore America. Explorers including John Cabot and Francis Drake challenged Spain's claim to the Americas.

England did not act on these claims, however, until the reign of Queen Elizabeth I (1558–1603). Queen Elizabeth built England into a sea power. Then religious issues caused Spain and England to go to war.

In 1588 the Spanish king sent a fleet of 130 ships, known as the Spanish Armada, to invade England. But England's superior navy actually defeated the Spanish Armada. The defeat was a major blow to Spain because it meant that England could start building its own colonies in North America.

READING CHECK Identifying the Main Idea
What were the main goals of Spanish explorers?

The English in Virginia

After the defeat of the Spanish Armada, England began to set up colonies in North America. English colonists came for many reasons. For some people, economic problems made them eager for new opportunities. In the lower classes in England, farmworkers and farmers were not making much money. In the upper classes, younger sons who did not inherit land were looking for new adventures.

In 1606 King James I issued a charter that divided North America between two groups of investors, the London Company and the Plymouth Company. Both were joint-stock companies, which meant that investors pooled their money hoping to make a profit. The companies governed and maintained the colonies they established. In return, the investors received most of the profit.

ACADEMIC VOCABULARY
maintain to keep in an existing state

The Lost Colony of Roanoke In 1584 Sir Walter Raleigh sent a group of people to find a site for an English colony in America. They claimed land along the Atlantic seaboard, naming it Virginia. The group returned in 1587 and founded the colony of Roanoke.

Roanoke's story took a tragic turn, however. The leader of the colony went back to England. When he returned to Roanoke in 1590, the village was empty. Many explanations have been suggested, but the mystery of the colonists' disappearance has never been solved.

Jamestown Settled in 1607, Jamestown was the first English colony that survived, although it encountered many hardships along the way. Many settlers died from malaria or dysentery from contaminated water. Settlers also spent more time looking for gold than growing food. By 1608 many of them had died of starvation.

How, then, did Jamestown survive? Two men, John Smith and John Rolfe, helped rescue the failing colony. Smith, for his part, tried to impose military discipline on the Jamestown colonists. Then John Rolfe made a discovery that finally made Jamestown and the Virginia colony profitable—tobacco.

Tobacco was a native plant grown in both North America and the islands of the West Indies. It was important in Native American ceremonies. Rolfe was the first English tobacco grower in Virginia. He was taught the correct method for curing tobacco by his wife, a Native

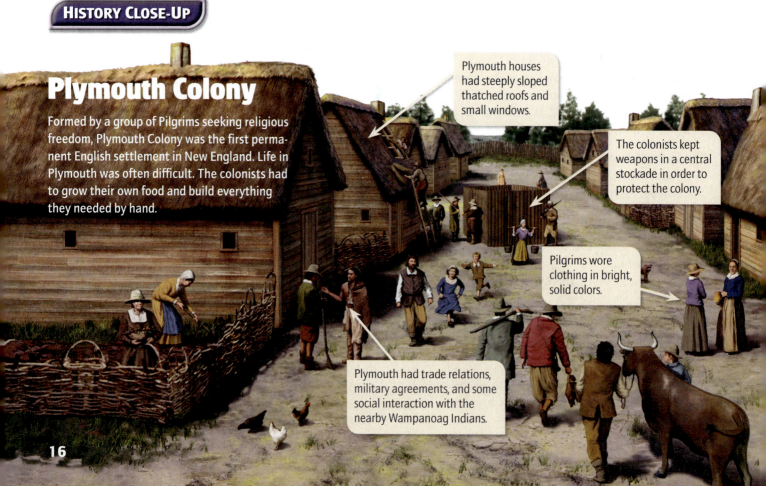

HISTORY CLOSE-UP

Plymouth Colony

Formed by a group of Pilgrims seeking religious freedom, Plymouth Colony was the first permanent English settlement in New England. Life in Plymouth was often difficult. The colonists had to grow their own food and build everything they needed by hand.

- Plymouth houses had steeply sloped thatched roofs and small windows.
- The colonists kept weapons in a central stockade in order to protect the colony.
- Pilgrims wore clothing in bright, solid colors.
- Plymouth had trade relations, military agreements, and some social interaction with the nearby Wampanoag Indians.

American woman named Pocahontas from the powerful Powhatan Confederacy.

The relationship with the Powhatan Confederacy was not always a peaceful one, however. Often the Powhatans and the English colonists clashed violently over land.

Virginia grows and changes During its 15-year existence, the Virginia Company struggled to attract settlers and create a viable economy. It faced hardships but its population grew dramatically. Key events in Virginia's history in the 1600s included:

- **Formation of the House of Burgesses** In 1619 the House of Burgesses became America's first legislature, or law-making body.
- **Use of indentured servants** Indentured servants agreed to work as servants for a certain number of years, in return for food, shelter, and a paid trip to America.
- **Transition to slave labor by the late 1600s** As it became more difficult to recruit indentured servants, planters turned to a new source of labor, enslaved Africans.

READING CHECK **Summarizing** How did the colony of Virginia succeed despite early difficulties?

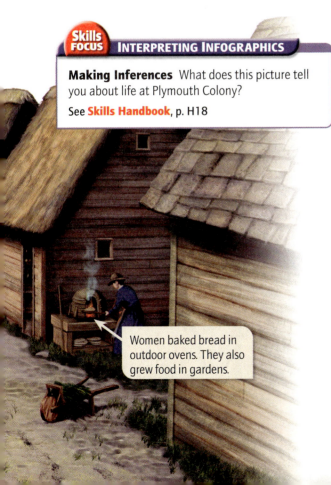

Skills FOCUS INTERPRETING INFOGRAPHICS

Making Inferences What does this picture tell you about life at Plymouth Colony?
See **Skills Handbook**, p. H18

Women baked bread in outdoor ovens. They also grew food in gardens.

The Northern Colonies

As you have read, the Protestant Reformation called for changes in the Catholic Church. But some English Protestants thought the Reformation did not go far enough. These people were known as Puritans, because they wanted to purify the church by making further changes. They wanted simpler church services, for example, and they objected to the wealth and power of bishops. Some of these Puritans wanted a total separation from the established church. They were known as Separatists.

The Pilgrims found Plymouth Colony

One group of Separatists set sail for America in September 1620, on a ship called the *Mayflower*. They wanted to form a colony where they could practice their religion freely. These Separatists who left England for America were known as the Pilgrims.

Two months later, the *Mayflower* reached land at present-day Massachusetts. There the Pilgrims signed the Mayflower Compact, a legal contract in which they agreed to make laws to protect the general good. It was one of the first attempts at self-government in the English colonies.

The Pilgrims then sailed to a nearby coast and established Plymouth Colony. There they built homes and grew their own food. Life at Plymouth was difficult, however. By spring of 1621, about half the group had died from hunger, cold, and sickness. The rest survived mainly because of the help of friendly local Wampanoag Indians.

Massachusetts Bay Colony Soon, thousands of Puritans moved to New England. Some Puritan merchants organized the Massachusetts Bay Company. Their goal was mainly to make a profit. But some of them wanted to create a religious haven. Their leader, John Winthrop, thought the colony should be a model for others, saying in a sermon, "For we must consider that we shall be as a City upon a hill. The eyes of all people are upon us."

Massachusetts Bay Colony grew quickly. The colony's success inspired what is called the Great Migration. From 1620 to 1643 some 16,000 English men, women, and children crossed the Atlantic Ocean in order to settle in New England.

BEGINNINGS OF AMERICA **17**

New colonies In time, the strict rules of Massachusetts Bay Colony caused dissent. Dissenters left the colony to settle new towns in other parts of New England. These new colonies included:

- **Connecticut** Led by Thomas Hooker, a group of settlers who believed in a more democratic government settled along the Connecticut River. There they settled the colony and wrote a constitution known as the Fundamental Orders of Connecticut.
- **Rhode Island** Roger Williams formed a new colony because he believed that church and state should be separate. Williams was also a friend to the Narragansett Indians and thought settlers should buy land, not take it. He built a settlement at Providence. Joining Williams was Anne Hutchinson, a woman from Massachusetts Bay Colony. Hutchinson had been banished because she had differed with church authorities.
- **New Hampshire** Anne Hutchinson's brother-in-law left Massachusetts Bay Colony in 1638 to form a new colony that became known as New Hampshire.

READING CHECK **Drawing Conclusions** What led to the founding of the northern colonies?

The Middle and Southern Colonies

Later in the 1600s, a new and different phase of colonization began in the middle and southern regions. A new king, Charles II, owed money and favors to many people. So, he established proprietary colonies—grants of American land to loyal friends. In this way, four new colonies began: New York, New Jersey, Carolina, and Pennsylvania. Unlike joint-stock colonies, these new colonies were ruled not by investors or colonial legislatures, but by their owners.

New Netherland becomes New York

One of Charles's first grants was to his brother James, duke of York. The grant included land that the Dutch had already claimed as New Netherland. In 1664 an English fleet sailed into the harbor and forced its surrender. The Dutch took it back briefly in 1673, but by 1674 New Netherland was firmly in English hands. James renamed the colony New York.

New York was unusual in the diversity of nationalities and religions among its settlers. They included not only the English and Dutch but also Scandinavians, Germans, French,

European Colonies in the Americas

British colonies
- Major explorers in North America included Cabot, Drake, and Raleigh.
- Thirteen colonies founded along Atlantic coast from 1607 to 1732.

French colonies
- Major explorers in North America included Cartier, Champlain, and La Salle.
- Colonies founded in Quebec and Louisiana.

Spanish colonies
- Major explorers in North America included Ponce de León, de Soto, and Coronado.
- Colonies founded in American Southeast and Southwest.

Dutch colonies
- Major explorer in North America was Hudson.
- Colonies founded in New Netherland and Delaware (both later became English colonies).

◀ Jamestown, 1607

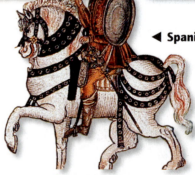
◀ Spanish conquistador

Native Americans, and enslaved Africans brought by the Dutch West India Company.

Later, James gave a large tract of land south of the Hudson River to two proprietors. This land became New Jersey.

The Carolinas and Georgia
Charles II also gave large land grants to other friends and supporters. In charters issued in 1663 and 1665, eight men became the co-owners of Carolina. The name came from *Carolus*, the Latin form of "Charles."

The southern and northern parts of Carolina developed very differently. In southern Carolina, rich rice plantations grew up along the rivers. The colony's economy soon depended heavily on slave labor. By contrast, the settlers in northern Carolina were mainly small farmers. Tensions grew between the two Carolina regions. In 1729 the king divided them into two royal colonies, North and South Carolina.

By this time, English colonies lined most of the Atlantic coast south of the French colony of New France. Colonists were moving westward steadily. But the Spanish Empire held the Southeast and Southwest, from Florida to California. Some people wanted a military buffer zone between the Carolinas and Spanish Florida. That led to the establishment of the last of the original thirteen colonies, Georgia.

Quakers settle Pennsylvania Another of King Charles's old debts led to the founding of the colony of Pennsylvania by a Quaker named William Penn. Quakers believed in personal communication with God, meaning no ministers and no set worship service.

Penn left for America in 1682 with a plan in mind for a "Holy Experiment" that would reflect his Quaker beliefs. He wanted Pennsylvania to be a haven for Quakers. Like Roger Williams in Rhode Island, Penn also recognized the Native Americans' right to the land. In 1682 he made an agreement with the Delaware Indians. The land from that agreement eventually became a separate colony, Delaware.

Maryland After the Church of England became the official English church, many Catholics in England were uncomfortable. They were a small minority but included some influential families. Some wanted to move to America in search of religious toleration. In 1634 George Calvert, the first Lord Baltimore, founded the colony of Maryland as a haven for English Catholics. The colony would also be a source of personal wealth for Lord Baltimore, who was its proprietor.

READING CHECK **Comparing** What did the middle and southern colonies have in common?

THE IMPACT TODAY

Culture

For many years, the statue of William Penn atop Philadelphia's City Hall remained the city's tallest structure, according to an informal "gentleman's agreement." In 1986 the 548-foot limit was broken and skyscrapers began to rise around Penn's statue. But pride in the city's founder remains strong.

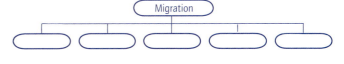

HSS 11.1.1

Reviewing Ideas, Terms, and People

1. **a. Identify** Name the areas covered by the following explorers: Ponce de León, de Soto, Coronado.
   b. Generalize What were two goals shared by Spanish explorers in the 1500s?
2. **a. Identify** Who were John Smith, John Rolfe, and Pocahontas?
   b. Summarize What factors led to hardships for the **Jamestown** settlers?
   c. Predict Why was the establishment of the **House of Burgesses** important?
3. **a. Describe** What was the **Mayflower Compact**?
   b. Explain Why did **Puritans** want to leave England?
   c. Identify What was the main cause of dissent in the New England colonies?
4. **a. Explain** What made New York different from other English colonies in North America?

   b. Compare How did the economies of North and South Carolina differ?
   c. Evaluate What was Charles II's pattern for establishing new colonies?

Critical Thinking

5. **Identifying Cause and Effect** Copy the chart below and identify the reasons for the migration of Puritans to New England.

   Migration

 ELA W1.1

6. **Narrative** As a new immigrant from England to the American colonies, write a letter home explaining what colony you would like to live in and why.

SECTION 3
Colonial Life

BEFORE YOU READ

MAIN IDEA
The American colonies developed politically, culturally, and economically.

READING FOCUS
1. How did political and economic events lead to the beginnings of self-government in the colonies?
2. How did the colonial economy differ in the North and South?
3. How did the Enlightenment and the Great Awakening contribute to America's emerging culture?
4. What were the causes and effects of the French and Indian War?

KEY TERMS AND PEOPLE
mercantilism
Navigation Acts
salutary neglect
plantation
Middle Passage
Enlightenment
Great Awakening
Jonathan Edwards
French and Indian War
Proclamation of 1763

HSS 11.1.1 Describe the Enlightenment and the rise of democratic ideas as the context in which the nation was founded.

HSS 11.3.2 Analyze the great religious revivals and the leaders involved in them, including the First Great Awakening.

THE INSIDE STORY

Why did molasses matter?
Colonial merchants and ship captains knew that the rugged coast of New England had thousands of bays and coves where small boats could come ashore. That made it easy for smugglers to bring in goods and avoid certain British taxes. Smuggling made life much harder for British customs officials trying to enforce trade laws.

One of those trade laws was the Molasses Act of 1733. Molasses is a dark, sweet syrup made when raw sugar is processed. Colonists used it in cakes and pies and poured it over pancakes. Molasses was also distilled to make rum, the most popular drink in the colonies. The yearly consumption of rum in the colonies averaged more than four gallons per person! Significantly, rum was also one of the northern colonies' most valuable products, with about a million gallons exported every year.

The Molasses Act made the colonists furious. They bought about half their molasses and sugar from planters on the Dutch, French, and Spanish islands in the Caribbean. The new law put a high tax on imports of such foreign sugar. Parliament's goal in enacting the law was to make Americans buy sugar from the British West Indies. Instead, smuggling became so widespread that tax revenues dropped. British officials eventually decided not to enforce the act.

SMUGGLING MOLASSES

▼ A merchant ship loaded with goods in Salem Harbor, Massachusetts
PEABODY ESSEX MUSEUM, SALEM, MASSACHUSETTS

The Beginning of Self-Government

Colonists began smuggling goods because they felt Great Britain was taxing them unfairly. From the British perspective, however, taxing the colonies was a good way to make money. After all, one of Great Britain's major reasons for establishing colonies in America was to obtain wealth.

Rising tensions During this time, Great Britain and its American colonies struggled to balance conflicting interests. They were divided on several issues, including:

- **Mercantilism** Guided by economic principles now called mercantilism, governments held that a nation's power was directly related to its wealth. But colonial merchants wanted to make money for themselves, not for Great Britain.
- **The Navigation Acts** To ensure that the colonies remained profitable to their home country, Great Britain passed the Navigation Acts, a series of laws to restrict colonial trade. The Navigation Acts angered the American colonists.
- **Role of the royal governors** Seeking greater control of the colonies, the king merged several colonies into one colony that he called the Dominion of New England. It was ruled by a royal governor, Edmund Andros. Andros was soon arrested and sent away by angry colonists.

Colonial self-government Local rebellions showed British officials that colonists would resist arbitrary rule like that of Governor Andros. As a result, some colonies regained their elected assemblies. However, many other colonies were now under tighter control as royal colonies.

Since the first settlements, American colonists had claimed their rights as British citizens. Now the colonies took small steps toward self-government. The colonies had even made an early move toward unification. In 1643 several formed the United Colonies of New England, commonly called the New England Confederation. A confederation is a group in which each member keeps control of internal affairs. They also cooperate on other actions, such as defense.

While many British officials were involved in colonial policy, in reality they did not rule the colonies very strictly. The British legislator Edmund Burke later termed this situation salutary neglect. That is, the colonies benefited by being left alone.

In the colonists' daily lives, local governments were more influential than faraway British officials. New Englanders were governed by town meetings. In other colonies, the county or parish was the local government. Colonists saw an elected assembly as one of their basic rights.

Each colony also had a governor. In royal colonies, the governor was appointed by the monarch. In proprietary colonies, the proprietor chose a governor. Members of the governor's council were chosen in the same way. They were usually rich and influential men.

Nearly all colonial assemblies were modeled on the British Parliament. They were bicameral, that is, with two houses. The governor's council was the upper house. The council had executive and legislative powers. It was also the supreme court of the colony.

The elected assembly was the lower house, much like Parliament's House of Commons. As the Commons gained more power after the Glorious Revolution, colonial assemblies sought more power as well. Gradually, they won important rights. Members had freedom of speech in debates. They also won the right to pass money bills. That meant the governor depended on the assembly for his salary.

READING CHECK **Making Inferences** Why was salutary neglect important in the development of self-government?

The Colonial Economy

Different economies developed in the northern and southern colonies. The North developed a commerce-based economy, while the South developed an agricultural economy.

Northern colonial economies Colonists in the north often found that crops did not grow well in rocky, forested New England. So many northern colonists practiced subsistence farming—or growing just enough food for one family. There was never enough to produce an export crop. This led northern colonists into

THE IMPACT TODAY

Government
Many New England communities still hold town meetings to discuss local matters. A few have even tried electronic town meetings, where citizens register their opinions via the Internet.

other ways of making a living. Farther south, the middle colonies had better land and a milder climate, so farmers had more success in that region.

The most valuable resources in the northern colonies came from its thick forests. The colonies exported timber, and many northern coastal towns became centers for shipbuilding. They also produced rum, textiles, and ironworks, among other goods.

Good harbors, inexpensive ships, and a tradition of seafaring also encouraged the development of commerce in the northern colonies. Commerce was concentrated in the port cities of Boston, New York, and Philadelphia. The northern colonies became a part of the triangular trade, which consisted of the trade routes that linked North America, the West Indies, Africa, and Great Britain.

Southern colonial economies The economies of the southern colonies were based on agrarianism, which means that they had many small farms and some large plantations. The southern colonies produced valuable cash crops—agricultural products grown to be sold. Among them were tobacco, rice, naval stores (such as tar), and indigo, a plant used to make a blue dye. Two agricultural systems developed in the South:

- **The plantation system** A **plantation** is a large farm, usually in a warm climate, with an unskilled labor force that grows one cash crop, such as sugar or tobacco. This system created a wealthy and influential class of planters. It was largely dependent upon slavery. A few huge plantations had hundreds of workers, who were either indentured servants or slaves.
- **Small independent farms** Southern economies relied on the plantation system and its valuable crops. Most farmers did not live on plantations, however, but on small farms. These independent yeoman farmers raised livestock and exported beef and pork. They grew corn, wheat, fruit, and vegetables for the home market.

The impact of slavery As British and Spanish settlers established their labor-intensive plantations and haciendas in the Americas, they needed more and more workers. Gradually, planters stopped using Native

American workers and indentured servants and came to depend on the labor of enslaved Africans instead.

As you have read, the slave trade caused tremendous human suffering. The difficult trip across the Atlantic became known as the **Middle Passage**. Kidnapped Africans were chained together in dark, foul-smelling quarters below the decks of the ship. In these filthy conditions, many died. The number of Africans in the British colonies grew quickly during the 1700s due to both births and the slave trade. As a result, the ratio of blacks to whites in the colonial population changed drastically. By 1760 the African population was about 325,000—more than 10 times what it had been in 1700.

Slavery existed both in the North and in the South, but the agricultural economy determined where most Africans lived. African American populations were largest in the colonies with plantation agriculture.

In spite of the difficulties of their lives, enslaved Africans created their own culture. This was especially true on larger plantations where the slave communities were large. Afri-

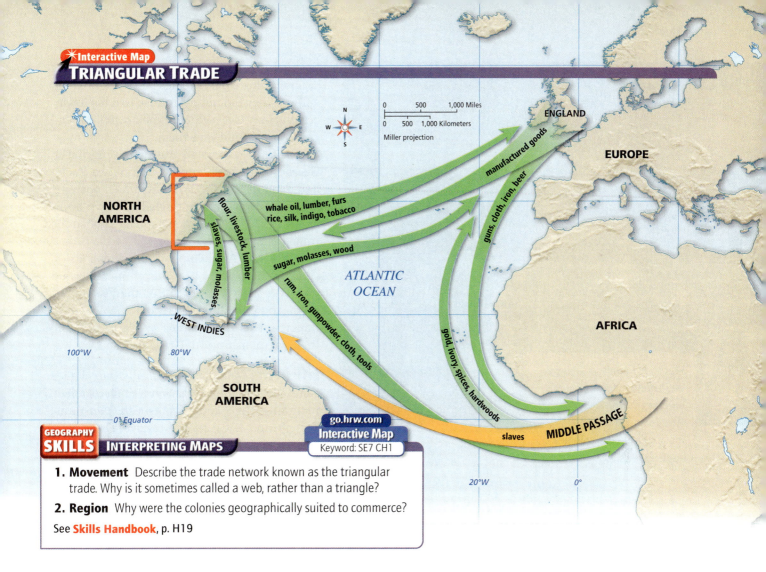

Interactive Map
TRIANGULAR TRADE

GEOGRAPHY SKILLS INTERPRETING MAPS

1. **Movement** Describe the trade network known as the triangular trade. Why is it sometimes called a web, rather than a triangle?
2. **Region** Why were the colonies geographically suited to commerce?

See **Skills Handbook**, p. H19

can Americans tried to build a strong family structure, and kinship networks were important. These networks became a way to look after those who had lost families.

Religion was another strength of the African American community. Many African Americans were Christians but also kept traditional African beliefs. The enslaved community preserved music and dance customs as well. African music, foods, and traditions gradually became a part of American culture.

READING CHECK **Contrasting** How did the economy differ in the North and in the South?

America's Emerging Culture

In the late 1600s, new ways of thinking changed ideas about government, human rights, science, and religion.

The Enlightenment Some thinkers in Europe thought that logic and reason—the tools of science—could also be used to improve society, law, and government. This period was known as the **Enlightenment**. In England, John Locke wrote *Two Treatises of Government* (1690), in which he said that it was the duty of government to protect the citizens' "natural rights." These natural rights were life, liberty, and property.

Locke also said that in a civil society people had a social contract with their government. Social contract theory held that if a government (or ruler) did not protect citizens and their rights, then they were justified in changing their government.

Not all Enlightenment thinkers were British. To limit the power of the monarchy, the French philosopher Baron de Montesquieu suggested that the powers of government be divided. He thought that would guarantee liberty by keeping any person or group from gaining too much power.

The ideas of the Enlightenment began in the educated upper classes of Europe but soon

BEGINNINGS OF AMERICA **23**

Methodist minister George Whitefield holds a religious meeting during the Great Awakening, a religious movement in the colonies.

spread beyond the European continent. Locke in particular was widely read in the American colonies. His ideas influenced Thomas Jefferson and Benjamin Franklin, among others. Later, in the Declaration of Independence, Jefferson would echo Locke's theories—and some of his words. Other Enlightenment ideas found their way into the U.S. Constitution, including limited government and divided powers.

The Great Awakening Enlightenment ideas also led some people in the colonies to question long-accepted religious beliefs. Most Enlightenment thinkers saw humankind as essentially good. However, several Christian denominations taught that humans were essentially wicked. These religious leaders worried that material values and concern for making money had displaced spiritual values.

Some clergy looked for new ways to bring people back to the church. That set the stage for one of the great social movements in American history.

The Great Awakening, a major religious revival in the colonies, began in the 1730s. One of its outstanding leaders was the Puritan clergy Jonathan Edwards. Trying to revive the old Puritan spirit, Edwards appealed to his listeners' fears and emotions. His most famous sermon pictured the agonies that sinners would suffer if they did not repent. He told his listeners that only God's grace or their own faith and good works could save them.

In 1739 a British Methodist minister, George Whitefield, traveled to America. As he had done in Britain, Whitefield held open-air meetings that were intended to move audiences to feel the religious spirit. Thousands came to hear him.

The Great Awakening made religion accessible to the people, and church membership grew. As with the Enlightenment's emphasis on the individual, this would become very important as the colonies began to redefine their relationship with Great Britain.

Life in the colonies Culturally, the colonies came of age in the 1700s. Non-British colonists, including the Scots, Scots-Irish, Germans, French, and Jews, began to arrive. These newcomers, along with British settlers, were creating a new American culture. It was not British or European, but something new.

Colonial cities were lively, exciting places. Some had paved streets and sidewalks lit by oil lamps. Ships from foreign ports anchored in the harbors. People waited eagerly for letters from relatives and for the latest British newspapers and magazines with gossip and drawings of new fashions.

Many colonial cities had libraries, bookshops, and impressive public buildings. City dwellers could go to plays or concerts. They shopped in markets for country produce and luxury goods from Europe. Schools taught music, dancing, drawing, and painting.

Colonial printers were also important. They printed and distributed newspapers, books, advertisements, and political announcements. Influential newspapers were published in Boston, New York, and Philadelphia.

READING CHECK **Drawing Conclusions**
What impact did the Enlightenment and the Great Awakening have on the colonies?

The French and Indian War

British colonies were thriving in the 1700s, but Britain was not the only European country with colonies. Spain and France also had

ACADEMIC VOCABULARY
displaced took the place of another thing

American colonies, and territorial struggles among the three countries eventually led to war. The **French and Indian War** got its name because France joined with some Indian nations to attack England. Spain and its American colonies were also involved.

To protect the fur trade, the French had made alliances with the Algonquins and Hurons. They also had built forts from the Great Lakes to the Mississippi Valley. The British built forts and alliances of their own. The power struggle between the two nations and their allies created constant battles along the frontier. Spain and Great Britain also had clashed over territory in North America.

The course of the war The French and Indian War broke out in 1754. The first part of the war went badly for the British army. The American landscape was unfamiliar territory. British soldiers were easy targets for an ambush by the French and their Native American allies. In one battle almost 1,000 British soldiers were wounded or killed.

Things changed when William Pitt took control. British officers in America began to force colonists into the army, seize supplies, and send soldiers to stay in colonists' houses. This allowed the British to recapture some forts from the French, but the Americans

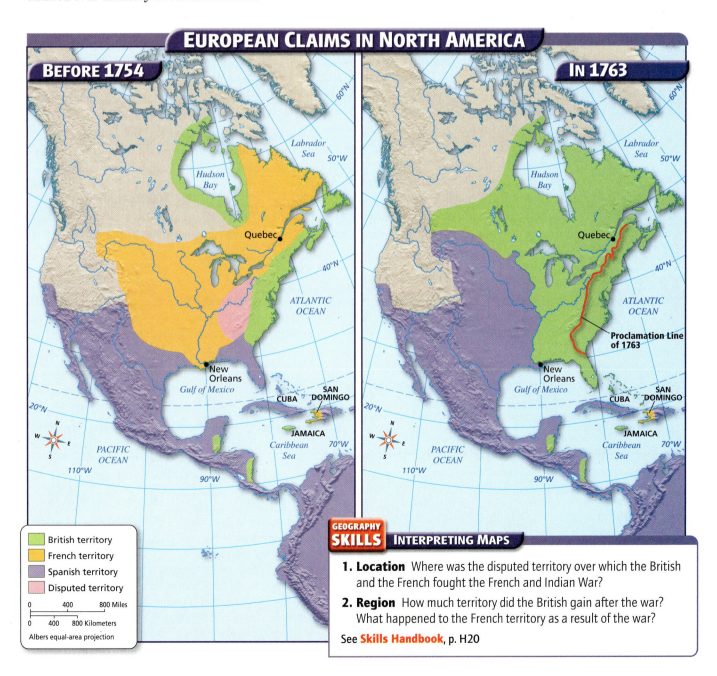

EUROPEAN CLAIMS IN NORTH AMERICA

BEFORE 1754 | **IN 1763**

Legend:
- British territory
- French territory
- Spanish territory
- Disputed territory

GEOGRAPHY SKILLS INTERPRETING MAPS

1. **Location** Where was the disputed territory over which the British and the French fought the French and Indian War?
2. **Region** How much territory did the British gain after the war? What happened to the French territory as a result of the war?

See **Skills Handbook**, p. H20

BEGINNINGS OF AMERICA

disliked the new policies. Then in a turning point of the war, the British besieged Quebec in New France. The city fell in September 1759. France surrendered the next year. The Treaty of Paris officially ended the war in 1763.

Impact of the French and Indian War

The French and Indian War is often said to be a precursor to the American Revolution. As the map on the previous page shows, it also dramatically changed territorial boundaries in North America. Effects of the war included:

- **Colonial unity** Thinking that bringing the colonies together would help Britain win the war, Benjamin Franklin proposed the Albany Plan of Union. Each colony would keep its own constitution, while a grand council would deal with military issues, Native American relations, and western settlement. Although the Albany Plan was never adopted, it is significant because it was the first plan for unifying the colonies.
- **New boundaries** Great Britain gained all of France's lands east of the Mississippi River—including much of what is now Canada. Spain, which had entered the war in support of the French, gave Florida to Britain. But Spain got a major prize from its ally France—the huge territory of Louisiana.
- **War debt** The war had cost England a lot of money. A new king, George III, took the throne in the midst of the war. His prime minister, George Grenville, thought the colonists should pay some of the costs of their own protection. Grenville's policies would push the colonists and Britain farther apart.
- **Effects on Native Americans** In 1762 an Ottawa chief named Pontiac put together an alliance of almost all the Native Americans in the Upper Midwest. He wanted to drive the British out. Pontiac's Rebellion lasted several bloody years. In 1766 Pontiac agreed to a peace treaty.

To avoid more conflicts with Native Americans on the frontier, British officials decided to stop colonists from moving further west. With the **Proclamation of 1763**, they drew a line along the Appalachian Mountains, reserving land on the western side for Native Americans. Colonists, however, resented the restriction on moving westward. Since the British government was unable to enforce the ban, the colonists continued to settle on these western lands.

READING CHECK **Making Inferences** How did the French and Indian War affect the relationship between Great Britain and its American colonies?

SECTION 3 ASSESSMENT

HSS 11.1.1, 11.3.2

Reviewing Ideas, Terms, and People

1. **a. Identify** What were the principles behind the policy of mercantilism?
   b. Analyze What were the causes and the effects of **salutary neglect** in the colonies?
   c. Predict Why might self-government in the colonies be important?
2. **a. Identify** What were the four major exports of the southern colonies?
   b. Explain Why did southern economies remain rural and agricultural?
   c. Evaluate In what ways was the ocean valuable to economies in the northern colonies?
3. **a. Recall** What was the **Enlightenment**?
   b. Compare How were the Enlightenment and the **Great Awakening** similar?
   c. Elaborate What were some other important aspects of colonial society?
4. **a. Identify** What was the central conflict of the **French and Indian War**?
   b. Explain What effects did the French and Indian War have upon the colonies?
   c. Evaluate How might the French and Indian War become a precursor to the American Revolution?

Critical Thinking

5. **Summarizing** Copy the chart below and list the different influences on colonial culture.

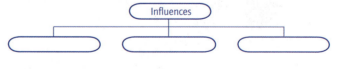

FOCUS ON WRITING

 ELA W1.1

6. **Expository** Write a brief paragraph in which you explain the triangular trade. Using details from this section, describe what goods were traded and which countries and regions were involved. Be sure to explain why the North American colonies were geographically suited to commerce.

Chapter Review

History's Impact video program
Review the videos to answer the closing question: Why was victory in the French and Indian War so important for the British?

Reviewing Key Terms and People

For each term or name below, write a sentence explaining its significance in the world before 1763.

1. agricultural revolution
2. Magna Carta
3. Reformation
4. Columbian Exchange
5. encomienda system
6. Fray Junípero Serra
7. Spanish Armada
8. Jamestown
9. Enlightenment
10. Great Awakening
11. French and Indian War

Comprehension and Critical Thinking

SECTION 1 *(pp. 6–12)* HSS 8.2.1

12. **a. Describe** Describe Columbus's career as an explorer and colonizer.
    b. Explain How did the actions of the Spaniards lead to enslavement of Caribbean Indians?
    c. Evaluate Who do you think benefited most from the Columbian Exchange, Native Americans or Europeans? Why?

SECTION 2 *(pp. 13–19)* HSS 11.1.1

13. **a. Define** What was the central agreement of the Mayflower Compact, and where were the settlers when they signed it?
    b. Contrast How did the Puritans' laws and government in the Massachusetts Bay Colony conflict with their reasons for moving to America?
    c. Elaborate How was Rhode Island different from most of the other colonies?

SECTION 3 *(pp. 20–26)* HSS 11.1.1, 11.3.2

14. **a. Identify** What was the central conflict of the French and Indian War?
    b. Summarize What impact did the war have on relations between Britain and its colonies?
    c. Predict How might the terms of the Proclamation of 1763 continue to affect the relationship between Great Britain and the American colonies?

Using the Internet

go.hrw.com
Practice Online
Keyword: SE7 CH1

15. The development of the original thirteen colonies was shaped by geographical factors and by the colonists themselves. Using the keyword above, research one of the colonies. Then from the viewpoint of a colonist, write a diary entry that discusses how the colony is changing over time. Consider factors such as religion, culture, values, family life, and work.

Critical Reading   HSS 11.1.1, 11.3.2; ELA R2.4

Read the passage in Section 3 that begins with the heading "America's Emerging Culture." Then answer the questions that follow.

16. According to the passage, which Enlightenment thinker was widely read in the colonies?
    A John Locke
    B Edmund Burke
    C Baron de Montesquieu
    D William Pitt

17. What was the Great Awakening?
    A A new trend toward education in the colonies
    B The beginning of self-government in the colonies
    C A religious revival that began in the 1730s
    D The beginning of a new American culture

 FOCUS ON WRITING   ELA W1.1

Persuasive Writing *Persuasive writing takes a position for or against an issue, using facts and examples as supporting evidence. To practice persuasive writing, complete the assignment below.*

Writing Topic Tensions between Great Britain and its colonies during the years 1650–1763

18. **Assignment** Given what you have read in the chapter, were the colonies justified in refusing to obey certain British laws and officials? Write a short essay in which you develop your position on this issue. Support your point of view with reasoning and examples from your reading and studies.

BEGINNINGS OF AMERICA **27**

CHAPTER 2

1763–1815

Forming a New Nation

THE BIG PICTURE After war broke out between Great Britain and the American colonies, the Patriots relied on their passion, strong leaders, and foreign allies to achieve victory. The work of defining the government of the new nation, however, was more difficult and would eventually lead to the emergence of political parties.

California Standards

History-Social Sciences

11.1 Students analyze the significant events in the founding of the nation and its attempts to realize the philosophy of government described in the Declaration of Independence.

READING LIKE A HISTORIAN

In the painting at right, George Washington holds his hat over his heart as two of his officers raise the American flag. Washington, who was commander of the Continental Army during the Revolutionary War, became the first president of the United States after the war ended.
Interpreting Visuals How does this painting depict Washington as a leader?

See **Skills Handbook**, p. H30

 U.S.

 World

1765
Stamp Act taxes Americans by requiring a stamp on certain printed materials.

1765

1768
The Ottoman Empire declares war on Russia.

History's Impact video program
Watch the videos to learn more about American history from 1763 to 1815.

1775 Revolutionary War begins with battles of Lexington and Concord.

1781 British surrender at Yorktown, ending the war.

1787 Constitutional Convention begins in Philadelphia.

1789 George Washington is inaugurated as the first president of the United States.

1803 France sells the territory of Louisiana to the United States.

1812 United States declares war on Great Britain.

1778 France formally recognizes the United States of America and promises military help.

1789 French Revolution begins with the capture of Bastille prison.

1814 French emperor Napoleon is defeated at the battle of Waterloo.

SECTION 1: The Revolutionary Era

BEFORE YOU READ

MAIN IDEA
America declared independence from Great Britain in 1776 and won the Revolutionary War in 1783.

READING FOCUS
1. What events led to the American Revolution?
2. Why did the colonists declare independence?
3. What key events took place as the Revolution continued?
4. How did Americans achieve victory?

KEY TERMS AND PEOPLE
Stamp Act
Boston Massacre
Battle of Lexington
Thomas Jefferson
George Washington
Common Sense
Declaration of Independence
Battle of Saratoga
Battle of Yorktown
Treaty of Paris

HSS 11.1.1 Describe the Enlightenment and the rise of democratic ideas as the context in which the nation was founded.

HSS 11.1.2 Analyze the ideological origins of the American Revolution, the Founding Fathers' philosophy of divinely bestowed unalienable natural rights.

▲ Colonists in crude disguises destroy tea at Boston Harbor.

THE INSIDE STORY

How did tea start a rebellion in Boston? In 1773 the British Parliament passed the Tea Act, which was designed to help a struggling British company and reduce smuggling. Because of colonial boycotts, the British East India Company had millions of pounds of unsold tea. Colonists instead were drinking smuggled Dutch tea. Under the new law, the East India Company was allowed to sell tea directly to the colonists. This meant its tea was actually cheaper than smuggled tea. Still, the colonists resisted.

In November 1773 three ships arrived in Boston Harbor. Bostonians allowed the ships to dock but not unload. On the night of December 16, 1773, a large and angry crowd gathered demanding that the ships be sent back to London. Then Samuel Adams and about 70 others arrived, disguised as Indians. Protected by the crowd, they boarded the ships and dropped the tea chests into the harbor. Hundreds of Bostonians watched the "Boston Tea Party." The loss of the tea infuriated British officials and brought more repressive laws.

The Road to Revolution

By the mid-1700s tensions had been rising between Britain and its colonies for some time. These tensions would intensify over the next decade and, eventually, lead the American colonies to revolution.

British laws anger the colonists The French and Indian War left the British with a huge debt. Britain decided the colonists should pay the costs of maintaining its North American empire. Over the next few years, Parliament passed several laws to raise money.

The Sugar Act (1764) was the first such law. It taxed sugar from the French and Spanish West Indies. This meant colonists would have to buy sugar from the British West Indies. Colonial leader Samuel Adams called the act "taxation without representation" because the colonies had no representative in Parliament.

The **Stamp Act** (1765) was more repressive. It required colonists to pay for an official government stamp on certain paper items. This was the first time Parliament had taxed the colonists directly, and Americans openly protested the stamp tax. Parliament eventually repealed the Stamp Act.

The Quartering Act was also enacted in 1765. This said that colonists must provide food, drink, fuel, living space, and transportation for British soldiers stationed

30 CHAPTER 2

in America. This was also the policy in Britain, but the colonists saw it as another attack on their rights.

The Stamp Act repeal left Britain with the need to raise money. The Townshend Acts were enacted in 1767. They taxed certain goods that were imported from England. The Townshend Acts also gave customs officers the right to search anyone's house for smuggled goods—without a search warrant. These laws aroused powerful opposition, and British troops were sent to the colonies to enforce the acts.

Continued unrest
Parliament partially repealed the Townshend Acts. But in 1773 it passed the Tea Act, giving the British East India Company nearly complete control over the tea market. As you read earlier, this led to the Boston Tea Party. British officials were furious over the incident. They enacted four laws to punish Massachusetts and to set an example for other colonies. The laws were so harsh they were called the Intolerable Acts. In response, a meeting of all the colonies was arranged to discuss what could be done.

The Boston Massacre
Boston was a center of protest. On March 5, 1770, five colonists died there when British soldiers fired into an angry crowd that had gathered outside a customs house. The best-remembered victim was Crispus Attucks, a sailor of African and Native American descent. Colonial leaders called the attack the Boston Massacre. They said it was a deliberate British attack on innocent civilians. This raised anger among many colonists.

The First Continental Congress
In September 1774 delegates from 12 colonies met in Philadelphia at the First Continental Congress. The delegates agreed to issue a Declaration of Rights, protesting Britain's actions. The Congress also agreed to boycott certain goods and formed a force of minutemen, colonial soldiers who would be ready to resist a British attack at short notice. The Congress agreed to meet again in the spring.

Battles of Lexington and Concord
Before the Continental Congress could meet again, however, war broke out. British general Thomas Gage was ordered to arrest local Patriot leaders, especially Samuel Adams and John Hancock, and capture gunpowder and weapons that Patriots had stored in Concord, near Boston. On the night of April 18, 1775, about 700 British troops set out for Concord.

Colonial alarm riders, including Paul Revere, rode to warn Adams, Hancock, and the minutemen. By the time the British reached Lexington, near Concord, about 70 minutemen were waiting for them. A shot rang out, and fighting began. Eight colonists were killed at the Battle of Lexington.

The British marched to Concord, where they were met by a stronger force of minutemen. On their retreat to Boston, many British soldiers were killed. The Revolutionary War had begun.

READING CHECK **Identifying Cause and Effect** Why did the new tax laws and other events lead to war?

ACADEMIC VOCABULARY
imported brought in from another country

THE IMPACT TODAY
Daily Life
Each year, the Boston marathon takes place on Patriot's Day, a day in April that commemorates the battles of Lexington and Concord.

Tensions between Britain and America, 1765–1775

STAMP ACT 1765	TOWNSHEND ACT 1767	BOSTON MASSACRE 1770
British Action Britain passed a law requiring colonists to pay tax—in the form of stamps—on certain commercial items.	**British Action** Britain passed a series of four laws declaring its authority over the colonies. The Townshend Acts suspended one colonial representative assembly and also set up strict measures for collecting taxes in the colonies.	**British Action** British troops quartered in Boston opened fire after being harassed by an angry mob of colonists. Five colonists died.
Colonists' Reaction Refusing to use the stamps, colonists burned them and started riots. In 1765 the colonists formed a Stamp Act Congress asking Parliament to repeal the law.	**Colonists' Reaction** The colonists resented the threat to self-government and protested what they saw as "taxation without representation."	**Colonists' Reaction** Boston colonists, including Samuel Adams, demanded the removal of British troops from Boston.

FORMING A NEW NATION 31

Declaring Independence

In May 1775, a few weeks after the battles at Lexington and Concord, the Second Continental Congress met as planned. During the next few months it made many crucial decisions. New members included Benjamin Franklin, John Hancock, and **Thomas Jefferson**.

Still, delegates' attitudes toward Britain were mixed. Many felt loyalty toward King George III. All delegates rejected Parliament's authority to tax the colonies, but only a few actually wanted full independence.

The Congress took several steps that reflected its divided nature. It created a Continental Army, with **George Washington** as leader. Meanwhile, other delegates sent the Olive Branch Petition to King George III, which asked for a "happy and permanent reconciliation" with Britain. The king refused to read it.

The battle for Boston
Even as the Congress was meeting, the fighting continued. The British at first treated these encounters as local rebellions. Then colonial forces expanded the war. Key battles included:

- **Battle of Bunker Hill** After the battles at Lexington and Concord, British troops withdrew to Boston, where they were met by 10,000 militia. Although the British won the first battle of the war on June 17, 1775, the colonists' brave defense encouraged resistance. It gave the colonists confidence in their ability to fight the better-trained and better-equipped British army.
- **Battle of Dorchester Heights** Two weeks after Bunker Hill, Washington took command of the Continental Army in Boston. The army was seriously short of artillery and gunpowder, so Washington sent Henry Knox to Fort Ticonderoga to bring back captured British weapons. As a result, Washington was able to retake Boston in March 1776. His troops captured and fortified Dorchester Heights, south of Boston. From there Washington forced the British troops to evacuate the city. This first test proved Washington's ability as a general.

The Declaration of Independence
The events of 1775 pushed more colonists toward support of independence. They were angry at the king's reaction to the Olive Branch Petition. Battles between the Americans and the British were intensifying. Then Thomas Paine issued an extremely influential pamphlet called **Common Sense.** (See excerpt on the next page.) In his pamphlet, Paine condemned the whole system of the monarchy and the rule of George III. He called not for protest but for a declaration of independence.

Paine's argument was based on Enlightenment thinking. Many American leaders had read the philosophy of Enlightenment writers such as John Locke. The idea of natural rights became part of their revolutionary ideology.

ACADEMIC VOCABULARY
philosophy
set of ideas

Tensions between Britain and America, 1765–1775 continued

TEA ACT 1773	INTOLERABLE ACTS 1774	BATTLES OF LEXINGTON AND CONCORD 1775
British Action Britain restructured the tax on tea to give a special advantage to the British East India Company. Under the Tea Act, colonial tea merchants would lose business.	**British Action** In response to colonial protests, Britain passed a series of laws designed to punish the colonies, especially Massachusetts. The laws essentially took away Massachusetts' power of self-government.	**British Action** 700 British troops advance toward Concord to seize the colonists' military supplies.
Colonists' Reaction In what became known as the Boston Tea Party, colonists dumped shiploads of British tea into Boston Harbor.	**Colonists' Reaction** The First Continental Congress convened in Philadelphia and sent a list of grievances to Great Britain.	**Colonists' Reaction** In Lexington, about 70 minutemen fight the British, and in Concord hundreds of colonists force the British troops to withdraw. It is the beginning of the Revolutionary War.

PRIMARY SOURCES

Common Sense

In January 1776 many colonists were divided about their future relationship with Great Britain. Then colonist Thomas Paine published *Common Sense*, a pamphlet that stated in clear, easy-to-understand terms why the colonies should break free from British rule. This widely read document strengthened support for the American Revolution.

"[A]ny submission to, or dependence on, Great Britain, tends directly to involve this continent in European wars and quarrels, and set us at variance [odds] with nations who would otherwise seek our friendship, and against whom we have neither anger nor complaint. As Europe is our market for trade, we ought to form no partial connection with any part of it. 'Tis the true interest of America to steer clear of European contentions, which she can never do while by her dependence on Britain she is made the weight in the scale of British politics."

Paine used direct language to make his arguments for independence from Great Britain.

Paine helped change the way many colonists viewed Great Britain, inspiring them to support independence.

Skills Focus: READING LIKE A HISTORIAN

1. **Analyzing Primary Sources** According to Paine, what is a major problem with remaining under British rule?
2. **Drawing Conclusions** Why do you think Paine named his pamphlet *Common Sense*?

See **Skills Handbook**, p. H12, H28–29

Under Locke's theory of the social contract, the present British government was failing to protect the rights and liberties of its citizens in North America. According to Locke, that justified a rebellion.

Then in June 1776 Virginia issued a declaration of citizens' rights. This was the first official call for American independence. Congress discussed the Virginia Declaration of Rights, and no one seriously objected.

Finally, a committee began to draft the **Declaration of Independence**. (The full text of the Declaration of Independence appears at the end of this section.) The Declaration formally announced the colonies' break with Great Britain. It expressed three main ideas. First, it stated that men possessed certain "inalienable rights" including "life, liberty, and the pursuit of happiness." Next, the Declaration explained that King George had passed unfair laws and taxed the colonies unfairly. Finally, it declared that the colonies had the right to break away from Great Britain because in passing these unfair laws, King George had violated the conditions of the social contract.

Jefferson wrote the first draft of the Declaration of Independence, but the Congress later made some changes. The members toned down some of what he wrote about the king. Also, because of pressure from some southern colonies, they cut out an entire section attacking the slave trade. Although the Declaration was a document about personal freedom, the colonial economy still depended upon the labor of enslaved Africans.

The final document was presented to the Congress on July 2, 1776, and it voted to declare independence. Two days later, on July 4, the members approved the entire document. Now, in the eyes of Britain, the colonists were all rebels and traitors.

Not all colonists were convinced of the need for independence and about a quarter of them remained loyal to Great Britain. These people were called Loyalists, or Tories. Those who supported independence were called Patriots.

READING CHECK **Identifying Cause and Effect** How did Enlightenment thinking influence the Declaration of Independence?

The Revolution Continues

After Washington's victory in Boston in March 1776, Revolutionary battles were centered in three of the colonies—New York, New Jersey, and Pennsylvania.

Defeats and victories Washington had moved his Continental Army to New York City, believing the British would attack there next. As expected, General Howe sailed into New York Harbor in August 1776 with more than 300 ships and 30,000 soldiers. With these reinforcements, Howe was able to defeat the colonists in several battles. The British managed to take control of New York City. They also forced Washington's troops to cross the Delaware River into Pennsylvania.

In traditional European warfare, it was customary not to fight in winter. As a result, Howe's men settled down in towns in New Jersey, including Trenton and Princeton. Hessians, German mercenary soldiers fighting for the British for pay, guarded Trenton, on the Delaware River.

Washington, however, did not follow European fighting methods. Instead, on Christmas night of 1776, he and his men crossed the icy Delaware River to reach Trenton. After spending the day celebrating, the Hessians were asleep. The colonists took them by surprise and captured British weapons and ammunitions.

Moving on, Washington then drove the British out of Princeton. The surprise attack had been a success and ended British hopes to conclude the war quickly.

British setback at Saratoga By mid-1777, the British were waging a campaign in upstate New York. General John Burgoyne and his troops were to invade from Canada and move south, while General Howe's forces would sail up the Hudson to meet them. This, the British hoped, would cut off New England from the rest of the colonies.

In the beginning, the British plan worked well. General Burgoyne recaptured Fort Ticonderoga in New York in July 1777. He then headed toward Albany, not knowing that General Howe had changed his plans and moved to Philadelphia instead.

Because Howe did not arrive in Albany as planned, the colonists were able to attack Burgoyne's army there. In early October, with fewer than 6,000 men left, Burgoyne found himself in Saratoga, New York, surrounded by a Continental force of about 17,000 troops. Burgoyne twice tried to break through the Continental lines, but failed. On October 17, 1777, he surrendered.

The **Battle of Saratoga** in New York is considered the turning point of the Revolutionary War. The colonists' victory encouraged them. General Howe later resigned, in part because of his role in the British defeat.

Winter at Valley Forge In the winter of 1777–1778, Washington and his exhausted troops settled into winter quarters at Valley Forge, about 20 miles north of Philadelphia, Pennsylvania. That winter was a low point for the Americans. The weather was bitterly cold, and some 12,000 men were housed in makeshift huts and tents. Food was scarce and soldiers had only worn, ragged uniforms. Many had no shoes. Thousands became ill, and more than 2,500 died of the cold, of diseases such as smallpox, and of malnutrition.

Valley Forge was a tough test of Washington's leadership, but he met the challenge. His firm character and common sense helped hold his troops together. Washington enforced discipline strictly. At the same time, he was always insisting that the Continental Congress treat the army better.

FACES OF HISTORY
George WASHINGTON
1732–1799

Many years before he became the first president of the United States, George Washington earned a reputation as an exceptional military leader. In 1752 he joined the Virginia militia and led troops in the French and Indian War. Years later, as an early supporter of American independence, Washington began to recruit and train a militia when tensions rose with the British.

Leading the Continental Army, Washington made some early tactical mistakes, such as allowing the British to occupy New York City. Nevertheless, his ability to inspire and manage his army helped the Americans achieve victory in the end.

Predict How do you think Washington's military experience prepared him for the presidency?

Strengths and Weaknesses of the Continental and British Armies

Continental Army	British Army
Strengths • Strong military leadership • Soldiers fighting for a cause they believed in • Fighting on home territory	**Strengths** • Well-trained military • Ample resources • Alliances with Native Americans, colonial Loyalists, and some American slaves
Weaknesses • Small, untrained military • Shortages of resources • Weak central government	**Weaknesses** • Fighting in unfamiliar territory • Fighting far from home • Soldiers fighting for a cause they didn't necessarily believe in

People in the Revolution British soldiers during the Revolutionary War were known as Redcoats because of their red uniforms. The British Redcoats were a well-trained, well-equipped fighting force. They were assisted by paid, foreign troops, and they formed alliances with some American Loyalists.

In contrast, finding and paying for supplies and military equipment for the Continental Army was hard. Congress was always short of money, so the army depended heavily on captured British guns and ammunition. Soldiers and their commanders complained about the shortages of food, clothes, and gunpowder.

Still, the Continental soldiers had some advantages of their own. Although often poorly equipped, they were fighting for a cause in which they believed. They were also fighting on familiar territory.

African Americans had fought at Lexington, Concord, and Bunker Hill. Despite this, Washington barred the enlistment of black soldiers when he assumed command of the Continental Army in 1775. After Valley Forge, however, the need for manpower was too great, and Washington approved the recruitment of African Americans. About 5,000 fought on the Patriot side.

While men were fighting on the battlefields, women played important roles at home. Some ran farms and businesses, and others made clothing for the troops. A number served as couriers, scouts and spies. A few, such as Deborah Sampson, even disguised themselves as men to fight as soldiers in the Continental Army.

READING CHECK **Summarizing** What advantages and disadvantages did the colonial army have?

An American Victory

After Saratoga, the Revolutionary War changed in several ways. Action shifted to the South and the western frontier. More importantly, the Americans' victories gained them the support of several European nations. These allies would eventually help the colonists win the war. Bernardo de Gálvez, governor of Spanish Louisiana, was one key ally. From France, Washington acquired an invaluable aide, the 20-year-old Marquis de Lafayette.

Interactive Map
BATTLES OF THE AMERICAN REVOLUTION, 1778–1781

GEOGRAPHY SKILLS INTERPRETING MAPS

1. **Human-Environment Interaction** How did Clark, a frontiersman, move his troops west?
2. **Place** Which battles did the colonists win in the West?
3. **Region** Where did the British concentrate their attacks?

See **Skills Handbook**, p. H19

War in the West and South Americans won some important victories in the region north and west of the Ohio River. This included the present-day states of Ohio, Indiana, Illinois, Michigan, Wisconsin, and part of Minnesota.

Then in 1778, the British shifted their strategy. Instead of sending more troops and supplies, British officials hoped that the many Loyalists in America would rise up to support them. Loyalist sympathies were stronger in the South, so they planned to campaign there.

Although the British did have some success in the South, they were hindered by frequent surprise raids by small groups of Patriots. These fighters struck quickly, then disappeared into the woods. The most famous was Francis Marion, who was nicknamed the Swamp Fox for his daring raids from the Carolina marshes.

Washington's second in command, General Nathanael Greene, took charge in the South. In March 1781 Greene and Lafayette's troops met British commander Lord Cornwallis's army in a brutal battle at Guilford Court House, North Carolina. Cornwallis won, but British losses were so great that he stopped the campaign.

Victory at Yorktown Lafayette's troops gradually forced the British to the coast. In July 1781 Cornwallis took his army to the Yorktown Peninsula in Chesapeake Bay. There they built a fort and waited for British ships

36 CHAPTER 2

The Revolutionary Era

The Road to Revolution
- Britain and the American colonies clash over "taxation without representation."
- The First Continental Congress meets.
- Battle of Lexington is "The shot heard 'round the world."

Declaring Independence
- The Second Continental Congress meets.
- Violence continues in Boston.
- Colonists draft and sign the Declaration of Independence.

The Revolution Continues
- Major battles take place in the North.
- The war turns in the colonies' favor at the Battle of Saratoga.
- Washington's troops regroup during the winter at Valley Forge.

An American Victory
- Colonists win major victories in the West and South.
- France and Spain become allies of the colonists.
- The Battle of Yorktown ensures American victory.

to rescue them and bring them to Charleston or New York. Washington then saw his chance to trap Cornwallis at Yorktown. He planned to establish a blockade in Chesapeake Bay, preventing the British ships from rescuing Cornwallis's men.

Washington ordered Lafayette to keep Cornwallis's army trapped on the peninsula. Meanwhile, Washington moved south with a combined French and colonial army of more than 17,000 troops. The Battle of Yorktown lasted about three weeks, but Cornwallis had little chance. His army was being bombarded by land and sea. On October 19, 1781, Cornwallis surrendered. The **Battle of Yorktown** was the last major battle of the Revolutionary War. When it ended, some British officials still hoped that America would remain part of the British Empire. But the colonial diplomats, who were sent to negotiate a peace treaty, insisted on independence.

The **Treaty of Paris** was signed on September 3, 1783. In it, Britain recognized the independence of the United States.

 READING CHECK **Summarizing** Explain how the Revolutionary War came to an end.

SECTION 1 ASSESSMENT

go.hrw.com
Online Quiz
Keyword: SE7 HP2

HSS 11.1.1, 11.1.2

Reviewing Ideas, Terms, and People

1. **a. Identify** What was the First Continental Congress?
   b. Summarize What actions did the First Continental Congress take?
   c. Predict Was the meeting of the Congress a final step toward independence? Why or why not?

2. **a. Recall** What British actions in 1775 moved the colonists toward independence?
   b. Identify Cause and Effect What was the effect of Paine's *Common Sense* on colonial thinking?
   c. Elaborate How did ideas from the Enlightenment become part of revolutionary ideology?

3. **a. Describe** What was Burgoyne's strategy for cutting New England off from the other colonies?
   b. Make Generalizations In general, what was the year 1776 like for the Continental Army?
   c. Draw Conclusions What effect did **George Washington's** leadership at Valley Forge have?

4. **a. Recall** Who was the Marquis de Lafayette?
   b. Identify Cause and Effect How did European allies affect the Revolutionary War?
   c. Predict What challenges do you think the colonists faced after the **Treaty of Paris**?

Critical Thinking

5. **Sequencing** Copy the chart below and make a time line of the events and laws leading up to the battles at Lexington and Concord.

   ———— ———— ———— ———— Battles at Lexington and Concord

 FOCUS ON SPEAKING ELA W1.1

6. **Persuasive** As a delegate to the First Continental Congress meeting before the Battles of Lexington and Concord, make a speech explaining what course you think the colonies should take next.

The Declaration of Independence

EXPLORING THE DOCUMENT Thomas Jefferson wrote the first draft of the Declaration in a little more than two weeks. **How is the Declaration's idea about why governments are formed still important to our country today?**

Vocabulary

impel force
endowed provided
usurpations wrongful seizures of power
evinces clearly displays
despotism unlimited power
tyranny oppressive power exerted by a government or ruler
candid fair

In Congress, July 4, 1776
The unanimous Declaration of the thirteen united States of America,

When in the Course of human events, it becomes necessary for one people to dissolve the political bands which have connected them with another, and to assume among the Powers of the earth, the separate and equal station to which the Laws of Nature and of Nature's God entitle them, a decent respect to the opinions of mankind requires that they should declare the causes which **impel** them to the separation.

We hold these truths to be self-evident, that all men are created equal, that they are **endowed** by their Creator with certain unalienable Rights, that among these are Life, Liberty, and the pursuit of Happiness. That to secure these rights, Governments are instituted among Men, deriving their just powers from the consent of the governed, That whenever any Form of Government becomes destructive of these ends, it is the Right of the People to alter or to abolish it, and to institute new Government, laying its foundation on such principles and organizing its powers in such form, as to them shall seem most likely to effect their Safety and Happiness. Prudence, indeed, will dictate that Governments long established should not be changed for light and transient causes; and accordingly all experience hath shown, that mankind are more disposed to suffer, while evils are sufferable, than to right themselves by abolishing the forms to which they are accustomed. But when a long train of abuses and **usurpations**, pursuing invariably the same Object **evinces** a design to reduce them under absolute **Despotism**, it is their right, it is their duty, to throw off such Government, and to provide new Guards for their future security.—Such has been the patient sufferance of these Colonies; and such is now the necessity which constrains them to alter their former Systems of Government. The history of the present King of Great Britain is a history of repeated injuries and usurpations, all having in direct object the establishment of an absolute **Tyranny** over these States. To prove this, let Facts be submitted to a **candid** world.

He has refused his Assent to Laws, the most wholesome and necessary for the public good.

He has forbidden his Governors to pass Laws of immediate and pressing importance, unless suspended in their operation till his Assent should be obtained; and when so suspended, he has utterly neglected to attend to them.

EXPLORING THE DOCUMENT Here the Declaration lists the charges that the colonists had against King George III. **How does the language in the list appeal to people's emotions?**

He has refused to pass other Laws for the accommodation of large districts of people, unless those people would **relinquish** the right of Representation in the Legislature, a right **inestimable** to them and **formidable** to tyrants only.

He has called together legislative bodies at places unusual, uncomfortable, and distant from the depository of their Public Records, for the sole purpose of fatiguing them into compliance with his measures.

He has dissolved Representative Houses repeatedly, for opposing with manly firmness his invasions on the rights of the people.

He has refused for a long time, after such dissolutions, to cause others to be elected; whereby the Legislative Powers, incapable of **Annihilation**, have returned to the People at large for their exercise; the State remaining in the mean time exposed to all the dangers of invasion from without, and **convulsions** within.

He has endeavored to prevent the population of these States; for that purpose obstructing the Laws of **Naturalization of Foreigners**; refusing to pass others to encourage their migration hither, and raising the conditions of new **Appropriations of Lands**.

He has obstructed the Administration of Justice, by refusing his Assent to Laws for establishing Judiciary Powers.

He has made Judges dependent on his Will alone, for the **tenure** of their offices, and the amount and payment of their salaries.

He has erected **a multitude of** New Offices, and sent hither swarms of Officers to harass our people, and eat out their substance.

He has kept among us, in times of peace, Standing Armies without the Consent of our legislature.

He has affected to render the Military independent of and superior to the Civil Power.

He has combined with others to subject us to a jurisdiction foreign to our constitution, and unacknowledged by our laws; giving his Assent to their Acts of pretended legislation:

For **quartering** large bodies of armed troops among us:

For protecting them, by a mock Trial, from Punishment for any Murders which they should commit on the Inhabitants of these States:

For cutting off our Trade with all parts of the world:

For imposing taxes on us without our Consent:

For depriving us in many cases, of the benefits of Trial by Jury:

For transporting us beyond Seas to be tried for pretended offences:

Vocabulary

relinquish release, yield
inestimable priceless
formidable causing dread
annihilation destruction
convulsions violent disturbances
naturalization of foreigners the process by which foreign-born persons become citizens
appropriations of lands setting aside land for settlement
tenure term
a multitude of many
quartering lodging, housing

EXPLORING THE DOCUMENT Colonists had been angry over British tax policies since just after the French and Indian War. **Why were the colonists protesting British tax policies?**

Vocabulary

arbitrary not based on law
render make
abdicated given up
foreign mercenaries soldiers hired to fight for a country not their own
perfidy violation of trust
insurrections rebellions
petitioned for redress asked formally for a correction of wrongs
unwarrantable jurisdiction unjustified authority
magnanimity generous spirit
conjured urgently called upon
consanguinity common ancestry
acquiesce consent to
rectitude rightness

EXPLORING THE DOCUMENT Here the Declaration calls the king a tyrant. What do you think *tyrant* means from this passage?

For abolishing the free System of English Laws in a neighboring Province, establishing therein an **Arbitrary** government, and enlarging its Boundaries so as to **render** it at once an example and fit instrument for introducing the same absolute rule into these Colonies:

For taking away our Charters, abolishing our most valuable Laws, and altering fundamentally the Forms of our Governments:

For suspending our own Legislature, and declaring themselves invested with Power to legislate for us in all cases whatsoever.

He has **abdicated** Government here, by declaring us out of his Protection and waging War against us.

He has plundered our seas, ravaged our Coasts, burnt our towns, and destroyed the lives of our people.

He is at this time transporting large armies of **foreign mercenaries** to complete the works of death, desolation and tyranny, already begun with circumstances of Cruelty & **perfidy** scarcely paralleled in the most barbarous ages, and totally unworthy the Head of a civilized nation.

He has constrained our fellow Citizens taken Captive on the high Seas to bear Arms against their Country, to become the executioners of their friends and Brethren, or to fall themselves by their Hands.

He has excited domestic **insurrections** amongst us, and has endeavored to bring on the inhabitants of our frontiers, the merciless Indian Savages, whose known rule of warfare, is an undistinguished destruction of all ages, sexes and conditions.

In every stage of these Oppressions We have **Petitioned for Redress** in the most humble terms: Our repeated Petitions have been answered only by repeated injury. A Prince, whose character is thus marked by every act which may define a Tyrant, is unfit to be the ruler of a free People.

Nor have We been wanting in attention to our British brethren. We have warned them from time to time of attempts by their legislature to extend an **unwarrantable jurisdiction** over us. We have reminded them of the circumstances of our emigration and settlement here. We have appealed to their native justice and **magnanimity**, and we have **conjured** them by the ties of our common kindred to disavow these usurpations, which, would inevitably interrupt our connections and correspondence. They too have been deaf to the voice of justice and of **consanguinity**. We must, therefore, **acquiesce** in the necessity, which denounces our Separation, and hold them, as we hold the rest of mankind, Enemies in War, in Peace Friends.

We, therefore, the Representatives of the united States of America, in General Congress, Assembled, appealing to the Supreme Judge of the world for the **rectitude** of our intentions, do, in the Name, and by Authority of the good People of these Colonies, solemnly publish and declare, That these United Colonies are, and of Right ought to be Free and Independent States; that they are Absolved from all Allegiance to the British Crown, and that all political connection between them and the State of Great Britain, is and ought to be totally dissolved; and that as Free and Independent States, they have full Power to levy War, conclude Peace, contract Alliances, establish Commerce, and to do all other Acts and Things which Independent States may of right do. And for the support of this Declaration, with a firm reliance on the Protection of Divine Providence, we mutually pledge to each other our Lives, our Fortunes and our sacred Honor.

John Hancock
Button Gwinnett
Lyman Hall
George Walton
William Hooper
Joseph Hewes
John Penn
Edward Rutledge
Thomas Heyward, Jr.
Thomas Lynch, Jr.
Arthur Middleton
Samuel Chase
William Paca
Thomas Stone
Charles Carroll of Carrollton
George Wythe
Richard Henry Lee
Thomas Jefferson
Benjamin Harrison
Thomas Nelson, Jr.
Francis Lightfoot Lee
Carter Braxton
Robert Morris
Benjamin Rush
Benjamin Franklin
John Morton
George Clymer
James Smith
George Taylor
James Wilson
George Ross
Caesar Rodney
George Read
Thomas McKean
William Floyd
Philip Livingston
Francis Lewis
Lewis Morris
Richard Stockton
John Witherspoon
Francis Hopkinson
John Hart
Abraham Clark
Josiah Bartlett
William Whipple
Samuel Adams
John Adams
Robert Treat Paine
Elbridge Gerry
Stephen Hopkins
William Ellery
Roger Sherman
Samuel Huntington
William Williams
Oliver Wolcott
Matthew Thornton

Yale University Art Gallery

EXPLORING THE DOCUMENT Here is where the document declares the independence of the colonies. **Whose authority does the Congress use to declare independence?**

EXPLORING THE DOCUMENT The Congress adopted the final draft of the Declaration of Independence on July 4, 1776. A formal copy, written on parchment paper, was signed on August 2, 1776.

EXPLORING THE DOCUMENT The following is part of a passage that the Congress removed from Jefferson's original draft: "He has waged cruel war against human nature itself, violating its most sacred rights of life and liberty in the persons of a distant people who never offended him, captivating and carrying them into slavery in another hemisphere, or to incur miserable death in their transportation thither." **Why do you think the Congress deleted this passage?**

DECLARATION OF INDEPENDENCE 41

SECTION 2
Creating a New Government

BEFORE YOU READ

MAIN IDEA
After the Revolution, American leaders struggled to form a national government and eventually wrote the Constitution.

READING FOCUS
1. What were the weaknesses of the Articles of Confederation?
2. What did the founders discuss when drafting the Constitution?
3. What was involved in ratifying the Constitution?

KEY TERMS AND PEOPLE
Articles of Confederation
James Madison
checks and balances
legislative branch
executive branch
judicial branch
Federalists
Antifederalists
ratification
Bill of Rights

 HSS 11.1.1 Describe the rise of democratic ideas as the context in which the nation was founded.

HSS 11.1.2 Analyze the debates on the drafting and ratification of the Constitution, and the addition of the Bill of Rights.

HSS 11.3.5 Describe the principles of religious liberty found in the Establishment and Free Exercise clauses of the First Amendment, including the debate on the issue of separation of church and state.

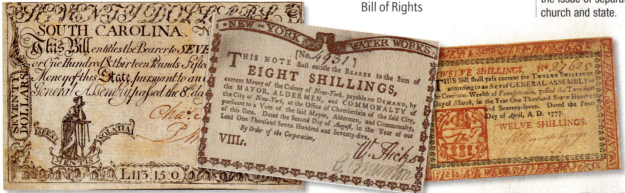

COLLECTION OF THE AMERICAN NUMISMATIC SOCIETY, NEW YORK

▲ Some states, like nations, had their own currencies.

The States, United

 Why was Pennsylvania money worthless in New York? In 1774, at the First Continental Congress, Patrick Henry declared, "The distinctions between Virginians, Pennsylvanians, New Yorkers, and New Englanders are no more. I am not a Virginian but an American."

Some 13 years later, however, state loyalty was still stronger than any feeling of national unity in the United States. In many ways, each state behaved like a small country. States imposed tariffs, or import taxes, on goods shipped from other states. Some states had their own navies and made treaties with foreign nations. Many states printed their own paper money. This meant if you had a pocket full of paper money printed in Pennsylvania, you could not spend it in New York or Virginia!

The Articles of Confederation

After the Declaration of Independence, the United States was an independent nation, so American leaders needed to create their own political system. Americans did not want a king or other supreme authority ruling them. Going back to the ideas of John Locke, they wanted a republic, a political system without a monarch. It would rule "with the consent of the governed."

No government in the world at that time was based on this idea. The ideal of republicanism was that hard-working, property-owning citizens would be active in their government. Reality, of course, was different. African Americans and Native Americans were not citizens, and most African Americans were enslaved. The right to vote or to own property was not extended to them. In addition, women had few property rights and poor white men had more limited civil rights.

The states had formed their new governments quickly. After independence had been declared, each wrote its own constitution. But the Second Continental Congress found it harder to agree on a structure for a national government. It was apparent that some kind of central government was needed to carry on the war and make agreements with foreign governments.

A weak central government Congress had adopted the Articles of Confederation back in November 1777. This was America's first national constitution. As its name says, the document established a confederation—an association of independent, sovereign states with certain common goals.

Under the Articles, the central government had power to set national policies and carry on foreign relations, including relations with Native American nations. The government could also borrow and coin money and set up post offices. Finally, it could establish an army and declare war.

But the Articles of Confederation had many weaknesses. Congress was the chief agency of the government because there was no executive branch. It proved difficult, and often impossible, for Congress to put its policies into effect. Nine of the 13 states had to agree on any law. All 13 had to agree to amend the Articles of Confederation.

The government also did not have the power to impose or collect taxes, which made it very difficult to pay for the Revolution. The Confederation could not pay back money it had borrowed. Some soldiers who had fought in the Revolution also went unpaid.

Because its central government was so weak, the Confederation had trouble taking advantage of what the United States had won in the 1783 Treaty of Paris. For example, the British continued to occupy their forts in the Great Lakes region. With the help of Native American allies, they kept American settlers out of parts of the Northwest Territory.

Shays's Rebellion It was not only the government that had money problems. Economic problems faced people in every state. The end of the war was a disaster for New England's valuable trade with Britain and the British West Indies. Traders lost the advantage of being part of the British Empire and now had to pay high customs duties.

In addition, the paper money issued during the war was not backed up with gold or silver. That led to inflation—a huge rise in prices as the value of paper money fell. The Confederation could not collect taxes, but the states could and did. Some required that people pay their taxes in "hard currency," not the almost-worthless paper money. People who could not pay their debts were jailed. The laws especially hurt poor farmers who were already in debt. That led to riots in several places.

The most famous was Shays's Rebellion in Massachusetts in 1786. Angry farmers, led by Daniel Shays, a former Continental Army captain, shut down debtor courts. The rebellion was crushed by Massachusetts militiamen, but it illustrated the weakness of the Articles.

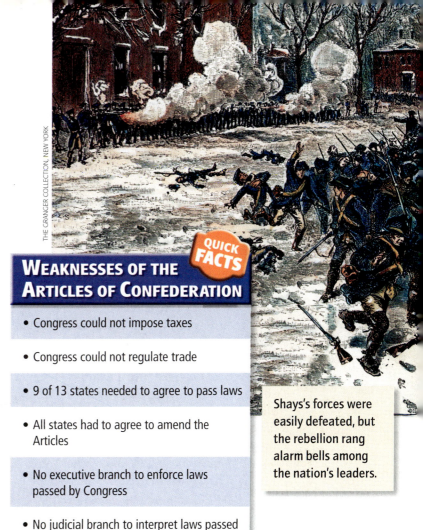

WEAKNESSES OF THE ARTICLES OF CONFEDERATION
QUICK FACTS

- Congress could not impose taxes
- Congress could not regulate trade
- 9 of 13 states needed to agree to pass laws
- All states had to agree to amend the Articles
- No executive branch to enforce laws passed by Congress
- No judicial branch to interpret laws passed by Congress

Shays's forces were easily defeated, but the rebellion rang alarm bells among the nation's leaders.

ACADEMIC VOCABULARY
constitution document outlining basic laws and principles
amend make changes

Settling the western territories Even though the Confederation established a weak central government, some of its actions did have long-lasting effects. One notable accomplishment was establishing a pattern for settlement in western lands.

The Articles of Confederation did not cover the question of new states. In 1784 Thomas Jefferson proposed a plan to divide the Northwest Territory—the land north and west of the Ohio River. It would set up 10 districts. When population in any district reached 20,000, its people could send a representative to Congress. Later, it could be admitted as a new state. This plan never went fully into effect.

The next year, in the Land Ordinance of 1785, Congress drew up a plan for surveying, selling, and settling the territory. Land would be surveyed and divided into a neat grid of townships, each six miles square. Within a township were 36 sections, each one mile square. The government would own four of them, while a fifth would be sold to support public schools. This changed the landscape of the Midwest into the checkerboard pattern still seen today.

Then in 1787, Congress passed another law for western settlement, the Northwest Ordinance. It was meant to encourage orderly settlement and the formation of new states, all controlled by law. The states of Ohio, Indiana, Illinois, Michigan, and Wisconsin were eventually carved out of the Northwest Territory.

The Ordinance also promised settlers religious freedom and other civil rights. Significantly, slavery was not allowed.

READING CHECK **Summarizing** Under the Articles of Confederation, what powers did the central government have?

Drafting the Constitution

Frustration with the Articles of Confederation had been building for years among farmers, veterans, merchants doing business between states, and many other Americans. In the fall of 1786 Washington and **James Madison** convened a meeting of the states in Annapolis, Maryland, to discuss the situation, but delegates from only five states attended.

The Constitutional Convention

Key Delegates at the Constitutional Convention
1. Roger Sherman
2. Alexander Hamilton
3. Benjamin Franklin
4. James Madison
5. George Washington

After the Annapolis meeting, Congress called all the states to meet in Philadelphia in May 1787 for a Constitutional Convention. This was a turning point in American history. The best account of the Convention is the detailed diary kept by James Madison. Because of the role he played in planning and writing the final document, Madison is often called the Father of the Constitution.

Other key delegates to the Constitutional Convention—now known as the Framers—included Roger Sherman, Alexander Hamilton, and James Wilson. Leading the group were George Washington and Benjamin Franklin. The convention unanimously chose Washington as its president.

Compromises at the Convention The major issues at the Constitutional Convention centered on how to find a balance between large and small states and between northern and southern interests. There was also a battle between those who wanted a strong national government and those who wanted to protect states' rights.

Edmund Randolph of Virginia presented the Virginia Plan, which proposed a completely new form of government. There would be three separate branches: an executive branch, a legislative branch, and a judicial branch. The legislature would choose an executive to carry out the laws. It would also set up a court system. The legislature would be bicameral, or made up of two houses, or groups of representatives. Members of the legislature would be chosen in proportion to each state's population.

Smaller states quickly objected to the Virginia Plan. Because their large neighbors would have more representatives in the legislature they would have more power. One delegate from a small state, William Paterson of New Jersey, proposed a "small state" plan. The New Jersey Plan kept many features of the Confederation, although it gave Congress additional powers. Among other proposals, the plan suggested a one-house legislature with equal representation for each state.

Finally, the Connecticut delegates came up with a plan for a compromise that would

ACADEMIC VOCABULARY
proportion proper or equal share

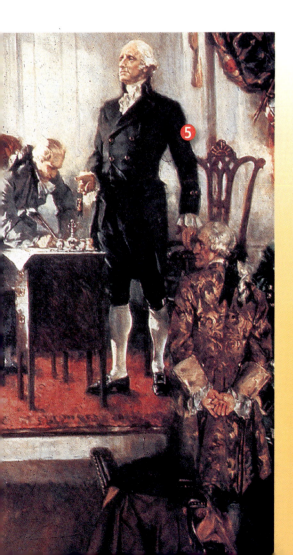

This painting shows the Framers signing the Constitution on September 17, 1787. A key accomplishment of the Convention was an agreement to create a bicameral, or two-house, legislature. This agreement is called the Great Compromise.

THE GREAT COMPROMISE

Virginia Plan
(Large state plan)
- Gave more power in national government to large states
- Bicameral legislature
- Each state's number of representatives would be based on population

New Jersey Plan
(Small state plan)
- Gave equal power in national government to all states
- Unicameral legislature
- Each state would have an equal number of representatives

THE GREAT COMPROMISE
- Bicameral legislature
- In the lower house, each state's number of representatives is determined by population
- In the upper house, each state has an equal number of representatives

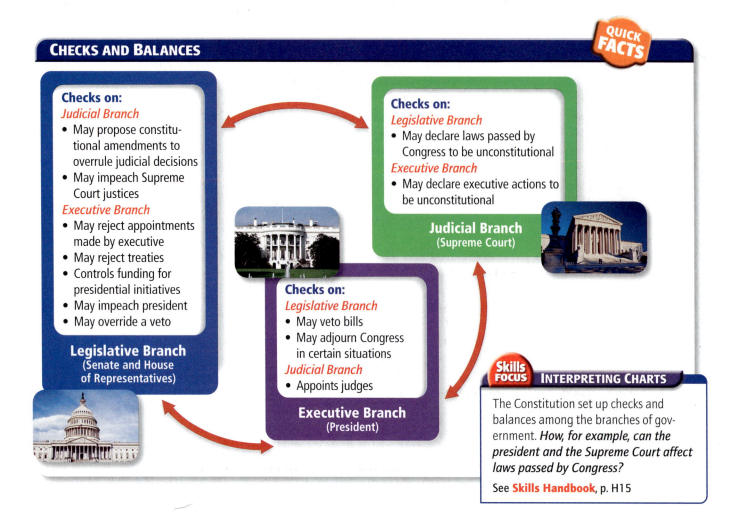

CHECKS AND BALANCES

Checks on:
Judicial Branch
- May propose constitutional amendments to overrule judicial decisions
- May impeach Supreme Court justices

Executive Branch
- May reject appointments made by executive
- May reject treaties
- Controls funding for presidential initiatives
- May impeach president
- May override a veto

Legislative Branch
(Senate and House of Representatives)

Checks on:
Legislative Branch
- May declare laws passed by Congress to be unconstitutional

Executive Branch
- May declare executive actions to be unconstitutional

Judicial Branch
(Supreme Court)

Checks on:
Legislative Branch
- May veto bills
- May adjourn Congress in certain situations

Judicial Branch
- Appoints judges

Executive Branch
(President)

INTERPRETING CHARTS

The Constitution set up checks and balances among the branches of government. *How, for example, can the president and the Supreme Court affect laws passed by Congress?*

See **Skills Handbook**, p. H15

ACADEMIC VOCABULARY
federal national

balance the interests of both large and small states. They said, "The two ideas . . . ought to be combined; that in one branch the people ought to be represented; in the other the States." That is, the upper house of the legislature, the Senate, would have two representatives from each state. In the lower house, representation would be based on population. All spending bills would begin in the lower house, where large states had more power.

Today this answer seems obvious. But it was such a major step for the convention that it became known as the Great Compromise. It is also called the Connecticut Compromise. As part of the Great Compromise, delegates also had to decide on how to count population.

Enslaved African Americans made up a large proportion of the population in several southern states—as much as 30 to 40 percent. Counting them would give those states greater representation in Congress. But because some taxes were based on population, it would also increase taxes. Southern states at first wanted to count all slaves for representation but none for taxation. Northern states objected.

In the Three-Fifths Compromise, delegates agreed that all whites plus three-fifths of the slave population (referred to as "all other persons") would be counted for both representation and taxation. Native Americans would not be counted.

Providing checks and balances Once the first draft of the Constitution was written, there were still other points to consider. One major point of discussion was the balance between the powers of Congress and those of the president (as the executive was by then being called). One underlying question was that of states' rights against the power of the federal, or national, government.

The outcome was another compromise. Instead of people directly electing the president, the state legislatures would select electors, who would then choose a president. These last-minute changes were important in setting up **checks and balances** among the three branches of government.

The committee gave the president the power to make treaties and nominate judges and ambassadors. But the Senate had to give its "advice and consent" to these actions. The president could veto a law passed by Congress. But Congress could pass it over his veto if two-thirds of each house agreed to do so.

At last, the Convention had a final document. It set out a plan of government that had never been tried before. It had three separate branches. The **legislative branch** (Congress) makes the laws. The **executive branch** (the president and the departments that help run the government) carries out those laws. The **judicial branch** (the Supreme Court and lower courts) interprets the laws as they relate to the Constitution.

As the diagram on the facing page shows, there were checks and balances between the three branches of government. Each branch could delay or stop an action taken by one of the other branches. This ensured that no one branch of the government would dominate the others or become too powerful.

Despite all of the compromises, a few of those who had worked hardest to draft a constitution could not bring themselves to sign the final document. In all, 39 delegates from 12 states signed the Constitution. Then the Constitutional Convention adjourned on Monday, September 17, 1787. Now it was time for the American people to ratify, or approve, the document.

READING CHECK **Drawing Conclusions** How did small states and large states reach compromise over the issue of representation in Congress?

Ratifying the Constitution

The proceedings of the Philadelphia Convention had been secret. As the meeting continued through the summer of 1787, people wondered what it would produce. When the document was finally published, supporters and opponents of the new Constitution immediately began to present their arguments.

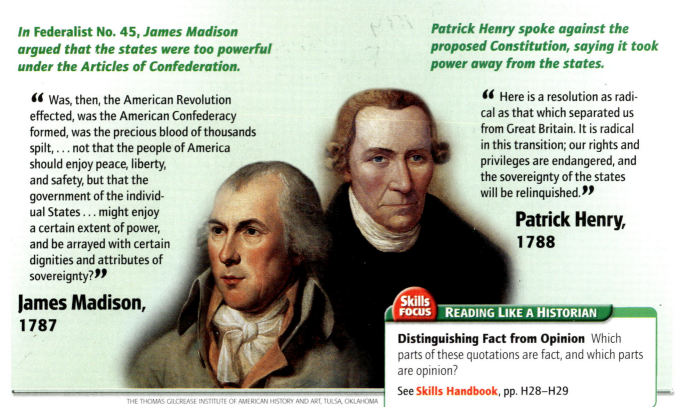

COUNTERPOINTS

Federalist vs. Antifederalist

In Federalist No. 45, James Madison argued that the states were too powerful under the Articles of Confederation.

"Was, then, the American Revolution effected, was the American Confederacy formed, was the precious blood of thousands spilt, ... not that the people of America should enjoy peace, liberty, and safety, but that the government of the individual States ... might enjoy a certain extent of power, and be arrayed with certain dignities and attributes of sovereignty?"

James Madison, 1787

Patrick Henry spoke against the proposed Constitution, saying it took power away from the states.

"Here is a resolution as radical as that which separated us from Great Britain. It is radical in this transition; our rights and privileges are endangered, and the sovereignty of the states will be relinquished."

Patrick Henry, 1788

Skills Focus **READING LIKE A HISTORIAN**

Distinguishing Fact from Opinion Which parts of these quotations are fact, and which parts are opinion?

See **Skills Handbook**, pp. H28–H29

THE THOMAS GILCREASE INSTITUTE OF AMERICAN HISTORY AND ART, TULSA, OKLAHOMA

Federalists and Antifederalists

Supporters of the Constitution, once called nationalists, were now referred to as **Federalists**. Their name comes from the term *federalism*, which is a sharing of power between a national government and its subdivisions (such as states). The people who opposed the Constitution were called **Antifederalists**. These two groups would battle over **ratification**, or official approval, of the Constitution.

Most Federalists believed that a strong national government was necessary for the survival of the nation. They wanted government to end chaos and be a check on the kind of mob rule shown by Shays's Rebellion. At the same time, they pointed out that the separation of powers in the Constitution limited government power. The Federalist cause was generally popular in the cities and among the wealthy.

On the other hand, Antifederalists feared that a strong national government would lead to a kind of tyranny—just what they had fought against in the Revolutionary War. The Antifederalists worried that the central government would abuse both states' rights and individual liberties. They did not trust any government to protect its people's rights.

Many Antifederalists also thought the new government favored the educated and the wealthy over ordinary people. The Antifederalists came from different economic backgrounds and social classes. Many, however, were farmers and planters.

The Federalist Papers

Some of the most important support for the Constitution appeared in a series of 85 essays known as the Federalist Papers. Published anonymously in a New York newspaper, they were eventually collected in a book called *The Federalist*.

In the essays, the anonymous writer who called himself Publius discussed and defended each part of the Constitution. The main goal of the essays was to persuade New York delegates to ratify the document by explaining its advantages. But they were also brilliant explanations of the principles of federalism.

Publius was in fact three leading Federalists—James Madison, Alexander Hamilton, and John Jay. Madison, on whose ideas the Constitution was based, wrote on political theory. Hamilton was leading the Federalist campaign in New York. He offered practical arguments for a strong government.

Creating a New Government

The Articles of Confederation (ratified 1781)
- America's first written constitution
- A loose union of sovereign states
- States intentionally made the central government weak because they feared tyranny
- The weak central government under the Articles of Confederation was ineffective

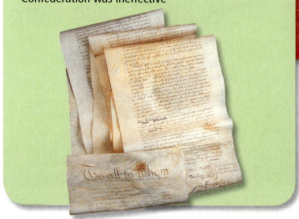

The United States Constitution (ratified 1788)
- Replaced the Articles of Confederation
- Provided representation for all states
- Established three branches of government (executive, legislative, judicial) with separation of powers to avoid tyranny
- Created checks and balances between the three branches
- Included a Bill of Rights (ratified in 1791)

The Bill of Rights Before agreeing to ratify the Constitution, most Antifederalists first wanted a **Bill of Rights**. They wanted to see basic rights added to the document to be sure that individual liberties would be protected. Adding a Bill of Rights to the Constitution became the main focus of the struggle over ratification.

Article VII of the Constitution explained what must be done to bring the document into effect and make the new government a reality. The Framers knew that getting unanimous agreement would be difficult. Therefore, only nine of the thirteen states needed to ratify the Constitution.

In the end, several crucial states ratified the Constitution only because they were promised a Bill of Rights. Once the new Congress was elected, it had to begin work on such legislation quickly. Article V of the Constitution gave either Congress or state conventions the right to propose amendments. Amendments then would go to the states for approval.

Madison took charge of getting a Bill of Rights through Congress. By the end of 1791, 10 amendments were approved. These first 10 amendments to the Constitution became the Bill of Rights.

The Bill of Rights protected both individuals and states against what people feared might be too much government power. The first eight amendments dealt with individual civil liberties. The Ninth Amendment stated that listing certain rights given to the people did not mean that others did not exist.

Most of the amendments that form the Bill of Rights listed things that no government, state or federal, could do. The final amendment addressed the actions that states could take. It addressed the Antifederalists' fears about the loss of states' rights and sovereignty.

The Tenth Amendment defined two kinds of government powers. The Constitution gives certain powers to each branch of the national, or federal, government. Those are known as the delegated powers. Some are expressly stated and others are implied. The Tenth Amendment also defined the reserved powers. Those are powers not specifically given to the federal government or denied to the states. Reserved powers belong to the states or to the people. This compromise opened the way to putting the Constitution in force.

Most of the amendments in the Bill of Rights echoed the rights listed in the Virginia Declaration of Rights, written by George Mason. The First Amendment, for example, guaranteed basic civil liberties, such as freedom of speech, the press, and religion. You can read the complete text of the Bill of Rights in the Constitution Handbook at the end of this chapter.

READING CHECK **Making Inferences** Why did Madison lead the fight for a Bill of Rights?

THE IMPACT TODAY

Government
The free-speech protection of the First Amendment has also been applied to "symbolic" speech— non-verbal communication that expresses an idea, such as wearing a protest button.

SECTION 2 ASSESSMENT

go.hrw.com
Online Quiz
Keyword: SE7 HP2

HSS 11.1.1, 11.1.2, 11.3.5

Reviewing Ideas, Terms, and People

1. **a. Describe** What kind of government did the **Articles of Confederation** create?
   b. Explain Why was it so difficult to amend the Articles of Confederation?
   c. Evaluate Do you think the farmers in Shays's Rebellion were justified in rebelling? Explain your answer.

2. **a. Identify** Identify the three branches of government and the role of each of them.
   b. Explain How did the Great Compromise balance the wishes of small states and large states?
   c. Develop How did delegates' opinions change during the course of the Constitutional Convention?

3. **a. Recall** What is the **Bill of Rights**?
   b. Summarize What kinds of rights were promised in the first eight amendments to the Constitution?
   c. Evaluate How has the Bill of Rights been important in American history since 1791?

Critical Thinking

4. **Comparing** Copy the chart below and list the powers and the weaknesses of the Confederation government.

Powers	Weaknesses

FOCUS ON WRITING ELA W1.1

5. **Persuasive** As a Federalist or Antifederalist during the 10 months after the Constitutional Convention, write a paragraph arguing for or against ratification.

SECTION 3
Forging the New Republic

BEFORE YOU READ

MAIN IDEA
Under presidents Washington, Adams, and Jefferson, the United States continued to shape its new government while facing both foreign and domestic challenges.

READING FOCUS
1. What actions did Washington take when he became president?
2. What challenges did the United States face in the 1790s?
3. What were the main events of Jefferson's presidency?
4. What were the causes and effects of the War of 1812?

KEY TERMS AND PEOPLE
Alexander Hamilton
Democratic-Republicans
Judiciary Act of 1789
strict constructionist
loose constructionist
Whiskey Rebellion
John Adams
Marbury v. *Madison*
Louisiana Purchase
War of 1812

HSS 11.1.3 Understand the history of the Constitution after 1787 with emphasis on federal versus state authority and growing democratization.

A Born LEADER

 How did Americans welcome the new president? On April 16, George Washington left his home in Virginia to attend his presidential inauguration in New York City. His trip north was one long celebration. As Washington's coach passed through towns and villages on the way, enthusiastic crowds cheered him. Men on horseback rode alongside the coach, stirring up dust from the dirt roads. Washington stopped in small towns to make speeches. He led parades and went to lavish dinners. The emotions of the people seemed almost overwhelming. At last Washington reached New York, and the joyful celebrations reached a peak on the historic day of his inauguration, April 30, 1789.

◀ Washington's stately image has come to symbolize the presidency.

50 CHAPTER 2

Washington Becomes President

In his inaugural address, Washington spoke modestly, saying that he was not experienced in civil administration. But the former commander in chief was used to being a leader. His dignity and air of quiet power along with his impressive height clearly commanded authority. He knew that what he did as president would set a pattern for later administrations.

Washington's cabinet One of the first things Washington did was set up the cabinet, a group of advisers to the president. The Constitution mentions the "heads of the executive departments" but does not mention the cabinet by name. In 1789 Congress created the first three executive departments—state, treasury, and war. To lead these new departments, Washington chose men he knew and trusted.

Henry Knox, who had been in charge of artillery in the Revolution, was secretary of war. Thomas Jefferson was secretary of state, while **Alexander Hamilton** was secretary of the treasury. Edmund Randolph of Virginia was attorney general, the president's legal adviser.

There were political divisions between the cabinet members. Hamilton and Jefferson were both brilliant but disagreed about policies. They were also very different in personality and grew to dislike each other intensely.

The Federalists, led by Hamilton, still saw the country growing into a strong centralized nation with prospering cities and businesses and a role in world affairs. But others saw a more rural than urban country, with power residing closer to the people, in the state governments. Led by Jefferson and Madison, they took the name **Democratic-Republicans**.

Another precedent set by the first government was setting up the structure of the court system. In the **Judiciary Act of 1789**, Congress organized the judicial branch. It had a six-person Supreme Court with one chief justice and five associates. It also set up district courts and circuit courts of appeal. Washington named John Jay as the first chief justice of the Supreme Court.

Hamilton's financial plan The first secretary of the treasury, Alexander Hamilton, faced enormous problems. The new government had no money to pay everyday expenses. It also owed money to foreign nations, to private lenders, and even to former soldiers. Hamilton did not share the belief in republican ideals. He thought that a wealthy, aristocratic class was the secret of a stable government.

Hamilton's financial plan recommended three major steps:
- The federal government should take on both state and national debt.
- The government should raise revenue by passing tariffs.
- The United States should create a national bank and a national mint to stabilize the banking system.

Hamilton's debt repayment plan was controversial. For one, many felt it would unfairly reward wealthy people who bought Revolutionary War bonds from the original bondholders. These bondholders, mostly merchants, farmers, and soldiers, had sold their bonds at low prices believing the government would not repay. Secondly, many southern states had already paid their debts. They resented that the federal government would take on state debts.

In part, the disagreement between northern and southern states was solved by moving the capital. Southerners had long felt that a capital in New York City would give the northern states too much influence. In 1791 the capital moved to Philadelphia with a plan to move south in ten years to a site on the Potomac River, later called Washington, D.C.

FACES OF HISTORY
Thomas JEFFERSON
1743–1826

Thomas Jefferson is best known as the writer of the Declaration of Independence as well as being the nation's third president. His most important accomplishment as president was the Louisiana Purchase.

Jefferson was a man of many talents and contradictions. He was not only a politician but also a gifted architect, scholar, scientist, and writer. Even though he was a wealthy and educated Virginia planter, he truly believed in republican simplicity. His actions reflected this belief. Jefferson was casual in the way he dressed and acted. He walked to and from his inauguration and kept state dinners informal.

Analyze What was Jefferson's most important accomplishment as president?

Government
The Supreme Court today consists of a chief justice and eight associate justices. Chief Justice William Rehnquist served as the nation's 16th chief justice until his death in 2005. He was succeeded by Chief Justice John Roberts.

The Bank of the United States By far, the most controversial part of Hamilton's plan was the idea of a national bank. Some people, such as Jefferson, believed that the government did not have the power to create a national bank. These people thought that the government only had the powers specifically granted in the Constitution. A person who held this belief was called a **strict constructionist**.

Alexander Hamilton, on the other hand, was a **loose constructionist**. When he proposed the national bank, he said that the Constitution also allows actions that are not specifically mentioned—as long as they are not specifically prohibited. He pointed to the clause that allows Congress to pass all laws that are "necessary and proper" to carry out its assigned powers.

Jefferson urged Washington to veto the bank bill. While Washington admitted that he was "greatly perplexed," he did not want to use the veto. Hamilton eventually persuaded him that it was necessary to be flexible. In February 1791 Washington signed the bill to charter the first Bank of the United States.

The differences of opinion between Hamilton and Jefferson had another consequence. Those who supported Jefferson became known as Democratic-Republicans, while supporters of Hamilton were known as Federalists. The Constitution did not anticipate political parties because most of the Framers thought political parties were dangerous to national unity. However, in the 1790s that was the way national politics was developing. The Democratic-Republicans and the Federalists became the nation's first two political parties.

READING CHECK **Identifying Problem and Solution** Why did Washington decide to sign the bank bill?

Challenges in the 1790s

Washington's presidency had a productive start. Still, the United States would continue to face challenges during the 1790s from groups both at home and abroad.

PRIMARY SOURCES

Washington's Farewell Address

In 1796 George Washington announced that he would not seek a third term in office. In his famous Farewell Address, Washington prepared the country for new leadership. Among other things, he warned Americans to avoid divisions based on political parties and geography.

"I have already intimated to you the danger of parties in the state, with particular reference to the founding of them on geographical discriminations. Let me now take a more comprehensive view, and warn you in the most solemn manner against the baneful [harmful] effects of the spirit of party, generally . . .

The alternate domination of one faction over another, sharpened by the spirit of revenge natural to party dissension . . . is itself a frightful despotism . . .

It serves always to distract the public council and enfeeble the public administration. It agitates the community with ill-founded jealousies and false alarms, kindles the animosity of one party against another, foments [promotes] occasionally riot and insurrection . . ."

The word *despotism* means "a system of government in which the ruler has unlimited power."

By "geographical discriminations," Washington meant differences based on where different sections of the country are located.

Skills Focus **READING LIKE A HISTORIAN**

1. **Making Inferences** What does Washington mean by the phrase "the spirit of party"?
2. **Analyzing Primary Sources** According to Washington, what are the dangers of political parties?

See **Skills Handbook**, p. H17, H28–H29

The French Revolution
In early 1789 France exploded into revolution. French citizens protested against food shortages, high prices, and taxes. On July 14, 1789, a crowd of angry Parisians stormed the Bastille prison, which was a hated symbol of royal power. Soon, a revolutionary government took over. It limited the king's power and made France a constitutional monarchy.

In 1793 radicals called Jacobins took power in France and declared a republic. They imposed a Reign of Terror. Thousands of people were arrested and imprisoned or sent to the guillotine to be beheaded, including the king and queen. Then moderates regained control.

Many Democratic-Republicans supported the French Revolution, thinking that it was a turn toward liberty in France. Hamilton's Federalists, however, were displeased that the revolution had overthrown the French government and that France was at war with European nations, including Britain.

President Washington was convinced that the growth and prosperity of the United States depended on staying neutral. In April 1793, he issued the Neutrality Proclamation. He held to that policy for the rest of his presidency.

Jay's Treaty and Pinckney's Treaty
Some ongoing disputes between Great Britain and the United States were resolved in 1794 in Jay's Treaty, negotiated by Chief Justice John Jay. Britain agreed to pay damages for American ships they had seized. They also agreed to vacate their forts in the Northwest Territory. The treaty was unpopular in the United States, where many felt Great Britain should have been punished more severely for seizing American ships.

Then in Pinckney's Treaty (1795), the United States peacefully settled boundary disputes with Spain over Spanish Florida. Americans considered this treaty a success because it opened the frontier to further settlement.

The Whiskey Rebellion
At home, the first major challenge was the **Whiskey Rebellion**. In 1794 farmers in western Pennsylvania objected violently to Hamilton's excise tax on whiskey. They attacked tax collectors and burned the barns of people who gave away the location of stills where whiskey was made. Washington responded quickly, sending militia to put down the rebellion. He wanted to make it clear that armed rebellion against the national government would not be tolerated. No blood was shed, and the farmers backed down.

Conflict in the Northwest Territory
As the Whiskey Rebellion was taking place, Americans were also facing conflicts with Native Americans in the Northwest Territory. In 1794 General Anthony Wayne defeated a confederacy of Native Americans at the Battle of Fallen Timbers. Then in the Treaty of Greenville, the United States claimed most of the Indian land in the Northwest Territory.

Challenges for President Adams
In 1796 Washington refused to consider a third term as president. As his Farewell Address, he published a long letter in a Philadelphia newspaper. (See the excerpt on facing page.) In it he continued to warn against getting involved in party politics and the affairs of foreign countries. Washington's vice president, **John Adams**, was elected president. Thomas Jefferson became vice president.

Adams wanted to improve the relationship between the United States and France, but some angry Federalists wanted war. In 1797 Adams sent three diplomats to France—Charles Cotesworth Pinckney, Elbridge Gerry, and John Marshall. Rather than meeting with them, the French foreign minister sent three minor diplomats who demanded bribes and a loan.

An angry President Adams sent a report to Congress, naming the three French agents as X, Y, and Z. When the XYZ affair became public, many Americans wanted war. A popular slogan was "Millions for defense but not one cent for tribute!"

The XYZ affair brought new suspicions about the Republicans' pro-French sympathies and a general resentment of foreigners. That allowed Congress to pass several repressive laws, including the Alien and Sedition Acts, which prohibited criticism of the federal government. In the Kentucky and Virginia Resolutions, Jefferson and Madison argued that these laws were unconstitutional.

READING CHECK **Sequencing** List, in order, the domestic and foreign challenges the United States faced in the 1790s.

Jefferson's Presidency

The election of 1800 was the first American election in which power passed from one political party to another. President Adams ran for re-election as a candidate of the Federalist Party, with Charles Cotesworth Pinckney nominated as his vice president. Running against Adams was Thomas Jefferson, the Democratic-Republican candidate. Jefferson's party nominated Aaron Burr to run as his vice president.

The election of 1800 was also unique because it was a tied election. At that time, the candidate who received the most electoral votes became president, and the candidate who received the second most electoral votes became vice president. Jefferson and Burr received the same number of electoral votes.

Eventually the House of Representatives decided that Jefferson would be president. To ensure that the problem never happened again, Congress also passed the Twelfth Amendment to the Constitution. This set up separate ballots for president and vice president, a system that remains in effect today.

Jefferson's inaugural address spoke of unity and tolerance. "We are all Republicans, we are all Federalists," he said. Jefferson's presidency was guided by two essential principles:
- reducing the size and influence of the federal government
- cutting back the taxes passed under Hamilton's financial plan

Marbury v. Madison A key event of Jefferson's presidency was strengthening the powers of the Supreme Court. This happened in an interesting turn of events. Jefferson's inauguration was not until March 1801. That gave Federalists in Congress time to create several new judgeships. Because Adams worked late into the night of March 3, 1801, appointing Federalists to these positions, they were known as the midnight judges.

Secretary of State James Madison, however, refused to deliver a commission to one of the midnight judges. In **Marbury v. Madison**, the Supreme Court ruled that the Constitution did not give the Court power to make Madison deliver the commission. Therefore, the law

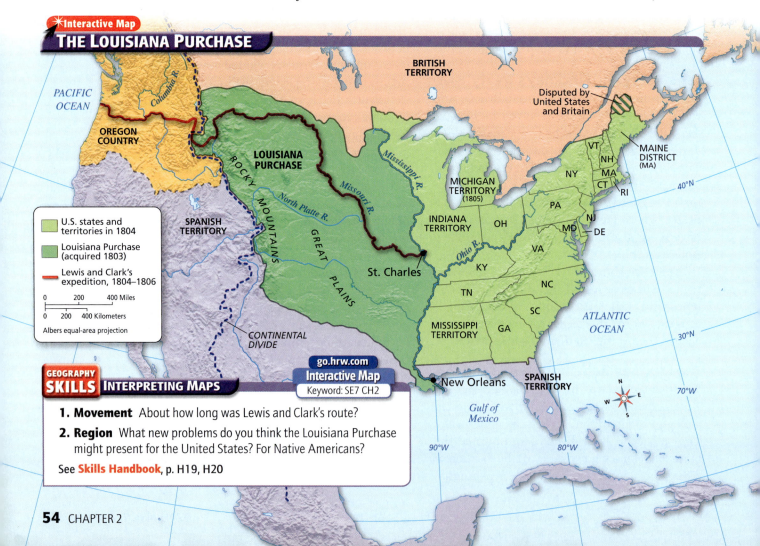

THE LOUISIANA PURCHASE

GEOGRAPHY SKILLS INTERPRETING MAPS
1. **Movement** About how long was Lewis and Clark's route?
2. **Region** What new problems do you think the Louisiana Purchase might present for the United States? For Native Americans?

See **Skills Handbook**, p. H19, H20

54 CHAPTER 2

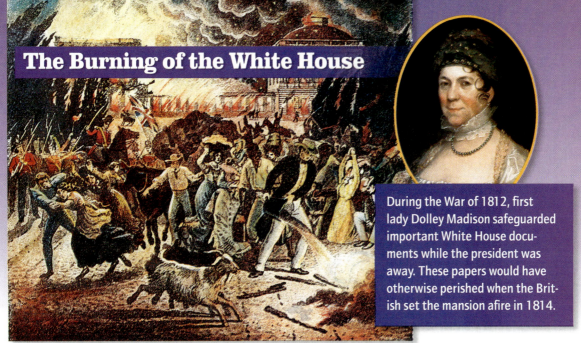

The Burning of the White House

During the War of 1812, first lady Dolley Madison safeguarded important White House documents while the president was away. These papers would have otherwise perished when the British set the mansion afire in 1814.

THE GRANGER COLLECTION, NEW YORK

that gave the Court that power—the Judiciary Act of 1801—was unconstitutional. *Marbury* v. *Madison* thus established the Supreme Court's right to declare that a law violates the Constitution. This power is known as judicial review.

The Louisiana Purchase One of Jefferson's major achievements was purchasing Louisiana from France. This transfer was known as the Louisiana Purchase, and it roughly doubled the size of the United States.

The Louisiana Purchase looked like a remarkable bargain, but it raised questions, especially for Jefferson. He had to consider his long-held position in favor of strict construction of the Constitution. Nowhere did the Constitution give him the authority to buy new territory. Yet he felt the purchase was a good idea. Jefferson and his advisers finally decided that the right to acquire territory was implicit in the constitutional power to make treaties.

Once the Louisiana Purchase was approved by Congress, Jefferson sent out a number of expeditions. The most famous was the Lewis and Clark expedition (1804–1806), led by Meriwether Lewis, Jefferson's secretary, and William Clark, an experienced frontiersman.

The ultimate destination of the Lewis and Clark expedition was the Pacific Ocean. Jefferson wanted the expedition to map the country and survey its natural history—plants, animals, and landforms. Lewis, Clark, and their men paddled along rivers, trekked across plains, and tramped through thick forests. Along the way, they acquired an invaluable guide—a young Shoshone woman, Sacajawea, whose name means Canoe Launcher. In November 1805 the expedition finally reached the Pacific Ocean.

READING CHECK Identifying Problem and Solution What constitutional question did the Louisiana Purchase raise?

The War of 1812

Most Americans were enthusiastic about the Louisiana Purchase, bringing a landslide victory for Jefferson in 1804. Then world events pushed the United States toward war.

Causes of the War of 1812 In 1803 the Napoleonic Wars broke out between France and Great Britain. Once again, the United States was caught in the middle. Both French and British warships would stop American merchant ships. The British even began a policy of impressment, or seizing Americans at sea and drafting them into the British navy. This angered many Americans.

Americans also discovered that the British were helping the Native Americans in the Northwest in their fight against American settlers. In response to these events, a group of young Congressmembers known as the War Hawks began calling for war with Britain to protect American interests. Soon, the War of 1812 began.

ACADEMIC VOCABULARY
implicit true but unexpressed

FORMING A NEW NATION 55

Causes and Effects of The War of 1812

QUICK FACTS

CAUSES
- British impressment of American sailors
- International conflicts over commerce
- British military aid to Native Americans on the Northwest Territory frontier

EFFECTS
- Foreign respect for the United States
- National pride
- Increase in American manufacturing
- Less Native American resistance

The **War of 1812** was the second war between British and American forces in North America. It was fought on land and sea, from Canada in the north to Louisiana in the south. Much of the war took place along the border between Canada and the United States. The British also set up a naval blockade along the Atlantic coast.

In the final battle of the war, Americans won a decisive victory. On January 8, 1815, General Andrew Jackson led American troops against a large British force in New Orleans and defeated it. The battle made Jackson a hero and was the last major conflict of the War of 1812.

Effects of the War of 1812 By the time Jackson won at New Orleans, however, the peace treaty had already been signed. Slow methods of communication prevented Jackson from receiving the message in time to prevent the battle.

In 1814 American and British diplomats met in Ghent, Belgium, to finalize a treaty that had been signed in December. No territory changed hands, but the United States felt it had proved itself as a nation.

Other effects of the war included the end of the Federalist Party, whose members had opposed the war. The war also weakened Native American resistance in the Northwest, and it gave a boost to American manufacturing. Above all, the war increased American pride. The new nation had again successfully defended itself against a foreign threat.

READING CHECK **Making Inferences** Why did the War Hawks want war?

SECTION 3 ASSESSMENT

HSS 11.1.3

go.hrw.com
Online Quiz
Keyword: SE7 HP2

Reviewing Ideas, Terms, and People

1. **a. Identify** Who were the members of Washington's first cabinet?
   b. Explain How did Washington influence the role of the president?
   c. Summarize What is the difference between **strict constructionist** and **loose constructionist** interpretations of the Constitution?

2. **a. Describe** How did Washington's retirement influence party politics?
   b. Explain What was the XYZ affair, and how did it affect American public opinion?
   c. Rate Were the Alien and Sedition Acts an effective weapon against outside interference?

3. **a. Recall** What was the purpose of passing the Twelfth Amendment?
   b. Summarize What were major issues in the election of 1800?
   c. Predict Why was the election of 1800 significant?

4. **a. Recall** Who were the War Hawks?
   b. Explain What were the causes of the **War of 1812**?
   c. Evaluate Why did Americans see the end of the war as a victory?

Critical Thinking

5. **Comparing** Copy the chart below and compare the points of view of Federalists and Democratic-Republicans.

Federalists	Democratic-Republicans

FOCUS ON SPEAKING ELA W1.1

6. **Persuasive** As a political campaign worker in 1800, write a speech persuading people to support the presidential campaign of either John Adams or Thomas Jefferson.

CHAPTER 2 Chapter Review

History's Impact video program
Review the videos to answer the closing question:
How has the American spirit of exploration affected the history of the nation?

Reviewing Key Terms and People

For each term or name below, write a sentence explaining its significance.

1. Stamp Act
2. Boston Massacre
3. Battle of Lexington
4. *Common Sense*
5. Articles of Confederation
6. checks and balances
7. ratification
8. Bill of Rights
9. Judiciary Act of 1789
10. Louisiana Purchase
11. War of 1812

Comprehension and Critical Thinking

SECTION 1 *(pp. 30–37)* HSS 11.1.1, 11.1.2

12. **a. Identify** What objects required stamps under the Stamp Act?

    b. Sequence Create a brief time line of the events leading up to the Battles of Lexington and Concord.

    c. Analyze How did the colonists eventually win the Revolutionary War?

SECTION 2 *(pp. 42–49)* HSS 11.1.1, 11.1.2, 11.3.5

13. **a. Identify** What did the Federalists believe? What did the Antifederalists believe?

    b. Contrast How was the Constitution different from the Articles of Confederation?

    c. Evaluate Why was the Bill of Rights necessary for ratification of the Constitution?

SECTION 3 *(pp. 50–56)* HSS 11.1.3

14. **a. Describe** What actions of Great Britain and France pushed the United States into fighting the War of 1812?

    b. Contrast What were the different opinions about the Louisiana Purchase?

    c. Evaluate What was ultimately accomplished by the War of 1812?

Using the Internet

go.hrw.com
Practice Online
Keyword: SE7 CH2

15. Revolutionary War battle sites still exist across the eastern seaboard of the United States. Using the keyword above, do research on a Revolutionary War site that tourists can visit today. Then create a brochure that teaches tourists the significance of your site and encourages them to visit.

Critical Reading HSS 11.1.1; ELA R2.4

Read the passage in Section 2 that begins with the heading "The Articles of Confederation." Then answer the questions that follow.

16. What was one notable accomplishment of the Articles of Confederation?

    A establishing a bicameral legislature
    B establishing a pattern for settlement in western lands
    C raising money through taxes
    D paying war debts

17. Which of the following was a weakness of the Articles of Confederation?

    A The executive branch was too strong.
    B The judicial branch had too much power.
    C Congress imposed high taxes.
    D All states had to agree to amend the Articles.

WRITING FOR THE SAT ELA W2.4

Think about the following issue:

After the U.S. Constitution replaced the Articles of Confederation, the government of the United States was very different.

18. **Assignment** How was the Constitution an improvement upon the Articles of Confederation? Write a short essay in which you develop your position on this issue. Support your point of view with reasoning and examples from your reading and studies.

FORMING A NEW NATION 57

The Constitution of the UNITED STATES

THE BIG PICTURE The Constitution has remained the central document of American government for more than two centuries. It established three branches of government—legislative, executive, and judicial. The first 10 amendments, known as the Bill of Rights, focus on personal liberties.

California Standards

History-Social Sciences

11.1 Students analyze the significant events in the founding of the nation and its attempts to realize the philosophy of government described in the Declaration of Independence.

11.10 Students analyze the development of federal civil rights and voting rights.

Skills FOCUS READING LIKE A HISTORIAN

Tourists line up to view the Declaration of Independence and the Constitution of the United States in the rotunda of the National Archives Building in Washington, D.C. Above them hangs a mural depicting the Founders. **Interpreting Visuals** How does this photograph link the past with the present?

See **Skills Handbook**, p. H30

The Constitution of the United States

Preamble
The short and dignified preamble explains the goals of the new government under the Constitution.

We the People of the United States, in Order to form a more perfect Union, establish Justice, insure domestic Tranquility, provide for the common defense, promote the general Welfare, and secure the Blessings of Liberty to ourselves and our Posterity, do ordain and establish this Constitution for the United States of America.

Note: The parts of the Constitution that have been lined through are no longer in force or no longer apply because of later amendments. The titles of the sections and articles are added for easier reference.

Article I The Legislature

Section 1. Congress

All legislative Powers herein granted shall be vested in a Congress of the United States, which shall consist of a Senate and House of Representatives.

Section 2. The House of Representatives

1. Elections The House of Representatives shall be composed of Members chosen every second Year by the People of the several States, and the Electors in each State shall have the Qualifications requisite for Electors of the most numerous Branch of the State Legislature.

2. Qualifications No Person shall be a Representative who shall not have attained to the Age of twenty five Years, and been seven Years a Citizen of the United States, and who shall not, when elected, be an Inhabitant of that State in which he shall be chosen.

3. Number of Representatives Representatives and direct Taxes shall be apportioned among the several States which may be included within this Union, according to their respective Numbers, ~~which shall be determined by adding to the whole Number of free Persons, including~~ those bound to Service[1] ~~for a Term of Years, and excluding Indians not taxed, three fifths of~~ all other Persons.[2] The actual Enumeration[3] shall be made within three Years after the first Meeting of the Congress of the United States, and within every subsequent Term of ten Years, in such Manner as they shall by Law direct. The Number of Representatives shall not exceed one for every thirty Thousand, but each State shall have at Least one Representative; ~~and until such enumeration shall be made, the State of New Hampshire shall be entitled to choose three, Massachusetts eight, Rhode-Island and Providence Plantations one, Connecticut five, New-York six, New Jersey four, Pennsylvania eight, Delaware one, Maryland six, Virginia ten, North Carolina five, South Carolina five, and Georgia three.~~

4. Vacancies When vacancies happen in the Representation from any State, the Executive Authority thereof shall issue Writs of Election to fill such Vacancies.

5. Officers and Impeachment The House of Representatives shall choose their Speaker and other Officers; and shall have the sole Power of impeachment.

Legislative Branch

Article I explains how the legislative branch, called Congress, is organized. The chief purpose of the legislative branch is to make laws. Congress is made up of the Senate and the House of Representatives.

The House of Representatives

The number of members each state has in the House is based on the population of the individual state. In 1929 Congress permanently fixed the size of the House at 435 members.

Vocabulary

[1] **those bound to Service** indentured servants

[2] **all other Persons** slaves

[3] **Enumeration** census or official population count

Vocabulary

[10] **Bills** proposed laws

EXPLORING THE DOCUMENT The Framers felt that because members of the House are elected every two years, representatives would listen to the public and seek its approval before passing taxes. *How does Section 7 address the colonial demand of "no taxation without representation"?*

EXPLORING THE DOCUMENT The veto power of the president is one of the important checks and balances in the Constitution. *Why do you think the Framers included the ability of Congress to override a veto?*

Section 7. How a Bill Becomes a Law

1. Tax Bills All **Bills**[10] for raising Revenue shall originate in the House of Representatives; but the Senate may propose or concur with Amendments as on other Bills.

2. Lawmaking Every Bill which shall have passed the House of Representatives and the Senate, shall, before it become a Law, be presented to the President of the United States: If he approve he shall sign it, but if not he shall return it, with his Objections to that House in which it shall have originated, who shall enter the Objections at large on their Journal, and proceed to reconsider it. If after such Reconsideration two thirds of that House shall agree to pass the Bill, it shall be sent, together with the Objections, to the other House, by which it shall likewise be reconsidered, and if approved by two thirds of that House, it shall become a Law. But in all such Cases the Votes of both Houses shall be determined by yeas and Nays, and the Names of the Persons voting for and against the Bill shall be entered on the Journal of each House respectively. If any Bill shall not be returned by the President within ten Days (Sundays excepted) after it shall have been presented to him, the Same shall be a Law, in like Manner as if he had signed it, unless the Congress by their Adjournment prevent its Return, in which Case it shall not be a Law.

3. Role of the President Every Order, Resolution, or Vote to which the Concurrence of the Senate and House of Representatives may be necessary (except on a question of Adjournment) shall be presented to the President of the United States; and before the Same shall take Effect, shall be approved by him, or being disapproved by him, shall be repassed by two thirds of the Senate and House of Representatives, according to the Rules and Limitations prescribed in the Case of a Bill.

How a Bill Becomes a Law

1. A member of the House or the Senate introduces a bill and refers it to a committee.

2. The House or Senate Committee may approve, rewrite, or kill the bill.

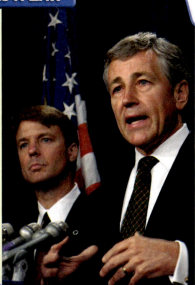

3. The House or the Senate debates and votes on its version of the bill.

4. House and Senate conference committee members work out the differences between the two versions.

5. Both houses of Congress pass the revised bill.

Section 8.
Powers Granted to Congress

1. Taxation The Congress shall have Power To lay and collect Taxes, **Duties**,[11] **Imposts**[12] and **Excises**,[13] to pay the Debts and provide for the common Defense and general Welfare of the United States; but all Duties, Imposts and Excises shall be uniform throughout the United States;

2. Credit To borrow Money on the credit of the United States;

3. Commerce To regulate Commerce with foreign Nations, and among the several States, and with the Indian Tribes;

4. Naturalization and Bankruptcy To establish an uniform **Rule of Naturalization**,[14] and uniform Laws on the subject of Bankruptcies throughout the United States;

5. Money To coin Money, regulate the Value thereof, and of foreign Coin, and fix the Standard of Weights and Measures;

6. Counterfeiting To provide for the Punishment of counterfeiting the **Securities**[15] and current Coin of the United States;

7. Post Office To establish Post Offices and post Roads;

8. Patents and Copyrights To promote the Progress of Science and useful Arts, by securing for limited Times to Authors and Inventors the exclusive Right to their respective Writings and Discoveries;

9. Courts To constitute Tribunals inferior to the supreme Court;

10. International Law To define and punish Piracies and Felonies committed on the high Seas, and Offences against the Law of Nations;

Linking to Today

Native Americans and the Commerce Clause

The commerce clause gives Congress the power to "regulate Commerce with . . . the Indian Tribes." The clause has been interpreted to mean that the states cannot tax or interfere with businesses on Indian reservations, but that the federal government can. It also allows Native American nations to develop their own governments and laws. These laws, however, can be challenged in federal court. Although reservation land usually belongs to the government of the Indian group, it is administered by the U.S. government.

Drawing Conclusions How would you describe the status of native American nations under the commerce clause?

Vocabulary

[11] **Duties** tariffs

[12] **Imposts** taxes

[13] **Excises** internal taxes on the manufacture, sale, or consumption of a commodity

[14] **Rule of Naturalization** a law by which a foreign-born person becomes a citizen

[15] **Securities** bonds

❻ The president signs or vetoes the bill.

❼ Two-thirds majority vote of Congress is needed to approve a vetoed bill. Bill becomes a law.

ANALYSIS SKILL **ANALYZING INFORMATION**
Why do you think the Framers created this complex system for adopting laws?

Vocabulary

[16] **Letters of Marque and Reprisal** documents issued by governments allowing merchant ships to arm themselves and attack ships of an enemy nation

11. War To declare War, grant **Letters of Marque and Reprisal**,[16] and make Rules concerning Captures on Land and Water;

12. Army To raise and support Armies, but no Appropriation of Money to that Use shall be for a longer Term than two Years;

13. Navy To provide and maintain a Navy;

14. Regulation of the Military To make Rules for the Government and Regulation of the land and naval Forces;

15. Militia To provide for calling forth the Militia to execute the Laws of the Union, suppress Insurrections and repel Invasions;

16. Regulation of the Militia To provide for organizing, arming, and disciplining, the Militia, and for governing such Part of them as may be employed in the Service of the United States, reserving to the States respectively, the Appointment of the Officers, and the Authority of training the Militia according to the discipline prescribed by Congress;

17. District of Columbia To exercise exclusive Legislation in all Cases whatsoever, over such District (not exceeding ten Miles square) as may, by Cession of particular States, and the Acceptance of Congress, become the Seat of the Government of the United States, and to exercise like Authority over all Places purchased by the Consent of the Legislature of the State in which the Same shall be, for the Erection of Forts, Magazines, Arsenals, dock-Yards, and other needful Buildings;—And

18. Necessary and Proper Clause To make all Laws which shall be necessary and proper for carrying into Execution the foregoing Powers, and all other Powers vested by this Constitution in the Government of the United States, or in any Department or Officer thereof.

The Elastic Clause

The Framers of the Constitution wanted a national government that was strong enough to be effective. This section lists the powers given to Congress. The last portion of Section 8 contains the so-called elastic clause.

THE ELASTIC CLAUSE

The elastic clause has been stretched (like elastic) to allow Congress to meet changing circumstances.

Section 9. Powers Denied Congress

1. Slave Trade The Migration or Importation of such Persons as any of the States now existing shall think proper to admit, shall not be prohibited by the Congress prior to the Year one thousand eight hundred and eight, but a Tax or duty may be imposed on such Importation, not exceeding ten dollars for each Person.

2. Habeas Corpus The Privilege of the **Writ of Habeas Corpus**[17] shall not be suspended, unless when in Cases of Rebellion or Invasion the public Safety may require it.

3. Illegal Punishment No **Bill of Attainder**[18] or **ex post facto Law**[19] shall be passed.

4. Direct Taxes No **Capitation**,[20] or other direct, Tax shall be laid, unless in Proportion to the Census or enumeration herein before directed to be taken.

5. Export Taxes No Tax or Duty shall be laid on Articles exported from any State.

6. No Favorites No Preference shall be given by any Regulation of Commerce or Revenue to the Ports of one State over those of another; nor shall Vessels bound to, or from, one State, be obliged to enter, clear, or pay Duties in another.

7. Public Money No Money shall be drawn from the Treasury, but in Consequence of Appropriations made by Law; and a regular Statement and Account of the Receipts and Expenditures of all public Money shall be published from time to time.

8. Titles of Nobility No Title of Nobility shall be granted by the United States: And no Person holding any Office of Profit or Trust under them, shall, without the Consent of the Congress, accept of any present, Emolument, Office, or Title, of any kind whatever, from any King, Prince, or foreign State.

Section 10. Powers Denied the States

1. Restrictions No State shall enter into any Treaty, Alliance, or Confederation; grant Letters of Marque and Reprisal; coin Money; emit Bills of Credit; make any Thing but gold and silver Coin a Tender in Payment of Debts; pass any Bill of Attainder, ex post facto Law, or Law impairing the Obligation of Contracts, or grant any Title of Nobility.

2. Import and Export Taxes No State shall, without the Consent of the Congress, lay any Imposts or Duties on Imports or Exports, except what may be absolutely necessary for executing it's inspection Laws: and the net Produce of all Duties and Imposts, laid by any State on Imports or Exports, shall be for the Use of the Treasury of the United States; and all such Laws shall be subject to the Revision and Control of the Congress.

3. Peacetime and War Restraints No State shall, without the Consent of Congress, lay any Duty of Tonnage, keep Troops, or Ships of War in time of Peace, enter into any Agreement or Compact with another State, or with a foreign Power, or engage in War, unless actually invaded, or in such imminent Danger as will not admit of delay.

EXPLORING THE DOCUMENT Although Congress has implied powers, there are also limits to its powers. Section 9 lists powers that are denied to the federal government. Several of the clauses protect the people of the United States from unjust treatment. *In what ways does the Constitution limit the powers of the federal government?*

Vocabulary

[17] **Writ of Habeas Corpus** a court order that requires the government to bring a prisoner to court and explain why he or she is being held

[18] **Bill of Attainder** a law declaring that a person is guilty of a particular crime

[19] **ex post facto Law** a law that is made effective prior to the date that it was passed and therefore punishes people for acts that were not illegal at the time

[20] **Capitation** a direct uniform tax imposed on each head, or person

Executive Branch

The president is the chief of the executive branch. It is the job of the president to enforce the laws. The Framers wanted the president's and vice president's terms of office and manner of selection to be different from those of members of Congress. They decided on four-year terms, but they had a difficult time agreeing on how to select the president and vice president. The Framers finally set up an electoral system, which differs greatly from our electoral process today.

Presidential Elections

In 1845 Congress set the Tuesday following the first Monday in November of every fourth year as the general election date for selecting presidential electors.

Article II The Executive

Section 1. The Presidency

1. Terms of Office The executive Power shall be vested in a President of the United States of America. He shall hold his Office during the Term of four Years, and, together with the Vice President, chosen for the same Term, be elected, as follows:

2. Electoral College Each State shall appoint, in such Manner as the Legislature thereof may direct, a Number of Electors, equal to the whole Number of Senators and Representatives to which the State may be entitled in the Congress: but no Senator or Representative, or Person holding an Office of Trust or Profit under the United States, shall be appointed an Elector.

3. Former Method of Electing President ~~The Electors shall meet in their respective States, and vote by Ballot for two Persons, of whom one at least shall not be an Inhabitant of the same State with themselves. And they shall make a List of all the Persons voted for, and of the Number of Votes for each; which List they shall sign and certify, and transmit sealed to the Seat of the Government of the United States, directed to the President of the Senate. The President of the Senate shall, in the Presence of the Senate and House of Representatives, open all the Certificates, and the Votes shall then be counted.~~

THE ELECTORAL COLLEGE

11 Number of Electors

WA 11, MT 3, ND 3, MN 10, NH 4, ME 4, VT 3, OR 7, ID 4, WI 10, MI 17, NY 31, MA 12, SD 3, IA 7, PA 21, RI 4, CT 7, WY 3, NE 5, IL 21, IN 11, OH 20, NJ 15, DE 3, NV 5, UT 5, CO 9, KS 6, MO 11, KY 8, WV 5, VA 13, MD 10, CA 55, TN 11, NC 15, Washington, D.C. 3, AZ 10, NM 5, OK 7, AR 6, SC 8, MS 6, AL 9, GA 15, TX 34, LA 9, FL 27, AK 3, HI 4

GEOGRAPHY SKILLS INTERPRETING MAPS

Place Which two states have the most electors?

~~The Person having the greatest Number of Votes shall be the President, if such Number be a Majority of the whole Number of Electors appointed; and if there be more than one who have such Majority, and have an equal Number of Votes, then the House of Representatives shall immediately choose by Ballot one of them for President; and if no Person have a Majority, then from the five highest on the List the said House shall in like Manner choose the President. But in choosing the President, the Votes shall be taken by States, the Representation from each State having one Vote; A quorum for this purpose shall consist of a Member or Members from two thirds of the States, and a Majority of all the States shall be necessary to a Choice. In every Case, after the Choice of the President, the Person having the greatest Number of Votes of the Electors shall be the Vice President. But if there should remain two or more who have equal Votes, the Senate shall choose from them by Ballot the Vice President.~~

4. Election Day The Congress may determine the Time of choosing the Electors, and the Day on which they shall give their Votes; which Day shall be the same throughout the United States.

5. Qualifications No Person except a natural born Citizen~~, or a Citizen of the United States, at the time of the Adoption of this Constitution~~, shall be eligible to the Office of President; neither shall any Person be eligible to that Office who shall not have attained to the Age of thirty five Years, and been fourteen Years a Resident within the United States.

6. Succession In Case of the Removal of the President from Office, or of his Death, Resignation, or Inability to discharge the Powers and Duties of the said Office, the Same shall devolve on the Vice President, and the Congress may by Law provide for the Case of Removal, Death, Resignation or Inability, both of the President and Vice President, declaring what Officer shall then act as President, and such Officer shall act accordingly, until the Disability be removed, or a President shall be elected.

7. Salary The President shall, at stated Times, receive for his Services, a Compensation, which shall neither be increased nor diminished during the Period for which he shall have been elected, and he shall not receive within that Period any other Emolument from the United States, or any of them.

8. Oath of Office Before he enter on the Execution of his Office, he shall take the following Oath or Affirmation:—"I do solemnly swear (or affirm) that I will faithfully execute the Office of President of the United States, and will to the best of my Ability, preserve, protect and defend the Constitution of the United States."

EXPLORING THE DOCUMENT The youngest elected president was John F. Kennedy; he was 43 years old when he was inaugurated. (Theodore Roosevelt was 42 when he assumed office after the assassination of McKinley.) *What is the minimum required age for the office of president?*

Presidential Salary

In 1999 Congress voted to set future presidents' salaries at $400,000 per year. The president also receives an annual expense account. The president must pay taxes only on the salary.

Commander in Chief

Today the president is in charge of the army, navy, air force, marines, and coast guard. Only Congress, however, can decide if the United States will declare war.

Appointments

Most of the president's appointments to office must be approved by the Senate.

Vocabulary

[21] **Reprieves** delays of punishment

[22] **Pardons** releases from the legal penalties associated with a crime

The State of the Union

Every year the president presents to Congress a State of the Union message. In this message, the president introduces and explains a legislative plan for the coming year.

Section 2. Powers of Presidency

1. Military Powers The President shall be Commander in Chief of the Army and Navy of the United States, and of the Militia of the several States, when called into the actual Service of the United States; he may require the Opinion, in writing, of the principal Officer in each of the executive Departments, upon any Subject relating to the Duties of their respective Offices, and he shall have Power to grant **Reprieves**[21] and **Pardons**[22] for Offences against the United States, except in Cases of Impeachment.

2. Treaties and Appointments He shall have Power, by and with the Advice and Consent of the Senate, to make Treaties, provided two thirds of the Senators present concur; and he shall nominate, and by and with the Advice and Consent of the Senate, shall appoint Ambassadors, other public Ministers and Consuls, Judges of the supreme Court, and all other Officers of the United States, whose Appointments are not herein otherwise provided for, and which shall be established by Law: but the Congress may by Law vest the Appointment of such inferior Officers, as they think proper, in the President alone, in the Courts of Law, or in the Heads of Departments.

3. Vacancies The President shall have Power to fill up all Vacancies that may happen during the Recess of the Senate, by granting Commissions which shall expire at the End of their next Session.

Section 3. Presidential Duties

He shall from time to time give to the Congress Information of the State of the Union, and recommend to their Consideration such Measures as he shall judge necessary and expedient; he may, on extraordinary Occasions, convene both Houses, or either of them, and in Case of Disagreement between them, with Respect to the Time of Adjournment, he may adjourn them to such Time as he shall think proper; he shall receive Ambassadors and other public Ministers; he shall take Care that the Laws be faithfully executed, and shall Commission all the Officers of the United States.

Section 4. Impeachment

The President, Vice President and all civil Officers of the United States, shall be removed from Office on Impeachment for, and Conviction of, Treason, Bribery, or other high Crimes and Misdemeanors.

Article III — The Judiciary

Section 1. Federal Courts and Judges

The judicial Power of the United States shall be vested in one supreme Court, and in such inferior Courts as the Congress may from time to time ordain and establish. The Judges, both of the supreme and inferior Courts, shall hold their Offices during good Behavior, and shall, at stated Times, receive for their Services a Compensation, which shall not be diminished during their Continuance in Office.

Section 2. Authority of the Courts

1. General Authority The judicial Power shall extend to all Cases, in Law and Equity, arising under this Constitution, the Laws of the United States, and Treaties made, or which shall be made, under their Authority;—to all Cases affecting Ambassadors, other public Ministers and Consuls;—to all Cases of admiralty and maritime Jurisdiction;—to Controversies to which the United States shall be a Party;—to Controversies between two or more States ~~—between a State and Citizens of another State;~~—between Citizens of different States;—between Citizens of the same State claiming Lands under Grants of different States~~, and between a State, or the Citizens thereof, and foreign States, Citizens or Subjects~~.

2. Supreme Authority In all Cases affecting Ambassadors, other public Ministers and Consuls, and those in which a State shall be Party, the supreme Court shall have original Jurisdiction. In all the other Cases before mentioned, the supreme Court shall have appellate Jurisdiction, both as to Law and Fact, with such Exceptions, and under such Regulations as the Congress shall make.

Federal Judicial System — Quick Facts

- **Supreme Court**: Reviews cases appealed from lower federal courts and highest state courts
- **Courts of Appeals**: Review appeals from district courts
- **District Courts**: Hold trials

> **Judicial Branch**
>
> The Articles of Confederation did not set up a federal court system. One of the first points that the Framers of the Constitution agreed upon was to set up a national judiciary. In the Judiciary Act of 1789, Congress provided for the establishment of lower courts, such as district courts, circuit courts of appeals, and various other federal courts. The judicial system provides a check on the legislative branch: It can declare a law unconstitutional.

3. Trial by Jury The Trial of all Crimes, except in Cases of Impeachment, shall be by Jury; and such Trial shall be held in the State where the said Crimes shall have been committed; but when not committed within any State, the Trial shall be at such Place or Places as the Congress may by Law have directed.

Section 3. Treason

1. Definition Treason against the United States, shall consist only in levying War against them, or in adhering to their Enemies, giving them Aid and Comfort. No Person shall be convicted of Treason unless on the Testimony of two Witnesses to the same overt Act, or on Confession in open Court.

2. Punishment The Congress shall have Power to declare the Punishment of Treason, but no Attainder of Treason shall work **Corruption of Blood**,[23] or Forfeiture except during the Life of the Person attainted.

Vocabulary

[23] **Corruption of Blood** punishing the family of a person convicted of treason

Article IV Relations among States

Section 1. State Acts and Records

Full Faith and Credit shall be given in each State to the public Acts, Records, and judicial Proceedings of every other State. And the Congress may by general Laws prescribe the Manner in which such Acts, Records and Proceedings shall be proved, and the Effect thereof.

Section 2. Rights of Citizens

1. Citizenship The Citizens of each State shall be entitled to all Privileges and Immunities of Citizens in the several States.

2. Extradition A Person charged in any State with Treason, Felony, or other Crime, who shall flee from Justice, and be found in another State, shall on Demand of the executive Authority of the State from which he fled, be delivered up, to be removed to the State having Jurisdiction of the Crime.

3. Fugitive Slaves No Person held to Service or Labour in one State, under the Laws thereof, escaping into another, shall, in Consequence of any Law or Regulation therein, be discharged from such Service or Labour, but shall be delivered up on Claim of the Party to whom such Service or Labour may be due.

EXPLORING THE DOCUMENT The Framers wanted to ensure that citizens could determine how state governments would operate. *How does the need to respect the laws of each state support the principle of popular sovereignty?*

FEDERALISM

National
- Declare war
- Maintain armed forces
- Regulate interstate and foreign trade
- Admit new states
- Establish post offices
- Set standard weights and measures
- Coin money
- Establish foreign policy
- Make all laws necessary and proper for carrying out delegated powers

Shared
- Maintain law and order
- Levy taxes
- Borrow money
- Charter banks
- Establish courts
- Provide for public welfare

State
- Establish and maintain schools
- Establish local governments
- Regulate business within the state
- Make marriage laws
- Provide for public safety
- Assume other powers not delegated to the national government or prohibited to the states

ANALYSIS SKILL **ANALYZING INFORMATION**
Why does the power to declare war belong only to the national government?

Section 3. New States

1. Admission New States may be admitted by the Congress into this Union; but no new State shall be formed or erected within the Jurisdiction of any other State; nor any State be formed by the Junction of two or more States, or Parts of States, without the Consent of the Legislatures of the States concerned as well as of the Congress.

2. Congressional Authority The Congress shall have Power to dispose of and make all needful Rules and Regulations respecting the Territory or other Property belonging to the United States; and nothing in this Constitution shall be so construed as to Prejudice any Claims of the United States, or of any particular State.

Section 4. Guarantees to the States

The United States shall guarantee to every State in this Union a Republican Form of Government, and shall protect each of them against Invasion; and on Application of the Legislature, or of the Executive (when the Legislature cannot be convened), against domestic Violence.

The States
States must honor the laws, records, and court decisions of other states. A person cannot escape a legal obligation by moving from one state to another.

EXPLORING THE DOCUMENT In a republic, voters elect representatives to act in their best interest. *How does Article IV protect the practice of republicanism in the United States?*

THE CONSTITUTION OF THE UNITED STATES 73

EXPLORING THE DOCUMENT America's founders may not have realized how long the Constitution would last, but they did set up a system for changing or adding to it. They did not want to make it easy to change the Constitution. **By what methods may the Constitution be amended? Under what sorts of circumstances do you think an amendment might be necessary?**

Article V — Amending the Constitution

The Congress, whenever two thirds of both Houses shall deem it necessary, shall propose Amendments to this Constitution, or, on the Application of the Legislatures of two thirds of the several States, shall call a Convention for proposing Amendments, which, in either Case, shall be valid to all Intents and Purposes, as Part of this Constitution, when ratified by the Legislatures of three fourths of the several States, or by Conventions in three fourths thereof, as the one or the other Mode of Ratification may be proposed by the Congress; Provided that no Amendment which may be made prior to the Year One thousand eight hundred and eight shall in any Manner affect the first and fourth Clauses in the Ninth Section of the first Article; and that no State, without its Consent, shall be deprived of its equal Suffrage in the Senate.

Article VI — Supremacy of National Government

National Supremacy

One of the biggest problems facing the delegates to the Constitutional Convention was the question of what would happen if a state law and a federal law conflicted. Which law would be followed? Who would decide? The second clause of Article VI answers those questions. When a federal law and a state law disagree, the federal law overrides the state law. The Constitution and other federal laws are the "supreme Law of the Land." This clause is often called the supremacy clause.

All Debts contracted and Engagements entered into, before the Adoption of this Constitution, shall be as valid against the United States under this Constitution, as under the Confederation.

This Constitution, and the Laws of the United States which shall be made in Pursuance thereof; and all Treaties made, or which shall be made, under the Authority of the United States, shall be the supreme Law of the Land; and the Judges in every State shall be bound thereby, any Thing in the Constitution or Laws of any State to the Contrary notwithstanding.

The Senators and Representatives before mentioned, and the Members of the several State Legislatures, and all executive and judicial Officers, both of the United States and of the several States, shall be bound by Oath or Affirmation, to support this Constitution; but no religious Test shall ever be required as a Qualification to any Office or public Trust under the United States.

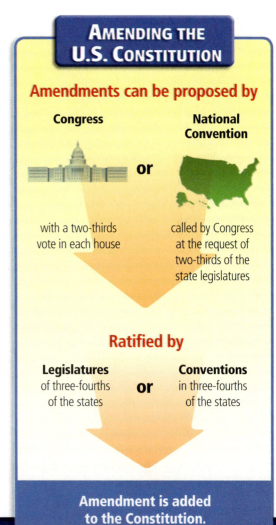

AMENDING THE U.S. CONSTITUTION

Amendments can be proposed by

Congress — with a two-thirds vote in each house

or

National Convention — called by Congress at the request of two-thirds of the state legislatures

Ratified by

Legislatures of three-fourths of the states

or

Conventions in three-fourths of the states

Amendment is added to the Constitution.

Article VII Ratification

The Ratification of the Conventions of nine States, shall be sufficient for the Establishment of this Constitution between the States so ratifying the Same.

Done in Convention by the Unanimous Consent of the States present the Seventeenth Day of September in the Year of our Lord one thousand seven hundred and Eighty seven and of the Independence of the United States of America the Twelfth In witness whereof We have hereunto subscribed our Names,

George Washington—
President and deputy from Virginia

> **Ratification**
>
> The Articles of Confederation called for all 13 states to approve any revision to the Articles. The Constitution required that 9 out of the 13 states would be needed to ratify the Constitution. The first state to ratify was Delaware, on December 7, 1787. Almost two-and-a-half years later, on May 29, 1790, Rhode Island became the last state to ratify the Constitution.

Delaware
George Read
Gunning Bedford Jr.
John Dickinson
Richard Bassett
Jacob Broom

Maryland
James McHenry
Daniel of St. Thomas Jenifer
Daniel Carroll

Virginia
John Blair
James Madison Jr.

North Carolina
William Blount
Richard Dobbs Spaight
Hugh Williamson

South Carolina
John Rutledge
Charles Cotesworth Pinckney
Charles Pinckney
Pierce Butler

Georgia
William Few
Abraham Baldwin

New Hampshire
John Langdon
Nicholas Gilman

Massachusetts
Nathaniel Gorham
Rufus King

Connecticut
William Samuel Johnson
Roger Sherman

New York
Alexander Hamilton

New Jersey
William Livingston
David Brearley
William Paterson
Jonathan Dayton

Pennsylvania
Benjamin Franklin
Thomas Mifflin
Robert Morris
George Clymer
Thomas FitzSimons
Jared Ingersoll
James Wilson
Gouverneur Morris

Attest:
William Jackson, Secretary

Constitutional Amendments

Note: The first 10 amendments to the Constitution were ratified on December 15, 1791, and form what is known as the Bill of Rights.

Amendments 1–10. The Bill of Rights

Amendment I
Congress shall make no law respecting an establishment of religion, or prohibiting the free exercise thereof; or abridging the freedom of speech, or of the press; or the right of the people peaceably to assemble, and to petition the Government for a redress of grievances.

Amendment II
A well regulated Militia, being necessary to the security of a free State, the right of the people to keep and bear Arms, shall not be infringed.

Amendment III
No Soldier shall, in time of peace be **quartered**[24] in any house, without the consent of the Owner, nor in time of war, but in a manner to be prescribed by law.

Amendment IV
The right of the people to be secure in their persons, houses, papers, and effects, against unreasonable searches and seizures, shall not be violated, and no **Warrants**[25] shall issue, but upon probable cause, supported by Oath or affirmation, and particularly describing the place to be searched, and the persons or things to be seized.

Amendment V
No person shall be held to answer for a capital, or otherwise **infamous**[26] crime, unless on a presentment or **indictment**[27] of a Grand Jury, except in cases

Bill of Rights
One of the conditions set by several states for ratifying the Constitution was the inclusion of a bill of rights. Many people feared that a stronger central government might take away basic rights of the people that had been guaranteed in state constitutions.

EXPLORING THE DOCUMENT The First Amendment forbids Congress from making any "law respecting an establishment of religion" or restraining the freedom to practice religion as one chooses. *Why is freedom of religion an important right?*

Rights of the Accused
The Fifth, Sixth, and Seventh Amendments describe the procedures that courts must follow when trying people accused of crimes.

Vocabulary
[24] **quartered** housed

[25] **Warrants** written orders authorizing a person to make an arrest, a seizure, or a search

[26] **infamous** disgraceful

[27] **indictment** the act of charging with a crime

FUNDAMENTAL LIBERTIES

Freedom of Religion

Freedom of Speech

arising in the land or naval forces, or in the Militia, when in actual service in time of War or public danger; nor shall any person be subject for the same offence to be twice put in jeopardy of life or limb; nor shall be compelled in any criminal case to be a witness against himself, nor be deprived of life, liberty, or property, without due process of law; nor shall private property be taken for public use, without just compensation.

Amendment VI

In all criminal prosecutions, the accused shall enjoy the right to a speedy and public trial, by an impartial jury of the State and district wherein the crime shall have been committed, which district shall have been previously ascertained[28] by law, and to be informed of the nature and cause of the accusation; to be confronted with the witnesses against him; to have compulsory process for obtaining witnesses in his favor, and to have the Assistance of Counsel for his defence.

Amendment VII

In suits at common law, where the value in controversy shall exceed twenty dollars, the right of trial by jury shall be preserved, and no fact tried by a jury, shall be otherwise reexamined in any Court of the United States, than according to the rules of the common law.

Amendment VIII

Excessive bail shall not be required, nor excessive fines imposed, nor cruel and unusual punishments inflicted.

Amendment IX

The enumeration in the Constitution, of certain rights, shall not be construed to deny or disparage others retained by the people.

Amendment X

The powers not delegated to the United States by the Constitution, nor prohibited by it to the States, are reserved to the States respectively, or to the people.

Trials
The Sixth Amendment makes several guarantees, including a prompt trial and a trial by a jury chosen from the state and district in which the crime was committed.

Vocabulary
[28] **ascertained** found out

EXPLORING THE DOCUMENT The Ninth and Tenth Amendments were added because not every right of the people or of the states could be listed in the Constitution. *How do the Ninth and Tenth Amendments limit the power of the federal government?*

Freedom of the Press

Freedom of Assembly

Freedom to Petition the Government

ANALYSIS SKILL — ANALYZING INFORMATION
Which amendments guarantee these fundamental freedoms?

Amendments to the U.S. Constitution

The Constitution has been amended only 27 times since it was ratified more than 200 years ago. Amendments help the structure of the government change along with the values of the nation's people. Read the time line below to learn how each amendment changed the government.

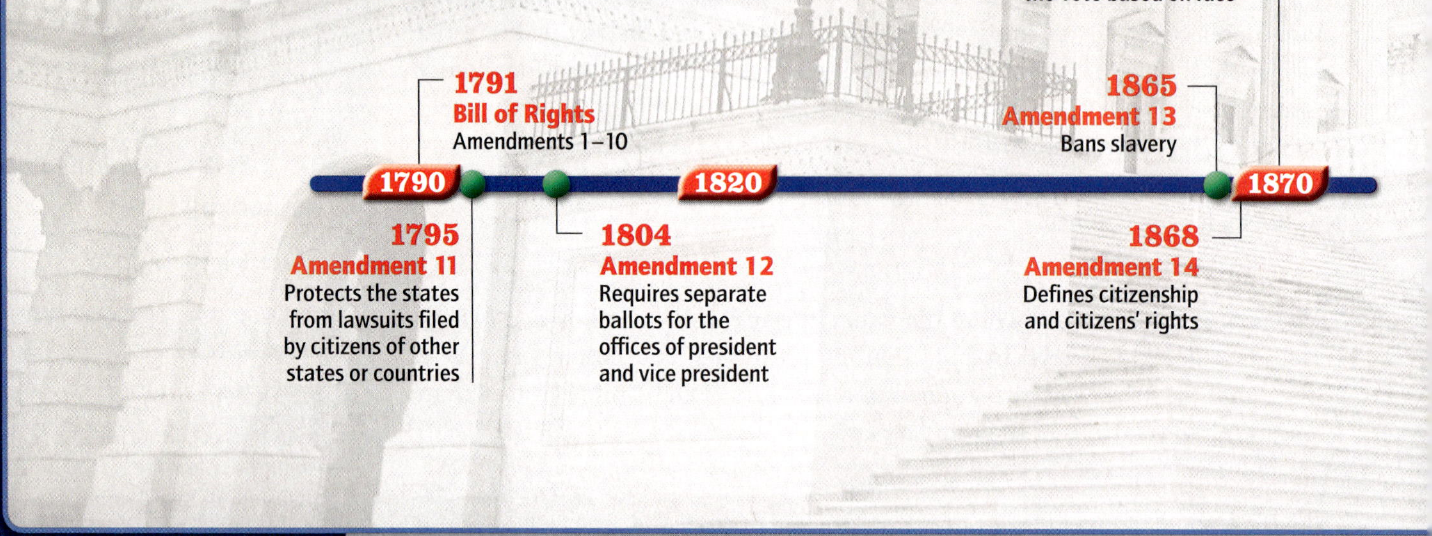

1790

1791 Bill of Rights Amendments 1–10

1795 Amendment 11 Protects the states from lawsuits filed by citizens of other states or countries

1804 Amendment 12 Requires separate ballots for the offices of president and vice president

1820

1865 Amendment 13 Bans slavery

1868 Amendment 14 Defines citizenship and citizens' rights

1870 Amendment 15 Prohibits national and state governments from denying the vote based on race

1870

Amendments 11–27

Amendment XI

Passed by Congress March 4, 1794. Ratified February 7, 1795.

The Judicial power of the United States shall not be **construed**[29] to extend to any suit in law or equity, commenced or prosecuted against one of the United States by Citizens of another State, or by Citizens or Subjects of any Foreign State.

Amendment XII

Passed by Congress December 9, 1803. Ratified June 15, 1804.

The Electors shall meet in their respective states and vote by ballot for President and Vice-President, one of whom, at least, shall not be an inhabitant of the same state with themselves; they shall name in their ballots the person voted for as President, and in distinct ballots the person voted for as Vice-President, and they shall make distinct lists of all persons voted for as President, and of all persons voted for as Vice-President, and of the number of votes for each, which lists they shall sign and certify, and transmit sealed to the seat of the government of the United States, directed to the President of the Senate;—the President of the Senate shall, in the presence of the

---

Vocabulary

[29] **construed** explained or interpreted

President and Vice President

The Twelfth Amendment changed the election procedure for president and vice president.

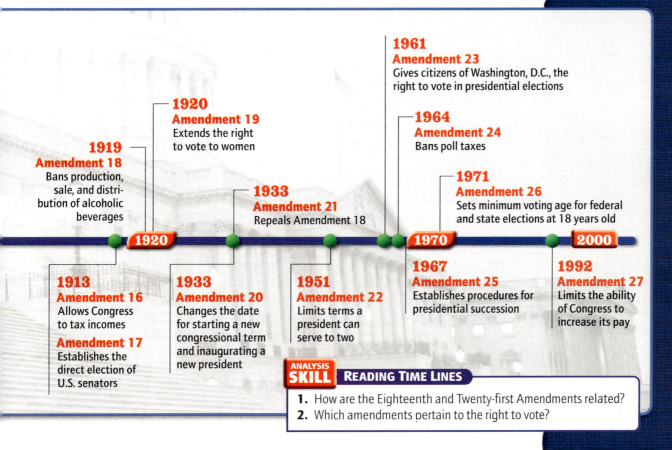

ANALYSIS SKILL — READING TIME LINES
1. How are the Eighteenth and Twenty-first Amendments related?
2. Which amendments pertain to the right to vote?

Senate and House of Representatives, open all the certificates and the votes shall then be counted;—The person having the greatest number of votes for President, shall be the President, if such number be a majority of the whole number of Electors appointed; and if no person have such majority, then from the persons having the highest numbers not exceeding three on the list of those voted for as President, the House of Representatives shall choose immediately, by ballot, the President. But in choosing the President, the votes shall be taken by states, the representation from each state having one vote; a quorum for this purpose shall consist of a member or members from two-thirds of the states, and a majority of all the states shall be necessary to a choice. ~~And if the House of Representatives shall not choose a President whenever the right of choice shall devolve upon them, before the fourth day of March next following, then the Vice-President shall act as President, as in case of the death or other constitutional disability of the President.~~—The person having the greatest number of votes as Vice-President, shall be the Vice-President, if such number be a majority of the whole number of Electors appointed, and if no person have a majority, then from the two highest numbers on the list, the Senate shall choose the Vice-President; a quorum for the purpose shall consist of two-thirds of the whole number of Senators, and a majority of the whole number shall be necessary to a choice. But no person constitutionally ineligible to the office of President shall be eligible to that of Vice-President of the United States.

Abolishing Slavery

Although some slaves had been freed during the Civil War, slavery was not abolished until the Thirteenth Amendment took effect.

Protecting the Rights of Citizens

In 1833 the Supreme Court ruled that the Bill of Rights limited the federal government but not the state governments. This ruling was interpreted to mean that states were able to keep African Americans from becoming state citizens and keep the Bill of Rights from protecting them. The Fourteenth Amendment defines citizenship and prevents states from interfering in the rights of citizens of the United States.

Vocabulary

[30] **involuntary servitude** being forced to work against one's will

Amendment XIII

Passed by Congress January 31, 1865. Ratified December 6, 1865.

1. Slavery Banned Neither slavery nor involuntary servitude,[30] except as a punishment for crime whereof the party shall have been duly convicted, shall exist within the United States, or any place subject to their jurisdiction.

2. Enforcement Congress shall have power to enforce this article by appropriate legislation.

Amendment XIV

Passed by Congress June 13, 1866. Ratified July 9, 1868.

1. Citizenship Defined All persons born or naturalized in the United States, and subject to the jurisdiction thereof, are citizens of the United States and of the State wherein they reside. No State shall make or enforce any law which shall abridge the privileges or immunities of citizens of the United States; nor shall any State deprive any person of life, liberty, or property, without due process of law; nor deny to any person within its jurisdiction the equal protection of the laws.

2. Voting Rights Representatives shall be apportioned among the several States according to their respective numbers, counting the whole number of persons in each State, ~~excluding Indians not taxed~~. But when the right to vote at any election for the choice of electors for President and Vice-President of the United States, Representatives in Congress, the Executive and Judicial officers of a State, or the members of the Legislature thereof, is denied to any of the ~~male~~ inhabitants of such State, ~~being twenty-one years of age~~, and citizens of the United States, or in any way abridged, except for participation in rebellion, or other crime, the basis of representation therein shall be reduced in the proportion which the number of such ~~male~~ citizens shall bear to the whole number of ~~male~~ citizens ~~twenty-one years of age~~ in such State.

3. Rebels Banned from Government No person shall be a Senator or Representative in Congress, or elector of President and Vice-President, or hold any office, civil or military, under the United States, or under any State, who, having previously taken an oath, as a member of Congress, or as an officer of the United States, or as a member of any State legislature, or as an executive or judicial officer of any State, to support the Constitution of the United States, shall have engaged in insurrection or rebellion against the same, or given aid or comfort to the enemies thereof. But Congress may by a vote of two-thirds of each House, remove such disability.

4. Payment of Debts The validity of the public debt of the United States, authorized by law, including debts incurred for payment of pensions and bounties for services in suppressing insurrection or rebellion, shall not be questioned. But neither the United States nor any State shall assume or pay

The Reconstruction Amendments

The Thirteenth, Fourteenth, and Fifteenth Amendments are often called the Reconstruction Amendments. This is because they arose during Reconstruction, the period of American history following the Civil War. A key aspect of rebuilding the Union was extending the rights of citizenship to former slaves.

The Thirteenth Amendment banned slavery. The Fourteenth Amendment required states to respect the freedoms listed in the Bill of Rights, thus preventing states from denying rights to African Americans. The Fifteenth Amendment gave African American men the right to vote.

African Americans vote in an election during Reconstruction.

ANALYSIS SKILL — ANALYZING INFORMATION
Why were the Reconstruction Amendments needed?

any debt or obligation incurred in aid of insurrection or rebellion against the United States, or any claim for the loss or emancipation of any slave; but all such debts, obligations and claims shall be held illegal and void.

5. Enforcement The Congress shall have the power to enforce, by appropriate legislation, the provisions of this article.

Amendment XV

Passed by Congress February 26, 1869. Ratified February 3, 1870.

1. Voting Rights The right of citizens of the United States to vote shall not be denied or abridged by the United States or by any State on account of race, color, or previous condition of servitude.

2. Enforcement The Congress shall have the power to enforce this article by appropriate legislation.

Amendment XVI

Passed by Congress July 2, 1909. Ratified February 3, 1913.

The Congress shall have power to lay and collect taxes on incomes, from whatever source derived, without apportionment among the several States, and without regard to any census or enumeration.

Amendment XVII

Passed by Congress May 13, 1912. Ratified April 8, 1913.

1. Senators Elected by Citizens The Senate of the United States shall be composed of two Senators from each State, elected by the people thereof, for six years; and each Senator shall have one vote. The electors in each State shall have the qualifications requisite for electors of the most numerous branch of the State legislatures.

2. Vacancies When vacancies happen in the representation of any State in the Senate, the executive authority of such State shall issue writs of election to fill such vacancies: *Provided*, That the legislature of any State may empower the executive thereof to make temporary appointments until the people fill the vacancies by election as the legislature may direct.

3. Future Elections This amendment shall not be so construed as to affect the election or term of any Senator chosen before it becomes valid as part of the Constitution.

> **EXPLORING THE DOCUMENT** The Seventeenth Amendment requires that senators be elected directly by the people instead of by the state legislatures. *What principle of our government does the Seventeenth Amendment protect?*

Amendment XVIII

Passed by Congress December 18, 1917. Ratified January 16, 1919. Repealed by Amendment XXI.

1. Liquor Banned After one year from the ratification of this article the manufacture, sale, or transportation of intoxicating liquors within, the importation thereof into, or the exportation thereof from the United States and all territory subject to the jurisdiction thereof for beverage purposes is hereby prohibited.

2. Enforcement The Congress and the several States shall have concurrent power to enforce this article by appropriate legislation.

3. Ratification This article shall be inoperative unless it shall have been ratified as an amendment to the Constitution by the legislatures of the several States, as provided in the Constitution, within seven years from the date of the submission hereof to the States by the Congress.

> **Prohibition** Although many people believed that the Eighteenth Amendment was good for the health and welfare of the American people, it was repealed 14 years later.

WOMEN FIGHT FOR THE VOTE

To become part of the Constitution, a proposed amendment must be ratified by three-fourths of the states. Here, suffragists witness Kentucky governor Edwin P. Morrow signing the Nineteenth Amendment in January 1920. By June of that year, enough states had ratified the amendment to make it part of the Constitution. American women, after generations of struggle, had finally won the right to vote.

ANALYSIS SKILL — **ANALYZING INFORMATION**

What right did the Nineteenth Amendment grant?

Amendment XIX

Passed by Congress June 4, 1919. Ratified August 18, 1920.

1. Voting Rights The right of citizens of the United States to vote shall not be denied or abridged by the United States or by any State on account of sex.

2. Enforcement Congress shall have power to enforce this article by appropriate legislation.

Amendment XX

Passed by Congress March 2, 1932. Ratified January 23, 1933.

1. Presidential Terms The terms of the President and the Vice President shall end at noon on the 20th day of January, and the terms of Senators and Representatives at noon on the 3d day of January, of the years in which such terms would have ended if this article had not been ratified; and the terms of their successors shall then begin.

Women's Suffrage

Abigail Adams and others were disappointed that the Declaration of Independence and the Constitution did not specifically include women. It took many years and much campaigning before national suffrage for women finally was achieved.

Taking Office

In the original Constitution, a newly elected president and Congress did not take office until March 4, which was four months after the November election. The officials who were leaving office were called lame ducks because they had little influence during those four months. The Twentieth Amendment changed the date that the new president and Congress take office. Members of Congress now take office during the first week of January, and the president takes office on January 20.

2. Meeting of Congress The Congress shall assemble at least once in every year, and such meeting shall begin at noon on the 3d day of January, unless they shall by law appoint a different day.

3. Succession of Vice President If, at the time fixed for the beginning of the term of the President, the President elect shall have died, the Vice President elect shall become President. If a President shall not have been chosen before the time fixed for the beginning of his term, or if the President elect shall have failed to qualify, then the Vice President elect shall act as President until a President shall have qualified; and the Congress may by law provide for the case wherein neither a President elect nor a Vice President shall have qualified, declaring who shall then act as President, or the manner in which one who is to act shall be selected, and such person shall act accordingly until a President or Vice President shall have qualified.

4. Succession by Vote of Congress The Congress may by law provide for the case of the death of any of the persons from whom the House of Representatives may choose a President whenever the right of choice shall have devolved upon them, and for the case of the death of any of the persons from whom the Senate may choose a Vice President whenever the right of choice shall have devolved upon them.

5. Ratification Sections 1 and 2 shall take effect on the 15th day of October following the ratification of this article.

6. Ratification This article shall be inoperative unless it shall have been ratified as an amendment to the Constitution by the legislatures of three-fourths of the several States within seven years from the date of its submission.

Amendment XXI

Passed by Congress February 20, 1933. Ratified December 5, 1933.

1. 18th Amendment Repealed The eighteenth article of amendment to the Constitution of the United States is hereby repealed.

2. Liquor Allowed by Law The transportation or importation into any State, Territory, or Possession of the United States for delivery or use therein of intoxicating liquors, in violation of the laws thereof, is hereby prohibited.

3. Ratification This article shall be inoperative unless it shall have been ratified as an amendment to the Constitution by conventions in the several States, as provided in the Constitution, within seven years from the date of the submission hereof to the States by the Congress.

Amendment XXII

Passed by Congress March 21, 1947. Ratified February 27, 1951.

1. Term Limits No person shall be elected to the office of the President more than twice, and no person who has held the office of President, or acted as President, for more than two years of a term to which some other person was elected President shall be elected to the office of President more than once. But this Article shall not apply to any person holding the office of President when this Article was proposed by Congress, and shall not prevent any person who may be holding the office of President, or acting as President, during the term within which this Article becomes operative from holding the office of President or acting as President during the remainder of such term.

2. Ratification This article shall be inoperative unless it shall have been ratified as an amendment to the Constitution by the legislatures of three-fourths of the several States within seven years from the date of its submission to the States by the Congress.

EXPLORING THE DOCUMENT From the time of President George Washington's administration, it was a custom for presidents to serve no more than two terms in office. Franklin D. Roosevelt, however, was elected to four terms. The Twenty-second Amendment restricted presidents to no more than two terms in office. *Why do you think citizens chose to limit the power of the president in this way?*

After Franklin D. Roosevelt was elected to four consecutive terms, limits were placed on the number of terms a president could serve.

Amendment XXIII

Passed by Congress June 16, 1960. Ratified March 29, 1961.

1. District of Columbia Represented The District constituting the seat of Government of the United States shall appoint in such manner as Congress may direct:

A number of electors of President and Vice President equal to the whole number of Senators and Representatives in Congress to which the District would be entitled if it were a State, but in no event more than the least populous State; they shall be in addition to those appointed by the States, but they shall be considered, for the purposes of the election of President and Vice President, to be electors appointed by a State; and they shall meet in the District and perform such duties as provided by the twelfth article of amendment.

2. Enforcement The Congress shall have power to enforce this article by appropriate legislation.

Voting Rights

Until the ratification of the Twenty-third Amendment, the people of Washington, D.C., could not vote in presidential elections.

POLL TAX AMENDMENT

Poll taxes were used to deny impoverished Americans, including many African Americans and Hispanic Americans, the right to vote. Poll taxes were outlawed by the Twenty-fourth Amendment.

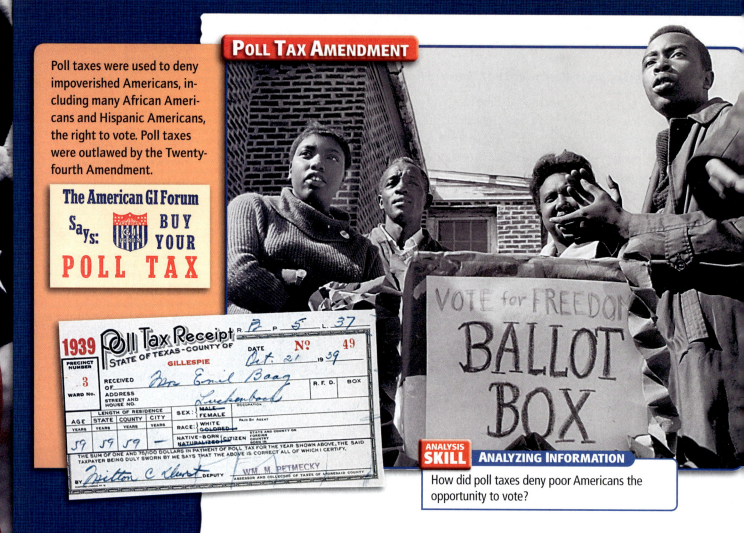

ANALYSIS SKILL — ANALYZING INFORMATION
How did poll taxes deny poor Americans the opportunity to vote?

Presidential Disability

The illness of President Eisenhower in the 1950s and the assassination of President Kennedy in 1963 were the events behind the Twenty-fifth Amendment. The Constitution did not provide a clear-cut method for a vice president to take over for a disabled president or upon the death of a president. This amendment provides for filling the office of the vice president if a vacancy occurs, and it provides a way for the vice president—or someone else in the line of succession—to take over if the president is unable to perform the duties of that office.

Amendment XXIV

Passed by Congress August 27, 1962. Ratified January 23, 1964.

1. Voting Rights The right of citizens of the United States to vote in any primary or other election for President or Vice President, for electors for President or Vice President, or for Senator or Representative in Congress, shall not be denied or abridged by the United States or any State by reason of failure to pay poll tax or other tax.

2. Enforcement The Congress shall have power to enforce this article by appropriate legislation.

Amendment XXV

Passed by Congress July 6, 1965. Ratified February 10, 1967.

1. Succession of Vice President In case of the removal of the President from office or of his death or resignation, the Vice President shall become President.

2. Vacancy of Vice President Whenever there is a vacancy in the office of the Vice President, the President shall nominate a Vice President who shall take office upon confirmation by a majority vote of both Houses of Congress.

3. Written Declaration Whenever the President transmits to the President pro tempore of the Senate and the Speaker of the House of Representatives his written declaration that he is unable to discharge the powers and duties of his office, and until he transmits to them a written declaration to the contrary, such powers and duties shall be discharged by the Vice President as Acting President.

4. Removing the President Whenever the Vice President and a majority of either the principal officers of the executive departments or of such other body as Congress may by law provide, transmit to the President pro tempore of the Senate and the Speaker of the House of Representatives their written declaration that the President is unable to discharge the powers and duties of his office, the Vice President shall immediately assume the powers and duties of the office as Acting President.

Thereafter, when the President transmits to the President pro tempore of the Senate and the Speaker of the House of Representatives his written declaration that no inability exists, he shall resume the powers and duties of his office unless the Vice President and a majority of either the principal officers of the executive department or of such other body as Congress may by law provide, transmit within four days to the President pro tempore of the Senate and the Speaker of the House of Representatives their written declaration that the President is unable to discharge the powers and duties of his office. Thereupon Congress shall decide the issue, assembling within forty-eight hours for that purpose if not in session. If the Congress, within twenty-one days after receipt of the latter written declaration, or, if Congress is not in session, within twenty-one days after Congress is required to assemble, determines by two-thirds vote of both Houses that the President is unable to discharge the powers and duties of his office, the Vice President shall continue to discharge the same as Acting President; otherwise, the President shall resume the powers and duties of his office.

Amendment XXVI

Passed by Congress March 23, 1971. Ratified July 1, 1971.

1. Voting Rights The right of citizens of the United States, who are eighteen years of age or older, to vote shall not be denied or abridged by the United States or by any State on account of age.

2. Enforcement The Congress shall have power to enforce this article by appropriate legislation.

Amendment XXVII

Originally proposed September 25, 1789. Ratified May 7, 1992.

No law, varying the compensation for the services of the Senators and Representatives, shall take effect, until an election of representatives shall have intervened.

Expanded Suffrage

The Voting Rights Act of 1970 tried to lower the voting age from 21 to 18. However, the Supreme Court ruled that the act applied to national elections only, not to state or local elections. The Twenty-sixth Amendment set the minimum voting age for all elections at 18.

Constitution Review

Visual Summary: The Constitution of the United States

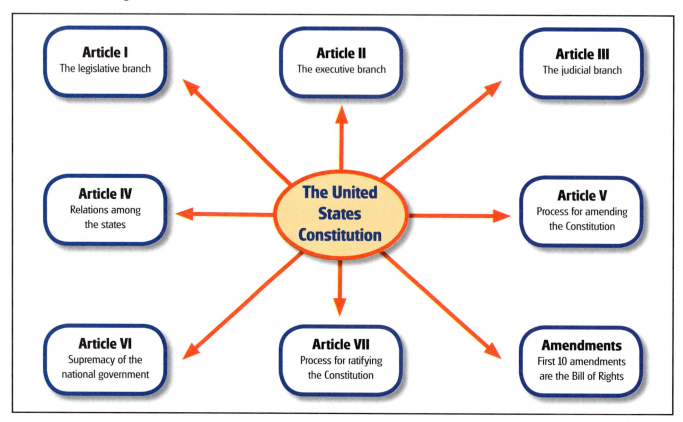

Reviewing Key Terms and People

For each term or name below, write a sentence explaining its significance to the U.S. Constitution.

1. pro tempore
2. quorum
3. bills
4. elastic clause
5. writ of habeas corpus
6. ex post facto law
7. executive branch
8. State of the Union
9. federalism
10. national supremacy
11. Bill of Rights

Comprehension and Critical Thinking

ARTICLE I *(pp. 61–67)*

12. **a. Recall** What is the focus of Article I?

    b. Make Inferences Why do you think Congress fixed the size of the House of Representatives at 435 members in 1929?

    c. Elaborate Describe how a bill becomes a law, explaining how the process is an example of checks and balances in the Constitution.

ARTICLE II *(pp. 68–70)*

13. **a. Identify** Which branch of government is the focus of Article II of the U.S. Constitution?

    b. Compare What are the main powers of the president, and how do they compare to the main powers of the legislature?

    c. Evaluate Do you think the electoral college is the best way to elect the president? Explain.

ARTICLE III (pp. 71–72)

14. a. Describe Which branch of government is the focus of Article III of the U.S. Constitution?

b. Analyze How are cases appealed to the Supreme Court in the federal judicial system?

c. Elaborate How does the judicial system provide a check on the legislature?

ARTICLE IV (pp. 72–73)

15. a. Describe What is the focus of Article IV of the U.S. Constitution?

b. Analyze Why must states honor the laws of other states?

c. Evaluate How well does the system of federalism balance the powers of states and the national government?

ARTICLE V (p. 74)

16. a. Identify What does Article V of the U.S. Constitution discuss?

b. Explain What is the process for amending the U.S. Constitution?

ARTICLE VI (p. 74)

17. a. Describe What happens if a state law and a federal law conflict with each other?

b. Analyze Why do you think the idea of national supremacy was included in the Constitution?

ARTICLE VII (p. 75)

18. a. Recall How many states are needed to ratify the Constitution?

b. Compare Why was the number of states needed to ratify the Constitution different from the number of states needed to revise the Articles of Confederation?

Using the Internet

19. Each of the 50 states sends representatives to the Senate and the House of Representatives. Using the keyword above, locate congressmembers representing your state or your congressional district. Then conduct research to find out if they have sponsored a bill, how they voted on recent legislation, issues that interest them, or their viewpoints on pending legislation. Create a chart to display your research.

go.hrw.com
Practice Online
Keyword: SE7 CH2

Analyzing Primary Sources

Reading Like a Historian This poll tax receipt was issued in 1939 to a voter in Texas. Poll taxes were later outlawed by the Twenty-fourth Amendment.

20. Recall What was a poll tax?

Explain Why were poll taxes outlawed by the Twenty-fourth Amendment?

Critical Reading

Review the timeline in this section titled "Amendments to the U.S. Constitution." Consider the 27 amendments on the time line and then answer the questions that follow.

21. The purpose of Amendment 15 was

A to prohibit national and state governments from denying the vote based on race.

B to extend voting rights to women.

C to repeal Amendment 14.

D to ban production, sale, and distribution of alcoholic beverages.

22. What do the amendments have in common?

A Each amendment gave a different group of people the right to vote.

B Each amendment helped the structure of government change along with the values of the nation's people.

C Each amendment helped the Constitution remain unchanged for 200 years.

D Each amendment was eventually repealed.

FOCUS ON WRITING

Expository Writing *Expository writing gives information, explains why or how, or defines a process. To practice expository writing, complete the assignment below.*

Writing Topic The preamble to the Constitution

23. What does the preamble state? What does it tell you about the Framers' intentions? Write a brief paragraph that answers these questions. Include quotations from the text of the preamble.

CHAPTER 3

1815–1860

Developing a National Identity

THE BIG PICTURE At the end of the War of 1812, Americans had a growing sense of nationalism. A religious revival helped spur reform movements that sought to improve the lives of the poor in an increasingly urban and industrialized nation. Americans also continued to settle in the West, and by 1848 the nation's borders extended to the Rio Grande and the Pacific Ocean.

California Standards

History-Social Sciences

8.8 Students analyze the divergent paths of the American people in the West from 1800 to the mid-1800s and the challenges they faced.

11.1 Students analyze the significant events in the founding of the nation and its attempts to realize the philosophy of government described in the Declaration of Independence.

11.3 Students analyze the role religion played in the founding of America, its lasting moral, social, and political impacts, and issues regarding religious liberty.

READING LIKE A HISTORIAN

An early steam engine pulls a train in New Jersey. The Camden and Amboy Railroad, chartered in 1830, was one of the first railroads in the country. It ran from the Delaware River to the Raritan River.
Interpreting Visuals What kind of service did the railroad provide?
See **Skills Handbook**, p. H30

U.S.

1819 The United States acquires Florida from Spain.

1820

World

1821 Mexico wins independence from Spain.

History's Impact video program
Watch the videos to learn more about American history from 1815 to 1860.

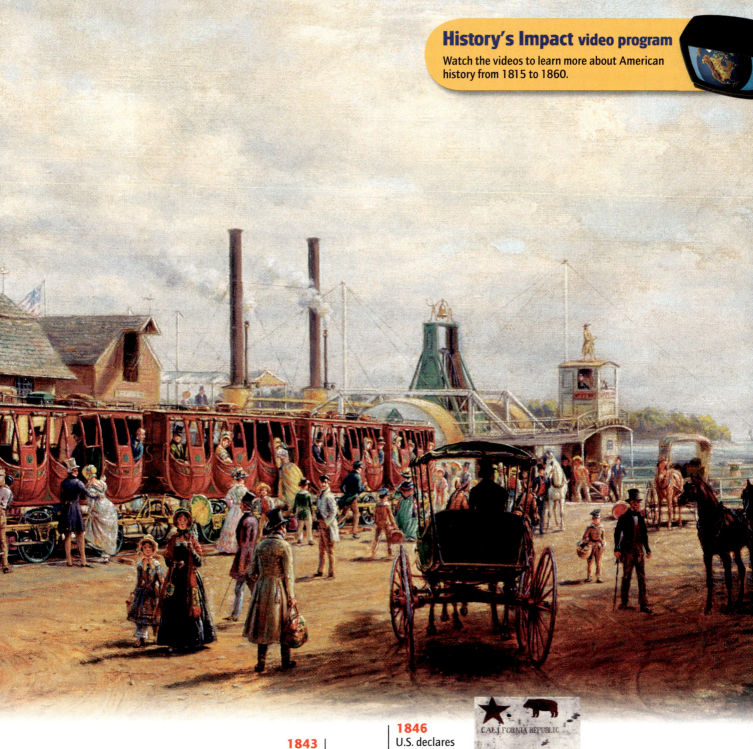

1830 Andrew Jackson signs the Indian Removal Act.

1833 Slavery is abolished throughout the British Empire.

1836 Texas gains independence from Mexico.

1843 Marcus Whitman leads at least 900 people over the Oregon Trail.

1845 Ireland's potato crop is devastated by blight.

1846 U.S. declares war on Mexico; the same year, American settlers declare a Republic of California.

1853 The Gasden Purchase further expands U.S. southwestern lands.

1857 A new constitution returns Mexico to a federal system of government.

1859 Charles Darwin's *On the Origin of Species* is published.

SECTION 1
From Nationalism to Sectionalism

BEFORE YOU READ

MAIN IDEA

In the early 1800s, feelings of nationalism grew, although conflicts between different regions of the United States were also emerging.

READING FOCUS

1. What events reflected the rise of nationalism in the United States?
2. What was the Age of Jackson?
3. How did the Industrial Revolution affect the North?
4. What was the importance of cotton in the South?

KEY TERMS AND PEOPLE

James Monroe
Monroe Doctrine
nationalism
McCulloch v. Maryland
Missouri Compromise
sectionalism
Indian Removal Act
Trail of Tears
Second Bank of the United States
Industrial Revolution

 HSS 11.1.3 Understand the history of the Constitution after 1787 with emphasis on federal versus state authority and growing democratization.

A BOLD MOVE

THE INSIDE STORY

How did the United States defy the monarchs of Europe? Between 1803 and 1815, a series of wars fought by or against France under the French emperor Napoleon had seriously threatened the monarchs of Europe. Soon after Napoleon's final defeat in 1815, the major European powers, including Great Britain and Russia, formed a loose alliance known as the Concert of Europe. Their goals were to keep a balance of power in Europe and to suppress revolutionary ideas.

At the same time, revolutions were breaking out in South America as colonies declared their independence from Spain. Although the United States declared neutrality, it supplied the rebels with ships and supplies. In 1822 President **James Monroe** was the first leader to give diplomatic recognition to the new nations. But both Great Britain and the United States were worried that France would send troops to reconquer Spain's colonies.

John Quincy Adams, Monroe's secretary of state, was an experienced diplomat. He was worried about territorial threats from European nations. Adams wanted to stand up to the monarchs of Europe. He declared "that the American continents are no longer subjects for any new European colonial establishments." Those strong words led to the statements made in the **Monroe Doctrine**, which declared the Americas off-limits to European colonization.

Lady Liberty and the liberty cap and pole she carries were powerful revolutionary symbols that citizens of the young nation could rally behind. ▲

The Rise of Nationalism

The Monroe Doctrine was a bold statement for such a young country to make. It showed a growing spirit of **nationalism**, which is the belief that the interests of the nation as a whole are more important than regional interests or the interests of other countries.

92 CHAPTER 3

Nationalism and domestic policy In 1816 voters elected James Monroe to the presidency. Monroe served as president from 1817 to 1825. During his presidency, the economy grew rapidly, and a spirit of nationalism and optimism prevailed. One Boston newspaper called the time the "era of good feelings." This new sense of nationalism was soon reflected in two landmark Supreme Court decisions:

- *McCulloch v. Maryland* (1819) In the landmark Supreme Court case **McCulloch v. Maryland**, Chief Justice John Marshall sided with the national government on the issue of a national bank. The Court's decision made it clear that national interests were to be put above state interests.
- *Gibbons v. Ogden* (1824) This Supreme Court case gave the national government the sole right to regulate interstate commerce, or trade between states.

Nationalism and foreign policy American foreign policy in the early 1800s also reflected the growth of nationalism. Americans were proud of their accomplishment in the War of 1812 and confident in the strength of their young but growing country. They were determined to take their place on the world stage. Monroe's presidency was characterized by good diplomacy abroad, including:

- **The Adams-Onís Treaty** (1819) Under this treaty, the United States acquired Florida and established a firm boundary between the Louisiana Purchase and Spanish territory. The treaty also allowed American settlers to travel to Oregon for 10 years.
- **The Monroe Doctrine** (1823) As you read in the "Inside Story," the Monroe Doctrine stated that the United States was off-limits to European colonization. According to the doctrine, the United States would view further colonization "as dangerous to our peace and safety." In essence, the Monroe Doctrine stated that the United States would stay out of European affairs and that it expected Europe to stay out of American affairs.

The Missouri Compromise American nationalism was fueled by pride in the rapid spread of settlement. But rapid settlement also caused some controversy.

When the Missouri Territory petitioned to join the union as a state, it caused an uproar.

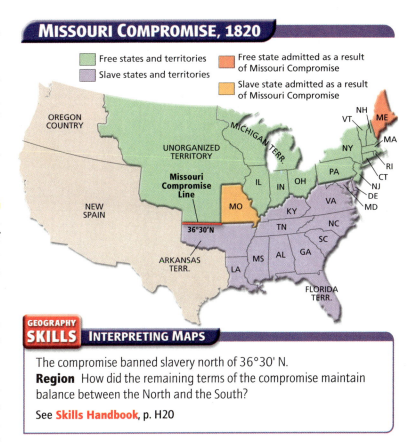

MISSOURI COMPROMISE, 1820

GEOGRAPHY SKILLS INTERPRETING MAPS

The compromise banned slavery north of 36°30' N.
Region How did the remaining terms of the compromise maintain balance between the North and the South?
See **Skills Handbook**, p. H20

In 1819 there were 22 states in the Union. In half of the states (the slave states of the South), slavery was legal. In the other half of the states (the free states of the North), slavery was illegal. This exact balance between slave states and free states gave them equal representation in the Senate. If Missouri were admitted as a slave state, the balance would be upset. Northerners were outraged.

In 1820 the situation was resolved by the **Missouri Compromise.** Under this agreement, Missouri was admitted to the Union as a slave state and Maine was admitted as a free state. Thus, the balance between the number of free states and slave states was preserved. The agreement also banned slavery in the northern part of the Louisiana Territory.

The Missouri Compromise kept the balance between slave and free states. It was clear, however, that feelings of sectionalism in the North and the South were emerging again. In contrast to nationalism, **sectionalism** is the belief that one's own section, or region, of the country is more important than the whole.

READING CHECK **Identifying Cause and Effect** Why was the Missouri Compromise adopted?

DEVELOPING A NATIONAL IDENTITY

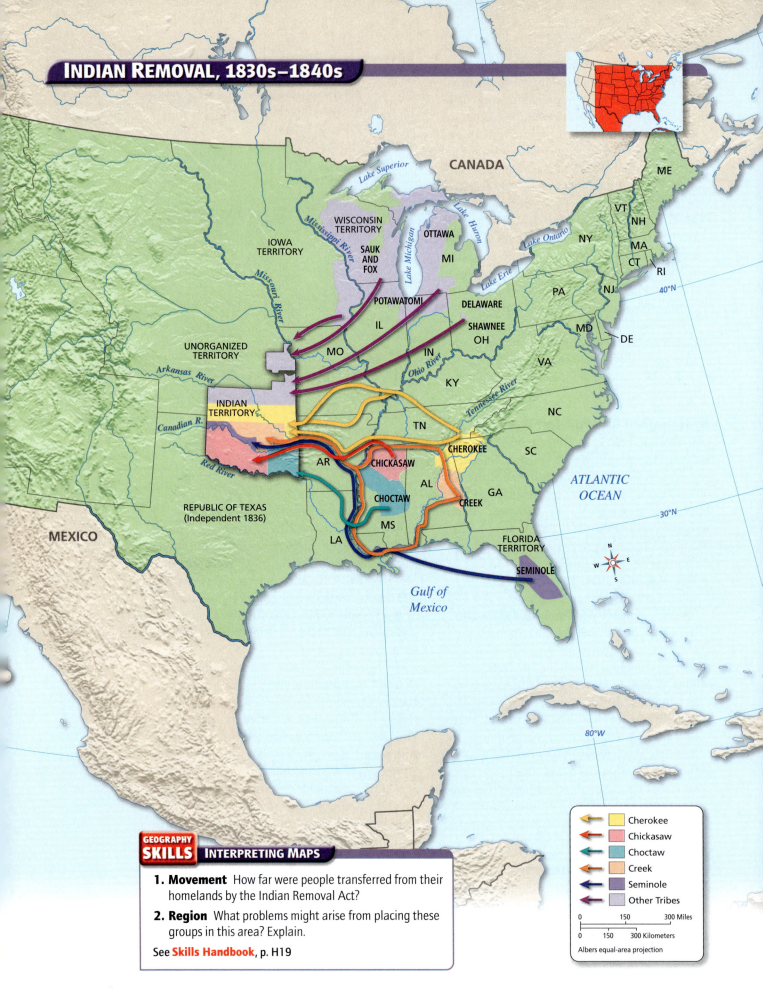

The Age of Jackson

In 1824 Andrew Jackson, a popular hero of the War of 1812, ran for president. It was a close election, ultimately decided in the House of Representatives. Jackson lost to John Quincy Adams but vowed to defeat him in the next election. Jackson and his supporters created a new political party that eventually came to be known as the Democratic Party. Adams and his supporters became known as the National Republicans.

Adams was not a popular president. His administration was weakened by scandal and by relentless criticism from Jackson's supporters. Many Americans also believed Adams was out of touch with the people. After one term in office, he lost the presidency to Jackson in the election of 1828.

Jackson's presidency is often called the Age of Jackson. It was characterized by conflict with Native Americans, conflict over the national bank, and increasing sectionalism.

The Indian Removal Act Five major Native American groups lived in the southeast when Jackson became president: the Cherokee, Choctaw, Chickasaw, Seminole, and Creek. White settlers wanted to acquire their land. President Jackson concluded that the best action was to relocate the Indian nations. In 1830 Congress passed, and Jackson signed into law, the Indian Removal Act, which called for the relocation of the five nations to an area west of the Mississippi River called Indian Territory.

Under the supervision of the U.S. Army, many Native American groups were forced to march west, hundreds of miles, to Indian Territory. Conditions on the marches were miserable. Exposure, malnutrition, and disease took their toll. So many Cherokee people suffered and died that their journey became known as the Trail of Tears, a term that symbolizes the suffering of all of the nations.

About 3,000 Seminole were forced to move west, but many more fought on. They were never completely defeated, and some of their descendants still live in Florida today.

The national bank One hotly contested issue during Jackson's presidency was the Second Bank of the United States, a national bank overseen by the federal government. Congress had established the bank in 1816, giving it a 20-year charter. The purpose of the bank was to regulate state banks, which had grown rapidly since the First Bank of the United States went out of existence in 1811.

Jackson and other Americans opposed the Second Bank of the United States. They thought that the Constitution did not give Congress the authority to create a national bank. They also knew that state banks made it easier for poor farmers in the South and West—people who supported Jackson—to get loans.

Jackson later sealed the fate of the bank, ordering his secretary of the treasury to take the money out of the national bank and deposit it in select state banks. Critics called them pet banks because they were loyal to Jackson.

Conflict over states' rights The controversy over the national bank was largely a dispute over how power should be divided between the federal government and state governments. Those who favored giving more power to the states invoked the concept of states' rights, based on the Tenth Amendment's provision that powers "not delegated to the United States by the Constitution, nor prohibited by it to the States" are reserved to the states.

In the early 1800s northern states and southern states clashed over tariffs on foreign goods. Northerners liked tariffs because they made northern goods more competitive. But southerners resented having to pay more for manufactured goods. In 1832 Congress passed another tariff, leading to what is known as the nullification crisis. Nullification theory held that states have the right to reject federal laws. In 1832 South Carolina declared the new tariff law "null and void" and then threatened to secede, or separate, from the Union if the federal government tried to enforce the tariff.

In response, President Jackson at first tried to use military force to collect the tariff. Eventually, Henry Clay worked out a compromise in which tariffs would be reduced for 10 years. But the issues of nullification and of states' rights would be raised again and again in the years to come.

> **READING CHECK** Identifying the Main Idea
> How did events in Jackson's presidency reflect conflict between federal and state authority?

THE IMPACT TODAY

Government
The Democratic Party is the oldest continuous political party in the United States. It traces its roots to 1792, when Thomas Jefferson and his followers called themselves Democratic-Republicans. Andrew Jackson's followers held the first Democratic national convention in 1832.

ACADEMIC VOCABULARY
acquire to get

TIME LINE

Industrial Revolution

1793 Eli Whitney patents the cotton gin, a machine for cleaning cotton, revolutionizing cotton production.

1793 Samuel Slater builds the nation's first successful textile mill, harnessing river water to power the machinery.

1797 Eli Whitney begins manufacturing muskets with interchangeable parts, devising the basis for mass production.

The Industrial North

The **Industrial Revolution** is the name for the birth of modern industry and the social changes that accompanied the resulting industrial growth. It occurred from the mid-1700s to the mid-1800s.

The Industrial Revolution first began in the British textile industry when British inventors created machines that used power from running water and steam engines to spin and weave cloth. This radically transformed the textile industry. Work that had once been done by hand or on simple machines became a machine-powered industry based in huge mills. The Industrial Revolution had begun.

The steam engine was a crucial part of the British Industrial Revolution. It had been invented in Great Britain in 1698. Steam engines became more efficient and reliable in the late 1700s, however, when James Watt radically improved the existing engine. It was Watt's steam engine design that powered the Industrial Revolution in Great Britain and, not long after, in the United States.

The North industrializes
To keep their economic advantage, the British made it illegal for anyone with knowledge of industrial machines to leave the country or for anyone to export any industrial machine.

A mechanic named Samuel Slater violated these laws when he brought knowledge of the new industrial machines to America. Slater and a partner built a water-powered spinning mill in Rhode Island. Their mill was the first successful textile mill in the country, and its construction marks the beginning of the Industrial Revolution in the United States.

By 1810 there were more than 60 textile mills along streams in New England. These early mills spun thread, but they did not weave it into cloth. That innovation took place in the city of Lowell, Massachusetts, where the textile industry boomed.

Industrialization in the North also led to urbanization. People left their farms and moved to cities where they could work in the mills and factories. In 1820 only 7 percent of Americans lived in cities. Within 30 years, the percentage more than doubled.

Transportation and communication
The development of American industry in the early 1800s went hand-in-hand with the development of transportation networks and communication advances including:

- **Roads** By 1840 a network of roads connected most cities and towns in the United States, promoting travel and trade.
- **Canals** In 1825 the 363-mile-long Erie Canal opened, connecting the Great Lakes with the Atlantic Ocean. The canal provided a quick, economical way to ship goods. Over the next 15 years, more than 3,000 canals were built in the Northeast.

1807 Robert Fulton launches the *Clermont*—and the first successful steamboat passenger service.

1844 Samuel Morse uses this telegraph key to send the world's first telegraph message.

c. 1830 The textile mills of Lowell, Massachusetts, kept working thanks to the innovation of employing farm girls.

SKILLS FOCUS: INTERPRETING TIME LINES

What was one common feature of the technological advances made during the Industrial Revolution?

See **Skills Handbook**, p. H14

- **Railroads** In 1830 the first steam-powered train ran in the United States. By 1840 there were about 3,000 miles of track in the country. The railroad became a important means of travel and transport.
- **The telegraph** In 1840 Samuel Morse patented the first practical telegraph. A telegraph is a device that sends messages using electricity through wires. Communication by telegraph was instantaneous, and newspapers, railroads, and other businesses were quick to grasp its advantages. It was the most important communication advance of the Industrial Revolution.

READING CHECK **Summarizing** What key advancements in industry, transportation, and communication were made in the early 1800s?

Cotton and the South

Cotton revolutionized the South, but only after a machine called the cotton gin made large-scale cotton production possible. Eli Whitney invented the cotton gin, which separated the seeds from the usable part of the cotton (*gin* is short for *engine*). Formerly, separating the seeds from the fluffy cotton fibers had been slow and expensive. Now it was much faster.

The cotton gin was actually quite a simple machine, but it had a major impact on life in the South. In the United States, the booming textile industry of the North bought cotton to weave into cloth to sell to the growing American population. Overseas, the greatest demand for cotton came from Great Britain. There, the newly mechanized textile industry, exploding in the midst of the Industrial Revolution, demanded ever-increasing amounts of cotton to feed its hundreds of mills. The combination of the cotton gin and the huge demand for cotton encouraged many Americans to become cotton farmers.

Slavery spreads Even with the use of the cotton gin, farming cotton was a labor-intensive enterprise. The land had to be prepared, and the cotton seeds had to be planted. The growing plants had to be tended. Of course, the crop also had to be picked and baled.

The first cotton farms were small, and they were run by families who didn't own slaves. Soon, however, wealthier planters bought huge tracts of land and used enslaved African Americans to raise and pick the cotton that made the planters rich. These wealthier planters grew cotton and other crops on plantations. As the amount of money made by growing cotton increased, so did the number of plantations. Some plantations were huge, covering thousands of acres. Others were more modest.

The growth of cotton farming led directly to an increase in demand for enslaved African Americans. In 1810 there were about 1 million enslaved African Americans in the United States. By 1840 that number had more than

THE IMPACT TODAY

Science and Technology
The telegraph has been replaced in most developed countries by digital information transmission that uses computer technology. Telegrams that once were sent by telegraph are now sent over the Internet.

ACADEMIC VOCABULARY
impact effect

Nationalism and Sectionalism

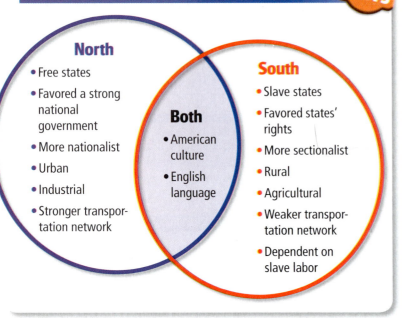

Differences in North and South The economic differences between the increasingly industrial North and the primarily agricultural South led to even greater differences between the two regions. Trade and industry encourage urbanization, and so cities grew faster in the North than in the South. Moreover, the Industrial Revolution and the revolutions in transportation and communication had the greatest impact on the North, where new technology was seized by businesses in pursuit of efficiency and growth.

The greatest difference between North and South, however, centered around slavery. In the South, slavery was legal, and most white people viewed it as an absolutely vital part of the economy, a natural situation. In the North, however, slavery was illegal, and increasing numbers of people viewed it as a problem.

Americans of the time were well aware of the differences between North and South. Yet few could know that these differences would eventually lead the two regions to fight each other in a bloody conflict that would become known as the Civil War.

READING CHECK **Identifying Supporting Details** Why was the cotton gin an important invention in the South?

doubled, to nearly 2.5 million. Overall, enslaved African Americans accounted for about one-third of the South's population.

Planters knew that the more slaves they used as laborers, the more cotton they could grow, and the more money they could make. Thus there was a powerful economic incentive to maintain slavery in the South.

SECTION 1 ASSESSMENT

HSS 11.1.3

go.hrw.com
Online Quiz
Keyword: SE7 HP3

Reviewing Ideas, Terms, and People

1. **a. Identify** What is **nationalism**?
   b. Compare What did *McCulloch* v. *Maryland* and *Gibbons* v. *Ogden* have in common?
   c. Analyze What was the purpose of the **Monroe Doctrine**?

2. **a. Recall** What was Jackson's position on the **Second Bank of the United States**?
   b. Draw Conclusions What does the passage of the **Indian Removal Act** indicate about American attitudes toward Native Americans?
   c. Evaluate Do you think states should be allowed to nullify federal laws?

3. **a. Identify** Name three major advances in transportation and communication during the **Industrial Revolution**.
   b. Draw Conclusions Why do you think that rail lines became more important than roads and canals?
   c. Evaluate Do you think transportation advances or communication advances were more important during the Industrial Revolution? Why?

4. **a. Recall** What was the significance of the cotton gin?
   b. Analyze How did cotton affect attitudes toward slavery in the South?
   c. Predict How do you think the differences between North and South led to the Civil War?

Critical Thinking

5. **Comparing and Contrasting** Copy the diagram and identify similarities and differences between the North and the South.

North	South

FOCUS ON WRITING

ELA W1.1

6. **Expository** Write a paragraph that explains why cotton became fundamental to the economy of the South. Use details from the section in your explanation.

98 CHAPTER 3

SECTION 2: A Push for Reform

BEFORE YOU READ

MAIN IDEA
The Reform Era led to some improvements in American society as well as the beginning of the women's movement and the abolition movement.

READING FOCUS
1. How did religion spark reform in the early nineteenth century?
2. How did early immigration lead to urban reform?
3. What was the role of women in the Reform Era?
4. What was the abolition movement?

KEY TERMS AND PEOPLE
Second Great Awakening
Dorothea Dix
transcendentalism
Know-Nothings
Seneca Falls Convention
Lucretia Mott
Elizabeth Cady Stanton
Underground Railroad
Harriet Tubman
Frederick Douglass

HSS 11.3.1 Describe the contributions of religious groups to social reform movements (e.g., civil and human rights, individual responsibility and the work ethic).

HSS 11.3.2 Analyze the Second Great Awakening and the rise of Christian liberal theology in the nineteenth century.

HSS 11.3.3 Cite incidences of religious intolerance in the United States (e.g., anti-Catholic sentiment).

THE INSIDE STORY

What was happening in western New York? In the 1820s and 1830s it seemed that people in every small town were finding a new interest in religion. Crowds flocked to prayer meetings to hear fiery preachers every evening. So many religious revivals took place that the area became known as the Burned-Over District—scorched by the flames of religion.

Revival meetings were personal, public, and emotional. The preacher prayed for people by name. People wept publicly and confessed their sins. Unlike in many traditional churches, women were welcome to pray and even preach in public during these revival meetings.

Several new religious movements began in the Burned-Over District. Joseph Smith published the Book of Mormon, based on golden plates that he said an angel had given him. Smith's revelations led to the founding of the Church of Jesus Christ of Latter-day Saints, or the Mormons. Another revivalist was William Miller, who prophesied the second coming of Christ. His followers developed into the Seventh-day Adventist Church. Western New York was also home to Shaker farms, utopian communities like Oneida, and advocates of Spiritualism.

Other social reform movements found support, too. Western New York was a stronghold for the antislavery movement. Homes and churches were stations on the Underground Railroad, which helped slaves escape to Canada. The movement for women's rights also took root in New York.

FUELED BY THE Fires of Religion

▼ American Methodists flock to a camp meeting.

Religion Sparks Reform

It was not only in New York that preachers found willing audiences. Across the country, but especially in the North, Americans attended revival meetings and joined churches in record numbers during the 1820s and 1830s. This new religious movement was called the Second Great Awakening. A similar movement, the First Great Awakening, had taken place in the American colonies in the 1700s.

Preachers of the Second Great Awakening were Protestant. They did not teach strict adherence to church rules or obedience to a minister. Rather, preachers told people that their destiny lay in their own hands. They were admonished to live well and to work hard.

Followers were also told that they had the opportunity and the responsibility to do God's work on earth. Through dedication and hard work, they were told, they could create a kind of heaven on earth. As a result, tens of thousands of Americans began to reform, or reshape, American life.

The Reform Era The Second Great Awakening helped launch a remarkable period in American history. The Reform Era, which lasted from about 1830 to 1860, was a time when Americans made many attempts to reshape American society. The men and women who participated in the many different movements of the Reform Era are called reformers. Key reforms of this period included:

- **The temperance movement** One of the first goals of the reformers was to eliminate or lessen the use of alcoholic beverages. This movement is called the temperance movement. Temperance means "moderation." Reformers wrote about the evils of alcohol, which they linked to sickness, poverty, and the breakup of families.
- **Education reforms** In 1830 not all children attended school. Most schools of the time were common schools—free public schools where children learned reading, writing, and mathematics. American reformers wanted more children to be educated. They believed that educated people made better decisions and that widespread education was fundamental to a democratic country. These reformers worked to improve American education.
- **Prison reforms** In 1841 Dorothea Dix visited a jail in Cambridge, Massachusetts. What she saw there appalled her. Prisoners, some mentally ill, were held in horribly crowded, unsanitary conditions. Dix began a campaign for prison reform. Because of her actions, the Massachusetts legislature created state-supported institutions to house and treat mentally ill people, separate from criminals. Dix and her supporters also convinced other states to do the same.

Transcendentalism One of the most remarkable movements of the Reform Era took place in New England. It was called the transcendental movement. Transcendentalism is the belief that knowledge is not found only by observation of the world but also through reason, intuition, and personal spiritual experiences. Key transcendentalists were Ralph Waldo Emerson and Henry David Thoreau.

READING CHECK **Identifying Cause and Effect** How did the Second Great Awakening have a lasting moral, social, and political impact?

Early Immigration and Urban Reform

Many people immigrated to the United States during the early 1800s to escape poor conditions in their home countries. Irish and German immigrants were two of the first groups to come to the United States in large numbers. By 1860 the United States was home to about 3 million Irish and German immigrants.

Immigrants' lives in the United States varied widely. Wealthy people, with family or other connections in the United States, did well. The majority of immigrants, however, had little or no money and no one to turn to for help. They struggled to survive in a country that was to them foreign and often hostile.

The Know-Nothings Anti-immigrant sentiment was promoted by well-funded and organized social and political groups. The best known of these was a secret fraternal organization called the Know-Nothings. They were called Know-Nothings because their members, when asked about their group's activities, answered by saying, "I know nothing." The

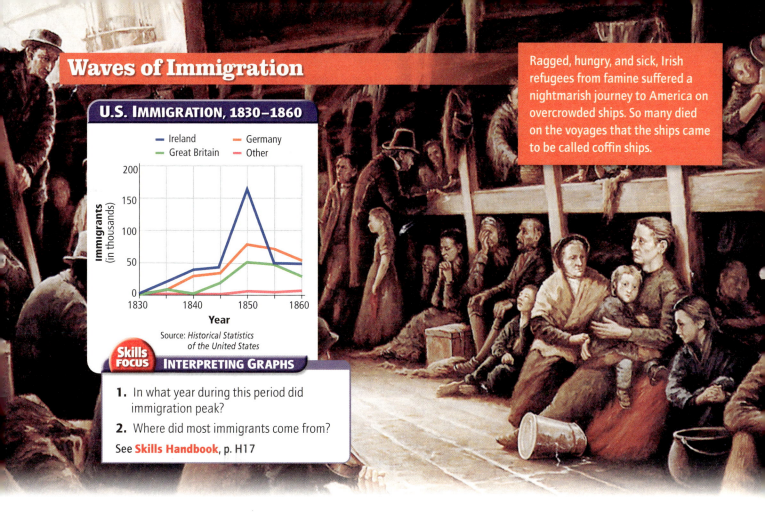

Waves of Immigration

U.S. IMMIGRATION, 1830–1860

Source: Historical Statistics of the United States

SKILLS FOCUS: INTERPRETING GRAPHS
1. In what year during this period did immigration peak?
2. Where did most immigrants come from?

See **Skills Handbook**, p. H17

Ragged, hungry, and sick, Irish refugees from famine suffered a nightmarish journey to America on overcrowded ships. So many died on the voyages that the ships came to be called coffin ships.

Know-Nothings organized themselves into a political party, the American Party, which had more than 1 million members by the 1850s.

Many German and Irish immigrants came to the United States in the mid-1800s. Fortunately for the Germans, they did not encounter the same hostility that greeted Irish immigrants. Why not? Whereas Irish immigrants were mainly poor and Catholic, German immigrants usually had more money. They also tended to be Protestant, like most Americans.

German immigrants spread across the country. They could afford to travel far inland, seeking land and other opportunities in the heartland. Many settled in the Midwest, but large German immigrant communities were found from New York to Texas. German immigrants worked as farmers, as artisans, in factories, and in many other occupations.

Reform in cities and industries Immigrants to the United States in the mid-1800s arrived in a country undergoing two dramatic changes, urbanization and industrialization. Growing cities and increasing industrialization led to further reforms.

Many city-dwellers lived in tenements, or poorly made, crowded apartment buildings. Lacking adequate light, ventilation, and sanitation, tenements were very unhealthy places to live. The plight of tenement dwellers sparked preliminary efforts at reform. In some cities, local boards of health were established to set sanitation rules. But conditions in the poorer districts of American cities would remain unsatisfactory throughout the mid-1800s. Serious efforts at reform would not begin until late in the century.

Between 1820 and 1860 the percentage of Americans who worked in manufacturing and related fields soared from 5 percent to about 30 percent. This fundamental shift in the economy had far-reaching social results.

As a rule, the relatively wealthy and educated business owners looked down on workers. The results were low wages, long hours, unsafe working conditions, and other abuses. In response, workers began to organize into groups to demand higher wages, shorter hours, and safer working conditions. This was the beginning of the American labor movement. It faced fierce opposition from business owners.

ACADEMIC VOCABULARY
preliminary first or early

DEVELOPING A NATIONAL IDENTITY

Labor did enjoy some victories, however. One successful campaign was the Ten-Hour Movement, which sought to limit the working day to 10 hours. In 1837 President Andrew Jackson declared a 10-hour workday for some federal employees. President Martin Van Buren extended the rule to other employees in 1840. Despite this success, it would be decades before the labor movement made substantial progress in improving work conditions.

READING CHECK **Identifying the Main Idea** What reforms arose in response to urbanization and industrialization?

Women in the Reform Era

A combination of legal, economic, and cultural factors limited what American women in the early 1800s could achieve. With few exceptions, women could not vote, hold public office, or serve on juries. Married women were not allowed to own property. Despite the limits placed on their lives, American women took the lead in reshaping life in the country. Women played a leading role in all of the great reform movements of the Reform Era, including education reforms, prison reforms, and the temperance movement. The modern women's movement also began during this era.

Women reformers All of the reform movements were rooted, to some degree, in the Second Great Awakening. This religious revival opened many doors for women. The movement de-emphasized obedience to a minister and celebrated doing good works. Women were therefore able to participate more fully in religious affairs. Many formed groups, such as Bible-reading and missionary societies, that served as extensions of their churches. These women's church societies evolved into reform societies, groups organized to promote social reforms. The number of reform societies grew rapidly in the 1830s and 1840s. Tens of thousands of women joined. They focused on issues ranging from education to urban reform.

The Seneca Falls Convention In July 1848 the Seneca Falls Convention was held in Seneca Falls, New York. It was the first women's rights convention held in America. By the time the Seneca Falls Convention was held, two generations of American women had led Reform Era movements.

Despite their Reform Era accomplishments, women were still prohibited from participating in American government by voting or by holding public office. These limits on women's lives severely restricted their influence. Many American women wanted to obtain political power in order to advance the reforms that mattered to them.

The Seneca Falls Convention was organized by **Lucretia Mott** and **Elizabeth Cady Stanton**, two key people in the nation's history. Mott was a leading abolitionist who had helped organize several antislavery groups and conventions. Stanton, too, was a dedicated abolitionist.

The major product of the convention was the Seneca Falls Declaration, written by Elizabeth Cady Stanton. Exactly 100 participants—68 women and 32 men—signed the Declaration of Sentiments, which publicly stated their belief that "all men and women are created equal."

The Seneca Falls Declaration was widely ridiculed. The women who supported it were also ridiculed. The handful of men who dared to speak out for the equal treatment of women were treated with even worse disdain.

Working Conditions
A cotton mill boss whips a young worker in this 1853 woodcut. Workers in this period also faced long hours, low wages, and unsafe conditions. *How did workers try to improve their conditions?*

Despite its limited short-term effects, the Seneca Falls Convention raised an important issue, one that would continue to be discussed for years to come. The convention also marked the beginning of the modern women's movement. The struggle for the equality of American women had begun.

READING CHECK **Drawing Conclusions** How do you think the Seneca Falls Convention will affect the women's movement for equal rights?

The Abolition Movement

Enslaved African Americans were denied a basic human right—freedom. Men, women, and children had no choice but to work whenever the slaveholder demanded it. For most enslaved people, this meant virtually every day of their lives, from the time they were old enough to perform chores until they were too old to be of any more use to the slaveholder.

Life as an enslaved person Most enslaved people lived on farms or plantations in the South. Cotton farming, which established slavery throughout the region, required many workers doing many different tasks. Some slaves worked as field hands, planting, tending, picking, processing, and loading cotton. Other jobs included constructing and repairing buildings and fences, hauling water, clearing land, and doing the countless other tasks needed to keep a farm or plantation running.

Other plantation slaves worked in the slaveholder's house, performing a wide variety of servant duties, like cooking and cleaning. Some enslaved people were skilled artisans, and many worked as blacksmiths, bricklayers, or carpenters.

Many slaves worked in cities. There, they worked in factories and mills, in offices, and in homes. Other enslaved people worked in mines or in the forest as lumberjacks.

Enslaved people lived, for the most part, in barely tolerable conditions. The food and clothing provided to slaves were typically as inadequate as the shelter. Medical care was virtually nonexistent. Slaves had no rights under the law, which viewed them as property. A nightmarish reality for slaves was the threat of being separated from their families. Slaveholders and slave dealers routinely separated children from their parents, brothers from their sisters, and husbands from their wives, when they were sold to different holders.

Despite lives of backbreaking work and their lack of freedom, many enslaved African Americans found some comfort in community and culture. Family and community bonds were important, as were religious beliefs.

FACES OF HISTORY

Elizabeth Cady STANTON
1815–1902

When Elizabeth Cady Stanton's only brother died, her father sighed, "Oh, my daughter, I wish you were a boy." Stanton tried to live up to her father's expectations. She got the best education available to women at the time and studied law in his office.

As an adult, Stanton organized the first women's rights convention at Seneca Falls, New York, in 1848. At the meeting, she presented the Declaration of Sentiments. It echoed the Declaration of Independence—but with an important difference: "We hold these truths to be self-evident, that all men and women are created equal . . ." Although Stanton did not live to see women gain the right to vote, she continued to work for women's rights for the rest of her life.

Interpret Why did Stanton use wording from the Declaration of Independence?

Antislavery efforts in the South Not all African Americans in the South were held in slavery. By the mid-1800s, about 250,000 were freemen, or free African Americans. They had been emancipated, or freed, by slaveholders or because their ancestors had been emancipated. These men and women faced harsh legal and social discrimination. Still, freemen played a leading role in antislavery activities. Many helped others escape slavery, and many bravely spoke out for freedom. Some even told stories about enslaved friends revolting against their oppressors.

Between 1776 and 1860, there were about 200 slave uprisings in the United States. Most were small and short-lived. But in 1831, an uprising led by Nat Turner became the deadliest slave revolt in American history. Turner and six accomplices murdered a slaveholder and his family. They then marched through the countryside of Southampton County, Virginia, gaining some 75 followers and killing dozens

DEVELOPING A NATIONAL IDENTITY

more white people. A local militia captured the rebels and hanged 20 of them, including Turner. Other white people in the area killed about 100 other slaves suspected of sympathizing with the revolt.

Far more enslaved people chose a nonviolent way to end their enslavement—they escaped. From the South they tried to reach the free states of the North or Canada or Mexico, where slavery was illegal.

No one knows exactly how many enslaved people escaped during the mid-1800s. Perhaps 40,000 or more had fled the United States by 1860. Other estimates put the number at 100,000. Certainly, thousands of enslaved people attempted escape, and although most were soon captured, many others did make it to freedom.

Over the years, an informal, constantly changing network of escape routes developed. Known as the **Underground Railroad**, it had no formal organization. Sympathetic white people and freemen provided escapees with food, hiding places, and directions to their next destination. Each hiding place was closer to free territory. One famous conductor on the Underground Railroad was **Harriet Tubman**. Tubman had escaped slavery herself, and she helped many others on their journey to freedom.

The abolition movement in the North

The number of slaves attempting to escape increased sharply during the 1830s. They may have been encouraged by a movement that was gaining supporters in the free states of the North. The abolition movement was formed to help abolish, or end, slavery. Its supporters were called abolitionists.

The Second Great Awakening formed another root of the abolitionist cause. Most religious people in the North saw slavery as a clear moral wrong that went directly against their religious beliefs. They joined reform societies to campaign against slavery. By 1830 some 50 such groups existed.

In 1833 an outspoken abolitionist named William Lloyd Garrison founded the American Anti-Slavery Society. It was the first major abolitionist group to call for the immediate end to slavery in the United States. By 1940 the American Anti-Slavery Society had more than 1,500 chapters throughout the North and an estimated 150,000 to 200,000 members.

Like the other movements of the time, the abolition movement was largely the work of American women. Two abolitionist leaders were Sarah Grimké and Angelina Grimké, the daughters of a southern slaveholder. They moved north to Philadelphia, Pennsylvania,

Enslaved African Americans in South Carolina take a Sunday rest by their cabins in this rare 1860 photograph. Most slaves worked sunrise to sunset every day except Sunday and perhaps a day or two at Christmas or New Year's. Many attended church on Sundays. Some slave narratives report that slaveholders reserved Sundays for jail time to punish workers for displeasing them during the week.

to work for the abolitionist cause. The Grimké sisters also supported the movement for women's rights.

Like the Grimkés, **Frederick Douglass** supported the women's rights movement. He was a featured speaker at the Seneca Falls Convention in 1848. Douglass is best remembered, however, for his role as a leading abolitionist. Born into slavery, he escaped to freedom as a young man. His intelligence and oratory skills eventually earned him a place as a popular antislavery speaker.

In 1845 Douglass published his autobiography, *Narrative of the Life of Frederick Douglass*. In writing about his escape from slavery to freedom, Douglass stated, "You have seen how a man was made a slave; you shall now see how a slave was made a man."

Opposition to abolition The majority of white southerners did not own slaves. To the minority who were slaveholders, however, the abolition movement was outrageous. They viewed the movement as an attack on their livelihood, on their way of life, and even on their religion. Southern ministers constructed elaborate arguments that attempted to justify slavery in Christian terms.

Slaveholders and politicians also argued that slavery was essential to cotton production. To many, even in the North, this economic argument was powerful. By 1860 cotton accounted for about 55 percent of American exports.

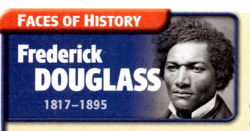

FACES OF HISTORY
Frederick DOUGLASS
1817–1895

After escaping slavery on his second attempt, Frederick Douglass made his way to Massachusetts where he gave a speech on the horrors of slavery, which instantly made him a leading spokesperson for the abolitionist cause. For the next 50 years, he used his sharp intellect, gift for writing, and strong public-speaking skills to campaign against slavery and racial prejudice in America.

During the Civil War, Douglass recruited African Americans to fight for the Union Army. He also met with President Abraham Lincoln to protest discrimination against black soldiers. In later years, Douglass focused on land rights for former slaves, women's rights, and the fight against lynching.

Explain What skills made Douglass a persuasive abolitionist?

Indeed, most northerners supported slavery as well. To northern workers, freedom for the slaves might mean increased competition for certain jobs. Still, the pressure to abolish slavery in the United States was undeniable. As Frederick Douglass put it, the issue of slavery was "the great, paramount, imperative, and all-commanding question for this age and nation to solve."

READING CHECK **Contrasting** What were the major arguments of abolitionists and their opponents?

SECTION 2 ASSESSMENT

HSS 11.3.1, 11.3.2, 11.3.3

go.hrw.com
Online Quiz
Keyword: SE7 HP3

Reviewing Ideas, Terms, and People
1. **a. Recall** What was the **Second Great Awakening**?
   b. Analyze How did the Second Great Awakening help launch the Reform Era?
2. **a. Describe** What was life like for poor city residents?
   b. Evaluate What factors limited the success of the early labor movement?
3. **a. Identify** Who organized the **Seneca Falls Convention**?
   b. Analyze What was the purpose of the Seneca Falls Convention?
   c. Evaluate Do you think the Declaration of Sentiments changed attitudes toward women? Why or why not?
4. **a. Describe** What was life like for enslaved African Americans?
   b. Elaborate How did enslaved people maintain their hope?
   c. Predict What do you think brought an end to slavery in the United States?

Critical Thinking
5. **Summarizing** Copy the chart below and identify the major movements of the Reform Era.

Movement			
Leader			

FOCUS ON WRITING **ELA** W1.1

6. **Expository** Write a paragraph that explains what the Underground Railroad was and why it was named that.

SECTION 3: Expansion Leads to Conflict

BEFORE YOU READ

MAIN IDEA
As the United States pushed westward, conflict erupted between Texas and Mexico.

READING FOCUS
1. How did the idea of manifest destiny influence Americans' western migration?
2. How did Texas achieve independence from Mexico?
3. What were the causes and effects of the Mexican-American War?

KEY TERMS AND PEOPLE
manifest destiny
gold rush
Oregon Treaty
Stephen F. Austin
Antonio López de Santa Anna
Alamo
Sam Houston
Mexican-American War
Bear Flag Revolt
Treaty of Guadalupe Hidalgo

HSS 8.8.2 Describe the purpose, challenges, and economic incentives associated with westward expansion, including the concept of Manifest Destiny and the territorial acquisitions that spanned numerous decades.

HSS 8.8.6 Describe the Texas War for Independence and the Mexican-American War.

▲ A westward-bound family poses with their prairie schooners, or small wagons.

A Day on the Trail

What challenges did westward-bound pioneers face? Oregon Territory was the goal of many pioneer families. Thousands of people traveled there on the Oregon Trail. Harriet Buckingham, who was just 19 years old, kept a diary of her trip to Oregon in 1851. She was a good observer, describing the landscape and the Native American peoples she met.

Buckingham's wagon train included seven wagons and a carriage, along with oxen, cows, horses, and mules. They carried tents, cookstoves, and a coop full of chickens. On May 13, 1851, they reached the Platte River. The wagon train had to cross the river, but it would be difficult to get everyone across safely. The weather also posed a challenge.

"We were quickly wakened this morning by the singing of the Indians. Our men all went to work with the three other companies [of wagons] building a bridge. It was completed by afternoon when we crossed. It is a matter of surprise that over 500 head of cattle & fifty wagons should cross without accident. The Waggons were all drawn over by hand & the cattle & horses swam... We encamped a mile from the creek. The Evening was delightful, the moon shone so clearly but before morning, it clouded up and one of the most terrifine [terrifying] storms I ever witnessed... The rain fell in torrents. The lightning was most vivid. We were obliged to move as soon as possible for fear of being overflown... we traveled on some 3 miles in water up to the axletrees."

Manifest Destiny

Like Harriet Buckingham, hundreds of thousands of Americans migrated to the West in the 1840s and 1850s. They went for many different reasons, and they settled in many different places. Yet they all shared the dream of new opportunities and a better life.

To Americans, westward expansion seemed inevitable. In fact, some people believed that it was America's God-given right to settle land all the way to the Pacific Ocean. This belief is called **manifest destiny**. Several major western trails were well established by 1850:

- **The Santa Fe Trail** The Santa Fe Trail led from Independence, Missouri, to Santa Fe, New Mexico.
- **The Oregon Trail** The longest and most famous trail used by the migrants was the Oregon Trail. The 2,000-mile-long trail stretched from Independence, Missouri, to the rich farming lands of the Willamette Valley in the Oregon Country.
- **The Mormon Trail** In 1830 Joseph Smith founded a church called The Church of Jesus Christ of Latter-day Saints, commonly called the Mormon Church. Because the Mormon faith differed from other Christian faiths, Mormons were persecuted and forced from their homes. Many Mormons migrated West to find a place where they could practice their religion freely. The route they followed became known as the Mormon Trail.

The California gold rush In 1848 a carpenter discovered gold in the American River at John Sutter's sawmill in northern California. Sutter tried to keep the discovery a secret, but word soon spread. People as far away as Asia, South America, and Europe heard the news. Many headed to California, dreaming of striking it rich.

The mass migration to California of miners—and businesspeople who made money from the miners—is known as the California **gold rush**. The migrants who left for California

GEOGRAPHY SKILLS INTERPRETING MAPS

1. **Movement** What trails did the Old Spanish Trail link together?
2. **Human-Environment Interaction** For what reasons was overland travel to and from the West difficult?

See **Skills Handbook**, p. H19

DEVELOPING A NATIONAL IDENTITY 107

California Gold Rush, 1849

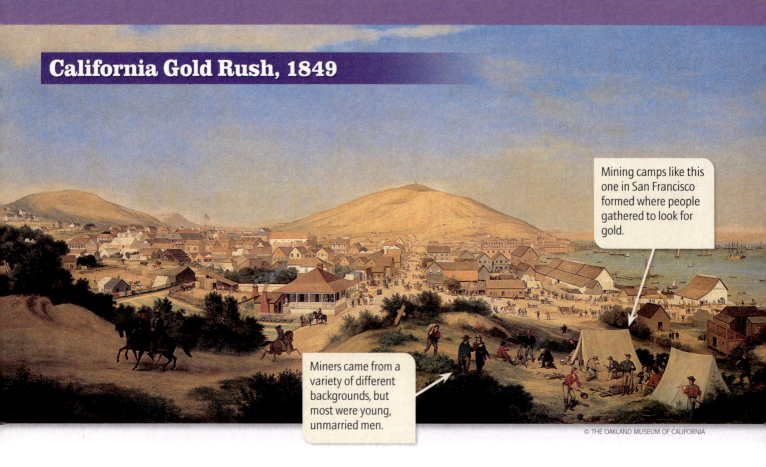

Mining camps like this one in San Francisco formed where people gathered to look for gold.

Miners came from a variety of different backgrounds, but most were young, unmarried men.

© THE OAKLAND MUSEUM OF CALIFORNIA

in 1849 were called forty-niners. A stunning 80,000 people moved to California in the year 1849 alone. This population boom made California eligible for statehood. A year later, in 1850, California became the 31st state.

Many more people moved to California in the 1850s. Although the dream of finding gold brought people from all around the world, 80 percent of the people arriving in California came from the United States. To reach California, most people traveled overland, following the California Trail. Others booked passage on ships that sailed all the way around the southern tip of South America. Still others sailed south to Panama, crossed Central America by mule train, and then sailed north to California. By 1854 as many as 300,000 people had migrated to California.

Upon reaching California most miners moved into camps in the gold fields. Many others—especially businesspeople—settled in cities. San Francisco, the port nearest the gold fields, had a population of about 800 in 1848. One year later, 25,000 people lived there. By 1860 it was home to 60,000 people.

The town of Stockton, located on the San Joaquin River on the way to the southern gold fields, boomed as well. Sacramento, located on the Sacramento River between San Francisco and the northern gold fields, also grew very rapidly. Sacramento became the capital of California in 1850.

Major effects of western migration

Use of the western trails declined sharply after 1869 when railroad tracks finally ran unbroken from the East Coast to the West Coast. By that time, however, more than 350,000 migrants had followed the overland trails to the West. Such a huge migration—equal to about 1.5 percent of the total American population in 1850—had significant effects:

- **The Oregon Treaty** The presence of so many Americans in the Oregon Country prompted presidential candidate James K. Polk to attempt to secure Oregon for the United States. Since 1818 the United States had jointly controlled the region with Great Britain. Later, President Polk signed the Oregon Treaty with Great Britain, which set the boundary between the United States and British Canada at the forty-ninth parallel. This boundary, now between the United States and Canada, still exists today.
- **Communication links** Western migration also created a need for communications over

Many mining camps, like the one in the painting at left, sprang up during the California gold rush. Over 80,000 people from many backgrounds came to California in 1849. Above, black and white miners work together in El Dorado County.

long distances. Mail was the first way messages traveled from East to West. For about 18 months, the Pony Express offered somewhat quicker mail service between Missouri and California using relays of young riders on fast horses. Then in 1861 the telegraph linked the East and the West. The telegraph made the Pony Express obsolete by delivering important news much more quickly.

In time, the greatest effect of westward migration would be on the original inhabitants of the West: Native Americans. Their lives would be forever changed as more and more American settlers moved west.

READING CHECK **Identifying Cause and Effect** What were some major causes and effects of westward migration?

Texas Independence

Americans who came to Texas in the 1820s were far from the first people to call the region home. Hundreds of Native American groups had lived in Texas for thousands of years. They belonged to the Plains, the Southwest, and the Southeast culture groups.

Then in the 1500s, Europeans explorers from Spain crossed Texas several times. Spain claimed Texas based on these explorations. Later, Spain set up a system of missions in Texas both to convert the Native Americans to Christianity and to counter the threat of French settlement. By 1800 Spain still claimed Texas, but there were only three Spanish settlements in the entire region. Soon, Americans would begin to settle in Texas.

Americans move into Texas
In 1820 Moses Austin, a banker from Missouri, approached Spanish officials in Texas with a plan he called the Texas Venture. Austin proposed that, in exchange for land, he would build a colony in Texas. The Spanish, eager to have the land settled, agreed. Austin died before he could organize his colony. One of his last wishes was that his son, **Stephen F. Austin**, carry out his plans for a colony in Texas.

In 1823 Austin's Colony was officially established. Austin then directed the building of a small town called San Felipe de Austin. San Felipe, as it came to be called, was the administrative, commercial, and social center of the colony. By 1824 about 300 families lived on farms and ranches throughout the colony. The total population of the colony was about 1,800. About 400 of those Texas colonists were African Americans.

Moses Austin had approached Spanish officials with his original plan for settlement. However, by the time his son Stephen had established the colony, Mexico was no longer part of Spain. Mexico had become an independent country in 1821 after a decade-long struggle with Spain.

By 1830 there were more than a dozen colonies in Texas and about 30,000 settlers, including several thousand enslaved African Americans and 4,000 Tejanos (Texans of Mexican heritage). This was a dramatic change: Just a decade earlier, there were only about 2,000 non-Indian people in Texas. Almost all of the settlers were from the United States.

The Texas Revolution
American settlers in Texas had to agree to certain things in exchange for receiving land. They had to surrender their American citizenship, swear allegiance to Mexico, adopt the Roman Catholic religion, and hold the land for seven years.

DEVELOPING A NATIONAL IDENTITY **109**

In practice, the settlers did not think of themselves as Mexicans but as Americans who lived in Mexico. The Mexican government grew concerned and took steps to decrease American influence in the region.

In response, Texans decided they wanted to gain independence from Mexico. This led to the Texas Revolution. Stephen F. Austin traveled to Mexico City to present the Texans' plan to the Mexican government. But Austin's visit to Mexico City went badly because the Mexican government felt he was a threat.

Meanwhile, political strife within Mexico had produced a new president, **Antonio López de Santa Anna**. In an effort to centralize the Mexican government, Santa Anna suspended some powers of Texas and other Mexican states. On March 2, 1836, Texas declared its independence from Mexico.

The Alamo The most famous battle of the Texas Revolution was at a fort called the Alamo. In December, forces under Ben Milam had captured the town of San Antonio, which contained the Alamo. In the 1700s the Alamo had been a mission, but after its closure it had been converted to military use.

Santa Anna was furious. He personally led a force of 6,000 soldiers north into Texas and demanded that the Texans surrender. But the commander of the Texans, William Travis, responded with a cannon shot. The Mexican army laid siege. For 12 days and nights they pounded the Alamo with cannon fire.

In the early hours of March 6, 1836, approximately 1,800 Mexican soldiers stormed the fort. Among the Americans defending the Alamo was David Crockett, who bravely helped hold back the Mexicans until he ran out of ammunition. Within four hours, the Mexicans had killed nearly all of the nearly 200 Alamo defenders. The Alamo remains one of the most famous battles in American history.

On April 21, in the Battle of San Jacinto, Texans captured Santa Anna and forced him to sign treaties recognizing Texan independence. The rallying cry at the Battle of San Jacinto was "Remember the Alamo!" Texas was now a new, independent country: It was named the Republic of Texas.

READING CHECK **Summarizing** What were the major events of the Texas Revolution?

War with Mexico

The troubles between Texas and Mexico were far from over, however. Because Santa Anna was a prisoner when he signed the treaties, the Mexican government refused to honor Texas independence. The Texas Revolution was over, but the fighting over Texas was not.

The annexation of Texas In Texas's first election, **Sam Houston**, who had led the Texans to victory at San Jacinto, won the presidency. Interestingly, the election was for more than the presidency. It was also for whether Texas should join the United States. By an overwhelming margin, Texans voted to join the union. They wanted the United States to annex, or add, Texas as a state.

In the United States, many Americans were in favor of annexation. As you have read previously, they believed in manifest destiny, and annexing Texas would add a large piece of land to the United States. Americans admired Texans for fighting for their freedom from Mexico. Many viewed the Texas Revolution as being fought in the spirit of the American Revolution. Southerners supported annexation because Texas allowed slavery.

Some other Americans opposed annexing Texas. They were concerned that the United States should not have to bear the substantial Texas debt. In addition, northerners opposed the annexation of Texas because it would spread slavery westward, increasing the slave states' power in Congress.

Texas remained an independent republic for nine years. The annexation question became an issue in the 1844 presidential election. When the pro-annexation candidate James Polk won, the outgoing president John Tyler offered a solution: Texas could join the union, but under certain conditions. Accepting those conditions, Texans overwhelmingly approved a new state constitution. On December 29, 1845, Texas joined the Union.

Causes of the Mexican-American War
Immediately after annexation, Mexico broke off diplomatic relations with the United States. The Mexican government still considered Texas to be Mexican territory.

James K. Polk became U.S. president in March 1845. Polk was an enthusiastic sup-

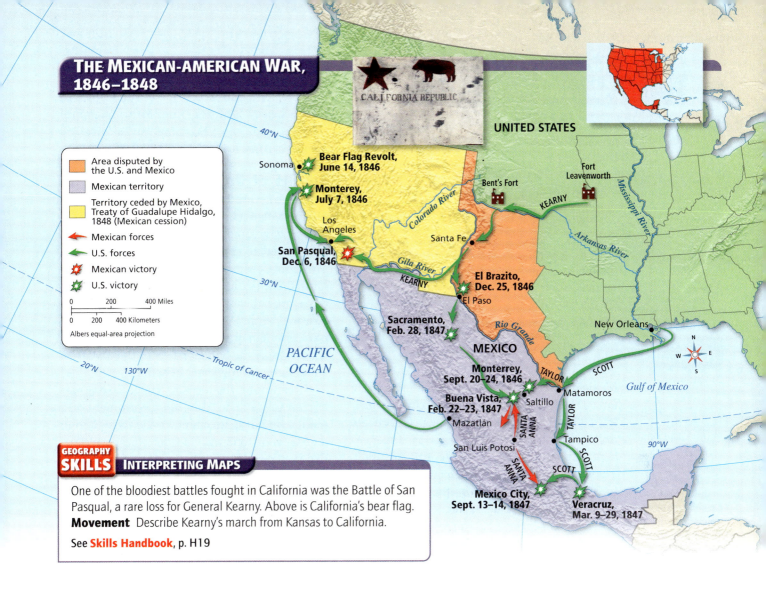

GEOGRAPHY SKILLS INTERPRETING MAPS

One of the bloodiest battles fought in California was the Battle of San Pasqual, a rare loss for General Kearny. Above is California's bear flag.

Movement Describe Kearny's march from Kansas to California.

See **Skills Handbook**, p. H19

porter of annexation. In fact, he had set his sights on even more territory. He wanted the United States to acquire the land between Texas and the Pacific Ocean. These territories, New Mexico and California, belonged to Mexico. But Polk thought that they should belong to the United States.

Only a handful of Americans lived in New Mexico and California. Yet there were very few Mexican citizens, either. The Mexican government and army had very little presence in these remote regions. Polk sought an opportunity to acquire these lands.

In the fall of 1845, President Polk sent a special envoy, or messenger, to Mexico. The envoy's name was John Slidell. Slidell was going to offer to cancel some of Mexico's debts to the United States. In exchange, he wanted Mexico to recognize the Rio Grande as the boundary between the United States and Mexico. Slidell was also authorized to pay up to $30 million to purchase New Mexico and California. No one in Mexico would meet with Slidell. Furious, he recommended to Polk that Mexico be punished.

Then following a boundary dispute, the United States declared war on Mexico on May 13, 1846. The **Mexican-American War** had begun.

The Republic of California

The United States used an aggressive strategy to win the Mexican War. Within weeks, General Stephen Kearny marched west from Kansas, bound for the New Mexico territory. When he arrived, he easily captured the town of Santa Fe and thus took control of New Mexico. Kearny then headed west, hoping to repeat his victory and gain control of California.

In California, a small group of American citizens revolted against the Mexican govern-

DEVELOPING A NATIONAL IDENTITY 111

Causes and Effects of the Mexican-American War

CAUSES
- annexation of Texas
- boundary dispute
- manifest destiny and expansionism

↓

EFFECTS
- Treaty of Guadalupe Hidalgo
- Mexican Cession
- Gadsden Purchase

THE IMPACT TODAY

Government A 2004 government study found that the United States failed to recognize Mexican titles to million of acres of land in the Mexican Cession, despite agreeing to do so in the Treaty of Guadalupe Hidalgo. The resulting land disputes remain a major political issue in New Mexico.

ment. The rebels easily defeated the small Mexican force in the village of Sonoma. They forced the Mexican leader to sign a treaty turning California over to the rebels. The rebels declared that California was now the independent Republic of California on June 14, 1846. They made a crude flag with a picture of a bear for their country. Thus, the incident became known as the **Bear Flag Revolt**.

A month later, U.S. forces arrived and soon gained control of California. Meanwhile, American forces under General Zachary Taylor advanced into northern Mexico and captured important towns in the region.

Another force under General Winfield Scott landed on the eastern coast of Mexico near Veracruz. In September 1846 Scott led his forces inland and marched into Mexico City. In a matter of months, U.S. forces had captured New Mexico, California, and Mexico's capital city. The Mexican government was forced to give in to American demands.

Results of the War Signed in 1848, the **Treaty of Guadalupe Hidalgo** ended the Mexican-American War. Under the treaty, Mexico gave up its claim to Texas. Mexico was also forced to cede a huge tract of land, the Mexican Cession, to the United States. The United States received land in the present-day states of New Mexico, California, Nevada, Arizona, Utah, Colorado, and Wyoming. As you read previously, California was discovered to have gold in the same year that the Treaty of Guadalupe Hidalgo was signed.

In return for the territory, the United States agreed to pay the Mexican government $15 million and drop its claim for the $3 million in damages. In 1853 the Gadsden Purchase clarified the treaty boundary and transferred more land to the United States.

Debate continues over whether the Mexican-American War was justified. Hard feelings exist to this day. Most people agree, however, that the war was a clear expression of America's belief in its manifest destiny.

READING CHECK **Drawing Conclusions** Why was the Bear Flag Revolt a significant part of the Mexican-American War?

SECTION 3 ASSESSMENT

HSS 8.8.2, 8.8.6

go.hrw.com
Online Quiz
Keyword: SE7 HP3

Reviewing Ideas, Terms, and People

1. **a. Recall** What is manifest destiny?
   b. Analyze Why did migrants head west in the 1840s and 1850s?
   c. Evaluate How large of a role do you think the belief in manifest destiny played in migrants' decisions to head west?

2. **a. Identify** Who was Stephen F. Austin?
   b. Evaluate Do you think it was wise for the Spanish and then the Mexican government to allow Americans to settle in Texas? Explain.

3. **a. Identify** What were the effects of the Mexican-American War?
   b. Explain How did California become a republic?

   c. Evaluate Do you think Mexico was wise to break off diplomatic relations with the United States? Explain.

Critical Thinking

4. **Identifying Cause and Effect** Copy the diagram below and identify the causes of the Texas Revolution.

FOCUS ON WRITING

ELA W1.1

5. **Persuasive** As an American living in 1844, write a paragraph arguing for or against Texas annexation. Use details from the section to support your position.

112 CHAPTER 3

CHAPTER 3 Chapter Review

History's Impact video program
Review the videos to answer the closing question:
How has the history of Texas and the Southwest been affected by different groups?

Reviewing Key Terms and People

For each term below, write a sentence explaining its significance.

1. Monroe Doctrine
2. nationalism
3. sectionalism
4. Missouri Compromise
5. Second Great Awakening
6. Seneca Falls Convention
7. Underground Railroad
8. Frederick Douglass
9. manifest destiny
10. gold rush
11. Alamo
12. Mexican-American War

Comprehension and Critical Thinking

SECTION 1 *(pp. 92–98)* HSS 11.1.3

13. **a. Recall** What replaced feelings of sectionalism in the early 1800s?
    b. Analyze How did growing nationalism affect foreign and domestic policies?
    c. Elaborate How did the Missouri Compromise reflect growing sectionalism in the United States?

SECTION 2 *(pp. 99–105)* HSS 11.3.1, 11.3.2, 11.3.3

14. **a. Recall** What was the Second Great Awakening?
    b. Describe What was the relationship between the Second Great Awakening and the Reform Era?
    c. Evaluate Which movement of the Reform Era do you think was the most important? Why?

SECTION 3 *(pp. 106–112)* HSS 8.8.2, 8.8.6

15. **a. Recall** Why was the Mexican government angry about the annexation of Texas?
    b. Make Inferences How did Slidell's recommendation to Polk reflect his feelings about his treatment in Mexico?
    c. Elaborate How did the United States take advantage of its military victories over Mexico?

Using the Internet

go.hrw.com
Practice Online
Keyword: SE7 CH3

16. With the exception of Native Americans, all people who live in the United States today can trace their history back to another country. Using the keyword above, do research to learn about your family's history regarding immigration. Then write a report that presents this information.

Critical Reading HSS 11.1.3; ELA R2.0

Read the passage in Section 1 that begins with the heading "The Missouri Compromise." Then answer the questions that follow.

17. What led to the Missouri Compromise?
    A the fact that slavery was illegal in Missouri
    B the effort to abolish slavery in the South
    C the desire to maintain a balance in the Senate
    D the need to admit Maine as a slave state

18. How did the Missouri Compromise affect the Louisiana Territory?
    A It forbid slavery in the territory.
    B It allowed slavery in the territory.
    C It forbid slavery in part of the territory and allowed it in another.
    D It left the question of slavery in the territory undecided.

FOCUS ON WRITING ELA W1.1

Persuasive Writing *Persuasive writing takes a position for or against an issue, using facts and examples as supporting evidence. To practice persuasive writing, complete the assignment below.*

Writing Topic The annexation of Mexican land by the United States

19. **Assignment** Based on what you have read in this chapter, write a paragraph that either supports or opposes the way the United States acquired land from Mexico.

DEVELOPING A NATIONAL IDENTITY

CHAPTER 4
1850–1877
The UNION in CRISIS

THE BIG PICTURE
The conflict over slavery divided North and South. In 1861 the Civil War erupted. Four years of fighting left over 600,000 American soldiers dead. In the end the Union was restored, and 4 million enslaved people gained their freedom. After the war, however, Reconstruction plans for the South were only partially successful.

California Standards

History-Social Sciences

11.1 Students analyze the significant events in the founding of the nation and its attempts to realize the philosophy of government described in the Declaration of Independence.

11.3 Students analyze the role religion played in the founding of America, its lasting moral, social, and political impacts, and issues regarding religious liberty.

Skills Focus: READING LIKE A HISTORIAN

In early March 1862, some 26,250 soldiers clashed in the Battle of Pea Ridge in Arkansas. Nearly 6,000 were killed or wounded in what one soldier described as a "harvest of death." On the left side of the painting are the victorious northern forces.
Interpreting Visuals What advantage did the northern forces have in this battle?

See **Skills Handbook**, p. H30

U.S.

March 1850 California is admitted to the Union as a free state; Fugitive Slave Act passes.

May 1854 Kansas-Nebraska Act becomes law.

1850

World

1852 South African Republic is established.

114

History's Impact video program
Watch the videos to learn more about American history from 1850 to 1877.

March 1861 Abraham Lincoln becomes the 16th president.

April 1861 The Civil War begins when Confederate troops open fire on Fort Sumter.

April 1865 Lee surrenders to Grant at Appomattox; Lincoln is assassinated.

June 1866 Congress passes the Fourteenth Amendment, granting citizenship to former slaves.

1877 Compromise of 1877 puts Rutherford B. Hayes in the White House and removes federal troops from the South.

1857 Indian uprising against British rule begins with Sepoy Rebellion.

1861 Italy becomes a unified nation under king Victor Emmanuel II.

1867 Canada becomes a self-governing dominion.

1877 The last Russo-Turkish war begins.

SECTION 1: The Nation Splits Apart

BEFORE YOU READ

MAIN IDEA
By 1850 the issue of slavery dominated national politics, leading to sectional divisions and, finally, the secession of the southern states.

READING FOCUS
1. How did the issue of slavery influence expansion in the 1850s?
2. How did other sectional conflicts influence national politics in the 1850s?
3. What was Abraham Lincoln's path to the White House?
4. How and why did the South secede and form the Confederacy?

KEY TERMS AND PEOPLE
Compromise of 1850
Fugitive Slave Act
Stephen A. Douglas
popular sovereignty
Kansas-Nebraska Act
James Buchanan
Abraham Lincoln
Lincoln-Douglas debates
Jefferson Davis
Confederate States of America

HSS 11.1.3 Understand the history of the Constitution after 1787 with emphasis on federal versus state authority and growing democratization.

Bleeding KANSAS

How did the conflict over slavery result in violence? Nowhere was the fight over slavery more pronounced than in the Kansas Territory. There the government left the issue of slavery to be decided by the residents. Some residents were firmly in favor of slavery while others were firmly opposed.

During the 1850s large bands of pro-slavery and antislavery forces ranged over the territory. Several violent battles took place. Many settlers on both sides saw their property looted or destroyed. In the Marais des Cygnes Massacre, named for a river in Kansas, a gang of 30 pro-slavery men rounded up a group of 11 antislavery settlers and gunned them down in a small ravine. Five people died.

By 1856 so much violence had occurred in the territory that it was often called Bleeding Kansas. Northerners and southerners alike realized what Kansas meant for the nation. "We are playing for a mighty stake," Missouri senator David Atchison noted. "If we win we carry slavery to the Pacific Ocean, if we fail we lose . . . all the territories." Northerners were just as eager to keep Kansas free. "We will engage in competition for the virgin soil of Kansas," said New York senator William Seward. "God give the victory to the side which is stronger in numbers as it is in right."

▲ A pro-slavery gang guns down 11 unarmed antislavery settlers, May 19, 1858, in what became known as the Marais des Cygnes Massacre.

Expansion and Slavery

The struggle over Kansas illustrated the deep divisions that existed in the United States during the 1850s. Victory in the Mexican-American War in 1848 had raised the question of expansion. The Mexican Cession added more than 500,000 square miles of territory to the United States. New states would eventually be formed. Would they allow slavery?

The issue of slavery also affected control of Congress. At the time, the number of free and slave states was equal. New states would mean additional pro-slavery or antislavery seats in Congress. Neither side wanted the other to gain control in Congress because it could mean new national policy on slavery.

The Compromise of 1850 The gold rush had swelled the population of California. The settlers quickly approved a constitution banning slavery, and in March 1850 California applied to Congress to become a state. That led to a historic debate between pro-slavery and antislavery legislatures.

In January 1850 Kentucky senator Henry Clay introduced a compromise plan that would preserve the balance of power. Two political giants—Daniel Webster of Massachusetts and John C. Calhoun of South Carolina—led the debate. Webster opposed slavery but believed that preserving the Union was more important. After months of debate, Congress passed the **Compromise of 1850**.

One provision, the **Fugitive Slave Act**, was highly controversial. The law made it a federal crime to aid runaway slaves and allowed the arrest of escaped slaves. Many northerners openly broke the law, angering slaveholders.

A book by Harriet Beecher Stowe added to public tensions. Her stories about slavery's cruelties were published in a novel called *Uncle Tom's Cabin*. Although it outraged most southerners, the book became a huge success.

The Kansas-Nebraska Act Another issue was the proposed railroad to link California with the rest of the nation. Illinois senator **Stephen A. Douglas** thought that a northern route would make Chicago an urban center. He proposed organizing the western lands into two territories, Kansas and Nebraska. To win southern support, he suggested dropping the Missouri Compromise's ban on slavery. Instead, **popular sovereignty**—the vote of the residents—would decide the issue.

In May 1854 the **Kansas-Nebraska Act** became law. It outraged northerners, weakened the Democrats, and destroyed the Whig Party. Soon after, northern Whigs joined the Free-Soil Party and other antislavery parties to found the Republican Party.

READING CHECK **Summarizing** How did the Kansas-Nebraska Act affect political parties?

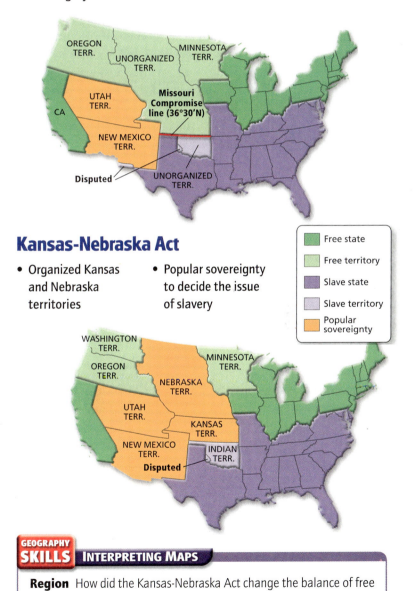

The Conflict over Slavery

During the 1850s Congress attempted to solve the conflict over slavery by compromise. But the Compromise of 1850 and the Kansas-Nebraska Act of 1854 only fueled sectional divisions.

The Compromise of 1850

- Admitted California to the Union as a free state
- Set Texas–New Mexico border
- Organized New Mexico and Utah territories with slavery to be decided by popular sovereignty
- Imposed heavy penalties on persons who aided runaway slaves (Fugitive Slave Act)
- Outlawed the buying and selling of slaves, but not slavery itself, in the nation's capital

Kansas-Nebraska Act

- Organized Kansas and Nebraska territories
- Popular sovereignty to decide the issue of slavery

GEOGRAPHY SKILLS INTERPRETING MAPS

Region How did the Kansas-Nebraska Act change the balance of free and slave states?
See **Skills Handbook**, p. H20

THE UNION IN CRISIS 117

Sectional Conflicts and National Politics

As you read in the "Inside Story," the Kansas-Nebraska Act made Kansas Territory the center of the struggle over slavery. Pro-slavery forces and free-soilers—advocates of territories free from slavery—were fighting for control.

In what became known as the Sack of Lawrence, a sheriff's posse attacked antislavery newspapers and burned buildings in free-soil Lawrence, Kansas. In response, John Brown, a committed abolitionist, led an attack that killed five pro-slavery settlers on Pottawatomie Creek in Kansas.

There were also political struggles in the territory. Before Kansas could apply for statehood, voters had to approve a constitution to allow or ban slavery. To win votes, both sides raised money and organized to bring in more settlers. Fraud and violence marked early elections. Armed pro-slavery Missourians crossed into Kansas to vote. By 1856 Kansas had two governments—one pro-slavery, the other led by free-soilers.

The election of 1856 Events in Kansas dominated the election of 1856. Disgusted northern Democrats refused to support either Stephen Douglas or President Franklin Pierce for the presidential nomination. They eventually nominated **James Buchanan**, a former senator and diplomat. The new Republican Party nominated explorer and war hero John C. Frémont. The American Party (the Know-Nothings) nominated former president Millard Fillmore. The Democrats won the election of 1856 by characterizing the Republicans as extremists on the slavery issue. Buchanan became president.

Dred Scott decision Buchanan had pledged not to interfere with slavery where it existed, but events during his term made tensions worse. The first was a controversial Supreme Court case, *Dred Scott* v. *Sandford*. Scott, a slave, had lived on free soil for many years. He sued for freedom, arguing that living on free soil made him free. In 1857 the Court ruled against him, saying the Fifth Amendment protected the property rights of slaveholders.

THE IMPACT TODAY

Government
Two constitutional amendments overturned the *Dred Scott* decision. The Fourteenth Amendment granted citizenship to people born in the United States, regardless of race, and the Fifteenth Amendment granted voting rights to African American men. Today the Voting Rights Act of 1965 enforces and expands the voting protections of the Fifteenth Amendment.

PRIMARY SOURCES

Political Cartoon

As tensions over slavery increased, violence even broke out in Congress. In 1856 South Carolina representative Preston Brooks attacked Massachusetts senator Charles Sumner over an antislavery speech Sumner had made. It took Sumner three years to recover from the beating.

Although the Senate chamber was nearly empty when the attack occurred, the artist added observers in this portrayal.

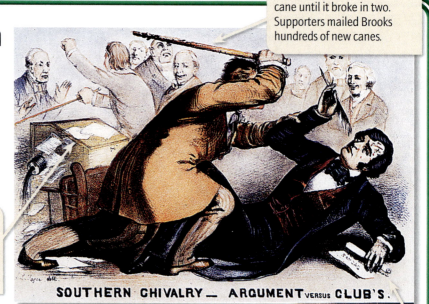

Brooks beat Sumner with a cane until it broke in two. Supporters mailed Brooks hundreds of new canes.

SOUTHERN CHIVALRY — ARGUMENT versus CLUB'S.

Sumner was writing at his desk when the attack occurred.

Skills Focus READING LIKE A HISTORIAN

1. **Identifying Points of View** What does the caption suggest about the artist's opinion of Sumner's actions?
2. **Interpreting Visuals** Why do you think the artist added observers to the scene?

See **Skills Handbook**, pp. H28–H29, H30

Meanwhile, Kansas was still in turmoil. Late in 1857 a pro-slavery convention tried to push through a state constitution that would allow slavery in Kansas. The Lecompton constitution, named for a town in Kansas, protected slavery and also included a bill of rights that excluded freed slaves. It was never ratified. A deadlock in Congress eventually led to the admission of Kansas as a free state. The debate deepened sectional divisions.

John Brown's raid At the same time, abolitionist John Brown was planning a raid on the U.S. arsenal at Harpers Ferry, Virginia, to get guns for a slave revolt. Brown and his followers easily captured the arsenal but failed to start a revolt. A company of U.S. Marines later stormed the arsenal and captured Brown and his surviving followers. They were tried for murder and treason against Virginia and sentenced to death. Brown was executed on December 2, 1859. While some people questioned Brown's sanity, many northerners saw him as a hero.

READING CHECK **Identifying the Main Idea** Why did the slavery debate center in Kansas?

Lincoln's Path to the Presidency

Abraham Lincoln was born in 1809 in a one-room cabin near Louisville, Kentucky. His family's attitudes and his own experiences as a young man had a lifelong effect on his feelings about slavery.

A frontier upbringing Lincoln once summarized his early life as "the short and simple annals [record of events] of the poor." His parents were poor, and like many white southerners, they held no slaves. Their opposition to slavery was one of the reasons the Lincoln family moved from Kentucky to the Indiana Territory in 1816.

In 1828 Lincoln took a job on a riverboat moving farm produce from Indiana to New Orleans. There he had his first contact with slavery when he observed a slave auction.

Lincoln's early political career As a young man, Lincoln moved to New Salem, a village near Springfield, Illinois. He took a job as

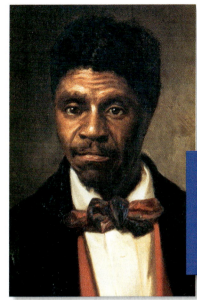

Dred Scott (left) "had no rights which the white man was bound to respect," Chief Justice Roger Taney ruled in the controversial Supreme Court case *Dred Scott* v. *Sandford*.

a store clerk and then ran for a seat in the state legislature. In December 1834 Lincoln began the first of four terms in the Illinois General Assembly, while at the same time studying law at home. In 1842 he married Mary Todd, the daughter of a Kentucky slaveholder.

In 1846 Lincoln was elected to Congress. During his first year in Congress, the Mexican-American War ended. Though Lincoln did not take part in the debates on the Wilmot Proviso to ban slavery in the territory gained from Mexico, he did vote in favor of the proposal. Lincoln believed that Congress could regulate slavery in the territories and in Washington, D.C. However, he felt that only the states had the right to end slavery within their borders.

Lincoln proposed ending slavery in the nation's capital by paying slaveholders to free their slaves. This approach was called compensated emancipation. It answered the argument that the Constitution protected slaveholders' property rights. In the late 1840s, however, this idea was still a bit too radical to gain widespread support.

Lincoln also worked hard campaigning for the Whigs' presidential candidate, Zachary Taylor, in 1848. He expected a job in the new administration as a reward for his hard work and was disappointed when he was not offered the position he sought. Lincoln resigned from Congress in 1849 and returned home to Illinois to practice law.

COUNTERPOINTS

Lincoln-Douglas Debates

Democratic senator Stephen A. Douglas believed that each state or territory should decide for itself whether or not to allow slavery.

" When this government was established by Washington and Madison and Jay and Hamilton ... it was composed of free States and slave States, bound together by our common Constitution. We have existed and prospered from that day to this, divided into these free and slave States. "

Stephen A. Douglas,
September 18, 1858

Republican Abraham Lincoln challenged Douglas for his seat in the Senate. He countered that the framers had intended a gradual end to slavery.

" [T]he fathers of the government intended and expected [slavery] to come to an end ... It is not true ... that [they] made this government part slave, and part free ... The exact truth is that they found the institution existing among us and they left it as they found it ... because of the ... absolute impossibility of the immediate removal of it. "

Abraham Lincoln,
October 15, 1858

SKILLS FOCUS: READING LIKE A HISTORIAN

Analyzing Primary Sources According to Senator Douglas, what united the states when the government was established?

See **Skills Handbook**, pp. H28–H29

The Lincoln-Douglas debates Lincoln had come home to practice law but said he was "thunderstruck and stunned" by the passage of the Kansas-Nebraska Act. He then decided to return to politics. Because the new Republican Party seemed to be in line with his beliefs, he helped organize the Illinois party. In 1858 he decided to oppose Douglas, who was seeking re-election to the Senate. Lincoln's acceptance speech focused on the divisive controversy over slavery. Quoting from the Bible, he said:

HISTORY'S VOICES

" 'A house divided against itself cannot stand.' I believe this government cannot endure, permanently half slave and half free. I do not expect the Union to be dissolved—I do not expect the house to fall—but I do expect it will cease to be divided. It will become all one thing or all the other. "
—Abraham Lincoln, June 16, 1858

Many people saw this statement as a threat to slavery. For months afterward, Lincoln tried to explain its <u>context</u>—that he was making a prediction, not stating a position. But many slaveholders were convinced that Lincoln was a secret abolitionist.

Lincoln's "house-divided" speech attracted national attention. National newspapers reported on the **Lincoln-Douglas debates**, which took place from late August to mid-October 1858 in towns across Illinois. Thousands of people gathered to hear the debates. Lincoln and Douglas were very different in their debating styles. Douglas spoke dramatically, clenching his fists and stamping his feet. In contrast, Lincoln spoke mildly, sprinkling his remarks with humor.

Lincoln challenged Douglas on the workability of popular sovereignty. In what became known as the Freeport Doctrine, Douglas said that people could exclude slavery simply by refusing to pass laws allowing it. Douglas also tried to characterize Lincoln as a dangerous radical. Lincoln frequently spoke about the immorality of slavery but at the same time denied proposing racial equality.

ACADEMIC VOCABULARY
context related or surrounding conditions

The election of 1860 Two years later, Lincoln and Douglas would meet again in the presidential race of 1860. Both candidates faced hard battles to win their party's nomination.

The Democrats were so divided that they soon split completely. Many southern Democrats walked out of their nominating convention. The remaining delegates met again and nominated Douglas. Southern Democrats then chose John Breckinridge of Kentucky as their candidate. Southern moderates formed the Constitutional Union Party, nominating Tennessee senator John Bell for president.

At the Republican convention, William Seward seemed to be the leading candidate for the nomination, but his abolitionist views were too radical for most voters. The Republicans chose Lincoln as the candidate with the best chance to win.

As in 1856, the election of 1860 was really two sectional elections. In the North it was Lincoln versus Douglas. In the South the contest was between Breckinridge and Bell. The vote was almost completely along sectional lines. Lincoln carried the more populous North and won the presidency. Many northerners celebrated, but many southerners were dismayed.

READING CHECK **Summarizing** What were Lincoln's beliefs on regulating slavery?

The South Secedes

A week after Lincoln's election, the South Carolina legislature called a convention to consider leaving the Union. On December 20, 1860, they passed a resolution stating that "the union now subsisting between South Carolina and the other states under the name of the 'United States of America' is hereby dissolved."

The rest of the Lower South quickly followed. By February 1, Mississippi, Florida, Alabama, Georgia, Louisiana, and Texas had all seceded. Four other states—Virginia, North Carolina, Tennessee, and Arkansas—warned that they might also secede.

Reactions to secession Many southerners opposed secession. The decision to secede was made by state conventions, not directly by the voters in each state. In some states, 30 to 40 percent of delegates voted against secession. Still, the radical secessionists prevailed.

CAUSES AND EFFECTS OF SECESSION

CAUSES

The Compromise of 1850
- Admits California as a free state, ending the equal number of free and slave states
- Tries to settle the dispute over expansion of slavery into the Mexican Cession by using popular sovereignty

The Kansas-Nebraska Act (1854)
- Uses popular sovereignty to decide the question of slavery in Kansas and Nebraska territories
- Causes the North and the South to compete to settle the territory
- Leads to guerrilla warfare between pro-and antislavery settlers

The Lincoln-Douglas Debates (1858)
- Emphasize the divisions over the Kansas-Nebraska Act and the *Dred Scott* decision
- Bring Lincoln's opposition to slavery's spread to a national audience
- Cause Douglas to lose support in the North and the South

The Election of 1860
- Northern and southern Democrats split over running Douglas for president
- Democratic Party splits, allowing Lincoln's election as president
- Both houses of Congress are in northern hands, and an opponent of slavery now will head the executive branch

EFFECTS

Secession (1860–1861)
- South Carolina fears a northern-controlled government will act against slavery and withdraws from the Union
- Several other slave states follow South Carolina's lead and form the Confederate States of America

Northern reactions to secession were also varied. Some northerners felt the nation would be better off without the slave states. Others wanted to let the South secede in peace. "If the Cotton States shall become satisfied that they can do better out of the Union than in it, we insist on letting them go," wrote Horace Greeley in the *New York Tribune*.

But other northerners worried about the long-term effects of letting Southern secession take place. President Lincoln told the leaders of the Republican Party, "We must settle this question now, whether in a free government the minority have the right to break up the government whenever they choose."

Buchanan, the outgoing president, agreed that secession was illegal but said that the Constitution gave the federal government no power to prevent it. He also questioned whether a Union held together by force was worth saving.

Forming the Confederacy In February 1861, representatives of the seven seceded states met in Montgomery, Alabama, to form a new nation. They quickly wrote a constitution that specifically recognized slavery and guaranteed the rights of citizens to own slaves. They chose **Jefferson Davis**, a former United States senator from Mississippi, as president, with Alexander Stephens of Georgia as vice president. The new constitution created an association of states called the **Confederate States of America**, also known as the Confederacy.

The Confederacy soon faced challenges and many internal disagreements. It had no currency, and the job of printing Confederate money was at first contracted out to a company in New York. President Davis had to hold the first meeting of his cabinet in a hotel room. He named one man from each state to the cabinet so that all seven Confederate states would be equally represented.

Attempts at compromise fail As the North and the South drew further apart, some Americans desperately sought ways to resolve the crisis and avoid war. In December 1860 both the House and Senate appointed special committees to suggest possible solutions.

One plan, the Crittenden Compromise, proposed several constitutional amendments. One would ban slavery north of the old Missouri Compromise line and guarantee that slavery would not be interfered with south of that line. Others would compensate slaveholders for escaped slaves and would stop Congress from interfering with the transport of slaves between states.

Powerful leaders in both North and South opposed the Compromise. For many southerners, no compromise could undo their main reason for secession—Lincoln's election. Lincoln remained publicly silent on the suggested compromises but privately opposed any plan that allowed the extension of slavery. The Senate defeated it and other compromise plans.

On March 4, 1861, Lincoln became president. In his inaugural address, he again promised not to interfere with slavery where it existed. Would this promise save the Union?

READING CHECK Identifying the Main Idea What was the principle behind the Confederacy?

SECTION 1 ASSESSMENT

HSS 11.1.3

Reviewing Ideas, Terms, and People

1. **a. Define** Briefly define each of these terms: **Compromise of 1850, Fugitive Slave Act, Kansas-Nebraska Act**
   b. Analyze What effect did the Mexican War have on the issue of slavery in the United States?
   c. Evaluate Was **popular sovereignty** a good solution to the question of slavery in new states?

2. **a. Identify** Who were John Brown, Dred Scott, and James Buchanan?
   b. Explain How did the Fourteenth and Fifteenth Amendments affect the *Dred Scott* decision?

3. **a. Recall** What were the **Lincoln-Douglas debates**, and why were they important?
   b. Explain How did **Abraham Lincoln**'s background influence his views on slavery?
   c. Predict Was Lincoln an abolitionist? Explain.

4. **a. Identify** Who was **Jefferson Davis**?
   b. Analyze Why did the states of the Lower South secede and form the **Confederate States of America**?
   c. Evaluate How did attitudes toward secession vary in northern and southern states?

Critical Thinking

5. **Sequencing** Copy the chart below and use it to trace Lincoln's rise from state legislator to president.

FOCUS ON SPEAKING

6. **Expository** As a senator from a northern state, write and present a speech explaining your views on the principle of popular sovereignty.

SECTION 2 The Civil War

BEFORE YOU READ

MAIN IDEA
The Civil War broke out following a Confederate attack on Fort Sumter, leading to widespread fighting, heavy casualties, and the eventual defeat of the Confederacy.

READING FOCUS
1. How did the Civil War begin, and what were some early battles?
2. What was life like during the Civil War?
3. How did continued fighting turn the tide of the war?
4. What happened in the final phase of the war?

KEY TERMS AND PEOPLE
Fort Sumter
Robert E. Lee
Battle of Bull Run
Ulysses S. Grant
Battle of Shiloh
Battle of Antietam
Emancipation Proclamation
Battle of Chancellorsville
Battle of Gettysburg
Thirteenth Amendment

HSS 11.1.4 Examine the effects of the Civil War and Reconstruction and of the industrial revolution, including demographic shifts and the emergence in the late nineteenth century of the United States as a world power.

HSS 11.3.2 Analyze the great religious revivals, including the Civil War revivals.

SHOWDOWN at Fort Sumter

◀ Confederate cannons fire upon Fort Sumter.

THE INSIDE STORY *Where was the first shot of the Civil War fired?* Fort Sumter, in Charleston harbor in South Carolina, was one of the few places in the South still in Union hands in April 1861. It had become a symbol of the South's rebellion against the federal government, and Confederate leaders demanded its surrender. Abraham Lincoln, the new president, faced a dilemma. The fort was desperately short of supplies. If Lincoln surrendered the fort, it might reassure the South that the North did not want war. On the other hand, it would anger northerners who did not want to treat the Confederacy as a separate nation.

So, Lincoln said that he would send in only nonmilitary supplies. That left the decision to fight up to Confederate president Jefferson Davis. Davis decided on action, and on April 12, 1861, Confederate artillery opened fire on Fort Sumter. The fort's defenses were no match for the massive guns, and it quickly surrendered. On April 14, Confederates hauled down the American flag and raised a Southern flag in its place.

The Civil War Begins

The shots fired at **Fort Sumter** marked the beginning of the Civil War. In response, Lincoln called for 75,000 volunteers to serve in the army for 90 days. Northerners rushed to enlist. The call for volunteers forced slave

THE UNION IN CRISIS **123**

FACES OF HISTORY

Abraham LINCOLN
1809–1865

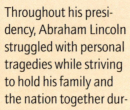

Throughout his presidency, Abraham Lincoln struggled with personal tragedies while striving to hold his family and the nation together during the Civil War. In 1862 Abraham and Mary Todd Lincoln's 11-year-old son William died of typhoid fever in the White House.

Struck with grief over the loss of their son, the Lincolns sunk into depression. The First Lady took William's death especially hard. The president struggled in the midst of a war that was going badly to care for his wife and to grieve for the loss of his son. Lincoln often resorted to humor and storytelling to overcome his grief. He explained to a friend that "if it were not for these stories [and] jokes . . . I should die."

Summarize Why was Lincoln's presidency especially difficult?

states still in the Union to choose a side. All refused to provide troops to fight against fellow southerners. Then on April 17, Virginia seceded. In May, the Confederate states Arkansas, Tennessee, and North Carolina followed.

Border states choose sides Leaders on both sides wondered what Delaware, Kentucky, Maryland, and Missouri would do. They were border states—slaveholding states still in the Union, on the border of the Confederacy. Delaware had few slaveholders, and most people believed it would stay in the Union. In the other border states, however, secessionist sympathies were strong.

Maryland was the most critical state. If it seceded, Washington, D.C., would be surrounded by Confederate territory. Lincoln took strong steps. He sent federal troops to guard sites with military value and placed parts of Maryland temporarily under military rule. In November 1861, the military oversaw new elections in which a pro-Union state legislature was elected.

Missouri was important because it could control the lower Mississippi River, while Kentucky controlled some 500 miles of the Ohio River, its northern border. Loyalties were divided in both states. Missouri secessionists never were politically strong enough to force the state to withdraw from the Union. Kentucky joined the Union side after Confederate troops invaded it in September 1861.

Goals of the North and South As war began, the North and South had different goals. Lincoln defined the Union goals very carefully. To keep the support of border states and non-abolitionists, he avoided making slavery the central issue. Instead, he asked northerners to fight to save the Union.

The South's war goals were simple: to be left alone with slavery unchanged. The Confederates were ready for a defensive war. That meant northern armies would have to invade the South. Still, the North was better equipped for war than the South. It had a larger population. The Northern also contained most of the nation's factories and most of its railroad lines.

The Confederates had fewer resources than the North, but they were fighting to preserve their way of life. They also believed in their military superiority. Many of the nation's best army officers were from the South. Many, like **Robert E. Lee** of Virginia, chose to side with their home states and fight for the Confederacy.

Some southerners thought the South's greatest advantage was its huge cotton exports to textile mills in Britain and France. They thought that if war disrupted that supply, both nations would come to their aid. Foreign aid and the recognition of southern independence became important goals in the Confederate war strategy.

When Britain and France did not recognize the Confederacy, the South stopped exporting cotton to them. Nonetheless, efforts to gain or block foreign help remained important in the strategies of both sides during the Civil War.

Tactics and technology Most of the top generals on both sides had been trained at the U.S. Military Academy at West Point. They had learned tactics from earlier wars, and many had used them in the Mexican-American War.

The weapons on Civil War battlefields, however, were far more deadly than in earlier wars. Weapons makers had redesigned gun barrels, increasing the range and accuracy of the new rifles. Other new weapons were exploding shells, flamethrowers, and machine guns. The Civil War also saw the first use of observation balloons. Camouflage was used to disguise tents and guns from airborne observers.

The telegraph, invented by Samuel Morse in the 1840s, allowed officers in the field to communicate quickly with government leaders. For the first time in history, railroads were used to move large numbers of troops and supplies. This collision of tactics and technology is why some historians call the Civil War the last of the old-time wars and the first of the modern ones.

The Battle of Bull Run The first major battle of the Civil War came in July 1861 at the Bull Run, a small stream about 25 miles from Washington, D.C. Confederate troops waited at the small town of Manassas Junction. Neither army was trained nor ready for battle, and inexperienced troops could not carry out their generals' plans.

The battle soon became chaos. The Union retreat turned into a panicky stampede as soldiers and onlookers fled the battlefield. The **Battle of Bull Run** ended both sides' hopes for a short war.

War in the West Gaining control of the Mississippi River Valley would split the Confederacy in two. In early 1862 Union forces under General **Ulysses S. Grant** opened two important water routes into the western Confederacy. Then Grant moved south, winning a major victory at the **Battle of Shiloh** in Tennessee. But the fierce battle ended northern hopes that the rebellion would collapse on its own.

A Union fleet under Admiral David Farragut moved north along the Mississippi. They captured New Orleans and other river cities.

War in the East Union general George B. McClellan had a plan to attack the Confederate capital at Richmond, but he delayed, asking for more troops. In May 1862 Confederate general Robert E. Lee took command of the Confederacy's Army of Northern Virginia. Lee took advantage of McClellan's caution. In August

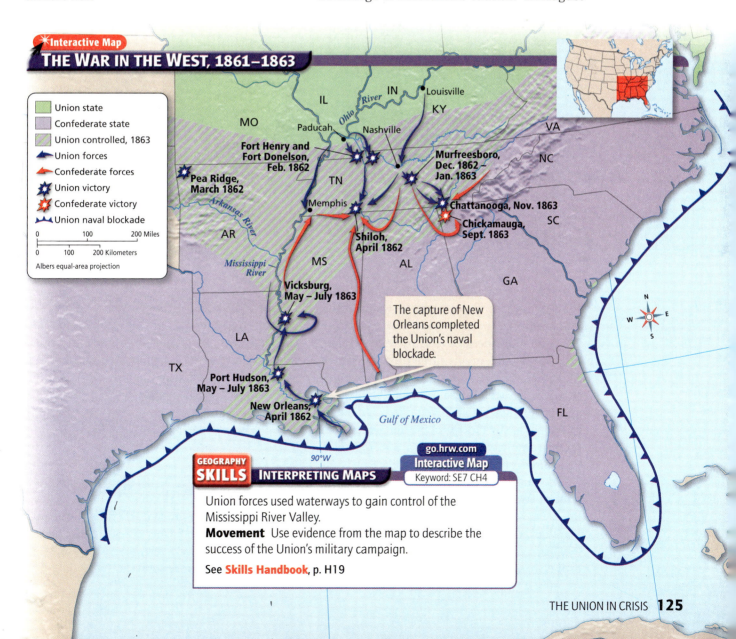

THE WAR IN THE WEST, 1861–1863

GEOGRAPHY SKILLS INTERPRETING MAPS

Union forces used waterways to gain control of the Mississippi River Valley.
Movement Use evidence from the map to describe the success of the Union's military campaign.
See **Skills Handbook**, p. H19

The capture of New Orleans completed the Union's naval blockade.

THE UNION IN CRISIS

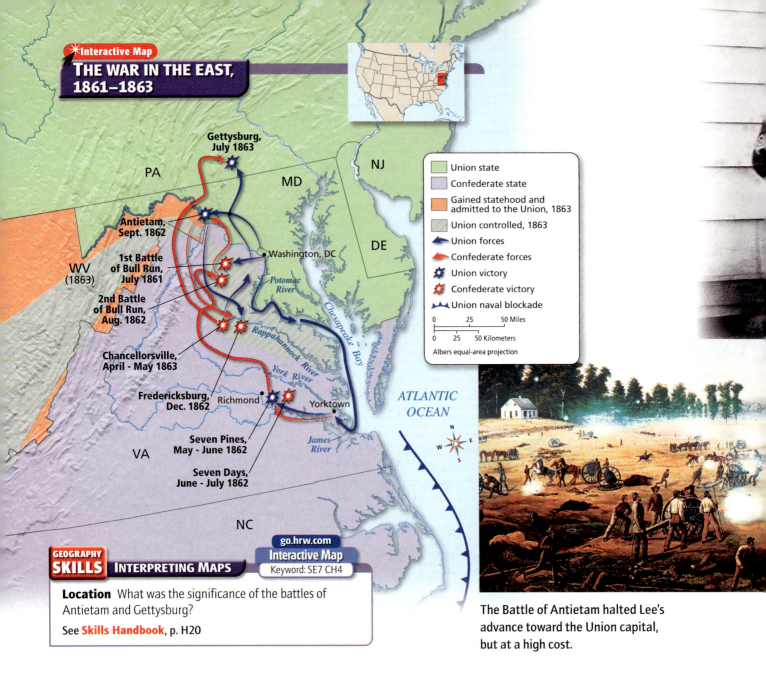

Interactive Map
THE WAR IN THE EAST, 1861–1863

GEOGRAPHY SKILLS INTERPRETING MAPS

Location What was the significance of the battles of Antietam and Gettysburg?

See **Skills Handbook**, p. H20

The Battle of Antietam halted Lee's advance toward the Union capital, but at a high cost.

1862 he lured a Union force into battle near Manassas, Virginia. In the Second Battle of Bull Run, Confederates won another victory.

The defeats in Virginia hurt morale in the North. Lee suggested to President Davis that it was time to take an offensive strategy and invade Maryland. A victory on Union soil might force the North to ask for peace, or it might convince Great Britain and France to recognize Confederate independence.

In early September 1862, Lee's army crossed the Potomac River into western Maryland. The 70,000 Union troops there dwarfed Lee's army of 40,000. But the always-cautious McClellan again delayed, giving the Confederates time to organize their defenses. The **Battle of Antietam**, on September 17, 1862, was the bloodiest day of the Civil War. Union and Confederate casualties combined exceeded 23,000. In the end Antietam was considered a Union victory, but only because Lee's invasion was stopped and he returned to Virginia.

READING CHECK Drawing Conclusions Why did Lee want to invade the North?

Life during the Civil War

The Civil War presented challenges, hardships, and opportunities for people in the North and the South. Both soldiers and civilians were affected as the war progressed.

African American Union Soldiers
Company E of the District of Columbia 4th U.S. Colored Infantry defends Fort Lincoln. About 10 percent of the Union forces were African American.

African Americans and the war In the South, the labor of enslaved African Americans helped to provide the food the South needed and allowed white males to fight in Confederate armies. Thousands of slaves, however, escaped to join invading Union troops. Many were hired to drive wagons, build forts, or serve as guides.

As the fighting continued, some northerners came to believe that preserving the Union was not enough. They wanted to punish the South and free its enslaved workers. On January 1, 1863, President Lincoln issued the Emancipation Proclamation. This document freed enslaved people in all areas that were in rebellion against the United States. Reactions in the North were mixed. Some northerners opposed the Emancipation Proclamation; others believed it did not go far enough.

The Emancipation Proclamation encouraged freedmen (the term for emancipated slaves) to join the Union forces. African American soldiers served in segregated units, usually commanded by white officers. Nearly 180,000 African Americans served in the Union armies during the war.

Conditions for soldiers Most soldiers who died during the Civil War did not die from wounds. Disease was by far the greatest killer. Epidemics of mumps, measles, and smallpox swept through army camps. Other illnesses were caused by poor sanitation and polluted water. Volunteers in the new U.S. Sanitary Commission, mostly women, worked as nurses and ambulance drivers. They distributed food, clothing, and medical supplies to Union troops and inspected hospitals and army camps.

Civil War soldiers spent most of their time in camp. Days were long and frequently boring. The men took part in drills, practicing battlefield maneuvers. Between drills, they wrote letters and played card games or baseball. In both the North and the South, prayer meetings were held in army camps, and a religious revival took place.

Conditions for prisoners of war were far worse than conditions in the camps. A large number of major battles in 1863 and 1864 overwhelmed camps that were already inadequate. The most notorious prisons were the Confederate stockade near Andersonville, Georgia, and the Union prison camp near Elmira, New York.

The home front The Civil War meant sacrifice and hardship for people on both sides. Conditions in the South, however, were quite different than they were in the North.

Since most Civil War battles were fought in the South, there was widespread property damage there. Also, shortages of both food and goods made life extremely difficult. Food riots took place in Richmond and other cities. Southerners also faced serious inflation, an increase in prices as the value of money fell. To pay for the war, the Confederate government had printed a great deal of paper money, which soon lost its value.

The Generals QUICK FACTS

Ulysses S. Grant
- Graduated West Point in 1843
- Rank: 21 in a class of 39
- Age in May 1864: 42
- Previous major victories: Battle of Shiloh, Siege of Vicksburg, Battle of Lookout Mountain, Battle of Missionary Ridge
- Grant's wife was a cousin of Confederate general James Longstreet.

Robert E. Lee
- Graduated West Point in 1829
- Rank: 2 in a class of 46
- Age in May 1864: 57
- Previous major victories: Second Battle of Bull Run, Battle of Fredericksburg, Battle of Chancellorsville
- Lee's great uncle, Richard Henry Lee, proposed and signed the Declaration of Independence.

In 1862 the Confederate Congress enacted the first military draft in United States history. In 1863 the Union also began to draft soldiers, causing riots across the North. The unrest added to an antiwar movement led by some Democrats in Congress and state legislatures. Their supporters called them Peace Democrats, but critics compared them to poisonous snakes, calling them Copperheads. Copperhead propaganda seriously threatened the Union war effort. The federal government arrested and jailed without trial some of the most vocal Copperheads.

Women and the war Women in both North and South contributed to the war in many ways. Some disguised themselves as men and enlisted in the army. A few served as spies. Women took over farms, plantations, stores, and businesses while men went to fight. Some did factory work or staffed government offices. About 3,000 women served the Union army as nurses. Some women, like Clara Barton, who later began the American Red Cross, cared for the wounded on the battlefield.

READING CHECK **Making Inferences** How did the Emancipation Proclamation affect the war?

Fighting Continues

The Civil War tore apart American society, but it was also an international event. Union naval blockades disrupted the South's trade with the rest of the world. At the beginning of the war, it was fairly easy to run, or slip through, the Union blockade. Gradually, the blockade of southern ports became tighter and tighter.

Blockade runners To get scarce goods, southerners depended on blockade runners. These low, sleek ships carried southern cotton to Caribbean ports, where it was unloaded and shipped to Europe. They returned with silk, soap, pepper, and other needed goods, making large profits. Later, blockade runners brought medicine and military supplies.

Hoping to break the Union blockade, the Confederates made an ironclad ship, which could withstand cannon fire. They covered a captured Union ship, the USS *Merrimack*, with thick iron plates and renamed it the *Virginia*. Union officials then built their own ironclad. On March 9, 1862, the Union's ironclad *Monitor* confronted the *Virginia* in the world's first battle between ironclads. The battle ended with no winner but changed naval warfare forever.

West of the Mississippi While most action was in the East, Union and Confederate forces also clashed west of the Mississippi River. There they fought over natural resources and additional soldiers for their armies. In 1861 Congress admitted Kansas to the Union as a free state, followed by Dakota, Colorado, and Nevada territories. It then created Idaho, Arizona, and Montana territories.

Lincoln appointed pro-Union officials to head the new territorial governments. To help ensure western loyalty, he did not enforce the draft in the West. Still, some 17,000 Californians joined the Union army. Moreover, western mines provided gold and silver to pay Union war costs.

More than 10,000 Native Americans took part in the Civil War, but issues of loyalty and slavery made the war controversial. Some nations saw it as a chance to take back land they had lost. Confederate agents negotiated treaties with the Cherokee, Creek, Choctaw, and others. But many Indian units fought with the Union army.

Three major battles After a disastrous loss at Fredericksburg in December 1862, the Union forces were ready to fight again by spring. General Joseph Hooker was now in command. Three major battles followed in 1862 and 1863:

- **Chancellorsville** Hooker hoped to surprise the Confederates from behind and take Richmond. But Lee marched most of his army west. He left 10,000 troops in Fredericksburg, ordering them to light campfires so Union forces would think a larger army was still there. Lee then ordered a surprise attack at dinnertime on May 2, 1862. The Battle of Chancellorsville was Lee's greatest victory (see illustration below).
- **Gettysburg** Lee then decided to invade the North again. The two armies met near Gettysburg, Pennsylvania. The skirmish that took place on July 1, 1863, developed into the historic three-day Battle of Gettysburg.

For two days, the armies held their positions facing each other on opposite ridges. Casualties were high. Then Lee ordered General George Pickett to take his 15,000 troops to attack the center of the Union lines on Cemetery Ridge. As Pickett's men charged across the open field, a storm of bullets and artillery shells tore huge holes in their ranks. Less than half returned to the Confederate lines.

The next day, the Confederates began their retreat to Virginia. Lee's 75,000 troops had suffered 28,000 casualties. The Union had about 23,000 casualties out of some 85,000 soldiers.

- **Vicksburg** Meanwhile, Grant was carrying on a siege of Vicksburg, a Confederate stronghold on the Mississippi. He aimed to starve its residents and defenders into surrender. For weeks, Union artillery and gunboats shelled the city. On July 4, as Lee began his retreat from Gettysburg, the Confederates at Vicksburg surrendered.

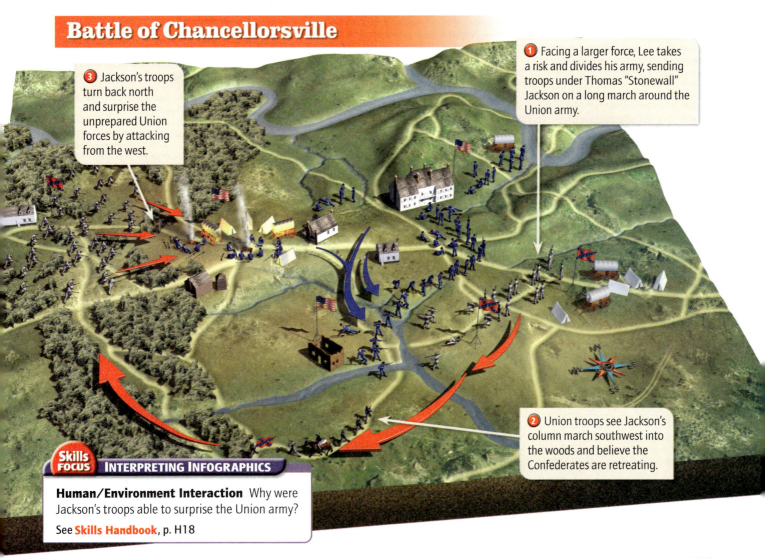

Battle of Chancellorsville

① Facing a larger force, Lee takes a risk and divides his army, sending troops under Thomas "Stonewall" Jackson on a long march around the Union army.

② Union troops see Jackson's column march southwest into the woods and believe the Confederates are retreating.

③ Jackson's troops turn back north and surprise the unprepared Union forces by attacking from the west.

Skills Focus INTERPRETING INFOGRAPHICS

Human/Environment Interaction Why were Jackson's troops able to surprise the Union army?
See Skills Handbook, p. H18

CAUSES AND EFFECTS OF THE CIVIL WAR

CAUSES
- Conflicts over slavery and states' rights
- Lincoln's election as president
- The secession of southern states
- The attack on Fort Sumter

EFFECTS
- The end of slavery
- More than 600,000 deaths
- Physical and economic devastation of the South
- The reuniting of the nation

Chattanooga campaign The Confederate losses at Gettysburg and Vicksburg were a turning point, pointing toward a Confederate defeat in the war. Then in September 1863, the Union army retreated to Chattanooga, an important railroad center in Tennessee, after being defeated at the Battle of Chickamauga in northwest Georgia. A Confederate siege trapped them in the city.

Confederate general Braxton Bragg prepared to starve the Union troops out. But in late October, Grant arrived with reinforcements and opened a supply line to the troops in Chattanooga. By late November 1863, Grant had enough troops to end the siege. Control of Chattanooga was an important step in his plan to invade Georgia, the heart of the Lower South.

READING CHECK **Drawing Conclusions** Why were Gettysburg and Vicksburg significant battles?

The Final Phase

Grant's victory at Chattanooga convinced Lincoln that the Union finally had a general who could win. In March 1864, Lincoln gave him command of all Union armies. Grant named General William T. Sherman to take his place on the western front.

Campaigns of 1864 Grant's first campaign moved the Army of the Potomac toward Richmond. Union and Confederate armies met in a dense forest near Chancellorsville. In May 1864 the fighting in the Battle of the Wilderness was so fierce that the woods caught fire. Despite heavy losses, Grant continued to push south. The two armies soon met again in a long and bloody series of clashes known as the Battle of Spotsylvania.

Fierce fighting and heavy loss of life continued. In June the armies met at the Battle of Cold Harbor. After a month of marching and fighting—without a victory—the Union soldiers' high spirits were gone. But Grant pressed on. Although he failed to capture Petersburg, a rail center south of Richmond, he began a siege of the city. This siege would cut supplies to the Confederate capital.

The next phase of the war began when Sherman set out on the long-expected invasion of Georgia. His army marched toward Atlanta, the South's second-most important manufacturing and rail center. By mid-July, they were just eight miles from Atlanta. Sherman laid siege to the city, and his artillery shelled it daily. Finally, he was able to close the last railroad line into Atlanta, forcing Confederate general Hood's troops to abandon the city. On September 2 the Union army entered Atlanta.

The election of 1864 While Sherman was besieging Atlanta, the Democratic Party was holding its national convention in Chicago. It chose George McClellan, a popular general, as its candidate and adopted a platform calling for an immediate end to the war.

The Republicans, hoping to broaden Lincoln's appeal, chose Andrew Johnson, a pro-Union Democrat from Tennessee as their vice-presidential candidate. But many believed it would not be enough. The Emancipation Proclamation and the mounting casualties from Grant's Virginia campaign had made the war highly unpopular in the North. Lincoln himself expected to lose the election.

Then word of Sherman's capture of Atlanta turned opinions around. The president easily defeated McClellan in the election. Lincoln's victory enabled Congress to finally pass the **Thirteenth Amendment**, which ended slavery in the United States.

As Lincoln began his second term in March 1865, the war seemed nearly over. He announced his intention to be forgiving to the South: "With malice toward none, with charity for all ... let us strive on to finish the work we are in, to bind up the nation's wounds."

The war ends After the November 1864 election, Sherman and some 60,000 troops set out to march across Georgia—Sherman's March to the Sea. As they left Atlanta, his troops burned much of the city. It was Sherman's belief that he had to strike at the enemy's economic resources. Over the next three weeks, Sherman's soldiers slaughtered livestock, destroyed crops, and looted homes and businesses. The army captured Savannah in December and then moved on to South Carolina.

In April 1865, the long siege of Petersburg succeeded. Confederate leaders fled Richmond. Union troops entered the city the next day. Lee tried to escape with what was left of his army, but he found himself surrounded. He surrendered rather than lose more lives.

Lee and Grant met in a home in Appomattox Court House, Virginia, on April 9. The two generals chatted briefly, then Grant presented the terms of the surrender. They were very generous for such a long, bitter conflict. Lee's troops merely had to turn over their weapons and leave. In cities across the North, news of Lee's surrender brought wild celebrations. Fireworks filled the sky in Washington, D.C. Tragically, President Lincoln did not live to see the official end of the war, when the last Confederates surrendered. Lincoln's assassination in April 1865 would change the course of American history.

Lee, in a quiet exchange, formally surrenders. He remarked that the generous terms would "have a very happy effect on my army."

READING CHECK **Summarizing** What were the major events of Sherman's invasion of the South?

SECTION 2 ASSESSMENT

HSS 11.1.4, 11.3.2

Reviewing Ideas, Terms, and People

1. a. Recall Why was **Fort Sumter** important to both the North and the South?
b. Identify Identify **Ulysses S. Grant** and **Robert E. Lee**.
c. Evaluate What was the strategic importance of the border states?

2. a. Identify What did the **Emancipation Proclamation** do?
b. Compare Which region—North or South—experienced greater hardship during the war? Why?
c. Evaluate Did conditions on the home front have an effect on the Civil War? Why or why not?

3. a. Recall Explain the importance of these battles: **Chancellorsville**, **Gettysburg**, Vicksburg, Chattanooga.
b. Explain How did Lincoln encourage loyalty to the Union in the West?
c. Elaborate Why do you think the Battle of Chancellorsville was considered Robert E. Lee's greatest victory?

4. a. Identify Who was William T. Sherman, and what was his role in the final phase of the war?

b. Sequence What events led to Lee's final surrender?
c. Elaborate Why do you think Grant offered Lee such generous surrender terms?

Critical Thinking

5. Identifying Cause and Effect Copy the graphic organizer below and use it to identify causes and effects of the South's surrender.

Causes → The South Surrenders

FOCUS ON WRITING ELA W1.1

6. Expository As President Lincoln, write a letter to a friend describing your thoughts about issuing the Emancipation Proclamation. Use details from the section to help explain your position on slavery.

THE UNION IN CRISIS 131

SECTION 3
Reconstruction

BEFORE YOU READ

MAIN IDEA
Conflicting plans for dealing with the post–Civil War South had long-lasting effects on government and the economy.

READING FOCUS
1. What were the differing plans for presidential Reconstruction?
2. What was congressional Reconstruction?
3. What happened when Radical Republicans took charge of Reconstruction?
4. Why did Reconstruction end, and what were its effects on American history?

KEY TERMS AND PEOPLE
Reconstruction
Ku Klux Klan
Civil Rights Act of 1866
Fourteenth Amendment
Fifteenth Amendment
scalawag
carpetbagger
sharecropping
tenant farming
Liberal Republicans

HSS 11.1.3 Understand the history of the Constitution after 1787 with emphasis on federal versus state authority and growing democratization.

HSS 11.1.4 Examine the effects of the Civil War and Reconstruction and of the industrial revolution, including demographic shifts and the emergence in the late nineteenth century of the United States as a world power.

Rebuilding the South

THE INSIDE STORY *What was the state of the South after the Civil War?* The nation faced great challenges at the end of the Civil War. The postwar recovery period, known as Reconstruction, lasted from 1865 to 1877. In the South the land had been ravaged; Richmond and other southern cities lay in ruins. Widespread fighting had devastated farms and plantations. Railroad lines had been destroyed. More than one-fifth of the South's white male population had perished.

The nearly 4 million African Americans living in the former Confederacy had won their freedom, but they faced an uncertain future with few job opportunities. Most had no money or education.

The nation also needed to answer many legal and political questions. What place would African Americans have in political life in the South? Were the former Confederate states conquered territories, or were they once again states in the Union? Should Confederates be forgiven or punished for starting the war?

▼ Southern cities such as Richmond needed rebuilding after the Civil War.

FINANCIAL COST OF THE CIVIL WAR
Southern livestock killed: **40%**
Southern farm machinery destroyed: **50%**
Drop in South's total property wealth: **66%**
Total national wealth held by the South, 1860: **30%**
Total national wealth held by the South, 1870: **12%**

Presidential Reconstruction

In December 1863 Lincoln issued a Proclamation of Amnesty and Reconstruction. It offered forgiveness to all southerners (except high-ranking Confederate leaders) who pledged loyalty to the Union and support for emancipation. When 10 percent of a southern state's voters had taken this oath, they could organize a new state government, which had to ban slavery. Under this Ten-Percent Plan, Lincoln readmitted three southern states—Arkansas, Louisiana, and Tennessee—before the war ended.

Lincoln's plan upsets Congress Lincoln's actions set off a debate in Congress over the best way to help the South after the war. The period of time when the United States made policies to rebuild the South is known as Reconstruction. Lincoln's Reconstruction plans were controversial for several reasons. Some Congressmembers noted that re-admitting states to the Union was a power of Congress, not the president. Others said that since secession was unlawful, Confederate states had never legally left the Union. Still others thought the states should go through the same admission process as territories.

In 1864 Congress responded with its own Reconstruction plan, the Wade-Davis Bill. It required a majority of a state's white male citizens to pledge loyalty to the Union before elections could be held. Lincoln killed the Wade-Davis Bill with a pocket veto—that is, by ignoring the bill for 10 days.

Lincoln is assassinated Abraham Lincoln did not live to see the war end or to carry out his Reconstruction plans. On April 14, 1865, John Wilkes Booth, a southerner, shot Lincoln while the president sat watching a play at Ford's Theater in Washington, D.C. Lincoln died the following morning.

Johnson's plan Lincoln's vice president, Andrew Johnson, was sworn in as president a few hours after Lincoln's death. Even though he was a Democrat, Republican leaders in Congress at first thought they could work with him. He did not seem to share Lincoln's forgiving attitude.

But Republican leaders did not understand his views. A Tennessean from a poor family, Johnson held no ill will toward the South but hated the wealthy planter class. In turn, many white southerners considered him a traitor. Johnson was determined to keep control of Reconstruction. His plan was similar to Lincoln's, but he added wealthy southern men to those who had to apply for a presidential pardon.

Charles Sumner, Thaddeus Stevens, and other powerful Republicans in Congress were troubled by Johnson's plan. One reason was that they felt it did not provide any role in government for freedmen, those who had been freed from slavery.

READING CHECK **Making Inferences** How did Johnson's background influence his views on Reconstruction?

Congressional Reconstruction

White southerners welcomed Johnson's plan, which let them form state governments on their own terms. They hoped to restore their old way of life. Former Confederates took state offices and were even sent to Congress.

Southern reaction Although southern leaders could not restore slavery, they passed laws called Black Codes. These gave freedmen certain rights, but their intent was to keep the former slaves in a dependent position and give planters a supply of cheap labor.

Black Codes varied from state to state. In most states, for example, former slaves—and sometimes whole families—had to sign one-year work contracts as plantation workers, which they could not break. In some states, freedmen could not own guns.

Throughout the South, local sheriffs and war veterans enforced the enactment of the Black Codes, invading homes and seizing property. Other white citizens formed private groups to maintain white control in the South. One such group was the Ku Klux Klan, which formed in 1866 and began terrorizing African Americans and whites who supported their rights.

Congress takes control At first, most northerners also supported Johnson's Reconstruction plan. They were eager to put the Civil War behind them and reunite the nation. But soon they were upset by Black Codes and the return of former Confederates to power.

ACADEMIC VOCABULARY
contract legal agreement

THE UNION IN CRISIS 133

That strengthened the Radical Republicans, members of Congress who wanted a stronger Reconstruction program. They favored tougher rules for restoring state governments. They wanted to reshape southern society, giving freedmen political and economic equality.

After Congress reconvened in 1866, moderate Republicans, who controlled both the House and the Senate, proposed two bills. One supported the Freedmen's Bureau, the organization created by Congress in 1865 to help former slaves and poor whites in the South. The new bill allowed the Freedman's Bureau to continue building schools and providing other aid. The second bill was the **Civil Rights Act of 1866**. This bill gave African Americans citizenship and guaranteed them the same legal rights as white Americans.

Both bills easily passed Congress, but President Johnson vetoed them. This dispute ended attempts by moderate Republicans to work with the president. They decided instead to help the Radical Republicans take control of Reconstruction plans.

Radical Reconstruction Worried that the Civil Rights Act of 1866 might be overturned, Republicans in Congress passed the **Fourteenth Amendment**. This amendment required states to grant citizenship to "all persons born or naturalized in the United States" and promised "equal protection of the laws." In effect, it wrote the Civil Rights Act of 1866 into the Constitution.

Johnson tried to make control of Reconstruction an issue in the 1866 congressional elections. But race riots in Memphis and New Orleans weakened his arguments. The election gave the Radicals enough votes in Congress to take control of Reconstruction. During 1867–1868 they passed, over Johnson's veto, four Reconstruction Acts.

These acts divided the South into five military districts. Three conditions for readmission were set: (1) ratify the Fourteenth Amendment; (2) write new state constitutions that guarantee freedmen the right to vote; (3) form new governments to be elected by all male citizens, including African Americans.

COUNTERPOINTS

Views on Reconstruction

Representative Thaddeus Stevens, a Radical Republican leader, insisted that the South be treated as a conquered territory.

❝ [W]e hold it the duty of the Government to inflict … punishment on the rebel belligerents, and so weaken their hands that they can never again endanger the Union … This can be done only by treating and holding them as a conquered people. ❞

Thaddeus Stevens, 1865

President Andrew Johnson, a southerner, argued that the southern states should not be denied their rights.

❝ [T]he policy of military rule over a conquered territory [implies] that the States [who took] part in the rebellion had by the act … ceased to exist. But the true theory is that all pretended acts of secession were from the beginning null and void. ❞

Andrew Johnson, 1865

SKILLS FOCUS READING LIKE A HISTORIAN

Recognizing Bias Why might President Johnson have been biased in favor of the South?

See **Skills Handbook**, p. H33

American Civil Liberty

Voting Rights

The Thirteenth Amendment ended slavery, and the Fourteenth Amendment granted citizenship to former slaves. Voting, however, remained under the control of the states. Although southern states had to grant African Americans voting rights in order to rejoin the Union, many southern whites objected. Many northern states also avoided granting voting rights to blacks.

In 1870 the Fifteenth Amendment established that "the right of citizens of the United States to vote shall not be denied or abridged by the United States or by any State on account of race, color, or previous condition of servitude."

Still, many states set other requirements that kept many African Americans from voting. Also, the Fifteenth Amendment did not give the vote to women. Native Americans could not vote because they were not considered citizens. Women were not granted the vote nationwide for another 50 years, and Native Americans did not have suffrage until after World War II.

Making Generalizations Why was the Fifteenth Amendment necessary?

Freedmen cast their votes, 1867

Afraid that Johnson might use his authority over the military to interfere with Reconstruction, Congress also passed the Tenure of Office Act in 1867. It required the Senate's permission to remove any official whose appointment it had approved.

This law set off the final battle between the president and Congress. Its focus was Secretary of War Edwin Stanton, an ally of congressional Republicans. Johnson believed the law was unconstitutional and to test it, fired Stanton. The House of Representatives then voted in February 1868 to impeach him for violating the act. After a six-week trial, the Senate fell one vote short of the two-thirds majority needed to convict Johnson and remove him from office.

READING CHECK **Making Inferences** Why was President Johnson impeached?

Republicans in Charge

Because Republicans had lost some support following the impeachment fight, they chose the hero of the Civil War, Ulysses S. Grant, as their presidential candidate in the election of 1868. The popular vote was close, but about a half million African American votes in the South gave Grant the victory.

To protect African American voting rights, Republicans quickly pushed the **Fifteenth Amendment** through Congress in February 1869. It protected the voting rights of African American males and went into effect in 1870.

New governments in the South As Congress took control of Reconstruction, political power in the South shifted. White southerners who supported the changes were labeled **scalawags**, or scoundrels, by ex-Confederates. The supporters were a varied group. Some were farmers who had not owned slaves and had opposed secession. They hoped to take power from the planter class. But some were planters who had been ruined by the war. Others were business leaders who wanted to end the South's dependence on agriculture.

Scalawags had allies—northerners who came south to take part in the region's political and economic rebirth. Southern critics called these northerners **carpetbaggers**, referring to a type of suitcase made of carpet fabric. They came from varied backgrounds, including politicians, teachers, Freedmen's Bureau officers, and former soldiers. Some of them were African American.

As carpetbaggers and scalawags took control of new state governments, they were joined by freedmen who wanted to utilize their new

ACADEMIC VOCABULARY
utilize make use of

ACADEMIC VOCABULARY
prejudice unfair judgments

rights. Nearly 700 African Americans served in southern state legislatures during Reconstruction. Sixteen were elected to Congress.

The new governments brought many changes to the South. They created the region's first public school systems and eliminated property requirements for voting and holding office. New laws made it illegal for railroads, hotels, and other public facilities to discriminate against African Americans. The Black Codes were repealed in every state.

Responses to freedom Freedom meant different things to formerly enslaved African Americans. For some, it meant the chance to search for long-lost relatives. For others it meant owning land or having a job. Many freedmen moved to urban areas, mainly in the South, but met prejudice and low-paying jobs. Some went West, becoming business owners, miners, soldiers, or cowboys. But most African Americans remained in the rural South.

Freed African American slaves eagerly sought education. The Freedmen's Bureau alone started more than 4,000 schools. Other groups, both black and white, founded schools and colleges in the South.

African Americans were now able to establish churches, which became centers of community life. They also created trade associations, fire companies, employment agencies, and mutual aid societies.

Economic changes For many freedmen, owning land was a symbol of freedom. But even freedmen with money found landowners unwilling to sell land to them because land would give former slaves economic independence. A new labor system gradually arose. Instead of working for wages, freedmen could receive a share of their employer's crop, a system known as **sharecropping**. By the end of the 1870s, most freedmen and many poor white southerners were sharecroppers. In this system, the employer provided land, seed, tools, a mule, and a cabin. The sharecropper provided labor.

A sharecropper who saved some money might switch to **tenant farming**. Tenant farmers rented their land from the landowner and could grow any crop. Many grew food crops, not cotton, to provide both food and income. It was hard for sharecroppers and tenant farmers to get out of poverty.

While the rural South suffered economic hardship, southern cities grew rapidly during Reconstruction. As railroads linked North and South, cities like Atlanta became business centers. Southern business leaders and northern investors joined to build textile mills and other ventures. But this industrial growth did not greatly benefit freedmen or other poor southerners.

READING CHECK **Contrasting** How did sharecropping and tenant farming differ?

Sharecropping and Poverty

HOPES RAISED AND DENIED

Slavery
- No rights
- Forced labor
- No freedom of movement without permission
- Family members sold away from one another
- No representation in government

Freedom
- Slavery banned
- Free to work for wages
- Could move and live anywhere
- Many families reunited
- Could serve in political office

Rights Denied
- Sharecropping system put in place
- Ability to vote and hold office restricted
- White leadership regained control of southern state governments

Much of Atlanta had been burned during the Civil War, but after the war it became the center of Reconstruction activity and Georgia's new state capital.

Reconstruction Ends

Violence plagued the South throughout the Reconstruction era. The hooded night riders of the Ku Klux Klan were the most active terrorists, but there were many similar groups. Many planters, merchants, and poor white farmers and laborers were united by a common desire to restore the old political and social order. Only a small minority of white southerners were active members, but others supported their goals.

African American leaders were the main targets of terrorist groups, but those groups threatened people of both races with house burnings and violence. They beat Freedmen's Bureau teachers and murdered public officials. Frightened state and local officials resigned.

When state governments could not control the violence, Congress passed three Enforcement Acts during 1870 and 1871. These laws set heavy penalties for anyone trying to prevent a qualified citizen from voting. The Enforcement Acts also gave the army and federal courts the power to punish Klan members.

Discontent with Reconstruction
Eventually, almost everyone became dissatisfied with Reconstruction. Many people were dismayed that the army was still needed to keep peace in the South and that the Republican state governments appeared to be ineffective.

African Americans were unhappy about their poverty and lack of land reform. Both white and black southerners were discouraged by the South's poor economic condition, in spite of costly building programs and other reforms. Southern critics also charged that Reconstruction governments were inefficient and corrupt.

Conditions in the South strengthened the Liberal Republicans, those who broke with the party over the Enforcement Acts and corruption scandals in the Grant administration. They helped Democrats regain power in Congress in 1872. Then a depression that began in 1873 turned Republican leaders' attention away from Reconstruction.

Impact of Reconstruction
By the mid-1870s it was clear that Reconstruction was on the decline. Its fiercest leaders, Thaddeus Stevens and Charles Sumner, had died. Supreme Court decisions had weakened its protections. In the Slaughterhouse Cases (1873), the Court said that most civil rights were under state control and so were not protected by the Fourteenth Amendment.

As support for Reconstruction declined, southern Democratic leaders and their supporters grew bolder. Lawlessness increased, and terrorists openly threatened and even murdered Republican candidates. When Mississippi's governor asked for help from the

Causes and Effects of Reconstruction

CAUSES
- President Johnson allows ex-Confederates to take control of southern states.
- Ex-Confederates treat freedmen badly.
- Congress and Radical Republicans take charge of southern states and help freedmen.
- Freedmen join northern Republicans to control state governments.
- White southerners resist and regain control.

EFFECT
Freedmen lose many of their gains.

federal government in 1875, President Grant refused, saying that the South's continuing problems had tired the northern public.

Divided rule in the South also directly affected the disputed presidential election of 1876. In the election, Ohio's Republican governor, Rutherford B. Hayes, ran against Democratic candidate Samuel J. Tilden, who was the governor of New York. Tilden narrowly won the popular election and also finished ahead in the electoral college vote. Yet because of several disputed votes, Tilden was one vote short of the majority he needed to win the presidency.

The election of 1876 was finally resolved by a compromise. A Republican-dominated commission gave the disputed votes to Hayes. In return, Republicans agreed to withdraw the remaining federal troops from the South. Without federal protection, the last Republican state governments collapsed. Reconstruction came to an end.

Despite its failures, Reconstruction did affect the nation's future development. The Fourteenth and Fifteenth Amendments, which were part of the Radical program to give former slaves citizenship and the right to vote, also gave those rights to African Americans in the North. The passage of the Fifteenth Amendment also increased calls for women's voting rights.

After Reconstruction ended some southerners referred to their region as the New South. Nevertheless, while the late 1800s and early 1900s were a time of industrialization and economic change in the South, in other ways the region remained just as it had been before the Civil War.

READING CHECK **Making Inferences** In what ways did states' rights issues affect civil rights laws during Reconstruction?

SECTION 3 ASSESSMENT

HSS 11.1.3, 11.1.4

go.hrw.com
Online Quiz
Keyword: SE7 HP4

Reviewing Ideas, Terms, and People

1. **a. Identify** Who was John Wilkes Booth?
   b. Explain What legal and political questions had to be answered after the war ended?
   c. Elaborate What were some objections to Lincoln's original plan for **Reconstruction**?

2. **a. Describe** Write a brief description of each term: Black Codes, Freedmen's Bureau, **Ku Klux Klan**
   b. Explain What was the relationship between the **Civil Rights Act of 1866** and the **Fourteenth Amendment**?
   c. Evaluate How valid were Congress's reasons for trying to impeach President Johnson?

3. **a. Recall** Who were **scalawags** and **carpetbaggers**?
   b. Compare What were the differences between sharecropping and **tenant farming**?
   c. Predict What did freed African Americans do to improve their own futures?

4. **a. Recall** What groups in the South wanted a return to prewar conditions?
   b. Make Inferences Why were violent acts against African Americans often not punished?
   c. Predict What were the lasting effects of the **Fourteenth** and **Fifteenth Amendments**?

Critical Thinking

5. **Identifying Cause and Effect** Copy the flowchart below and record the events that led to the end of Reconstruction.

Reconstruction ends

FOCUS ON WRITING ELA W1.1

6. **Persuasive** As a newspaper editor in the South in the 1870s, write an editorial criticizing or defending Reconstruction.

CHAPTER 4

Chapter Review

History's Impact video program
Review the videos to answer the closing question: How did the three amendments passed after the Civil War help the civil rights movement a century later?

Reviewing Key Terms and People

Match each numbered definition with the correct term from the chapter.

1. Five laws to preserve the nation based on Henry Clay's resolutions
2. A law making it illegal to help runaway slaves
3. The winner of the 1860 presidential election
4. The president of the Confederacy
5. Announcement freeing enslaved African Americans in all areas that were in rebellion against the United States
6. Southern general in command at Gettysburg
7. A farming system that replaced the wage labor system
8. Group of white citizens that terrorized African Americans
9. Northern Republicans who came to the South to take part in the region's rebirth
10. Southerners who supported changes brought by Reconstruction
11. Amendment requiring states to grant citizenship to "all persons born or naturalized in the United States," promising "equal protection of the laws"

Comprehension and Critical Thinking

SECTION 1 (pp. 116–122) HSS 11.1.3

12. **a. Identify** What political issue was behind the question of the expansion of slavery after the Mexican War?
    b. Analyze How did the Fugitive Slave Act cause more divisions between the North and South?

SECTION 2 (pp. 123–131) HSS 11.1.4, 11.3.2

13. **a. Identify** What major events of the Civil War occurred in 1863?
    b. Predict How might the war have been different if Lee had decided not to fight at Gettysburg?

SECTION 3 (pp. 132–138) HSS 11.1.3, 11.1.4

14. **a. Describe** How did legal challenges contribute to the decline of Reconstruction?
    b. Draw Conclusions In what ways was the election of 1876 a victory for the Democrats?

Using the Internet

go.hrw.com
Practice Online
Keyword: SE7 CH4

15. The Civil War was a long, complicated conflict marked by many complex battles. Using the keyword above, do research to learn more about one of the most important battles of the war. Then create a report on the fighting, people involved, or consequences of the Battle of Gettysburg.

Critical Reading HSS 11.1.4; ELA R2.4

Read the passage in Section 3 that begins with the heading "Economic changes." Be sure also to look at the accompanying visual, titled "Sharecropping and Poverty." Then answer the question that follows.

16. According to the passage, instead of working for wages, some freedmen could
    A receive benefits from the government.
    B receive a share of their employer's crop.
    C buy land of their own.
    D move to another state.

WRITING FOR THE SAT ELA W1.1

Think about the following issue:

Three important amendments—the Thirteenth, Fourteenth, and Fifteenth—were passed during Reconstruction. Under Johnson's Reconstruction program, however, the southern states passed Black Codes restricting the rights of African Americans. Subsequent laws continued to weaken the impact of the Reconstruction amendments.

17. **Assignment** Did Reconstruction ultimately help African Americans gain more rights? Write a short essay in which you develop your position on this issue. Support your point of view with reasoning and examples from your reading and studies.

THE UNION IN CRISIS 139

CHAPTER 5
1860–1920
An Industrial NATION

THE BIG PICTURE In the 60 years following the Civil War, the United States became the world's leading industrial nation. New inventions drove a Second Industrial Revolution, in which new systems of transportation and communication transformed American life. Economic opportunity drew millions of immigrants, and the United States expanded its territories westward.

California Standards

History-Social Sciences

11.2 Students analyze the relationship among the rise of industrialization, large-scale rural-to-urban migration, and massive immigration from Southern and Eastern Europe.

11.3 Students analyze the role religion played in the founding of America, its lasting moral, social, and political impacts, and issues regarding religious liberty.

 READING LIKE A HISTORIAN

This factory in Springfield, Massachusetts, filled tracks all over the world with railroad cars. It was one factory that supplied the growing United States with everything from steam engines and freight trains to trolley cars.
Interpreting Visuals What opportunities does such a large-scale industry represent?

See **Skills Handbook**, p. H30

The Granger Collection, New York

 U.S.

1864 U.S. troops kill 150 Cheyenne in Sand Creek Massacre.

1871 600,000 cattle travel on the Chisholm Trail.

1860 — **1870**

 World

1864 China's Taiping Rebellion ends, leaving 20 million Chinese dead and causing mass emigration.

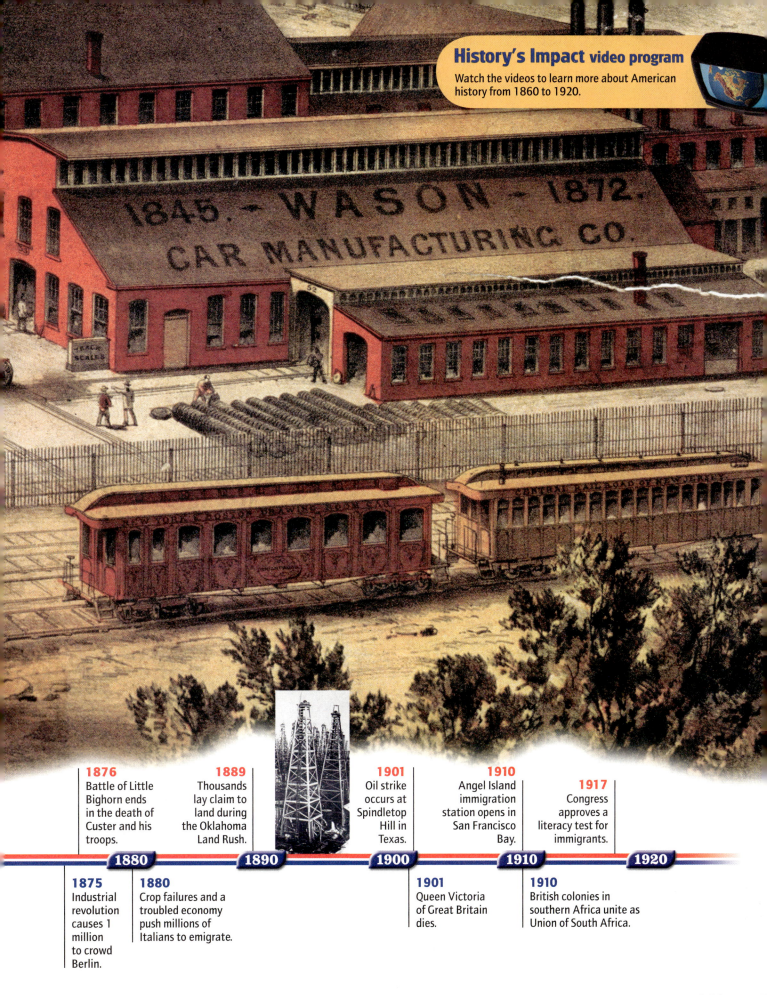

History's Impact video program
Watch the videos to learn more about American history from 1860 to 1920.

1876 Battle of Little Bighorn ends in the death of Custer and his troops.

1889 Thousands lay claim to land during the Oklahoma Land Rush.

1901 Oil strike occurs at Spindletop Hill in Texas.

1910 Angel Island immigration station opens in San Francisco Bay.

1917 Congress approves a literacy test for immigrants.

1880 | 1890 | 1900 | 1910 | 1920

1875 Industrial revolution causes 1 million to crowd Berlin.

1880 Crop failures and a troubled economy push millions of Italians to emigrate.

1901 Queen Victoria of Great Britain dies.

1910 British colonies in southern Africa unite as Union of South Africa.

SECTION 1
The American West

BEFORE YOU READ

MAIN IDEA
As Native Americans gradually lost their battle for their lands in the West, settlers brought in new enterprises—mining, ranching, and farming.

READING FOCUS
1. How did changing government policies lead to conflicts with Native Americans in the West?
2. How did mining and ranching influence the development of the West?
3. What opportunities and challenges did farmers face on the Great Plains?

KEY TERMS AND PEOPLE
Sand Creek Massacre
Battle of the Little Bighorn
Sitting Bull
George Armstrong Custer
Wounded Knee Massacre
Chief Joseph
Geronimo
Dawes Act
Chisholm Trail
Homestead Act

HSS 11.2.2 Describe the changing landscape, including the growth of cities linked by industry and trade.
HSS 11.2.3 Trace the Americanization movement.
HSS 11.2.5 Discuss corporate mergers that produced trusts and cartels and the economic and political policies of industrial leaders.

◀ Some Plains Indians hoped the Ghost Dance would help them reclaim their former way of life.

THE INSIDE STORY

What would you do to save your culture? By the 1890s Native American cultures were dying. People had lost their homes and their way of making a living. The Sioux, especially, were starving. In despair, many Indians turned to traditional religion and a prophet who gave them hope.

The prophet was Wovoka, also called Jack Wilson, a shaman of the Northern Paiute in Nevada. He was believed to have the power to heal and to bring rain. Working for white farmers, Wovoka learned the beliefs of several Christian sects, including the Presbyterians, Mormons, and Shakers. In 1889 during a solar eclipse, he had a vision. In his dream, he spoke with God in heaven, where he saw many who had died. He was told to bring the Indians a message and a special sacred dance. Most accounts say that his message told people not to steal or lie or go to war. People were to perform the Ghost Dance five nights in a row. Wovoka promised that a messiah, a savior, would save them.

The Ghost Dance movement spread widely in the central Plains. In their visions, dancers saw the great buffalo herds returning and settlers leaving the West. But while the Ghost Dance offered many Indians hope, when it reached the Sioux it led to a tragedy at Wounded Knee.

Conflicts with Native Americans

The Ghost Dance was an expression of deepest grief about the loss of Native Americans' ways of life. As white settlers began streaming into the West, Native Americans and white settlers clashed over control of the land. U.S. government actions compounded the tensions.

The Sioux, Blackfoot, and Cheyenne of the northern Plains and the Kiowa and Comanche of the southern Plains thrived thanks to the abundance of wild buffalo, their main source of food and clothing. The Plains Indians traveled the great grasslands on horseback, following the migrations of the buffalo. They did not believe that land should be bought and sold.

Most white settlers were farmers or town dwellers. They believed that land should be divided and claims given to people to farm or establish businesses. If Native Americans would not settle down in one place, many settlers believed, then their lands were available for the taking.

142 CHAPTER 5

Government policy In the mid-1800s the U.S. government's Indian policy underwent a major change. Previously the army had forcibly removed Native Americans from the East and relocated them farther west. But by the 1850s growing numbers of white settlers wanted to move into those western lands as well.

So instead of pushing the Native Americans farther westward, the government began seizing their land and sending them to reservations. The goal was to break the power of the Plains Indians and open up their lands for settlement. Americans generally agreed with this new policy.

For Plains Indians, being confined to these reservations threatened their buffalo-centered way of life. The vast buffalo herds that had supported them for countless generations were now being driven to extinction as more settlers moved west.

The Indian Wars Tensions between Plains Indians, settlers, and the U.S. Army grew into a long period of violence known as the Indian Wars. Settlers often broke treaties. Many army commanders believed that the Indians must simply be wiped out.

- **Sand Creek Massacre (1864)** The U.S. Army had persuaded a group of Cheyenne to stop raiding farms and return to their Colorado reservation peacefully. But then army troops attacked, killing about 150 people, and burned the camp. Congress condemned the actions but did not punish the commander.
- **Battle of the Little Bighorn (1876)** To stop raids on settlers in Sioux territory, the government ordered all Sioux to leave. Instead, led by **Sitting Bull**, thousands of Sioux, Cheyenne, and Arapaho gathered near the Little Bighorn River. There a young cavalry officer, **George Armstrong Custer**, led a headlong attack

ACADEMIC VOCABULARY
policy settled plan or procedure

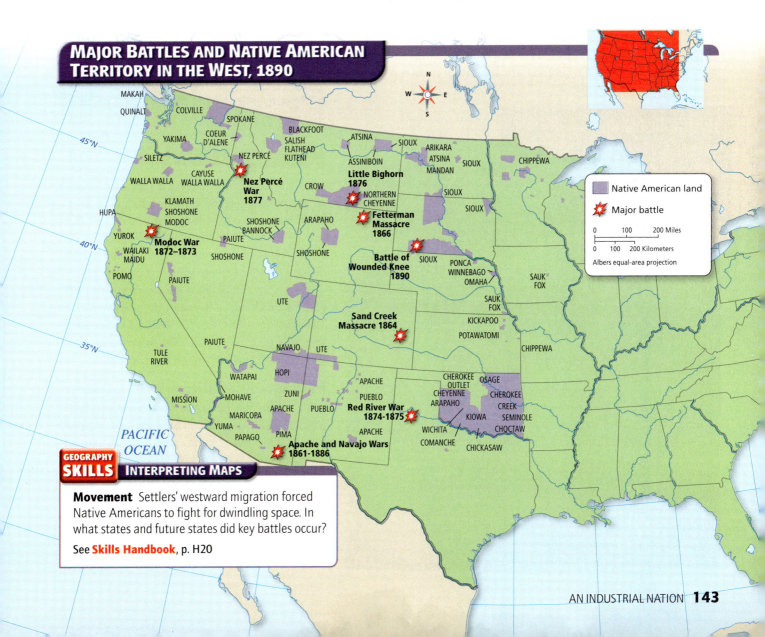

MAJOR BATTLES AND NATIVE AMERICAN TERRITORY IN THE WEST, 1890

GEOGRAPHY SKILLS INTERPRETING MAPS

Movement Settlers' westward migration forced Native Americans to fight for dwindling space. In what states and future states did key battles occur?

See **Skills Handbook**, p. H20

AN INDUSTRIAL NATION 143

ACADEMIC VOCABULARY
traditional dealing with inherited customs

THE IMPACT TODAY
Daily Life
To this day Wounded Knee remains a symbol of injustice toward Native Americans. In 1973 so-called Wounded Knee II, a standoff between the federal agents and Indians protesting discrimination, ended in the deaths of two Indian activists.

against the far larger force. Custer and his men were slaughtered. It was a great victory for the Sioux, but it was their last.

- **Wounded Knee Massacre** (1890) In December 1890, Army troops captured some of Sitting Bull's followers and took them to a camp at Wounded Knee Creek. The next morning soldiers demanded the Indians' rifles, and fighting broke out. The soldiers had machine guns and quickly killed many Sioux warriors. Women and children fled, but soldiers pursued them. In the end, some 300 Sioux men, women, and children lay dead in the snow. The massacre shocked Americans and broke Native American resistance on the Plains.

Resistance ends in the West In 1877 the government ordered the Nez Percé to move to a smaller reservation in Idaho. On the way, a few angry young men killed several white settlers. The Nez Percé and their leader, **Chief Joseph**, fled toward Canada with the army in pursuit. When they finally had to surrender, the chief said: "My heart is sick and sad. From where the sun now stands, I will fight no more forever."

Meanwhile, in the Southwest, the government had moved the Apache to a reservation in Arizona. The Apache leader **Geronimo** fled the reservation and led raids on the Arizona-Mexico border for years. He and his followers were captured one last time in September 1886 and held as prisoners of war.

Reservation life One goal in creating Indian reservations was the policy of Americanization. Officials wanted Indians to abandon traditional culture and identity and to live like white Americans. The Bureau of Indian Affairs, the federal agency that managed Native American reservations, set up government schools for Indian children, often far from their homes. Students had to speak English and could not wear traditional clothing.

The **Dawes Act** (1887) broke up some reservations and divided the land among individuals. But often the government sold the best land and gave the rest to the Indians. Even when Indians received good land, many could not afford the supplies needed for farming.

READING CHECK **Making Inferences** Why did the government adopt a policy of Americanization?

Mining and Ranching

After the California gold rush, each new gold or silver strike inspired a new rush to the West. In 1859 prospectors found silver in the Carson River valley in Nevada Territory. This rich mine, the Comstock Lode, yielded about $500 million worth of silver in the next 20 years.

The last major gold strike came in 1896 along the Klondike River in the remote Yukon Territory on the Canada-Alaska border. Over the next year, some 100,000 Americans made the treacherous journey to the Klondike.

Mining communities Most prospectors were men, though some families and single women also came. They came from the United States and other countries. Mining camps were usually just groups of tents or shacks. Some camps grew into towns with dirt streets, wooden sidewalks, stores, and saloons. As more families arrived, towns turned into thriving communities with churches, schools, and newspapers. A few of these communities, grew into major cities, such as Denver, Colorado.

Hydraulic Mining
Large-scale operations used high-pressure hoses to loosen dirt. Hydraulic mining was banned in 1884 because of its negative effects on the environment.

CATTLE TRAILS AND THE RAILROADS, 1870s

GEOGRAPHY SKILLS INTERPRETING MAPS

Movement Describe how cattle made their way from Texas to markets in the north. Use the map key to help you.

See **Skills Handbook**, p. H19

Mining as a business At first, individual prospectors worked the mines with hand tools. Some found gold by simple methods such as panning—washing gold out of loose sand or gravel. When the surface deposits of gold ran out, machinery was needed. By the 1880s mining was dominated by large companies.

Most miners then went to work for mining companies instead of hoping to strike it rich on their own. They dug mine shafts, built tunnels, and drilled out the ore. It was dangerous, with an constant threat of cave-ins, explosions, and flooded mines. In some places miners tried to organize unions to negotiate for better working conditions, but mining companies resisted.

Ranching on the Plains In the decades after the Civil War, a new business came to dominate the economy of the Plains—cattle ranching. The first cattle ranchers in the West were the Spanish, who brought cattle from Spain in the 1500s. The Spanish, and later the Mexicans, became skilled at raising cattle in a harsh environment. They interbred Spanish and English cattle to develop a new breed—the Texas longhorn—that thrived on the Plains. Longhorns were hardy, did not need much water, and could live on grass alone.

The Spanish also brought sheep ranching to the Plains. In the Southwest, Navajos and Pueblos took up raising sheep. Sheep ranching expanded after the Civil War as New England mills increased their demand for raw wool. However, cattle ranchers believed that sheep destroyed the grasslands by eating the roots. Conflicts between sheep owners and cattle owners became violent as they competed for grazing land on the open range.

Cattle drives After the Civil War, the East's demand for beef grew as city populations expanded. By 1866 a steer worth about $4 in Texas sold for $40 in the East. So ranchers hired cowboys to drive a herd of cattle to a railroad town, where they would be shipped to meat-packing centers such as Chicago.

AN INDUSTRIAL NATION **145**

Several major cattle trails ran from Texas cattle country to rail centers in the North. One of the most important of these trails was the Chisholm Trail, which began in San Antonio and ended in Kansas.

Cattle drives usually lasted three months. Cowboys gently urged the cattle along the trail for 10 or 12 miles a day. Pushing the herd faster could cause a stampede. About two-thirds of the cowboys were white teenage boys aged 12 to 18, but there were many African American and Hispanic cowboys and even a few women.

Ranching as big business Cattle owners often had trouble managing their herds on the open range. Then an inventor patented barbed wire, a fencing material made of twisted wire with sharp barbs. Ranchers enclosed their grazing land with barbed-wire fences.

Between 1882 and 1886, more than 400 cattle corporations, financed by outside investors, sprang up in Wyoming, Montana, Colorado, and New Mexico. Cattle ranching became big business. However, the enclosure of the open range led to conflicts between landless cattle owners and the ranchers and farmers who fenced their land.

READING CHECK **Identifying Cause and Effect** Why did sheep and cattle ranchers clash?

THE IMPACT TODAY
Science and Technology
Today land-grant colleges make higher education widely accessible. Famous universities such as Michigan State and Texas A&M are at the forefront of technological research and innovation.

Farmers on the Great Plains

An early visitor to the Great Plains called the region the Great American Desert, saying it was "unfit for cultivation." But a few decades later, with encouragement from the government, people began pouring onto the Great Plains to build farms.

In 1862 Congress passed three acts to encourage settlement. The Homestead Act allowed any head of household over age 21 to claim 160 acres of land. Each homesteader was required to build a home on the land, make improvements, and farm the land for five years before receiving full ownership. Nearly 2 million people attempted to claim land under the Homestead Act.

Under the Pacific Railway Act, governments gave millions of acres to railroad companies to encourage them to build railroads and telegraph lines. The railroads used some of the land and sold the rest to settlers. To attract settlers, railroads ran newspaper ads in the East and in Europe, praising the wonders of the West.

Finally, a new law called the Morrill Act gave the states land to build colleges to teach "agriculture and the mechanic arts." This was the first federal government assistance for higher education.

HISTORY CLOSE-UP
Oklahoma Land Rush

Between 1889 and 1895, five land runs drew thousands of new settlers to Oklahoma. The largest land run occurred in 1893. Settlers claimed seven million acres of land in an area known as the Cherokee Outlet on September 16, 1893.

Around 100,000 settlers rushed to claim land in the Cherokee Outlet.

Homesteaders await the trumpet calls, gunshots, and even cannon blasts that will signal the start of the land run.

The Oklahoma Land Rush As you read in a previous chapter, a number of Native American nations had been moved to Indian Territory (present-day Oklahoma). In 1879, however, a lobbyist discovered that some 2 million acres had not been assigned to any nation. A presidential order banned entry into Indian Territory, but settlers still tried to claim the land. Political pressure grew, and in 1889, it was opened to settlers.

On April 22, 1889, would-be settlers lined up on the Oklahoma border. At a signal, some 50,000 people rushed into the Oklahoma interior, staking claims on some 11,000 homesteads. Towns sprang up overnight, though not all settlers remained.

The new settlers Most of the people moving West after the Civil War came because of certain push-pull factors. The push factors are the reasons they left their homes. The pull factors are the reasons they moved to the West.

- **White settlers** White settlers came mainly from states in the Mississippi Valley, which had once been considered the frontier. They were mostly middle-class farmers or businesspeople, who could afford supplies and transportation.
- **African American settlers** In the late 1870s African Americans began a massive migration West. Some left because of the discriminatory Black Codes and violence by groups such as the Ku Klux Klan.

  Rumors spread that the federal government would set Kansas aside for former slaves. While it was not true, some 15,000 African Americans moved there. They became known as Exodusters.
- **European settlers** Economic opportunity attracted thousands of northern Europeans, especially land-poor Scandinavians and Germans. Irish who had come to work on the railroads settled on the Plains. Mennonites (a Protestant sect) from Russia brought their experience of farming on the steppes to the Great Plains.
- **Chinese settlers** By the 1880s some of the Chinese who had immigrated for the California gold rush or railroad jobs turned to farming. They helped establish California's fruit industry. Because laws often barred Asians from owning land, many became farmworkers, not owners.

Challenges and solutions Farming on the Plains presented new challenges and hardships.

Like many frontier towns, Perry, Oklahoma, began to emerge within days of the opening of the Cherokee Outlet.

Skills Focus: INTERPRETING VISUALS

Chaotic settlement patterns led to some conflicts between homesteaders and the people known as boomers and sooners. These were people who staked claims before the territory was legally opened to settlers.
Making Inferences What other types of conflicts do you think might have arisen in the land rush?

See **Skills Handbook**, p. H7

AN INDUSTRIAL NATION **147**

Cause and Effects of Western Migration

CAUSE
- Americans continue moving west in large numbers.

EFFECTS
- Traditional Native American ways of life are destroyed.
- Mining communities are established.
- Ranches are established, and the cattle industry booms.
- Farmers settle on the Plains.

ACADEMIC VOCABULARY
thesis central idea

The climate was harsh, with bitter cold weather, high winds, and snow. Summer weather was fiercely hot, and water was scarce. Many families had to depend on wells with pumps powered by windmills. In the Southwest, some settlers learned irrigation techniques from Hispanic and Native American farmers.

Wood for houses was in limited supply, so many settlers used the earth itself. At first they quickly built dugouts, which were shelters dug into the sides of hills. More comfortable were sod houses, homes built from blocks of tough prairie soil.

New machinery helped farmers meet the challenge of farming on the Great Plains. The new technology included a new plow with a sharper edge as well as combine harvesters that cut wheat, separated out the grains, and removed the husks.

Large companies started giant bonanza farms, which were like factories with expensive machinery, professional managers, and specialized workers. They were profitable in good growing years but too expensive to survive bad years.

In 1890 the U.S. Census Bureau issued a momentous report that declared the frontier closed. There had been so many new settlements that they had broken up the open land, meaning that there no longer was a frontier area to be settled.

In 1893 the historian Frederick Jackson Turner wrote an essay on the thesis that the existence of the frontier had given the United States a unique history. Historians debated Turner's idea for decades afterward.

READING CHECK **Making Generalizations** What motivations brought settlers to the West?

SECTION 1 ASSESSMENT

go.hrw.com
Online Quiz
Keyword: SE7 HP5

HSS 11.2.2, 11.2.3, 11.2.5

Reviewing Ideas, Terms, and People

1. **a. Identify** Briefly explain the importance of each of these events: **Battle of the Little Bighorn, Wounded Knee Massacre, Dawes Act**
   b. Analyze What was at stake for each side in the Indian Wars?
   c. Evaluate What is your opinion about the process of Americanization carried out by the Bureau of Indian Affairs?

2. **a. Identify** What role did each of these play in the development of the West? **Comstock Lode, Texas longhorn, barbed wire**
   b. Summarize How did mining lead to the establishment of new towns in the West?
   c. Predict How would fencing in grazing lands change future development in the West?

3. **a. Recall** What was the intent of each of these laws? **Homestead Act, Pacific Railway Act, Morrill Act**
   b. Explain Which groups of people decided to move West? Why did they move?
   c. Develop What role, if any, do you think the frontier played in American history?

Critical Thinking

4. **Identifying Cause and Effect** Make a chart like the one below and list the effects of each of the government policies listed.

Policy	Effects
Americanization (BIA)	
Homestead Act	
Morrill Act	
Oklahoma Land Rush	

FOCUS ON WRITING ELA W1.1

5. **Narrative** As a homesteader who moved westward, write a letter to your family back East telling about your life on the Great Plains.

SECTION 2
The Second Industrial Revolution

BEFORE YOU READ

MAIN IDEA
During the late 1800s, new technology and inventions led to the growth of industry, the rise of big business, and revolutions in transportation and communication.

READING FOCUS
1. How did industry and railroads lead to the Second Industrial Revolution?
2. How did entrepreneurs and public attitudes help the rise of big business in the late 1800s?
3. What conditions prompted workers to organize in the late 1800s?
4. What advances in transportation and communication were made in the late 1800s?

KEY TERMS AND PEOPLE
entrepreneur
capitalism
laissez-faire
social Darwinism
John D. Rockefeller
Andrew Carnegie
Cornelius Vanderbilt
George Pullman
Sherman Antitrust Act
Thomas Alva Edison

HSS **11.2.1** Know the effects of industrialization on living and working conditions.

HSS **11.2.2** Describe the changing landscape, including the growth of cities linked by industry and trade and the development of cities.

HSS **11.2.6** Trace the economic development of the United States and its emergence as a major industrial power.

THE INSIDE STORY

How did oil fuel the Second Industrial Revolution? For years, people had found oil on the surface of coastal waters and lakes. In the mid-1800s people began to refine oil into kerosene to light lamps. In August 1859 in Pennsylvania, Edwin L. Drake drilled into the ground to try to extract oil. His crew hit a crevice deep in the rock, and oil seeped up. Drake had drilled the first commercial oil well. He was soon steadily pumping oil to the surface.

Wildcatters, or oil prospectors, went looking for oil in other places. In January 1901, some struck oil at Spindletop Hill near Beaumont, Texas. The discovery kicked off an oil boom in Texas. Spindletop produced more than 17 million barrels of oil in 1902, but its output soon declined.

The oil boom in Texas lasted less than 20 years but had long-term consequences. Many of the world's leading oil companies got their start at Spindletop. Later, they would refine crude oil into gasoline and other petroleum products, fueling a revolution in transportation and industry.

OIL BOOM

▶ Wooden derricks line Spindletop's Boiler Avenue in Texas in 1903.

AN INDUSTRIAL NATION **149**

Industry and Railroads

The boom in the oil industry was only one part of what became known as the Second Industrial Revolution. During this period of time, new technology led production to skyrocket, particularly in the steel and oil industries. This increased production in turn created advances in technology and transportation, most notably the American railroad system.

Making steel In the 1850s a new method called the Bessemer process made steel-making faster and cheaper. In 1873 American steel mills turned out about 115,000 tons of steel. By 1910 output had soared to 24 million tons, making the United States the world's top producer of steel.

Steel helped transform the United States into a modern industrial economy. It was used to make railroad locomotives and rails, bigger bridges, and taller buildings. Factories equipped with steel machinery could turn out more manufactured goods. The low cost of steel also made it practical for everyday items such as nails and wire.

Railroads expand In the 1850s train tracks already crisscrossed the Northeast and reached into the Southeast and the Great Lakes area. Between 1865 and 1890 the number of miles of railroad track jumped nearly fivefold. The federal government helped by giving the railroads millions of acres of land. Cheap steel also helped the railroads expand.

Congress authorized two companies to build rail lines to the West Coast. For six and a half years, workers raced to complete the first transcontinental railroad—one that crossed

GEOGRAPHY SKILLS INTERPRETING MAPS

1. **Region** How many time zones was the continental United States divided into?
2. **Place** What region had the most railroads? Why do you think this might have been so?

See **Skills Handbook**, p. H20

the country. The Union Pacific laid tracks westward from Omaha. The work went fairly quickly because much of the land was prairie or gently rolling hills. Central Pacific workers laid track from the west, starting in Sacramento, California. These workers labored on tough terrain, crossing deserts and blasting tunnels through mountains on the California-Nevada border. They also faced Indian attacks.

On May 10, 1869, the two rail lines met at Promontory Summit in Utah Territory, linking east and west. Throughout the country, railroads expanded, creating a vast railroad network. Railroads promoted trade and provided jobs. The railroads also speeded up settlement of the West, cutting travel time from months to days. Wherever railroads were built, new towns sprang up.

Railroads led to the adoption of standard time. Until then, people kept time according to the position of the sun. When it was noon in Chicago, it was 12:07 p.m. in Indianapolis and 12:31 p.m. in Pittsburgh. Michigan had at least 27 different local times. Running a railroad, though, required accurate timekeeping. A New York school principal proposed dividing the earth into time zones. All communities within a single time zone would set their clocks alike. Railroad officials enthusiastically embraced this idea. In 1918 Congress adopted standard time for the nation.

READING CHECK **Making Inferences** How did the railroads help westward expansion?

The Rise of Big Business

Big business prospered in the late 1800s because of **entrepreneurs**—risk takers who started new ventures within the economic system called free enterprise or **capitalism**, in which most businesses are privately owned. Under **laissez-faire** capitalism (French for "allow to do" or "leave alone"), companies operated without government interference.

There were huge inequalities under capitalism, but some people explained them by a philosophy known as **social Darwinism**. In studying nature, British scientist Charles Darwin had concluded that members of a species compete for survival. Stronger members adapt to the environment and thrive while weaker ones gradually die out in a process called natural selection. Social Darwinists believed that natural selection also applied to society. Stronger people, businesses, and nations would prosper. Weaker ones would fail.

New business organization In response to changes in industry, a new type of business organization developed. The corporation is a business with the legal status of an individual. Corporations are owned by people who buy stock, or shares, in the company. A board of directors makes decisions; corporate officers run day-to-day operations.

Corporate organization had advantages. To expand, a corporation can raise money by selling stock. Stockholders can lose only the amount of money they have invested in the business. Finally, a corporation can continue to exist after its founders leave.

Competition in the 1800s was fierce. To gain dominance, some competing companies merged to form a trust. A board of trustees ran the companies like a single corporation. When a trust gained complete control over an industry—such as sugar—it held a monopoly. It had no competition and could raise prices or lower quality at will.

Industrial tycoons As businesses grew ever larger, some corporate leaders amassed staggering fortunes. Historians refer to this time period as the Gilded Age.

John D. Rockefeller's company, Standard Oil, started as an oil refinery. To increase profits, he used vertical integration—acquiring companies that supplied the oil business, such as pipelines and railroad cars. He also practiced horizontal integration by taking over other refineries. By 1875 Standard Oil refined half of all the oil in the United States. Rockefeller gave away huge amounts of his wealth to colleges and other good causes.

Andrew Carnegie was a poor boy from Scotland who came to the United States when he was 12. He worked for the Pennsylvania Railroad, began to invest, then founded his own company and rose to the top of the steel business. By 1899 the Carnegie Steel Company dominated the American steel industry. In 1901 Carnegie sold the company to banker J. P. Morgan for $480 million and retired. He devoted his time and fortune to building public libraries and financing education.

COUNTERPOINTS

Social Darwinism

William Graham Sumner was the leading proponent of social Darwinism in the United States.

" If . . . men were willing to set to work with energy and courage . . . all might live in plenty and prosperity. But if they insist on remaining in the slums of great cities . . . there is no device . . . which can prevent them from falling victims to poverty and misery or from succumbing in the competition of life to those who have greater command of capital. "

William Graham Sumner, c. 1885

Walter Rauschenbusch lived among the poor in New York City. He found fault with the attitude of the rich toward the working class.

" Competitive commerce exalts selfishness to the dignity of a moral principle. It pits men against one another in a gladiatorial game in which there is no mercy and in which ninety percent of the combatants finally strew the arena . . . If the rich had only what they earned, and the poor had all that they earned . . . life would be more sane. "

Walter Rauschenbush, 1908

Skills Focus — READING LIKE A HISTORIAN

Identifying Points of View How does each man find fault with either the working class or the wealthy?
See **Skills Handbook**, pp. H28–H29

Cornelius Vanderbilt began investing in railroads during the Civil War. Soon his holdings stretched west to Michigan and north to Canada. Vanderbilt also gave money to education. **George Pullman** made his fortune by designing and building sleeper cars that made long-distance rail travel more comfortable. In 1881 he built a company town near Chicago for his employees. The town of Pullman had comfortable homes, shops, a church, and a library, but the company controlled many aspects of life.

Some Americans viewed the tycoons of the late 1800s as robber barons, destroying competitors with tough tactics. Others, however, saw them as captains of industry, using their business skills to strengthen the economy.

Mass marketing Retail merchants were also looking for new ways to maximize their profits. They turned to new forms of marketing—including clever brand names and advertising aimed at women.

In the cities, the department store made shopping easier. Instead of going from store to store, shoppers could find many different goods under one roof in separate departments for clothing, cookware, and so on. In rural areas, people could now purchase a huge variety of goods—from shoes to entire houses—from the catalogs sent out by mail-order companies.

READING CHECK **Summarizing** What were the advantages of forming a corporation?

Workers Organize

In the laissez-faire climate of the late 1800s, the government had little concern for workers. Many industrial workers were scraping by on less than $500 per year. Meanwhile, the rich were very, very rich. By 1890 an estimated 10 percent of the population held 75 percent of the nation's wealth.

The government grew uneasy about the power of corporations. In 1890 Congress passed the **Sherman Antitrust Act**, which made it illegal to form trusts that interfered with free trade. The act was ineffective, however, since the government prosecuted only a few companies.

ACADEMIC VOCABULARY
maximize make as large as possible

The American workforce Many factory workers were European immigrants; others were rural Americans who came to the cities for work. African Americans generally held lower-paying jobs as laborers or household help.

Many industrial workers were children. By 1900 about one in six children ages 10 to 15 held a job outside the home. Workers often worked 12 to 16 hours a day, six days a week, in unhealthy conditions. They had no paid vacation, no sick leave, and no compensation for workplace injuries, which were common.

By the late 1800s working conditions were so bad that more workers began to organize. By banding together, organized labor hoped to pressure employers into giving better pay and safer workplaces. The first effective group was the Knights of Labor, founded in Philadelphia in 1869. Under the leadership of Terence V. Powderly, the Knights accepted unskilled workers, women, African Americans, and even employers. The Knights campaigned for an eight-hour workday, the end of child labor, and equal pay for equal work. At first, the union preferred boycotts and negotiation to strikes. But strikes soon became a common tactic.

- **The Great Railroad Strike** The first major rail strike came in 1877. Protesting against cuts in wages, workers for two railroads blocked the movement of trains. Strikes spread, stopping most freight traffic for over a week. Clashes between strikers and militia led to numerous deaths. Mob violence in Pittsburgh caused millions of dollars in damage. The army finally ended the Great Railroad Strike.
- **The Haymarket Riot** In 1886 there were about 1,500 different strikes over wage cuts, some involving violent clashes with employers and police. In Chicago, crowds gathered in Haymarket Square to protest police action. Someone threw a bomb, and people panicked. Before the riot ended, 11 people were dead and more than 100 injured.

People immediately blamed foreign-born unionists for the violence. Police eventually charged eight men—all with foreign-sounding names—with conspiracy and murder. With little evidence, all eight were convicted and sentenced to death. Four of the men were hanged, and one killed himself in prison. The others were later pardoned.

Setbacks for organized labor Employers then struck back. They forced employees to sign documents saying they would not join unions. They blacklisted troublemakers. But unions kept on organizing. In 1886 a group of workers led by Samuel Gompers formed the American Federation of Labor (AFL). The AFL won wage increases and shorter workweeks.

In a labor dispute in 1892, at the Carnegie Steel Company in Homestead, Pennsylvania, workers seized the plant. Private guards hired by the company tried to take control, and a 14-hour battle left 16 people dead. The Homestead strike seriously hurt the steelworkers' union.

Other unions suffered setbacks, too. In 1893 the Pullman Company laid off a third of its employees and severely cut the wages of the rest. Eugene V. Debs, head of the American Railway Union, urged his members not to work on trains that included Pullman cars. The government ordered the union to call off the strike because it interfered with delivering the U.S. mail. Federal troops moved in, and the Pullman strike collapsed. Workers who had taken part were fired or blacklisted. The late 1800s remained the era of big business.

READING CHECK Identifying the Main Idea
Why did factory workers organize unions?

THE IMPACT TODAY

Daily Life
The federal government and all 50 states now have child labor laws to protect minors. These laws set minimum ages for different kinds of work and limit the hours that children may work.

ACADEMIC VOCABULARY

labor workers considered as a group

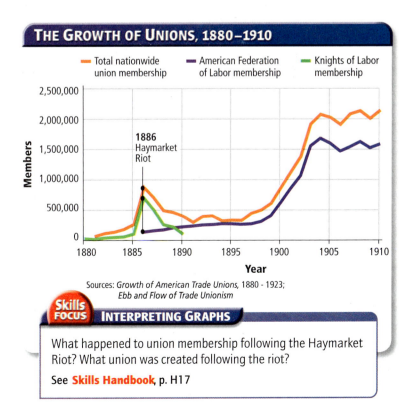

THE GROWTH OF UNIONS, 1880–1910

Sources: *Growth of American Trade Unions, 1880 - 1923; Ebb and Flow of Trade Unionism*

Skills Focus INTERPRETING GRAPHS

What happened to union membership following the Haymarket Riot? What union was created following the riot?

See **Skills Handbook**, p. H17

Advances in Transportation and Communication

Railroads made long-distance travel easier, but Americans also needed ways to travel locally. Growth of cities led to developments in mass transit—public transportation systems that carry large numbers of people along established routes. At the same time, Americans invented ways to communicate over long distances.

A transportation revolution Important advances in transportation during the Second Industrial Revolution included:
- **Streetcars** Horse-drawn passenger vehicles were the earliest mass transit. By the 1830s, horsecars, or streetcars, were rolling along rails in the street. In cities with steep hills, such as San Francisco, cable cars were built, which latched onto a moving cable underground. By 1900 most cities had electric streetcars, or trolleys, powered by overhead electrical wires.
- **Subways** As American cities grew, street traffic became a serious problem, especially in urban centers such as Boston and New York. The city of Boston found a solution — the subway. Boston opened the first subway line in the United States in 1897; the New York subway opened in 1904.
- **Automobiles** While mass transit was growing, inventors were also experimenting with vehicles for personal use. A German engineer invented the internal combustion engine, and soon inventors were trying to use it in a "horseless carriage." In 1893 Charles and Frank Duryea built the first practical American motorcar. The early automobiles were for the wealthy few who could afford them.
- **Airplanes** For centuries human beings had dreamed of flying. Two American brothers were the first to build a successful airplane. On December 17, 1903, Orville and Wilbur Wright flew their tiny airplane at Kitty Hawk, North Carolina.

A communications revolution Inventors also changed the way Americans communicated in the 1800s.
- **Telegraph** In 1837 Samuel F. B. Morse patented his method for sending messages instantly over wires with electricity. Telegraph operators tapped out patterns of long and short signals—now called Morse code—that stood for letters of the alphabet. After the Civil War, the telegraph grew with the railroads. Telegraph wires were strung on poles along the railroad tracks. Train stations had telegraph offices. The telegraph became the fastest way to send messages.

The First Flight

Brothers Orville and Wilbur Wright developed the first successful motorized aircraft in 1903, opening up the skies to travel.

Orville Wright flew 10 feet into the air for a distance of 120 feet. His 12-second flight made history.

Later that same day, Wilbur Wright flew the plane 852 feet in a flight lasting 59 seconds.

- **Telephone** Though two inventors devised ways to transmit voices by electricity, Alexander Graham Bell patented his design first, in 1876. By 1900 there were more than a million telephones in offices and households.
- **Typewriter** Many inventors tried to create a writing machine. Christopher Latham Sholes, a Milwaukee printer, developed the first practical typewriter in 1867. He later improved it by designing the keyboard that is still standard for computers today. The typewriter could produce legible documents very quickly. Businesses began to hire women as typists, opening up new job opportunities for many American women.

Thomas Edison One of America's most amazing inventors was **Thomas Alva Edison**. In 1876 Edison opened his own research laboratory in Menlo Park, New Jersey. He hired assistants with scientific and technical expertise, encouraging them to think creatively and work hard. Edison spent hours testing ideas. He and his team soon invented the first phonograph and a telephone transmitter. Edison became known as the Wizard of Menlo Park.

Edison was the first to come up with a safe electric lightbulb that could light homes and street lamps. He then undertook a new venture—bringing an electricity network to New York City. In 1882 he installed a lighting system powered by his own electric power plant. Similar electric power plants were built all over the country. Edison and his team later invented a motion picture camera and projector. In all, Edison had more than 1,000 U.S. patents.

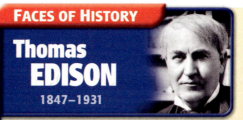

FACES OF HISTORY
Thomas EDISON
1847–1931

Thomas Edison attended school for only a few months. He began work at the age of 13, selling newspapers. Edison spent his spare time reading about science. At the age of 20, he created his first invention, an electric vote recorder, but few people were interested. Edison vowed to only invent things people would use.

Edison made good on his word. His next invention, a new stock ticker, earned him $40,000. He used the money to set up a laboratory. Edison generated hundreds of new inventions including the phonograph, the lightbulb, and movies. He also established businesses to manufacture his new gadgets for Americans to use and enjoy.

Explain Why did Edison decide to invent things people would use?

READING CHECK **Identifying the Main Idea** How did technology change communication in the late 1800s?

SECTION 2 ASSESSMENT

HSS 11.2.1, 11.2.2, 11.2.6

go.hrw.com
Online Quiz
Keyword: SE7 HP5

Reviewing Ideas, Terms, and People

1. **a. Describe** How did new steel-making technology help American industry grow?
   b. Explain What was the importance of oil to the Industrial Revolution?
   c. Develop What would be the long-term effects of the transcontinental railroad?
2. **a. Recall** What was **laissez-faire capitalism**?
   b. Analyze What was innovative about the department store?
   c. Predict Why would business leaders welcome the philosophy of **social Darwinism**?
3. **a. Identify** Explain the significance of the Knights of Labor, Samuel Gompers, and Eugene V. Debs.
   b. Analyze What groups of people worked in factories during the late 1800s?
4. **a. Recall** What types of mass transit were used in the 1800s?
   b. Make Inferences Why did railroads and the telegraph expand together?
   c. Evaluate How important are Edison's inventions in American life today?

Critical Thinking

5. **Comparing and Contrasting** Copy the chart below and analyze the similarities and differences between streetcars and private automobiles.

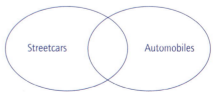

FOCUS ON WRITING ELA W1.1

6. **Expository** As an admirer of the inventor Thomas Edison, write a letter explaining why you would like to work in his research laboratory.

AN INDUSTRIAL NATION

SECTION 3
Life at the Turn of the Twentieth Century

BEFORE YOU READ

MAIN IDEA
A new wave of immigrants came to America in the late 1800s and settled in rapidly changing cities where political corruption was common and minorities faced discrimination.

READING FOCUS
1. Who were the new immigrants of the late 1800s, and what challenges did they face?
2. What was urban life like at the turn of the twentieth century?
3. How did political scandals lead to reform in the late 1800s?
4. What types of segregation and discrimination did African Americans and other minorities encounter?

KEY TERMS AND PEOPLE
Ellis Island
Americanization
tenement
settlement house
Jane Addams
social gospel
Populist Party
Jim Crow laws
lynching
Booker T. Washington
W. E. B. Du Bois

HSS **11.2.3** Trace the Americanization movement.
HSS **11.2.4** Analyze the effect of urban political machines.
HSS **11.2.7** Analyze the ideologies of Social Darwinism and Social Gospel.
HSS **11.2.8** Examine the effect of political programs and activities of Populists.
HSS **11.3.4** Discuss the expanding pluralism that resulted from immigration.

THE INSIDE STORY *What was it like to move to the United States at the turn of the century?* For many years, immigrants had been moving to the United States in search of new homes and better lives. At the turn of the twentieth century, a new wave of immigration to the United States was well underway. Between 1880 and 1910, millions of immigrants came to America, mostly from southern and eastern Europe. In American cities they built tight-knit communities that reflected the communities they had left in Europe.

In 1900 New York City's Mulberry Street, shown below, was home to a large population of Italian immigrants. At the turn of the century, it was common for families from the same town in Italy to move to the same street in an American city. These new Italian American communities maintained many of the same cultural traditions they had back home in Italy. Although immigrant groups faced difficult living conditions, families joined together to help one another. Mulberry Street remains part of New York City's Little Italy neighborhood today.

A Snapshot of 1900

▼ Italian immigrants pose for a photograph on New York City's Mulberry Street in 1900.

PRIMARY SOURCES

Political Cartoon

This cartoon appeared in 1893. Its caption reads: "They would close to the new-comer the bridge that carried them and their fathers over." The shadow figures in the cartoon represent previous immigrants.

These characters represent wealthy "old immigrants" opposed to new immigrants.

The clothing and items carried by this immigrant are typical of a poor person from Eastern Europe.

SKILLS FOCUS: READING LIKE A HISTORIAN

1. **Interpreting Political Cartoons** What do the shadow figures look like?
2. **Making Inferences** Was the artist a nativist?

See **Skills Handbook**, p. H31

New Immigrants

The United States has been called a nation of immigrants. Of all the groups who made America, only Native Americans have not come from somewhere else. Between 1800 and 1880, more than 10 million immigrants came to the United States. These "old immigrants" were mainly from northern and western Europe. Chinese immigrants also arrived for the Gold Rush or to work on the railroads.

Between 1880 and 1910, however, a new wave of immigration brought some 18 million newcomers to America. Most came from places in southern and eastern Europe, including Greece, Italy, Poland, and Russia. Because of severe immigration laws, smaller numbers came from East Asia.

These "new immigrants" made America more diverse in ethnicity and religion. They included people of Roman Catholic, Greek Orthodox, Russian Orthodox, and Jewish faiths. By 1910 nearly one out of every seven Americans was foreign-born.

Coming to America People came to America in search of a better life, but they left their homelands for various reasons. Jews in particular fled Russia and eastern Europe to escape religious persecution. Emigrants left southern and eastern Europe because of desperate poverty and little economic opportunity.

The U.S. government opened an immigration station in 1892 on **Ellis Island** in New York Harbor. Over the next 62 years, some 12 million Europeans passed through Ellis Island.

After 1910 newcomers from Asia passed through Angel Island, an immigration station in San Francisco Bay. Because of discriminatory laws, many Chinese immigrants were held in prison-like conditions for weeks or months, awaiting a ruling on whether they could stay.

While many immigrants found a better life in the United States, they also met hardships. Many lived in crowded tenements and took low-paying, unskilled jobs. Many settled near others from their homeland, who spoke their language and shared their culture.

AN INDUSTRIAL NATION **157**

HISTORY CLOSE-UP

Early Skyscrapers

The Reliance Building To people in Chicago in the 1890s, the Reliance Building almost appeared to defy gravity. Supported by a steel skeleton, the light and airy exterior was made almost entirely of windows. The Reliance Building, and others like it, ushered in a new era of urban construction—the era of the skyscraper.

Steel beams provide strength and support for taller buildings.

Windows could be larger because steel beams, not exterior walls, supported the structure.

Mechanical elevators allow people to reach upper floors easily.

People in ethnic neighborhoods worked to keep their cultures alive and build a sense of community. They established churches and synagogues and formed organizations that helped immigrants with money, jobs, health care, and education.

Reactions to immigrants Some native-born Americans, known as nativists, saw immigrants as a threat. Nativists blamed immigrants for increases in crime and poverty and said they took American jobs.

On the West Coast, prejudice was directed against Asians. California had restrictions against Chinese holding jobs or even living in certain places. On the federal level, Congress passed the Chinese Exclusion Act in 1882. It banned immigration for 10 years, with a few exceptions, and barred Chinese immigrants from becoming citizens. In 1906 San Francisco required Japanese students to attend separate schools from white students, although the policy was later dropped.

Some nativists called for all immigrants to pass a literacy test, an exam to determine whether they could read in English or their native language. Congress approved a literacy test bill over President Woodrow Wilson's veto.

Other native-born Americans, driven by a mixture of fear and charity, wanted to help the new immigrants assimilate, or blend in, to American society. This process became known as **Americanization**. Schools and voluntary organizations taught immigrants English literacy skills and subjects needed for citizenship, such as American history and government. Many immigrants from southern and eastern Europe gained valuable skills. However, the process often involved a loss of cultural heritage.

READING CHECK Summarizing Why did nativists oppose immigration?

Skills Focus INTERPRETING INFOGRAPHICS

With an internal steel structure for support, the Reliance Building could be taller and more decorative. Larger windows let in more light and air. Exterior details, such as the bands of terra-cotta ornamentation, became more delicate.

Making Inferences How did new steel construction techniques make urban buildings different?

See **Skills Handbook**, p. H18

Urban Life in America

Before industrialization, American cities were compact, with buildings only a few stories high. People could walk to workplaces, schools, shops, and churches. In the late 1800s cities changed dramatically. As buildable space grew limited, architects began to build up. Strong steel frames let them design taller buildings. The mechanized elevator, invented by Elisha Otis, made taller buildings practical.

As cities grew more crowded, some people worried that urban areas would no longer have any green space. Specialists in the new field of urban planning looked at the use of space in cities. Landscape architects such as Frederick Law Olmsted designed city parks such as Central Park in New York City.

How different classes lived Lifestyles and opportunities varied tremendously with status in society.

- **The wealthy** Most wealthy people of the late 1800s had made their money in industry and business. They showed off their wealth in many ways, especially in their homes. On New York City's stylish Fifth Avenue, they built houses resembling medieval castles and Italian Renaissance palaces.
- **The middle class** The urban middle class was made up of corporate employees such as accountants and managers, and professionals such as teachers, engineers, lawyers, and doctors. During the 1870s and 1880s, professional organizations began to set standards for certain occupations such as medicine, education, and the law.
- **The working class** Most people in the cities lived in poverty. Wages were low, and housing shortages meant that many people lived in crowded tenements, or rundown apartment buildings. Tenements were usually within walking distance of the factories, stockyards, and ports where many poor urban dwellers worked. Tenement life was unhealthy. Buildings did not have sufficient light or ventilation. The few windows overlooked streets and alleys filled with trash and sewage. With no indoor plumbing, women and children had to haul water from an outdoor water pump. In addition, many working-class women held jobs outside the home.

The settlement house movement A reform movement in Great Britain inspired some Americans to try a new approach to helping people overcome poverty. In 1883 London reformers founded the first settlement house, a place where volunteers offered immigrants services such as English-language and job-training courses. They also provided social activities such as clubs and sports.

One of the first American settlement houses was Hull House in Chicago, founded by Jane Addams and Ellen Gates Starr in 1889. In New York City, Lillian Wald founded the Henry Street Settlement. In Richmond, Virginia, Janie Porter Barrett began the Locust Street Social Settlement, the first for African Americans. By 1910 U.S. cities had 400 settlement houses.

Most settlement-house workers were college-educated women. Many believed in the concept of social gospel, the idea that faith should be expressed through good works. These people believed churches had a moral duty to help solve social problems.

READING CHECK Summarizing How did cities change in the late 1800s?

Political Scandal and Reform

By the late 1800s many American cities had problems such as crime, bad housing, and poor sanitation. In some cities, control of local government passed to a political machine, which was an organization of professional politicians. Political machines made cities run better, but they were often corrupt.

Machine bosses won support by giving people jobs or helping their families. In return, they expected votes. They also won elections by fraudulent means and used their positions to gain money, demanding bribes in exchange for city contracts.

The most notorious political machine was Tammany Hall in New York City. William Marcy Tweed, known as Boss Tweed, became head of Tammany Hall in 1863. He used his position to make himself and his friends, the Tweed Ring, very rich. Tweed's power seemed unbreakable until 1871, when his corruption was made public. He was convicted of fraud and sent to prison.

ACADEMIC VOCABULARY
sufficient enough

The Populist Movement

Farmers joined organizations such as the Grange and the Farmers' Alliances to protect their economic interests. The Farmer Alliances formed the Populist Party in 1892 to further their impact on government policy.

Scandal in the government Political corruption extended all the way to the nation's capital. Civil War hero Ulysses S. Grant became president in 1869, but scandals marred his presidency. One such scandal involved the Crédit Mobilier, a company set up by the Union Pacific Railroad. It was actually a scheme to funnel federal railroad money to Crédit Mobilier stockholders, who included members of Congress and the vice president.

Attempts at reform split the Republican Party. In 1880 the Republicans chose a reformer, Ohio senator James A. Garfield, as their candidate. But four months into his term, Garfield was assassinated. His successor, Chester A. Arthur, surprised many people by supporting government reforms. In 1883 he helped secure passage of the Pendleton Civil Service Act, which required that promotions be based on merit, not political connections.

Farmers' reform movements Times were desperate for farmers in the late 1800s. Crop prices were falling. Merchants, banks, and railroads were getting richer, but farmers were in debt. They organized to help themselves. The first major group of farmers was the Order of Patrons of Husbandry, known as the National Grange. Its first political goal was to persuade state legislatures to regulate railroad rates. Railroads challenged these laws in court. The Supreme Court first upheld the laws but later ruled that the federal government, not the states, could regulate traffic across state lines. This led Congress to pass the Interstate Commerce Act in 1887, which called for reasonable railroad rates. It was the first time that the federal government had passed a law to regulate an industry.

Silver versus gold Another farmers' group, the Farmers' Alliance, formed in the 1870s. The Alliance wanted the government to print more paper money. It believed that farmers could charge more for farm goods if there were more money in circulation.

Paper money was originally redeemable for either gold or silver. Then in 1873 Congress put the U.S. dollar on the gold standard, meaning that a dollar could be redeemed only for gold in the U.S. Treasury. That reduced the amount of money in circulation and hurt farmers. Farmers wanted money to be backed by silver.

Farmers' Alliance policies gained support, and its leaders decided to form a national political party. The People's Party, usually called the Populist Party, was a coalition of Alliance members, farmers, labor leaders, and reformers. It lasted only a few years, but its stand against powerful interests influenced later politicians.

It called for bank regulation, government ownership of railroads, and free (unlimited) coinage of silver.

Soon after the 1892 election, a major railroad company failed, triggering the Panic of 1893. Stock prices fell, and millions lost their jobs. This depression had many causes. President Cleveland blamed the Sherman Silver Purchase Act, which required the government to purchase silver with paper money redeemable in either gold or silver.

The election of 1896 Silver was still an issue in the 1896 election. The Republicans nominated Ohio governor William McKinley, who supported the gold standard. Democrats chose William Jennings Bryan. In a famous speech, Bryan defended the free coinage of silver. He concluded dramatically: "...we will answer their demand for a gold standard by saying to them: You shall not press down upon the brow of labor this crown of thorns, you shall not crucify mankind upon a cross of gold!"

The "cross of gold" speech won Populist support for Bryan. Terrified business leaders contributed millions of dollars to the Republican campaign, and McKinley won the election.

READING CHECK Summarizing What were the goals of the Populist Party?

Segregation and Discrimination

After Reconstruction ended, Southern legislatures passed laws that restricted the rights of African Americans. However, the prejudice that led to such laws existed nationwide.

Legalized discrimination Some white southerners were determined to prevent African Americans from using the right to vote. Tactics included making voters pay a poll tax and pass a literacy test. Most African Americans were too poor to pay the tax and had been denied the education to pass a literacy test.

Southern state legislatures also passed laws—known as Jim Crow laws—to create and enforce segregation in public places. (The name Jim Crow came from a character in a minstrel song.) The first, passed in Tennessee in 1881, required separate railway cars for African Americans and whites. By the 1890s southern states had segregated many public places, including schools.

In 1890 the Louisiana legislature passed a law requiring African Americans to ride in separate railway cars from whites. Homer Plessy, an African American man, sat in a whites-only train compartment to test the law. He was arrested, and his case finally went to the U.S. Supreme Court.

In the case of *Plessy* v. *Ferguson* (1896), the Court upheld segregation. It ruled that "separate but equal" facilities did not violate the Fourteenth Amendment. Justice John Marshall Harlan disagreed, saying, "Our Constitution is color-blind, and neither knows nor tolerates classes among citizens." But the *Plessy* decision allowed legalized segregation for nearly 60 years.

In addition to legalized discrimination, many strict rules of behavior were understood to govern the social and business interactions of white and black Americans. In every encounter, African Americans were supposed to confirm their lower status in society. If they did not do this, the consequences could be serious, even deadly.

The worst outcome of this discrimination was lynching—murder of an individual by a group or mob. Between 1882 and 1892, nearly 900 African Americans lost their lives to lynch

ACADEMIC VOCABULARY
consequence result

mobs. Lynchings could be sparked by even the most minor offenses, or perceived offenses. They declined after 1892 but continued into the early 1900s.

Opposing discrimination Two different approaches to fighting racism emerged. Born into slavery, **Booker T. Washington** believed that African Americans had to accept segregation for the moment. He believed they could improve their situation best through acquiring farming and vocational skills. He founded the Tuskegee Institute to teach African Americans practical skills.

On the other hand, **W. E. B. Du Bois** believed that African Americans should strive for full rights immediately. Du Bois helped found the Niagara Movement in 1905 to fight for equal rights. Members of the Niagara Movement later founded the National Association for the Advancement of Colored People (NAACP).

Other groups face discrimination Hispanic Americans, Asian Americans, and Native Americans also experienced discrimination.

- **Hispanic Americans** Many Mexican immigrants encountered strong anti-Mexican feelings. Most Mexicans were farmers, but there were not enough farm jobs to go around. Spanish-speaking people often had to take menial jobs for little pay. Many were trapped in their jobs by a system brought from Mexico called debt peonage. They could not leave a job until they paid debts they owed their employer. Debt peonage was made illegal in 1911.
- **Asian Americans** In some places, Chinese and Japanese Americans lived in segregated neighborhoods. Many landlords would not rent to Asian tenants. Other laws limited or prevented Asian immigration. In the early 1900s, California legislators passed laws prohibiting marriages between whites and Asian Americans.
- **Native Americans** Native Americans had to endure the government's Americanization policy, which tried to stamp out their traditional cultures. Living on reservations gave them few economic opportunities. Many Native Americans did not even have American citizenship until the passage of the Indian Citizenship Act of 1924.

READING CHECK Identifying the Main Idea What was the intent of southern legislators toward African American voters?

SECTION 3 ASSESSMENT

go.hrw.com
Online Quiz
Keyword: SE7 HP5

HSS 11.2.3, 11.2.7, 11.2.8, 11.3.4

Reviewing Ideas, Terms, and People

1. **a. Recall** Who were the new immigrants, and where did most come from?
   b. Identify How were Ellis and Angel islands similar, and how were they different?
   c. Predict Of all the differences between new and old immigrants, which ones do you think would cause the most tensions between the two groups?

2. **a. Identify** What part did each of these people play in the changing cities? Elisha Otis, Frederick Law Olmsted, **Jane Addams**, Lillian Wald
   b. Contrast How were living conditions different for the wealthy and the working class in cities?
   c. Develop Why might educated, middle class women get involved in the settlement house movement?

3. **a. Identify** Briefly identify each of these political figures: William Marcy Tweed, Ulysses S. Grant, William McKinley, William Jennings Bryan
   b. Explain How did the scandals of the Grant administration have an impact on reformers?
   c. Predict What might be the lasting impact of the ideas put forth by the Populist Party?

4. **a. Identify** Identify each of these tactics and explain how they prevented African Americans from voting: poll tax, literacy test.
   b. Contrast How did **Booker T. Washington** and **W. E. B. Du Bois** differ in their views of the best way to combat discrimination?
   c. Evaluate In what ways was the discrimination against Native Americans different from that faced by Hispanic Americans and Asian Americans?

Critical Thinking

5. **Sequencing** Copy the chart below and record the sequence of events from the passage of the first Jim Crow law in Tennessee to the Supreme Court decision in *Plessy v. Ferguson*.

☐ → ☐ → ☐ → Plessy v. Ferguson

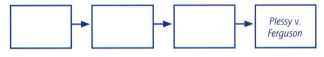

6. **Persuasive** As someone wanting to open a settlement house, write a speech explaining your reasons why it is needed.

Chapter Review

History's Impact video program
Review the video to answer the closing question: How did *Plessy* v. *Ferguson* affect African Americans?

Reviewing Key Terms and People

Identify the correct term or person from the chapter that best fits each of the following descriptions.

1. The law that divided reservation land among individual Native Americans
2. A cattle trail that went from San Antonio, Texas, to rail centers in Kansas
3. The law that allowed any head of household over age 21 to claim 160 acres of land
4. The term for companies operating without government interference
5. System in which most businesses are privately owned
6. Belief that stronger people, businesses, and nations would prosper, while weaker ones would fail
7. Law that made it illegal to form trusts that would interfere with free trade
8. Immigration station opened in New York Harbor in 1892
9. The idea that faith should be expressed through good works
10. Party that called for bank regulation, government ownership of railroads, and unlimited coinage of silver
11. Laws created to enforce segregation

Comprehension and Critical Thinking

SECTION 1 (pp. 142–147) HSS 11.2.2, 11.2.3, 11.2.5

12. **a. Describe** What did the Pacific Railway Act and the Morrill Act do?
    b. Make Inferences Why was the government interested in helping railroads expand westward?
    c. Evaluate What effect did the expansion of railroads have on the West?

SECTION 2 (pp. 148–155) HSS 11.2.1, 11.2.2, 11.2.6

13. **a. Describe** What was the Haymarket Riot?
    b. Make Generalizations What were working conditions like for factory workers? What goals did union organizers have?
    c. Evaluate Why do you think employers and government officials were generally unsympathetic to the labor movement in the late 1800s?

SECTION 3 (pp. 156–162) HSS 11.2.3, 11.2.7, 11.2.8, 11.3.4

14. **a. Identify** What was the gold standard?
    b. Analyze Information Why did farmers oppose the gold standard?
    c. Evaluate Why do you think the issue of the free coinage of silver was too weak to produce a Populist victory in 1896?

Using the Internet

go.hrw.com
Practice Online
Keyword: SE7 CH5

15. During the gold and silver rushes of the late 1800s, people often abandoned mining towns as soon as the minerals were gone. Using the keyword above, do research to learn about ghost towns of the West. Then create a report that tells the story of one town, from its founding to its decline.

Critical Reading HSS 11.2.2; ELA R2.4

Read the passage in Section 1 that begins with the heading "The Oklahoma Land Rush." Then answer the question that follows.

16. Why was land made available to settlers in 1889?
    A The federal government had purchased the land from Native Americans.
    B The Homestead Act made the land available.
    C The government gave in to political pressure from settlers to open the unassigned lands.
    D Railroad companies sold the land to pay for expansion of the railroads.

FOCUS ON WRITING ELA W1.1

Expository Writing *Expository writing gives information, explains why or how, or defines a process. To practice expository writing, complete the assignment below.*

Writing Topic The settlement of the West

17. Based on what you have read in this chapter, write a paragraph that explains how Americans settled the West in the late 1800s.

AN INDUSTRIAL NATION **163**

# UNIT 1 IN BRIEF

Below is a chapter-by-chapter summary of the main ideas covered in Unit 1.

Chapter 1: Beginnings of America
Beginnings–1763

MAIN IDEA Native Americans were the first to inhabit the Americas. Later, Europeans built American colonies, including the thirteen colonies that would eventually become the United States.

SECTION 1 Native Americans inhabited the Americas for thousands of years before the arrival of Europeans. Then, in the 1400s, an age of exploration began in Europe, which led to European sailors traveling to Asia, Africa, and the Americas.

SECTION 2 Spain was the first European nation to claim land in the Americas. By 1733, Great Britain claimed thirteen colonies in North America.

SECTION 3 Life in the colonies was shaped by the policies enforced by Great Britain and the economies that emerged in the various regions. Territory struggles eventually led to the French and Indian War.

Chapter 2: Forming a New Nation
1763–1815

MAIN IDEA The United States fought and won its independence and created a new government based on the ideals of democracy.

SECTION 1 Angered by a series of new British laws, the colonists fought the Revolutionary War and eventually gained independence from Great Britain.

SECTION 2 American leaders drafted the Constitution, which remains the central document of American government today.

SECTION 3 In its early years, the United States faced many challenges, including the emergence of political parties and military conflicts.

Chapter 3: Developing a National Identity
1815–1860

MAIN IDEA A new American identity emerged through religious revivals, reform movements, and territorial expansion. Meanwhile, differences between North and South continued to grow.

SECTION 1 The outcome of the War of 1812 filled Americans with a sense of national pride. Yet sectional divisions over economic issues and slavery also grew.

SECTION 2 The mid-1800s were a time of great reform in the United States. Inspired by religion, Americans worked to make improvements in American society.

SECTION 3 As more Americans moved West, the United States expanded its borders. By 1850 the nation stretched from the Atlantic Ocean to the Pacific.

Chapter 4: The Union in Crisis
1850–1877

MAIN IDEA The tensions between the states erupted into the Civil War. After the war, Reconstruction attempted to rebuild the South.

SECTION 1 Despite efforts to find compromises between the North and the South over slavery, southern states eventually seceded from the Union and created the Confederate States of America.

SECTION 2 The Civil War pitted the North against the South in the bloodiest war the United States had yet seen. The Union defeated the Confederacy in 1865.

SECTION 3 Reconstruction of the South following the Civil War went through many phases and brought many changes to the region.

Chapter 5: An Industrial Nation
1860–1920

MAIN IDEA The years after the Civil War were characterized by industrialization, urbanization, and a new wave of immigration.

SECTION 1 In the late 1800s, Americans moved West in increasing numbers. They established mining, ranching, and farming operations, but in the process, they also destroyed the traditional way of life of the Native Americans they encountered.

SECTION 2 In the late 1800s, many innovations in business and industry occurred. Business leaders made vast sums of money, but ordinary workers continued to work and live under difficult conditions.

SECTION 3 In the late 1800s, waves of immigrants were arriving from southern and eastern Europe. Discrimination was a daily reality for many Americans. Meanwhile the government was plagued by corruption, although reformers began to make efforts toward change.

UNIT 2
Becoming a World Power

1898–1920

Chapter 6
The Progressives
1898–1920

Chapter 7
Entering the World Stage
1898–1917

Chapter 8
The First World War
1914–1920

Themes

Government and Democracy
Movements for social, moral, economic, and political reform responded to changes that had been brought on by industrialization, the growth of cities, and immigration.

Economic Development
Claiming Alaska, Hawaii, and new territories in the Pacific made the United States a growing economic power.

Global Relations
The United States became increasingly involved in foreign affairs, claiming new territories after the Spanish-American War, and entering the fighting in World War I.

Sixteen U. S. battleships, together known as the Great White Fleet, sailed around the globe in 1907–1908 in a proud display of American naval power.

Prepare to Read

Comparing and Contrasting
Find practice for **Comparing and Constrasting** in the **Skills Handbook,** p. H10

Historians can describe people and events by comparing and contrasting them. Good readers identify similarities and differences in the text and use them to gain better understanding of a passage's overall context.

Before You Read
Skim the headings and visuals to determine what you will be reading about.

While You Read
Compare and contrast the reading with the headings and visuals. How are they alike or different?

After You Read
Compare and contrast what you previously knew about the subject matter with what you have learned about it.

Political Organizing

The failure of women to gain the vote urged suffragists to action. In 1869 Elizabeth Cady Stanton and Susan B. Anthony helped form the National Woman Suffrage Association (NWSA). The NWSA focused its efforts on campaigning for a constitutional amendment to give women the vote. But it also dealt with other issues that concerned women, such as labor organizing. In 1872 the NWSA supported Victoria Woodhull, the first woman candidate for U.S. president.

Similarly, the American Woman Suffrage Association (AWSA) was founded in 1869 with Henry Ward Beecher as its president. Unlike the NWSA, the American Woman Suffrage Association focused exclusively on winning the right to vote on a state-by-state basis. It also aligned itself with the Republican party.

READING CHECK **Comparing** In what ways was the NWSA similar to the AWSA?

Compare Both the NWSA and the AWSA were founded in 1869 and worked for suffrage.

Identify signal words such as *similarly* and *likewise* for comparison and *but* and *unlike* for contrast.

Contrast Unlike the NWSA, which dealt with various issues affecting women, the AWSA focused solely on suffrage.

Test Prep Tip
Some essay questions on tests will ask you to compare and contrast historical people, places, and events. As a prewriting activity, create and complete a word web or Venn diagram about the subject matter. Then use your findings to develop an outline for the essay.

History's Impact video program
Watch the video to understand the impact of labor laws.

1904 Muckraker Lincoln Steffens exposes government corruption in *The Shame of the Cities*.

1906 Workers form the British Labour Party.

May 1909 Civil rights activists found the NAACP.

1913 Dr. Albert Schweitzer opens hospital in the French Congo to battle diseases such as leprosy and the plague.

1913 Anti-Defamation League is formed to fight anti-Semitism.

1915 Mohandas K. Gandhi returns to India after leading a nonviolent campaign against discrimination in South Africa.

January 1919 Eighteenth Amendment bans alcoholic beverages.

August 1920 Nineteenth Amendment gives women the right to vote.

1923 Mustafa Kemal establishes the Republic of Turkey.

169

SECTION 1
Progressivism

BEFORE YOU READ

MAIN IDEA
Progressives focused on three areas of reform: easing the suffering of the urban poor, improving unfair and dangerous working conditions, and reforming government at the national, state, and local levels.

READING FOCUS
1. What issues did Progressives focus on, and what helped energize their causes?
2. How did Progressives try to reform society?
3. How did Progressives fight to reform the workplace?
4. How did Progressives reform government at the national, state, and local levels?

KEY TERMS AND PEOPLE
Jacob Riis
progressivism
muckrakers
Ida Tarbell
Lincoln Steffens
Robert M. La Follette
Seventeenth Amendment
initiative
referendum
recall

HSS 11.2.1 Know the effects of industrialization on living and working conditions.

HSS 11.2.9 Understand the effect of political programs and activities of the Progressives (e.g., federal regulation of railroad transport, Children's Bureau, the Sixteenth Amendment, Hiram Johnson).

MUSEUM OF THE CITY OF NEW YORK

How the OTHER HALF Lives

THE INSIDE STORY *How did a photographer help the nation's urban poor?* When **Jacob Riis** wrote about the lives of impoverished immigrants in New York City, he was telling a familiar story: his own. Riis emigrated from Denmark in 1870, at the age of 21. He had trouble finding jobs and lived in poverty. By 1877, however, he was a police reporter for the *New York Tribune,* a voice for social reform.

Riis went to places that were comfortably out of view of most Americans: the tenements of the Lower East Side. "Someone had to tell the facts; that is one reason I became a reporter," he said. He described a room where six adults and five children lived: "One, two, three beds are there, if the old boxes and heaps of foul straw can be called by that name; a broken stove with crazy pipe from which the smoke leaks at every joint . . . piles of rubbish in the corner. The closeness and smell are appalling."

Words could barely describe the squalor. So Riis learned to use a camera. With a new invention, flash powder, he photographed dingy rooms and hallways. He showed his photos in public lectures. His 1889 article in *Scribner's Magazine,* "How the Other Half Lives," became a best-selling book. Riis's fame helped him press the city to improve living conditions for the poor and to build parks and schools.

◀ Jacob Riis photographed a part of America that people did not know existed—or did not want to know.

What Was Progressivism?

Jacob Riis's book *How the Other Half Lives* stunned Americans with its photographs of desperate urban poverty. In the late 1800s, a reform movement known as **progressivism** arose to address many of the social problems that industrialization created. The reformers, called Progressives, sought to improve living conditions for the urban poor. They questioned the power and practices of big business. Progressives also called for government to be more honest and responsive to people's needs.

Reform-minded writers were the first to expose many of the social ills that Progressives targeted. Popular magazines printed journalists' firsthand accounts of injustices and horrors they had witnessed. These journalists were known as **muckrakers** because they "raked up" or exposed the filth of society.

Most of the muckrakers' articles focused on business and political corruption. **Ida Tarbell** wrote a scathing report condemning the business practices of the Standard Oil Company in *McClure's Magazine*. Tarbell revealed how John D. Rockefeller crushed his competition in his quest to gain control over the oil business. Tarbell's reports appealed to a middle-class readership increasingly frightened by the unchecked power of large businesses such as Standard Oil.

Other muckrakers wrote about insurance and stock manipulation, the exploitation of child labor, slum conditions, and racial discrimination. **Lincoln Steffens** exposed the corruption of city governments in *The Shame of the Cities* (1904). Frank Norris described the strangling power of a monopolistic railroad in his 1901 novel *The Octopus: A Story of California*. The muckrakers helped prepare the way for many reforms in the United States.

READING CHECK **Sequencing** How important were the writings of the muckrakers in the Progressive movement, and what did they write about?

Reforming Society

By 1920, more than half of all Americans lived in cities. As cities continued to grow, they were increasingly unable to provide the services people needed: garbage collection, safe housing, and police and fire protection.

PRIMARY SOURCES

Ida Tarbell

Journalist Ida Tarbell's 1903 exposé of the business practices of the Standard Oil Company was one of the triumphs of muckraking. Here Tarbell comments on the company's 1880 victory over independent oil producers who were pressured into giving up their lawsuits against Standard Oil.

> "Now, what was this loose and easily discouraged organization [of independent oil producers] opposing? A compact body of a few able, cold-blooded men—men to whom anything was right that they could get, men knowing exactly what they wanted, men who loved the game they played because of the reward... The withdrawal of the [law]suits was a great victory for Mr. Rockefeller. There was no longer any doubt of his power in defensive operations. Having won a victory, he quickly went to work to make it secure."

Skills FOCUS **READING LIKE A HISTORIAN**

1. **Analyzing Primary Sources** How does Tarbell describe the leaders of Standard Oil?
2. **Identifying Points of View** What do you think Tarbell hoped to achieve by publishing her articles?

See **Skills Handbook**, pp. H28–H29

Housing reforms For the reformers, these conditions provided an opportunity. In New York City, for example, activists such as Lillian Wald worked vigorously to expand public health services for the poor. Progressives scored an early victory in New York State with the passage of the Tenement Act of 1901. This law forced landlords to install lighting in public hallways and to provide at least one toilet for every two families. Outhouses were eventually banned from New York City slums.

These simple steps helped create a healthier environment for impoverished New Yorkers. Within 15 years, the death rate in New York dropped dramatically. Housing reformers in other cities and states pushed for legislation similar to New York's law.

Fighting for civil rights Some progressives also fought prejudice in society. In 1909 Ida Wells-Barnett, W. E. B. Du Bois, Jane Addams,

THE PROGRESSIVES

and other activists formed the multiracial National Association for the Advancement of Colored People (NAACP). Its purpose was to fight for the rights of African Americans.

The NAACP fought on a number of fronts. In 1913 it protested the introduction of segregation into the federal government. Two years later, the NAACP protested the film *Birth of a Nation*, by D.W. Griffith, because of its hostile stereotyping of African Americans. Attempts to ban or censor the film met with little success.

In 1913 Sigmund Livingston, a Jewish man living in Chicago, founded the Anti-Defamation League (ADL). The mission of the ADL was to fight anti-Semitism, or hostility toward Jews.

ADL began by combatting the use of negative stereotypes of Jews in print, on stage, and in films. Adolph S. Ochs, publisher of *The New York Times* and a member of the ADL, wrote a memo to newspaper editors nationwide discouraging the use of negative references to Jews. By 1920 the practice in newspapers had nearly stopped.

> **ACADEMIC VOCABULARY**
> concrete specific, particular

READING CHECK **Comparing** How were the missions of the NAACP and the ADL similar?

Reforming the Workplace

By the end of the 1800s, labor unions were actively campaigning for the rights of adult male workers. Progressive reformers took up the cause of working women and children. In 1893 Florence Kelley helped persuade Illinois to prohibit child labor and to limit the number of hours women were forced to work.

In 1904 Kelley helped found the National Child Labor Committee. The committee's mission was to persuade state legislatures to ban child labor. Yet many employers continued hiring children, and not all states enforced child labor laws.

Progressives also organized state-by-state campaigns to limit women's workdays. Kelley led a successful effort in Oregon that limited the workday in laundries to 10 hours. Utah also passed a law limiting workdays to eight hours in some women's occupations.

But unskilled workers, men and women alike, were still paid extremely low wages. In 1900 about 40 percent of working-class families lived in poverty. Labor unions and Progressives both worked to secure laws ensuring workers a minimum wage. In 1912 Massachusetts became the first state to pass such a law. Congress did not pass a national minimum-wage law until 1938.

Courts and labor laws
Business owners began to fight labor laws in the courts. In the early 1900s, the Supreme Court ruled on several cases concerning state laws that limited the length of the workday. In the 1905 case *Lochner* v. *New York*, the Supreme Court sided with business owners. The Court refused to uphold a law limiting bakers to a 10-hour workday on the grounds that it denied workers their right to make contracts with employers.

But in 1908 the Court sided with workers. In the case *Muller* v. *Oregon*, the Court upheld a state law establishing a 10-hour workday for women in laundries and factories. Louis D. Brandeis, the attorney for the state of Oregon and a future Supreme Court justice, argued the state's case. He maintained that concrete evidence showed that working long hours harmed the health of women. This research convinced the Supreme Court to uphold the Oregon law.

His defense, known as the Brandeis brief, became a model for the defense of other labor laws. It was used in the 1917 case *Bunting* v. *Oregon*, in which the Court upheld a law that extended the protection of a 10-hour workday to men working in mills and factories.

The Triangle Shirtwaist Company Fire
A gruesome disaster in New York in 1911 galvanized Progressives to fight for safety in the workplace. About 500 young women worked for the Triangle Shirtwaist Company, a high-rise factory that made women's blouses. One Saturday, just as these young workers were ending their six-day workweek, a fire erupted, probably from a discarded match.

Within moments, the eighth floor was ablaze, and the flames quickly spread to two other floors. Escape was nearly impossible. Many doors were locked to prevent theft. The flimsy fire escape broke under the weight of panic-stricken people, sending its victims tumbling to their deaths. With flames at their backs, dozens of workers leaped from the windows.

More than 140 women and men died in the Triangle Shirtwaist Company fire. Union organizer Rose Schneiderman commented on the senseless tragedy.

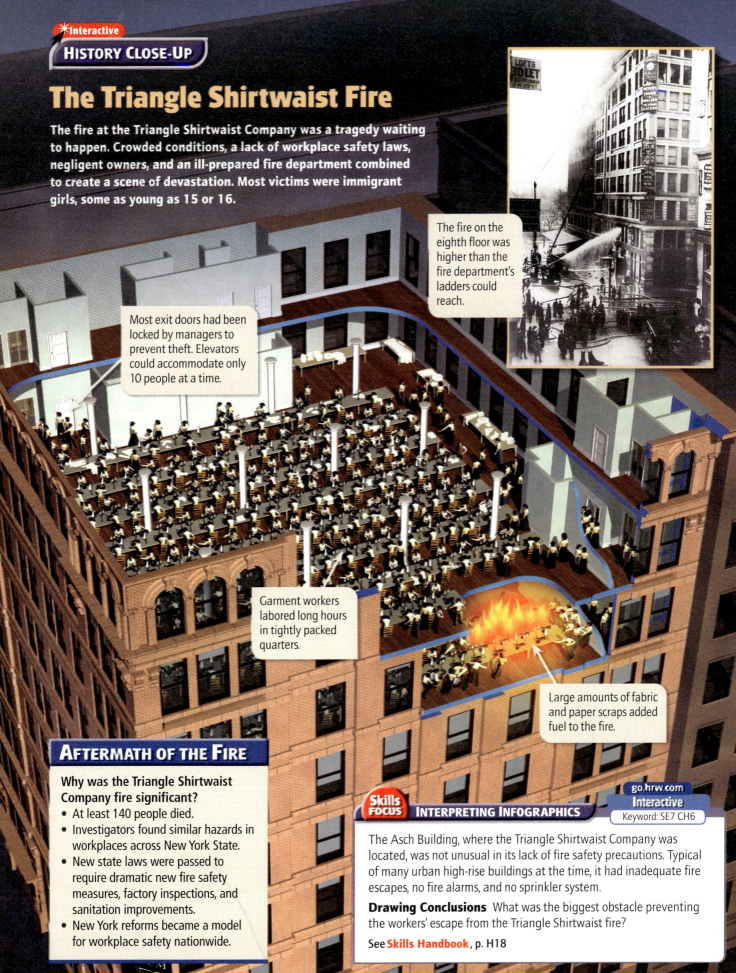

Interactive HISTORY CLOSE-UP

The Triangle Shirtwaist Fire

The fire at the Triangle Shirtwaist Company was a tragedy waiting to happen. Crowded conditions, a lack of workplace safety laws, negligent owners, and an ill-prepared fire department combined to create a scene of devastation. Most victims were immigrant girls, some as young as 15 or 16.

The fire on the eighth floor was higher than the fire department's ladders could reach.

Most exit doors had been locked by managers to prevent theft. Elevators could accommodate only 10 people at a time.

Garment workers labored long hours in tightly packed quarters.

Large amounts of fabric and paper scraps added fuel to the fire.

AFTERMATH OF THE FIRE

Why was the Triangle Shirtwaist Company fire significant?
- At least 140 people died.
- Investigators found similar hazards in workplaces across New York State.
- New state laws were passed to require dramatic new fire safety measures, factory inspections, and sanitation improvements.
- New York reforms became a model for workplace safety nationwide.

Skills Focus INTERPRETING INFOGRAPHICS

go.hrw.com
Interactive
Keyword: SE7 CH6

The Asch Building, where the Triangle Shirtwaist Company was located, was not unusual in its lack of fire safety precautions. Typical of many urban high-rise buildings at the time, it had inadequate fire escapes, no fire alarms, and no sprinkler system.

Drawing Conclusions What was the biggest obstacle preventing the workers' escape from the Triangle Shirtwaist fire?

See **Skills Handbook**, p. H18

HISTORY'S VOICES

"This is not the first time girls have been burned alive in the city. Every week I must learn of the untimely death of one of my sister workers. Every year thousands of us are maimed. The life of men and women is so cheap and property is so sacred."

—Rose Schneiderman, April 2, 1911

THE IMPACT TODAY

Government
In 1970, about 60 years after the Triangle Shirtwaist fire, the federal Occupational Safety and Health Administration (OSHA) was created.

The Triangle Shirtwaist fire was a turning point for reform. With the efforts of Schneiderman and others, New York State passed the toughest fire-safety laws in the nation.

The unions During the Progressive Era, energetic new labor unions joined the fight for better working conditions. The International Ladies' Garment Workers Union (ILGWU) was founded in 1900. Unlike the American Federation of Labor (AFL), which allowed only skilled workers as members, the ILGWU organized unskilled workers. In 1909 the garment workers called a general strike known as the "Uprising of the 20,000." The strikers won a shorter workweek and higher wages. They also attracted thousands of workers to the union.

Meanwhile, the Industrial Workers of the World (IWW), founded in 1905, opposed capitalism altogether. Under the leadership of William "Big Bill" Haywood, the IWW organized the unskilled workers that the AFL ignored. Known as "Wobblies," IWW members not only used traditional strategies such as strikes and boycotts but also engaged in more radical tactics, including industrial sabotage.

At the height of its strength in 1912, the IWW led some 20,000 textile workers on strike in Lawrence, Massachusetts, to protest pay cuts. After a bitter, well-publicized 10-week strike, the mill owners gave in and raised wages.

But the IWW's success was brief. Several later strikes were terrible failures. Fearing the union's revolutionary goals, the government cracked down on the IWW's activities. Disputes among its leaders also weakened the union. Within a few years, it declined in power.

READING CHECK **Identifying Cause and Effect** What factors produced reforms in wages and workplace safety?

Reforming Government

Progressives targeted government for reform as well. They wanted to eliminate political corruption and make government more efficient.

City government reforms Cleaning up government often meant winning control of it. One of the most successful reform mayors was Tom Johnson of Cleveland, Ohio. He set new rules for the police, released debtors from prison, and supported a fairer tax system. In Toledo, Ohio, Mayor Samuel M. Jones overhauled the police force, improved municipal services, set a minimum wage for workers, and opened kindergartens for children.

Progressives also promoted new government structures as a means to improve efficiency. In 1900 a massive hurricane struck Galveston, Texas. The traditional city government proved unable to cope with the disaster, so the Texas legislature set up a five-member commission to govern the city. The commissioners were experts in their fields rather than party loyalists. Galveston's city commission was more honest and efficient than its previous government. By 1918 some 500 American cities adopted the commission plan of city government.

Another new form of government, the council-manager model, began in Staunton, Virginia, in 1908. The city council appoints a professional politician to run the city. The reform inspired cities nationwide to follow suit.

Women march in a Labor Day parade in 1912. Although not considered "ladylike behavior," some women protested their unhealthy and dangerous working conditions.

State government reforms The fight for Progressive reforms extended to the state level. In Wisconsin, a progressive governor named **Robert M. La Follette** pushed through an ambitious agenda of reforms that became known as the Wisconsin Idea.

Elected in 1900, La Follette called for electoral reforms, such as limits on campaign spending. He created state commissions to regulate railroads and utilities. He also formed commissions to oversee transportation, civil service, and taxation.

Other governors pushed for reforms in their states. In New York Charles Evans Hughes regulated public utilities and pushed through a worker safety law. In Mississippi James Vardaman limited the use of convict labor. Vardaman's reforming spirit, however, was marred by extreme racism. He exploited prejudices of poor white farmers toward African Americans to gain support for his policies.

Election reforms Progressives wanted to reform elections to make them fairer and to make politicians more accountable to voters. They pushed for the direct primary, an election in which voters choose candidates to run in a general election. Mississippi adopted the direct primary in 1903. Most other states followed.

Progressives also backed the **Seventeenth Amendment**, ratified in 1913. The amendment gave voters, rather than state legislatures, the power to directly elect their U.S. senators. Progressives believed that direct elections would undermine the influence of party bosses.

Progressives also fought for the use of the secret ballot, which printed all candidates' names on a single piece of paper. Previously, each political party printed its own ballot on colored paper, making it easy to see how people voted and to pressure them to support certain candidates. By 1900 almost all states had adopted the secret ballot.

Finally, Progressives urged states to adopt three additional election reform measures: the initiative, the referendum, and the recall. These measures have become powerful tools with which voters can influence public policy.

An **initiative** allows voters to put a proposed law on the ballot for public approval. The **referendum** allows citizens to place a recently passed law on the ballot, allowing voters to approve or reject the measure. The **recall** enables citizens to remove an elected official from office by calling for a special election. Each measure was designed to make politicians more accountable to voters.

READING CHECK **Contrasting** How does the city commission form of government differ from the city manager form?

QUICK FACTS

PROGRESSIVE ELECTION REFORMS

- **direct primary** voters select a party's candidates for public office
- **17th Amendment** voters elect their senators directly
- **secret ballot** people vote privately without fear of coercion
- **initiative** allows citizens to propose new laws
- **referendum** allows citizens to vote on a proposed or existing law
- **recall** allows voters to remove an elected official from office

---

SECTION 1 ASSESSMENT

go.hrw.com
Online Quiz
Keyword: SE7 HP6

HSS 11.2.1, 11.2.9

Reviewing Ideas, Terms, and People

1. **a. Identify** What was **progressivism**?
   b. Summarize What were some areas of reform that the Progressives targeted?
   c. Evaluate If the **muckrakers** had not done their work, do you think reforms would have occurred? Explain.

2. **a. Explain** Why was the Triangle Shirtwaist fire important?
   b. Contrast How did the tactics of the **ILGWU** differ from those of the IWW?

3. **a. Recall** What are the differences between an **initiative**, a **referendum**, and a **recall**?
   b. Rank Which of the election reforms do you think had the greatest impact on American voters? Explain.

Critical Thinking

4. **Identifying Cause and Effect** Copy the chart below and record the effects of the work of the Progressives in three broad categories: society, workplace, and government.

FOCUS ON WRITING
ELA W1.1, 1.3

5. **Descriptive** Suppose you are a New York newspaper reporter in 1911. Describe the events of the Triangle Shirtwaist fire.

American Literature

UPTON SINCLAIR (1878–1968)

About the Reading The muckraking novel *The Jungle* exposed the horrific working conditions and unsanitary manufacturing practices in the meatpacking industry. The book prompted a huge federal probe and the passage of the Meat Inspection Act of 1906.

AS YOU READ Think about the risks these factory workers dealt with on the job every day.

Excerpt from

The Jungle

by Upton Sinclair

There was no heat upon the killing-floor. The men might exactly as well have worked out of doors all winter. For that matter, there was very little heat anywhere in the building, except in the cooking-rooms and such places—and it was the men who worked in these who ran the most risk of all, because whenever they had to pass to another room they had to go through ice-cold corridors, and sometimes with nothing on above the waist except a sleeveless undershirt. In summer time the chilling-rooms were counted deadly places, for rheumatism and such things; but when it came to winter the men envied those who worked there—at least the chilling rooms were kept at a precise temperature, and one could not freeze to death. On the killing-floor you might easily freeze, if the gang for any reason had to stop for a time. You were apt to be covered with blood, and it would freeze solid; if you leaned against a pillar you would freeze to that, and if you put your hand upon the blade of your knife, you would run a chance of leaving your skin on it. The men would tie up their feet in newspapers and old sacks, and these would be soaked in blood and frozen, and then soaked again, and so on until by night time a man would be walking on great lumps the size of feet of an elephant. Now and then, when the bosses were not looking, you would see them plunging their feet and ankles into the steaming hot carcass of the steer, or darting across the room to the hot-water jets. The cruelest thing of all was that nearly all of them—all of those who used knives—were unable to wear gloves, and their arms would be white with frost and their hands would grow numb, and then of course there would be accidents. Also the air would be full of steam, from the hot water and the hot blood, so that you could not see five feet before you; then, with men rushing about at the speed they kept up on the killing-floor, and all with butcherknives, like razors, in their hands—well, it was to be counted as a wonder that there were not more men slaughtered than cattle.

Sinclair exposed the nation's meatpacking plants, where workers operated in dangerous, grueling, disease-ridden conditions.

Skills Focus HSS 11.2.1, ELA 3.5

READING LIKE A HISTORIAN

1. **Identifying Supporting Details** What dangers to workers and to food does Sinclair describe?
2. **Literature as Historical Evidence** What does *The Jungle* suggest about reasons workers formed unions?

See **Skills Handbook**, pp. H5, H32

SECTION 2
Women and Public Life

BEFORE YOU READ

MAIN IDEA
Women during the Progressive Era actively campaigned for reforms in education, children's welfare, temperance, and suffrage.

READING FOCUS
1. What opportunities did women have for education and work outside the home during the late 1800s?
2. How did women gain political experience through participation in reform movements?
3. How did the women's suffrage movement campaign for the vote?

KEY TERMS AND PEOPLE
Prohibition
Woman's Christian Temperance Union
Frances Willard
Carry Nation
Eighteenth Amendment
National Association of Colored Women
Susan B. Anthony
National American Woman Suffrage Association

HSS 11.10.7 Analyze the women's rights movement from the era of Elizabeth Stanton and Susan Anthony and the passage of the Nineteenth Amendment to the movement launched in the 1960s, including differing perspectives on the roles of women.

THE INSIDE STORY

How did some African American women break barriers in the late 1800s? Most African American women of the 1800s could only dream of going to college. Two women dreamed it, and then did it. Alberta Virginia Scott (1875–1902) and Otelia Cromwell (1874–1972) both graduated from prestigious women's colleges.

Scott was the first known African American to graduate from Radcliffe College in Cambridge, Massachusetts. She entered Radcliffe in 1894, studying science and classics. After graduating, Scott felt she should teach in the South. In 1900 Booker T. Washington invited her to teach at Tuskegee Institute, but sadly, after a year she became ill and died.

Otelia Cromwell had a long and distinguished career as an educator. She transferred from Howard University to Smith College in Northampton, Massachusetts. After graduating in 1900, she taught public school in Washington, D.C. She then went back to school, earning a master's degree from Columbia University and a Ph.D. from Yale.

Professor Cromwell became head of the literature department at Miner Teachers College in Washington. She wrote and edited several books and articles, including a respected biography of suffragist Lucretia Mott. She retired in 1944, and in 1950 she received an honorary degree from Smith. Today Smith College hosts an annual Otelia Cromwell Day, featuring lectures, films, and workshops.

Educational PIONEERS

▶ Otelia Cromwell was honored for her career in education.

THE PROGRESSIVES

Opportunities for Women

By the late 1800s, women were finding more opportunities for education and employment. With greater opportunities came a desire for greater involvement in the life of the community. Many women turned outward, beyond the home, to work for change and reform in society. They sought to use their talents and skills to make life better for others as well as for themselves. In the process, women became a greater political force.

Higher education Throughout the early 1800s, women had limited opportunities for higher education. It wasn't until 1833, for example, that a college, Oberlin College in Ohio, began admitting women as well as men. Later in the century, more colleges opened their doors to women. By 1870 about 20 percent of all college students were women. By 1900 that number had increased to more than one-third.

Most of the women who attended college at this time were members of the middle or upper classes. They wanted to be able to use their knowledge and skills after graduating. However, many professional opportunities were still denied them. The American Medical Association, for example, did not admit women members until 1915. Denied access to their professions, many of these women put their talents and skills to work in various reform movements. These movements would be the training grounds for later political activism.

Employment opportunities Job opportunities for educated middle class women expanded in the late 1800s. Women worked as teachers and nurses—the traditional "caring professions"—but they also entered the business world as bookkeepers, typists, secretaries, and shop clerks.

In addition, businesses such as newspapers and magazines began to hire more women as artists and journalists. The businesses wanted to cater to the interests of the growing consumer group formed by educated and employed women. By 1900 the census counted 11,207 female artists, up from 412 in 1870, and 2,193 female journalists, up from a mere 35 some three decades years before.

Working class women and those without high school educations found jobs available to them in industry. Women poured into the garment industry, where they took positions that paid less than men's jobs did. Employers usually assumed that women were single and were being supported by their fathers. They also

TRACING HISTORY

Women's Rights

Efforts to expand women's rights began long before the Progressive Era and continued beyond it. Study the time line to learn about key events in the history of women's rights.

1776 Shortly before the Declaration of Independence was drafted, Abigail Adams wrote her husband, John, urging that the new nation protect women's liberties.

1848 Delegates to the historic Seneca Falls Convention, led by Elizabeth Cady Stanton (right), issue a bold declaration calling for equal rights for women.

1869 Women living in Wyoming Territory become the first American women to win the right to vote.

assumed that male employees were supporting families. Employers used these assumptions as reasons to pay women lower wages.

By the late 1800s these opportunities in public life began to change the way many middle-class women viewed their world. They began to see that they had a role to play in their communities and in society beyond the home.

READING CHECK **Summarizing** What new opportunities did women find outside the home in the late 1800s?

Gaining Political Experience

As in earlier times, women became the backbone of many reform movements during the Progressive Era. Women learned how to organize, how to persuade other people, and how to publicize their cause. Furthermore, participation in these movements taught women that they had the power to improve life for themselves, their families, and their communities.

Children's health and welfare Some women gained experience while campaigning for the rights of children. Many Progressive reformers worked to end child labor, improve children's health, and promote education. Lillian Wald, founder of the Henry Street Settlement in New York City, believed the federal government had a responsibility to tend to the well being of children. She campaigned tirelessly for the creation of a federal agency to meet that goal. She was successful when the Federal Children's Bureau opened in 1912.

Prohibition Progressive women also gained political experience by participating in the **Prohibition** movement, which called for a ban on making, selling, and distributing alcoholic beverages. Reformers believed alcohol was often responsible for crime, poverty, and violence against women and children.

Two major national organizations, the **Woman's Christian Temperance Union** (WCTU) and the Anti-Saloon League, led an organized crusade against alcohol. **Frances Willard** headed the WCTU from 1879 to 1898. Willard made the WCTU a powerful force for temperance and for the rights of women.

Many reformers spread the anti-alcohol message in Protestant churches. Billy Sunday, a former baseball player turned Presbyterian evangelist, preached that the saloons were "the parent of crimes and the mother of sins." Starting in 1900, evangelist **Carry Nation** took her campaign right to the source. With a hatchet

1920 The Nineteenth Amendment is ratified, guaranteeing women the right to vote.

2004 Some 73 percent of women were registered to vote in the 2004 election, and a high proportion of them, about 65 percent, did vote.

1972 Congress approves the women's Equal Rights Amendment to the Constitution, but it fails to win ratification by the required 38 states.

Carry Nation's theatrical hatchet-wielding protests made her a big attraction. This poster spelled her name as "Carrie."

in one hand and a Bible in the other, she smashed up saloons in Kansas and urged other women to do the same. Nation's fiery speeches, dramatic raids, and canny sense of publicity made her a national figure in the temperance cause.

Prohibitionists eventually won Congress to their cause. In 1917 Congress proposed the **Eighteenth Amendment**, which prohibited the manufacture, sale, and distribution of alcoholic beverages.

The states ratified the amendment in 1919. The Eighteenth Amendment proved so unpopular, however, that it was repealed in 1933.

Civil rights African American women fought for many of the same causes as white women, such as ending poverty, promoting child welfare, fighting for better wages and safer workplace conditions, and fighting alcohol abuse. Yet these women had the added burden of waging their battles in an atmosphere of discrimination.

Many African American women discovered that they were not welcome in most reform organizations. So they formed their own.

One of the largest organizations of African American women was founded in 1896. The **National Association of Colored Women** (NACW) included some of the most prominent women within the African American community, such as antilynching activist Ida B. Wells-Barnett and Margaret Murray Washington of the Tuskegee Institute. Harriet Tubman, the famous conductor on the Underground Railroad during the 1850s, who had remained active in civil rights causes, also became a member. By 1916 the organization had more than 100,000 members.

The NACW campaigned against poverty, segregation, and lynchings. It fought against the persistence of Jim Crow laws that denied African Americans the right to vote. Eventually, the NACW also began to campaign for temperance and women's suffrage. The organization formed settlement houses, hospitals, and schools.

READING CHECK Identifying the Main Idea
What did women learn through their reform work that would be useful to them politically?

Rise of the Women's Suffrage Movement

When the delegates to the Seneca Falls Convention met in 1848 to campaign for women's rights, little did they know how long it would take for women to win the right to vote. It took 72 more years of organizing, campaigning, and persuading before they won the right to vote.

The Fifteenth Amendment After the Civil War, suffragists, who had supported abolition, called for granting women the vote as well as newly freed African American men. They were told that women would have to wait. Abolitionist Horace Greeley urged them to "remember that this is the Negro hour and your first duty is to go through the state and plead his claims." Suffragists waited.

Many of these suffragists were not satisfied by the ratification of the Fifteenth Amendment in 1868. The amendment gave the vote to African American men but not to women. It prohibited denying the right to vote "on account of race, color, or previous condition of servitude."

Women organize Now suffragists were spurred to action. In 1869 Elizabeth Cady Stanton and **Susan B. Anthony** formed the National Woman Suffrage Association. The NWSA campaigned for a constitutional amendment to give women the vote. It dealt with other issues that concerned women as well, such as labor organizing. In 1872 some NWSA members supported Victoria Woodhull, the first woman presidential candidate.

Meanwhile, the American Woman Suffrage Association (AWSA) was founded in 1869, with Henry Ward Beecher as its president. Unlike the NWSA, the American Woman Suffrage Association focused exclusively on winning the right to vote on a state-by-state basis. It also aligned itself with the Republican Party.

Very soon, suffragists began to rejoice at some victories in the West. In 1869 Wyoming

Territory became the first to grant women the vote. Utah Territory followed a year later. Before women nationwide won the vote, legislators in 12 states granted women the right to vote.

Susan B. Anthony tests the law A tireless campaigner for the women's suffrage cause, Susan B. Anthony wrote pamphlets and made speeches. She also testified before every Congress between 1869 and 1906 on behalf of women's suffrage. In 1872 she and three of her sisters staged a dramatic protest. They registered to vote, and on Election Day they voted in Rochester, New York. Two weeks later they were arrested for "knowingly, wrongfully and unlawfully" voting for a representative to the Congress of the United States.

Before her trial began, Anthony delivered an address in which she spelled out many reasons that justice required that women be given the right to vote.

HISTORY'S VOICES

"One-half of the people of this nation to-day are utterly powerless to blot from the statute books an unjust law, or to write there a new and a just one. The women, dissatisfied as they are with this form of government, that enforces taxation without representation—that compels them to obey laws to which they have never given their consent—that imprisons and hangs them without a trial by a jury of their peers, that robs them, in marriage, of the custody of their own persons, wages and children—are this half of the people left wholly at the mercy of the other half, in direct violation of the spirit and letter of the declarations of the framers of this government, every one of which was based on the immutable [undeniable] principle of equal rights to all."

—Susan B. Anthony, 1872

At her trial, the judge refused to allow Anthony to testify on her own behalf, ruled her guilty, and fined her $100. Anthony refused to pay the fine, hoping to force the judge to

THE IMPACT TODAY

Government
Some 65 women served as representatives and 14 as senators in the 2005–2006 U.S. Congress. Representative Nancy Pelosi of California was minority leader in the House, the highest-ranking position ever held by a woman in Congress.

PRIMARY SOURCES

Political Cartoon

In 1912 cartoonist Laura E. Foster addressed an issue faced by even more women today: the tough choices relating to careers and home life.

The prize of Fame at the top of the stairs represents the goal that some people believed suffragists sought.

The woman climbing the stairs represents women seeking career success.

The words at the bottom imply the traditional women's values—home, children, marriage—the woman is leaving behind. The children represent those left behind by the woman's search for personal success.

READING LIKE A HISTORIAN

1. **Interpreting Political Cartoons** How do the words change as the stairs lead up to the top?
2. **Identifying Points of View** What point is the cartoonist trying to make with this cartoon?

See **Skills Handbook**, pp. H28–H29, H31

THE PROGRESSIVES 181

arrest her and create a case that could be tried through the courts. The judge, however, did not imprison Anthony for refusing to pay the fine, thus denying her the right to appeal her case to a higher court.

In 1875 the Supreme Court ruled that even though women were citizens, citizenship did not give them the right to vote. The Court decided it was up to the states to grant or withhold that right. Suffrage associations therefore continued their strategy of trying to persuade each state legislature to grant women the vote.

Anti-suffrage arguments Opponents of the suffrage movement put forth a variety of arguments. Some believed that voting would interfere with women's duties at home or would destroy families altogether. Others claimed that women did not have the education or experience to be competent voters. Still others believed the notion that most American women did not want to vote. They said that it was unfair for suffragists to try to force the vote on those unwilling women.

Significant business interests also opposed women's suffrage. The liquor industry feared that women would vote for Prohibition. As women became more active in other reform movements—such as food and drug safety, worker safety, and child labor—business owners feared that women would vote for regulations that would drive up business costs.

Even some churches and clergy members spoke out against women's suffrage. They argued that marriage was a sacred bond in which the entire family was represented by the man. In that case, they believed that women did not need the vote.

Two organizations merge In 1890 the National Woman Suffrage Association and the American Woman Suffrage Association merged. They formed the **National American Woman Suffrage Association** (NAWSA) under the leadership of Elizabeth Cady Stanton. Susan B. Anthony served as NAWSA's president from 1892 to 1900. Anthony died in 1906. Her final public statement was "Failure is impossible."

Like Susan B. Anthony, most of the early suffragists did not live long enough to cast their ballots. In fact, when women nationwide finally won the vote in 1920, only one signer of the Seneca Falls Declaration—Charlotte Woodward, age 92—was still alive.

READING CHECK **Identifying Cause and Effect** What effect did the passage of the Fifteenth Amendment have on suffragists?

ACADEMIC VOCABULARY
notion idea

SECTION 2 ASSESSMENT

HSS 11.10.7

Reviewing Ideas, Terms, and People

1. **a. Describe** In the 1800s, what new opportunities did women in various social classes have outside the home?
   b. Explain How did new opportunities change the way many women viewed their place in the public world?

2. **a. Identify** Write a sentence describing each of the following: **Prohibition, Carry Nation, Frances Willard, National Association of Colored Women**.
   b. Analyze Why did many women choose to join the temperance movement?
   c. Elaborate How were women's reform causes related to traditional roles in the home?

3. **a. Recall** What happened to **Susan B. Anthony** when she attempted to vote?
   b. Analyze What effect did the Fifteenth Amendment have on the women's rights movement?
   c. Elaborate Why do you think many suffragists decided to adopt a state-by-state strategy, rather than campaign for a constitutional amendment?

Critical Thinking

4. **Comparing and Contrasting** Copy the Venn diagram below and fill it out to show the ways in which the National Woman Suffrage Association and the American Woman Suffrage Association were similar and different.

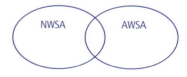

FOCUS ON WRITING ELA W1.1, 1.3

5. **Persuasive** Suppose you are a woman who has gained political experience in the abolitionist movement. Write a letter to the editor explaining your opposition to the exclusion of women from the proposed Fifteenth Amendment. Be sure to provide details to support your argument.

SECTION 3
Theodore Roosevelt's Square Deal

BEFORE YOU READ

MAIN IDEA
Theodore Roosevelt used the power of the presidency to push for progressive reforms in business and in environmental policy.

READING FOCUS
1. What was Theodore Roosevelt's view of the role of the president?
2. How did Roosevelt attempt to regulate big business?
3. What was Roosevelt's philosophy about conserving the environment, and how did he carry out his philosophy?

KEY TERMS AND PEOPLE
Theodore Roosevelt
bully pulpit
Square Deal
Elkins Act
Hepburn Act
Upton Sinclair
Meat Inspection Act
Pure Food and Drug Act
John Muir
Newlands Reclamation Act
Gifford Pinchot

HSS 11.2.1 Know the effects of industrialization on living and working conditions, including the portrayal of working conditions and food safety in Upton Sinclair's *The Jungle*.

HSS 11.2.9 Understand the effect of political programs and activities of the Progressives (e.g., federal regulation of railroad transport, Theodore Roosevelt).

THE INSIDE STORY

Cowboy or politician? No one who knew "Teedie" Roosevelt at age 9 would have recognized the sturdy athlete who later cleaned up a corrupt New York City police department and led the Rough Riders in Cuba during the Spanish-American War. The young Roosevelt was sickly and shy. Family doctors forbade any sports or strenuous activity, so Teedie spent his time reading and studying natural history. Then as a teenager, **Theodore Roosevelt** energetically set about making himself into a new person. He took up boxing, tennis, horseback riding, and rowing. He fashioned an optimistic, vigorous personality that was to make him a successful politician.

Roosevelt came from a prominent New York family and attended Harvard University, but he grew to love the outdoors. He spent time in northern Maine and in the rugged Badlands of the Dakota territory, where he rode horses and hunted buffalo. When Roosevelt was 26, tragedy struck. Both his wife and his mother died unexpectedly. Trying to forget his grief, Roosevelt returned to his ranch in Dakota Territory.

For two years, Roosevelt lived and worked with cowboys, who came to admire his toughness as he rode in roundups and hunted bear, elk, and mountain lions. The westerners also liked the way he stood up to bullying rustlers who called him "four eyes" because of his thick glasses. After two years, Roosevelt's western adventure was over. He returned to New York and to politics.

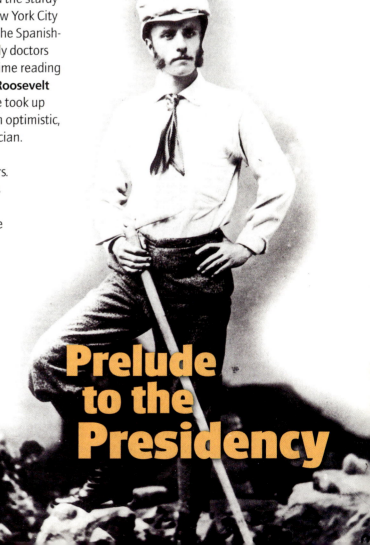

▶ A young Theodore Roosevelt in 1880

Prelude to the Presidency

Roosevelt's View of the Presidency

Theodore Roosevelt's rise to the governorship of New York in 1898 spelled big trouble for the Republican political machine in New York. To rid themselves of the Progressive reformer, party bosses came up with a clever plan: They got Roosevelt nominated as vice president, a job with little power at the time.

Taking office However, the party bosses—and the nation—were shocked when anarchist Leon Czolgosz (CHAWL-gawsh) fatally shot President William McKinley in 1901. Theodore Roosevelt, the energetic reformer, now held the highest office in the land.

Roosevelt was just 42 years old when he took office—the youngest person ever to become president. During the late 1800s, most presidents had taken a hands-off approach to governing. Not Teddy Roosevelt. He saw the White House as a **bully pulpit**—a powerful platform to publicize important issues and seek support for his policies. With great enthusiasm and energy, Roosevelt brought new momentum to the Progressive movement.

The coal strike of 1902 Soon after the new president took office, some 150,000 Pennsylvania coal miners struck for higher wages, shorter hours, and recognition of their union. The strike gave Roosevelt an opportunity to define his view of the presidency.

As winter neared, Roosevelt feared what might happen if the strike were not resolved. Northern cities depended on Pennsylvania coal for heating. The president felt compelled to use his influence "to bring to an end a situation which has become literally intolerable."

Roosevelt urged the mine owners and the striking workers to accept arbitration. In the arbitration process, two opposing sides agree to allow a third party to settle a dispute. The workers agreed to accept arbitration, but the mine owners refused. As winter drew nearer, Roosevelt threatened to take over the mines. The threat finally convinced the mine owners to agree to his arbitration plan.

After a three-month investigation, the arbitrators announced their decision. They gave the workers a shorter workday and higher pay but did not require the mining companies to recognize the union. For the first time, the federal government had intervened in a strike to protect the interests of the workers and the public. Satisfied, Roosevelt pronounced the compromise a "square deal."

The Square Deal The **Square Deal** became Roosevelt's 1904 campaign slogan and the framework for his entire presidency. He promised to "see that each [person] is given a square deal, because he is entitled to no more and should receive no less." Roosevelt's promise revealed his belief that the needs of workers, business, and consumers should be balanced. Roosevelt's Square Deal called for limiting the power of trusts, promoting public health and safety, and improving working conditions.

The popular president faced no opposition for the nomination with his party. In the general election Roosevelt cruised to victory, easily defeating his Democratic opponent, Judge Alton Parker of New York.

READING CHECK Identifying the Main Idea What was Roosevelt's Square Deal?

Regulating Big Business

Roosevelt believed that big business was essential to the nation's growth, but he also believed companies should behave responsibly.

HISTORY'S VOICES

"We demand that big business give the people a square deal; in return we must insist that when anyone engaged in big business honestly endeavors to do right he shall himself be given a square deal."

—Theodore Roosevelt

Roosevelt focused a great deal of attention on regulating large corporations. Addressing Congress in 1902, Roosevelt stated, "We are . . . determined that they [corporations] shall be so handled as to subserve [serve] the public good. We draw the line against misconduct, not against wealth."

Trust-busting In 1901 tycoons J. P. Morgan, James J. Hill, and E. H. Harriman joined their railroads together to eliminate competition. Their company, the Northern Securities Company, dominated railroad shipping from Chicago to the Northwest.

ACADEMIC VOCABULARY
framework the basic concepts that constitute a way of viewing reality

The following year, President Roosevelt directed the U.S. attorney general to sue the Northern Securities Company for violating the Sherman Antitrust Act. In 1904 the Supreme Court ruled that the monopoly did violate the Sherman Antitrust Act, and it ordered the corporation dissolved.

The ruling proved to be a watershed. An encouraged Roosevelt administration launched a vigorous trust-busting campaign. It filed dozens of lawsuits against monopolies and trusts that it believed were not in the public interest.

The size of the trust was not the issue. What mattered was whether a particular trust was good or bad for the American public. The Roosevelt administration went after the bad trusts: the ones that sold inferior products, competed unfairly, or corrupted public officials.

Regulating the railroads Another way to ensure that businesses competed more fairly was through regulation. Railroads commonly granted rebates to their best customers. This meant that huge corporations

Bully Pulpit

NO MOLLY-CODDLING HERE

THE GRANGER COLLECTION, NEW YORK

SKILLS FOCUS   READING LIKE A HISTORIAN

Far left, Roosevelt is making good use of the bully pulpit. The cartoon shows Roosevelt as a man who will not "mollycoddle," or indulge, big business.

1. **Interpreting Political Cartoons** What does the reference to big business mean?
2. **Identifying Points of View** What does the cartoon say about Roosevelt's efforts? Explain.

See **Skills Handbook**, p. H28–H29, H31

FACES OF HISTORY

Theodore ROOSEVELT
1858–1919

Author, athlete, and Nobel Prize–winning statesman, Theodore Roosevelt forged a presidential style that was an extension of the fascinating life he had led. Doing battle with corporate trusts and crusading for the environment were just other adventures for the battle-ready hero and nature lover.

Roosevelt embraced the "strenuous life" in what he called "the arena" of public service. Whether reforming the New York City police department, defying corrupt party bosses, or leading soldiers in the Spanish-American War, Roosevelt was always, in his words, "daring greatly." As president, Roosevelt focused on "trust-busting" and environmental conservation at home and pursued a "muscular" foreign policy, using an enlarged U.S. Navy to project American power. His intervention in Central America led to the founding of Panama and, later, the building of the Panama Canal.

"TR" even survived a brush with death in 1912. Shot in the chest by a would-be assassin, he proceeded to give a 90-minute campaign speech. He told the stunned crowd, "It takes more than that to kill a bull moose."

Interpret How did Roosevelt's life affect his style of leadership?

---

paid significantly less to ship their products than small farmers or small businesses. In 1903 Congress passed the **Elkins Act**, which prohibited railroads from accepting rebates. The Elkins Act ensured that all customers paid the same rates for shipping their products.

The **Hepburn Act** of 1906 strengthened the Interstate Commerce Commission (ICC), giving it the power to set maximum railroad rates. It also gave the ICC the power to regulate other companies that were engaged in interstate commerce.

Protecting consumers Roosevelt also responded to growing public dismay about practices of the food and drug industries. Some food producers, drug companies, and meat packers were selling dangerous products to an unknowing public.

Food producers, for example, resorted to clever tricks to pass off tainted foods. Some poultry sellers added formaldehyde, a chemical used in embalming dead bodies, to old eggs to hide their foul odor. Unwary consumers bought the tainted food and were tricked into thinking it was healthy.

Many drug companies were equally unconcerned for their customer's welfare. Some sold medicines that simply did not work. Others marketed patent, or nonprescription, medicines containing dangerous narcotic drugs. Products such as Dr. James' Soothing Syrup, intended to soothe babies' teething pain, contained the drug heroin. Gowan's Pneumonia Cure contained the addictive painkiller opium.

Few industries fell into greater public disrepute than the meatpacking business. The novelist **Upton Sinclair** exposed the wretched and unsanitary conditions at meatpacking plants in his 1906 novel *The Jungle*.

HISTORY'S VOICES

> "There would be meat stored in great piles in rooms; and the water from leaky roofs would drip over it, and thousands of rats would race about on it.... A man could run his hand over these piles of meat and sweep off handfuls of the dried dung of rats.... The packers would put poisoned bread out for them; they would die, and then rats, bread, and meat would go into the hoppers together."
>
> —Upton Sinclair, *The Jungle*, 1906

Sinclair's novel ignited a firestorm of criticism aimed at meatpackers. Reformers and an outraged public called for change. Roosevelt ordered Secretary of Agriculture James Wilson to investigate the conditions in the packing houses. Wilson's final report made for gruesome reading.

"We saw meat shoveled from filthy wooden floors, piled on tables rarely washed, pushed from room to room in rotten box carts. In all of which processes it [the meat] was in the way of gathering dirt, splinters, floor filth, and the expectoration [saliva] of tuberculous and other diseased workers."

The Wilson report shocked the U.S. Congress into action. In 1906 it enacted two groundbreaking consumer protection laws. The first, the **Meat Inspection Act**, required federal inspection of meat shipped across state lines. The **Pure Food and Drug Act** forbade the manufacture, sale, or transportation of food and patent medicine containing harmful ingredients. The law also required food and medicine containers to carry accurate ingredient labels.

READING CHECK **Summarizing** What measures did the Roosevelt administration take to regulate business and protect consumers?

THE IMPACT TODAY

Government
The Pure Food and Drug Act was the forerunner of today's Food and Drug Administration, which regulates food, drugs, cosmetics, and medical products.

Environmental Conservation

In the late 1800s people acted as if the United States had an unending supply of natural resources. Lumber companies cleared large tracts of forest lands. Farmers plowed up the Great Plains. Ranchers' cattle and sheep overgrazed the prairies. Mining companies clogged rivers and cluttered the land with their refuse. Cities dumped sewage into rivers and garbage onto the land.

Roosevelt, however, believed that each generation had a duty to protect and conserve natural resources for future generations.

HISTORY'S VOICES

> "We of an older generation can get along with what we have, . . . but in your full manhood and womanhood you will want what nature once so bountifully supplied and man so thoughtlessly destroyed; and because of that want you will reproach us, not for what we have used, but for what we have wasted."
> —Theodore Roosevelt

Before Roosevelt's presidency, the federal government had left the nation's natural resources largely unregulated. Business needs had always taken priority over the environment. But Roosevelt recognized that natural resources were limited, and he believed their use needed to be controlled.

In 1903 Roosevelt joined famed naturalist **John Muir** for a camping trip in Yosemite National Park in California. Muir had played a pivotal role in convincing the government to protect and preserve Yosemite. "Unfortunately, God cannot save trees from fools," Muir had observed. "Only the government can do that."

Despite their friendly camping trip, Muir and Roosevelt held different views about conservation. Muir wanted the entire wilderness to be preserved in its natural state. Roosevelt believed that conservation involved the active management of public lands for a variety of uses. Some lands should be preserved as wilderness. Other lands should be put to more directly economical productive uses.

The **Newlands Reclamation Act** of 1902 reflected Roosevelt's beliefs. It allowed the federal government to create irrigation projects to make dry lands productive. The projects would be funded from money raised by selling off public lands. The Roosevelt administration launched more than 20 reclamation projects.

Linking to Today

National Park System

Theodore Roosevelt will be remembered as the first champion of conservation. Yet before him, some Americans worked to protect natural wonders.

In 1872 Congress passed a law that set aside land in Wyoming, Montana, and Idaho as Yellowstone National Park. Yellowstone became the world's first national park.

Over time, the federal government founded more national parks across the country. In 1919 parts of the Grand Canyon in Arizona became a national park. Shenandoah National Park in Virginia was founded in 1935. Biscayne National Park in Florida was established in 1980, and Cuyahoga Valley National Park in Ohio was created in 2000.

While many parks preserve land and wildlife, other parks throughout the world preserve cultural history. Mesa Verde National Park in Colorado is famous for its Cliff Palace, a settlement built by ancestral Pueblo Indians about 800 years ago. In the Caribbean, Virgin Islands National Park is home to ancient ruins and Danish sugar plantations from the 1700s and 1800s.

In the Yellowstone tradition, national parks have been created in many countries. Meanwhile, debate continues over how to both save and use public lands.

Making Generalizations Why do some national parks preserve cultural elements as well as natural ones?

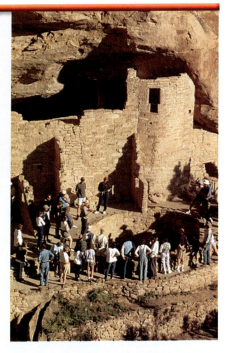

Visitors enjoy the wonders of Colorado's Mesa Verde National Park.

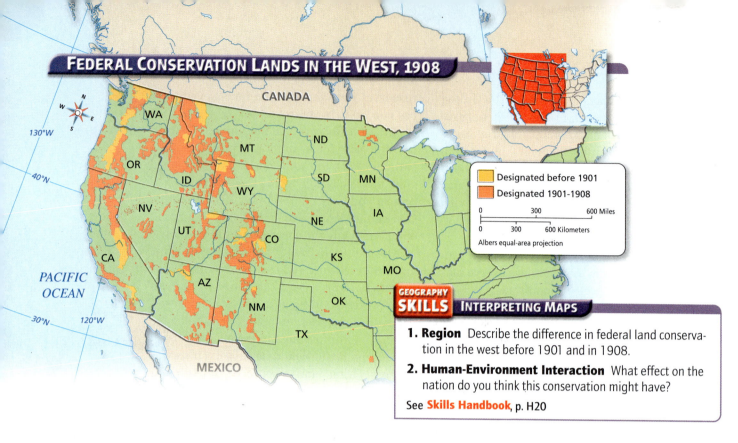

GEOGRAPHY SKILLS INTERPRETING MAPS

1. **Region** Describe the difference in federal land conservation in the west before 1901 and in 1908.
2. **Human-Environment Interaction** What effect on the nation do you think this conservation might have?

See **Skills Handbook**, p. H20

Another conservationist, **Gifford Pinchot** (PIN-shoh), shared Roosevelt's view. Pinchot first came up with the word *conservation* to describe the need to protect the country's natural environment. He wrote: "The conservation of natural resources is the key to the future. It is the key to the safety and prosperity of the American people." Pinchot believed scientific management of natural resources was crucial to sustaining them to serve the nation's needs.

In 1905 the Roosevelt administration established the U.S. Forest Service with Pinchot as its chief. During Roosevelt's presidency, the Forest Service added nearly 150 million acres to the national forests, controlled their use, and regulated their harvest.

The Antiquities Act of 1906 led to the creation of 18 national monuments during Roosevelt's presidency. For many historians, environmental conservation is Roosevelt's greatest legacy.

READING CHECK **Contrasting** How did Roosevelt's and Muir's views of natural resources differ?

SECTION 3 ASSESSMENT

go.hrw.com
Online Quiz
Keyword: SE7 HP6

HSS 11.2.1, 11.2.9

Reviewing Ideas, Terms, and People

1. **a. Recall** How did Roosevelt use the **bully pulpit** to promote the **Square Deal**?
   b. Evaluate How was Roosevelt's response to the coal strike symbolic of his view of the presidency?
2. **a. Describe** How did Roosevelt engage in trust-busting?
   b. Draw Conclusions Why did the food companies knowingly sell spoiled food?
   c. Predict What impact would Roosevelt's policies have on consumer protection in America?
3. **a. Identify** Who was **Gifford Pinchot**?
   b. Contrast How did Roosevelt's view of natural resources differ from the policies of past presidents?

Critical Thinking

4. **Summarizing** Copy the chart below and record major legislation regulating business during Roosevelt's presidency.

Law	Purpose

FOCUS ON WRITING  ELA W1.1, 1.3

5. **Persuasive** As a consumer in 1906, write a letter to Congress supporting the Pure Food and Drug bill.

188 CHAPTER 6

SECTION 4: Taft and Wilson

BEFORE YOU READ

MAIN IDEA
Progressive reforms continued during the Taft and Wilson presidencies, focusing on business, banking, and women's suffrage.

READING FOCUS
1. How did Taft's approach to progressivism split the Republican Party?
2. What was Wilson's New Freedom reform plan?
3. How did women gain the right to vote in national elections?
4. How did progressivism affect African Americans?

KEY TERMS AND PEOPLE
William Howard Taft
Sixteenth Amendment
Hiram W. Johnson
Woodrow Wilson
New Freedom
Federal Reserve Act
Clayton Antitrust Act
Alice Paul
Nineteenth Amendment
Brownsville incident

HSS 11.2.9 Understand the effect of the Progressives (e.g., the Sixteenth Amendment).

HSS 11.5.4 Analyze the passage of the Nineteenth Amendment.

HSS 11.10.7 Analyze the women's rights movement and the passage of the Nineteenth Amendment.

THE INSIDE STORY

Can politics and friendship mix? In 1904 Theodore Roosevelt told the country he would not seek re-election as president. He kept his word. Instead, when the 1908 election approached, Roosevelt put forth a successor: his friend and close adviser **William Howard Taft**.

The two men were very different. Roosevelt was an energetic crusader for reform. He held an expansive view of the president's powers and was not afraid to set new precedent. Taft was an easygoing, cautious lawyer with a more restrained view of the presidency. He expressed some discomfort at Roosevelt's activism, saying that Roosevelt "ought more often to have admitted the legal way of reaching the same ends." Still, he served the president loyally for four years as secretary of war, and though his main ambition was to become the chief justice of the Supreme Court, he agreed to run.

Taft didn't enjoy the campaign. He called it "one of the most uncomfortable four months of my life." But he pledged loyalty to the Roosevelt program, and with the president's strong backing he won the 1908 election. In March of 1909 the reluctant candidate found himself living in the White House.

Roosevelt soon regretted his decision. He believed that Taft departed from Progressive ideals on tariffs and the environment. Roosevelt charged that Taft "completely twisted around the policies I advocated." The onetime friends were to become bitter foes.

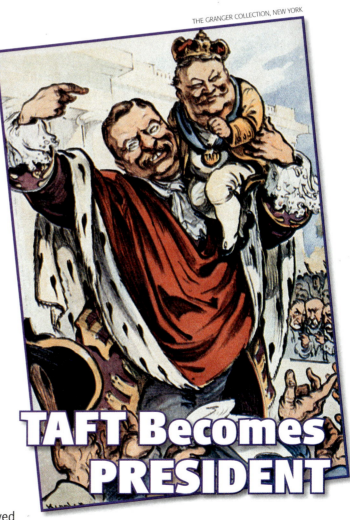

▲ Roosevelt crowns his successor, believing Taft will carry on his work.

TAFT Becomes PRESIDENT

Progressivism under Taft

In the election of 1908, Taft faced three-time Democratic candidate William Jennings Bryan. The Democrats lost the election by a wide margin in the electoral college and by nearly 1.27 million popular votes.

A cautious man, President Taft worked to secure Roosevelt's progressive reforms rather than to build upon them. Still, he supported several reforms, such as creating a Department of Labor to enforce labor laws and increasing national forest reserves.

The Taft administration also is credited with passage of the **Sixteenth Amendment**. Introduced during the Taft years but ratified in 1913 after Taft left office, the Sixteenth Amendment granted Congress the power to levy taxes based on an individual's income. Progressives had supported a nationwide income tax as a way to pay for government programs more fairly.

Despite these reforms, President Taft lost the support of most Progressive Republicans.

The trouble began early, in April 1909, with the passage of a bill on tariffs, or taxes charged on imports or exports.

The House had passed a version of the bill, which lowered tariffs on imported goods. When the bill went to the Senate, though, Senator Nelson Aldrich of Rhode Island and others added so many amendments that it became a high-tariff bill. Nevertheless, Taft signed the Payne-Aldrich Tariff into law. Progressives were outraged because they saw tariff reduction as a key step in lowering the prices of consumer goods.

Taft also alienated Progressive supporters of conservation. His secretary of the interior, Richard Ballinger, was accused of impeding a government fraud investigation of public coal-land deals in Alaska. When Gifford Pinchot, head of the U.S. Forest Service, charged Ballinger with sabotaging conservation efforts, Taft fired Pinchot.

Progressives believed that the Ballinger-Pinchot affair showed Taft's lack of commitment to conservation. Theodore Roosevelt, who had put forth Taft for the presidency, refused to support Taft after the Ballinger-Pinchot affair.

Split in the Republican Party In the 1910 congressional elections, Roosevelt campaigned for Progressive Republicans who opposed Taft. Roosevelt proposed a program called New Nationalism, a set of laws to protect workers, ensure public health, and regulate business.

Some reformers saw the New Nationalism as a revival of the progressive spirit. Roosevelt's help on the campaign trail was not enough to ensure a Republican victory, though. Republicans lost control of the House of Representatives for the first time in 16 years.

THE ELECTION OF 1912

Candidate	Political Affiliation	Electoral Votes	Popular Votes
Woodrow Wilson	Democratic	435	6,293,454
Theodore Roosevelt	Progressive	88	4,119,538
William Howard Taft	Republican	8	3,484,980

GEOGRAPHY SKILLS INTERPRETING MAPS

Taft made the poorest showing of any president seeking reelection. Wilson won with only about 42 percent of the popular vote.

Region In comparison, how did Wilson fare in the electoral vote?

See **Skills Handbook**, p. H21

By the presidential election of 1912, the Republican Party was badly fractured. Many Republicans continued to support Taft. When the Republican Party nominated Taft as its presidential candidate, the more Progressive Republicans broke away to form the new Progressive ("Bull Moose") Party. Theodore Roosevelt led the ticket, and the popular governor of California, **Hiram W. Johnson**, was their candidate for vice president.

With the Republicans split between Taft and Roosevelt, Democrat **Woodrow Wilson** glided to victory. Wilson received 435 electoral votes, while Roosevelt received 88 and Taft received 8. Socialist candidate Eugene V. Debs won more than 900,000 popular votes but no electoral votes.

READING CHECK **Identifying Cause and Effect** What effect did the split in the Republican Party have on the election of 1912?

Wilson's New Freedom

Wilson came to office with a reputation as a zealous reformer. As governor of New Jersey, he had fought political machines, approved a law permitting direct primaries, and enacted a program to compensate injured workers. During the campaign, he proposed an ambitious plan of reform that he called the **New Freedom**. The New Freedom platform called for tariff reductions, banking reform, and stronger antitrust legislation—causes dear to the hearts of Progressives.

Tariff reduction Wilson's first priority as president was to lower tariffs. Wilson waged a tireless campaign to persuade Congress. He even appeared at a joint session of Congress, the first president since John Adams to do so. In October 1913 Congress passed the Underwood Tariff Act. This law reduced tariffs to their lowest levels in more than 50 years.

Tariff reduction meant that the government had less income, however. How would the nation make up the shortfall?

The answer was an income tax. The Underwood Tariff Act also introduced a graduated income tax, which would assess people at different rates according to their income levels. Wealthier people would pay more; poorer people would pay less.

Banking reform President Wilson's next target for reform was the banking system. Historically bank failures had been common. Banks collapsed when too many people withdrew their deposits at the same time. What could be done to keep the banks' doors open, while still allowing people to withdraw their money when they wanted to?

The answer was the **Federal Reserve Act**. This law, passed in 1913, created a central fund from which banks could borrow to prevent collapse during a financial panic.

The Federal Reserve Act created a three-tier banking system. At the top was the Federal Reserve Board, a group of officials appointed by the president and charged with running the system. On the second level were 12 Federal Reserve banks, which served other banks rather than individuals. On the third level were the private banks, which could borrow from the Federal Reserve banks as they needed to. The Federal Reserve Act put the nation's banking system under the supervision of the federal government for the first time.

Stronger antitrust laws Congress had passed the Sherman Antitrust Act in 1890 to limit the power of monopolies. But lax enforcement and loopholes in the law allowed a number of unfair business practices to persist.

At President Wilson's urging, Congress passed the **Clayton Antitrust Act**, which clarified and extended the Sherman Antitrust Act. Passed in 1914, the Clayton Antitrust Act prohibited companies from buying the stock of competing companies in order to form a monopoly. The law also supported workers by making strikes, boycotts, and peaceful picketing legal for the first time.

In another effort to make business fairer, Wilson supported the creation of the Federal Trade Commission (FTC) by Congress in 1915. The FTC enforced antitrust laws and got tough on companies that used deceptive advertising. It also had the power to undertake special investigations of businesses. Progressives were displeased, however, when Wilson appointed to the commission a number of people who were sympathetic to business.

READING CHECK **Identifying Problems and Solutions** What were the three major areas of reform in Wilson's New Freedom?

COUNTERPOINTS

How to Win the Vote

Alice Paul believed that picketing, imprisonment, and hunger strikes would win suffrage.

" Every day that the Government sends women to prison for holding harmless banners... makes the position of the Government more indefensible and therefore strengthens our position. "

Alice Paul,
1917

Suffragist Carrie Chapman Catt believed that women had to work with lawmakers to win the vote.

" When thirty-six state associations... [agree] to get the Amendment submitted by Congress and ratified by their respective state legislatures; when they live up to their compact by running a red-hot, never ceasing campaign... we can get the Amendment through. "

Carrie Chapman Catt,
1916

SKILLS FOCUS — READING LIKE A HISTORIAN

Identifying Points of View Summarize each woman's approach to the struggle for voting rights.
See **Skills Handbook**, p. H28–H29

Women Gain the Vote

The struggle for women's suffrage took some dramatic turns during Wilson's time in office, highlighted by a split in the ranks of suffrage supporters over the best way to win the vote. The National American Woman Suffrage Association (NAWSA) favored a state-by-state approach. But by 1901 just four western states had given women full voting rights.

Frustrated by this slow progress, in 1913 two activists, **Alice Paul** and Lucy Burns, broke away from NAWSA and formed the Congressional Union for Woman Suffrage. Renamed the National Woman's Party (NWP) in 1916, the group focused on passage of a federal constitutional amendment for women's suffrage. Paul and Burns used new tactics learned from the British suffrage movement. The NWP members picketed the White House in January 1917, chaining themselves to the railings. Many were arrested. Some went on hunger strikes in prison. The dramatic efforts of the NWP protesters brought renewed attention to the suffrage cause.

Meanwhile, the state-by-state approach was gaining momentum. In 1915 Massachusetts, New Jersey, New York, and Pennsylvania held special referendums on women's suffrage. The motions were all defeated, but NAWSA's membership grew to nearly 2 million.

Under the energetic leadership of Carrie Chapman Catt, NAWSA launched a new strategy in 1916 to campaign for suffrage on both the state and federal levels. When the United States entered World War I in 1917, leaders of the movement—along with millions of American women—lent strong support to the war effort. Women's patriotism helped weaken opposition to suffrage.

The work of suffragists convinced members of the House and Senate to support a constitutional amendment. Even President Wilson lent his support, in a speech in 1918. Proposed by Congress in 1919 and ratified in 1920, the **Nineteenth Amendment** finally gave women full voting rights.

READING CHECK **Contrasting** Explain how the tactics used by NAWSA and the NWP differed.

Progressivism and the Rights of African Americans

The Progressive movement achieved some remarkable successes. But progressive efforts at reform had limits, particularly when it came to securing the rights of African Americans.

Theodore Roosevelt compiled a mixed record concerning the treatment of African Americans. In 1901 he invited Booker T. Washington to the White House, becoming the first U.S. president to entertain an African American as a dinner guest there. Roosevelt also refused to bow to pressure to withdraw his appointment of an African American collector of tariffs in South Carolina.

HISTORY'S VOICES

> "I cannot consent to take the position that the doorway of hope—the door of opportunity—is to be shut upon any man, no matter how worthy, purely upon the grounds of race or color. Such an attitude would, according to my contentions, be fundamentally wrong."
> —Theodore Roosevelt

However, Roosevelt's reaction to an event in 1906 in Brownsville, Texas, disappointed African Americans. Twelve members of the African American 25th Infantry were accused of going on a shooting spree in town. The members of the 25th were told that if no one accepted responsibility, they would all be dishonorably discharged. None came forward. Roosevelt signed the papers discharging 167 African American soldiers, denying them all back pay and canceling their pensions. Years later, the truth came out that the soldiers involved in the **Brownsville incident** had been falsely accused. It wasn't until 1972 that their records were corrected to read "honorable discharge."

President Woodrow Wilson had a worse record on civil rights. He opposed a federal antilynching law and maintained that the matter should be dealt with at the state level. He also allowed cabinet members to segregate their offices, which had been desegregated since Reconstruction. In addition, during Wilson's administration, Congress passed a law making it a felony for blacks and whites to marry in the District of Columbia.

The outbreak of World War I in Europe in 1914 brought an end to the Progressive Era. As the United States edged closer to war, reformers found that Americans were more interested in the war and less eager to devote their energies to the reform movement. World War I, not progressivism, dominated President Wilson's second term in office.

READING CHECK **Drawing Conclusions** How would you characterize Roosevelt's and Wilson's records in regard to African Americans' rights?

SECTION 4 ASSESSMENT

HSS 11.2.9, 11.5.4, 11.10.7

Reviewing Ideas, Terms, and People

1. **a. Identify** What was the **Sixteenth Amendment**?
   b. Explain What did Progressives like and not like about Taft?
   c. Evaluate Do you think Roosevelt should have run for a third term, run as the Bull Moose candidate, or not run again?

2. **a. Recall** What was the **New Freedom**?
   b. Compare How did the **Clayton Antitrust Act** expand on the Sherman Antitrust Act?
   c. Predict How might the Federal Reserve Act protect the nation in the future?

3. **a. Identify** What was the **Nineteenth Amendment**?
   b. Elaborate How did the tactics of both NAWSA and the NWP succeed?

4. **a. Recall** What was the **Brownsville incident**?
   b. Make Inferences What do you suppose Wilson's reasons were for not supporting an antilynching law?

Critical Thinking

5. **Analyzing Information** Copy the chart below and record examples of the major elements of Wilson's New Freedom.

Wilson's New Freedom		
Tariff reduction	Banking reform	Antitrust legislation

FOCUS ON SPEAKING ELA W1.1; LS2.0

6. **Persuasive** In 1913 Congress debated the bill that would become the Underwood Tariff Act. Suppose you are a member of Congress. Write a short speech in which you support or oppose a graduated income tax. Provide specific examples to support your argument.

CHAPTER 6 DOCUMENT-BASED INVESTIGATION

Impact of Progressivism

HSS 11.2.1, 11.2.9

Historical Context The documents below provide different types of information about the muckrakers, turn-of-the-century journalists and activists who publicized corruption and urban problems.

Task Examine the documents and answer the questions that follow. Then you will be asked to write an essay about the goals of muckrakers, using facts from the documents and from the chapter to support the position you take in your thesis statement.

DOCUMENT 1

The muckrakers got their nickname from a tool used to scrape up sewage and other unwanted garbage. The cartoon below reflects President Theodore Roosevelt's investigation into unsanitary conditions in meat packing plants. The investigation was sparked by muckraker Upton Sinclair's book *The Jungle*.

A NAUSEATING JOB, BUT IT MUST BE DONE
(President Roosevelt takes hold of the investigating muck-rake himself in the packing-house scandal.)

DOCUMENT 2

One leading muckraker was Lincoln Steffens, who wrote several articles on city corruption between 1902 and 1904. He published the collection as a book titled *The Shame of the Cities*. In this introduction to the book, he reflects on the central problem that faced all of the cities he studied.

"[P]olitics is business. That's what's the matter with it... But there is hope, not alone despair, in the commercialism of our politics. If our political leaders are to be always a lot of political merchants, they will supply any demand we may create. All we have to do is to establish a steady demand for good government... If we would leave parties to the politicians, and would vote not for the party, not even for men, but for the city, and the State, and the nation, we should rule parties, and cities, and States, and nation. If we would vote in mass on the more promising ticket, or, if the two are equally bad, would throw out the party that is in, and wait till the next election and then throw out the other party that is in—then, I say, the commercial politician would feel a demand for good government and he would supply it. That process would take a generation or more to complete, for the politicians now really do not know what good government is. But it has taken as long to develop bad government, and the politicians know what that is. If it would not 'go,' they would offer something else, and, if the demand were steady, they, being so commercial, would 'deliver the goods.'"

DOCUMENT 3

Florence Kelley was a social worker and lawyer who published numerous studies on urban problems. The following is from a study she conducted with Alzina P. Stevens on child labor in Chicago. It led to the first Illinois laws limiting work hours for women and children.

"The Ewing Street Italian colony furnishes a large contingent to the army of bootblacks and newsboys; lads who leave home at 2:30 A.M. to secure the first edition of the morning paper, selling each edition as it appears, and filling the intervals with blacking boots and tossing pennies, until, in the winter half of the year, they gather in the Polk Street Night-School, to doze in the warmth, or torture the teacher with the gamin [street kid] tricks acquired by day. For them, school is "a lark," or a peaceful retreat from parental beatings and shrieking juniors at home during the bitter nights of the Chicago winter.

There is no body of self-supporting children more in need of effective care than these newsboys and bootblacks. They are ill-fed, ill-housed, ill-clothed, illiterate, and wholly untrained and unfitted for any occupation. The only useful thing they learn at their work in common with the children who learn in school, is the rapid calculation of small sums in making change; and this does not go far enough to be of any practical value."

Skills Focus: READING LIKE A HISTORIAN

HSS Analysis HR4, HI1, HI4

1. **a. Describe** Look at the political cartoon in Document 1. Describe what is going on.
   b. Interpret Do you think the artist sees the work of muckrakers as positive or negative? Explain.
2. **a. Compare** Refer to Document 2. To what does Steffens compare politics?
   b. Interpret Steffens blames the public for urban problems. Why?
   c. Evaluate Would Steffens's reform work? Explain.
3. **a. Recall** Refer to Document 3. What kinds of work do the boys do?
   b. Analyze Why do you think the boys see no importance in going to school?
4. **Document-Based Essay Question** Consider the question below and form a thesis statement. Using examples from Documents 1, 2, and 3, create an outline and write a short essay supporting your position.
   How did muckrakers change government and society?

See **Skills Handbook**, p. H28–H29, H31–H33

CHAPTER 6 Chapter Review

Visual Summary: The Progressives

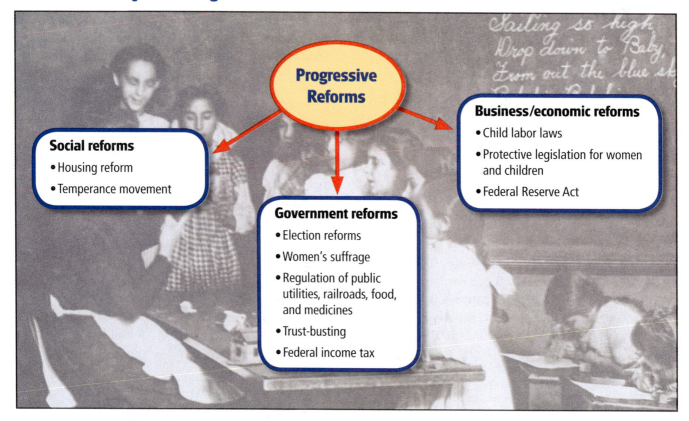

Progressive Reforms

Social reforms
- Housing reform
- Temperance movement

Government reforms
- Election reforms
- Women's suffrage
- Regulation of public utilities, railroads, food, and medicines
- Trust-busting
- Federal income tax

Business/economic reforms
- Child labor laws
- Protective legislation for women and children
- Federal Reserve Act

Reviewing Key Terms and People

Match each lettered definition with the correct numbered item.

a. A law that gave American women the right to vote

b. A reform that gives voters the power to put a proposed law on the ballot for public approval

c. A law that allowed Congress to levy taxes based on an individual's income

d. A law giving voters power to elect senators directly

e. A law that banned the manufacture and sale of alcoholic beverages in the United States

f. A women's organization that fought poverty, segregation, lynchings, and Jim Crow laws

g. Theodore Roosevelt's plan to balance the needs of workers, business, and consumers fairly

h. A law that created a central fund from which banks could borrow to prevent collapse

i. A women's suffrage group that favored a state-by-state approach

1. Eighteenth Amendment
2. Federal Reserve Act
3. initiative
4. National Association of Colored Women
5. National American Woman Suffrage Association
6. Sixteenth Amendment
7. Seventeenth Amendment
8. Nineteenth Amendment
9. Square Deal

History's Impact video program

Review the video to answer the closing question: What impact have labor laws had on American workers and industries?

Comprehension and Critical Thinking

SECTION 1 (pp. 170–175) HSS 11.2.9

12. a. **Analyze** How did the commission plan make city government more effective?

    b. **Evaluate** Why do you think that the city manager plan of government eventually became more popular than the commission plan?

SECTION 2 (pp. 177–182) HSS 11.10.7

13. a. **Recall** What strategy did major women's suffrage organizations use to campaign for the vote?

    b. **Draw Conclusions** How did the Supreme Court influence the decision to use this strategy?

    c. **Evaluate** What were some possible advantages and disadvantages of adopting this strategy?

SECTION 3 (pp. 183–188) HSS 11.2.9

14. a. **Define** What was the Elkins Act?

    b. **Analyze** Why did the U.S. attorney general sue the Northern Securities Company?

    c. **Elaborate** Why do you think that regulating the railroads was such a high priority for Roosevelt?

SECTION 4 (pp. 189–193) HSS 11.2.9, 11.5.4, 11.10.7

15. a. **Identify** What were the three main reforms called for in the New Freedom?

    b. **Make Inferences** How did all of those reforms relate to business in the United States?

    c. **Evaluate** Why would the president be so concerned about business practices?

Using the Internet

go.hrw.com
Practice Online
Keyword: SE7 CH6

16. Upton Sinclair's novel *The Jungle* had a powerful effect on readers, including President Roosevelt. Using the keyword above, research Roosevelt's reaction to the novel. Then write a paragraph explaining how the novel moved Roosevelt to act.

Analyzing Primary Sources HSS HR4

Reading Like a Historian

This political cartoon shows President Theodore Roosevelt's support for William Howard Taft as his successor.

17. **Describe** What relationship does the cartoon show?

18. **Analyze** Do you think the cartoonist supports Roosevelt's action?

Critical Reading ELA R3.8

Read the passage in Section 4 that begins with the heading "Women Gain the Vote." Then answer the question that follows.

19. How did Alice Paul and Lucy Burns change the American women's suffrage movement?

    A Their decision to adopt a state-by-state approach split the main suffrage organization.

    B Their support of NAWSA led to success.

    C Their use of tactics from the British movement focused new attention on the suffragists' cause.

    D Their attention-getting tactics turned supporters away from the women's suffrage movement.

WRITING FOR THE SAT ELA W1.1

Think about the following issue:

Roosevelt believed in achieving a balance between conservation and management of the nation's wilderness areas. He thought that some land should be kept in its natural state and some should be used to meet the nation's needs.

20. **Assignment** Do you agree with Roosevelt's beliefs about the proper use of the nation's wilderness areas? Write a short essay in which you develop your position on this issue. Support your point of view with reasoning and examples from your reading and studies.

CHAPTER 7

1898–1917
Entering the WORLD STAGE

THE BIG PICTURE U.S. foreign relations took a new turn at the end of the nineteenth century. Global competition for empire led the United States into war against Spain and into military conflicts in Mexico. The United States had forged a new role as a world power.

California Standards

History-Social Sciences

11.1 Students analyze the significant events in the founding of the nation and its attempts to realize the philosophy of government described in the Declaration of Independence.

11.4 Students trace the rise of the United States to its role as a world power in the twentieth century.

Skills FOCUS READING LIKE A HISTORIAN

In the Battle of San Juan Hill, future president Theodore Roosevelt leads a band of rough-and-ready volunteers in a famous charge in a war against Spain.
Interpreting Visuals What kind of leader does this painting suggest Roosevelt was? What kind of president do you think he would make?

See **Skills Handbook**, p. H30

U.S.

February 1898 *USS Maine* explodes in Havana Harbor, triggering the Spanish-American War.

1900

World

1900 Radicals in China stage the Boxer Rebellion to drive away foreigners.

198

History's Impact video program
Watch the video to understand the impact of the Panama Canal.

1904 The United States begins construction of the Panama Canal.

1911 President Taft promotes "dollar diplomacy."

April 1914 U.S. troops intervene in the Mexican Revolution, occupying Veracruz, Mexico.

August 1914 Panama Canal opens.

1903 — 1906 — 1909 — 1912 — 1915 — 1918

1903 Panama declares independence from Colombia.

1905 Japan wins the Russo-Japanese War.

1910 The Mexican Revolution begins.

1917 Russian Revolution begins.

199

SECTION 1
The Lure of Imperialism

BEFORE YOU READ

MAIN IDEA

The United States entered the imperialist competition late, but it soon extended its power and influence in the Pacific region.

READING FOCUS

1. What inspired the imperialist activity of the late 1800s?
2. How did the United States take control of Hawaii?
3. How did the United States gain influence in China?
4. How did the United States exert influence in Japan?

KEY TERMS AND PEOPLE

imperialism
bayonet constitution
Liliuokalani
Sanford B. Dole
sphere of influence
Open Door Policy
Boxer Rebellion
Russo-Japanese War

HSS 11.1.4 Examine the effects of the Civil War and Reconstruction and of the industrial revolution, including demographic shifts and the emergence in the late nineteenth century of the United States as a world power.

HSS 11.4.1 List the purpose and the effects of the Open Door policy.

▲ Uncle Sam did not have to look far to pluck new territories. This political cartoon suggests that the nation continued to eye neighboring countries.

THE INSIDE STORY

Why did the United States buy Alaska? In the 1890s the United States seemed to be off to a late start in the scramble for colonial possessions. European nations were already busily adding new colonies to their empires. The United States, though, had actually taken its first step toward imperialism back in 1867. While European nations were looking toward Africa and Asia, the United States was expanding in North America and the Pacific.

The huge Alaska landmass lies at the northwestern edge of North America, almost touching northeastern Russia. Russian fur traders were the first foreigners to settle there, in 1784. With a charter from Czar Paul I, the Russian-American Company served as Alaska's government after 1799. Russian, British, and American fur traders all competed amicably. But by 1867, sea otters, which had the most valuable fur, were becoming scarce. In addition, Russia was struggling to recover from the Crimean War. Russia offered to sell the territory to the United States.

At the time, William H. Seward was secretary of state for President Andrew Johnson. He had visions of an American empire and was eager to buy Alaska. He thought it had potential as a resource for fur, timber, and metals. He faced opposition from Congress, though. Unaware of Alaska's rich mineral resources, many people regarded the territory as a frozen wasteland.

Seward finally succeeded in buying Alaska for $7.2 million. Critics joked about Seward's Folly and Seward's Icebox. Later, though, after gold and oil were discovered in Alaska, Americans came to appreciate the bargain they'd gotten.

Alaska was not Seward's only smart acquisition. The very same year—1867—he snapped up the Midway Islands, strategically located west of Hawaii.

200 CHAPTER 7

Imperialist Activity

From the 1870s to the 1910s, a few industrialized nations actively competed for territory in Africa, Asia, and Latin America. This scramble for territorial control was part of the imperialist mind-set. **Imperialism** involves the extension of a nation's power over other lands.

By the late 1800s, nations such as Great Britain, France, Belgium, Germany, and Japan had all embraced the imperialist spirit. Soon, beginning in Hawaii, the United States would also pursue imperialist policies. What led to this quest for empire?

Economic interests The Industrial Revolution had brought great prosperity to the Western powers. Industrialized nations had flooded their own countries with goods and investment capital. Now they looked to other nations for new customers and new places to invest. Industrialists also began to look to Africa, Asia, and Latin America for new sources of raw materials for their factories.

Military needs Industrialized nations created strong navies to defend their shores and protect their trading interests. But navies needed bases where ships could refuel and make repairs. Industrialized nations sought foreign territory so they could build these coaling stations in strategic places.

Ideology Two popular ideologies also contributed to imperialism. One was a strong sense of nationalism, or love of one's country. Many people felt that territorial conquests enhanced a nation's power and prestige.

The other ideological motive was a feeling of cultural superiority. Because Africa, Asia, and Latin America had less industry and urban development, they seemed "backward" to many Europeans and Americans in the late 1800s.

Social Darwinism fed into this view. Social Darwinists believed that when nations competed against one another, only the fittest would survive. Some people therefore considered it a social responsibility to "civilize" the inhabitants of less developed countries and spread the benefits of Western society. In addition, Protestant Christian missionaries felt they had a moral duty to convert others to their beliefs.

The scramble for territory By the late 1800s, European imperial powers had taken control of vast territories in Africa and Asia, and dominated the economy of Latin America. The British Empire alone ruled about one-quarter of the world's land and population. France, Belgium, Germany, and Japan also controlled huge areas overseas.

Many Americans began to believe it was time for the United States to claim its own territories abroad. The prospect of new markets and military advantages was a powerful attraction. Some Americans, too, wanted to spread the Christian faith and democratic values. Josiah Strong, a Protestant clergyman, expressed this viewpoint eloquently.

HISTORY'S VOICES

"The two great needs of mankind . . . are, first, a pure, spiritual Christianity, and second, civil liberty. Without controversy, these are the forces which, in the past, have contributed most to the elevation of the human race . . . It follows, then, that the Anglo-Saxon [person of British descent], as the great representative of these two ideas . . . is divinely commissioned to be, in a peculiar sense, his brother's keeper."
—Josiah Strong, *Our Country*, 1885

In the mid-1800s, Americans had believed it was their manifest destiny to expand westward to the Pacific Ocean. Now people sought to move even beyond the shoreline, to claim distant islands farther west.

READING CHECK **Summarizing** What were the three main reasons that industrialized nations became imperialist nations?

ACADEMIC VOCABULARY
ideology set of ideas about human life or culture

CAUSES OF U.S. EXPANSIONISM — QUICK FACTS

CAUSES
- **Economic** Desire for new markets and raw materials
- **Military** Desire for naval bases and coaling stations
- **Ideological** Desire to bring Christianity, western-style culture, and democracy to other peoples

→ United States expansionism

ENTERING THE WORLD STAGE

Taking Control of Hawaii

American expansionists became interested in acquiring Hawaii in the late 1800s. Located some 2,000 miles west of California, Hawaii was an ideal spot for coaling stations and naval bases for ships traveling to and from Asia.

Early contact Americans were not the first outsiders to show interest in Hawaii. A British explorer, Captain James Cook, had visited the islands in 1778. Great Britain did not claim Hawaii then, but Captain Cook's voyage brought Hawaii to the attention of the outside world.

Shortly after Cook's arrival, Hawaii's Chief Kamehameha (kah-MAY-hah-MAY-hah) united the eight major islands under his leadership. He established a monarchy and began a profitable trade in sandalwood. In the 1820s U.S. ships began arriving with some frequency, bringing traders and missionaries. Many of the missionaries had come from New England to convert Hawaiians to Christianity. Soon, the missionaries and their families began to settle down and raise crops, particularly sugarcane.

The foreigners also brought diseases, to which Hawaiians had no immunity. The population of Hawaii declined from about 300,000 in the 1770s to about 40,000 by 1893.

Sugar interests gain power As more and more Americans came to the islands, investors in the sugar industry began increasing their control. Americans had a sweet tooth, and sugar planters grew very rich. To keep the sugarcane plantations running, planters needed workers. With so few native Hawaiians left, planters brought in workers from China, Japan, and the Philippines.

Kalakaua became king in 1874. By this time, Americans had gained control over Hawaii's land and economy. But Kalakaua was strongly nationalistic. He resented the Americans' influence over his government and promised to put native Hawaiians back into power.

HISTORY'S VOICES

"Do not be led by the foreigners; they had no part in our hardships, in gaining the country. Do not be led by their false teachings."
—Kalakaua, "Proclamation," 1872

Early in his reign, King Kalakaua allied himself with landowners in his desire to strengthen the Hawaiian economy. He negotiated a treaty in 1875 that allowed Hawaiian sugar to enter the United States tax free. This

Pineapple Industry

James Dole, Sanford Dole's cousin, began growing pineapples in Hawaii in 1901. By the 1930s Dole supplied 90 percent of the world's canned pineapple.

made Hawaiian sugar cheaper than sugar from other places. The treaty gave a real boost to the Hawaiian sugar industry. But the more money that the sugar tycoons made, the more power they wanted over Hawaiian affairs.

Plotting against the king A group of American business leaders, planters, and traders formed a secret society called the Hawaiian League. Its purpose was to overthrow the monarchy and establish a democracy in Hawaii under the control of Americans.

Conflicts between these American business leaders and the king escalated in 1886. The United States wanted the port of Pearl Harbor in exchange for renewing the sugar treaty. But King Kalakaua refused to give up the independence of any part of Hawaii.

Angered, the Hawaiian League forced King Kalakaua to sign a new constitution at gunpoint in July 1887. The king angrily called it the **bayonet constitution**. It severely restricted his power and deprived most Hawaiians of the vote. King Kalakaua was now forced to give Pearl Harbor to the United States. This gave U.S. warships a permanent port in Hawaii.

American sugar planters now had political control over Hawaii. But the economy suffered a heavy blow in 1890. The United States revoked the sugar treaty in order to support sugar producers on the U.S. mainland. American sugar producers in Hawaii believed they had only one option to protect their businesses—become part of the United States. Secretly, they began talks with U.S. officials about annexation.

End of the monarchy When King Kalakaua died in 1891, his sister **Liliuokalani** (LI-lee-uh-woh-kuh-LAHN-ee) became queen. Queen Liliuokalani was a Hawaiian nationalist who wanted to do away with the bayonet constitution. In January 1893, she announced her plan to restore the power of the Hawaiian monarchy. In response, members of the business community plotted to overthrow her. They wanted the islands to be governed as a territory of the United States.

John L. Stevens, the American minister to Hawaii, decided he would help the rebel sugar planters. Without authorization, he ordered four boatloads of U.S. Marines to go ashore. They took up positions around the royal palace, aiming machine guns and cannons at the building. The rebels then declared an end to the monarchy. Queen Liliuokalani surrendered under protest on January 17, 1893.

FACES OF HISTORY
Queen LILIUOKALANI
1838–1917

Born into a royal Hawaiian family, Lydia Liliuokalani grew up proud of her heritage. Although she studied with foreign missionaries, learned to speak English, and married the son of a Boston sea captain, she did not want Hawaii to become part of the United States.

After ascending to the throne in 1891, Liliuokalani tried to fortify the islands through a political movement called Oni Pa'a (Stand Firm). Nonetheless, she was soon overthrown by American business owners. Accused of attempting to revolt against the new government, Liliuokalani was arrested in 1895 and jailed for more than a year. After being released, the queen continued to live quietly in Hawaii, a beloved figure to her people.

Make Inferences What can you infer about the goals of Queen Liliuokalani's Oni Pa'a movement?

The rebel leaders quickly formed a new regime with **Sanford B. Dole**, a sugar tycoon, as president. John L. Stevens, acting on his own once again, formally recognized the new Republic of Hawaii. He also proclaimed Hawaii to be under U.S. protection, while the Senate considered a treaty to annex the islands.

Annexation Troubled by the events in Hawaii, President Grover Cleveland put the treaty on hold and ordered an investigation. The investigator's report condemned the revolt against Liliuokalani and proposed restoring her to the throne. Cleveland agreed, but Dole refused to step down.

Cleveland was unwilling to use military force to back Liliuokalani. Yet he would not support annexation, either. The matter remained at a standstill until the next president, William McKinley, took office. McKinley favored annexation, and Congress narrowly voted its approval in 1898. Hawaii became an American territory and eventually—in 1959—the fiftieth state. In 1993 Congress apologized for the U.S. role in overthowing Liliuokalani.

READING CHECK Sequencing How did American sugar interests gain so much power in Hawaii?

THE BOXER REBELLION

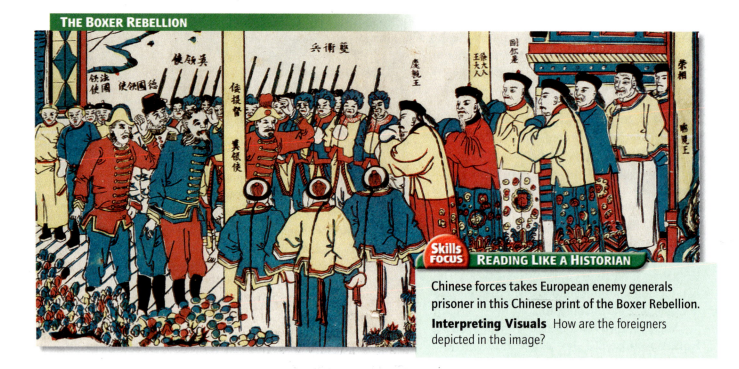

Skills Focus: READING LIKE A HISTORIAN

Chinese forces takes European enemy generals prisoner in this Chinese print of the Boxer Rebellion.
Interpreting Visuals How are the foreigners depicted in the image?

Influence in China

Early on, Hawaii had attracted American interest because it was a convenient place to stop for fuel and supplies on the journey to China. American traders had been traveling to China since 1784.

Even so, China stayed nearly isolated from the rest of the world. It strictly controlled foreign trade, allowing foreigners only in the port of Guangzhou. Then in 1842, the British forced China to open five ports to British trade. Two years later, the United States received broader trading privileges as well. For the next 50 years, China's rulers struggled to keep foreign interests from overrunning the country.

The threat was not just from Western nations, however. In 1895 Japan took over the island of Taiwan and tried to seize the Liaotung Peninsula too. European powers—Russia, France, Germany, and Great Britain—quickly carved out their own **spheres of influence** in China. A sphere of influence is a geographic area where an outside nation exerts special economic or political control.

The United States was too late to secure a sphere of influence in China. American leaders feared that the United States would be shut out of the valuable China trade. As a result, Secretary of State John Hay proposed the **Open Door Policy** in 1899. The aim was to give all nations equal trading rights in China. As Senator Henry Cabot Lodge of Massachusetts declared, "We ask no favors; we only ask that we shall be admitted to that great market upon the same terms with the rest of the world."

Hay sent notes recommending the Open Door Policy to Great Britain, Germany, Russia, Japan, France, and Italy. None of them agreed to it, but none rejected it outright. Therefore, Hay felt he could announce in March 1900 that the Open Door Policy had been approved.

With foreign countries now vying for business in China, antiforeigner sentiments grew. A secret group called the Society of Righteous and Harmonious Fists—known to westerners as Boxers—began attacking foreign missionaries and Chinese Christians. In June 1900 the Boxers laid siege to the capital city of Beijing in what became known as the **Boxer Rebellion**.

Western nations rushed 20,000 troops—including 2,000 Americans—to China. They soon quelled the rebellion, and a year later, in September 1901, China signed a humbling settlement agreement.

The Boxer Rebellion increased support for Hay's Open Door Policy. Western nations realized that competition among themselves would hurt their ability to exploit the China trade.

READING CHECK **Identifying Problem and Solution** Why did Hay propose the Open Door Policy?

Influence in Japan

Until Japan seized Taiwan from China in 1895, no one would have thought of the Japanese as imperialists. Since the late 1630s, the country had been inward-looking, shutting itself off from nearly all foreign contact.

By the mid-1800s, though, Japan came under U.S. pressure to open its ports to trade. In 1853 President Millard Fillmore sent Commodore Matthew Perry with a fleet of four ships into Edo (Tokyo) Bay. Japan was not yet industrialized, and Japanese people had never seen steamships before. They were awed by the demonstration of American naval strength.

The Japanese government knew that it could not defend itself against a modern navy. It also realized that it could no longer maintain its isolated position in the world. So in 1854 its leaders agreed to a treaty that opened Japan to trade with the United States.

Japan then embarked on a program of rapid modernization. It transformed itself into an industrial power and built a strong military. After taking over Taiwan, Japan began eyeing Korea and the Chinese province of Manchuria. Russia, meanwhile, also wanted these lands.

In 1904 the **Russo-Japanese War** broke out. The conflict took a toll on both sides, and by the following spring, both sides had had enough. At Japan's request, President Theodore Roosevelt helped negotiate a peace treaty. He met with representatives of the two countries in Portsmouth, New Hampshire, and hammered out a compromise. Roosevelt received the Nobel Prize for Peace for his efforts in negotiating the Treaty of Portsmouth.

Japan was the clear victor in the war with Russia, and it emerged as a major power. It was now the strongest power in East Asia and a rival to the United States for influence in China and the Pacific region. American leaders knew that Japan remained hungry for territory. It had fewer natural resources than the other imperialist nations. In addition, the Japanese government wanted to expand territorially in order to counterbalance U.S. expansion in the Pacific.

Roosevelt decided to impress upon Japan—and the rest of the world—just how powerful the U.S. military was. In 1907 he sent four squadrons of battleships, known as the Great White Fleet, on a 43,000-mile, around-the-world journey. Led by Rear Admiral Charles Sperry, the fleet stopped at 20 ports on six continents, including a port in Japan, before returning home in 1909.

READING CHECK Identifying the Main Idea
How did the United States influence Japan's economic policies and its imperialist ambitions?

SECTION 1 ASSESSMENT

HSS 11.1.4, 11.4.1

Reviewing Ideas, Terms, and People

1. **a. Define** What is **imperialism**?
   b. Summarize What were the main incentives for countries to seek new territories?
   c. Evaluate Do you think imperialists who wanted to spread western culture were arrogant or well meaning? Explain.

2. **a. Recall** Why did its location make Hawaii attractive to Americans?
   b. Draw Conclusions What role did sugar play in the desire of many Americans to control Hawaii?
   c. Elaborate How did American sugar planters go outside the law to gain control over Hawaii?

3. **a. Describe** What was the **Open Door Policy**?
   b. Explain Why did Americans think they might be at a disadvantage in trading with China?
   c. Predict What would have been the likely consequences for the United States if other western powers had divided China into colonies instead of accepting the Open Door Policy?

4. **a. Identify** Who was Commodore Perry?
   b. Analyze Why did the United States want to impress Japan in particular with the Great White Fleet?

Critical Thinking

5. **Identifying Cause and Effect** Copy the chart below and record the effects of key events in Hawaii's history.

Event	Effect

FOCUS ON WRITING ELA W1.1

6. **Expository** Write an essay about the different perspectives that a Chinese native and a Christian missionary might have had on the Boxer Rebellion. Explain how each might have viewed the Boxers' goals and their means of achieving them.

SECTION 2

The Spanish-American War

BEFORE YOU READ

MAIN IDEA
A quick victory in the Spanish-American War gave the United States a new role as a world power.

READING FOCUS
1. How did simmering unrest in Cuba lead to rebellion?
2. Why did Americans get war fever?
3. What happened in the course of the Spanish-American War?
4. Why was annexing the Philippines controversial?

KEY TERMS AND PEOPLE
José Martí
William Randolph Hearst
Joseph Pulitzer
yellow journalism
de Lôme letter
George Dewey
Emilio Aguinaldo
Rough Riders
Battle of San Juan Hill

HSS 11.1.4 Examine the effects of the Civil War and Reconstruction and of the industrial revolution, including demographic shifts and the emergence in the late nineteenth century of the United States as a world power.

HSS 11.4.2 Describe the Spanish-American War and U.S. expansion in the South Pacific.

"You Furnish the PICTURES, I'll Furnish the WAR"

Did a telegram start a war? In the 1890s rival newspapers owned by William Randolph Hearst and Joseph Pulitzer were competing fiercely. They tried to woo readers with sensational stories and blaring banner headlines.

How far would Hearst go? In January 1897 he sent an artist and reporter team to cover the Cuban rebellion against Spanish rule. Frederic Remington was to send drawings of war scenes. Richard Harding Davis would write the dramatic stories. According to one account, Remington spent some time in Cuba and found that not much was happening in the way of a war. He sent this telegram: "W. R. Hearst, *New York Journal*, N.Y.: Everything is quiet. There is no trouble here. There will be no war. I wish to return. Remington."

Supposedly Hearst answered: "Remington, Havana: Please remain. You furnish the pictures, and I'll furnish the war. W. R. Hearst."

Is the story true? One historian points out that the only source was a journalist named James Creelman, who wrote a book about his life as a foreign correspondent for Hearst. Hearst always denied a role in "manufacturing" the war, but the tale fit with people's belief that he would do anything for a good story. Certainly both the *Journal* and its rival, the *New York World*, played up every incident in Cuba. But Americans were already sympathetic to the Cuban rebels, and perhaps they did not need a push toward war.

▶ War news draws a crowd outside the *New York Journal* offices.

Simmering Unrest in Cuba

By the 1890s Spain had lost all of its colonies in the Western Hemisphere except for Cuba and Puerto Rico. Cubans in particular were not happy to be part of Spain's empire. Since 1868, Cubans had launched a series of revolts against Spanish rule. Spain responded by exiling leaders of the independence movement.

José Martí was one such leader, exiled in 1878. He moved to New York City, where he continued to promote independence and inspire his fellow Cubans. Through newspaper articles and poetry, Martí urged Cubans to fight for their freedom. He also founded the Cuban Revolutionary Party in 1892 and made preparations to return to his homeland.

Cubans rose once more in revolt against Spain in February 1895. Martí joined them in April, but a month later he was killed in battle. By dying for his country, José Martí immediately became one of Cuba's greatest heroes.

As the revolt raged on, Spain sent General Valeriano Weyler to suppress the rebels in 1896. Weyler forced thousands of civilians into camps controlled by the Spanish army to keep them from aiding the rebels. However, nearly one-third of the Cubans in the camps died from starvation or disease. Weyler's mistreatment of these civilians shocked Americans.

READING CHECK Summarizing How did José Martí inspire other Cubans to seek independence?

Americans Get War Fever

Many Americans were already sympathetic to the Cuban cause. They believed the Cubans' struggle was similar to their own during the American Revolution. They became even more supportive after learning how Cuban civilians were suffering under General Weyler.

The media's role In this era before radio, television, or the Internet, most people got their news from daily or weekly newspapers. At one point, New York City had as many as 15 daily newspaper editions.

Two of the most widely read papers were the *New York Journal*, published by **William Randolph Hearst**, and the *New York World*, published by **Joseph Pulitzer**. Both papers told scandalous stories and splashed large, shocking illustrations across their pages. This style of sensationalist reporting became known as **yellow journalism**, named after the "Yellow Kid," a popular comic strip that ran in the *World*. Determined to compete with the *World* in every way, the *Journal* created its own "yellow kid" comic, and the rivalry between the two papers became a competition between the two "yellow kids."

The *Journal* threw its support behind the Cuban rebels and refused to use any Spanish sources for news stories. Relying only on Cuban sources made the *Journal*'s stories biased, but it also made for exciting reading—and sold more papers.

Not to be left behind, the *World* abandoned all attempts at objectivity. It used the same strategy as the *Journal*, and newspaper sales went up. People could not get enough of the dramatic stories printed daily.

The explosion of the *Maine* Hearst felt strongly that the United States should intervene in Cuba. As a result, the *Journal* continued the drumbeat for war. In 1897 Hearst sent artist Frederic Remington to Cuba to create illustrations showing Spanish cruelty. Hearst printed those drawings in his papers to stir up more support for war with Spain.

President William McKinley was reluctant at first to involve the United States in the conflict. Events soon changed McKinley's

THE IMPACT TODAY

Culture
Today's most prestigious award in journalism is the Pulitzer Prize, funded by Joseph Pulitzer in his will.

FACES OF HISTORY

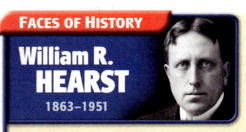

William R. HEARST 1863–1951

An outgoing and controversial man, William Randolph Hearst built a vast publishing empire. He began his career managing the *San Francisco Examiner*. At the height of his success, he owned 28 major newspapers and 18 magazines, along with various news services, radio stations, and movie companies. Hearst even served in the House of Representatives but was defeated in his efforts to become the mayor of New York City, and later the governor of New York State.

Orson Welles's 1941 film *Citizen Kane* depicted Hearst's extravagant life. It became one of the most popular films of all time.

Drawing Conclusions Many film critics consider *Citizen Kane* to be one of the best movies ever made. Why might Hearst's life make an interesting story?

PRIMARY SOURCES

Editorial

The *New York Journal* published this editorial on February 17, 1898, after the *Maine* exploded.

"To five hundred thousand Cubans starved or otherwise murdered have been added an American battleship and three hundred American sailors lost as the direct result of the dilatory [slow] policy of our government toward Spain. If we had stopped the war in Cuba when duty and policy alike urged us to do[,] the *Maine* would have been afloat today . . .

It was an accident, they say. Perhaps it was, but . . . it was an accident of a remarkably convenient kind for Spain. Two days ago we had five battleships in the Atlantic. Today we have four. A few more such accidents will leave us at the mercy of a Spanish fleet."

Skills Focus — READING LIKE A HISTORIAN

1. **Analyzing Primary Sources** Whom does the *Journal* blame for the deaths on the *Maine*?
2. **Recognizing Bias** What suggests that the *Journal* is biased against Spain?

See **Skills Handbook**, pp. H28–H29, H33

---

mind. On February 9, 1898, the *Journal* published a letter written by Enrique Dupuy de Lôme, Spain's minister to the United States. The letter had fallen into the hands of a Cuban spy who sold it to Hearst. The **de Lôme letter** ridiculed McKinley for being "weak and catering to the rabble." Americans were outraged at the remarks. The *Journal* called it "the worst insult to the United States in its history."

Furious Americans began clamoring for war with Spain. Then came the final straw: a violent tragedy in Havana Harbor that brought relations with Spain to a breaking point. The battleship USS *Maine* had been sent to Havana to protect American lives and property. On February 15, 1898, the *Maine* mysteriously blew up, killing 260 sailors.

"DESTRUCTION OF THE WAR SHIP MAINE WAS THE WORK OF AN ENEMY!" screamed the *Journal*'s headline, although there was no proof of this. Some historians now believe that a fire in a coal storage room caused the explosion. At the time, however, Americans blamed Spain. "Remember the *Maine*!" became the rallying cry of war supporters.

At the time, an inquiry into the explosion confirmed public perceptions, blaming a Spanish mine for destroying the *Maine*. In late March, President McKinley demanded that Spain grant Cuba its independence. When Spain refused, Congress declared a state of war on April 25, 1898. The Spanish-American War had begun.

READING CHECK **Making Inferences** Why did the *Journal* jump to the conclusion that the Spanish were responsible for the explosion of the *Maine*?

The Course of the War

Although its impact would be felt for years, the Spanish-American War lasted only about four months. It was fought on two fronts: Cuba and the Philippines.

War in the Philippines The Philippines are a group of islands located east of Vietnam between the Philippine Sea and the South China Sea. Spain had claimed the islands since the 1500s.

Before the United States declared war on Spain, Theodore Roosevelt (then the assistant secretary of the navy) sent secret orders to Commodore **George Dewey**, the commander of the U.S. Navy's Asiatic Squadron. If war broke out between the United States and Spain, Dewey's assignment was to attack the Spanish fleet in the Philippines.

Once Dewey received word that war had been declared, his squadron rushed to Manila Bay in the Philippines. Early on the morning of May 1, 1898, the Spanish fleet opened fire, but the American forces were out of range. Dewey had his sailors hold their fire for nearly half an hour, until they came within striking distance of the Spanish ships. Dewey did not want to waste ammunition, because the nearest American point of resupply was in California, some 7,000 miles away.

Finally, Commodore Dewey quietly told Charles Gridley, the captain of the flagship *Olympia*, "You may fire when ready, Gridley." The Americans had the advantage of modern ships with iron and steel hulls, as well as superior weaponry. They were soon inflicting heavy damage on the old-fashioned wooden ships of the enemy.

Then two hours into the battle, Captain Gridley reported that the *Olympia* was low on ammunition. Dewey decided to withdraw from battle so that the ships could redistribute their remaining supplies. To keep morale up, he told his men they were taking a break to eat breakfast. During the break, however, Dewey learned that the report about the ammunition was incorrect. The *Olympia* had plenty of supplies for the rest of the battle.

The Americans continued fighting shortly before noon. Soon the entire Spanish fleet was ablaze and sinking. In a matter of hours, the United States had won a decisive victory. Not a single American life was lost, but nearly 400 Spaniards were injured or killed in the Battle of Manila Bay.

Dewey then began planning an attack on the capital city of Manila. He found a willing partner in **Emilio Aguinaldo**, leader of a rebel army of Filipino patriots. Filipinos had been fighting for independence from Spain for two years. While Dewey's warships remained in the harbor, Aguinaldo's army captured Manila. Cut off by Dewey's fleet and surrounded by Aguinaldo's rebels, Spanish forces in the Philippines surrendered on August 14, 1898.

The war in Cuba Days before declaring war, Congress had recognized Cuba's independence and adopted the Teller Amendment. This stated that once Cuba freed itself from Spanish rule, the United States would "leave the government and control of the Island to its people."

Victory in Cuba proved difficult to achieve, however. The U.S. War Department was not as prepared as it should have been for the conflict.

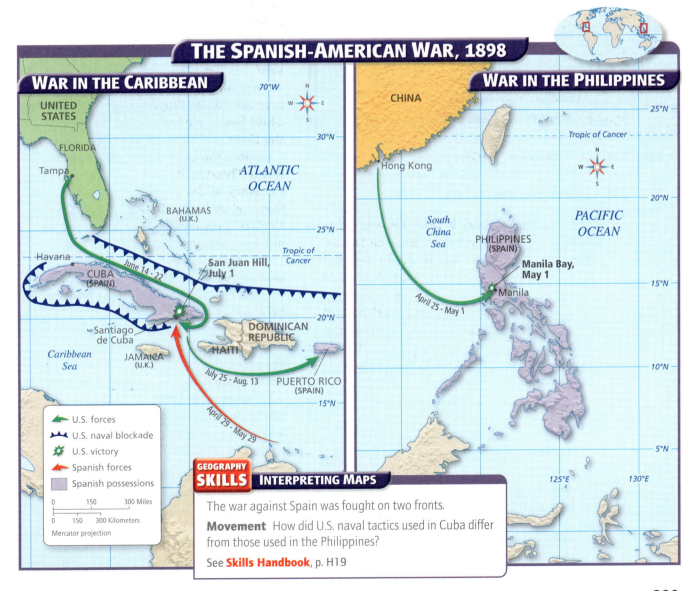

GEOGRAPHY SKILLS INTERPRETING MAPS

The war against Spain was fought on two fronts.

Movement How did U.S. naval tactics used in Cuba differ from those used in the Philippines?

See **Skills Handbook**, p. H19

ENTERING THE WORLD STAGE **209**

BUFFALO SOLDIERS AND ROUGH RIDERS

Skills Focus: READING LIKE A HISTORIAN

Some 10 African American regiments were called to serve in the Spanish-American War. The Ninth and Tenth Cavalries are shown here with the Rough Riders at the Battle of Kettle Hill.

Interpreting Visuals What marks these soldiers as Americans?

For example, it equipped soldiers with woolen uniforms for a summer war in a tropical climate. The mess pans—tin plates issued to soldiers—were left over from the Civil War. The canned meat in Cuba was so sickening that soldiers called it "embalmed beef."

Most of the soldiers who fought in Cuba were enlisted men (also called regulars), but there were many volunteers as well. The most famous volunteers were the **Rough Riders**, a regiment organized by Theodore Roosevelt after he left his navy post. Adventurous college athletes, cowboys, ranchers, and miners all joined the Rough Riders. They expected to fight on horseback, but because the transport ships to Cuba were overbooked, they had to leave their horses behind in America. The Rough Riders ended up functioning as foot soldiers instead of as a cavalry.

The American strategy in Cuba was to capture the port city of Santiago. U.S. troops needed to control the hills around the city. On July 1, one U.S. division seized the hill at El Caney after a four-hour fight.

That same day, some 8,000 U.S. soldiers fought to take control of Kettle and San Juan hills. Experienced African American soldiers of the Ninth and Tenth Cavalries—known as Buffalo Soldiers—led the charge, supported by the Rough Riders and regulars. Theodore Roosevelt described how the Rough Riders stayed the course.

HISTORY'S VOICES

> "We were still under a heavy fire and I got together a mixed lot of men and pushed on..., driving the Spaniards through a line of palm-trees, and over the crest of a chain of hills. When we reached these crests we found ourselves overlooking Santiago."
> —Theodore Roosevelt, *The Rough Riders*, 1902

By nightfall, U.S. troops controlled the ridge above Santiago. For their heroic actions in the **Battle of San Juan Hill**, six of the Buffalo Soldiers and two Rough Riders—including Theodore Roosevelt—received the Medal of Honor.

On July 3, the U.S. Navy sank the entire Spanish fleet off the coast of Cuba in the Battle of Santiago. Two weeks later, Spanish troops in Cuba surrendered. Soon after, U.S. troops defeated Spanish forces in Puerto Rico.

Consequences of the war The terms of the peace treaty proved costly for Spain. The Spanish had to give up all claims to Cuba and cede Puerto Rico and the Pacific island of Guam to the United States. Spain also turned control of the Philippines over to the United States in exchange for a $20 million payment.

For Americans, the victory in the Spanish-American War was sweet. John Hay, the ambassador to Great Britain, summed up his view in a letter to Theodore Roosevelt.

HISTORY'S VOICES

> "It has been a splendid little war; begun with the highest motives, carried on with magnificent intelligence and spirit, favored by that fortune which loves the brave."
> —John Hay, letter to Theodore Roosevelt

Still, the United States paid a heavy toll for the war. The monetary costs amounted to roughly $250 million. In addition, some 2,000 soldiers died, not from battle wounds but from yellow fever.

Despite the lives lost and the dollars spent, the Spanish-American War had a huge payoff for the United States. Senator Henry Cabot Lodge of Massachusetts noted that although the war was very brief, "its results were many, startling, and of world-wide meaning."

The United States now moved into the ranks of imperialist nations. Its new overseas territories gave it more bases for trade and for resupplying its navy. Within a year, it would capitalize on its new economic and military strength to acquire the Pacific island of Samoa. Expansionists expressed delight over the country's growing power, but the quest for empire troubled many Americans.

READING CHECK **Making Generalizations** How did the United States benefit from the war?

Annexing the Philippines

After the Spanish-American War, a controversy raged in the United States over whether to annex the Philippines. Some Americans were uneasy with the idea of controlling overseas territories. Others believed that imperialism not only made the United States stronger but also benefited those under colonial rule.

Arguments for annexation Some people who favored annexation believed that the United States had a duty to spread its values overseas. President McKinley, for example, spoke of the need "to educate the Filipinos, and uplift and civilize and Christianize them."

Other Americans wanted the Philippines for their economic and strategic value. Located on the route to China, the Philippines would be useful as a place to refuel and resupply ships. For that reason, many expansionists wanted to annex the Philippines before they fell into the hands of Germany, Japan, or another nation.

COUNTERPOINTS

Annexation of the Philippines

Senator Henry Cabot Lodge argued that the United States should annex the Philippines.

" The taking of the Philippines does not violate the principles of the Declaration of Independence, but will spread them among a people who have never known liberty and who in a few years will be ... unwilling to leave the shelter of the American flag. "

Henry Cabot Lodge, 1900

Senator George F. Hoar favored independence for the Philippines.

" Now, I claim that under the Declaration of Independence you cannot govern ... a foreign people ... against their will, because you think it is for their good, when they do not ... You have no right at the cannon's mouth to impose on an unwilling people ... your notions of freedom and notions of what is good. "

George F. Hoar, 1899

Skills Focus **READING LIKE A HISTORIAN**

Comparing How does each senator invoke the Declaration of Independence in his argument?

See **Skills Handbook**, p. H10

ACADEMIC VOCABULARY
foundation underlying principle

Opponents' views Americans who opposed annexing the Philippines felt strongly, too. Some reasoned that annexation would violate the ideal of self-government—the foundation of the American system. They formed the Anti-Imperialist League in June 1898.

Many African Americans worried about exporting oppression to the Philippines. A group of activists called the Colored Citizens of Boston argued that with racism and violence still painfully common at home, "the duty of the President and country is to reform these crying domestic wrongs and not attempt the civilization of alien peoples by powder and shot."

Other Americans feared that annexing the Philippines would open the doors to a flood of new immigrants. Samuel Gompers, the leader of the American Federation of Labor, believed that this would hurt American workers.

American rule After a fierce debate, the Senate narrowly approved the treaty calling for annexation of the Philippines. The measure passed on February 6, 1899.

Filipino nationalists were infuriated. They had been fighting for independence from Spain for years. Now they had exchanged one set of rulers for another.

Emilio Aguinaldo had already set up a government and proclaimed himself president of the new Philippine Republic. He warned that he was prepared to take military action if the United States tried to assume control of the Philippines.

To no one's surprise, fighting broke out. For three years, Filipino independence fighters battled U.S. soldiers. Aguinaldo was finally captured by the Americans and forced from power in 1901. By the time the rebellion ended, more than 4,000 U.S. soldiers and some 220,000 Filipinos had died, many from disease.

In taking over the Philippines, the stated goal of the United States was to prepare the islands for independence. Therefore, although Congress put a U.S.-appointed governor in charge, Filipinos were also allowed a voice in governing. At first they could only elect members to the lower house of their legislature. Then in 1916, Filipino voters won the right to elect both houses of their legislature. Three decades later, on July 4, 1946, the United States finally granted full independence to the Philippines.

READING CHECK **Identifying Cause and Effect** What were some of the effects of American annexation of the Philippines?

SECTION 2 ASSESSMENT

Online Quiz Keyword: SE7 HP7

HSS 11.1.4, 11.4.2

Reviewing Ideas, Terms, and People

1. **a. Recall** By the 1890s, how did Cubans view Spanish rule?
   b. Explain How did José Martí promote the Cuban cause from New York City?
   c. Evaluate Did General Weyler's actions toward civilians help or hinder the Spanish cause? Explain.

2. **a. Define** What was yellow journalism?
   b. Draw Conclusions Why was the sinking of the USS Maine significant?
   c. Elaborate Was the press irresponsible in covering the buildup to the Spanish-American War? Why or why not?

3. **a. Identify** What were the key battles during the Spanish-American War?
   b. Summarize What were the terms of the peace treaty?
   c. Predict If the United States had lost the Spanish-American War, do you think it would have been more or less likely to continue its quest for empire? Explain.

4. **a. Recall** Why were the Philippines of strategic importance to the United States?

   b. Make Inferences Why might Emilio Aguinaldo and other Filipino nationalists have felt betrayed by the United States?
   c. Evaluate Was the United States justified in not granting immediate independence to the Philippines? Why or why not?

Critical Thinking

5. **Contrasting** Copy the chart below and record the reasons why some Americans supported annexation of the Philippines and others opposed it.

Supporters	Opponents

FOCUS ON WRITING  ELA W1.1, 1.3

6. **Narrative** Imagine that you were aboard the *Olympia* during the Battle of Manila Bay or that you were with the Rough Riders during the Battle of San Juan Hill. Write a letter to a friend back home telling about your experiences and your feelings.

SECTION 3
Roosevelt and Latin America

BEFORE YOU READ

MAIN IDEA
The United States began to exert its influence over Latin America in the wake of the Spanish-American War.

READING FOCUS
1. How did the United States govern Cuba and Puerto Rico?
2. Why and how was the Panama Canal built?
3. What was the Roosevelt Corollary?
4. How did Presidents Taft and Wilson reshape U.S. diplomacy?

KEY TERMS AND PEOPLE
Platt Amendment
protectorate
Foraker Act
Roosevelt Corollary
dollar diplomacy

HSS 11.1.4 Examine the emergence in the late nineteenth century of the United States as a world power.

HSS 11.4.3 Discuss America's role in the Panama Revolution and the building of the Panama Canal.

HSS 11.4.4 Explain Theodore Roosevelt's Big Stick diplomacy, William Taft's Dollar Diplomacy, and Woodrow Wilson's Moral Diplomacy, drawing on relevant speeches.

"Speak Softly and Carry a Big Stick"

THE GRANGER COLLECTION, NEW YORK

▲ Roosevelt uses a "big stick" to control the Caribbean region.

THE INSIDE STORY

How did President Roosevelt get the Canal Zone?

Theodore Roosevelt was a man of action with a vigorous foreign policy. He often quoted a West African proverb: "Speak softly and carry a big stick; you will go far."

Roosevelt's "big stick" was naval power. As president, he built up the Great White Fleet. It helped achieve his dream—a canal that would let ships sail between the Atlantic and the Pacific without going around South America. The canal site was in Panama, which was then a province of Colombia.

Under pressure, Colombian diplomats agreed to lease a canal zone across Panama for a one-time payment of $10 million and a yearly fee of $250,000. The Colombian senate, however, rejected the deal and demanded more money.

Then various groups with a stake in the canal stepped in to encourage a revolution in Panama. In November 1903, the USS *Nashville* lingered off the coast. American marines landed to "maintain order," preventing Colombian troops from stopping the rebels. Within three days, the government of newly independent Panama agreed to the original treaty. Work on the canal could begin!

ENTERING THE WORLD STAGE 213

Cuba and Puerto Rico

After the Spanish-American War, the United States began to expand its power in Latin America. To restore order in Cuba and Puerto Rico after the war—and to protect American investments—President William McKinley set up military governments on each island.

Yellow fever in Cuba President McKinley appointed Leonard Wood as governor of Cuba in 1899. During Wood's term in office, scientists made significant steps toward eliminating yellow fever. The disease had reached epidemic levels among American troops in Cuba. As many as 85 percent of the people infected with yellow fever died.

U.S. Army doctors Walter Reed and William C. Gorgas studied the problem. Cuban doctor Carlos Juan Finlay had theorized that mosquitoes spread yellow fever. Within a year, Reed and Gorgas had proven Finlay's theory. Then Gorgas organized a plan to drain all pools of standing water, where mosquitoes bred. Within six months, yellow fever had been virtually eliminated from the city of Havana.

THE IMPACT TODAY

Government
Since the terrorist attacks of September 11, 2001, the base at Guantánamo has housed prisoners suspected of terrorist activity.

U.S. control over Cuba Wood also oversaw the drafting of a new Cuban constitution in 1901. The United States had already declared with the Teller Amendment of 1898 that it would not annex Cuba. After the Spanish-American War, however, the United States feared that other imperialist nations might try to take control of Cuba or undercut American business interests there.

As a result, the United States forced Cuba to include the **Platt Amendment** as part of its new constitution. The amendment limited Cuba's ability to sign treaties with other nations. At the same time, it gave the United States the right to intervene in Cuban affairs. The amendment also required Cuba to sell or lease land to the United States for naval and coaling stations. This last clause led to the establishment of a U.S. naval base at Guantánamo Bay.

The Platt Amendment made Cuba a U.S. **protectorate**—a country under the control and protection of another country. After Cuba accepted the Platt Amendment, U.S. troops withdrew. The amendment was eventually repealed, but the United States retained its lease on the naval base at Guantánamo Bay.

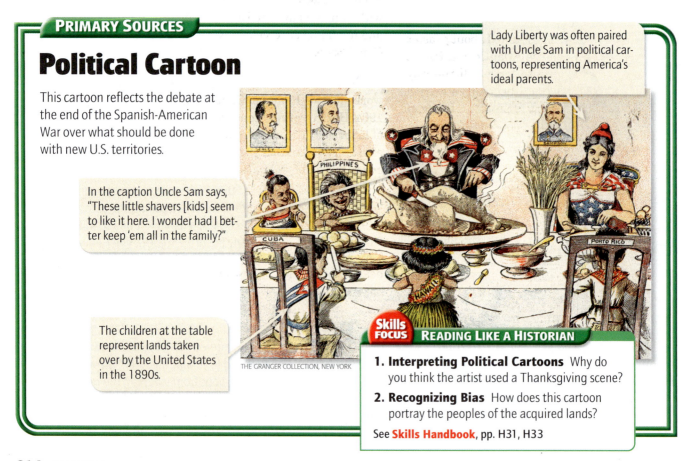

PRIMARY SOURCES

Political Cartoon

This cartoon reflects the debate at the end of the Spanish-American War over what should be done with new U.S. territories.

In the caption Uncle Sam says, "These little shavers [kids] seem to like it here. I wonder had I better keep 'em all in the family?"

The children at the table represent lands taken over by the United States in the 1890s.

Lady Liberty was often paired with Uncle Sam in political cartoons, representing America's ideal parents.

THE GRANGER COLLECTION, NEW YORK

Skills Focus — READING LIKE A HISTORIAN

1. **Interpreting Political Cartoons** Why do you think the artist used a Thanksgiving scene?
2. **Recognizing Bias** How does this cartoon portray the peoples of the acquired lands?

See **Skills Handbook**, pp. H31, H33

Governing Puerto Rico The United States did not make Puerto Rico a protectorate. Instead, it governed Puerto Rico as a territory, as it did the Philippines. The **Foraker Act** of 1900 established that the United States would appoint Puerto Rico's governor and the upper house of its legislature. Puerto Rican voters would elect the lower house.

A 1917 law granted U.S. citizenship to Puerto Ricans. It also allowed Puerto Rican voters to elect all of their legislative representatives. In 1952 Puerto Rico became a self-governing commonwealth of the United States. Today the Puerto Rican government has power over most of its domestic affairs. The U.S. government still controls certain matters though—interstate trade, immigration, and military affairs—just as it does for U.S. states.

READING CHECK **Summarizing** How did Cuba become a U.S. protectorate?

The Panama Canal

For decades, people had dreamed about a faster way to move between the Atlantic and Pacific oceans without having to travel all the way around South America. In the 1880s a French company tried to solve this problem. It began building a canal across the 50-mile-wide Isthmus of Panama, which was then part of the Republic of Colombia. Facing many obstacles, the company eventually went bankrupt and abandoned the canal.

U.S. interest in a canal In 1902 the United States bought the rights to the French canal property and equipment. Secretary of State John Hay began negotiations with Colombia to gain permanent use of the strip of land that the canal would cut through. By 1903 a treaty for a canal zone had been drafted, but Colombia's senate would not ratify it.

Panama's revolution President Theodore Roosevelt had a keen interest in building the canal. Meanwhile, Panamanian revolutionaries were plotting to break free of Colombian rule. Roosevelt supported the rebellion, and on November 2, it began. The next day, Panama declared its independence, and the United States swiftly recognized the Republic of Panama. Soon afterward, a new treaty with Panama gave the United States complete and unending sovereignty over a 10-mile-wide Canal Zone.

Building the Panama Canal American work on the Panama Canal began in May 1904. Harsh working conditions and shortages of labor and materials hampered construction efforts. The situation grew worse when a serious outbreak of yellow fever hit.

To put the project back on track, Roosevelt appointed John F. Stevens as chief engineer and architect. Stevens tackled the technical problems while the army colonel Dr. William C. Gorgas focused on improving sanitation and health. Wiping out yellow fever was one goal, but malaria was an even greater threat. Unlike yellow fever, which gave survivors immunity, malaria could strike people again and again. During the first month of U.S. construction activity, nearly the entire workforce had been stricken with malaria.

Eliminating the mosquitoes that spread malaria was a huge task. Sanitation workers drained swamps, cleared vegetation, spread oil

Hardships Faced by Canal Workers
- Yellow fever and malaria
- Accidents
- Lost equipment
- Extreme heat
- Estimated death toll of more than 30,000 workers

on pools of standing water, and bred spiders, ants, and lizards to feed on the adult mosquitoes. By 1913 malaria was almost eliminated.

Meanwhile, John F. Stevens resigned in 1907, and Lt. Col. George W. Goethals continued the mammoth task of coordinating the construction—not just the canal but all the housing and other facilities needed for workers. His efforts led him to be called the Genius of the Panama Canal.

More than 60 giant steam shovels bit into the land, digging out hundreds of train-car loads of earth each day. Up to 44,000 workers, many recruited from the British West Indies, labored on the project at a time. There were frequent accidents, lost equipment, and deaths—but there was also progress. In August 1914 the SS *Ancon* became the first ship to pass officially through the Panama Canal.

READING CHECK **Drawing Conclusions** Why did the United States get involved in Panama's rebellion against Colombian rule?

The Roosevelt Corollary

The Monroe Doctrine, proclaimed in 1823, declared the Western Hemisphere off-limits to further colonization by European nations. For much of the 1800s, however, the Monroe Doctrine was only an idle threat.

After the Spanish-American War, however, presidents began to back up the Monroe Doctrine with military strength. They wanted to protect American economic interests in Latin America.

In the late 1800s Europeans and Americans invested large sums of money in Latin America, which had a wealth of laborers, consumers, and raw materials. Much of this investment came in the form of high-interest bank loans, which many Latin American countries found difficult to repay. Foreign powers often intervened to collect the loans.

In 1904 the Dominican Republic was unable to repay its European lenders. Fearing that the Europeans would use force to collect

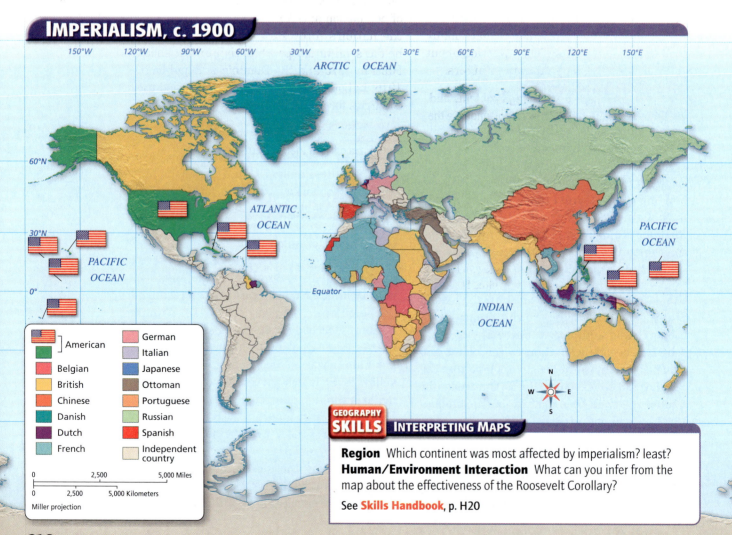

IMPERIALISM, c. 1900

GEOGRAPHY SKILLS INTERPRETING MAPS

Region Which continent was most affected by imperialism? least?
Human/Environment Interaction What can you infer from the map about the effectiveness of the Roosevelt Corollary?

See **Skills Handbook**, p. H20

the debts, President Roosevelt decided to take a tough policy stand. Without seeking approval from any Latin American nation, he issued the **Roosevelt Corollary** to the Monroe Doctrine.

HISTORY'S VOICES

> "Chronic wrongdoing . . . in the Western Hemisphere . . . may force the United States, however reluctantly . . . to the exercise of an international police power."
> —Theodore Roosevelt, Roosevelt Corollary, 1904

Roosevelt was putting into practice one of his favorite proverbs: "Speak softly and carry a big stick; you will go far." Applying this "big stick" policy to the situation in the Dominican Republic, the United States pledged to use armed forces to prevent any European country from seizing Dominican territory.

Roosevelt hoped to avoid a military confrontation. To ensure that the Europeans were repaid, the United States took control of collecting all Dominican customs duties.

The Roosevelt Corollary succeeded in bringing more stability to the region and keeping other nations out. But America's willingness to use its police power made many Latin Americans uneasy. They worried about continued U.S. involvement in their affairs.

READING CHECK **Identifying Problems and Solutions** Why did Roosevelt decide to announce the Roosevelt Corollary?

Reshaping U.S. Diplomacy

During the presidency of William H. Taft, U.S. influence in Latin America deepened. Taft believed in advancing U.S. interests in other countries through **dollar diplomacy**, a policy of promoting American economic interests in other countries and using that economic power to achieve American policy goals.

To reduce the chances of European interference in Latin America, Taft suggested that Americans buy out European loans. By 1914 Americans had invested more than $1.6 billion in Latin America, mainly in mines, railroads, and banana and sugar plantations.

Dollar diplomacy, however, caused resentment. In Nicaragua, for example, American banks made loans to the government and became heavily involved in the economy. In 1912 President Taft had to send in U.S. troops to quell an uprising against the authorities.

President Woodrow Wilson, who succeeded Taft in 1913, rejected the concept of dollar diplomacy in favor of moral diplomacy, the use of persuasion and American ideals to advance the nation's interests abroad. Nonetheless, he did send in troops when civil unrest shook Haiti in 1915 and the Dominican Republic in 1916. In both cases, U.S. Marines occupied the countries for years.

ACADEMIC VOCABULARY
concept abstract notion or idea

READING CHECK **Contrasting** How did Taft and Wilson differ in their patterns of diplomacy?

SECTION 3 ASSESSMENT

HSS 11.1.4, 11.4.3, 11.4.4

go.hrw.com
Online Quiz
Keyword: SE7 HP7

Reviewing Ideas, Terms, and People

1. **a. Recall** How did the United States govern Puerto Rico?
   b. Draw Conclusions Why did the United States make Cuba a **protectorate**?
2. **a. Identify** What was the Panama Canal Zone?
   b. Explain Why was it important to control malaria and yellow fever in Panama?
   c. Predict What effect do you think the Panama Canal had on American military capabilities?
3. **a. Identify** What was the **Roosevelt Corollary**?
   b. Contrast What did the Roosevelt Corollary do that the Monroe Doctrine had not done?
4. **a. Recall** Which president favored **dollar diplomacy**?
   b. Evaluate How effective do you think dollar diplomacy was in Nicaragua?

Critical Thinking

5. **Organizing Information** Copy the table below and fill in the names of Latin American lands discussed in this chapter. Then briefly note how the United States became involved in each.

Country or Territory	U.S. Involvement

FOCUS ON WRITING ELA W1.1

6. **Descriptive** Imagine you are a worker helping to build the Panama Canal. Write a diary entry giving details about the task you're doing, the hardships you face, and why you think the project is worthwhile.

ENTERING THE WORLD STAGE 217

Interactive HISTORY & Geography

Caribbean Sea

Lake Gatún
Created by damming the Chagres River, this lake's water feeds the lock system and was once the world's largest human-made lake.

Gaillard Cut
At the continental divide, the canal route cuts through the lowest point between two hills, 335.5 feet above sea level. For nearly 9 miles, workers blasted loose the rock. Steam shovels loaded the spoil onto railroad cars to be hauled away.

Building the Panama Canal

Sailors had dreamed of a canal through Central America since the 1500s, but it wasn't until the early 1900s that engineers had the technology to build it. The canal's planners and builders faced considerable geographic obstacles along the 50-mile path.

218

SECTION 4
Wilson and the Mexican Revolution

BEFORE YOU READ

MAIN IDEA
American intervention in Mexico's revolution caused strained relations between the two neighbors.

READING FOCUS
1. How did the Díaz dictatorship spark a revolution in Mexico?
2. How and why did the United States intervene in the Mexican Revolution?
3. How did the Mexican Revolution conclude?

KEY TERMS AND PEOPLE
Porfirio Díaz
Francisco Madero
Mexican Revolution
Emiliano Zapata
Francisco "Pancho" Villa
Victoriano Huerta
Tampico incident
Battle of Veracruz
John J. Pershing

HSS 11.1.4 Examine the emergence in the late nineteenth century of the United States as a world power.

HSS 11.4.4 Explain Theodore Roosevelt's Big Stick diplomacy, William Taft's Dollar Diplomacy, and Woodrow Wilson's Moral Diplomacy, drawing on relevant speeches.

THE INSIDE STORY

Why did Wilson send troops into Mexico? To many people, Francisco "Pancho" Villa was a bandit, a cattle rustler, even a murderer. To many others, he was a folk hero, a kind of Mexican Robin Hood. Legends and ballads told about his deeds. Villa was a brilliant horse rider, leading a cavalry force called Los Dorados ("Golden Ones") in northern Mexico. In 1911 he helped drive Mexico's dictator out of power.

Two years later, Villa was again at the center of a power struggle. This time he was vying with Venustiano Carranza to lead Mexico. When U.S. president Woodrow Wilson recognized Carranza as president, Villa was furious. In 1916 Villa and his men killed a group of American mining engineers in Mexico, and then crossed the border to Columbus, New Mexico. In an attack there, Villa's followers killed more Americans.

Wilson was outraged by the raid on American territory. He sent General John J. Pershing into Mexico with a "punitive expedition." With vehicles and even airplanes, they chased Villa through northern Mexico for almost a year. They never caught him.

By 1917 the United States was preoccupied with war in Europe. American forces left Mexico, and Pancho Villa retired to his ranch. In 1923, however, Villa was ambushed and killed. He died as dramatically as he had lived.

PANCHO VILLA
WAGES WAR

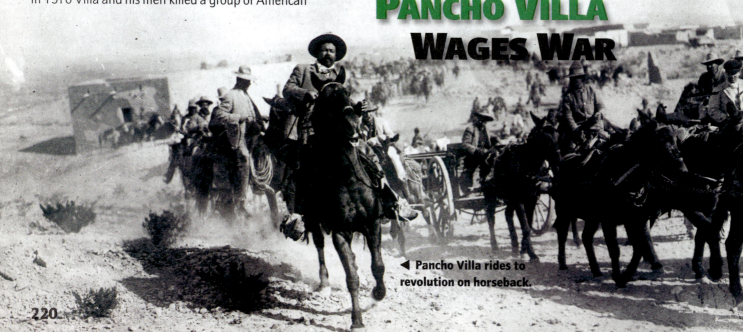

◀ Pancho Villa rides to revolution on horseback.

Dictatorship Sparks a Revolution

When Mexico erupted in revolution in the early 1900s, the United States was drawn into the conflict because of its economic ties with Mexico. But what led to the revolution in the first place?

The Díaz dictatorship For most of the period from 1877 to 1910, the dictator **Porfirio Díaz** ruled Mexico. When Díaz came to power, he brought order to Mexico, which had endured decades of war and unrest. However, order came at a price. Díaz jailed his opponents. He did not permit freedom of the press. He used the army to maintain peace at any cost.

Díaz also got money from foreign investors, including many Americans. Their investments helped modernize Mexico very quickly. Railroads expanded. Production of factory goods doubled. Cotton production also doubled. Still, most Mexicans did not enjoy the benefits of modernization. Wealth became concentrated in the hands of foreign investors and a small Mexican elite. Most Mexicans lived in poverty, and opposition to Díaz grew steadily.

Overthrowing Díaz In 1910 Porfirio Díaz ran for re-election. As in earlier elections, Díaz controlled the outcome. Just before the voting began, he jailed his opponent **Francisco Madero**, a wealthy landowner but a reform-minded idealist. When the ballots were counted, Díaz claimed he had earned a million votes and Madero had earned fewer than 200.

After being released from jail in September 1910, Madero fled over the border to Texas. There he declared himself president of Mexico and called for a revolution. When Madero returned to Mexico in November, he found bands of rebels already active.

The <mark>Mexican Revolution</mark> unfolded as a series of uprisings in different parts of the country. In the south, **Emiliano Zapata** and his army of mostly Native American peasants—known as Zapatistas—wanted land to be returned to the native peoples. They began to seize land by force. Meanwhile, in northern Mexico, **Francisco "Pancho" Villa** and Pascual Orozco led a large-scale revolt against Díaz. Rebellion spread, and in May 1911, Díaz resigned and went into exile in France.

Shaky leadership In November 1911, Francisco Madero was elected president of Mexico. He tried to establish a democratic government, but he was quickly overwhelmed by the very forces he had unleashed in toppling Díaz. Madero faced challenges from all sides. Even the commander of the government troops, **Victoriano Huerta** (WEHR-tah), proved disloyal. In 1913 Huerta overthrew Madero, imprisoned him, and had him executed soon thereafter. Huerta named himself president of Mexico, but immediately four armies rose up to fight him. The situation in Mexico grew dire.

READING CHECK **Sequencing** What major events occurred between the Mexican election of 1910 and the declaration of Huerta as president?

Turmoil in Mexico

Conflicting visions for Mexico's future led to a series of violent government overthrows.

Porfirio Díaz ruled Mexico as an oppressive dictator from 1877 to 1910. He modernized the country, but kept most of the people impoverished.

Emiliano Zapata led the revolt against Díaz in the south. He and his fellow Zapatistas wanted land returned to Native Americans.

After Díaz fled in the face of revolt, Francisco Madero became president of Mexico. He tried to establish a democratic government.

Victoriano Huerta executed Madero and named himself president. He faced opposition from Mexicans and the United States.

The United States Intervenes

Many European nations recognized Huerta's government, but the United States did not. President Woodrow Wilson viewed Huerta as an assassin with no legitimate claim to power. In February 1914 Wilson authorized arms sales to Huerta's enemies. For a time, Wilson followed a policy of "watchful waiting." Then came an incident that let him move openly against Huerta.

The Tampico incident On April 9, 1914, nine crew members of the USS *Dolphin* went ashore for supplies in the Mexican port of Tampico. There they were arrested by soldiers loyal to Huerta. The Americans were quickly released unharmed, and Mexican officials apologized. However, U.S. Admiral Henry Mayo demanded more than a formal apology from the Mexican government. He also insisted that the Mexicans give the American flag a 21-gun salute within 24 hours. Huerta refused this humiliating demand.

Because of the **Tampico incident**, the president asked Congress on April 20 to authorize the use of armed forces against Mexico. Congress approved the request on April 22, but events in Mexico moved faster.

Occupying Veracruz While waiting for Congress to act, President Wilson learned some alarming news. A German ship loaded with weapons for Huerta was heading for the Mexican port city of Veracruz. Without deliberating further, Wilson ordered the U.S. Navy to seize the city.

Under the cover of a naval bombardment, U.S. Marines then landed at Veracruz. They were met by gunfire from Mexican soldiers, and a violent battle erupted. The Americans had expected to seize control with little bloodshed. Instead, 17 Americans and some 300 Mexicans died during the **Battle of Veracruz**.

For the next six months, U.S. troops occupied the city. The occupation threatened to plunge the United States and Mexico into war. Crisis was avoided, though, thanks to mediation by Argentina, Brazil, and Chile.

Meanwhile, Huerta struggled to stay in power. In June the mediators called for Huerta's resignation and for the creation of a provisional government. Huerta refused. Pressure mounted against him within Mexico and beyond. In July he resigned and fled to Spain.

READING CHECK **Identifying Cause and Effect** Why did the United States take action against Huerta's government?

The Battle of Veracruz
American sailors aboard a battleship use field artillery to attack Veracruz from their position off the coast.
What prevented the Battle of Veracruz from turning into a full-scale war between the United States and Mexico?

The Revolution Concludes

With Huerta gone from Mexico, Venustiano Carranza stepped in and declared himself the leader of the Mexican Revolution in August 1914. He faced opposition from Pancho Villa and Emiliano Zapata, however. For some time, it appeared that Villa and Zapata would triumph. This worried American leaders, who feared that U.S. economic interests would be harmed by the land redistribution that Zapata and Villa wanted. President Wilson decided to support the more moderate Carranza.

Pancho Villa retaliated with violence. In March 1916 he led hundreds of troops across the U.S. border to the small, isolated town of Columbus, New Mexico. Striking at dawn, Villa's troops burned the town and killed 17 Americans. This was the first armed invasion of the continental United States since the War of 1812.

Pursuing Pancho Villa President Woodrow Wilson quickly ordered a military expedition to hunt down Villa. Within a week, General **John J. Pershing** led more than 10,000 U.S. troops into Mexico. They searched for 11 months but were never able to capture Pancho Villa. The farther Pershing went into Mexican territory, the more the Mexicans resented the Americans.

By early September 1916, nearly 150,000 U.S. National Guard members were stationed along the Mexican border. Wilson realized that the threat of war increased each day that U.S. troops remained in Mexico. Furthermore, America's attention was shifting to Europe, where World War I was raging. In late January 1917, the president called off the search for Pancho Villa and withdrew U.S. troops from Mexico. Nonetheless, for the rest of Wilson's presidency, relations between Mexico and the United States remained strained.

A new constitution for Mexico In December 1916, Venustiano Carranza called a constitutional convention. A new constitution went into effect on February 5, 1917. The constitution contained the ideas of all the revolutionary groups. It protected the liberties and rights of citizens.

Despite the new constitution, fighting continued in Mexico until 1920. Mexico's economy suffered terribly. Agriculture was disrupted, mines were abandoned, and factories were destroyed. Many Mexican men and women immigrated to the United States in search of work and a more stable life.

READING CHECK **Summarizing** How did Pancho Villa cause trouble for the United States?

THE IMPACT TODAY
Daily Life
More than 25 million people of Mexican descent now live in the United States.

SECTION 4 ASSESSMENT

HSS 11.1.4, 11.4.4

Reviewing Ideas, Terms, and People

1. **a. Identify** Who was **Porfirio Díaz**?
   b. Explain Why did Mexicans rise up against Díaz?
   c. Elaborate Why do you think that **Francisco Madero** and **Victoriana Huerta** both faced challenges after they claimed Mexico's presidency?

2. **a. Recall** What was the **Tampico incident**?
   b. Analyze How did the Tampico incident draw the United States into armed conflict with Mexico?
   c. Evaluate Was the United States justified in launching the **Battle of Veracruz**? Why or why not?

3. **a. Describe** What made **Pancho Villa** decide to lead a raid into New Mexico?
   b. Draw Conclusions Why was President Wilson so eager to capture Pancho Villa?
   c. Predict How do you think the expedition to find Pancho Villa affected relations between Mexicans and Americans?

Critical Thinking

4. **Sequencing** Copy the flowchart below and record the major sequence of events of the Mexican Revolution, from the overthrow of Díaz to the Constitution of 1917. Add as many boxes as you need.

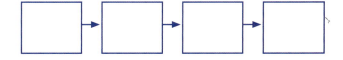

FOCUS ON SPEAKING W1.1

5. **Persuasive** Imagine that you are a Mexican revolutionary in 1911, while Porfirio Díaz is still clinging to power. Prepare a speech to give to people in your community, explaining why you oppose Díaz and whom you support in his place. Encourage your listeners to join you in the fight to overthrow Díaz and bring better leadership to Mexico.

CHAPTER 7 DOCUMENT-BASED INVESTIGATION

Views on American Expansionism

HSS 11.4.2

Historical Context The documents below provide information about attitudes regarding American expansion in the late 1800s.

Task Examine the documents and answer the questions that follow. Then write an essay about interaction between imperialists and local peoples. Use facts from the documents and the chapter to support the position you take in your thesis statement.

DOCUMENT 1

Princess Kaiulani, niece of Hawaii's Queen Liliuokalani, visited Washington, D.C., in 1893 to plead for a restoration of the monarchy.

"Seventy years ago, Christian Americans sent over Christian men and women to give religion and civilization to Hawaii. Today, three of the sons of the missionaries are at your capitol, asking you to undo their fathers' work. Who sent them? Who gave them the authority to break the constitution which they swore they would uphold? Today, I, a poor, weak girl, with not one of my people near me and all these statesmen against me, have the strength to stand up for the rights of my people. Even now I can hear their wail in my heart, and I am strong . . . strong in the faith of God, strong in the knowledge that I am right, strong in the strength of seventy million people who in this free land will hear my cry and will refuse to let their flag cover dishonor to mine!"

DOCUMENT 2

John L. Stevens was the U.S. minister to Hawaii in 1893, when Queen Liliuokalani was forced from the throne. That year, he wrote "The Hawaiian Situation. II. A Plea for Annexation."

"The Hawaiian monarchy being thus extinct, and the Hawaiian Islands being not sufficient to constitute an independent nation, all who really understand their situation know that good government is now the first and imperative need . . . [T]hese Islands have become thoroughly Americanized . . . For sixty years the Islands have had the American school system . . . The two principal daily newspapers are edited, owned, and published by Americans. The principal lawyers at the bar and on the bench are Americans . . . and educated in American colleges. More than eighty percent of the trade, amounting to more than twenty million dollars per year, is with the United States. American newspapers, magazines, and books are in as familiar use in the Islands as in the United States . . .

A paramount reason why annexation should not be long postponed is that, if it soon takes place, the crown and government lands will be cut up and sold to American and Christian Caucasian people, thus preventing the Islands from being submerged and overrun by Asiatics, putting an end to Japanese ambitions stimulated by our strong European rival."

DOCUMENT 3

Puck was a political magazine that often used humor and satire to address social and political issues. In this magazine cover, the annexation of Hawaii is shown as a marriage between a Hawaiian woman and Uncle Sam. President William McKinley is depicted as a minister, and Alabama senator John T. Morgan stands behind the couple with a shotgun.

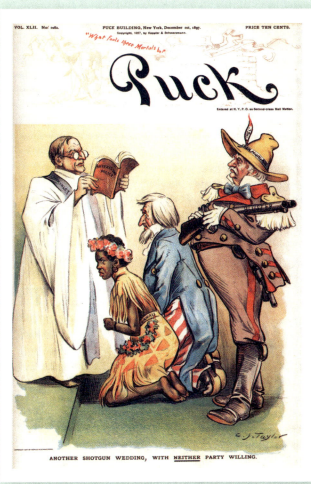

READING LIKE A HISTORIAN

HSS Analysis HR4, HI1

1. **a. Recall** Refer to Document 1. Why does Kaiulani feel that she will be successful?
   b. Contrast In Kaiulani's view, how are the sons of the early missionaries different from their fathers?
2. **a. Identify** Refer to Document 2. What reasons does Stevens give for annexing Hawaii to the United States?
   b. Predict How might Stevens have responded to a statement like that made by Kaiulani?
3. **a. Identify** Refer to Document 3. What expression is shown on the woman's face?
   b. Evaluate How would you describe the cartoonist's opinion of annexation?
4. **Document-Based Essay Question** Consider the question below and form a thesis statement. Using examples from Documents 1, 2, and 3, create an outline and write a short essay supporting your position.
   What factors influenced the decision to annex Hawaii?

See **Skills Handbook**, pp. H28–H29, H31

CHAPTER 7 Chapter Review

Visual Summary: Entering the World Stage

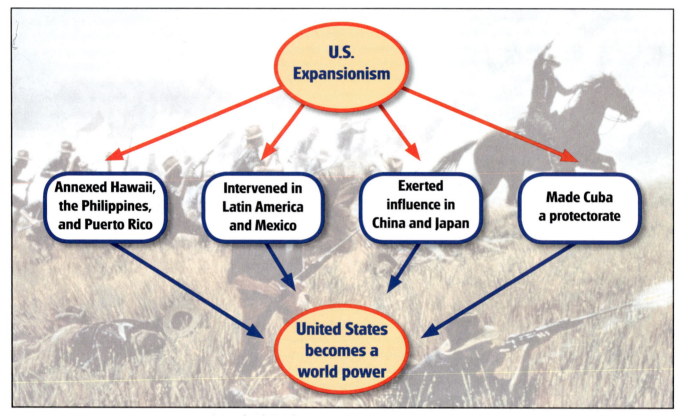

Reviewing Key Terms and People

Complete each sentence by filling the blank with the correct term or name.

1. In 1887 King Kalakaua was forced to sign the _____, which severely restricted his power and denied most Hawaiians the right to vote.
2. Imperialist nations carved out _____ in China—geographic areas where they dominated politics or the economy.
3. The _____ was intended to give all nations equal trading rights in China.
4. The sensationalist style of news coverage called _____ helped sway U.S. public opinion in favor of war with Spain.
5. The _____ gave the United States the right to intervene in Cuban affairs and to buy or lease land for naval and coaling stations.
6. In Latin America and Asia, President Taft practiced _____, a policy of substituting economic power for military force.
7. The Mexican Revolution began as an effort to overthrow the dictator _____.
8. The _____ occurred on April 9, 1914, when nine U.S. sailors were mistakenly arrested by Mexican soldiers.
9. The _____ took place after the United States seized a German ship that was carrying weapons to Mexican president Victoriano Huerta.

Comprehension and Critical Thinking

SECTION 1 *(pp. 200–205)* HSS 11.4.4

10. **a. Identify** Who was Queen Liliuokalani?
    b. Explain Why did Liliuokalani's plans for strengthening the monarchy alarm the American business community in Hawaii?
    c. Predict How do you think the Japanese reacted to the Great White Fleet? Do you think the fleet had the effect that President Roosevelt wished?

226 CHAPTER 7

History's Impact video program
Review the video to answer the closing question: What are two benefits the Panama Canal has provided for the United States?

SECTION 2 (pp. 206–212) HSS 11.4.2

11. **a. Recall** What was the de Lôme letter?
    b. Summarize What were the consequences of the Spanish-American War?
    c. Evaluate How much influence did the media have in building public support for the Spanish-American War? Explain.

SECTION 3 (pp. 213–217) HSS 11.4.4

12. **a. Describe** What was the Roosevelt Corollary?
    b. Analyze In what various ways did the United States exert its power in Latin America?
    c. Evaluate How did the acquisition of overseas territory affect the way the United States viewed its role in the world?

SECTION 4 (pp. 220–223) HSS 11.4.4

13. **a. Identify** Who was Pancho Villa?
    b. Contrast As government leaders, how did Porfirio Díaz and Francisco Madero differ?
    c. Elaborate Why do you think President Wilson wished to avoid war with Mexico?

Using the Internet

go.hrw.com
Practice Online
Keyword: SE7 CH7

14. On December 31, 1999, the United States returned control of the Panama Canal and the 10-mile-wide Canal Zone to the government of Panama. Using the keyword above, do research to learn about the events that led to this historic handover. Then create a report that analyzes the reasons why the United States gave up the canal and the Canal Zone to Panama.

Analyzing Primary Sources HSS HR4

Reading Like a Historian This painting shows a pineapple plantation in Hawaii, where pineapples were typically harvested by hand.

15. **Analyzing Visuals** How are the pickers protecting themselves against the tropical heat?

16. **Making Inferences** Why do you suppose one man is on horseback?

Critical Reading ELA R2.2

Read the passage in Section 1 that begins with the heading "Influence in China." Then answer the questions that follow.

17. Why did the United States propose the Open Door Policy?
    A The United States wanted to prevent China from refusing to trade with western nations.
    B The United States was protesting Japan's seizure of Taiwan.
    C The United States hoped the Open Door Policy would help resolve the Boxer Rebellion.
    D Without a sphere of influence of its own, the United States was afraid of being cut out of the China trade.

18. Which of the following is a true statement about the Boxer Rebellion?
    A Members of a secret martial arts group in China demanded more respect for their sport.
    B Foreign missionaries and Chinese Christians in Beijing came under attack.
    C An large international military force stopped the rebellion in 1900 and occupied China for many years afterward.
    D The Boxer Rebellion caused western nations to reject the Open Door Policy.

FOCUS ON WRITING ELA W1.1, 2.4

Persuasive Writing Persuasive writing takes a position for or against an issue, using facts and examples as supporting evidence. To practice persuasive writing, complete the assignment below.

Topic U.S. imperialism in the late 1800s and early 1900s

19. **Assignment** Write a paragraph in which you take a position on the overseas activities of the United States in the late 1800s and early 1900s. Was the United States justified in annexing foreign territories and expanding its control over other nations during this period? Support your point of view with reasoning and examples from your reading and studies.

ENTERING THE WORLD STAGE

CHAPTER 8

1914–1920

The First WORLD WAR

THE BIG PICTURE The United States tried to stay neutral when war swept Europe. After the United States joined the Allies in 1917, however, the government quickly mobilized the economy and built public support for the war.

California Standards

History-Social Sciences
11.4 Students trace the rise of the United States to its role as a world power in the twentieth century.

 READING LIKE A HISTORIAN

Artist Frank Schoonover captured a spirit of optimism and determination in the faces of these young Allied soldiers in *Doughboys First*. (A "doughboy" is an infantry member.) The painting was one of a series painted for *The Ladies' Home Journal*.
Interpreting Visuals What do you think the artist wanted to accomplish with this painting?

See **Skills Handbook**, p. H30

 U.S.

August 1914 President Wilson declares American neutrality in World War I.

1914

 World

June 1914 Archduke Franz Ferdinand is killed in Sarajevo.

August 1914 German troops invade Belgium, and Great Britain declares war on Germany.

History's Impact video program
Watch the video to understand the impact of *Schenck* v. *United States*.

May 1915 German U-boat sinks the *Lusitania*, killing 128 Americans.

April 1917 President Wilson asks Congress to declare war against Germany.

January 1918 President Wilson presents his 14-point plan for world peace.

August 1920 The Nineteenth Amendment, giving women the right to vote, is ratified.

1915 | 1916 | 1917 | 1918 | 1919 | 1920

February 1915 Germany sets up a submarine blockade of England.

November 1917 Lenin's Bolsheviks take control of Russia.

November 11, 1918 The Allies and Germany sign an armistice.

June 1919 The Treaty of Versailles officially ends World War I.

SECTION 1
A World Crisis

BEFORE YOU READ

MAIN IDEA
Rivalries among European nations led to the outbreak of war in 1914.

READING FOCUS
1. What were the causes of World War I?
2. How did the war break out?
3. Why did the war quickly reach a stalemate?

KEY TERMS AND PEOPLE
Archduke Franz Ferdinand
Kaiser Wilhelm II
militarism
Triple Alliance
Triple Entente
balance of power
Central Powers
Allied Powers
trench warfare

 HSS 11.4.5 Analyze the political, economic, and social ramifications of World War I on the home front.

◀ Soldiers arrest Archduke Ferdinand's young assassin.

A WRONG TURN INTO History

THE INSIDE STORY

How does a 19-year-old start a world war? In 1912 Serbian teenager Gavrilo Princip joined the Black Hand terrorist organization. Princip wanted to free his home country, Bosnia and Herzegovina, from Austro-Hungarian rule. He was already a good shot with a pistol—a handy skill for a terrorist.

After years of training and planning, the Black Hand leaders came up with a terrorist plot that they hoped could lead to an independent Bosnia. They heard that **Archduke Franz Ferdinand** of Austria was going to visit the Bosnian city of Sarajevo. The Black Hand ordered a team of assassins to kill the archduke.

On June 28, 1914, Princip and six other terrorists positioned themselves around Sarajevo as Ferdinand and his wife toured the city in a convertible sedan. Princip was hungry, so he went to buy a sandwich. As he stepped out of the sandwich shop, he could not believe his eyes. There, stopped in front of him, was the car carrying the archduke. Princip dropped his sandwich, reached for his pistol, and fired, killing the archduke and his wife. This single act would propel most of Europe into war within weeks.

230 CHAPTER 8

Causes of World War I

Some 3,000 miles away from Sarajevo, most Americans cared little about the news of Archduke Franz Ferdinand's death. A North Dakota newspaper reported, "One archduke more or less makes little difference." In Europe, however, the death of this archduke made a huge difference. Most of Europe plunged into war within five short weeks. But how could one assassination start a world war?

Long before Princip fired his pistol, a series of political changes in Europe made war almost unavoidable. By 1914 Europe was ripe for war.

Nationalism Nationalism is an extreme pride or devotion that people feel for their country or culture. The spirit of nationalism led to the formation of new nations, such as Germany and Italy during the 1870s. It also led to competition for power.

This struggle for greater power was most visible in the Balkans, a region of southeastern Europe populated by a great number of ethnic groups. The Ottoman Empire, which had ruled the Balkans for hundreds of years, was starting to fall apart during the 1800s. The Austro-Hungarian Empire saw an opportunity to expand and began to push into the region, annexing provinces such as Bosnia and Herzegovina. Many Slavic peoples there, such as the Serbs, rejected the rule of these outsiders.

Some Serbs encouraged other Slavic peoples to revolt against Austria-Hungary, and they received support from Russia, another European power. Russia saw itself as the protector of the Slavs and argued with the Austro-Hungarian rulers about the future of Serbia and control of the Balkans. By the early 1900s tensions in the region were high.

Imperialism Austria-Hungary was not the only nation trying to expand during the late 1800s. Growing nationalism also led nations to compete for overseas colonies. This quest for colonial empires was known as imperialism.

By the late 1800s Great Britain and France already had colonial empires in Africa, the Middle East, and Asia. Colonies provided markets and rich natural resources, so the German emperor, **Kaiser Wilhelm II**, wanted colonies for Germany, too. And to get them, Germany would need a stronger military.

Militarism The world soon also saw the rise of **militarism**—the policy of military preparedness and building up weapons. In 1900 Germany began to build a navy that could take on the world's strongest sea power—Great Britain's Royal Navy.

At the same time, Germany had also enlarged its army. It supplied its troops with the latest weapons, including machine guns and larger artillery.

German army officials also began to draw up war strategies. One such strategy, the Schlieffen Plan, provided precise instructions for waging a two-front war against France and Russia at the same time. The Schlieffen Plan also called for a surprise invasion of France by passing through Belgium, with a subsequent attack on Russia.

Aware of Germany's growing supply of weapons, Great Britain, France, and Russia worried about Germany's intentions. Each country began to build its own military in order to defend itself should war break out.

Many Europeans believed that strong military forces would prevent countries from attacking one another. British admiral Jackie Fisher explained, "I am not for war, I am for peace. That is why I am for a supreme Navy. The supremacy of the British Navy is the best security for the peace of the world."

Alliances For protection, some nations formed alliances, or partnerships. These alliances were created to maintain peace, but they would lead Europe directly into war.

Germany formed a military alliance with Austria-Hungary and Italy. This alliance became known as the **Triple Alliance**. Fearful of Germany's growing power, France and Russia formed a secret alliance with each other. Meanwhile, Great Britain also began to worry about Germany's expanding navy and allied itself with France. Soon Britain, France, and Russia formed the **Triple Entente** (AHN-TAHNT).

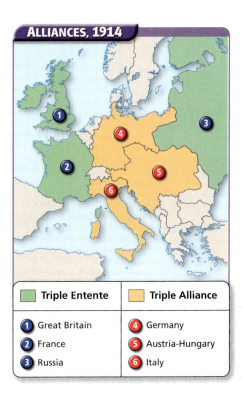

ALLIANCES, 1914

Triple Entente
1. Great Britain
2. France
3. Russia

Triple Alliance
4. Germany
5. Austria-Hungary
6. Italy

ACADEMIC VOCABULARY
subsequent following in time or order

The word *entente* come from French and means "understanding.")

Some European leaders believed that these alliances created a **balance of power**, in which each nation or alliance had equal strength. Many leaders thought that the alliance system would help decrease the chances of war. They hoped that no single nation would attack another out of fear that the attacked nation's allies would join the fight.

The assassination of Archduke Franz Ferdinand exposed the flaws in this thinking. The major European powers' long history of national tensions, imperial rivalries, and military expansion proved too great for alliances to overcome. After this single attack on Austria-Hungary, Europe exploded into war.

READING CHECK **Summarizing** What issues led Europe to the brink of war in 1914?

War Breaks Out

After the assassination, Princip was immediately arrested. While investigating Princip's background, Austro-Hungarian officials learned that the Serbian government had supplied the assassins with bombs and weapons. Furious, Austria-Hungary blamed Serbia for Ferdinand's murder and declared war.

Russia had promised to protect Serbian Slavs. Therefore, the Russian army quickly began to mobilize, or prepare for war. Germany viewed Russia's mobilization as an act of aggression against its ally Austria-Hungary and declared war on Russia. Then Germany declared war on France, Russia's ally. All-out war was about to begin.

The Germans take Belgium Germany made the first move in the war, following the Schlieffen Plan. On August 4, 1914, German troops crossed the border into the neutral country of Belgium. Kaiser Wilhelm II believed Germany needed to make this first move in order to catch Belgium and France by surprise.

Germany's invasion of Belgium drew a new, powerful nation into the conflict. Because the British had pledged to defend Belgium, Great Britain declared war on Germany.

With the entry of Great Britain into the war, most of the major powers of Europe had chosen sides. On one side were Germany, Austria-Hungary, and the Ottoman Empire, fighting together as the **Central Powers**.

On the other side of the conflict were Great Britain, France, and Russia, who united as the **Allied Powers**, or Allies. Before the conflict's end, another 30 nations, including Italy, would join in what became known as the Great War. Later generations would call it World War I.

At first the Schlieffen Plan worked well for Germany. With only six divisions of troops, Belgian forces were no match for the 38 divisions of the German army, totaling a massive 700,000 soldiers. The tiny Belgian army fought bravely and put up an unexpectedly strong defense, but they were only able to delay the German advance briefly.

The German attack on Belgium was fierce. Germans burned entire villages to the ground. Civilians caught in the fighting, including women and children, were executed. German field marshall Helmuth von Moltke admitted,

Major Battles

 Battle of Tannenberg, Aug. 1914
Russia's worst defeat in World War I

 1st Battle of the Marne, Sept. 1914
Allies halted the German advance and saved Paris from occupation

 1st Battle of Ypres, Oct.–Nov. 1914
Last major German offensive until 1918

 3rd Battle of Ypres (Passchendaele), July–Nov. 1917
British forces advanced just five miles at a cost of about 300,000 lives

 Battle of Gallipoli, April–Dec. 1915
Failed attempt of the Allies to knock the Ottoman Empire out of World War I

 Battle of Verdun, Feb.–Dec. 1916
Longest battle of World War I with huge loss of life

 Battle of the Somme, July–Nov. 1916
First major offensive for the British; remembered for its staggering loss of life

 Battle of Caporetto, Oct.–Nov. 1917
Tremendous victory for the Central Powers

"Our advance in Belgium is certainly brutal... all who get in the way must take the consequences."

A new kind of warfare Word of the German invasion of Belgium quickly spread to France and other European countries. French troops mobilized and rushed to meet the approaching German divisions. The French troops who marched to the front looked much as French soldiers had looked more than 40 years earlier, wearing bright red uniforms and heavy brass helmets. The Germans, on the other hand, dressed in gray uniforms that worked as camouflage to help them blend into the battlefield.

French war strategy had also not changed much since the 1800s. In Belgium, French soldiers marched row by row onto the battlefield. With bayonets mounted to their field rifles,

GEOGRAPHY SKILLS INTERPRETING MAPS

Location Where was the Western Front of the war located at this time? What were the outcomes of the major battles fought there?
Movement Describe the movement of the Central Powers. Why did the war have two fronts?

See **Skills Handbook**, p. H20

THE FIRST WORLD WAR 233

they were prepared for close combat with the Germans. But when French officers drew their swords and ordered their troops to charge, they were met by a hail of machine gun bullets.

The French military had purchased a small number of machine guns and other new weapons such as the 75-millimeter artillery gun. They were not prepared for Germany's massive firepower.

A well-trained German machine gun team could set up its equipment in just four seconds, and each machine gun's firepower equaled that of 50 to 100 French rifles. Machine guns could fire up to 600 bullets per minute and mow down thousands of troops. In early battles, some 15,000 French soldiers died per day. In short, the Germans were prepared to fight a new kind of war. The French were not.

Many European leaders thought that these modern advances in military technology would result in a short war. German military advisers confidently predicted that France would be defeated in two months.

When the war began in midsummer, Kaiser Wilhelm II promised his German soldiers that they would be home "before the leaves had fallen." The European powers would soon learn that this new kind of war would last much longer than expected, and its devastation would be much more terrible.

The First Battle of the Marne The German army quickly advanced through northern France. After only one month of fighting, the German army was barely 25 miles from Paris. Still, the French troops refused to surrender.

Fighting in the Trenches

Protected by rows of barbed wire, sandbags, and armed soldiers, trenches were very difficult to capture. Neither side could advance on the Western Front without losing thousands of men in the attack.

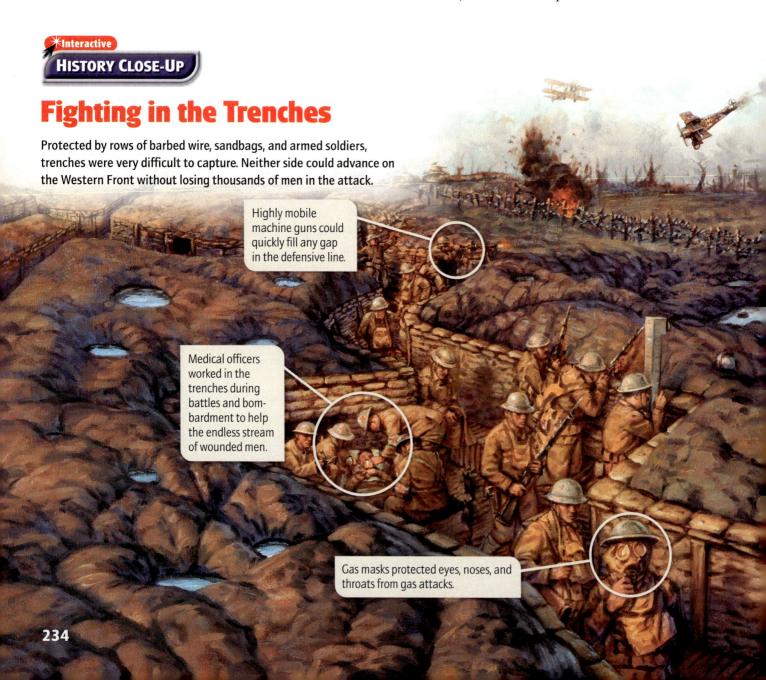

Highly mobile machine guns could quickly fill any gap in the defensive line.

Medical officers worked in the trenches during battles and bombardment to help the endless stream of wounded men.

Gas masks protected eyes, noses, and throats from gas attacks.

Desperate for a victory, the French launched a daring counterattack along the Marne River east of Paris on September 7, 1914. In what became known as the First Battle of the Marne, 2 million men fought along a battlefront that stretched 125 miles. After five days and 250,000 lives lost, the French had rallied and pushed the Germans back some 40 miles.

The French had paid a heavy price. A French journalist walking on the battlefield saw what he thought was a field of red poppies. However, these bright patches of red were actually the uniforms of countless fallen French troops.

Despite the cost of the French counterattack, it helped the Allies by giving Russia more time to mobilize for war. Once Russia mobilized, Germany had to pull some of its troops out of France. It needed those troops to fight Russia along the Eastern Front, which stretched from the Black Sea to the Baltic Sea.

READING CHECK **Drawing Conclusions** Why was World War I considered a new kind of war?

The War Reaches a Stalemate

The First Battle of the Marne ended in a standoff. Both French and German soldiers dug trenches, or deep ditches, to seek protection from enemy fire and to defend their positions. By the late fall of 1914, two massive systems of trenches stretched for some 400 miles across western Europe. These battle lines of the Western Front extended from Switzerland to the North Sea.

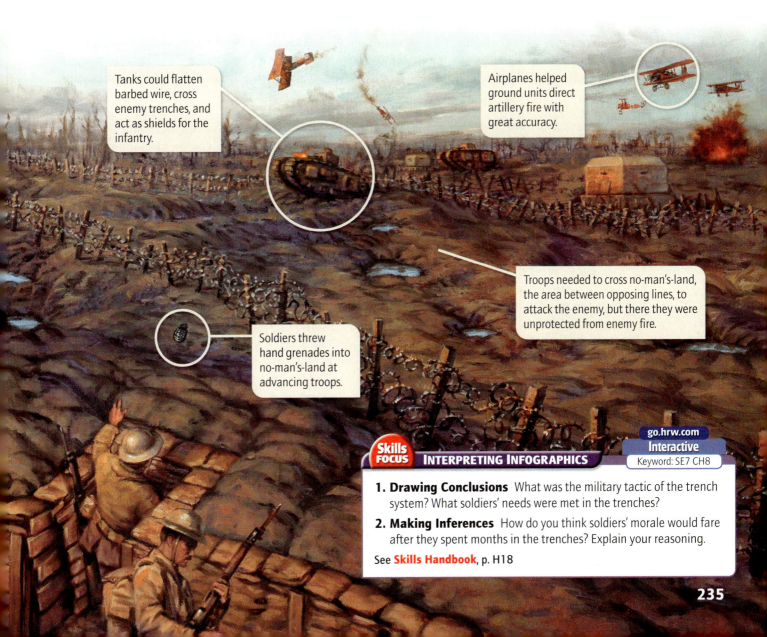

Tanks could flatten barbed wire, cross enemy trenches, and act as shields for the infantry.

Airplanes helped ground units direct artillery fire with great accuracy.

Troops needed to cross no-man's-land, the area between opposing lines, to attack the enemy, but there they were unprotected from enemy fire.

Soldiers threw hand grenades into no-man's-land at advancing troops.

Skills Focus **INTERPRETING INFOGRAPHICS**

go.hrw.com
Interactive
Keyword: SE7 CH8

1. **Drawing Conclusions** What was the military tactic of the trench system? What soldiers' needs were met in the trenches?
2. **Making Inferences** How do you think soldiers' morale would fare after they spent months in the trenches? Explain your reasoning.

See **Skills Handbook**, p. H18

The Battle of the Somme

The British made little progress against the Germans' heavy barbed wire and trenches during the Battle of the Somme. After months of fighting, they had advanced only six miles, and hundreds of thousands of soldiers had lost their lives (see table below).

SOMME STATISTICS
- **Duration of battle:** July 1–Nov. 18, 1916
- **Total Allied casualties:** about 630,000
- **British casualties on day 1:** about 57,000
- **Total German casualties:** about 650,000

THE IMPACT TODAY
Science and Technology
Since World War I, improvements in technology have made trench warfare nearly obsolete. Because the military today uses long-distance weapons, radar, and air surveillance, there is less direct combat.

Fighting in the trenches Trench warfare, or fighting from trenches, was not a new strategy. Years earlier American armies had dug trenches during some Civil War battles, including Petersburg. In other wars, armies had dug some trenches in Asia decades before World War I.

However, no soldiers had ever experienced trench warfare on the scale that European forces now did. All across the Western Front, soldiers lived in the trenches, surrounded by machine gun fire, flying grenades, and exploding artillery shells.

Many European military officers thought that a well-motivated army could easily capture the enemy's trenches. They were wrong. Opposing forces had their machine guns aimed at enemy trenches at all times. Any time a helmet or rifle appeared along the trench line, the opposing troops would fire.

Occasionally, soldiers would go over the top to fire at the enemy, but this meant they also lost the protection the trench provided. Soldiers would jump out of their trenches and run across the area between opposing trenches—called no-man's-land—as quickly as they could to attack the other side. But as they ran, thousands of men were chopped down by enemy machine gun fire. No-man's-land became littered with bodies.

As a result, neither the Allies nor the Germans were able to make significant advances. Trench warfare created a stalemate, or deadlock. With the fighting bogged down, both the Allied and Central Powers began looking for new ways to gain an advantage. Many of these new strategies involved the use of new weapons and technology.

New weapons Scientists for both the Allied and Central Powers developed new weapons during World War I in an attempt to win an advantage. German military scientists had been experimenting with poisonous gas as a possible weapon to defeat the Allies.

Although gas seemed to be a breakthrough in military technology, actually using the poisonous gas as a weapon on the battlefield remained a very risky maneuver. Soldiers did not know how much gas to use in an attack. Moreover, a quick change in wind direction could blow the gas back into the troops who had launched it.

The German military eventually found ways to overcome these obstacles, however. In April 1915 German soldiers fired canisters of poisonous gas into Allied trenches. A yellow-green cloud of chlorine gas miles wide enveloped the Allied soldiers. The gas quickly destroyed the soldiers' lungs, and many of them panicked.

Some traditional military officers felt that using poisonous gas was an unfair and barbaric way to fight the war. Even the German commander at the April 1915 attack regretted using the gas, saying, "The plan of poisoning the enemy with gas just as if they were rats . . . disgusted me."

Nevertheless, the Allies could not let the Germans gain an advantage. So British and French forces soon began to develop and use the poisonous gas in their attacks against the Germans as well.

Gas, however, had little effect on the outcome of battles. Soldiers on both sides began to carry gas masks for protection against this new kind of chemical warfare. The gas masks worked well. As long as the soldiers could see the colored gas cloud approaching, they could survive a poisonous gas attack simply by putting on their gas masks.

Once again facing a stalemate, both the Allied and Central Powers began to look for other weapons that could help them win the war. British forces soon developed a motorized armored tank which could maneuver through the dangerous no-man's-land.

These tanks, however, had limited success. In the first battle in which tanks were used, 18 out of 48 tanks became stuck in the mud. Although the tanks frightened the German troops, German military planners were not as impressed. They soon developed strategies to destroy the tanks with artillery fire.

Airplanes proved to be even more useful than tanks. Both sides used airplanes to map enemy positions and trenches and to attack the trenches from above. At first, airplane pilots dropped bricks and heavy objects on enemy troops. Soon, mechanics also figured out how to mount machine guns on planes and launch bombs from the air.

Skilled French and British pilots, or aces, fought German pilots in spectacular air battles called dogfights. Using daring rolls and dives, Allied pilots dueled German aces such as the notorious Baron Manfred von Richthofen, who was known as the Red Baron. The Red Baron shot down 80 Allied planes before he himself was finally shot down in 1918.

Nevertheless, none of the new technologies used in battle gave the Allied or Central Powers the advantage they hoped for. The miserable form of battle known as trench warfare continued. Clearly something would have to change before either side could declare victory in the war.

READING CHECK **Summarizing** Why were the new weapons not very effective in ending trench warfare?

SECTION 1 ASSESSMENT

HSS 11.4.5

Reviewing Ideas, Terms, and People

1. **a. Identify** What was **militarism**?
   b. Explain How did the assassination of **Archduke Franz Ferdinand** lead so many nations into war?
   c. Elaborate Why do you think that European nations were willing to go to war so quickly?

2. **a. Recall** What kinds of military technology were new in World War I?
   b. Draw Conclusions At the beginning of the war, how did the new military technology affect the way European leaders thought about the war?
   c. Evaluate Was it reasonable for European leaders to believe the war would be quick? Why or why not?

3. **a. Identify** What was **trench warfare**?
   b. Draw Conclusions How did trench warfare affect the progress of the war?
   c. Elaborate How did soldiers try to overcome the limitations of trench warfare?

Critical Thinking

4. **Identifying Cause and Effect** Copy the chart below and record the four main causes of World War I. Below each cause list two supporting examples.

Cause			
Example			
Example			

FOCUS ON WRITING

ELA W1.1

5. **Persuasive** Write a letter to the editor of a newspaper that argues either for or against using poison gas and other new military technologies in World War I. Write your letter as if you are a soldier in the war. Use information from the chapter to support your position.

SECTION 2
The United States in World War I

BEFORE YOU READ

MAIN IDEA
The United States helped turn the tide for an Allied victory.

READING FOCUS
1. Why did the United States try to stay neutral in the war?
2. Which events showed that America was heading into war?
3. What contributions did Americans make in Europe?
4. How did the war end?

KEY TERMS AND PEOPLE
Lusitania
isolationism
U-boats
Sussex pledge
Zimmermann Note
Selective Service Act
convoy system
Communists

HSS 11.4.4 Explain Woodrow Wilson's Moral Diplomacy, drawing on relevant speeches.
HSS 11.4.5 Analyze the political, economic, and social ramifications of World War I on the home front.

THE INSIDE STORY

Would you travel into a war zone? In New York Harbor on Saturday, May 1, 1915, some 1,900 passengers and crew boarded the British luxury ship *Lusitania* and headed for a war zone. The ship's destination was Great Britain. A spokesperson for the ship's company reassured the nervous passengers, "The *Lusitania* ... is too fast for any German submarine."

In the early afternoon of May 7, 1915, the *Lusitania* approached the British Isles. Crew member Leslie Morton spotted ominous air bubbles and streaks in the water below. He grabbed a megaphone and shouted, "Torpedoes coming!" But it was too late. A torpedo slammed into the ship's right side. Passengers scrambled for life jackets and lifeboats when the ship began to lean and take on water. As the *Lusitania* slid beneath the waves, parents tried to hold their children above water. Some even tied their children to deck chairs and wreckage in a futile attempt to save them. As Morton later described the scene, "The turmoil of passengers and life jackets, many people losing hold on the deck and slipping down and over the side ... [created] a horrible and bizarre orchestra of death."

The *Lusitania* sank only 18 minutes after it was torpedoed. About 1,200 people died. Among the dead were 128 Americans.

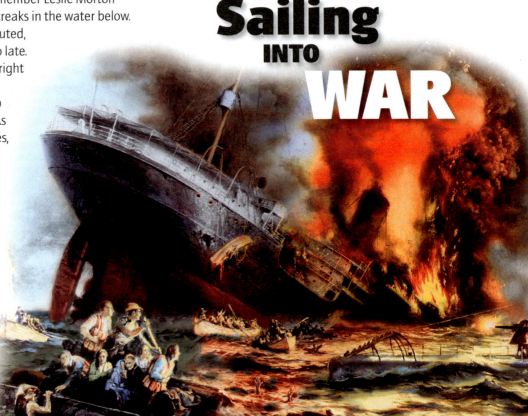

▶ The sinking of the *Lusitania* killed more than 1,200 people.

Sailing INTO WAR

238 CHAPTER 8

United States Stays Neutral

Before the sinking of the *Lusitania*, Americans thought of the war as a European conflict that had little effect on life in the United States. Just after the war began, President Woodrow Wilson declared that the United States would remain neutral. Wilson's response to the war reflected a long-standing American tradition of isolationism—a policy of not being involved in the affairs of other nations.

Leaning toward the Allies Privately, Wilson favored the Allied cause. He was extremely concerned about Germany's war tactics and its invasion of Belgium. Furthermore, the United States historically had greater political, cultural, and commercial ties to Great Britain and France than to Germany.

Financially, the United States was far from neutral. The British fleet had blockaded German ports and transportation routes, and few American businesses could sell goods to German forces. It was far easier, however, to supply the Allies. By 1917 Britain was purchasing nearly $75 million worth of war goods from American businesses each week.

German submarine warfare Germany suffered greatly under the British blockade, and the German navy began to develop a plan to strike back at Great Britain. Germany planned to wage its naval war with U-boats—small submarines named after the German word *Unterseeboot*, which means "undersea boat."

In February 1915 the German government announced that the waters around Great Britain would be a war zone in which Germany would destroy all enemy ships. Germany warned the United States that neutral ships might be attacked as well. This policy of having submarines attack all ships was called unrestricted submarine warfare.

The German plan for unrestricted submarine warfare angered most Americans. Wilson believed that Germany's actions violated the laws of neutrality. He warned Germany that he would hold the nation responsible if American lives were lost. Tensions between the United States and Germany were rising.

READING CHECK Drawing Conclusions Why did American businesses do more business with the Allies than with Germany?

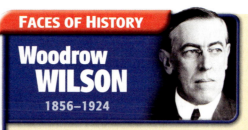

FACES OF HISTORY
Woodrow WILSON
1856–1924

Woodrow Wilson is best known for his peace-making efforts during and after World War I. In fact, Wilson wanted to avoid entering the war at all, but Germany soon challenged American neutrality. In stirring words, Wilson asked Congress for a declaration of war. "The world must be made safe for democracy," he said. "Its peace must be planted upon the tested foundations of political liberty."

After the war Wilson once again addressed Congress, this time with a plan for keeping peace in the postwar world. His Fourteen Points speech called for a League of Nations, an organization for cooperation between countries. Wilson's support of the League of Nations earned him the Nobel Prize for Peace in 1919.

Interpret What did Wilson want to accomplish after World War I?

Heading Toward War

As you read in the "Inside Story," the American public was outraged by the 1915 sinking of the *Lusitania*. President Wilson demanded an end to unrestricted submarine warfare.

Facing international criticism, the German government agreed to attack only supply ships. But less than one year later, Germany attacked the French passenger ship *Sussex* on March 24, 1916, killing about 80 people. After this attack, Wilson threatened to end diplomatic relations with Germany unless it stopped killing innocent civilians. German officials feared that the United States might enter the war, so Germany issued the **Sussex pledge**, which included a promise not to sink merchant vessels "without warning and without saving human lives."

Wilson's re-election As he campaigned during the election of 1916, Wilson assured Americans that he would not send their sons to die in Europe. Wilson's chief rival, Republican candidate Charles Evans Hughes, took a stronger pro-war stance. The election was very close. In the end, Wilson won by little more than 3 percent of the popular vote.

Once re-elected, Wilson began to work for a peace settlement. In January 1917 he asked the Allied and Central Powers to accept a "peace without victory." This request angered

ACADEMIC VOCABULARY
neutral not aligned with either side in a war or dispute

the Allies. They blamed the Central Powers for starting the war and wanted them to pay for wartime damage and destruction.

Any hope for peace ended when Germany resumed unrestricted submarine warfare on February 1, 1917. Two days later, the United States ended diplomatic relations with Germany. Wilson asked Congress for the authority to install guns on U.S. merchant ships.

The Zimmermann Note Meanwhile, German foreign secretary Arthur Zimmermann sent a telegram to a German official in Mexico. The Zimmermann Note proposed an alliance between Germany and Mexico. "We shall make war together, make peace together," the telegram offered. "[In exchange] Mexico is to reconquer the lost territory in New Mexico, Texas, and Arizona." The Germans hoped that an American war with Mexico would keep the United States out of the war in Europe. Since Mexico expressed no interest in fighting, this German strategy backfired.

The British had intercepted the Zimmermann Note, decoded it, and sent it to American officials. On March 1, American newspapers printed excerpts from the telegram. More Americans began to call for war against Germany. Yet Wilson continued to resist, hoping to bring about a lasting peace in Europe.

The United States declares war In mid-March, dramatic events in Russia raised new questions for the United States. An uprising in Russia forced Czar Nicholas II to give up his absolute power over the government. Rebel leaders set up a government based on republican ideals.

These changes made Russia more democratic but also raised questions about how long the new Russian government would continue to fight on the Eastern Front. Many Americans—who believed that the American role in world politics should be to promote democracy—became more supportive of the Allies and the war after the Russian czar lost power.

Then in mid-March 1917, German U-boats sank three American merchant ships. Outraged about the violation of American neutrality, President Wilson called a meeting with his cabinet. Each cabinet member argued for war. On April 2, Wilson asked Congress to declare war on Germany so that the world could "be made safe for democracy."

HISTORY'S VOICES

> "We shall fight for the things which we have always carried nearest our hearts, for democracy … [and to] bring peace and safety to all nations and make the world itself at last free."
>
> —Woodrow Wilson, Speech to Congress, April 2, 1917

From Neutrality to War

Remaining Neutral

Below, a German U-boat prowls the seas. President Wilson opposed the use of unrestricted submarine warfare, but he campaigned for re-election in 1916 (right) with promises to keep America out of the war.

Congress approved President Wilson's request. On April 6, 1917, the United States joined the war on the side of the Allies.

READING CHECK **Drawing Conclusions** How did the United States respond to war in Europe?

Americans in Europe

Now the United States military began quickly preparing for battle. An army needed to be raised, new recruits needed to be trained for combat, and troops and supplies needed to be shipped to the front.

Raising an army On May 18, 1917, Congress passed the Selective Service Act, which required men between the ages of 21 and 30 to register to be drafted into the armed forces. Most young men willingly participated in the draft. A small number of men asked to be classified as conscientious objectors—members of certain religious groups, such as the Quakers, whose moral or religious beliefs prevented them from fighting in a war. But few local draft boards accepted their applications. Once rejected, these men had to take combat positions or face prison.

In the summer of 1917, the new recruits reported for training but found almost nothing ready for them. Many soldiers slept in tents until barracks could be hastily built. Supplies had been ordered but had not yet arrived.

Nevertheless, the training was intense. New recruits spent most of their days learning military rules and practices, marching, and preparing for inspections. Because of a shortage of rifles, they practiced with wooden sticks. Instead of horses, the trainees pretended to ride wooden barrels.

African American soldiers were segregated into separate divisions and trained in separate camps. Many white Army officers and southern politicians objected to the training of African American soldiers to use weapons. They feared that these black soldiers might pose a threat after the war. Because of these beliefs, only a few black regiments were trained for combat.

Latinos also experienced discrimination. Some Hispanic soldiers faced scorn from other American troops and were often assigned menial tasks. Some Latinos who were eager to serve in the war did not speak English fluently. The federal government did not reject them. Instead, the military established special programs in New Mexico and Georgia to help them improve their English skills. After completing such training, the soldiers would fight alongside other American troops.

THE IMPACT TODAY

Government
The Selective Service Act remains in effect today. All men between the ages of 18 and 25 must register to be selected randomly for military service. However, the draft has not been instituted since 1973.

Joining the War

After the United States declared war in 1917, General John J. Pershing led U.S. forces in Europe. Below, Pershing arrives in France with the first soldiers. He spent months establishing the American Expeditionary Forces (right) and setting up communications and supply lines.

Arriving in Europe The American soldiers who went overseas formed the American Expeditionary Forces (AEF), led by General John J. Pershing. The AEF included soldiers from the regular army, the National Guard, and a new larger force of volunteers and draftees.

The first U.S. troops arrived in France in late June 1917. To transport forces safely, Pershing relied on the **convoy system**, in which troop-transport ships were surrounded by destroyers or cruisers for protection. The convoy system reduced the number of ships sunk and limited the loss of troops and supplies.

When American troops arrived in France, the Allies' situation was grim. German troops occupied all of Belgium and part of northeastern France. Along the Eastern Front, Russia was struggling to defend itself against Germany. The Russians were facing famine and civil war. If Russia fell, many German troops could be sent to fight in France. The Allies desperately needed help and wanted the Americans to start fighting as soon as they arrived.

General Pershing had other plans. He wanted his soldiers to fight as American units and not as individuals in different European regiments. Pershing also wanted to give his troops more training. The American general believed that sending inexperienced soldiers into battle was the same as sending them to die. As a result, Pershing sent his troops to training camps in eastern France.

Allied setbacks Meanwhile, the Allies suffered another blow. In November 1917 a group known as the Bolsheviks took control of Russia's government. The Bolsheviks were **Communists**—people who seek the equal distribution of wealth and the end of all private property. The new government, led by Vladimir Ilich Lenin, withdrew the Russian army from the Eastern Front and signed a peace agreement with the Central Powers. Now Germany was free to focus on fighting in the west.

In March 1918, German soldiers launched a series of tremendous offensives against the Allies. The Germans were backed by some 6,000 artillery pieces, including "Big Berthas"—massive guns capable of firing a 2,100-pound shell almost 75 miles. By late May the Germans had pushed the Allies back to the Marne River, just 70 miles northeast of Paris.

U.S. troops in action Almost 12 months after arriving in France, American troops finally saw combat. Reaching the front lines, they quickly learned the Allied war strategy. They dug extensive trenches to protect themselves from German gunfire. When Company A

From Neutrality to War, *continued*

Fighting in the War

In June 1918, Belleau Wood, France, became the proving grounds for American soldiers (below). Although a U.S. victory, 8,000 American casualties at the Battle of Belleau Wood made it America's bloodiest battle thus far in the war.

of the 82nd Division reached the front lines, for example, its members had to dig 3,000 yards of trenches and set up 12,000 yards of barbed wire. The soldiers worked in the middle of the night to avoid detection by the enemy. As dawn broke, the exhausted soldiers returned to their temporary shelters. They were covered in mud, and their uniforms were torn to shreds by barbed wire.

Life in the trenches was a painful ordeal. The soldiers stood in deep mud as rats ran across their feet. Enemy planes dropped bombs, artillery shells exploded nearby, and clouds of mustard gas floated into the trenches. "It was an eerie feeling down in that dugout [trench]," one soldier recalled. "No one knew what was going to happen next."

The American troops were a major factor in the war. While defending Paris in June 1918, U.S. troops helped the French stop the Germans at Chateau-Thierry. In northern France, a division of U.S. Marines recaptured the forest of Belleau Wood and two nearby villages. After fierce fighting, the Allies finally halted the German advance. Paris was saved.

American military women The vast majority of Americans who served in the military were men, but some women also signed up to serve overseas. The U.S. Army Signal Corps recruited French-speaking American women to serve as switchboard operators. Known as the Hello Girls, they served a crucial role in keeping communications open between the front line and the headquarters of the American Expeditionary Forces.

During the war, more than 20,000 nurses served in the U.S. Army in the United States and overseas. Women also served in the navy and marines, usually as typists and bookkeepers, although some became radio operators, electricians, or telegraphers.

READING CHECK Identifying the Main Idea
Why did it take so long for U.S. troops to enter combat?

The War Ends

On July 15, 1918, the Germans launched their last, desperate offensive at the Second Battle of the Marne. During the fighting, the U.S. 3rd Division blew up every bridge the Germans had built across the Marne. The German army retreated on August 3, having suffered some 150,000 casualties.

The Allies began a counterattack in September 1918. For the first time, Americans fought as a separate army. The AEF defeated German troops at Mihiel, near the French-German border.

ACADEMIC VOCABULARY
factor something that contributes to a result

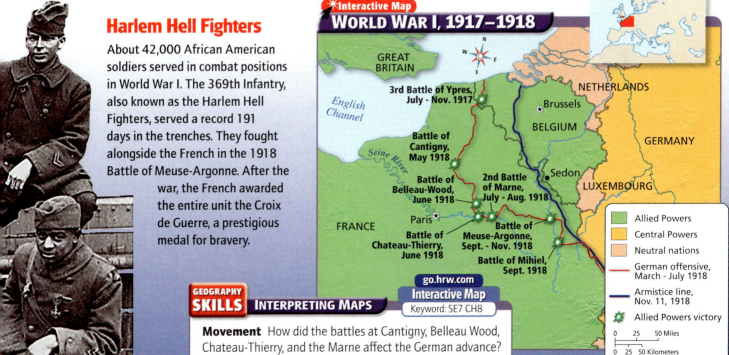

Harlem Hell Fighters
About 42,000 African American soldiers served in combat positions in World War I. The 369th Infantry, also known as the Harlem Hell Fighters, served a record 191 days in the trenches. They fought alongside the French in the 1918 Battle of Meuse-Argonne. After the war, the French awarded the entire unit the Croix de Guerre, a prestigious medal for bravery.

GEOGRAPHY SKILLS INTERPRETING MAPS
Movement How did the battles at Cantigny, Belleau Wood, Chateau-Thierry, and the Marne affect the German advance?
See **Skills Handbook**, p. H20

Alvin York's bravery—and capture of 132 Germans—made him the most famous hero of the war.

After the victory, the Allies continued their advance toward the French city of Sedan on the Belgian border. The railway there was the main supply line for German forces. Other Allied forces advanced all along the front.

For more than a month the Allies pushed northward through the rugged Argonne Forest, facing artillery explosions and deadly machine gun fire every step of the way. In the Battle of the Argonne Forest the Americans suffered some 120,000 casualties. By November, however, the Allies reached and occupied the hills around Sedan.

The armistice By late 1918 the war was crippling the German economy; many civilians lacked food and supplies. Food riots and strikes erupted in Germany, and revolution swept across Austria-Hungary. The Central Powers had difficulty encouraging their soldiers to fight. Some soldiers even ran away.

Lacking the will to keep fighting, the Central Powers began to surrender. In early November, Austria-Hungary signed a peace agreement with the Allies. On November 7 a German delegation entered French territory to begin peace negotiations.

The Allies demanded that Germany leave all territories it had occupied. Germany surrendered its aircraft, heavy artillery, tanks, and U-boats. The Allies also forced Germany to allow Allied troops to occupy some German territory. On November 11, 1918, the armistice went into effect, and the guns of war fell silent. An Allied soldier later described the moment when the Great War ended.

HISTORY'S VOICES

" There came a second of expectant silence, and then a curious rippling sound … It was the sound of men cheering from the Vosges [mountain range] to the sea. "
—John Buchan, *The King's Grace*, 1935

War tragedies muted some of the celebration. When asked what the armistice meant, one British soldier replied, "Time to bury the dead." People around the world had grown weary of death. Some 8.5 million people had been killed. People everywhere hoped that the Great War would be "the war to end all wars." World leaders soon turned their attention to healing what the American writer W.E.B. Du Bois referred to as the "wounded world."

READING CHECK Sequencing What events led to the armistice?

SECTION 2 ASSESSMENT

HSS 11.4.4, 11.4.5

Keyword: SE7 HP8

Reviewing Ideas, Terms, and People

1. **a. Define** What was **isolationism**?
   b. Explain Why did the United States pursue a policy of isolationism?
   c. Elaborate How did Germany's actions make the United States begin to consider abandoning isolationism?
2. **a. Recall** What was the **Zimmermann Note**?
   b. Draw Conclusions How did the Zimmermann Note affect American public opinion about the war?
   c. Evaluate Which event do you think was the most significant in convincing Americans to join the war? Why?
3. **a. Identify** What was the **convoy system**?
   b. Explain What effect did U.S. troops have on the outcome of the war?
4. **a. Describe** What was the Battle of the Argonne Forest?
   b. Analyze How did the economic effects of the war help bring an end to the fighting?

Critical Thinking

5. **Identifying Cause and Effect** Copy the timeline below. Using information from the section, place on the timeline the major events that led the United States to declare war against Germany.

FOCUS ON WRITING ELA W1.1

6. **Expository** What caused the United States to enter World War I? Write a short paragraph in which you explain the events that led the United States to declare war.

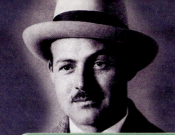

American Literature

Ernest Hemingway (1899–1961)

About the Reading Ernest Hemingway based his novel *A Farewell to Arms* (1929) on his experiences as an ambulance driver for the American Red Cross in World War I. His novel tells the story of Frederic Henry, an American serving with the Italian ambulance service, who falls in love with Catherine Barkley, a British nurse. In the following passage Frederic describes an atmosphere of confusion and uncertainty as he works to help the wounded.

AS YOU READ Notice how the narrator remains distant from the "great battle."

Excerpt from
A Farewell to Arms
by Ernest Hemingway

American snipers on the outskirts of a French town take potshots at German soldiers from the shelter of a shattered building.

The wounded were coming into the post, some were carried on stretchers, some walking and some were brought on the backs of men that came across the field. They were wet to the skin and all were scared. We filled two cars with stretcher cases as they came up from the cellar of the post and as I shut the door of the second car and fastened it I felt the rain on my face turn to snow. The flakes were coming heavy and fast in the rain.

When daylight came the storm was still blowing but the snow had stopped. It had melted as it fell on the wet ground and now it was raining again. There was another attack just after daylight but it was unsuccessful. We expected an attack all day but it did not come until the sun was going down. The bombardment started to the south below the long wooded ridge where the Austrian guns were concentrated. We expected a bombardment but it did not come. It was getting dark. Guns were firing from the field behind the village and the shells, going away, had a comfortable sound.

We heard that the attack to the south had been unsuccessful. They did not attack that night but we heard that they had broken through to the north.

In the night word came that we were to prepare to retreat. The captain at the post told me this. He had it from the Brigade. A little while later he came from the telephone and said it was a lie. The Brigade had received orders that the line of the Bainsizza should be held no matter what happened. I asked about the break through and he said he had heard at the Brigade that the Austrians had broken though the twenty-seventh arms corps up toward Caporetto. There had been a great battle in the north all day.

Skills Focus **READING LIKE A HISTORIAN**

1. **Drawing Conclusions** How reliable is the information about the distant battle that the narrator receives?
2. **Literature as Historical Evidence** What larger statement do you think Hemingway is trying to make about the nature of warfare in the twentieth century?

See **Skills Handbook**, pp. H12, H32.

SECTION 3: The Home Front

Before You Read

MAIN IDEA
The United States mobilized a variety of resources to wage World War I.

READING FOCUS
1. How did the government mobilize the economy for the war effort?
2. How did workers mobilize on the home front?
3. How did the government try to influence public opinion about the war?

KEY TERMS AND PEOPLE
Liberty bonds
Bernard Baruch
National War Labor Board
Committee on Public Information
George Creel
propaganda
Schenck v. *United States*

 HSS 11.4.5 Analyze the political, economic, and social ramifications of World War I on the home front.

Pocketbook PATRIOTISM

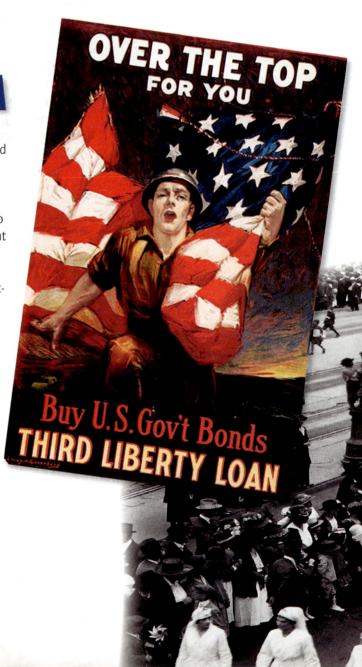

THE INSIDE STORY

What was a Liberty bond? When the United States entered the war in 1917, President Wilson called on everyone to join the war effort. To help pay for the war, he launched four drives to sell **Liberty bonds**. The bonds, like today's government savings bonds, were a form of loan to the government. In schools, children filled Liberty Books with 25-cent stamps until they were full and could be exchanged for a bond. The slogan was "Lick a Stamp and Lick the Kaiser."

Campaigns to sell bonds were intense. Organizers sent out workers to sell in workplaces, neighborhoods, and theaters. Celebrities from movie stars to baseball players to opera singers appeared at rallies flanked by doughboys in uniform and asked their audiences to buy bonds. Some of the largest rallies were held in Manhattan. In one skit, movie actor Douglas Fairbanks—known for playing swashbuckling heroes—wore boxing gloves labeled Victory and Liberty Bonds as he knocked out the Kaiser.

Artists and advertising experts produced slogans and colorful propaganda posters. They appealed to patriotism, fear, or sympathy for war victims in Europe. One famous poster showed a woman refugee and her children. It read: "Must Children Die and Mothers Plead in Vain—Buy More Liberty Bonds." Another showed a smiling little girl hugging a bond: "My daddy bought me a government bond of the Third Liberty Loan. Did Yours?" In all, the bond drives brought in almost $17 billion.

246 CHAPTER 8

Mobilizing the Economy

Going to war was an enormous—and enormously expensive—undertaking. One of the first things that President Wilson and his advisers had to do after joining the war was figure out how to pay for it. First, Congress passed the War Revenue Act of 1917. This law established very high taxes and taxed the wealthiest Americans as much as 77 percent of their annual incomes. It increased federal revenues by 400 percent within two years.

The government also borrowed money to pay for the war. The national debt grew from $1.2 billion in 1916 to $25.5 billion in 1919. More than $20 billion of that debt was owed to Americans who had purchased Liberty bonds. These bonds were essentially a loan from the American people to the federal government.

Regulating industry To make sure that the troops received all the supplies they needed, the Wilson administration prepared the nation's industries for war. Congress created hundreds of administrative boards to regulate both industrial and agricultural production and distribution.

One of the most powerful boards was the War Industries Board (WIB). It had the authority to regulate all materials needed in the war effort. Wall Street business leader **Bernard Baruch**, head of the WIB, explained the board's power: "No steel, copper, cement, rubber, or other basic materials could be used without our approval."

The policies and rules of the WIB managed to increase American industrial production by about 20 percent. The military could select any of the goods that were produced. Once the military's needs were met, any remaining goods could be used by civilians.

Regulating food To make sure that the troops would have plenty of food and supplies, Congress passed the Lever Food and Fuel Control Act. This law gave the government the power to set prices and establish production controls for food and for the fuels needed to run military machines.

Wilson's administration also created agencies to manage and increase food production. Herbert Hoover led the Food Administration, whose slogan was "Food Can Win the War." Hoover's goals were to increase the production of crops and to conserve existing food supplies for the military and for American allies.

Financing the War
Colorful posters that spoke to Americans' sense of patriotism (left), parades (below), and appeals by movie stars such as Charlie Chaplin, Mary Pickford, and Douglas Fairbanks (right), all encouraged the purchase of war bonds. *What other attempts did the government make to finance the war?*

In order to encourage wartime production, he promised farmers higher prices for their crops. Farm production soared.

Hoover asked Americans to plant vegetables at home in "victory gardens." He also urged Americans to eat less by participating in "meatless Mondays" and "wheatless Wednesdays." His efforts paid off. By 1918 the United States had so much surplus food that it exported three times as much food as it had prior to the war.

Another proposal to conserve food supplies was a prohibition, or ban, on alcohol. Most alcohol is made with food crops such as grapes and wheat. Days after entering the war, Congress limited the alcohol content of wine and beer so that these crops could be used for food production instead.

Some progressives tried to discourage Americans from drinking beer by linking German Americans to the brewing industry. The progressives hoped that anti-German feelings would lead Americans to stop drinking beer.

As the war continued, the temperance, or anti-alcohol, movement gained strength. In 1919 the Eighteenth Amendment was ratified, banning the "manufacture, sale or transportation" of alcohol in the United States. In 1919 Congress passed the Volstead Act, giving the government the authority to enforce this prohibition on alcohol.

Regulating fuel After the passage of the Lever Food and Fuel Control Act, the Fuel Administration was established to set production goals and prices for fuels. Its purpose was to make sure that military needs for fuel could always be met.

Harry Garfield, the son of former president James A. Garfield, headed the Fuel Administration. To encourage fuel conservation, Garfield introduced daylight saving time in order to extend daylight hours for those who worked long shifts in the factories. He promoted fuel conservation in other ways, such as through publicity campaigns calling for "gasless Sundays" and "heatless Mondays."

Supplying U.S. and Allied troops By creating these various boards and agencies, the federal government was quickly able to produce and collect the supplies needed for the

Working for the War Effort

war effort. It was not just American soldiers who benefited from these supplies. The United States also became the major supplier for the Allied Powers. During the war Great Britain alone received more than 1 billion rounds of ammunition, 1.2 million rifles, and more than half a million tons of explosives from the United States. The power of U.S. manufacturing and farming became a much-needed boost for the struggling Allies and a boost for the American economy as well.

READING CHECK **Drawing Conclusions** How did the Wilson administration change the U.S. economy for the war effort?

Mobilizing Workers

During the war, the profits of many major industrial corporations skyrocketed. This was because the corporations sold their products to the federal government. In turn, the federal government used those products in the war effort. In this way the war created enormous profits for stockholders of industries such as chemicals, oil, and steel.

Wages for factory workers increased as well. The rising cost of food and housing, however, meant that workers were hardly better off than they had been before the war.

Meanwhile, war demands led to laborers working long hours, sometimes in increasingly dangerous conditions. The urgent need to produce materials for the war—and the great financial incentive for companies to do so—led to a faster pace of production.

These harsher working conditions led many workers to join labor unions. Union membership increased by about 60 percent between 1916 and 1919. Union activities boomed as well, with more than 6,000 strikes being held during the war.

National War Labor Board Massive industrial production was essential to the war effort. Leaders feared that industrial protests such as strikes would disrupt the war effort. To keep disruptions to a minimum, the Wilson administration created the National War Labor Board in 1918. This board judged disputes between workers and management. During the short time that the board was in operation (less than a year), it handled some 1,200 cases involving 700,000 workers.

The National War Labor Board also set policies that sought to improve working conditions for all Americans. The board established the eight-hour workday, urged that businesses recognize labor unions, and promoted equal pay for women who did equal work.

Women's war efforts As men left their jobs to fight on the war front, women moved into those jobs to keep the American economy moving. Women took on many jobs traditionally held by men. They worked on railroads, at docks, and in factories. They also built ships and airplanes.

Other women filled more traditional jobs, working as teachers and nurses. Some took on volunteer positions that ranged from helping to sell Liberty bonds to digging victory gardens. In all, about 1 million women entered the workforce during World War I. After the war ended, however, most women left the jobs they had taken. Many women left by choice, but others were forced to leave by employers who wanted to return the jobs to men who had served in the war.

Women in a gun factory (left) assemble soldiers' pistols in 1918. Below, men at a steel plant make shell casings in 1917. After many male workers went off to fight in the war, women supplied much-needed labor. **How did Wilson aid this transition?**

Linking to Today

Epidemics

In 1918 and 1919, an influenza epidemic killed millions of people, including some 675,000 Americans. Influenza also spread around the world, killing at least 20 million, and perhaps as many as 40 million people. Travelers carried the disease between countries.

In 2002 a respiratory virus called Severe Acute Respiratory Syndrome (SARS) emerged in China. It also spread to the United States. As with influenza in 1918, travelers are believed to have carried the disease.

Making Inferences How can travel affect the spread of disease?

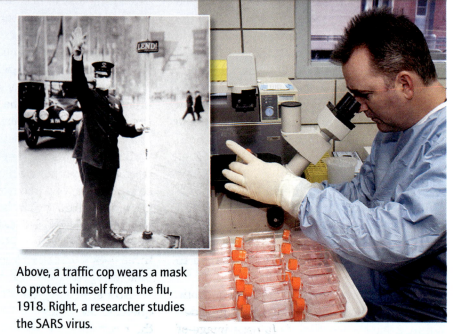

Above, a traffic cop wears a mask to protect himself from the flu, 1918. Right, a researcher studies the SARS virus.

The contributions that women made to the war effort did not go unnoticed. Women's suffrage advocates used these contributions as further justification for granting women the vote. President Wilson also acknowledged women's role in the war effort.

HISTORY'S VOICES

> "This war could not have been fought … if it had not been for the services of women rendered in every sphere."
>
> —President Woodrow Wilson, 1918

Influenza epidemic on the home front

The war's efffort was seriously affected by an extremely severe flu epidemic that broke out between 1918 and 1919. In Europe the disease quickly spread across the Western Front, where crowded and unsanitary trenches were perfect breeding grounds for the disease. In fact, of all the American troops who lost their lives in World War I, about half of them died from influenza.

Soldiers on the front lines, however, were not the only ones to suffer from influenza. On March 11, 1918, an army private in Kansas complained of flulike symptoms. By the end of that week, more than 500 soldiers had come down with influenza. By August, influenza was reported in Philadelphia and Boston.

This was no ordinary flu. Most forms of influenza were simply uncomfortable and unpleasant. But this form of influenza was deadly. It killed healthy people within days. During the month of October 1918 alone, influenza killed nearly 200,000 Americans.

Panicked city leaders canceled public gatherings, but the disease still spread. Rumors spread almost as quickly. Many people, such as Lieutenant Colonel Philip Doane, wrongly blamed Germans for causing the disease. Doane remarked, "It would be quite easy for one of these German agents to turn loose influenza germs in a theater or some other place where large numbers of persons are assembled."

By the time this wave of influenza passed, some 675,000 Americans had lost their lives. It was the deadliest epidemic in U.S. history.

READING CHECK **Identifying the Main Idea** Why did the Wilson administration create the National War Labor Board?

Influencing Public Opinion

President Wilson moved quickly to build public support after Congress declared war. Many Americans had been in favor of the U.S. position of neutrality. Now Wilson had to convince these

THE IMPACT TODAY

Science and Technology

Scientists have reconstructed the 1918 influenza virus and found it to be a bird flu that was transmitted directly to humans. The research team analyzed lung tissue from two people who died in the 1918–1919 epidemic.

Americans that it was their duty to support the war. "It is not an army that we must shape for war … it is a nation," he said.

Winning American support Wilson created the **Committee on Public Information** (CPI) less than two weeks after the United States declared war. He appointed newspaper reporter and political reformer **George Creel** to head the CPI.

Creel began a nationwide campaign of **propaganda**—posters, newspaper stories, speeches, and other materials designed to influence people's opinions. This campaign was meant to encourage Americans to support the war. Creel hired popular movie stars such as Mary Pickford and Douglas Fairbanks to speak on behalf of the war effort.

The CPI also hired artists to create patriotic posters and pamphlets. These posters included James Montgomery Flagg's famous image of Uncle Sam pointing to the viewer and demanding, "I Want You for the U.S. Army."

As many Americans became more patriotic and supportive of the war, some began to distrust all things German as well. Some tried to eliminate all German influence from American culture. Many schools stopped teaching the German language to their students. Many symphonies stopped playing music written by German composers. Even German-sounding items were renamed to sound patriotic. For example, sauerkraut became liberty cabbage, dachshunds became liberty pups, and hamburger became known as liberty steak.

Anti-German feelings continued to grow after reports spread that secret agents from Germany were operating in the United States. In one of the worst acts of sabotage, German agents planted a bomb at a ship-loading terminal in New York City. The bomb destroyed $20 million worth of supplies for the war, killed three dock workers, and shattered windows in buildings across lower Manhattan.

Acts such as these led some Americans to question the loyalty of German Americans in their communities. As a result, some German Americans experienced discrimination and violence. In April 1918, for example, a mob in Illinois lynched socialist coal miner Robert Prager because townspeople suspected him of being a German spy.

PRIMARY SOURCES

Propaganda Poster

To gain support for the war effort, officials in the United States hired skilled artists to create posters that would build public support and increase recruitment. This poster was designed by artist James Montgomery Flagg.

The use of the word *you* as well as Uncle Sam looking and pointing at the viewer makes it clear that the U.S. Army is asking each individual to serve.

Uncle Sam's red, white, and blue clothing tells young men that joining the army is an act of patriotism.

Skills Focus — READING LIKE A HISTORIAN

1. **Drawing Conclusions** What is the main message of this propaganda poster?
2. **Interpreting Visuals** How effective do you think this poster was?

See **Skills Handbook**, p. H30

Limiting antiwar speech Prominent Americans, such as reformer Jane Addams and Senator Robert La Follette, spoke out against the war. Addams, a pacifist, also founded the Women's International League for Peace and Freedom. As the Wilson administration built public support, it also tried to limit this public opposition to the war.

In 1917 Congress passed the Espionage Act, which punished people for aiding the enemy or refusing military duty. The next year, Congress passed a related law called the Sedition Act. This law made it illegal for Americans to "utter, print, write, or publish any disloyal … or abusive language" criticizing the government, the flag, or the military.

More than 1,000 opponents of the war were jailed under these laws. Robert Goldstein, who directed a film on the American Revolution called *The Spirit of '76*, was jailed for three years because he refused to remove scenes of British brutality from the movie.

In another case, Socialist Party leader Eugene V. Debs was sentenced to prison for 10 years for criticizing the United States government's prosecution of Americans under the Espionage Act. After the war ended, however, Debs was released from prison by a presidential order.

Some Americans believed that the Espionage Act and the Sedition Act violated the First Amendment. Others, however, thought these laws were essential to protect military secrets, the safety of American soldiers, and the overall U.S. war effort.

The Supreme Court also struggled to interpret the Espionage Act and the Sedition Act. The defining case came when Charles Schenck, an official of the American Socialist Party, was convicted of violating the Espionage Act. Schenck had organized the printing and distribution of some 15,000 leaflets opposing government war policies. He challenged the conviction as a violation of his constitutional right to free speech.

In its first decision interpreting the First Amendment, the Supreme Court upheld Schenck's conviction. Justice Oliver Wendell Holmes Jr. wrote the Court's unanimous opinion in *Schenck v. United States*, explaining the limits to free speech.

In his written opinion, Holmes went on to explain that many things that can safely be said in peacetime can cause problems for the government and danger for soldiers in wartime. For that reason, Holmes argued, some limits needed to be placed on individual free-speech rights during wartime to ensure the country's overall safety. You will read more about *Schenck v. United States* on the following page.

READING CHECK **Drawing Conclusions** Why did the Wilson administration place wartime limitations on free speech?

SECTION 3 ASSESSMENT

HSS 11.4.5

Reviewing Ideas, Terms, and People

1. **a. Identify** What were **Liberty bonds**?
   b. Explain In what two ways did the United States pay for its war effort?

2. **a. Describe** What happened to the profits of many major corporations during the war?
   b. Compare and Contrast Did workers prosper in the same way that major companies did during the war? Why or why not?
   c. Elaborate Why would the government consider it necessary to get involved in disputes between workers and management?

3. **a. Recall** What was the **Committee on Public Information**?
   b. Contrast How did the government try to persuade people to support the war and discourage them from opposing it?

   c. Evaluate Was the government justified in trying to suppress opposition to the war? Why or why not?

Critical Thinking

4. **Identifying Supporting Details** Copy the chart below and record the ways in which the United States managed its food supply for the war effort.

FOCUS ON WRITING ELA W1.1

5. **Expository** Write a short paragraph in which you explain the contributions American women made to the war effort.

LANDMARK SUPREME COURT CASES
Constitutional Issue: Freedom of Speech

Schenck v. United States (1919)

Why It Matters Schenck was the first major Supreme Court case to consider limits on the First Amendment right of free speech. According to the decision, speech can be limited when it poses a "clear and present danger."

Background of the Case
During World War I, the Espionage Act made it a crime to interfere with the war effort. Charles Schenck, general secretary of the American Socialist Party, distributed thousands of leaflets urging men to oppose the draft. Schenck was convicted of violating the Espionage Act, and he appealed. He argued that the First Amendment protected his right to speak out on this subject.

The Decision
The Supreme Court ruled unanimously against Schenck. Writing for the Court, Justice Oliver Wendell Holmes Jr. looked both at what Schenck said and at the circumstances in which he said it. The Constitution does not protect speech that causes danger to others. For example, the First Amendment

> "... would not protect a man in falsely shouting 'Fire' in a theatre and causing a panic. ... The question in every case is whether the words used ... create a clear and present danger ..."
>
> — Justice Oliver Wendell Holmes Jr.

Certain things that might safely be said during peacetime could be dangerous when the country was at war. Congress can place some limits on the right of free speech in order to protect the country's safety. Schenck's intent was to interfere with the draft, and the First Amendment does not protect this activity.

THE IMPACT TODAY War protesters march in California to mark the first anniversary of the 2003 invasion of Iraq. If this demonstration had taken place in 1919 or 1920, the group could have been arrested under the Espionage Act or the Sedition Act.

CRITICAL THINKING
go.hrw.com
Research Online
Keyword: SS Court

1. **Analyze the Impact** Using the keyword above, research the decision in *Texas* v. *Johnson*. How do the facts in *Johnson* differ from those in *Schenck*? Why did the Court decide in Johnson's favor?

2. **You Be the Judge** While U.S. troops were fighting in Vietnam, Afghanistan, and Iraq, some Americans argued that it is unpatriotic to oppose an ongoing war. Others said that the right to disagree with government policy is essential to democracy. Can Congress constitutionally restrict Americans' right to speak against military actions? Explain your answer.

SECTION 4: Peace without Victory

BEFORE YOU READ

MAIN IDEA:
The Allies determined the terms for peace in the postwar world.

READING FOCUS
1. What was President Wilson's Fourteen Points plan for peace?
2. What was resolved at the Paris Peace Conference?
3. Why did Congress fight over the treaty?
4. What was the impact of World War I on the United States and the world?

KEY TERMS AND PEOPLE
Fourteen Points
self-determination
League of Nations
David Lloyd George
Georges Clemenceau
Big Four
reparations
Treaty of Versailles
Henry Cabot Lodge

HSS 11.4.4 Explain Woodrow Wilson's Moral Diplomacy, drawing on relevant speeches.

HSS 11.4.5 Analyze the political, economic, and social ramifications of World War I on the home front.

THE INSIDE STORY

Will the treaty pass? President Woodrow Wilson had to make many compromises at the peace conference after World War I. The Treaty of Versailles did, however, include his greatest dream—a League of Nations, an international organization that would work to ensure peace. "America shall in truth show the way," Wilson told the Senate, which still had to approve the treaty.

Although he was worn out, Wilson decided to go to the people for support. He set out on an exhausting cross-country speaking tour. In three weeks he traveled 8,000 miles by train from city to city, speaking several times a day. His speeches were eloquent, but they ignored some of the harsh provisions of the treaty. Western audiences were welcoming, which encouraged Wilson to push himself harder.

After speaking in Pueblo, Colorado, on September 25, 1919, Wilson collapsed. A few days later, after returning to Washington, he suffered a stroke that left him partially paralyzed. He carried on some duties but was an invalid, often angry and bitter, for the rest of his presidency. He cut off ties with old friends and political allies. He was openly angry at his opponents. He refused to compromise on changes, and the treaty was defeated. The United States never joined the League of Nations. Perhaps Wilson's only real reward was the 1919 Nobel Peace Prize, which called the League "a design for [bringing] a fundamental law of humanity into present-day international politics."

A Plan for Peace

▶ President Wilson rides through the streets of San Francisco on his tour to promote the League of Nations.

The Fourteen Points

As World War I drew to a close, the scale of destruction and massive loss of life was shocking. President Woodrow Wilson wanted a "just and lasting peace" to ensure that a war like the Great War would never happen again.

Wilson outlined his vision of world peace in a speech he made to the U.S. Congress in January 1918, before the war ended. His plan for peace was called the **Fourteen Points**.

HISTORY'S VOICES

> "What we demand ... is that the world be made fit and safe to live in; and particularly that it be made safe for every peace-loving nation which, like our own, wishes to live its own life, determine its own institutions, be assured of justice and fair dealing by the other peoples of the world as against force and selfish aggression."
>
> —President Woodrow Wilson, Fourteen Points speech, 1918

Wilson's first four points called for open diplomacy, freedom of the seas, the removal of trade barriers, and the reduction of military arms. The fifth point proposed a fair system to resolve disputes over colonies. The next eight points dealt directly with **self-determination**, or the right of people to decide their own political status. For example, Wilson wanted the different ethnic groups within Austria-Hungary to be able to form their own nations.

The fourteenth point, which Wilson believed was the most important, called for the establishment of the **League of Nations**. The League would be an organization of nations that would work together to settle disputes, protect democracy, and prevent future wars.

The components of the Fourteen Points expressed a new philosophy for U.S. foreign policy. The Fourteen Points applied the principles of progressivism to foreign policy. The ideals of free trade, democracy, and self-determination sprang from the same ideals that Progressive reformers supported within the United States. Most importantly, the Fourteen Points declared that the foreign policy of a democratic nation should be based on morality—not just on what was best for that nation.

READING CHECK **Identifying the Main Idea** What did President Wilson hope to accomplish with his Fourteen Points?

Paris Peace Conference

President Wilson led the group of American negotiators who attended the peace conference that began in Paris in January 1919. By doing so, he became the first U.S. president to visit Europe while in office.

Republicans and others back home criticized Wilson's decision to leave the country. They argued that it was more important for Wilson to stay and help the nation restore its economy after the war than to work toward peace in Europe.

Wilson had a dream of international peace, though, and he wanted to make that dream a reality. He believed that a lasting peace required a fair and unbiased leader, such as himself, to attend the Paris Peace Conference. Otherwise he felt sure that the European powers would continue to squabble over land and colonial rights.

The American delegation arrived in France a few weeks before the conference was scheduled to begin. President Wilson enjoyed a hero's welcome in Paris, when thousands of Parisians lined the streets to cheer his arrival. Before the conference began, Wilson also traveled to London and Rome, and in each city, he received the same heartfelt welcome.

The conference opens The Paris Peace Conference began on January 12, 1919. Leaders from 32 nations—representing about three-quarters of the world's population—attended the conference.

The leaders of the victorious Allies dominated the negotiations. Those leaders—President Woodrow Wilson of the United States, British prime minister **David Lloyd George**, French premier **Georges Clemenceau**, and Italian prime minister Vittorio Orlando—became known as the **Big Four**. Germany and the other Central Powers nations, however, were not invited to participate.

Conflicting needs The delegates arrived at the Paris Peace Conference with competing needs and desires. President Wilson had a vision of a better world where nations dealt with each other openly and traded with each other fairly, while at the same time reducing their arsenals of weapons. Many of the other Allies, however, wanted to punish Germany

THE IMPACT TODAY

Government The League of Nations failed to prevent future wars, in part because the United States and Germany were not members. After World War II, the United Nations (UN) formed to solve many of the same problems. The United States has been a member of the UN since 1945.

ACADEMIC VOCABULARY

component a part of something

THE FIRST WORLD WAR **255**

for its role in the war. Georges Clemenceau explained the French view in a speech at the conference in June 1919.

HISTORY'S VOICES

"The conduct of Germany is almost unexampled in human history. The terrible responsibility which lies at her doors can be seen in the fact that not less than seven million dead lie buried in Europe, while more than twenty million others carry upon them the evidence of wounds and sufferings, because Germany saw fit to gratify her [desire] for tyranny by resort to war."

—Georges Clemenceau

Other leaders came to the Paris Peace Conference seeking independence. Some wanted to build new nations, such as Yugoslavia and Czechoslovakia. Delegates from Poland, which had been divided between Germany and Russia during the war, wanted to re-establish their nation. A young Vietnamese chef named Ho Chi Minh who worked at the Paris Ritz hotel asked the peacemakers to grant his nation independence from France. Ho Chi Minh would later lead his people in taking Vietnamese independence by force.

The Treaty of Versailles The Allies eventually reached an agreement and presented their peace treaty to Germany in May. The final treaty was much harsher than Wilson had wanted. The treaty forced Germany to disarm its military forces. It required Germany to pay the Allies **reparations**—payments for damages and expenses caused by the war. This amount far exceeded what the German government could actually afford to pay. The Allies also demanded that Germany accept sole responsibility for starting the war.

The treaty did include some of Wilson's Fourteen Points. It would establish a League of Nations. Some ethnic groups in parts of

Wilson's Fourteen Points and the Treaty of Versailles

Some—but not all—of President Wilson's Fourteen Points were reflected in the Treaty of Versailles.

THE FOURTEEN POINTS

1. Public diplomatic negotiations and an end to secret treaties
2. Freedom of navigation on the seas
3. Free trade among nations
4. Reduction of armaments to the level needed for domestic safety
5. Fair resolution of colonial claims that arose because of the war
6. Evacuation of Russia and restoration of its conquered territories
7. Preservation of Belgium's sovereignty
8. Restoration of France's territory, including Alsace-Lorraine
9. Redrawing Italy's borders according to nationalities
10. Divide up Austria-Hungary according to nationalities
11. Redraw the borders of the Balkan states according to nationalities
12. Self-determination for Turks and the other nationalities under Turkish rule
13. Creation of an independent Polish nation
14. Creation of a League of Nations

MAJOR PROVISIONS OF THE TREATY OF VERSAILLES

Military Changes
- Limited the German army to 100,000 men, with no tanks or heavy artillery.
- Limited the German navy to 15,000 men.
- Banned Germany from having an air force.

Territory Changes
- Required Germany to cede land to France, Denmark, Poland, Czechoslovakia, and Belgium.
- Required Germany to surrender all colonies to the control of the League of Nations.
- Germany and Austria were prohibited from uniting.

War-Guilt Provisions
- Held Germany solely responsible for all losses and damages suffered by the Allies during the war.
- Required Germany to pay reparations of 269 billion gold marks, later reduced to 132 billion.

Establishment of the League of Nations
- Did not initially permit Germany to join the League.

COUNTERPOINTS

The League of Nations

President Wilson exhausted himself traveling the country to win support for the League.

“ Why, my fellow citizens, this is one of the great charters of human liberty, and the man who picks flaws in it ... forgets the magnitude of the thing, forgets the majesty of the thing, forgets that the counsels of more than twenty nations combined ... in the adoption of this great instrument. ”

Woodrow Wilson, 1919

The man who most strongly voiced the opposition to the League was Senator Henry Cabot Lodge.

“ We would not have our politics distracted and embittered by the dissensions of other lands. We would not have our country's vigour exhausted or her moral force abated, by everlasting meddling and muddling in every quarrel, great and small, which afflicts the world. ”

Henry Cabot Lodge, 1919

Skills Focus: READING LIKE A HISTORIAN

Identifying Points of View Wilson and Lodge had very different views on the role of the United States in the world. How does each quotation about the League of Nations reflect the speaker's view of relationships between nations?

See **Skills Handbook**, p. H28–H29

Germany, Austria-Hungary, and Russia would receive the right of self-determination. The treaty would create nine new nations, including Czechoslovakia, Poland, and Yugoslavia. The Central Powers also had to surrender control of their colonies to the Allies. The treaty placed some of the colonies under the temporary control of Allied nations until the colonies were deemed ready for independence.

Germany strongly protested the terms of the treaty. Threatened with French military action, however, German officials signed the **Treaty of Versailles** on June 28, 1919. Wilson was disappointed at the treaty's harshness but believed that the League of Nations could resolve any problems the treaty had created.

READING CHECK **Summarizing** How did the Allied leaders at the Paris Peace Conference react to the Fourteen Points?

The Fight over the Treaty

President Wilson returned to the United States on July 8, 1919, and formally presented the treaty to the U.S. Senate two days later. Wilson needed the support of both Republican and Democratic senators to ratify, or approve, the treaty. The Republicans had won control of the Senate in 1918, and getting their support proved difficult for the Democratic president.

The senators quickly divided into three groups. The first consisted of Democrats who supported immediate ratification of the treaty. The second group was the so-called irreconcilables, who urged the outright rejection of U.S. participation in the League of Nations. The last group was the reservationists, who would ratify the treaty only if changes were made.

The reservationists focused their criticism on the part of the League of Nations charter that required its members to use military force to carry out the League's decisions. Some Republicans believed that this conflicted with the constitutional power of the United States Congress to declare war. Senator **Henry Cabot Lodge**, head of the Committee on Foreign Relations, led the reservationists.

Wilson refused to compromise with the reservationists. He took his case directly to the

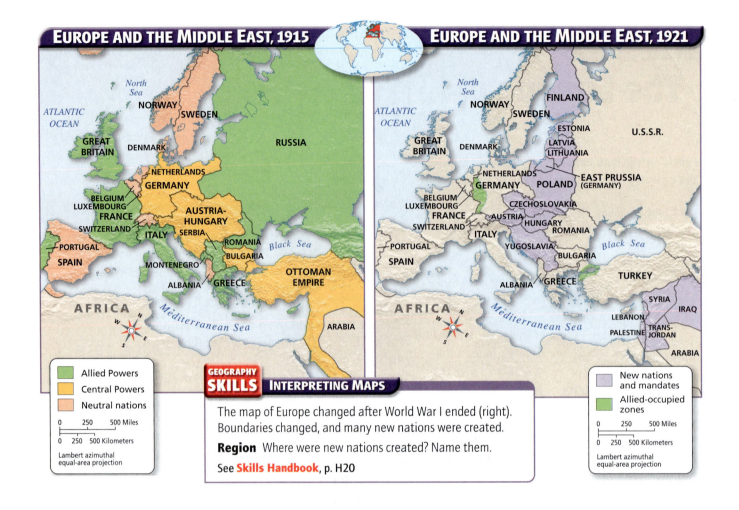

GEOGRAPHY SKILLS INTERPRETING MAPS

The map of Europe changed after World War I ended (right). Boundaries changed, and many new nations were created.

Region Where were new nations created? Name them.

See **Skills Handbook**, p. H20

American people. In 22 days Wilson traveled 8,000 miles and gave 32 major speeches, urging the public to pressure Republican senators to ratify the treaty. He warned of serious consequences if the world's nations did not work together in the future.

HISTORY'S VOICES

"I can predict with absolute certainty that within another generation there will be another world war if the nations of the world do not concert [agree upon] the method by which to prevent it."
—President Woodrow Wilson

As you read in the "Inside Story," Wilson's speaking schedule took a heavy toll on his health. After a speech in Pueblo, Colorado, on September 25, 1919, he collapsed. He suffered a stroke in early October and never fully recovered. Wilson spent the rest of his term living privately in the White House, cut off from everyone except his wife and his closest aides.

In November 1919, Senator Lodge presented the treaty to the U.S. Senate for ratification. He included a list of 14 reservations, or concerns about the treaty. Wilson was unwilling to compromise. Following Wilson's instructions, the Senate rejected Lodge's revised treaty on November 19 and again in March 1920.

After Wilson left office in 1921, the United States signed separate peace treaties with Austria, Germany, and Hungary. The United States never joined the League of Nations. Without the United States, the League's ability to keep world peace was uncertain.

READING CHECK   Making Inferences Why did some Americans oppose the Treaty of Versailles?

The Impact of World War I

World War I was a devastating conflict that shocked the world with its staggering cost. By the end of the war, combat, disease, and starvation had killed more than 14 million people. The war left some 7 million men permanently disabled. The war had cost more than $280 billion—significantly more than any previous war in history.

When the war ended, Americans were eager to return to normal life. But the war had changed the world, and there was no going back to the way things had once been.

Political impact The consequences of World War I were felt far beyond the battlefield. The war led to the overthrow of the monarchies in Russia, Austria-Hungary, Germany, and the Ottoman Empire. It contributed to the rise of the Bolsheviks to power in Russia in 1917. It fanned the flames of revolts against colonialism in the Middle East and in Southeast Asia.

Economic impact World War I devastated European economies. As a result, the United States emerged as the world's leading economic power.

Despite this new financial power, the United States still faced economic challenges at home. The demand for consumer goods increased as Americans raced to buy items that had been in short supply during the war. This increased demand led to inflation, and many Americans struggled to afford ordinary, day-to-day items.

Farmers, who had increased production to meet the needs of European markets during the war, were particularly hard hit when postwar markets no longer need to buy their food. Despite these economic setbacks, most Americans looked forward to the new decade as a time of peace and prosperity.

Social impact The war had drawn more than a million women into the American workforce. Their service to the nation contributed to the passage of the Nineteenth Amendment in 1919, which gave women the right to vote. In 1920 the states ratified the amendment.

The war also encouraged many African Americans to move to northern cities in search of factory work. This changed the population patterns of northern cities and led to new and often uneasy race relations.

Impact in Europe The effects of the war in Europe were devastating. European nations had lost almost an entire generation of young men. France, where most of the combat took place, was in ruins. Great Britain was deeply in debt to the United States and lost its position as the world's financial center. The reparations imposed on Germany by the Treaty of Versailles were crippling.

World War I would not be the "war to end all wars," as many had hoped. Too many issues were left unresolved, and too much anger and hostility would remain. Within a generation, conflict would again break out in Europe, pulling the United States and the rest of the world back into war.

READING CHECK **Summarizing** What economic effects did World War I have on the United States?

SECTION 4 ASSESSMENT

HSS 11.4.4, 11.4.5

Reviewing Ideas, Terms, and People

1. **a. Define** What was Wilson's **Fourteen Points** plan?
   b. Explain Why did Wilson believe the Fourteen Points should be the basis for peace talks?
   c. Elaborate How did the Fourteen Points explain a new philosophy of U.S. foreign policy?

2. **a. Recall** What are **reparations**?
   b. Contrast Why did the other Allies reject much of Wilson's plan?
   c. Evaluate Whose plan do you believe was most justified—Wilson's or the other Allies'? Explain.

3. **a. Identify** Who were the reservationists in the U.S. Senate?
   b. Drawing Conclusions Why did the reservationists believe that some provisions of the League of Nations were dangerous?
   c. Predict What might be the consequence of the United States not joining the League of Nations?

4. **a. Describe** What are two ways in which World War I made a political impact on the world?
   b. Analyzing Information How did World War I propel the United States into a position of greater power in the world?

Critical Thinking

5. **Compare** Copy the chart below and record examples of the major ways in which World War I had a lasting impact.

	Political Impact	Economic Impact	Social Impact
United States			
The World			

6. **Persuasive** Should the United States have joined the League of Nations? Write a paragraph supporting your position.

CHAPTER 8 DOCUMENT-BASED INVESTIGATION

Perspectives on Trench Warfare

HSS 11.4.5

Historical Context The three documents below provide different perspectives of trench warfare in World War I.

Task Read the selections and answer the questions that follow. Then write an essay about soldiers' experiences in trench warfare, using facts from the documents provided and from the chapter to support the position you take in your thesis statement.

DOCUMENT 1

In 1929 German author Erich Maria Remarque wrote *All Quiet on the Western Front*, an autobiographical account of the war that became the most celebrated novel of its time. Remarque immigrated to the United States in 1939 after his books were banned by the Nazis and his citizenship was revoked. In the excerpt below, the book's main character, a soldier in whose voice the novel is told, describes a visit home on a leave. Here, he is visiting his mother who is ill in bed.

> Suddenly my mother seizes hold of my hand and asks falteringly: "Was it very bad out there, Paul?"
> Mother, what should I answer to that! You would not understand, and never realize it. And you never should realize it. Was it bad, you ask.—You, Mother,—I shake my head and say: "No, Mother, not so very. There are always a lot of us together so it isn't so bad."
> "Yes, but Heinrich Bredemeyer was here just lately and he said it was terrible out there now, with the gas and all the rest of it."
> It is my mother who says that. She says: "With the gas and all the rest of it." She does not know what she is saying, she is merely anxious for me. Should I tell her how we once found three enemy trenches with their garrison all stiff as though stricken with apoplexy? Against the parapet, in the dug-outs, just where they were, the men stood and lay about, with blue faces, dead.
> "No, Mother, that's only talk," I answer, "there's not very much in what Bredemeyer says."

DOCUMENT 2

Stull Holt was an American soldier in World War I, fighting in the trenches of France. Below is a letter he wrote home after a frightening experience in which he left his trench and was knocked down by a shell. His gas mask fell off and he was affected by the poison gas.

> Sept. 1, 1917
> Dear Lois,
> At last the long delayed and promised letter. You mustn't complain tho because I wrote to no one . . .
> I had a very close call with gas . . . I and this other fellow crawled in a trench alongside the road and waited. We huddled there a long time getting splashed several times by mud thrown by shells exploding, when gas shells started to come in great numbers . . . We started crawling throwing ourselves flat, crawling again (gas masks on of course) . . . I was about buried by a shell and a few seconds later a big gas shell went off within 20 ft of me. Something hit me on the head, making a big dent in my helmet . . . I was dazed, knocked down and my gas mask knocked off. I got several breathes of the strong solution right from the shell before it got diluted with much air. If it hadn't been for the fellow with me I probably wouldn't be writing this letter because I couldn't see, my eyes were running water and burning, so was my nose and I could hardly breathe. I gasped, choked and felt the extreme terror of the man who goes under in the water and will clutch at a straw. The fellow with me grabbed me and led me the hundred yards or so to the post . . . where I felt alright again in a few hours . . . I think the hardest thing I ever did was to go back alone the next night."

DOCUMENT 3

This photograph from March 17, 1918, shows U.S. troops of the 168th infantry in the trenches near the town of Badonville, France.

READING LIKE A HISTORIAN
HSS Analysis HI1, HI3

1. **a. Recall** Refer to Document 1. What does the soldier think to himself and not tell his mother?
   b. Interpret *All Quiet on the Western Front* is a novel, but its author, Erich Maria Remarque, drew upon his experiences as a German soldier to write it. In your opinion, which parts of this excerpt might be based on Remarque's own experiences, and which parts of the excerpt might be fiction?

2. **a. Recall** Refer to Document 2. How was Stull Holt's gas mask knocked off?
   b. Make Inferences Why do you think Stull Holt says that walking back alone was the hardest thing he had ever done?

3. **a. Identify** Refer to Document 3. Then review the labeled illustration of trench warfare in Section 1. Identify the following items in Document 3: machine gun, no-man's-land.
   b. Make Inferences What is happening in this photograph? Is there a battle under way? Explain your answer using information in the photograph.

4. **Document-Based Essay Question** Consider the question below and form a thesis statement. Using examples from Documents 1, 2, and 3, create an outline and write a short essay supporting your position.
   What challenges might soldiers face when they returned to peacetime life at home?
   See **Skills Handbook**, p. H28–29, H30, H32

Chapter 8 Chapter Review

Visual Summary: The First World War

European rivalries lead to the outbreak of war in 1914.
- Nationalism
- Militarism
- Imperialism
- Alliances

The United States enters the war in 1917 and helps turn the tide for an Allied victory.
- Victory in the Battle of Chateau-Thierry
- Stopped German advance at Belleau Wood
- Defeated Germans' last offensive in the Second Battle of the Marne

With the Treaty of Versailles, the Allies determine the terms for peace in the postwar world.
- Forced Germany to pay massive reparations
- Created the League of Nations
- Treaty not ratified by U.S. Senate
- United States did not join the League of Nations

Reviewing Key Terms and People

Match each lettered definition with the correct numbered item below at right.

a. a communication that proposed an alliance between Germany and Mexico to help the Central Powers in case the United States declared war on Germany

b. a military alliance among Germany, Austria-Hungary, and Italy

c. a policy of not being involved in the affairs of other nations

d. payments for damages and expenses caused by the war

e. a military alliance among Great Britain, France, and Russia

f. an extreme pride or devotion that people feel for their country or culture

g. the expansion of arms and the policy of military preparedness

h. posters, newspaper stories, speeches, and other materials designed to influence people's opinions, often during wartime

i. the right of people to decide their own political status

j. the name given to Germany, Austria-Hungary, and the Ottoman Empire during World War I

k. the German promise not to sink merchant vessels without warning

l. the name given to Great Britain, France, and Russia during World War I

1. Allied Powers
2. isolationism
3. Central Powers
4. militarism
5. propaganda
6. Triple Alliance
7. Zimmermann Note
8. *Sussex* pledge
9. self-determination
10. Triple Entente
11. nationalism
12. reparations

History's Impact video program

Review the video to answer the closing question: How does the Supreme Court's decision in *Schenck v. United States* explain the limits to free speech?

Comprehension and Critical Thinking

SECTION 1 *(pp. 230–237)* HSS 11.4.5

13. a. Identify What were the main causes of World War I?

   b. Analyze How did European leaders discover that a balance of power did not decrease the chances for war among them?

   c. Evaluate Which cause of World War I do you believe was the most dangerous? Explain.

SECTION 2 *(pp. 238–244)* HSS 11.4.4, 11.4.5

14. a. Recall What did Germany do with its U-boats that violated laws of neutrality?

   b. Sequencing Which German actions helped shift U.S. public opinion toward supporting the Allies in the war?

   c. Elaborate What effect did U.S. troops have on the Allied fight against the Central Powers?

SECTION 3 *(pp. 246–252)* HSS 11.4.5

15. a. Describe What did the Lever Food and Fuel Control act do?

   b. Analyze Why did the U.S. government impose so many regulations on industrial and food production during the war?

   c. Elaborate What impact did U.S. industrial and food production have on the war effort for the Allies?

SECTION 4 *(pp. 254–259)* HSS 11.4.4, 11.4.5

16. a. Recall What are reparations?

   b. Contrasting How did Wilson's goal for the peace treaty differ from that of the other Allies?

   c. Elaborate What provisions from Wilson's Fourteen Points were included in the Treaty of Versailles?

Using the Internet

go.hrw.com Practice Online Keyword: SE7 CH8

17. The influenza epidemic of 1918 was the deadliest in U.S. history. Using the keyword above, do research to learn about the origins, progression, and final conclusion of this tragic epidemic. Then create a time line of the major events in the progression of the epidemic.

Analyzing Primary Sources HSS HR4

Reading Like a Historian
Propaganda posters like this one encouraged Americans to buy Liberty bonds to support the war effort.

18. Identify What does "Over the Top" mean?

19. Analyze Do you think this was an effective poster? Why or why not?

Critical Reading ELA R2.2

Read the passage in Section 1 that begins with the heading "War Breaks Out." Then answer the following question.

20. What was one effect of the German invasion of Belgium?

   A It led Russia to join the Central Powers.

   B It failed miserably, as Belgium pushed the German forces back across the border.

   C It drew Britain into the war against Germany.

   D It led the French to surrender to Germany out of fear of being attacked like Belgium.

WRITING FOR THE SAT   ELA W1.1, 2.4

Think about the following issue:

The United States had a long-standing foreign-policy tradition of isolationism. As European nations went to war, the United States tried to stay neutral. Eventually, it began leaning toward the Allied side, until in 1917 it joined the war on the side of the Allies.

21. Assignment Given its history of neutrality, was the United States justified in going to war against Germany and the other Central Powers? Write a short essay in which you develop your position on this issue. Support your point of view with reasoning and examples from your reading and studies.

THE FIRST WORLD WAR   263

UNIT 2 IN BRIEF

Below is a chapter-by-chapter summary of the main ideas covered in Unit 2.

CHAPTER 6: The Progressives
1898–1920

MAIN IDEA During the early 1900s, the Progressive movement arose to redress the negative impact of industrialization. Progressives achieved many wide-reaching reforms affecting American political, social, and economic life.

SECTION 1 Progressives focused their attentions on improving the lives of the urban poor, changing dangerous and unfair working conditions, and reforming government.

SECTION 2 Most American women did not have the right to vote in national elections. Nevertheless, many were politically active in reform campaigns for education, children's welfare, temperance, and the vote.

SECTION 3 President Theodore Roosevelt pushed for many Progressive reforms in business and the environment. His program, called the Square Deal, sought to balance the needs of business and industry leaders, and those of workers and consumers.

SECTION 4 Progressive reforms continued during the Taft and Wilson presidencies, focusing on business, banking, and certain civil rights reforms. During this time, women won the vote. Despite the many reforms that Progressives campaigned for, they did not fight for the civil rights of African Americans.

CHAPTER 7: Entering the World Stage
1898–1917

MAIN IDEA Global competition for empire led the United States into war against Spain and into military conflicts in Mexico. The United States emerged with a new role as a world power.

SECTION 1 The United States joined other industrialized nations in the scramble for empire. For economic, military, and nationalistic reasons, the United States annexed Hawaii and extended its influence in China and Japan.

SECTION 2 The Spanish-American War resulted in a resounding defeat for Spain and the relinquishing of Cuba, Puerto Rico, Guam, and the Philippines to United States control. In the aftermath of war, American expansionists and anti-imperialists debated whether to annex the Philippines.

SECTION 3 The United States began to exert its influence over Latin America in the wake of the Spanish-American War. It made Cuba a protectorate and governed Puerto Rico as a territory. Meanwhile, the United States undertook the mammoth task of building the Panama Canal.

SECTION 4 When Mexico exploded into revolution, the United States became drawn into the conflict to protect its economic interests.

CHAPTER 8: The First World War
1914–1920

MAIN IDEA The United States stayed neutral when European nations went to war in 1914. But after the United States joined the Allies in 1917, the U.S. government quickly mobilized the economy and built public support for the war.

SECTION 1 Rivalries among European nations led to the outbreak of war in 1914. The assassination of an Austrian archduke led to rapid declarations of war, and soon most of Europe was drawn into World War I. Changes in military technology and strategies made World War I a new and deadlier kind of war.

SECTION 2 The United States tried to stay neutral in World War I, but hostile German acts soon convinced President Wilson and Congress that war was inevitable. The United States sent troops to France, where they helped turn the tide for the Allies. The Central Powers agreed to an armistice on November 11, 1918.

SECTION 3 The U.S. government mobilized its resources for the war effort. It sold Liberty bonds to pay for the war, and regulated industry to fulfill the needs of the troops overseas. It encouraged women to take on the jobs left vacant by men who joined the military. And the government campaigned to win the support of public opinion and minimize dissent.

SECTION 4 At the Paris Peace Conference, the Allies hammered out a peace treaty. Some, but not all, of Wilson's Fourteen Points were included in the Treaty of Versailles. But the treaty also called for Germany to pay heavy reparations for its role in the war. In the United States, the Senate hotly debated the treaty. Many senators objected to the idea of the United States joining the League of Nations, and eventually the Senate rejected the treaty.

UNIT 3
A Modern Nation

1919–1940

Chapter 9
From War to Peace
1919–1928

Chapter 10
The Roaring Twenties
1920–1929

Chapter 11
The Great Depression Begins
1929–1933

Chapter 12
The New Deal
1933–1940

Themes

Government and Democracy
The nation struggled with postwar labor unrest, radical political ideas, and later, high unemployment brought on by the Great Depression.

Economic Development
Americans experienced a period of great productivity and prosperity, followed by a devastating economic downturn.

Cultural Expressions
The growth of mass media and popular culture, a rebirth in the arts, and the development of a consumer society marked a period of cultural change.

New York City's Times Square is ablaze with electric lights and other signs of progress and prosperity in this 1925 painting.

Prepare to Read

Identifying Problems and Solutions

Find practice for **Identifying Problems and Solutions** in the **Skills Handbook,** p. H11

Historical texts frequently discuss problems that people in the past encountered and the solutions they adopted. Identifying problems and solutions can help you understand what you are reading.

Before You Read
Skim headings to determine a passage's content. What problem do you think will be discussed in this passage?

While You Read
Note the problem cited in the text and the reasons it occurred.

After You Read
Review the problem and the solutions offered.

Bank Failures

As you have read, the collapse of the stock market strained the financial resources of many banks. In the weeks following the crash, a number of banks failed. For ordinary Americans, the collapse of banks was unnerving. Most people did not have money invested in banks, but many had entrusted their savings to banks.

Today, insurance from the federal government protects most people's deposits in the event of bank failure. That is, most Americans do not have to worry that they will lose their savings if their bank goes out of business. In addition, laws today require that a bank keep a greater percentage of its assets in cash, to be paid out to depositors on request.

READING CHECK **Identifying Problems and Solutions** What precautions has the federal government taken to safeguard people's money in banks?

Identify the problem If the problem is large, organize it in smaller parts.

Problem The collapse of banks unnerved many Americans who had entrusted their savings to them.

Solution Federal insurance and laws help protect people's finances today.

Test Prep Tip

Some tests may require you to identify a problem and its solution. In such instances, first try to recognize the problem and its cause and then to identify possible options and solutions for that problem. Then evaluate the effectiveness of the solution.

Reading like a Historian

California Standards
HSS Analysis CS3, HR2

Interpreting Literature as Historical Evidence

Find practice for **Interpreting Literature as Historical Evidence** in the **Skills Handbook,** p. H32

Literature can be an important source of historical information. It can tell us what life was like in the past and what people believed. But it needs to be read with caution. The author is creating a fictional story not recording facts. Be sure to use your prior knowledge and information from reliable primary and secondary sources when assessing literature as historical evidence.

Strategies historians use:
- Look for descriptive passages that help you understand what life was like in that time and place.
- Examine the author's point of view and any biases by contrasting the types of words used to describe different events.
- Determine whether the literature is meant to describe a certain historical event or to elicit an emotional response.

> Steinbeck is describing the migration of people from the Plains to California in the 1930s along Route 66, "the great cross-country highway."

The cars of the migrant people crawled out of the side roads onto the great cross-country highway, and they took the migrant way to the West. In the daylight they scuttled like bugs to the westward; and as the dark caught them, they clustered like bugs near to shelter and to water. And because they were lonely and perplexed, because they had all come from a place of sadness and worry and defeat, and because they were all going to a new mysterious place, they huddled together; they talked together; they shared their lives, their food, and the things they hoped for in the new country. Thus it might be that one family camped for the spring and for company, and a third because two families had pioneered the place and found it good. And when the sun went down, perhaps twenty families and twenty cars were there.

—from *The Grapes of Wrath* by John Steinbeck, 1939

> Words like *lonely* and *perplexed* describe how the migrants heading west to California felt. You could check these words against other sources.

> The description of families gathering together is fairly neutral. It doesn't seem to betray any bias.

Reading Like a Historian

As You Read List historical evidence found in the literature. Then compare the evidence with known facts to arrive at the most complete account of history.

As You Study Use literature to help you understand political and social movements in history. Determine whether the literature recounts history, makes an activist appeal, or has some other purpose.

CHAPTER 9

1919–1928
From WAR to PEACE

THE BIG PICTURE The end of the war brought peace to Americans, but not peace of mind. Dangers seen and unseen troubled the nation—until a new president in the White House and a booming economy seemed to smooth the transition from war to peace.

California Standards

History-Social Sciences
11.5 Students analyze the major political, social, economic, technological, and cultural developments of the 1920s.

Skills Focus **READING LIKE A HISTORIAN**

This photo, taken in 1924 by the Electric Club of Louisville, Kentucky, shows a few of this appliance store's products. These people are members of the club or employees of the store.
Analyzing Primary Sources What does the fact that Louisville had an Electric Club tell you about how American consumers felt about modern electrical appliances during the 1920s?
See **Skills Handbook**, pp. H28–H29

 U.S.

1919 Attorney General Palmer launches anti-radical raids.

1918

 WORLD

1918–1919 Influenza epidemic kills millions of people worldwide.

History's Impact video program
Watch the video to understand the impact of women's suffrage.

1920 Promising normalcy, Warren G. Harding wins the presidency.

1920 Bolsheviks win a civil war and take control of Russia.

1922 Benito Mussolini establishes a Fascist regime in Italy.

1924 The U.S. government imposes strict limits on immigration.

1927 The German stock market collapses.

1928 Coolidge opts not to seek re-election.
The United States signs the Kellogg-Briand Pact.

1928 Scottish doctor Alexander Fleming discovers penicillin.

SECTION 1

Before You Read

MAIN IDEA
Although the end of World War I brought peace, it did not ease the minds of many Americans, who found much to fear in the postwar years.

READING FOCUS
1. What were the causes and effects of the first Red Scare?
2. How did labor strife grow during the postwar years?
3. How did the United States limit immigration after World War I?

KEY TERMS AND PEOPLE
Bolshevik
communism
Red Scare
A. Mitchell Palmer
Palmer raids
alien
deportation
anarchist

 HSS 11.5.2 Analyze the international and domestic events, interests, and philosophies that prompted attacks on civil liberties, including the Palmer Raids, the Ku Klux Klan, and immigration quotas and the responses of organizations such as the American Civil Liberties Union, and the Anti-Defamation League to those attacks.

A DEADLY Epidemic

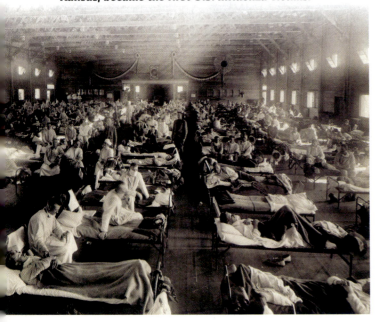

▼ In March 1918, soldiers in Camp Funston, Kansas, became the first U.S. influenza victims.

THE INSIDE STORY

How did peace in Europe bring death to the United States? Influenza found breeding grounds in the military camps and the trenches, where soldiers lived in close quarters. It invaded the United States, traveling on troop ships among the healthy and the wounded. In the streets, as hopeful Americans gathered to celebrate the end of World War I, the infection spread quickly. Soon, many were sick and dying—victims of a worldwide influenza epidemic in 1918 and 1919 that would kill some 10 times as many Americans as died in battle in World War I.

Even in the early 1900s, the flu was not generally a serious disease. It caused unpleasant symptoms, and it could be dangerous to the very old and very young. Healthy adults might feel ill for a few days, but they usually recovered quickly. In 1918, however, a powerful new strain of influenza struck with deadly force, eventually infecting more than 1 in 4 Americans. It took an especially heavy toll on men and women in their twenties and thirties. Some victims died within a day or two of getting sick.

The nation's hospitals, already strained with large numbers of wounded soldiers, suddenly had thousands of new patients at their doorsteps. Cities and towns suffered shortages of doctors, nurses, and beds for the sick.

As the winter of 1919 passed, the number of new flu cases began to drop. The crisis had passed, but more than half a million Americans had perished.

As society began to return to normal in the postwar world, many people remained fearful and uneasy. The world was at peace, but Americans were not. As you will read, this feeling would continue for some time.

The First Red Scare

The end of World War I in 1918 brought great rejoicing in America, but it was just the beginning of new problems at home. Besides a terrifying medical crisis, the nation faced economic and political turmoil that cast a dark shadow over the postwar recovery.

Farms and factories that had buzzed with activity during the war now lay silent, as demand for their products suddenly fell. In the slowing economy, returning soldiers had difficulty finding jobs. People began to

Linking to Today

Terrorism in the United States

Around noon on September 16, 1920, a horse-drawn cart stopped in front of the offices of financier J.P. Morgan, on Wall Street in New York City. Suddenly, the cart—which had been packed with dynamite—exploded. More than 30 people were instantly killed, and some 300 were injured. Of the cart and horse, only hooves remained.

Detectives took the horseshoes to thousands of stables, but they found no more evidence. Some officials suspected labor organizers and political radicals. Although many people were questioned and even arrested, no one was ever brought to trial.

At about 9 a.m. on April 19, 1995, a homemade bomb exploded inside a truck parked in front of the Alfred P. Murrah Federal Building in Oklahoma City. Nearly 170 people were killed, including children, and more than 500 were injured.

Investigators learned that the Oklahoma City bombing was carried out by two men who opposed earlier government actions against an armed group in Texas. Both were tried and convicted. One received the death penalty, and the other was sentenced to life in prison.

Contrasting How did the outcomes of the two investigations differ?

The 1995 Oklahoma City bombing collapsed the front of the federal building. At the time the bombing was the worst terrorist attack that had occurred on American soil.

---

realize that in many ways, they had traded a painful war for a troubling peace.

HISTORY'S VOICES

> "I felt that when peace came we'd all be so joyful that nothing would weigh upon us again. I find, however, the problems of reconstruction loom so large that we are as much occupied with them as we have been with the problems of war."
>
> —Illinois governor Frank Lowden, quoted in *The Harding Era* by Robert K. Murray

The emotional turmoil of the times had disturbing political effects. While World War I had stirred deep feelings of patriotism, it had also ignited hatred toward Germans. These sentiments gave rise to a movement known as 100 Percent Americanism. It celebrated all things American while it attacked ideas—and people—it viewed as foreign or anti-American.

The rise of the Bolsheviks Americans worried about a new foreign enemy. In 1917 a violent revolution had ripped across Russia. The Red Army of the **Bolsheviks**, which was led by Vladimir I. Lenin, eventually gained control. Five years later Russia would become part of a new nation called the Soviet Union.

Lenin and the Bolsheviks dreamed of establishing a new social system for their people—and for the world. This system, called **communism**, would have no economic classes and no private property. Lenin believed all people should share equally in society's wealth.

American reaction Many Americans were baffled and frightened by communism. The Soviets called for the overthrow of capitalism. But most Americans embraced the ideals of capitalism, including the freedom to own property. They valued the opportunity to better themselves by hard work or ingenuity.

Lenin predicted that communism would inspire workers throughout the world to rise up and crush capitalism. To some Americans, the threat seemed more ominous than the traditional conflicts of the past.

Throughout World War I, the American public had focused its fear and hatred on "the Hun." Now, public anxiety became fixed on a new target: Communists and others who held radical ideas. They were known as Reds.

Communist parties formed in the United States after the war. Some of their members promoted the violent overthrow of the government. In fact, radicals may have played a role in a 1919 plot in which bombs were mailed to government officials. The plot failed, however. Most historians agree that an internal

Primary Sources

Political Cartoon

Hundreds of political cartoons, including this one titled "Put Them Out and Keep Them Out," fueled Red Scare fears. This cartoon originally appeared in the *Philadelphia Inquirer* in October 1919, when the U.S. government was trying to deport many suspected Communist sympathizers.

Political cartoonists often portrayed Communist sympathizers as bearded, sinister-looking characters carrying torches and sometimes weapons.

The torch of anarchy represents the destructive nature of communism. The knife represents the dangers of Bolshevism.

Skills Focus: Reading Like a Historian

1. **Drawing Conclusions** What do you think the title "Put Them Out and Keep Them Out" means?
2. **Interpreting Political Cartoons** Why do you think the artist showed the character peeking out from under the American flag?

See **Skills Handbook**, p. H12, H31

Communist threat to the nation was probably never great. Yet at the time, the threat seemed very real.

A **Red Scare**, or widespread fear of communism, gripped the nation. One official noted, "I believe it has been 'scared up' considerably by the newspapers, which relate every arrest and incident . . . by printing large scary headlines."

The government took the threat seriously. New York state legislators voted to bar five legally elected socialists from office. New York also passed a law making it a crime to call for the overthrow of the government. The Supreme Court found the law unconstitutional in the 1925 case of *Gitlow* v. *New York*.

The Palmer raids A. Mitchell Palmer, a former Progressive, had been one of the targets of the 1919 bombing plot. Later that year, as attorney general of the United States, Palmer became a key leader of the federal government's anti-Communist campaign. He led an attack on suspected radicals known as the **Palmer raids**.

To justify the raids, Palmer used wartime laws that gave the government broad powers against suspected radicals. For **aliens**—citizens of other countries living in the United States—just belonging to certain groups considered radical could lead to deportation. **Deportation** means removing an alien from one country and sending him or her to another country.

In late 1919 Palmer's forces arrested thousands of members of suspected radical groups. In December 1919, a naval vessel named the *Buford* set sail carrying nearly 250 aliens who were being deported. Many Americans cheered Palmer's actions. Said Leonard Wood, a Republican leader, "I believe we should place them all in ships of stone, with sails of lead."

In time, the Red Scare died down. It became clear that predictions about the radical threat to the country were not coming true. At the same time, Communist movements in Germany and Hungary were failing. These failures dampened fears of worldwide revolution. The nation's anxiety was reduced, but it was not eliminated.

READING CHECK Sequencing Who replaced "the Hun" as the object of American fear and hatred?

THE IMPACT TODAY

Government
Between 1917 and 1920, many Americans were willing to give up some civil liberties in order to achieve security. The American Civil Liberties Union (ACLU), founded in 1920, works to defend the constitutional rights of citizens. The ACLU has fought to protect civil liberties, even in times of national emergencies.

Labor Strife Grows

The year 1919 was one of the most explosive times in the history of the American labor movement. Some 4 million workers took part in more than 3,000 strikes nationwide. In nearly every case, labor lost. Wartime successes and peacetime disappointments set the stage for this catastrophic year for workers.

Postwar difficulties Workers' raised expectations helped create the crisis. During the war, President Wilson had sought good relations with workers who were keeping the troops clothed and equipped. Organized labor won many gains, including shorter hours and higher wages. When the war ended, labor leaders hoped to build on what they had achieved. They were disappointed.

A number of factors combined to frustrate labor's high hopes. Wilson, now focused on promoting his peace plan, paid less attention to events at home and did little to promote workers' causes. Meanwhile, the sinking postwar demand for factory goods hurt many industries. Returning soldiers expected to take their place on the factory floor, but the jobs just weren't there. Unhappy workers, especially strikers, were replaced.

The Red Scare further weakened labor by damaging its reputation. Communism's call to workers to rise up and overthrow their government made many people suspicious of organized labor. Opponents linked labor with the radical ideas that so many people feared.

Labor's losses The showdown between labor and management in 1919 devastated organized labor. Unions lost members and national political power. It would take another decade—and another national crisis—to restore organized labor's reputation, status, and bargaining power in the United States.

Major strikes of the era Among the thousands of union strikes that rocked the country in 1919, a few hold a place in labor history. In Seattle, Washington, labor unrest at the shipyards spread citywide, igniting what became the nation's first major general strike—one in which workers in all industries take part.

The conflict virtually shut down the city. Yet the Seattle general strike of 1919 failed to achieve any gains for workers. In fact, it did great harm. For years afterward, industry, and its jobs, stayed away from Seattle.

On the opposite coast, the city of Boston descended into chaos when its police force went on strike in September 1919 to protest low wages and poor working conditions. Eventually, Massachusetts governor Calvin Coolidge called in the state's militia to end the strike.

ACADEMIC VOCABULARY
status one's standing in society relative to that of others

Major Strikes, 1919
- Seattle general strike— February 6–11
- Boston police strike— September 9–13
- Nationwide steelworkers strike— September 22, 1919– January 1920

It was another loss for labor, but a great political boost for the Republican governor. In a telegram to the famous labor leader Samuel Gompers, Coolidge wrote, "There can be no right to strike against the public safety by anybody, anywhere, anytime."

The words echoed across a nervous country and made Coolidge a hero. His sudden fame as a champion of law and order elevated his career to the national stage and eventually landed him in the White House.

Other notable strikes hit the steel industry and the coalfields of the eastern United States. The United Mine Workers had kept a "no strikes" pledge during the war. Under the tough new leadership of John L. Lewis, the striking union won a large wage increase.

The workers failed, however, to win other key demands, such as a reduction of their workweek to five days. Lewis recognized the limitations of the union's power at that time.

"We cannot fight the government," the labor leader declared. His miners, like union members throughout the country, would have to wait to press their demands for shorter hours and safer workplaces.

READING CHECK **Summarizing** How successful were the postwar labor strikes?

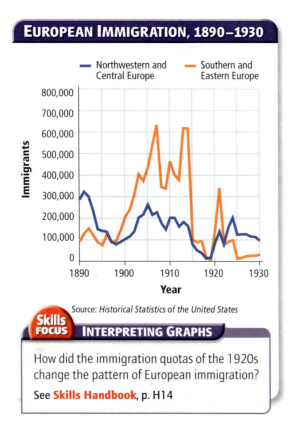

EUROPEAN IMMIGRATION, 1890–1930

Source: *Historical Statistics of the United States*

Skills Focus INTERPRETING GRAPHS

How did the immigration quotas of the 1920s change the pattern of European immigration?

See **Skills Handbook**, p. H14

Limiting Immigration

Competition for scarce jobs, combined with the Red Scare, triggered an ugly backlash against foreigners in the postwar period. The rise of nativism, or distrust of foreigners, produced a culture clash between the nation's earlier immigrants and its newer ones.

Many nativists were Protestant Christians who had their roots in northern and western Europe, the source of most immigration before 1900. The nativists targeted newer arrivals from southern and eastern Europe, many of whom were Catholics and Jews. Immigrants from these areas of Europe, nativists argued, were less willing to become "Americanized," and should not be welcomed.

Labor leaders, along with the nativists, pushed for immigration restrictions on these groups. New arrivals, often poor and alone, were willing to work for low wages. Unions saw them as a threat.

Immigration control The federal government responded to nativist concern by passing laws to limit immigration. A 1921 law established a quota—an established number—of immigrants to be allowed into the United States from various nations.

The National Origins Act of 1924 went even further. It set quotas for each country at 2 percent of the number of people from that country living in the United States in 1890. The goal was clearly to reduce immigration to the United States from certain countries—mainly southern and eastern European countries. The act also nearly eliminated all immigration from Asian countries.

Nativism also produced a revival in the 1920s of the Ku Klux Klan. The Klan had started as a terror group that targeted African Americans in the South. It reemerged in the postwar years with a broader mission. The hate group now targeted Jews, Catholics, and radicals of all types.

A Klan slogan of the 1920s characterized the group's vision of the nation: "Native white, Protestant supremacy." The new Ku Klux Klan of the 1920s also moved out of the South into other parts of the United States.

Sacco and Vanzetti In the 1920s a court case in Massachusetts dramatically illustrated the nation's struggle with nativist and anti-radical feelings. In May 1920, two men, Nicola Sacco and Bartolomeo Vanzetti, were arrested for armed robbery and murder. The two men were Italian immigrants. More importantly, they proclaimed that they were **anarchists**—radicals who sought the destruction of government.

At the trial, it became clear that the evidence against the two men was weak. It also was apparent that Sacco and Vanzetti were on trial for their political beliefs as well as for bank robbery and murder.

Amid great publicity and protests in Europe and South America as well as in the United States, the two men were convicted and sentenced to die. They were executed in 1927.

Historians still argue over the guilt or innocence of Sacco and Vanzetti. Many agree, however, that the men's political ideas played a prominent role in the trial.

Bartolomeo Vanzetti expressed these same ideas before his trial.

READING LIKE A HISTORIAN

The artist Ben Shahn based this painting of Sacco and Vanzetti, like many subjects of his paintings, on a newspaper photograph.

Making Inferences Why do you think Shahn chose to use newspaper images?

HISTORY'S VOICES

"My conviction is that I have suffered for things I am guilty of. I am suffering because I am a radical, and indeed I am a radical; I have suffered because I was an Italian, and indeed I am Italian."
—Bartolomeo Vanzetti in court, 1927

The executions of Sacco and Vanzetti were highly controversial at the time. By then, however, the nation had largely recovered from the Red Scare and the turmoil of the postwar years. The 1920s would be very different from the previous decade.

READING CHECK **Identifying Cause and Effect** How did Congress respond to the growing concern about immigration?

SECTION 1 ASSESSMENT

HSS 11.5.2

Reviewing Ideas, Terms, and People

1. **a. Define** What was the Red Scare?
   b. Compare How did American attitudes toward "the Hun" relate to attitudes toward Reds?
   c. Evaluate Why do you think Americans were able to quickly transfer their feelings about Germans to Communists and radicals?

2. **a. Describe** Why did labor strife increase after the war?
   b. Contrast How did labor fare after the war compared to during the war?

3. **a. Define** Write a brief definition for each of the following terms: alien, anarchist
   b. Explain What change in immigration in recent decades appeared to concern many Americans in the postwar years?
   c. Elaborate How do you think nativism might have related to the Red Scare?

Critical Thinking

4. **Comparing and Contrasting** Copy the chart below and compare and contrast the public attitudes about radicals, organized labor, and immigrants in the post–World War I era.

FOCUS ON WRITING ELA W1.1, 1.3

5. **Persuasive** Write a letter to a member of Congress in which you argue for or against the idea that simply holding a "radical" idea should be against the law.

SECTION 2
A New Economic Era

BEFORE YOU READ

MAIN IDEA
New products, new industries, and new ways of doing business expanded the economy in the 1920s, although not everyone shared in the prosperity.

READING FOCUS
1. What role did the Ford Motor Company and Henry Ford play in revolutionizing American industry?
2. How did both the auto industry and the nation change during the 1920s?
3. What were some qualities of the new consumer of the 1920s?
4. What were some weak parts of the economy in the 1920s?

KEY TERMS AND PEOPLE
Henry Ford
assembly line
productivity
welfare capitalism
suburb
installment buying
credit

 HSS 11.5.7 Discuss the rise of mass production techniques, the growth of cities, the impact of new technologies (e.g., the automobile, electricity), and the resulting prosperity and effect on the American landscape.

THE INSIDE STORY

How did a department store create an American tradition?

In 1924 Americans were on a shopping spree. The U.S. economy was on the rise, spurred by the American consumer, who was busy spending money on a wide range of exciting new products.

In the middle of this national buying frenzy was Macy's department store in New York City. By 1924 Macy's aisles and displays filled some 1 million square feet of New York real estate. It was said to be the largest store in the world.

In 1924 some Macy's employees came up with the idea to hold a Christmas parade. Many of the employees were recent immigrants from Europe, and they wanted to share their holiday traditions as a gift to the people of their new country. It wasn't a bad idea for the store, either. The parade would provide an opportunity for Macy's to unveil its enormous Christmas window displays along 34th Street.

The parade kicked off on Thanksgiving Day, 1924, featuring about a thousand employees of the store. Brass bands, clowns, and zoo animals enlivened the scene. Along the route, a quarter million potential shoppers took in the sights and sounds.

The first Macy's parade was a great success. In 1925, on Thanksgiving Day, marchers once again delighted the crowds and welcomed the holiday season. Soon the parade—and the department store itself—was a tradition shared not just by the people of New York but also by visitors from around the world.

Meanwhile, the American consumers who had helped make Macy's a success in New York continued their postwar shopping spree. Indeed, as you will read, for Macy's and other American businesses, the 1920s provided much to be thankful for and to celebrate.

▼ Macy's first big Christmas parade was held on November 27, 1924.

Let the PARADE Begin

Ford Revolutionizes Industry

The black automobiles that chugged and sputtered their way down the streets of New York and other cities represented the latest in American technology. During the 1920s, the Ford Model T automobile, like the Macy's parade, would become a fixture of American life.

The first cars appeared in America in the late 1800s, but they remained a toy for the rich through the early 1900s. That changed when a young entrepreneur, **Henry Ford**, began selling his Model T in 1908. It wasn't much to look at. However, it changed American society forever. Ford spelled out his revolutionary vision:

HISTORY'S VOICES

> "I will build a motor car for the great multitude. It will be large enough for the family but small enough for the individual to run and care for. It will be constructed of the best materials, by the best men to be hired, after the simplest designs that modern engineering can devise. It will be so low in price that no man making a good salary will be unable to own one."
>
> —Henry Ford, announcing plans for his Model T

The assembly line Imagine how expensive cars would be today if every one were custom-made! Ford began by making his cars identical and simple. That brought the cost down, but not enough. So he studied manufacturing processes, from interchangeable parts to the moving belts in meatpacking plants that brought the work to the workers. Then he hired scientific management expert Frederick Winslow Taylor to determine how workers should move, and at what speed, to be most productive.

These ideas combined to produce the first large-scale moving **assembly line**, a production system in which the item being built moves along a conveyor belt to various workstations. On Ford's assembly line, each worker had one of 84 specific jobs, often requiring simple skills.

Ford explained, "The man who puts on a bolt does not put on a nut. The man who puts on the nut does not tighten it." In its first year, the Ford assembly line produced a car every hour and a half.

The car sold for under $500, about half the cost of the first Model Ts. The price was not cheap in its day, but many people could afford it. By the 1920s Ford was rolling out a car every minute, and the price had dropped even lower. By 1929 about 22 million cars bumped along the nation's mostly unpaved roads. People loved the Model T. They wrote songs about it. They formed automobile driving clubs.

Ford realized that his workers also were potential car buyers. He raised his workers' pay to $5 a day, far above average factory wages. This enabled his workers to buy cars.

Workers did pay a price, however. Ford bitterly opposed unions and dealt ruthlessly with anyone who tried to organize workers. Organizers pointed out the boring, repetitive tasks in Ford's clockworklike assembly lines. One labor leader remarked, "Ford workers are not really alive, they are half dead."

The effect on industry During the first quarter of the century, the Ford Motor Company dominated automaking. In the 1920s, more than half the cars in the United States were Fords. Competitors such as General Motors and Chrysler tried to improve on Ford's formula. In an effort to keep costs low, Ford refused to change the Model T's design until 1927, after some 15 million had rolled off the assembly line. New competitors General Motors and Chrysler arose to challenge that formula, bringing out new designs and colors each year. Competition helped the entire industry grow.

Other industries also learned from Ford. Manufacturers of all kinds of consumer goods

THE IMPACT TODAY

Science and Technology

Automakers still use assembly lines to make cars. Industrial robots, instead of people, perform much of the repetitive work. Each machine performs a specific task, much as in Ford's assembly line.

FACES OF HISTORY

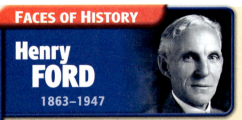

Henry FORD 1863–1947

Since he was a young boy, Henry Ford loved to tinker with machines. As a young man, Ford worked as a machinist at the Edison Company plant in Detroit. In 1896 Ford built his first automobile. A few years later, Ford quit his machinist job to start an automobile company. Ford wanted to make cars more affordable. By developing the assembly line and using standardized parts, Ford drastically lowered the cost of manufacturing cars. In turn, he sold his cars at a price the average American could afford. Ford's strategy worked. In 1908 Ford designed the Model T. By 1927, Ford sold more than 15 million Model Ts, transforming American life.

Explain How did Ford build more affordable cars?

History Close-Up

Autos Drive the Modern Age

The automobile fostered many changes in American industry, business, and culture.

Service stations gassed up American cars, and the gasoline tax, levied by most states, helped pay for new roads.

The Model T had its competitors—as many as 107 at one time. By the end of the 1920s, however, three competitors dominated the market: General Motors, Chrysler, and Ford.

By 1925 America was producing about five times the number of car and truck tires that it was making a decade earlier.

Like many Americans in the 1920s, these beach-goers in Jacksonville, Florida, took to their cars in pursuit of leisure. America's romance with the open road had its tragic side, too. The rate of traffic fatalities more than doubled during the decade.

Skills Focus · Interpreting Infographics

Mass production of the automobile affected Americans' lives in many ways. *How many can you identify by examining these pictures?*

See **Skills Handbook**, p. H30

began using assembly-line techniques to make goods in large quantities and at lower costs. In the 1920s productivity rose by 60 percent. **Productivity** is a measure of output per unit of input such as labor. American workers were producing more in less time.

The success of business in the 1920s led to a growth of what is called **welfare capitalism**, a system in which companies provide benefits to employees in an effort to promote worker satisfaction and loyalty. For example, many companies offered company-paid pensions—payments made to workers when they retire. Others set up recreation programs for workers. In return, business owners hoped that welfare capitalism would encourage workers to shun unions and accept lower pay. Many did.

READING CHECK Drawing Conclusions What innovation by Henry Ford helped transform American industry?

Industry Changes Society

Every time motorists turned the crank handle to start their cars, other industries benefited. Demand for steel, glass, rubber, and other automobile materials soared. Automobile repair shops and filling stations sprang up in cities and towns. Motels and restaurants arose to meet the needs of car travelers.

The simple engines ran on gasoline, a by-product of petroleum. A few of the landowners who found petroleum on their property became rich practically overnight.

Automaking put the city of Detroit, Michigan, on the map. Henry Ford based his manufacturing operations there, and other carmakers followed. In 1910 fewer than 500,000 people lived in Detroit. Within 20 years the population had tripled.

The growth in manufacturing caused a boom in other Midwest cities. Akron, Ohio, the center of the rubber and tire industry, grew from fewer than 70,000 people in 1910 to nearly 210,000 in 1920. For the decade, it was the fastest-growing city in the United States.

As cities grew, so did their **suburbs**, the smaller towns located outside urban areas. Many suburbs had been established since the late 1800s, thanks in part to the construction of trolley lines that carried workers back and forth between home and workplace. Car travel, however, allowed people to live at even greater distances from their jobs. Trolley enterprises, however, suffered during the 1920s, even as suburbs expanded.

Freedom to travel also produced a new tourist industry. Before the auto boom, Florida had a few resorts that attracted mainly wealthy visitors. Automobiles brought tourists by the thousands to discover warm, sunny Florida. Buyers snatched up land, causing prices to rise sharply. Some Florida swamps were drained to put up new housing.

READING CHECK Identifying Cause and Effect How did the growth of the auto industry affect related industries?

The New Consumer

During the 1920s Americans witnessed an explosion of new products, new experiences, and new forms of mass communication on a scale never seen before. People were getting into the buying habit and liking it. Companies were happy to supply more new products for them to buy.

New products Using cost-efficient, new manufacturing processes, factories turned out a variety of new electrical appliances, such as refrigerators and vacuum cleaners. The electrification of new areas of the country enabled more people to use the latest home conveniences.

Perhaps the favorite new electronic home technology was the radio. By the end of the 1920s, 4 homes in 10 had a radio. Like the televisions and computers that followed it, the radio opened new worlds to American families. Now, families gathered in the evenings to hear news from around the world as well as dramas and comedy shows.

Radio connected the world as never before. So did a new form of public transportation: the airplane. Aviation had made great advances during World War I. The first passenger airlines appeared over American skies in the 1920s.

The early flights offered little comfort—some passengers wore goggles and helmets. Planes were uninsulated and unpressurized; they couldn't fly over mountains or at night. In fact, for cross-country travel, trains were more comfortable as well as cheaper. For some Americans, though, the thrill of air travel outweighed the early discomforts.

Creating demand Buy! Buy! Buy! On the sidelines of the great American spending spree, advertisers became the cheerleaders. During the 1920s, persuasive advertising gained a major role in the economy. Advertisers paid for space in publications. Companies sponsored popular radio shows, such as the Palmolive Hour and the Maxwell House Concert. Advertising money made these publications and shows available to the public, and advertising gave wide exposure to consumer products.

New ways to pay In the early 1900s, most Americans paid for items in full when they bought them. They might borrow money to buy a house, a piano, or a sewing machine. But as one economist noted, "People who made such purchases didn't talk about them." Borrowing money was not considered respectable.

Setting the stage for today's credit-card society, the generation of the 1920s turned to installment buying—paying for an item over time in small payments. They bought on credit, which is, in effect, borrowing money.

Consumers took quickly to installment buying to purchase the new products on the market. By the end of the decade, 90 percent of durable goods, or long lasting goods such as cars and appliances, were bought on credit. Advertisements encouraged the use of credit, telling consumers they could "get what they want now" and assuring them that with small payments they would "barely miss the money."

READING CHECK **Summarizing** How did life change for consumers in the 1920s?

Consumer Culture

The advertising industry expanded after World War I. With the help of psychologists, advertising produced glamorous ads that tempted Americans with exciting new products. New payment methods convinced people they could afford to buy them. *What image of Americans is the advertisers portraying?*

Weaknesses in the Economy

The era that brought the boom in cars, consumer goods, radio, and advertising earned the nickname the Roaring Twenties. The name captured a certain excitement of the times. Today, however, historians tend to avoid that nickname because it gives the false impression that all Americans were prosperous and freewheeling. In fact, many Americans suffered deeply in the postwar period.

American farmers had experienced good times during World War I. Demand for their products was high, and competition from European farmers was low. After the war, however, demand slowed. European farmers returned to their fields. A glut of farm products hit the market. As a result, U.S. farm prices plunged, and American farmers entered a decade of extreme hardship. Farm failures increased. The income of farmers and even the value of farmland declined.

The federal government tried to help. A 1921 tariff made foreign farm products more expensive, which helped raise prices for U.S. products. Yet these measures failed to fully relieve the problems.

In some places, nature added to farmers' woes. An infestation of an insect called the boll weevil destroyed cotton crops throughout the South. As a popular song of the era observed, this plague hit struggling sharecroppers especially hard.

HISTORY'S VOICES

"Well, the merchant got half the cotton.
The boll weevils got the rest.
Didn't leave the poor farmer's wife
but one old cotton dress.
And it's full of holes, all full of holes."
—Carl Sandburg, the Boll Weevil Song

Disaster also struck the South in 1927, when the great Mississippi River flooded. Up to a thousand people died, and countless more were left homeless.

In Florida the wild land boom came to a sudden and disastrous end. Demand for land peaked, then collapsed. Then came "The Big Blow"—the strongest hurricane recorded up to that time. The hurricane had winds of 150 miles per hour, and it killed 243 people. Few people heard the warning on South Florida's only radio station. The hurricane was one of the most destructive ever. As a result, Florida sunk into an economic depression even as other parts of the nation enjoyed prosperity.

READING CHECK **Making Generalizations** What was one group that missed out on the booming economy of the 1920s?

SECTION 2 ASSESSMENT

HSS 11.5.7

Reviewing Ideas, Terms, and People

1. **a. Define** What was the **assembly line**?
   b. Explain How did the assembly line affect Ford's ability to make automobiles?
   c. Predict What potential problems might result from industry's rapid increase in **productivity**?

2. **a. Describe** What was the effect of the boom in the auto industry on other industries?
   b. Interpret Why could industrial changes be said to change the map of the United States?
   c. Predict How do you think the rise of the automobile will affect rural areas?

3. **a. Define** Write a brief definition for each of the following terms: **installment buying, credit**
   b. Contrast What change occurred in consumer attitudes in the 1920s compared to earlier times?
   c. Elaborate How did the changes in consumer behavior make possible the growth of the American economy in the 1920s?

4. **a. Identify** What part of the American economy did not enjoy prosperity in the 1920s?
   b. Summarize What factors explain the economic plight of farmers?

Critical Thinking

5. **Sequencing** Copy the chart below and then place events in the chapter in the diagram in the order in which they occurred.

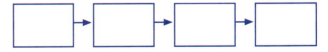

FOCUS ON WRITING  ELA W1.1, 1.3

6. **Persuasive** Write a letter to the editor of your local newspaper arguing for or against the use of credit for the purchase of desired goods, such as cars and appliances.

SECTION 3
The Harding and Coolidge Presidencies

BEFORE YOU READ

MAIN IDEA
The nation's desire for normalcy and its support for American business was reflected in two successive presidents it chose—Warren G. Harding and Calvin Coolidge.

READING FOCUS
1. What political events and ideas marked the Warren G. Harding presidency?
2. What political events and ideas marked the Calvin Coolidge presidency?
3. What were the lingering effects of World War I on politics in the 1920s?

KEY TERMS AND PEOPLE
Warren G. Harding
Teapot Dome
Calvin Coolidge
reparation
arms race
Charles Evans Hughes
Billy Mitchell
Kellogg-Briand Pact

HSS 11.5.1 Discuss the policies of Presidents Warren Harding, Calvin Coolidge, and Herbert Hoover.

A New Time and a New PRESIDENT

▲ In a 1920 speech, Harding spoke about America's need for "normalcy."

 How did one word help Warren G. Harding become president? The Ohio senator was not known for being an intellectual giant. But behind his appearance of lazy good humor, Warren G. Harding had political smarts. In 1920 he sensed something about the country. He sensed the longing that people have, in times of fear and chaos, for the things that seem familiar and safe. With typical Harding flair, he used a word coined shortly before the Civil War, *normalcy,* rather than the more accepted word *normality.*

Harding was running in the 1920 presidential race when he made a speech in May, in Boston. To recover from World War I, he said, the nation needed healing, restoration, and... "normalcy." What did he mean by normalcy? What did it mean to Americans?

People were weary of the great sacrifices they had made during World War I. Soldiers had witnessed unspeakable horrors in the trenches and on the battlefields, and many citizens wondered what the country had gained from it all. After a year of violent labor conflicts and fears of Communist revolution, with factories and family farms in trouble, normalcy—whatever it meant—sounded good to many Americans.

Democrats made fun of what they called Harding's "pompous phrases." But voters wanted a "return to normalcy" nonetheless. They swept Harding into office and inaugurated a decade of Republican rule.

282 CHAPTER 9

The Harding Presidency

In Marion, Ohio, where newspaper publisher **Warren G. Harding** grew up, people were proud of their small-town values. They did not expect or want the government to solve their problems. They believed in taking care of one another and working hard.

In his political career, however, Harding is not remembered for his work ethic. In fact, his notorious love of leisure produced quite a casual approach to governing. Elected as the U.S. senator from Ohio in 1914, Harding actually skipped more sessions than he attended. He missed historic Senate debates on Prohibition and on women's suffrage. As president, he regarded the job as largely ceremonial and told friends that the job was beyond his skills. On the other hand, his friendly, backslapping manner—and his tendency to avoid taking positions on issues—made him quite popular.

The election of 1920 As Woodrow Wilson's term came to a chaotic end, Republicans knew they had an opportunity to win the White House. At first, Harding was not a leading candidate for his party's nomination. However, he offered a coherent message, one highly appealing to the public. A high point for Harding was inventing the normalcy slogan in his campaign speech in Boston. Harding's candidacy also was aided by the lack of a dominant leader among the Republicans. Theodore Roosevelt, the heart and soul of the party in the early 1900s, had died the year before. Teddy Roosevelt had no clear successor.

Out of this uncertainty, the Republicans named Harding as their candidate. Democrats nominated James Cox, also of Ohio. In the campaign, voters overwhelmingly preferred Harding's vision of normalcy. Harding also helped himself by skillfully avoiding taking a firm stand for or against the League of Nations. The result was a landslide. Harding won more than 60 percent of the vote.

Harding's policies President Harding's answer to the nation's postwar economic troubles was his campaign slogan, "Less government in business and more business in government." To help achieve his pro-business goal, Harding sought to cut the federal budget and to reduce taxes on the wealthiest Americans. Harding and his advisers believed that

ACADEMIC VOCABULARY
coherent clear and logical

PRIMARY SOURCES

Political Cartoon

As the Teapot Dome scandal unfolded, many people began to take a closer look at the illegal activities of the Harding cabinet. This cartoon, titled "Juggernaut," was published in 1924 during the height of the scandal. A "juggernaut" is an indestructible force that crushes everything in its path.

The oil scandal at the heart of Teapot Dome is portrayed as a steamroller.

The steamroller is headed towards the White House.

SKILLS FOCUS: READING LIKE A HISTORIAN

1. **Identifying Points of View** What does the artist's choice of title and imagery say about the power of the scandal?
2. **Making Inferences** What effect does the artist think the scandal might have on the Republican administration?

See **Skills Handbook**, p. H7, H28–H29

it was the wealthy who started and expanded businesses. By taxing them less, the thinking went, business would grow and pull the nation out of the hard times.

To farmers, Harding offered little. He did sign the high Fordney-McCumber Tariff soon after taking office. His motive was to help American farmers by raising the cost of foreign-grown farm products. As the costs for foreign products rose, so did the prices for American products. This helped U.S. farmers in the short term. Yet it also hurt Europeans by making it harder for them to pay back war debts.

The tariff was the only measure Harding would take to help American agriculture. "The farmer," he said, "requires no special favors at the hands of government."

Scandal and sudden death Whatever he lacked in governing skills, Harding attempted to compensate for by appointing highly skilled people to his cabinet. One of his most gifted and respected advisers was Treasury Secretary Andrew Mellon, a multimillionaire business person and philanthropist. Mellon proceeded to reform the nation's tax system during more than a decade in the office. Harding's cabinet included two other highly respected men: Secretary of State Charles Evans Hughes and Commerce Secretary Herbert Hoover.

ACADEMIC VOCABULARY
motive reason to take action

Unfortunately, not all of Harding's choices were so wise. He named a number of old friends from Ohio to lower-level government posts. Some members of this so-called Ohio Gang were later convicted of taking bribes.

The worst Harding-era scandal involved Secretary of the Interior Albert Fall. Fall accepted bribes in return for allowing oil companies to drill federal oil reserves on a piece of federal land known as Teapot Dome in Wyoming. Fall was eventually convicted and sent to jail.

Harding was never found to be personally connected to Teapot Dome or the Ohio Gang incidents, and he did not live to see their effects. Distressed by the rumors of scandals, Harding and his wife took a trip to Alaska.

While giving a speech in Seattle at the end of his trip, Harding collapsed. His doctor first diagnosed indigestion. The *New York Times* reassured readers "Harding . . . Rallies From a Slight Indigestion." He had, however, suffered a heart attack. Harding himself expressed concern. "I am worn out," he told his sister at the Palace Hotel in San Francisco, "can't stand the heavy responsibilities and physical work too." In bed that evening, he shuddered and died.

At the time of his death, Harding's popularity was high. Over time, however, the corruption of his administration and Harding's own failings soured his reputation.

READING CHECK **Drawing Conclusions** What was Harding's goal with regard to business when he became president?

The Coolidge Presidency

"I was awakened by my father coming up the stairs calling my name. I noticed his voice trembled," **Calvin Coolidge** later recalled. To the vice president and the whole country, the news of Harding's death was a shock.

Coolidge received the message after he had gone to bed on the evening of August 2. He walked across town to the nearest telephone to call Secretary of State Charles Evans Hughes, who urged Coolidge to take the oath of office. In the early hours of the morning, by the light of an oil lamp, John Coolidge, a notary public, administered the oath of office to his son, John Calvin Coolidge—now the thirtieth president of the United States.

FACES OF HISTORY
Calvin & Grace COOLIDGE
1872–1933 and 1879–1957

When Calvin Coolidge was only 12 years old, his mother died. Coolidge had to take over many duties on the family farm while going to school. He had another setback when he failed a college entrance exam. He studied hard and finally passed. Coolidge's determination helped him rise in politics from city council member in Northampton, Massachusetts, to president of the United States.

Grace Coolidge's warm, outgoing personality greatly benefited her husband's political career. As first lady, Grace had a striking memory for names and faces. She enjoyed entertaining artists, actors, and writers at the White House. Grace's colorful personality was a welcome contrast to Calvin's quiet demeanor.

Summarize What challenges did Calvin Coolidge overcome?

American Civil Liberty

Native Americans and Citizenship

President Coolidge (left) poses with members of the Blackfoot nation.

Citizenship and voting rights have expanded throughout U.S. history. By 1869 nearly everyone born in the United States, except Native Americans, was a citizen.

The 1887 Dawes Act granted citizenship to some Native Americans, and the Indian Naturalization Act, passed in 1890, allowed Indians to apply for citizenship. In 1901 Congress granted citizenship to Native Americans living on reservations in Oklahoma.

At this time, possibly one-third of Native Americans were not U.S. citizens. In spite of this, thousands of Indians served in the U.S. military during World War I or supported the war effort at home. Still it was not until 1924 when President Coolidge signed the Indian Citizenship Act, that all Indians born in the United States were granted citizenship.

Sequencing What steps did Congress take toward granting citizenship to all Native Americans?

Coolidge's background The Coolidges' rural Vermont home was modest. Calvin Coolige's father ran a store and was active in the local Republican Party. These two interests, business and politics, would stick with Calvin Coolidge throughout his life.

After graduating from college in Amherst, Massachusetts, Coolidge took up law and politics, working his way up the ranks of the Republican Party. Elected governor of Massachusetts in 1918, he achieved national fame for his role in the Boston police strike, as you read in Section 1. The event ignited Coolidge's national career, earning him the vice presidential slot on the 1920 Republican ticket with Harding.

Coolidge in office Coolidge's reputation for honesty helped him deal with the erupting Harding administration scandals. He quickly got rid of officials suspected of corruption. His success overcoming the scandals was proven when he easily defeated Democrat John W. Davis in the 1924 election.

Coolidge's presidency was characterized by his unshakable faith in the power of business and industry. "Those who build a factory build a temple of worship," he said. "Those who work in the factory, worship there."

Business, he believed, would provide the energy and resources to fuel America's growth. Business would promote the arts and sciences. It would fund charities to help society.

The president's faith in the positive power of business was matched by his strong belief that the role of government should be strictly limited. Government, he thought, did not produce things of value and only took away resources that could be used to build businesses. Coolidge believed in lowering taxes and reducing the federal budget. In fact, there were no major budget increases between 1923 and 1929.

One observer noted Coolidge's "active inactivity." Indeed, the president proposed few laws or policies. Among his chief initiatives were efforts to stop congressional plans to help farmers. He also vetoed a bill to provide a bonus to World War I veterans. The costs, he felt, were too great. Coolidge also worked to weaken regulations on industry.

Coolidge the man Serious and straightforward, Coolidge was known as "Silent Cal." He hated small talk, although he did enjoy playing practical jokes on White House staff. His style—and the fairly good times of his era—made him popular at the time.

In his quiet, no-nonsense fashion, Coolidge stunned the nation as the presidential election of 1928 approached. While on vacation he declared, "I do not choose to run for President in 1928."

READING CHECK **Comparing** How did Coolidge's basic beliefs compare to Harding's?

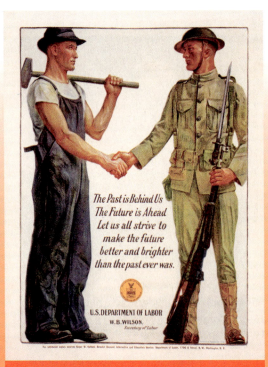

This 1918 poster expressed the hope of many Americans that postwar life would soon return to normal.

Effects of World War I

IMMEDIATE EFFECTS
- Nation desires "normalcy."
- Farmers struggle to recover from postwar slump.
- European countries unable to pay war debts.
- Desire to avoid future wars remains strong.

LONG TERM EFFECTS
- Harding and then Coolidge—who each harken back to an earlier, simpler time—are elected.
- Harding and Congress pass the Fordney-McCumber Tariff. European countries unable to pay war debts.
- United States becomes banker to the nations of Europe.
- United States sponsors Washington Naval Conference and signs the Kellogg-Briand Pact.

The Lingering Effects of World War I

The fighting on the battlefields of World War I ended in 1918, yet the war's effects on national and international politics endured throughout a whole generation and several presidencies. The fight over Wilson's peace plans and the League of Nations consumed the final years of Wilson's presidency. Other questions about the peace played a major role in 1920s politics.

The question of war debt During World War I, the warring nations of Europe had borrowed more than $10 billion from the United States. Americans expected that, when the fighting stopped, the Europeans would repay the money. For the war-torn nations of Europe, this proved very difficult.

The high Fordney-McCumber Tariff made the task that much harder. Europeans had trouble selling their goods in the United States and so could not earn the dollars they needed to pay off their debts. Instead, countries turned to Germany and demanded that it pay extremely high **reparations**, or payments designed to make up for the damage of the war.

Germany was unable to pay what the Allies demanded. This, in turn, left the Allies unable to pay off their war debts. To solve this problem, the United States began to lend money to Germany. In this way, the United States assumed the role of banker to Europe. The loans continued throughout the 1920s, until the German reparations were sharply reduced.

The Washington Naval Conference
Peacetime brought considerable public pressure to reduce the size of U.S. armed forces to save money and reduce the threat of war. On the other hand, people feared that the naval powers of the world, especially Great Britain and Japan, were on the verge of a naval arms race. In an **arms race**, competing nations build more and more weapons in an effort to avoid one nation gaining a clear advantage.

Hoping to head off an arms race, the U.S. government organized the Washington Naval Conference in 1921. The major naval powers of the world were invited. At the conference, the parties agreed to cut back sharply on the size of their navies. Countries actually scrapped existing ships and some that were under construction. The conference also led to agreement on several issues that threatened world peace. These included plans to avoid competition among the world's military powers for the control of China.

Many Americans considered the conference a great success. Secretary of State **Charles Evans Hughes** reported, "We are taking perhaps the greatest forward step in history to establish the reign of peace." As you will read, however, it would not be long before world tensions were rising and nations were again building ships of war.

Billy Mitchell argues for air power

While the United States was scuttling some of its fleet, Brigadier General **Billy Mitchell** was arguing that the United States should invest more in building up its air power. Mitchell had commanded the U.S. air combat operations in World War I. He was a firm believer in the military potential of aircraft.

To demonstrate his point, Mitchell conducted tests in which he used planes to sink two battleships. This, Mitchell thought, proved the superiority of air power over naval power. Other military officials were not convinced. Mitchell's confrontational style hurt him. He was eventually punished for accusing them of "almost treasonable administration of the national defense." He left the military and continued to promote air power until his death in the 1930s.

The Kellogg-Briand Pact

Though the United States had refused to join the League of Nations, a strong interest remained in preventing another catastrophic war. So, when the French proposed a treaty with the United States that would outlaw war between two nations, the United States responded with a bigger idea. Secretary of State Frank Kellogg proposed an agreement that would involve many countries.

The **Kellogg-Briand Pact** was the result. It stated the following:

HISTORY'S VOICES

> "The High Contracting Parties solemnly declare in the names of their respective peoples that they condemn recourse to war for the solution of international controversies, and renounce it, as an instrument of national policy in their relations with one another."
>
> —Kellogg-Briand Pact, Article I, 1928

In a world where war had raged across continents throughout human history—a world that had viewed war as a necessity, even a game—the pact represented a high ideal. More than 60 nations signed on. Yet the pact had no system for enforcement. The only thing holding nations to their promise was their word. As you will read, that would not be enough.

THE IMPACT TODAY

Science and Technology

Today the U.S. Air Force is central to the nation's military capability and security. Air power has been a decisive factor in military conflicts such as Afghanistan and Iraq.

READING CHECK **Summarizing** How did America demonstrate its wish to disarm in the 1920s?

SECTION 3 ASSESSMENT

HSS 11.5.1

go.hrw.com
Online Quiz
Keyword: SE7 HP9

Reviewing Ideas, Terms, and People

1. **a. Identify** What was **Teapot Dome**?
   b. Analyze What do you think Harding meant when he said that the United States needed "normalcy"?
   c. Evaluate Why do you think so many voters were drawn to Harding's message of normalcy and a return to values of the past?

2. **a. Recall** Why is **Calvin Coolidge** known as "Silent Cal"?
   b. Compare How did Coolidge's policies compare to those of Harding?
   c. Rank Who do you think would have had a more positive impression of Coolidge: a farmer or a business owner? Explain.

3. **a. Define** Write a brief definition for the following term: reparation
   b. Make Inferences Why do you think **Billy Mitchell** was unable to get a strong commitment to air power in the 1920s?

   c. Evaluate Why do you think the United States signed the **Kellogg-Briand Pact** but did not join the League of Nations?

Critical Thinking

4. **Sequencing** Copy the chart below, using information from the chapter to complete the diagram.

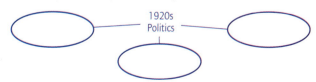

FOCUS ON WRITING ELA W1.1, 1.3

5. **Persuasive** Write a memo to the president in which you argue for or against the agreements made in the Washington Naval Conference.

CHAPTER 9 DOCUMENT-BASED INVESTIGATION

Tactics of the Red Scare

HSS 11.5.2

Historical Context The documents below provide several different perspectives on the U.S. government's actions during the Red Scare.

Task Examine the documents and answer the questions that follow. Then, you will be asked to write an essay about the government's tactics during the Red Scare, using facts from the documents and from the chapter to support the position you take in your thesis statement.

DOCUMENT 1

Attorney General A. Mitchell Palmer led the government's attack on suspected radicals. He was one of several public officials who had been targeted by bombs suspected of being sent by violent radicals. Among his more controversial policies was the jailing or deportation of people for speech or writings that might lend support for radical actions. In the following magazine article, he explained why people should be arrested for speech, not just actions, against the government.

> Like a prairie-fire, the blaze of revolution was sweeping over every American institution of law and order a year ago. It was eating its way into the homes of the American workman, its sharp tongues or revolutionary heat were licking the altars of the churches, leaping into the belfry of the school bell, crawling into the sacred corners of American homes . . . burning up the foundations of society. . . .
>
> Upon these two basic certainties, first that the "Reds" were criminal aliens, and secondly that the American Government must prevent crime, it was decided that there could be no nice distinctions between the theoretical ideals of the radicals and their actual violations of our national laws. . . . Any theory which excuses crime is not wanted in America.

DOCUMENT 2

Not all government officials supported the tactics used to crackdown on suspected Communists. Georgia Senator Thomas W. Hardwick had also been a target of radical bombings. He, his wife, and a maid had all been injured when a mailed bomb exploded in his home. Although Hardwick supported tightening some immigration laws to keep suspected radicals out of the country, he spoke out against Red Scare laws aimed mainly at weakening the power of labor unions, especially the Industrial Workers of the World (IWW). Laws against radical speech were often used against union members who criticized anything about the capitalist system.

> I understand that the real, in fact practically the only, object of this [legislation] is to get some men called I.W.W.'s who are operating in a few of the Northwestern states, and you Senators from those states have been exceedingly solicitous [concerned] to have legislation of this kind enacted . . . I dislike to be confronted by a situation in which in the name of patriotism we are asked to justify the fundamental rights and liberties of 100,000,000 American people in order to meet a situation in a few Northwestern states."

DOCUMENT 3

This political cartoon refers to the deportation of alien radicals that occurred in December 1919. The ship, the USS *Buford,* pictured in the cartoon, was nicknamed the "Soviet Ark." The bear in the lower left hand corner was a feature that the artist Clifford K. Berryman used in all his cartoons.

A. Mitchell Palmer and J. Edgar Hoover spent four months rounding up alleged alien radicals and others for deportation. In the end, fewer than 300 of the thousands detained were deported. Because they were not citizens, aliens could be deported without a trial or indictment. Most, but not all, of those deported were members of the Union of Russia Workers and supported the Bolshevik revolution in Russia. Emma Goldman, a well known radical and publisher of *Mother Earth* magazine, was among those deported.

READING LIKE A HISTORIAN

HSS Analysis HI1, 4

1. **a. Describe** Refer to Document 1. To what does Palmer compare the spread of revolution in the United States?
   b. Analyze What is his main justification for the jailing of people for speech?
2. **a. Identify** Refer to Document 2. What region of the country does Hardwick argue will be affected the most from Red Scare laws targeted at labor?
   b. Analyze Why does Hardwick oppose such laws?
3. **a. Identify** Refer to Document 3. How does the cartoonist depict the people on the boat?
   b. Interpret What is the message the cartoonist is trying to send?
4. **Document-Based Essay Question** Consider the question below and form a thesis statement. Using examples from Documents 1, 2, and 3, create an outline and write a short essay supporting your position.
   Were the Red Scare policies of the U.S. government appropriate responses to fears of a Bolshevik revolution?

See **Skills Handbook**, p. H28–H29, H31

CHAPTER 9

Chapter Review

Visual Summary: From War to Peace

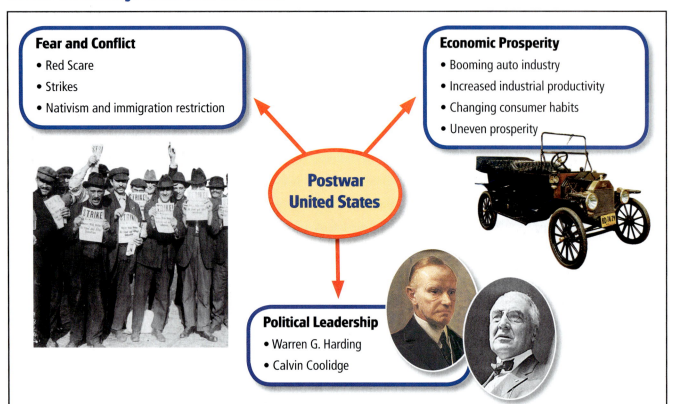

Fear and Conflict
- Red Scare
- Strikes
- Nativism and immigration restriction

Economic Prosperity
- Booming auto industry
- Increased industrial productivity
- Changing consumer habits
- Uneven prosperity

Postwar United States

Political Leadership
- Warren G. Harding
- Calvin Coolidge

Reviewing Key Terms and People

Complete each sentence by filling the blank with the correct term or person.

1. Following World War I, a heightened fear of radicals, or a _____ , gripped the nation.
2. Increasingly, consumers in the 1920s paid for purchases with _____ rather than with cash.
3. _____ became president in 1920 by promising a return to normalcy.
4. The United States government helped Germany pay its high _____ .
5. Vice President _____ skillfully avoided being tainted by the scandals of the Harding administration.
6. The _____ allowed cars to be made in large numbers and at a relatively low cost.
7. The _____ wanted to establish a new social system in their country and in the world.
8. A. Mitchell Palmer's raids led to the _____ of many aliens.
9. _____'s dream was to build a car that the average American could afford.
10. Harding's secretary of the interior was involved in a scandal over a place called _____ .

Calvin Coolidge
Bolsheviks
deportation
Teapot Dome
Henry Ford
credit
Warren G. Harding
reparations
assembly line
Red Scare

290 CHAPTER 9

History's Impact video program
Review the video to answer the closing question:
How did American women win the right to vote?

Comprehension and Critical Thinking

SECTION 1 *(pp. 270–275)* HSS 11.5.2

11. **a. Describe** What are some examples of postwar havoc in the United States?

   b. Summarize What factors contributed to the postwar havoc?

   c. Evaluate Why do you think many Americans reacted to the difficulties of the postwar years by targeting immigrants?

SECTION 2 *(pp. 276–281)* HSS 11.5.7

12. **a Describe** Describe the significance of the following terms in the 1920s economy: assembly line, welfare capitalism, installment buying.

   b. Compare How did the economic performance of agriculture compare to that of industry in the 1920s?

   c. Evaluate What was the role of consumer credit in the expansion of the 1920s economy, and why might this pose a problem in the future?

SECTION 3 *(pp. 282–287)* HSS 11.5.1

13. **a. Recall** Who were the two U.S. presidents who served between 1920 and 1928?

   b. Make Generalizations What kind of relationship did the American political leaders of the 1920s promote between business and government?

   c. Evaluate Why do you think many people in the United States were so willing to support the pro-business policies of the federal government in the 1920s?

Using the Internet

go.hrw.com Practice Online Keyword: SE7 CH9

14. The decade after World War I was a turbulent one. Americans feared the spread of communism. They also were experiencing many political, social, and economic changes at home. Using the keyword above, do research to learn about the changes that were occuring in the United States during the years 1919–1928. Then create a report that describes how political, social, and economic forces combined to create such a sense of uneasiness in the decade after World War I.

Analyzing Primary Sources
HSS HR4

Reading Like a Historian
The vacuum cleaner was one of the many new products sold to consumers, often on installment plans, in the 1920s.

15. **Identify** Who was the primary audience for this advertisement?

16. **Analyze** Based on the woman's facial expression in the ad, what do you think the ad is claiming the vacuum cleaner will do?

Critical Reading ELA R2.2

Read the passage in Section 1 that begins with the heading "American Reaction." Then answer the questions that follow.

17. According to the passage, the fear of Reds in the United States was a continuation of

   A wartime prosperity.
   B the fight over the League of Nations.
   C hatred of "the Hun."
   D the rise of labor.

18. In the fourth paragraph of the passage, the text reads, "Some of their members promoted the violent overthrow of the government." In this sentence, the word *promoted* means

   A opposed.   **C** achieved.
   B stopped.   **D** advocated.

FOCUS ON WRITING ELA W1.1

Expository Writing *Expository writing gives information, explains why or how, or defines a process. To practice expository writing, follow the directions below.*

Writing Topic The impact of the assembly line

19. **Assignment** Based on what you have read in this chapter, write a paragraph that explains how Ford's assembly line revolutionized the automobile industry and other industries.

FROM WAR TO PEACE 291

CHAPTER 10
1920–1929
THE ROARING Twenties

THE BIG PICTURE American culture underwent rapid and radical change in the 1920s. Signs of this change were everywhere—in the music and fashions of the day, in the habits and pastimes of Americans, in the art and literature of the country's most creative minds. Large population shifts and new technologies transformed the nation from rural to urban and from traditional to modern.

California Standards

History-Social Sciences

11.5 Students analyze the major political, social, economic, technological, and cultural developments of the 1920s.

11.8 Students analyze the economic boom and social transformation of post-World War II America.

11.10 Students analyze the development of federal civil rights and voting rights.

Skills FOCUS READING LIKE A HISTORIAN

This jazz band is supplying not only music but also some food and drink to competitors in a Charleston endurance contest. The Charleston was a new dance that was all the rage in the 1920s. **Interpreting Visuals** What words would you use to describe the mood of the scene captured in this photograph?

See **Skills Handbook**, p. H30

U.S.

World

1920 First corporate radio station offers music and news.

1920

1920 League of Nations holds first meeting in Paris, France.

History's Impact video program
Watch the video to understand the impact of younger generations.

1924 Nellie Tayloe Ross is elected in Wyoming as the nation's first woman governor.

1926 Langston Hughes publishes *The Weary Blues*, his first book of poetry.

1927 Charles Lindbergh completes his solo flight across the Atlantic Ocean.

1924 Soviet leader Vladimir Lenin dies.

1926 Ruins of Mayan cities reported found in Mexico.

1929 The National Revolutionary Party is established in Mexico.

1922 | 1924 | 1926 | 1928 | 1930

SECTION 1
American Life Changes

BEFORE YOU READ

MAIN IDEA
The United States experienced many social changes during the 1920s.

READING FOCUS
1. What were the new roles for American women in the 1920s?
2. What were the effects of growing urbanization in the United States in the 1920s?
3. In what ways did the 1920s reveal a national conflict over basic values?
4. What was Prohibition, and how did it affect the nation?

KEY TERMS AND PEOPLE
flapper
values
Billy Sunday
fundamentalism
Aimee Semple McPherson
evolution
Clarence Darrow
William Jennings Bryan
bootlegger
speakeasy

HSS 11.5.3 Examine the passage of the Eighteenth Amendment and the Volstead Act (Prohibition).

HSS 11.10.7 Analyze the women's rights movement from the era of Elizabeth Stanton and Susan Anthony and the passage of the Nineteenth Amendment, including perspectives on the roles of women.

THE INSIDE STORY

Who put the car and the radio together? By the early 1920s cars and radio were well on their way to becoming key features of American life. For young people especially, cars meant freedom. Radio meant access to music, news, sports, and a blossoming American popular culture.

Inventors William Lear and Elmer Wavering were two young Americans who enjoyed cars and music. It was their girlfriends, however, who gave them the idea to put a radio inside a car. The two couples liked to park at a scenic spot in their little Illinois town to watch the sun go down. When the young women suggested that it would be wonderful to have music on these evenings, Lear and Wavering decided to figure out how to install a radio inside a car in such a way that it could be heard over the car's engine and would not interfere with the car's electrical system. The result was the invention of the first practical car radio.

Within a few years the car radio would become standard equipment in millions of automobiles. The world of the American teenager would never be the same.

A Match Made in Heaven

◄ Before radios were installed into cars, people used portable radios powered by the car's battery. The bulky size didn't stop people from carrying them along.

294 CHAPTER 10

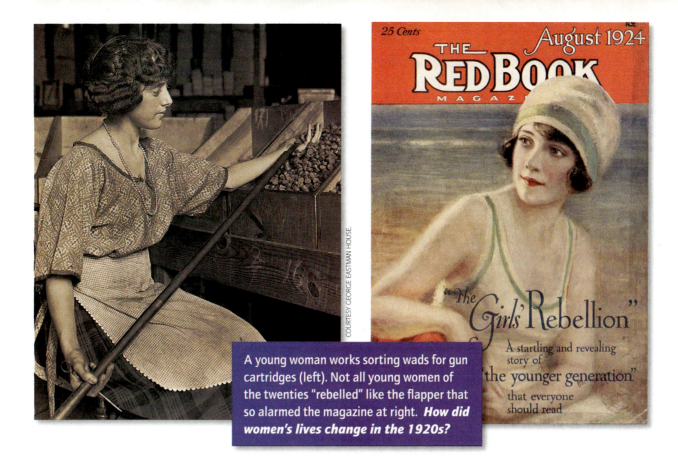

A young woman works sorting wads for gun cartridges (left). Not all young women of the twenties "rebelled" like the flapper that so alarmed the magazine at right. **How did women's lives change in the 1920s?**

New Roles for Women

The invention of the car radio was just one example of the many cultural changes that took place in the 1920s. The decade itself became known as the Roaring Twenties for the speedy social change it brought to the United States. Women were especially affected.

New opportunities As you have read, the states ratified the Nineteenth Amendment in 1920. After a decades-long struggle, women could finally vote. As a result, women were soon elected to state and local offices. In Wyoming, Nellie Tayloe Ross became the nation's first woman governor when she won election in 1924 to complete the term of her husband, William B. Ross, who had died in office. Miriam "Ma" Ferguson was elected governor of Texas that same year.

In general, however, women voters did not make their presence felt at the ballot box and bring about sweeping changes in the national government, as some advocates for women's suffrage had expected. In fact, women in the 1920s tended to vote much as their husbands, fathers, or other men in their lives voted. As a result, they did not yet represent a unique group of voters with a distinct point of view.

American women also saw changes in their workplace roles during the 1920s. While many women had taken jobs outside the home during World War I, most lost these wartime jobs when the troops returned to the United States. During the economic boom of the 1920s, however, women again joined the workforce in large numbers. They filled a greater range of jobs than ever before. Still, nearly all women in the workforce held jobs in a handful of the lowest-paying professions, including nurses, teachers, and domestic servants.

Also during the 1920s, Americans began attending college in greater numbers than ever before. Many of these new students were women from middle- and upper-class families.

New family roles In part because of these changing opportunities for women, the 1920s brought about a shift in many people's attitudes concerning the relationship between men and women. The basic rules that defined proper female behavior were beginning to change. American women did continue to have primary responsibility for caring for the home and children, and most still depended on men for financial support. An increasing number, however, sought a greater sense of equality in their relationships with men.

THE ROARING TWENTIES **295**

The flapper One popular image that reflects many of the changes affecting women in the 1920s is the flapper. The term refers to young women of the era who defied traditional ideas of proper dress and behavior. Flappers shocked society by chopping off their hair, raising their hemlines, wearing makeup, smoking cigarettes, drinking alcohol, and going dancing in nightclubs. Not all flappers did all of these things, of course. The new mode of dress, however, was particularly popular among rebellious girls.

ACADEMIC VOCABULARY
mode style or fashion

HISTORY'S VOICES

"Not since 1820 has feminine apparel been so frankly abbreviated [shortened] as at present ... Nor is this merely the sensible half of the population dressing as everyone ought to, in hot weather. Last winter's styles weren't so dissimilar, except that they were covered up by fur coats and you got the full effect only indoors."
—Bruce Bliven, *The New Republic,* September 9, 1925

In general, the term *flapper* suggested a certain lifestyle of great independence and freedom. As writer Dorothy Parker slyly noted about the modern woman, "She's not what Grandma used to be."

Although flappers became a symbol of the 1920s, they were hardly representative of all women of their time. Not all American women were flappers. In fact, in many parts of the United States, including small towns and rural areas, women merely read about flappers in magazine. They either disapproved of them or would not dare to be so bold or reckless. Indeed, many older supporters of women's rights believed that the flappers were more interested in having fun than in advancing the cause of women.

Disapproving of the face powder that flappers wore, Charlotte Perkins Gilman wrote, "A generation of white-nosed women who wear furs in summer cannot lay claim to any real progress." So while the flapper did represent some very real shifts taking place in American society, she certainly did not represent all American women.

READING CHECK **Summarizing** In what ways did flappers represent the changes American women were experiencing in the 1920s?

Effects of Urbanization

The flapper craze took hold mainly in American cities. In many ways the flapper phenomenon represented the growing divide between the nation's booming cities and the countryside.

As you have read, the 1920s was a time of great economic prosperity in the United States. One segment of the economy, however, did not share in the good times. Farming took a hard

URBAN AND RURAL POPULATION, 1890–1930
Source: *Historical Statistics of the United States*

hit in the post-World War I years, as wartime demand for food dropped off. Hard times in agriculture contributed to a loss of rural population, as people sought jobs in the cities. The 1920 census showed that for the first time ever, more Americans lived in urban areas than in rural areas. Three fourths of all workers worked somewhere other than a farm.

The rise of the automobile also helped shift the geographic borderline between rural and urban America. As more rural people acquired cars, the distances that had once separated them from the cities shrank. Rural people were now more likely to spend time in town interacting with each other and joining in the urban culture. Even if they continued to live in the country, they became less isolated and more urban in their outlook and attitudes.

Related to the rural-to-urban population shift was an increase in education in the United States. By the 1920s many states had passed laws requiring young people to attend school. These laws helped force children out of the workplace and into the classroom. Requiring children to attend school was also a way to teach immigrants about American life.

Interestingly, school attendance increased along with the growth of American industry. Why? As industry grew, the earnings of American workers also rose. More families could afford to send their children to school instead of sending them to the textile mills and other factories. As a result, high school and college enrollment increased.

READING CHECK **Contrasting** How did the relationship between rural America and urban America change in the 1920s?

Conflicts Over Values

The shift from a mostly rural America to a mostly urban one was highly significant. Americans were living in larger communities. This population change also produced important shifts in **values**, the key ideas and beliefs a person holds. The values of many urban Americans in the 1920s differed greatly from the traditional values of rural dwellers.

Urban and rural America differed significantly in the kinds of values that were dominant in those places. In the minds of some people, rural America represented the traditional spirit of the nation: hard-working, self-reliant, religious, and independent. Cities, on the other hand, represented changes that threatened those values.

As you read in an earlier chapter, the Ku Klux Klan grew dramatically in the 1920s. The new Klan drew many of its new members from rural America. Most new Klan members were workers, farmers, and small business owners. They saw their own status declining while the size and cultural influence of urban America was increasing. They believed the Klan could help them preserve their place in society.

Members of the new Klan continued to use violent tactics. The Klan targeted not only African Americans but also recent immigrants, especially Catholics and Jews. In the 1920s, however, the Klan also focused on influencing politics. Although founded in the South, the Klan had members nationwide in the 1920s. At its peak, membership was in the millions. Membership declined in the late 1920s because of a series of scandals affecting top Klan leaders. But the social divisions that the Klan had taken advantage of still remained.

The rise of fundamentalism
The uncertainty that comes with changing times caused many Americans to turn to religion for answers. One key religious figure of the time was a tough-talking former ballplayer named

THE IMPACT TODAY

Daily Life
Urbanization continued throughout the century. According to the 2000 U.S. Census, the country's population was 79.2 percent urban and 20.8 percent rural.

America Moves to the Cities
Los Angeles, California, shown here in a 1920s postcard, grew from a city of just over 50,000 in 1890 to a city with a population of more than 1 million by 1930. *According to the chart, during what decade did the United States become a nation of urban dwellers?*

The Scopes Trial

Key figures in the Scopes trial were Clarence Darrow (above left), representing John Scopes, and William Jennings Bryan (above right), leading the prosecution. At right, Scopes stands to receive his guilty verdict. Political cartoons like the one at left portrayed the case as a "monkey trial" because it focused on a theory that humans may have descended from an ape-like species.

Billy Sunday. Ordained as a minister in 1903, Sunday rose to national prominence as a powerful revivalist preacher. Reflecting the values of many white, rural Americans, Sunday condemned radicals and criticized the changing attitudes of women.

Sunday's Christian beliefs were based on a literal interpretation of the Bible, which is called **fundamentalism**. While many people believe that certain stories in the Bible were meant to be symbolic rather than literal, fundamentalists believe that historic events occurred exactly as the Bible describes.

Another leading fundamentalist preacher of the time was **Aimee Semple McPherson**. McPherson presented a much more sophisticated image than Billy Sunday did. In fact, she seemed to embrace the kind of glamour that many other fundamentalists warned about. Her religion, however, was firmly in the fundamentalist tradition. She was especially well known for healing the sick through prayer.

The Scopes trial As fundamentalism gained strength in the 1920s, it came into sharper conflict with the teachings of modern science. A leading example of this conflict centered on the theories of the 19th-century scientist Charles Darwin. The most controversial of Darwin's ideas is known as **evolution**. The theory of evolution holds that inherited characteristics of a population change over generations and that as a result of these changes, new species sometimes arise.

According to Darwin, the human species may have developed from an ape-like species that lived long ago. Fundamentalists believed that this theory went against the biblical account of how God created humans. Further, many fundamentalists believed that teaching evolution undermined religious faith.

Fundamentalists worked hard to prevent evolution from being taught in public schools. In several states, they succeeded in having laws passed which outlawed the teaching of Darwin's ideas or the inclusion of evolution in classroom materials. One of these states was Tennessee, where a 1925 law made it a crime to teach evolution to students.

Opponents of the Tennessee law were quick to challenge it. One group persuaded a young science teacher named John Scopes to agree to violate the law and get himself arrested. This set the stage for one of the most dramatic trials in American history.

THE IMPACT TODAY

Science and Technology
The teaching of evolution in public schools continues to be a controversial issue. More than 80 years after the Scopes trial, debate continues about what to teach in the public schools about the origin of life.

The trial took place in the little town of Dayton, Tennessee, but people around the country followed the events. The nation riveted its attention on the two distinguished, colorful lawyers who squared off against one another.

Representing Scopes was **Clarence Darrow**, perhaps the most famous criminal lawyer in the country. **William Jennings Bryan**, the three-time candidate for president, led the prosecution. Beloved as an orator who championed farmers and rural values, Bryan had become a major figure in the fundamentalist movement. In fact, he had influenced public opinion in Tennessee against evolution.

The guilt of John Scopes was never really in doubt. In the trial, both sides focused on larger issues. Bryan called it a contest between the competing ideas of Christianity and evolution. The defense openly stated that it was trying to make a point about freedom of speech.

The key moment in the trial occurred when Darrow called Bryan to testify as an expert witness on religion. Darrow asked Bryan an exhausting series of questions about events described in the Bible. Bryan said that in his view, some biblical events may not have happened exactly as described. Yet he stood by his basic beliefs. "If I am not able to explain it, I will accept it," he declared.

The trial ended, as expected, with Scopes's conviction. He was fined $100. Scopes's fate, however, was not the only story. This occurred five days after the trial, when Bryan died in his sleep. To many fundamentalists, he died a hero, giving his life for a sacred cause.

Darrow's team had hoped to appeal the decision and test the constitutionality of the Tennessee law. They never got the chance. A higher court overturned Scopes's conviction because the judge had committed a technical violation of the law.

The Tennessee law remained in place into the 1960s. Meanwhile, other states that passed similar laws soon repealed them.

> **READING CHECK** **Identifying the Main Idea**
> For what crime was Scopes tried and convicted?

Prohibition

Throughout the history of the United States, groups such as the Woman's Christian Temperance Union had fought to outlaw alcohol. To many people, alcohol was the source of much unhappiness. It hurt families, and it promoted crime, they said. Outlawing alcohol, they argued, would promote family stability. Over the years, a number of states passed anti-alcohol laws.

The drive to outlaw alcohol gained strength in the early 1900s, as Progressives joined the effort to curb the harmful effects of liquor on society. World War I aided the cause. The wartime need for discipline among the troops—and the need for grain, from which different types of alcohol are made—were two arguments in favor of banning alcohol nationally.

The fight against alcohol also borrowed from the bias against immigrants that was increasing in the World War I era. Some people who opposed immigration portrayed certain immigrant groups as abusers of alcohol. Small-town Americans also tended to view alcohol and its evils as a city problem—one that was growing more serious as the nation became more urban. Protestant religious groups and fundamentalists were among those who favored a liquor ban.

The Eighteenth Amendment
For these and other reasons, by 1917 more than half the states had passed some form of law restricting alcohol use. In that year, Congress proposed an amendment to the Constitution that made it illegal to manufacture, transport, or sell alcohol in the United States. Ratification of this amendment—the Eighteenth Amendment—followed in 1919. Congress then passed

ACADEMIC VOCABULARY
stability
consistency; resistance to change

a law known as the Volstead Act to enforce the amendment. Prohibition, as the new ban on alcohol was known, became the law of the land in 1920.

Prohibition in practice Supporters of Prohibition believed it would have many positive effects on American society. To be sure, Prohibition did reduce the amount of alcohol Americans consumed. Enforcing the new law, however, proved to be virtually impossible.

While making, transporting, and selling alcohol was illegal, drinking it was not. Many people continued to drink liquor during Prohibition—and those who wanted alcohol had little trouble getting it.

Prohibition gave rise to huge smuggling operations. Large amounts of alcohol slipped into the country through seaports and across the border from Canada. It was said that in Detroit, Michigan, located on the Canadian border, liquor smuggling was the second largest industry after automobile manufacturing. Newspaper headlines followed the high drama of the hunt for **bootleggers**, or liquor smugglers. Bootleggers—from the slang term for smuggling items inside boots—were highly skilled at avoiding capture. Government officials estimated in 1925 that they had stopped only 5 percent of all the liquor entering the country illegally.

In addition to smuggled liquor, many people simply made their own illegal alcohol using homemade equipment. Others drank alcohol that was intended for use in medicines or other products. At the time, doctors were allowed to prescribe alcohol to their patients for medical reasons.

The illegal liquor business also became the foundation of great criminal empires. The most notorious Prohibition-era gangster was Chicago's Al Capone. After brutally destroying

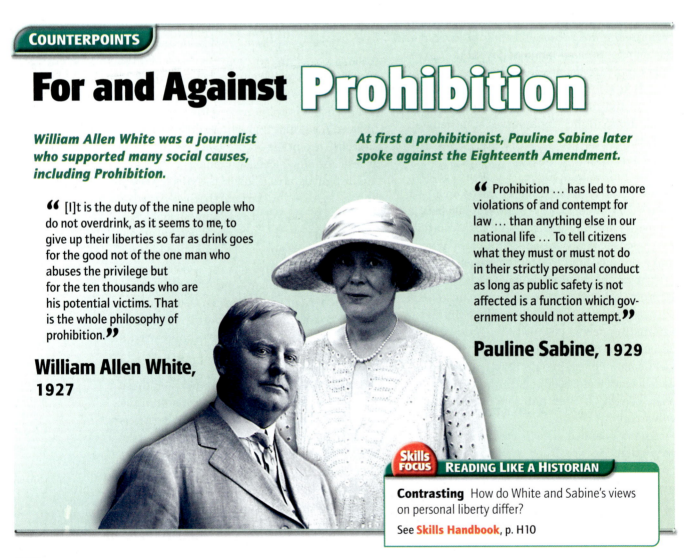

COUNTERPOINTS

For and Against Prohibition

William Allen White was a journalist who supported many social causes, including Prohibition.

❝ [I]t is the duty of the nine people who do not overdrink, as it seems to me, to give up their liberties so far as drink goes for the good not of the one man who abuses the privilege but for the ten thousands who are his potential victims. That is the whole philosophy of prohibition. ❞

William Allen White, 1927

At first a prohibitionist, Pauline Sabine later spoke against the Eighteenth Amendment.

❝ Prohibition ... has led to more violations of and contempt for law ... than anything else in our national life ... To tell citizens what they must or must not do in their strictly personal conduct as long as public safety is not affected is a function which government should not attempt. ❞

Pauline Sabine, 1929

SKILLS FOCUS READING LIKE A HISTORIAN

Contrasting How do White and Sabine's views on personal liberty differ?

See **Skills Handbook,** p. H10

his competition, he used the alcohol trade to build a business that earned tens of millions of dollars a year.

With these resources, Capone and other gangsters were able to frighten off and pay off the law-enforcement agents who threatened them. The federal government, which never had more than 3,000 Prohibition agents working nationwide, found it difficult to compete with the criminals. Still, many agents worked diligently to enforce the law. They shut down **speakeasies**, the illegal bars where alcohol was served. They destroyed barrels of captured liquor and the equipment that gangsters used to make alcohol. Yet they could not keep up with the criminals.

In spite of its problems, Prohibition continued through the 1920s. More and more people, however, questioned whether this experiment was succeeding. The scientist Albert Einstein voiced the concerns of many Americans:

HISTORY'S VOICES

"The prestige of government has undoubtedly been lowered considerably by the Prohibition law. For nothing is more destructive of respect for the government and the law of the land than passing laws which cannot be enforced."
—Albert Einstein, "My First Impression of the U.S.A.," 1921

Agents created a red river in the streets of Los Angeles as they destroyed 900 gallons of wine one day in 1920. *How effective were agents in controlling the distribution of alcohol?*

Even as millions of Americans violated the spirit of the Eighteenth Amendment, Prohibition remained in force. It would be several more years before it came to an end.

READING CHECK Making Generalizations
In what ways did Prohibition cause more problems than it solved?

SECTION 1 ASSESSMENT

HSS 11.5.3, 11.10.7

Online Quiz Keyword: SE7 HP10

Reviewing Ideas, Terms, and People

1. **a. Define** What was a flapper?
   b. Make Generalizations How were women's roles changing in the 1920s?
   c. Evaluate How do you think people who did not embrace the changes of the 1920s might have reacted to the flappers?

2. **a. Recall** What significant change in the distribution of the American population became known in 1920?
   b. Analyze How did rural and urban areas of the United States differ in terms of **values**?

3. **a. Define** Write a brief definition for each of the following terms: **fundamentalism, evolution**
   b. Make Inferences Why did fundamentalism gain popularity in the 1920s?
   c. Elaborate How did the Scopes trial reflect the tensions and conflicts taking place in American society in the 1920s?

4. **a. Identify** What was **Prohibition**?
   b. Sequence Briefly trace the history of the effort to outlaw alcohol in the United States.

   c. Predict Do you think Prohibition would have been different if drinking alcohol had been outlawed completely?

Critical Thinking

5. **Identifying the Main Idea** Copy the chart below and place events in the chapter in the diagram that support the main idea.

FOCUS ON WRITING
ELA W1.1, W1.3

6. **Persuasive** Write a letter to one of your government representatives that argues either for or against a prohibition on alcohol. Use information from the chapter to support your position.

SECTION 2
The Harlem Renaissance

BEFORE YOU READ

MAIN IDEA
Transformations in the African American community contributed to a blossoming of black culture centered in Harlem, New York.

READING FOCUS
1. What was the Great Migration, and what problems and opportunities faced African Americans in the post–World War I era?
2. What was Harlem, and how was it affected by the Great Migration?
3. Who were the key figures of the Harlem Renaissance?

KEY TERMS AND PEOPLE
Zora Neale Hurston
Great Migration
Harlem Renaissance
Marcus Garvey
James Weldon Johnson
Langston Hughes
Paul Robeson
jazz
Louis Armstrong
Bessie Smith

HSS 11.5.2 Analyze Marcus Garvey's "back-to-Africa" movement.
HSS 11.5.5 Describe the Harlem Renaissance and new trends in literature, music, and art (e.g., Zora Neale Hurston, Langston Hughes).
HSS 11.8.8 Discuss forms of popular culture (e.g., jazz and other forms of popular music, and artistic styles).

Zora Neale HURSTON

▲ Hurston wanted "a busy life, a just mind and a timely death."

THE INSIDE STORY *How could one person write such a wide variety of works?* If a "Renaissance man" is a person with a wide range of knowledge and abilities, **Zora Neale Hurston** was a Renaissance woman. As an African American girl living in Florida in the late 1800s and early 1900s, she overcame long odds to get a good education and eventually leave the South.

In 1925 Hurston won acclaim in the literary world by writing short stories and plays. After that success, she attended Barnard College in New York City, where she studied anthropology, the study of human cultures. With this training, she did important scholarly work on the subject of African American folklore. In the 1930s she moved on to writing novels, including the celebrated *Their Eyes Were Watching God*. Later still, she wrote nonfiction, including an autobiography and essays about politics.

Zora Neale Hurston's life is remarkable for the quality, quantity, and variety of the work she produced. Indeed, she was one of the leading figures in a major cultural movement that was centered in New York City's Harlem neighborhood in the 1920s: the Harlem Renaissance.

The Great Migration

Beginning around 1910 Harlem, a neighborhood in upper Manhattan, became a favorite destination for black Americans migrating from the South. Life in the South was very difficult for African Americans. Many had little choice but to work as sharecroppers or in other low-paying jobs. Segregation laws kept southern African Americans in a separate and unequal world. For these people, racial violence was a constant threat.

302 CHAPTER 10

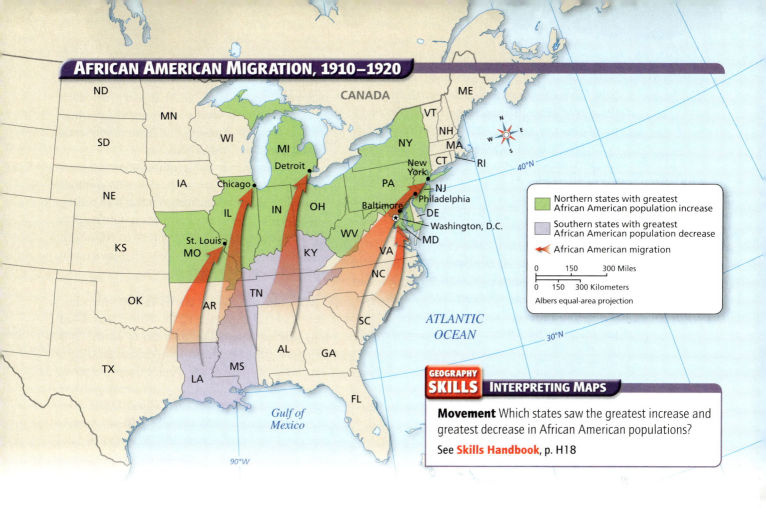

AFRICAN AMERICAN MIGRATION, 1910–1920

GEOGRAPHY SKILLS INTERPRETING MAPS

Movement Which states saw the greatest increase and greatest decrease in African American populations?

See **Skills Handbook**, p. H18

Many African Americans looked to the North with hope of finding the freedom and economic opportunities unavailable to them in the South. These hopes came true with the outbreak of World War I. Suddenly, demand for war equipment and supplies surged, and northern factories had more jobs than they could fill. Employers eagerly looked to the South for a new supply of workers. African American newspapers, such as the *Chicago Defender*, helped spread the word about the economic opportunities. The papers, in turn, fielded many requests for information. "I don't want you to loan me another 1 cent," wrote one Mississippi man, "but help me to find an occupation there in your town."

By the thousands, southern African Americans streamed into northern cities such as Chicago and Detroit. Black populations of these communities rose sharply. This major relocation of African Americans is known as the **Great Migration**.

African Americans after World War I

African Americans moved North with high hopes. Many found opportunities there, but they did not escape the effects of racism.

Racial tensions were especially severe after World War I. You have read about the economic adjustments that followed the return home of American soldiers. The shortage of jobs created tension between whites and African American workers.

This tension contributed to a wave of racial violence in the summer of 1919. The deadliest riot occurred in Chicago, Illinois. There, a dispute at a public beach led to rioting that left 38 people dead and nearly 300 people injured. Racially motivated riots occurred in some two dozen other cities in 1919.

Another factor that added to racial conflict was the changing expectations of African Americans. Many believed that they had earned greater freedom by helping fight for freedom overseas in World War I.

Unfortunately for African Americans, not everyone agreed that their war service had earned them greater freedom. In fact, some whites were determined to strike back against the new African American attitude.

READING CHECK **Identifying Cause and Effect** Why did many African Americans decide to move to the North in the early 1900s?

Life in Harlem

New York City was one of the northern cities to which African Americans moved in large numbers during the Great Migration. By the early 1920s, about 200,000 African Americans lived in the city. Most of these people lived in a single neighborhood known as Harlem. This neighborhood soon became the unofficial capital of African American culture and activism in the United States.

The role of W.E.B. Du Bois
A key figure in the rise of Harlem was W.E.B. Du Bois, about whom you read earlier. Born in Massachusetts, the well-educated Du Bois had been a leading voice in the African American community for many years. In 1909 he helped found the National Association for the Advancement of Colored People—the NAACP—in New York City. This group worked to end discrimination and mistreatment of African Americans throughout the United States.

Du Bois also served as editor of a magazine called *The Crisis*. The magazine was a major outlet for African American writing and poetry. Du Bois and *The Crisis* helped promote a great African American arts movement in New York City in the 1920s. The movement was known as the **Harlem Renaissance**.

The rise of Marcus Garvey
Another famous Harlem figure of the World War I era was **Marcus Garvey**. A Jamaican by birth, Garvey took great pride in his African heritage. Through his Universal Negro Improvement Association, or UNIA, he encouraged other African Americans to do the same. Unlike the NAACP, which was founded by African Americans and whites, Garvey's UNIA promoted self-reliance for African Americans. Garvey believed that African Americans could and should look out for their own interests, without involvement from whites. Garvey looked forward to the day when Africans from around the world could return to Africa and create a new empire. UNIA's slogan was "Back to Africa."

"We have no animus [hatred] against the white man," Garvey said. "All that we have as a race desired is a place in the sun."

In order to achieve that goal, Garvey declared, African Americans needed to build a base of economic success. This he hoped to achieve by operating a number of business enterprises. The most significant was the Black Star Line, which promoted trade among Africans around the world.

Some 2 million people, mostly impoverished African Americans, joined UNIA. Garvey held colorful parades and wore military-style uniforms to help build enthusiasm.

Garvey was highly critical of W.E.B. Du Bois and the NAACP. Garvey believed that the NAACP undermined and discouraged African American pride and self-confidence. He felt that the NAACP goal of breaking down the barriers between blacks and whites threatened the racial purity of Africans.

For their part, Du Bois and the NAACP were suspicious of Garvey and his organization.

The Crisis Magazine
First published by the NAACP in 1910, *The Crisis* was a forum for African American literary talent as well as discussion of race relations. It helped launch the careers of such Harlem Renaissance figures as Langston Hughes and Countee Cullen. It remains the official publication of the NAACP today.

Du Bois published in *The Crisis* the results of a thorough investigation of the UNIA. The Federal Bureau of Investigation (FBI) kept the UNIA under close watch. In 1923 the FBI had collected enough evidence to charge Garvey with mail fraud. Garvey went to prison in 1925. When he was released in 1927 he was forced to leave the country. With Garvey gone, the UNIA collapsed as an organization. The Harlem it left behind, however, remained a vital and exciting place.

READING CHECK **Contrasting** How did the views of W.E.B. Du Bois and Marcus Garvey differ?

A Renaissance in Harlem

Harlem in the 1920s bristled with creative energy. The growing New York City neighborhood became home to tens of thousands of African Americans. To some, Harlem was their first experience living outside of the South. They felt a strong sense of racial pride and identity. This spirit attracted a historic influx of talented African American writers, thinkers, musicians, and artists.

The result was a flowering of African American arts that came to be known as the Harlem Renaissance. The term *renaissance* comes from a French word that means "rebirth" or "revival."

Harlem writers and poets A great number of African American poets and writers burst onto the scene during the Harlem Renaissance. Their literary achievements were astounding. This is especially true given the fact that before this era, little African American literature had been published. But in 1924 the National Urban League's magazine *Opportunity* sponsored a dinner at the New York Civic Club to bring together prominent publishers and editors with up-and-coming black writers. This helped propel African American writers into the mainstream of American literature.

One notable Harlem Renaissance figure was **James Weldon Johnson**. A man of many talents, he had worked early in life as a journalist, educator, and lawyer. Johnson expressed a musical side as well: In 1900 he and his brother wrote the song "Lift Every Voice and Sing." Two decades later, Johnson had risen to the top leadership post of the NAACP, and his song became that organization's official anthem. In addition to his NAACP work, Johnson continued to write and to collect and publish the work of other poets of the Harlem Renaissance. In 1927 he published a book of poetry called *God's Trombones*, which many regard as his finest work.

A common theme among Harlem Renaissance writers was defiance or resistance in the face of white prejudice. The great poet Claude McKay wrote this poem, one of his most famous, following the 1919 race riots.

FACES OF HISTORY
Langston HUGHES
1902–1967

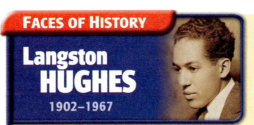

Langston Hughes began writing poetry as a teenager. As a young man, he traveled to Mexico, Africa, and Europe, writing about the things he saw. In 1926 he published *The Weary Blues,* his first book of poetry. He used the money he earned to complete college.

After college, Hughes settled in Harlem, where he soaked up the rhythms of jazz music and incorporated them into his writing. In characteristic images and jangling language, Hughes's poetry described the rich culture of African American life, capturing the joys, suffering, and speech of the people he knew. Hughes had a major impact on the Harlem Renaissance and on American literature.

Predict How might Hughes's travels affected his view of America?

HISTORY'S VOICES

"If we must die, let it not be like hogs
Hunted and penned in an inglorious spot,
While round us bark the mad and hungry dogs,
Making their mock at our accursed lot.
If we must die, O let us nobly die,
So that our precious blood may not be shed
In vain; then even the monsters we defy
Shall be constrained to honor us though dead!
O kinsmen! we must meet the common foe!
Though far outnumbered let us show us brave,
And for their thousand blows deal one deathblow!
What though before us lies the open grave?
Like men we'll face the murderous, cowardly pack,
Pressed to the wall, dying, but fighting back!"
—Claude McKay, "If We Must Die," 1919

Langston Hughes, another celebrated Harlem Renaissance poet and writer, wrote of black defiance as well, but he also wrote of hope. His works recorded the distinctive culture of Harlem during the 1920s itself.

HISTORY CLOSE-UP

The Harlem Renaissance

During the 1920s, the numerous African American writers, artists, and musicians in Harlem inspired one another to reach new heights of creativity. The work produced during this time of enormous literary and artistic achievement often reflected a strong and growing sense of racial pride and confidence.

Literature

Claude McKay's *Home to Harlem*, a novel about daily life in Harlem, was published in 1928 and quickly became a bestseller. It was the first novel by a Harlem writer to reach the bestseller list.

Performing Arts

Paul Robeson, Bessie Smith, and Louis Armstrong (from left to right) were just a few of the influential performers and musicians of the Harlem Renaissance.

Fine Arts

Artist Aaron Douglas used elements of African design and subject matter in his murals for public buildings, illustrations for publications, and paintings such as "Into Bondage" (below). Douglas also created the cover for *Home to Harlem*.

AARON DOUGLAS, "INTO BONDAGE," 1936. OIL ON CANVAS, 60 3/8 X 60 1/2 IN. CORCORAN GALLERY OF ART, WASHINGTON, D.C.

Skills Focus: INTERPRETING INFOGRAPHICS

African American writer and philosopher Alain Locke said of Harlem that "culturally and spiritually it focuses a people."

Drawing Conclusions How many art forms are represented in these pictures? How do you think this flourishing of the arts affected African Americans in general?

See **Skills Handbook**, p. H30

Harlem artists Black American artists also won fame and recognition during the Harlem Renaissance. Among the best known were William H. Johnson, Aaron Douglas, and Jacob Lawrence. Each of these artists often focused on the experiences of African Americans in their work. Later artists such as Loïs Mailou Jones drew inspiration from the works of the Harlem Renaissance.

Performers and musicians The Harlem Renaissance helped create new opportunities for African American stage performers. Historically, black actors, musicians, and other performers were not given serious roles on the American stage. That began to change in the 1920s. One of the key figures in this development was the multitalented **Paul Robeson**.

Robeson had originally come to New York to practice law but won fame on the stage. He performed in a number of movie and stage productions, the most famous of which was Shakespeare's *Othello*, in which he played the lead character. This role won him acclaim around the country and the world.

Robeson also had a rich singing voice. One of his earliest performances was in the groundbreaking 1921 musical show *Shuffle Along*, which featured an all-black cast. Another cast member was a young woman named Josephine Baker. She would go on to a remarkable career as a singer and dancer, much of it in Europe. Audiences in France and elsewhere in Europe tended to be more accepting of black performers than white Americans were.

Harlem was also a vital center for **jazz**. This music blended several different musical forms from the Lower South into a wholly original American form of music that was new, different, and very exciting. While a jazz song might start with a known melody or theme, much of the music was improvised, or composed on the spot. Jazz could be fast or slow, and it was easy to dance to. In short, jazz was not defined by clear rules but rather by its spirit and creativity. "Man, if you have to ask what it is," said legendary jazz musician **Louis Armstrong**, "you'll never know."

Louis Armstrong was a leading performer on the Harlem jazz scene, which was centered at clubs such as the Savoy Ballroom and the Cotton Club. The audience was made up in large part of white jazz fans. They flocked to Harlem to hear Armstrong and other leading performers, including Cab Calloway, composers Duke Ellington and Fats Waller, and the great blues singer **Bessie Smith**.

Jazz music was not limited to Harlem. As you will read, it was part of a wider cultural movement spreading throughout the United States in the 1920s.

READING CHECK **Identifying the Main Idea** What happened during the Harlem Renaissance?

THE IMPACT TODAY
Daily Life
The Cotton Club closed its doors in 1940 and the site was later demolished. After decades of decline, Harlem is again on the rise, and a new, relocated Cotton Club serves up jazz, swing, and gospel music to multi-ethnic audiences.

SECTION 2 ASSESSMENT

HSS 11.5.2, 11.5.5, 11.8.8

go.hrw.com
Online Quiz
Keyword: SE7 HP10

Reviewing Ideas, Terms, and People

1. **a. Recall** What was the **Great Migration**?
   b. Draw Conclusions Why do you think the Great Migration occurred when it did?
   c. Design Create an poster that would encourage southern African Americans to move to the North in the early 1900s.
2. **a. Identify** What was the role of the **NAACP** and **UNIA** in the growth of Harlem?
   b. Contrast How did W.E.B. Du Bois and **Marcus Garvey** differ in their views about the future of African Americans?
   c. Elaborate Why do you think Du Bois and Garvey were so critical of each other's ideas?
3. **a. Identify** Briefly describe the contributions of **James Weldon Johnson** and **Zora Neale Hurston**.
   b. Explain What role did *The Crisis* play in the **Harlem Renaissance**?
   c. Evaluate Why do you think there were so few published African American writers prior to the Harlem Renaissance?

Critical Thinking

4. **Sequence** Copy the chart below and place events in the chapter in the diagram to complete the sequence of events.

FOCUS ON WRITING **ELA** W1.1

5. **Persuasive** Write a letter to a publisher urging him or her to publish more African American writers. Write your letter as if you are living in the 1920s. Use information from the section to support your argument.

SECTION 3
A New Popular Culture Is Born

BEFORE YOU READ

MAIN IDEA
New technologies helped produce a new mass culture in the 1920s.

READING FOCUS
1. How did mass entertainment change in the 1920s?
2. Who were the cultural heroes of the 1920s?
3. How was the culture of the 1920s reflected in the arts and literature of the era?

KEY TERMS AND PEOPLE
D. W. Griffith
Charlie Chaplin
Charles A. Lindbergh
transatlantic
Amelia Earhart
F. Scott Fitzgerald
George Gershwin

HSS 11.5.6 Trace the growth and effects of radio and movies and their role in the worldwide diffusion of popular culture.

HSS 11.5.7 Discuss the impact of new technologies and the resulting prosperity and effect on the American landscape.

HSS 11.8.8 Discuss forms of popular culture, with emphasis on their origins and geographic diffusion (e.g., jazz and other forms of popular music, professional sports, architectural and artistic styles).

How did one movie revolutionize the movie industry? In the 1920s, Americans by the millions flocked to movie theaters to watch films. For most of the decade these films were silent. Printed words on the screen narrated the story and gave the dialogue.

Then in 1927 filmgoers watched in awe and amazement as actor Al Jolson appeared on screen, moved his lips to speak, and the words "You ain't heard nothin' yet!" came right out of his mouth.

▼ *The Jazz Singer* premiered at Warners' Theatre in New York City.

The Jazz Singer Talks

That sentence was one of only a few spoken lines of dialogue in the film, called *The Jazz Singer*. The movie also included many songs and the traditional onscreen printed explanations of events. But to the moviegoing public, the "talkies" had arrived. *The Jazz Singer* was a huge success and made millions of dollars for its producers. It also helped change the movie industry forever. As you will read, the introduction of sound in movies was one of the major developments in a decade of enormous change in American popular culture.

Mass Entertainment in the 1920s

The American people have always sought ways to entertain and inform themselves. In the 1920s, new media created whole new types of entertainment. These technologies were able to reach a growing share of the nation's population. Increasingly, people all across the country were sharing the same information and enjoying the same pastimes. A new American popular culture was emerging.

Radio One driving force in the development of this popular culture was the radio. During the 1920s, this device went from being a little-known novelty to being standard equipment in the American home.

Guglielmo Marconi invented radio in the late 1800s. In the early 1900s the military and ships at sea used the technology to aid in communications. Radio was also popular with a small number of hobbyists around the country. As the 1920s dawned, however, few Americans owned a radio. No regular programming was on the airwaves for people to listen to.

Radio's breakthrough occurred in 1920. In that year a radio hobbyist living near Pittsburgh, Pennsylvania, began to play records over his radio. His audience was made up of the small but growing number of people with radios within range of his equipment.

The growing popularity of these simple broadcasts caught the attention of the Westinghouse Company, which manufactured radios. Westinghouse realized that more people would buy its product if there was good programming on the airwaves. In October 1920 Westinghouse started the first corporate radio station in the United States. The station's call letters were KDKA. The station played music and provided news—including the results from the 1920 presidential election.

KDKA was quickly joined by hundreds of radio stations across the nation. By 1922 the United States had 570 stations broadcasting all types of programming. Listeners enjoyed music, news, and broadcasts of religious services and sporting events. Children tuned in to hear bedtime stories.

Technical improvements in radios increased their popularity. A new device called the vacuum tube greatly increased the quality of radio sound. Radios became portable with the invention of battery-powered units.

Like the automobile, the radio helped break down barriers that had once separated country people from city folk. Now Americans everywhere could hear the same news and listen to the same music. They heard the same advertisements and bought the same products. In short, the radio helped create a shared culture that included a growing number of Americans.

Movies Movies were another form of mass entertainment that exploded in popularity during the 1920s. Several factors explain this development. One was a change in the type of films available to viewers. In earlier years

ACADEMIC VOCABULARY
media forms of communication

Mass Media in the 1920s

Radio was a smashing success. By the end of the decade, about 13 million households tuned into the airwaves. Print media reached a wide audience, too. Some 202 million periodicals (right) and 92 million newspapers were in circulation by 1929.

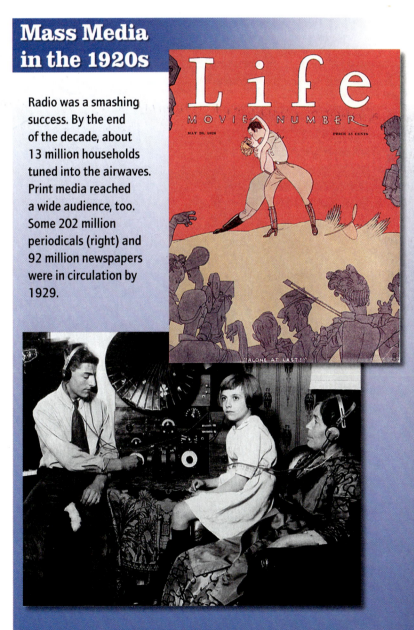

309

THE IMPACT TODAY

Daily Life
Movies help diffuse popular culture worldwide. American films are translated into foreign languages and widely distributed overseas, often reaching much larger audiences than in the United States.

most movies were short, simple pieces. During World War I, however, filmmaker **D. W. Griffith** produced the powerful *The Birth of a Nation*. This film's content was, and still is, highly controversial. By standards then and today, it includes themes and images that many people consider racist. Yet the film's impact on the movie industry is undeniable. *The Birth of a Nation* introduced many advanced filmmaking techniques. It helped establish film as an art form and widened the audience for movies. Viewers included President Woodrow Wilson. "It's like writing history with lightning," he is said to have remarked after a screening of the movie.

Another important movie innovation of the 1920s was the introduction of films with sound. In 1928, a year after the release of *The Jazz Singer*, a filmmaker named Walt Disney released an animated film called *Steamboat Willie*. It featured a character named Mickey Mouse, and a new type of movie star—a cartoon character—was born.

The popularity of the movies was enormous. By the end of the decade, experts estimated that Americans bought 100 million tickets a week. At the time, the entire population of the United States was about 123 million people. As with radio, movies provided the nation with a shared experience.

READING CHECK **Comparing** What qualities did movies and radio have in common?

An Era of Heroes

The great popularity of movies in the 1920s helped to create a new type of celebrity: the movie star. Indeed, the 1920s produced a whole new group of heroes for Americans to follow. The public responded with enthusiasm.

Film stars One of the brightest stars of the 1920s was the silent film actor **Charlie Chaplin**. Millions loved his signature character, a tramp with ragged clothes and a derby hat.

Rudolph Valentino was also a superstar of the silent movies. This dashing leading man made his name in romantic films such as *The Sheik*. When he died unexpectedly in 1926, tens of thousands of women visited the funeral home where his body lay.

Like Valentino, Clara Bow became a movie sex symbol. Nicknamed the "It Girl," she starred in a number of films that helped her build a highly popular image. Actress Mary Pickford was beloved as "America's Sweetheart." She was married to Douglas Fairbanks Jr., a major star of swashbuckling action films. Their magnificent home, called Pickfair, was located in Hollywood, California, the center of the motion picture industry.

Lucky Lindy On May 21, 1927, a small, single-engine airplane touched down on an airfield in Paris, France. In the cockpit was a lone pilot, **Charles A. Lindbergh**. Thirty three and one-half hours earlier, he had taken off from a muddy airfield in New York on a nonstop flight across the Atlantic Ocean.

Several pilots had attempted this daring <mark>transatlantic</mark> flight, but no one had succeeded—until Lindbergh. With his triumph, Lindbergh achieved what one newspaper called "the greatest feat of a solitary man in the history of the human race."

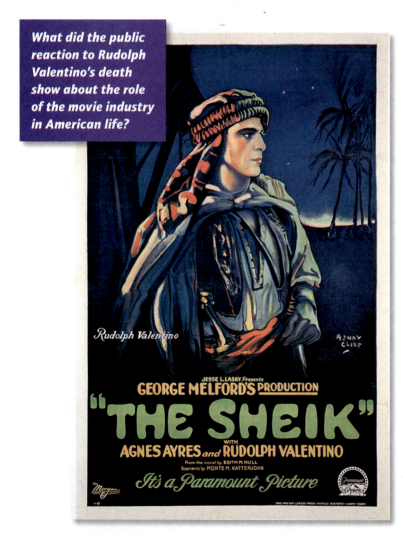

What did the public reaction to Rudolph Valentino's death show about the role of the movie industry in American life?

The Spirit of St. Louis

Lindbergh modified the *Spirit of St. Louis* for his transatlantic flight. He lightened the aircraft as much as he could to compensate for the weight of the fuel needed for the long voyage. He even replaced the leather pilot's seat with a wicker one.

Because he placed the main fuel tank in front of the pilot's seat, Lindbergh needed a periscope to see ahead.

Extra fuel tanks occupied the cabin space.

The wingspan was increased to accommodate the weight of the fuel.

Lindbergh became perhaps the most beloved American hero in an era of heroes. There were many reasons for his popularity. Young, tall, and handsome, Lindbergh simply looked like a hero. His down-to-earth, humble manner seemed to represent many of the qualities Americans admired. A true pioneer, he had triumphed alone against overwhelming odds. He had achieved his goal with a powerful combination of skill, daring, and determination.

The public adoration of Lindbergh was astounding. Songwriters published hundreds of songs about him and his flight.

HISTORY'S VOICES

> "Lucky Lindy, up in the sky
> Fair or windy,
> He's flying high
> Peerless, fearless, knows every cloud,
> The kind of a son makes a mother feel proud."
> —"Lucky Lindy!" by L. Wolfe Gilbert and Abel Baer, 1927

Before attempting his famous flight, Lindbergh had won some fame as a daredevil pilot. He had practiced his skills working as an airmail pilot, a dangerous job that had claimed the lives of 31 of the first 40 pilots employed in the service. When he learned about a $25,000 prize for the first aviator to fly nonstop between New York and Paris, he resolved to win. He rejected the commonly held belief that this flight would require a large plane with multiple engines. Instead, he developed a single-engine craft with room for only one pilot. Then he removed every ounce of unnecessary weight and added as much gasoline as the plane could carry.

The myth of Lindbergh was not far from the reality. He truly was a courageous man who risked much to expand the nation's frontiers.

Amelia Earhart A little over a year after Lindbergh's famous flight, **Amelia Earhart** became the first woman to fly across the Atlantic. She too returned to the United States as a hero. Earhart went on to a legendary career as a pilot in which she set a number of speed and distance records. In 1937 she was most of the way through another record-breaking attempt—a flight around the world—when she disappeared over the Pacific Ocean. No definitive trace of her remains has ever been found.

Sports heroes The American people's fascination with movie stars was matched in the 1920s by their devotion to sports heroes.

THE IMPACT TODAY

Technology
On March 3, 2005, millionaire Steve Fossett landed his Virgin Atlantic GlobalFlyer at the Kansas airport where he had taken off 67 hours before, becoming the first person to fly nonstop, solo, around the world without refueling. Fossett flew 23,000 miles (36,800 kilometers).

Sports Heroes of the 1920s

◀ The "Galloping Ghost" swept like a shadow across college football fields. Red Grange turned professional after college—a bit shocking for the time.

▶ Helen Wills played powerful tennis, winning 31 major tournaments and two Olympic gold medals. Nerves of steel earned her the nickname "Little Miss Poker Face."

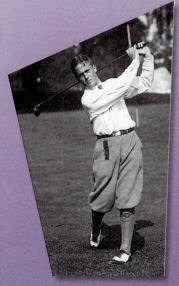

◀ Bobby Jones won golf's first Grand Slam—that is, he won the game's four major tournaments. He remains the only golfer to earn a Grand Slam for tournaments won in the same calendar year.

▶ The "Sultan of Swat," Babe Ruth, was legendary on the field for his home runs.

Radio helped inflame public passion for sports. Americans by the millions tuned in to broadcasts of ballgames and prize fights. Millions more attended events in person. In the process, American athletes were the top performers among the most famous and wealthy individuals in the world.

READING CHECK **Identifying the Main Idea** What types of heroes did Americans idolize in the 1920s?

Arts of the 1920s

The 1920s was a decade of great economic and social change. These themes offered novelists a rich source of material. You have read already about the writers of the Harlem Renaissance. A number of other American authors produced important works in this decade.

F. Scott Fitzgerald may be the writer most closely linked with the 1920s. His works include stories such as "Bernice Bobs Her Hair," which helped create the image of the flapper, and *Tales of the Jazz Age*, which provided a lasting nickname for the decade. His novel *The Great Gatsby* explored the lives of the rich and critically examined the values of the wealthy.

Sinclair Lewis's novel *Babbitt* also underscored the costs of success in America. Unlike Fitzgerald's glamorous characters, however, Lewis's Babbitt illustrated the emptiness of middle-class life.

HISTORY'S VOICES

❝He was forty-six years old now, in April, 1920, and he made nothing in particular, neither butter nor shoes nor poetry … He who had been a boy very credulous of life was no longer greatly interested in the possible and improbable adventures of each new day.❞
—Sinclair Lewis, *Babbitt*, 1922

Edna St. Vincent Millay wrote beautiful poetry that ranged from celebrations of youthful spirit to concern over leading social issues of the day. For example, she was deeply involved in the effort to prevent the executions of Italian immigrants Sacco and Vanzetti, which you read about earlier.

Women also held a prominent place in the field of fiction writing. Willa Cather and Edith Wharton produced some of the era's most notable works of literature.

World War I had a deep impact on American writers, including Ernest Hemingway and John Dos Passos. Both were war veterans, and both wrote powerfully about their experiences. Hemingway's *A Farewell to Arms* and Dos Passos's *Three Soldiers* are major works of the era. Hemingway and Dos Passos were also included among the so-called Lost Generation. The term, invented by writer Gertrude Stein, referred to the group of American writers who chose to live in Europe following World War I. It included F. Scott Fitzgerald, who lived part time in Paris in the 1920s.

Some literature celebrated the booming business and popular culture of the time period. In 1925 advertising executive Bruce Barton published *The Man Nobody Knows*. In it, he compared the biblical figure of Jesus to a modern-day business executive. Hard-driving business and advertising, Barton argued, was consistent with Christianity.

George Gershwin was another writer, but of music rather than of literature. He is especially remembered for his composition *Rhapsody in Blue*. This orchestral piece showed the powerful impact of jazz music, which was gaining great popularity in the 1920s. Gershwin is also beloved for his popular songs, many of which were written with his brother, Ira.

READING CHECK **Contrasting** How did the writings of Fitzgerald and Lewis differ?

PRIMARY SOURCES

The Great Gatsby

F. Scott Fitzgerald published *The Great Gatsby* in 1925. The novel details the selfish, reckless, and ultimately meaningless lives of the very rich—an image that became associated with the Jazz Age. Here he describes a party on a Long Island estate.

"By seven o'clock the orchestra has arrived, no thin five-piece affair, but a whole pitful of oboes and trombones and saxophones and viols and cornets and piccolos, high and low drums. The last swimmers have come in from the beach now and are dressing upstairs; the cars from New York are parked five deep in the drive, and already the halls and salons and verandas are gaudy with primary colors, and hair shorn in strange new ways … The bar is in full swing, and floating rounds of cocktails permeate the garden outside, until the air is alive with chatter and laughter, and casual innuendo and introductions forgotten on the spot, and enthusiastic meetings between women who never knew each other's names."

Skills Focus READING LIKE A HISTORIAN

1. **Drawing Conclusions** What details indicate showy excess at the party?
2. **Interpreting Literature** What message is Fitzgerald conveying about the Jazz Age?

See **Skills Handbook**, p. H28–H29

SECTION 3 ASSESSMENT

HSS 11.5.6, 11.5.7, 11.8.8

Reviewing Ideas, Terms, and People

1. **a. Recall** What two major developments in mass entertainment took place in the 1920s?
   b. Make Generalizations How did the development of mass entertainment affect American culture?
   c. Evaluate Do you think the new mass entertainment would have a greater effect in urban areas or in rural ones?

2. **a. Identify** Briefly describe the significance of the following: Charlie Chaplin, Charles A. Lindbergh, Amelia Earhart
   b. Make Inferences What can you infer from the fact that some 300 songs were written about Lindbergh's 1927 flight?
   c. Rate Judge which of the heroes discussed in this chapter had the most lasting influence on life in the United States.

3. **a. Identify** Briefly describe the contributions of the following: F. Scott Fitzgerald, George Gershwin
   b. Contrast Contrast the points of view of Sinclair Lewis and Bruce Barton as described in the section.
   c. Evaluate Why do you think economic and social changes in the 1920s affected American literature?

Critical Thinking

4. **Support the Main Idea** Copy the diagram below. Complete the diagram using details that support the main idea.

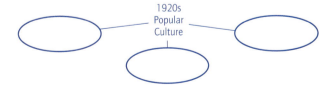

FOCUS ON WRITING ELA W1.1, 1.3

5. **Persuasive** Write an advertisement for a radio. The ad should seek to persuade potential buyers of the possible benefits of owning a radio in the 1920s.

THE ROARING TWENTIES **313**

CHAPTER 10 DOCUMENT-BASED INVESTIGATION

The 1920s Flapper

Historical Context The documents below provide different perspectives on new fashions of the 1920s. As you read in this chapter, some young American women of the era were captivated by new trends in nightlife, fashion, and music.

Task Examine the documents and answer the questions that follow. Then you will be asked to write an essay about American reactions to new styles in the 1920s, using facts from the documents and from this chapter to support the position you take in your thesis statement.

HSS 11.10.7

DOCUMENT 1

Well-known poet Dorothy Parker lived from 1893 to 1967. Her poetry is known for its witty, quotable lines and its insightful social criticism. Below is the first stanza of Parker's poem "The Flapper." You will notice the French phrase *au contraire*, which means "on the contrary" or "just the opposite."

> The Playful flapper here we see,
> The fairest of the fair.
> She's not what Grandma used to be, –
> You might say, au contraire.
> Her girlish ways may make a stir,
> Her manners cause a scene,
> But there is no more harm in her
> Than in a submarine.

DOCUMENT 2

Not all women during the 1920s were flappers, and not everyone was captivated by the flapper lifestyle. Below is an excerpt from a 1923 commentary in a newspaper called *The New York World*.

> There is nothing inspiring in seeing an extremely tired pretty girl in a worn bathrobe, dingy white stockings in rolls about scruffy felt slippers, her eyes held shut, her arms hung over her partner's shoulders, drag aching feet that seemed glued to the floor in one short, agonizing step after another, dancing to the sounds of what they call jazz . . .

DOCUMENT 3

John Held Jr. was an artist and cartoonist who is best known for his cartoons depicting the flappers of the 1920s. Below is a cover from *Life* magazine. The woman shown here is dressed in typical flapper style, with short (bobbed) hair, a loose dress, and heavy makeup.

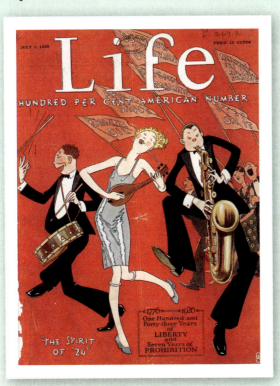

DOCUMENT 4

This 1925 article was printed in a magazine called *The New Republic*. The author describes a 19-year-old woman named Jane who dresses in the flapper style. Part of the article is an interview with Jane, in which she describes her reasons for dressing the way she does.

> Jane's a flapper. That is a quaint, old-fashioned term, but I hope you remember its meaning....
> Let us take a look at the young person as she strolls across the lawn of her parents' suburban home, having just put the car away after driving sixty miles in two hours. She is, for one thing, a very pretty girl. Beauty is the fashion in 1925. She is frankly, heavily made up, not to imitate nature, but for an altogether artificial effect—pallor mortis [deathly paleness], poisonously scarlet lips, richly ringed eyes . . .
> "In a way," says Jane, "it's just honesty. Women have come down off the pedestal lately. They are tired of this mysterious-feminine-charm stuff. Maybe it goes with independence, earning your own living and voting and all that."

Skills Focus — Reading Like a Historian
HSS Analysis HI1, HI3

1. **a. Identify** Refer to Document 1. What does the line "She's not what Grandma used to be" tell you about the differences between flappers and women of previous generations?
   b. Analyze Does the poem present a positive or negative view of the flapper?

2. **a. Describe** Refer to Document 2. What activity is this passage criticizing?
   b. Analyze What is the main argument the writer makes against the flapper lifestyle?

3. **a. Describe** Refer to Document 3. Name three characteristics of the woman in the cartoon.
   b. Interpret What message does this cartoon present about flappers?

4. **a. Describe** What does Jane look like?
   b. Judge Do you think flapper fashions were connected to women's growing independence? Why or why not?

5. **Document-Based Essay Question** Consider the question below and form a thesis statement. Using examples from Documents 1, 2, 3, and 4, create an outline and write a short essay supporting your position.
   Did American reactions to flappers in the 1920s reflect tensions between old attitudes and new trends?

See **Skills Handbook**, pp. H31, H32

CHAPTER 10 Chapter Review

Visual Summary: The Roaring Twenties

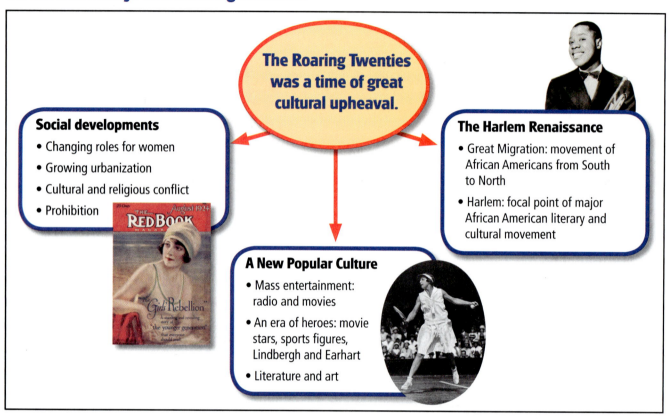

Reviewing Key Terms and People

Match each numbered definition with the correct numbered item from the list below.

a. African American literary flowering during the 1920s

b. a system of religious belief based on a strict interpretation of the Bible

c. pilot whose solo crossing of the Atlantic Ocean made him a national hero

d. the large-scale movement of African Americans from the South to the North in the early 1900s

e. founder of the Universal Negro Improvement Association (UNIA)

f. an African American woman writer who produced novels and many works of nonfiction

g. the lawyer who defended John Scopes in the trial about teaching evolution in Tennessee schools

h. writer from the 1920s who wrote *The Great Gatsby*

i. term for the nation's experiment with outlawing the manufacture and sale of alcohol

j. a young woman of the 1920s who adopted a certain style of dress and behavior

1. Zora Neale Hurston
2. Marcus Garvey
3. Prohibition
4. Harlem Renaissance
5. Charles A. Lindbergh
6. Clarence Darrow
7. Great Migration
8. flapper
9. F. Scott Fitzgerald
10. fundamentalism

History's Impact video program
Review the video to answer the closing question: How did young Americans change society during the 1920s?

Comprehension and Critical Thinking

SECTION 1 (pp. 294–301) HSS 11.5.3, 11.10.7

11. **a. Recall** What was the significance of the fact that the 1920 census showed that the United States population was more urban than rural?
    b. Analyze Identify at least two events that represent the conflict over values taking place in America in the 1920s.
    c. Evaluate How was rising fundamentalism related to changing American values in the 1920s?

SECTION 2 (pp. 302–307) HSS 11.5.2, 11.5.5, 11.8.8

12. **a. Describe** How did the Great Migration relate to the development of the Harlem Renaissance?
    b. Draw Conclusions Why do you think so few African Americans had achieved literary success before the Harlem Renaissance?
    c. Evaluate Why was *renaissance* an appropriate term to describe what took place in Harlem in the 1920s?

SECTION 3 (pp. 308–313) HSS 11.5.6, 11.5.7, 11.8.8

13. **a. Identify** What effects did the development of radio and motion pictures have on American culture?
    b. Analyze Why did the development of mass culture contribute to the creation of widespread adoration of heroes, such as movie stars, sports figures, and Charles Lindbergh?
    c. Evaluate Why do you think Charles Lindbergh captured the imagination of the American people perhaps more than other heroes of the age?

Using the Internet

go.hrw.com
Practice Online
Keyword: SE7 CH10

14. American movies became incredibly popular during the 1920s, as films added sound and grew more sophisticated. Using the keyword above, do research to learn more about changes in American films during the 1920s. Then create an illustrated report that describes these changes, including references to important films, actors, and directors.

Analyzing Primary Sources HSS HR4

Reading Like a Historian During the 1920s radio went from being a little-known novelty to standard equipment in the American home. The photograph at right shows a family listening to their radio.

15. **Describe** How is this radio different from modern radios?

16. **Interpret** What does the placement of chairs and people around the radio suggest about its importance to the family?

Critical Reading ELA R2.2

Read the passage in Section 1 under the heading "Effects of Urbanization." Then answer the questions that follow.

17. Which of the following is true of rural America in the 1920s?
    A It was prospering economically.
    B It was losing population compared with urban America.
    C It was gaining population compared with urban America.
    D It was attracting millions of immigrants.

 ELA W1.1

Think about the following issue.

The 1920s in the United States was a time of much social change. To some people, rural America represented the traditional spirit of the nation, while cities represented changes that threatened traditional values.

18. **Assignment** Did the social changes of the 1920s threaten traditional American values? Write a short essay in which you develop your position on the issue. Support your point of view with reasoning and examples from your readings and studies.

THE ROARING TWENTIES 317

CHAPTER 11
1929–1933
The Great DEPRESSION Begins

THE BIG PICTURE The boom times of the 1920s had never reached into all sectors of the economy. Much of the prosperity rested on shaky foundations. In 1929 the economy's underlying weaknesses were exposed. The stock market collapsed, and the nation plunged into the worst economic depression in its history.

California Standards

History-Social Sciences

11.5 Students analyze the major political, social, economic, technological, and cultural developments of the 1920s.

11.6 Students analyze the different explanations for the Great Depression and how the New Deal fundamentally changed the role of the federal government.

Skills Focus — READING LIKE A HISTORIAN

Employees of the *Chicago Defender*, an African American newspaper, prepare food supplies to donate to needy families at Thanksgiving, 1931. Thousands of hungry, homeless, and jobless Americans had to rely on such generosity to survive the Great Depression.
Interpreting Visuals Do these workers seem to be victims of the Great Depression? Explain.

See **Skills Handbook**, p. H30

U.S.

World

March 1929
President Herbert Hoover takes office.

1929

August 1929
German dirigible *Graf Zeppelin* begins round-the-world flight.

History's Impact video program
Watch the video to understand the impact of the 1929 stock market crash.

October 29, 1929 Stock market crashes on "Black Tuesday."

1931 Drought that helps produce the Dust Bowl begins on the Great Plains.

June 1932 World War I veterans' "Bonus Army" sets up camp in Washington, D.C.

1931 Japanese army invades Manchuria.

1932 Ibn Saud proclaims himself king of newly created Saudi Arabia.

January 1933 Adolf Hitler becomes chancellor of Germany.

SECTION 1: The Great Crash

BEFORE YOU READ

MAIN IDEA
The stock market crash of 1929 revealed weaknesses in the American economy and helped trigger a spreading economic crisis.

READING FOCUS
1. What economic factors and conditions made the American economy appear prosperous in the 1920s?
2. What were the basic economic weaknesses in the American economy in the late 1920s?
3. What events led to the stock market crash of October 1929?
4. What were the effects of the crash on the economy of the United States and the world?

KEY TERMS AND PEOPLE
gross national product
Herbert Hoover
buying on margin
Federal Reserve System
Black Tuesday

HSS 11.5.1 Discuss the policies of Presidents Harding, Coolidge, and Hoover.

HSS 11.6.1 Describe the monetary issues that gave rise to the establishment of the Federal Reserve and the weaknesses in the economy in the late 1920s.

HSS 11.6.2 Understand the causes of the Great Depression and the steps taken by the Federal Reserve, Congress, and President Herbert Hoover to combat the economic crisis.

Calm Before the Storm

THE INSIDE STORY

How did Americans behave on the eve of disaster? For many people in the 1920s, investing in the stock market was one big joyride. Week after week, month after month, stock prices steadily rose. After a while, it seemed like making money on Wall Street was a sure thing.

With so many fortunes being made, it was easy to ignore the warning signs that began to appear in the fall of 1929. The economy had began to slump. Consumers weren't buying as much. Products were piling up on factory floors. A handful of experts whispered that trouble lay in store for the stock market.

On Thursday, October 24, 1929, those whispers became reality. By the end of the day, the value of the stocks traded on the New York Stock Exchange had plunged by 9 percent. Years of investment gains—billions of dollars—were wiped out in a few hours.

Major banks and stockbrokers tried to rally the market on Friday. They bought large numbers of stocks, hoping to keep prices from dropping still more. Over the anxious weekend of October 26 and 27, stockbrokers worked quietly to reassure investors. They made phone calls and wrote letters to major investors urging them to buy stocks when the markets reopened on Monday. But nothing could answer the questions on everyone's minds. On Monday morning, which way would prices go—up or down? Were the good times about to come to an end?

▲ Stockholders anxiously gather outside the New York Stock Exchange after news of the crash on October 29, 1929.

An Appearance of Prosperity

The 1920s may not have been good times for everyone. Most farmers, for instance, saw their incomes drop. But for the economy as a whole, the "Roaring Twenties" were a period of impressive and sustained growth. Between 1922 and 1928, the **gross national product** (GNP)—the total value of goods and services produced in a nation during a specific period—rose by 30 percent. At a time when most people's understanding of the economic matters was relatively limited, such rapid growth triggered a feeling of optimism that proved contagious. That optimism, however, led to reckless activities.

The explosive growth of American manufacturing, particularly the new automobile industry, helped drive the expansion of the American economy. By 1929 one in five Americans owned a car. Industries that made products related to automobile production—including steel, oil, and rubber—enjoyed unprecedented business opportunities. Overall, the automobile industry and related industries employed nearly 4 million workers.

As corporate profits swelled, companies hired additional factory workers to keep up with production needs. Unemployment between 1923 and 1929 remained very low, averaging around 3 percent. Low unemployment, in turn, slowed the growth of organized labor. Union membership dropped as employers expanded welfare capitalism programs.

As you read earlier, welfare capitalism is a term for various benefits, such as employer-paid insurance, which companies provide to employees as a way of improving worker loyalty and satisfaction. Such programs helped increase workers' sense of prosperity and well-being in the 1920s.

This feeling of prosperity encouraged many workers to purchase the new products coming off the nation's assembly lines. With their shorter work hours and bigger paychecks, Americans flocked to movie theaters, sporting events, and other leisure activities. Times, it seemed, were good.

ACADEMIC VOCABULARY
specific particular

Stock market expansion
While Americans generally were feeling good about the economy in the 1920s, those who invested in the stock market were overjoyed. The stock market is a place where stocks are bought and sold. *Stock* is ownership in a company, and it is sold in *shares*. In other words, by buying shares of stock, a person is able to buy a piece of a corporation. If the corporation succeeds, its value may rise. This means that the value of its stock also rises. If the corporation does not do well, it may lose value. This would drive the value of the stock down.

The False Sense of Security
Positive economic trends masked the trouble that lay ahead.
- The stock market had been booming for a decade.
- Corporate profits soared.
- Unemployment was low.
- Welfare capitalism and credit increased workers' buying power.

The American stock market performed spectacularly during the 1920s. Although stocks increased at different rates, the general trend in stock prices was sharply upward. Between 1920 and 1929 the overall value of stocks traded at the nation's stock markets quadrupled.

The steep rise in stock prices changed the way many people thought about buying stocks. Since the market never seemed to go down in the 1920s, many people began to act as though it never would.

A growing number of ordinary Americans began to make stock investments. To *invest* means to put money into stocks, land, or some other location in the hope that the value of this money will grow.

The number of shares being traded in the United States rose sharply during the 1920s. The number rose from 318 million in 1920 to more than 1 billion in 1929. Many investors were encouraged by the words of men such as John Raskob, a leader of General Motors.

HISTORY'S VOICES

"If a man saves $15 a week and invests in good common stocks . . . at the end of 20 years, he will have at least $80,000 and . . . $400 a month. He will be rich. And because income can do that, I am firm in my belief that anyone not only can be rich, but ought to be rich."

—John J. Raskob, "Everyone Ought to Be Rich," *Ladies' Home Journal,* August 1929

Faith in business and government For many Americans, the prosperity of the 1920s demonstrated the triumph of American business. Presidents Harding and Coolidge favored policies that gave businesses the maximum freedom to achieve and succeed. As Coolidge once famously remarked, "The chief business of the American people is business."

This approach was popular with the majority of voters. Harding had won a clear victory in the 1920 election, and Coolidge did the same in 1924. Coolidge in particular remained widely popular throughout his term in office. Public confidence in the federal government and in its pro-business policies remained very high.

The election of 1928 Coolidge decided not to run for reelection in 1928, so the Republicans chose **Herbert Hoover** as their candidate. Hoover had never held elective office, but he had an impressive record of public service. He had overseen America's food production during World War I and later directed relief efforts in Europe. He also served as the secretary of commerce under Harding and Coolidge.

By 1928 Hoover had built an outstanding reputation as a businesslike administrator—just the sort of leader who could guide the prosperous nation. Indeed, people thought so highly of Hoover that it troubled him. "They have a conviction that I am sort of superman, that no problem is beyond my capacity," he once said. "If some unprecedented calamity should come upon the nation . . . I would be sacrificed to the unreasoning disappointment of a people who expected too much."

Hoover and the Democratic candidate, Al Smith, presented the nation with a stark contrast. Smith was an outgoing and natural politician. Hoover was quiet and shy by comparison. Smith was a Catholic—the first ever to run for president—and drew much of his support from Catholic urban immigrant

THE ELECTION OF 1928

Candidate	Political Affiliation	Electoral Votes	Popular Votes
Herbert C. Hoover	Republican	444	21,391,381
Alfred E. Smith	Democratic	87	15,016,443

GEOGRAPHY SKILLS INTERPRETING MAPS

The nation was experiencing an era of prosperity under a Republican administration during 1928 presidential election.

Region Most of the nation voted for the candidate of what party affiliation? In what region was Smith's support concentrated?

See **Skills Handbook**, p. H20

populations. Hoover was a Quaker, and many of his supporters did not trust Catholics. His support was strongest in small towns.

The two men also differed on Prohibition. Smith supported alcohol sales, while Hoover supported Prohibition. In short, the contest represented many of the cultural conflicts that had divided the nation in the 1920s. Hoover won an easy victory.

READING CHECK **Identifying Cause and Effect** How did the rise of the stock market affect American investors?

Economic Weaknesses

The economic prosperity of the 1920s helped define the decade. Yet while many Americans celebrated their financial good fortune, a number of serious problems bubbled just beneath the surface.

Wealth distribution One troubling aspect of the American economy was the vastly uneven distribution of the new wealth that was being created. Despite the boom in business in the 1920s, a surprisingly small number of people had truly prospered. As a group, the wealthiest 1 percent of the population had seen their share of the national income grow 60 percent between 1920 and 1929. Most workers, however, experienced much smaller pay increases—about 8 percent for most job categories.

Workers in certain industries, such as farming and coal mining, were hit particularly hard. By 1929 more than 70 percent of the nation's families had an income below the level they needed for a good standard of living. The personal savings rate declined noticeably during the decade as well.

For much of the decade, the easy availability of credit had allowed many Americans to buy the automobiles, radios, vacuum cleaners, and other products rolling quickly off the nation's assembly lines. By the end of the decade, however, many consumers were reaching the limits of their credit. The pace of purchases slowed. Warehouses became filled with factory goods that no one could afford to buy.

Credit and the stock market Installment credit was not just a tool for buying consumer products. Investors also used credit to purchase

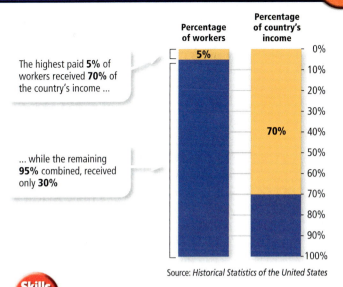

DISTRIBUTION OF WEALTH, 1929

The highest paid **5%** of workers received **70%** of the country's income ...

... while the remaining **95%** combined, received only **30%**

Source: *Historical Statistics of the United States*

Skills Focus **INTERPRETING GRAPHS**

The 1920s prosperity was more illusion than reality. The uneven distribution of the nation's wealth is shown in this bar graph. *What share of the nation's wealth did the top 5 percent of workers own? What did the remaining 95 percent own?*

See **Skills Handbook**, p. H16

stocks. This risky practice increased during the 1920s as the stock market rose sharply.

Here is how it worked: Imagine an investor wanted to buy 100 shares of stock in Company A at $10 a share. The total purchase price would be $1,000. To make this purchase, the investor would pay just a portion of the $1,000—say, for example, $500. The investor would borrow the other $500 from a stockbroker. The understanding was that the investor would pay off the loan when he or she sold the stock. Buying stocks with loans from stockbrokers is known as **buying on margin.**

As enthusiasm for investing in the stock market grew, brokers began to require lower and lower margins for stock purchases, giving bigger and bigger loans to investors. In 1929 an investor could purchase a stock with as little as a 10 percent margin. In a time when many stocks were gaining value by the day, margin buying seemed like an easy way to make money.

Buying on margin, however, involved enormous risks. Returning to the example of Company A, say its stock price rose to $15 a share. The investor then could sell the stock

THE GREAT DEPRESSION BEGINS **323**

for $1,500. In this case, the investor would get back the original $500 investment, be able to repay the $500 loan, and still have a $500 profit—doubling the original investment. But if the stock price dropped to $5 a share, the sale then would bring in just $500. All of this would go to pay off the loan. The investor would have no profit and be out the original $500 as well.

The terms of a margin loan made the gamble even riskier for the investor. Under these terms, brokers could force investors to repay their loans if the stock's value fell below a certain point. Such a demand was called a margin call. In theory, margin calls ensured that brokers would get their loans repaid. Margin calls also meant that investors could be in big trouble if their stocks lost value suddenly.

The Federal Reserve The nation's fascination with stocks and with buying on margin drew the concern of the governing board of the **Federal Reserve System**, which serves as the nation's central bank. The Federal Reserve Board takes actions and sets policies to regulate the nation's money supply in order to promote healthy economic activity. In the late 1920s, the Federal Reserve Board decided to make it more difficult and more costly for brokers to offer margin loans to investors.

The Federal Reserve's move was partly successful, at least at first. Borrowing from banks by brokers began to decrease, but it was replaced by money from a new source. Large American corporations began providing brokers with the cash to make margin loans to investors. As a result, the run-up of the stock market continued despite the Federal Reserve's actions.

In September 1929, economist Roger Babson sounded a warning note. "Sooner or later," he said, "a crash is coming, and it may be terrific." The crash he was anticipating was a sudden drop in stock prices, which could devastate those who had borrowed heavily to buy stock.

Many experts, however, dismissed Babson's worries. In October, banker Charles E. Mitchell responded to the warnings of people such as Babson. Mitchell said, famously, "I see no reason for the end-of-the-year slump which some people are predicting." He could not have been more wrong.

READING CHECK **Summarizing** What were some of the weaknesses of the economy in the 1920s?

THE IMPACT TODAY
Economics
Today the Federal Reserve Board places strict limits on the practice of buying on margin.

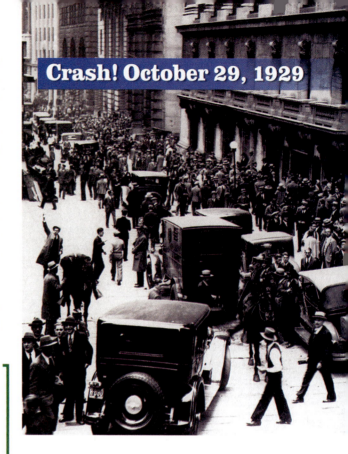

Crash! October 29, 1929

The Stock Market Crashes

While Babson and Mitchell were making their contrasting predictions about the future of the stock market, American investors looked back on several years of fantastic success. The steady growth of the early and mid-1920s had given way to truly astounding gains as the decade neared its end. One leading measure of the market's value showed a 50 percent gain in 1928 alone. During the following year, 1929, the market gained another 27 percent before reaching its high point on September 3.

Many people in the financial world, however, were beginning to recognize increasing signs of trouble in the economy. Sales of some manufactured goods were sagging badly. Rumors spread that some big investors were getting ready to take their money out of the market. Fears began to grow that current stock prices could soon collapse. The stage was set for an economic disaster.

On Thursday, October 24, 1929, some nervous investors began selling stocks. As others noticed the increased activity, they joined in the selling, afraid to be left behind. A huge sell-off had begun. With few people willing to buy the millions of stocks flooding the market,

Weaknesses in the general economy, combined with unsound financial practices, set the stage for the stock market crash. Worried investors (at left) crowded Wall Street on Black Tuesday to await news.

CAUSES OF THE 1929 STOCK MARKET CRASH

Economic Factors
- Poor distribution of wealth
- Many consumers relied on credit
- Credit dried up
- Consumer spending dropped
- Industry struggled

Financial Factors
- Stock markets rise in mid-1920s
- Speculation in stock increases
- Margin buying encouraged by Federal Reserve policies
- Stock prices rise to unrealistic levels

↓

Stock Market Crash

---

stock prices plunged, triggering an even greater panic to sell. One newspaper described it as "the most terrifying stampede of selling ever experienced on the New York Stock Exchange."

HISTORY'S VOICES

❝Traders on the floor of the Stock Exchange shrieked and howled their offers for desperate minutes before they found takers. Such a roar arose from the Stock Exchange floor that it could be heard for blocks up and down Broad and Wall Streets.❞
—*Seattle Post-Intelligencer,* October 25, 1929

Toward the end of this terrible day, a number of leading bankers joined together to buy stocks and prevent a further collapse in their prices. This effort succeeded in stopping the panic—for a time. The market returned to normal trading on Friday, and some stocks actually gained value.

When traders returned to work on Monday, however, the good feelings from Friday had completely evaporated. As trading began that day, the market sank like a stone. The next day—Tuesday, October 29—was the worst of all. As panic completely overcame the markets, investors dumped more than 16 million shares of stock. While the sell-offs of earlier days had affected mainly the stocks of weaker businesses, the collapse on Black Tuesday affected the stock of even the most solid companies.

The damage was widespread and catastrophic. During October, the stock market dropped in value by about $16 billion. This represented nearly one-half of the market's pre-crash value.

"It was like a thunderclap," one investment banker recalled. "Everybody was stunned."

Devices called ticker-tape machines communicated a steady stream of falling stock prices. One reporter described the scene on October 29 as horrified investors watched the ticker tape.

HISTORY'S VOICES

❝[T]he crowds about the ticker tapes, like friends about the bedside of a stricken friend, reflected in their faces the story the tape was telling. There were no smiles. There were no tears either. Just the camaraderie of fellow-sufferers. Everybody wanted to tell his neighbor how much he had lost. Nobody wanted to listen. It was too repetitious a tale.❞
—*The New York Times,* October 30, 1929

READING CHECK **Sequencing** Briefly describe the events of the stock market crash from October 24 through October 29, 1929.

Gross National Product In the aftermath of the crash, U.S. GNP fell by nearly one half—from $103.1 billion in 1929 to $55.6 billion in 1933.

Banking Crisis The stock market crash triggered a banking crisis. By 1933 more than 5,000 banks had shut their doors.

World Economy The effects of stock market crash rippled through the world economy. In Germany, industrial productivity plunged by more than 40 percent.

Fallen on Hard Times
A Wall Street speculator (above) tries to sell his car after losing his wealth in the stock market crash. Margin calls left many such investors desperate for cash. *What other effects did the stock market crash have on individuals?*

The Granger Collection, New York

The Effects of the Crash

In the aftermath of the crash, business and political leaders rushed to calm the panic and reassure the nation. One business executive wrote optimistically in the days following Black Tuesday, "The recent collapse of stock market prices has no significance as regards the real wealth of the American people as a whole." President Hoover also downplayed the effects of the crash. He and many others firmly believed that the economy would soon recover from the shock and return to prosperity.

The impact on individuals No one denied, however, that the stock market collapse had ruined many individual investors. Some had lost years of gains. Huge fortunes disappeared before their eyes.

Margin buyers were particularly hard hit. When stock prices began to fall, brokers demanded that they pay back the borrowed money. To meet these margin calls, investors were forced to sell their shares for far less than they had paid for them. Some lost their entire savings trying to make up the difference. In the end, investors often owed enormous amounts of money to their brokers for stocks they had been forced to sell below cost.

Effects on banks The stock market crash triggered a banking crisis. Frightened depositors rushed to withdraw their money, draining banks of funds. Worse, many banks had themselves invested, directly or indirectly, in the stock market. They had purchased stock in companies whose shares were now crumbling in value. In addition, banks had made loans to stockbrokers, who in turn had loaned the money to investors on margin. When individual investors failed to cover their margins, the banks absorbed losses, too.

These loan failures eventually drove many banks out of business. As you will read in the next section, the struggles of the banks would have a deep impact on the American people.

326 CHAPTER 11

Effects on business The crash delivered a crushing blow to already struggling businesses. With money scarce, banks and investors were suddenly unwilling or unable to provide industry with the money it needed to grow and expand.

At the same time, consumers cut back their spending on everything but essential purchases. With consumers spending less, many companies began to lay off workers. Unemployed workers had even less money to make purchases, and the cycle of layoffs and reduced consumer spending accelerated quickly.

In the year that followed the great crash, Americans saw their wages drop by a total of $4 billion. Nearly 3 million people lost their jobs. Faced with an uncertain future and lower incomes, consumers, who had driven the prosperity of the 1920s, simply stopped spending.

Effects overseas The crisis that began in the United States soon rippled throughout the industrialized world. The fragile economies of Europe, still recovering from World War I, were thrown backward. American banks that had lent heavily to European businesses and governments now called in those loans.

In many cases businesses and governments alike simply did not have the money to pay back the loans. Moreover, with buying power down in the United States, foreign businesses were less able to export their products here. They responded by laying off workers. Just as in the United States, laying off workers in Europe meant that there was less money in the hands of consumers to buy products.

Governments in the United States and in countries around the world moved to protect their own industries by passing high tariffs. A high tariff would make imported goods more expensive than those made at home. Leaders in each country hoped that high tariffs would benefit their local manufacturers.

Unfortunately, the high tariff actually did more harm than good to the American and world economies. As you will read, the decline in world trade that took place in the 1930s created misery around the world. It was one of the several factors that contributed to the nation's slide into what came to be called the Great Depression.

READING CHECK **Identifying Cause and Effect** How did the stock market crash affect banks?

THE IMPACT TODAY
Economics
Today an international organization called the World Trade Organization (WTO) oversees many trade agreements between nations. Its goal is to reduce trade barriers such as tariffs.

SECTION 1 ASSESSMENT

HSS 11.5.1, 11.6.1, 11.6.2

Reviewing Ideas, Terms, and People

1. **a. Define** Write a brief definition for the following term: gross national product
   b. Identify Cause and Effect What effect did America's mood have on individuals' financial decisions?
   c. Evaluate Defend the widespread American investment in stocks in the 1920s.

2. **a. Recall** Name two signs of weakness in the American economy in the 1920s.
   b. Analyze Why is it significant that much of the nation's wealth was owned by a small number of people?
   c. Predict How might the lack of available credit hurt the nation's economy in the 1930s?

3. **a. Identify** What was Black Tuesday?
   b. Sequence Describe how the drop in the stock market brought ruin to so many investors.
   c. Elaborate Why would an investor who had not bought stocks on margin have been in a better position to survive the crash than one who had?

4. **a. Describe** How did the crash affect individual investors, brokers, and banks?

   b. Summarize Why did the stock market crash have such a powerful impact on the overall economy?
   c. Evaluate Defend Hoover's belief that the economy would soon recover.

Critical Thinking

5. **Understanding Cause and Effect** Copy the chart below and use information from the section to identify effects of the stock market crash on the American economy.

FOCUS ON WRITING ELA W1.1

6. **Persuasive** Write a letter to a friend in which you urge him or her to be careful about making stock market investments. Use information from the chapter to support your position.

SECTION 2
Americans Face Hard Times

BEFORE YOU READ

MAIN IDEA
The Great Depression and the natural disaster known as the Dust Bowl produced economic suffering on a scale the nation had never seen before.

READING FOCUS
1. How did the Great Depression develop?
2. What was the human impact of the Great Depression?
3. Why was the Dust Bowl so devastating?

KEY TERMS AND PEOPLE
hobo
Great Depression
foreclosure
Hooverville
drought
Dust Bowl
Okie
Woody Guthrie

HSS 11.6.2 Understand the principal causes of the Great Depression and the steps taken to combat the crisis.

HSS 11.6.3 Discuss the human toll of the Depression, natural disasters, and unwise agricultural practices on the depopulation of rural regions and on political movements, with particular attention to the Dust Bowl refugees and their social and economic impacts in California.

Teenage HOBOES

THE INSIDE STORY

Where do you go when you have no place to go? Some of them decided on their own to leave home. Others were told to leave by their parents because there simply was no money to care for them. In either case, tens of thousands of teenagers faced a stark reality during the Great Depression. They had to find their future on the road.

At the height of the Great Depression, as many as a quarter of a million teenagers were wandering the nation, riding the railroads from town to town. With no families to support or protect them, they joined the ranks of the jobless, homeless wanderers known as **hoboes**.

For the young hoboes of the Depression—boys and girls, black and white, some less than 16 years old—the daily task was to survive. The lucky ones found or formed communities with other homeless people, who were primarily adults. The unlucky ones fell prey to abuse and violence.

Young women often disguised themselves as boys in order to reduce the dangers they faced. African Americans often had the threat of racial violence added to the hardships of the road.

Homeless teenagers riding the rails or walking the back roads became a familiar sight in the years of the Great Depression. Along with millions of others, they formed part of the human face of the economic catastrophe that followed the crash.

◀ Thousands of youths experienced the grim life of a hobo.

The Development of the Great Depression

With the crash of the stock market, the boom times of the 1920s came to an end. The crash and its aftermath revealed serious flaws in the American economy. These flaws helped transform a stock market crisis into the Great Depression, the most severe economic downturn in the history of the United States.

Bank failures As you have read, the collapse of the stock market strained the financial resources of many banks. In the weeks following the crash, a number of those banks failed. For ordinary Americans, the collapse of banks was an especially unnerving new development. Most people did not have money invested in stocks, but many had entrusted their savings to banks.

Today, most Americans do not have to worry that they will lose their savings if their bank goes out of business. Insurance from the federal government protects most people's deposits in the event of bank failure. In addition, laws today require that a bank keep a greater percentage of its assets in cash, to be paid out to depositors on request.

In 1929 there was no such deposit insurance, and with little cash on hand, banks were vulnerable to "runs." A run occurred when nervous depositors, suspecting a bank might be in danger of failing, rushed to withdraw their savings. A run could quickly drain a bank of its cash reserves and force the bank to close.

In the months following October 1929, bank runs struck across the country. Hundreds of banks failed. In late 1930 the rate of failures turned from frightening to disastrous. In December alone almost 350 banks closed. Included was the enormous Bank of the United States, which once had boasted about 400,000 depositors. By 1933 U.S. bank failures had wiped out billions of dollars in savings, on top of losses from the stock market crash.

Farm failures The hard times farmers had faced in the 1920s only worsened with the onset of the Great Depression. Widespread joblessness and poverty reduced Americans' ability to buy food. Many people simply went hungry. With farmers producing more than they could sell, farm prices sank. By 1933 prices were down more than 50 percent from their already low 1929 levels. Lower prices meant lower income for farmers.

ACADEMIC VOCABULARY
asset financial holdings or resources

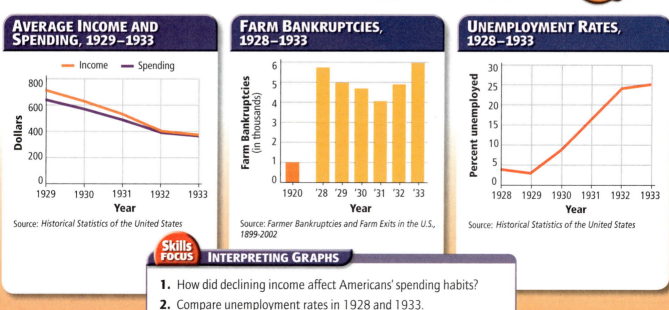

Economic Impact of the Great Depression

Interpreting Graphs

1. How did declining income affect Americans' spending habits?
2. Compare unemployment rates in 1928 and 1933.

See Skills Handbook, p. H16, H17

It was typical for farmers to borrow money from banks to pay for land and equipment. As their incomes dropped, many farmers were unable to make the payments on their loans. In 1933 alone, some 364,000 farms went bankrupt or suffered foreclosure. **Foreclosure** occurs when a bank or other lender takes over ownership of a property from an owner who has failed to make loan payments.

Unemployment The year following the crash of October 1929 saw a sharp drop in economic activity and a steep rise in unemployment. Such negative trends are not uncommon in a time of economic downturn. What made the Great Depression different was the extent and the stubborn duration of these trends.

By 1933 the gross national product had dropped more than 40 percent from its pre-crash levels. Unemployment reached a staggering 25 percent. In some places and among some groups, the number was even higher. In the African American neighborhood of Harlem in New York City, for example, unemployment reached 50 percent in 1932.

READING CHECK **Making Generalizations** What happened to the economy in the early 1930s?

The Human Impact of the Great Depression

The Great Depression was an economic catastrophe. Yet statistics tell only part of the story. The true measure of the disaster lies in how it affected the American people.

Hoovervilles and hoboes With millions of people out of work, the competition for jobs became fierce. Thousands of workers would apply for a handful of jobs, and the winners knew they were lucky.

HISTORY'S VOICES

"I'd get up at five in the morning and head for the waterfront. Outside the Spreckles Sugar Refinery, outside the gates, there would be a thousand men. You know dang well there's only three or four jobs. The guy would come out … 'I need two guys for the bull gang. Two guys to go into the hole.' A thousand men would fight like a pack of Alaskan dogs to get through there."

—Ed Paulson, quoted in Studs Terkel's *Hard Times*

For millions of Americans during the Great Depression, the loss of a job meant a quick slide into poverty. To survive, some people begged from door to door. Unable to provide food for

HISTORY CLOSE-UP

Life in a Hooverville

As desperate poverty engulfed people from coast to coast, many formed makeshift communities that they nicknamed Hoovervilles.

The lack of running water and power made tasks such as cooking and cleaning much more difficult and messy.

Most male residents of Hoovervilles had been used to a life of work. For many, idleness led to deep feelings of uselessness and despair.

themselves, some relied on soup kitchens or breadlines—or simply went without.

In the early 1930s, no federal government programs provided food or money to the poor. Local charities and some municipal and state governments provided relief, but these programs were unable to meet the need. In 1932 only 1 in 4 families needing unemployment relief received it.

With no jobs or income, many Americans lost their homes. Property owners evicted tenants who couldn't pay rent, and banks foreclosed on homeowners. In many communities, sprawling neighborhoods of shacks sprang up on the outskirts of town or in public parks to house the newly homeless. These shantytowns came to be known as **Hoovervilles**. This was a bitter reference to President Hoover, whom many people blamed for the Great Depression.

On the streets of America's great cities, some unemployed workers took to selling apples. Charging a nickel an apple, a seller might earn $1.15 on a good day. In the fall of 1930 more than 6,000 unemployed workers sold apples on the streets of New York City alone.

Other Americans took to the road in search of work. Hoboes hopped trains to travel from town to town, often taking their lives in their hands. Not only was boarding a moving train very dangerous, it was also illegal. Many railroads hired "bulls," or guards, to chase hoboes off the trains.

Wherever hoboes went, finding food was a constant challenge. Townspeople often had little food to spare. Approaching homes to beg or steal, hoboes were sometimes met with violence. Across the country, hoboes developed a system of sign language to alert each other to good opportunities—and warn of possible dangers—in a particular town or home.

Most hoboes were men. Many had left behind families that they could no longer care for. During the Great Depression, some families simply broke apart under the strains of poverty and homelessness.

The emotional toll The greatest toll of the Great Depression may have been on the minds and spirits of the American people. Even though millions of people shared the same fate, many of the unemployed saw their situation as a sign of a personal failure. Accepting handouts deeply troubled many proud Americans.

"Shame? You tellin' me?" recalled one person who lived through the Depression. "The only scar it left on me was my pride, my pride." The

MUSEUM OF THE CITY OF NEW YORK

For people living in a Hooverville, reminders of their former homes and the lives they used to lead often were important. Here, pictures provide a touch of beauty to an otherwise grim environment.

Hooverville shacks were generally thrown together with whatever building materials could be found. They were often leaky and drafty.

INTERPRETING INFOGRAPHICS

Hoovervilles, like this one in New York, were cobbled together with whatever people could salvage.

Drawing Conclusions What hardships might the men in this photograph have endured?

See **Skills Handbook**, p. H18

The Dust Bowl

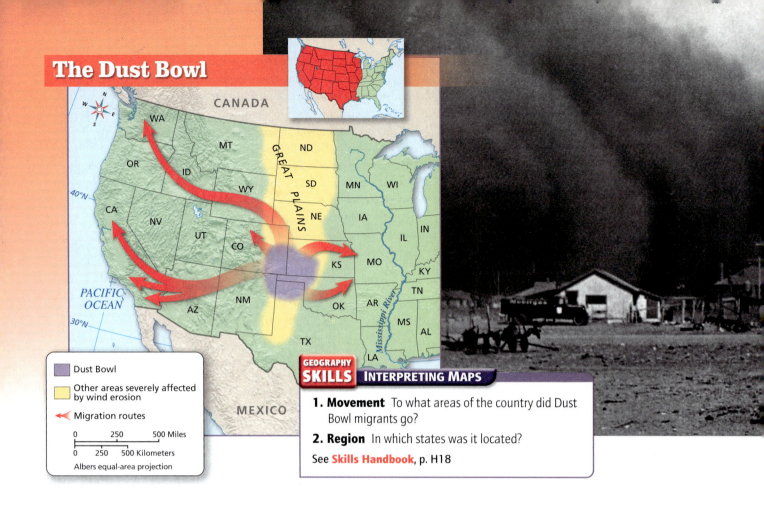

GEOGRAPHY SKILLS INTERPRETING MAPS

1. **Movement** To what areas of the country did Dust Bowl migrants go?
2. **Region** In which states was it located?

See **Skills Handbook**, p. H18

grim despair people felt was reflected in a rise in suicide rates in the early 1930s.

Other people were simply angry. There was a widespread feeling that the nation had failed its hardworking citizens. One popular song of the era summed up the mixture of defiance and shame this way:

HISTORY'S VOICES

❝Once I built a railroad, I made it run, made it race against time,

Once I built a railroad; now it's done. Brother, can you spare a dime?❞

—"Brother, Can You Spare a Dime,"
Yip and Gorney Harburg, 1931

READING CHECK **Summarizing** In what ways did the Great Depression affect many Americans?

Devastation in the Dust Bowl

In the midst of the economic disaster, nature delivered a cruel blow. Around 1931 much of the Great Plains region entered a long, severe dry spell. This **drought**, or period of below-average rainfall, lasted for several years. By the time it lifted, millions of people had fled the area.

The great dust storms Drought is a part of a weather cycle, naturally occurring on the Great Plains every few decades. By the 1930s, however, careless agricultural practices had left the region vulnerable. Land once covered with grasses now lay bare to the sky with no vegetation to hold the soil in place.

When wind storms came, they stripped away the topsoil and blew it hundreds of miles away. In some of the worst storms, dust reached as far as the Atlantic Coast. Drifting mounds of dust choked crops and buried farm equipment. The fine dust blew into homes through drafty windows and under doors. Year after year, storms came and wreaked destruction. The hardest hit area—including parts of Oklahoma, Kansas, Colorado, New Mexico, and Texas—became known as the **Dust Bowl**.

Fleeing the Plains The terrible drought and dust storms robbed many farmers of their livelihood. Some simply packed up what little they had and moved. By the end of the 1930s, about 2.5 million people had left the Great Plains states. Many headed west along Route 66 to California, where they settled in camps and sought work in farms and orchards.

Pitch-black dust storms, like this one in Springfield, Colorado, drove people out of the Plains on migration routes shown by the arrows on the map. Decades of farming had removed the natural vegetation that had held the soil in place.

The plight of the migrants captured the imagination of some of America's greatest writers and artists, including author John Steinbeck and singer-songwriter **Woody Guthrie**. Guthrie's songs about the Dust Bowl describe the disaster's effect on the people it touched.

ACADEMIC VOCABULARY

plight bad situation

HISTORY'S VOICES

> It's a mighty hard row my poor hands have hoed;
> My poor feet have traveled this hot dusty road
> Out of your dustbowl and westward we rolled,
> Your desert was hot and your mountains were cold.
> I've worked in your orchards of peaches and prunes,
> Slept on the ground by the light of the moon
> On the edge of your city you've seen us and then,
> We come with the dust and we're gone with the wind.
>
> —Woody Guthrie, "Pastures of Plenty"

Guthrie's lyrics speak to the hardships and struggles not only of the migrants who left the Dust Bowl but also of all Americans hit hard by the Great Depression. For much of the decade the Depression seemingly defied most government efforts to defeat it. The American people were forced to fend for themselves.

The migrants were called **Okies**, after the state of Oklahoma. The term was inaccurate, since the migrants came from a number of different states. It was also meant to be insulting. The Great Plains migrants were often met by resistance and outright discrimination.

READING CHECK **Identifying the Main Idea** How did the Dust Bowl affect Americans?

SECTION 2 ASSESSMENT

HSS 11.6.2, 11.6.3

Reviewing Ideas, Terms, and People

1. **a. Identify** Briefly describe the **Great Depression** and its main effects.
   b. Explain What is the significance of the fact that there were few government relief programs in the early 1930s?
   c. Predict How do you think the federal government will respond to the Great Depression?
2. **a. Define** Write a brief definition for the following term: Hooverville
   b. Make Inferences What can you infer from the fact that the shantytowns of homeless Americans came to be known as Hoovervilles?
   c. Predict What do you think the political effect of the Great Depression on President Hoover will be? Explain.
3. **a. Identify** Who were the **Okies**?
   b. Compare How were the Okies similar to **hoboes**?
   c. Elaborate Do you think those affected by the Dust Bowl were victims of nature or responsible for their own fate?

Critical Thinking

4. **Understand Cause and Effect** Copy the chart below and use information from the section to identify effects of the Great Depression.

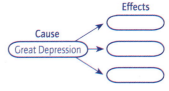

FOCUS ON WRITING ELA W1.1

5. **Expository** Write an essay in which you describe the causes and effects of the Great Depression. Use details from the section to support your account.

American Literature

JOHN STEINBECK (1902–1968)

About the Reading Drought, dust storms, and new technology combined to displace tenant farmers during the 1930s. In his Pulitzer Prize-winning 1939 novel *The Grapes of Wrath*, John Steinbeck tells the story of the Joads, a family who lost everything during the Great Depression. Like many other families, the Joads begin migrating from Oklahoma toward California in search of work and a fresh start.

AS YOU READ Think about the challenges facing farmers and their families as they leave their homes in search of new beginnings.

Excerpt from
The Grapes of Wrath
by John Steinbeck

The cars of the migrant people crawled out of the side roads onto the great cross-country highway, and they took the migrant way to the West. In the daylight they scuttled like bugs to the westward; and as the dark caught them, they clustered like bugs near to shelter and to water. And because they were lonely and perplexed, because they had all come from a place of sadness and worry and defeat, and because they were all going to a new mysterious place, they huddled together; they talked together; they shared their lives, their food, and the things they hoped for in the new country. Thus it might be that one family camped for the spring and for company, and a third because two families had pioneered the place and found it good. And when the sun went down, perhaps twenty families and twenty cars were there.

In the evening a strange thing happened: the twenty families became one family, the children were the children of all. The loss of home became one loss, and the golden time in the West was one dream. And it might be that a sick child threw despair into the hearts of twenty families, of a hundred people; that a birth there in a tent kept a hundred people quiet and awestruck through the night and filled a hundred people

Migrant workers, like this family on the road in California's San Joaquin Valley in 1935, were the lowest paid in the nation.

with birth-joy in the morning. A family which the night before had been lost and fearful might search its goods to find a present for a new baby. In the evening, sitting about the fires, the twenty were one. They grew to be units of the camps, units of the evenings and the nights. A guitar unwrapped from a blanket and tuned–and the songs, which were all of the people, were sung in the nights.

HSS 11.6.3

SKILLS FOCUS **READING LIKE A HISTORIAN**

Analyze Do you think Steinbeck was a social activist?

Literature as Historical Evidence In the 1930s many people believed that collective action could be more effective than individual action. How does the excerpt express that point of view?

See **Skills Handbook**, p. H32

SECTION 3
Hoover as President

BEFORE YOU READ

MAIN IDEA
Herbert Hoover came to office with a clear philosophy of government, but the events of the Great Depression overwhelmed his responses.

READING FOCUS
1. What was President Hoover's basic philosophy about the proper role of government?
2. What actions did Hoover take in response to the Great Depression?
3. How did the nation respond to Hoover's efforts?

KEY TERMS
associative state
Hoover Dam
cooperative
Reconstruction Finance Corporation
Smoot-Hawley Tariff Act

HSS 11.5.1 Discuss the policies of Presidents Warren Harding, Calvin Coolidge, and Herbert Hoover.

HSS 11.6.2 Understand the causes of the Great Depression and the steps taken by the Federal Reserve, Congress, and President Herbert Hoover to combat the economic crisis.

Hoover Seals his DOWNFALL

 How did a ragtag army help defeat President Hoover? In 1932 the United States was nearing the low point of the Great Depression. By now Americans had become used to scenes of homeless, jobless people camped out in cardboard shacks in public areas. But the group of some 15,000 World War I veterans who set up camp near the nation's capital in May 1932 was not just another group of men who were down on their luck.

These veterans had come to Washington for a reason. They were trying to put pressure on the federal government to pay them the veteran's bonus, a cash award they had been promised for their service during the war. The bonus, $1.25 for each day served overseas and $1 a day for U.S. service, was not supposed to be paid until 1945. But the men needed the money now, and they believed their request was fair.

The campers settled in, laying out orderly streets and sanitation facilities. As May turned to June, the numbers of so-called Bonus Marchers grew. When Congress failed to agree to their demands, some of the Bonus Marchers left town, but a core of them remained, along with women and children. In July police and U.S. Army soldiers began clearing the area of the veterans. Violence erupted, and soon the Bonus Marchers' main camp was in flames. Hundreds were injured, and two of the veterans were killed.

Many Americans were deeply disturbed by the sight of U.S. soldiers using weapons against homeless veterans. For President Herbert Hoover, who was already facing complaints that he did not care enough about the plight of the nation's poor, the impact was devastating. As you will read, the Bonus Marchers incident helped complete the public view of Hoover as heartless and helpless in the face of the nation's suffering.

▼ Bonus Army marchers from Columbus, Georgia, begin their trek to Washington, D.C.

Herbert Hoover's Philosophy

Herbert Hoover came to the presidency with a set of core beliefs that he had formed over a long career in business and government service. He knew just how he planned to run the country. Yet after less than a year in office, Hoover's plans were upset by the massive stock market collapse. In responding to the growing crisis, Hoover drew on his experience and on the core beliefs that had guided him.

THE IMPACT TODAY

Government
In modern times, Republican presidents from Ronald Reagan to George W. Bush have also sought to limit government regulation on businesses.

"Rugged individualism" Hoover had served in the administrations of both Warren G. Harding and Calvin Coolidge. He shared many of their ideas about the proper relationship among government, business, and the people. In short, he favored a federal government that played as little role as possible in the affairs of business.

Hoover believed that unnecessary government not only threatened prosperity but also dimmed the very spirit of the American people. A key part of this spirit was what he called "rugged individualism."

The Hoover Dam took 21,000 men five years to complete at a cost of $165 million. *How did the project exemplify the associative state?*

HISTORY'S VOICES

❝One of the great problems of government is to determine to what extent the Government itself shall interfere with commerce and industry and how much it shall leave to individual exertion... By adherence to the principles of... opportunity and freedom to the individual, our American experiment has yielded a degree of well-being unparalleled in all the world.❞

—Herbert Hoover, speech, October 1928

Hoover did not reject the idea of government oversight or regulation of certain business. Nor did he advocate letting people and businesses do exactly as they pleased. Yet he believed deeply that it was vital for the nation's well-being not to destroy people's belief in their own responsibility and power.

The associative state Individualism did not rule out cooperation in Hoover's view. Businesses, he believed, should form voluntary associations that would make the economy fairer and more efficient. Skilled government specialists would then "cooperate with these various associations for the accomplishment of high public purposes." Hoover had a term for his vision of voluntary partnerships between business associations and government. He called it the **associative state**.

As secretary of commerce in the Harding and Coolidge administrations, Hoover had put these beliefs into practice. He often called together meetings of business leaders and experts to discuss ways to achieve key national goals. He continued to call such conferences after he became president.

Hoover's beliefs were dramatically tested in the construction of what came to be called the **Hoover Dam**. The dam would harness the Colorado River to provide electricity and a safe, reliable water supply to a vast area that included parts of seven states. The federal government provided funding for the project, which was approved in the 1920s and built in the 1930s. A group of six independent companies joined together to design and construct it. For Hoover, the project's success demonstrated the creative power of partnerships between private business and the federal government.

READING CHECK **Identifying the Main Idea** Briefly describe the two key features of President Hoover's main beliefs about government.

Hoover's Response to the Great Depression

Hoover's core beliefs shaped many of his early actions as president. Government, Hoover believed, should not provide direct aid. It should find ways to help people help themselves.

Voluntary cooperation Hoover put these beliefs into practice before the stock market crash, when he looked for ways to assist the nation's struggling farmers. He pushed for a program of loans to create and strengthen farm cooperatives. A **cooperative** is an organization that is owned and controlled by its members, who work together for a common goal. The idea behind farmers' cooperatives was that large groups of farmers could buy materials such as fertilizer at lower prices than individual farmers could. Cooperatives also could help farmers market crops in ways that would raise crop prices and increase farmers' income.

After the stock market crash, Hoover continued to rely on his basic belief in voluntary action and cooperation between business and government. He called together many of the nation's top business and government leaders and urged them not to lay off workers or cut wages. If these groups cooperated, Hoover reasoned, workers would have plenty of money to spend on consumer goods, and the worst of the economic crisis would soon pass.

Direct action Unfortunately, the president found it difficult to rally cooperation. In the face of economic disaster, individuals made decisions according to their own economic interests. Businesses cut jobs and wages. State and local governments stopped their building programs, throwing many people out of work. Consumers stopped spending. As a result, the economy plunged into the Great Depression.

The growing crisis eventually persuaded Hoover to break somewhat with his beliefs. At his urging, Congress created in early 1932

PRIMARY SOURCES

Political Cartoon

Most Hoover officials believed the effects of the Great Crash would eventually ease without drastic government action. Treasury Secretary Ogden L. Mills was especially reluctant to fund relief programs. This cartoon appeared three weeks before the 1932 presidential election.

Treasury Secretary Ogden L. Mills attempts to reassure the driver, "U.S. public," that repairs are underway.

President Herbert Hoover, an engineer by training, is unsure how to put the car back together again.

"IT WON'T BE LONG NOW?" —By Jerry Doyle

READING LIKE A HISTORIAN

Interpreting Political Cartoons What message is the cartoonist trying to convey, and what details in the drawing support that message?

See **Skills Handbook**, p. H31

THE GREAT DEPRESSION BEGINS

ACADEMIC VOCABULARY
clause separate section of writing

the **Reconstruction Finance Corporation** (RFC). A key clause in the RFC legislation authorized up to $2 billion in direct government loans to struggling banks, insurance companies, and other institutions. Later that year, Hoover asked Congress to create the Federal Home Loan Bank. The new program encouraged home building and reduced the number of home foreclosures. These measures marked a historic expansion of the role of the federal government in the business of the American people. Still, for many citizens, Hoover's actions were too little, too late.

The Smoot-Hawley Tariff Act One of Hoover's major efforts to address the economic crisis backfired badly. In 1930 he signed the **Smoot-Hawley Tariff Act**. The new tariff raised the cost of imported goods for American consumers, making it more likely that they would purchase the cheaper American goods.

The Smoot-Hawley Tariff Act was a disaster. The tariff rates were set at historically high levels. When European nations responded with tariffs on American goods, trade plunged. By 1934 global trade was down roughly two thirds from 1929 levels.

READING CHECK **Summarizing** What actions did Hoover take to improve the economy during the Great Depression?

The Nation Responds to Hoover

Hoover had entered office believing that government should seek to avoid direct involvement in the lives of individuals and businesses. Under the pressure of events, he modified his beliefs and began to push for some forms of direct relief. In spite of his efforts, however, Hoover increasingly came under attack for his handling of the Great Depression.

The president loses favor Hoover's frequent optimistic claims about the economy slowly undermined his credibility with voters. Early in the crisis, as millions of people were losing their jobs, he proclaimed the basic economic foundation of the nation to be sound. "I am convinced," he told the nation, "that we have passed the worst." In fact, the worst was yet to come.

Hoover later spoke glowingly about the efforts being made to deal with the Depression. "Industry and business have recognized their social obligation," he said in February 1931. "Never before in a great depression has there been so systematic a protection against distress." Millions of jobless Americans did not share Hoover's assessment of the situation.

Worse, many Americans came to question Hoover's compassion. As economic conditions grew worse, his unwillingness to consider giving direct relief to people became harder and harder for Americans to understand. When Hoover finally broke with his stated beliefs and pushed for programs such as the Reconstruction Finance Corporation, many people wondered why he was willing to give billions of dollars to banks and businesses but nothing to individuals.

Bonus March The Bonus March incident further damaged Hoover's reputation. The photographs of armed soldiers fighting with unarmed, unemployed veterans deeply troubled many observers. As one newspaper of the time observed, "If the Army must be called upon to make war on unarmed citizens, this is no longer America."

Hoover's opposition to paying the Bonus Army marchers stemmed partly from a concern about the federal budget. Hoover believed that the government must have a balanced

FACES OF HISTORY
Herbert HOOVER
1874–1964

Few presidents have entered office seemingly as well prepared and qualified as Herbert Hoover, yet the Great Depression proved too great a challenge for him to master. As an engineer, successful businessman, and humanitarian, Hoover had never met a problem he could not solve through sheer brilliance and dogged hard work. But his failure to make headway against the Depression combined with his reluctance to provide public relief spelled electoral disaster.

Following his defeat, Hoover wrote books and continued to serve with distinction on various government commissions into the 1950s. His work streamling the executive branch for presidents Truman and Eisenhower demonstrated a still potent talent for administration.

Rate How did Hoover's performance as president compare with his earlier public service?

budget—that is, it must spend no more money than it takes in—in order to achieve financial health. To meet this goal, Hoover pushed for and got a large tax increase in 1932. At a time when people were suffering and asking for government relief, a larger tax burden was highly unpopular.

The voters react The 1930 midterm congressional elections provided an early sign that the public was growing dissatisfied with Hoover's policies. The Republican Party had controlled Congress during the boom years of the 1920s. In 1930, however, Democrats managed to win a majority of the seats in the U.S. House of Representatives. They also came within one seat of matching the Republicans in the Senate.

By the 1932 presidential election, it seemed certain that the voters would reject Hoover at the polls. The Great Depression showed little sign of ending, and Hoover's ability to influence events was nearly gone. The president didn't even bother campaigning until October, little more than a month before the election. The main question now was who the Democrats would pick to run against him, and what that candidate would do to end the nation's grief.

After Congress refused to approve payment to the Bonus Army marchers, stunned protestors began a "Death March" in front of the Capitol. Finally Hoover moved to disband the camp, and violence broke out. *How did the public respond?*

READING CHECK **Identifying Supporting Details** What were some actions—taken or not taken—that made voters believe Hoover did not care?

SECTION 3 ASSESSMENT

HSS 11.5.1, 11.6.2

Reviewing Ideas, Terms, and People

1. **a. Identify** What were two key ideas that helped shape Hoover's core beliefs?
   b. Compare In what ways were Hoover's basic beliefs similar to those of Presidents Harding and Coolidge?
   c. Evaluate What is your opinion about Hoover's belief in the importance of rugged individualism?

2. **a. Define** Write a brief definition for each of the following terms: **cooperative, Reconstruction Finance Corporation, Smoot-Hawley Tariff Act**
   b. Analyze How effective was President Hoover's preferred approach to government in responding to the hardships of the Great Depression?
   c. Rate Defend Hoover's commitment to avoiding direct relief to individuals.

3. **a. Describe** What was the general reaction of the American people to Hoover's performance?
   b. Contrast How did Hoover's core beliefs contrast with what many Americans wanted?

   c. Design What are some relief programs that Hoover's Democratic opponent might suggest?

Critical Thinking

4. **Understanding Cause and Effect** Copy the chart below and use information from the section to identify effects of Hoover's personal philosophy on government.

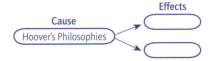

FOCUS ON WRITING ELA W1.1, 1.3

5. **Persuasive** Write a letter to the editor in which you either defend or criticize Herbert Hoover's approach to the stock market crash and the depression that followed. Use details from the section to support your position.

THE GREAT DEPRESSION BEGINS **339**

CHAPTER 11 DOCUMENT-BASED INVESTIGATION

Life During the Great Depression

HSS 11.6.3

Historical Context The documents below provide different types of information on the life during the Great Depression.

Task Examine the documents and answer the questions that follow. Then you will be asked to write an essay about life during the Great Depression, using facts from the documents and from the chapter you just read to support the position you take in your thesis statement.

DOCUMENT 1

During the Depression many families found themselves standing helplessly in lines to get donated food and clothing. A great many of these people never imagined they would be in such a situation. The photograph below shows people standing in a relief line in San Antonio, Texas, to receive aid.

DOCUMENT 2

Charities did what they could to help the needy, but it was often not enough. Social worker Nell Blackshear of Atlanta, Georgia, recalled the relief lines in her city and her experiences providing help to others through a government program.

"That was a sad time when there was a soup line. Men, women, and children would come and go through the soup line once a day—it was bad. They had a black soup line, of course. There was no such thing as just hungry people. Even on relief you had to remember that you were black and they were white. They would have hot soup and sometimes just coffee and bread that was donated from some of the bakeries . . .

[As part of a government program,] I had to buy milk for the families. Even had to buy clothes. We would take the mothers to the stores on Edgewood Avenue . . . We would buy the clothing, then order and pay for the coal, twenty-five-cent bags of coal.

I remember the rear of 210 Butler Street. This was a long tenement house. I would have to go get some groceries in the house, or take coal to give them to make a fire in those little rooms. Sometimes seven or eight people would live in one room. They had a communal toilet outside. It was a deplorable [horrible] sort of thing. And that's where our clients lived, this is the kind of relief and work with families that I started off doing."

DOCUMENT 3

Like African Americans, Asian Americans were targets of discrimination. In California, many Asian American communities were segregated from their white neighbors. They relied heavily on one another. During the 1930s many survived by sharing resources. The photograph at right shows Japanese American migrant workers picking broccoli in Guadalupe, California.

DOCUMENT 4

People showed remarkable generosity during the hard times. Kitty McCulloch, a young seamstress, recalled her experiences.

"There were many beggars, who would come to your back door, and they would say they were hungry. I wouldn't give them money because I didn't have it. But I did take them in and put them in my kitchen and give them something to eat.

One elderly man that had white whiskers and all, he came to my back door. He was pretty much of a philosopher. He was just charming. A man probably in his sixties. And he did look like St. Nicholas, I'll tell you that. I gave him a good, warm meal. He said, 'bring me a pencil and paper and I'll draw you a picture.' So he sketched. And was really good. He was an artist.

A man came to my door... He said, 'You don't suppose you could have a couple of shirts you could give me, old shirts of your husband's?' I said, 'Oh, I'm so very sorry, my husband hasn't anything but old shirts, really. That's all he has right now and he wears those.' He said, 'Lady, if I get some extra ones, I'll come back and give them to you.'"

Skills Focus — READING LIKE A HISTORIAN
HSS Analysis HI2, HI3

1. **a. Describe** Refer to Document 1. Describe the expressions on the people's faces.
   b. Elaborate How do you think these people felt about having to go on relief?

2. **a. Identify** Refer to Document 2. What did Blackshear do as part of her job with the government?
   b. Interpret What did Blackshear mean when she said, "There was no such thing as just hungry people?"

3. **a. Identify** Refer to Document 3. What are the people in the photograph doing?
   b. Analyze How do the field workers reflect the community spirit of Japanese Americans in the 1930s?

4. **a. Identify** Refer to Document 4. What were the beggars who came to McColluch's door seeking?
   b. Elaborate How did the beggars' responses to McColluch reflect the spirit of the times?

5. **Document-Based Essay Question** Consider the question below and form a thesis statement. Using examples from Documents 1, 2, 3, and 4, create an outline and write a short essay supporting your position.
   How did the Great Depression bring people together?

See **Skills Handbook**, p. H28–29, H30

CHAPTER 11 Chapter Review

Visual Summary: The Great Depression Begins

Great Depression Begins
- Stock market crashes; banks, businesses fail
- Widespread joblessness and suffering occur
- Drought and dust storms add to suffering

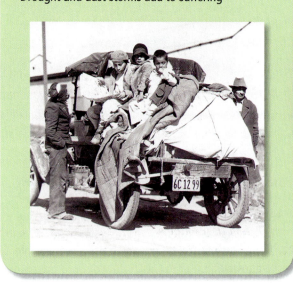

Hoover Responds
- Relies on cooperation, voluntary action
- Later begins using power of government
- Fails to curb spreading economic crisis

Reviewing Key Terms and People

Identify the correct term or person from the chapter that best fits each of the following descriptions.

1. The term for the decisive drop in the stock market at the end of October 1929
2. Hoover's vision of a partnership between private business associations and government
3. The nickname given to a settlement of homeless people during the Great Depression
4. An organization owned and controlled by its members, who work together for a common goal
5. A person who rode the railroads from town to town in search of work
6. The nickname given to refugees from the dust storms of the early 1930s
7. Law originally meant to protect American businesses but that ended up harming the United States and world economies
8. The nickname for the central Plains region struck by a terrible drought and dust storms in the 1930s
9. The widespread practice during the 1920s that increased the danger to investors from a drop in the stock market
10. An organization created by the Hoover administration to aid struggling banks
11. The central bank of the United States
12. A prolonged period of below-normal rainfall
13. What can happen to a home or farm when the owner fails to pay off loans taken to buy the property
14. A singer who described the effects of the Dust Bowl
15. the total value of goods and services produced in a nation during a specific period of time

342 CHAPTER 11

History's Impact video program
Review the video to answer the closing question: How do changes made after the 1929 stock market crash help protect the American economy today?

Comprehension and Critical Thinking

SECTION 1 (pp. 320–327) HSS 11.6.1, 11.6.2

16. **a. Recall** What was the general experience of investors in stocks in the United States in the mid-1920s?
    b. Explain How did the success of the American stock market also increase the dangers of investing in the market?
    c. Elaborate How did the collapse of the stock market come to hurt so many people who did not have money invested in stocks?

SECTION 2 (pp. 328–333) HSS 11.6.3

17. **a. Describe** How did the Great Depression affect ordinary Americans?
    b. Summarize How did victims of the Great Depression cope with the effects of homelessness and joblessness?
    c. Evaluate Why do you think so many people blamed themselves for their misfortune during the Great Depression, in spite of the fact that millions of Americans were in a similar situation?

SECTION 3 (pp. 335–339) HSS 11.5.1, 11.6.2

18. **a. Identify** What was President Hoover's basic belief about the proper relationship of citizens to their government?
    b. Analyze Why did the Great Depression greatly test Hoover and his fundamental philosophy about how to govern?
    c. Evaluate Do you think it was reasonable to expect Hoover to change his philosophy and tactics in response to the crisis the nation faced in the Great Depression? Explain.

Using the Internet

go.hrw.com
Practice Online
Keyword: SE7 CH11

19. The worst day of the Great Crash of 1929 was "Black Tuesday," October 29. During a catastrophic series of workdays preceding Black Tuesday, the American stock market lost nearly one half of its value. Using the keyword above, do research to learn more about what happened to the American economy in October 1929. Then create a report that traces the aftereffects of the stock market crash and explains how it quickly came to affect people throughout the nation, even those who had not invested in stocks.

Analyzing Primary Sources HSS HR4

Reading Like a Historian
This photograph shows an automobile being sold by an investor following the stock market crash of October 1929.

20. **Describe** What is the significance of the moment shown in this photograph?

21. **Draw Conclusions** What does this image tell you about how Americans were affected by the crash?

Critical Reading ELA R2.2

Read the passage in Section 1 that begins with the heading "An Appearance of Prosperity." Then answer the question that follows.

22. The heading "An Appearance of Prosperity" suggests that
    A. there was no prosperity in the United States at all.
    B. every American prospered in the 1920s.
    C. overall, the economy seemed to be performing very well.
    D. in fact, only the auto industry was performing well.

FOCUS ON WRITING ELA W1.1

Expository Writing *Expository writing gives information, explains why or how, or defines a process. To practice expository writing, complete the assignment below.*

Writing Topic Herbert Hoover's Response to the Great Depression

23. **Assignment** Based on what you have read in this chapter, write a paragraph that discusses why so many Americans were dissatisfied with Hoover's response to the Great Depression.

THE GREAT DEPRESSION BEGINS **343**

CHAPTER 12
1933–1940
The NEW DEAL

THE BIG PICTURE The New Deal was President Franklin D. Roosevelt's plan for overcoming the Great Depression. His plan gave government jobs to the unemployed and increased government regulation of the economy. Although New Deal programs achieved varied levels of success, they did represent a basic change in American society.

California Standards

History-Social Sciences

11.6 Students analyze the different explanations for the Great Depression and how the New Deal fundamentally changed the role of the federal government.

11.8 Students analyze the economic boom and social transformation of post–World War II America.

11.10 Students analyze the development of federal civil rights and voting rights.

 READING LIKE A HISTORIAN

Artist Ben Shahn painted this mural for the community center of Jersey Homesteads. The panel shown here celebrates the planning of the New Jersey town, which was built as part of a New Deal program for garment workers.
Interpreting Visuals Why do you think Shahn included a poster of Roosevelt among the symbols in the mural?

See **Skills Handbook**, p. H30

 U.S.

 World

March 1933 President Franklin Delano Roosevelt is inaugurated.

1933 | 1934

March 1933 Germans elect Adolf Hitler as chancellor.

History's Impact video program
Watch the video to understand the impact of the Tennessee Valley Authority.

August 1935 Congress passes Social Security Act.

December 1936 United Auto Workers stage a sit-down strike against General Motors.

July 1937 Farm Tenancy Act gives tenant farmers the opportunity to buy their own land.

October 1938 Radio broadcast of H.G. Wells's *The War of the Worlds* frightens listeners.

1935 — **1936** — **1937** — **1938** — **1939**

September 1935 Germany passes Nuremberg Laws, discriminating against Jews.

1936 Spanish Civil War begins.

1937 The German airship *Hindenburg* explodes at Lakehurst, New Jersey.

September 1938 Mexico nationalizes foreign oil companies.

1939 Germany invades Poland.

SECTION 1: Launching the New Deal

BEFORE YOU READ

MAIN IDEA
In 1933 Franklin Delano Roosevelt became president of a suffering nation. He quickly sought to address the country's needs, with mixed results.

READING FOCUS
1. What were the key events of the presidential election of 1932?
2. What was the nature of Franklin and Eleanor Roosevelt's political partnership?
3. What initial actions did Roosevelt take to stabilize the economy?
4. How did the New Deal run into trouble in Roosevelt's first term?

KEY TERMS AND PEOPLE
Franklin Delano Roosevelt
public works
fireside chat
Eleanor Roosevelt
Hundred Days
New Deal
subsidy
Huey P. Long
Father Charles Coughlin
Dr. Francis Townsend

HSS 11.6.2 Understand the steps taken by the Congress and Presidents Hoover and Roosevelt to combat the economic crisis.

HSS 11.6.4 Analyze the effects of and the controversies arising from New Deal policies.

HSS 11.8.5 Describe the increased powers of the presidency in response to the Great Depression.

▲ Roosevelt's "forgotten man" speech was as powerful as Maynard Dixon's 1934 painting of the same name.

THE INSIDE STORY

How did it feel to be a forgotten victim of the Great Depression?

Franklin Delano Roosevelt seemed to know. In 1932 Roosevelt was one of several candidates seeking the Democratic presidential nomination. Some critics dismissed him as "an amiable man... without very strong convictions." But in an April 1932 speech, Roosevelt took a strong stand. He criticized the policies of President Hoover as ineffective and wrongly directed at only the "top of the social and economic structure." By contrast, Roosevelt pledged to help the "forgotten man at the bottom of the economic pyramid." Only by helping these people, Roosevelt claimed, would the nation's economic ills be cured.

Roosevelt's speech included few specific proposals. Yet that did not seem to matter to the Depression-weary citizens reading his words or watching the newsreels at the movie houses. Here at last was someone who understood the plight of ordinary citizens. He remembered them, he cared about them, and he seemed to understand that their fate was key to the nation's recovery.

The personal connection Roosevelt established was something few Americans felt they had with Herbert Hoover. It would serve Roosevelt well in the months and years ahead.

The Election of 1932

The 1932 presidential election presented the Democrats with a great opportunity to recapture the White House for the first time in 12 years. With joblessness mounting and banks collapsing in record numbers, many Americans placed the blame squarely on President Hoover. Eager to unseat him, Democrats competed fiercely for their party's nomination. **Franklin Delano Roosevelt** emerged the victor.

Roosevelt's rise Franklin Roosevelt was a distant relative of former president Theodore Roosevelt. He had served as assistant secretary of the navy under Woodrow Wilson. He had also run unsuccessfully for vice president in 1920.

Soon after, the ambitious young politician was stricken with polio. The disease nearly killed him and left him without full use of his legs. Yet Roosevelt rebounded from that experience to become governor of New York in 1929. Many considered Roosevelt's record as governor impressive. He launched a groundbreaking relief program to aid the state's many victims of the Great Depression. By 1932 Roosevelt's program had provided help to 1 of every 10 New York families. His record stood in stark contrast to Hoover's insistence on limited government action.

The 1932 campaign During the campaign, Roosevelt offered some general ideas about what he would do as president. He promised relief for the poor and more **public works** programs—government-funded building projects—that would provide jobs. He also talked about lowering tariffs.

Mainly, though, Roosevelt attacked Hoover and the Republicans for their response to the Great Depression. "For at least two years after the crash," Roosevelt railed in an October 1932 speech, "the only efforts made by the national administration to cope with the distress of unemployment were to deny its existence." At the same time, Roosevelt criticized Hoover for spending too much money, and he promised to cut the federal budget. In general, his speeches laid out the case for change at the White House without tying him down to specific promises or policies.

Though Roosevelt's speeches were vague and sometimes contradictory, they alarmed Hoover. Considering the prospect of Roosevelt's election, he predicted disaster. "The grass will grow in the streets of a hundred cities," cried Hoover. "The weeds will overrun the fields of millions of farms."

A landslide victory Hoover's warnings failed to stir many voters. On election day, the voters handed Roosevelt a clear victory. Roosevelt received more than 57 percent of the popular vote and swept the electoral vote in all but six states. In addition, the Democrats gained 90 seats in the House of Representatives and 13 seats in the Senate to take control of both houses of Congress.

READING CHECK **Making Generalizations**
What was Franklin Roosevelt's campaign strategy in the election of 1932?

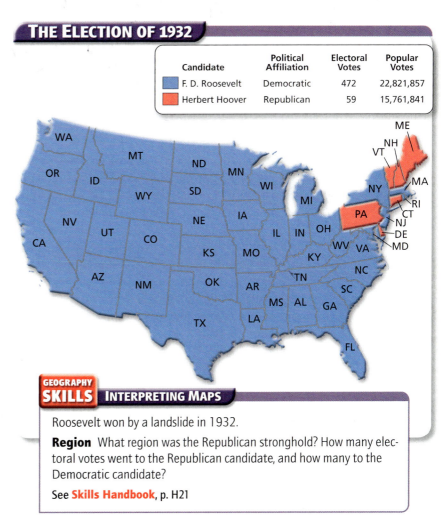

THE ELECTION OF 1932

Candidate	Political Affiliation	Electoral Votes	Popular Votes
F. D. Roosevelt	Democratic	472	22,821,857
Herbert Hoover	Republican	59	15,761,841

GEOGRAPHY SKILLS INTERPRETING MAPS

Roosevelt won by a landslide in 1932.

Region What region was the Republican stronghold? How many electoral votes went to the Republican candidate, and how many to the Democratic candidate?

See **Skills Handbook**, p. H21

THE NEW DEAL 347

FACES OF HISTORY

Franklin Delano ROOSEVELT
1882–1945

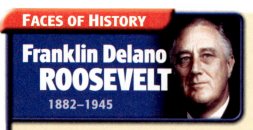

Raised in a wealthy New York family, Franklin Roosevelt had private tutors and traveled to Europe frequently. He won election in 1910 to the New York State Senate, but he resigned in 1913 to serve as President Wilson's assistant secretary of the navy.

Roosevelt's career seemed over when he contracted polio in 1921. With the help of his wife, Eleanor, Roosevelt returned to public service. In 1928 he won the race for governor of New York, serving during the early years of the Depression. His work in easing New Yorkers' suffering helped him win the 1932 Democratic presidential nomination.

Explain How did Roosevelt's experience in New York help him nationally?

A Political Partnership

As a politician, Roosevelt's greatest asset may have been his personality. He had an appealing blend of cheerfulness, optimism, and confidence. These qualities were illustrated by his response to the illness that had left him unable to walk without assistance.

Rather than giving in to his disability, Roosevelt had worked tirelessly to regain strength in his legs and to continue his public career. In this era before television, most Americans were unaware of Roosevelt's handicap. However, his personal struggle gave him a strength that many found very reassuring. In this way, Roosevelt took a personal challenge and turned it into one of his greatest political strengths.

Roosevelt also possessed a warmth and charm that made him an effective communicator. As president, he used the radio to great effect, particularly in his **fireside chats**. As the name suggests, these addresses were meant to sound as though Roosevelt were in the listener's living room, speaking personally with the family. He spoke calmly and clearly and in a way that ordinary people could understand. He conveyed real concern and gave reassurance to millions of troubled Americans.

"I never saw him," recalled one Depression survivor, "but I knew him." This ability to help people feel better during their time of hardship won Roosevelt lasting support with voters.

Roosevelt's philosophy As you have read, Roosevelt sent some unclear signals during his 1932 presidential campaign. Sometimes he attacked Hoover for not doing enough to fight the Depression—and sometimes for doing too much. At heart, however, Roosevelt was a reform-minded Democrat in the tradition of Woodrow Wilson and the Progressives who came before him.

As he had demonstrated as governor of New York, Roosevelt believed that it was the government's job to take direct action to help its people. His basic faith in the ability of government to solve economic and social problems and to help people in need ran deep.

HISTORY'S VOICES

> "I assert that modern society, acting through its Government, owes the definite obligation to prevent the starvation or the dire want of any of its fellow men and women who try to maintain themselves but cannot."
>
> —Franklin D. Roosevelt, Campaign Speech, October 13, 1932

Eleanor Roosevelt While still in law school, Franklin Roosevelt had married his distant cousin, **Eleanor Roosevelt**. Their marriage would play a central role in Franklin Roosevelt's political success.

Throughout her husband's career, but especially following his bout with polio in the 1920s, Eleanor served as her husband's "eyes and ears." With his mobility impaired, Franklin Roosevelt relied on his wife to collect and share information gained in her wide travels. He deeply valued his wife's keen insight.

In her own right, Eleanor became a powerful political force. She threw her energies into several major social issues, including the campaign to stop the lynching of African Americans. In the process, she helped change the role of First Lady.

During her husband's presidency, Eleanor began writing her own newspaper column, called "My Day." She received thousands of letters every week. These letters demonstrate the trust and affection many Americans held for the First Lady. They also revealed people's faith in her influence. "Thank you very much for helping me to keep my house," wrote one admirer. "If it wasn't for you, I know I would have lost it."

Not everyone was a fan of Eleanor Roosevelt and her active political role. She was a frequent target of the enemies of her husband's administration. Yet even her critics agreed that no First Lady had ever played such an important role in the government of the nation.

READING CHECK **Summarizing** What did President Roosevelt believe was the proper role of government in the lives of American citizens?

Roosevelt Takes Action

By the time Roosevelt was inaugurated in March 1933, four months had passed since the election. Hoover had struggled during that time to prevent a worsening of the economy. As the loser of the presidential race, however, Hoover had little power to accomplish anything. The crisis deepened.

Rescuing the nation's banking system presented the most immediate challenge facing Roosevelt when he took office. The problems facing the nation's banks had gotten so bad that when leaders gathered in Washington, D.C., for Roosevelt's March 4 inauguration, hotels would not accept checks from out-of-town guests. The hotels feared that the guests' banks might fail before the hotels were able to receive payment.

The banking crisis Roosevelt could see that the nation faced a critical loss of confidence. He wasted no time in addressing the situation. In his inaugural address, the new president sought to calm the public.

HISTORY'S VOICES

"So, first of all, let me assert my firm belief that the only thing we have to fear is fear itself—nameless, unreasoning, unjustified terror which paralyzes needed efforts to convert retreat into advance."

—Franklin D. Roosevelt, First Inaugural Address, March 4, 1933

Two days later, Roosevelt took action. The shaky state of the nation's banks had led many people to withdraw all their money from their accounts. They feared losing their savings if the bank collapsed. Such large-scale withdrawals could—and did—ruin even healthy banks. This created more panic, more withdrawals—and more bank failures. To stop this cycle, Roosevelt issued an executive order temporarily closing all of the nation's banks. The president called it a bank holiday.

Next, the president called Congress into emergency session and pushed through the Emergency Banking Act. The law gave government officials power to examine each bank,

"Hoover sent the army; Roosevelt sent his wife."
A World War I veteran

When a second Bonus Army came to Washington in 1933, Roosevelt sent Eleanor to investigate. Her tour of their camp in Virginia ended in a sing-along.

FACES OF HISTORY

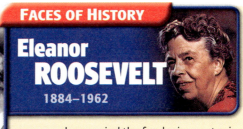

Eleanor ROOSEVELT
1884–1962

Orphaned at the age of 10, Eleanor Roosevelt was raised by her mother's relatives. A sad and shy teenager and a serious and scholarly young woman, she married the fun-loving, outgoing Franklin D. Roosevelt.

Eleanor grew into her roles in life, becoming one of the most respected women in America. With dynamic energy, she labored for charities, traveled the world making speeches, and spoke out for women's rights and against racial discrimination. After her husband died in office, Eleanor began a new chapter in life. She served as a delegate to the United Nations, chaired President John F. Kennedy's Commission on the Status of Women, and remained active in American politics.

Make Inferences What choices did Eleanor Roosevelt make in life, and what did those choices reflect about her character?

Relief, Reform, Recovery

determine its soundness, take steps to correct problems, and, if necessary, close it. To explain to the worried public what was going on, Roosevelt gave the first of his famed fireside chats.

The plan worked. Within days, banks began to reopen with government assurances that they were on solid footing. Ordinary people, who had been frantically taking money out of their banks, started to return funds. Some banks never did reopen, but the crisis was over. In just over a week, the nation had regained crucial confidence in its financial system.

In the days ahead, Congress enacted additional banking reforms. The Glass-Steagall Act of 1933 created the Federal Deposit Insurance Corporation, or FDIC. This provided government insurance for depositors' savings. Individual depositors no longer needed to fear losing their savings if their bank collapsed.

Reassured by the new law, even more depositors took the money they had stuffed in home safes and under their mattresses and returned it to the banking system. Within a month, about $1 billion in new deposits flowed into the system.

The Hundred Days The resolution of the banking crisis was just the beginning of a critical period of government activity that came to be known as the **Hundred Days**. During this time, Roosevelt pushed Congress to put in place many of the key parts of his program—what he called the **New Deal**.

Roosevelt first used the phrase in a campaign speech in which he promised "a new deal for the American people." The New Deal came to include a wide range of measures aimed at accomplishing three goals:

(1) *relief* for those suffering the effects of the Great Depression;

(2) *recovery* of the depressed economy;

(3) *reforms* that would help prevent serious economic crises in the future.

The Civilian Conservation Corps, or CCC, was typical of the reform programs passed during the Hundred Days. Established in March 1933, it sought to address an immediate problem: unemployment among young men 18 to 25 years old.

Americans enrolled in the CCC were paid to work on a variety of conservation projects, such as planting trees and improving parks. CCC workers lived in army-style camps and were required to send most of their earnings to their families.

Two key recovery programs sought to reinforce the twin pillars of the economy—agriculture and industry. The Agricultural Adjustment Act, or AAA, gave farmers a **subsidy**, or government payment, to grow fewer crops. A smaller

Civilian Conservation Corps workers replant a clear-cut Oregon hillside with seedlings in 1939 (left). The CCC brought immediate relief to families and provided work for 3 million young men. Businesses following fair-practice business codes displayed the NRA's blue eagle emblem (above).

supply of crops on the market would increase demand for those crops. This would drive prices up and help farmers earn more.

The National Industrial Recovery Act (NIRA) mandated that businesses in the same industry cooperate with each other to set prices and levels of production. In the days of Theodore Roosevelt, government had viewed such cooperation as a violation of antitrust laws. Now, with the NIRA, government sought to promote it as a way of helping business.

The NIRA also included $3.3 billion for public-works programs. These were managed through a new agency called the Public Works Administration, or PWA. (The New Deal was famous for creating an "alphabet soup" of government agencies known by their initials.) Labor unions benefited, too, from the NIRA. For the first time, labor got federal protection for the right to organize.

The Federal Securities Act emerged as a major reform effort of the Hundred Days. The measure forced companies to share certain financial information with the public. The purpose was to help investors and to restore confidence in the fairness of the markets.

In 1934 Congress established the Securities and Exchange Commission. The SEC would serve as a government watchdog over the nation's stock markets.

One of the most far-reaching and ambitious programs of the New Deal was the Tennessee Valley Authority, or TVA. Created in May 1933, this massive program was charged with developing the resources of the entire Tennessee River Valley, a vast region in the Southeast United States.

The TVA built dams and other projects along the Tennessee River and its tributaries. These dams controlled floods, aided navigation and shipping along the river, and provided hydroelectric power to be used by industries. (See the History and Geography feature on the TVA at the end of this section.)

Beyond the Hundred Days President Roosevelt had campaigned promising action and "bold, persistent experimentation." He had delivered. Many Americans applauded his efforts. Journalist and former Roosevelt critic Walter Lippmann wrote, "In the hundred days from March to June we became again an organized nation confident of our power."

Amid the successes, there was also much to criticize. Even Roosevelt admitted in a fireside chat, "I do not deny that we make mistakes." Comparing himself to a baseball player, he said, "I have no expectation of making a hit every time we come to bat."

Yet FDR and the Congress kept trying, passing significant legislation in the period after the Hundred Days. In November 1933, for example, the Civil Works Administration (CWA) was created. This agency provided winter employment to 4 million workers. CWA crews built miles of highways and sewer lines, hundreds of airports, and more.

In June 1934 Congress passed the Indian Reorganization Act. It reversed previous policies by recognizing the tribe as the key unit of social organization for Native Americans. It limited the sale of Indian lands and provided assistance to native groups in developing their resources, economy, and culture. It also granted some limited rights of self-rule.

Many Native Americans hailed the new direction. Others viewed it more skeptically, as just another instance of outsiders telling them what to do.

ACADEMIC VOCABULARY
mandate
require

READING CHECK Identifying Supporting Details What were the three main categories of the programs and actions of Roosevelt's New Deal?

ACADEMIC VOCABULARY
significant meaningful

Trouble for the New Deal

The New Deal marked a significant shift in the relationship between government and the American people. Never before had government assumed such a central role in the business and personal lives of its citizens. Not surprisingly, this shift triggered strong reactions.

Some reformers and radicals believed the New Deal had not gone far enough in reforming the economy. They wanted a complete overhaul of capitalism. The New Deal, they complained, merely propped up the old banking system and gave new freedoms to business. These, critics charged, were the same people and powers that had led the nation into the Great Depression in the first place.

Conservatives, on the other hand, attacked the New Deal as a radical break with traditional American ideals. Senator Carter Glass of Virginia lamented in 1933 that "Roosevelt is driving this country to destruction faster than it has ever moved before."

Leading critics of the New Deal Over time, several leading critics of the New Deal emerged. Perhaps the most powerful of these was Senator **Huey P. Long** of Louisiana, who believed Roosevelt's policies were too friendly to banks and businesses.

In 1934 Long set up his own political organization, the Share Our Wealth Society. Long's idea, reflected in the slogan "Every Man a King," was to give every family $5,000 to buy a home, plus an income of $2,500 a year. To pay for this, Long proposed heavy taxes on wealthy Americans. Long's organization attracted millions of followers. Roosevelt's advisers feared his possible role in the 1936 election.

Father Charles Coughlin, a Catholic priest, was another one-time Roosevelt supporter who turned against the president. At the peak of Coughlin's popularity, one-third of the nation tuned in to the weekly radio broadcasts of the "radio priest." His program, featuring religious messages and political commentary, was sharply critical of the nation's bankers and financial leaders. When Coughlin concluded that the president was not doing enough to curb their power, he called the president "Franklin Double-Crossing Roosevelt."

Coughlin also began to attack leading Jewish figures in the administration and elsewhere. As his speeches became more extreme,

---

PRIMARY SOURCES

Political Cartoon

The New Deal represented a great change in the role of the federal government in the lives of Americans. Government agencies became involved in people's business and personal lives in many new ways—and not everyone was pleased with the results.

This long line of eager scholars represent government officials carrying out New Deal programs.

The United States is depicted as a patient under anesthesia.

SKILLS FOCUS — READING LIKE A HISTORIAN

1. **Interpreting Political Cartoons** What does this cartoon suggest is happening to Uncle Guinea Pig?
2. **Drawing Conclusions** Does this cartoon present a positive view of the New Deal? Explain.

See **Skills Handbook**, p. H31

Coughlin began to lose influence with the American people. Eventually, the Catholic Church forced him to end his radio program.

Dr. Francis Townsend criticized the New Deal for not doing enough for older Americans. He proposed a plan for providing pensions to people over the age of 60. Like Long and Coughlin, Townsend attracted millions of followers. Some of his ideas would later help shape the thinking and policies of President Roosevelt.

The American Liberty League spoke for many conservatives who felt the New Deal had gone too far. The League drew members from both parties, including former Democratic presidential candidate Al Smith. It also included a number of wealthy business leaders, who believed the New Deal's policies were antibusiness. But despite spending thousands of dollars to defeat New Deal candidates in elections, the League met with little success.

Opposition from the courts The American people supported the New Deal's attempts to bring change to the economy. The courts, however, were more skeptical.

The New Deal changed in basic ways the relationship between the American people and their government. It also threatened to alter the balance of power among the president, the Congress, and the courts. Critics feared that the New Deal gave the president too much power over other branches of government. Presidentially appointed administrators, rather than Congress, were now making rules affecting millions of people. Some critics argued that these changes violated the Constitution.

By 1935 New Deal cases were making their way to the Supreme Court. Their decisions delivered a series of sharp blows to Roosevelt's program. For example, in May 1935, the Supreme Court issued a ruling in *Schechter Poultry Corporation* v. *United States* that destroyed key parts of the NIRA. (See the Landmark Supreme Court Cases feature at the end of this section.) In 1936 the court's ruling in *United States* v. *Butler* found a key part of the AAA—the tax used to raise the money for farmer subsidies—unconstitutional.

The courts managed do what the New Deal's critics had failed to accomplish over the course of two years. As Roosevelt faced re-election in 1936, he continued to enjoy wide popularity among voters. Yet parts of his ambitious economic program were in shambles. Meanwhile, the Great Depression remained a grim fact of life for millions of Americans.

READING CHECK **Summarizing** What were the two major types of complaints about the New Deal during Roosevelt's first term in office?

SECTION 1 ASSESSMENT

HSS 11.6.2, 11.6.4, 11.8.5

Reviewing Ideas, Terms, and People

1. **a. Define** Write a brief definition for the following term: public works
   b. Explain What factors made Roosevelt a good choice for the Democratic nomination in 1932?
   c. Evaluate Defend Roosevelt's campaign strategy in 1932.

2. **a. Describe** What were Roosevelt's **fireside chats**?
   b. Analyze How did Franklin Roosevelt's beliefs about government represent a change from those of Hoover?
   c. Compare Compare **Eleanor Roosevelt** to First Ladies who came before her.

3. **a. Define** Write a brief definition of the following terms: Hundred Days, New Deal, subsidy
   b. Draw Conclusions Why do you think Roosevelt's first act as president was to try to restore confidence in the nation's banking system?
   c. Rank Of the three main goals—relief, recovery, and reform—which do you think was most important? Explain.

4. **a. Identify** Identify at least three major critics of the New Deal in its early years.
   b. Compare What viewpoint did **Huey P. Long, Father Coughlin,** and **Dr. Francis Townsend** share in common?
   c. Predict How do you think the decisions of the Supreme Court will affect Roosevelt in the future?

Critical Thinking

5. **Sequence** Copy the chart below and use information from the section to record events in sequence.

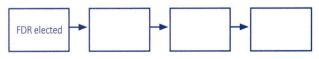

 Persuasive Write a letter to the editor in which you either defend or criticize Roosevelt's New Deal programs. Use details from the section to support your position.

Interactive
HISTORY & Geography

The Tennessee Valley Authority

The Tennessee Valley Authority (TVA) was one of the New Deal's largest projects. It brought affordable electricity to thousands of rural citizens, improved river navigation, controlled flooding, and introduced modern farming techniques to failing farmers. It fit with President Roosevelt's interests in conservation, government-owned utilities, agricultural development, and improving the lives of "Forgotten Americans."

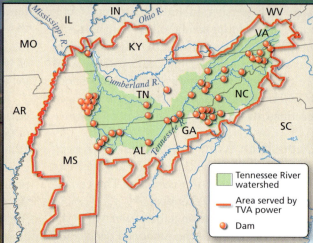

Tennessee Valley The Tennessee River basin includes parts of seven states.

Locks
Locks allow boats to travel past the dams on the river. Today, about 34,000 barges carrying 50 million tons navigate through the locks annually.

Navigational Dams
The dams in the Tennessee River serve to manage navigation and flooding. Droughts, floods, fast currents, and rocky shoals were hazards to earlier shipping. Now nine river dams maintain a water level deep enough for the barges.

Electricity for Farms

By the 1930s, only 10 percent of rural dwellers had electricity, while 90 percent of urbanites did. Isolated farmers couldn't keep food cold or turn on a light. The Roosevelt Administration thought the government should provide electricity to citizens not yet served by private companies.

Hydroelectric Dams

The dams built on the rivers that flow into the Tennessee River are high dams backed by huge reservoirs. These dams generated the cheap electricity needed to improve lives and lure industries that would provide jobs to the region.

Farming Practices

Many Tennessee Valley farmers used methods that depleted and eroded the soil. The TVA taught farmers how to use crop rotation and plants like alfalfa and clover to enrich and conserve the soil.

HSS 11.6.4
HSS Analysis CS3, HI1

GEOGRAPHY SKILLS INTERPRETING MAPS

go.hrw.com
Interactive Map
Keyword: SE7 CH12

1. **Location** Why was the Tennessee Valley a good location for this New Deal project?
2. **Movement** How did the TVA help boats navigate the river?

See **Skills Handbook**, p. H20

LANDMARK SUPREME COURT CASES

Constitutional Issue: Powers of the President

Schechter Poultry Corporation v. United States (1935)

Why It Matters Can Congress broadly delegate its lawmaking authority to the administrative agencies of the executive branch? That was the question the Court faced in *Schechter*. The Court's negative ruling temporarily derailed President Franklin D. Roosevelt's New Deal program. However, it also forced Roosevelt and Congress to tailor future legislation more narrowly.

Background of the Case

In 1933 President Roosevelt created the National Recovery Administration (NRA). The NRA supervised the development of mandatory industry-wide codes for production, prices, and wages. The standards carried the force of law. The Schechter Corporation appealed after it was convicted of violating the minimum wage and maximum hour provisions of the code for the live poultry industry.

The Decision

In its unanimous decision, the Court cited two grounds for finding the mandatory code system unconstitutional. First, it ruled that the delegation of rule-making authority to an agency of the executive branch violated the constitutional separation of powers. The Constitution places all legislative power in the Congress. Rules or codes having the force of law could only be made by Congress, not by the executive branch.

Second, the Court ruled that the activities of the Schechter Corporation were not subject to congressional regulation. Under the commerce clause, Congress can regulate interstate commerce (conducted in more than one state), not intrastate commerce (conducted entirely within a single state). The Schechter Corporation bought and sold its chickens almost exclusively within New York State. So the commerce clause did not apply to the way that Schecter conducted business.

THE IMPACT TODAY The Supreme Court later took an expanded view of the commerce clause and gave Congress more authority to delegate lawmaking authority to administrative agencies. Today there is widespread governmental regulation of business and economic matters. Much of the regulation is done by administrative agencies within the executive branch. Above, President George W. Bush meets with Senate leaders to discuss energy policy.

CRITICAL THINKING

go.hrw.com
Research Online
Keyword: SS Court

1. **Analyze the Impact** Using the keyword above, read about the Interstate Commerce Commission. What does the Commission do? If *Schechter* had been ruled differently, what aspects of the commission today would have created constitutional problems?

2. **You Be the Judge** The Gun Free School Zones Act of 1990 made it a federal crime for an individual knowingly to possess a firearm in a school zone. Does the act exceed Congress's power to legislate under the Commerce Clause? State the arguments for and against the law's constitutionality.

SECTION 2: The Second New Deal

BEFORE YOU READ

MAIN IDEA
A new wave of government initiatives starting in 1935 resulted in some strong successes and stunning defeats for President Roosevelt.

READING FOCUS
1. What were the key programs in the Second Hundred Days?
2. How did New Deal programs help to revive organized labor?
3. What were the key events of the 1936 election?
4. Why was 1937 a troubled year for Roosevelt and the Second New Deal?

KEY TERMS AND PEOPLE
Second New Deal
Social Security
John L. Lewis
CIO
sit-down strike
deficit
John Maynard Keynes

HSS 11.6.2 Understand the steps taken by Congress and President Roosevelt to combat the economic crisis.

HSS 11.6.4 Analyze the effects of and the controversies arising from New Deal policies and the expanded role of the federal government.

HSS 11.8.5 Describe the increased powers of the presidency in response to the Great Depression.

 How do you restore hope to the hopeless? The New Deal did not end the Great Depression. Yet the sense of forward movement it created helped give people hope.

Starting in 1935, government increased its commitment to work relief. Earlier programs such as the Civilian Conservation Corps (CCC) had shown how such programs provided not just a source of income but also a sense of purpose and dignity. One worker described how hard work in the CCC transformed his body and mind: "[Y]ou must go through the actual experience before you can really understand the hopeless state of mind most of the prospective members of the CCC were in when we put on our 'G.I.' clothing and tramped half-heartedly into the forests and fields to plant and cut trees, build dams,… fire breaks and trails, control insect pests, tree diseases, and risk our lives… protecting the forests from the most efficient of destructive forces—Fire. But our don't-care-what-happens attitude didn't last long.… I am making my own way and that is sufficient for the present. What is probably more important is the fact that I am not the undernourished, furtive-eyed, scared kid that went in … over five years ago. Instead, my eyes are clear and my mind is receptive to whatever the future has in store. In short, the CCC has equipped me with the weapons necessary to cope with the innumerable problems that are bound to obstruct my path through life and that must be surmounted before success can be attained."

Working for Dignity

▼ Millions of Americans were uplifted by New Deal work-relief programs.

The Second Hundred Days

With public support for the president and the New Deal running high, the Democratic Party rolled to an unprecedented victory in the congressional elections of 1934. For the first time in U.S. history, the party in control of the White House gained seats in both houses of Congress in a midterm election.

When the new Congress took office in 1935, Democrats held three-quarters of all seats. It was a clear vote of confidence in Roosevelt. As one journalist remarked, "He has been all but crowned by the people."

Roosevelt's victory, however, threatened to be a hollow one. The courts were in the process of finding major parts of the New Deal unconstitutional. The economy was proving stubbornly resistant to recovery. Meanwhile, more-liberal elements in the country were clamoring for the president to do more.

And he did do more. In a flurry of activity in the spring of 1935, during a period called the Second Hundred Days, Roosevelt launched the so-called **Second New Deal**. In short order, Congress passed laws extending government oversight of the banking industry and raising taxes for the wealthy. It funded new relief programs for the still-struggling population.

Emergency relief The major relief legislation of the Second New Deal marked a shift from Roosevelt's earlier programs. The Emergency Relief Appropriations Act largely did away with direct payments to Americans in need. As you have read, the Second New Deal expanded on what had been a small but successful part of the first New Deal: work relief. From now on, said the president, people should work for pay.

HISTORY'S VOICES

" [C]ontinued dependence upon relief [brings about] a spiritual and moral disintegration . . . destructive to the national fiber. To dole out relief in this way is to administer a narcotic, a subtle destroyer of the human spirit. "

—Franklin Delano Roosevelt,
State of the Union Address, 1935

The new Works Progress Administration (WPA), created in 1935, was the largest peacetime jobs program in U.S. history. It eventually employed 8.5 million Americans on all kinds of public-works projects at a cost of about $11 billion.

WPA workers built roads, subways, airports, even zoos. They worked in offices, schools, museums, and factories. They ventured into the fields to record the oral histories of former

Murals of the New Deal

Men operating air drills and rope work the dangerously steep slopes of the canyon.

Workers operating a heavy crane hoist a huge conduit above a canyon.

slaves. The WPA even funded the efforts of artists, writers, composers, and actors. A number of soon-to-be-famous figures got their starts in the program, including artist Jackson Pollock and writers Ralph Ellison, Richard Wright, and Eudora Welty.

At its peak, the WPA employed some 3.4 million formerly jobless Americans. This amounted to nearly a fourth of the unemployed people in the country.

As Roosevelt had hoped, getting the opportunity to earn a paycheck rather than get a handout lifted people's spirits. As one worker put it, "You worked, you got a paycheck and you had some dignity."

Social Security A centerpiece of the Second New Deal was the Social Security Act, signed in August 1935. This law created a system called **Social Security**, which provided a pension, or guaranteed, regular payments, for many people 65 and older.

With the creation of Social Security, many retired workers no longer needed to fear hunger and homelessness once they became too old to work. The Social Security Act also included a system of unemployment insurance run jointly by the federal government and the states. This program provided payments to workers who lost their jobs, giving them a financial cushion while they looked for new work. To fund the programs, Congress passed new taxes that affected both workers and employers.

In promoting Social Security, Roosevelt responded to a number of his critics. For example, in helping older Americans, Roosevelt hoped to undermine the attacks of Dr. Francis Townsend, the California doctor whose plan for older Americans had attracted so many supporters. The president hinted to nervous lawmakers that his own plan was preferable to Townsend's more radical design.

Funding Social Security, however, posed problems. To avoid a huge tax hike that could hamper economic recovery, Roosevelt agreed to exclude certain workers from the new program. "Everybody ought to be in on it," Roosevelt had argued. In the end, millions of Americans, including farmworkers, household workers, and government employees, were left out of Social Security.

READING CHECK Summarizing What were two major elements of the Second New Deal?

Reviving Organized Labor

After setbacks during the 1920s, the passage of the NIRA during the first New Deal marked a major step forward for organized labor. It guaranteed workers the right to form unions and bargain collectively. Yet many businesses ignored the new rules, vigorously battling the growth of unions. In 1934, unions lost a number of major strikes, as labor-related violence increased.

A cautious FDR was unwilling to push business too hard to accept labor's new powers. In addition, under NIRA's terms, government had little power to force business cooperation.

When NIRA was fatally weakened by the Supreme Court's ruling in *Schechter*, Roosevelt recognized the need to act on behalf of labor. He threw his support behind a new labor law, the Wagner Act (named for its sponsor, Senator Robert Wagner of New York).

The law, also known as the National Labor Relations Act, was stronger than NIRA. The act outlawed a number of antilabor practices, such as the creation of company-sponsored unions. It also established a powerful new National Labor Relations Board. The NLRB was given

The WPA paid artists to create public art. *Construction of the Dam*, a mural by William Gropper, shows workers on a WPA construction project.

A group of muscular men put together a large section of steel framework.

THE IMPACT TODAY

Government
The public today has come to depend heavily on Social Security. The cost to workers and employers for funding this program have risen steadily, and payments have risen as more and more Americans live longer and longer lives.

THE NEW DEAL **359**

MAJOR NEW DEAL PROGRAMS

Relief

Civilian Conservation Corps (CCC), 1933 Provided jobs on conservation projects to young men whose families needed relief

Federal Emergency Relief Administration (FERA), 1933 Provided grants to states for direct relief to the needy

Public Works Administration (PWA), 1933 Provided public-works jobs for many of those needing relief

Civil Works Administration (CWA), 1933 Provided public-works jobs for many of those needing relief

Works Progress Administration (WPA), 1935 Provided public-works jobs on a wide range of projects for many of those needing relief

Social Security Act, 1935 Established pensions for retirees, unemployment insurance, and aid for certain groups of low-income or disabled people

Farm Security Administration (FSA), 1937 Provided assistance to tenant farmers to help them purchase land or establish cooperatives

Reform

Emergency Banking Act, 1933 Gave federal government power to reorganize and strengthen banks

Federal Deposit Insurance Corporation (FDIC), 1933 Established an insurance program for deposits in many banks

Securities and Exchange Commission (SEC), 1934 Provided increased government regulation of the trading on stock exchanges

National Labor Relations Act (NLRB), 1935 Established the National Labor Relations Board to enforce labor laws

Fair Labor Standards Act (Wages and Hours Law), 1938 Established minimum wages and maximum hours for many workers

Recovery

Agricultural Adjustment Administration (AAA), 1933 Encouraged farmers to cut production in return for a subsidy

Tennessee Valley Authority (TVA), 1933 Promoted development projects for the Tennessee River Valley—for example, to improve navigation, produce electricity, and control floods

National Industrial Recovery Act (NIRA), 1933 Encouraged cooperation among businesses in establishing production and labor practices

Federal Housing Administration (FHA), 1934 Encouraged loans for renovating or building homes

Rural Electrification Administration (REA), 1935 Encouraged the delivery of electricity to rural areas

Programs in red are still in existence.

---

the authority to conduct voting in workplaces to determine whether employees wanted union representation. The NLRB could require businesses to accept the voting results. With these new legal tools, organized labor membership surged by millions in the years to come.

The CIO is born The passage of the Wagner Act roughly coincided with a major change in the American labor movement. A new union devoted to the interests of industrial workers arose to challenge the traditional hold of the nation's largest union, the American Federation of Labor (AFL).

The AFL was created as a collection, or federation, of smaller unions representing the interests of skilled workers. These smaller unions were organized within specific crafts rather than across broad industries, such as the auto or steel industries. In general, the AFL looked down on unskilled factory workers, many of whom were immigrants.

The growth of mass production in the 1920s, however, greatly swelled the ranks of unskilled workers. **John L. Lewis,** head of the United Mine Workers, recognized this opportunity. He sought to take advantage of it.

A fiery speaker and organizer, Lewis led a group that broke away from the AFL in 1935 to form the Committee for Industrial Organization, or CIO. (The CIO later changed its name to the Congress of Industrial Organizations.) It was not long before Lewis and his new organization would make their mark.

The GM sit-down strike In December 1936 the United Auto Workers, which was part of the CIO, launched a new kind of strike. Workers at the General Motors (GM) plant in Flint, Michigan, simply sat down inside the factory and stopped working.

A **sit-down strike,** as it was called, required the strikers to stay at the factory day and night until the dispute was resolved. They relied on supporters outside the factory to provide food and to look after their families at home.

The sit-down strike created a complicated situation for GM. It could not use traditional methods of strike breaking—bringing in security forces to scatter the picket line and hiring non-union "scab" labor to run the factory. Any effort to take back the factory might turn violent. Valuable property inside the factory could be destroyed, and the risk of negative publicity, such as images of workers being beaten or killed, was too high.

GM asked the state government for help in removing the workers, but Michigan's governor refused. The company tried shutting off heat and water to the factory, but the strikers stayed on. When the police tried shutting off food deliveries to the factory, workers rioted. A brief battle raged between striking workers and the police until the police withdrew.

The sit-down strike was hard on the workers, but it was harder still on GM. The shutdown cost the automaker tens of millions of dollars a week in sales. After a tense six weeks, GM finally gave in and agreed to recognize the union. The workers had won.

It was an enormous victory for labor—and for the CIO. Along with a successful action against the United States Steel Corporation in 1937, the General Motors strike helped establish the CIO as a major force in American organized labor.

HISTORY'S VOICES

"When [GM executive William] Knudsen put his name to a piece of paper and says that General Motors recognizes UAW-CIO—until that moment we were non-people, we didn't even exist. That was the big one."

—Bob Stinson, sit-down striker, recorded in *Hard Times*

The CIO and other labor unions did not win every confrontation with American business in the 1930s. Indeed, unions suffered some serious losses later in the decade. Yet union membership continued to grow. By the early 1940s, nearly one-fourth of the American workforce was unionized.

READING CHECK Identifying Cause and Effect How did the Wagner Act work to revive labor?

GM Sit-Down Strike
Strikers make themselves as comfortable as possible on the floor of the GM plant at Flint, Michigan.

GROWTH OF UNION MEMBERSHIP, 1933–1940

Source: *Historical Statistics of the United States*

INTERPRETING GRAPHS

The NLRB and the CIO strengthened unions. **Compare** What was union membership in 1933? What was it in 1939?

See **Skills Handbook,** p. H17

The Election of 1936

As President Roosevelt entered the election year of 1936, he could look back on a productive 1935. He also knew there was more to be done before he faced the voters in November.

Rural electricity One goal was to provide additional help to rural Americans. Toward this end, Roosevelt in May signed the Rural Electrification Act. It empowered the Rural Electrification Administration (REA) to loan money to farm cooperatives and other groups trying to bring electricity to people living outside of cities and towns. In many areas, for-profit power companies had been unwilling to put in the miles of power lines needed to serve remote, sparsely settled areas. Under the REA, the numbers of rural homes with electricity grew from 10 percent to 90 percent in about a decade. Millions of farmers were finally able to enjoy the benefits of electricity.

THE IMPACT TODAY
Technology
In what is seen as a parallel to rural electrification in the 1930s, Congress has earmarked funds to help bring high-speed Internet service to rural America today.

Americans re-elect Roosevelt President Roosevelt campaigned on a solid record of legislative achievement. He also pointed to significant improvements in the economy. Unemployment, though still high, had been sliced in half. Personal incomes and corporate earnings were up sharply. New Deal programs had given hope and help to millions, even if they had not brought about full economic recovery.

In the 1936 campaign, Roosevelt virtually ignored the Republican nominee, Governor Alf Landon of Kansas. Landon's mildly reformist positions supporting organized labor and aid to the unemployed and elderly posed no serious threat. Roosevelt also faced no serious competition from the Union Party, a new party formed by Father Charles Coughlin and Dr. Francis Townsend.

Appealing to potential Union Party supporters, Roosevelt gave speeches thundering against big business. Business leaders responded with alarm, again pouring money into the American Liberty League. To some of them, the New Deal amounted to a revolution.

HISTORY'S VOICES

❝The history of these past three years will be written in the future as the history of an American revolution which was engineered and carried on under the unseeing eyes of one hundred and thirty million citizens.❞
—Senator Lester Dickinson, *The American Mercury,* February 1936

In a bitterly waged campaign, Republicans attacked Roosevelt's New Deal for being overly bureaucratic and creating a planned economy.

On election day, however, the American voters again handed Roosevelt a tremendous victory. Landon carried only two states. The ineffective Union Party candidate polled less than 2 percent of the popular vote. The Democrats again gained in both houses of Congress. They also won 26 of the 33 races for governor.

The electoral landslide also confirmed a momentous shift in American politics. African Americans in the North switched from the party of Lincoln to the Democratic Party.

READING CHECK **Identifying Supporting Details** What evidence can you find to suggest that the 1936 election showed widespread support for Roosevelt and the New Deal?

Historically, African Americans had supported the Republicans, the party of Lincoln. In 1936, however, a majority of African American voters chose Roosevelt and the Democrats—a shift in loyalty that has continued to this day.

PRIMARY SOURCES

Political Cartoon

President Roosevelt was very upset when the Supreme Court struck down some of the key provisions of the New Deal. To protect his new reforms, he attempted to "pack" the Court by adding more justices. Congress stopped this effort, marking one of the few great political defeats for the popular president. Many critics feared that such a change would threaten the balance of powers as spelled out in the U.S. Constitution. The following political cartoon originally included a caption that read, "Oh, So That's the Kind of a Sailor He Is!"

Skills Focus: READING LIKE A HISTORIAN

1. **Contrasting** How do the expressions of the captain and the sailor reflect different views of the court-packing plan?
2. **Interpreting Political Cartoons** Why do you think the artist chose this imagery?

See **Skills Handbook**, pp. H10, H31.

A Troubled Year

Never before had Roosevelt seemed more in command than when he began his second term. His determination to overcome obstacles to his programs, however, led to a serious misstep.

The court-packing plan Frustrated that the courts had struck down many New Deal programs, Roosevelt surprised Congress with a plan to reorganize the nation's courts. The plan would give the president power to appoint many new judges and expand the Supreme Court by up to six justices. The president argued that changes were needed to make the courts more efficient. Most observers, however, saw it as a clumsy effort to "pack" the Supreme Court with friendly justices—and a dangerous attempt to upset the constitutional balance of power. Even the president's supporters were troubled.

The battle over Roosevelt's proposal occupied Congress for much of 1937. Even members of the president's own party began to desert him. In the end, the president who had begun the year looking invincible ended it with a crushing loss.

HISTORY'S VOICES

"Roosevelt moved against the court more boldly and directly than any other President had ever done. Public opinion then swung to the defense of the court, and F. D. R. suffered the most humiliating defeat of his career."

—Merlo J. Pusey, *American Heritage,* April 1958

Moving forward President Roosevelt lost much of the year in his doomed battle over expanding the Supreme Court. Congress, however, did enact some major legislation in 1937.

The Farm Tenancy Act aided some of the poorest of the nation's poor—tenant farmers and sharecroppers. Many had been forced off the land as a result of New Deal programs that paid landowners to take fields out of production. The new law gave tenants and sharecroppers a chance to buy land of their own.

Roosevelt also won some important victories in an unlikely place—the Supreme Court. Even as he was trying to push through his court-packing plan, the Court handed down rulings that favored key New Deal programs. In March 1937 the Court upheld a rather

THE NEW DEAL 363

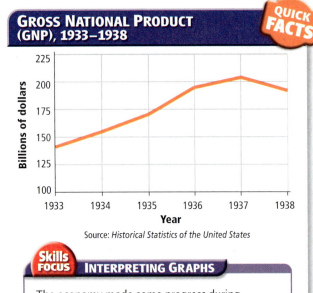

GROSS NATIONAL PRODUCT (GNP), 1933–1938

Source: Historical Statistics of the United States

SKILLS FOCUS: INTERPRETING GRAPHS

The economy made some progress during Roosevelt's time in office. Which year between 1933 and 1938 saw the worst performance?

See **Skills Handbook**, p. H17

ACADEMIC VOCABULARY

classical well known, original

controversial Washington State law requiring a minimum wage for workers. The ruling signaled a new willingness to let legislatures regulate the economy—a decision with clear implications for the New Deal.

In April the Court also ruled clearly in favor of a key element of the Wagner Act. In May it declared Roosevelt's Social Security plan to be constitutional.

The favorable rulings pleased Roosevelt. They effectively killed any remaining support for his court-packing plan, however.

Recovery in doubt In the fall of 1937, the nation's economy suffered another setback. It began in a familiar way with a sharp drop in the stock market. By the time the year was over, about 2 million more Americans had lost their jobs.

The return of hard times changed Roosevelt's plans. He had hoped to cut back on government spending, fearing the growing federal budget **deficit**. A deficit occurs when a government spends more money than it takes in through taxes and other income. But as unemployment rose in late 1937 and early 1938, Roosevelt again found himself seeking large sums of money to help the unemployed.

Roosevelt may have been troubled by deficits, but the new spending was supported by the theories of British economist **John Maynard Keynes**. Contrary to classical economic theory, which stressed balanced budgets, Keynes argued that deficit spending could provide jobs and stimulate the economy.

In fact, the economy did begin to rebound in the summer of 1938. By then, however, the positive feelings about Roosevelt and the New Deal had begun to fade.

READING CHECK Sequencing What events made 1937 a troubled year for President Roosevelt?

SECTION 2 ASSESSMENT

HSS 11.6.2, 11.6.4, 11.8.5

go.hrw.com
Online Quiz
Keyword: SE7 HP12

Reviewing Ideas, Terms, and People

1. **a. Identify** Identify the significance of the following terms: Second New Deal, Social Security
   b. Make Inferences What lessons did Roosevelt draw from the 1934 election?
   c. Evaluate What do you think of Roosevelt's decision to cut back on programs that provided relief without work?

2. **a. Identify** What was the CIO?
   b. Explain What factors contributed to labor's growth after 1935?
   c. Rank Which do you think was more important in labor's success: the passage of the Wagner Act or the success of the sit-down strikes? Explain.

3. **a. Recall** What was Roosevelt's 1936 election strategy?
   b. Summarize What were the results of the 1936 election?

4. **a. Identify** Identify the significance of the following: deficit, John Maynard Keynes
   b. Summarize Why did the court-packing plan cause so much damage to Roosevelt?

Critical Thinking

5. **Understand Cause and Effect** Copy the chart below and use information from the section to fill it in.

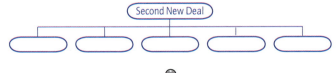

FOCUS ON SPEAKING ELA W1.1, 1.3

6. **Persuasive** Deliver a speech in which you argue for or against Roosevelt's court-reorganization plan.

SECTION 3
Life during the New Deal

BEFORE YOU READ

MAIN IDEA
The Great Depression and the New Deal had a deep impact on American culture during the 1930s.

READING FOCUS
1. How did the public roles of women and African Americans change during the New Deal?
2. How did artists and writers of the era tell the story of the Great Depression?
3. What forms of popular entertainment were popular during the Great Depression?

KEY TERMS AND PEOPLE
Frances Perkins
Black Cabinet
Mary McLeod Bethune
Dorothea Lange
swing

HSS **11.6.3** Discuss the human toll of the Depression.

HSS **11.10.7** Analyze the women's rights movement, including differing perspectives on the roles of women.

The Best Woman for the Job

▼ Labor Secretary Frances Perkins on the job

THE INSIDE STORY *How did one woman help to change public views of women in government?* "[M]en will take advice from a woman, but it is hard for them to take orders from a woman." That was a bit of counsel Franklin Roosevelt received when he was considering naming Frances Perkins to a key post in his administration.

Women's suffrage was not yet a decade old when Roosevelt, as New York's governor, made Perkins the top labor official in the state. When Roosevelt became president, he named Perkins to be his secretary of labor—the first woman ever to serve in the cabinet.

Born in Boston, Massachusetts, Perkins was already a social reformer when she witnessed the Triangle Shirtwaist Factory fire in New York City in 1911. That gruesome tragedy, in which 146 people died, spurred her interest in working to improve conditions in the workplace.

During her time in Washington, her tireless efforts and great skill won her many admirers—and the grudging respect of her enemies. Perkins played a central role in the creation of many New Deal programs, and she led the White House team that created the Social Security system.

Perkins served in Roosevelt's cabinet from 1933 until after his death in 1945. Her example advanced the cause of women in government.

THE NEW DEAL **365**

FACES OF HISTORY

Mary McLeod BETHUNE
1875–1955

The fifteenth child of former slaves, Mary McLeod Bethune rose from the cotton fields of South Carolina to be a pioneer in several fields.

In 1902, with borrowed furniture and $1.50, Bethune opened a school for African American girls in Daytona, Florida. This effort reflected her belief in the power of education as a means of advancement. Her little school later became Bethune-Cookman College.

Fiercely determined, a stirring speaker, and a tireless fundraiser, Bethune eventually gained national prominence. She worked for the voting rights of African Americans and women. An adviser to four presidents, she was the first African Amercan woman to head an agency of the federal government

Summarize How did Mary McLeod Bethune make a lasting impact?

New Roles for Women and African Americans

The New Deal brought great change in American life and society. Under the pressure of an economic emergency, old ways of doing things gave way to new. For women and African Americans, these changes brought hope for an expanded role in public life.

Women in the New Deal As you read in Section 1, Eleanor Roosevelt played a major role in her husband's administration. In addition to her tireless support for her husband's programs, she actively pursued issues of importance to women, helping leaders of women's groups gain access to the president.

THE IMPACT TODAY

Government
Today it is commonplace for women, African Americans, and members of other minorities to fill cabinet and other top government posts. They continue, however, to hold a relatively small share of these positions.

HISTORY'S VOICES

❝When I wanted help on some definite point, Mrs. Roosevelt gave me the opportunity to sit by the president at dinner and the matter was settled before we finished our soup.❞
—Molly Dewson, quoted in *Beyond Suffrage* by Susan Ware, 1981

Other women besides the First Lady served in prominent government posts during the New Deal, none more so than Secretary of Labor **Frances Perkins**. As the first woman to head an executive department, Perkins played a leading role in the formation of major New Deal policies. This included, as you have read, the Social Security system. Perkins, however, was not the only prominent woman in the government. Ruth Bryan Owen, daughter of three-time presidential candidate William Jennings Bryan, served as minister to Denmark. Roosevelt also appointed women to such posts as director of the U.S. Mint and assistant secretary of the Treasury. Women served as leaders in several New Deal agencies. In short, Roosevelt's record at promoting and recognizing women was simply unmatched for his time.

Still, women faced challenges and discrimination. New Deal programs, for example, generally paid men higher wages than women in work-relief jobs. Men continued to enjoy far more work opportunities. The attitude in the wider world to women in the workforce ranged from grudging acceptance to outright hostility. For example, one journalist put forward his idea for solving unemployment: "Simply fire the women, who shouldn't be working anyway, and hire the men. Presto! No unemployment."

African Americans in the New Deal
Roosevelt's administration also broke new ground in appointing African Americans. William Hastie, for example, became the first black federal judge in U.S. history. African Americans were also hired to fill posts in the government. A group of these officials, known as the **Black Cabinet,** met under the leadership of **Mary McLeod Bethune**, director of Negro Affairs in the National Youth Administration.

The Black Cabinet acted as unofficial advisers to the president. They stood as a powerful symbol of rising African American influence in government. In addition, First Lady Eleanor Roosevelt visibly championed civil rights, frequently staking out bold positions in advance of what her husband felt he could take.

Still, African Americans continued to face tremendous hardships in the 1930s. New Deal programs left largely unchallenged the discrimination that African Americans faced in the larger society. In addition, thousands of African American sharecroppers and tenant farmers suffered terribly. Many never saw real benefit from any New Deal program.

Roosevelt often explained his record with respect to African Americans by saying he was at the mercy of southern Democrats in Congress. Many of these legislators strongly opposed efforts to aid African Americans.

Roosevelt felt that angering southern Democrats would jeopardize the entire New Deal. "They will block every bill I ask Congress to pass to keep America from collapsing," he told the head of the NAACP when he was pressed to support an antilynching law. "I just can't take that risk."

Although President Roosevelt's record was not perfect, African American voters apparently decided that their best hopes lay with the Democratic Party. Staunchly Republican since the Civil War, a majority of African Americans for the first time in history voted Democratic in the 1934 midterm elections. As you have read, this support continued in the 1936 presidential election as well.

READING CHECK **Making Generalizations** What was the overall effect of Roosevelt's policies on women and African Americans in the 1930s?

Telling the Story of the Depression

Responding to unprecedented economic calamity, artists showed a new interest in social problems and activism. Painters and sculptors fashioned works depicting the struggles of the working class. Authors and playwrights focused on the plight of the rural and urban poor. For example, you read in the last chapter about John Steinbeck's moving tale of Dust Bowl refugees, *The Grapes of Wrath*. Songwriter Woody Guthrie celebrated the grandeur of America and the lives of ordinary people.

The work of Dorothea Lange
Photographer **Dorothea Lange** was another celebrated chronicler of the Great Depression. In her hometown of San Francisco, Lange recorded images of jobless people. Yet her most famous subjects were the rural poor, who were especially hard hit in the 1930s.

Starting in 1935, Lange worked on behalf of the Farm Security Administration. This organization focused on the lives of tenant farmers and sharecroppers. One of her most famous photographs appears at right. These and other pictures helped raise awareness about the poorest of the poor. Indeed, in 1937 the federal government finally began to provide help to tenant farmers and sharecroppers.

IMAGES OF THE GREAT DEPRESSION

Ella Watson, a Washington, D.C. charwoman, with her three children

Gordon Parks

Dorothea Lange

Destitute mother of seven children in California

Skills Focus **READING LIKE A HISTORIAN**

Photographers like Gordon Parks and Dorothea Lange were hired to document the plight of the poor and, through their images, gain public support for Roosevelt's New Deal programs.

Interpreting Visuals Do you think these photographs succeed in showing a sympathetic view of their subjects? Explain.

THE NEW DEAL **367**

HISTORY CLOSE-UP
Going to the Movies

At an average of 25 cents a ticket, movies were one of the most affordable forms of entertainment in the 1930s. More than that, movies served the public's emotional needs.

▲ Comedian Charlie Chaplin wrestles with machinery in *Modern Times*, a film that criticized the dehumanizing effects of industry.

Agee, Evans, and *Famous Men* Writer James Agee and photographer Walker Evans also depicted the lives of sharecroppers in the Lower South. Their work, *Let Us Now Praise Famous Men*, focused on a group of families in rural Alabama. This work received little notice when it was first published. Yet Evans's compassionate and unblinking images and Agee's powerful descriptions form a moving record of the reality of rural poverty and the great dignity of those who struggled against it.

READING CHECK Comparing How did artists such as Lange, Parks, Agee, and Evans seek to tell the story of the Great Depression?

Popular Entertainment in the 1930s

Despite the hard times of the 1930s, Americans still found the handful of pennies it cost to go to a movie theater. Radio also continued to grow in popularity in the 1930s. A large majority of American households had a radio, and a wide range of programming, including sports, was available.

Movies One study in 1935 showed that nearly 80 million of the nation's 127 million Americans attended a movie each week. Throughout the decade, movie studios produced some 5,000 feature-length films.

A few of these movies focused on the hardships of life during the Great Depression. For example, Steinbeck's *The Grapes of Wrath* was turned into a successful Hollywood film in 1940. Another example of a successful Depression-themed film was *I Am a Fugitive from a Chain Gang*. This told the tale of a jobless man who is lured into a life of crime. *Make Way for Tomorrow* portrayed the financial hardships of an older couple.

For the most part, however, films of the 1930s steered clear of troubling reminders of the hard times gripping the nation. Indeed,

▲ *King Kong* roared into movie theaters with state-of-the-art special effects in March 1933. In the film's opening week, about 150,000 American moviegoers flocked to the theaters to be frightened by the giant ape.

▼ Ginger Rogers and Fred Astaire were the picture of glamour and grace for a downtrodden public.

▲ The Fabulous Fox San Francisco Theatre opened in 1929 with 5,000 seats. Such grand theaters could make moviegoers feel rich, if only for an hour or two at a time.

Skills Focus: INTERPRETING INFOGRAPHICS

Making Inferences How do you think attending movies like the examples above helped people through the Great Depression? Discuss each example separately, including the theater.

See **Skills Handbook**, p. H7

filmmakers seemed to realize that most Americans went to the movies in an attempt to escape from their own problems—even if only for a couple of hours.

Highly popular in the 1930s were grand musicals featuring glamorous dancers gliding across lavish sets or living it up at posh nightclubs. In the exciting, imaginary lives of characters played by actors such as Fred Astaire and Ginger Rogers, viewers got a glimpse of a life they could only dream about.

Comedy was another popular choice for the public. The Marx Brothers used a zany style to produce a string of hits in the 1930s. Charlie Chaplin continued to be popular. Not only did he make the transition to talkies successfully but he also continued to produce silent movies. The classic *Modern Times* took a hilarious look at a serious subject—the dehumanizing effect of industrial life.

Director Frank Capra captured the spirit of the times in films that combined social themes with a sentimental and comic view of life. Films such as *Mr. Deeds Goes to Town* and *Mr. Smith Goes to Washington* told of the triumph of the "little guy."

The 1930s also saw the introduction of some new moviemaking techniques. For example, Walt Disney's *Snow White and the Seven Dwarfs* was history's first full-length animated feature. It drew huge audiences. *The Wizard of Oz* delighted audiences not only with its charming story and performances but also with the use of color photography and special effects. *Gone with the Wind*, which came out the same year as *The Wizard of Oz*, was also a color blockbuster.

Radio Radio had an important role in American politics. From President Roosevelt's fireside chats to Father Coughlin's rants against the New Deal, radio brought a variety of news and views into millions of American homes.

Of course, radio also provided listeners with religion, music, sports, and other forms of entertainment. Though by today's standards the sound quality was poor, families in living rooms across the country were enthralled by action shows such as *The Lone Ranger* and comedies such as *Fibber McGee and Molly*.

Radio's power to captivate listeners was dramatically demonstrated in October 1938. The actor Orson Welles produced a radio broadcast of the H. G. Wells science fiction tale *The War of the Worlds* that was so realistic, it convinced many panicked listeners that Earth was actually under attack by spaceships from Mars.

Radio helped broaden the appeal of jazz. This vibrant form of music had its roots in African American communities in New Orleans and other big cities. It had spread northward and taken root in cities such as New York. There, performers such as Louis Armstrong dazzled audiences with their ability at improvising.

A new, highly orchestrated type of jazz known as **swing** swept the country in the 1930s. This music tended to feature larger groups of musicians known as big bands. Audiences often danced to the music, performing such steps as the jitterbug or the Lindy Hop (named after Charles Lindbergh).

Swing had its share of African American stars. Duke Ellington and Count Basie were two famous big-band leaders. At the same time, white big-band leaders such as Benny Goodman and the Dorsey Brothers reached audiences that had been untouched by the jazz masters of the 1920s.

Joyous or soulful, the unrestrained moods of jazz were medicine for the times. Said one critic, "This was the Depression. It was not an easy period. And this was a music that was just pure pleasure. Pure physical pleasure."

Sports in the 1930s The 1920s is widely regarded as the golden age of sports. The Great Depression did limit the ability of many Americans to buy tickets and attend events in person. Nevertheless, interest in sports remained quite strong.

Baseball remained a popular attraction. The legendary Babe Ruth, who had become a huge star in the 1920s, continued his career until the mid-1930s. He was soon replaced on the roster of the New York Yankees by a new star—the great Joe DiMaggio.

Meanwhile, former Ruth teammate Lou Gehrig stirred the emotions of the nation when, stricken with a terrible illness that would soon end his life, he ended his record streak of consecutive games played.

Sports fans also thrilled to the exploits of Babe Didrikson Zaharias. A multisport star, Zaharias won fame for her talents in softball, golf, basketball, and track and field.

Boxing was hugely popular in the 1930s. The big star was heavyweight fighter Joe Louis. His 1938 bout against German Max Schmeling came to represent the growing conflict between Germany and the United States. You will read more about this contest in the next chapter.

READING CHECK **Identifying the Main Idea** How did popular entertainment help Americans cope with the stresses of the Great Depression?

SECTION 3 ASSESSMENT

HSS 11.6.3, 11.10.7

Reviewing Ideas, Terms, and People

1. **a. Identify** Who were **Frances Perkins** and **Mary McLeod Bethune**?
   b. Make Generalizations How did women and African Americans fare under the policies of the Roosevelt administration?
2. **a. Identify** Who was **Dorothea Lange**?
   b. Make Generalizations Why do you think Lange, Evans, and Agee focused on the plight of sharecroppers and tenant farmers?
3. **a. Define** Write a brief definition of the following term: **swing**
   b. Draw Conclusions What can you conclude about the importance of movies in American life based on the average weekly audience in the 1930s?

Critical Thinking

4. **Find Supporting Details** Copy the chart below and use information from the section to find supporting details for the main idea given.

FOCUS ON WRITING ELA W1.1

5. **Descriptive** Write a brief description of American popular entertainment in the 1930s, using examples from your reading of the chapter.

SECTION 4
Analyzing the New Deal

BEFORE YOU READ

MAIN IDEA
The New Deal had mixed success in rescuing the economy, but it fundamentally changed Americans' relationship with their government.

FOCUS QUESTIONS
1. What was the impact of the New Deal on the nation in the 1930s?
2. In what ways was the impact of the New Deal limited?
3. How did the New Deal come to an end?

KEY TERMS AND PEOPLE
Marian Anderson
minimum wage
incumbent

HSS 11.6.2 Understand the causes of the Great Depression and the steps taken to combat the crisis.

HSS 11.6.4 Analyze the controversies arising from New Deal policies and the expanded role of the federal government since the 1930s.

HSS 11.6.5 Trace the advances and retreats of organized labor.

How far would white society go to battle racial discrimination in the 1930s? As a musically gifted African American child, **Marian Anderson** got her vocal training the only way she could: singing in the choir at the local church. In time, her talents took her from the choir box to some of the world's most famous concert halls.

Like many African American performers of her day, Anderson went to Europe first to build up her reputation. She returned to America as an international star. But success did not protect her from discrimination at home.

In 1939 Anderson's manager tried to book a concert for her at Constitution Hall in Washington, D.C. The owners of the hall, a prestigious group called the Daughters of the American Revolution (DAR), turned him down, citing a contract clause that said "concert by white artists only."

Many Americans were outraged. Eleanor Roosevelt and other prominent women resigned from the DAR. The First Lady then arranged for Anderson to hold a concert on the steps of the Lincoln Memorial in Washington. Some 75,000 people turned out, hearing Anderson's glorious voice sing the words, "My country, 'tis of thee, sweet land of liberty." Millions heard the national radio broadcast. Anderson later gave a private concert at the White House.

Eleanor Roosevelt's actions on behalf of Marian Anderson were typical of her efforts to aid African Americans. However, the incident also illustrated just how widespread racism was in 1930s America. A principled stand, a public cry of outrage, and groundbreaking symbolism went far in changing attitudes. Indeed, within four years, Constitution Hall changed its whites-only policy and invited Anderson to sing there. Meanwhile, however, there was no move to legally challenge the injustice done to Anderson or the racism it represented. The architects of the New Deal, including President Roosevelt, chose not to fight that battle.

▶ **Marian Anderson performs on the steps of the Lincoln Memorial.**

QUICK FACTS

UNEMPLOYMENT, 1933–1940

Source: *Historical Statistics of the United States*

DEFICIT SPENDING, 1933–1940

Source: *Historical Statistics of the United States*

Skills Focus: INTERPRETING GRAPHS

1. What was the overall trend of unemployment between 1933 and 1940?
2. What was significant about 1938?

See **Skills Handbook**, p. H17

The Impact of the New Deal

From the moment he took office, Franklin Roosevelt knew he faced an economic crisis—and a crisis of spirit. Though he could not hope to please everyone, he knew he had to take action. "Take a method and try it," he said, describing his approach. "If it fails, admit it frankly and try another. But above all, try something."

Relief, recovery, and reform What was the record of the New Deal? Was the promise of relief, recovery, and reform met?

Certainly, the relief programs enacted in 1933 and 1935 put billions of dollars into the pockets of poor Americans. Millions of people enjoyed some form of help, from direct relief to jobs that provided a steady paycheck. Programs such as Social Security and unemployment insurance, moreover, became a fixture of American government.

The New Deal was less successful in delivering economic recovery. Joblessness initially fell from a high of 13 million in 1933 to about 9 million by 1936. Wages, factory output, and other economic indicators rose to levels at or even above those of 1929. Unfortunately, many early gains were wiped out in the downturn of 1937 and 1938. At decade's end, some 10 million workers remained unemployed.

Historians continue to debate the reasons for the New Deal's mixed results. Some argue that Roosevelt's policies, which were never popular with big business, hurt business confidence and slowed the pace of recovery. Others believe that the New Deal was too timid and that real unemployment reduction would have required spending billions more.

New Deal reforms proved more successful—and long-lasting. For example, the Federal Deposit Insurance Corporation helped restore public confidence in the safety of the nation's banks. This was a critical step in stopping the nation's slide into chaos in 1933. The FDIC has continued to serve the nation's economy ever since. Similarly, the Securities and Exchange Commission, established in 1934, helped the public regain faith in the stock markets. Investors today continue to rely on SEC oversight.

The New Deal also left an impressive legacy in the form of thousands of roadways, bridges, dams, and public buildings. The WPA built 2,500 hospitals and nearly 6,000 schools. WPA artists painted over 2,500 murals and erected nearly 18,000 sculptures in public places.

Changing relationships Americans have long argued about whether the New Deal was good or bad for the nation. What is undeniable is that the New Deal changed some basic relationships in American society.

In general, the New Deal changed the link between the American people and their government. The leaders of the 1920s had promoted business as the best way to achieve progress, and they generally viewed government as a barrier to progress. Roosevelt believed that government could help businesses and individuals achieve a greater level of economic security.

The new role for government meant a much bigger government. Dozens of new programs and agencies put people in contact with their government in ways they had not experienced before. Americans now began to look regularly to government for help. Roosevelt and the New Deal were both praised and hated for this. For some, this change brought a welcome shift from the laissez-faire policies of the 1920s. To others, it threatened the basic character that had always held the country together.

HISTORY'S VOICES

" It cannot be successfully denied that whatever the merits of the New Deal policies, they have, as a whole, caused an appreciable drift away from individual responsibility and self-reliance. They have brought about an excessive, utterly [false] and dangerous reliance upon government. "

—*Saturday Evening Post,* November 6, 1936

READING CHECK **Making Generalizations** How did the New Deal impact relationships among important segments of American society?

Limits of the New Deal

The New Deal was never as sweeping as its supporters or its opponents claimed. In practice, New Deal programs often compromised—some might say contradicted—Roosevelt's desire to build "a country in which no one is left out."

Relief programs provide a clear example. While they gave aid to millions of people, these programs were never meant to be a permanent solution to joblessness. Nor were they able to provide jobs to all those who needed them.

Roosevelt had hoped the federal government would assist all but about 1.5 million "unemployable" people, who would be left to the states to care for, but some 4.7 million went unserved. Work-relief programs could only provide temporary help. In addition, pay scales were very low. An unskilled worker might make a mere third of what the government deemed a minimum family income. Government leaders did not want wages to be so high that workers would be discouraged from seeking nongovernment jobs.

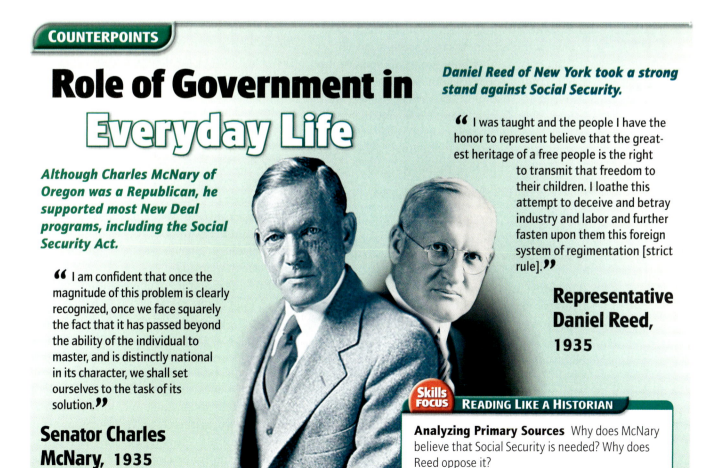

COUNTERPOINTS

Role of Government in Everyday Life

Although Charles McNary of Oregon was a Republican, he supported most New Deal programs, including the Social Security Act.

" I am confident that once the magnitude of this problem is clearly recognized, once we face squarely the fact that it has passed beyond the ability of the individual to master, and is distinctly national in its character, we shall set ourselves to the task of its solution. "

Senator Charles McNary, 1935

Daniel Reed of New York took a strong stand against Social Security.

" I was taught and the people I have the honor to represent believe that the greatest heritage of a free people is the right to transmit that freedom to their children. I loathe this attempt to deceive and betray industry and labor and further fasten upon them this foreign system of regimentation [strict rule]. "

Representative Daniel Reed, 1935

Skills FOCUS **READING LIKE A HISTORIAN**

Analyzing Primary Sources Why does McNary believe that Social Security is needed? Why does Reed oppose it?

See **Skills Handbook,** pp. H28–29

Limits of the New Deal

The New Deal did not lift everyone out of poverty. Many working families, such as these migrant workers in Minnesota (right) or these homesteaders in New Mexico (far right) had little choice but to make the best out of the cramped and impoverished conditions in which they lived.

The level of government assistance also varied by state. For example, under Aid to Families with Dependent Children, a child in Massachusetts might receive more than $60 a month, while one in Arkansas might get $8.

In addition, New Deal programs sometimes permitted discrimination against African Americans, Hispanic Americans, women, and others. New Deal leaders, Roosevelt included, were unwilling to irritate local populations by requiring programs to go against "local standards"—including discriminatory ones.

READING CHECK **Summarizing** What were some of the limits of the New Deal?

The End of the New Deal

The sense of optimism accompanying Roosevelt's victory in 1936 withered by 1937. The fight over court-packing cost the president some of his support within his party and with the American public. The economic downturn of 1937–1938 delivered a further blow to his efforts. By the end of 1938, the New Deal era of reform launched in 1933 was, in reality, over.

Weakening support Roosevelt's setbacks emboldened his opponents in Congress. In late 1937, a group of anti–New Deal senators made up of Republicans and southern Democrats issued a direct challenge to Roosevelt's policies. They called on the president to cut taxes, balance the budget, and return more power to the states. This group was strong enough to stop most legislation they disliked.

One target of this group's opposition was the president's plan to reorganize the executive branch of the government. Roosevelt said his goal was to help make the executive branch work more smoothly.

Critics, however, complained that the measure gave too much power to the president. As one member of Congress stated, "This is just a step to concentrate power in the hands of the president and set up a… form of dictatorship." Such a charge carried real weight after the court-packing episode.

Only one major piece of legislation emerged from Congress in 1938: the Fair Labor Standards Act. This law established a **minimum wage**—the lowest wage an employer can legally pay a worker. It also set the maximum number of required hours for a work week at 44. (This was later lowered to 40.) The Fair Labor Standards Act also included a requirement that workers receive the overtime rate of time-and-a-half—payment at one-and-a-half times their normal rate for any hours over the weekly maximum.

The new law did not cover many large groups, such as farmworkers. Still, it marked a major victory for millions of workers.

Southern Democrats opposed the bill. Southern industry, they argued, depended on paying workers less than in other parts of the country. But Roosevelt worked hard to win passage of the bill. Although he did not know it, the bill would be the last major New Deal law.

The 1938 elections Facing opposition in Congress, President Roosevelt decided his best hope lay in defeating his opponents in the 1938 congressional elections. This included opponents within his own party. He handpicked candidates to fight for the Democratic nominations in several southern states.

President Roosevelt traveled to the South to tell voters he needed new senators to help pass his program. The embattled senators responded by enflaming white fears that African Americans were becoming political empowered, sponsored by Roosevelt.

Georgia senator Walter George was among those targeted by Roosevelt. He compared the president's attempt to influence the election to the U.S. Army's occupation of the South during post–Civil War Reconstruction. "We answered this question before when federal bayonets stood guard over the ballot box," he observed.

Roosevelt's efforts backfired. In each case, his candidate lost, and the **incumbent** senator—the one presently in office—won the nomination and the November election. In addition, Republicans made gains in the House and Senate, further swelling the ranks of New Deal opponents.

After the New Deal Following the 1938 elections, President Roosevelt lacked the support he needed to pass more New Deal–style laws. Opposition was simply too strong for Roosevelt to overcome.

At the same time, Congress, the president, and the American public turned their attention away from the long struggle against the Great Depression. The possibility of a different kind of struggle lay ahead.

Now Europe appeared to be marching relentlessly toward another war. American factories now began to gear up to arm those who would fight the battles. By the millions, workers returned to the assembly lines and workshops. In a period of months in 1939 and 1940, international conflict produced what years of political struggle had failed to achieve: an end to the Great Depression.

READING CHECK Sequencing What events marked the end of the New Deal?

SECTION 4 ASSESSMENT

HSS 11.6.2, 11.6.4, 11.6.5

Reviewing Ideas, Terms, and People

1. **a. Describe** On what grounds did people praise and criticize the New Deal?
   b. Contrast How did Roosevelt's views about the role of government differ from presidents of the 1920s?
   c. Rate Do you think the positive impact of the New Deal outweighed the negative impact? Explain.

2. **a. Recall** Did the New Deal bring an end to the Depression?
   b. Make Inferences Why were New Deal programs able to provide only limited support to the needy?
   c. Evaluate Defend the New Deal's approach of honoring local customs in establishing levels of aid.

3. **a. Define** Write brief definitions of the following terms: minimum wage, incumbent
   b. Explain How did Roosevelt's effort to get rid of disloyal Democrats backfire?
   c. Elaborate How might Roosevelt have tried to improve relations with Congress and win more support for his efforts?

Critical Thinking

4. **Find Supporting Details** Copy the chart below and use information from the section to find supporting details for the main idea given.

FOCUS ON WRITING ELA W1.1, 1.3

5. **Narrative** Write a narrative account of the final year of the New Deal. Be sure to include details from the section about the failures and rare successes of Roosevelt as well as the reasons for the end of the New Deal.

CHAPTER 12 DOCUMENT-BASED INVESTIGATION

Perceptions of Roosevelt

HSS 11.6.2, 11.6.5

Historical Context The documents below provide different information on perceptions of Franklin Roosevelt.

Task Examine the documents and answer the questions that follow. Then you will be asked to write an essay about perceptions of Franklin Roosevelt, using facts from the documents and from the chapter to support the position you take in your thesis statement.

DOCUMENT 1

To his admirers, Franklin Roosevelt's appeal lay in both his policies and his personality. His energy and enthusiasm helped reassure a country that was going through hard times. Tom Vinciguerra, who grew up during the Great Depression, recalled his family's perceptions of Roosevelt.

"'Depression' was fast becoming a household word to all six of us children. Mother's pretty and usually smiling face now turned grim almost daily. The '29 crash destroyed my father's car-repair business. Survival was dependent on Dad's intermittent part-time jobs, plus welfare. Coal money ran out fast, and we weren't always warm. Hand-me-downs and leftover store bread warded off stark desperation.

In 1931, my nonpolitical mother surprised us with an announcement that the family would attend an election eve rally for Roosevelt in Camden, N.J. At the rally, I watched my mother smile and sing. I was so happy for her. As the troubled '30s rolled on, Roosevelt's alphabet soup—PA, CCC, etc.—worked its magic. Our lives improved.

In 1939, at age 13, I heard the loud wail of sirens while walking to my part-time busboy job in downtown Camden. It was Roosevelt's reelection motorcade. As it reached me, the president doffed his famous hat in my direction. Thrilled, I ran home. When I told my mother, she hugged me. I felt her tremble as she sobbed. Then she looked at me as if through me she could express her deep gratitude to the president. My brothers and sisters treated me like a celebrity. I did not bus dishes that day."

DOCUMENT 2

Some critics argued that Roosevelt's charisma sometimes gave people false hope and hid the details of his political plans. The following editorial appeared in *The Nation* magazine after one of Roosevelt's 1936 speeches, as he was preparing for his re-election.

"Mr. Roosevelt's amazing radio message to Congress has undoubtedly strengthened his campaign fortunes, but leaves his program as unclear as ever. Politically adroit [skilled], and from the standpoint of radio oratory a magnificent achievement, it was intellectually a confused and straddling performance... The common man wanted to be let in on a dramatic occasion, and he had his wish. He wanted a fighting speech, and he got it. He was tuning in on history-in-the-making, and the President took pains to make it a good show... The President has again used some sort of magic to increase his stature, and by comparison every Presidential possibility on the Republican side seems puny and frustrate[d]....

But a sober rereading of the speech shows how consummately Mr. Roosevelt displayed his talent for leaving almost all the important things unsaid....

In the domestic field Mr. Roosevelt's message was better as a manifesto [a public statement] than as a preface [introduction] to legislative action. It was here that the speech became... a political rally, with the business of state being transacted under the klieg lights [bright lights used in making motion pictures]."

DOCUMENT 3

Although he grew up wealthy and privileged, President Roosevelt had a strong appeal among many poor Americans, who felt he understood their suffering. The following cartoon reflects this idea.

"Yes, you remembered me."

DOCUMENT 4

Some of Franklin Roosevelt's harshest critics were the wealthy, who resented his efforts to redistribute wealth by taxing the rich to help the poor. Some accused him of betraying his class. In this cartoon, a group of wealthy New Yorkers are going to the Trans-Lux, a popular movie theater on Madison Avenue in New York City that showed newsreels about the president.

"Come along. We're going to the Trans-Lux to hiss Roosevelt."

Skills Focus: READING LIKE A HISTORIAN

HSS Analysis HR4, HI1

1. **a. Identify** Refer to Document 1. What was the writer's impression of Roosevelt?
   b. Analyze How did Roosevelt change this family's life in multiple ways?
2. **a. Describe** Refer to Document 2. According to the writer, what was the main purpose of Roosevelt's speech?
   b. Interpret Why was the writer critical of the president for having strong speaking abilities?
3. **a. Identify** Refer to Documents 3 and 4. What are the two different types of people responding to Roosevelt?
   b. Contrast What do these two cartoons reflect about the personal appeal of President Roosevelt?
4. **Document-Based Essay Question** Consider the question below and form a thesis statement. Using examples from Documents 1, 2, 3, and 4, create an outline and write a short essay supporting your position. How did President Franklin Roosevelt's personality shape public perceptions of his presidency?

See **Skills Handbook**, pp. H28–H29, H31

THE NEW DEAL

CHAPTER 12 Chapter Review

Visual Summary: The New Deal

The New Deal
- Two major plans—in 1933 and 1935
- Established many new government programs
- Popular at first, but limited in its success

Criticism and Resistance
- Political opposition from right and left
- Supreme Court opposition

Lasting Impact
- Forever changes relationship between people and government
- Introduces programs such as Social Security that are still functioning today
- Still controversial

Reviewing Key Terms and People

For each term or name below, write a sentence explaining its significance to the New Deal.

1. public works
2. fireside chat
3. Hundred Days
4. Huey P. Long
5. Social Security
6. CIO
7. deficit
8. John Maynard Keynes
9. Black Cabinet
10. Frances Perkins
11. Mary McLeod Bethune
12. minimum wage

Comprehension and Critical Thinking

SECTION 1 *(pp. 346–353)* **HSS** 11.6.2, 11.6.4

13. **a. Recall** Who did the Democratic Party choose as its candidate in 1932?

    b. Contrast What did the American people seem to like most about Roosevelt's programs? What did they find fault with?

    c. Evaluate What can you conclude from the fact that Roosevelt and the New Deal were criticized both for doing too much and for doing too little?

SECTION 2 *(pp. 357–364)* **HSS** 11.6.4

14. **a. Identify** What was the Second New Deal?

    b. Draw Conclusions What factors undermined support for Roosevelt and his programs?

    c. Evaluate Explain this statement: In some ways, President Roosevelt's success contributed to his failure in the late 1930s.

History's Impact video program
Review the video to answer the closing question: How did the Tennessee Valley Authority change life in much of the rural South?

SECTION 3 (pp. 365–370) HSS 11.10.7

15. **a. Recall** How did the Roosevelt administration treat women and African Americans?

    b. Make Inferences Why do you think Eleanor Roosevelt was able to take a firmer stand for the rights of women and African Americans than her husband did?

    c. Rate How do you think Franklin Roosevelt should be evaluated historically in terms of his treatment of women and minorities?

SECTION 4 (pp. 371–375) HSS 11.6.4

16. **a. Describe** What effects did New Deal programs have on the major problems of the Great Depression, such as unemployment?

    b. Summarize On what grounds can the New Deal be considered a success? a failure?

    c. Rate In your opinion, was the New Deal a success or a failure? Explain.

Using the Internet

go.hrw.com Practice Online Keyword: SE7 CH12

17. Photographer Dorothea Lange used a camera to tell stories of life during the Great Depression. Her photographs convey many different moods, show different groups of people and different types of circumstances. Yet the pictures have much in common. Using the keyword above, research Lange's life and study some of her photographs. Then answer these questions: (a) How did Lange's own life affect her work? (b) What do her photographs reveal about the lives of people during the Depression? In your answers, refer to at least two specific photographs by their titles.

Analyzing Primary Sources HSS HR4

Reading Like a Historian This photograph shows Eleanor Roosevelt meeting with several members of the Bonus Army that formed during the early years of the Roosevelt administration.

18. **Describe** How would you describe the interaction between Eleanor Roosevelt and the Bonus Army marchers?

19. **Contrast** How did Eleanor Roosevelt's interaction with the Bonus Army differ from Hoover's treatment of the Bonus Army of 1932?

Critical Reading ELA R2.2

Read the passage in Section 2 that begins with the heading "The Second Hundred Days." Then answer the question that follows.

20. The issue of Social Security is most closely associated with the criticisms of

    A Congress.

    B Dr. Francis Townsend.

    C voters in 1936.

    D African Americans.

WRITING FOR THE SAT ELA W1.1

Think about the following issue.

Franklin Roosevelt and the New Deal set off one of the most fundamental debates about government in the nation's history. Not since the debates between the Federalists and Antifederalists had the country seen such diverging viewpoints as those between Roosevelt and his conservative opponents. The debate is as strong as ever today.

21. **Assignment** How far should government go to try to improve the lives of citizens? Is it appropriate to use deficit spending when necessary to relieve suffering? What standards would you apply to decide how much help is too little or too much? Support your point of view with reasoning and examples from the chapter.

UNIT 3 IN BRIEF

Below is a chapter-by-chapter summary of the main ideas covered in Unit 3.

CHAPTER 9 — From War to Peace
1919–1928

MAIN IDEA The years following World War I brought unease over the apparent spread of radical influences. The American people sought leaders who offered a return to peaceful times—and they eagerly contributed to a booming, consumer-driven economy.

SECTION 1 Far from feeling safe and at peace, many Americans in the postwar years saw threats in a variety of forms, including labor unrest, rising immigration, and radical political ideas.

SECTION 2 The increasing availability of consumer goods—from cars to household appliances—helped inspire a growing economic boom in the 1920s.

SECTION 3 Warren Harding captured the national mood—and the White House—with his calls for normalcy. His pro-business agenda was expanded upon by his successor, Calvin Coolidge.

CHAPTER 10 — The Roaring Twenties
1920–1929

MAIN IDEA The 1920s was a time of widespread cultural change. Music, art, literature, and popular culture reflected dramatic demographic and cultural developments.

SECTION 1 The changing American culture of the 1920s was reflected in new roles for women and an increase in urbanization.

SECTION 2 Centered in New York City's Harlem community, African American culture experienced a renaissance of literature, music, and art.

SECTION 3 The growing popularity of the radio and the movies helped contribute to the rise of a mass popular culture in the 1920s. Americans idolized the stars, both on the screen and off, that emerged from these new forms of entertainment.

CHAPTER 11 — The Great Depression Begins
1929–1933

MAIN IDEA Following an era of apparent prosperity, the Great Depression began in 1929. Soon millions of Americans were suffering, and the political landscape of the United States stood on the brink of great change.

SECTION 1 The American stock markets, which had ballooned in value and helped fuel the economic optimism of the 1920s, collapsed in 1929. The crash had effects far beyond the losses by investors.

SECTION 2 In the Great Depression that followed the 1929 stock market crash, millions of people lost their jobs, their savings, and their homes. In some parts of the country, environmental catastrophe added to the suffering.

SECTION 3 President Herbert Hoover believed in limited government action to address the growing national crisis. For many Americans, he came to be the target of much anger and unhappiness.

CHAPTER 12 — The New Deal
1933–1940

MAIN IDEA Swept into office in 1932 on his promises to help the victims of the Great Depression, Franklin Delano Roosevelt pushed forward a series of programs that came to be called the New Deal. These programs met with some success, as well as some criticism.

SECTION 1 As president, Roosevelt quickly sought to address the fears of the nation. New Deal laws helped repair the banking system and provide relief for the jobless, though they met with significant criticism.

SECTION 2 The Emergency Relief Appropriation Act and Social Security helped set the pace for the Second New Deal, which helped Roosevelt win re-election as president in 1936.

SECTION 3 The New Deal provided some new opportunities for women and minority groups. It also helped shape the popular and artistic culture of the decade.

SECTION 4 The New Deal had mixed results in solving the economic problems of the Great Depression. However, it unquestionably changed the relationships between the people and their government.

UNIT 4: A Champion of Democracy

1939–1960

Chapter 13
World War II Erupts
1939–1941

Chapter 14
The United States in World War II
1941–1945

Chapter 15
The Cold War Begins
1945–1953

Chapter 16
Postwar America
1945–1960

Themes

Global Relations
The United States and the Allies defeated the Axis Powers in World War II, but tensions between the United States and its former ally the Soviet Union led to a long-running Cold War.

Government and Democracy
The United States fought against regimes that opposed democracy during World War II and the Cold War.

Japan formally surrendered aboard the USS *Missouri* on September 2, 1945, bringing World War II to an end.

Prepare to Read

Drawing Conclusions

Find practice for **Drawing Conclusions** in the **Skills Handbook,** p. H12

Good readers can use clues and their own prior knowledge to draw conclusions about various people places, and events mentioned in text. Drawing conclusions helps you remember what you read.

Before You Read
Skim chapter titles, section headings, and visuals to determine what the chapter will be about. Make a mental list of what you already know about the subject matter.

While You Read
Identify facts and ideas in the text. Then look for connections between those facts, ideas and what you already know.

After You Read
Briefly summarize what you have read. Then form a conclusion that makes a decision, judgment, or opinion about what the facts and ideas mean to you.

Mobilizing Industry and Science

The enthusiasm of American fighting forces was important. In order to defeat the Axis armies, however, American troops would need the proper equipment. The nation responded quickly to this need. Many factories that made consumer goods were quickly converted to the production of war supplies.

Rosie the Riveter Producing enough supplies to fight the war required many workers. At the same time, American men were leaving their factory jobs by the millions to join the armed forces.

Women helped provide a solution to this problem. During the war, the number of women working outside the home rose dramatically. Many of these eight million new workers took industrial jobs that had never been open to women before.

READING CHECK **Drawing Conclusions**
How were working women important to the war effort?

The section head tells you that the passage will be about how science and industry were mobilized for war.

Fact To win, American troops needed equipment.

Fact Factories needed workers, but men were leaving to be soldiers.

Test Prep Tip

Short answer and essay questions on tests frequently ask you to draw a conclusion about something you have read. But conclusions are not always stated directly. Try restating a passage from the text as a question that begins, "Why was it important that...?" For example, "Why was it important that many of the eight million new [women] workers took industrial jobs?"

382 UNIT 4

History's Impact video program
Watch the video to understand the impact of isolationism.

March 1941 Congress establishes the lend-lease program to deliver arms to Great Britain on credit.

December 1940 President Roosevelt declares the United States an "arsenal of democracy."

December 7, 1941 Japanese bomb the U.S. Navy's Pacific Fleet at Pearl Harbor, Hawaii.

1940 | **1941**

May 1940 Winston Churchill becomes UK prime minister.

May–June 1940 Germany conquers the Netherlands, Belgium, and France.

October 1940 Battle of Britain ends with Hitler's forces rebuffed.

September 1940 Japan joins Axis alliance with Germany and Italy.

October 1941 General Hideki Tojo becomes Japanese prime minister.

385

SECTION 1
The Rise of Dictators

BEFORE YOU READ

MAIN IDEA
The shattering effects of World War I helped set the stage for a new, aggressive type of leader in Europe and Asia.

READING FOCUS
1. How did the aftermath of World War I contribute to political problems in Europe?
2. How did the problems facing Europe in the postwar years lead to the rise of totalitarian leaders?
3. What events exemplify the growing use of military force by totalitarian regimes in the 1930s?
4. What alarming actions did Adolf Hitler take in the mid-1930s?

KEY TERMS AND PEOPLE
inflation
Benito Mussolini
fascism
dictatorship
totalitarian
Adolf Hitler
Francisco Franco
Joseph Stalin
Haile Selassie
Neville Chamberlain

 HSS 11.7.1 Examine the origins of American involvement in the war, with an emphasis on the events that precipitated the attack on Pearl Harbor.

THE INSIDE STORY

How can one man shatter a hateful myth? The 1936 Summer Olympic Games were held in the German capital of Berlin. For German leader Adolf Hitler, the event presented a golden opportunity. Hitler had risen to power telling of the greatness of the German people—and of the racial inferiority of certain other groups, such as Africans. The Olympic Games, many Germans believed, would provide proof of this racist idea for the whole world to see.

The U.S. Olympic team included many African American athletes. Among them was track star Jesse Owens. In an amazing performance, he captured gold medals in the 100- and 200-meter dashes, the long jump, and a relay. As he stood on the podium before the German crowd, he was living proof that Hitler's views on race were wrong.

Unfortunately, Hitler and Germany failed to learn the lessons of Owens's example. Hitler's hold on the German people was strong, and his message of hate, anger, and false pride had taken firm root. As you will read, he was merely one of several powerful and ruthless leaders to emerge during this time of turmoil and uncertainty.

The "Master Race" Loses the Race

► Jesse Owens (center) stands above his competitors at the 1936 Olympic Games.

386 CHAPTER 13

Europe after World War I

In an earlier chapter, you read about some of the difficulties facing the United States after World War I. Economic problems, social change, and the threat of communism helped produce a Red Scare—a fear of aliens and radicals.

Europe faced even more challenges at the end of the war. The war had caused the deaths of millions and the destruction of numerous cities and farms. The European economy was in ruins. It would take years to recover.

Problems with peace The Treaty of Versailles (ver-SY), which had brought the war to an end, left many European nations dissatisfied. France in particular had hoped to use the peace settlement to severely weaken Germany. They felt the treaty was not harsh enough on the Germans. Italy was also unhappy with the treaty. The Italians had been on the winning side in the war. They had hoped to be rewarded with territory as part of the treaty. Instead, they were largely ignored during the peace talks.

German outrage Germany suffered the most as a result of the Treaty of Versailles. Its terms did serious damage to the German economy. It also left the German people—and the German military—feeling humiliated. This helped usher in a period of political upheaval.

The treaty forced Germany to give up control of some of its land, including major industrial regions. As you read earlier, the treaty also required Germany to make heavy reparation payments to other countries. In the early 1920s, these factors helped bring about a period of severe **inflation,** or rising prices. Prices for goods increased at an incredible rate. The chart on this page shows the effects of this economic disaster. By 1923 German currency had simply ceased to have any meaningful value. For millions of Germans, a lifetime's worth of hard work and savings had vanished.

Germany also experienced political turmoil after the war. As you have read before, Communists and Socialists tried to take control of Germany in 1918 and early 1919. This effort failed, and Germany soon established a democratic system of government led by less radical elements. This government was known as the Weimar (VY-mahr) Republic, after the German city where it was established.

German money lost so much value in the early 1920s that children used currency as building blocks.

TALES OF GERMAN HYPERINFLATION

One American dollar could buy about 9 German marks in 1919. At the height of the panic, a dollar could buy more than 4 trillion marks.

By 1923, some 300 paper mills and 2,000 printing presses were working around the clock to print money.

Prices rose extremely fast. One customer at a cafe ordered a cup of coffee at 5,000 marks. By the time he ordered his second, the price had risen to 7,000 marks.

A typical loaf of bread cost about 1 mark in 1920. By November 1, 1923, that bread might cost 3 billion marks. Two weeks later, the price for the bread would have risen to 80 billion marks.

The Weimar Republic, however, was not a very strong government. It faced opposition from the political far left—Communists—and from the far right, which was antidemocratic. Another problem was unhappiness in the German military. It had been greatly reduced in size and power as part of the Treaty of Versailles. These factors helped make the Weimar Republic weak and unstable.

READING CHECK Identifying Cause and Effect How did the Treaty of Versailles affect Europe after World War I?

Totalitarian Leaders Arise

European struggles and dissatisfaction during the postwar years had a major effect on European politics. In some countries, a certain type of leader emerged—one who reflected and expressed the people's bitterness and anger. These leaders promised a return to greatness for their nations. This vision was so appealing to their unhappy people that many were willing to give up basic freedoms in return for the hope of future glory.

Mussolini and the birth of fascism
The first of these new leaders to emerge in Europe was the Italian **Benito Mussolini**. He had begun his public life in the early 1900s as a member of a Socialist party in Italy. Unlike many of his fellow Socialists, however, he supported Italy's entry into World War I. By the war's end, Mussolini had moved to the far right of Italian politics. He strongly opposed socialism and communism.

Outraged by the Treaty of Versailles, Mussolini founded a new Italian political party—the National Fascist Party. The term *fascist* comes from a Latin word for "a bundle of rods tied together." The ancient Romans had used this bundle as a symbol of their state. The single rod, Roman thinking went, could be easily broken. When tied together with other rods, however, it was strong.

For Mussolini, **fascism** was a system of government that stressed the glory of the state. He summed up the principle of fascism with the slogan, "Everything in the State, nothing outside the State, nothing against the State." The rights and concerns of individuals were of little importance.

HISTORY'S VOICES

> "Anti-individualistic, the Fascist conception of life stresses the importance of the State and accepts the individual only in so far as his interests coincide with those of the State."
>
> —Benito Mussolini and Giovanni Gentile, *The Doctrine of Fascism*, 1932

After World War I, Mussolini used his dynamic public speaking skill to win a seat in Italy's parliament. His vision of a strong, orderly Italy appealed to many people. He also encouraged the use of violence against Communists and Socialists, whom many Italians blamed for the disorder of postwar Italy. By these means, Mussolini gained wide support. In 1922 he became leader of the government.

Europe's New Dictators

Once in power, Mussolini established a **dictatorship**—government by a leader or group that holds unchallenged power and authority. He allowed no other political parties and ruthlessly crushed opponents. His government controlled newspapers, schools, and businesses. All power flowed through the man Italians referred to as *Il Duce* (il DOO-chay)—"the leader." Under this **totalitarian** regime, Mussolini had total control over daily life in Italy.

Hitler's rise to power
Another of Europe's aggressive new leaders was Austrian-born **Adolf Hitler**, who had an unremarkable early life. An unsuccessful art student, he was rejected by the Austrian military because they thought him too weak to carry a weapon. With the start of World War I, however, Hitler volunteered for the German army. There he built a solid record as a soldier.

Hitler's anger about the Treaty of Versailles led him into politics. He joined a small political party known as the National Socialists, or Nazis. The party attracted many former soldiers and others who were unhappy with conditions in Germany. It was during this time that Hitler discovered his talent for public speaking and leadership. Under his guidance, the Nazis gained influence in German politics.

Hitler, however, was impatient for change. In 1923 he organized an effort to seize power in Germany by force. This revolt failed. As a result, Hitler was imprisoned for nine months of a five-year sentence.

While in prison, he produced a book called *Mein Kampf*—German for "My Struggle." The book outlined Hitler's major political ideas. Like Mussolini, Hitler stressed nationalism and devotion to the state. He dreamed of uniting all the Germans of Europe in a great empire. "Germany will either be a world power or there will be no Germany," he wrote.

In *Mein Kampf*, Hitler expressed a belief in the racial superiority of Germanic peoples, whom he called Aryans. In addition, he blamed Jews for many of Germany's problems and believed that they threatened the purity of the Aryan race. (You will read more about Hitler's beliefs in the next chapter.)

HISTORY'S VOICES
> "If we pass all the causes of the German collapse in review, the ultimate and most decisive remains the failure to recognize the racial problem and especially the Jewish menace."
> —Adolf Hitler, *Mein Kampf*, 1924

When he got out of prison, Hitler was determined to gain power through peaceful means. Seizing on public discontent and offering an appealing vision of German greatness, Hitler gradually built support. By 1933 the Nazis were the most powerful party in the nation. Hitler became Germany's chancellor, a top position in the government.

Hitler now moved to establish himself as a totalitarian dictator. Using his political skills—and violence when necessary—he managed to eliminate his political opponents. Meanwhile, Hitler continued to spread the myth of Aryan greatness and the coming German empire. At the center of this myth was Hitler himself. As with Mussolini in Italy, Hitler the man was glorified above all other Germans.

Hitler also began secretly to build up the German armed forces. He knew that these would be useful to him as he sought to fulfill his goal of expanding German territory. The German people, Hitler explained, needed more "living space" in which to grow and prosper.

Hitler (left) and Mussolini (above) both used cunning, violence, and repression to achieve and maintain power. Both also possessed a theatrical speaking style that enabled them to achieve great influence over their audiences.

Linking to Today

Totalitarian Dictators

Totalitarian governments are not just a part of the historical past. Today a number of countries are controlled by dictatorial governments.

In Africa, the former British colony of Rhodesia became the independent nation of Zimbabwe in 1980. A guerrilla fighter turned politician named Robert Mugabe gained power.

At first, many people saw him as a reformer. As time passed, however, Mugabe came under sharp criticism. His land-redistribution policies drove out white farm owners and broke up large farms into small plots of land. In recent years, Mugabe has used fear and violence to limit voting rights.

North Korea also has a totalitarian government. Ruled by Kim Jong Il, the government controls all television and radio broadcasts. It does not permit any criticism of the nation's so-called Dear Leader. Rigid economic policies have led to more than 10 years of famine.

In Myanmar, also called Burma, the totalitarian government is run by a group of military officers. The government has suppressed prodemocracy movements since 1988 and ignored the results of a legislative election in 1990.

Drawing Conclusions Would you expect a country with a totalitarian government to have a thriving economy? Explain.

North Korean leader Kim Jong Il

THE IMPACT TODAY

Government

In 2003 the American-led attack on Iraq was meant in part to remove the totalitarian dictator Saddam Hussein. Like Mussolini, Hitler, and Stalin, Saddam glorified himself with statues and portraits throughout Iraq.

Other regimes Some of the same forces that helped Mussolini and Hitler gain totalitarian power also helped create powerful regimes in other countries. For example, Spain erupted in civil war in the 1930s. Out of this conflict, Fascist general **Francisco Franco** came to power. You will read more about the Spanish Civil War shortly.

In the Soviet Union, communism was already established when **Joseph Stalin** came to power in the mid-1920s. Communism and fascism represent opposite political extremes. Yet there were similarities between the Soviet system under Stalin and the Fascist systems. Like the Fascists, Stalin violently crushed his political opponents.

Also like Hitler and Mussolini, Joseph Stalin created a myth of his own greatness. Throughout the Soviet Union, towns and cities were renamed for him. His portrait was displayed everywhere. "[W]e regard ourselves as the happiest of mortals," gushed one writer in the newspaper *Pravda*, "because we are the contemporary of a man who never had an equal in world history." Stalin's domination of all aspects of Soviet life made him one of the era's most notorious totalitarian dictators.

Japan was another country torn by political and economic conflict. In the early 1930s, military leaders used violence to gain control over the government. They, too, were inspired by nationalistic dreams of Japanese greatness. Such dreams would soon lead to war.

READING CHECK **Comparing** What common factors contributed to the rise of the totalitarian leaders who emerged after World War I?

Totalitarian Governments and Military Force

A common feature of the powerful postwar leaders was a willingness to use violence to gain power. Many were also willing to use military force against other nations.

Japan and Manchuria Among the problems facing Japan in the 1920s was the limited size of its territory. The islands of Japan were growing crowded. Many Japanese wanted to expand their territory and gain greater access to wealth and resources. This desire grew even stronger as a result of the worldwide economic depression of the 1930s.

390 CHAPTER 13

At this time, Japan's government was under civilian control. Many Japanese, however, were unhappy with their leaders. Dissatisfaction was especially high among members of the military who held strong nationalist beliefs.

Some Japanese generals decided it was time to act. In 1931 the army invaded the Chinese province of Manchuria—without the approval of the Japanese government. The goal was to seize Manchuria's land and resources for the use of the Japanese people. Japan's government ordered the army to end the action. The army officers simply refused to obey the order.

The takeover of Manchuria demonstrated the weakness of the Japanese government and the strength of Japan's nationalists. Over the next several years, the military would expand its influence over the government, in part by assassinating its political enemies. In general, the Japanese public supported the increasingly powerful military. As in Germany and Italy, the Japanese people were beginning to believe in the nationalists' dream of expansion.

The League of Nations strongly criticized Japan for the invasion of Manchuria. In response, Japan simply withdrew from the League of Nations, which was unable or unwilling to take any strong action against Japan. The powerlessness of the League was clear for the world to see.

Italy Invades Ethiopia

The weakness of the League was soon confirmed by events elsewhere. In 1935 Mussolini's Italy invaded the East African nation of Ethiopia.

Italy's history with Ethiopia was several decades old. Italian efforts to establish a colony there in the late 1800s had ended in a crushing military defeat at the hands of the Ethiopians.

Italy did manage to keep several smaller colonies in East Africa. Some Italians, however, held on to bitter feelings toward Ethiopia for decades.

Those feelings resurfaced when Mussolini came to power with grand plans to rebuild an Italian empire. In 1935 he used a dispute about the border between Ethiopia and an Italian colony as an excuse to launch an invasion.

The Ethiopians were unable to resist the more powerful Italian forces, and Italy soon conquered the country. Ethiopian emperor **Haile Selassie** personally asked the League of Nations for help.

HISTORY'S VOICES

> "It is collective security. It is the very existence of the League of Nations. It is the confidence that each State is to place in international treaties. It is the value of promises made to small States that their integrity and their independence shall be respected and ensured.... In a word, it is international morality that is at stake."
>
> —Haile Selassie, Speech to League of Nations, June 1936

Selassie's words failed to sway the League. Again, the international community was unwilling to take a strong stand against aggression.

American leaders, meanwhile, spoke out against Italy's actions, but there was little public support for doing more. President Franklin Roosevelt was unwilling to take formal steps to punish Mussolini.

The Spanish Civil War

Spain in the mid-1930s was troubled by fierce political conflict. On the left were Communists. On the right were Fascists and Nationalists. Most Spaniards held political views somewhere in between these extremes.

In 1936 this conflict led to civil war. The war soon attracted interest and involvement from

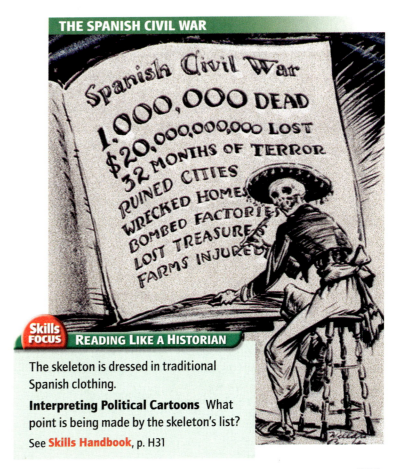

THE SPANISH CIVIL WAR

READING LIKE A HISTORIAN

The skeleton is dressed in traditional Spanish clothing.

Interpreting Political Cartoons What point is being made by the skeleton's list?

See **Skills Handbook**, p. H31

WORLD WAR II ERUPTS **391**

COUNTERPOINTS

Appeasement

Prime Minister Chamberlain declared himself "a man of peace to the depths of my soul."

" [W]e should seek by all means in our power to avoid war, by analyzing possible causes, by trying to remove them, by discussion in a spirit of collaboration and good will. I cannot believe that such a programme would be rejected by the people of this country, even if it does mean the establishment of personal contact with dictators. "

Neville Chamberlain, 1938

When Chamberlain returned from his meeting with Hitler declaring "peace for our time," Churchill voiced a quite different opinion of events.

" The Prime Minister desires to see cordial relations between this country and Germany.... You must have diplomatic and correct relations, but there can never be friendship between the British democracy and the Nazi Power. "

Winston Churchill, 1938

SKILLS FOCUS: READING LIKE A HISTORIAN

Drawing Conclusions How does Chamberlain's comment hint at why Churchill's warnings went unheeded in 1938?

See **Skills Handbook**, p. H12

---

many other countries in Europe and in North America. For example, Fascist Italy and Nazi Germany sent forces and equipment to fight for the Nationalists, who were led by General Francisco Franco. Opposing the Nationalists were the the so-called Republicans, who controlled the government at the start of the war. They had the support of the Soviet Union, which provided arms and equipment. In addition, volunteers from the United States and many other countries joined the fight on the Republican side.

The fighting in the Spanish Civil War was bloody and brutal. Many hundreds of thousands of people died. This included several hundred American participants in the fighting. By 1939, however, Franco's Nationalists had defeated the Republicans. Spain came under the control of a Fascist dictator.

READING CHECK **Summarizing** How did the League of Nations respond to Japan's and Italy's use of military force?

Hitler Takes Action

As soon as Hitler gained power in Germany, he secretly began to rebuild the German military. Before long, however, he was openly stating his plan to re-arm Germany. This was in direct violation of the Treaty of Versailles. Despite this, Hitler managed to convince Great Britain and France to tolerate his actions. In 1935, for example, the British agreed to allow Germany to rebuild its naval forces, including submarines. Hitler claimed that he was building German military strength in order to resist the spread of communism. This was a goal the British supported. In fact, he was already committed to using war to expand his nation.

Militarizing the Rhineland Under the Treaty of Versailles, Germany was required to keep its troops out of an area in the Rhine River valley along the French border. This was meant to protect France against possible German aggression. In 1936, however, Hitler violated the treaty by sending German troops into the Rhineland. As an excuse, Hitler claimed that a recent French military agreement with the Soviet Union threatened Germany.

France was greatly alarmed by the German action. It was unwilling, however, to take military action against Germany. Britain, for its part, had no interest in going to war over the matter. Germany's troops remained in the Rhineland, and Hitler grew bolder.

The Anschluss Two years later, Hitler took action to gain control of neighboring Austria. Hitler was an Austrian by birth. He had long dreamed of uniting all ethnic Germans, including the Austrians. In 1938 he tried to force the Austrian government to agree to *Anschluss* (AHN-shloos)—union with Germany. When the Austrian government refused, Hitler sent troops into the country.

The *Anschluss* was popular among the people of Austria. It was, however, another German violation of the Treaty of Versailles. Germany's neighbors issued strongly worded protests. But they did nothing more to stop Hitler.

The Sudetenland By now, Hitler was confident that no one would act to stop him. Soon after the *Anschluss*, he began plans to gain control of a German-speaking portion of Czechoslovakia called the Sudetenland. First, he encouraged Germans in the Sudetenland to protest against Czechoslovakian rule. Then he began threatening a military attack.

Hoping to end the crisis, British prime minister **Neville Chamberlain** and French premier Edouard Daladier met with Hitler. As in the past, the British and French seemed most interested in avoiding armed conflict. At a meeting in Munich, Chamberlain and Daladier agreed to allow Hitler to annex the Sudetenland—that is, make it part of Germany. Czechoslovakia, which had no representative at the Munich meeting, protested the agreement. Chamberlain, however, boasted of having achieved "peace for our time." In reality, the world was on the verge of war.

ACADEMIC VOCABULARY

ethnic relating to a large group of people sharing a common racial, national, linguistic, or cultural heritage

READING CHECK **Summarizing** Explain how France and Great Britain responded to Hitler's actions in the early to mid-1930s.

SECTION 1 ASSESSMENT

HSS 11.7.1

Reviewing Ideas, Terms, and People

1. **a. Describe** How did the conclusion of World War I affect the political climate in Europe?
   b. Make Inferences How did the severe **inflation** in Germany affect the population?
   c. Evaluate Why do you think it is important for a peace agreement, such as the Treaty of Versailles, to be regarded as fair by all sides?

2. **a. Define** Write a brief definition for each of the following terms: **fascism, dictatorship, totalitarian**
   b. Compare What did **Mussolini, Hitler,** and **Stalin** all share in common?
   c. Elaborate Why do you think the three totalitarian dictators worked so hard to build public adoration of themselves?

3. **a. Identify** What was the significance of Manchuria, Ethiopia, and Spain in the 1930s?
   b. Make Generalizations How did other nations react to the aggression of the Japanese and the Italians?
   c. Evaluate Why do you think the League of Nations was unwilling to stand up to the aggression of the Japanese and the Italians?

4. **a. Describe** How did Hitler respond to Germany's obligations under the Treaty of Versailles when he became Germany's leader?

   b. Compare How did the reaction of Great Britain and France toward Germany compare to their reaction toward Italy and Japan?
   c. Predict How do you think the failure to enforce rules of the League of Nations and the Treaty of Versailles will affect Germany in the future?

Critical Thinking

5. **Identifying Cause and Effect** Copy the chart below and use information from the section to identify the effects of the rise of dictators.

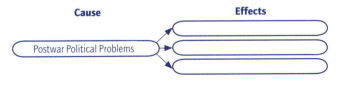

FOCUS ON WRITING ELA W1.3, LS2.0

6. **Persuasive** Assume the position of a delegate to the League of Nations and deliver a speech in which you argue for or against firm action to enforce the League's promises of protection for places such as Manchuria and Ethiopia.

SECTION 2
Europe Erupts in War

BEFORE YOU READ

MAIN IDEA
Far from being satisfied by the actions of France and Great Britain, Germany turned to force and triggered the start of World War II.

READING FOCUS
1. How did Germany's actions in 1939 trigger the start of World War II?
2. Where did German forces turn after overrunning Poland in 1939?
3. What developments increased tensions between the United States and Japan in East Asia?

KEY TERMS AND PEOPLE
appeasement
Winston Churchill
blitzkrieg
the Allies
Vichy France
Charles de Gaulle
Luftwaffe
Axis Powers
Hideki Tojo

HSS 11.7.1 Examine the origins of American involvement in the war, with an emphasis on the events that precipitated the attack on Pearl Harbor.

THE INSIDE STORY

How do you stop an attack that is as fast as lightning? The German war machine began its attack from the air and without warning. Bombers struck at cities, transportation systems, and airfields. Roads became choked with panicked citizens.

Next came the fast-moving columns of German tanks and motorized forces, stabbing deep into the enemy countryside. Defending troops who went out to meet the armored German forces often were attacked by air.

After the tanks came German foot soldiers, fanning out across the land their tanks had just rumbled through. They destroyed or scattered any remaining resistance.

The German method of attack was devastating. The combined effect of speed and armor represented a major innovation over battle techniques used just two decades before in World War I. Starting in 1939, Europe would come to dread the German blitzkrieg, or lightning war.

Blitzkrieg

Aircraft bombed airfields, transportation systems, and cities, crippling defenses.

Fast-moving armored columns struck quickly, driving deeply into enemy territory.

394

World War II Starts

British prime minister Neville Chamberlain believed that his policy toward Hitler of **appeasement**, or giving in to aggressive demands to maintain peace, had prevented the outbreak of a needless war. "How horrible, fantastic, incredible it is," Chamberlain said after meeting Hitler in Munich, "that we should be digging trenches and trying on gas masks here because of a quarrel in a faraway country." Yet others believed that Hitler was not going to stop after gaining the Sudetenland, as he had promised Chamberlain. One such critic was a rival politician named **Winston Churchill**. He condemned Chamberlain's appeasement as cowardly and likely to lead to war.

Hitler's early moves Churchill was correct. In March 1939 Hitler sent his troops into what remained of Czechoslovakia, capturing it without a fight. Now even Chamberlain realized that Hitler could not be trusted—and that his aggression was far from over.

Hitler's next move was to build alliances that he hoped would help him in the future. First, he established a pact with Italy. Then in August 1939, he announced a nonaggression pact with Stalin's Soviet Union.

With this pact, Hitler had shrewdly won Stalin's agreement to stay out of Germany's way as it continued to expand. In return, Hitler promised not to attack the Soviet Union. He also secretly agreed to give the Soviet Union parts of soon-to-be-conquered territory in Eastern Europe. "I have the world in my pocket!" Hitler triumphantly declared when Stalin agreed to the deal.

This development shocked many in Europe. The British and French had thought that tensions between the Soviets and Germans were rising. They had hoped that Stalin would stand with them against a possible German attack. In fact, the Soviets did fear Hitler's intentions. Stalin, however, believed the deal with the Nazis offered the greatest security.

Hitler attacks Poland Within days of the Nazi-Soviet agreement, Hitler was ready to launch his next strike—the invasion of Poland. To provide an excuse for the attack, Hitler had a German criminal dressed in a Polish military uniform. The man was taken to the German-Polish border and shot. The next morning—September 1, 1939—Germany claimed it had been attacked by Poland, using the dead criminal as proof. German troops immediately launched a massive invasion of Poland.

ACADEMIC VOCABULARY
security the promise of safety

INTERPRETING INFOGRAPHICS

The speed of a German blitzkrieg attack had a devastating effect on a population—both physically and emotionally.

Drawing Conclusions What was the main element on which this type of warfare depended?

See **Skills Handbook**, p. H18

Behind the armor came foot soldiers. They crushed any resistance behind the armor advance.

Earlier you read about German military tactics. The **blitzkrieg**, German for "lightning war," featured an overwhelming combination of air attack and fast-moving armored strikes to drive deep into enemy territory.

The well-trained Germans used the blitzkrieg to devastating effect in Poland. Although the Poles fought bravely, they could not resist the German onslaught. The Polish landscape offered few natural barriers to slow the speedy invasion, and Polish troops were no match for German armor. In some battles, Polish soldiers on horseback carried swords into battle against German tanks. By the end of the month, Poland was in German hands.

> **READING CHECK** **Sequencing** Outline Hitler's actions in 1939 which led to war.

German Forces Turn to the West

On September 3, 1939, Great Britain and France declared war on Germany. They became known as **the Allies**. There was little they could do, however, to slow Hitler in Poland. And even before the fighting there had ended, Hitler was planning his attack on his new enemies.

The Allies, meanwhile, had been forming their own strategy. They decided not to attack Germany. Instead, they would wait for Hitler's next move. They hoped German forces would weaken by trying to break through what they thought were France's strong defenses.

Allied leaders were surprised that Germany did not attack in the winter of 1939–1940. This period of inaction came to be known as the *sitzkrieg*, or the phony war. In fact, German military leaders were busily making plans for an invasion through the dense Ardennes (ahr-DEN) Forest in northern France and Belgium. Thinking that the forest was too rugged for an army to pass through, the French had concentrated their defenses elsewhere. Some troops were stationed to the north of the Ardennes, along France's border with Belgium. French defenses to the south of the Ardennes featured the famed Maginot (MA-zhuh-noh) Line. This was a string of bunkers and fortresses that lined part of the French-German border.

The lull in the fighting ended in April 1940, when Hitler sent his forces into Denmark and Norway. This move was aimed at improving Germany's access to the Atlantic Ocean. Both countries fell with little resistance. The surprised Allies were unable to do much to help. With Denmark and Norway secured, Hitler was now ready to focus on France.

The Netherlands and Belgium fall The Germans finally made their expected strike toward France in May 1940. Their plan worked to perfection. One group of German troops quickly conquered the Netherlands and stormed into Belgium. There they were met by Belgian, British, and French units.

These forces, however, were unable to stop the German assault. By early June, the Germans had trapped hundreds of thousands of Allied soldiers at the French port of Dunkirk. Included were nearly all British forces in France. In a heroic rescue, Allied ships and hundreds of civilian boats plucked nearly 340,000 troops from the coast and carried them to Great Britain. These rescued forces would prove vital to Great Britain's defense.

France falls France, however, was doomed. While Hitler's troops were capturing the Netherlands and Belgium, more German soldiers were carrying out the planned surprise attack through the Ardennes. When they broke through the forest, they easily overwhelmed the thin French force waiting there. The Maginot Line had simply been bypassed.

Having shattered France's defensive plan, Hitler's troops now raced toward Paris, the capital. By the end of June, France had surrendered to Germany and Italy, which had joined the war earlier that month. German forces now occupied much of France. The rest was placed under the control of French officials who cooperated with Hitler. This unoccupied part of France was known as **Vichy** (VEE-shee) **France**. Many other French leaders, led by General **Charles de Gaulle**, fled to Great Britain. There they organized resistance to German and Vichy control of France.

The Battle of Britain Now Great Britain stood alone against what appeared to be an unstoppable German war machine. The nation was now led by Winston Churchill, who had a great gift for inspiring courage and confidence among the British people.

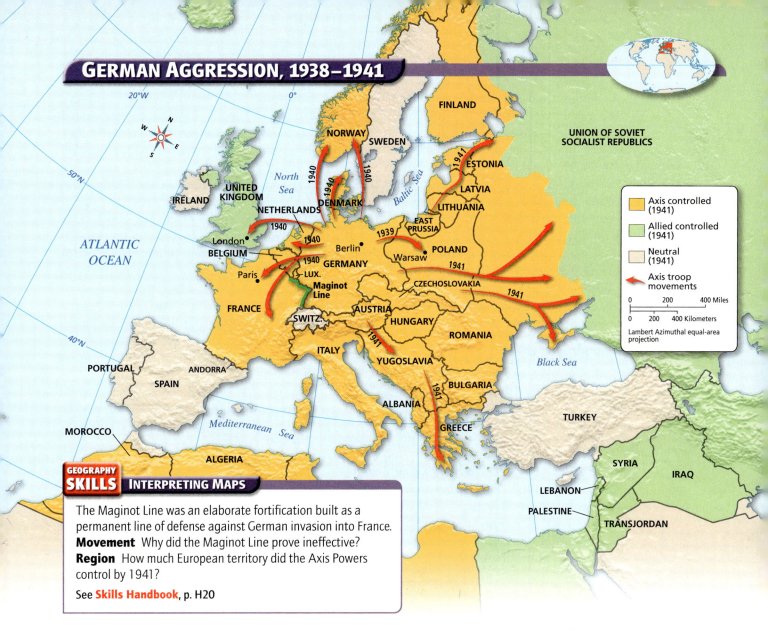

GERMAN AGGRESSION, 1938–1941

GEOGRAPHY SKILLS   INTERPRETING MAPS

The Maginot Line was an elaborate fortification built as a permanent line of defense against German invasion into France.
Movement Why did the Maginot Line prove ineffective?
Region How much European territory did the Axis Powers control by 1941?

See **Skills Handbook**, p. H20

HISTORY'S VOICES

"We shall defend our island whatever the cost may be; we shall fight on beaches, landing grounds, in fields, in streets and on the hills. We shall never surrender…"

—Winston Churchill, speech before the House of Commons, June 4, 1940

As promised, Churchill refused even to consider trying to negotiate a peace agreement with Germany. Hitler, meanwhile, prepared to invade Great Britain.

The first stage of the German plan was to destroy the British Royal Air Force, or RAF. For the first time in the war, the Germans failed. Using radar, a new technology that used radio waves to detect approaching airplanes, the RAF inflicted heavy damage on German planes. As the battle wore on, the German air force, or **Luftwaffe**, began bombing London. The goal was to terrorize the public so that they would lose the will to fight. Though thousands of civilians died in the raids, Churchill helped keep the nation's spirits up. "Little does [Hitler] know the spirit of the British nation," he said, "or the tough fiber of the Londoners."

Americans followed the Battle of Britain through the thrilling radio reports of Edward R. Murrow. He was an American reporter stationed in London. His live broadcasts described the air raids as bombs exploded around him.

By late 1940, the Battle of Britain was over. The British had stopped the Luftwaffe. Hitler was forced to call off the attempted invasion.

 Summarizing What was Hitler's experience when he turned his forces to the West in 1940?

THE IMPACT TODAY

Science and Technology

Radar continues to be a major tool in modern armies and navies. Radar allows not only the tracking of enemy aircraft, but also other functions, including detailed weather prediction and guidance for missile systems.

WORLD WAR II ERUPTS   397

Tensions in East Asia

As you have read, Japanese nationalists expanded their influence in the 1930s. Japan increasingly viewed itself as a great imperial power. In 1934 it began expanding its naval forces. This violated promises made at the Washington Naval Conference in the early 1920s. In 1936 it signed an anticommunism pact with Germany that clearly linked Japan with Europe's Fascist menace.

Then in 1937, Japan began a war against China. The attack was marked by great brutality. For example, Japanese troops massacred an estimated 200,000 to 300,000 Chinese in the capital of Nanjing.

HISTORY'S VOICES

"There is probably no crime that has not been committed in this city today.... How many thousands were mowed down by guns or bayoneted we shall probably never know."
—Minnie Vautrin, recorded in her diary, 1937

In 1940 Japan formed a military alliance with Germany and Italy. The three nations became known as the **Axis Powers**.

The next year, Japanese forces, with the agreement of the French Vichy government, moved to take control of French Indochina. This was a French colony in Southeast Asia that included the modern-day countries of Vietnam, Laos, and Cambodia. Japan's takeover of French Indochina threatened British and American interests in the region. It signaled Japan's intention to seek the oil and other resources of the Dutch East Indies (today known as Indonesia), the Philippines, and other parts of Southeast Asia.

The United States reacted quickly to this move. President Roosevelt took steps to punish Japan economically and to deny it access to vital oil supplies. This was a serious threat to Japan's future plans.

Representatives of the two nations met to try to settle their growing differences. In Japan, a powerful group led by the minister of war, General **Hideki Tojo**, pushed the government not to accept any compromise.

Tojo was a strong nationalist. He was quite willing to go to war in order to build a Japanese empire. In October 1941, strong pressure from Tojo forced Japan's government to resign. Tojo took control of the country. American leaders did not yet realize it, but the time for compromise with Japan was over.

READING CHECK **Identifying Cause and Effect** How did rising tension between the United States and Japan affect politics in Japan?

SECTION 2 ASSESSMENT

HSS 11.7.1

Reviewing Ideas, Terms, and People

1. **a. Define** Write a brief definition for each of the following terms: **appeasement, blitzkrieg**
   b. Compare What factor made Germany's blitzkrieg so different from the tactics used in World War I?
   c. Develop Based on what you have read about the blitzkrieg, how do you think the Poles might have better defended against it?

2. **a. Identify** What was the significance of the **Allies, Vichy France**, and **Luftwaffe**?
   b. Compare Why do you think the British were able to defend themselves against the Germans but the French were not?
   c. Rate Why do you think the leadership abilities of Winston Churchill were so important to the British during the Battle of Britain?

3. **a. Describe** Briefly describe the relationship between Japan and the United States in the late 1930s and early 1940s.
   b. Make Inferences Why do you think the United States was so concerned about Japanese expansion into Southeast Asia?

   c. Evaluate Do you think the United States did the right thing by drawing a firm line against Japanese aggression? Explain.

Critical Thinking

4. **Identifying the Main Idea** Copy the chart below and use information from the section to identify and record key details about the early stages of World War II.

 ELA W1.1, 1.3

5. **Descriptive** Write a description of what you imagine life was like in Great Britain just before and during the Battle of Britain.

SECTION 3: The United States Enters the War

BEFORE YOU READ

MAIN IDEA
Isolationist feeling in the United States was strong in the 1930s, but Axis aggression eventually destroyed it and pushed the United States into war.

READING FOCUS
1. Why was a commitment to isolationism so widespread in the 1930s?
2. How did Roosevelt balance American isolationism with the need to intervene in the war?
3. What did the United States do to prepare for war in 1940 and 1941?
4. What were the causes and effects of the Japanese attack at Pearl Harbor?

KEY TERMS AND PEOPLE
pacifist
Neutrality Act
neutral
Quarantine Speech
cash-and-carry
Wendell Willkie
Lend-Lease Act
Atlantic Charter

HSS 11.7.1 Examine the origins of American involvement in the war, with an emphasis on the events that precipitated the attack on Pearl Harbor.
HSS 11.7.4 Analyze Roosevelt's foreign policy during World War II (e.g., Four Freedoms speech).

Lindbergh and "AMERICA FIRST"

THE INSIDE STORY

What threat made even Lucky Lindy nervous? Ever since his historic 1927 solo flight across the Atlantic, Charles Lindbergh held a place as perhaps the greatest of all American heroes. People admired him not just for his bravery but also for his knowledge about aviation. When he spoke, people listened.

In the early days of World War II, Lindbergh was speaking a lot. Back in the United States after several years living in Europe, the great American flying hero was working hard to keep the country out of the war.

Getting involved in the fighting would be a disaster for the United States, Lindbergh argued. We were safe here in the United States as long as we built our own defenses and minded our own business, he claimed. Danger waited if we got mixed up in the bloody affairs of Europe. There, Lindbergh argued, the mighty German nation, with its superior air force, was poised to win. Lindbergh himself had inspected their aircraft and came away deeply impressed. He concluded that lending support to Hitler's foes was a lost cause that might end up costing us dearly. Americans, Lindbergh insisted, should put "America first." It must avoid giving in to the cries for help from the British and the other doomed people of Europe.

Lindbergh was a powerful voice in American society. His message was well received by millions of people, including many leading politicians. It would take one of the most shocking events in American history to drown it out.

◀ A soldier snatches a sign from an antiwar demonstrator at the White House in 1941.

WORLD WAR II ERUPTS **399**

American Isolationism

Many Americans had questioned what the Allies' costly victory in World War I had actually achieved. These feelings helped explain why the U.S. Senate was unwilling for America to join the League of Nations. Many feared that the League might drag the United States into future wars. Anti-League feelings remained strong in the 1920s and 1930s.

The desire to avoid involvement in foreign wars was known as isolationism. This view view shared by both liberals and conservatives in the 1930s. Isolationists were not necessarily pacifists, or people who do not believe in the use of military force. Most Americans remained ready to defend their country and its interests. Isolationists simply wanted to preserve America's freedom to choose the time and place for such action.

Franklin D. Roosevelt was not an isolationist. After World War I, for example, he had supported entry into the League of Nations. Though this remained an unpopular position in 1932, Roosevelt easily defeated the staunch isolationist Herbert Hoover in that year's election. This was largely because voting took place in the depths of the Great Depression. Most voters were more concerned with economic issues than with foreign policy.

In his first term, Roosevelt only rarely focused on foreign-policy matters. The United States did establish diplomatic relations with the Soviet Union in 1933. Nearly all of Roosevelt's attention, however, went to his New Deal programs. Meanwhile, when Congress discussed foreign affairs, it was generally to pass isolationist measures, such as the first Neutrality Act. Passed in 1935, this law was meant to prevent the nation from being drawn into war as it had been in 1917.

HISTORY'S VOICES

"Upon the outbreak or during the progress of war between, or among, two or more foreign states…it shall thereafter be unlawful to export arms, ammunition, or [tools] of war to any port of such [warring] states."
—Neutrality Act, 1935

Over the next several years, Congress strengthened the Neutrality Act. For example, it outlawed making loans to warring countries.

READING CHECK Summarizing Why was isolationism widespread in the years after World War I?

Academic Vocabulary
liberal favoring political reform; progressive

conservative tending to preserve established traditions or policies

---

TRACING HISTORY

Isolationism

From the nation's founding, many American leaders have sought to isolate the nation from international politics. Since World War II, however, the United States has increasingly formed alliances with other nations. Study the time line to learn how international events challenged American isolationist impulses.

The USS *Maine* blows up in Havana Harbor.

1898 United States gains control of Puerto Rico, Guam, and the Philippines in the Spanish-American War.

1800

THE GRANGER COLLECTION, NEW YORK

1823 Monroe Doctrine pledges neutrality in European disputes but warns European nations not to interfere in the Western Hemisphere.

Political cartoon supporting the Monroe Doctrine

Balancing Isolationism and Intervention

While many Americans focused on their own problems in the 1930s, circumstances overseas were taking an alarming turn. Italy's 1935 invasion of Ethiopia disturbed Roosevelt deeply. He viewed Italy as a dangerous aggressor. Citing the Neutrality Act, he halted arms sales to the two warring countries. This, Roosevelt knew, would hurt only Italy, for Ethiopia was unable to afford weapons. He further urged businesses to voluntarily end oil shipments to Italy. Few listened. Roosevelt, however, could do little more. He feared that taking a stronger stance against Italy would anger isolationists, whose political support he still needed. The isolationists wanted the United States to remain neutral—that is, not aid one side or the other.

Other events of the mid-1930s also challenged Roosevelt and his relationship with the isolationists. During the Spanish Civil War, strict neutrality meant not supplying either warring party with arms. Remaining truly neutral, however, was not a simple matter for the United States. Not aiding either side clearly gave an advantage to the Fascists, who were being well supplied by the Italians and Germans. Even the isolationists were unclear how to solve this dilemma.

Another problem was that deep down, President Roosevelt did not want to be neutral. He was deeply disturbed by the increasingly aggressive actions of the world's new group of totalitarian dictators. His willingness to avoid conflict with isolationists in the government was beginning to fade.

After Japan invaded China in 1937, President Roosevelt decided that it was time to speak out. In a speech he delivered in Chicago, he offered his views on recent world events.

ACADEMIC VOCABULARY
circumstances happenings or facts, especially those that affect other people or events

HISTORY'S VOICES

"The peace, the freedom, and the security of 90 percent of the population of the world is being jeopardized by the remaining 10 percent who are threatening a breakdown of all international order and law."
—Franklin D. Roosevelt, October 5, 1937

Roosevelt compared the spread of war to the spread of a contagious disease. Such diseases can be stopped, he said, by a quarantine. This means identifying the sick and separating them from the healthy. Roosevelt urged the United

1918 World War I ends. Isolationists in Congress defeat President Wilson's plan to join the League of Nations.

President Woodrow Wilson

1945 World War II ends. The United States leads the effort to create the United Nations.

1949 To contain Soviet expansion during the Cold War, the United States joins eleven other nations to form the North Atlantic Treaty Organization (NATO).

2004 NATO expands to include several countries that had once been part of the Soviet Union.

President George W. Bush and NATO Secretary General Lord Robertson

Primary Sources

Political Cartoon

After the outbreak of World War II, many Americans were sympathetic to the Allies, but few wanted to get involved in another global war. *Chicago Tribune* cartoonist Carey Orr produced this cartoon recommending the American course of action.

The character of Uncle Sam represents the government of the United States.

The character of Democracy pleads with Uncle Sam to stay out of the war.

Across the Atlantic lies Europe.

THE GRANGER COLLECTION, NEW YORK

SKILLS FOCUS: READING LIKE A HISTORIAN

1. **Interpreting Political Cartoons** What is the artist recommending the United States do?
2. **Drawing Conclusions** Why do you think the artist took this position?

See **Skills Handbook**, pp. H12, H28–H29, H31

States to work with peace-loving countries to quarantine aggressive nations and stop the spread of war. For this reason, the speech was referred to as the **Quarantine Speech**.

READING CHECK **Identifying Problems and Solutions** How did Roosevelt strike a balance between isolationism and intervention in the 1930s?

Preparing for War

Roosevelt's Quarantine Speech upset many isolationists. They predicted that his policies would lead to war. North Dakota senator Gerald P. Nye attacked the speech as a "call...upon the United States to police a world that chooses to follow insane leaders." Still, others applauded Roosevelt. Indeed, the president seemed to be gaining strength against the isolationists.

In early 1938, for example, Roosevelt sought from Congress money for building new naval vessels. Isolationists saw warships mainly as a means of fighting wars far from the United States. Some complained about this proposal. Nevertheless, Congress approved the request.

But Adolf Hitler's aggressive actions strengthened Roosevelt's position. Isolationists had cheered Chamberlain's appeasement at Munich. When German forces later invaded Poland, however, Roosevelt got Congress to change the nation's neutrality laws. The change established a new policy known as **cash-and-carry**. Under this policy, countries at war were allowed to purchase American goods as long as they paid cash and picked up their orders in American ports.

Roosevelt had hoped that the cash-and-carry policy would allow the Allies to slow Hitler's advances. German victories in 1940, however, convinced the president that he needed to do more.

As a result, Roosevelt urged a policy of "all aid short of war." The president agreed to trade fifty aging American warships for eight British military bases. Isolationists opposed the deal but were too weak to stop it.

402 CHAPTER 13

The election of 1940 As Europe was erupting into war, Roosevelt decided to seek a third term as president. Though no one had ever been elected to more than two terms, Roosevelt felt that the world situation required experience in the White House. His opponent was business leader **Wendell Willkie**. In terms of foreign policy, Willkie's views were similar to Roosevelt's. The voters decided to stick with Roosevelt for another term.

Following his re-election, Roosevelt continued his drive to provide aid to the Allies in their fight against Hitler's armies. In a speech at the end of December 1940, Roosevelt declared his goal of making the United States the "arsenal of democracy." An arsenal is a place where weapons are stored. Soon afterward, Congress passed the **Lend-Lease Act**. This allowed the nation to send weapons to Great Britain regardless of its ability to pay.

Ties between the United States and Britain were further strengthened in August 1941. Roosevelt and British leader Winston Churchill met secretly on a ship off the coast of Canada. There the two leaders agreed to the **Atlantic Charter**. This agreement proclaimed the shared goals of the United States and Britain in opposing Hitler and his allies.

Isolationists reacted strongly to these developments. They viewed them as steps leading directly to war. Charles Lindbergh and the America First Committee, which you read about earlier, became leading critics of the president's actions.

In spite of their complaints, however, the United States was looking more and more like a nation at war. Indeed, armed conflict was already taking place on the open seas. As the United States sought to deliver war supplies under the terms of the Lend-Lease Act, German U-boats tried to stop them. In October 1941, torpedoes struck the American destroyer USS *Kearny*. Eleven Americans died. Two weeks later, a German U-boat sank the USS *Reuben James*, killing more than 100 sailors.

Despite the attacks on their ships, many Americans continued to oppose entry into to the war. That, however, was about to change.

READING CHECK Identifying Cause and Effect Why did the conflict between Roosevelt and the isolationists grow as the United States prepared for the coming war?

Japan Attacks Pearl Harbor

While the situation in Europe troubled many Americans, an even bigger threat to peace was taking shape in the Pacific Ocean. Indeed, by late fall of 1941, American leaders were convinced that war between the United States and Japan was likely. The two nations had earlier come into conflict over French Indochina. Japan had also forged an alliance with Germany and Italy, and Japan's new prime minister, Hideki Tojo, was hostile toward the United States.

The key remaining question was how and where the fighting would start. American officials believed that Japan might attack American bases in the Philippines or British territory in Southeast Asia. In any case, American officials were determined not to fire the first shot. They continued to negotiate with the Japanese. At the same time, they warned American forces throughout the world to be prepared for a possible Japanese attack.

The attack on Pearl Harbor American officials were correct: Japan had decided on war. For months, Japanese military leaders had been developing plans for a surprise attack on the American naval base at Pearl Harbor, Hawaii. This base was home to the United States Navy's Pacific Fleet. The Japanese plan called for aircraft carriers to approach the island of Oahu, where Pearl Harbor was located, from the north. Japanese war planes loaded with bombs and torpedoes would lift off from the carriers and destroy as many American ships and planes as possible.

American military planners had for months believed that an attack on Pearl Harbor was a possibility. In December 1941, however, forces at the base were unready to defend it. This was in part because no single commander was in charge of Pearl Harbor's defenses. In the resulting confusion, routine defensive steps, such as using airplanes to watch for approaching ships, were not in place. The Japanese attack force was able to approach Pearl Harbor undetected.

As the sun rose on Sunday morning, December 7, 1941, the Japanese strike force went into action. The raid was a complete surprise to the Americans. Most American fighter planes in Hawaii never got off the ground. Hundreds were severely damaged or

HISTORY CLOSE-UP

Attack on Pearl Harbor

In December 1941 military officials throughout the Pacific were on alert for a possible Japanese attack. Yet Pearl Harbor was not considered the most likely target, and the Japanese strike force approached Hawaii undetected. In one stroke, they destroyed the American Pacific battleship fleet. Below, the USS *West Virginia* sinks as sailors rescue a survivor in the water.

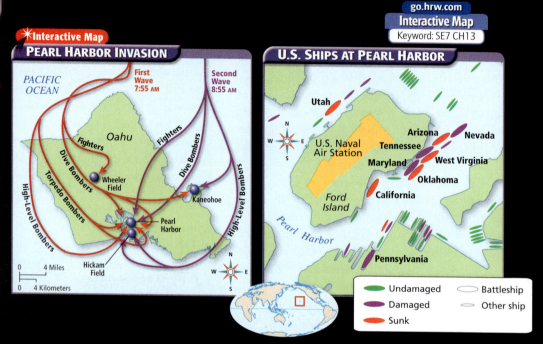

Skills Focus: INTERPRETING INFOGRAPHICS

1. **Making Inferences** What types of ships do you think the Japanese were targeting in their attack?
2. **Interpreting Visuals** How do you think the images of the destruction to the American fleet may have affected the American public?

See **Skills Handbook**, pp. H7, H18, H30

destroyed where they sat. Meanwhile, Japanese bombs and torpedoes took a heavy toll on the American warships anchored in the harbor.

The Japanese attack lasted barely two hours. By the time it was over, however, the Pacific Fleet was a tangled mass of smoking metal. "We felt like crying," said one sailor who survived the raid. "We could see our beautiful fleet upside down and burning up."

The destruction was enormous. All eight battleships in the harbor suffered damage. Four were sunk. Nearly 200 aircraft were completely destroyed, and more were damaged. Some 2,400 Americans were dead. Japan, meanwhile, lost only a handful of submarines and fewer than 30 aircraft. It was a complete defeat for the United States.

American reaction Americans reacted to the devastating attack with anger and fear. Rumors spread that Japanese troops would soon invade the West Coast. Nervous Californians reported seeing submarines off their shores. They strung beaches with barbed wire. As you will read in the next chapter, some people became afraid that Japanese Americans would secretly assist an invasion of the United States mainland.

Roosevelt had expected a Japanese strike, but he also expected a formal declaration of war by Japan. Indeed, Japan's ambassadors had scheduled an appointment to deliver just such a message on the day of the attack. By the time they arrived, however, Pearl Harbor was in flames. Roosevelt was furious that Japan had meant to deceive the United States. On December 8, 1941, he asked Congress for a declaration of war.

HISTORY'S VOICES

> "Yesterday, December 7, 1941—a date which will live in infamy—the United States of America was suddenly and deliberately attacked by naval and air forces of the Empire of Japan.... Always will we remember the character of the onslaught against us. No matter how long it may take us to overcome this..., the American people in their righteous might will win through to absolute victory."
>
> —Franklin Roosevelt, December 8, 1941

America was now at war with Japan. Three days later, Germany and Italy declared war on the United States. The nation had entered World War II as one of the Allies.

READING CHECK **Drawing Conclusions** What made Japan's attack on Pearl Harbor so devastating?

THE IMPACT TODAY

Daily Life
The terrorist attacks of September 11, 2001 in the United States are often compared to the attack on Pearl Harbor. Both took the nation completely by surprise and caused reactions of fear and anger. Both triggered strong surges of patriotism and a commitment to defeat our foes.

SECTION 3 ASSESSMENT

HSS 11.7.1, 11.7.4

Reviewing Ideas, Terms, and People

1. **a. Define** Write a brief definition for each of the following terms: **pacifist**, **Neutrality Act**
   b. Analyze How did World War I contribute to isolationist feeling in the 1920s and 1930s?

2. **a. Describe** Why were some isolationists skeptical of Roosevelt's foreign policy during his campaign for president?
   b. Sequence How did Roosevelt's position toward isolationism change over time?
   c. Elaborate Why do you think Roosevelt increasingly came into conflict with isolationists?

3. **a. Recall** What events explain Roosevelt's continuing shift away from isolationism in the late 1930s?
   b. Compare Describe **cash-and-carry** and the **Lend-Lease Act** and how they differed from one another.
   c. Evaluate Do you think the isolationists were correct in arguing that Roosevelt's policies, including lend-lease, would increase the likelihood of war? Explain.

4. **a. Describe** What was the attack on Pearl Harbor?
   b. Summarize What was the significance of this battle?

Critical Thinking

5. **Sequencing** Copy the chart below and use information from the section to identify and record the sequence of events that led the United States away from its isolationist position and into World War II.

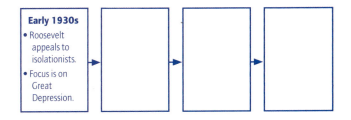

FOCUS ON WRITING ELA W1.1, 1.3

6. **Persuasive** Write a letter to the editor of a local newspaper from the perspective of a citizen in October 1941, in which you argue either for or against isolationism. Be sure to refer to information from this section and elsewhere in the chapter to support your view.

SECTION 4: Mobilizing for War

BEFORE YOU READ

MAIN IDEA
The outbreak of World War II spurred the mobilization of American military and industrial might.

READING FOCUS
1. How did the U.S. armed forces mobilize to fight World War II?
2. What role did American industry and science play in mobilizing to fight World War II?
3. How did mobilization challenge the nation's ideals of freedom?

KEY TERMS AND PEOPLE
George C. Marshall
Oveta Culp Hobby
Rosie the Riveter
Manhattan Project
atomic bomb
J. Robert Oppenheimer
A. Philip Randolph
Bracero Program
zoot suit riots

HSS 11.7.3 Identify the roles and sacrifices of American soldiers, as well as the unique contributions of special fighting forces.

HSS 11.7.6 Describe the war's impact on American industry and use of resources.

HSS 11.10.1 Explain how demands of African Americans helped produce a stimulus for civil rights, including Roosevelt's ban on racial discrimination in defense industries in 1941.

Can you fight a war by assembly line? Reporters had never seen anything like Willow Run. Inside the giant structure, a person could scarcely see from end to end. "Like infinity," noted an observer, "it stretches everywhere into the distance."

The building these people were describing was the brainchild of business pioneer Henry Ford. Built in the tradition of the great Ford auto factories, Willow Run was a giant, mile-long assembly line for airplanes. As the United States entered World War II, the plant stood as a symbol of the nation's great industrial might. Indeed, the tremendous power of American industry would provide the key to victory against the Axis menace.

It took time for Willow Run to get up to speed. Finding tens of thousands of employees was difficult. Lack of housing was another issue. Over time, however, Ford and the government resolved these problems. Willow Run and its 42,000 workers kicked into high-speed production. By the end of the war, 650 aircraft per month were coming off the Willow Run line.

Willow Run demonstrated the enormous power of American industry—and the mighty effort of American business and government leaders to harness it. As you will read, this was just one part of the nationwide effort to get ready to fight World War II.

▲ B-24 bombers roll off the assembly line in the Willow Run factory.

406 CHAPTER 13

Mobilizing the Armed Forces

The Japanese bombs and torpedoes that fell on Pearl Harbor had destroyed not only ships and planes, but also most of the remaining isolationist feeling in the United States. Now that the country had entered the war, it had to mobilize, or bring its forces into readiness. This was a huge job.

Fortunately, the United States had made something of a head start. Starting in 1940 the government had sharply increased military spending. This spending, in fact, was largely responsible for ending the Great Depression. Thousands found work in the now-busy factories, making supplies for the military.

The leader of the mobilization effort was Army Chief of Staff, General **George C. Marshall**. Marshall worked closely with President Roosevelt to plan for war. He ensured that American soldiers were well equipped and properly trained. Marshall would also play an important role in developing the nation's military strategy.

Finding soldiers In addition to equipment and supplies, the United States needed soldiers and sailors to fight the Axis Powers. Following Pearl Harbor, the government expanded the draft, which Roosevelt had reinstated in 1940. Many young men, however, did not wait to be called into service. Eager to defend their country, they volunteered by the millions.

HISTORY'S VOICES

> "I wanted to be in it. I was fifteen.... I lied about my age and tried to get in in '43. I was sixteen now. My mother wouldn't sign. ... Then I passed the air corps test at Oak Park High.... Then I figured... you're gonna be two years training, the war'll be over. Go in the Marine Corps."
>
> —Roger Tuttrup, quoted in *"The Good War": An Oral History of World War Two*, by Studs Terkel

Eventually, some 16 million Americans would enter the armed forces.

Women and the armed forces Although they were not permitted to take part in combat, American women filled a variety of vital roles in the military. Their service helped make more men available for fighting. For example, 10,000 women joined the Women Accepted for Volunteer Emergency Service, or WAVES. This was a navy program in which women did

PRIMARY SOURCES
Propaganda Poster

During World War II the U.S. government produced a wide variety of posters to encourage recruitment and support for the war. This poster for the Army Air Corps was created by artist James Montgomery Flagg, who also created the famous image of Uncle Sam during World War I.

P-38 Lightnings were one of the most popular fighter aircraft used in the war.

The man is clearly enthusiastic to join the fight.

This man's gear identifies him as a pilot.

SKILLS FOCUS — READING LIKE A HISTORIAN

1. **Analyzing Primary Sources** What was the purpose of this image?
2. **Interpreting Visuals** Do you think the image accurately reflects fighter pilots during World War II? Explain.

See **Skills Handbook**, pp. H28–H29, H30

necessary clerical work that would otherwise have to be performed by men. Some 1,000 women joined the Women Airforce Service Pilots, or WASPs. They tested and delivered aircraft. Nearly 40 WASPs gave their lives serving the country.

By far the largest women's unit was the Women's Army Corps, or WAC, in which 150,000 women served. At the start of the war, the unit was known as the Women's Army Auxiliary Corps, or WAAC. Its members worked with, but were not part of, the army. The WAACs repaired equipment, worked as electricians, and performed many other jobs.

By 1943 demand for their services was so great that the army created the Women's Army Corp. WACs were full-fledged members of the army. As such, they were entitled to full army protection and benefits and could serve overseas on nearly every task except combat. They were led by **Oveta Culp Hobby**, who was given the rank of colonel.

New military bases The millions of Americans entering the armed forces all needed training and housing. This required building hundreds of new military bases.

In general, the military looked to build new bases in rural areas where there was plenty of open land. Life on a rural, isolated base often required a big adjustment, especially for those who came from larger cities. It also required some getting used to by local citizens. They had to cope with the presence of thousands of young men in their once quiet neighborhoods.

The military buildup transformed many parts of the country. California became home to more military bases than any other state. Florida, with its warm weather and plentiful land, was also an excellent location for military training. Camp Blanding, with its 55,000 soldiers, became the fourth largest city in Florida almost overnight.

Texans saw 1.2 million troops train at their army bases, including Camp Hood. Some 200,000 air pilots trained at Texas air bases, such as Randolph Air Field. In addition, Texas was a temporary home to over 50,000 German, Italian, and Japanese prisoners of war.

READING CHECK **Identifying Problem and Solution** What were the challenges of mobilizing the armed forces?

Mobilization

Women were essential to the war mobilization effort. They filled many jobs once reserved for men, such as riveting (above).

Mobilizing Industry and Science

The enthusiasm of American fighting forces was important. In order to defeat the Axis armies, however, American troops would need the proper equipment. The nation responded quickly to this need. Many factories that made consumer goods were quickly converted to the production of war supplies.

The federal government spent tens of billions of dollars on weapons and supplies in the months following the outbreak of war. Shortly after Pearl Harbor, Roosevelt set the ambitious goal of building 60,000 new planes in 1942 and a further 125,000 aircraft the following year. He asked for 120,000 new tanks over the same time period. Thanks to the efforts of people such as Henry Ford and the workers of Willow Run, American industry met these goals.

The United States not only had to produce all of these war supplies, it also had to ship them to the armed forces overseas. Cargo

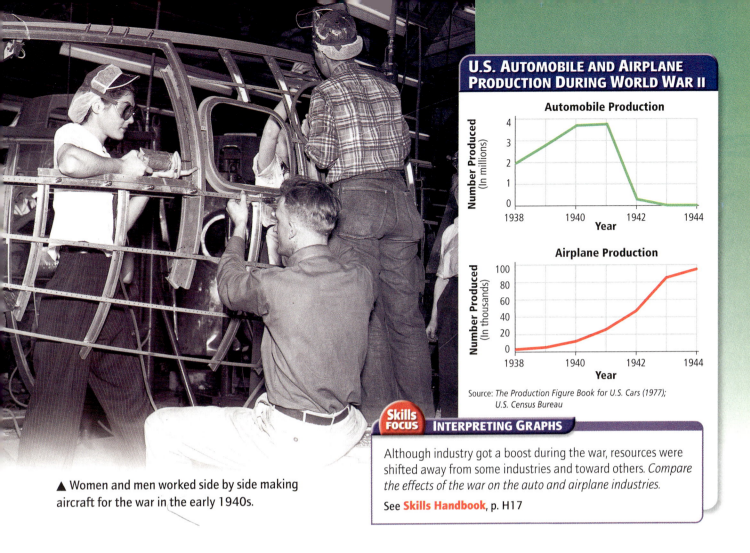

▲ Women and men worked side by side making aircraft for the war in the early 1940s.

U.S. Automobile and Airplane Production During World War II

Automobile Production

Airplane Production

Source: *The Production Figure Book for U.S. Cars* (1977); U.S. Census Bureau

SKILLS FOCUS — INTERPRETING GRAPHS

Although industry got a boost during the war, resources were shifted away from some industries and toward others. *Compare the effects of the war on the auto and airplane industries.*

See **Skills Handbook**, p. H17

ships, however, were a main target of enemy submarines. Early in the war, submarines took a terrible toll on American shipping. To replace these losses, American shipyards turned out 5,500 vessels over the course of the war.

About half of these ships were the so-called liberty ships built by Henry Kaiser. Before the war, Kaiser was known for such projects as Hoover Dam. He had never built a ship. Yet he created a shipyard in California and used assembly-line techniques to produce massive cargo ships at an astounding rate. His workers once produced a liberty ship in a mere four and a half days.

The federal government created several new agencies to help ensure that American industry would be able to meet the needs of the armed forces. These agencies regulated what products factories produced, what prices they could charge, and how the nation's raw materials would be used. The wartime agencies were staffed in part by American business and labor leaders. Key figures included William Knudsen and Sidney Hillman, who led the Office of Production Management, and Donald Nelson, who headed the government's War Production Board.

Rosie the Riveter Producing enough supplies to fight the war required many workers. At the same time, American men were leaving their factory jobs by the millions to join the armed forces.

Women helped provide a solution to this problem. During the war, the number of women working outside the home rose dramatically. Many of these 6.5 million new workers took industrial jobs that had never been open to women before.

"I was a woman doing a 'man's job'!" recalled one of these women workers. "I was also very proud of the fact that I was contributing, even in a small way, to the war efforts." Working women of the war came to be represented by the symbolic figure known as **Rosie the Riveter**.

Labor in World War II Government spending during World War II helped end the Great Depression and created millions of new jobs. Many of these workers joined labor unions, but the federal government was concerned that strikes might hamper the war effort.

Just weeks after the nation declared war on Japan, President Roosevelt established the National War Labor Board to help settle labor disputes. In 1943 Congress passed the Smith-Connally Act, giving the president power to take over vital industries in the event of strikes. These measures helped reduce—but not end—labor disputes in the early war years.

Mobilizing science War planners knew that technology would play an important role in World War II. The Manhattan Project, with laboratories in Los Alamos, New Mexico, was the most significant scientific program of World War II. This was a top-secret American program to build an atomic bomb, a powerful weapon that used energy released by the splitting of atoms.

Research into building an atomic bomb had begun in 1939, motivated by concern that Germany was already working on such a weapon. As you will read later, American scientists led by physicist J. Robert Oppenheimer would win this race. The result would shape world history for decades to come.

READING CHECK **Identifying the Main Idea** What steps did the U.S. government take to mobilize industry and science?

Fighting for Freedom at Home

As in World War I, the United States faced the challenge of fighting for freedom overseas. The nation also faced the challenge of ensuring freedom for Americans at home.

African Americans in the military Hundreds of thousands of African Americans served with honor during World War II. In the process, they broke down barriers that had long blocked their way. For example, the war saw the enlistment of the first African American marines in U.S. history. The navy commissioned the first African American officers during the war.

At the same time, African Americans continued to suffer discrimination. They were forced to serve in segregated units. Their bravery often went unrecognized. Not a single African American soldier of World War II received the prestigious Medal of Honor. This oversight was corrected nearly 50 years after the fact, when seven African Americans received recognition for their remarkable bravery in battle.

African Americans in the workforce The war created an enormous demand for factory workers. White women took many of these jobs. African Americans found new opportunities as well. As factories increased

Seeking Equal Opportunity
African American workers wanted an equal opportunity to contribute to the nation's mobization effort and to benefit from the opportunities it created. *How did President Roosevelt respond to African American demands for fair treatment?*

war production, thousands found jobs that had in the past been unavailable to them. Yet even with these new opportunities came harsh reminders of widespread racist attitudes. For example, African Americans were often forced to take the lowest-paying jobs, regardless of their skills or experience.

Union leader **A. Philip Randolph**, head of the Brotherhood of Sleeping Car Porters, noted these developments. In 1941 he called for a march on Washington, D.C., to protest unfair treatment of African Americans. Only after President Roosevelt issued an order outlawing discrimination in government or defense jobs did Randolph call off the march.

Challenges for Hispanic Americans Hispanic Americans experienced opportunities and challenges during World War II. For example, the demand for farm labor led the U.S. and Mexican governments to establish the **Bracero Program** in 1942. This gave some Mexican workers the chance to work temporarily in the United States.

In some communities, unfortunately, the arrival of thousands of Hispanic workers led to increased ethnic tensions. In California, such tensions boiled over into violence. In the **zoot suit riots** of June 1943, white sailors stationed in Los Angeles fought with groups of Mexican American youths during a week of terrible violence. The riot was named after the zoot suit, a flashy style of clothing favored by some Mexican American young men.

In spite of the conflicts, Hispanic Americans remained deeply loyal to the United States and sought opportunities to serve.

HISTORY'S VOICES

"We know that us Mexican-American boys and girls can do a lot of things to win the war if someone will give us a chance.... [D]iscrimination is the thing that makes the other Americans divide from us."
—Letter from Youth Committee for the Defense of Mexican American Youth to Vice President Henry Wallace

Like members of other minority groups, many Hispanic Americans served bravely in the armed forces. They also shared a strong commitment to victory and freedom.

READING CHECK **Identifying Cause and Effect** Explain how mobilization triggered a fight for freedom among minority groups in the United States.

SECTION 4 ASSESSMENT

HSS 11.7.3, 11.7.6, 11.10.1

Reviewing Ideas, Terms, and People

1. a. Describe Briefly describe the significance of the following to the mobilization effort during World War II: **George C. Marshall**, **Oveta Culp Hobby**
   b. Explain What effect did the bombing of Pearl Harbor have on the nation's mobilization effort?
   c. Evaluate How do you think the changing roles of women in the United States were reflected in their experiences during wartime?

2. a. Define Write a brief definition of each of the following terms: **Rosie the Riveter**, **Manhattan Project**, and **atomic bomb**
   b. Summarize Why was mobilization of American industry considered so important to the war effort?
   c. Evaluate Do you think the decision of the U.S. government to expand its oversight of American industry would help or hurt industry's ability to meet its goals? Explain

3. a. Recall How did African American military personnel and workers fare during World War II?

b. Draw Conclusions Why do you think World War II created so many opportunities for women and members of minority groups?
   c. Predict How do you think the end of the war, when it comes, will affect minority groups? Explain your answer.

Critical Thinking

4. Identifying Supporting Details Copy the chart below and use information from the section to identify and record the details that support the main idea.

FOCUS ON WRITING ELA W1.1, 1.3

5. Descriptive The preparations for World War II brought major changes to life in the United States. Assume the point of view of an American citizen in late 1941 to early 1942. Write a journal entry in which you describe the changes taking place around you.

CHAPTER 13 DOCUMENT-BASED INVESTIGATION

Reactions to Pearl Harbor

HSS 11.7.1

Historical Context The documents below provide information on different reactions to the Japanese bombing of Pearl Harbor in Hawaii.

Task Examine the documents and answer the questions that follow. Then you will be asked to write an essay about reactions to the Pearl Harbor attack, using facts from the documents and information from the chapter to support the position you take in your thesis statement.

DOCUMENT 1

The day after the attack on Pearl Harbor, President Franklin Roosevelt asked Congress to declare war on Japan. His simple speech reflected the shock that most Americans felt about the attack.

> "Yesterday, December 7, 1941—a date which will live in infamy—the United States of America was suddenly and deliberately attacked by naval and air forces of the Empire of Japan....
>
> Always will we remember the character of the onslaught against us. No matter how long it may take us to overcome this premeditated invasion, the American people in their righteous might will win through to absolute victory.
>
> I believe I interpret the will of the Congress and of the people when I assert that we will not only defend ourselves to the uttermost but will make very certain that this form of treachery shall never endanger us again.
>
> Hostilities exist. There is no blinking at the fact that our people, our territory and our interests are in grave danger.
>
> With confidence in our armed forces—with the unbounded determination of our people—we will gain the inevitable triumph—so help us God."

DOCUMENT 2

The government used memories of Pearl Harbor to encourage support for the war. The poster below was created to encourage support for war-related work, such as making munitions.

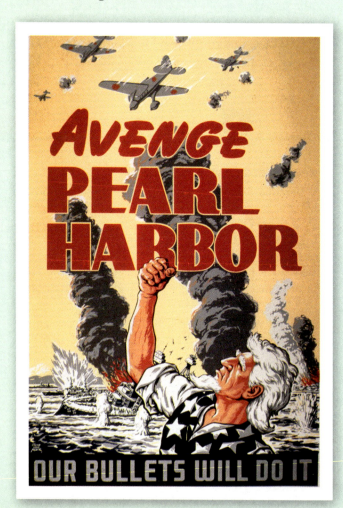

DOCUMENT 3

Most Americans found out about the Pearl Harbor attacks from the radio. Duane T. Brigstock of Battle Creek, Michigan, recalled his reactions upon hearing the news.

"Along with a large contingent [group] of Battle Creek bowlers, I was participating in the Central States tournament in Toledo, Ohio, that fateful Sunday afternoon. As the news broke, the message was relayed to us over the P.A. system: 'The Japanese are bombing Pearl Harbor!' We listened in shocked disbelief and activity halted on the busy alleys. Our first reaction was anger—followed by a great surge of patriotism. Bowling scores were quickly forgotten. As we checked out of our hotel, someone softly started to sing "God Bless America" and soon everyone joined in.

We were a quiet group driving home as we listened to bits of information on our car radios. We dug out our draft registration cards from our billfolds to recheck our numbers and wonder when we would be called up. There was no question in our minds that we would serve—only when."

DOCUMENT 4

While many people reacted to the war by joining the military, those who worked on the home front never forgot the event. Just a few weeks after the attack, these war-production workers took a break from their night shift on New Year's Eve to celebrate the coming year. Instead of shouting "Happy New Year," they shouted "Remember Pearl Harbor!"

HSS Analysis HR4, HI1, HI4

Skills Focus: READING LIKE A HISTORIAN

1. **a. Identify** Refer to Document 1. Why does Roosevelt call December 7, 1941, a "date which will live in infamy?"
   b. Analyze How does Roosevelt try to warn and also to reassure the nation after the attack?

2. **a. Describe** Refer to Document 2. What is going on in this image?
   b. Interpret What kind of effect do you think this image had on wartime workers?

3. **a. Identify** Refer to Document 3. What feelings did the attack immediately stir up for this writer?
   b. Elaborate How do you think that day changed the lives of those who heard about it on the radio?

4. **a. Identify** Refer to Document 4. How did these workers celebrate the new year?
   b. Analyze Why do you think the workers chose that cheer to mark the new year?

5. **Document-Based Essay Question** Consider the question below and form a thesis statement. Using examples from Documents 1, 2, 3, and 4, create an outline and write a short essay supporting your position.
   How did Americans react to the attack on Pearl Harbor?

See **Skills Handbook**, pp. H28–H29, H30

Chapter 13 Chapter Review

Visual Summary: World War II Erupts

Rise of Dictators
- Dictators, taking advantage of widespread fear, uncertainty and despair, emerge in the post–World War I era.

Aggression and War
- Aggressive dictators use war to promote their tyrannical goals.

The United States: From Isolationism to War
- Isolationism gives way to the call for war when the United States comes under direct attack.

Mobilizing for War
- The United States musters its tremendous industrial and human might to fight the war.

Reviewing Key Terms and People

Complete each sentence by filling in the blank with the correct term or person.

1. Benito Mussolini introduced a political philosophy known as _Facism_.
2. In the 1930s, many Americans supported _isolationism_ rather than an active involvement in affairs overseas.
3. Neville Chamberlain is associated with the _appeasement_ of Hitler at Munich.
4. The German attack of Poland demonstrated a tactic known as _blitzkrieg_.
5. The symbol for women factory workers during the war was _Rosie The Riviter_.
6. Germany, Italy, and Japan formed the _Axis Powers_.
7. In order to aid the British, Roosevelt promoted the policy of _Lend-Lease_.
8. In 1933 _Adolf Hitler_ became the chancellor of Germany.
9. The _Manhattan Project_ was a top-secret program to build an atomic bomb.
10. In the _quarentine speech_, Roosevelt likened the spread of aggression to the spread of disease.
11. The _Bracero program_ provided an opportunity for workers from Mexico to work in the United States temporarily.

Comprehension and Critical Thinking

SECTION 1 (pp. 386–393) **HSS** 11.7.1

12. **a. Identify** Who were the major totalitarian dictators to emerge following World War I?

    b. Summarize What were the key features of the postwar totalitarian regimes?

    c. Elaborate What do you think was the appeal of fascism, and why did it spread in the post–World War I era?

414 CHAPTER 13

History's Impact video program
Review the video to answer the closing question: Why did so many Americans favor isolationism before the United States entered World War II?

SECTION 2 *(pp. 394–398)* HSS 11.7.1

13. **a. Recall** What countries did Germany attack in 1939 and 1940?

    b. Make Inferences Based on the events of 1940, what can you infer about the Allies' evaluation of German military strength at the start of World War II?

    c. Evaluate Do you think Hitler would have behaved differently had the British and French not appeased him in Munich? Explain.

SECTION 3 *(pp. 399–405)* HSS 11.7.1

14. **a. Describe** During the 1930s, what was the general attitude among the American public toward events taking place in Europe, Africa, and Asia?

    b. Sequence Describe the change in American attitudes toward world events in the period between the late 1930s and the end of 1941.

    c. Develop How would you counter the isolationist argument in the late 1930s? Write a brief statement to explain your idea.

SECTION 4 *(pp. 406–411)* HSS 11.7.6

15. **a. Describe** Describe the key steps in mobilizing the nation for war.

    b. Explain What does it mean to say that mobilzation created "opportunities and challenges" for minority groups?

    c. Predict How do you think a mobilization effort such as the one that occurred in the early 1940s would affect the United States today? Explain your answer.

Using the Internet

16. Why did people put their faith in totalitarian dictators who propelled their nations into war? Using the keyword above, do some research on the Internet to find some answers to this question. Then create a chart to compare and contrast the reasons why many German, Italian, and Japanese people supported totalitarian dictators in their nations.

go.hrw.com
Practice Online
Keyword: SE7 CH13

Analyzing Primary Sources HSS HR4

Reading Like a Historian
This photograph shows a worker at a defense plant during World War II.

17. **Identify** What term was used to identify the type of worker shown in this picture?

18. **Analyze** What is the significance of the fact that this worker is a woman?

Critical Reading ELA R3.8

Read the passage in Section 2 that begins with the heading "World War II Starts." Then answer the questions that follow.

19. Winston Churchill believed that
    A. appeasement would lead to war.
    B. it was foolish to get involved in foreign conflicts.
    C. Hitler would stop at the Sudetenland.
    D. Chamberlain correctly handled Hitler.

20. The passage suggests that in return for giving into Chamberlain's demands, Hitler
    A. threatened to invade Great Britain.
    B. promised to support Chamberlain.
    C. promised not to seek further territorial gains.
    D. agreed that Chamberlain was a coward.

FOCUS ON WRITING ELA W1.1

Narrative Writing *Narrative writing tells a story. It uses precise detail and often describes events in sequence. To practice narrative writing, complete the assignment below.*

Writing Topic Isolationism in the 1930s

21. **Assignment** Based on what you have read in this chapter, write a narrative paragraph that retells the story of the rise and fall of isolationist feeling in the United States between World War I and World War II.

CHAPTER 14
1941–1945
The United States in WORLD WAR II

THE BIG PICTURE The United States—including its military forces and its civilian population—succeeded along with the Allies to defeat the Axis powers in Europe and the Pacific. Yet the cost of victory and the discovery of the full horrors of World War II were staggering.

California Standards

History-Social Sciences
11.7 Students analyze America's participation in World War II.

SKILLS FOCUS — READING LIKE A HISTORIAN

U.S. soldiers in Germany pose on top of an enormous cannon captured from the Germans, pleased to have removed this monster from the enemy's arsenal. These guns were called railway guns because they required one or even two sets of railroad tracks to move their bulk.
Interpreting Visuals What do the soldiers' poses tell you about their attitudes?

See **Skills Handbook**, p. H30

 U.S.

January 6 Roosevelt delivers the Four Freedoms speech about the future of the world.

December 7 Japan attacks Pearl Harbor.

1941

 World

June 22 Germany begins its invasion of the Soviet Union.

416

The Battle of the Atlantic

For the United States and the Allies, defeating the Axis Powers depended largely on control of the seas. It was only by sea that the United States could deliver soldiers and supplies to the hard-pressed opponents of Hitler. If the Atlantic was not kept safe for shipping, the Axis would soon win the war.

Germany entered World War II with a navy powerful enough to challenge for control of the seas. It featured several new surface ships. Foremost among these was the giant *Bismarck*, the pride of the German fleet. After Great Britain managed to sink the *Bismarck* in 1941, however, Germany began to rely on a familiar weapon—the U-boat.

U-boat attacks In World War I the Allies had learned to protect ships against U-boats by forming convoys. Early in World War II, however, the British (and the Americans) did not have enough vessels to form effective convoys. This made it easy for U-boats to attack supply ships bound for Great Britain. The Germans also developed new tactics to increase U-boat effectiveness. One example was the so-called **wolf pack**, in which U-boats hunted in groups and often attacked at night.

The German U-boat fleet enjoyed what it referred to as the "happy time" in 1940 and 1941. U-boats sent hundreds of ships and tons of supplies to the bottom of the sea. At the same time, the German navy lost only a few dozen U-boats.

After Germany declared war on the United States, U-boat attacks on American shipping increased. German submarines even patrolled the waters off the East Coast of the United States. There they made easy pickings of merchant ships that sailed from American ports without the protection of a full convoy. In a few short months, 360 American ships were sunk compared to just eight German U-boats.

The Allies fight back Despite early losses, America's entry into the war would help turn the tide in the Battle of the Atlantic. Energized American shipyards began producing new ships at an amazing rate. These were used to form larger, better-equipped convoys, which helped cut down on the effectiveness of U-boat

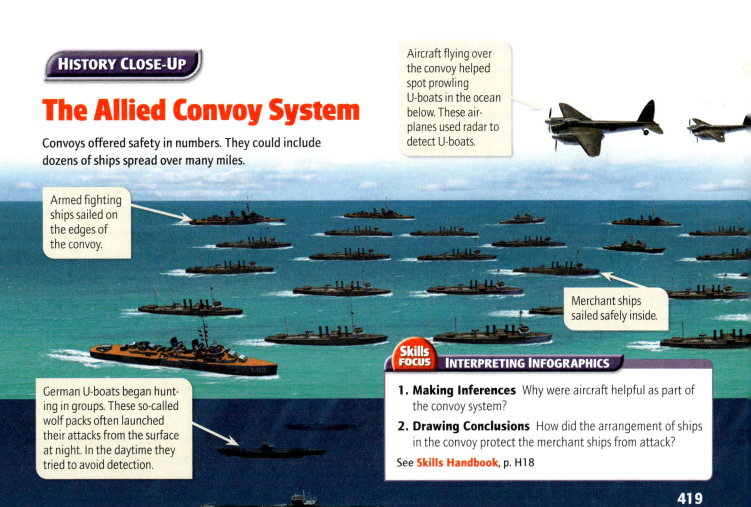

HISTORY CLOSE-UP

The Allied Convoy System

Convoys offered safety in numbers. They could include dozens of ships spread over many miles.

Aircraft flying over the convoy helped spot prowling U-boats in the ocean below. These airplanes used radar to detect U-boats.

Armed fighting ships sailed on the edges of the convoy.

Merchant ships sailed safely inside.

German U-boats began hunting in groups. These so-called wolf packs often launched their attacks from the surface at night. In the daytime they tried to avoid detection.

Skills Focus: INTERPRETING INFOGRAPHICS

1. **Making Inferences** Why were aircraft helpful as part of the convoy system?
2. **Drawing Conclusions** How did the arrangement of ships in the convoy protect the merchant ships from attack?

See **Skills Handbook**, p. H18

attacks. At the same time, new Allied aircraft protected convoys from the air. The aircraft and escort ships used radar and other technologies to find and destroy more U-boats.

Another factor in the Allied success was the breaking of Germany's code system, which was called Enigma. After cracking Enigma in 1941, the Allies began to gain vital information about the locations and plans of U-boat formations.

These factors began to give the Allies an advantage over German U-boats. German sailors were soon referring to their ships as "iron coffins." By war's end, some 70 percent of the Germans who had served on a submarine were dead. The Atlantic belonged to the Allies.

READING CHECK **Identifying Problems and Solutions** How did the Allies overcome the German U-boats and win the Battle of the Atlantic?

The War in the Soviet Union

In the summer of 1941, Hitler broke his nonaggression pact with Stalin and sent his forces into the Soviet Union. (The Soviets thus joined the Allies as enemies of the Axis Powers.) For the next several months, German forces stormed across the Soviet countryside. As they had in Poland and France, German tanks, planes, and soldiers steadily pressed the attack. Stalin's forces seemed unable to stop the blitzkrieg.

Though the Soviet Union appeared close to collapse, it did not fall. As autumn came and went, the Soviets were joined by a new ally—the bitterly cold Russian winter. German soldiers and equipment performed poorly in the freezing temperatures, and their invasion slowed.

Still, the Germans held a huge portion of the western Soviet Union. They had also besieged the city of Leningrad. The suffering of the people there was extreme. With little food and fuel, some 200,000 residents died in January and February alone. Hundreds of thousands more would perish in the months ahead.

The Battle of Stalingrad
When spring returned to the Soviet Union, the German armies renewed their assault. One major target was the city of Stalingrad, a major industrial center on the Volga River. The Germans attacked Stalingrad in August 1942. In some of the bloodiest fighting in the history of warfare, the Soviets refused to let Stalingrad fall.

Not only did the Germans fail to take Stalingrad, they also exposed themselves to a Soviet counterattack. In the fighting that followed, 250,000 Axis soldiers were trapped by Soviet forces. The surviving Axis troops were forced to surrender in early 1943. Hitler had suffered a stunning defeat.

Stalingrad marked the beginning of Germany's collapse in the Soviet Union. Thereafter, Soviet forces began to push German forces back toward Germany. The fighting took a terrible toll. Hitler's forces suffered losses of some 2 million, and the Soviets paid an even higher price—12 million soldiers. Millions of civilians also died. In Leningrad alone, as many as 800,000 civilians perished before the siege there was finally lifted in January 1944. Yet the Soviet Union had survived. Now it was fighting toward the final defeat of the Axis.

READING CHECK **Sequencing** Briefly describe the sequence of events of the war in the Soviet Union.

American Forces in North Africa and Italy

Soon after the fall of France in June 1940, the British and Italians began a battle for North Africa. This territory was vital to the Allies. By controlling it, the British could protect shipping on the Mediterranean Sea against Italian attack. This shipping was a lifeline by which the British could efficiently get oil through the Suez Canal from the Middle East. Without oil Great Britain would not be able to defend itself, much less defeat the Axis.

In the early fighting, Italian forces based in Libya tried to drive the British from their stronghold in Egypt. They failed. In fact, the Italians were beaten badly and driven backwards. Hitler was forced to send troops to support the Italians in early 1941. At the head of these forces was the famed German general **Erwin Rommel**. Throughout 1941 and 1942, Rommel's forces and the British fought a back-and-forth battle for control of North Africa. Though Rommel led brilliantly—it was here he earned the nickname Desert Fox—the British ultimately gained control. At the battle of El Alamein (el-a-luh-MAYN), fought about the same time as the Battle of Stalingrad, the British handed the Germans a major defeat.

GEOGRAPHY SKILLS INTERPRETING MAPS

1. **Regions** What was the extent of Axis control in 1942?
2. **Movement** Describe the major Allied advances in Africa and the Mediterranean.

See **Skills Handbook**, p. H20

Operation Torch When the United States entered the war in late 1941, President Roosevelt was anxious to make a contribution quickly. Stalin wanted the Allies to invade Europe, to help divide Hitler's attentions. Other Allied leaders, however, resisted calls to rush into Europe unprepared. North Africa, it was decided, was the logical place for American soldiers to enter the fray.

The commander of what came to be called **Operation Torch** was a U.S. lieutenant general named **Dwight D. Eisenhower**. The plan called for American forces to invade the North African countries of Morocco and Algeria in November 1942. France had controlled this territory before 1940. After the fall of France, Vichy leaders were installed there. Still, the Allies hoped that the French in North Africa would side with them in battle. Indeed, the Allies met little resistance upon landing, and French forces soon joined them.

After landing, Allied forces turned east to fight the Germans. In battles at places such as Kasserine Pass, Americans gained valuable combat experience. Some 20,000 Americans were killed or wounded in the six months of North Africa fighting. But by May 1943, they had helped defeat Rommel's forces.

While this fighting was taking place, Allied leaders focused on the war's next phases. Stalin continued to push for a European invasion, and in the planning stages was a massive invasion of France. In early 1943, however, such an operation was still a year away. For now, Allied leaders prepared to cross the Mediterranean and knock the Italians out of the war.

ACADEMIC VOCABULARY

logical based on correct reasoning

THE UNITED STATES IN WORLD WAR II   **421**

On to Italy The first major step in this assault was the July 1943 invasion of the island of Sicily. Soon after the attack began, Roosevelt and Churchill issued a message to the Italian people asking them "whether they want to die for Mussolini and Hitler or live for Italy and civilization." The Italians chose life. By the end of the month, they had turned against dictator Benito Mussolini and forced him from power. The Allies took Sicily a few weeks later. They planned next to occupy the Italian Peninsula.

Hitler, however, was not going to let the Allies simply march through Italy and into Europe. German forces rushed to stop them.

Despite German resistance, the Allies made steady progress at first. Taking part in the fighting were the **Tuskegee Airmen**. This was a segregated unit of African Americans, the first ever to receive training as pilots in the U.S. military.

After its early success, the Allied invasion slowed as it approached Rome. To keep it moving, the Allies planned to land a large force behind enemy lines. The site they chose for this landing was a seafront resort called Anzio.

In late January, the first of some 100,000 Allied soldiers went ashore at Anzio. Fighting raged for the next four months as the Allies were unable to break out of their small coastal beachhead. Finally, Allied forces from the south fought their way to Anzio and freed the trapped soldiers. By then, from 25,000 to 30,000 Allied soldiers had been killed or wounded.

The end of the battle at Anzio, however, did not end the fighting in Italy. It continued for nearly a year. Some 300,000 Allied troops were killed or wounded there.

READING CHECK **Summarizing** What did American forces experience in North Africa and Italy?

Americans in North Africa and Italy

The Tuskegee Airmen's 99th Pursuit Squadron (left) provided air support in both North Africa and Italy. Among their numerous awards, their fighter group was honored for "outstanding performance and extraordinary heroism." In all, the Tuskegee Airmen completed 15,500 missions. Below, elite U.S. Army Rangers charge up an Italian hillside. Rangers, specially trained volunteers who had been serving in Northern Ireland, spearheaded the push through Italy.

D-Day: The Invasion of France

The fighting in Italy was slow and difficult partly because the Allies could not devote all their fighting resources to the battle. Many of these resources were being held for the planned invasion of France. This plan came to be known as **Operation Overlord**.

Planning Operation Overlord To end the war as quickly as possible, the Allies wanted to launch a large invasion of mainland Europe. Careful planning was vital. The Allies worked for months to select a location for Operation Overlord. They finally settled on the beaches of Normandy, in northern France.

The Allies had to assemble huge numbers of troops, weapons, and other equipment necessary for an invasion. Eisenhower commanded the mission and chose General **Omar Bradley** to lead the American troops. The top British commander was Bernard Montgomery.

While good planning was important, speed was also vital. Of particular concern to the Allies was the expected introduction of two new German weapons, the V1 flying bomb and the V2 rocket. The Allies were able to destroy some rocket-launch sites, but fears of these dangerous weapons forced the Allies onward.

The landing at Normandy By early June 1944, the Allied force of 3.5 million soldiers was ready for action. Tension ran high. The soldiers knew they had to succeed—and that success was uncertain. They knew that at Normandy they would meet a determined German force.

After a short delay caused by bad weather, **D-Day** finally arrived on June 6, 1944. The attack began with soldiers parachuting behind the German lines to try to secure key sites. Ships offshore rained shells on the coastline to destroy German defenses. Allied aircraft filled the sky to provide cover for the wave of troops to come. A variety of amphibious craft helped deliver equipment and soldiers to the beaches.

In the end, however, the success of Operation Overlord came down to the courage of the individual soldiers who would make the landing. Their job was to wait for their landing-craft gate to open—then to move forward toward shore. By the thousands, they waded through the surf till they hit the sand and then raced through obstacles, wounded and dead comrades, and a hail of gunfire to find something to hide behind. Then those who managed to get that far gathered their courage, got to their feet, and went forward again. All was chaos and confusion. Little went according to plan. Still, soldiers stuck to their assigned tasks.

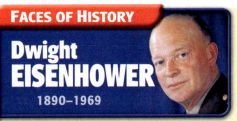

FACES OF HISTORY
Dwight EISENHOWER
1890–1969

Dwight D. Eisenhower was known for his logical mind, a talent for organizing, and an outgoing yet diplomatic attitude. He proved to be the ideal person to lead the Allied military force in World War II.

From his humble childhood in the small farm town of Abilene, Kansas, Eisenhower rose steadily through the ranks of the army. During World War II, General George C. Marshall chose Eisenhower to be Supreme Allied Commander in Europe. In this position Eisenhower planned and commanded Operation Overlord (D-Day), the invasion of France. He also accepted Germany's surrender in 1945.

Explain In what ways do you think Eisenhower's personality helped make him a good leader in World War II?

HISTORY'S VOICES

"It's amazing what you can do when you're called upon to do it. There was just an overwhelming demand for me to do my duty. Patriotism—that was there. But more, I was filled with a sense of duty. This was my duty, my assigned duty. This is what was expected of me."

—Frank Walk, recorded in *War Stories*, by Elizabeth Mullener

Fortunately for the Allies, the Germans were slow to respond to the invasion. Thanks in part to Allied deceptions, Hitler feared that the assault on Normandy was just a trick and that another invasion would take place elsewhere. For precious days, German leaders delayed in sending backup forces to the area. By the time they realized their mistake, the Allies had established a beachhead.

Though the costs were high—an estimated 10,000 Allied casualties, including 6,600 Americans—D-Day had been a success. With each day, more troops and equipment came ashore. By early July, the Allies had landed almost a million soldiers and nearly 180,000 vehicles. The landing area was considered secure enough to send in members of the Women's

Interactive HISTORY CLOSE-UP

D-Day, June 6, 1944

Allied forces landed at five separate sites at Normandy on D-Day of the invasion of France. Omaha Beach was one of two beaches invaded by U.S. forces (see map opposite). As American soldiers moved toward the nearly 100-foot-high cliffs, German guns at the top rained a deadly fire down on them.

Allied aircraft provided cover for the invading forces.

Allied warships fired shells on German positions before and during the landing.

Army Corp. They were to supply support for the forces that would soon fight their way past German defenses at Normandy. This breakthrough occurred in late July. As the German commander reported, "The whole western front has been ripped open."

The Allies were now on the march in France. By the end of August, Paris had been freed from the Germans. Hitler's once mighty war machine was now in full retreat.

The Battle of the Bulge Throughout the fall of 1944, the Allies moved eastward. The Germans fought well in places. For example, the Battle of Hürtgen Forest claimed thousands of Allied lives. Overall, however, the Germans appeared near collapse. As one of Eisenhower's advisers put it in early December, "The battle is over and the German army has had it."

This judgment, it turned out, was premature. On December 16, 1944, the Germans launched a surprise offensive of their own. The attack was known as the **Battle of the Bulge**. This referred to the bulge in the Allied battle lines created by the German advance. For several days, Hitler's forces threatened to win back vital ground from the Allies.

A key moment in the battle came at the Belgian city of Bastogne. This was an important crossroads, and the Germans were determined to take it. Even more determined was the small force of American defenders. Surrounded by Germans, shivering in below-zero temperatures and low on supplies, the Americans clung to survival. But survive they did. On December 26, troops led by Lieutenant General **George S. Patton** arrived to provide relief for the American force. The victory at Bastogne helped blunt the German offensive. It also became a symbol of American strength and determination.

By the end of January 1945, the bulge created by the German offensive had been rolled back. Once again the Allies set their sights on Germany and the defeat of Hitler. Victory was close at hand.

READING CHECK **Drawing Conclusions** Why did the planning for D-Day take so long?

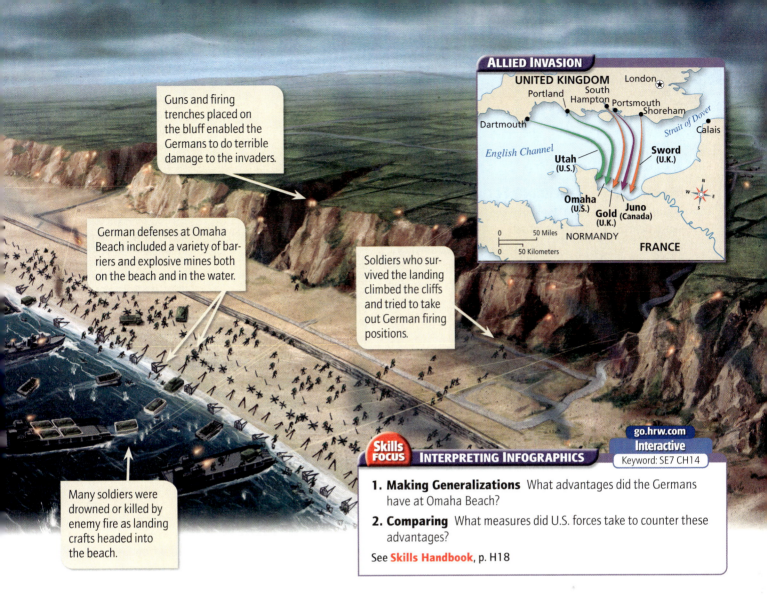

Guns and firing trenches placed on the bluff enabled the Germans to do terrible damage to the invaders.

German defenses at Omaha Beach included a variety of barriers and explosive mines both on the beach and in the water.

Soldiers who survived the landing climbed the cliffs and tried to take out German firing positions.

Many soldiers were drowned or killed by enemy fire as landing crafts headed into the beach.

Skills Focus: INTERPRETING INFOGRAPHICS

1. **Making Generalizations** What advantages did the Germans have at Omaha Beach?
2. **Comparing** What measures did U.S. forces take to counter these advantages?

See **Skills Handbook**, p. H18

SECTION 1 ASSESSMENT

HSS 11.7.2, 11.7.3

Reviewing Ideas, Terms, and People

1. **a. Describe** Briefly describe the Battle of the Atlantic.
   b. Explain Why was control of the seas so important for the Allies and the Axis?
2. **a. Identify** Why was the Battle of Stalingrad significant?
   b. Summarize Write one sentence that summarizes the fighting in the Soviet Union between 1941 and 1944.
3. **a. Define** Write brief definitions of the following terms: **Operation Torch, Tuskegee Airmen**
   b. Make Inferences What can you infer from the fact that the Americans' initial battles with the Germans can be described as "learning experiences"?
4. **a. Define** Write brief definitions of the following terms: **Operation Overlord, D-Day, Battle of the Bulge**
   b. Contrast How did Operation Overlord compare to the landing at Anzio?

Critical Thinking

5. **Identifying Cause and Effect** Copy the chart. Use it to identify major battles in the Soviet Union, North Africa, and Europe between 1941 and 1944 and the result of each battle.

Battle	Result
1.	
2.	
3.	
4.	

FOCUS ON WRITING ELA W1.1

6. **Expository** Was Operation Overlord a major turning point in the European war? Write a short essay in which you develop your position on this issue.

THE UNITED STATES IN WORLD WAR II **425**

SECTION 2

HSS **11.7.4** Analyze Roosevelt's foreign policy during World War II (e.g., Four Freedoms speech).

HSS **11.7.5** Discuss the constitutional issues and impact of events on the U.S. home front, including the internment of Japanese Americans (e.g., *Fred Korematsu* v. *United States of America*) and the restrictions on German and Italian resident aliens; the response of the administration to Hitler's atrocities against Jews and other groups; the roles of women in military production; and the roles and growing political demands of African Americans.

BEFORE YOU READ

MAIN IDEA
During the Holocaust, Germany's Nazi government systematically murdered some 6 million Jews and 5 million others in Europe.

READING FOCUS
1. What was the history of Nazi anti-Semitism?
2. What was the Nazi government's Final Solution?
3. How did the United States respond to the Holocaust?

KEY TERMS AND PEOPLE
anti-Semitism
Kristallnacht
concentration camp
ghetto
genocide
Final Solution
War Refugee Board
Holocaust
Hermann Göering

◀ During the Holocaust, the Nazi government targeted European Jews.

A Life-Saving EFFORT

 How did people in a French village save the lives of thousands of Jews? In 1940 Hitler's German army was rampaging across Europe. By June it had conquered France. The Jewish population there found itself facing what Jews in Germany and Poland had already come to know—government-sponsored persecution, hatred, and brutal mistreatment at the hands of Germany's Nazi Party. Scenes like the one shown above took place throughout France, as Nazis and their followers rounded up Jews and sent them to prison camps far from home. These Jews' futures—and their chances of survival—were extremely grim.

During World War II, thousands of non-Jews risked their lives to help save Jews from the Nazis. One such rescue took place in the village of Le Chambon-sur-Lignon (luh shahm-BOHN-soor-leen-yohn) in southern France. In 1942 André Trocmé, the pastor of a local church, called on village residents to give shelter to Jews who asked for help. The residents began to hide Jews in their homes and farms and help them escape to safety in Switzerland. France's Nazi-controlled government demanded that the pastor end the rescue effort. He responded by saying, "These people came here for help and for shelter. I am their shepherd. A shepherd does not desert his flock . . . We do not know what a Jew is; we only know people."

Over the course of the war, the people of Le Chambon helped some 5,000 Jews escape Nazi capture. This was a life-saving effort. As you will read in this section, the persecution of Jews was part of a terrible Nazi plan to murder the entire Jewish population of Europe.

In 1963 the government of Israel began a program to honor those who risked their lives to save Jews. Among those honored were the people of Le Chambon. ◾

426 CHAPTER 14

Nazi Anti-Semitism

Why did the Nazi government single out Jews especially for mistreatment? The answer has to do with **anti-Semitism**, which is hostility toward or prejudice against Jews.

As you have read, Germany after World War I suffered blows to its economy and pride. Adolf Hitler rose to power in part by promising to return Germany to its former glory. He also told the Germans that they came from a superior race—the Aryans. The idea that Germans had descended from the mythical Aryan people was not new. It was found in German folktales and music. Hitler, however, was effective at using the notion to build support.

In addition to appealing to German pride, Hitler also provided a scapegoat—someone to blame for Germany's woes. The group he singled out was the Jews.

In fact, Jews had lived in Germany for 1,600 years. Christian hostility toward Jews had existed since the Middle Ages. Indeed, many of the anti-Jewish Nazi laws recalled medieval efforts to humiliate Jews. For example, a Nazi law that forced Jews to wear the Jewish Star of David was similar to a 1215 decree that told Jews to dress differently than Christians.

Nazi anti-Semitism combined this medieval Christian hostility with modern—but false—scientific ideas about racial inferiority. Another Nazi law defined anyone with a Jewish grandparent as a Jew, even if the person had no connection with Judaism. Under the Nazis, anti-Semitism changed from prejudice based on religion to hatred based on ancestry.

Hitler in power Hitler began his campaign against Germany's Jews soon after becoming chancellor in 1933. Over the next few years, his Nazi government <u>established</u> a series of anti-Semitic laws. The purpose was to drive the Jews from Germany. For example, in 1935, the Nuremberg Laws stripped Jews of German citizenship and took away most civil and economic rights. The laws also defined who was a Jew and who was an Aryan German.

Attacks on Jews Some Germans were repelled by Hitler's actions. Yet many other people supported his anti-Semitic ideas. Discrimination against Jews continued. Violent attacks against Jews also increased.

In 1938, on the nights of November 9 and 10, anti-Jewish riots broke out across Germany. The attack came to be called **Kristallnacht** (KRIS-tahl-nahkt)—the "night of broken glass." The Nazis claimed the attacks were a spontaneous reaction to the assassination of a Nazi official by a Jewish teenager. In fact, the Nazis encouraged the violence. During the rampage, thousands of Jewish businesses and places of worship were damaged. Thugs killed nearly 100 Jews. Over 26,000 more were sent to **concentration camps**—labor camps meant to hold what Hitler called enemies of the state. The Nazis blamed the Jews for Kristallnacht and held them financially responsible. Jews were fined a total of 1 billion marks.

Flight from Germany Kristallnacht sent a strong message to those Jews still in Germany: "Get out!" Over 100,000 managed to leave Germany in the months following the attacks. Many others, however, found it difficult to leave the country. Nazi laws had left many German Jews without money or property, and most countries were unwilling to take in poor immigrants. Other countries, such as the United States, had limited the number of Germans who could enter the country.

READING CHECK **Summarizing** Briefly trace the history of Nazi anti-Semitism.

Jewish shopkeepers in Berlin pick up the pieces of their shattered businesses after the destruction of Kristallnacht. **What prompted Germans to attack their Jewish neighbors?**

ACADEMIC VOCABULARY
established created, or brought into being

Toward the Final Solution

When Hitler came to power, Europe was home to 9 million Jews. Few of these people lived under German control. That changed with the outbreak of World War II. As Hitler's armies blazed across Europe, many European Jews came under the control of the Nazi SS. This was the feared police and military force that carried out terror activities for the Nazis. SS treatment of the Jews was overwhelmingly brutal. In the words of one SS leader, the goal was to "incarcerate [jail] or annihilate" the Jews.

Concentration camps and ghettos The first concentration camps were created in Germany before the start of World War II. These were basically prisons for Jews and others who were considered enemies of Hitler's regime. After the outbreak of World War II, the Nazis established many more camps to hold Jews from the countries that Germany had invaded and occupied. Camps were also set up to house prisoners of war.

As German forces took control of an area, they would arrest the Jews living there. The local population sometimes helped shelter their Jewish neighbors. *The Diary of Anne Frank* is a famous book that tells the story of a young Jewish girl living in the Netherlands whose family hid successfully for two years with the help of neighbors. Like many Jews in German-occupied lands, the Franks were eventually discovered and sent to concentration camps.

Conditions in the Nazi camps were horrific. Inmates received little food and were often forced to perform grueling labor. This combination of overwork and starvation was deliberately designed to kill. Punishment for even the most minor offenses was swift, sure, and deadly. In short, there were many ways to die in a concentration camp. Yet as you will read, the Nazis had only just begun to develop their ghastly killing methods.

Another tactic used by the Nazis to control and punish Jews was to establish **ghettos**. These are neighborhoods in a city to which a group of people are confined. As in the concentration camps, life in a Jewish ghetto was desperate. Walls or fences kept Jews inside. Those trying to get out were shot. Food was scarce. Diseases spread quickly in the crowded conditions, and many Jews fell ill.

The worst ghetto was in Warsaw, Poland. There, a half-million Jews were crammed into an area less than 1.5 miles square. They lived on a daily ration of thin soup and a slice of bread. In 1941 alone, 43,000 died of hunger. Recalled one survivor, "Every day was men with hand wagons picking up the dead ones from the corners who died of hunger or cold."

In 1943, most of the ghetto residents were sent off to Treblinka, a concentration camp. Those who remained decided to fight back. A group called the Jewish Fighting Organization attacked the Germans with crude weapons. For many Jews it was a proud moment.

HISTORY'S VOICES

"For the first time since the occupation, we saw Germans clinging to walls, crawling on the ground, running for cover, hesitating before taking a step in the fear of being hit by a Jewish bullet."

—Tuvia Borzykowski, recorded in *The Second World War: A Complete History*, by Martin Gilbert

The Warsaw uprising lasted nearly a month. In the end, however, it was crushed. The residents were killed or shipped to concentration camps, where most would die.

The Final Solution From the first days of World War II, instances of Nazi mass-killings of Jews and other civilians occurred. In many Polish towns, German soldiers rounded up Jews and shot them on the spot. In Bedzin, soldiers forced several hundred Jews into the local synagogue, or Jewish house of worship, and set it on fire. Stories such as these were repeated across Poland.

The German invasion of the Soviet Union in 1941 raised the killing of Jews to a new level. Now Hitler called for the total destruction of all of Europe's Jews. What he proposed—the killing of an entire people—is called **genocide**. At first, the bloody work was carried out by mobile killing units—*Einsatzgruppen* (EYEN-sahtz-GROOP-uhn). In one incident in the fall of 1941, over 33,000 people were massacred in two days. The bodies were piled into a ravine at Babi Yar, near the Ukrainian city of Kiev.

As bloody as the work of the *Einsatzgruppen* was, Nazi leaders were not satisfied. For them, the killing was not going quickly enough. It was also proving difficult on the men who performed it. Thus, Nazi officials adopted a plan known as the **Final Solution**. This involved

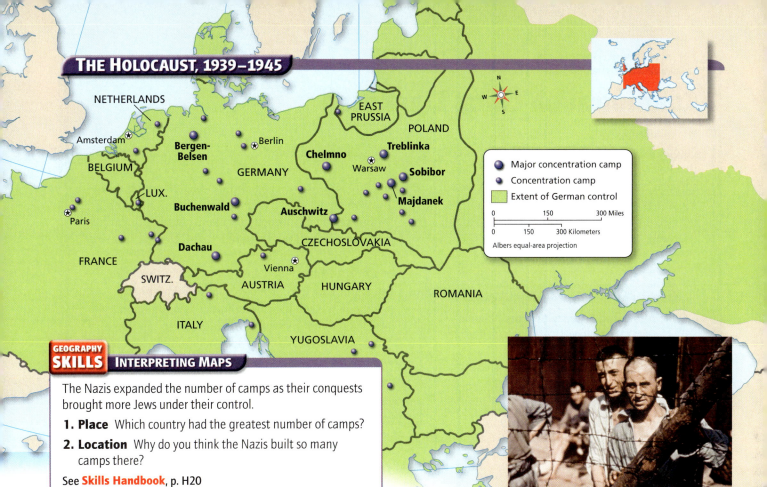

THE HOLOCAUST, 1939–1945

GEOGRAPHY SKILLS: INTERPRETING MAPS

The Nazis expanded the number of camps as their conquests brought more Jews under their control.

1. **Place** Which country had the greatest number of camps?
2. **Location** Why do you think the Nazis built so many camps there?

See **Skills Handbook**, p. H20

the establishment of six new camps. These were to be extermination camps for the widespread murder of Jews. Unlike the concentration camps you read about earlier, nearly all inmates at the extermination camps were murdered upon their arrival. The method of killing was by exposure to poison gas in specially built gas chambers. Inmates might also be selected for cruel medical experiments, which often ended in death. Some were also forced to perform labor.

Some 3 million Jews died in Nazi extermination camps. Another 3 million died at Nazi hands by other means. Nazis murdered men, women, and children alike. Wrote Nazi leader Heinrich Himmler, "I did not feel justified in exterminating the men… while allowing the avengers, in the form of their children, to grow up."

In addition to the Jews, the Nazi death machine killed about 5 million others. Among these victims were prisoners of war, disabled people, and the Romany, an ethnic group also known as Gypsies.

READING CHECK Identifying the Main Idea What was the purpose of the Final Solution?

JEWISH LOSSES IN THE HOLOCAUST

	c. 1933	c. 1950	Percent Decrease
Europe	9,500,000	3,500,000	63
Selected Countries			
Poland	3,000,000	45,000	98.5
Romania	980,000	28,000	97
Germany	565,000	37,000	93.5
Hungary	445,000	155,000	65
Czechoslovakia	357,000	17,000	95
Austria	250,000	18,000	93
Greece	100,000	7,000	93
Yugoslavia	70,000	3,500	95
Bulgaria	50,000	6,500	87

Source: *United States Holocaust Memorial Museum*

PRIMARY SOURCES

Concentration Camp Liberation

As the Allied forces pushed westward across Europe, they came upon the concentration camps that held victims of the Holocaust. Many of the survivors were barely alive. Gerda Weissman was a Jewish prisoner in a Czechoslavakian camp. She recalled the day that American soldiers liberated her camp.

"All of a sudden I saw a strange car coming down the hill, no longer green, not bearing the swastika, but a white star. It was sort of a mud-splattered vehicle but I've never seen a star brighter in my life. And two men sort of jumped out, came running toward us and one came toward where I stood. He was wearing battle gear... I would say it was the greatest hour of my life. And then he asked an incredible question. He said, 'May I see the other ladies?' You know, what... what we have been addressed for six years and then to hear this man. He looked to me like a young god... He held the door open for me and let me precede him and in that gesture restored me to humanity."

Skills Focus: READING LIKE A HISTORIAN

1. **Analyzing Primary Sources** Why was Gerda Weissman so surprised by the soldier's question?
2. **Drawing Conclusions** What did Weissman mean when she said the soldier's gesture "restored me to humanity"?

See **Skills Handbook**, pp. H28–H29

The American Response

THE IMPACT TODAY

Government
American leaders continue to face pressure to help populations under attack by their own governments. In the early 2000s, the United States worked to end what was seen as a government-supported effort to destroy the population in Darfur, a region of the African nation of Sudan.

In the 1930s American immigration rules limited the number of Jews who could move to the United States. Although many Americans had read of Kristallnacht and knew about Hitler's policies toward the Jews, they were unwilling to allow large numbers of foreign workers enter the United States during a time when jobs were already scarce. At the time, few truly understood that millions of lives were at stake.

The start of the war eventually brought an end to the economic problems facing American workers, but it did not change American feelings about immigration. That began to change in 1942, when American officials started to learn the horrifying details of what was taking place in Europe. The head of a major Jewish organization in Switzerland told American officials what he had heard about Hitler's Final Solution. The Americans were doubtful at first. One official wrote to another, "The report has earmarks of war rumor inspired by fear." Soon, however, the reality began to sink in.

The fate of Europe's Jews was just one of many issues that preoccupied the United States and its leaders. As you have read, 1943 was a year of difficult fighting in Italy and a time for planning the D-Day invasion. The United States was also fighting hard in the Pacific. These were vital steps in the effort to defeat Hitler and the Axis Powers, which, some argued, might help save millions of lives.

It was not until January 1944 that President Roosevelt announced the creation of the **War Refugee Board**. This organization was told to "take all measures to rescue victims of enemy oppression in imminent [immediate] danger of death." Through the board, the United States was able to help 200,000 Jews who might otherwise have fallen into the hands of the Nazis.

Liberating the Nazi camps As you have read, Allied forces in 1942 started to push back the German advances gained in the beginning of the war. The Soviets made the greatest early progress. In 1944 Soviet troops began to discover some of the Nazi camps that had been set up to house and kill Jews in Poland. In early 1945, they reached the huge extermination camp at Auschwitz. Their reports of the conditions at these camps finally gave the American people proof of Hitler's terrible plan.

American and British forces also encountered death camps. In April 1945 American soldiers came upon several, including the camp at Buchenwald. This was one of the first and largest concentration camps established in Germany. During its existence, some 240,000 prisoners spent time at the camp. Of those, at least 43,000 died. Another 10,000 were shipped elsewhere to be killed.

The Nazis had abandoned Buchenwald shortly before the Americans arrived. Many of the camp's prisoners, however, remained behind. The scenes were appalling. The bodies of victims lay in piles throughout the camp. Many of the survivors were themselves barely alive. One American soldier who was among the first to enter the camp recalled, "They were just one step from their last breath. They weren't able to feel happy. They were so skinny—just skin and bones." Many of these rescued victims were so ill that they could not be saved. At the Bergen-Belsen concentration camp, 13,000 inmates died after they were set free by the British.

Some of the inmates were strong enough to celebrate their freedom. At Dachau, surviving inmates broke out of their prison to meet the approaching American tanks. "Everybody was running—everybody who could run," recalled one survivor. "It looked like somebody from heaven came." Yet within the camp fences was the same horror—the piles of bodies and a great many starving inmates.

HISTORY'S VOICES

"I was a hardened soldier. I had been in combat since 1944, and I had seen death and destruction that was unparalleled in modern times. But this—there are no words to describe this."

—Reid Draffen, recorded in *War Stories*, by Elizabeth Mullener

The Nuremberg trials Following World War II, many Nazis faced trial for their roles in what is now called the Holocaust—the genocidal campaign against the Jews during World War II. The court, located at Nuremberg, Germany, was called the International Military Tribunal. It was organized by the United States, Great Britain, France, and the Soviet Union.

A total of twenty two Nazis were tried for war crimes. Included were some of the leading Nazis, such as **Hermann Göering** (GEH-ring). Twelve were sentenced to die. Several others served long prison terms.

After Nuremberg, several Nazis have been captured and tried in different courts, including in Israel. These trials demonstrate the commitment of people around the world to remember the Holocaust and the millions of victims of Nazi brutality during World War II.

READING CHECK **Summarizing** How did the United States respond to the reports that the Nazis were attempting to kill all of Europe's Jews?

THE IMPACT TODAY

Government After World War II, many surviving European Jews were sent to displaced persons' camps. Many made their way to Palestine, where in the late 1940s they took part in the creation of the Jewish nation of Israel.

SECTION 2 ASSESSMENT

HSS 11.7.4, 11.7.5

Online Quiz Keyword: SE7 HP14

Reviewing Ideas, Terms, and People

1. **a. Recall** What term describes Hitler's racist attitudes toward the Jews?
   b. Explain Why do you think the German people supported Hitler's anti-Semitic attitudes?
   c. Evaluate Why do you think observers of events in Germany did not do more to help Germany's Jews?

2. **a. Define** Write brief definitions of the following terms: ghetto, Final Solution
   b. Make Generalizations What was the experience of Jews living in territories conquered by the Germans?
   c. Develop How can you explain the participation of so many Germans in the campaign to destroy the Jews?

3. **a. Identify** What was the significance of the War Refugee Board?
   b. Make Inferences Why did it take the United States so long to offer direct help to Europe's Jews?

   c. Evaluate Do you think that the best way to help Europe's Jews was to defeat Hitler as quickly as possible? Or should the United States have taken a different approach? Explain.

Critical Thinking

4. **Identifying Supporting Details** Copy the chart below and use information from the section to find supporting details for the main idea given.

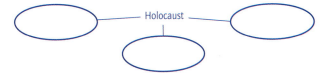

FOCUS ON SPEAKING ELA W1.1, 1.3

5. **Persuasive** Could the United States have done more to prevent the Holocaust? Write a persuasive speech in which you present your position.

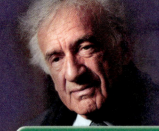

American Literature

ELIE WIESEL (1928–)

About the Reading Elie Wiesel was born in the small town of Sighet, Romania, in 1928. In 1944 the Nazis began deporting Jewish families from his hometown. In his autobiography, *Night* (1958), he recounts his experiences during his time in Nazi concentration camps. Wiesel became an American citizen in 1963. In this excerpt from *Night*, he describes his journey by train to the camp in Auschwitz, Poland.

AS YOU READ Think about the reasons why we study the Holocaust today.

Excerpt from

by Elie Wiesel

Survivors at Buchenwald after their liberation in 1945. Elie Wiesel is on the second bunk from the bottom, seventh from the left.

Pressed up against the others in an effort to keep out the cold, head empty and heavy at the same time, brain a whirlpool of decaying memories. Indifference deadened the spirit. Here or elsewhere—what difference did it make? To die today or tomorrow, or later? The night was long and never ending.

When at last a gray glimmer of light appeared on the horizon, it revealed a tangle of human shapes, heads sunk upon shoulders, crouched, piled one on top of the other, like a field of dust-covered tombstones in the first light of the dawn. I tried to distinguish those who were still alive from those who had gone. But there was no difference. My gaze was held for a long time by one who lay with his eyes open, staring into the void. His livid face was covered with a layer of frost and snow.

My father huddled near me, wrapped in his blanket, his shoulders covered with snow. And was he dead, too? I called him. No answer. I would have cried out if I could have done so. He did not move.

My mind was invaded suddenly by this realization—there was no more reason to live, no more reason to struggle. The train stopped in the middle of a deserted field. The suddenness of the halt woke some of those who were asleep. They straightened themselves up, throwing startled looks around them.

Outside, the SS went by, shouting:

"Throw out all the dead! All corpses outside!"

The living rejoiced. There would be more room. Volunteers set to work. They felt those who were still crouching.

"Here's one! Take him!"

They undressed him, the survivors avidly sharing out his clothes, then two "gravediggers" took him, one by the head and one by the feet, and threw him out of the wagon like a sack of flour.

From all directions came cries:

"Come on! Here's one! This man next to me. He doesn't move."

Skills Focus: READING LIKE A HISTORIAN

Literature as Historical Evidence How does the personal testimony of survivors such as Wiesel help us understand the Holocaust?

See **Skills Handbook**, p. H32

432 CHAPTER 14

SECTION 3: The War in the Pacific

BEFORE YOU READ

MAIN IDEA
After early defeats in the Pacific, the United States gained the upper hand and began to fight its way island by island to Japan.

READING FOCUS
1. Why did the Allies experience a slow start in the Pacific?
2. How did the Allies bring about a shift in their fortunes in the Pacific?
3. What were the major events that marked Allied progress in the late stages of the Pacific war?

KEY TERMS AND PEOPLE
Douglas MacArthur
Bataan Death March
James Doolittle
Chester Nimitz
Battle of Midway
code talker
kamikaze
Battle of Iwo Jima
Battle of Okinawa

HSS 11.7.2 Explain U.S. and Allied wartime strategy, including the major battles of Midway, Normandy, Iwo Jima, Okinawa, and the Battle of the Bulge.

HSS 11.7.6 Describe major developments in aviation, weaponry, communication, and medicine and the war's impact on the location of American industry and use of resources.

Raising the Flag at Iwo Jima

Why was it so hard to capture a tiny island? Iwo Jima lies 750 miles south of Japan. It is a small island of rock and sand, covering barely eight square miles. Yet during World War II over 100,000 soldiers fought for a month to capture this tiny scrap of land. It was some of the heaviest fighting of the war.

On February 19, 1945, the U.S. Marines stormed the beaches of Iwo Jima (EE-woh-JEE-muh). They made easy targets for the Japanese, who had dug miles of tunnels and built dozens of hidden concrete bunkers throughout the island. From these hiding places they could pick off American troops without being exposed.

Also deadly for the Americans were the Japanese guns mounted high on the slopes of Mount Suribachi, an extinct volcano on the southern tip of the island. The Americans knew that they must capture Suribachi or be blown off the island.

On the morning of February 23, a group of Marines finally made it to the top of Mount Suribachi and raised the American flag as thousands of soldiers below watched and cheered. A few hours later a larger flag was raised. This second flag raising is shown in the famous photograph on this page.

The American flag now flew over Iwo Jima, but fierce fighting lasted for another month before the Americans finally captured the island. An estimated 25,000 American soldiers were killed or wounded. Among the dead were three of the six men who raised the flag atop Mount Suribachi.

◀ **U.S. Marines claim Mount Suribachi with a proud display of the Stars and Stripes.**

A Slow Start for the Allies

The attack on Pearl Harbor had been a tremendous success for the Japanese. They had dealt a blow to the U.S. Pacific Fleet that would take months to overcome. The damage to American sea power—combined with the Allies' decision to focus their energy and resources on defeating the Axis in Europe—would for a time limit the ability of the United States to strike back at the Japanese.

Pearl Harbor also had an enormous emotional impact. For the Japanese, it provided a major boost to national pride and encouraged them to continue their assault. For Americans, it inspired a firm resolve to fight. Some Japanese leaders seemed to sense the dual danger of Japanese confidence and American anger.

HISTORY'S VOICES

> "The fact that we have had a small success at Pearl Harbor is nothing . . . Personally, I do not think it is a good thing to whip up propaganda to encourage the nation. People should think things over and realize how serious the situation is."
>
> —Japanese admiral Isoroku Yamamoto, quoted in *The Second World War: Asia and the Pacific*, Thomas E. Griess, Ed.

Japanese advances In the early days of the war, the Japanese saw little reason to heed Admiral Yamamoto's warning. After all, following Pearl Harbor, Japanese forces won a quick string of impressive victories. In late 1941 they drove American forces from Wake Island and Guam. Elsewhere, they captured the British stronghold at Hong Kong. Then they launched a campaign against the British base at Singapore. The British had believed that this mighty fortress would never fall to invaders. It took the Japanese just two weeks to capture it. In the process, they handed the British what Winston Churchill called "the greatest disaster and capitulation [surrender] in British history."

At the same time, other Japanese forces were easily taking control of the Dutch East Indies (today known as Indonesia) and British Borneo. In the Battle of Java Sea, they caused much damage to the Allied navies. The Japanese also conquered British-controlled Burma as well as a number of key positions in the South Pacific. In this way, they gained control of rich oil reserves, which were vital to their military plans. They also established strategic bases for future operations.

Bataan Death March
Some 70,000 American and Filipino prisoners were force-marched 63 miles in tropical heat with little food or water in the Bataan Death March. Some 7,000 to 10,000 died. The surrender at Bataan was the largest in U.S. history. *Why were the forces defending Bataan so vulnerable?*

The Allies were stunned by the rapid success of the Japanese military in the months after Pearl Harbor. They had not realized that Japanese soldiers were so highly skilled and well trained. The Japanese military also had excellent equipment. For example, Japanese fighter aircraft were as good as—or better than—anything the Allies could produce. Japanese ships and torpedoes were also of high quality. These factors gave the Japanese an important advantage early in the war.

The British were the first to discover the true strength of Japan's military in Hong Kong, Singapore, and Burma. American soldiers were about to learn the same lesson.

The Philippines Japan's attacks on Hong Kong, Singapore, the Dutch East Indies, and Burma were part of a large offensive that had one other major target: the American-controlled islands of the Philippines. General **Douglas MacArthur** led the defense of that island chain. He commanded a small force of Americans, plus a number of poorly trained and equipped Filipino soldiers. In fact, MacArthur's troops were no match for the Japanese invaders, who came ashore in December 1941.

As the Japanese gained ground, MacArthur planned a retreat to the Bataan Peninsula. There he hoped to hold off the Japanese for as long as possible. Simply getting his troops into this defensive position, however, took hard fighting and brilliant leadership. Once there, the soldiers found that food, medicine, and other supplies were terribly short. MacArthur urged Allied officials to send ships to help relieve his starving troops. War planners, however, decided that such a move was too risky. As Secretary of War Henry Stimson grimly noted, "There are times when men have to die."

MacArthur and his forces fought on bravely. Soon, however, illness and hunger began to take their toll. In March 1942 MacArthur was ordered to leave his men. He did so reluctantly, promising, "I shall return." Less than a month later, 10,000 American and 60,000 Filipino troops on Bataan surrendered.

The fighting was over, but the suffering of the soldiers was just beginning. For five days and nights, the Japanese forced the already starving and sick soldiers to march through the steaming forests of Bataan. Those who dropped out of line were beaten or shot. Those who fell were left for dead. The Japanese provided little food or water. Thousands of soldiers perished on this so-called **Bataan Death March**. Those who completed this terrible journey did not fare much better. In the Japanese prison camp, lack of food and medicine claimed hundreds more American and Filipino lives.

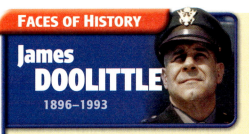

FACES OF HISTORY
James DOOLITTLE
1896–1993

James Doolittle left college to join the army when the United States entered World War I. He became an expert pilot and flight instructor. After the war he tested and raced aircraft for the Army Air Corps.

Doolittle left the army in 1930 to work as an aviation consultant, but he returned to active duty when World War II began. He led air operations throughout the war, including a courageous bombing attack on Japan in 1942, immortalized in the famous movie *Thirty Seconds Over Tokyo*. The raid was the first attack on the Japanese mainland during the war. Doolittle later commanded bombing raids on Germany, which helped lead to the end of the war in Europe.

Make Inferences Why do you think Doolittle returned to active duty when World War II began?

READING CHECK **Drawing Conclusions** Why did the Allies experience a slow start in the war in the Pacific?

Fortunes Shift in the Pacific

The loss of the Philippines was a low point for the United States in the Pacific war. Days later, however, Americans finally got some good news. On April 18, 1942, Army Lieutenant Colonel **James Doolittle** led a group of 16 American bombers on a daring air raid of Tokyo and several other Japanese cities. The airplanes had been launched from an aircraft carrier several hundred miles off the coast of Japan.

Doolittle's raid, as the event came to be known, did not do major damage to the Japanese targets. It did, however, have some significant effects. One was to finally give the American people something to celebrate. The other effect was to worry and anger Japan's leaders. Their outrage—and their concern about future attacks—would cloud their judgment and lead to major military mistakes in the months ahead.

The Battle of Coral Sea Americans got something else to cheer about in May 1942, when news reached home about the Battle of Coral Sea. This battle featured the one part of the Pacific fleet that had not been badly damaged at Pearl Harbor—the aircraft carriers.

The Battle of Coral Sea took place as Japanese forces were preparing to invade the British controlled Port Moresby on the island of New Guinea. To prevent this attack, U.S. Admiral **Chester Nimitz** sent two aircraft carriers on the attack. In the battle that followed, the American and Japanese navies both suffered damage. For the Americans, this included the loss of an aircraft carrier and several dozen aircraft. Yet they had stopped the Japanese attack. For the first time, the Japanese advance had been halted.

The Battle of Midway As you have read, Doolittle's raid had troubled Japan's leaders. They were determined to stop any future attacks on the Japanese mainland. To do this, they knew they had to destroy what remained of the United States naval power.

Japanese military planners decided to try to lure the Americans into a large sea battle. The first step would be to attack the American-held Midway Island, which sat in the middle of the Pacific Ocean. They hoped the attack would pull the American fleet into the area. Then the Japanese could destroy it.

The Japanese had a large advantage in the number of ships and carriers they could bring to the battle. The Americans, however, had one great advantage. Naval intelligence officers had broken a Japanese code and learned about the plans for attacking Midway. Americans knew the date for the planned attack—June 3, 1942. They also knew the direction from which the Japanese ships would approach.

The Americans also benefited from the carelessness of Japanese war planners. These planners had recognized possible flaws in their plan. Yet they chose to ignore them. It seemed as though their recent success had led them to believe they could not be defeated.

They were wrong. Using his advance knowledge of Japanese plans, Admiral Nimitz placed his three available aircraft carriers carefully. His goal was to stop a Japanese landing at Midway and to avoid contact with the larger Japanese fleet.

Nimitz's plan worked perfectly. Just as he had expected, the Japanese launched their attack in the early morning hours of June 4, 1942. The first stage was an air attack, meant to prepare Midway Island for a future landing by Japanese forces. The attacking Japanese planes took off from a group of four aircraft carriers that were leading the assault on Midway. American air defenses were waiting and managed to fight off the air raid.

The surviving Japanese planes raced back to their carriers to refuel and rearm. They were followed by American aircraft. The Japanese desperately fought off dozens of American bombers. Finally, several planes from the USS *Enterprise* broke through the Japanese defenses.

HISTORY'S VOICES

> "The terrifying scream of the dive bombers reached me first, followed by the crashing of a direct hit. There was a blinding flash and then a second explosion, much louder than the first... I watched the fires spread, and I was terrified at the prospect of induced explosions, which would surely doom the ship."
>
> —Mitsuo Fuchido, quoted in *The Pacific War*, by John Costello

The American bombs severely damaged three of the four carriers. The decks of these ships had been cluttered with returning planes, bombs and torpedoes, and fuel, which blew up in the American attack. As Fuchido had predicted, these fires and explosions destroyed all three ships. American aircraft later destroyed the fourth carrier in this group.

During the battle, Japanese planes did manage to destroy one of the American carriers, the USS *Yorktown*. Nimitz, however, had placed the rest of his ships perfectly. The surviving ships of the Japanese battle fleet were too far away to threaten them. As the **Battle of Midway** ended, it was clear the Americans had won a tremendous victory.

The plan to invade Midway had been stopped, and Japan's navy had suffered a terrible blow. Japan's once great advantage on the seas no longer existed.

READING CHECK **Sequencing** What events helped shift the Americans' fortunes in the Pacific?

The Allies Make Progress

The Battle of Midway had changed the entire balance of power in the Pacific. Japanese naval power, which had been a key to its early success, was greatly reduced. Now on a more equal footing with the Japanese, the Americans began to make plans of their own in the Pacific.

Guadalcanal A first step was to win control of territory in the Solomon Islands. The Japanese had moved into these islands in the spring of 1942. This threatened nearby Australia, which was fighting alongside the Allies in the Pacific. An Allied presence in the Solomons would help protect Australia. It would also provide a base for further efforts to push back the Japanese.

A key goal in the Solomons was the capture of an island called Guadalcanal (GWAHD-uhl-KUH-NAL). The Japanese had nearly completed an airfield there, making it a tempting target. The rest of the island, however, offered little. It was covered by swamps and dense jungles. Daytime temperatures regularly reached into the 90s. Millions of disease-carrying insects filled the air. It was a miserable place to fight.

In spite of this, American forces came ashore on Guadalcanal in August 1942. For the next six months, they fought in bloody combat with Japanese forces. The battle took place on land, at sea, and in the air. Each side won small victories until finally, in February 1943, Japanese forces fled the island. It was a key moment in the war. "Before that," recalled one soldier, "we weren't looking for the Japanese, they were looking for us. . . . But from there on out, the Japanese were on the run."

The Allies press on The Allied victory at Guadalcanal set a pattern that was repeated in the coming months. The Allies would use a powerful combination of land, sea, and air forces to capture key islands. These would then

The American Victory at the Battle of Midway

Devastator torpedo bombers lie in wait for the Japanese fleet aboard the USS *Enterprise* (left). Above, a Japanese battle cruiser is destroyed by a hail of American bombs. After Midway, the *Enterprise* received the first Presidential Unit Citation ever awarded to a carrier, the Navy Unit Commendation, and 20 battle stars.

Geography Skills: Interpreting Maps

1. **Location** Why did the United States want to control Iwo Jima and Okinawa?
2. **Movement** Describe U.S. strategy in the Pacific as shown on this map. What role did the tiny Pacific islands play?

See **Skills Handbook**, p. H20

become the stepping-stones for future military actions. The Allies focused on Japanese weak spots and simply skipped over strongholds. In this way, the Allies made steady progress in the Southwest Pacific in 1943. In 1944 the Allies captured locations in the Gilbert, Marshall, Caroline, and Mariana islands. You can trace this progress in the map above.

The Allies also began to take advantage of America's tremendous industrial power. The fighting in the Pacific was extremely costly, and both sides lost dozens of ships and thousands of aircraft. These were losses the Japanese were unable to replace. Busy American factories, meanwhile, produced planes and ships at an amazing rate.

438 CHAPTER 14

American fighters in the Pacific also benefited from Allied gains in Europe. Early in the war, Allied leaders had followed the strategy of focusing their efforts on Europe first. This cut down on the numbers of soldiers, sailors, and supplies available for the Pacific war. Then the Soviets began to push back German advances, and the Allies made gains in North Africa, Italy, and France. This allowed Allied war planners to send more resources to the Pacific.

American ingenuity and diversity also played a role in the Allied success. One example was the hundreds of Native Americans of the Navajo nation who served in the Marines as **code talkers**. Their main job was translating messages into a coded version of the Navajo language. This unwritten language is so complex that the Japanese code-breakers were never able to figure it out. Navajo code talkers could quickly and accurately transmit vital information about troop movements, enemy positions, and more. Their contributions helped the Allies win many major battles.

Back to the Philippines Ever since leaving the Philippines in early 1942, General MacArthur had looked forward to the day when he could fulfill his promise to return. By the middle of 1944, that day was at hand. Allied forces had fought to within striking distance of the Philippines. After much planning, MacArthur was ready to attack.

The first major action took place on the seas—the Battle of Leyte (LAY-tee) Gulf. Here nearly 300 ships took part in the largest naval battle ever fought. By this time, the Allies held a huge advantage in numbers of ships. When the battle was over, the Japanese had lost four carriers, three battleships, and a number of other vessels. What little was left of their fleet would play no major role in the rest of the war.

The Battle of Leyte Gulf also saw the first major use of a new Japanese weapon—the **kamikaze** attack. The term *kamikaze* is a Japanese word meaning "divine wind." It refers to a famous event in Japanese history—a sudden storm that drove off a fleet preparing to invade Japan in the 1200s. In World War II, however, a kamikaze was a pilot who loaded his aircraft with bombs and deliberately crashed it into an enemy ship. It was understood that the attack would lead to the death of the pilot. As a Japanese admiral explained, such tactics were "the only way of assuring our meager strength will be effective to the maximum degree." The kamikaze attacks did not change the outcome of the Battle of Leyte Gulf, but the Allies would come to fear these suicidal attacks.

In late October 1944, MacArthur waded ashore to fulfill his promise to return to the Philippines. It would take his soldiers many more months of tough fighting to gain full control of the islands.

ACADEMIC VOCABULARY
strategy plan of action

THE IMPACT TODAY
Recent Scholarship
The work of the Navajo code talkers was kept secret for years. It was not until recently that they received public recognition. In 2001 the 29 original code talkers received the Congressional Gold Medal for their service.

Linking to Today

Return to Iwo Jima

Iwo Jima was one of the bloodiest battles of the war in the Pacific. On the 60th anniversary of the battle, it was the site of a reunion of former enemies.

After the month-long battle in early 1945, nearly 7,000 Americans had been killed, along with three times as many Japanese fighters. Around 1,000 Japanese soldiers were captured.

In 2005 American and Japanese veterans returned to Iwo Jima to remember the battle and show how the world has changed. Following World War II, Japan and the United States became close allies. The two nations have a strong trade relationship and work together on international issues.

"Today, 60 years after the battle of Iwo Jima, it gives me deep awe to see Japan and the United States cooperate in fighting terrorism," said Yoshitaka Shinda, whose grandfather was the island's last Japanese commander.

Drawing Conclusions Would Yoshitaka Shinda's grandfather agree with his statement? Explain.

Honoring the war dead on the 60th anniversary of the Battle of Iwo Jima

Iwo Jima and Okinawa Beginning in late 1944 the massive new American B-29 bomber began making regular raids on Japanese cities. Allied bombers dropped many tons of explosives on Tokyo and other centers.

In order to provide a better base from which to launch these raids, American forces set out in February 1945 to capture Iwo Jima. This tiny volcanic island lay some 750 miles south of Tokyo, the capital of Japan. The island's rugged terrain was heavily guarded by Japanese soldiers. American troops greatly outnumbered the defenders. For the first time in the war, however, the Japanese troops were fighting for land that was actually part of Japan. Hidden in caves and tunnels and protected by concrete bunkers, they fought ferociously.

Early in the **Battle of Iwo Jima**, marines managed to capture the island's tallest point, Mount Suribachi. You read about this moment earlier in this section. Some Americans thought that the capture of Mount Suribachi meant that the battle was over, but the Japanese troops refused to surrender. The fighting raged on for several more weeks. By the time it was over, nearly 7,000 Americans were dead and many more were wounded. More than 20,000 Japanese defenders had been on Iwo Jima when the Americans landed. All but a thousand of them fought to the death.

The next American target was Okinawa (OH-kee-NAH-wah). Only 350 miles from Japan, this island was to be the launching pad for the final invasion of Japan itself. First, however, it had to be captured. This would be the bloodiest task the Americans would face in the Pacific.

Allied troops invaded Okinawa on April 1, 1945. The Japanese forces retreated to the southern tip of the island to plan their response. Five days later, they attacked. The island of Okinawa was filled with caves and tunnels. Japanese soldiers used these skillfully to hide and to launch deadly assaults. Over 12,000 Americans died in the **Battle of Okinawa**, and thousands more were injured.

The Japanese lost a staggering 110,000 troops in the fighting. As on Iwo Jima, their willingness to fight on when death was certain filled the Americans with amazement—and dread. "I see no way to get them out," noted one American general, "except to blast them out yard by yard."

In spite of the terrible losses, the Americans finally gained control of the island in June 1945. As you will read, the lessons learned on Okinawa would have a major impact on the final days of the war.

READING CHECK **Summarizing** What factors allowed the Allies to advance in 1944 and 1945?

SECTION 3 ASSESSMENT

go.hrw.com
Online Quiz
Keyword: SE7 HP14

HSS 11.7.2, 11.7.6

Reviewing Ideas, Terms, and People

1. **a. Recall** What events led up to the **Bataan Death March**?
   b. Analyze What were the key reasons for the early success of the Japanese?
   c. Evaluate How do you think the fighting in Europe may have affected events taking place in the Pacific?

2. **a. Identify** Describe the significance of the following people in World War II: James Doolittle, Chester Nimitz
   b. Explain What was the importance of the American victory at the **Battle of Midway**?
   c. Predict At **Iwo Jima** and **Okinawa**, Japanese troops refused to surrender even when facing certain defeat. How might this reluctance to give in affect the end of the war?

3. **a. Identify** Describe the significance of the following: **code talkers, kamikaze**
   b. Make Generalizations How would you describe the performance of the Japanese in the later battles of the war in the Pacific?

   c. Elaborate What is your opinion about the actions of the kamikaze?

Critical Thinking

4. **Identifying Supporting Details** Copy the chart below and use information from the section to find supporting details for the main idea given.

Slow start	Fortunes shift	Progress

FOCUS ON WRITING  ELA W1.1, 1.3

5. **Persuasive** In the early years of the war, should the Allies have committed more resources to the fighting in the Pacific? Write a short essay in which you develop your position on the issue. Include references to events in Europe.

SECTION 4: The Home Front

HSS 11.7.5 Discuss the constitutional issues and impact of events on the U.S. home front, including the internment of Japanese Americans (e.g., *Fred Korematsu v. United States of America*) and the restrictions on German and Italian resident aliens; and the roles of women in military production.

HSS 11.7.6 Describe major developments in aviation, weaponry, communication, and medicine and the war's impact on the location of American industry and use of resources.

Before You Read

MAIN IDEA
While millions of military men and women were serving in World War II, Americans on the home front were making contributions of their own.

READING FOCUS
1. What sacrifices and struggles did Americans at home experience?
2. How did the U.S. government seek to win American support for the war?
3. What was Japanese internment?
4. How did World War II help expand the role of the government in the lives of the American people?

KEY TERMS AND PEOPLE
rationing
Ernie Pyle
Bill Mauldin
internment

Gardening for Victory

THE INSIDE STORY

How did vegetable gardens help to win a war? World War II placed huge demands on the United States. Not only did millions of Americans serve in the armed forces, but people at home had to make do with less—including less food and less fuel for harvesting and transporting crops.

To help overcome these shortages and preserve precious resources for the military, Americans by the millions planted "victory gardens." In small towns and large cities, any spare piece of land was likely to be used to grow food. People gardened on the rooftops of apartment buildings and in flower boxes outside their windows. School yards, ball fields, and vacant lots were plowed under. Government agencies and private businesses encouraged the effort with posters, seeds, and instructions for gardening.

Many victory gardens were small and humble but combined they produced big results. In 1943 the nation's 20 million victory gardens yielded an astounding 8 million tons of produce. Grace Bracker's Wisconsin garden was typical. She canned over 400 quarts of fruits and vegetables her first year—more than she and her family could eat.

Victory gardens also helped unite communities. Very young children and older men and women could all help in the preparation, planting, weeding, and harvesting of vegetables. Indeed, the victory gardens became a popular expression of patriotism. They helped Americans at home stay strong during the difficult days of the bloodiest war in human history.

▶ A few simple tools, some seed, some fertilizer, and a patriotic spirit were nearly all a person needed to grow a victory garden.

THE UNITED STATES IN WORLD WAR II **441**

Sacrifice and Struggle at Home

You have read about the amazing courage and sacrifice of the Allied soldiers, sailors, and pilots. By the millions, they risked life and limb so that others could enjoy freedom. Many spilled their blood so that others could live.

World War II, however, made demands of every American. The women, children, and men who remained in the United States played a key role in ensuring success overseas.

HISTORY'S VOICES

> "Not all of us can have the privilege of fighting our enemies in distant parts of the world ... But there is one front and one battle where everyone in the United States is in action. That front is right here at home."
>
> —Franklin D. Roosevelt, radio address, April 28, 1942

As you read earlier, millions of Americans made contributions to the war effort by taking jobs in factories or offices. In addition, life in the American home changed significantly as citizens of all ages did their part to help the cause of victory in Europe and the Pacific.

Conserving food and other goods Meeting the food needs of the military took top priority in the United States. The planting of victory gardens, which you read about in the "Inside Story," was one way in which Americans filled these needs.

Victory gardens alone did not solve all the nation's food needs. Some foods could not be produced in home gardens, and there was simply not enough of certain products to go around. As a result, the United States began rationing food shortly after the nation entered the war. **Rationing** means limiting the amount of a certain product each individual can get.

During the war, the government rationed products such as coffee, butter, sugar, and meat. Each member of the family received a ration book, which entitled that person to a certain amount of certain foods. Most people willingly accepted the system. Penalties for breaking the rationing rules could be severe.

The war effort also meant shortages of other materials, such as metal, glass, rubber, and gasoline. Gasoline was rationed. Americans helped meet the demand for other materials by holding scrap drives, in which citizens col-

American Support for the War Effort

These children (right) drum up support for the war with a scrap metal drive. Communities enthusiastically responded to such drives by contributing everything from old pots and pans to the statues in their town squares. People also turned out for war bond rallies, such as this one at a navy shipyard in Chicago in 1944 (below). The promotional efforts of movie stars and artists helped sell war bonds to tens of millions of Americans.

lected waste material of all sorts that might be used in the war efforts. Empty tin cans, bits of rubber and glass—anything that could be useful was salvaged. Even women's silk and nylon stockings were recycled to make parachutes.

Scrap drives provided a way for young Americans to help with the war effort. Scouts and other youth organizations helped lead the way in this important national effort.

Investing in victory Americans supported the war effort not just with their trash but also with their treasure. They did this by buying billions of dollars worth of war bonds. The money invested by millions of ordinary citizens helped pay for the the vast quantities of shipping, aircraft, and other weaponry being produced in American factories.

Throughout the war, magazines and newspapers were filled with ads encouraging people to do their civic duty and support the war effort. Inspirational pictures and messages helped promote patriotism and self-sacrifice. "Our fighting forces will do their stuff," promised one ad, "but we at home must do ours."

The result of these appeals was amazing. By war's end, 85 million Americans had purchased war bonds. This represented well over half of the entire population of the country. The total raised was nearly $185 billion. This amount was twice what the entire federal government spent in the year 1945.

Paying the personal price Americans willingly put up with many hardships and made do without many comforts during the war. For many, the hardest part was dealing with the absence of loved ones.

HISTORY'S VOICES

> " At first you feel abandoned and you feel angry because they took him when you needed him more at home ... [B]ut he went and he was doing his duty, and we figured that was part of our job to give our husband to the war effort and to do the best we could without him. "
>
> —Jean Lechnir, quoted in *Women Remember the War*, Michael E. Stevens, Ed.

Across the country, families with loved ones in the service showed their sacrifice by displaying a flag with a blue star. If the service member was killed, the blue star was replaced with a gold one.

Families followed the news of the war with great interest. Millions of Americans read the newspaper columns of writer **Ernie Pyle**, who covered the war from the point of view of the men in the field. **Bill Mauldin**, whose cartoons featured two ordinary soldiers named Willie and Joe, also gave folks on the home front a soldier's view of life in the army.

READING CHECK Identifying Problems and Solutions What were some of the sacrifices and struggles facing people on the home front?

Winning American Support for the War

American leaders were well aware that public support for the war effort was vital to its success. In the words of one government publication of the time, "Each word an American utters either helps or hurts the war effort." For this reason, the government made a great effort to shape public attitudes and beliefs.

This effort to win American support for the war effort began even before the United States entered the war. In January 1941, President Roosevelt gave a speech in which he observed that the challenge facing the world was a struggle for basic American values. By supporting its allies overseas, Roosevelt argued, the nation would be working to protect what he called the "four freedoms." These were the freedom of speech, freedom of worship, freedom from want, and freedom from fear.

The Office of War Information When the United States officially entered the war, the federal government's need to influence the thoughts, feelings, and actions of the public became even greater. In June 1942, the government created the Office of War Information (OWI). This agency was responsible for spreading propaganda, or information and ideas designed to promote a cause.

The OWI produced dozens of posters and films during the war. Many of these encouraged a positive vision of the United States and stressed positive actions. For example, many posters and films encouraged men to join the fighting forces and women to take jobs in war industries. Others encouraged positive goals, such saving gasoline and working for racial

ACADEMIC VOCABULARY
civic public or community

harmony. Another famous poster series illustrated the four freedoms that Roosevelt had talked about. These featured paintings by the popular artist Norman Rockwell.

The OWI also issued stark warnings to the public about the dangers they faced. Drawings of Nazi or Japanese soldiers threatening small children were meant to inspire fear in Americans—and the desire to take action against the Axis nations. "We're fighting to prevent this," declared one headline. Below the words was a picture of a giant Nazi boot crushing a little white church.

Another technique was to show the harmful outcomes of improper actions and attitudes, such as talking about sensitive military information. "Someone talked!" accused a drowning American sailor in one poster, moments before he slipped beneath the waves. Films such as *Safeguarding Military Information* dramatized the same ideas.

Hollywood helps out Movies remained enormously popular during the war years. In the early 1940s, some 90 million Americans visited the movie theater each week. As a result, the nation's film industry became a major producer of wartime propaganda.

In general, Hollywood was a willing helper in the war effort. The big movie studios made a series of patriotic films that featured soldiers and workers on the home front. To assist the studios, the OWI produced a guide called "The Government Information Manual for the Motion Picture." This offered tips to ensure that Hollywood films helped promote what the government felt were the right attitudes about the war. The OWI also reviewed movie scripts for the proper messages.

Many leading movie stars devoted time and energy to the war cause. They helped sell war bonds and provided entertainment to the troops at home and overseas.

PRIMARY SOURCES

Propaganda Poster

Office of War Information propaganda posters used bold graphics and simple text to convey their messages. This poster was issued in 1943. It addressed a key priority: the need to safeguard sensitive war-related information when nearly everyone in society was involved in the war effort.

- The hand with the swastika suggests that Nazi spies might be hidden in America.
- The poster compares bits of information with puzzle pieces that, if combined, could reveal a damaging secret.

Skills FOCUS — **READING LIKE A HISTORIAN**

1. **Interpreting Visuals** What is the hand doing, and why?
2. **Drawing Conclusions** What is the main message of this poster?

See **Skills Handbook**, p. H12, H30

The *Barnette* ruling While most Americans willingly supported the war effort, the drive to influence public attitudes sometimes led to conflict. For example, in West Virginia, members of the Jehovah's Witness religious group challenged a law that required students in school to salute the American flag. The Jehovah's Witnesses felt that this requirement went against their religious teachings. In 1943 the Supreme Court of the United States agreed that Americans could not be forced to salute the flag. In *West Virginia Board of Education v. Barnette*, the Court wrote that "no official … can prescribe [require] what shall be orthodox [standard or required belief] in politics, nationalism, religion or other matters of opinion."

READING CHECK **Identifying Supporting Details** What was the mission of the Office of War Information in influencing public opinion?

Japanese Internment

After Pearl Harbor, government officials began to fear that people of German, Italian, and especially Japanese descent would help the enemy. Many Italians and Germans who had immigrated to the United States were forced to carry identification cards. Thousands were placed in prison camps. But the worst treatment was reserved for Japanese Americans.

Executive Order 9066 Right after the bombing of Pearl Harbor, military officials began to investigate the Japanese American community for signs of spying or other illegal activity. They found no evidence of wrongdoing. In spite of this finding, General John L. DeWitt, the Army officer in charge of the western United States, still recommended that all people of Japanese background be removed from the West Coast. "The very fact that no sabotage or espionage has taken place," he warned, "is disturbing and confirming indication that such action will take place."

In response to warnings such as this, President Roosevelt issued Executive Order 9066 on February 19, 1942. This order gave the armed forces the power to establish military zones. It also gave them the power to force people or groups to leave these zones. The clear goal of the order was to remove people of Japanese heritage from the western United States.

The order affected all people of Japanese heritage living in the military zone. Within weeks of the order, soldiers were rounding up Japanese Americans in California, Washington, Oregon, and Arizona. Two-thirds of the 110,000 people affected were American citizens. Many had been born in the United States and had lived here for decades. No hearings or trials were conducted to determine if an individual posed a real threat. The only factor considered was the person's racial background. The Japanese Americans were told they would be taken to one of several camps somewhere in the West. There they would be forced to live for as long as the military decided it was necessary.

This forced relocation and confinement to the camps was called **internment**. It placed many hardships on Japanese Americans. They were allowed to bring only those belongings they could carry. Everything else—homes, businesses, and other property—had to be left behind or sold. Sometimes people were given just days to get rid of their property. As a result, they were forced to accept very low prices for their belongings or were unable to sell them at all. In this way, many Japanese Americans lost their homes and businesses. Confined to camps they were unable to work and pay off loans.

Life in the camps was hard. Many camps were located in barren desert areas with a harsh climate. Barbed wire and armed guards surrounded the facility. Families lived in cramped quarters with few furnishings. Facilities for education and health care were poor.

Japanese American loyalty While interned, Japanese Americans were required to answer questions about their loyalty to the United States. Though German Americans and Italian Americans also faced restrictions during the war, they were not forced to answer such questions.

For many Japanese in America, the desire to prove their loyalty to the country was strong. A number of young people from the camps joined the armed forces to help fight the Axis powers. Many became part of the 442nd Regimental Combat Team, made up entirely of Japanese Americans. This unit fought in Europe and had an outstanding record in battle. For the length of time it served, this unit received more medals and awards than any other of its size in American military history.

Japanese American Internment
Once an elegant race track, California's Santa Anita Assembly Center held Japanese Americans during the war. Internees were instructed to bring personal effects and small household goods, such as plates, utensils, and linens. Here they awaited transportation to more permanent relocation centers. *Why did the government intern Japanese Americans?*

Other inmates of the internment camps demonstrated their loyalty in different ways. For some, the greatest statement they could make was in keeping faith in the future and in the promise of the country that had imprisoned them.

HISTORY'S VOICES

"We are ever hoping that the time will come soon when we can all re-enter the America beyond the relocation camps in order that we make our contributions and be considered as an integral part of the American way of living."
—Yoshiko Uchiyama, letter reprinted in the *University of Washington Daily*, January 1943

Not all Japanese Americans accepted their internment peacefully. Incidents of violence and resistance occurred at the camps. In addition, a number of legal challenges were mounted against Japanese internment. One was *Korematsu* v. *United States*, a landmark Supreme Court case that you will read about at the end of this section.

After the war some Japanese Americans continued to speak out against the injustice of their internment. Decades later, the federal government formally acknowledged that it had acted unjustly. Survivors of the internment received letters of apology and a payment from the government.

READING CHECK **Identifying Supporting Details** What was life like in the internment camps?

A New Role for the Federal Government

During the 1930s, the federal government faced the crisis of the Great Depression. With the New Deal, the government grew to have a much larger role in the lives of average Americans than it had in the past. The trend that began in the Great Depression continued during World War II.

You have read about wartime rationing. This program was run by the Office of Price Administration (OPA). The OPA also placed limits on the prices businesses could charge for products and materials.

The War Production Board was another agency involved in the war effort. It was created to make sure that the military got the products and resources it needed to fight the war. As part of this effort, the board promoted the scrap drives you read about earlier. The War Production Board also placed limits on clothing manufacturers in order to ensure a supply of fabrics, such as cotton, wool, silk, and nylon. Jackets were only allowed to be a certain length. Skirts and dresses were limited in size as well. It was these restrictions on clothing that played a role in the zoot suit riots you read about in the last chapter.

Government spending during the war rose sharply. As you can see from the graph on this page, the high cost of waging war meant a steep increase in the federal budget. Almost all of this increase went to the armed forces.

To help pay for the war effort, the federal government increased income tax rates. Before the war, income taxes had been just for the wealthy, but now millions of Americans paid income taxes for the first time. As one observer noted, "the Kansas wheat farmer, the lumberjack, and the boys around the cracker barrel in the corner grocery are going to have to pay the tax bill this time." As a result American tax revenues jumped from $7.4 billion in 1941 to $43 billion in 1945.

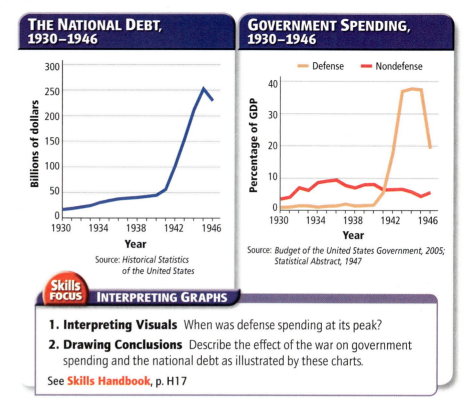

Skills Focus: INTERPRETING GRAPHS

1. **Interpreting Visuals** When was defense spending at its peak?
2. **Drawing Conclusions** Describe the effect of the war on government spending and the national debt as illustrated by these charts.

See **Skills Handbook**, p. H17

READING CHECK **Identifying Supporting Details** Why did income tax rates increase during World War II?

SECTION 4 ASSESSMENT

HSS 11.7.5, 11.7.6

Reviewing Ideas, Terms, and People

1. **a. Recall** What were the purposes of **rationing** and **scrap drives**?
   b. Summarize What kinds of sacrifices were required of people on the home front?
   c. Predict What might have happened had people on the home front been unwilling to support the war?
2. **a. Describe** What did the Office of War Information seek to do?
   b. Draw Conclusions What can you conclude from the fact that the federal government had an organization in charge of propaganda?
3. **a. Recall** What concern led to the **internment** of Japanese Americans?
   b. Explain What factors made the experience of interned Japanese Americans so difficult?
4. **a. Identify** Name two actions the federal government took to support the war effort during World War II.
   b. Compare How did the changes in the federal government during the Great Depression compare to the changes during World War II?

Critical Thinking

5. **Identifying Supporting Details** Copy the chart below and use information from the section to find supporting details for the main idea given.

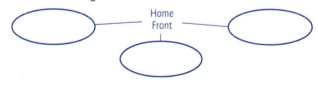

FOCUS ON WRITING ELA W1.1

6. **Narrative** Based on what you have read in this section, write a one-paragraph account about the internment of Japanese Americans on the West Coast in World War II.

LANDMARK SUPREME COURT CASES
Constitutional Issue: Equal Protection

Korematsu v. United States (1944)

Why It Matters In wartime, citizens are sometimes fearful of those who have common ancestry with the enemy. But the American population includes people from all over the world, and almost all people who live here are loyal to this country. In *Korematsu v. United States,* the U.S. Supreme Court tried to find the right balance between the rights of Japanese Americans and wartime needs.

Background of the Case

In February 1942 President Roosevelt signed an executive order that resulted in the relocation of 110,000 Japanese Americans to internment camps. Fred Korematsu refused the order and was arrested. Korematsu was in his 20s. He was of Japanese ancestry but had been born in Oakland, California, and was an American citizen. In court, Korematsu was found guilty of violating the executive order. He appealed his case to the Supreme Court.

The Decision

The Supreme Court ruled against Korematsu. Writing for the majority, Justice Hugo Black began by noting that "all legal restrictions which curtail [limit] the civil rights of a single racial group are immediately suspect" and must be given "rigid scrutiny." In this wartime situation, however, there was no easy way to separate loyal Americans of Japanese descent from those who might not support the country. The Court ruled that the relocation order was justified as a temporary wartime measure. Black rejected the argument that the relocation was racially motivated.

> "Korematsu was excluded because we are at war with the Japanese Empire … [W]hen under conditions of modern warfare our shores are threatened by hostile forces, the power to protect must be commensurate [equal] with the threatened danger."

THE IMPACT TODAY Although Fred Korematsu lost his case, he continued to work for civil rights. He finally succeeded in having his conviction overturned in 1983, and in 1998 he received the Presidential Medal of Freedom from President Bill Clinton. Korematsu died in 2005.

CRITICAL THINKING

go.hrw.com
Research Online
Keyword: SS Court

1. **Analyze the Impact** *Korematsu* v. *the United States* established the idea that classifications based on race are "suspect" and have to be supported by a compelling government interest. Using the keyword above, read about *Loving* v. *Virginia,* a case in which the Supreme Court used "strict scrutiny" to decide whether a state law prohibiting interracial marriage was constitutional. What individual interests did the law violate?

2. **You Be the Judge** The USA Patriot Act, enacted shortly after the terrorist attacks of September 11, 2001, authorizes the Immigration and Naturalization Service to detain immigrants suspected of terrorism for lengthy, or even indefinite, periods. Is this a violation of civil rights or an appropriate use of military authority? Explain your answer in a short paragraph.

SECTION 5
World War II Ends

HSS 11.7.2 Explain U.S. and Allied wartime strategy, including the major battles of Midway, Normandy, Iwo Jima, Okinawa, and the Battle of the Bulge.

HSS 11.7.6 Describe major developments in aviation, weaponry, communication, and medicine and the war's impact on the location of American industry and use of resources.

HSS 11.7.7 Discuss the decision to drop atomic bombs and the consequences of the decision.

BEFORE YOU READ

MAIN IDEA
While the Allies completed the defeat of the Axis Powers on the battlefield, Allied leaders were making plans for the postwar world.

READING FOCUS
1. How did the Allies defeat Germany and win the war in Europe?
2. How did the Allies defeat Japan and win the war in the Pacific?
3. What challenges faced the United States after victory?

KEY TERMS AND PEOPLE
Yalta Conference
occupy
V-E Day
Harry S Truman
Enola Gay
V-J Day
United Nations
Potsdam Conference

THE INSIDE STORY

What happened when the Soviet and American forces met? By April 1945, American forces had crossed Germany's western border and were moving steadily eastward. At the same time, their Soviet allies were driving westward toward the German capital of Berlin. Each side knew that when they met, Hitler's fate would be sealed.

Sometime around noon on April 25, a group of American troops spotted a Soviet force on the other side of the Elbe River. The Americans identified themselves as friendly forces. Once they had made contact, the Americans headed across the Elbe. Some swam and others took boats to the other side. There they met a group of Soviet soldiers for the first time.

The soldiers shook hands, embraced, and offered toasts to the leaders of their countries. They danced and sang. All present promised that they would do everything they could to make sure that their nations would build a lasting peace.

News of the meeting on the Elbe River set off celebrations in the United States and in the Soviet Union. There were still several days of fighting ahead before Germany surrendered, but everyone was convinced that the linking of the two main Allied forces doomed the Germans.

In the days ahead, the scene from that first meeting at the Elbe was repeated many times, as American and Soviet units linked up, posed for pictures and enjoyed their success in the war. Yet these moments of friendship and joy would soon fade away. American forces still had fighting to do in the Pacific. At the same time, tension between the Soviet Union and the United States was growing.

A HISTORIC Meeting

◀ American (left) and Soviet brothers in arms reach out across the Elbe River.

THE UNITED STATES IN WORLD WAR II **449**

Winning the War in Europe

In the first section of this chapter you read about the Battle of the Bulge. In those few desperate days of combat, over 80,000 Allied troops were killed, wounded, or captured. As bad as those figures were, the result for the German army was even worse. It had risked much in the attack and suffered a crushing defeat. Germany now had few soldiers left to defend the homeland from the 4 million Allied troops poised on its western border. To the east were millions of Soviet soldiers, who had been pushing the Germans westward since the heroic Soviet stand at Stalingrad. They stood waiting to launch a final assault.

The Yalta Conference In January 1945 Franklin D. Roosevelt took the presidential oath of office for the fourth time. He had run in 1944 believing that he needed to see the nation through to victory. A majority of the American voters had agreed.

Shortly after Roosevelt's inauguration, the president left for a conference of the Allied leaders. The meeting was held in the resort town of Yalta, in the Soviet Union. The so-called Big Three—Roosevelt, Winston Churchill, and Joseph Stalin—met to make plans for the end of the war and the peace that was to follow.

A key goal of the **Yalta Conference** was to reach an agreement on what to do with the soon-to-be-conquered Germany. The three leaders agreed to divide the country into four sectors. The Americans, Soviets, British, and French would each occupy one of these sectors. To **occupy** means to take control of a place by placing troops in it. The Soviet Union, which had the largest army, was given the largest zone. It covered most of the eastern half of

ACADEMIC VOCABULARY
sector a part or division

Toward Victory in Europe

By the spring of 1945, the Allies were closing in on Hitler. At left, U.S. army infantrymen blast their way through a German city. Below, an American soldier is lifted into the air by Russians celebrating their liberation from a German camp.

Germany. The American, British, and French zones covered the western half. The capital city of Berlin, which lay in the Soviet zone, was similarly divided into four sectors.

Another agreement at Yalta had to do with the fate of Poland and other Eastern European countries now occupied by the Soviets. Stalin agreed to hold elections in these countries following the war. As you will read, this was an promise Stalin would not keep.

Stalin also committed to a third major decision. He said that the Soviet Union would declare war on Japan three months after Germany was defeated.

Though all the participants at Yalta had been allies in the fight to defeat the Axis, the conference had been tense. Friction between the Soviet Union and the other Allies was growing. Nevertheless, Roosevelt cheerfully reported the success of the meeting to the Congress.

HISTORY'S VOICES

"Of course we know that it was Hitler's hope… that we would not agree, that some slight crack might appear in the solid wall of Allied unity… But Hitler has failed. Never before have the major Allies been more closely united—not only in their war aims but also in their peace aims."
—Franklin D. Roosevelt, March 1, 1945

Crossing the Rhine As the Big Three were meeting in Yalta, Allied forces to the west of Germany were preparing to cross the Rhine River. This represented a key barrier to the center of Germany—at least in the minds of the German people. For this reason, Hitler ordered his forces to make a stand there. He refused to allow them to fall back to a better defensive position. This turned out to be another of Hitler's military mistakes.

German troops began blowing up bridges over the Rhine in order to slow the Allies. On March 7, 1945, however, American forces managed to capture a bridge at Remagen. They did this while the Germans were still moving their own forces to the eastern side. The Germans fought desperately to destroy the bridge and keep it out of American hands. They used every weapon in their arsenal against it, including the powerful V-2 rocket. Yet the bridge stood even under this vicious bombardment. Meanwhile, Allied troops and tanks rumbled steadily across.

Once the Allies crossed the Rhine, the foolishness of Hitler's order to defend the river became clear. The Allies were able to surround and capture a quarter million German soldiers. Tens of thousands more were killed.

The question of Berlin With the Rhine crossed, German resistance weakened. Allied planes roamed the skies freely, raining bombs down on German targets. Allied troops began moving speedily across Germany.

Now some Allied leaders, knowing that the Soviets would claim any German land they captured, hoped to claim the prize of Berlin before the Soviets did so. The possibility of beating the Soviets to Berlin had once seemed unlikely. Just days before, the western lines were 200 miles away from the German capital, while the Soviets rested just 30 miles outside the city. Since the Rhine crossing, however, the situation had changed. It was no sure thing the Soviets would get there first.

In spite of these facts, General Eisenhower decided not to make a drive toward Berlin itself. Although German defenses were crumbling, he believed the battle for the city would be a bloody one. He also knew that Allied leaders had already reached an agreement with the Soviets about how to divide Berlin. This meant that some of the territory American soldiers might fight and die for would be turned over to the Soviets anyway. In addition, Eisenhower knew that the war in the Pacific was still raging. He felt it was most important to preserve American forces and supplies and make it as easy as possible to send them to the Pacific when the fighting in Europe was done.

With the decision to leave Berlin to the Soviets made, Eisenhower's forces moved rapidly through Germany. They did receive a blow on April 12, 1945, when President Roosevelt died. Although the president had not been in good health, his death was unexpected. Many American soldiers had known no other president during their adult lives. Roosevelt's death saddened the troops. It did not, however, slow the drive to victory.

American Civil Liberty

Women and Minorities in the Military

At the beginning of World War II, only two African Americans had been line officers in the army. One was Benjamin O. Davis Sr., the first African American general. The other was his son, Benjamin O. Davis Jr., who commanded the famous Tuskegee Airmen, a squadron of African American fighter pilots who flew wartime missions in North Africa and Europe. Like his father, Davis Jr. was eventually promoted to general.

The Davises and other African Americans in World War II served in segregated units. In 1948 President Harry S Truman signed legislation that began racial integration in the military.

Members of women's military units also wanted fair treatment. In most branches of the armed services, women's units did not receive veterans' benefits. Leaders such as Oveta Culp Hobby and Mary Agnes Hallaren fought to change this.

In 1948 Truman signed the Women's Armed Services Integration Act. Still, American women continued to serve in separate units until 1978. Today women make up about 20 percent of the U.S. military.

Drawing Conclusions Why did events in World War II lead Truman to end segregation in the military?

Members of the U.S. Air Force in Iraq during Operation Iraqi Freedom

Hitler's death In the final weeks of April 1945 the steady destruction of the German resistance continued. One by one, units from the Soviet Union met up with other Allied forces. At the same time, Berlin was under heavy bombardment. On April 30 Hitler finally recognized that all hope was lost. He committed suicide in his Berlin bunker.

As news of Hitler's death spread, fighting came to a halt. Berlin surrendered on May 2. The German armies scattered elsewhere gave up the fight. Finally, Karl Dönitz, who had taken over for as Germany's leader following Hitler's death, agreed to a surrender on May 7. The surrender was to take effect on May 8. In the United States, this was proclaimed **V-E Day**—Victory in Europe Day.

Celebrations erupted in the United States and throughout Europe. "I was alive! And I was going to stay alive," recalled one soldier of his joyful reaction to the German surrender. This fortunate young American could enjoy the Allied victory. Yet many others still had work to do. This was especially true for those still fighting for their lives in a place called Okinawa.

READING CHECK **Identifying the Main Idea** What was the significance of crossing the Rhine in winning the war in Europe?

Winning the War in the Pacific

As you have read, the Allies did capture Okinawa—but at a terrible cost. The horrors of this combat were reflected in the high rates of battle-related psychological casualties. Thousands of Allied soldiers and sailors suffered from battle fatigue and other disorders. These conditions were serious enough to require medical treatment.

The experience of the Allies in fighting the Japanese made many of them dread the prospect of invading the major islands of Japan. Nevertheless, General MacArthur and Admiral Nimitz went forward with developing plans for a massive invasion. The costs would be enormous. Some officials believed that capturing Japan might produce as many as 1 million Allied casualties.

Japan continues fighting Other Allied military leaders hoped to force Japan to surrender by putting a blockade in place or by bombing Japan heavily. In fact, Allied bombs had already caused severe damage to Japanese cities. In March 1945 Major General Curtis LeMay had experimented with a bombing tactic that was designed to produce a tremendous firestorm in the bombed area. The first of LeMay's raids, on Tokyo, killed nearly 84,000 Japanese and destroyed nearly 270,000 buildings. One American compared the effect of the bombs to "a tornado started by fires." The flames were so intense that river water was heated to the boiling point.

The bombing of Tokyo stunned the people of Japan. The defeat at Okinawa was another blow. Still they vowed to fight on.

Some leaders within the Japanese government saw the need for peace. During June and July of 1945 these officials began to seek contact with the Soviet Union. They hoped that the Soviets could help arrange an agreement for peace with the other Allies. These talks went slowly. Meanwhile, American war plans moved steadily forward.

The atomic bomb You have already read about the U.S. program to build an atomic bomb. The Manhattan Project continued throughout the war. In late 1944 leaders of the project declared that the bomb would be ready by the summer of 1945.

Vice President **Harry S Truman** had become president after Roosevelt's death in April. The new president had known nothing about the bomb prior to assuming the presidency. Now he had to decide whether the United States should use this fearsome new weapon.

Truman formed a group to advise him about using the bomb. This group debated where the bomb should be used and whether the Japanese should be warned. After carefully considering all the options, Truman decided to drop the bomb on a Japanese city. There would be no warning.

Truman and the Allies did, however, give the Japanese one last chance to avoid the bomb. On July 26 they issued a demand for Japan's surrender. Failure to give up, the demand read, would lead to "prompt and utter destruction." The Japanese failed to respond. The plan to drop the atomic bomb went forward.

On August 6, 1945, an American B-29 named the *Enola Gay* flew over the city of Hiroshima (hee-roh-SHEE-mah) and dropped its atomic bomb. Seconds later, the bomb exploded.

HISTORY'S VOICES

"I witnessed a yellowish scarlet plume rising like a candle fire high in the sky surrounded by pitch black swirling smoke... At the same moment... houses levitated [rose] a little and then crushed down to the ground like domino pieces. It was just like a white wavehead coming toward me."

—Memoir of Takeharu Terao, Hiroshima survivor

Hiroshima

Nearly everything within a one-mile radius of the blast was destroyed when an atomic bomb hit Hiroshima. Heavy damage extended three miles out. Lighter damage reached as far as 12 miles out from the center of the blast.

COUNTERPOINTS

Dropping the Atomic Bomb

It fell to Secretary of War Henry Stimson to advise President Truman on whether or not to drop the atomic bomb.

" The face of war is the face of death ... The decision to use the atomic bomb was a decision that brought death to over a hundred thousand Japanese. No explanation can change that fact and I do not wish to gloss it over. But this deliberate, premeditated destruction was our least abhorrent choice. **"**

Henry Stimson, 1947

Physicist Leo Szilard's work on nuclear reactions was key to the development of the bomb, and he felt a moral responsibility to speak against its use.

" Using atomic bombs against Japan is one of the greatest blunders of history. Both from a practical point of view on a ten-year scale and from the point of view of our moral position. I went out of my way and very much so in order to prevent it. **"**

Leo Szilard, 1945

Skills FOCUS — READING LIKE A HISTORIAN

Identifying Points of View Henry Stimson focuses on the immediate need to end the war. What consideration does Leo Szilard emphasize?

See **Skills Handbook**, pp. H28–H29

In a single terrible blast, most of Hiroshima was reduced to rubble. Some 80,000 residents died immediately, and 35,000 were injured. Two-thirds of the city's 90,000 buildings were destroyed. Fires raged everywhere.

In spite of the horror of Hiroshima, Japan's leaders took no action to end the war. For three days, they debated their next step. On August 9 the United States dropped a second bomb on Nagasaki (nah-gah-SAH-kee). The death toll there was 40,000.

Amazingly, even this did not bring an end to the war. Japanese emperor Hirohito (hir-oh-HEE-toh) favored surrender, but military leaders resisted. Some even tried to overthrow the Japanese government and continue the war. They failed. Finally, on August 15—known from then on to the Allies as **V-J Day**—Hirohito announced the end of the war in a radio broadcast. It was the first time the Japanese people had ever heard the emperor's voice.

 **READING CHECK Summarizing** What finally brought victory for the Allies in the war against Japan?

The Challenges of Victory

Winning World War II had been a monumental effort for the United States and its allies. Peace would bring its own challenges.

You have read about the Yalta Conference, where the Allies began to discuss postwar plans for Europe. This planning continued throughout the spring and summer of 1945.

The creation of the United Nations In June 1945 representatives from 50 countries, including the United States, met in San Francisco, California, to establish a new organization—the **United Nations**. Like the League of Nations formed after World War I, the United Nations (UN) was meant to encourage cooperation among nations and to prevent future wars. You will read more about the UN in future chapters.

The Potsdam Conference The next month, leaders of the Allied nations met to carry on the work begun at Yalta. They met at

THE IMPACT TODAY
Government
The United States remains part of the United Nations, an organization it was instrumental in creating, and is a member of the UN Security Council.

454 CHAPTER 14

the German city of Potsdam. There was growing American concern that communism and Soviet influence might spread in the postwar world. Truman had hoped that if he met with Stalin, he could get the Soviet leader to live up to his promises from Yalta. In this regard, the **Potsdam Conference** was not a success.

Rebuilding Europe and Japan The United States also faced the difficult task of helping to rebuild Europe and Japan. In Japan, General Douglas MacArthur directed the effort to create a new, democratic government and rebuild the nation's economy. MacArthur skillfully walked a fine line between showing respect for Japanese traditions and insisting on democratic values. He helped the Japanese create a new constitution that reflected many American ideals, such as equality for women.

As with the Nazis in Europe, Japanese war crimes did not go unpunished. Seven key figures in wartime Japan, including leader Hideki Tojo, were tried and executed for their crimes.

The United States also faced a difficult task in rebuilding war-torn Europe. As you will read in the next chapter, this process resulted in increasing tensions with America's wartime ally, the Soviet Union. In the coming years, this relationship would only grow worse.

READING CHECK **Identifying Problems and Solutions** What was the UN meant to accomplish?

CAUSES AND EFFECTS OF WORLD WAR II

CAUSES
- Isolationism had helped lead the United States not to resist German, Japanese, and Italian aggression in the 1930s.
- Germany invaded Poland, and Japan attacked the United States.

EFFECTS
- The Allies occupied Japan and parts of Europe.
- War led to renewed commitment to the idea of collective security and creation of the United Nations.
- Conflict began between the Soviet Union and the other Allies over the fate of conquered European areas.
- The United States emerged as the world's strongest military power.

SECTION 5 ASSESSMENT

HSS 11.7.2, 11.7.6, 11.7.7

Reviewing Ideas, Terms, and People

1. **a. Identify** What is the significance of the following terms: Yalta Conference, V-E Day
   b. Explain What were the issues surrounding Eisenhower's decision not to push to Berlin?
   c. Evaluate What do you think Eisenhower's greatest responsibility was as the war wound down in Europe? Did he fulfill this responsibility?

2. **a. Define** Write a brief definition of the following term: V-J Day
   b. Make Inferences What can you infer about the atomic bomb from the fact that some people felt that it should not have been dropped without warning?
   c. Predict How do you think the decision to drop the bomb will affect the United States in the future?

3. **a. Identify** What is the significance of the following terms: United Nations, Potsdam Conference

   b. Elaborate Why do you think that rebuilding a war-torn country is so difficult?

Critical Thinking

4. **Identifying Supporting Details** Copy the chart below and use information from the section to find supporting details for the main idea given.

FOCUS ON WRITING
ELA W1.1, 1.3

5. **Descriptive** Write a paragraph in which you describe the circumstances of the end of the war in either Europe or in the Pacific theater.

Interactive HISTORY & Geography

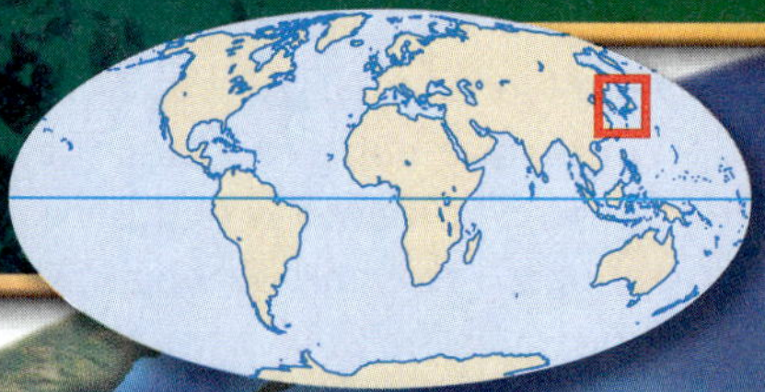

ISLAND HOPPING
The Route to Japan

In the early weeks of the war, Japan seized key islands in the Pacific to form a defensive barrier. To end the war, the United States planned to bomb and invade the Japanese mainland, but getting there proved enormously difficult and costly. It took nearly four years for the United States to push back the Japanese defenses, one island at a time. Each island captured served as a base to launch air raids or to protect American naval forces, who then moved on to attack the next island. The U.S. strategy was known as "island hopping." This map shows some of the islands that the U.S. forces captured on route to Japan.

HOKKAIDO

Sea of Japan

Tokyo

JAPAN

KYUSHU

Moving into Range Aircraft carriers were crucial for fighting in the vast Pacific Ocean. U.S. carriers transported fighter planes, torpedo bombers, and dive-bombers, many of which had only a 200-mile range, to battle sites.

CHINA

OKINAWA

TAIWAN

Okinawa, April–June, 1945
Okinawa was the southernmost of the Japanese home islands. After costly fighting, U.S. forces seized the island as a base for launching the final invasion of Japan.

Island Invasions

Bombing Runs The B-29 Superfortress's 5000-mile range was essential in the Pacific Ocean. Air raids on Japan, from the Marianas, began in October 1944.

Aerial Bombing Bombers from aircraft carriers or nearby land bases "soften up" islands before amphibious assaults.

Iwo Jima, February–March, 1945
In one of the most costly battles in the Pacific, U.S. forces attacked Japanese forces well entrenched in caves and tunnels carved into the island's volcanic rock.

Iwo Jima

Pacific Ocean

Storming the Beach Behind further bombardment from offshore battleships, marines storm the beaches.

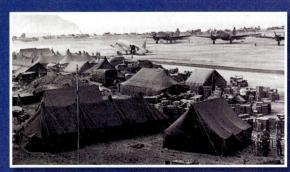

Establishing Air Bases Once an island was secured, engineers rapidly transform it into a staging area for aerial attacks on nearby islands or on Japan itself.

Mariana Islands, June–August, 1944
The conquest of the Mariana Islands put American B-29 bombers within reach of Japan. Still, numerous planes were shot down during the 5,000 mile round-trip to Japan. The reason was Iwo Jima—home to a Japanese radar station and fighter planes.

Northern Mariana Islands

GEOGRAPHY SKILLS INTERPRETING MAPS

HSS 11.7.2, 11.7.6
HSS Analysis CS2, HI2

go.hrw.com
Practice Online
Keyword: SE7 CH14

1. **Location** What challenges did Iwo Jima's location offer the American invaders?
2. **Movement** What strategy did the U.S. follow in moving toward Japan?

See **Skills Handbook**, p. H20

Saipan

THE UNITED STATES IN WORLD WAR II 457

CHAPTER 14 DOCUMENT-BASED INVESTIGATION

Perspectives on Life in Uniform

HSS 11.7.3

Historical Context The documents below provide different information on the hardships and sacrifices of American military personnel during World War II.

Task Examine the documents and answer the questions that follow. Then write an essay about the hardships U.S. soldiers faced. Use facts from the documents and from this chapter to support the position you take in your thesis statement.

DOCUMENT 1

Cartoonist Bill Mauldin chronicled the sufferings of the everyday soldier in *Stars and Stripes,* a newspaper published by the U.S. Army. His gritty cartoons featured the characters Willie and Joe, who stood for all ordinary soldiers. Mauldin served during the entire war and was wounded in battle in Sicily.

"Joe, yestiddy ya saved my life an' I swore I'd pay ya back. Here's my last pair of dry socks."

DOCUMENT 2

Army nurses saw much of the worst suffering of the war up close. June Wandrey served as a combat nurse during some of the bloodiest battles in North Africa and western Europe. She helped save many lives and was awarded eight battle stars for her service under fire. She wrote this letter to her family in Wautoma, Wisconsin, in January 1944.

"We now have a mix of wounded, medical patients, and battle-fatigued soldiers . . . The wounded were happy to be missing only one arm or leg . . . I have a terrible earache but as usual I have to work. The patients need me."

DOCUMENT 3

For many Americans, the war was draining both physically and spiritually. Paul Curtis was from a small town in Tennessee. Fighting in the Italian campaign was unlike anything he had ever experienced. In this letter home from May 1944, he tried to explain his reactions to his brother. Curtis was killed in action shortly after writing this letter.

"Take a combination of fear, anger, hunger, thirst, exhaustion, disgust, loneliness, homesickness, and wrap that all up in one reaction and you might approach the feelings a fellow has. It makes you feel mighty small, helpless, and alone . . . Without faith, I don't see how anyone could stand this."

DOCUMENT 4

Many African American soldiers faced an extra hardship during the war. In addition to the dangers and shortages experienced by all soldiers, African Americans also encountered racial discrimination. Corporal Rupert Trimmingham wrote the following letter to *Yank,* a weekly magazine published by the U.S. Army. In the letter, Trimmingham refers to "Old Man Jim Crow," a name for the discriminatory laws then in force across much of the United States.

"Myself and eight other Negro soldiers were on our way from Camp Claiborne, La., to the hospital here at Fort Huachuca, Arizona . . . We could not purchase a cup of coffee at any of the lunchrooms around there . . . As you know, Old Man Jim Crow rules. But that's not all; 11:30 A.M. about two dozen German prisoners of war, with two American guards, came to the station. They entered the lunchroom, sat at the tables, had their meals served, talked, smoked, in fact had quite a swell time. I stood on the outside looking on . . . Are we not American soldiers, sworn to fight for and die if need be for this our country?"

DOCUMENT 5

Popular comedian Bob Hope never served in the armed forces, but he traveled throughout the war zones entertaining the troops for the United Service Organizations (USO). In 1944 he wrote *I Never Left Home,* a memoir of his experiences during the war. In the preface he told the public about the soldiers he encountered. President Lyndon Johnson awarded Hope the Presidential Medal of Freedom in 1969. Hope was still entertaining American troops far from home at the age of 90, when he took his act to the Persian Gulf on the eve of the first Persian Gulf War.

"I saw your sons and your husbands, your soldiers and your sweethearts. I saw how they worked, fought, and lived. I saw some of them die. I saw more courage, more good humor in the face of discomfort, more love in an era of hate, and more devotion to duty than could ever exist under tyranny.
 I saw American minds, American skill, and American strength breaking the backbone of evil . . . And I came back to find people exulting over the thousand plane raids over Germany . . . and saying how wonderful they are! Those people never watched the face of a pilot as he read a bulletin board and saw his buddy marked up missing . . .
 Dying is sometimes easier than living through it . . ."

Skills Focus
HSS Analysis HR2, HR4, HI1
READING LIKE A HISTORIAN

1. **a. Identify** Refer to Document 1. What does the character of Willie offer to Joe in exchange for saving his life?
 b. Interpret What does this cartoon say about the living conditions and supplies for soldiers?

2. **a. Identify** Refer to Document 2. What was Wandrey's job?
 b. Analyze Why were the wounded soldiers happy to be missing only one arm or leg?

3. **a. Identify** Refer to Document 3. What is the overall impression that Curtis gives of his experience?
 b. Elaborate How do you think Curtis's faith helped him during the war?

4. **a. Identify** Refer to Document 4. Why could the African American soldiers not buy coffee at the southern bases?
 b. Analyze How might seeing the German soldiers being treated better than African American soldiers have affected Trimmingham's views of the war?

5. **a. Identify** Refer to Document 5. What was Bob Hope's role in the war?
 b. Explain What did Hope mean when he wrote, "Dying is sometimes easier than living through it"?

6. **Document-Based Essay Question** Consider the question below and form a thesis statement. Using examples from Documents 1, 2, 3, 4, and 5, create an outline and write a short essay supporting your position.
 What kinds of hardships and suffering did American soldiers face during World War II?

See **Skills Handbook**, pp. H28–H29, H31

THE UNITED STATES IN WORLD WAR II

CHAPTER 14 Chapter Review

Visual Summary: The United States in World War II

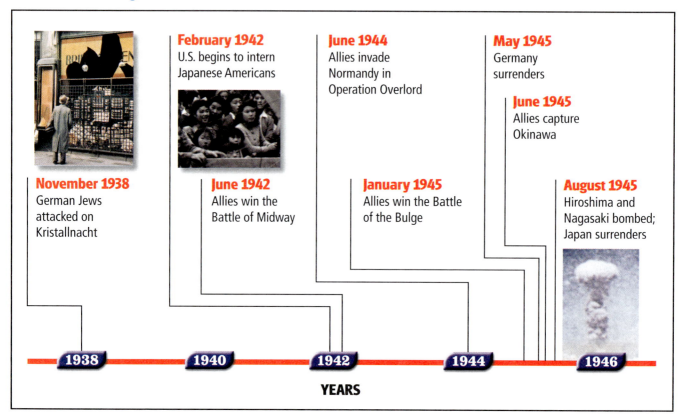

Reviewing Key Terms and People

For each term or name below, write a sentence explaining its significance to World War II.

1. ghetto
2. Operation Overlord
3. Dwight D. Eisenhower
4. internment
5. Final Solution
6. Battle of Okinawa
7. Douglas MacArthur
8. rationing
9. Battle of Midway
10. Tuskegee Airmen
11. Harry S Truman
12. kamikaze

Comprehension and Critical Thinking

SECTION 1 *(pp. 418–425)* HSS 11.7.2, 11.7.3

13. **a. Recall** What were Operation Torch and Operation Overlord, and what was their significance?

    b. Sequence Create a brief time line of U.S. involvement in Europe between 1941 and 1944.

    c. Elaborate Explain how American success in the Battle of the Atlantic may have affected the outcome of Operation Overlord.

SECTION 2 *(pp. 426–431)* HSS 11.7.4, 11.7.5

14. **a. Describe** What was the Holocaust?

    b. Compare Did Hitler's attitudes toward Jews change over time? Explain.

    c. Evaluate What do you think of Roosevelt's decision to focus all his energy on defeating the Germans and Japanese rather than trying to rescue the Jews in Nazi camps?

History's Impact video program
Review the video to answer the closing question: Why did the United States emerge as a global superpower after World War II?

SECTION 3 (pp. 433–440) HSS 11.7.2, 11.7.6

15. **a. Recall** Why did the Japanese have early success against the United States in the Pacific?

    b. Explain Why was the Battle of Midway such an important victory for the United States?

    c. Elaborate Why do you think air and sea power were so important in the Pacific?

SECTION 4 (pp. 441–447) HSS 11.7.5, 11.7.6

16. **a. Recall** What sacrifices did Americans on the home front have to make for the war effort?

    b. Summarize How did the federal government try to encourage Americans to support the war effort?

    c. Elaborate In what ways did World War II increase the power of the American government and its influence in everyday life?

SECTION 5 (pp. 449–455) HSS 11.7.2, 11.7.6, 11.7.7

17. **a. Identify** Write a brief explanation of the significance of the following terms: V-E Day, V-J Day

    b. Contrast How did the behavior of German soldiers compare to the behavior of Japanese soldiers in the final months before each side surrendered?

    c. Evaluate How do you think the experience of World War I affected the decisions made at the end of World War II?

Using the Internet

go.hrw.com
Practice Online
Keyword: SE7 CH14

18. The Allied invasion of France, often called D-Day, began on June 6, 1944. Within a few weeks, the Allies had landed nearly a million soldiers on the beaches of Normandy, and Germany's forces were in serious trouble. Using the keyword above, do research to learn more about the events of D-Day. Then create a report that describes the invasion and its importance in ending the war in Europe.

Analyzing Primary Sources HSS HR4

Reading Like a Historian
This photograph was taken after the capture of Mount Suribachi on Iwo Jima. It was soon printed in newspapers all across the United States and became one of the most recognizable images of the war.

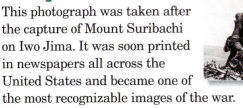

19. **Describe** What is the significance of the moment captured in this photograph?

20. **Draw Conclusions** Why do you think this image had such a powerful impact on the public?

Critical Reading ELA R2.4

Read the passage in Section 4 under the heading "Winning American Support for the War." Then answer the questions that follow.

21. The government demonstrated its need to influence public opinion on the war by

    A making Hollywood movies.

    B establishing the Office of War Information.

    C outlawing religious services.

    D forbidding negative talk about the war effort.

22. In the *Barnette* ruling, the Supreme Court held that

    A people could be forced to listen to patriotic speeches.

    B it was illegal to make movies that did not support the war effort.

    C religious groups had to support the war effort.

    D people could not be forced to salute the flag.

 ELA W1.1, 1.3

Think about the following issue.

Following the Japanese attack on Pearl Harbor, some military and government officials worried about a Japanese attack on the mainland of the United States. Though they had no evidence of any plot, they were especially concerned that such an attack would be aided by some of the many residents of Japanese ancestry then living in the western states.

23. **Assignment** Was the government right to single out residents of Japanese ancestry as a special threat to the United States? Write a short essay in which you develop your position on this issue. Support your point of view with reasoning and examples from your reading and studies.

THE UNITED STATES IN WORLD WAR II **461**

CHAPTER 15
1945–1953
The COLD WAR Begins

THE BIG PICTURE The Cold War was born in the uneasy World War II alliances between the Soviet Union and democratic nations. After the war, the struggle between democracy and communism led to a long war of ideas with occasional outbreaks of fighting.

California Standards

History-Social Sciences

11.4 Students trace the rise of the United States to its role as a world power in the twentieth century.

11.7 Students analyze America's participation in World War II.

11.8 Students analyze the economic boom and social transformation of post-World War II America.

11.9 Students analyze U.S. foreign policy since World War II.

 READING LIKE A HISTORIAN

A group of Berliners gaze up at a U.S. military cargo plane bringing them supplies during the Soviet blockade of their city in 1948. The Berlin Airlift, as it was known, lasted until 1949.
Interpreting Visuals What do you think it was like, for Berliners and Americans, during the heightened tensions of this Cold War incident?

See **Skills Handbook**, p. H30

U.S.

World

February 1945
President Roosevelt meets with Allied leaders at the Yalta Conference to discuss postwar issues.

1945

June 1945
Delegates from 50 nations meet in San Francisco to found the United Nations.

History's Impact video program
Watch the video to understand the impact of defense spending.

April 1949 The United States joins the North Atlantic Treaty Organization (NATO).

June 1947 Marshall Plan is established to help Europe rebuild after World War II.

September 1950 UN forces under General MacArthur land at Inchon, South Korea.

April 1951 President Truman fires General MacArthur over Korean War strategy.

1947 — **1949** — **1951** — **1953**

March 1947 International Monetary Fund begins operation.

June 1949 Chinese Communists take control of the country.

October 1950 Chinese troops pour into North Korea.

June 1950 North Korean troops invade South Korea.

July 1953 Fighting in Korea ends. United States, North Korea, and China sign an armistice.

463

SECTION 1
The Iron Curtain Falls on Europe

HSS 11.4.6 Trace the expanding role of the United States in world affairs after World War II.

HSS 11.7.8 Analyze the effect of massive aid given to Western Europe under the Marshall Plan and the importance of a rebuilt Europe to the U.S. economy.

HSS 11.9.2 Understand the role of military alliances, including NATO, in deterring communist aggression and maintaining security during the Cold War.

BEFORE YOU READ

MAIN IDEA
At the end of World War II, tensions between the Soviet Union and the United States deepened, leading to an era known as the Cold War.

READING FOCUS
1. What were the roots of the Cold War?
2. What was the Iron Curtain?
3. How did the United States respond to Soviet actions in Europe?
4. What was the crisis in Berlin in the late 1940s, and how was it resolved?

KEY TERMS AND PEOPLE
Cold War
Iron Curtain
containment
George F. Kennan
Truman Doctrine
Marshall Plan
Berlin Airlift
NATO

 What does a "man of steel" look like in the flesh? When the Potsdam Conference began in the summer of 1945, President Truman already knew the legend of Soviet leader Joseph Stalin, whose last name meant "man of steel." Stalin's brutal repression of his own people was thought to have led to millions of deaths. His brutality was rivaled perhaps only by Hitler's. Now, on July 17, 1945, this man of steel stood in the doorway across the room from Truman.

As Truman sized up Stalin, he began to realize why Franklin Roosevelt had referred to him as Uncle Joe. The five-foot, five-inch-tall leader was "a little bit of a squirt," Truman would later recall. As Stalin discussed the matters facing the Allied leaders in the days ahead—including the possibility of Soviet entry into the war with Japan and the future of Poland and the rest of Eastern Europe—Truman even found himself admiring the man.

Truman would soon learn that dealing with Stalin was more difficult than he first expected. As you will read, in the months after the Potsdam Conference, Truman would have to deal with Stalin's efforts to expand Soviet power.

President Truman Sizes Up STALIN

▲ President Truman (center) shoulder to shoulder with Stalin

464 CHAPTER 15

The Roots of the Cold War

Following World War II, the United States and the Soviet Union entered an era of high tension and bitter rivalry known as the **Cold War**. The roots of the Cold War reached back many years. As far back as the 1920s and 1930s, the United States had viewed the Soviet Union as a potential enemy. Americans were hostile to the ideas of communism and had at times feared its spread in the United States.

World War II alliances Despite the American fear of communism, the United States and the Soviet Union joined as allies against Nazi Germany during World War II. The two countries were not truly friends, however. Indeed, after the Germans and Soviets signed their nonaggression pact in 1939, President Roosevelt had worried that the Germans and the Soviets might join forces. He feared the United States might one day be fighting against Stalin and his armies.

Nevertheless, when Hitler's forces invaded the Soviet Union in 1941, the Americans offered to help Stalin by providing military equipment. This was not an expression of support for the Soviet dictator. It was a practical move aimed at helping defeat Hitler, who was seen as a bigger threat. Over time, the Soviets received many tons of American shipments under the Lend-Lease program.

Yet even as the United States sent supplies to the Soviet Union, the two countries argued over military strategy. Early in World War II, Stalin urged the United States and Great Britain to launch an immediate invasion of Europe. This, Stalin believed, would force the Germans to remove some of their troops from the Soviet Union. Several times Roosevelt promised Stalin that the invasion was on its way. With each delay, Stalin fumed. The American and British inaction, he complained, "leaves the Soviet Army . . . to do the job alone." Hard feelings between the Soviets and the Americans and British grew.

The atomic bomb Another issue that created mistrust between the United States and the Soviet Union was the development of the atomic bomb by the United States. As you have read previously, the Manhattan Project was a tightly guarded secret. Nevertheless,

CAUSES OF THE COLD WAR

CAUSES

Philosophical Differences
- Soviet Union: communism, totalitarian dictatorship
- United States: free-enterprise capitalism, republic

World War II Conflicts
- Soviets wanted British and Americans to open a second European front earlier in war.
- United States secretly developed atomic bomb.

Postwar Conflicts
- Soviet Union refused to live up to wartime promises of elections in Eastern Europe.
- United States made efforts to resist Soviet expansion.

The Cold War
- An era of high tension between the United States and the Soviet Union.

Soviet spies had managed to steal the plans and Soviet scientists followed them closely. The Soviets saw the weapon as a threat and soon began to develop an atomic bomb of their own.

READING CHECK *Identifying the Main Idea* What were the roots of the conflict between the United States and the Soviet Union?

The Iron Curtain Descends

After World War II, the United States and Britain were worried about what the Soviet Union might do. In particular, they were concerned that Stalin aimed to gain control of Eastern Europe. This was not a new concern. As you have read, in the Yalta and Potsdam conferences during World War II, American and British leaders pressed Stalin to hold free elections in Soviet-occupied lands, such as Poland.

The Americans and British had good reason to be concerned about Stalin's plans. He had no intention of giving up political and economic control over Eastern Europe. In Stalin's view, he was fully justified in wanting to control Eastern Europe. The Soviet Union had just

ACADEMIC VOCABULARY
justified based on sound reasoning

emerged from a terrible war in which as many as 30 million or more Soviets had died. To Stalin, the German invasion from the West had been part of a long history of attacks originating from Europe. Stalin believed that he could increase the security of his country by creating a line of Soviet-friendly nations between the Soviet Union and its historic enemies in Western Europe.

Communism spreads To achieve his goal in Eastern Europe, Stalin used whatever means necessary. In some cases, he outlawed political parties or newspapers that opposed the Communists. The Soviets also jailed or killed some political opponents and sometimes even rigged elections to ensure the success of Communist candidates. In these ways, the Soviets managed to install Communist governments throughout Eastern Europe during the postwar years.

Soon, every nation in Eastern Europe had a Soviet-friendly Communist government in place. Most of these governments were under the direct control of Stalin and the Soviet Union. The lone exception was the nation of Yugoslavia. There, Josip Broz Tito, who won fame fighting the Nazis during World War II, was firmly in control. Though he was a Communist, Tito refused to take orders from the Soviet Union. His wide popularity in Yugoslavia helped him remain in power.

The United States was also alarmed by the Soviet treatment of Germans living in Poland and the other countries of Eastern Europe. During the war, the Allies had agreed that Germans living in these areas should be removed in an "orderly and humane manner." After the war, however, the Soviets relocated the Germans with great brutality. Several hundred thousand Germans died, as millions were forced to relocate to the western section of Germany, which was occupied by the United States, Britain, and France.

The Iron Curtain American and British leaders were saddened to see Eastern Europeans, who had already suffered greatly during World War II, fall under the control of a dictator. They were also concerned that the Soviet Union would not stop at Eastern Europe.

In response, President Truman urged his secretary of state, James Byrnes, to get tough with the Soviets. "Unless Russia is faced with an iron fist and strong language," Truman wrote, "another war is in the making."

In 1946 former British prime minister Winston Churchill traveled to the United States.

The Iron Curtain in Europe

After World War II, Stalin helped install Communist governments throughout Eastern Europe. Here, a poster of Stalin (center) hangs above a doorway in newly Communist East Germany in 1946. The spread of communism concerned American and British leaders. In a famous speech, British Prime Minister Winston Churchill (far right) described a sharp division between Europe's Communist and non-Communist nations—a division that he famously termed "the Iron Curtain."

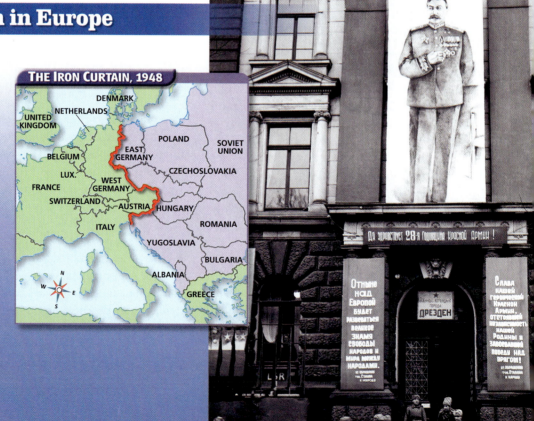

On March 5 he delivered a speech in Fulton, Missouri, in which he sharply attacked the Soviet Union for creating what he called an **Iron Curtain**. The term reflected Churchill's belief that communism had created a sharp division in Europe.

HISTORY'S VOICES

" A shadow has fallen upon the scenes so lately lighted by the Allied victory. Nobody knows what Soviet Russia and its Communist international organization intends to do in the immediate future, or what are the limits, if any, to their expansive . . . tendencies . . . It is my duty to place before you certain facts about the present position of Europe. From Stettin in the Baltic to Trieste in the Adriatic an iron curtain has descended across the Continent. "
—Winston Churchill, Speech at Westminster College

In the Soviet Union, Stalin's reaction to Churchill's speech was harsh. He used Churchill's words to help persuade his people that the United States and Great Britain were enemies of the Soviet Union. This became his excuse to rebuild the Soviet Union's military strength—which slowed the pace of rebuilding the shattered Soviet countryside.

READING CHECK **Making Inferences** Why did Churchill use the term *Iron Curtain*?

"An iron curtain has descended upon the Continent."
—Winston Churchill, March 1946

The United States Responds

The end of World War II and the start of the Cold War presented American leaders with a challenge. The United States was now one of the world's two most powerful nations. The other was an increasingly hostile Soviet Union.

American leaders felt they needed a new policy to deal with the situation. That is, the United States had to become the leader of all nations committed to democratic ideals and freedoms, even as the Soviet Union sought to expand its power and influence.

Containment and the Truman Doctrine

The policy that the United States adopted in the late 1940s was known as **containment**. The creator of the containment policy was an American diplomat and expert on the Soviet Union named **George F. Kennan**. Kennan believed the United States should resist Soviet attempts to expand its power and influence wherever those attempts occurred. To Kennan, containment was not limited to military force. It also involved providing economic aid to other countries in order to strengthen them against the Soviet Union.

Kennan's containment policy was put to the test in 1947. That year, President Truman informed Congress of an urgent need to provide emergency economic and military aid to Greece and Turkey. Both countries were facing Soviet pressure. In Greece, Soviet-supported Communists were trying to take advantage of postwar economic problems to gain power. In Turkey, the Soviet government was trying to gain more control.

President Truman argued that providing aid would help both the Greek and Turkish governments resist Soviet expansion. In the process, he issued what came to be called the **Truman Doctrine**:

HISTORY'S VOICES

" I believe it must be the policy of the United States to support free peoples who are resisting subjugation [forced control] by armed minorities or outside pressures . . .
I believe that our help should be primarily through economic and financial aid which is essential to economic stability and orderly political processes. "
—Harry S Truman, speech to joint session of Congress, March 12, 1947

THE IMPACT TODAY

Government
Kennan's containment policy guided U.S. foreign affairs for decades, including the decision to send troops to Vietnam in the 1960s.

THE COLD WAR BEGINS

The Marshall Plan

THE MARSHALL PLAN

Purpose: A U.S. financial aid program to rebuild the economies of European countries in order to create stable conditions for democratic governments.

Total amount of aid: $13.4 billion

Number of countries that received aid: 17

Countries that received the most aid: Great Britain, France, and Italy

Residents lined the streets as the millionth ton of Marshall-Plan goods were paraded through Athens, Greece, in December 1949. The Marshall Plan focused its efforts on struggling countries such as Greece, which was in the midst of a civil war against Communist rebels. The plan, originally called the European Recovery Program, is credited with boosting Western Europe's gross national product by 15 to 25 percent. In 1953 George Marshall received the Nobel Peace Prize for crafting the plan that, noted the prize presenter, "has become inseparably connected with his name."
How would economic recovery discourage communism?

Following Truman's speech, a bipartisan Congress voted in favor of the United States providing hundreds of millions of dollars in aid to Greece and Turkey, to fight Communist influence. In both countries, the Soviets did not succeed in gaining control.

The Marshall Plan The war-related economic problems facing Greece were severe. They were not, however, unusual. Across Europe, World War II had devastated cities and ruined farms. Railroads, factories, and mines lay idle. Though the fighting was over, people were continuing to suffer, and hunger and poverty were widespread.

Many Americans felt moved to help the people of Europe, who had already suffered so much from the war. Americans also realized that, if conditions grew worse, more Europeans might turn to communism. Indeed, as the people of Europe became more desperate, the influence of Soviet communism grew. In several European nations, strong Communist movements were beginning to appear.

In June 1947, George C. Marshall, the former World War II military leader and now secretary of state, gave a speech at Harvard University. In it he called for a massive American program of aid to help Europe rebuild and get back on its economic feet.

HISTORY'S VOICES

> "Our policy is directed not against any country or doctrine but against hunger, poverty, desperation, and chaos. Its purpose should be the revival of working economy in the world so as to permit the emergence of political and social conditions in which free institutions can exist."
>
> —George C. Marshall, commencement address, Harvard University, June 5, 1947

The **Marshall Plan**, as this vision came to be known, was an enormous undertaking. Between 1948 and 1951, the U.S. government spent over 13 billion dollars in 17 different countries. This aid bought food and farm equipment. It also rebuilt factories and homes. Marshall's original plan even offered aid to the Soviet Union and its allies. But Stalin refused the aid.

With the help of the Marshall Plan, Western Europe was soon feeding its hungry and providing jobs for its workers. Western European countries were also able to buy products from American factories, which helped the postwar economy grow in the United States. Finally, the Marshall Plan helped the United States build strong political support in Western Europe. This support would be vital in the Cold War years to come.

READING CHECK **Identifying Cause and Effect** How did the United States respond to the growing tension with the Soviets in the late 1940s?

The Crisis in Berlin

After World War II, the Allies had divided Germany into four zones of occupation—British, French, and American in the western area and Soviet in the east. The capital of Berlin, which lay within the Soviet zone, was also divided into four zones.

With the start of the Cold War, the lines dividing Germany became sharper. It became clear that the Soviets planned to keep their zone under Communist control. The British and Americans, meanwhile, began to take steps to set up a free, democratic government within their zones. The French would later join this effort. The western zone eventually became known as the Federal Republic of Germany, or West Germany. The British and the Americans also took steps to set up a democratic government in West Berlin.

The Soviets block traffic The Soviets were not pleased by the idea of a Western-style government and economy in the middle of the Soviet zone of occupation. In June 1948 they decided to take drastic action. The Soviets announced that they would block any road, rail, or river traffic into West Berlin. Suddenly, West Berlin's 2.1 million residents had been cut off from sources of food, coal, and other basic necessities.

In fact, West Berlin was not completely cut off because there were airstrips in the city. The Western powers could try to supply West Berlin by air. It was a risky plan. Some officials did not believe it was even possible to supply all the needs of a major city by aircraft. Another danger was that the Soviets might try to stop the planes or shoot them down. This could lead to war.

In the end, the Western leaders decided that they had to take the risk. Their only hope for keeping West Berlin free was a massive airlift. The plan went forward.

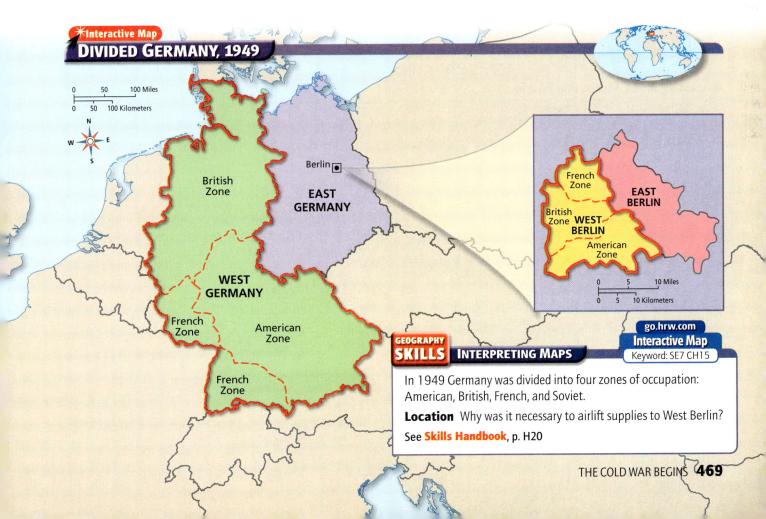

DIVIDED GERMANY, 1949

GEOGRAPHY SKILLS INTERPRETING MAPS

In 1949 Germany was divided into four zones of occupation: American, British, French, and Soviet.

Location Why was it necessary to airlift supplies to West Berlin?

See **Skills Handbook**, p. H20

THE COLD WAR BEGINS **469**

The Berlin airlift begins Within days of the Soviet blockade, British and American airplanes began making deliveries to the people of West Berlin. Every day, the planes flew an average of 7,000 tons of supplies into West Berlin. Hundreds of flights landed, unloaded, and took off again.

To the amazement of the Soviet leaders, the **Berlin airlift** continued week after week, month after month. The airlift also got bigger. To allow more planes to land, the Allies built another airfield in the French sector of Berlin. In the month of April 1949, nearly 1,400 separate flights took place and nearly 400,000 tons of supplies were delivered.

There were tragedies, however. Some 70 American and British citizens died in airplane crashes. At least five German civilians on the ground were also killed.

In spite of these problems, the airlift continued. Finally, in the face of Allied determination, the Soviet Union lifted its blockade on May 12, 1949. By that time, American, British, and French planes had made nearly 280,000 flights into Berlin. American pilots flew two-thirds of them, leading the way.

NATO forms The widening conflict with the Soviet Union made many Western Europeans very uncomfortable. They realized that if war were to break out, they would be no match for the huge Soviet army. In order to provide a measure of security, Belgium, France, Luxembourg, the Netherlands, and the United Kingdom joined together in a system of common defense in 1948.

The crisis in Berlin helped make other Western nations aware of the wisdom of this action. In April 1949 the United States and six other nations joined the original five to create a new military alliance—the North Atlantic Treaty Organization, or **NATO**. (The other six nations were Canada, Denmark, Iceland, Italy, Norway, and Portugal.) According to the North Atlantic Treaty, an armed attack against one of the member nations would be considered an attack against all.

In the mid-1950s, Greece, Turkey, and the newly created West Germany joined NATO. Today 26 countries, including several former Communist nations, are NATO members.

READING CHECK **Summarizing** What was the crisis in Berlin?

SECTION 1 ASSESSMENT

HSS 11.4.6, 11.7.8, 11.9.2

Reviewing Ideas, Terms, and People

1. **a. Define** Write a brief definition for the following term: **Cold War**
   b. Make Inferences What can be inferred from the fact that the United States did not share its plans for building the atomic bomb with the Soviets during the war?
   c. Evaluate Do you think the United States should have done more to improve relations with the Soviet Union during World War II? Explain.

2. **a. Recall** What was the **Iron Curtain**, and why was that term chosen?
   b. Draw Conclusions Why do you think western leaders were so concerned about the Iron Curtain?
   c. Elaborate Do you think the United States was right to be concerned about the fate of the people of Eastern Europe? Explain.

3. **a. Define** Write a brief definition for each of the following terms: **containment, Truman Doctrine, Marshall Plan**
   b. Analyze What were two different ways that the Marshall Plan benefited the United States?
   c. Predict How do you think the Marshall Plan will affect relationships between the United States and the countries of Western Europe who received the aid? Support your answer with details from the section.

4. **a. Recall** What was the **Berlin Airlift**, and why was it necessary?
   b. Explain What were the risks in attempting to supply West Berlin by air?

Critical Thinking

5. **Identifying Cause and Effect** Copy the chart below and use information from the section to identify causes and effects of the Cold War.

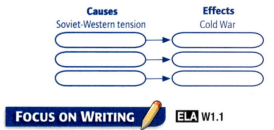

FOCUS ON WRITING ELA W1.1

6. **Expository** Write a paragraph explaining whether or not you think George F. Kennan's containment policy was a good idea for the United States.

SECTION 2
Healing the Wounds of War

BEFORE YOU READ

MAIN IDEA
Following the end of World War II, U.S. military forces—and the rest of the country—faced the challenge of returning to life during peacetime.

READING FOCUS
1. What was life like in America after World War II?
2. What happened in politics in postwar America?
3. How did the United States and other countries try to build a better world after the war?

KEY TERMS AND PEOPLE
GI Bill
baby boom
Fair Deal
Universal Declaration of Human Rights
World Bank
International Monetary Fund
General Agreement on Tariffs and Trade

HSS 11.8.3 Examine Truman's labor policy and congressional reaction to it.

HSS 11.9.1 Discuss the establishment of the United Nations and International Declaration of Human Rights, International Monetary Fund, World Bank, and General Agreement on Tariffs and Trade (GATT) and their importance in shaping modern Europe and maintaining peace and international order.

Challenges for RETURNING SOLDIERS

▲ Returning soldiers fight for jobs at a coal-mining operation in 1946.

THE INSIDE STORY

What did the veterans of World War II have to worry about? In 1946 a popular song told the tale of a soldier returning home from World War II. "Not so long ago when the bullets screamed," went one of the verses, "many was the happy dream I dreamed." Indeed, millions of soldiers had survived the terror of combat by looking forward to their return to a bright future in the United States. Yet as the song continued, it told of a different sort of homecoming for the World War II veteran.

"Now the mighty war over there is won,
Troubles and trials have just begun
As I face that terrible enemy sign, 'No Vacancy.'"

This song tells of just one of the challenges facing veterans of the war, who returned to America by the millions within a few short months of V-J and V-E days. These men and women found shortages of housing—and, as the picture shows above, difficulty finding work. For these veterans who had given so much to their country, the bumpy transition back to life in the United States was a bitter one.

As you will read, however, this troubled transition period was remarkably brief. The federal government did much to help returning soldiers resume their lives and move the country forward beyond the war. American consumers did the rest.

Life in America after World War II

The end of World War II was a joyous occasion for Americans. Yet it was also a time of concern. During the war, the nation's factories had worked overtime to supply the Allied forces. Now the orders for tanks, planes, ships, and weapons dropped sharply. Some experts predicted serious economic trouble.

At the same time, nearly all of the 12 million men and women who had been serving in the armed forces at the end of the war were returning to civilian life. Many of these returning veterans would be looking for jobs. But often jobs simply were not available. In addition, some women workers were pressured to leave their jobs so a male veteran could take their places. In general, however, most veterans did eventually find jobs.

The GI Bill This shift actually began before World War II ended. In June 1944, President Roosevelt signed the Servicemen's Readjustment Act of 1944. The act became known as the GI Bill. GI, which stood for "government issue," was a nickname for members of the armed forces.

The GI Bill included several features aimed at helping veterans make a smooth entry into civilian life. For example, it provided money for veterans to attend college or receive advanced job training. It helped arrange for loans for those wishing to buy a home, farm, or business. The GI Bill also provided help in finding work as well as a year's worth of unemployment benefits for those who could not find work. As you have read, the government had promised financial bonuses to World War I veterans but had not delivered. Now, after World War II, veterans were not receiving cash bonuses, but they were receiving immediate benefits.

Increasing demand The GI Bill helped millions of GIs make a successful return to civilian life. At the same time, civilians helped spur the postwar economy. During the war, the federal government took steps to control what products American industry could make. For example, car production stopped so that factories could turn out tanks and equipment.

After the war, demand for consumer goods rose sharply. People who had delayed purchases during the war now decided to buy. Returning veterans built houses, which increased the demand for furniture and appliances.

THE IMPACT TODAY

Government
The GI Bill remains in effect today. Since 1944, about 21 million Americans have received GI Bill tuition benefits, and about 17.5 million Americans have received GI Bill home loans.

The GI Bill in Action

The GI Bill helped millions of World War II veterans earn college degrees. Many attended college while raising their families. Here, veterans celebrate after graduating from the University of Colorado. GI Bill benefits included

- money for college or job training
- loans for homes, farms, or businesses
- unemployment pay of $20 a week for up to a year
- assistance finding jobs

Many more Americans also began having families. The two decades following World War II marked the beginning of the **baby boom**, a dramatic rise in the birthrate. Larger families created demand for larger cars. In this way, the postwar economy made an unexpectedly smooth shift from providing the tools of war to providing the products of peace.

Labor unions after the war During the war, the government had sought to prevent labor disputes that might affect wartime production. After the war, unions began seeking the increases in wages that had been limited during the war. Starting in 1946, the number of strikes rose sharply. In 1947 Congress passed the Taft-Hartley Act over President Truman's veto. This law greatly reduced the power of labor unions. For example, it empowered the president to stop strikes when the national interest was at stake.

Racial minorities after the war You have read about efforts early in the war to ensure equal opportunity for African Americans in wartime government and industry jobs. These efforts continued after the war. President Truman was committed to expanding opportunities for African Americans. After meeting strong opposition from members of Congress, he decided to take action on his own. In June 1948, Truman issued Executive Order 9981.

HISTORY'S VOICES

"It is hereby declared to be the policy of the President that there shall be equality of treatment and opportunity for all persons in the armed services without regard to race, color, religion, or national origin."
—Harry S Truman, Executive Order 9981, July 26, 1948

Truman's order ended segregation in the U.S. armed forces. This was a major step forward for African Americans. It would also help pave the way for future gains.

Hispanic Americans were another group seeking opportunities after the war. Several hundred Hispanic veterans joined together in the American GI Forum. This group worked hard to win full access for Hispanic veterans to the benefits they had earned for their military service. In 1948 they won national attention for their efforts on behalf of Felix Longoria, a Mexican American soldier who had been killed

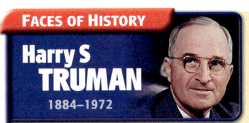

FACES OF HISTORY
Harry S TRUMAN
1884–1972

Harry S Truman served less than three months as vice president before President Roosevelt died in April 1945. As the new president, Truman quickly took over the U.S. effort in World War II. He oversaw Germany's surrender and made the decision to drop atomic bombs on Japan to end the war in the Pacific. After the war, he worked to limit the spread of communism. His Truman Doctrine was a plan to provide aid to countries that might otherwise have fallen to communism.

On the home front, Truman attempted to extend New Deal social reforms in a plan he called the Fair Deal. However, he did not have the same success Roosevelt had with the New Deal. Only a few of Truman's Fair Deal provisions actually became policy.

Analyze In what ways did Truman succeed, and in what ways did he fail?

in the last days of World War II. When his body was returned to his Texas hometown, the local funeral home refused to provide services because of Longoria's Mexican background. The GI Forum and its Texas leader, Hector Garcia, accepted Senator Lyndon Johnson's offer that Longoria be buried at Arlington National Cemetery. The case helped highlight the contributions of Hispanic Americans.

READING CHECK Summarizing What challenges did the United States face after World War II?

Politics in Postwar America

When President Roosevelt died suddenly in April 1945, Harry S Truman had been vice president for less than three months. In fact, Truman barely knew Roosevelt and had little knowledge of the many issues and decisions the president had been dealing with. After he was sworn in as the new president, Truman told reporters:

HISTORY'S VOICES

"[I]f you ever pray, pray for me now. I don't know if you fellas ever had a load of hay fall on you, but when they told me what happened yesterday, I felt like the moon, the stars, and all the planets had fallen on me."
—Harry S Truman to reporters, April 13, 1945

American Civil Liberty

Integration and the Military

During World War II, about 1 million African Americans were drafted into the military. All of these soldiers, sailors, and marines served in segregated units.

In 1946 President Harry S Truman appointed the President's Committee on Civil Rights. The committee said that segregation made the armed forces less effective than they would be if they were integrated.

Backed by the committee's report, Truman decided to end racial segregation in the United States military. On July 26, 1948, he signed Executive Order 9981. This executive order required "equality of treatment and opportunity for all persons in the armed services without regard to race, color, religion, or national origin."

Although some military leaders resisted, by 1949 all branches had developed plans for integration. Today all positions in the military are open to people who are qualified, regardless of race or ethnicity.

Making Inferences What might Truman have hoped to gain by ending segregation in the military?

In October 1948, James Leroy Brown (center) became the first African American to receive his wings as a Navy pilot.

Truman faced huge challenges. He had to lead the Allies through the end of the war while guiding the nation through the shift from wartime to peace. He also had to deal with political criticism that came from all sides. Many Democrats compared him unfavorably to their hero, Roosevelt. Republicans saw in Truman someone they thought they could finally defeat.

The 1946 elections in Congress

The attacks on Truman grew stronger as the 1946 elections in Congress approached. One key complaint was inflation, or a rise in prices. During the war, the government had acted to keep prices low. After the war, price controls were relaxed. Prices shot up as a result, and Truman took the blame.

The 1946 elections were a disaster for the Democrats. Republicans gained so many seats that they were now the majority in Congress for the first time since 1930. With this majority, Republicans fought against Truman with increased strength. Truman found it difficult to put in place his own programs. One exception was the Marshall Plan, which you read about in Section 1. His handling of the Berlin Crisis was another of his few accomplishments.

The 1948 presidential election

As the presidential election of 1948 approached, Truman appeared to be in trouble. His popularity with voters was low. Even his fellow Democrats did not fully support him. Liberals broke off to back former vice president Henry Wallace, who ran under the banner of the Progressive Party. Many southern Democrats were angry at Truman's support for civil rights. They supported South Carolina governor Strom Thurmond, who ran as a Dixiecrat.

With his popularity low and his party divided, Truman seemed certain to lose the election. In a poll of 50 political writers published in a leading newsmagazine a few weeks before election day, every single one predicted a Republican victory. Newspapers made fun of him openly. "Mr. Truman is the most complete fumbler and blunderer this nation has seen in high office in a long time," wrote the *Los Angeles Times*. The Republican candidate, Governor Thomas Dewey of New York, was confident of victory.

Refusing to give up, Truman set off on a whirlwind campaign across the country. His tough-talking, plainspoken style had made him the target of many jokes in Washington, D.C. But elsewhere people responded well to Truman's style. He made a special point of criticizing Republicans in the House and Senate. When he complained about the "do-nothing Congress," crowds cheered in support.

In spite of Truman's efforts, most experts did not think he had a chance. Yet on election day, the voters handed Truman a victory. It was one of the most surprising election outcomes in American history.

Having won the election, Truman finally felt strong enough to put forward his own plan for the country. It was called the **Fair Deal**. It included a number of programs in the tradition of the New Deal. This included a federal health insurance program and new funding for education. Congress, however, did not support Truman's program. Few of his Fair Deal ideas ever became law. Meanwhile, new problems in Korea came to dominate the president's attention. You will read about the Korean War in Section 4.

READING CHECK   Drawing Conclusions Why do you think the Democrats faced problems in the politics of the postwar era?

Trying to Build a Better World

World War II helped give rise to the political tensions of the Cold War. It also gave rise to a strong desire to understand and prevent the causes of war. After two catastrophic conflicts, many people were anxious to find new ways to prevent a third.

One result was the establishment of the United Nations (UN). Its creation started in the final days of the war. Representatives of 50 nations met in June 1945 to create the UN Charter, the written agreement that outlines its aims and principles. The UN Charter was ratified in October 1945. The UN was officially born. Over the years, it would welcome many new members.

The UN Charter committed its members to "save succeeding generations from the scourge of war" and to "reaffirm faith in fundamental human rights." It called for members to respect treaties and agreements and to promote the progress and freedom of all people. Member nations agreed to live in peace and to unite to maintain security. Force would be used only to serve the common interests of the membership. The charter also called for the use of international organizations to promote economic and social advancement.

Human rights Soon after its formation, the United Nations established the Commission on Human Rights. The U.S. representative to this commission was the former first lady Eleanor Roosevelt. She became the chairperson of the commission, helping to soothe tensions between members from different countries. Different countries sometimes had very different ideas about what kinds of human rights all people ought to have and how to achieve them.

PROGRAMS FOR A SAFER WORLD

As World War II came to an end, the countries of the world began seeking ways to prevent the problems and conflicts that helped lead to war. Leaders in the United States and other countries paved the way in establishing the following:

World Bank (1944)	• Organization for providing loans and advice to countries for the purpose of reducing poverty
International Monetary Fund (1944)	• System for promoting orderly financial relationships between countries • Designed to prevent economic crises and to encourage trade and economic growth
United Nations (1945)	• Organization in which member nations agree to settle disputes by peaceful means • Replaced the League of Nations
General Agreement on Tariffs and Trade (1946)	• Agreement among member nations on rules and regulations for international trade • Focused on reducing tariffs and other trade barriers

THE COLD WAR BEGINS

The democratic United States and Communist Soviet Union, for instance, had different ideas about how to secure basic economic rights.

In December 1948, the commission presented to the UN General Assembly the **Universal Declaration of Human Rights**. This document set high goals for all member nations of the UN. For example, it declared a belief that all human beings are born free and equal. It called for an end to slavery, torture, and inhumane punishment. It demanded a variety of civil rights, including the right to assembly and the right to access to courts. It also stated that elementary education should be free and available to all. The UN General Assembly adopted the declaration and directed member countries to publicize it.

Trade and economic development

World War II had raised a number of concerns about the financial relationships between countries. These problems had helped bring about the Great Depression. Now they threatened to limit trade and create conflict between nations. Many leaders hoped that solving these problems would lead to greater prosperity around the world. This, in turn, would promote peace.

Even before the war was over, representatives of many of the world's great powers met at a conference in Bretton Woods, New Hampshire. Out of this conference came an agreement to create two new organizations—the **World Bank** and the **International Monetary Fund** (IMF).

The World Bank aimed to help poor countries build their economies. It provided grants of money and loans to help with projects that could provide jobs and wealth.

Economic policy was the focus of the International Monetary Fund. Prior to the creation of the IMF, countries often followed economic policies that served their own interests, regardless of whether they hurt other countries. Such practices often had a harmful effect on world trade, which hurt everyone. The IMF was designed to encourage economic policies that promoted international trade. For example, the IMF helped build confidence in the values of different countries' currencies.

The **General Agreement on Tariffs and Trade** (GATT) was another international organization created to promote economic cooperation. The GATT, which took effect in 1948, was designed to reduce barriers to trade.

READING CHECK **Identifying Problems and Solutions** Name some international organizations that aimed to build a better world in the years after World War II.

SECTION 2 ASSESSMENT

Reviewing Ideas, Terms, and People

1. **a. Define** Write a brief definition for each of the following terms: **GI Bill, baby boom**
   b. Explain Following World War II, how did the United States manage to avoid the severe economic problems that some people had expected?
   c. Predict How do you think Truman's decision to desegregate the U.S. armed forces will affect African Americans and their growing demands for civil rights?

2. **a. Recall** What was the outcome and significance of the elections of 1946?
   b. Make Inferences What can you infer about Truman's successful tactic of attacking the "do-nothing Congress"?
   c. Elaborate How do you explain the fact that so many political observers were wrong about Truman and the presidential election of 1948?

3. **a. Identify** What was the UN, and why was it created?
   b. Summarize By what means did the United States and other countries seek to make the world better during the postwar era?

   c. Elaborate Based on what you have read here and in other chapters, how do you think efforts to improve countries' economies and international trade will help promote peace in the future?

Critical Thinking

4. **Identifying the Main Idea** Copy the chart below and use information from the section to identify details that support the main idea given.

5. **Persuasive** From the point of view of a member of the Commission of Human Rights, write and present a speech in favor of the Universal Declaration of Human Rights. Use details from the section in your speech.

SECTION 3: The Second Red Scare

BEFORE YOU READ

MAIN IDEA
The start of the Cold War and events at home helped trigger a second Red Scare in the late 1940s and early 1950s.

READING FOCUS
1. Why was the fear of communism growing in the late 1940s?
2. What methods and actions did the government use to fight the spread of communism at home?
3. Who was Senator Joseph McCarthy, and what was his role in the second Red Scare?

KEY TERMS AND PEOPLE
Chiang Kai-shek
Mao Zedong
House Un-American Activities Committee
Hollywood Ten
Alger Hiss
Joseph McCarthy
McCarthyism

HSS 11.9.3 Trace the origins and geopolitical consequences (foreign and domestic) of the Cold War and containment policy, including the following:
• The era of McCarthyism, instances of domestic Communism (e.g., Alger Hiss) and blacklisting

 How did the White House find out that the Soviets had the atomic bomb? Everyone realized the day would eventually come, though many did not expect it so soon. They even had a code name for describing the situation—Vermont. Still, the realization that the Soviet Union had likely exploded an atomic weapon came as a tremendous shock to most Americans.

For David Lilienthal, head of the Atomic Energy Commission, the news came in the form of a visit from an army general. Lilienthal was on vacation on the island of Martha's Vineyard off the coast of Massachusetts. As he was returning to his home on the evening of September 19, 1949, the general was waiting for him with a grave message: The Soviets had the atomic bomb and had conducted a test explosion.

The next morning, Lilienthal flew to Washington, D.C., to meet with President Truman and several of his advisers. The group debated how to handle the news. Should the public be told? How would they react?

Truman decided that the public must be informed. He presented the information himself several days later. As you will read, the news hit the nation hard. Soon, Americans were in the grips of another Red Scare.

▲ The news that the Soviet Union had tested an atomic bomb sent shock waves of fear through the nation.

THE COLD WAR BEGINS 477

THE SPREAD OF COMMUNISM, 1945–1949

GEOGRAPHY SKILLS INTERPRETING MAPS

Notice the pattern of Communist nations in Europe.

Place Look at the chart at right. Why do you think the Communist takeover of China worried the United States?

See **Skills Handbook**, p. H20

Growing Fear of Communism

The postwar years were a tense time in the United States. American leaders worried about the spread of communism in Europe. In 1948 the crisis over Berlin drove the tension level even higher.

Then in 1949, two events added greatly to the nation's anxiety. First came the discovery that the Soviet Union possessed an atomic weapon. Then came the news that Communists had gained control of China, the most populous country in the world.

Soviet atomic weapons The first hint of trouble occurred in late August 1949. U.S. aircraft flying over the North Pacific Ocean picked up signs of unusual radioactivity in the atmosphere. American scientists quickly figured out what had happened. In September, President Truman issued a short, terse statement that confirmed the Soviet Union had detonated an atomic bomb.

Truman's announcement came as a great shock to the nation. No longer could the country rely on this terribly destructive weapon as the basis of its defense against the Soviets. Soon, Truman would seek to strengthen the nation's military against a possible Soviet threat.

The threat of Communist China Within days of the announcement that the Soviets had atomic weapons, the United States learned that Communists in China had gained nearly full control of the country. The so-called Nationalist government of **Chiang Kai-shek** had fled mainland China for the island of Taiwan. Chiang had been a loyal friend to the United States during World War II. He—and the United States—continued to claim that the Nationalist Party represented the one true government of all China. Now, outside of Taiwan, the Nationalists had no power. China was in the hands of the Communist Party. A new People's Republic of China had been born.

The Communist takeover of China had been many years in the making. At the end of World War II, the defeated Japanese had withdrawn from China. Led by **Mao Zedong**, Chinese Communists used this opportunity to gain control of large areas, especially in northern China.

In a civil war between Nationalists and Communists, the United States supported the Nationalists' effort to defeat communism. Chiang's Nationalist government, however, was riddled with corruption and poor leadership. As a result, Mao's Communists steadily gained power in China.

ACADEMIC VOCABULARY
detonate to cause an explosion

Quick Facts

Population, 1950

NATO Members		Communist Nations	
The United States and Canada	171,550,000	Soviet Union	180,980,000
Western Europe	173,882,000	Eastern Europe	106,055,000
		China	554,760,000
Total	**345,432,000**	**Total**	**841,795,000**

The Communist victory in China delivered another shock to the American people. Americans did not yet know if Chinese communism was equivalent to Soviet communism. Many worried that China would increase the Communist threat to the United States.

READING CHECK **Identifying Cause and Effect** What events helped increase the fear of communism for the American public in the late 1940s?

Fighting the Spread of Communism at Home

The events of 1949 fed an already strong anti-Communist feeling in the United States. Indeed, for several years, concern had been growing about possible Communist influence in American government. Efforts were already underway to root out disloyal people.

Investigating communism Since the 1930s, the House of Representatives had had a House Un-American Activities Committee, or HUAC. This committee's original purpose was to investigate the full range of radical groups in the United States, including Fascists and Communists. Over time, however, it came to focus only on the possible threat of communism in the United States. This focus existed even before the start of the Cold War. It sharpened significantly as the Soviets emerged as the chief enemy of the United States.

The most famous HUAC investigation began in 1947. Its goal was to explore possible Communist influence in the American film industry. The committee collected the names of Hollywood writers and directors who were thought to hold radical political views. Ten of these people, when called before HUAC, refused to answer questions about their beliefs or those of their colleagues. As a result of this refusal, the Hollywood Ten were found guilty of contempt of Congress and were sentenced to a year in jail.

The case alarmed others in Hollywood. Many now agreed to provide names of possible Communists to HUAC. Others refused to provide names, and for this they were placed on a blacklist—a list from which all the major Hollywood employers refused to hire. The careers of several hundred writers, actors, directors, and producers were damaged.

In another case that attracted widespread attention, the Atomic Energy Commission accused atomic bomb scientist J. Robert Oppenheimer of Communist sympathies. The commission stripped him of his top-secret security clearance.

Truman and loyalty The public fear of communism also put pressure on American leaders. No leader wanted to appear weak when dealing with communism. This included the president. Truman felt he had to take action because Republicans in Congress were claiming that Communists were working in the federal government. To help address this charge, Truman created a new plan for ensuring the loyalty of government officials. Under the plan, all federal employees would be investigated. Those found to be disloyal to the United States could be barred from federal employment.

The investigations turned up little evidence of disloyalty. Over the next few years, 3 million people were investigated. A few thousand federal workers resigned, and about 200 were judged disloyal. The investigations troubled some Americans. They made it clear, however, that the Truman administration was serious about fighting communism.

ACADEMIC VOCABULARY
equivalent equal in importance

THE COLD WAR BEGINS **479**

Major Spy Cases

Alger Hiss, 1948
Accused of being a spy for the Soviets, Alger Hiss prepares to testify to HUAC in 1948. Although he denied the charges, evidence later showed Hiss had lied to HUAC. In 1950 he was convicted of perjury, or lying under oath, and sentenced to prison. Soviet documents decoded by American intelligence and declassified in the 1990s confirmed Hiss's guilt in the case.

Klaus Fuchs, 1950
Fuchs, a nuclear physicist, worked on the Manhattan Project. During his work on the development of the atomic bomb, he transmitted information to the Soviet Union, including detailed drawings of "Fat Man," the bomb the United States dropped on Nagasaki, Japan, in World War II. After serving nine years in prison, Fuchs settled in East Germany.

Ethel and Julius Rosenberg, 1951
The Rosenbergs were convicted of passing military secrets to the Soviets, including information from Ethel's brother, who was an employee on the Manhattan Project. They received the death sentence and were executed in 1953. The Rosenbergs were the first U.S. civilians to be executed for espionage.

The Smith Act In 1949 Truman made another show of his commitment to fight communism at home. The government charged several leaders of the Communist Party in the United States under the Smith Act. This 1940 law made it a crime to call for the overthrow of the U.S. government or belong to an organization that did so.

The Communist Party officials were convicted. These convictions, and the Smith Act itself, were upheld in the 1951 Supreme Court ruling in *Dennis v. United States*. The Court considered that the domestic danger posed by Communists was "grave and probable" and justified limits on their free speech. (Later, in *Yates v. United States,* the Court held that it was a crime only when a person called for specific actions to overthrow the government.)

The McCarran Act In 1950 Congress took further action to fight communism in the United States. The McCarran Internal Security Act required Communist organizations to register with the government and established a special board to investigate Communist involvement. The act also made it illegal to plan for a creation of a totalitarian dictatorship and prevented Communists or other radicals from entering the United States.

Truman vetoed the bill, stating that it "would delight the Communists, for it would make a mockery of the Bill of Rights and of our claims to stand for freedom in the world." But Congress easily overrode Truman's veto.

Spy cases Fear of communism was also fueled by a series of spy cases in the late 1940s. One case involved a former government official named **Alger Hiss**. In 1948 former Communist spy Whittaker Chambers accused Hiss of being part of a 1930s plot to place Communists inside the government. Hiss denied the charges. Then in a dramatic move, Chambers led investigators to his Maryland farm. There, hidden in a hollowed-out pumpkin, they found several rolls of top-secret government microfilm. Chambers said the stolen film had come from Hiss.

Hiss could not be charged with spying—many years had passed since his alleged crime. He was charged, however, with lying under oath. Hiss was eventually convicted and served some years in prison. Future president Richard Nixon played a key role in the investigation.

Another famous case involved the theft of atomic secrets. Klaus Fuchs was a German-born scientist who had worked on the Manhattan Project during World War II. Investigators learned that he gave American atomic secrets to the Soviet Union, including detailed drawings. Fuchs was sentenced to 14 years in prison though he served just 9 years.

The Fuchs case raised fears about atomic spies operating inside the United States. Indeed, investigators soon found several Americans who admitted providing atomic secrets to the Soviets. One of them charged that his sister and brother-in-law—Ethel and Julius Rosenberg—were leaders of the spy ring.

At the trial, the Rosenbergs denied the charges. They also refused to answer questions about their political activities, which included past involvement with communism. They were convicted of conspiracy to commit espionage, or spying. The Rosenbergs received the death sentence and were executed in 1953.

READING CHECK **Identifying the Main Idea** Name some examples of efforts to fight communism in the United States in the late 1940s and early 1950s.

Senator Joseph McCarthy

On February 9, 1950, a U.S. senator named **Joseph McCarthy** visited Wheeling, West Virginia to deliver a speech before a Republican women's group. His topic was a familiar one to Americans of that day—the dangers of communism. In his speech, McCarthy claimed that there were 205 known Communists working for the U.S. Department of State. In a later speech, he went a step further. Waving a list before the crowd, he said it contained the names of 57 Communists in the State Department.

The rise of McCarthyism
McCarthy's charges created a sensation. For many Americans, his claim was all too easy to believe. It helped explain recent events, such as the loss of China and the Soviet development of the atomic bomb. But McCarthy never produced the list of names he claimed to be holding in his speech. A Senate committee looked into his charges and found no evidence of Communists in the State Department.

By that time, however, many frightened Americans did not need any evidence. Even if he had been wrong with his first list, they

THE IMPACT TODAY

Recent Scholarship
In 1995 the National Security Agency released information on Soviet spy communications during the Cold War. These files provided further evidence that the Rosenbergs were guilty.

The McCarthy Hearings

Senator Joseph McCarthy presents a map of alleged Communist Party organization to Army counsel Joseph Welch as part of the Army-McCarthy hearing in 1954. *How does McCarthy's use of a map give support to his claims?*

figured, he was clearly on the right track. In this way, just by making accusations, McCarthy had earned for himself a reputation as the nation's top Communist fighter.

With his newfound fame, McCarthy went on the attack. He made many new charges, but none were backed up with any evidence. When people complained about his methods, McCarthy suggested that maybe they had secrets to hide. Truman dismissed him as a "ballyhoo artist who has to cover up his shortcomings by wild charges." One critic, the political cartoonist Herblock, dubbed McCarthy's tactic of spreading fear and making baseless charges **McCarthyism**. The public, however, seemed willing to believe McCarthy.

Then in the 1950 elections, McCarthy made a special effort to bring about the defeat of Maryland senator Millard Tydings. Tydings was one of President Truman's strongest supporters. It was his committee that had investigated McCarthy's first claims and found them to be false. In the Tydings campaign, McCarthy produced faked photographs showing Tydings talking to the head of the American Communist Party. Tydings was defeated.

McCarthyism quickly spread beyond the Senate. In other branches of government, at universities, in labor unions, and in private businesses, the hunt for Communists geared up. The FBI and even private investigators produced names of people with questionable political views. People who refused to help with investigations were also named.

Officials and employers feared that failure to take action would open them to charges of being "soft on communism," in other words, weak in dealing with it. Across the United States, thousands of people were fired for political reasons.

McCarthy's fall Meanwhile, Senator McCarthy continued his campaign from the Senate. He became increasingly wild in his charges. After winning re-election in 1952, he began to go after fellow Republicans. In 1954 he attacked the U.S. Army, claiming that it was protecting Communists. His Senate hearings were televised, which spread his anti-Communist message widely. Still, the public increasingly came to view McCarthy's tactics as unfair. As you will read, the fear of communism in the United States would remain for some time. But the career of Senator Joseph McCarthy—and McCarthyism—would soon fade away.

READING CHECK Making Generalizations What did Joseph McCarthy aim to do?

SECTION 3 ASSESSMENT

HSS 11.9.3

Reviewing Ideas, Terms, and People

1. **a. Recall** How did the Communist takeover of China and the Soviet explosion of an atomic bomb affect the United States?
   b. Draw Conclusions Do you think that it was reasonable to conclude from the advance of communism in the late 1940s that communism was "winning"?
   c. Predict How do you think the events of 1949 would affect the U.S. policy toward communism in the future?

2. **a. Identify** Who were the **Hollywood Ten**, and what was their significance in the late 1940s?
   b. Summarize What was the effect of the growing fear of communism at home?
   c. Elaborate Why do you think Julius and Ethel Rosenberg received the death sentence?

3. **a. Define** Write a brief definition of the following term: McCarthyism
   b. Explain Why was Senator McCarthy able to win recognition as a great fighter of communism without actually identifying any Communists?

   c. Elaborate Why do you think some people were unwilling to stand up to McCarthy and his hunt for Communists?

Critical Thinking

4. **Identifying the Main Idea** Copy the chart below and use information from the section to identify details that support the main idea given.

FOCUS ON WRITING ELA W1.1

5. **Expository** Do you think Truman's investigation of federal employees was justified? Write a short essay in which you explain your position on this issue. Use details from the section to support your explanation.

SECTION 4: The Korean War

BEFORE YOU READ

MAIN IDEA
Cold War tensions finally erupted in a shooting war in 1950. The United States confronted a difficult challenge defending freedom halfway around the world.

READING FOCUS
1. What was the situation in Korea before the war began in 1950?
2. What were the circumstances that led to the start of the Korean War?
3. What were the key battles of the Korean War?
4. How did the fighting in the Korean War end?

KEY TERMS AND PEOPLE
38th parallel
Kim Il Sung
Syngman Rhee
police action
Inchon
Panmunjom

HSS 11.9.3 Trace the origins and geopolitical consequences (foreign and domestic) of the Cold War and containment policy, including the following:
• The Korean War

▲ These soldiers became the first ground troops to enter into combat in Korea.

Crisis in Korea

THE INSIDE STORY

How did the Korean War begin for American troops? The soldiers of Task Force Smith—a group of some 400 soldiers shipped to Korea in 1950—never really had time to be afraid. Just days before, they had been a half-equipped and undertrained unit stationed in Japan. Few of their members had any combat experience—a fact that concerned no one since there was no combat for them to take part in.

That changed with the sudden, surprise invasion of South Korea by North Korean forces in late June 1950. As the North Koreans drove deep into South Korean territory, President Truman authorized the use of American ground forces to stop the advance. That meant Task Force Smith would be transferred from Japan to Korea.

General Douglas MacArthur referred to the soldiers as "that arrogant display of strength." Upon their arrival in South Korea, the troops were greeted with cheers. They drove out to meet the enemy, each soldier carrying two days worth of food and ammunition. They expected that the North Koreans would never dare to do battle with the mighty Americans.

Of course, the North Koreans were not impressed. As you will read, they quickly pushed aside the ill-prepared Task Force Smith. The bloody Korean War was on.

THE COLD WAR BEGINS **483**

KOREA

GEOGRAPHY SKILLS | INTERPRETING MAPS

1. **Location** Why was the 38th parallel chosen as a dividing line?
2. **Place** What nation shares a border with North Korea, besides South Korea? Why is this significant?

See **Skills Handbook**, p. H20

THE IMPACT TODAY
Government
Today Kim Il Sung's son, Kim Jong Il, is the leader of North Korea. North Korea remains a Communist country, while South Korea has a democratic government.

Korea before the War

The 600-mile-long Korean Peninsula lies between China and Japan. The peninsula is also close to Russia, which in 1950 was part of the Soviet Union. China, Japan, and Russia have long held a strong influence over the Korean people. After 1905 Korea came under the control of the Japanese. Japan dominated and occupied the peninsula.

Then in 1945 the Allies defeated the Japanese in World War II. As you have read, the Allies had agreed to divide control of the conquered Germany among several Allied nations. A similar sort of agreement was reached regarding Japanese-occupied Korea. At the Yalta Conference in February 1945, the Allies agreed that Korea should be free following the war. For purposes of accepting the Japanese surrender and providing postwar security in Korea, however, the Allies also agreed to temporarily divide Korea into northern and southern parts. The dividing line was to be the parallel at 38° north latitude. The Soviet Union would control Korea north of the **38th parallel**. South of it, the Americans would be in charge. In fact, the Soviets played virtually no role in the military defeat of Japan. Stalin did not declare war on Japan until after the dropping of the first atomic bomb at Hiroshima. Nevertheless, after the Japanese surrender, the Soviets took control of North Korea.

The presence of the Soviets and Americans in Korea was meant to be temporary. As in Germany, however, the start of the Cold War led to problems. In North Korea, the Soviet Union tried to establish a Communist system of government. The North called itself the Democratic People's Republic of Korea. Its first leader was **Kim Il Sung**, who sought to reunify North and South Korea under Communist control.

In South Korea, the United States promoted a democratic system. South Korea, known as the Republic of Korea, was led by president **Syngman Rhee**. Although an elected leader, Rhee held dictatorial control over South Korea. Like Kim Il Sung, he hoped the two halves of Korea would be reunified.

Both the North and the South held the goal of bringing together the two Korean halves into one whole, but they had different ideas of how best to reunify the country. Efforts toward unification continued in the late 1940s. In the end, however, these efforts led to war.

READING CHECK Summarizing How did the status of Korea prior to June 1950 lead to its division into northern and southern halves?

The Start of the Korean War

In the dark, early hours of June 25, 1950, more than 100,000 North Korean troops crossed the 38th parallel and invaded South Korea. Kim Il Sung had ordered the invasion, hoping to reunify all of Korea under his rule.

The troops carried Soviet-made weapons and drove Soviet-made tanks. In the recent past, some border skirmishes had occurred between North and South Korean troops, but this was different. From the outset it was clear that this was a major attack. The future of South Korea was at stake.

The attack came as a surprise to most leaders in the United States. Tensions on the peninsula had been high, and some observers had noticed a buildup of North Korean forces along the 38th parallel. Still, nobody in the Truman administration had anticipated serious fighting there. In fact, American troops stationed in South Korea since the end of the war had recently completed their withdrawal from the country. This had been part of a large-scale decrease in the size of U.S. armed forces that had been taking place in recent years. Because of this, the United States was not well prepared to fight in Korea. Nevertheless, the decision to fight was made quickly.

The role of the United States
In President Truman's mind, South Korea was where the United States had to take a stand against Communist aggression. South Korea was a small country, unable to defend itself against an enemy supported by the Soviet Union or Communist China. Failure to defend South Korea might send a signal to other nations that the United States would not help defend their freedom. It was even feared that a failure to act could lead to a wider war. In a message to Congress about the situation in Korea, Truman said:

HISTORY'S VOICES

"For ourselves, we seek no territory or domination over others... We are concerned with advancing our prosperity and our well-being as a Nation, but we know that our future is inseparably joined with the future of other free peoples."
—Harry S Truman, July 1950

Truman's viewpoint was shared by many others, including World War II hero General Dwight D. Eisenhower. "We'll have a dozen Koreas soon," Eisenhower declared, "if we don't take a firm stand."

Meanwhile, on the battlefield, the situation was getting more serious by the hour. Within days of the invasion, the North Korean force had pushed back the South Korean defenses and captured the capital city of Seoul. Truman realized something had to be done, and it had to be done soon. He ordered American naval and air forces to support South Korean ground troops. Then he asked the United Nations to approve the use of force to stop the North Korean invasion.

The role of the UN
The United Nations Security Council voted unanimously in favor of the use of force. Under the UN rules, five key countries held the power to veto UN Security Council decisions. That is, those five countries could single-handedly vote against a measure and defeat it.

One of the countries holding a veto was the Soviet Union. However, at the time of the UN vote on North Korea, the Soviet representative was absent, in protest over the UN's admission of Nationalist China. Therefore, the soviet representative was not there to veto the use of force against North Korea.

This twist, however, would not be enough to save the South Koreans. It soon became clear that American ground troops were needed. This was a step Truman had been reluctant to take. He feared that sending ground troops might trigger the start of another world war. It soon became clear, however, that there was no other way to stop the North Korean onslaught. On June 30 Truman ordered American ground troops into action.

The military force sent to Korea would be a United Nations force. Technically, the whole effort was referred to as a UN **police action**. The United States never declared war. Its commander was to be none other than General Douglas MacArthur. American soldiers made up the largest part of the force. Some 15 other nations contributed a total of 40,000 troops. This combined force then joined what was left of the South Korean military in a desperate fight to save the country.

READING CHECK **Sequencing** What events occurred at the beginning of the war in Korea?

Key Battles of the Korean War

American soldiers had entered the battle in South Korea. Unfortunately, North Korean troops greatly outnumbered and outgunned South Korea's defenders. Fighting conditions were miserable. Summer heat and heavy rains sapped what little strength the soldiers had after days of desperate combat.

Throughout the month of July, the news from Korea was discouraging. By the end of the month, the North Koreans had pushed UN forces all the way to the southeastern tip of South Korea. Here the UN forces formed a line around the port city of Pusan. This 130-mile-long line, soldiers were told, needed to be held at all costs.

The Inchon landing In fact, UN forces held the port of Pusan. By early September, the Communist attack had stalled. Meanwhile, thousands of UN troops and tons of equipment were unloading at Pusan daily. Now MacArthur wanted to go on the offensive.

MacArthur's plan was daring and brilliant. It called for UN forces to make an amphibious landing behind North Korean lines at the port city of Inchon, on South Korea's western coast. Inchon was an unlikely place for such an assault. Its natural features made an attack by sea very risky. Chief among these features were the extremely high tides in Inchon's waters.

To MacArthur, the disadvantages of attacking at Inchon only meant that the North Koreans would not expect it. Surprise would be the key to his success. "We shall land at Inchon," he promised, "and I shall crush them."

MacArthur's plan worked beautifully. Within 24 hours of the September 15 invasion at Inchon, a 70,000-troop force had secured a solid landing and regained some ground. See the History Close-Up feature opposite to learn more about the Inchon landing.

North Korea on the run The Inchon landing helped bring about an amazing change in fortunes in South Korea. UN forces quickly moved out from Inchon to recapture Seoul. The North Koreans had stretched themselves too thin chasing the UN forces all the way south to Pusan. They were powerless to stop the force moving out of Inchon.

Meanwhile, the UN launched another offensive from Pusan. This attack broke through the North Korean line and started marching northward. Huge numbers of North Korean troops were destroyed or forced to surrender.

The turnaround was startling. The UN had been facing defeat in August. Only a few months later, by October 1, all of South Korea was back in UN hands.

American leaders now faced the question of whether to stop at the 38th parallel. North Korea's forces were in tatters. MacArthur favored taking all of North Korea. One concern about this plan, however, was the possibility that the Chinese or Soviets might come to the defense of North Korea. A top Chinese official issued just such a warning. But the Americans decided the risk was worth taking. Truman also supported the plan.

Moving into North Korea continued to seem like a good idea through the days of October and November. UN forces made solid progress. There were some reports of Chinese troops filtering into North Korea and joining the battle. By the end of November, however, MacArthur was preparing for a major push. He said his new plan would end the Korean War. Then just as the general's plan was getting under way, it happened: A huge force of 260,000 Chinese troops poured across the Yalu River, which was North Korea's border with China. Again there had been an unexpected turnaround, but this time it favored the North Koreans.

UN forces retreat With the Chinese attack, MacArthur's promise of a quick victory disappeared. In fact, the UN forces suddenly faced defeat. According to MacArthur, the size of the Chinese force was simply too large. Just as in the early days of the war, UN forces were soon in full retreat.

In the case of the 8th Army, this retreat went all the way back south of Seoul. It was the longest such fallback in U.S. military history. To make matters worse, the brutal Korean winter had arrived. Temperatures in some areas dropped well below 0°F. In places such as the Chosin Reservoir, American soldiers suffered terribly under the wintry conditions.

MacArthur is fired As 1951 began, the situation in Korea once again seemed dire for the Americans and the UN. In MacArthur's view, the UN faced a choice between defeat by the Chinese or a major war with them. He called for expanding the war by bombing the Chinese mainland and bringing Nationalist Chinese forces into the fighting. He even called for the use of atomic weapons.

MacArthur, as it turned out, was wrong. In January 1951, a force led by Lieutenant General Matthew Ridgway not only stopped the Chinese onslaught but actually went on the offensive. By April 1951 Ridgway's men had pushed the Chinese back to the 38th parallel.

Interactive HISTORY CLOSE-UP

Assault on Inchon

The September, 1950 invasion at Inchon was a key victory for UN forces in Korea, helping regain territory in South Korea. Territory changed hands frequently during the Korean War (see inset maps at right). UN forces pushed all the way into North Korea but were forced back to the 38th parallel by January 1951.

Controlled by North Korea
Controlled by South Korea
North Korean forces
United Nations forces

0   200   400 Miles
0   200   400 Kilometers
Albers equal-area projection

The tides near Inchon were extreme, and only for short windows of time was water deep enough to allow landing craft to reach the beaches.

The three landing "beaches" were code-named "red," "green," and "blue." They were muddy and rocky and, in some places, had tall sea walls attackers had to climb.

Over 250 ships took part in the assault on Inchon. They had to navigate tricky, swift-moving currents.

THE KOREAN WAR, 1950–1951

June 1950

Sept. 1950

Sept.–Oct. 1950

Nov. 1950–Jan. 1951

Skills Focus INTERPRETING INFOGRAPHICS

go.hrw.com
Interactive
Keyword: SE7 CH15

Drawing Conclusions How did UN forces overcome geographic obstacles in their invasion of Inchon?

See **Skills Handbook**, p. H18

THE COLD WAR BEGINS   **487**

FACES OF HISTORY

Douglas MACARTHUR
1880–1964

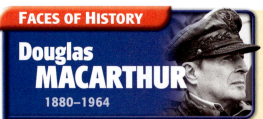

Born to a Civil War veteran who became a high-ranking army officer and raised on a series of military bases across the United States, Douglas MacArthur naturally chose a career in the military. He wrote in his memoirs, "My first memory was the sound of bugles." In 1903 he graduated first in his class at the U.S. military academy at West Point. During World War I he fought in France, where he was promoted to the rank of brigadier general. Known for his bravery and daring on the battlefield, he became the most decorated American soldier of World War I.

As supreme Allied commander in occupied Japan, MacArthur made one of his most important contributions to history—he helped Japan rebuild itself as a democratic nation. After President Truman removed him from command in the Korean War, MacArthur returned home. He died in 1964, still admired for his World War II victories and his leadership in occupied Japan.

Analyze What experiences prepared MacArthur for his leadership roles during World War II and after?

ACADEMIC VOCABULARY
scope extent or size

Ridgway's success called into question MacArthur's harsh warnings about the need to expand the war. It especially called into question MacArthur's recommendation to use atomic weapons. Truman began to believe that peace was possible without losing South Korea or triggering a larger war with China or even the Soviets.

MacArthur was dismayed by Truman's attitude. He wanted to see communism defeated in Asia even if meant expanding the scope of the war. Increasingly, he made public statements that challenged the authority of the president. He made threats against the Chinese government even as American officials were exploring ways to stop the fighting in Korea.

Truman faced a serious challenge. To many Americans, MacArthur was a major hero of World War II. They supported his goal of taking the war to the Chinese. Truman, though, wanted to avoid widening the war. Further, he could not allow a general to disobey the president and make his own policy. Truman decided he had to fire MacArthur.

The American public swiftly reacted to the MacArthur firing. While a few leaders supported the president's action, many Americans were outraged. "The American nation has never been in a greater danger," warned the *Chicago Tribune*. "It is led by a fool who is surrounded by knaves."

This anger only grew when MacArthur appeared before Congress for a dramatic farewell address. Some 30 million Americans watched his speech on television.

HISTORY'S VOICES

" In war, there is no substitute for victory. There are some who for varying reasons would appease Red China. They are blind to history's clear lesson, for history teaches with unmistakable emphasis that appeasement but begets new and bloodier war."

—General Douglas MacArthur, April 19, 1951

MacArthur closed with the emotional words, "Old soldiers never die; they just fade away." Americans everywhere wept and cheered for their World War II hero.

READING CHECK **Sequencing** What was the sequence of the fighting in Korea from the start of the war through April 1951?

Fighting Ends in Korea

Before long, the uproar over the MacArthur firing died down. Congress investigated the matter. The nation's leading military officers testified that Truman had been right in firing MacArthur.

Meanwhile, in July 1951, the United States entered into peace talks to end the fighting. By this point, 80,000 Americans had been wounded and nearly 14,000 were dead. South Korea and other UN forces had also suffered greatly. So had the Chinese and North Koreans.

Unsuccessful negotiations for peace

One major obstacle during the peace talks was the location of the boundary between North Korea and South Korea. UN forces by that point had actually managed to fight a short distance north of the 38th parallel. The UN wanted the boundary to be there. But the Communists insisted on setting the boundary precisely at the 38th parallel. This dispute helped break off negotiations at the end of the summer.

Meanwhile, the two military forces strengthened their positions. Now and then one side or the other would launch an attack. The goal was not to gain territory but to improve position.

Examples of such actions were the battles of Bloody Ridge and Heartbreak Ridge. These were fought in the late summer and early fall of 1951. Both battles followed a similar pattern: The two forces took turns winning, then losing, key hilltops. Though little was gained, losses were heavy. In these and other battles during this time, the UN suffered 40,000 casualties.

Negotiations resumed in October but again hit a major snag. This time the issue was prisoners of war. Hoping that the UN would continue to fight for unification, Syngman Rhee refused to send North Korean or Chinese prisoners back to Communist countries. This hindered the peace negotiations. Few major moves were happening on the battlefield, but the steady shelling and sniping was a deadly threat.

All of 1952 passed in a similar way. Negotiators meeting in the town of **Panmunjom** (PAHN-MOOHN-JAWM) argued over details of a peace agreement. At the same time, small-scale fighting claimed thousands of casualties.

Events of 1953 Meanwhile, 1952 was a presidential election year in the United States. American voters elected the World War II hero Dwight D. Eisenhower. Eisenhower would be inaugurated in January 1953. You will read more about Eisenhower's presidency in the next chapter.

In his campaign, Eisenhower had promised to end the Korean War. Once in office, he set about achieving this goal. At the same time, the Communists also seemed to want the war to end. Negotiators at Panmunjom worked toward agreement.

Though the end of the conflict was coming, the fighting remained deadly. Indeed, the Communists seemed to step up the fighting in the hope of gaining a last-minute advantage. During the final two months, UN forces suffered 57,000 casualties. The Communists lost 100,000. Finally, however, the guns fell silent on July 27. On that day, negotiators reached an armistice agreement.

The Korean War had left the map of Korea looking much as it had in early 1950, before the war began. The North Koreans had lost only a small amount of territory. The human costs, however, were much more significant. Some 37,000 American soldiers had died. Almost 60,000 UN troops from other countries were killed. Communist forces suffered some 2 million casualties. Perhaps as many as 3 million North and South Korean civilians were killed or injured.

READING CHECK Sequencing What events helped bring about the end of the fighting in the Korean War?

SECTION 4 ASSESSMENT

HSS 11.9.3

Reviewing Ideas, Terms, and People

1. **a. Identify** Identify the significance of the following term: 38th parallel
   b. Explain Why were there two different views about the way in which Korea might be reunified?

2. **a. Describe** What were the events that started the Korean War?
   b. Draw Conclusions Why did Truman believe it was important to defend a small country such as South Korea?
   c. Elaborate Why do you think the fighting in Korea was referred to as a **police action**?

3. **a. Recall** What was the significance of **Inchon** in the war?
   b. Make Generalizations How would you describe the major pattern of fighting in the first year of the Korean War?
   c. Rate Consider the arguments of both MacArthur and Truman about the possibility of a wider war with China. Which argument do you think was stronger? Explain.

4. **a. Identify** What is the significance of **Panmunjom**?

   b. Make Generalizations What happened to the kind of fighting that took place in the final phase of the war?
   c. Evaluate Considering the cost of the war and what was gained, do you think the United States was right to fight in Korea? Explain.

Critical Thinking

5. **Sequencing** Copy the chart below and use information from the section to sequence the events following the information provided.

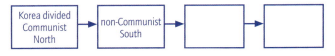

6. **Expository** Write a paragraph in which you explain the events that led to the beginning of the Korean War.

CHAPTER 15 DOCUMENT-BASED INVESTIGATION

The Cold War at Home

Historical Context The documents below provide different perspectives on the domestic impact of the Cold War.

Task Examine the documents and answer the questions that follow. Then you will be asked to write an essay about the domestic impact of the Cold War, using facts from the documents and from the chapter to support the position you take in your thesis statement.

HSS 11.9.3

DOCUMENT 1

In the aftermath of World War II, the House Un-American Activities Committee, or HUAC, investigated possible Communist subversion everywhere, from schools to labor unions to the entertainment industry. The political cartoon below was published in the *Washington Post* in 1947.

"IT'S OKAY—WE'RE HUNTING COMMUNISTS"
from *The Herblock Book* (Beacon Press, 1952)

DOCUMENT 2

In 1947 President Truman signed Executive Order 9835 in order to ban Communists and Fascists from federal employment. The order outlined procedures for investigating the background of federal employees. Although no actual espionage was discovered among government workers, many people were investigated in the years following Executive Order 9835. Below is an excerpt of the order.

> "Part I
> INVESTIGATION OF APPLICANTS
> There shall be a loyalty investigation of every person entering the civilian employment of any department or agency of the executive branch of the Federal Government. ...
>
> Part V
> STANDARDS [for Employment]
> Activities and associations of an applicant or employee which may be considered in connection with the determination of disloyalty may include one or more of the following:
>   Membership in, affiliation with or sympathetic association with any foreign or domestic organization, association, movement, group or combination of persons, designated by the Attorney General as totalitarian, fascist, communist, or subversive, or as having adopted a policy of advocating or approving the commission of acts of force or violence to deny other persons their rights under the Constitution of the United States, or as seeking to alter the form of government of the United States by unconstitutional means ..."

DOCUMENT 3

This photograph shows a man building a bomb shelter in the backyard of a private home in 1951. These reinforced underground rooms were built for protection in the event of an atomic attack. During the 1950s and 1960s, bomb shelters became increasingly popular as Americans' fears of nuclear war grew.

SKILLS FOCUS: READING LIKE A HISTORIAN

HSS Analysis HI1, HI2

1. **a. Describe** Refer to Document 1. What does the car symbolize in this political cartoon?
   b. Identify What is happening to the people who are in the car's path?
   c. Analyze What point of view does this cartoon present about the House Un-American Activities Committee?

2. **a. Identify** Refer to Document 2. Name three activities that would exclude a person from working for the federal government in 1947.
   b. Interpret Why might President Truman have considered this executive order necessary?

3. **a. Identify** Refer to Document 3. When finished, how would this structure protect people from a bomb?
   b. Analyze What does this photograph suggest about the impact of the Cold War on American society?

4. **Document-Based Essay Question** Consider the question below and form a thesis statement. Using examples from Documents 1, 2, and 3, create an outline and write a short essay supporting your position.
   How did the Cold War affect domestic policy and American society?

See **Skills Handbook**, pp. H28–H29, H30

THE COLD WAR BEGINS 491

CHAPTER 15 Chapter Review

Visual Summary: The Cold War Begins

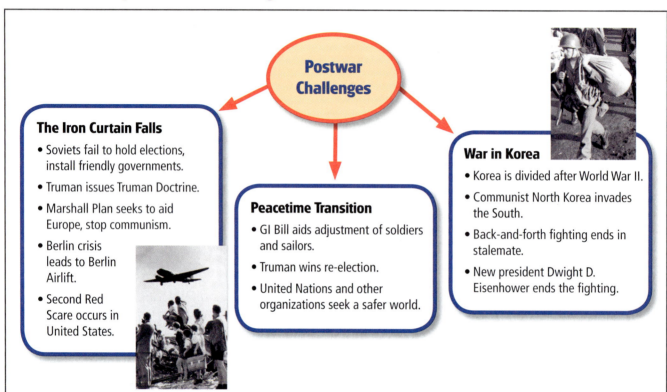

Postwar Challenges

The Iron Curtain Falls
- Soviets fail to hold elections, install friendly governments.
- Truman issues Truman Doctrine.
- Marshall Plan seeks to aid Europe, stop communism.
- Berlin crisis leads to Berlin Airlift.
- Second Red Scare occurs in United States.

Peacetime Transition
- GI Bill aids adjustment of soldiers and sailors.
- Truman wins re-election.
- United Nations and other organizations seek a safer world.

War in Korea
- Korea is divided after World War II.
- Communist North Korea invades the South.
- Back-and-forth fighting ends in stalemate.
- New president Dwight D. Eisenhower ends the fighting.

Reviewing Key Terms and People

Identify the correct term or person from the chapter that best fits each of the following descriptions.

1. Truman policy for limiting spread of communism
2. Alliance formed after World War II
3. Postwar rise in U.S. birthrate
4. Effort to help rebuild Europe after World War II
5. Helped many former soldiers get a college education, start a business, or buy a home
6. Term for method of making reckless attacks on people's reputations
7. A major turning point of the Korean War occurred here
8. Communist leader in China
9. Group blacklisted for refusing to help in effort to uncover Communists
10. Accused of spying against the United States
11. The period of high tension between the United States and Soviet Union

a. GI Bill
b. baby boom
c. McCarthyism
d. Inchon
e. containment
f. Mao Zedong
g. Alger Hiss
h. Marshall Plan
i. Cold War
j. Hollywood Ten
k. NATO

492 CHAPTER 15

History's Impact video program
Review the video to answer the closing question: How did the Cold War and the increase in American defense spending affect life during the 1950s?

Comprehension and Critical Thinking

SECTION 1 (pp. 464–470) HSS 11.4.6, 11.7.8, 11.9.3

12. a. Identify What was the term that described the dividing line between Communist Eastern Europe and non-Communist Western Europe?

b. Sequence What were the events that led up to and marked the beginning phases of the Cold War?

c. Rate What do you think was the most important benefit of the Marshall Plan? Explain your answer.

SECTION 2 (pp. 471–476) HSS 11.9.1

13. a. Describe What difficult adjustments faced the people of the United States after the war?

b. Draw Conclusions Why do you think there was so much interest after the war in creating organizations to improve conditions for people in the United States and around the world?

c. Elaborate What was the common idea behind the GI Bill and programs such as the International Monetary Fund and the World Bank established after World War II?

SECTION 3 (pp. 477–482) HSS 11.9.3

14. a. Recall What was the second Red Scare?

b. Sequence Identify the sequence of events discussed in the section that contributed to the rising Red Scare.

c. Evaluate How was the second Red Scare similar to and different from the Red Scare of 1919?

SECTION 4 (pp. 483–489) HSS 11.9.3

15. a. Describe What events led to the Korean War?

b. Sequence Describe the major events of the war in the order in which they occurred.

c. Rate Do you think the United States and the United Nations in Korea made an effective defense against the spread of communism?

Using the Internet

go.hrw.com
Practice Online
Keyword: SE7 CH15

16. During the twentieth century, the history of the city of Berlin was closely connected with the history of the Cold War. Using the keyword above, do research to learn about Berlin in the twentieth century, beginning after World War II and ending with the fall of the Berlin Wall. Then create a report that explains the significance of Berlin in the Cold War.

Analyzing Primary Sources   HSS HR4

Reading Like a Historian
This photograph depicts a parade celebrating the millionth ton of Marshall-Plan goods delivered to Europe.

17. Identify Study the photograph. In what country was it taken?

18. Draw Conclusions Why do you think a parade was held to celebrate this shipment of goods?

Critical Reading   ELA R3.8

Read the passage in Section 3 that begins with the heading "Truman and loyalty." Then answer the questions that follow.

19. Based on this passage, it seems that
   A. Truman was deeply anti-Communist.
   B. Truman did not care about communism
   C. Truman took action against communism mainly to satisfy the public.
   D. communism was a serious threat.

20. Truman's loyalty investigations produced
   A. little evidence of Communist influence in government.
   B. thousands of Communists in government.
   C. complete support from the public.
   D. widespread anger among the public.

FOCUS ON WRITING   ELA W1.1

Expository Writing *Expository writing gives information, explains why or how, or defines a process. To practice expository writing, complete the assignment below.*

Writing Topic The Korean War

21. Assignment Based on what you have read in this chapter, write a paragraph that explains why the United States became involved in the Korean War.

CHAPTER 16
1945–1960
Postwar America

THE BIG PICTURE In the years following World War II, the nation experienced tremendous economic growth and prosperity. Many Americans bought new homes, cars, and televisions as fast as they came on the market, transforming the way middle-class people lived. The Cold War arms race with the Soviet Union, however, cast a dark cloud of anxiety over the Eisenhower years.

California Standards

History-Social Sciences

11.8 Students analyze the economic boom and social transformation of post-World War II America.

11.9 Students analyze U.S. foreign policy since World War II.

11.11 Students analyze the major social problems and domestic policy issues in contemporary American society.

 READING LIKE A HISTORIAN

After the war, Americans eagerly bought products that were denied them during the war years. Many people also moved to newly created suburbs. A neat home with a white picket fence came to symbolize middle-class prosperity in the postwar years.
Interpreting Visuals What signs of prosperity can you identify for this family of five?

See **Skills Handbook**, p. H30

U.S.

1947 Bell Laboratories invents the transistor.

1945

World

1945 Nuremberg trials of Nazi leaders begins.

History's Impact video program
Watch the video to understand the impact of television.

June 1951 The first computer comes on the market.

October 1952 The United States tests a hydrogen bomb.

June 1956 Congress approves funds for the Interstate Highway System.

May 1960 Soviets shoot down an American U-2 spy plane.

1948 The nation of Israel is founded.

March 1953 Soviet leader Joseph Stalin dies.

1956 Egypt takes control of the Suez Canal.

1957 Soviets launch *Sputnik*, the first artificial satellite.

SECTION 1
The Eisenhower Era

BEFORE YOU READ

MAIN IDEA
The presidency of Dwight D. Eisenhower was shaped in large part by the Cold War and related conflicts.

READING FOCUS
1. What were the circumstances of Eisenhower's election in 1952?
2. How did the continuing Cold War affect the Eisenhower administration?
3. What were the Cold War "hot spots" of the 1950s?

KEY TERMS AND PEOPLE
Richard M. Nixon
John Foster Dulles
brinkmanship
massive retaliation
CIA
Nikita Khrushchev
Warsaw Pact
summit
SEATO
Eisenhower Doctrine

HSS 11.9.2 Understand the role of military alliances, including NATO and SEATO, in deterring communist aggression and maintaining security during the Cold War.

HSS 11.11.2 Discuss the significant domestic policy speeches of Truman, Eisenhower, Kennedy, Johnson, Nixon (e.g., with regard to education, civil rights, economic policy, environmental policy).

THE INSIDE STORY

Which party would Eisenhower pick in 1952?

If there was one thing on which Republicans and Democrats could agree in 1952, it was that General Dwight D. Eisenhower would make an excellent president. The World War II hero had an outstanding reputation with voters on both sides of the political divide. Yet as the election year approached, Eisenhower refused to announce whether he would seek the White House. In fact, no one really knew for certain which political party he might belong to.

President Truman seemed to think that Eisenhower might run as a Democrat. After all, the general had worked closely with Truman and with Franklin Roosevelt before that. In 1948 Truman had reportedly even offered to run with Eisenhower—as the vice presidential candidate on a ticket headed by the general. What's more, Truman and Eisenhower shared a strong opposition to the isolationist views of the leading Republican figure of the day, Senator Robert Taft of Ohio. In late 1951 Truman questioned Eisenhower on his willingness to run. He reportedly offered his help in getting Eisenhower the Democratic nomination. Eisenhower replied that he was not interested in politics.

Days later, the nation received startling news. Eisenhower would in fact be seeking the presidency—as a Republican. The entry of the popular war hero into the 1952 presidential race greatly changed the campaign. As you will read, there would be more surprises to follow.

▲ "Likeable Ike" on the campaign trail in 1952

496 CHAPTER 16

The Election of 1952

Truman's admiration for Eisenhower may have affected his decision not to seek re-election in 1952. The year before, the states had ratified the Twenty-second Amendment. This set a 10-year limit on the number of years a president could serve. Truman was specifically excluded from the amendment's limits. Still, he felt he had served long enough. "In my opinion," he declared, "eight years as president is long enough and sometimes too much for any man to serve in this capacity."

Stevenson vs. Eisenhower

With the race wide open, Democrats nominated Illinois governor Adlai Stevenson. Republicans chose Eisenhower, known to the public as "Ike."

On the campaign trail, Eisenhower sharply criticized the Democrats for their handling of the Korean War. Peace talks had been dragging on for months, and soldiers were dying by the thousands. Eisenhower vowed that if elected he would go to Korea to end the war. In response, Democrats noted that if Eisenhower knew how to end the Korean war, he should have done so long ago.

American voters, however, seemed to trust and admire Eisenhower. As election day neared, polls showed him well in the lead.

Nixon and the Checkers speech

The Eisenhower campaign did hit one major snag. It involved Ike's vice presidential running mate, **Richard M. Nixon**. Nixon was a senator from California who had made his name as a strong anti-Communist, having led the investigation of Alger Hiss.

During the 1952 campaign, reporters alleged that Nixon had an $18,000 fund made up of gifts from political supporters. At the time, such a fund was not illegal. Nixon's critics, however, implied that he was dishonest.

In a dramatic move, Nixon went on television to defend his conduct. His outstanding performance in the so-called Checkers speech saved his spot on the Republican ticket. With the issue behind them, the Eisenhower campaign moved on to a solid election-day victory.

READING CHECK **Summarizing** What were the key events of the presidential campaign of 1952?

PRIMARY SOURCES

Speech

In what became known as the Checkers speech, Richard M. Nixon admitted having a secret political fund but denied using it improperly. He detailed his personal finances—and admitted to having accepted one special gift in 1952. The speech was well received, and it saved his political career.

"We did get something, a gift, after the election. A man down in Texas heard [my wife] Pat on the radio mention the fact that our two youngsters would like to have a dog, and ... the day before we left on this campaign trip we got a message from Union Station down in Baltimore, saying they had a package for us. We went down to get it. You know what it was? It was a little cocker spaniel dog, in a crate that he had sent all the way from Texas, black and white, spotted, and our little girl, Tricia, the six-year-old, named it Checkers. And, you know, the kids, like all kids, loved the dog, and I just want to say this, right now, that regardless of what they say about it, we're going to keep it."

Nixon used the image of his daughter and her puppy to build sympathy.

Skills Focus **READING LIKE A HISTORIAN**

1. **Analyzing Primary Sources** What was the gift that Nixon admitted to having received?
2. **Drawing Conclusions** Why do you think the speech was effective at ending the scandal?

See **Skills Handbook**, pp. H12, H28–H29

The Cold War Continues

True to his promise, Eisenhower traveled to Korea in December 1952. There he began the task of getting the stalled peace talks going. The effort proved difficult. A cease-fire was not achieved until July 1953. Even with the end of the fighting in Korea, the Cold War continued to rage throughout the 1950s and to dominate Eisenhower's presidency.

Eisenhower's Cold War policies

At the center of Eisenhower's foreign policy team was Secretary of State **John Foster Dulles**. Dulles had played a role in the Truman administration.

ACADEMIC VOCABULARY
imply to express indirectly

Like Eisenhower, he was sharply critical of the Democrats' foreign policy. In particular, Dulles wanted to revise the nation's approach to communism. Rather than merely containing it, as Truman had called for, Dulles spoke of rolling it back.

To stand against the Soviets, Dulles favored building more nuclear weapons. Only the threat of nuclear war, he believed, would stop the Soviets. Dulles's belief was a part of the policy known as **brinkmanship**, the diplomatic art of going to the brink of war without actually getting into war. The practice of brinkmanship involved making threats that were strong enough to bring results without having to follow through on the threats.

Related to this notion was Dulles's concept of **massive retaliation**. This was the pledge that the United States would use overwhelming force against the Soviet Union, including nuclear weapons, to settle a serious conflict.

While Dulles presented the public face of American foreign policy, there was also a secret side. The Central Intelligence Agency, or **CIA**, was formed in 1947 to collect information about—and spy on—foreign governments. The CIA was increasingly active in the 1950s. In addition to collecting information, CIA agents also took part in secret actions against hostile governments. For example, during Eisenhower's first term CIA agents helped overthrow governments in Guatemala and Iran.

Changes in the Soviet Union In March 1953 longtime Soviet leader Joseph Stalin died. His death brought an end to a terrible period in Soviet history. A ruthless dictator, he had been responsible for the deaths of millions of his own citizens. He had also led the Soviet Union in its domination of Eastern Europe and the start of the Cold War.

Stalin's death raised many questions in the United States. Observers were unsure what policies his successor would pursue. Eventually, **Nikita Khrushchev** emerged as the new leader. Many political prisoners jailed under Stalin were freed. Nevertheless, the Soviet Union remained a Communist dictatorship—and a bitter rival of the United States.

The Warsaw Pact forms In 1955 the Soviets established a new organization called the **Warsaw Pact**. This was a military alliance with the Soviet-dominated countries of Eastern Europe. It was roughly similar in purpose to NATO. The Warsaw Pact, however, was entirely under the control of the Soviet Union. Warsaw Pact nations stood ready to defend each other and the Soviet Union. At the same time, the pact was a tool that helped the Soviets solidify control in Eastern Europe.

Communist control was firm—and when necessary, ruthless. For example, in June 1956 soldiers violently put down an anti-Communist protest in Poland. Dozens were killed.

Several months later, a larger uprising occurred in Hungary. There, many citizens rose up to demand changes to their harsh, Soviet-style government. Some also sought the return of a former leader, Imre Nagy. Nagy was a Communist, but he favored a more democratic system of government.

Height of the Cold War

In the 1950s Cold War tensions reached new heights as the United States and the Soviet Union maneuvered for power and influence.

This cartoon of Khrushchev and Eisenhower appeared on the cover of *Newsweek* in 1959.

November 1952
Eisenhower is elected president, in part on the strength of his tough anti-Communist stance.

March 1953
Stalin dies; eventually Nikita Khrushchev emerges as the new Soviet leader.

July 1953
Fighting in Korea ends in a stalemate.

In response to public demands, Nagy was named prime minister in late October. Once in office, he promised new reforms for Hungary. He also tried to force the withdrawal of Soviet troops from his country. When these efforts failed, he declared that Hungary would withdraw from the Warsaw Pact.

As demonstrations continued in the Hungarian capital of Budapest, the Soviets used the unrest as an excuse to send in military forces. Soviet tanks rolled through the streets, and planes bombed the city. The Hungarians fought back, but they could not resist the Soviets. The Soviets had sent a powerful message: They were in control in Eastern Europe.

U.S.-Soviet relations Although the 1950s were a time of Cold War tension, the Americans and Soviets did meet in the first postwar U.S.-Soviet summit in 1955. A **summit** is a meeting of the heads of government. The summit took place in Geneva, Switzerland.

Eisenhower proposed an "open skies" treaty. Under it, both the Soviets and the Americans could fly over each other's territory to learn more about the other's military abilities. Eisenhower believed this would help lower tensions because neither side would have to imagine the worst about the other's military strength. The Soviets, however, rejected the proposal.

This setback did not shake voters' faith in Eisenhower and his handling of international affairs. He easily won re-election in 1956, again defeating Adlai Stevenson.

The Soviet rejection of the open skies proposal did not prevent Eisenhower from seeking information about the Soviet military. The United States sent U-2 aircraft into Soviet airspace to inspect their military facilities. The U-2s carried advanced spying equipment and flew at altitudes thought to be out of reach of Soviet defenses. In 1960, however, the Soviets shot down pilot Francis Gary Powers's U-2 spy plane and captured Powers. Powers was freed in 1962 in exchange for the U.S. release of a captured Soviet spy. The incident greatly damaged U.S.-Soviet relations.

READING CHECK **Identifying Cause and Effect** Identify several events that represent the continuation of the Cold War in the 1950s.

Cold War "Hot Spots"

The Cold War had led to armed conflict in Korea. Cold War tensions also flared in several other spots around the world in the 1950s.

Vietnam and the seeds of war In 1954 France lost a bloody struggle to keep control of its Southeast Asian colony in Vietnam. After a terrible defeat in the battle of Dien Bien Phu, the French sought peace with the Vietnamese rebels who had been fighting to oust them. Among these rebels were many Communists.

The peace talks between the French and Vietnamese reflected Cold War rivalries. The final agreement divided Vietnam in northern and southern halves. The north came under the control of Communist leader Ho Chi Minh. As in Korea, this division was supposed to be temporary. The peace agreement called for a

Peace talks in Panmunjom stall as the partition between the two Koreas is negotiated.

The military used high-altitude aircraft on spying missions.

September 1954 The Southeast Asia Treaty Organization is formed to stop communism in Southeast Asia.

May 1955 The Warsaw Pact is formed between the Soviet Union and the countries it dominated in Eastern Europe.

1956 Poland and Hungary rebel against Communist rule; Egypt seizes the Suez Canal, and Israel, Great Britain, and France attack.

January 1957 The President issues the Eisenhower Doctrine, intended to resist communism in the Middle East; he later sends troops into Lebanon.

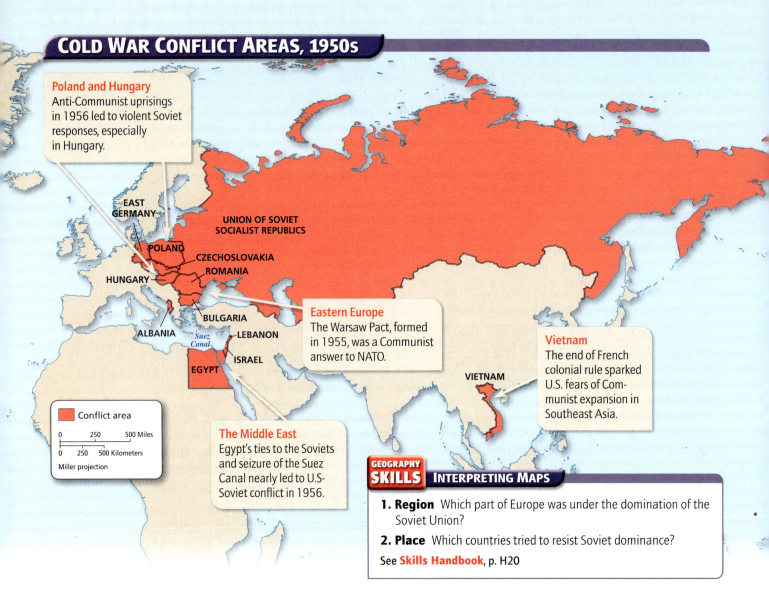

COLD WAR CONFLICT AREAS, 1950s

Poland and Hungary
Anti-Communist uprisings in 1956 led to violent Soviet responses, especially in Hungary.

Eastern Europe
The Warsaw Pact, formed in 1955, was a Communist answer to NATO.

Vietnam
The end of French colonial rule sparked U.S. fears of Communist expansion in Southeast Asia.

The Middle East
Egypt's ties to the Soviets and seizure of the Suez Canal nearly led to U.S.-Soviet conflict in 1956.

GEOGRAPHY SKILLS INTERPRETING MAPS

1. **Region** Which part of Europe was under the domination of the Soviet Union?
2. **Place** Which countries tried to resist Soviet dominance?

See **Skills Handbook**, p. H20

1956 election. Vietnamese voters would then get to choose for themselves what kind of government they would have.

For Eisenhower, this agreement was unacceptable: An election might lead to a Communist victory. Communism in Vietnam could lead to the spread of communism in the region.

HISTORY'S VOICES

"You have a row of dominoes set up, you knock over the first one, and what will happen to the last one is the certainty that it will go over very quickly . . .

But when we come to the possible sequence of events, the loss of [Vietnam], of Burma, of Thailand, of the Peninsula, and Indonesia following . . . the possible consequences of the loss are just incalculable to the free world."

—Dwight D. Eisenhower, press conference, April 7, 1954

To address this danger, the United States and its anti-Communist allies created a new organization. This was called the Southeast Asia Treaty Organization, or **SEATO**. Members included Australia, Great Britain, France, New Zealand, Pakistan, the Philippines, Thailand, and the United States. SEATO nations agreed to work together to resist Communist aggression.

SEATO and the United States supported the creation of a new anti-Communist nation in 1955: South Vietnam. In the coming years, the United States provided much military and economic support to this government. Unfortunately, its president, Ngo Dinh Diem, angered his own people with his harsh leadership.

Meanwhile, the North Vietnamese were growing impatient. They still wanted to unite all of Vietnam under their control. This set the stage for later armed conflict.

Trouble in the Middle East The Middle East was another region troubled by Cold War tensions. These tensions were heightened by the conflict between Jews and Arabs. This conflict reached a crisis point in 1948, when Israel declared its independence. The creation of Israel followed a UN resolution dividing Palestine into a Jewish and an Arab state.

Israel's Arab neighbors—Egypt, Syria, Jordan, Lebanon, and Iraq—immediately attacked Israel. In the war that followed, Israel won. The land that had been set aside for the Palestinians came under the control of Israel and the nations of Jordan and Egypt.

In 1954 Gamal Abdel Nasser rose to power in Egypt. Nasser sought to unite and strengthen the Arab nations. Toward this goal, he was willing to seek the support of the Soviet Union.

U.S. leaders were unhappy with Nasser's growing relationship with the Soviet Union. In 1956 the United States withdrew its financial support for a major Egyptian building project, the Aswan High Dam.

In response, Nasser seized control of the Suez Canal, the vital waterway between the Mediterranean Sea and the Red Sea. A British-controlled company owned the canal, through which Europe received two-thirds of its petroleum. Britain and France wanted to continue to use the canal and to protect their oil supplies.

Egypt's action in the Suez also blocked Israel's only outlet to the Red Sea. In response, Israel launched a military attack on Egypt. The British and French quickly sent in their forces to take control of the canal. The Soviets then threatened to enter the fight on the side of Egypt. This, Eisenhower knew, might draw the United States into the conflict.

The Suez crisis ended when Eisenhower insisted that the invaders leave Egypt. A wider conflict was averted, although Egypt kept control of the canal. The incident also demonstrated the leadership of the United States over its European allies.

The Suez crisis had not resulted in a larger war over the Suez Canal. Eisenhower was worried, however, about the growing influence of the Soviets in the Middle East. In January 1957 he issued the **Eisenhower Doctrine**. This declared the right of the United States to help, on request, any nation in the Middle East trying to resist armed Communist aggression.

Using the doctrine, Eisenhower sent marines into Lebanon in 1958 to help put down a popular uprising against Lebanon's government. Though no Communists threatened Lebanon, Eisenhower wanted to prevent a wider crisis that might invite Soviet involvement.

READING CHECK **Identifying the Main Idea** What made the Cold War "hot spots" hot?

THE IMPACT TODAY
Economics
Some 25,000 ships pass through the Suez Canal annually, carrying about 14 percent of the world's shipping.

SECTION 1 ASSESSMENT

HSS 11.9.2, 11.11.2

go.hrw.com
Online Quiz
Keyword: SE7 HP16

Reviewing Ideas, Terms, and People

1. **a. Recall** What were the key issues and individuals of the 1952 presidential campaign?
   b. Elaborate How did Nixon's Checkers speech help the Eisenhower campaign?

2. **a. Define** Write a brief definition of each of the following terms: **brinkmanship, massive retaliation, Warsaw Pact**.
   b. Compare How was the Warsaw Pact similar to and different from NATO?
   c. Evaluate What do you think were the strengths and weaknesses of Dulles's policy of brinkmanship and massive retaliation?

3. **a. Describe** How did Cold War tensions contribute to conflicts in Vietnam and in Egypt?
   b. Explain What did President Eisenhower mean when he compared Vietnam to a domino?

   c. Elaborate Do you think Eisenhower was right to request that Great Britain, France, and Israel end their attack on Egypt during the Suez crisis? Explain.

Critical Thinking

4. **Identifying the Main Idea** Copy the chart below and use information from the section to record details that support the main idea of the section.

FOCUS ON SPEAKING ELA W1.1

5. **Persuasive** Assume the point of view of President Eisenhower. Make a speech to British, French, and Israeli leaders urging them to end their attack on Egypt.

SECTION 2
Atomic Anxiety

BEFORE YOU READ

MAIN IDEA
The growing power of, and military reliance on, nuclear weapons helped create significant anxiety in the American public in the 1950s.

READING FOCUS
1. What was the hydrogen bomb, and when was it developed?
2. What was the arms race, and what were its effects in the United States?
3. How did Americans react to the growing threat of nuclear war?

KEY TERMS AND PEOPLE
hydrogen bomb
ICBM
Sputnik
satellite
NASA
nuclear fallout

HSS 11.9.3 Trace the origins and geopolitical consequences (foreign and domestic) of the Cold War and containment policy, including the following:
• Atomic testing in the American West, the "mutual assured destruction" doctrine, and disarmament policies

HSS 11.11.2 Discuss the significant domestic policy speeches of Truman, Eisenhower, Kennedy, Johnson, Nixon (e.g., with regard to education, civil rights, economic policy, environmental policy).

THE INSIDE STORY

Where would you go if the unthinkable happened?
To Americans of the 1950s, war was something that took place in faraway lands. Few people had seriously faced the threat of death and destruction in their own communities. The atomic bomb, however, changed that comfortable feeling. With the bomb came the realization that devastation could come to them with no more warning than the wail of an air-raid siren.

How could Americans living in such a world protect their families? Some sought protection in backyard bomb shelters. Homeowners across the country were urged to install underground bunkers, complete with supplies of food and water that would help them and their loved ones survive a nuclear attack. There were a number of models available on the market. Popular magazines included helpful plans for do-it-yourselfers. For those unable to install an underground shelter, the government provided tips on how to create a bomb-safe area within an existing structure.

Nuclear weapons had brought a kind of peace to the world. They also brought uneasiness. As you will read, this tension colored much of American life in the 1950s.

Three Rooms, Two Baths, One Bomb Shelter

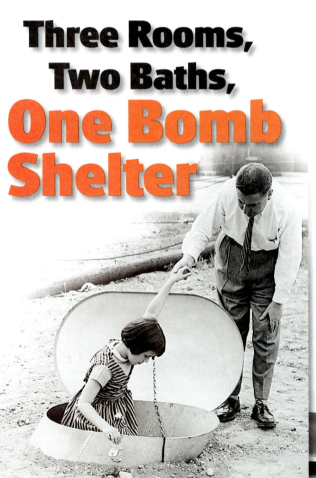

▶ In theory, a family could survive up to five days in one of these underground backyard shelters.

The Hydrogen Bomb

The atomic bombs that the United States used at the end of World War II had changed the world. Their terrible power persuaded Japanese leaders to do what millions of Allied soldiers had been unable to get them to do: surrender. Military strategy would never be the same.

American leaders chose not to use nuclear weapons during the Korean War. Nevertheless, these weapons were clearly a key part of the nation's military future. Even as soldiers were dying in Korea, the United States was building up its atomic stockpile and testing new and improved weapons. Nuclear testing took place in a variety of locations, including New Mexico, Nevada, Colorado, Mississippi, and Alaska.

Among the weapons being studied during this time was a different kind of nuclear device: the **hydrogen bomb**. The atomic bombs that destroyed Hiroshima and Nagasaki used energy that came from splitting apart atoms. The new hydrogen bomb would get its power from the fusing together of hydrogen atoms. Fusion is the same process that creates the energy of the sun and stars. Harnessed into a weapon, fusion had the potential to create a blast hundreds of times more powerful than an atomic bomb. Indeed, the hydrogen bomb—also known as the H-bomb or super bomb—was so potentially devastating that some scientists argued against ever building it.

HISTORY'S VOICES

> "In determining not to proceed to develop the super bomb, we see a unique opportunity of providing by example some limitations on the totality of war and thus of limiting the fear and arousing the hopes of mankind."
>
> —Report of the General Advisory Committee of the Atomic Energy Commission, October 1949

In spite of these concerns, development of the hydrogen bomb went forward in the late 1940s and early 1950s. President Truman had made the final decision. "It is part of my responsibility as commander-in-chief," he declared, "to see to it that our country is able to defend itself against any possible aggressor." Truman did not want to take the chance that the Soviet Union would develop its own hydrogen bomb. That would give the Soviet Union a significant military advantage over the United States.

The first hydrogen bomb, detonated in 1951, was code-named "Mike," for *megaton*.

THE FIRST HYDROGEN BOMB TEST

When detonated:	November 1, 1952, Eniwetak Atoll, Marshall Islands
Amount of energy released:	10.4 megatons, equivalent to 10.4 million tons of TNT
Size of fireball:	3 miles in diameter
Height of mushroom cloud:	more than 25 miles

By 1952 scientists had solved the difficult technical challenges of building a hydrogen bomb. On November 1 they tested it. The blast was beyond anything they had imagined. The island on which the bomb had been placed simply vanished. "I was stunned," recalled one observer of the explosion. "It looked as though it blotted out the whole horizon."

The explosion of the H-bomb once again put the United States ahead of the Soviet Union in weapons technology. This lead, however, was short-lived. In August 1953 the Soviets successfully tested a hydrogen bomb of their own.

READING CHECK **Drawing Conclusions** Why did President Truman decide to develop the hydrogen bomb?

The Arms Race

The United States and the Soviets again had roughly the same technology. Each side, however, remained concerned that the other would gain an advantage. To prevent this, both countries began to build stockpiles of weapons. They also sought new and better ways of delivering those weapons to potential targets.

Each improvement or technological advance by one country was met with some response by the other. Thus the United States and Soviet Union began an arms race—an international contest between countries seeking a military advantage over each other.

New military strategies The arrival and advance of nuclear weapons forced American leaders to reconsider the way the United States built its military defenses. When Eisenhower took office, he scaled back the nation's reliance on so-called conventional forces, such as soldiers and tanks. In their place, he increased reliance on nuclear weapons. This shift helped lead to the development of John Foster Dulles's policies of brinkmanship and massive retaliation. Instead of resisting its enemies with armies at the point of attack, the United States would seek to prevent its enemies from attacking in the first place by promising a devastating nuclear response.

Eisenhower and Dulles's strategies placed great importance on keeping the lead in the arms race. The American threat of massive retaliation would be more effective if its forces were superior to those of any adversary.

New bombs The first American hydrogen bomb was massive, not just in its destructive power but also in its size. It stood three stories tall and weighed a million pounds. It was so big, there would have been no way to actually use the weapon against an enemy.

Scientists therefore worked hard to reduce the size of the H-bomb. Before long, they had succeeded in making weapons that could be more easily delivered to enemy targets. The first such bomb was tested in 1954.

Early on, the United States focused on aircraft as the means of delivering nuclear weapons. As a result, the U.S. Air Force grew substantially in the 1950s. While Eisenhower was cutting budgets in many other parts of the military, he spent large amounts on new long-range bomber aircraft, such as the B-52. These bombers had the ability to deliver nuclear weapons anywhere in the world.

The U.S. fleet of bombers was spread across dozens of locations in Europe, Africa, and elsewhere. The American nuclear arsenal was constantly on the move. Bombers were always in the air, and those on the ground were ready to take off within 15 minutes. This helped ensure that no enemy would be able to destroy the American ability to launch an attack.

While the United States at first relied on aircraft to carry its nuclear weapons, scientists were hard at work developing missiles that could be equipped with these weapons. The effort involved reducing the size of the weapons themselves. It also involved developing missiles that could reach enemy targets accurately.

The development of missiles represented a major technological challenge. In the early 1950s, American rockets were capable of carrying a small nuclear weapon only a short distance. By the end of the 1950s, Americans had developed intercontinental ballistic missiles, or **ICBMs**. The ICBMs could travel thousands of miles and strike very close to their intended targets. They could also deliver powerful nuclear weapons.

Other new technologies While scientists were exploring the atom's destructive power, they were also learning to use it for other purposes. In 1954 the U.S. Navy launched the first nuclear-powered submarine. On this vessel, the USS *Nautilus*, nuclear fuel heated water to create steam. This steam powered the engine.

Unlike earlier submarines, the *Nautilus* could travel for months without needing to refuel. Thus, vessels such as the *Nautilus* could perform missions over greater distances. Nuclear-powered submarines were also capable of traveling at high speeds underwater.

ACADEMIC VOCABULARY
equipped fitted with; possessing certain equipment

THE IMPACT TODAY
Science and Technology
In recent times, the United States and other nations have worked to prevent the spread of nuclear weapons to developing countries, including Iran and North Korea.

Several years after launching the *Nautilus*, the United States began fitting its nuclear-powered submarines with nuclear missiles. By sending some of its nuclear weapons underwater and out of reach of enemy attack, the United States had found another way to ensure that any enemy move could be met with a devastating nuclear response.

Nuclear power was put to use for peaceful purposes on land as well. Nuclear power plants in the United States began to produce electricity for homes and businesses in 1957.

Soviet advances in technology The Soviet Union was also improving and expanding its weapons. Throughout the 1950s, the Soviets built new and improved weapons and delivery systems. The Soviets did lag behind the United States in the number of weapons it possessed. Nevertheless, it was well understood that any nuclear attack would lead to terrible destruction for both sides.

Soviet technological skill was demonstrated in shocking fashion in 1957. On October 4 the

The Cold War Arms Race

During the Cold War, the United States and the Soviet Union competed vigorously to achieve superiority in the arms race.

United States

October 1952
Americans explode an H-bomb.

January 1954
United States launches a nuclear-powered sub.

April 1957
United States tests a missile with a 2,000-mile range.

January 1958
United States launches a satellite.

July 1958
NASA is formed to lead U.S. space exploration programs.

May 1960
Francis Gary Powers's U-2 is shot down by the Soviets.

Soviet Union

August 1953
Soviets explode an H-bomb.

August 1957
Soviets test a missile with a 4,000-mile range.

October 1957
Sputnik, the first artificial satellite, is launched.

November 1957
Sputnik II is launched, carrying a dog into space.

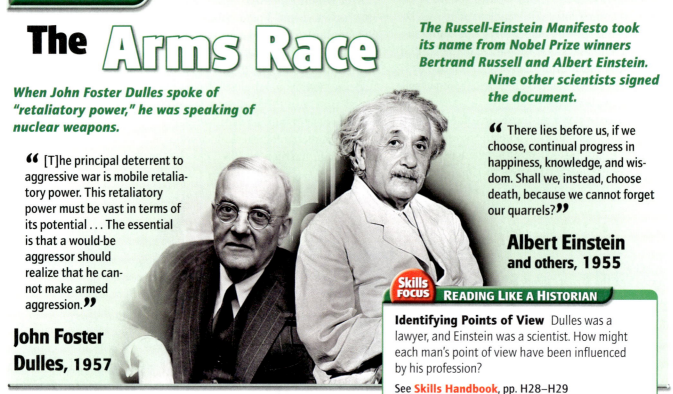

COUNTERPOINTS

The Arms Race

When John Foster Dulles spoke of "retaliatory power," he was speaking of nuclear weapons.

❝ [T]he principal deterrent to aggressive war is mobile retaliatory power. This retaliatory power must be vast in terms of its potential... The essential is that a would-be aggressor should realize that he cannot make armed aggression.❞

John Foster Dulles, 1957

The Russell-Einstein Manifesto took its name from Nobel Prize winners Bertrand Russell and Albert Einstein. Nine other scientists signed the document.

❝ There lies before us, if we choose, continual progress in happiness, knowledge, and wisdom. Shall we, instead, choose death, because we cannot forget our quarrels?❞

Albert Einstein and others, 1955

SKILLS FOCUS — READING LIKE A HISTORIAN

Identifying Points of View Dulles was a lawyer, and Einstein was a scientist. How might each man's point of view have been influenced by his profession?

See **Skills Handbook**, pp. H28–H29

Soviets launched the first-ever artificial satellite, named **Sputnik**. A **satellite** is an object that orbits around the Earth. *Sputnik* was small, only about the size of a basketball and weighed 200 pounds. The Soviets launched *Sputnik II* less than a month later. This satellite carried a dog, the first living creature to orbit Earth in space.

The *Sputnik* launches caused great concern in the United States. To many Americans, it signaled that the Soviets had surpassed American scientists in terms of technical skill and knowledge. Many worried this would translate into better, more accurate weaponry.

The United States was quick to respond to the *Sputnik* challenge. By January 1958, the United States was ready to launch a satellite of its own. In addition, in July of that year Congress established the National Aeronautics and Space Administration, or **NASA**. This new agency took charge of the nation's programs for exploring outer space. You will read more about NASA in future chapters.

The American people also took a hard look at their educational system. Many wondered whether a decline in the nation's schools had enabled the Soviet Union to surpass the United States in technological achievement. In response to this concern, Congress in 1958 passed the National Defense Education Act, which provided hundreds of millions of dollars for education in the United States.

READING CHECK **Identifying Cause and Effect** What was NASA, and how was its creation related to the arms race of the 1950s?

Americans React to the Threat of Nuclear War

After World War II, Americans had experience with the dangers of war. With the Japanese attack on Pearl Harbor, they had even experienced an attack by a foreign enemy. But the threat of nuclear attack was something new.

For the first time, Americans had to face the possibility that entire cities might be destroyed in the fireball of a nuclear explosion. Another fear was **nuclear fallout**, streams of radioactive particles produced by nuclear explosions. Such radiation drifts down through the atmosphere like rain to the ground. Exposure to nuclear fallout can cause burns and increase the risk of future health problems, such as cancer and birth defects. The environmental dangers from nuclear fallout can last for many years.

The American public was reminded of the terrible effects of nuclear fallout following the testing of a hydrogen bomb in the Marshall Islands in 1954. In that incident, bad weather spread a large cloud of nuclear fallout over a large area. The fallout harmed sailors on a Japanese fishing boat. One died as a result. In addition, many people living on the islands near the huge blast were forced to leave their homes—permanently. The levels of radioactivity left behind were too high for people to safely endure.

Strengthening civil defense American foreign policy was designed to prevent war. But there was no way to be sure that war would never come. As a result, American leaders also worked to prepare the nation for what to do in the event of a nuclear attack.

The Truman administration created the Federal Civil Defense Administration (FCDA) to help educate and prepare the public for nuclear emergencies. The FCDA stressed the key role of the average citizen in being ready to handle a crisis. In a nuclear war, the thinking went, the public might not be able to depend on the military to keep them safe.

In the words of FCDA leader Millard Caldwell, the "back yard may be the next front line." Indeed, during the Eisenhower administration, a strong civil defense program was seen as a good way to deter Soviet aggression.

To help educate the public, the FCDA issued materials, such as the booklet "How to Survive an Atomic Bomb." Educational films such as *Duck and Cover*, which featured a friendly turtle named Bert, taught schoolchildren techniques for protecting themselves from the deadly effects of a nuclear blast.

Air-raid sirens were installed in communities across the country. Tested on a regular basis, their haunting wail became a familiar sound to millions of Americans.

Women played a central role in the FCDA's civil defense program. They were seen as the keepers of the family and the guardians of the home. It became their job, according to the FCDA, to prepare the home for emergency—and to recognize the warning signals of attack.

The FCDA began staging tests of the nation's civil defense program in 1955. These tests, called Operation Alert, explored the

ACADEMIC VOCABULARY
issued officially distributed

Preparing for Attack

The government encouraged people to prepare for nuclear attack. At left, students practice the "duck and cover" drill, which was supposed to help protect them from injury in the event of a nuclear blast. *Why were Americans so fearful of attack?*

possible effects of a nuclear attack on major American urban areas. They took into account the results of the 1954 hydrogen bomb test, in which significant nuclear fallout spread over an area of 7,000 square miles.

The results of the 1955 Operation Alert were deeply disturbing. According to the FCDA's evaluation in the densely populated New York City area, a nuclear attack could leave millions dead and millions more injured and homeless.

In other cities, participation in the tests was inconsistent. In Washington, D.C., for example, the U.S. Congress simply ignored the exercise and continued its work.

In case anyone had had any doubt, Operation Alert made it clear that a true nuclear attack on a major urban area would have terrible, long-lasting results.

HISTORY'S VOICES

> "This demonstration gives new emphasis to President Eisenhower's dictum [statement] that war no longer presented the possibility of victory or defeat, but only the alternative of varying degrees of destruction."
>
> —*The New York Times*, June 16, 1955

Nuclear fears The government's efforts did raise preparedness. It also raised fears, leading many Americans to build bomb shelters in their yards. The public also began to express concern over the testing of nuclear weapons and the effects of nuclear fallout. These concerns eventually helped lead to negotiations with the Soviet Union for a treaty limiting nuclear testing. The Limited Test-Ban Treaty was ratified in 1963.

Nuclear fears also affected the culture of the times. A number of 1950s movies had plots that centered on the dangers of radiation. Comic books for young readers featured heroes and villains doing battle in a nuclear world.

The military-industrial complex While the public learned to live with the fear of nuclear attack, President Eisenhower used part of his farewell address in 1961 to inform them of a new danger: the "military-industrial complex." In the past, Eisenhower said, the United States had no permanent arms industry. When war came, factories changed from making cars, for example, to making tanks. By the 1950s, however, that had changed.

"We have been compelled to create a permanent armaments industry of vast proportions," Eisenhower said. While necessary, he noted, it was still a threat to freedom. "The potential for the disastrous rise of misplaced power exists and will persist," Eisenhower warned. Thus, as the 1950s ended and a new decade began, Americans had a new challenge to face.

READING CHECK **Identifying Supporting Details** How were the American people regularly reminded of the threat of nuclear war?

SECTION 2 ASSESSMENT

HSS 11.9.3, 11.11.2

Reviewing Ideas, Terms, and People

1. **a. Describe** How did the **hydrogen bomb** differ from the atomic weapons used on Hiroshima and Nagasaki?
   b. Draw Conclusions How do you think a more powerful weapon such as the hydrogen bomb would fit within the policies of brinkmanship and massive retaliation?

2. **a. Define** Write a brief definition of each of the following terms: **ICBM**, *Sputnik*, **NASA**
   b. Summarize Why was the Soviet development of a **satellite** so significant to the people of the United States?
   c. Predict How do you think the race to find an edge in nuclear weapons will affect the nature of nuclear weapons in the decades to come?

3. **a. Describe** What was the job of the FCDA?
   b. Contrast How did the nuclear threat differ from the kinds of threats that had faced the American people in the past?

Critical Thinking

4. **Identifying the Main Idea** Copy the chart below and use information from the section to record details that support the main idea of the section. Refer to the main idea at the beginning of this section.

FOCUS ON WRITING ELA W1.1

5. **Narrative** Write a brief narrative paragraph that tells the story of the arms race of the 1950s. Include details from this section.

SECTION 3: The Television Age

BEFORE YOU READ

MAIN IDEA
Television was a major influence on American culture in the 1950s, mirroring larger changes in technology and culture.

READING FOCUS
1. How did television change American life in the 1950s?
2. What other technological developments occurred during the 1950s?
3. How was American culture changing during the 1950s?

KEY TERMS AND PEOPLE
Lucille Ball
transistor
integrated circuit
Jonas Salk
vaccine
Levittown
Sunbelt
Interstate Highway System

 HSS 11.8.7 Describe the effects on society and the economy of technological developments since 1945, including the computer revolution, changes in communication, advances in medicine, and improvements in agricultural technology.

 THE INSIDE STORY

How did a redhead become a star in black-and-white? Television was still quite new in 1951 when the *I Love Lucy* show was first broadcast. The nation quickly fell in love with the zany antics of the show's characters: the redheaded Lucy Ricardo, played by Lucille Ball, and her bandleader husband Ricky, played by Desi Arnaz. At the peak of the show's success, two of three television sets in the country were tuned in for every episode.

The show helped shape the future of television itself. Prior to *I Love Lucy*, TV did not have its own style and distinctive art. Programs were little more than filmed versions of radio programs or vaudeville routines. But under the shrewd guidance of Ball and Arnaz, *I Love Lucy* pioneered new production techniques. For example, the show was filmed rather than broadcast live. This enabled the stars to perfect their comic routines—with hilarious results.

The program also broke ground with its casting. In 1951 Ball was a movie star in decline. Cuban-born Arnaz spoke with a thick Spanish accent. Neither fit the mold of the traditional star of the time. Yet their chemistry—the two were married in real life—was remarkable. Together they produced some of the most memorable moments in TV history. In the process, they helped television revolutionize American life.

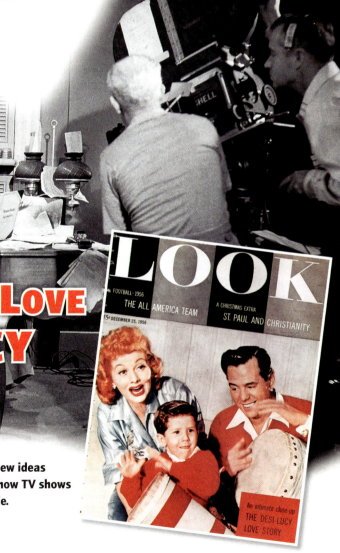

FOR THE LOVE OF LUCY

▲ Ball's new ideas changed how TV shows were made.

Television Changes American Life

Though broadcast television was still young when **Lucille Ball** captured the hearts of the nation, TV technology had existed for a number of years. Scientists had been working on it at least since the 1920s. By the end of World War II, television was ready for home use. Postwar consumers, eager to spend after years of wartime sacrifice, purchased the new devices. Between 1945 and 1950, some 5 million TV sets appeared in American homes.

That was just the beginning. During the 1950s, the number of Americans owning TVs continued to rise. By 1959 more than 40 million American homes had at least one set.

TV and politics One field in which television had an immediate impact was politics. America's leaders quickly learned that TV had great power to change their relationships with the voters. You have read how vice presidential candidate Richard Nixon used television in 1952 to appeal to the voting public. As you will read later, Nixon would also find that TV could do harm to a candidate's image.

Television also altered the career of Senator Joseph McCarthy, the Communist hunter. The televised 1954 Army-McCarthy hearings finally gave the public the chance to see his disgraceful, bullying behavior. The hearings left his once-lofty reputation ruined and his career in tatters.

Television advertising Advertisers were another group that quickly recognized the promise of television. TV's combination of picture and sound gave it more persuasive potential than radio. By 1960 television was the major method of advertising in the country.

Early TV advertising was patterned after radio advertising. A single advertiser sponsored the broadcast of an entire program. On programs such as the *Colgate Comedy Hour,* the line between program and advertisement was blurry. The product being sold was actually a part of the action.

As the cost of producing entire TV programs rose, advertisers shifted to buying just one- or two-minute segments during shows to sell their products. Ads were separated from programming, and the TV commercial was born.

Programming Of course, for most Americans, television was mainly about the programs. Each day and night, audiences tuned in to watch their favorites. The *I Love Lucy* show was only one example of many popular television programs.

Television's first big hit was the *Texaco Star Theater,* starring comedian Milton Berle, which later became the *Milton Berle Show*. Berle's great success earned him the nickname "Mr. Television." His hugely popular program of comedy and music is credited with helping television get established in its earliest days.

The hit show *American Bandstand* got its appeal from another cultural movement of the 1950s: rock and roll music. The show, which began in 1957, featured young people dancing to popular songs. *American Bandstand* remained on television until 1987.

The 1950s also saw the introduction of some of the many categories of programs popular today. Daytime dramas (known as soap operas), crime dramas, and game shows almost all got their start during this decade. To help people keep track of their favorite programs, a magazine called *TV Guide* began publishing.

Concerns about television As television's popularity ballooned, some people began to question its effects. Of special concern was TV's possible impact on children.

On several occasions in the 1950s, Congress looked into the effects of violent content on young viewers. To address this concern, the TV industry adopted its own voluntary standards. For example, the industry promised that law enforcement would always appear in a positive light and that criminals would always be presented as "bad guys." Satisfied, Congress took no formal action to limit television content during the 1950s. Still, Americans would continue to discuss the effect of television on children for years to come.

TV experienced a scandal in the late 1950s when the public learned that a popular game show had been rigged. Congress held hearings into the matter, and one of the contestants involved, Charles Van Doren, wound up leaving his job as a university professor.

READING CHECK **Identifying Cause and Effect** What were some of the effects of television on American life and culture in the 1950s?

ACADEMIC VOCABULARY
categories groups or classes with members that share common features

THE IMPACT TODAY
Science and Technology
Today most televisions are built to include a device called the V-chip. This device allows concerned adults to block the display of certain programs, such as those that contain violent content.

HISTORY CLOSE-UP

Milestones in Television History

Television has made history, and it has recorded history. Along the way, many changes have taken place in television. In the 1950s three major networks—ABC, CBS, and NBC—dominated TV broadcasting with shows aimed at the same general audience. Today the major networks share the television market with hundreds of cable networks airing programs tailored to specific age groups and interests.

A 1950 TV set ▲

1950 9 percent of U.S. households have televisions.

1951 Coast-to-coast live television broadcasts begin.

1954 CBS and NBC begin regular color broadcasting, even though just 1 percent of U.S. households own a color TV set. The NBC "peacock" logo is shown above. ▲

TV Guide magazine is published for the first time.

1960 The first televised presidential debate takes place.

87 percent of U.S. households have televisions. Programming is aimed at a family audience. ▼

1963 ABC, CBS, and NBC broadcast four days of continuous live coverage of the assassination and funeral of President John F. Kennedy. Millions of people around the world watch the state funeral on TV.

1969 *Sesame Street* airs for the first time, breaking new ground in children's educational programming.

An estimated 720 million people watch the first moon landing on live television. ▼

1970 The sitcom *Julia* is the first to feature an African American actor in the title role, played by Diahann Caroll. ▶

1971 Under federal law, cigarette advertising is banned on television and radio.

1972 The first cable network, Home Box Office (HBO), begins broadcasting.

1980 Cable News Network (CNN) offers the first 24-hour news service. ▼

1986 The *Challenger* space shuttle explodes just over a minute after takeoff. Millions of Americans witness the disaster on live TV.

1999 V-chip technology is introduced, allowing parents to block violent or unsuitable television programming from their children.

Today 98 percent of U.S. households have televisions. 76 percent of TV households have more than one set. About 68 percent of TV households have cable TV.

SKILLS FOCUS: INTERPRETING INFOGRAPHICS

Making Generalizations In what ways has television changed since the 1950s?

See **Skills Handbook**, p. H18

Other Technological Developments of the 1950s

Television was certainly the most popular technological innovation of the 1950s. A number of other breakthroughs, however, also helped to transform American life.

Transistors and computers Machines have been used to perform calculations for thousands of years. In the 1940s, however, researchers began to build the first of what we might recognize today as computers. These devices used electricity to perform complicated calculations. For example, in Great Britain, scientists used an early type of computer to help break communications codes during World War II.

To build the first computers, scientists used thousands of vacuum tubes. These were glass and metal devices that helped form the complicated electronic workings of the machines. Because computers used so many tubes, they took up hundreds of square feet of floor space. They also drew large amounts of electricity.

In 1947 scientists at Bell Laboratories developed a device called the **transistor**. These devices worked much like tubes but with several advantages. For one, they were smaller. They also did not break as often as tubes did. The invention of transistors led to the improvement of all kinds of electronics, from radios to televisions. Transistors also made possible smaller and more efficient computers.

In 1951 the first computer available for commercial use hit the market. It was called the UNIVAC, short for universal automatic computer. The UNIVAC earned fame for predicting the outcome of the 1952 presidential election based on early returns.

Use of computers continued to expand in the 1950s. New computer makers, such as International Business Machines (IBM), entered the market. The computers were still large. (A complete UNIVAC system could weigh 30,000 pounds.) Even relatively inexpensive systems cost up to $50,000 or more. Nevertheless, large companies and government agencies purchased computers. By the end of the decade, for example, banks were using computers to help process checks.

Meanwhile, computer technology continued to improve. In 1958 scientists developed the **integrated circuit**, a single piece of material that includes a number of transistors and other electronic components. Also known as computer chips, integrated circuits made possible the dizzying advancement of computer technology in the years ahead.

Linking to Today

The Computer Revolution

The first general-purpose electronic computer was developed in the 1940s. The Electronic Numerical Integrator and Computer (ENIAC) was about 80 feet long, 8 feet high, and 2 feet deep.

New developments allowed more people to use computers. By the 1980s, Apple Computer had popularized tools such as the mouse, and Compaq had developed a portable computer that weighed 28 pounds.

Today, laptop computers weigh just a few pounds and do not require wires. Powerful computing devices fit in the palm of your hand.

Drawing Conclusions Why was ENIAC not useful to most people?

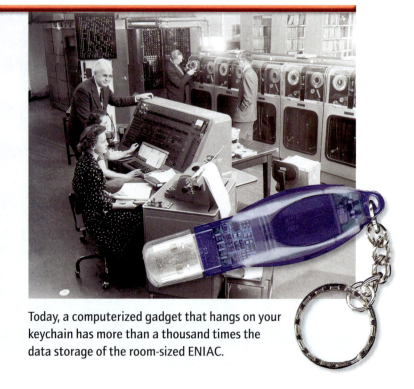

Today, a computerized gadget that hangs on your keychain has more than a thousand times the data storage of the room-sized ENIAC.

The Salk vaccine Earlier in this book, you read about Franklin D. Roosevelt and his bout with polio. The disease left him without the use of his legs. Another common effect of polio, which often struck children, was an impaired ability to breathe. Many victims died.

Polio was a contagious disease. Outbreaks were all too common in the early 1900s. When polio hit, it spread quickly. For weeks at a time, parents would keep their children out of school or other public places.

The worst year on record for polio in the United States came in 1952. More than 57,000 people came down with the dreaded disease. That year, scientist **Jonas Salk** developed a new polio vaccine. A **vaccine** is a preparation that uses a killed or weakened form of a germ to help the body build defenses against that germ. Vaccines are often given by injection.

The public announcement of the discovery of the polio vaccine came in 1955, and Salk became a hero. Children began receiving the shot, and the number of polio cases plunged.

READING CHECK **Summarizing** What were two major technological developments of the 1950s?

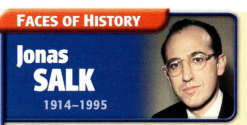

FACES OF HISTORY
Jonas SALK
1914–1995

Jonas Salk dedicated his career to fighting diseases that kill and maim people. After helping develop a vaccine for influenza for the Army during World War II, Salk turned his attention to fighting polio.

Salk worked for eight years to develop a polio vaccine. Confident of success, he tested his vaccine on himself, his wife, and their three sons in 1952. None of them became ill. After further testing, Salk's polio vaccine began to be used for mass vaccinations nationwide.

Salk refused to patent the vaccine. He did not want to profit from it. Rather, he wanted it made available to as many people as possible. Salk later served as a spokesperson for vaccinations. In 1995 he announced a new search—for an HIV vaccine.

Draw Conclusions In what ways was Salk's commitment to ending polio truly heroic?

Cultural Change in the 1950s

The 1950s in the United States is often viewed as a time of peace and prosperity. For some, this was true. At the same time, though, the richness and variety of American life formed a more complicated picture.

Boom times The threats of nuclear war and the spread of communism did cause unease for millions of Americans. At the same time, many people took comfort in the nation's stunning economic success. Indeed, in the 1950s the United States had clearly emerged as the world's greatest economic power. The American people made up just 6 percent of the world's population. Yet American workers and farmers produced about one-third of the world's goods and services.

As you have read, the years after World War II saw a sharp increase in birthrates—a baby boom. The baby boom continued throughout the 1950s. To house these growing families, builders such as Bill and Alfred Levitt created whole new communities of individual houses. (See the History Close-Up on the next page.)

New homes were filled with new stoves, refrigerators, and washing machines. New TVs ran ads urging people to want and buy even more.

Americans also purchased automobiles by the millions. To help fuel the desire of consumers, carmakers revised the styling of cars regularly. All this buying meant busy factories and high company profits. This, in turn, meant plentiful jobs. Employment was generally high in the 1950s. Wages rose steadily.

Indeed, a leading economist of the time, John Kenneth Galbraith, used the term "affluent society" to describe America in the postwar years. Yet Galbraith's view of the United States was not a positive one. In fact, he criticized an America overly focused on its own wealth.

ACADEMIC VOCABULARY
revise changing or modifying

HISTORY'S VOICES

"The family which takes its . . . air-conditioned, power-steered, and power-braked automobile out for a tour passes through cities that are badly paved, made hideous by litter, blighted buildings, billboards, and posts for wires that should long since have been put underground."
—John Kenneth Galbraith, *The Affluent Society,* 1958

Another critic of the 1950s was Michael Harrington. His book *The Other America,* published in 1962, described the plight of the nation's poor. In his view, people living in poverty had been forgotten amid the economic success of the 1950s.

Daily Life
The postwar baby boom is having a huge effect on society today, as this large population is entering retirement. Health care costs are expected to rise as the "boomers" age and require more services.

Still another critic of the 1950s was William H. Whyte. In his book *The Organization Man*, he observed the push toward "sameness" and the increasing loss of individuality among the growing class of business workers.

New communities Many new homes built in the 1950s were parts of new suburban developments. The most famous of these was the enormous Levittown, New York, started in 1947 by Bill and Alfred Levitt.

The key to the success of Levittown and the many similar communities built in the postwar years was affordability: A family could purchase a single-family home at a reasonable price, often financed with the help of the government under the terms of the GI Bill.

Levittown was not a diverse community. Like many builders at the time, the Levitts at first refused to sell to African Americans.

The Levitts later built other communities in New Jersey and Pennsylvania. Overall, however, the U.S. population was beginning a shift in settlement toward the warmer southern and western portions of the United States, the so-called Sunbelt. In the 1950s the wide availability of home air conditioning helped make this move practical. This population shift has continued to the present.

California was (and still is) a major Sunbelt destination. At the start of the 1950s, just over 10.5 million people called California home. Over the next 10 years, more than 5 million people moved to the state.

Northern population centers such as New York and Illinois grew much more slowly. The shift from the North to the South and West was dramatized in the late 1950s when two New York baseball teams, the Brooklyn Dodgers and New York Giants, moved to California.

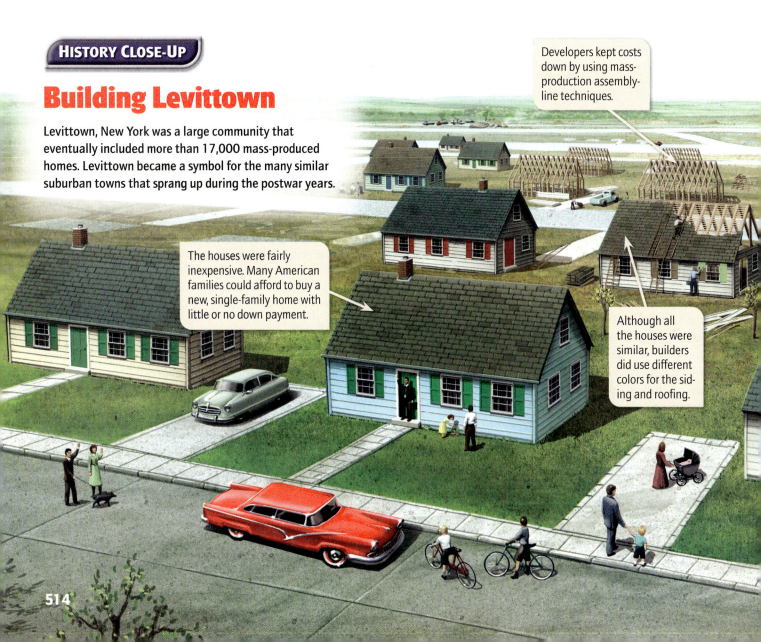

HISTORY CLOSE-UP

Building Levittown

Levittown, New York was a large community that eventually included more than 17,000 mass-produced homes. Levittown became a symbol for the many similar suburban towns that sprang up during the postwar years.

The houses were fairly inexpensive. Many American families could afford to buy a new, single-family home with little or no down payment.

Developers kept costs down by using mass-production assembly-line techniques.

Although all the houses were similar, builders did use different colors for the siding and roofing.

New highways During the 1950s the United States launched an ambitious building project: the **Interstate Highway System**. This system was designed to be a network of high-speed roads for interstate travel, all built on the same design.

President Eisenhower had long favored such a system. In 1956 Congress finally approved funding for a planned 40,000-mile system. With its construction, the United States reinforced its commitment to cars and trucks as its main means of ground transportation.

The art of rebellion Interestingly, the arts of the 1950s often stressed rebellion against sameness and conformity. Film stars such as Marlon Brando and James Dean built images as rebels who defied social norms. Jack Kerouac and other writers of the Beat generation also took the position of outsiders. They borrowed language from African American jazz music and rejected many social norms.

In popular music, rock and roll represented the rebellion of young people. Early stars such as Elvis Presley shocked many older Americans with his on-stage behavior. (Rock and roll was also influenced by African American musical forms, including jazz and rhythm and blues.)

If America seemed fascinated with the image of the rebel, it was mainly a male image. Women in film and literature tended to fill more traditional roles. It would be several years before women began to make their rebellion from the limits of American cultural norms.

READING CHECK **Summarizing** What were some key features of cultural change in the 1950s?

SECTION 3 ASSESSMENT

HSS 11.8.7

Reviewing Ideas, Terms, and People

1. **a. Recall** What was the significance of **Lucille Ball** and Milton Berle in the 1950s?
   b. Draw Conclusions Why do you think Richard Nixon used television as a means of persuading the public that he had done no wrong in 1952?

2. **a. Define** Write a brief definition of each of the following terms: transistor, integrated circuit, vaccine
   b. Make Inferences Why do you think the development of the computer was so important in spite of the fact that only large companies could afford computers in the 1950s?

3. **a. Identify** What was the significance of **Levittown** and the **Sunbelt** in the 1950s?
   b. Contrast How did the concepts of the "affluent society" and the "other America" relate to the general prosperity of the 1950s?

Critical Thinking

4. **Identifying the Main Idea** Copy the chart below and use information from the section to record details that support the main idea of the section.

American life in the 1950s

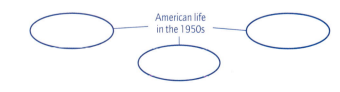 ELA W1.1

5. **Descriptive** Assume the point of view of a citizen of the United States in the 1950s. Write a letter to a friend in another country describing the changing life and culture in your country.

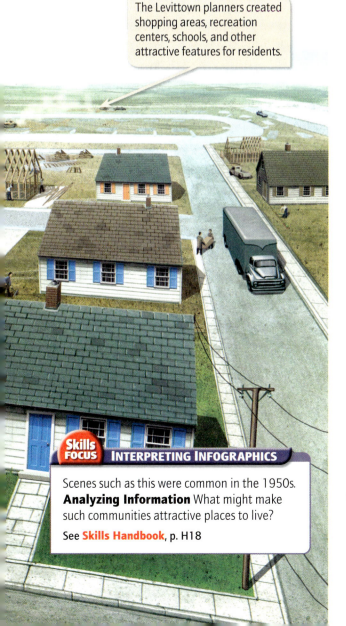

The Levittown planners created shopping areas, recreation centers, schools, and other attractive features for residents.

INTERPRETING INFOGRAPHICS

Scenes such as this were common in the 1950s.
Analyzing Information What might make such communities attractive places to live?

See **Skills Handbook**, p. H18

CHAPTER 16 DOCUMENT-BASED INVESTIGATION

Perspectives on Interstate Highways

HSS 11.8.7

Historical Context The documents below provide information on the impact of the Interstate Highway System.

Task Examine the documents and answer the questions that follow. Then you will be asked to write an essay about the impact of the Interstate Highway System, using facts from the documents and from the chapter to support the position you take in your thesis statement.

DOCUMENT 1

The Interstate Highway System was developed in response to public pressure to improve the nation's roads. In this excerpt from a speech given to Congress on February 22, 1955, President Eisenhower discusses the importance of U.S. highways.

> "Our unity as a nation is sustained by free communication of thought and by easy transportation of people and goods. The ceaseless flow of information throughout the Republic is matched by individual and commercial movement over a vast system of interconnected highways criss-crossing the Country and joining at our national borders with friendly neighbors to the north and south.
>
> Together, the uniting forces of our communication and transportation systems are dynamic elements in the very name we bear—United States. Without them, we would be a mere alliance of many separate parts.
>
> The Nation's highway system is a gigantic enterprise, one of our largest items of capital investment. Generations have gone into its building.... One in every seven Americans gains his livelihood and supports his family out of it. But, in large part, the network is inadequate for the nation's growing needs....
>
> To correct these deficiencies is an obligation of Government at every level. The highway system is a public enterprise. As the owner and operator, the various levels of Government have a responsibility for management that promotes the economy of the nation and properly serves the individual user."

DOCUMENT 2

Within a few short years of the creation of the Interstate Highway System, trucks replaced railroads as the major means of freight transportation. These charts show how the amount of available railroad and highway transportation changed within 50 years.

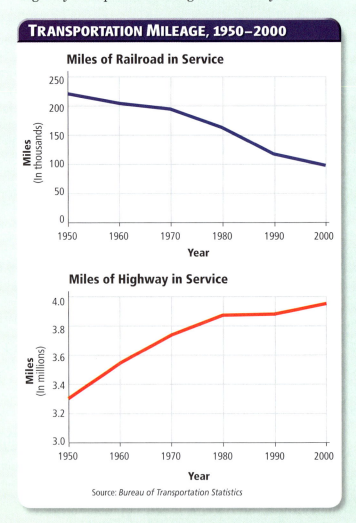

TRANSPORTATION MILEAGE, 1950–2000

Source: Bureau of Transportation Statistics

516 CHAPTER 16

DOCUMENT 3

Even with the expansion of air travel, driving by car is still the preferred means of getting around today. People routinely drive to destinations hundreds of miles away. In the year 2000 alone, domestic travelers spent nearly $500 billion visiting other places in the United States. The maps below show how U.S. highways expanded between 1950 and 2000. The red lines indicate interstate highways. Green lines are other highways.

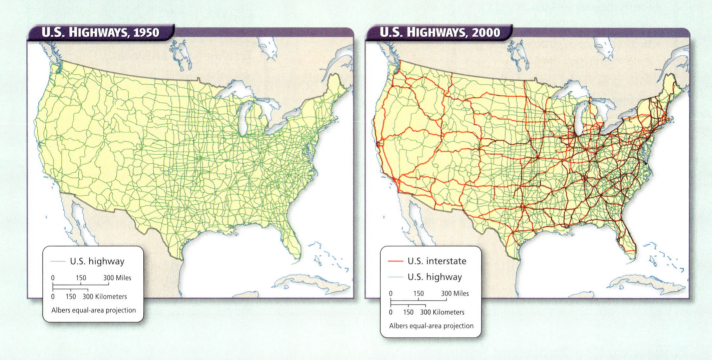

Skills Focus: READING LIKE A HISTORIAN

HSS Analysis CS1, CS3, HI1

1. **a. Identify** Refer to Document 1. What is Eisenhower's view of the highway system?
   b. Elaborate Why do you think Eisenhower thought it was the government's obligation to improve the highway system?

2. **a. Describe** Refer to Document 2. What happened to railroad and highway mileage during this period?
   b. Analyze What do you think were some of the reasons that highways came to replace railroads?

3. **a. Describe** Refer to Document 3. Where were most highways concentrated in 1950? in 2000?
   b. Elaborate What do you think a similar map of highways in 2050 will look like? Explain.

4. **Document-Based Essay Question** Consider the question below and form a thesis statement. Using examples from Documents 1, 2, and 3, create an outline and write a short essay supporting your position. How did the expansion of highways affect the United States?

See **Skills Handbook**, pp. H17, H20, H28–H29

POSTWAR AMERICA 517

CHAPTER 16
Chapter Review

Visual Summary: Postwar America

Arms race anxiety
- Soviets and Americans engage in an arms race.
- Foreign policies are built around the threat of nuclear weapons.
- New technologies emerge, including massive hydrogen bombs.
- Public prepares for worst.

The United States in the 1950s

Eisenhower's presidency
- Ike is elected in 1952 and 1956.
- His presidency is heavily focused on Cold War issues.
- "Hot spots" include Eastern Europe, Southeast Asia, and the Middle East.

Television and cultural change
- Television arrives in full force.
- Scientific advances, such as vaccines, change Americans' lives.
- Population grows and moves.

Reviewing Key Terms and People

For each of the following questions, choose the letter that corresponds to the best available answer.

1. Following the launch of *Sputnik*, the U.S. government established which of the following?
   a. SEATO
   b. NASA
   c. ICBM
   d. CIA

2. Brinkmanship and massive retaliation are both associated with which person?
   a. John Foster Dulles
   b. Jonas Salk
   c. Nikita Khrushchev
   d. Richard M. Nixon

3. This weapon raised the stakes in the conflict between the United States and the Soviet Union in the Cold War.
   a. integrated circuit
   b. transistor
   c. *Sputnik*
   d. H-bomb

4. Which of the following was under the influence of the Soviet Union?
   a. SEATO
   b. Warsaw Pact
   c. CIA
   d. Interstate Highway System

5. Which term represents the new suburban housing developments that appeared in the postwar years?
   a. Sunbelt
   b. Interstate Highway System
   c. Levittown
   d. integrated circuit

6. Jonas Salk is associated with which of these 1950s inventions?
   a. polio vaccine
   b. satellites
   c. transistor
   d. Sunbelt

518 CHAPTER 16

History's Impact video program
Review the video to answer the closing question: How did Americans' knowledge of other places change after the introduction of the television?

Comprehension and Critical Thinking

SECTION 1 (pp. 496–501) HSS 11.9.2, 11.9.3

7. **a. Identify** What is the significance of each of the following to the events described in this section? Hungary, Vietnam, Egypt

   b. Contrast How did Eisenhower claim to differ in his ideas about foreign policy compared with Truman?

   c. Evaluate Do you think that Eisenhower actually was different from Truman in the way that he claimed? Explain your answer.

SECTION 2 (pp. 502–508) HSS 11.9.3

8. **a. Describe** What was the arms race, and how did it evolve in the 1950s?

   b. Summarize How did the arms race in the 1950s change the concept of victory and defeat in war?

   c. Evaluate What were some effects of the government's efforts to educate people about how to respond to a nuclear attack? Why do you think people responded this way?

SECTION 3 (pp. 509–515) HSS 11.8.7

9. **a. Recall** What were some of the major technological advancements of the 1950s?

   b. Draw Conclusions How did the economic prosperity of the 1950s also present certain challenges to the country?

   c. Rank In your opinion, which was the most significant technological change of the 1950s in terms of its long-term impact on the nation? Explain your reasoning.

Using the Internet

go.hrw.com
Practice Online
Keyword: SE7 CH16

10. *I Love Lucy* and other programs captivated the attention of American television audiences during the 1950s. Some of those TV programs are still broadcast on cable and satellite channels today. Using the keyword above, do research to learn more about popular television programs of the 1950s. Then create a report that explains the appeal of those programs in the 1950s and why some of those programs remain popular among some audiences today. Refer to specific examples from your research.

Analyzing Primary Sources HSS HI1

Reading Like a Historian The photograph shows an example of a bomb shelter from the 1950s.

11. **Identify** Who do you think might be interested and able to buy and install a bomb shelter?

12. **Draw Conclusions** How long do you think someone could survive in the type of shelter shown here?

Critical Reading ELA R2.4

Read the passage from Section 1 under the heading "Cold War 'Hot Spots.'" Then answer the following question.

13. According to this passage, Eisenhower believed that

    A it would be foolish to fight over communism in Vietnam.

    B it was necessary to fight over communism in Vietnam.

    C the French had failed to hold the line against Communist aggression.

    D the United States would be better off waiting to see what happened in Vietnam and then reacting.

WRITING FOR THE SAT ELA W2.4

Think about the following issue:

In Vietnam, following the departure of the French, it appeared that a truly free election might lead to the election of a Communist regime that was friendly with the Soviet Union.

14. **Assignment** Was the United States correct to support the creation of an anti-Communist South Vietnam? Write a short essay in which you develop your position on this issue. Support your point of view with reasoning and examples from your reading and studies.

POSTWAR AMERICA **519**

UNIT 4 IN BRIEF

Below is a chapter-by-chapter summary of the main ideas covered in Unit 4.

CHAPTER 13: World War II Erupts
1939–1941

MAIN IDEA After World War I, unsettled conditions in Europe and beyond led to the rise of ruthless dictators. One of these leaders, Germany's Adolf Hitler, led Europe into another great war in 1939. The United States was eventually drawn into World War II after being attacked by Germany's ally, Japan.

SECTION 1 The Treaty of Versailles helped create conditions for the rise of powerful dictators.

SECTION 2 Appeasement failed to stop Hitler's aggression. On September 1, 1939, Germany invaded Poland, starting World War II. Within a year, only Great Britain stood between Hitler and control of Europe.

SECTION 3 As tensions grew in Europe and Asia in the 1930s, President Roosevelt slowly overcame isolationist feeling in the United States. That feeling was shattered completely with Japan's attack on Pearl Harbot on December 7, 1941.

SECTION 4 The United States mobilized its military forces and its industries to fight World War II. The effort changed the nation and gave new opportunities to women and minority groups.

CHAPTER 14: The United States in World War II
1941–1945

MAIN IDEA World War II was fought in two theaters. Hard fighting by the Allies brought victory first in Europe and then in the Pacific.

SECTION 1 With American entry into the war, the Allies focused first on Europe. As the Soviets fought desperately on their home soil, the rest of the Allies invaded North Africa and then, on D-Day, France.

SECTION 2 Adolf Hitler pursued first the persecution of Jews and then their systematic destruction. The resulting Holocaust claimed 6 million innocent lives.

SECTION 3 After early losses, the Allies won a key victory in the Battle of Midway. This was followed by a series of hard-fought victories, including battles at Iwo Jima and Okinawa.

SECTION 4 Americans at home worked hard to support the war. The attack on Pearl Harbor led the government to intern thousands of innocent Japanese Americans.

SECTION 5 By late 1944, the Germans were under pressure from both east and west by the Allies. They finally surrendered in May 1945. Meanwhile, the Japanese only surrendered after the Americans dropped two atomic weapons in early August 1945.

CHAPTER 15: The Cold War Begins
1945–1953

MAIN IDEA After World War II, the United States took its place as a world leader and an adversary of the Soviet Union in the Cold War.

SECTION 1 Tensions between the United States and the Soviet Union that had simmered during the war rose to the surface in the post-war years, resulting in the start of the Cold War.

SECTION 2 The United States helped its own people adjust to the return of peacetime with the GI Bill. It also helped lead the rest of the world toward a more peaceful future through the creation of the United Nations.

SECTION 3 A Communist takeover of China and the Soviet acquisition of an atomic bomb led to a Second Red Scare, headed by Senator Joseph McCarthy.

SECTION 4 Cold War tensions led to war in Korea, as the United States and its United Nations allies took a stand against Communist aggression.

CHAPTER 16: Postwar America
1945–1960

MAIN IDEA In the 1950s, Cold War conflict and a nuclear arms race worried many Americans, who nevertheless found diversion in television and other new ways of living.

SECTION 1 Dwight D. Eisenhower became president in 1952 and helped bring about a tough approach toward communism.

SECTION 2 The development of the hydrogen bomb and the growing arms race between the United States and the Soviet Union created great anxiety for many people in the United States.

SECTION 3 The introduction of the television and other new technologies led to significant changes in the way of life of many Americans.

UNIT 5
A Nation Facing Challenges

1954–1975

Chapter 17
The New Frontier and the Great Society
1961–1969

Chapter 18
The Civil Rights Movement
1954–1975

Chapter 19
The Vietnam War
1954–1975

Chapter 20
A Time of Social Change
1963–1975

Themes

Government and Democracy
Government enacted social and economic welfare programs, such as poverty relief, conservation, and urban renewal.

Rights and Responsibilities
Citizens called for racial equality for African Americans and other minorities, equality for women, and social and political reforms.

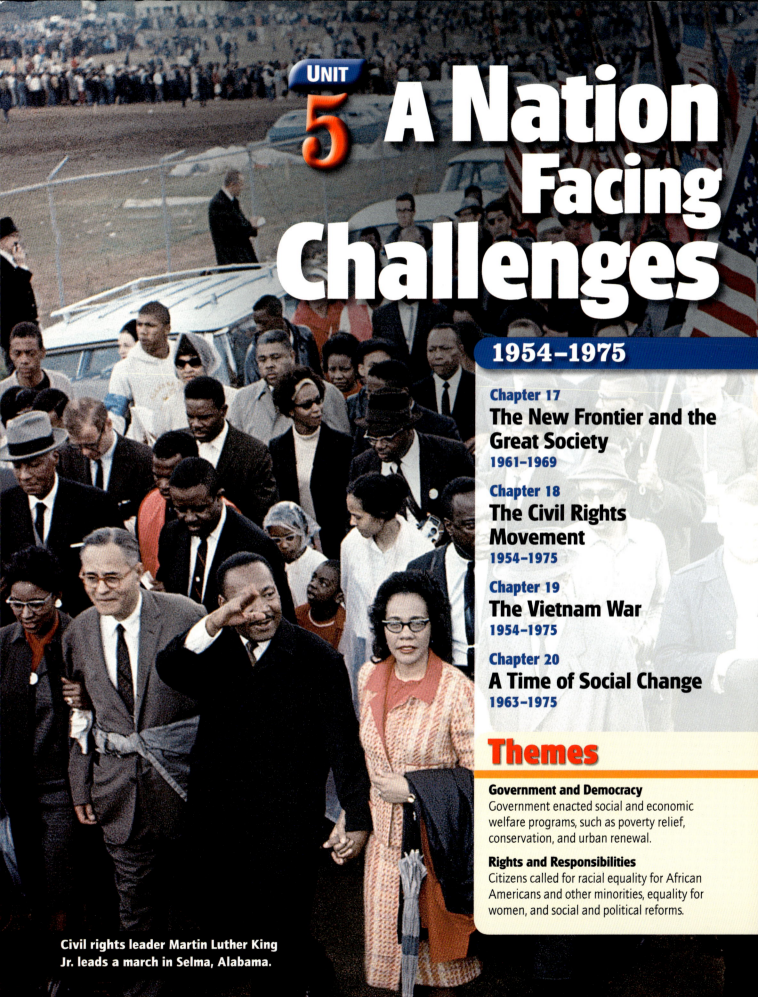

Civil rights leader Martin Luther King Jr. leads a march in Selma, Alabama.

Prepare to Read

Making Generalizations

Find practice for **Making Generalizations** in the **Skills Handbook,** p. H13

A generalization is a broad statement that tells how different examples are similar in some way. Experienced readers make generalizations that enable them to understand and remember what they are reading.

Before You Read
Read the headings to determine what the passage will be about. Then make a mental list of what you already know about the subject matter.

While You Read
List facts from the passage. How do they compare with your prior knowledge of the subject matter?

After You Read
Use your prior knowledge and facts from the reading to make a generalization about what the passage means to you.

Kennedy's Media Strategy

Presidents before and after Kennedy have been masters of the media. Franklin Delano Roosevelt used his radio "fireside chats" to inspire the nation during the Great Depression and World War II. Ronald Reagan, an experienced radio, television, and film actor, became known as the Great Communicator for his skill in conveying his messages directly to the voters. But Kennedy was the first president to consciously use access to the media as part of his strategy for governing the nation.

The passage mentions more than one president.

Image and reality Photographs of the president often showed him engaged in athletic activities like sailing, swimming, or playing touch football. Kennedy understood how such pictures would shape his image and boost his appeal. Like Roosevelt, he understood that images showing him in less-than-top physical shape might lessen the country's confidence in his abilities. In reality, Kennedy struggled with health problems most of his life. He suffered from Addison's disease, a sometimes fatal condition. A bad back kept him in nearly constant pain.

Kennedy and Roosevelt both tried to convey images of strength.

READING CHECK Making Generalizations
How is an effective use of the media important to presidents?

Test Prep Tip

Some tests may ask you to make generalizations from a given reading passage. Look for clue words such as *all, everyone, many, most, few, generally, never, often, always,* and *usually* that indicate generalizations. Then make sure that the facts in the passage support the entire generalization.

History's Impact video program
Watch the video to understand the impact of space technology.

November 1963 President Kennedy is assassinated. Lyndon B. Johnson becomes president.

July 1964 Congress passes Civil Rights Act of 1964.

July 1965 Congress funds Medicaid and Medicare.

January 1968 U.S. Navy spy ship *Pueblo* is captured by North Korea.

October 1964 Khrushchev is forced to resign as Soviet leader.

January 1966 Indira Gandhi becomes India's first woman prime minister.

August 1968 Soviet army crushes revolt in Czechoslovakia.

SECTION 1
Kennedy and the Cold War

BEFORE YOU READ

MAIN IDEA
President Kennedy continued the Cold War policy of resisting the spread of communism by offering help to other nations and threatening to use force if necessary.

READING FOCUS
1. In what ways did Kennedy's election as president suggest change?
2. Why did the Bay of Pigs invasion take place, and with what results?
3. Why did the Berlin crisis develop, and what was its outcome?
4. What caused the Cuban missile crisis, and how was war avoided?
5. How did Kennedy's foreign policy reflect his view of the world?

KEY TERMS AND PEOPLE
John F. Kennedy
Robert Kennedy
Fidel Castro
Bay of Pigs invasion
Lyndon B. Johnson
Cuban missile crisis
Peace Corps
Alliance for Progress
flexible response

HSS 11.9.3 Trace the origins and geopolitical consequences (foreign and domestic) of the Cold War and containment policy, including the following:
• The Bay of Pigs invasion and the Cuban Missile Crisis
HSS 11.11.2 Discuss the significant domestic policy speeches of Truman, Eisenhower, Kennedy, Johnson, Nixon, Carter, Reagan, Bush, and Clinton (e.g., with regard to education, civil rights, economic policy, environmental policy).

The Great Debates

How does television shape public opinion? On September 26, 1960, some 70 million Americans watched Vice President Richard Nixon and Senator John Kennedy in the first televised presidential debate. Nixon was just two weeks out of the hospital. During that time he had covered 15,000 miles, campaigning in 25 states. He had lost so much weight that his shirt collar sagged around his neck. On the day of the debate, he pored over his notes until just before air time.

Kennedy had a leisurely dinner and took a nap before the debate. Still tan from several days of campaigning in sunny California, he refused the traditional TV makeup. Nixon refused makeup too. In his gray suit, Nixon looked pale, ill, and tired. Kennedy's dark suit and deep tan added to his rested and fit appearance.

The hour-long debate was broadcast on both radio and television. Radio listeners thought Nixon narrowly won, while those watching on television gave Kennedy the edge. For days afterward, huge crowds turned out at campaign rallies to see the handsome candidate in the flesh. In contrast, Nixon's staff reassured his supporters that "Mr. Nixon is in excellent health and looks good in person."

Three more debates took place. Although some reporters at the time called them the Great Debates, the Kennedy-Nixon debates probably did not change the outcome of the 1960 election. They did increase the average American's interest in politics, however. The debates also set the standard for modern election campaigns. Voters today expect candidates for office at practically every level to appear in televised debates.

◀ Kennedy's appearance gave him great appeal to a television audience.

Kennedy Becomes President

The personal contrasts between **John F. Kennedy** and Richard Nixon were far greater than their political differences in the 1960 presidential campaign. Kennedy was born into a wealthy and politically powerful Massachusetts family, while Nixon was a self-made "common man" from a small town in southern California.

Although the two men were about the same age, Kennedy's movie-star good looks made him appear much younger. During their four television debates, he spoke with ease and authority. To many Americans, the 43-year-old senator represented America's future. Nixon's ties to the 70-year-old Eisenhower made him seem a part of America's past.

The election of 1960
Kennedy emphasized this contrast by adopting the term "new frontier" for his campaign. "There are new frontiers for America to conquer," he declared, "not frontiers on a map, but frontiers of the mind, the will, and the spirit of man."

During the election campaign, Kennedy played on the nation's Cold War fears by claiming the United States had fallen behind the Soviet Union in the development of nuclear missiles. He also claimed that the prosperity of the 1950s was not reaching the poor. "Seventeen million Americans go to bed hungry at night," Kennedy charged. Vice President Nixon defended President Eisenhower's record, which made him appear opposed to new ideas.

Despite Kennedy's personal appeal, some Protestant voters were concerned because he was a Roman Catholic. They feared that Kennedy might put the views of the Catholic Church over those of the American public. The election of 1960 was one of the closest in American history. Fewer than 120,000 votes separated the two candidates out of nearly 69 million ballots cast.

Kennedy's victory by a 303–219 margin in the electoral college was more comfortable. He became the youngest person and the first Catholic elected president. Fifteen southern electors, however, cast their ballots for Virginia's Democratic senator Harry Byrd, who was not even a candidate. This weakness in Kennedy's southern support coupled with his narrow victory in the popular vote would later cause problems for his presidency.

One incident in October might have helped Kennedy's election campaign. Civil rights leader Martin Luther King Jr. was arrested in Georgia during a protest. Kennedy telephoned King's wife, Coretta, to express his concern. **Robert Kennedy**, the candidate's brother, persuaded the judge to release King on bail.

King's father told the press he had planned to vote for Nixon but that Kennedy's call to his daughter-in-law had changed his mind. The Kennedy campaign printed 2 million leaflets that told the story of this incident. The leaflets were passed out in African American churches the Sunday before election day.

Kennedy takes office
Kennedy's inaugural address focused on his theme of change. It also took a strong anti-Communist tone.

HISTORY'S VOICES
" Let the word go forth from this time and place, to friend and foe alike, that the torch has been passed to a new generation of Americans—born in this century, tempered by war, disciplined by a hard and bitter peace . . . Let every nation know, whether it wishes us well or ill, that we shall pay any price, bear any burden, meet any hardship, support any friend, oppose any foe, in order to assure the survival and the success of liberty. "
—John F. Kennedy, Inaugural Address, January 20, 1961

ACADEMIC VOCABULARY
authority firm self-assurance

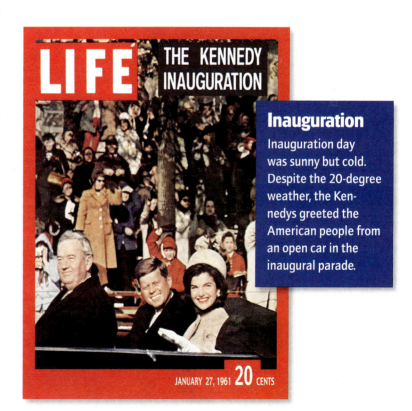

Inauguration
Inauguration day was sunny but cold. Despite the 20-degree weather, the Kennedys greeted the American people from an open car in the inaugural parade.

In his inaugural address, Kennedy did not specify his policy goals at home because so much division existed over domestic issues. However, he made accomplishing domestic goals a top priority. "If we are to regain . . . leadership on our domestic problems, it must be presidential leadership," he maintained.

To advance his programs, Kennedy gathered a group of advisers that some people called "the best and the brightest." National Security Adviser McGeorge Bundy had been a dean at Harvard University. Special Assistant Arthur Schlesinger had taught history there. Another adviser was a professor at Massachusetts Institute of Technology (MIT).

Most of Kennedy's advisers were young like he was—some were still in their 30s. Ted Sorensen, who helped develop domestic policies and programs, was just 32 years old. Kennedy called Sorensen his "intellectual blood bank." But no one was closer to the president than his own brother, Robert ("Bobby") Kennedy. He included his 36-year-old brother in his cabinet by making him attorney general.

Except for Bobby, cabinet members had less influence on President Kennedy than did his White House advisers. In foreign affairs, for example, Kennedy relied more on National Security Adviser Bundy than on Secretary of State Dean Rusk or Secretary of Defense Robert McNamara. Kennedy also held cabinet meetings less often than Eisenhower did—only once a month unless Kennedy cancelled the meeting. At an average age of 47, President Kennedy's cabinet was relatively young. Its members averaged 10 years younger than President Eisenhower's.

READING CHECK **Contrasting** How did Kennedy differ from Eisenhower as president?

The Bay of Pigs Invasion

Kennedy would soon need Rusk and McNamara's advice as well as that of Bundy. During the 1960 campaign, Kennedy learned that the Central Intelligence Agency (CIA) was secretly training about 1,500 Cuban exiles in Central America in order to invade Cuba. Many of the trainees were Cuban Americans the CIA had recruited in south Florida. President Eisenhower had authorized the project in the hope of overthrowing Cuba's dictator **Fidel Castro**.

Background to the invasion
Fidel Castro came to power in Cuba in 1959 after a two-year guerrilla war against Fulgencio Batista, the U.S.-backed dictator of Cuba. As Castro's followers increased in number, his tactics grew bolder. When his rebel force marched on Havana, Cuba's capital city, Batista fled the country. On January 8, 1959, Castro entered Havana and declared victory.

During his revolt, Castro gained the support of many Cubans by promising to restore people's rights and freedoms. Once in power, however, he

Communist Neighbor
Fidel Castro established the first Communist nation in the Western Hemisphere. He railed against the United States in speeches and forged ties between Cuba and the Soviet Union. *Why did the U.S. government find Castro's actions so alarming?*

followed a more radical course. His government seized private businesses, including American companies on the island. In addition, Castro began making anti-American speeches. U.S.-Cuban relations were further strained when Castro signed a trade agreement with the Soviet Union in February 1960. Eisenhower responded by cutting off American economic and diplomatic ties with Cuba.

The invasion of Cuba The CIA believed an invasion of Cuba would inspire its people to rise up against Castro. Eisenhower doubted this prediction, but he let planning continue to keep all options open. Besides, he knew that the new president would have to make the decision whether to approve an invasion.

Kennedy asked his advisers about the plan to invade Cuba. Opinions were mixed. Schlesinger was openly and strongly opposed. "You would dissipate [lose] all the extraordinary good will . . . toward the new administration throughout the world," he warned.

The president was in a bind. He considered Castro's communism a threat to all of Latin America. In fact, Kennedy had attacked Eisenhower during the campaign for not taking stronger action against Castro. He felt that he could not back down now. When the CIA assured Kennedy that the invasion would succeed, he gave the go-ahead.

The **Bay of Pigs invasion** was a disaster. The *New York Times* reported the plan a week before the invasion began. Kennedy publicly denied the story. Then on April 15, 1961, an air strike by old, unmarked U.S. bombers flown from Nicaragua by Cuban exiles failed to destroy Cuba's air force. Even worse, a bomber damaged in the attack landed at Key West, Florida, instead of returning to Nicaragua. With the U.S. connection now exposed, Kennedy cancelled additional air strikes on Cuba that had been planned for April 16 and 17.

The land invasion on April 17 had little chance of success. Warned by the air attack, Castro was prepared. When the force of Cuban exiles came ashore at the Bay of Pigs, Castro's troops rushed to the scene. Pinned down at their landing site, the invaders fought for nearly three days.

Former vice president Nixon and others urged Kennedy to send U.S. troops to Cuba to rescue the invasion force and overthrow

Skills Focus — READING LIKE A HISTORIAN

Interpreting Visuals What comment is the cartoonist making on Kennedy's dealings with Cuba? What specific incident do you think the cartoon is referencing?

Castro. Concerned about how such a response might affect U.S.-Soviet relations, the president rejected this advice.

Poor planning and the lack of U.S. air cover had doomed the Bay of Pigs invasion to failure. Also, the CIA had greatly underestimated Castro's support. The expected anti-Castro uprising in Cuba never took place. The nearly 1,200 surviving invaders were captured and put in prison. In December 1962 Kennedy obtained their release in return for $52 million in food and medical aid to Cuba.

Instead of eliminating the threat of communism so close to the United States, the Bay of Pigs incident actually strengthened Castro's ties to the Soviet Union. Increasingly, he looked to the Soviets for protection from the United States. Soviet leader Nikita Khrushchev welcomed the closer relations. "We shall render [the] Cuban government all necessary assistance," he declared.

READING CHECK Drawing Conclusions Why did Kennedy decide to go ahead with the CIA's plan to invade Cuba?

The Berlin Crisis

One reason Kennedy rejected sending U.S. forces into Cuba was that he feared it would cause Khrushchev to retaliate in Europe. Khrushchev, however, interpreted Kennedy's failure to intervene in Cuba as a sign of weakness. It encouraged Khrushchev to press the United States in Berlin.

The Vienna conference Kennedy invited Khrushchev to meet with him in Vienna, Austria, in June 1961. The president hoped to ease tensions with the Soviet Union. Instead, Khrushchev demanded that the United States and its allies recognize Communist East Germany as an independent nation. He also demanded that the United States withdraw from West Berlin.

Khrushchev said he would sign a treaty with East Germany in December if these demands were not met. He warned that East Germany could then decide for itself what to do about Berlin. Kennedy would not be bullied.

Berlin's significance Berlin had long been a problem for the Soviet Union. The western half of the city was an island of freedom surrounded by East Germany. In the first half of 1961 alone, about 200,000 East Germans escaped communism by slipping past guards to safety in West Berlin.

Some of Kennedy's advisers were concerned that East Germany might use force to gain control of West Berlin. All agreed that Khrushchev was using Berlin to test America's will in Europe and that any action East Germany took would have the approval and backing of the Soviet Union.

Determined to meet the Soviet test, Kennedy acted to show America's strength and resolve. He called reserve troops to active duty, launched a program to build shelters in the United States against nuclear attack, and began a troop buildup in West Germany. Khrushchev responded by threatening to mobilize troops. Realizing how dangerous the situation had become, Kennedy waited for the Soviet leader to make the next move.

The Berlin Wall Khrushchev's response came on August 13, 1961, when Communist forces closed the crossing points between East and West Berlin. Within hours, some 25,000 East German soldiers were in place to guard a hastily erected barbed wire barrier around West Berlin. The temporary fencing was soon replaced with a high concrete wall, to block further escapes to freedom.

Kennedy responded to the construction of the Berlin Wall by sending 1,500 troops from West Germany to West Berlin. Vice President **Lyndon B. Johnson** visited West Berlin to reassure its people that America would not abandon them. Kennedy, however, was relieved. He believed that Khrushchev would now not attempt to seize West Berlin. "A wall is a . . . lot better than a war," he concluded.

The Berlin Wall divided families, neighborhoods, streets, and even cemeteries. As time passed it was extended and fortified. The concrete sections eventually spanned most of the nearly 100 miles around West Berlin. Trenches were dug to keep vehicles from crashing though the wall. The East Germans later built a second wall parallel to the first one. The corridor between the two walls was patrolled by soldiers and attack dogs.

Nearly two years after the crisis was past, Kennedy went to West Berlin to renew his commitment to the city. At an outdoor rally near the Berlin Wall, he gave one of the greatest speeches of his presidency—his *"Ich bin ein Berliner"* ("I am a Berliner") speech. Speaking in English, he noted the wall's importance as a symbol of the failures of communism.

HISTORY'S VOICES

❝There are many people in the world who really don't understand . . . the great issue between the free world and the communist world. Let them come to Berlin. There are some who say that communism is the wave of the future. Let them come to Berlin. And there are some who say in Europe and elsewhere we can work with the communists. Let them come to Berlin.❞

—John F. Kennedy, June 26, 1963

As the huge crowd cheered wildly, Kennedy ended his speech by declaring, "All free men, wherever they may live, are citizens of Berlin, and, therefore, as a free man I take pride in the words 'Ich bin ein Berliner.'"

READING CHECK **Identifying Cause and Effect** Why was the Berlin Wall constructed?

ACADEMIC VOCABULARY
interpreted understood within the context of the circumstances

GEOGRAPHY SKILLS INTERPRETING MAPS
1. About how many miles is Cuba from the United States?
2. What was the extent of the U.S. blockade?

See **Skills Handbook**, p. H20

The Cuban Missile Crisis

Khrushchev's continued testing of Kennedy's resolve led to the Cold War's most dangerous crisis. For several days in October 1962, the United States and the Soviet Union teetered on the brink of nuclear war as Kennedy sought a peaceful solution to the **Cuban missile crisis**.

Buildup to the crisis The origins of the Cuban missile crisis can be found in the policies and politics of both the United States and the Soviet Union. U.S. actions in the Bay of Pigs and Berlin crises encouraged hard-line leaders in the Soviet Union. They pushed Khrushchev to be more aggressive.

Some Americans continued to call for an invasion of Cuba after the Bay of Pigs. This concerned Khrushchev because he had pledged to defend Cuba. The Soviets were also concerned about nuclear missiles the United States had placed in Turkey. Khrushchev thought this threat on the Soviet Union's southwestern border justified putting similar missiles near the southern border of the United States.

Kennedy faced similar pressures. Some American politicians blamed him for the Bay of Pigs disaster and accused him of being "soft on communism." Republicans announced that Cuba would be their main issue in the 1962 congressional election campaign. Khrushchev decided to upgrade Cuba's defenses with antiaircraft weapons called surface-to-air missiles (SAMs). He also convinced Castro to allow the secret installation of offensive nuclear missiles that would be controlled by the Soviet Union.

The crisis begins Republicans' pressure on Kennedy increased as Khrushchev pumped aid into Cuba. Kennedy responded by ordering U-2 spy-plane flights over the island. On August 29, 1962, one of these flights detected the SAMs.

The Soviets pointed out that the SAMs were defensive missiles. They denied charges they were placing offensive missiles in Cuba. Kennedy reported the Soviets' denial to the nation, warning that if it proved untrue, "the gravest issues would arise." Moscow replied that a U.S. attack on Cuba would mean war.

At a Cabinet briefing during the Cuban missile crisis, President Kennedy marked this map of Cuba with a series of X marks, the words *missile sites,* and a black arrow to show locations of Soviet activity as photographed by U-2 spy planes.

As administration officials continued to assure the American people, the spy flights continued. Then on October 14, photos taken from a U-2 plane provided the first solid evidence that the Soviets had lied.

Managing the crisis Kennedy assembled a group of advisers, known as the Ex Comm, to help him decide on a response. He usually did not attend the Ex Comm's daily meetings. He wanted to follow his normal schedule until he was ready to reveal what he knew to the Soviets and to the American people.

Ex Comm's military members favored an air strike against the missile sites, perhaps followed by an invasion of Cuba. Secretary of Defense McNamara and Robert Kennedy argued for a naval blockade instead. Like an air strike, the blockade would be an act of war, but it seemed less likely to provoke a missile launch from Cuba or the Soviet Union. A blockade would also give the Soviets the chance to avoid war by removing the missiles themselves. The president agreed with this reasoning.

On October 22, Kennedy went on television to tell Americans about the Soviet threat. He put U.S. forces on full alert. Some 550 bombers armed with nuclear weapons took to the air and 100,000 troops assembled in Georgia. He wanted to be prepared for war and to show Khrushchev the seriousness of the situation.

As the world nervously watched and waited, several Soviet ships carrying missile parts continued toward Cuba. Khrushchev warned that trying to stop them would mean war. Then on October 24, as they neared the U.S. blockade, they turned back.

Two days later, Kennedy received a letter from Khrushchev offering to remove the missiles if the United States pledged to never invade Cuba. The next day he received a tougher letter from Khrushchev demanding that the United States remove its missiles from Turkey. The Ex Comm advised Kennedy to ignore the second letter and accept the offer in the first letter. The president did so, and Khrushchev announced he would dismantle the missiles.

Effects of the crisis This incident is the closest the world has ever come to nuclear war. Kennedy and Khrushchev both took steps to ease tensions between their countries. In 1963 they set up a hotline to allow U.S. presidents and Soviet leaders to communicate directly in times of crisis. The United States, the Soviet Union, and Great Britain also signed the Limited Nuclear Test Ban Treaty to end the testing of nuclear weapons in the atmosphere and underwater.

 Drawing Inferences Why was the Cuban missile crisis such an important event?

THE IMPACT TODAY

Government

Kennedy's pledge that the United States would never invade Cuba caused many Cuban Americans to switch their support to the Republican Party. The Cuban American community remains strongly Republican today.

Kennedy's Foreign Policy

In a 1963 speech at American University in Washington, D.C., Kennedy answered those who criticized his foreign policy. He summarized the values he thought should guide America's relations with other nations.

HISTORY'S VOICES

> " What kind of peace do we seek? Not a [peace] enforced on the world by American weapons of war ... not merely peace for Americans but peace for all men and women ... For, in the final analysis, our most basic common link is that we all inhabit this small planet. We all breathe the same air. We all cherish our children's future. And we are all mortal. "
>
> —John F. Kennedy, June 10, 1963

Kennedy also tried to express these principles in his foreign policy through programs to help poorer nations. The **Peace Corps** was the most successful. This entity trained and sent volunteers to Africa, Asia, and Latin America to serve for two years as educators, health care workers, and agricultural advisers, or in other jobs that aided the host country's development. The Peace Corps encouraged women and African Americans to volunteer.

ACADEMIC VOCABULARY
entity something that has a separate and distinct existence

Most volunteers were young college graduates. They were instructed not to argue the merits of U.S. foreign policy and to respect the culture of their host country. The program increased goodwill toward the United States throughout the world.

Another of Kennedy's foreign-policy programs was the **Alliance for Progress**. It offered billions of dollars in aid to build schools, hospitals, roads, low-cost housing, and power plants in Latin America. The program was intended to counter communism's influence in the region. It never lived up to its hopes, partly because aid often went to anti-Communist dictators who had little support among their people.

In other areas Kennedy followed the Cold War policies of his predecessors. He continued the nuclear arms buildup begun by Eisenhower as well as Truman's practice of containment. He also developed the strategy of **flexible response**. This involved strengthening conventional American forces so the nation would have other options than nuclear weapons in times of crisis.

READING CHECK **Summarizing** How did the Peace Corps and the Alliance for Progress help other nations?

SECTION 1 ASSESSMENT

HSS 11.9.3, 11.11.2

go.hrw.com
Online Quiz
Keyword: SE7 HP17

Reviewing Ideas, Terms, and People

1. **a. Define** What did John F. Kennedy mean by the term "new frontier"?
   b. Analyze In what ways did Kennedy represent change to the American people?
   c. Elaborate How do you think Kennedy chose his advisers?

2. **a. Describe** Why were U.S.-Cuban relations strained when Kennedy took office?
   b. Make Inferences Why would a strong Soviet alliance with a Latin American nation make the United States uneasy?
   c. Predict Do you think the Bay of Pigs invasion could have been more successful? How?

3. **a. Identify** What demands did Khrushchev make at the conference in Vienna?
   b. Draw Conclusions Why was Kennedy relieved when he heard about the Berlin Wall?

4. **a. Recall** What was the immediate set of events that resulted in the Cuban missile crisis?
   b. Analyze Why did Kennedy choose a blockade over an air strike in dealing with Soviet missiles in Cuba?

   c. Evaluate Do you think Kennedy handled the Cuban missile crisis well? Is there anything he should have done differently?

Critical Thinking

5. **Identifying Cause and Effect** Review your notes on Cold War crises faced by President Kennedy's administration. Then copy the graphic organizer below and use it to identify the causes and effects of those crises.

Causes	Crisis	Effects

FOCUS ON WRITING ELA W1.1

6. **Expository** President Kennedy and many other Americans believed that the Peace Corps was a good way to aid other nations. Would you be interested in becoming a Peace Corps volunteer? Write a paragraph explaining why or why not.

SECTION 2: Kennedy's Thousand Days

BEFORE YOU READ

MAIN IDEA
John F. Kennedy brought energy, initiative, and important new ideas to the presidency.

READING FOCUS
1. What was Kennedy's New Frontier?
2. In what ways did the Warren Court change society in the early 1960s?
3. What impact did Kennedy's assassination have on the nation and the world?

KEY TERMS AND PEOPLE
Jacqueline Kennedy
New Frontier
mandate
Earl Warren
Warren Court
Lee Harvey Oswald
Warren Commission

HSS 11.9.4 List the effects of foreign policy on domestic policies and vice versa (e.g., protests during the war in Vietnam, the "nuclear freeze" movement).

HSS 11.11.2 Discuss the significant domestic policy speeches of Truman, Eisenhower, Kennedy, Johnson, Nixon, Carter, Reagan, Bush, and Clinton (e.g., with regard to education, civil rights, economic policy, environmental policy).

THE INSIDE STORY

How did the Kennedys bring style and glamour to the White House?

John F. Kennedy brought something to the White House that had not been seen since the early 1900s—young children. The press carried pictures of the president's toddlers playing in the Oval Office and stories of their pony strolling through the White House gardens. The young family was shown sailing on the blue waters off Cape Cod, in Massachusetts. The image of youth and vitality was unmistakable. It was visual reinforcement of what Kennedy had promised at the start of his campaign—a "new generation of leadership."

In addition to youth, the Kennedy White House was a picture of style. The handsome young president was complemented by his glamorous first lady, Jacqueline. The pair dazzled observers with their movie-star appearance. But beyond the glittery exterior was a genuine appreciation of beauty. Jacqueline Kennedy made the White House a showplace for art, music, and theater. State dinners became cultural events. Many Americans responded with enthusiasm to her grace, charm, and sense of style.

Of course, Kennedy could not lead the nation on style alone. As you will read, the outward image of youth and vigor helped set a tone for politics and change that pushed the nation in new directions.

▲ John and Jacqueline Kennedy brought youthful elegance to the White House.

THE NEW FRONTIER AND THE GREAT SOCIETY 535

Kennedy's New Frontier

Many Americans were struck by the youth and vitality of the Kennedy White House. Few presidents have been more available to the media. Even fewer have used it as successfully to obtain the public image they desired.

Image and reality Photographs of the president often showed him engaged in physical activities like sailing and swimming. Kennedy understood how such pictures would shape his image and boost his appeal. In reality, he struggled with health problems most of his life. He suffered from Addison's disease, a fatiguing and sometimes painful condition. A bad back kept him in nearly constant pain.

First lady **Jacqueline Kennedy** and the couple's two young children contributed to the sense of glamour and energy that surrounded Kennedy's presidency. Caroline and John Jr. were the first young children to live in the White House since 1908. Although Jacqueline Kennedy tried to protect the children's privacy, the president encouraged the press to photograph and write about them. He knew that this information also would help to create a favorable public opinion of his presidency.

Just 31 years old when Kennedy became president, Jacqueline was, like her husband, very attractive and from a wealthy family. "Jackie" was the more refined of the two and had a great interest in the arts. She made the White House the nation's unofficial cultural center by hosting elaborate events featuring world-famous artists and musicians.

Kennedy and Congress Americans seemed to like the Kennedys more than they liked his New Frontier. Because the president had spoken so often of a new frontier during the election campaign, this was the name given to his plans for changing the nation. Most Americans in the early 1960s were not reform minded, however.

The makeup of Congress reflected the American public's mood. Conservative southern Democrats often joined with Republicans to block many of Kennedy's proposals. In addition, Kennedy's narrow victory in the 1960 election denied him the clear mandate, or authorization to act, he needed to convince Congress that the people agreed with his plans.

For example, Kennedy asked Congress to reduce taxes to fight rising unemployment. This action would give consumers more money to

TRACING HISTORY

Exploration

Early explorers travelled the Earth in search of new places and experiences. Today such curiosity takes people into space and to robotic exploration of the oceans. Study the time line to learn about how key events in American history have transformed the nature of exploration over time.

1804–1806 Lewis and Clark explore the new territory acquired by the United States in the Louisiana Purchase of 1803. The expedition included Sacagawea, a Shoshone guide.

THE GRANGER COLLECTION, NEW YORK

1927 Charles A. Lindbergh makes the first nonstop transatlantic solo flight from New York to Paris.

1932 Amelia Earhart becomes the first woman to make a solo flight across the Atlantic Ocean. In 1937 she vanishes while attempting to fly around the world.

spend, which would lead businesses to produce more goods and hire more workers. Despite his urgings, Congress failed to act. Congressional leaders also ignored Kennedy's proposals to provide federal aid to education and to create a health care plan for older Americans.

In some cases Kennedy's popularity and presidential powers allowed him to solve problems without depending on Congress. For example, the nation's major steel producers announced big price increases in 1962. Kennedy was concerned this would lead to inflation. When some steel-company executives refused to roll back the price increases, he cancelled government contracts to buy steel from those companies. He also began a vigorous campaign against them in the media. The steel companies soon gave in to the president's pressure and cancelled their price increases.

Although Kennedy was among the nation's wealthiest presidents, he sought ways to help poor Americans. He convinced Congress to pass the Area Redevelopment Act in 1961, which gave financial assistance to economically distressed regions. Congress also created a program to retrain workers in areas with high unemployment and raised the minimum wage from $1.00 to $1.25 per hour.

The space program Kennedy's foreign-policy crises helped to create the program that came to symbolize the New Frontier—the exploration of space. In April 1961 the Soviet Union launched the first human into space in a one-orbit flight. It was nearly a year before U.S astronaut John Glenn matched the Soviet accomplishment.

Khrushchev claimed the Soviet lead in space showed the superiority of communism. Coupled with the Cold War embarrassment of the Bay of Pigs, Americans were dismayed. "Is there any place where we can catch them [the Soviets]?" President Kennedy asked his advisers. In May 1961 Kennedy made a bold proposal to Congress to restore America's world prestige.

HISTORY'S VOICES

> **"**This nation should commit itself to achieving the goal, before this decade is out, of landing a man on the moon and returning him safely to the earth. No single space project . . . will be more impressive to mankind, or more important for the long-range exploration of space . . . But in a very real sense, it will not be one man going to the moon . . . it will be an entire nation.**"**
>
> —John F. Kennedy, May 25, 1961

Science and Technology
In 2004, President George W. Bush announced that Americans would return to the moon by 2015 and establish a permanent U.S. base there by 2020.

1962 Astronaut John Glenn becomes the first American to orbit the Earth.

1983 Astronaut Sally Ride becomes the first American woman in space on the space shuttle *Challenger*.

2005 Space shuttle engineer John Phillips dazzles the world by repairing the *Discovery* in space.

1947 USAF Major Chuck Yeager breaks the sound barrier by flying faster than the speed of sound.

1969 Astronaut Neil Armstrong becomes the first person to set foot on the moon.

1985 Robert Ballard discovers the wreck of RMS *Titanic* and revolutionizes undersea exploration by using remotely controlled submersible devices.

THE NEW FRONTIER AND THE GREAT SOCIETY

FACES OF HISTORY

John and Jacqueline KENNEDY
1917–1963, 1929–1994

In November 1960 John F. Kennedy became the youngest elected U.S. president in history. John and his 31-year-old wife, Jacqueline, brought youth, energy, and style to the White House. Known for her sense of fashion, grace, and glamour as the first lady, Jacqueline promoted the arts and culture.

The first lady quickly rose to the top of the list of America's most admired women. Her popularity spread beyond U.S. borders and often exceeded that of the president. On a 1961 trip to Europe, President Kennedy introduced himself as "the man who accompanied Jacqueline Kennedy to Paris." When the Kennedys met Nikita Khrushchev, the Soviet leader said, "I'd like to shake her hand first."

The young couple also experienced tragedy during their years in the White House. In August 1963 the Kennedys' third child, Patrick, died just two days after his birth. Tragedy struck again with John Kennedy's assassination. The country mourned with Jacqueline and the two young Kennedy children.

Make Inferences For what reasons did Jacqueline Kennedy increase the president's appeal and prestige?

The president also asked Congress to fund the unmanned exploration of space. These proposals made the space race as much a part of the Cold War as the conflict over Cuba had been. This race, however, was one the United States would win.

READING CHECK **Identifying Cause and Effect** Why did Kennedy propose a mission to the moon and the unmanned exploration of space?

The Warren Court

During Kennedy's presidency, Supreme Court decisions were responsible for major changes in American society. Under the leadership of Chief Justice **Earl Warren**, controversial Court rulings greatly extended individual rights and freedoms. Many historians regard Warren as second only to John Marshall as the most important chief justice. The Supreme Court's influence on the nation increased greatly during Warren's nearly 16 years as chief justice.

Earl Warren did not have a positive record on civil rights when President Eisenhower appointed him chief justice in 1953. As California's attorney general, Warren had called for the internment of Japanese Americans during World War II. Later, as governor of California, he fought against an effort to make the state's Assembly more representative of the people.

Yet as chief justice, Warren led the Court in 1954 to one of the most significant civil rights advances in U.S. history. He persuaded the other justices in *Brown* v. *Board of Education* to ban racial segregation in the nation's schools. You will read more about this landmark case in the next chapter.

Then in the early 1960s, the **Warren Court** issued a series of decisions concerning other reforms. These decisions required some of the legislative reforms Warren had opposed when he had been governor of California.

Voting-rights reform One significant reform made important changes in the way that legislative representation was determined. In the mid-1900s it was standard practice for states not to redraw the boundaries of their legislative districts to reflect changes in the population.

As cities grew, however, their representation in state legislatures did not. In Tennessee, for example, the boundaries of legislative districts had not changed since 1901. By 1960 densely populated urban areas had the same number of state legislators as sparsely populated rural regions.

In *Baker* v. *Carr* (1962), the Court declared that this situation denied urban voters the equal protection of law required by the Fourteenth Amendment. The Court went further in *Westberry* v. *Sanders* (1964) and *Reynolds* v. *Sims* (1964) when it ruled that legislative districts must have equal populations. This reform guaranteed that each citizen's vote has equal weight, a principle known as "one person, one vote."

The rights of the accused The Warren Court also extended the Bill of Rights to the actions of state governments. In *Mapp* v. *Ohio* (1961), the Court established that the search warrants required by the Fourth Amendment apply to state and local police too, not just to searches conducted by federal agents. In *Gideon v. Wainwright* (1963), the Supreme Court ruled that states must provide free lawyers to poor persons being tried for crimes. In *Escobedo v. Illinois* (1964), the justices decided that a person has a right to a lawyer during police questioning. In 1966 the Court extended these rights again in the case of *Miranda v. Arizona*. You will read more about this case in Landmark Supreme Court Cases at the end of this chapter.

Religious freedom In other important cases, the Warren Court defined the religion guarantees of the First Amendment. In *Engel v. Vitale* (1962), for example, the justices banned formal prayers in public schools. A year later the Court prohibited daily Bible readings in school. The Supreme Court ruled that both activities violated the First Amendment's guarantee that government would not make any religion the nation's "official" religion.

READING CHECK **Summarizing** How did the Warren Court extend individual rights and freedoms?

The Kennedy Assassination

As 1964 approached, President Kennedy worked to build support for his re-election campaign. To help win the backing of southern Democrats, Kennedy flew to Texas in late 1963. On November 22, President Kennedy rode in an open car of a motorcade through the city of Dallas to the site where he was to deliver a speech. With the first lady by his side, the president waved to the cheering crowds that lined his route.

Then shots rang out from the sixth floor of a schoolbook depository building as the motorcade passed by. Kennedy slumped over, fatally wounded. Within hours, Vice President Johnson, who was with the Kennedys on the trip, was sworn in as president aboard Air Force One.

Kennedy's tragic death shocked the nation and the world. People today still remember what they were doing when they heard the terrible news. Donna Shalala, who later served in President Bill Clinton's cabinet, was working with the Peace Corps in Iran at the time.

Death of a President

Left, President and Mrs. Kennedy shortly before the assassin's bullets struck. Right, Kennedy's widow, Jacqueline, and their children, John and Caroline, wait for the president's funeral to begin. **Why do you think it was important for the nation to have a state funeral?**

HISTORY'S VOICES

"I . . . recall a beggar walking up to me in the street and I said 'No, I don't have any money.' He said, 'I don't want any money. I just want to tell you how sorry I am that your young president died.'"

—Donna Shalala, quoted in *Ordinary Americans*

White House correspondent Helen Thomas later remarked, "The legacy of hope died with him. You never had that same sense again that we were moving forward."

The Warren Commission Within hours of the shooting, Dallas police arrested **Lee Harvey Oswald**, a troubled loner with connections to the Soviet Union and Cuba. Two days later, as police were transferring Oswald from the Dallas Police Department to the county jail, Oswald was shot to death by Jack Ruby, a Dallas nightclub owner with ties to organized crime. These strange circumstances caused some people to question whether Oswald had acted alone in killing the president.

President Johnson named a commission headed by Chief Justice Earl Warren to investigate the assassination. The **Warren Commission**, after a 10-month investigation, reported that there was no conspiracy and that Oswald and Ruby had each acted alone. Despite lingering suspicions, additional government investigations and many private ones have never found credible evidence of a conspiracy.

An end and a beginning The Kennedy assassination deeply affected all Americans. The Kennedy family and supporters made a great effort to shape the nation's memory of the fallen president. Jacqueline Kennedy arranged a funeral to rival that of President Lincoln's nearly a century before. Broadcast live on national television, it concluded with the president's burial at Arlington National Cemetery, on a hillside overlooking the capital, with a continuously burning flame at the site.

"In many ways the drama of [Kennedy's] presidency outweighed its achievements," wrote Clark Clifford, an adviser to several presidents. Yet Clifford acknowledged that "[Kennedy] offered a vast promise to a whole new generation of Americans." In world affairs, that promise was realized by improved relations with the Soviet Union following the Cuban missile crisis and the goodwill toward America that the Peace Corps produced.

At home, Kennedy's accomplishments were less impressive. Yet, even during his presidency, Kennedy had acknowledged that the nation's social, economic, and environmental problems would take many years to solve. It remained up to his successor, Lyndon B. Johnson, to carry on his work. As president, Johnson would achieve greater legislative success than Kennedy.

READING CHECK **Drawing Conclusions** What was the purpose and conclusion of the Warren Commission?

SECTION 2 ASSESSMENT

HSS 11.9.4, 11.11.2

Reviewing Ideas, Terms, and People

1. **a. Describe** What public image did Kennedy project?
   b. Analyze How did Kennedy deal with the threat of increased steel prices?
   c. Evaluate Do you think the space race was an important part of the Cold War? Explain your answer.

2. **a. Define** What was the "one person, one vote" standard?
   b. Predict How do you think the **Warren Court's** decisions would expand people's rights in the future?

3. **a. Describe** What event made Lyndon Johnson president on November 22, 1963?
   b. Make Inferences Why did the fate of President Kennedy affect people so deeply?
   c. Evaluate Do you agree that "the drama of [Kennedy's] presidency outweighed its achievements"? Why or why not?

Critical Thinking

4. **Analyze Information** Review your notes on President Kennedy's proposed programs. Then copy the graphic organizer below and use it to show the results of those ideas.

Kennedy's Ideas	Results

FOCUS ON SPEAKING ELA W1.1

5. **Expository** Explain to a classmate what you see as President Kennedy's legacy to the American people. Support your opinion with facts, arguments, and examples.

SECTION 3: The Great Society

BEFORE YOU READ

MAIN IDEA
President Johnson used his political skills to push Kennedy's proposals through Congress and expanded them with his own vision of the Great Society.

READING FOCUS
1. Why was Lyndon Johnson's background good preparation for becoming president?
2. Why was Johnson more successful than Kennedy in getting Congress to enact Kennedy's agenda?
3. In what ways did Johnson's Great Society change the nation?
4. What foreign-policy issues were important in Johnson's presidency?

KEY TERMS AND PEOPLE
War on Poverty
Job Corps
VISTA
Great Society
Barry Goldwater
Medicaid
Medicare
Johnson Doctrine
Pueblo incident

HSS 11.8.4 Analyze new federal government spending on welfare.

HSS 11.11.2 Discuss the significant domestic policy speeches of Kennedy, Johnson (e.g., with regard to education, civil rights, economic policy, environmental policy).

HSS 11.11.6 Analyze the persistence of poverty and how different analyses of this issue influence welfare reform and other social policies.

THE INSIDE STORY

What made President Johnson an effective leader? Lyndon Johnson had an ability to get what he wanted that few others could match—or were able to resist. The skills that made Johnson a highly effective majority leader in the Senate helped him to quickly become a strong president following President Kennedy's death.

Knowledge was the basic element in Johnson's leadership style. To Lyndon Johnson, information was power. He made it a point to learn everything he could about his subject and about the people with whom he was dealing. He claimed to know the strengths and weaknesses of each senator—how far each could be pushed, in what direction, and by what means.

One of Johnson's most effective methods was what journalists called "The Treatment." One person who received The Treatment described it "as if a St. Bernard had licked your face for an hour [and] had pawed you all over."

First, Johnson closed in on his target, until his face was just a couple of inches away. Then words poured out of him in a torrent as his eyes widened and narrowed. If the target tried to say something, Johnson never allowed the chance. He countered objections before they could even be spoken. "He'd come on just like a tidal wave," one senator reported. "There was nothing delicate about him." Observers of The Treatment called it an almost hypnotic experience that rendered its targets stunned and helpless.

THE Johnson "TREATMENT"

▶ Johnson (right) overwhelmed friends and opponents alike.

Johnson Becomes President

As vice president, Lyndon B. Johnson had little opportunity to showcase his political talents. Those talents, however, were one reason John F. Kennedy wanted Johnson as his vice president. Another reason was that Kennedy needed a running mate in 1960 who would help the Democrats win the South. Kennedy might have been better served, however, had Johnson remained in the Senate, where his political skills might have helped to get Kennedy's programs enacted.

Kennedy and Johnson made an unlikely team. A large and intense man, Johnson shared none of Kennedy's good looks, polish, or charm. While Kennedy showed off his beautiful young children to reporters, Johnson was known to display the surgery scars on his abdomen. His often crude language reflected the macho ranching culture from which he came. Born and raised in the rural Hill Country of central Texas, he was hardworking and ambitious. In spite of his sometimes overbearing manner, he had a genuine desire to help others.

Johnson gave up school teaching for government work during the Great Depression. When President Franklin D. Roosevelt created the National Youth Administration (NYA) in 1935, a New Deal agency that found work for young people, Johnson sought the job of state director for Texas. At age 26 he was the youngest NYA director in the nation. Two years later he ran for Congress, where he served his Hill Country district until 1948. Then Texans statewide elected him to the U.S. Senate.

After just one term as a senator, Johnson's Democratic colleagues made him majority leader in the Senate. He soon developed a close relationship with the Republican president Dwight D. Eisenhower. Johnson used his powerful Senate position and Eisenhower's popularity to force compromises in Congress and pass the first civil rights laws since Reconstruction. By 1960 he had more influence in Washington, D.C., than any other Democrat.

Although Johnson campaigned hard for Kennedy's election in 1960, he was unhappy as vice president. He missed the power he had exercised as Senate majority leader. Even more than Kennedy, Johnson promoted an expanded role for government in making Americans' lives better. He also had a greater concern for the poor and underprivileged. These differences were probably due to the two men's differing backgrounds, including Johnson's experience as part of the New Deal.

Despite his sometimes crude behavior, Johnson was a compassionate man. He was saddened by his inability to comfort Jacqueline Kennedy on the plane ride back from Dallas following her husband's death. When he told the nation in his first speech as president, "All I have I would have given gladly not to be standing here today," he truly meant his words.

READING CHECK **Summarizing** Why was Lyndon Johnson well qualified to be president?

FACES OF HISTORY
Lyndon B. JOHNSON
1908–1973

A former Texas high school teacher and long-time member of Congress, Lyndon Johnson ran for the Democratic Party presidential nomination in 1960. Unable to defeat Senator John F. Kennedy of Massachusetts for the nomination, Johnson accepted Kennedy's offer of the vice presidency in order to unite the party.

As president, Johnson carried out an ambitious set of social reforms. After winning the presidential election in 1964, he soon escalated U.S. involvement in Vietnam. Unwilling to let communism advance, he sent American troops into battle. As the Vietnam War dragged on without success, Johnson's popularity with voters decreased. In March 1968 he decided not to run for re-election.

Make Inferences How would Johnson's acceptance of the vice presidency have helped to unite the Democratic Party?

Enacting Kennedy's Agenda

Johnson's mastery of the political process, along with his years of experience in Washington, allowed him to manage the transition of the presidency with great skill and tact. He reassured the nation by promising no great changes from the previous administration. Johnson demonstrated that intent by asking Kennedy's cabinet and advisers to continue serving in the new administration. "I constantly had before me the picture that Kennedy had selected me," he later recalled. "It was my duty to carry on and this meant his people as well as his programs. They were part of his legacy."

Linking to Today

The Job Corps

Among the programs created during the War on Poverty was the Job Corps, a program for young people age 16 to 24 who have not graduated from high school. Today some 60,000 students live on more than 120 Job Corps campuses, where they complete their education and learn a vocation and job-hunting skills.

One of the best-known Job Corps participants is boxer George Foreman. After leaving high school, he joined the Job Corps and learned construction and forestry. A Job Corps counselor also taught Foreman to box, and he went on to win an Olympic gold medal and the heavyweight championship of the world.

Although Foreman's achievements are not typical, Job Corps participants are more successful than other high school dropouts. One study found that Job Corps participants earn about 11 percent more income than dropouts who do not become part of the Job Corps program.

A Job Corps recruiter shares information with high school students in Miami, Florida.

Drawing Conclusions How does the Job Corps represent the ideas of President Johnson's War on Poverty?

The new president also pledged to carry on the New Frontier. Speaking to a joint session of Congress, he called on its members to pass Kennedy's programs, which they had blocked for so long. "Let us here highly resolve that John Fitzgerald Kennedy did not live—or die—in vain," Johnson declared.

HISTORY'S VOICES

❝John F. Kennedy told his countrymen that our national work would not be finished 'in the . . . life of this administration, nor even perhaps in our lifetime . . . But,' he said, 'let us begin.' Today, in this moment of new resolve, I would say to all my fellow Americans, let us continue. This is our challenge—not to hesitate, not to pause, not to turn about and linger over this evil moment, but to continue on our course so that we may fulfill the destiny that history has set for us.❞
—Lyndon B. Johnson, speech to Congress, November 27, 1963

The War on Poverty

After Congress passed the Area Redevelopment Act in 1961, Kennedy had told an adviser, "I want to go beyond the things that have already been accomplished." His interest in antipoverty programs was fueled in part by social activist Michael Harrington's influential book published in 1962. Harrington's *The Other America* was a study of poverty in the United States that shattered the popular belief that all Americans had benefited from the postwar prosperity.

HISTORY'S VOICES

❝They [the poor] exist within the most powerful and rich society the world has ever known. Their misery has continued while the nation talked of itself as being 'affluent' [wealthy] . . . In this way tens of millions of human beings became invisible. They dropped out of sight and out of mind . . . How long shall we ignore this underdeveloped nation in our midst?❞
—Michael Harrington, *The Other America*, 1962

Kennedy's staff had begun work on a series of antipoverty programs he wanted to present as part of his 1964 re-election campaign. Johnson was told of Kennedy's planned antipoverty proposals on November 23, 1963, his first full day in office. "Go ahead," the new president ordered. "Give it the highest priority. Push ahead full tilt."

In his first State of the Union Address in January 1964, Johnson declared "unconditional war on poverty" in America. To launch the **War on Poverty** he asked Congress to pass the Economic Opportunity Act. Congress granted his request in August 1964.

THE NEW FRONTIER AND THE GREAT SOCIETY

The Economic Opportunity Act funded several new antipoverty programs. The **Job Corps** offered work-training programs for unemployed youth. Volunteers in Service to America, or **VISTA**, was a domestic version of the Peace Corps that provided help to poor communities in the United States. Other programs provided basic education for adults, work opportunities for unemployed fathers and mothers, and help to fight rural poverty and assist migrants. These programs were run directly out of the White House by the newly created Office of Economic Opportunity (OEO). Congress gave the OEO $1 billion to operate them.

Other initiatives passed Johnson also pushed for passage of Kennedy's tax-cut bill and civil rights legislation, both of which had been stalled in Congress. Senate conservatives demanded that the president promise to hold government spending to $100 billion if taxes were cut. Johnson knew the government would not need even that much money. He cleverly told the press, however, how difficult it was to write a budget that met this requirement. Believing it had won a victory, Congress passed the Tax Reduction Act in February 1964.

The law had the effect that Kennedy had hoped for. The nation's economy grew by more than 10 percent, and unemployment declined. As a result, tax revenue actually increased.

The Tax Reduction Act illustrated the difference in the way Kennedy and Johnson approached getting legislation passed.

ACADEMIC VOCABULARY
revenue income from a specific source

"Kennedy felt that the way to get the tax cut was to educate the Congress and . . . persuade them to go for it," an aide to both presidents later recalled. "Johnson used his incomparable technique to get the thing through."

"No memorial . . . could more eloquently honor President Kennedy's memory than the earliest possible passage of the civil rights bill for which he fought so long," Johnson told Congress. "We have talked long enough in this country about equal rights . . . It is time now to . . . write it in the books of law." In July, after more than a year of division and debate, Congress passed the landmark Civil Rights Act of 1964. (You will read more about the Civil Rights Act and the circumstances surrounding its passage in the next chapter.)

READING CHECK Identifying the Main Idea
How did Johnson convince Congress to pass Kennedy's programs?

The Great Society

President Johnson wanted to do more than just follow in Kennedy's footsteps, however. He had ambitious plans of his own. "If you look at my record, you would know that I am a Roosevelt New Dealer," he told an adviser. "As a matter of fact, . . . John F. Kennedy was a little too conservative to suit my taste."

Johnson described his own plans for the nation in a commencement address at the University of Michigan in May 1964.

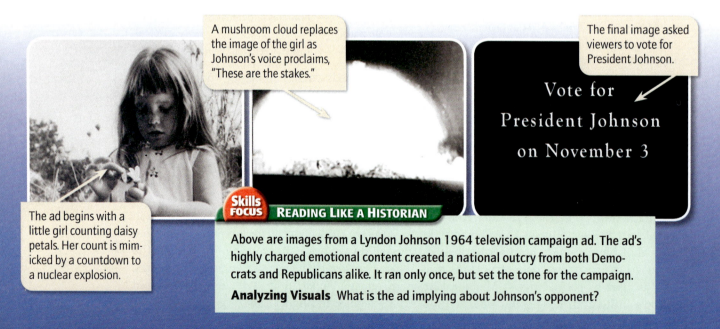

The ad begins with a little girl counting daisy petals. Her count is mimicked by a countdown to a nuclear explosion.

A mushroom cloud replaces the image of the girl as Johnson's voice proclaims, "These are the stakes."

The final image asked viewers to vote for President Johnson.

Skills Focus READING LIKE A HISTORIAN

Above are images from a Lyndon Johnson 1964 television campaign ad. The ad's highly charged emotional content created a national outcry from both Democrats and Republicans alike. It ran only once, but set the tone for the campaign.

Analyzing Visuals What is the ad implying about Johnson's opponent?

COUNTERPOINTS

Government's Role in Shaping Society

As senator and vice president, Hubert Humphrey acted on his belief that the government should play an active role in society.

" [W]e call upon all Americans to join us in making our country a land of opportunity for our young, a home of security and dignity for our elderly, and a place of . . . care for our afflicted . . . Let us take those giant steps forward . . . to build the great society."

Hubert Humphrey, 1964

Senator Barry Goldwater opposed President Johnson's Great Society—which Hubert Humphrey had played a large part in creating.

" I've always stood for government that is limited and balanced and against the ever increasing concentrations of authority in Washington . . . I believe we must . . . not continue drifting endlessly down and down for a time when all of us, our lives, our property, our hopes, and even our prayers will become just cogs in a vast government machine."

Barry Goldwater, 1964

SKILLS FOCUS — READING LIKE A HISTORIAN

Analyzing Primary Sources In what ways do both speakers try to win support by playing on the emotions of their listeners?

See **Skills Handbook**, pp. H28–H29

HISTORY'S VOICES

" We have the opportunity to move not only toward the rich society and the powerful society, but upward to the Great Society. The Great Society rests on abundance and liberty for all. It demands an end to poverty and racial injustice . . . I want to talk to you today about three places where we begin to build the Great Society—in our cities, in our countryside, and in our classrooms."

—Lyndon Johnson, May 22, 1964

The 1964 election The phrase Johnson used—Great Society—became the term for the domestic programs of his administration. To achieve his goals for the Great Society, Johnson worked hard to ensure his victory in the 1964 presidential election. He easily won the Democratic Party's nomination for president and chose Hubert Humphrey, a liberal senator from Minnesota, as his running mate. The Republicans selected Senator **Barry Goldwater**, a conservative from Arizona, as their nominee. The vast differences in the two candidates' views gave voters a clear choice.

Goldwater set the tone of the campaign in his acceptance speech at the Republican National Convention by declaring that "extremism in the defense of liberty is no vice." The Democrats portrayed him as a radical who would lead the country into a nuclear war and turn back the clock on the nation's social progress. When Goldwater suggested using nuclear weapons to end the growing war in Vietnam, he convinced many voters that he indeed was a dangerous extremist. (You will read about the Vietnam War in an upcoming chapter.)

Goldwater's attacks on the Great Society also seemed to prove the Democrats' claims about him. "We are all equal in the eyes of God," he proclaimed, "but we are equal *in no other respect*." He charged that government programs to help people were similar to communism and that they posed a threat to the nation's freedom.

In November, the voters provided Johnson with the mandate he sought. The president received 61 percent of the popular vote in the biggest election landslide of the century. His

486–52 victory in the electoral college was even more one-sided. Democrats also strengthened their majorities in both houses of Congress.

Creating the Great Society Now that he had been elected president in his own right, Johnson pushed even harder for his plans. He told aides at an inaugural ball, "Don't stay up late. There's work to be done. We're on our way to the Great Society."

Johnson had a personal interest in providing education for the children of the poor. In 1965 Congress passed the Elementary and Secondary Education Act, the first large-scale program of government aid to public schools. The Higher Education Act created the first federal scholarships for needy college students. In February 1965 the OEO launched Head Start, an education program for the preschool children of low-income parents.

The president also persuaded Congress to pass the Omnibus Housing Act in 1965. To oversee this and other federal housing programs, Congress created the Department of Housing and Urban Development (HUD). Johnson appointed Robert Weaver to head this new department, making him the first African American to be part of a president's cabinet.

In July 1965 Congress authorized funds for states to set up **Medicaid**—a program that provides free health care for poor people. At the same time it created **Medicare**, a health care program for people over age 65. Johnson traveled to Independence, Missouri, to sign the bill into law in front of Harry Truman, the 81-year-old former president who had first proposed such a program. "No longer will older Americans be denied the healing miracle of modern medicine," Johnson declared. "No longer will illness crush and destroy . . . [their] savings."

THE IMPACT TODAY
Economics
Today more than 12 percent of the U.S. population receives health care through Medicaid. Nearly half of those covered are children.

MAJOR GREAT SOCIETY PROGRAMS

Year Enacted	Legislation	Purpose and Provisions
1964	Economic Opportunity Act	Created the Job Corps, VISTA, and eight other programs to fight the "war on poverty"
1964	Tax Reduction Act	Cut income tax rates up to 30%, with the greatest cuts going to lower-income Americans
1964	Civil Rights Act	Outlawed discrimination in housing, employment, and public accommodations; authorized federal government to enforce desegregation
1964	Wilderness Preservation Act	Protected 9.1 million acres of national forest from development
1965	Elementary and Secondary Education Act	Provided aid to school systems based on number of students from low-income homes
1965	Social Security Amendments	Established Medicare and Medicaid
1965	Voting Rights Act	Ended the requirement that voters pass literacy tests and allowed federal supervision of voter registration
1965	Omnibus Housing Act	Provided housing for low-income Americans
1965	Water Quality Act	Required states to clean up rivers and lakes
1965	Clean Air Act Amendments	Established exhaust emission standards for new motor vehicles
1965	Higher Education Act	Provided scholarships and low-interest loans for college students
1966	National Traffic and Motor Vehicle Safety Act	Established safety standards for automobiles and tires
1967	Air Quality Act	Set guidelines on air pollution and increased the federal government's power to enforce clean-air standards

PRIMARY SOURCES

Political Cartoon

President Johnson's long-standing ties in the Senate and public sympathy after the assassination of President Kennedy helped win support for many issues that had been stalled for months or years. This cartoon, called "Maestro of the 88," reflects on Johnson's relationship with Congress.

Johnson's influence as a senator was so great that he has been called a Master of the Senate. A *maestro* is someone who is a master in the arts, especially music.

These "song lyrics" represent important legislation that Congress passed soon after Johnson became president.

The eighty-eighth Congress met from 1963 to 1965. A piano has 88 keys.

SKILLS FOCUS   READING LIKE A HISTORIAN

Interpreting Political Cartoons What message is the artist trying to convey about Johnson's influence over Congress?

See **Skills Handbook**, p. H31

Many programs of the Great Society were intended to promote a better life for Americans regardless of their economic status. For example, improving the environment was a major emphasis of Johnson's presidency. He signed laws to improve the quality of the air and water as well as other important environmental measures.

Preserving the outdoors and the nation's natural beauty was especially important to Lady Bird Johnson, the first lady. She asked her husband to push the Highway Beautification Act through Congress in October 1965. This law limited advertising along main highways and provided federal funds for landscaping and roadside rest areas. It came to be called Lady Bird's bill.

The decline of the Great Society
The peak years for the Great Society were 1965 and 1966. Congress passed 181 of the 200 major bills President Johnson requested during that period. However, some members of Congress expressed substantial concern over the rapid pace of reform called for by Johnson.

The outcome of the midterm elections of 1966 suggested that many Americans shared these concerns. The Democrats retained their majorities in both houses of Congress, but the Republicans gained 47 seats in the House of Representatives and 3 in the Senate. This shift enabled conservatives to slow down Johnson's legislative program.

The new Congress, however, did enact some Great Society proposals into law. One was the Public Broadcasting Act. This law, enacted in 1967, created the Corporation for Public Broadcasting (CPB) to provide public affairs, cultural, and educational programs. The CPB then created the Public Broadcasting System (PBS) for television and National Public Radio (NPR). The programming of PBS and NPR provide alternatives to the offerings of commercial television and radio.

The Truth-in-Lending Act, also passed in 1967, required lenders to inform consumers of actual costs of credit transactions. A 1968 law established the nation's wild and scenic rivers program. These and many other key Great Society reforms continue to provide benefits to Americans today.

READING CHECK   **Identifying the Main Idea** What was the overall goal of the Great Society?

THE NEW FRONTIER AND THE GREAT SOCIETY   **547**

Johnson's Foreign Policy

Another factor in the decline of the Great Society was the increasing involvement of the United States in the Vietnam War. You will read more details about the Vietnam War in an upcoming chapter.

At the end of 1966 some 385,000 U.S. combat troops were in Vietnam. The U.S. government was spending about $2.5 billion each month on the war. Budgetary pressures mounted as the nation tried to afford both a major war and expensive social programs at home. As one member of Congress put it, "We cannot have guns and butter."

Johnson chose guns over butter because, like Kennedy, he was fully committed to stopping the spread of communism. Johnson sent 22,000 U.S. troops in 1965 to end a revolt in the Dominican Republic. He justified his actions by declaring that revolutions in Latin America were not just local concerns when "the object is the establishment of a Communist dictatorship." This guideline for intervention became known as the **Johnson Doctrine**.

As he fought the spread of communism, President Johnson also continued Kennedy's efforts to improve relations with the Soviet Union. In March 1967 the first direct treaty between the two nations since 1917 took effect. The treaty protected each country's diplomats from harassment by authorities in the other country.

A month later, the United States and the Soviet Union joined 58 other nations to ban weapons in outer space. After war broke out between Israel and its Arab neighbors in June, Johnson met Soviet leader Aleksey Kosygin in New Jersey to discuss the situation.

A crisis developed in January 1968 when North Korean forces captured the *Pueblo*, a U.S. Navy spy ship, off the coast of Communist North Korea. U.S. officials claimed the *Pueblo* had been in international waters and demanded its return.

When the North Koreans refused, Johnson ordered the call-up of some 14,000 national guard, air force, and navy reserves. At the same time he sought a negotiated settlement to the **Pueblo incident**. The crisis was resolved in December when the North Koreans released the crew but kept the ship.

READING CHECK **Making Inferences** Why did Johnson involve the United States in the affairs of the Dominican Republic?

SECTION 3 ASSESSMENT

HSS 11.8.4, 11.11.2, 11.11.6

Reviewing Ideas, Terms, and People

1. **a. Identify** What were some of Johnson's political accomplishments before he became president?
   b. Compare and Contrast In what ways were Johnson and Kennedy alike and different?
   c. Predict How do you think Johnson's experiences would help him as president?

2. **a. Identify** What Kennedy programs did Johnson help pass?
   b. Analyze In what ways did the Economic Opportunity Act address poverty?
   c. Elaborate Which of the laws and programs Johnson enacted do you think is the most important? Why?

3. **a. Describe** What were Johnson's main goals for the Great Society?
   b. Make Inferences Why did some people find **Barry Goldwater's** views threatening?
   c. Evaluate How would you rate Johnson's domestic achievements? Explain your answer.

4. **a. Identify** What were Johnson's most significant foreign-policy concerns?
   b. Analyze How did the Vietnam War affect the growth of Johnson's Great Society?
   c. Evaluate Do you think Johnson's response to communism in the **Johnson Doctrine** was effective? Why or why not?

Critical Thinking

5. **Sequence** Review your notes on President Johnson's achievements. Then copy the graphic organizer below and use it to record those achievements in chronological order. You may need to add more boxes.

FOCUS ON WRITING ELA W1.1

6. **Persuasive** Suppose you live in the mid-1960s. Write a letter to your senator expressing support for the Great Society. Your letter should try to convince the senator to support President Johnson's programs.

LANDMARK SUPREME COURT CASES
Constitutional Issue: Due Process

Miranda v. Arizona (1966)

Why It Matters The Fifth Amendment protects a criminal defendant from being forced to be a witness against himself or herself. The Sixth Amendment gives the right to an attorney in criminal cases. If a suspect is unaware of these rights, the police cannot interrogate him or her without informing the suspect about his or her rights.

Background of the Case

In 1963 Mexican immigrant Ernesto Miranda was arrested in Arizona. Police questioned him for two hours. He confessed to a serious crime, was tried and convicted, and sentenced to jail. The Arizona Supreme Court upheld his conviction.

The U.S. Supreme Court had ruled in *Brown* v. *Mississippi* (1936) that confessions coerced, or forced, by state or local officials violated the due process clause of the Fourteenth Amendment. In *Gideon* v. *Wainwright* (1963), the Court held that a criminal defendant who cannot afford an attorney can have one appointed without charge. Miranda's lawyer argued that police must inform a suspect of these rights before questioning.

The Decision

The Supreme Court ruled that police must protect a suspect's right against self-incrimination before questioning him or her.

> [T]he person must be warned that he has a right to remain silent, that any statement he does make may be used as evidence against him, and that he has a right to the presence of an attorney, either retained or appointed.

Police may then question the suspect if he waives these rights. But they must stop if the suspect says he or she wants a lawyer or no longer wants to talk to police. If police do not follow these procedures, any confession or admissions that the suspect makes cannot be used as evidence against him or her at trial in court.

THE IMPACT TODAY *Miranda* was one of the Warren Court's most controversial decisions. Those who disagreed with the ruling warned it could allow guilty people to go free just because of police officers' errors. Today police in the United States carry cards with the Miranda warnings printed on them and routinely "Mirandize" suspects by "reading them their rights" prior to questioning.

CRITICAL THINKING

go.hrw.com
Research Online
Keyword: SS Court

1. **Analyze the Impact** The year after *Miranda* was decided, the Court was faced with the question of whether an accused person is entitled to have counsel present when being shown to prosecution witnesses for identification at a line-up. How is this like the situation in *Miranda*? How is it different? How would you decide this question?

2. **You Be the Judge** Many states have laws requiring a person suspected of committing a crime to identify himself to police. Based on *Miranda*, are such laws constitutional, or does the person have the right to refuse to give police any information? Explain your reasoning in a short paragraph.

CHAPTER 17 DOCUMENT-BASED INVESTIGATION

The New Frontier and Great Society

HSS 11.11.2

Historical Context The documents below provide information on President John F. Kennedy's New Frontier and President Lyndon Johnson's Great Society programs.

Task Examine the documents and answer the questions that follow. Then you will be asked to write an essay about Kennedy's New Frontier and Johnson's Great Society, using facts from the documents and from the chapter to support the position you take in your thesis statement.

DOCUMENT 1

President John F. Kennedy came into office with bold ideas and an agenda that came to be known as the New Frontier. He explained some of the goals of this program in his inaugural address.

"[M]an holds in his mortal hands the power to abolish all forms of human poverty and all forms of human life. And yet the same revolutionary beliefs for which our forebears fought are still at issue around the globe . . .

"We dare not forget today that we are the heirs of that first revolution. Let the word go forth from this time and place, to friend and foe alike, that the torch has been passed to a new generation of Americans . . .

"Let every nation know, whether it wishes us well or ill, that we shall pay any price, bear any burden, meet any hardship, support any friend, oppose any foe, to assure the survival and the success of liberty . . .

"To those people in the huts and villages of half the globe struggling to break the bonds of mass misery, we pledge our best efforts to help them help themselves . . . If a free society cannot help the many who are poor, it cannot save the few who are rich . . .

"In your hands, my fellow citizens, more than mine, will rest the final success or failure of our course . . .

"And so, my fellow Americans, ask not what your country can do for you; ask what you can do for your country."

DOCUMENT 2

One component of the New Frontier was the creation of the Peace Corps to help developing countries improve their economies, education, and infrastructure. Thousands of young volunteers heeded Kennedy's call and went to help the poor in foreign countries. Here a Peace Corps volunteer is helping to inoculate children in Bolivia.

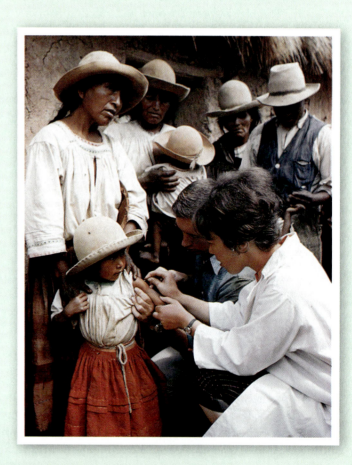

DOCUMENT 3

President Lyndon Johnson came into office with his own bold goals, namely the creation of the Great Society, in which problems such as poverty and racism would be wiped out. In the following speech, he explains his War on Poverty, a key element of creating the Great Society.

"We are citizens of the richest and most fortunate nation in the history of the world...

"The path has not been an easy one. But we have never lost sight of our goal—an America in which every citizen shares all the opportunities of his society, in which every man has a chance to advance his welfare to the limit of his capacities.

"We have come a long way toward this goal. We still have a long way to go. The distance which remains is the measure of the great unfinished work of our society. To finish that work I have called for a national war on poverty. Our objective: total victory...

"The war on poverty is not a struggle simply to support people, to make them dependent on the generosity of others. It is a struggle to give people a chance. It is an effort to allow them to develop and use their capacities, as we have been allowed to develop and use ours, so that they can share, as others share, in the promise of this nation.

"Because it is right, because it is wise, and because, for the first time in our history, it is possible to conquer poverty..."

DOCUMENT 4

Many conservatives opposed Lyndon Johnson's Great Society programs. His costly programs would increase the size of government, they argued. They feared a larger central government would rob people of their democratic freedoms. Actor Ronald Reagan was new to politics when he delivered the following speech in October 1964. He asked voters to support Republican Barry Goldwater in his campaign for the presidency. Goldwater lost the election to Johnson, but the speech made Reagan a rising star in politics. Reagan would one day become the 40th president of the United States.

In this vote-harvesting time, they use terms like the "Great Society," or as we were told a few days ago by the President, we must accept a greater government activity in the affairs of the people...

"This is the issue of this election: Whether we believe in our capacity for self-government or whether we abandon the American revolution and confess that [the government] can plan our lives for us better than we can plan them ourselves...

We have so many people who can't see a fat man standing beside a thin one without coming to the conclusion the fat man got that way by taking advantage of the thin one. So they're going to solve all the problems of human misery through government and government planning...

No government ever voluntarily reduces itself in size. So governments' programs, once launched, never disappear..."

Skills Focus — READING LIKE A HISTORIAN
HSS Analysis CS1, HI1

1. **a. Identify** Refer to Document 1. What goals of the New Frontier does Kennedy emphasize in this excerpt?
   b. Elaborate How do you think the Cold War influenced the ideas Kennedy expresses here?

2. **a. Describe** Refer to Document 2. What is happening in this image?
   b. Analyze How does this program help achieve Kennedy's goals?

3. **a. Identify** Refer to Document 3. What does Johnson hope to achieve?
   b. Elaborate Do you think his goal was realistic?

4. **a. Identify** Refer to Document 4. Who do the "fat man" and the "thin one" represent?
   b. Explain What did Reagan mean when he said "they're going to solve all the problems of human misery through government and government planning"?

5. **Document-Based Essay Question** Consider the question below and form a thesis statement. Using examples from Documents 1, 2, 3, and 4, create an outline and write a short essay supporting your position.
   How were some of the goal were President Kennedy's New Frontier and President Johnson's Great Society similar to and different from one another?

See **Skills Handbook**, p. H28, H30

Chapter 17 Chapter Review

Visual Summary: The New Frontier and the Great Society

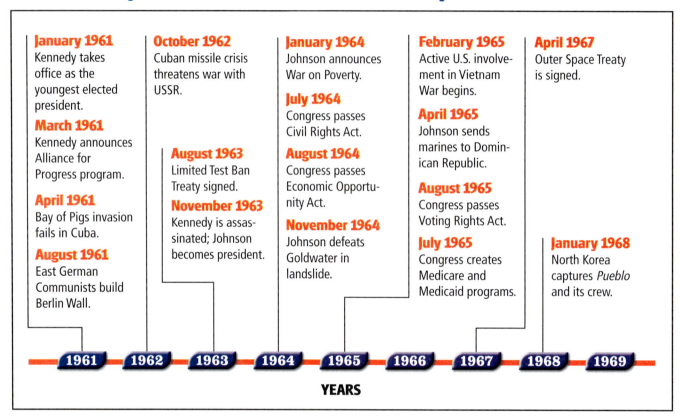

Reviewing Key Terms and People

Complete each sentence by filling in the blank with the correct term or person.

1. The dictator _____ came to power in Cuba in 1959.
2. A disastrous attempt by the CIA to invade Cuba became known as the _____.
3. The _____ brought the United States and the Soviet Union to the brink of nuclear war.
4. Kennedy's strategy of _____ involved strengthening conventional U.S. forces to avoid using nuclear weapons in times of crisis.
5. The _____ offered economic aid to Latin American countries.
6. Because of his narrow victory in 1960, Kennedy never had a strong _____ for his plans.
7. The chief justice of the Supreme Court during Kennedy's presidency was _____.
8. Dallas police arrested _____ for the assassination of President Kennedy.
9. The _____ reported that there was no conspiracy in the assassination of President Kennedy.
10. A domestic version of the Peace Corps called _____ helped poor communities in the United States.
11. Johnson's Republican opponent in the 1964 election was _____.
12. Under the Great Society, a government health care program for people over 65 called _____ was begun.
13. The _____ was resolved when North Korea kept the ship but released its crew.
14. The _____ was the president's justification for U.S. intervention in Latin America when there was the threat of a Communist dictatorship.

552 CHAPTER 17

History's Impact video program

Review the video to answer the closing question: How did advances in technology as a result of the space program change American life?

Comprehension and Critical Thinking

SECTION 1 *(pp. 526–534)* HSS 11.9.3, 11.11.2

15. **a. Describe** What happened at the Bay of Pigs invasion?
    b. Draw Conclusions In what ways did the Peace Corps increase goodwill for the United States?
    c. Evaluate How might the Berlin Wall affect the lives of people in East and West Berlin?

SECTION 2 *(pp. 535–540)* HSS 11.9.4, 11.11.2

16. **a. Identify** What was the Area Redevelopment Act of 1961?
    b. Make Inferences Why was Congress willing to fund the space race?
    c. Elaborate Why were the reforms of the Warren Court important to the nation?

SECTION 3 *(pp. 541–548)* HSS 11.8.4, 11.11.2, 11.11.6

17. **a. Recall** Why did Kennedy choose Johnson as his vice president?
    b. Analyze Why did Johnson decide to carry out Kennedy's initiatives?
    c. Elaborate Why do you think Americans voted so overwhelmingly for Johnson in the presidential election of 1964?

Using the Internet

go.hrw.com
Practice Online
Keyword: SE7 CH17

18. The Berlin Wall remained in place from 1961 to 1989, when it was finally torn down. Using the keyword above, do research on the significance of the Berlin Wall. Then write a report about the ways the construction and destruction of this barrier changed the world.

Analyzing Primary Sources HSS CS1, HR4

Reading Like a Historian In response to criticism of how he handled the Cuban missile crisis, Kennedy made a speech. Read an excerpt from that speech in the History's Voices passage in Section 1 that begins, "What kind of peace do we seek?"

19. **Identify** What kind of peace does Kennedy reject? What kind of peace does he want?
20. **Analyze** Why is it important to remember our "common link"?

Critical Reading ELA R2.4

Read the passage in Section 3 that begins with the heading "Creating the Great Society." Then answer the questions that follow.

21. According to the passage, one thing limited along major highways by the Highway Beautification Act was
    A landscaping.
    B rest areas.
    C billboards.
    D streetlights.

22. The appointment of Robert Weaver as secretary of the Department of Housing and Urban Development was significant because
    A he was the first African American to be part of a president's cabinet.
    B he was the youngest cabinet member ever.
    C Congress had originally rejected his nomination.
    D he was a conservative Republican who had previously opposed President Johnson.

FOCUS ON WRITING ELA W2.4

Expository Writing *Expository writing gives information, explains why or how, or defines a process. To practice expository writing, complete the assignment below.*

Writing Topic The New Frontier of John F. Kennedy

23. **Assignment** Based on what you have read in this chapter, write a paragraph that explains what the New Frontier was and how it was presented to the American people.

CHAPTER 18   1954–1975
The Civil Rights MOVEMENT

THE BIG PICTURE In the mid-1900s, many African Americans rose up against the treatment they had endured for decades. They fought discrimination through court cases and through nonviolent resistance, marches, boycotts, and "freedom rides." Their efforts resulted in meaningful government protections of basic civil rights.

California Standards

History-Social Sciences

11.10 Students analyze the development of federal civil rights and voting rights.

Skills Focus: READING LIKE A HISTORIAN

More than 200,000 civil rights demonstrators gathered peacefully at the Lincoln Memorial in Washington, D.C., in 1963. In his most famous speech, civil rights leader Martin Luther King Jr. told those gathered that "we have come here today to dramatize a shameful condition."
Interpreting Visuals How do you think this event affected public opinion? Explain.

See **Skills Handbook**, p. H30

U.S.

May 1954 Supreme Court rules that segregation in public schools is unconstitutional.

1954

World

1956 The Soviet army brutally crushes a revolt against Communist rule in Hungary.

History's Impact video program
Watch the video to understand the impact of equal rights and justice for all.

February 1960 Protesters in Greensboro, North Carolina, challenge racial segregation of public facilities.

August 1963 Civil rights protesters stage March on Washington.

July 1964 President Johnson signs the Civil Rights Act of 1964 into law.

April 1968 Civil rights leader Martin Luther King Jr. is killed.

April 1971 The Supreme Court upholds the use of busing to integrate schools.

1960 Nazi war criminal Adolf Eichmann is captured in Argentina.

1967 South African surgeon Christian Barnard performs first successful human heart transplant.

1970 Rhodesian prime minister declares the country an independent and racially segregated republic.

1975 Khmer Rouge leader Pol Pot takes over in Cambodia.

555

SECTION 1
Fighting Segregation

BEFORE YOU READ

MAIN IDEA
In the mid-1900s, the civil rights movement began to make major progress in correcting the national problem of racial segregation.

READING FOCUS
1. What was the status of the civil rights movement prior to 1954?
2. What were the key issues in the Supreme Court's ruling in *Brown v. Board of Education of Topeka, Kansas*, and what was its impact?
3. How did events in Montgomery, Alabama, help launch the modern civil rights movement?

KEY TERMS AND PEOPLE
CORE
Jackie Robinson
Thurgood Marshall
Little Rock Nine
Rosa Parks
Montgomery bus boycott
Martin Luther King Jr.
SCLC

HSS 11.10.2 Examine and analyze the key events, policies, and court cases in the evolution of civil rights, including *Plessy* v. *Ferguson*, *Brown* v. *Board of Education*.

HSS 11.10.4 Examine the roles of civil rights advocates (e.g., A. Philip Randolph, Martin Luther King, Jr., Malcom X, Thurgood Marshall, James Farmer, Rosa Parks).

Civil Rights PIONEERS

▼ Harry and Eliza Briggs (middle row, at either side of their child Catherine) with plaintiffs and supporters of *Briggs v. Elliott*.

THE INSIDE STORY

What does it take to turn ordinary people into activists? For Harry and Eliza Briggs, it was bad enough that their child had to attend a segregated school in their South Carolina community. But when the school board refused a request for school bus transportation—in spite of the fact that some African American children had to walk as much as 10 miles to school—they had had enough. Harry and Eliza Briggs joined 18 other parents in a legal challenge aimed at ending segregation of the local schools. With the help of the NAACP, they filed *Briggs* v. *Elliott* in 1950. Harry and Eliza Briggs paid dearly for their actions. Both of them lost their jobs. Harry had to leave the state to find work to support his family.

Yet their legal challenge went forward. Soon, it was joined together with four other cases, including a case from Topeka, Kansas, for argument before the Supreme Court of the United States. In 2004, Congressional Gold Medals of Honor were awarded posthumously to civil rights pioneers Harry and Eliza Briggs and two other South Carolina citizens, the Reverend Joseph S. DeLaine and Levi Pearson, who were part of their lawsuit.

556 CHAPTER 18

The Civil Rights Movement Prior to 1954

The Briggses played a key role in launching the modern civil rights movement in the United States. Yet this movement was not really new. You read in earlier chapters about the long struggle for African American rights. This fight had its start with the opposition to slavery in colonial days. It continued in the 1800s with the abolition movement and the Civil War. Slavery ended after the Civil War, and formerly enslaved people enjoyed some rights for a time during Reconstruction.

African American rights suffered setbacks after Reconstruction. In the late 1800s, legalized racism returned to the South. Supported by the Supreme Court's 1896 ruling in *Plessy* v. *Ferguson,* the segregation of African Americans and whites was the law of the land in much of the United States in the early 1900s.

In the late 1800s and early 1900s, a new group of champions joined the battle for civil rights. They included Booker T. Washington and W.E.B. Du Bois. You read about the role of Du Bois in the founding of the National Association for the Advancement of Colored People, or NAACP. This organization formed in 1909. In the decades ahead, it would be a powerful voice in the struggle to improve the legal rights of African Americans. The NAACP also fought to bring an end to racial violence.

The Great Depression of the 1930s presented new challenges to African Americans. Although the entire nation suffered, African Americans fared worse than others. President Roosevelt's New Deal helped win him the support of many African American voters. First Lady Eleanor Roosevelt was a staunch supporter of civil rights. Yet the president was unwilling to push too hard for greater rights for African Americans out of concern that it would anger his southern white supporters.

The 1940s: a decade of progress
In earlier chapters, you read about some of the civil rights gains of the 1940s. For example, during World War II, A. Philip Randolph managed to force a federal ban against discrimination

SCHOOL SEGREGATION, 1952

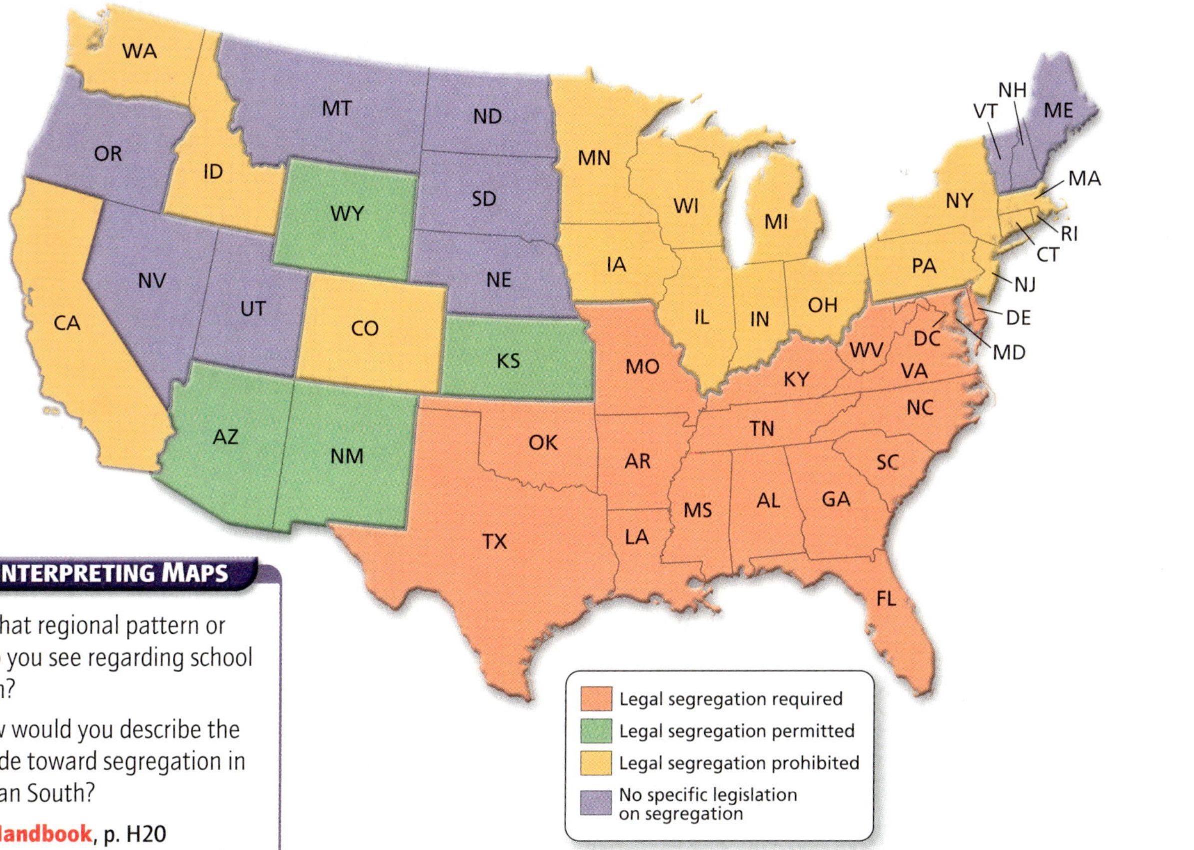

Legend:
- Legal segregation required
- Legal segregation permitted
- Legal segregation prohibited
- No specific legislation on segregation

GEOGRAPHY SKILLS INTERPRETING MAPS

Region What regional pattern or patterns do you see regarding school segregation?

Place How would you describe the legal attitude toward segregation in the American South?

See **Skills Handbook**, p. H20

THE CIVIL RIGHTS MOVEMENT

Early Civil Rights Victories

QUICK FACTS

Early efforts in the civil rights movement included the following gains:

1940	NAACP Legal Defense Fund founded by Thurgood Marshall
1941	Ban against discrimination in defense industry
1942	Founding of CORE
1947	Integration of Major League Baseball by Jackie Robinson (right)
1948	Desegregation of armed forces

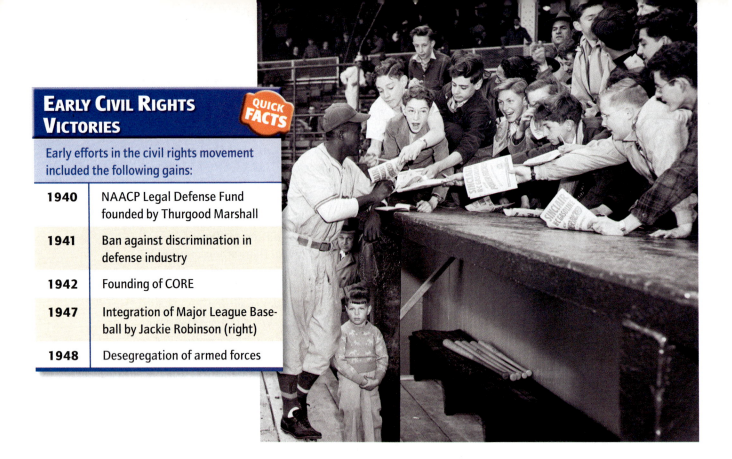

in defense-related work. Another key development in the 1940s was the founding of the Congress of Racial Equality, or **CORE**. This organization was dedicated to nonviolent protest. Its methods would have a strong effect on civil rights activists in the years ahead.

The end of the 1940s saw several key changes in the march toward greater civil rights. One was President Truman's order to desegregate the armed forces. Another came from popular culture. In 1947 the Brooklyn Dodgers became the first Major League Baseball team to put an African American on its roster. Millions admired **Jackie Robinson** for his great skill as an athlete. Millions more were inspired by his courage. Robinson bore with bravery and dignity the pressure of being an individual so many people wanted to see succeed—and so many others expected to see fail.

Seeking change in the courts While Randolph, Robinson, and others worked to bring change to American society, the NAACP continued its strategy of attacking racism through the courts. This was a method the organization had used from its earliest days to combat such discriminatory practices as the use of grandfather clauses to keep African Americans from voting.

In the 1930s Charles Hamilton Houston began an NAACP campaign to attack the concept of "separate but equal." Houston chose to focus on segregation in education. One of his former students, **Thurgood Marshall**, soon joined him. Marshall knew firsthand the effects of discrimination in education. He was once denied admission to the University of Maryland law school because of his race.

Under Houston and Marshall, NAACP lawyers began to chip away at the 1896 Supreme Court ruling in *Plessy* v. *Ferguson*, which served as the legal basis of segregation. In 1938, for example, in *Missouri ex rel. Gaines* v. *Canada, Registrar of the University of Missouri,* the NAACP successfully argued against Missouri's refusal to offer a law school education to African Americans.

In 1950 the Supreme Court ruled in *Sweatt* v. *Painter* that the separate law school for African Americans at the University of Texas was inferior to the one for whites. The Court also held that just being separate from the white school was likely to harm the preparation of African American students for a career in law.

READING CHECK **Identifying Problems and Solutions** What were some of the methods by which civil rights were expanded in the years before 1954?

Brown v. Board of Education

The NAACP's early success had focused on graduate schools, which affected only a small number of people around the country. In the 1950s Marshall began focusing on the nation's elementary and high schools. At the time, millions of students around the country attended segregated schools. For African Americans, these were almost always inferior schools.

To press its cause, the NAACP needed a case. As you read at the start of this section, it found one in South Carolina, with Harry and Eliza Briggs. NAACP lawyers found another one in the case of Linda Brown, in Topeka, Kansas. You will read about the details of the Kansas case in Landmark Supreme Court Cases later in this section.

The Supreme Court hears *Brown*

In both the *Briggs* and *Brown* cases, the lower courts upheld the practice of segregation. Yet these defeats did not stop Marshall and the NAACP. In fact, they provided an opportunity to bring the issue of school segregation to the Supreme Court. The Court combined the cases and several others from around the country into a single case. It was known as *Brown* v. *Board of Education of Topeka, Kansas*.

The Supreme Court was aware of the case's great significance. It heard arguments over a two-year period. The Court also considered research about segregation's effects on African American children. In one study, black children were shown dolls that were identical except for skin color. The children had more positive feelings about the white-skinned dolls than about the dark-skinned dolls they resembled. This and other tests suggested that segregation had harmed the self-image of young students.

In 1954 Chief Justice Earl Warren issued the Supreme Court's decision. All nine justices agreed that separate schools for African Americans and whites violated the Constitution's guarantee of equal protection of the law.

HISTORY'S VOICES

"Education is perhaps the most important function of state and local governments . . . It is doubtful that any child may reasonably be expected to succeed in life if he is denied the opportunity of an education. Such an opportunity . . . is a right that must be made available to all on equal terms . . . Does segregation of children in schools solely on the basis of race . . . deprive the children of the minority group of equal educational opportunities? We believe that it does."

—Chief Justice Earl Warren, *Brown v. Board of Education of Topeka, Kansas,* May 17, 1954

American Civil Liberty

Ending Legal Segregation

For many decades following the 1896 Supreme Court ruling in *Plessy* v. *Ferguson,* the concept of "separate but equal" was used to deny African Americans equal protection of the law. Segregation denied African Americans the education—and the dignity—they needed in order to achieve true social equality.

When the NAACP and its lawyers decided to attack the policy of "separate but equal," they knew it would be a long process. They understood that even if they were able to quickly overturn *Plessy,* it would take longer to destroy the attitudes that supported segregation. Instead, they sought to chip away at the *Plessy* ruling and slowly pave the way for true social change.

The strategy worked. By 1954 several cases had weakened the "separate but equal" policy and had in fact begun to break down the walls of segregation in education. The Supreme Court's forceful, unanimous decision in *Brown v. Board of Education of Topeka, Kansas,* showed clearly that legally enforced segregation could be challenged.

Identifying Problems and Solutions Why did the NAACP try to chip away at the *Plessy* ruling bit by bit?

Thurgood Marshall (center) and colleagues in front of the Supreme Court building after their victory

ACADEMIC VOCABULARY
integrate to combine two groups in such a way that one becomes fully part of the other

THE IMPACT TODAY
Government
In 1998 Central High School became a national historic site. It continues to educate students and is operated jointly by the Little Rock school district and the National Park Service.

The Little Rock crisis At the time of the *Brown* decision, 21 states had schools that were segregated by law. The Supreme Court's ruling declared segregation unconstitutional, but it offered no firm guidance about how or when desegregation should occur.

Some states quickly prepared to integrate their schools. In other states, however, there was strong opposition. Virginia Democratic senator Harry Byrd Jr. organized a movement known as massive resistance, under which officials at all levels pledged to block integration.

In Virginia, for example, the legislature passed laws forcing the closure of any school planning to integrate. Laws also assisted white students wishing to attend private schools. It was more than a year before the federal courts stopped this practice.

Little Rock, Arkansas, was another trouble spot. In 1957 Governor Orval Faubus violated a federal court order to integrate Little Rock's Central High School. Claiming that white extremists were threatening violence, he warned that "blood would run in the streets" if nine African Americans tried to attend the school. Just before the school year was to start, he ordered the Arkansas National Guard to keep them out.

On September 4, 1957, a crowd of angry whites harassed the black students as they arrived for the first day of school. When they reached the door, the soldiers turned them away. The Guard made no effort to protect them from the hostile crowd, who spat at them and tore their clothing.

For nearly three weeks the Guard prevented the African American students, now known as the **Little Rock Nine**, from entering the school. Meanwhile, President Eisenhower tried to persuade Faubus to back down. Finally, on September 24, Eisenhower went on national television to announce that he was sending federal troops to end the standoff. The next day, protected by U. S. soldiers with fixed bayonets, the Little Rock Nine entered Central High School.

For the rest of the school year, the African American students endured great abuse. Other students constantly shoved them in the halls. Their lives were threatened. The one senior among the Little Rock Nine had to be guarded at graduation. When his name was called at the ceremony, none of his classmates or their families clapped for him.

Meanwhile, Faubus continued to seek ways to stop school integration. In the end he failed. However, the events in Little Rock revealed to many Americans just how strong racism was in some parts of the nation.

READING CHECK **Identifying Problems and Solutions** What kinds of issues faced the Supreme Court in making its *Brown* decision?

Linking to Today

Integrating Central High School

The famous photograph at right shows Elizabeth Eckford, one of the Little Rock Nine, walking to Little Rock's Central High School on September 4, 1957. The white girl shouting at Eckford is Hazel Massery. Massery later regretted what she had done. She decided that she did not want to be, as she put it, the "poster child of the hate generation, trapped in the image captured in the photograph." In 1963 Massery apologized to Eckford. The two women later became friends and have spoken publicly together about their experiences.

Identifying the Main Idea Why did Hazel Massery apologize to Elizabeth Eckford?

Eckford and Massery in 1957 (above) and later, after becoming friends (left)

LANDMARK SUPREME COURT CASES
Constitutional Issue: Equal Protection

Brown v. Board of Education of Topeka, Kansas (1954)

Why It Matters By 1950 public schools in many parts of the United States were segregated. Under the Supreme Court's decision in *Plessy* v. *Ferguson*, separate schools for African American and white students were legally acceptable as long as the facilities were equal in quality. In practice, schools for African American children were generally far below the quality of schools for whites.

Background of the Case

Linda Brown, an African American third-grader in Topeka, Kansas, lived just blocks away from the nearest elementary school. However, that was a whites-only school, so she had to walk five blocks and then take a bus for two miles to reach the elementary school for blacks. The NAACP recruited Brown's parents and other Topeka residents to challenge segregation in the public schools. The Supreme Court recognized the harm segregation did to African American students. "The impact is greater when it has the sanction of law," it noted, "for the policy of separating the races is usually interpreted as denoting the inferiority of the Negro group."

The Decision

Chief Justice Earl Warren wrote an opinion for a unanimous Supreme Court that reversed the *Plessy* decision's "separate but equal" doctrine for public schools. Warren wrote that schools segregated by race were unconstitutional:

> ❝We conclude that in the field of public education the doctrine of 'separate but equal' has no place. Separate educational facilities are inherently [by their nature] unequal... Such segregation is a denial of the equal protection of the laws.❞

In 1955 the Supreme Court issued a follow-up decision, now called *Brown II*, ordering that desegregation proceed "with all deliberate speed."

THE IMPACT TODAY A decade after *Brown*, few schools had been integrated. In the early 1970s many communities turned to busing to integrate schools by force. But busing proved highly controversial, and many communities stopped busing by the late 1990s. Nevertheless, by the early 2000s, schools were much more integrated than they had been before *Brown*. Changing demographics were largely responsible for this trend.

CRITICAL THINKING

go.hrw.com
Research Online
Keyword: SS Court

1. **Analyze the Impact** Using the keyword above, read about the Supreme Court's 1971 decision in *Swann* v. *Charlotte-Mecklenburg Board of Education*. How was this case like *Brown*? In what way did the Court's decision in *Swann* move beyond the decision in *Brown*?

2. **You Be the Judge** *Brown* found that separate facilities were inherently unequal in education, but the case did not directly affect other types of legally imposed segregation. After *Brown*, how should a judge rule on a challenge to segregation in public transportation, restaurants, or hotels? Explain your answer in a short paragraph.

A Boycott Begins in Montgomery, Alabama

The Supreme Court's *Brown* decision had an enormous impact on society. Yet it directly affected only schools. Elsewhere in the South, a great variety of other public places and facilities remained segregated.

The Montgomery bus boycott One example of these segregated public facilities was the bus system in Montgomery, Alabama. African American riders, who made up two-thirds of bus passengers, had to pay their fare at the front of the bus, leave the bus, then enter again through the rear doors. They were forbidden from sitting in the front rows, which were reserved for white passengers. If those front rows filled, all African Americans riding in the next row had to give up their seats. Sharing a row with a white passenger was not allowed.

African Americans in Montgomery had endured these conditions for years. Even before the *Brown* ruling, local groups had sought to end segregation on the buses. It was not until 1955 that decisive action was taken, however.

In that year, a local NAACP member named **Rosa Parks** boarded a Montgomery bus after a day of work. She sat in the section reserved for African Americans. The white section soon filled, however. Parks was ordered to give up her seat and make her row available to white riders. She refused and was arrested.

The NAACP recognized the opportunity Parks's arrest presented. With her cooperation, the organization called for a one-day boycott of the city bus system. Some 90 percent of African American riders stayed off the buses that day. This response convinced community leaders to continue the Montgomery bus boycott. To lead this effort, they formed the Montgomery Improvement Association. The group selected as its leader a young minister of a local Baptist church named **Martin Luther King Jr.**

The boycott created hardship for Montgomery's African Americans. Many depended on the buses to get to work and to do errands.

The boycott also hurt the bus system and other white businesses. As a result, many of the city's whites tried to weaken it. Police harassed African Americans who took part in the boycott. When the city's black churches set up car pools to help their members get around, insurers cancelled the auto insurance policies of the cars' owners. King and other African American leaders became targets of violent threats.

Montgomery Bus Boycott

Rosa Parks was arrested for not surrendering her bus seat to a white passenger, setting in motion the Montgomery bus boycott. Below, boycotters wait for rides at a carpool station. The success of the boycott helped make Martin Luther King Jr. a nationally known civil rights leader.

As the boycott continued, court challenges to segregation of city buses also moved forward. The Supreme Court finally ruled on the subject in late 1956. By then, the boycott was a year old. The Court held that segregation on buses was unconstitutional.

Integration of the buses moved forward. There were some tense moments, including threats of violence against buses and local African American leaders. The tension, however, eventually faded. Integrated buses became a fact of life in Montgomery and elsewhere.

Birth of the SCLC The success of the Montgomery bus boycott inspired African Americans elsewhere. In communities across the South, groups organized boycotts of their own.

In January 1957, representatives of the Montgomery Improvement Association and several other groups met in Atlanta, Georgia. The goal was to form a new group that would organize protest activities taking place all across the region. This group became known as the Southern Christian Leadership Conference, or **SCLC**. Martin Luther King Jr., the leader of the successful Montgomery boycott, was elected leader of the SCLC.

As its name suggests, the SCLC was heavily influenced by the Christian faith. Many of its members, such as King, were members of the clergy. However, the SCLC was open to people of all races and faiths. At its heart was a commitment to mass, nonviolent action. You will read more about nonviolent protest in the next section. You will also read about the spread of the campaign to end segregation from the bus stops of Montgomery to other public places throughout the South.

FACES OF HISTORY
Rosa PARKS
1913–2005

When Rosa Parks refused to give up her seat on a bus in 1955, she already had a long history of community activism. In 1943 she became one of the first women to join the local NAACP chapter, where she served as its secretary. She also had experience protesting discrimination on the city's buses. In 1943 her protest of mistreatment on a bus resulted in the driver forcefully removing her from the bus.

In 1957 Parks and her family moved to Detroit. She joined the staff of Representative John Conyers Jr. in 1965, working there for 22 years. For her role in the civil rights movement, Parks received the Presidential Medal of Freedom in 1996 and the Congressional Gold Medal in 1999. After her death in 2005, she became the first woman to lie in honor in the U.S. Capitol rotunda, a tribute only given to the most significant national leaders.

Make Inferences Why was it significant that Rosa Parks had experience as an activist before her 1955 bus protest?

READING CHECK **Making Generalizations** What was the nature of the movement created by the successful Montgomery bus boycott?

SECTION 1 ASSESSMENT

HSS 11.10.2, 11.10.4

go.hrw.com
Online Quiz
Keyword: SE7 HP18

Reviewing Ideas, Terms, and People

1. **a. Describe** How did Jackie Robinson bring change to American society?
   b. Compare How were the NAACP and CORE similar?
   c. Predict What do you think will be the final result of Charles Hamilton Houston and Thurgood Marshall's challenges to segregated education?

2. **a. Identify** What Supreme Court decision had been the legal basis for the segregation of public schools?
   b. Make Inferences Why do you think African American students want to attend integrated schools, despite hardships?
   c. Evaluate How successful was the *Brown* v. *Board of Education of Topeka, Kansas* decision in desegregating schools?

3. **a. Describe** What was the goal of the SCLC?
   b. Analyze Why was Rosa Parks arrested?

   c. Evaluate Did the Montgomery bus boycott achieve its goals? Explain why or why not.

Critical Thinking

4. **Categorizing** Review your notes on the major events of the early civil rights movement. Then copy the graphic organizer below and use it to list legal and social civil rights victories.

Legal Victories	Social Victories

FOCUS ON WRITING

ELA W1.1

5. **Persuasive** Write a flyer encouraging African Americans to join in the Montgomery bus boycott. Make sure your flyer explains why it is important for people to participate.

SECTION 2
Freedom Now!

BEFORE YOU READ

MAIN IDEA
The quest for civil rights became a nationwide movement in the 1960s as African Americans won political and legal rights, and segregation was largely abolished.

READING FOCUS
1. What are sit-ins and Freedom Rides, and why were they important in the 1960s?
2. How was the integration of higher education achieved in the South?
3. What role did Albany, Georgia, and Birmingham, Alabama, play in the history of civil rights?
4. What concerns and events led to the passage of the Civil Rights Act of 1964?

KEY TERMS AND PEOPLE
Mohandas Gandhi
James Farmer
SNCC
Freedom Riders
James Meredith
Medgar Evers
Civil Rights Act of 1964

HSS **11.10.3** Describe the collaboration on legal strategy between African American and white civil rights lawyers to end racial segregation in higher education.

HSS **11.10.4** Examine the significance of Martin Luther King, Jr.'s "Letter from Birmingham Jail" and "I Have a Dream" speech.

HSS **11.10.6** Analyze the passage and effects of civil rights legislation (e.g., 1964 Civil Rights Act), with an emphasis on equality of access to education and to the political process.

SITTING DOWN FOR CIVIL RIGHTS

▲ Student protesters hold their ground at a lunch counter sit-in.

THE INSIDE STORY

How can you win by being beaten? On May 28, 1963, Anne Moody, Memphis Norman, and Pearlena Lewis, three students from Tougaloo College in Jackson, Mississippi, attempted to place an order at a whites-only lunch counter. The waitress told them to move to the back counter, which was for African Americans. "We would like to be served here," Moody replied. Instead, the waitress closed the counter. The three black students remained seated as a form of protest.

A hostile crowd gathered around the protesters. A man pulled Norman from his stool and beat him. Joan Trumpauer, one of Tougaloo's two white students, took his place. Lois Chaffee, a white faculty member, and John Salter, a Native American professor, soon joined the protesters.

The crowd dumped food on the protesters. Someone hit Salter with brass knuckles, and others poured table salt into his open wound. Still the protesters sat at the counter, refusing to leave or fight back. Finally, fearing greater violence, Tougaloo's president convinced the demonstrators to end their sit-in.

That night the protesters were honored at a huge rally for civil rights. Local NAACP leader Medgar Evers announced that the sit-in was the start of a campaign to end segregation not only in Jackson but throughout Mississippi.

Sit-ins and Freedom Rides

The events in Jackson, Mississippi, illustrate tactics that had become common in the civil rights movement in late 1950s and early 1960s. In addition to boycotts, such as the one in Montgomery you read about in Section 1, civil rights workers used other direct, nonviolent methods to confront discrimination and racism. These tactics frequently provoked a violent response from their opponents.

The strategy of nonviolence Many of the tactics used in the civil rights movement were based on those of **Mohandas Gandhi**. Gandhi, who died in 1948, had been a leader in India's struggle for independence from Great Britain. Gandhi organized actions in which protesters were willing to suffer harm instead of inflicting it. He taught that this nonviolent approach would expose injustice and force those in power to end it. Nonviolent resistance, he believed, was the best way to achieve change in a society in which others held most of the power.

American civil rights leaders such as **James Farmer** of CORE, Martin Luther King Jr. of SCLC, and others shared Gandhi's views. "There is more power in socially organized masses . . . than there is in guns in the hands of a few desperate men," King wrote. "We shall so appeal to your heart and conscience that we will win you in the process."

In the early 1950s, James Lawson, an African American minister, visited India and studied Gandhi's teachings. With King's encouragement, Lawson began conducting workshops on nonviolent methods in Nashville, Tennessee, and on the campuses of African American colleges across the South. He trained hundreds of students, including some whites who supported the civil rights movement. One participant described the weekly workshops.

HISTORY'S VOICES

> "We would practice such things as how to protect your head from a beating and how to protect each other. If one person was taking a severe beating, we would practice other people putting their bodies in between that person and the violence, so that the violence would be more distributed and hopefully no one would get seriously injured. We would practice not striking back if someone struck us."
>
> —Diane Nash in *Voices of Freedom* (1990)

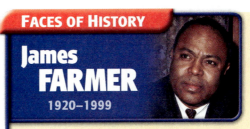

FACES OF HISTORY

James FARMER
1920–1999

Born in Marshall, Texas, James Farmer moved to Washington, D.C., to attend college at Howard University. After graduating, Farmer moved to Chicago, Illinois, where at age 22, he founded the Congress of Racial Equality (CORE) to push for an end to segregation. Farmer believed that direct, nonviolent action was the best way to achieve this goal.

CORE's first actions were sit-ins, in which African American and mixed-race groups tried to get service in Chicago restaurants. The tactic was so successful that years later it was copied by other civil rights activists. In 1947 Farmer organized an integrated bus trip through the South to challenge segregation on interstate buses. He used this tactic again in 1961, in the famous Freedom Rides.

Farmer retired from politics in 1971 but continued to lecture and teach. In 1998 he was awarded the Presidential Medal of Freedom.

Make Inferences What do Farmer's early sit-ins suggest about the civil rights of northern African Americans in the 1940s?

The sit-in movement Lawson was nearly ready to launch a sit-in campaign in Nashville when on February 1, 1960, four college students in Greensboro, North Carolina, began a sit-in of their own after ordering coffee at a lunch counter in a Woolworth's store. Denied service because of their race, the four young men stayed in their seats, expecting to be arrested. When they were not, they remained at the lunch counter until the store closed.

The next day, they returned with more students. By day three, protesters filled 63 of the lunch counter's 66 seats. The daily sit-ins soon attracted hundreds of supporters. The story of these dedicated and well-behaved students, who ended each day's protest with a prayer, quickly became national news. In mid-February, Lawson's Nashville sit-ins began.

The four students who began the sit-in at Greensboro had not attended Lawson's workshops. They had read about his methods, however. The Greensboro protest won important white support. "As long as those who seek a change . . . seek it in a peaceful manner, their power (and their haunting image on the white man's conscience) will not diminish," the *Greensboro Daily News* wrote in an editorial.

THE CIVIL RIGHTS MOVEMENT

During the next two months, protesters in about 50 southern cities began to use the sit-in tactic. In many places, white onlookers attacked the participants with food and other objects. Demonstrators, some of whom were white, were sometimes beaten. By April some 2,000 protesters had been arrested. "We do not consider going to jail a sacrifice but a privilege," a jailed demonstrator proclaimed. "Sixty days is not long to spend in jail. We will do it again for a cause as great as this one."

Despite the arrests and violence—or perhaps because of them—sit-ins were generally successful at getting business owners to change their policies. In May several stores in Nashville ended segregation at their lunch counters. The Greensboro sit-ins ended in July with the integration of lunch counters there. In October, Woolworth's and three other national chains integrated lunch counters nationwide.

The sit-ins marked a shift in the civil rights movement. They showed young African Americans' growing impatience with the slow pace of change. Sit-in leaders formed the Student Nonviolent Coordinating Committee, or **SNCC**, to conduct other nonviolent protests.

ACADEMIC VOCABULARY

enforce to require something to happen

The Freedom Rides The success of the student sit-ins inspired CORE to plan its own nonviolent action in 1961. In December 1960 the Supreme Court had ordered that facilities in bus stations serving interstate travelers be open to all passengers, regardless of race. The Court's order, however, was not being enforced. Newly elected president John F. Kennedy, though a supporter of civil rights, seemed unwilling to anger southern whites.

Members of CORE decided to draw attention to the situation by sending a group of **Freedom Riders** on a bus trip through the South. At each stop the African American riders would go into the whites-only waiting rooms and try to use facilities such as restrooms and lunch counters. "We felt we could count on the racists of the South to create a crisis so that the federal government would be compelled to enforce the law," James Farmer later explained.

On May 4, 1961, a group of 13 volunteers, including Farmer, left Washington, D.C., by bus, bound for New Orleans, Louisiana. They tried to use the facilities in bus stations in towns they passed through. At first they experienced only mild harassment. Then on May 14, one of the buses was swarmed by a mob outside of Anniston, Alabama. The mob firebombed the bus and beat the Freedom Riders as they escaped. Newspapers nationwide showed the incident on their front pages.

Another Freedom Ride bus reached Birmingham, Alabama, where it was attacked by a group armed with baseball bats and metal pipes. One Freedom Rider suffered permanent brain damage, and another required dozens of stitches to close the wounds to his head. No police arrived to stop the savage beatings. When the bus company refused to sell the Freedom Riders tickets to continue their journey, the CORE-sponsored Freedom Ride disbanded.

Federal intervention SNCC leader Diane Nash refused to give in to the violence, however. She gathered a group of SNCC members to continue the Freedom Rides from Nashville. Fearing death, several of them made out wills or wrote letters of farewell to loved ones before leaving for Birmingham.

Attorney General Robert Kennedy arranged with Alabama's governor to provide police protection for the SNCC volunteers. When their bus reached Montgomery, however, the police disappeared. The SNCC riders were attacked by yet another mob. An aide to President John Kennedy, at the scene as an observer, was among those beaten unconscious. Outraged at the governor's betrayal, the attorney general sent 600 federal marshals to Montgomery to protect the Freedom Riders.

On May 24 the SNCC riders reached Jackson, Mississippi. There they were arrested and jailed for using the bus station's whites-only facilities. The next day more volunteers arrived in Jackson, vowing to continue the rides. They were also arrested.

During the next four months, several hundred Freedom Riders rode buses through the lower South. The protest ended in September 1961, when the federal Interstate Commerce Commission finally issued tough new rules forcing integration of bus and train stations.

READING CHECK **Comparing** In what ways were the sit-ins and the Freedom Rides similar?

Integrating Higher Education

While SNCC and CORE attempted to achieve change using nonviolent protest, the NAACP pushed ahead with its legal campaign against school segregation. By 1960 it had expanded its efforts to include colleges and universities. White lawyers collaborated with the NAACP. In 1961 the organization obtained a court order requiring the University of Georgia to admit two African American students.

Charlayne Hunter and Hamilton Holmes were only in school a few days before they were suspended after white students rioted. A federal judge ordered their reinstatement. Robert Kennedy publicly praised the school for its respect for the law. He called the two students "freedom fighters" for returning to campus

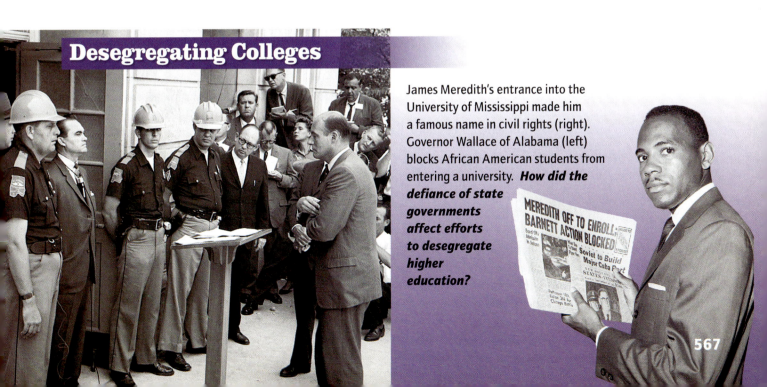

Desegregating Colleges

James Meredith's entrance into the University of Mississippi made him a famous name in civil rights (right). Governor Wallace of Alabama (left) blocks African American students from entering a university. *How did the defiance of state governments affect efforts to desegregate higher education?*

FACES OF HISTORY

Martin Luther KING Jr.
1929–1968

Martin Luther King Jr. entered Morehouse College in Atlanta, Georgia, at age 15 and graduated in 1948. He became an ordained minister while attending Morehouse. After religious training in Pennsylvania, King attended Boston University, where he completed a doctoral degree in religion in 1955. At all three schools, King studied the teachings on nonviolent protest of Indian leader Mohandas Gandhi.

The powerful speaking abilities for which King was known developed slowly. He received C's in his first public speaking courses in Pennsylvania. By his third year there, however, his professors were praising the impression he made in public speeches and discussions.

In 1953 King married Coretta Scott, an Alabamian he met in Boston. The next year they moved to Montgomery, Alabama, where King became pastor of a Baptist church. The Montgomery bus boycott boosted him to leadership in the civil rights movement. In 1964 King was awarded the Nobel Peace Prize for his work for civil rights.

Draw Conclusions How did King's education prepare him for his role in the civil rights movement?

---

amidst all the threats. Although Hunter especially suffered continuing hostility and taunts, both she and Holmes graduated in 1963.

Greater trouble erupted at the University of Mississippi when **James Meredith** attempted to enroll there in September 1962. A federal court ruled that the university had rejected Meredith's application "solely because he was a Negro," and ordered him to be admitted. On Sunday evening, September 30, Meredith arrived on campus. He was accompanied by 500 federal marshals that Robert Kennedy had ordered to protect him. A mob of 2,500 protesters, many of them nonstudents, met the group with violence.

As the riot worsened, President Kennedy went on national television to announce that he was sending in troops. "The eyes of the nation and the world are upon you," he told Mississippians. "The honor of your university and the state are in the balance." The troops arrived in the predawn hours of Monday morning and finally ended the protest. By then, however, hundreds of people had been injured and two killed. One of the dead was a journalist from France, sent to cover Meredith's enrollment.

In the months that followed, Meredith was frequently harassed by groups of white students. Yet a few students defied their peers and drank coffee with him or sat at his table at mealtimes. A small force of marshals remained at the university to protect Meredith until he graduated in the summer of 1963.

At the University of Alabama, Governor George Wallace in June 1963 physically blocked Vivian Malone and James Hood from enrolling. "This action is in violation of rights reserved to the state by the Constitution of the United States," Wallace proclaimed. However, after his speech and symbolic defiance of a court order to integrate the university, Wallace stepped aside.

READING CHECK Making Generalizations How were public universities in Georgia, Mississippi, and Alabama integrated?

Albany and Birmingham

In late 1961 Albany, Georgia, became a battleground in the civil rights movement. SNCC began a sit-in in Albany's bus station in November because local officials were ignoring the Interstate Commerce Commission's new integration rules. When demonstrators were arrested, SNCC notified the U.S. Justice Department. The federal government, however took no action.

The Albany Movement By mid-December more than 500 protesters had been jailed. Local civil rights leaders brought national attention to the situation by inviting Martin Luther King Jr. to lead more demonstrations. The campaign was called the Albany Movement. "We will wear them down with our capacity to suffer," King promised. He was soon arrested for leading a march on city hall. King refused to pay the fine. He vowed to remain in jail until the city agreed to desegregate. "I hope thousands [of others] will join me," he said.

Albany police chief Laurie Prichett had studied King's tactics, however. "His method was nonviolence . . . to fill the jails, same as Gandhi in India," Prichett said later. "And once they filled the jails, we'd have no capacity to arrest and then we'd have to give in to his demands." Prichett made arrangements with every jail in the surrounding area, so he was able to arrest all the protesters. In addition, when the national press arrived to cover King's sentencing, Prichett had King's fine paid, so King was released instead.

Opponents of integration also took advantage of divisions in the Albany Movement. The local leaders who began it became upset when the SCLC took control. Sensing this, city officials refused to negotiate with anyone but local leaders and would not negotiate at all as long as King was in town. In August 1962, King called off his demonstrations and left Albany. City officials then refused to meet with the local leaders. The protests resumed without King but failed to accomplish their goals.

The nine-month Albany Movement was a major defeat for King. It proved to be an important experience, however. After Albany, King vowed that the SCLC would organize its own campaigns rather than aid campaigns begun by others. His new strategy soon proved successful in Birmingham.

The Birmingham campaign King next focused his efforts on Birmingham, Alabama. Birmingham was known for its strict enforcement of segregation. With help from entertainer Harry Belafonte, King raised several hundred thousand dollars to fund a campaign against Birmingham's segregation laws. Volunteers taught local African Americans the techniques of nonviolence in the city's African American churches.

King's effort began in April 1963 with sit-ins and marches. Authorities quickly arrested the protesters. King had counted on this response to motivate more people to join the protests and focus national attention on the city. At first his strategy worked. On April 12 King and hundreds more were arrested and jailed.

The next day a group of local white clergy took out a full-page ad in the city's newspaper. They attacked King's actions as unwise and untimely. In his jail cell, King rejected these charges with a letter written in the margins of the newspaper. His response gained fame as the "Letter from a Birmingham Jail."

When King was released a few days later, he found fewer adult African Americans willing to risk losing their jobs by going to jail. Another SCLC leader urged King to use children instead. On May 2 demonstrators between the ages six and eighteen sang and chanted as they marched to lines of police set up to stop them. More than 900 were arrested and jailed.

The next day, Birmingham police chief Eugene "Bull" Connor used police and firefighters to break up a group of about 2,500

Witness to Violence

Images of peaceful protesters in Birmingham being attacked by police dogs and swept away by high-pressure fire hoses shocked the nation. *How did President Kennedy react?*

African American students as they gathered for another march. As television cameras and press photographers recorded the scene, the authorities struck. They blasted the protesters with fire hoses. The force of the water knocked the protesters down, tore their clothes, and left some of them bloody on the ground.

Connor repeated these actions for the next several days, as the nation watched on television. Finally, after hundreds of demonstrators had been jailed, federal negotiators succeeded in getting city officials to agree to many of King's demands. King called the agreement "the most magnificent victory for justice we've seen in the Deep South."

Some white people in Birmingham refused to accept the compromise. The motel where King was staying and the home of his brother were bombed. When some African Americans rioted, President Kennedy declared that he would not let extremists on either side destroy the agreement. He sent federal troops to Birmingham to restore order.

ACADEMIC VOCABULARY
restore to put something back into its former or original condition

READING CHECK **Comparing and Contrasting** How were the Albany and Birmingham campaigns alike, and how did they differ?

Major Civil Rights Reforms

Brown v. Board of Education of Topeka, Kansas (1954)	• declared segregated public schools unconstitutional
Civil Rights Act of 1957	• established a federal Civil Rights Commission to investigate violations of civil rights • created a civil rights division within the Justice Department to enforce civil rights laws • authorized the federal government to prosecute anyone interfering with another person's right to vote
Executive Order 11063 (November 20, 1962)	• banned racial and religious discrimination in housing built or purchased with federal aid
Civil Rights Act of 1964	• banned discrimination in public accommodations • outlawed unequal voting requirements • barred discrimination in employment based on race, gender, religion, or national origin • established the Equal Employment Opportunity Commission • applied federal power to speed integration of schools and other public facilities
Voting Rights Act of 1965	• suspended literacy tests and other devices used to exclude black voters • authorized federal supervision of voter registration • allowed federal workers to register voters
Civil Rights Act of 1968 (Fair Housing Act)	• banned racial discrimination in the sale, rental, or financing of housing • made harming civil rights workers a federal crime

The Civil Rights Act of 1964

You have read about Kennedy's approach on civil rights. He had believed that moving slowly was the best way to make progress. The events in Alabama, however, changed his mind.

HISTORY'S VOICES

"The fires of frustration and discord are burning in every city, North and South . . . We face . . . a moral crisis as a country and as a people . . . We cannot say to 10 percent of the population that . . . the only way . . . to get their rights is to go into the streets and demonstrate. I think we owe them and we owe ourselves a better country than that."
—John Kennedy, June 11, 1963

Kennedy announced that he would ask for sweeping legislation designed to finally end segregation in public accommodations—hotels, restaurants, theaters, and other establishments that serve the public.

The assassination of Medgar Evers A murder just hours after Kennedy's speech helped put the president's concerns into sharp focus. The head of the NAACP in Mississippi, **Medgar Evers**, was shot dead in his front yard. Evers was one of the movement's most effective leaders. His slaying shocked many Americans.

Police quickly arrested a Ku Klux Klan member named Byron De La Beckwith. All-white juries failed to reach a verdict in two trials, and De La Beckwith went free. Some 30 years later, however, authorities tried him yet a third time. In 1994, at the age of 73, De La Beckwith was finally convicted and sentenced to life in prison.

The March on Washington To build support for the civil rights movement, African American leaders planned a huge march on the nation's capital for August 1963. In June, when President Kennedy called for a civil rights law, African American leaders decided to include demands for its passage as one of the march's goals.

The March on Washington for Jobs and Freedom took place on August 28, 1963. It was the largest civil rights demonstration ever held in the United States. More than 200,000 people of all races covered the National Mall. Major civil rights figures addressed the crowd from the steps of the Lincoln Memorial. Gospel singer Mahalia Jackson, folk singer Joan Baez, and other popular entertainers of the day performed for the crowd.

Martin Luther King Jr. delivered the last speech at the day-long rally. He started by reviewing African Americans' long struggle throughout history for freedom. Then, urged on by Mahalia Jackson and other listeners nearby, King put aside his prepared remarks and began to speak from his heart. His speech became known as the "I Have a Dream" speech.

HISTORY'S VOICES

"I have a dream that one day this nation will rise up and live out the true meaning of its creed: 'We hold these truths to be self-evident; that all men are created equal.'... I have a dream that my four little children will one day live in a nation where they will not be judged by the color of their skin, but the content of their character. I have a dream today!"

—Martin Luther King Jr., August 28, 1963

Passing the Civil Rights Act The good feeling produced by the March on Washington was short-lived. The next month a bomb exploded in a Birmingham church, killing four young African American girls. Then in November, President Kennedy was assassinated. His vice president, Lyndon Johnson, took office.

President Johnson supported passage of a strong civil rights bill. Although some southerners in Congress fought hard to kill it, Johnson signed it into law on July 2, 1964. The **Civil Rights Act of 1964** banned discrimination in employment and in public accommodations.

READING CHECK **Summarizing** Why did a strong civil rights bill finally become law in 1964?

THE IMPACT TODAY

Government

The conviction in Evers's killing has encouraged the FBI to reopen other old cases from the civil rights movement. In 2002 a jury convicted a man long suspected in the Birmingham church bombing.

SECTION 2 ASSESSMENT

HSS 11.10.3, 11.10.4, 11.10.6

Reviewing Ideas, Terms, and People

1. **a. Identify** What civil rights tactic was based on the ideas and actions of **Mohandas Gandhi**?
   b. Summarize What was the basic belief behind the tactic of nonviolence?
   c. Elaborate Why do you think the sit-ins were successful?

2. **a. Describe** How did the NAACP work for the integration of colleges and universities?
   b. Make Inferences Why did so many federal marshals accompany **James Meredith** to the University of Mississippi?
   c. Predict Do you think the rioting at the University of Mississippi affected people's opinions about segregation? Why or why not?

3. **a. Identify** What began the Albany Movement?
   b. Make Inferences Why did Martin Luther King Jr. decide to focus on Birmingham?
   c. Elaborate Why did federal negotiators want Birmingham officials to agree to many of King's demands?

4. **a. Define** What was the goal of the March on Washington?
   b. Analyze What inspired President Kennedy to begin focusing on civil rights?

   c. Evaluate Do you think the **Civil Rights Act of 1964** went far enough? Explain why or why not. What substitute or additional provisions might the law have contained?

Critical Thinking

5. **Identify Cause and Effect** Review your notes on the Civil Rights Act of 1964. Then copy the graphic organizer below and use it to list the causes and effects of the law. You may need to add more circles.

FOCUS ON WRITING ELA W1.1

6. **Persuasive** Write a letter to your representative in Congress, explaining why he or she should vote for the Civil Rights Act of 1964. Be sure to include in your letter persuasive arguments that support your position.

American Literature

MARTIN LUTHER KING JR. (1929–1968)

About the Reading While protesting segregation in Birmingham, Alabama, Martin Luther King Jr. was arrested and held in a Birmingham jail. The following is an excerpt from a letter that King wrote in response to a full-page ad in a local newspaper. The ad, taken out by eight members of the clergy, denounced the protests. King's letter clearly presents his philosophy on nonviolence.

AS YOU READ Consider the dangers that Martin Luther King Jr. as well as other social activists faced by standing up for the causes they believed in.

Excerpt from

Letter from a Birmingham Jail

by Martin Luther King Jr.

Men drinking from segregated water fountains in the South

You express a great deal of anxiety over our willingness to break laws. This is certainly a legitimate concern. Since we so diligently urge people to obey the Supreme Court's decision of 1954 outlawing segregation in the public schools, at first glance it may seem rather paradoxical for us consciously to break laws. One may well ask: "How can you advocate breaking some laws and obeying others?" The answer lies in the fact that there are two types of laws: just and unjust. I would be the first to advocate obeying just laws. One has not only a legal but a moral responsibility to obey just laws. Conversely, one has a moral responsibility to disobey unjust laws. I would agree with St. Augustine that "an unjust law is no law at all."

Now, what is the difference between the two? How does one determine whether a law is just or unjust? A just law is a man-made code that squares with the moral law or the law of God. An unjust law is a code that is out of harmony with the moral law. To put it in the terms of St. Thomas Aquinas: An unjust law is a human law that is not rooted in eternal law and natural law. Any law that uplifts human personality is just. Any law that degrades human personality is unjust.

All segregation statutes are unjust because segregation distorts the soul and damages the personality. It gives the segregator a false sense of superiority and the segregated a false sense of inferiority. Segregation, to use the terminology of the Jewish philosopher Martin Buber, substitutes an "I-it" relationship for an "I-thou" relationship and ends up relegating persons to the status of things. Hence segregation is not only politically, economically and sociologically unsound, it is morally wrong and sinful. Paul Tillich said that sin is separation. Is not segregation an existential expression of man's tragic separation, his awful estrangement, his terrible sinfulness? Thus it is that I can urge men to obey the 1954 decision of the Supreme Court, for it is morally right; and I can urge them to disobey segregation ordinances, for they are morally wrong.

HSS 11.10.4, **ELA** R3.5

Skills Focus: READING LIKE A HISTORIAN

Literature as Historical Evidence How does King's letter show the importance of religious thought in the civil rights movement?

See **Skills Handbook**, p. H32

SECTION 3: Voting Rights

BEFORE YOU READ

MAIN IDEA
In the 1960s, African Americans gained voting rights and political power in the South, but only after a bitter and hard-fought struggle.

READING FOCUS
1. What methods did civil rights workers use to gain voting rights for African Americans in the South?
2. How did African American political organizing become a national issue?
3. What events led to passage of the Voting Rights Act?

KEY TERMS AND PEOPLE
Voter Education Project
Twenty-fourth Amendment
Freedom Summer
Mississippi Freedom Democratic Party
Fannie Lou Hamer
Voting Rights Act of 1965

HSS 11.10.4 Examine the roles of civil rights advocates.
HSS 11.10.5 Discuss the diffusion of the civil rights movement of African Americans from the churches of the rural South and the urban North, including the resistance to racial desegregation in Little Rock and Birmingham.
HSS 11.10.6 Analyze voting rights legislation (e.g., Voting Rights Act of 1965) and the Twenty-Fourth Amendment.

THE INSIDE STORY

What did the 2000 election in Selma symbolize? On March 7, 1965, about 600 people marching for voting rights were attacked and beaten by police as they crossed the Edmund Pettus Bridge in Selma, Alabama. The savage attack gained national attention and became one of the most notorious events of the civil rights movement.

Thirty-five years later, in 2000, Selma made national news again when James Perkins became the city's first African American mayor. Perkins was twelve years old when the march took place. He wanted to join, but his parents, fearing that violence might erupt, refused to let him go. However, like many other Selma residents, Perkins never forgot that fateful and bloody day.

The candidate Perkins defeated in 2000, Joe Smitherman, had been Selma's mayor in 1965. He did not take part in the beatings at the bridge. But back then, Smitherman opposed voting rights for African Americans. He later apologized for his views. This helped him stay in office for ten terms, as the number of African American voters in his city increased from 150 in 1964 to 9,000—some 65 percent of Selma's voters—in 2000.

Perkins focused his campaign in 2000 on economic issues instead of race, but some Selma residents organized their own effort to defeat Smitherman. For months, demonstrators stood at the Edmund Pettus Bridge holding signs reading "Remember the Blood" and shouting to passing cars, "Joe gotta go!"

Within minutes of the announcement of James Perkins's victory, thousands of his supporters poured back and forth across the bridge in cars and on foot, honking and cheering. "This is the final step of the march over the bridge," said one supporter about the election's significance. "This is the dream that Dr. King wanted."

SELMA, Now and Then

◀ Selma mayor James Perkins, with the Edmund Pettus Bridge in the background

Gaining Voting Rights

James Perkins and the many other African Americans who hold elective offices across the nation today owe much to the civil rights struggles of the 1960s. Voting rights for African Americans, like other victories of the civil rights movement, were achieved at great human cost and sacrifice.

Registering voters The nonviolent methods of the civil rights movement troubled the Kennedy administration because of the violent reactions they provoked. After the brutal attacks on the Freedom Riders in 1961, Attorney General Robert Kennedy met with SNCC leaders. He urged them to focus on voter registration rather than on protests. The vote was the key to changing things in the South, Kennedy claimed. He said that civil rights workers could count on federal government protection if they took this approach.

In 1962 SNCC, CORE, and other groups founded the **Voter Education Project** (VEP) to register southern African Americans to vote. However, the groups soon discovered that opposition to African American suffrage was as great as opposition to ending segregation. Marches to register voters were attacked by mobs or broken up by the police. Project workers routinely were beaten or jailed.

Mississippi presented the greatest challenge. VEP workers there lived in daily fear for their safety. A local farmer helping one voter registration drive was killed. The state legislator who shot him was aquitted. The lone African American witness to the crime was later found shot to death.

In spite of such terror tactics, the Voter Education Project was a success. In 1962 fewer than 1.4 million of the South's 5 million African American adults were registered to vote. By 1964 the VEP had registered more than a half million more African American voters. Only in Mississippi were results discouraging. "We are powerless to register people in significant numbers anywhere in the state," SNCC organizer Robert Moses told the VEP in a report.

The Twenty-fourth Amendment Congress passed the **Twenty-fourth Amendment** to the Constitution in August 1962 and submitted it to the states for ratification. The amendment banned states from taxing citizens to vote. Many southern states required these poll taxes as a way to keep African Americans from voting. Because the tax was not based on gender or race, it was constitutional. But since more African Americans than whites were poor, it affected them most.

Although the Twenty-fourth Amendment's ban on poll taxes applied only to elections

---

TRACING HISTORY

Civil Rights

The Declaration of Independence says that all people are born with "unalienable rights," but it took nearly 200 years to see that promise extended to all Americans. Study the time line to learn about key events in the struggle for civil rights.

1865–1870 The Thirteenth, Fourteenth, and Fifteenth Amendments abolish slavery, grant citizenship to African Americans, and give the vote to African American men.

1791 The First Amendment in the Bill of Rights guarantees freedom of religious worship.

An Islamic prayer service

for president or Congress, it increased hopes that change was on the way. As the proposed amendment worked its way through the ratification process, voting rights leaders planned more projects, concentrating on Mississippi.

Freedom Summer The Twenty-fourth Amendment became part of the Constitution in January 1964. A call went out for college students willing to spend their summer in Mississippi, registering African Americans to vote.

When school let out, hundreds of volunteers gathered at an Ohio college to train for a project called Freedom Summer. Most of the trainers—mainly SNCC workers—were from poor southern African American families. The student volunteers were mainly white, northern, and upper middle class. One volunteer later recalled why he took part.

HISTORY'S VOICES

❝I grew up in New York City. I had been raised in a family where being Jewish was important in terms of identifying with the underdog, with people who were suffering repression and discrimination . . . It was tremendously impressive and exciting. For me, it was a tremendous privilege to be allowed to participate in this movement for racial justice. At eighteen years old, to be able to be involved in this kind of a struggle was very important to me.❞

—Peter Orris in *Voices of Freedom* (1990)

Volunteers were trained to register voters or to teach at summer school. Mississippi spent about $82 per year to educate each white student but less than $22 per black student. In addition, many black schools in Mississippi closed during the cotton harvest to provide cheap child labor. The project's Freedom Schools offered African American students much-needed help in reading and math as well as instruction in black history and the civil rights movement.

Besides educating children and registering voters, project workers hoped to start a freedom movement in Mississippi that would continue after the volunteers left. Project leader Robert Moses had another goal: Just getting everyone through the summer alive would be an accomplishment, he said.

Crisis in Mississippi The first 200 volunteers arrived in Mississippi on June 20, 1964. The very next day one of them went missing. Andrew Goodman, a college student from New York, had gone with two CORE workers, James Chaney and Michael Schwerner, to inspect an African American church that had recently been bombed. They were arrested for speeding in Philadelphia, Mississippi, and held in jail until evening. After paying a fine, the three men drove off into the night. They were never heard from again.

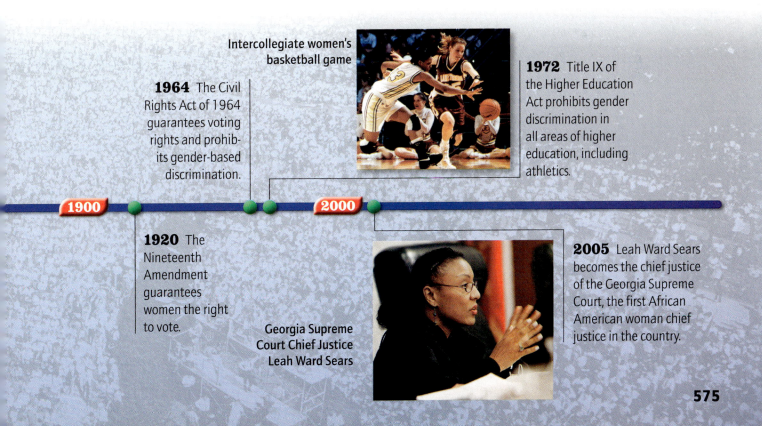

Intercollegiate women's basketball game

1900

1964 The Civil Rights Act of 1964 guarantees voting rights and prohibits gender-based discrimination.

1920 The Nineteenth Amendment guarantees women the right to vote.

2000

1972 Title IX of the Higher Education Act prohibits gender discrimination in all areas of higher education, including athletics.

Georgia Supreme Court Chief Justice Leah Ward Sears

2005 Leah Ward Sears becomes the chief justice of the Georgia Supreme Court, the first African American woman chief justice in the country.

American Civil Liberty

Twenty-fourth Amendment

In 1870 the Fifteenth Amendment granted African American men the right to vote in federal elections. Still, many states set requirements that made voting difficult for African Americans. One example was the poll tax. Many people could not afford this tax. Often, however, anyone whose father or grandfather had been eligible to vote did not have to pay it. In this way, many whites avoided the tax. Many African Americans could not.

One result of the civil rights movement of the 1950s and 1960s was a new amendment to the Constitution. The Twenty-fourth Amendment outlawed poll taxes in federal elections. This amendment was reinforced by a 1966 Supreme Court decision that poll taxes were illegal in state and local elections.

Identifying Cause and Effect In what ways would the Twenty-fourth Amendment increase the political power of African Americans?

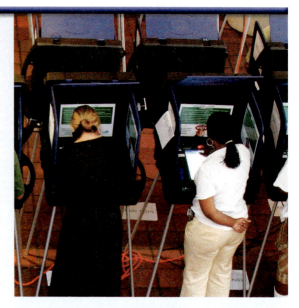
All Americans today cast their ballots free of the poll tax.

Government
In 2005 another of the killers was convicted and sentenced to prison for the murders of Goodman, Chaney, and Schwerner.

President Lyndon Johnson ordered a massive hunt for the three young men. In August their bodies were found in an earthen dam near Philadelphia, Mississippi. The incident cast gloom over Freedom Summer. Two-thirds of the volunteers went home. Many of those who remained suffered through shootings, beatings, bombings, and arrests.

In December the FBI arrested 21 suspects in the murders of Goodman, Chaney, and Schwerner. Most were members of the Ku Klux Klan. When the state dropped all charges, they were brought to trial in federal court for violating civil rights laws. Seven were convicted and received prison sentences ranging from 4 to 10 years. They were the first convictions ever in Mississippi for killing a civil rights worker.

In spite of the violence, organizers considered Mississippi's Freedom Summer project a success. The Freedom Schools taught 3,000 students, and more than 17,000 African Americans in Mississippi applied to vote. When state elections officials accepted only about 1,600 of these applications helped to show that a federal law was needed to secure voting rights for African Americans.

READING CHECK **Summarizing** What steps were taken to help African Americans register to vote?

Political Organizing

Freedom Summer was often overshadowed by the 1964 presidential election campaign. Most African American leaders wanted Johnson to defeat the Republican candidate Barry Goldwater, who had voted against the Civil Rights Act of 1964. You read about the election in the previous chapter. To help Johnson, Martin Luther King Jr. and other civil rights leaders agreed to suspend their protests until after election day.

SNCC, however, refused to agree. SNCC leaders wanted to protest segregation within the Democratic Party itself. "It is time for the Democratic Party to clean itself of racism," John Lewis, the head of SNCC, told the press.

As part of Freedom Summer, SNCC helped the **Mississippi Freedom Democratic Party** (MFDP) to organize. The MFDP elected sixty-eight delegates to the Democratic National Convention in August 1964. They arrived at the convention and asked to be seated instead of the all-white delegation sent by the state's Democratic Party.

The convention's credentials committee held a hearing to decide which delegates should represent Mississippi. **Fannie Lou Hamer**, an MFDP leader, presented her group's case. Her testimony was carried live on national television. Hamer, a poor sharecropper, told how on the day she registered to vote she was fired from the plantation where she had lived for 18 years. She described how she was beaten in jail after being arrested for attending a voter registration meeting. Hamer wept as she concluded her powerful statement.

HISTORY'S VOICES

> "All this on account of us wanting to register, to become first-class citizens, and if the Freedom Democratic Party is not seated now, I question America. Is this America, the land of the free and the home of the brave where we have to sleep with our telephones off the hooks because our lives be threatened daily because we want to live as decent human beings in America?"
>
> —Fannie Lou Hamer, August 22, 1964

While Hamer's powerful testimony was on the air, President Johnson was trying to control any political damage to the Democratic Party. In a quickly arranged news conference, he offered to compromise with the MFDP.

The compromise that party leaders proposed was to seat two members of the MFDP delegation and classify the rest as nonvoting "guests" of the convention. Although the NAACP and SCLC supported the compromise, SNCC and the MFDP opposed it. "We didn't come all this way for just two votes," Hamer declared. "We must stop playing the game of token recognition for real change," the MFDP said in a statement rejecting the compromise.

The MFDP's challenge failed in the end. It also helped widen a split that was developing in the civil rights movement. But it helped pave the way for future increases in the power of minorities and women in American politics.

READING CHECK **Identifying Problems and Solutions** How did the MFDP represent the drive for political organization among African Americans?

The Voting Rights Act

Following passage of the Civil Rights Act of 1964, the SCLC shifted its main focus to voting rights for African Americans. "The right to vote was the issue, replacing public accommodation as the mass concern of a people hungry for a place in the sun," Martin Luther King Jr. later wrote of the movement's new focus.

The Selma campaign In January 1965 King began a campaign to gain voting rights for African Americans by organizing marches in Selma, Alabama. "We will dramatize the situation to arouse the federal government by marching by the thousands to the places of registration," he declared.

By the end of January more than 2,000 marchers had been arrested. Police acted with restraint. They did not want to give King the confrontation he was seeking. King then repeated a tactic he had used earlier in Birmingham. He forced police to jail him along with several hundred other marchers, including many children.

King's arrest had the desired effect. The national media swarmed into Selma. The mass arrests and images of children being sent off to jail began appearing on the networks' evening news programs.

March from Selma

Above, police lay in wait for civil rights marchers as they cross the Edmund Pettus Bridge, March 7, 1965. Right, John Lewis, the SNCC leader who organized the first Selma march, is beaten by state troopers after crossing the bridge on what came to be known as Bloody Sunday.

THE CIVIL RIGHTS MOVEMENT **577**

Tensions rose in mid-February, when police attacked a march in nearby Marion, Alabama. Two state troopers shot and killed a marcher. A few days later King announced a four-day march from Selma to Montgomery, the state capital, to protest police brutality. Governor George Wallace issued an order prohibiting the march. "[It] will not be tolerated," he warned.

The Selma march On Sunday, March 7, 1965, about 600 African Americans began the 54-mile march. Just across the Edmund Pettus Bridge, on the way out of Selma, city and state police blocked their way. After firing tear gas at the marchers, police attacked with clubs, chains, and electric cattle prods. TV networks showed film of the savage violence.

King was not present on the March 7 march. He announced that it would resume on March 9. In a controversial decision, he led the group only to the base of the bridge—not across it. The pause was only temporary, however. After receiving promises of federal protection, the marchers finally reached Montgomery on March 25.

The Voting Rights Act of 1965 A week later, President Johnson gave a nationally televised address to a joint session of Congress. "At times history and fate meet . . . to shape a turning point in man's unending search for freedom," he observed. "So it was last week in Selma, Alabama." The president asked for quick passage of a tough voting rights law. "It is wrong—deadly wrong—to deny any of your fellow Americans the right to vote," Johnson declared. "Outside this chamber is the outraged conscience of a nation."

The **Voting Rights Act of 1965** passed in Congress by large majorities. King, James Farmer, Rosa Parks, and other civil rights leaders attended the president's signing ceremony on August 6.

The law proved to be one of the most important pieces of civil rights legislation ever passed. It gave the federal government powerful tools with which to break down longstanding barriers to African American voting rights. The impact was felt quickly. Within three weeks more than 27,000 African Americans in Mississippi, Alabama, and Louisiana registered to vote. African American candidates were soon elected to state and local offices, helping to break the long-held political power of those who supported segregation.

READING CHECK **Identifying Cause and Effect** How did the Selma march help to secure passage of the Voting Rights Act of 1965?

SECTION 3 ASSESSMENT

HSS 11.10.4, 11.10.5, 11.10.6

Reviewing Ideas, Terms, and People

1. **a. Identify** What was the goal of the **Voter Education Project**?
   b. Compare How were the obstacles faced by the Voter Education Project and **Freedom Summer** workers similar?
   c. Elaborate Why do you think African American voter registration efforts faced such fierce resistance?

2. **a. Describe** Who was **Fannie Lou Hamer** and what was her goal?
   b. Analyze Why did some civil rights groups suspend their protests before the election of 1964?
   c. Evaluate Do you think the **Mississippi Freedom Democratic Party** was right to reject President Johnson's compromise? Explain your viewpoint.

3. **a. Define** What was the Selma campaign?
   b. Make Inferences How did the media help the marchers' cause in Selma?
   c. Elaborate Why do you think so many members of Congress supported the **Voting Rights Act of 1965**?

Critical Thinking

4. **Analyze Information** Review your notes on African Americans' struggle for political equality. Then copy the graphic organizer below and use it to list the events in the struggle, what injustice each event targeted, and the effects of those actions.

Event	Injustice	Effects

FOCUS ON SPEAKING  ELA W1.1

5. **Expository** Make a short speech supporting either the Twenty-fourth Amendment or the Voting Rights Act of 1965. In your speech, explain the likely benefits of the new law.

LANDMARK SUPREME COURT CASES
Constitutional Issue: Equal Protection

Reynolds v. Sims (1964)

Why It Matters *Reynolds* v. *Sims* provided the Court's philosophy behind the "one person, one vote" standard. Because of this ruling, all states had to change their methods for electing state legislators.

Background of the Case

By 1960 about three-fourths of Alabama voters lived in cities, but rural voters still controlled both houses of the legislature. A group of Birmingham citizens sued, claiming that their votes had substantially less impact than the votes of people from rural counties.

In earlier cases the Supreme Court ruled that federal courts could not tell state legislatures how to handle representation issues. But in 1960 the Court struck down an Alabama law designed to keep African American votes from deciding elections. This case opened the door to judicial review of apportionment decisions. However, the Birmingham plaintiffs still had to convince the Court that Alabama's legislative districts were so unfair as to be unconstitutional.

The Decision

Chief Justice Earl Warren wrote the opinion of the Court. He emphasized that the individual citizen is the key component of a democratic society:

> "Legislators represent people, not trees or acres. Legislators are elected by voters, not farms or cities or economic interests . . . A citizen, a qualified voter, is no more nor no less so because he lives in the city or on the farm. This is the clear and strong command of our Constitution's Equal Protection Clause."

The Court held that seats in both branches of state legislatures had to be apportioned based on population. Each elected official in a particular state had to represent approximately the same number of voters. This "one person, one vote" standard has become a hallmark of democracy.

THE IMPACT TODAY Members of New York's state assembly wrap up a legislative session. Based on *Reynolds* v. *Sims*, seats in state legislatures must be apportioned based on population. The U.S. Census Bureau provides guidelines to assist states in gathering population data to redraw their district boundaries.

CRITICAL THINKING

1. **Analyze the Impact** Using the keyword above, read about the decision in *Baker* v. *Carr*, decided two years before *Reynolds*. What was the issue in *Baker*? How did that decision pave the way for the plaintiffs in *Reynolds* to bring their case?

2. **You Be the Judge** The New York Education Law said that only the parents or guardians of public school children—or the owners or renters of property—could vote in school district elections. A man living in the Union School District No. 15 brought suit after he was not allowed to vote in a school district election. He was not a parent of a student and he neither rented nor owned property in the district. Does New York's law deny him equal protection? How should the court rule on his claim? Explain your reasoning in a paragraph.

SECTION 4
Changes and Challenges

BEFORE YOU READ

MAIN IDEA
Continued social and economic inequalities caused many young African Americans to lose faith in the civil rights movement and integration and seek alternative solutions.

READING FOCUS
1. Why did the civil rights movement expand to the North?
2. What fractures developed in the civil rights movement, and what was the result?
3. What events led to the death of Martin Luther King Jr., and how did the nation react?

KEY TERMS AND PEOPLE
de jure segregation
de facto segregation
Kerner Commission
Stokely Carmichael
Black Power
Black Panther Party
Malcolm X

HSS 11.10.4 Examine the roles of civil rights advocates (e.g., Malcom X).

HSS 11.10.5 Discuss the diffusion of the civil rights movement of African Americans from the churches of the rural South and the urban North, including the resistance to racial desegregation in Little Rock and Birmingham.

The March Against Fear

THE INSIDE STORY

How did the March Against Fear widen a split in the civil rights movement? In June 1966 James Meredith, the University of Mississippi's first African American graduate, began a 27-day march from Memphis, Tennessee, to Jackson, Mississippi, to encourage African Americans to register to vote. On the second day of what he called his March Against Fear, Meredith was shot and wounded. About 150 SCLC and SNCC members gathered to finish his march. Among them were Martin Luther King Jr. of SCLC and SNCC's young new leader, Stokely Carmichael.

The march was a harrowing experience. Vehicles swerved at the marchers, forcing them off the highway. People threw bottles, rocks, and firecrackers. "What are we waiting for, till they kill some of us?" some marchers began to ask. "I'm not much for that nonviolence stuff any more," an angry marcher announced on the highway one day.

As they marched, demonstrators shouted the SCLC's familiar call-and-response chant: "What do we want?" "Freedom now!" Soon, however, SNCC marchers began offering a new response: "Black power!" Whenever the chant began, each side tried to drown out the other. Finally, King and Carmichael agreed to abandon the chant for the rest of the march. Journalists accompanying the march had already noticed the conflict, however. They reported this visible break in the unity of the civil rights movement.

▼ King (left) and Carmichael (right) on the March Against Fear in Mississippi

De Facto Segregation

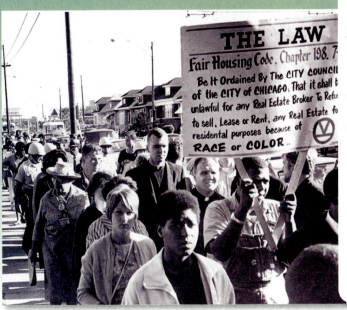

ECONOMIC CONDITIONS IN SELECTED CITIES, 1960

Percentage of population earning less than $3,000 per year

Note: In 1960, the U.S. Census Bureau did not collect data by race at the metropolitan level. Instead, they collected data by white and non-white.

Source: United States Census Bureau

SKILLS FOCUS: INTERPRETING GRAPHS

De facto segregation was reflected in the economic status of the population. How great was the difference in the incomes of whites and minorities in the cities shown in this graph?

See **Skills Handbook**, p. H16

About 350 demonstrators, guarded by police, march through an all-white Chicago neighborhood to protest housing discrimination in the Chicago real estate industry in 1966. Housing discrimination was a form of de facto segregation.

Expanding the Movement

The March Against Fear marked a turning point in the drive for civil rights. The movement had done much to bring an end to **de jure segregation**, or segregation by law, in the South. However, Meredith's shooting provided grim evidence that changes in laws had not altered attitudes. Especially outside the South, African Americans were challenging the movement's tactics. Many began to question whether nonviolent protest was the best means to genuine and permanent change.

Conditions outside the South African Americans in the South and outside the South faced similar but slightly different conditions. Most states did not deny African Americans voting rights. Nor did they require segregated public accommodations. Yet segregation was widespread in America. In most places it was **de facto segregation**—segregation that exists through custom and practice rather than by law. De jure segregation ends when the laws that create it are repealed. De facto segregation can be more difficult to overcome.

Most African Americans outside the South lived in cities. However, they often faced conditions like those faced by black southerners. For example, few real estate agents would take African Americans to homes for sale in white neighborhoods. White homeowners willing to show their house to African American buyers incurred the anger of their neighbors. As a result, African Americans often had no choice but to live in all-black parts of town.

In addition, discrimination by banks made it hard to borrow money to buy or improve property in African American neighborhoods. This caused homeownership there to be low and many buildings to decay. Job discrimination against African Americans led to high unemployment and poverty in these neighborhoods, making the situation worse.

Urban unrest Frustration over these conditions exploded into violence. From 1964 to 1967, racial unrest erupted in most of the nation's large cities. Some of the worst violence took place in the poor, African American neighborhood of Watts in Los Angeles. In 1965, about 35,000 African Americans took part in a six-day riot that destroyed entire city blocks. Some 3,000 people were arrested and 34 were killed before police and troops restored order.

A week of violence in Detroit in July 1967 resulted in 43 deaths and thousands of injuries and arrests. After the riot, President Johnson

Divisions within the Movement

Black Power
At the 1968 Summer Olympics, African American members of the U.S. track team Tommie Smith (left) and John Carlos (right) gave the Black Power salute as they received their medals. Many saw the Black Power movement as threatening because it abandoned the concept of non-violence.

Black Panther Party
The Black Panther Party formed in Oakland, California, in 1966 as a militant group that called for an armed revolution to achieve African American liberation.

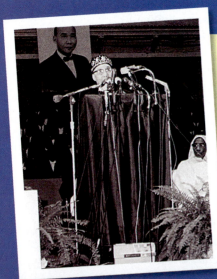

Nation of Islam
Elijah Muhammad led the Nation of Islam from 1934 to 1975. Here he is speaking to a group of followers. The Nation of Islam promoted economic independence for African Americans as well as racial separation.

appointed the **Kerner Commission** to study the causes of urban rioting. Its report placed the blame on poverty and discrimination. "Our nation," the report warned, "is moving toward two societies, one black and one white—separate and unequal."

The movement moves north The riots convinced King that the movement's gains in the South had bypassed millions of African Americans. This awareness spurred him to focus his attention on Chicago in 1966.

The SCLC's Chicago campaign lasted eight months. It was one of King's biggest failures. Chicago's African Americans did not share his civil rights focus. They had the right to vote, and they did not consider themselves segregated. Their concerns were mainly economic.

Chicago authorities also failed to provide the confrontations that worked so well for King in the South. Chicago police had strict orders against using force. Without such brutality, King found it hard to attract the media attention on which he relied to sway public opinion.

In July, King took his marches into Chicago's white neighborhoods. This tactic worked. Residents showered marchers with rocks and bottles. Unlike in the South, however, police protected the marchers. In addition, King's new strategy weakened his northern white support. He found that some whites who had criticized racism in the South had no interest in seeing it exposed in the North. In August, King hollowly declared victory and left Chicago.

READING CHECK **Summarizing** What did King hope to accomplish by expanding the civil rights movement into Chicago?

Fractures in the Movement

Most white Americans viewed the civil rights movement as a unified effort. In fact, it was made up of diverse groups united by the goal of ending racial discrimination. By the mid-1960s, however, conflicts among these groups had developed.

The first signs of trouble arose from Freedom Summer in 1964. As harassment of SNCC and CORE workers in Mississippi increased, some of them rejected the philosophy of non-violence. As you have read, unity was further weakened when the NAACP, CORE, and the

COUNTERPOINTS

Tactics of Change

Martin Luther King's commitment to nonviolence never wavered.

" [V]iolence ... seeks to annihilate rather than convert ... Nonviolence is a powerful and just weapon ... which cuts without wounding and ennobles the man who wields it."

Martin Luther King Jr., 1964

Malcolm X was blunt and uncompromising. He inspired hatred from some and respect from others.

" [N]ow you're facing a situation where the young Negro's coming up. They don't want to hear that 'turn-the-other-cheek' stuff, no. ... There's new thinking coming in. There's new strategy coming in ... It'll be ballots, or it'll be bullets. It'll be liberty, or it will be death."

Malcolm X, 1964

SKILLS FOCUS READING LIKE A HISTORIAN

Identifying Points of View What does King mean when he says that nonviolence "cuts without wounding"? To what is Malcolm X referring when he speaks of "ballots" or "bullets"?

See **Skills Handbook**, pp. H28–H29

SCLC favored the compromise offered the Mississippi Freedom Democratic Party at the Democratic National Convention. SNCC members accused the other groups of betrayal.

Black Power Cracks in the movement widened in May 1966, when **Stokely Carmichael** replaced the moderate John Lewis as head of SNCC. Under Carmichael's leadership, SNCC abandoned the philosophy of nonviolence.

Carmichael's support of aggressive action became clear during the March Against Fear in June 1966. The SNCC leader was among those arrested when the marchers stopped in Greenwood, Mississippi. After being released, Carmichael addressed a rally of about 3,000 protesters. With his arm raised in a clenched-fist salute, he shouted his defiance.

HISTORY'S VOICES

"This is the twenty-seventh time I have been arrested—and I ain't going to jail no more. The only way we're going to stop them white men from whippin' us is to take over. We been saying freedom for six years—and we ain't got nothin'. What we gonna start now is 'Black Power!'"

—Stokely Carmichael, June 17, 1966

As onlookers cheered, Carmichael yelled, "What do you want?" "Black power!" the crowd roared back. The next day the slogan became newspaper headlines across the nation.

Many critics believed the Black Power movement to be a call to violent action. Carmichael rejected this interpretation. He explained **Black Power** as African Americans' dependence on themselves to solve problems. "Integration is irrelevant," he declared. "Political and economic power is what black people have to have." He called on African Americans to form their own separate political organizations.

Like SNCC, CORE also abandoned nonviolence and endorsed Black Power in 1966. In 1967 CORE gave up its commitment to being a multiracial organization.

The Black Panthers Black Power appealed to many young African Americans. It inspired two young community activists, Huey Newton and Bobby Seale, to found a group called the **Black Panther Party** in Oakland, California, in October 1966. The Panthers rejected nonviolence and called for violent revolution as a means of African American liberation.

THE CIVIL RIGHTS MOVEMENT

To achieve some of their goals, the Panthers carried guns and monitored African American neighborhoods to guard against police brutality. Confrontations between Black Panthers and the police in the late 1960s led to several shootouts resulting in deaths on both sides.

Black Muslims One of the largest and most influential groups expressing the ideas of Black Power was the Nation of Islam. Based on the Islamic religion, it was founded in 1930. Its members were called Black Muslims.

The group's leader, the Honorable Elijah Muhammad, preached a message of black nationalism, self-discipline, and self-reliance. Rules forbade smoking, gambling, and alcohol and stressed cleanliness and thrift. Men and women dressed conservatively. During the Great Depression, Black Muslims would not accept any government assistance.

By the 1960s the Nation of Islam had as many as 65,000 followers. Young African Americans, especially from the North's urban slums, were drawn to the Black Muslims' image and to a fiery minister known as **Malcolm X**. (Some Black Muslims took the surname "X" to represent the loss of their original, African identities.) Malcolm X offered a message of hope, defiance, and black pride. "Revolutions are never based upon . . . begging a corrupt society or a corrupt system to accept us into it," Malcolm X said. "Revolutions overturn systems."

At first, Malcolm X was also critical of King and nonviolence. "Any Negro who teaches other Negroes to turn the other cheek is disarming the Negro . . . [of] his natural right to defend himself," he charged. Many white Americans found his message frightening. King and other civil rights leaders thought him an extremist.

In 1964, however, Malcolm X broke with Elijah Muhammad and the Black Muslims. He visited Islam's holy sites in Saudi Arabia and returned a changed man. Although Malcolm X continued to preach Black Power, he began cooperating with other civil rights leaders and called for racial harmony. "If the white people realize what the alternative is," he noted, "perhaps they will be more willing to hear Dr. King." In February 1965, a few weeks after making this observation, Malcolm X was assassinated by Black Muslims who considered him a traitor to their cause.

READING CHECK Identifying Supporting Details How did Black Muslims reflect fractures in the civil rights movement?

The Death of Martin Luther King Jr.

Moments after Martin Luther King Jr. was shot, his aides frantically pointed to the source of the gunshots (left).

The Assassination of King

King's disappointing Chicago campaign increased his awareness that economic issues must be part of the civil rights movement. With this in mind, he went to Memphis, Tennessee, in March 1968 to aid African American sanitation workers who were on strike against discrimination in the city's work and pay policies. King led a march to city hall on March 28 and then remained in Memphis to speak at a rally on April 3.

The next day James Earl Ray, a white sniper with a high-powered rifle, shot and killed King as he stood on the balcony of his motel. Within hours, rioting erupted in more than 120 cities as enraged African Americans across the nation responded to the assassination. Within three weeks, 46 people were dead, some 2,600 were injured, and more than 21,000 were arrested. Nearly 55,000 troops were required to restore order. One civil rights leader noted that King would have been outraged by the violent reaction to his death.

Robert Kennedy, who was running for president at the time, was about to give a campaign speech in an African American neighborhood of Indianapolis, Indiana, when he learned of the shooting. After informing the audience of the tragedy, he recalled King's message while making an impassioned appeal for calm.

HISTORY'S VOICES

"You can be filled with bitterness and with hatred and a desire for revenge. We can move in that direction as a country, in great polarization, black people amongst blacks and white people amongst whites, filled with hatred toward one another. Or we can make an effort, like Martin Luther King did, to understand and to comprehend, and replace that violence, that stain of bloodshed that has spread across the land, with . . . compassion and love."

—Robert Kennedy, April 4, 1968

READING CHECK **Summarizing** What were the circumstances of King's death?

King's widow, Coretta Scott King, mourns at his funeral (left). Below, mules pull King's casket, symbolizing his work on behalf of the poor. Some 50,000 mourners joined the procession.

SECTION 4 ASSESSMENT

go.hrw.com
Online Quiz
Keyword: SE7 HP18

HSS 11.10.4, 11.10.5

Reviewing Ideas, Terms, and People

1. **a. Describe** What did the **Kerner Commission** conclude?
   b. Contrast What is the difference between **de jure segregation** and **de facto segregation**?
   c. Predict How do you think urban unrest could have been prevented or stopped?

2. **a. Identify** What was the **Black Panther Party**?
   b. Contrast How were the goals of supporters of the **Black Power** movement different from those of other civil rights groups?
   c. Elaborate Why do you think many African Americans were drawn to leaders such as **Stokely Carmichael** and **Malcolm X**?

3. **a. Describe** Why did Martin Luther King Jr. go to Memphis, Tennessee, in March 1968?
   b. Make Inferences Why would King have been upset about the public reaction to his death?
   c. Predict What long-term effect do you think King's death will have on the civil rights movement?

Critical Thinking

4. **Categorizing** Review your notes on the Black Power movement. Then copy the graphic organizer below and use it to list traditional and Black Power civil rights groups and leaders.

Traditional	Black Power

FOCUS ON WRITING

ELA W1.1

5. **Expository** Write a paragraph either for or against Black Power. Explain why you would or would not have supported its goals and methods.

THE CIVIL RIGHTS MOVEMENT

SECTION 5
The Movement Continues

BEFORE YOU READ

MAIN IDEA
The civil rights movement was in decline by the 1970s, but its accomplishments continued to benefit American society.

READING FOCUS
1. How did the SCLC's goals change and with what results?
2. For what reasons did the Black Power movement decline?
3. What civil rights changes took place in the 1970s, and what were their results?

KEY TERMS AND PEOPLE
Poor People's Campaign
Ralph Abernathy
Civil Rights Act of 1968
affirmative action
John Lewis
Andrew Young
Jesse Jackson

HSS 11.10.5 Discuss the diffusion of the civil rights movement of African Americans from the churches of the rural South and the urban North.

HSS 11.10.6 Analyze the effects of civil rights and voting rights legislation, with an emphasis on equality of access to education and to the political process.

The Poor People's Campaign

THE INSIDE STORY *Would you endure miserable conditions to seek changes that you believed to be right?* A covered wagon pulled by mules would have attracted attention on the streets of Washington, D.C., even if not accompanied by tens of thousands of demonstrators protesting their poverty. Another strange sight was the community of tents and shacks that 2,500 of these protesters—African Americans, Native Americans, Hispanic Americans, and whites among them—occupied on the National Mall. They called their settlement Resurrection City.

Longtime SCLC leader Ralph Abernathy explained why the protesters were there. "The poor are no longer divided. We're not going to let the white man put us down any more," he declared. "It's not white power, and I'll give you some news, it's not black power, either. It's poor power and we're going to use it."

Unusually heavy spring rains quickly put Resurrection City ankle-deep in mud, making sanitation and trash collection difficult. Each day, however, determined groups of demonstrators organized marches from their miserable surroundings to federal agencies throughout the city. The marches were designed to demand that the government do more to combat poverty. "We have business on the road to freedom," Abernathy encouraged one group of protesters as they marched toward Capitol Hill: "We must prove to white America that you can kill the leader but you cannot kill the dream."

▶ The Poor People's Campaign set off to combat economic inequality as the next phase of the civil rights movement.

586 CHAPTER 18

A Change in Goals

The **Poor People's Campaign** marked an important expansion of the civil rights movement. By 1967 changes in the law had achieved basic rights for African Americans. Martin Luther King Jr. believed, however, that most African Americans were still prevented from achieving equality because they were poor. He decided to alert the nation to the economic plight not only of African Americans, but of all poor people.

King's death prevented him from leading this effort. That task fell to his successor as the head of the SCLC, **Ralph Abernathy**. In May 1968, thousands of protesters came to the nation's capital to be part of the Poor People's Campaign. A Mississippi woman explained why she joined the protest.

HISTORY'S VOICES

> "I'm here because when I was a child, I got taken out of school and put to work on the farm helping my family . . . Then I got married and had kids, and my husband worked in the cotton fields . . . But he got sick and don't work much no more and there ain't hardly no cotton to get picked by hand anyway . . . So I came here with the Campaign to tell people that we got to be treated like human beings—that we have a right to live because we've earned that right but we've yet to be paid."
>
> —Henrietta Franklin, quoted in the *Washington Post*, May 24, 1968

The Poor People's Campaign turned out to be a disaster. Besides bad weather, the SCLC experienced terrible media relations. Some Resurrection City residents harassed reporters. About 200 protesters turned out to be members of inner-city gangs. The campaign's organizers eventually sent them home. After six weeks of problems, police used tear gas to empty Resurrection City and then tore it down.

Without King's eloquence and leadership, the Poor People's Campaign also failed to express clearly the protesters' needs and demands. Some conservative members of Congress believed they saw elements of communism in the campaign's beliefs and goals. All these factors combined to cause the SCLC and its role in the civil rights movement to decline.

READING CHECK **Identifying the Main Idea** How did the Poor People's Campaign represent a change of goals for the civil rights movement?

The Decline of Black Power

The civil rights movement took place at the height of the Cold War, when the nation's fear of communism was at its height. FBI director J. Edgar Hoover was convinced that the major civil rights groups were led by Communists.

In 1956 Hoover created a secret program within the FBI to keep an eye on many types of groups that were involved in the unrest that was plaguing society. Spies and informers working for the FBI posed as supporters of these groups and reported the groups' plans and activities back to the government.

At first, King was Hoover's main target in the civil rights movement. As the Black Power movement grew, however, he instructed his agents to disrupt and otherwise interfere with the activities of other civil rights groups he considered a threat to American society.

For example, to disrupt SNCC—and at the same time weaken the Black Panthers—FBI spies in SNCC spread false rumors that the Panthers intended to kill SNCC leaders. The FBI also forged harmful posters, leaflets, and correspondence that appeared to come from the groups it had targeted.

Hoover was especially concerned about the Black Panthers. The FBI encouraged local authorities to combat the Panthers by any means possible. Police raided the Panthers'

The Congressional Black Caucus
Retired North Carolina Supreme Court Chief Justice Henry Frye swears in members of the Congressional Black Caucus of the 109th Congress. Founded in 1970 as an organization of African American members of the House of Representatives, the group's mission is to address legislative concerns of black and minority citizens.

AFRICAN AMERICAN GAINS IN THE CIVIL RIGHTS MOVEMENT

African American Elected Officials:
1,469 in 1970; 9,040 in 2000

African Americans Not Living in Poverty:
45% in 1960; 78% in 2000

African American College Graduates:
3.3% in 1960; 16.5% in 2000

---

headquarters in cities across the country. Since Black Panthers usually were armed, violent conflict sometimes resulted. Law enforcement authorities also sometimes shot Black Panther members whether they resisted or not. By the early 1970s, armed violence had led to the killing or arrest of many Black Panther leaders. Others had fled the United States in order to avoid arrest.

SNCC also collapsed with FBI help. In 1967, H. Rap Brown replaced Stokely Carmichael as head of SNCC. Urged on by his staff—many of whom were on the FBI's payroll—Brown took increasingly radical and shocking positions. As a result, SNCC's membership declined rapidly. The group disbanded in the early 1970s.

READING CHECK **Identifying Main Ideas**
How did federal action help lead to a decline of the Black Power movement?

New Changes and Gains

In spite of the challenges, the civil rights movement did make gains in the late 1960s. For example, just a week after Martin Luther King Jr.'s death, President Johnson signed the **Civil Rights Act of 1968**. Also called the Fair Housing Act, the law banned discrimination in the sale or rental of housing.

Busing and political change Despite the 1954 *Brown* decision, urban schools were still largely segregated in the late 1960s. This was a result of de facto segregation. Years of housing discrimination had contributed to segregated neighborhoods in many cities.

The Fair Housing Act was a step toward ending this situation. However, it would take years to overcome decades of discrimination and to achieve integrated neighborhoods. Meanwhile, many city schools would remain segregated.

To speed integration of city schools, courts began ordering that some students be bused from their neighborhoods to schools in other parts of the city. Busing met fierce opposition, especially in the North. Court-ordered busing in Boston in 1974, for example, led to two years of sometimes violent protests. Denver opponents of busing burned school buses.

Forced busing speeded the migration of whites from cities to suburbs. This development increased the political power of African Americans. By 1974 Cleveland, Detroit, Los Angeles, Washington, Atlanta, and several smaller cities had elected black mayors.

Affirmative action As you read in Section 2, the Civil Rights Act of 1964 banned discrimination in employment. By the late 1960s, the U.S. Justice Department was taking legal action against employers for violating this law. At the same time, the government helped businesses and colleges set up **affirmative action** programs that gave preference to minorities and women in hiring and admissions. These programs were designed to help make up for past discrimination against these groups.

Affirmative action and busing were divisive issues in the 1970s. It is difficult to assess clearly their contribution to the Republican Party's success in the late 1900s and early 2000s. However, backlash against these programs helped Republicans lure two important groups of voters away from the Democratic Party—white southerners and urban, working-class whites.

The new Black Power As African Americans in the South exercised their newly won voting rights—and were more politically active nationwide—it became clear that Black Power did not die in the 1970s. It merely took on a new form and meaning.

By 1970 the populations of more than 100 counties in the South were at least 50 percent African American. The African Americans who took over elected offices in these and other places governed as well as the white officials they replaced. In addition, many African Americans who played important roles in the civil rights movement later provided other services to the nation. For example, Thurgood Marshall, the NAACP lawyer who argued the *Brown* case before the Supreme Court, later became the Court's first African American justice.

John Lewis took part in some of the first sit-ins in 1960. He was also a Freedom Rider in 1961 and participated in the Selma march in 1965. The head of SNCC in the early 1960s, Lewis was elected in 1986 to the first of many terms representing the people of Atlanta, Georgia, in Congress.

As a staff member of the SCLC and a close adviser to King, **Andrew Young** played a key role in the 1963 Birmingham campaign and in the Selma march. In 1972 he became Georgia's first African American member of Congress since Reconstruction. Young later served as U.S. ambassador to the United Nations and as mayor of Atlanta. You will read more about Young's career later in this book.

Jesse Jackson was another young activist who went on to leave his own mark on the nation. Jackson founded his own civil rights organization, Operation PUSH, and became an international figure for his work on behalf of poor and oppressed peoples around the world. His campaigns for the Democratic presidential nomination in the 1980s raised the real possibility that the nation might one day have an African American president.

ACADEMIC VOCABULARY
assess determine the importance of

READING CHECK **Summarizing** What political changes did busing, affirmative action, and Black Power bring to America in the 1970s?

SECTION 5 ASSESSMENT

HSS 11.10.5, 11.10.6

Reviewing Idea, Terms, and People

1. **a. Identify** Who succeeded Martin Luther King Jr. as head of the SCLC?
   b. Analyze Why did the Poor People's Campaign fail?
   c. Elaborate Why did Martin Luther King Jr. treat poverty as a civil rights issue?

2. **a. Describe** How did J. Edgar Hoover and the FBI weaken the Black Panthers?
   b. Make Inferences How did the Cold War influence Hoover and the FBI's attitude about the Black Power movement?

3. **a. Define** What was busing, and what was its purpose?
   b. Contrast How was the role of Black Power different during and after the 1970s than before the 1970s?
   c. Elaborate Why do you think many people have opposed affirmative action?

Critical Thinking

4. **Identifying Supporting Details** Review your notes on the decline of the civil rights movement. Then copy the graphic organizer below and use it to list gains and losses for African Americans that accompanied the movement's decline.

Gains	Losses

FOCUS ON WRITING  ELA W1.1

5. **Expository** Write a statement suggesting ways to prevent the civil rights movement from declining. Include an assessment of whether the civil rights movement is needed today.

CHAPTER 18 DOCUMENT-BASED INVESTIGATION

The Government and Equal Rights

HSS 11.10.6

Historical Context The documents below provide information on views of government intervention for equal rights.

Task Examine the documents and answer the questions that follow. Then you will be asked to write an essay about the federal government's role in establishing equal rights for Americans, using facts from the documents and from the chapter to support the position you take in your thesis statement.

DOCUMENT 1

Many white southerners viewed integration as a social question that should not be answered by the federal government. Some argued that segregation would eventually end on its own. Federal intervention, they argued, would only create hostility and resentment. Robert Patterson was a white Mississippi native who opposed government-enforced integration. In the following interview, he explained his views on the integration of restaurants and motels.

> "That's not social integration, that's forced integration under the might of the federal government.... To be subjected to integration is one thing, but to submit to it is something else entirely. We are being subjected to integration; we're not submitting to it. And you will find that white people do not frequent places where there are a whole lot of Negroes through choice. And I think gradually . . . things will resegregate themselves."

DOCUMENT 2

Some people who supported civil rights cautioned that the federal government risked a backlash if it moved too fast to change society. Clifford H. Baldowski was a white editorial cartoonist for the *Atlanta Journal-Constitution* who supported civil rights. The following cartoon, published in 1963, depicts Attorney General Robert F. Kennedy trying to ensure the success of needed federal civil rights legislation.

"... Wait a minute ... Somebody has gotta keep this thing on the track!"

590 CHAPTER 18

DOCUMENT 3

Many African Americans did not believe that white officials in the South would protect equal rights unless the federal government forced them to do so. Fannie Lou Hamer called on the federal government to intervene in Mississippi, a state in which a majority black population was largely prevented from participating in local and state government. In the following interview, she recalled how Byron De La Beckwith, the assassin of civil rights leader Medgar Evers, was set free by two all-white juries.

> "America that is divided against itself cannot stand, and we cannot say that we have all this unity they say we have when black people are being discriminated against in every city in America I have visited.
>
> "I was in jail [for protesting] when Medgar Evers was murdered and nothing, I mean nothing has been done about that... We can no longer ignore the fact that America is NOT the 'land of the free and the home of the brave.'"

DOCUMENT 4

Some African American leaders warned the federal government that it needed to enforce equal rights not just because it was the right thing to do but in order to prevent violence. In the following speech from 1964, Malcolm X urged government leaders to enforce equal rights before people took matters into their own hands.

> "America is the only country in history in a position to bring about a revolution without violence and bloodshed. But America is not morally equipped to do so.
>
> Why is America in a position to bring about a bloodless revolution? Because the Negro in this country holds the balance of power and if the Negro in this country were given what the Constitution says he is supposed to have, the added power of the Negro in this country would sweep all of the racists and segregationists out of office. It would change the entire political structure of the country. It would wipe out the southern segregationism that now controls America's foreign policy, as well as America's domestic policy.
>
> And the only way without bloodshed that this can be brought about is that the black man has to be given full use of the ballot in every one of the 50 states. But if the black man doesn't get the ballot, then you are going to be faced with another man who forgets the ballot and starts using the bullet."

Skills Focus — HSS Analysis HI1
READING LIKE A HISTORIAN

1. **a. Identify** Refer to Document 1. To Patterson, what is the difference between "subjected" and "submitting"?
   b. Elaborate Do you think Patterson sees voluntary integration ever taking place without force? Explain.

2. **a. Describe** Refer to Document 2. Who is driving?
   b. Interpret What does this cartoon reflect about the role that Robert F. Kennedy played in civil rights legislation?

3. **a. Identify** Refer to Document 3. What is the main hypocrisy that Hamer sees?
   b. Analyze How does the example of Byron De La Beckwith support Hamer's call for federal intervention?

4. **a. Describe** Refer to Document 4. To Malcolm X, what was the most important right that the government needed to protect for African Americans?
   b. Elaborate Do you think Malcolm X's reasons for needing government intervention are valid? Explain.

5. **Document-Based Essay Question** Consider the question below and form a thesis statement. Using examples from Documents 1, 2, 3, and 4, create an outline and write a short essay supporting your position. What role should the government have in enforcing equal rights for Americans?

See **Skills Handbook**, pp. H28–H29, H30

Chapter Review

Visual Summary: The Civil Rights Movement

Fighting Segregation
- Early civil rights groups included the NAACP and CORE.
- In 1954 the Supreme Court ordered an end to racial segregation in public schools.
- A bus boycott in Montgomery, Alabama, launched the SCLC and the modern civil rights movement.

Freedom Now!
- Sit-ins and Freedom Rides provoked violent reactions from some white southerners.
- Violent response to marches in Birmingham, Alabama, shocked the nation.
- The March on Washington helped lead to the Civil Rights Act of 1964.

Voting Rights
- Some white southerners tried to block efforts of African Americans to vote.
- African Americans in Mississippi organized to increase their political power.
- A brutal attack on a protest in Selma, Alabama, helped win support for the Voting Rights Act of 1965.

Changes and Challenges
- Civil rights leaders began attacking de facto segregation in the North in the mid-1960s.
- Differences within the civil rights movement weakened it and led to the rise of Black Power.
- The assassination of Martin Luther King Jr. caused urban unrest.

The Movement Continues
- King's death and the Poor People's Campaign helped lead to the decline of SCLC.
- Internal divisions and an FBI campaign weakened some civil rights groups.
- The civil rights movement resulted in important gains for African Americans.

Reviewing Key Terms and People

Identify the correct term or person from the chapter that best fits each of the following descriptions.

1. Law banning discrimination in employment and in public facilities
2. Leader of SNCC in the 1960s who many years later was elected to Congress from the state of Georgia
3. A type of discrimination that exists through custom and practice instead of by law
4. Groups of people who traveled through the South challenging segregation at bus stations
5. Project for college students to spend their summer vacation registering African Americans to vote in Mississippi
6. African American politician and civil rights leader who campaigned for the Democratic presidential nomination in the 1980s
7. Minister and civil rights leader who supported nonviolent resistance
8. NAACP leader who was murdered at his home by a member of the Ku Klux Klan
9. Part of the Constitution banning states from taxing citizens to vote in elections

Comprehension and Critical Thinking

SECTION 1 *(pp. 556–563)* **HSS** 11.10.2, 11.10.4

10. **a. Recall** What civil rights gains were made in the 1940s?

    b. Analyze How did the African American community support the Montgomery bus boycott?

    c. Elaborate How did Thurgood Marshall and the NAACP's earlier work contribute to the *Brown* v. *Board of Education of Topeka, Kansas,* decision?

History's Impact video program
Review the video to answer the closing question: How did civil rights activists push for equality during the 1950s and 1960s?

SECTION 2 (pp. 564–571) HSS 11.10.3, 11.10.4

11. **a. Identify** What were the goals of SNCC?
    b. Draw Conclusions What effect did racial violence have on President Kennedy's approach to civil rights?
    c. Evaluate What do you think made the strategy of nonviolence effective?

SECTION 3 (pp. 573–578) HSS 11.10.5

12. **a. Describe** What did Freedom Summer accomplish?
    b. Draw Conclusions Why did Martin Luther King Jr. resume the march from Selma to Montgomery, Alabama after it met with violence?
    c. Predict How do you think the actions of the Mississippi Freedom Democratic Party affected the Democratic Party?

SECTION 4 (pp. 580–585) HSS 11.10.4, 11.10.5

13. **a. Identify** What slogan did Stokely Carmichael introduce at a SNCC rally?
    b. Compare How were conditions similar for African Americans in the South and in the North?
    c. Elaborate Why is the legacy of Martin Luther King Jr. so important?

SECTION 5 (pp. 586–589) HSS 11.10.5, 11.10.6

14. **a. Describe** How did civil rights leaders such as John Lewis and Andrew Young continue serving the nation after the 1960s?
    b. Analyze Why did SNCC collapse?
    c. Predict What could have made the Poor People's Campaign more successful?

Using the Internet

go.hrw.com
Practice Online
Keyword: SE7 CH18

15. The policy of affirmative action resulted from the civil rights movement, but it remains controversial today. Using the keyword above, do research to learn about court cases and controversies related to affirmative action. Then create a report that analyzes how these questions and decisions have shaped affirmative action policies today.

Analyzing Primary Sources HSS HR4

Reading Like a Historian Read the History's Voices passage in Section 2 from Diane Nash that begins: "We would practice such things …" Nash was training to take part in civil rights demonstrations.

16. **Identify** What were the civil rights workers practicing?

17. **Draw Conclusions** Why do you think civil rights workers needed this kind of training?

Critical Reading ELA R3.2

Read the passage in Section 4 that begins with the heading "Fractures in the Movement." Then answer the question that follows.

18. The first major signs of trouble in the civil rights movement occurred when some workers
    A rejected the philosophy of nonviolence.
    B split off and formed their own groups.
    C made speeches in favor of Black Power.
    D disagreed at the 1964 Democratic National Convention.

Think about the following issue.

Martin Luther King Jr. was an inspiring leader who was highly effective at communicating and motivating African Americans and whites. He was clearly the most important and influential leader of the civil rights movement in the mid-1950s through the late 1960s.

19. **Assignment** Did King's death bring an end to the civil rights movement? Write a short essay in which you develop your position on this issue. Support your point of view with reasoning and examples from your reading and studies.

THE CIVIL RIGHTS MOVEMENT

CHAPTER 19
1954–1975
The Vietnam War

THE BIG PICTURE It was the first war to invade American homes via television. For years TV brought the U.S. fight against the horrors of jungle warfare into American living rooms. Seemingly unwinnable, the U.S. war effort brought down a president and bitterly divided the nation.

California Standards

History-Social Sciences
11.9 Students analyze U.S. foreign policy since World War II.

Skills Focus **READING LIKE A HISTORIAN**

Members of the 1st Squadron, 9th Cavalry, burst out of their helicopter and into action in Chu Lai, South Vietnam, in 1967. While Americans at home may have been divided about the war, U.S. involvement was reaching its peak at this time.
Interpreting Visuals What does this photo suggest about soldiers' commitment to the war?

See **Skills Handbook**, p. H30

 U.S.
1953
United States aids France in Indochina War.

1954

 World
May 1954 French forces at Dien Bien Phu surrender to the Vietminh.

History's Impact video program
Watch the video to understand the impact of public opinion on foreign policy.

1960 The United States starts supplying military assistance to South Vietnam.

August 1964 Congress passes the Tonkin Gulf Resolution, expanding U.S. involvement in Vietnam.

April 1965 Antiwar demonstration in Washington, D.C., draws more than 200,000 protesters.

January 1973 The United States agrees to withdraw all troops from South Vietnam.

January 1959 Communist guerillas, led by Fidel Castro, take control of Cuba.

January 1968 Communist forces launch the Tet Offensive.

April 30, 1975 South Vietnam surrenders to North Vietnam.

SECTION 1
The War Develops

BEFORE YOU READ

MAIN IDEA
Concern about the spread of communism led the United States to become increasingly involved in Vietnam.

READING FOCUS
1. How did Southeast Asia's colonial history produce increased tensions in Vietnam?
2. What policies did Presidents Truman and Eisenhower pursue in Vietnam after World War II?
3. What events and conditions caused growing conflicts between North Vietnam and South Vietnam?
4. Why did Presidents Kennedy and Johnson increase U.S. involvement in Vietnam?

KEY TERMS AND PEOPLE
Ho Chi Minh
Vietminh
domino theory
Dien Bien Phu
Geneva Conference
Ngo Dinh Diem
Vietcong
Tonkin Gulf Resolution

HSS 11.9.3 Trace the origins and geopolitical consequences (foreign and domestic) of the Cold War and containment policy, including the following:
• The Vietnam War

THE INSIDE STORY

How did President Woodrow Wilson disappoint Ho Chi Minh? Paris in 1919 was an exciting place to be for 28-year-old Nguyen That Thanh (NY-uhn TAHT TAHN). He was one of some 50,000 Southeast Asians from the colony of French Indochina who were living in France at the end of World War I. Most of these Vietnamese worked in factories, aiding the French war effort.

Nguyen That Thanh, however, had come for a different reason: to convince the other Vietnamese in France to support Vietnam's independence. He was inspired by the Fourteen Points that U.S. president Woodrow Wilson had issued during World War I. Wilson's Fourteen Points called for self-determination for all people—that is, letting people decide how they want to be governed.

Wilson was among the leaders who met in Paris in 1919 to negotiate the peace treaty and plan the postwar world. Nguyen wrote to the president asking that his Fourteen Points be applied to the people of Southeast Asia. He hand-delivered his letter to American officials at the peace conference, but he was turned away.

There was little chance that Wilson could have convinced France to give up its control of Vietnam. Yet Nguyen was very disappointed that the president ignored his letter. He bitterly complained of being deceived by Wilson's "song of freedom." Nguyen left France in 1923. In 1941 he returned to Vietnam to lead its fight for independence. By then he was known by a new name: Ho Chi Minh.

▲ As a young man in France, Nguyen That Thanh began working toward Vietnamese independence.

The French Presidential Palace, located in the city of Hanoi, remains a powerful reminder of French colonial influence.

Colonial Vietnam

The Southeast Asian nation of Vietnam is bordered by China to the north and by Laos and Cambodia to the west. Rich agricultural resources have long made the country ripe for foreign invasion. China invaded northern Vietnam's Red River Delta around 200 BC. The Vietnamese people struggled for independence for centuries, finally driving out Chinese rulers in the early 1400s.

Vietnam's independence again was threatened in the mid-1800s, as European powers competed to build colonial empires. Despite fierce resistance from the Vietnamese, France gained control of Vietnam by 1883. The French later combined Vietnam with Laos and Cambodia to form French Indochina.

A nationalist leader Many Vietnamese were driven into poverty under French rule. The French raised taxes and gave the Vietnamese no civil rights under French authority.

These conditions helped to fuel a growing nationalist movement in Vietnam. Nguyen That Thanh emerged as one of its leaders. He came to be known by a new name, **Ho Chi Minh**, meaning "He Who Enlightens."

Ho Chi Minh was born in a village in central Vietnam in 1890. He participated in several tax revolts against the French before leaving home and traveling around the world in the early 1900s. After President Wilson declined to meet him at the Paris Peace Conference, Ho Chi Minh joined the French Communist Party. "It was patriotism, not communism, that inspired me," he claimed.

While living in China and the Soviet Union in the 1920s and 1930s, Ho Chi Minh continued to work for Vietnam's independence and to study communism. He came to believe that a Communist revolution was a way Vietnam could gain freedom from foreign rulers.

Changing rulers Control of Vietnam again changed hands during World War II, when the Japanese army occupied Indochina. Ho Chi Minh returned to Vietnam in 1941 and organized a group to resist the Japanese occupation. The group was called the League for the Independence of Vietnam, or the **Vietminh** (vee-eht-MIN). The Vietminh was led by Communists, but the group was open to non-Communists who were committed to independence. During World War II, the Vietminh attacked Japanese forces and were able to liberate parts of northern Vietnam.

In 1945 Japan surrendered to the Allies and withdrew from Indochina. The Vietminh took the opportunity to declare Vietnam an independent country. Thousands of people gathered in Hanoi, Vietnam's capital, to hear Ho Chi Minh speak on September 2. Hoping to gain American support for Vietnam's independence, he quoted from the Declaration of Independence.

FACES OF HISTORY

Ho Chi MINH
1890–1969

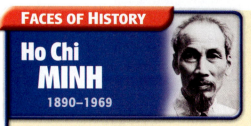

Ho Chi Minh was a rebel from a young age. The school he attended taught that France was trying to improve Vietnam. Ho Chi Minh told other students that France was actually an invader, a view he formed by reading banned books. He was soon kicked out of school.

When he was 21 he went to London, where he met Asian workers who he believed were overworked and underpaid. In France he became a Communist, but he criticized the French Communist Party for not opposing colonialism more strongly. He called for revolution in Southeast Asia and moved to south China to train Vietnamese exiles. He amassed an army of supporters who would eventually wage the twentieth century's longest and costliest battle against colonialism.

Draw Conclusions Why did Ho adopt Communist beliefs?

HISTORY'S VOICES

> "All men are created equal. They are endowed by their Creator with certain unalienable Rights; among these are Life, Liberty, and the pursuit of Happiness . . . The whole Vietnamese people, animated [driven to action] by a common purpose, are determined to fight to the bitter end against any attempt by the French colonialists to reconquer their country. We are convinced that the Allied nations, which . . . have acknowledged the principles of self-determination and equality of nations, will not refuse to acknowledge the independence of Vietnam."
>
> —Ho Chi Minh, September 2, 1945

Ho Chi Minh believed that Vietnam's fight for independence from France was similar to the American colonies' struggle for independence from Great Britain. He expected that the United States would support the Vietnamese nationalist movement.

READING CHECK **Drawing Conclusions** Why did Ho Chi Minh work for Vietnam's independence from France?

Vietnam after World War II

As Ho Chi Minh feared, the French reclaimed Vietnam as a colony after World War II. In December 1946 the Vietnamese people again began battling French rule.

The first Indochina war President Harry Truman disappointed Ho Chi Minh after World War II, just as Wilson had done after World War I. Truman saw the situation in Indochina in terms of the Cold War struggle against communism. He decided to support France, a key ally in the effort to block Communist expansion in Europe. He was also unwilling to back the Vietminh because many of its members were Communists.

Events in Asia soon revealed the extent of Communist expansion. The Communist army of Mao Zedong seized China in 1949. The next year, Communist North Korea invaded South Korea. At the same time, several Communist-led nationalist revolts were raging in Indonesia, Malaya, and the Philippines. These events strengthened the U.S. commitment to contain communism in Southeast Asia.

The domino theory After Dwight D. Eisenhower became president of the United States in 1953, he warned that if Vietnam fell to communism, other Southeast Asian countries would quickly follow. The belief that communism would spread to neighboring countries was called the **domino theory**. "You have a row of dominoes set up," Eisenhower explained. "You knock over the first one, and what will happen to the last one is a certainty that it will go over very quickly."

The United States sent arms, ammunition, supplies, and money to the French forces in Vietnam. By 1954 the United States was paying more than 75 percent of the cost of France's war. Despite the massive U.S. aid, the French were losing to the Vietnamese, suffering defeat after defeat.

The Vietminh used guerrilla tactics effectively. They attacked French forces without warning and then disappeared into the jungle. Ho Chi Minh compared this type of warfare to a fight between a tiger and an elephant.

HISTORY'S VOICES

> "If the tiger ever stands still, the elephant will crush him with his mighty tusks. But the tiger does not stand still . . . He will leap upon the back of the elephant, tearing huge chunks from his hide, and then the tiger will leap back into the dark jungle. And slowly the elephant will bleed to death. That will be the war of Indochina."
>
> —Ho Chi Minh, quoted in *America Inside Out*

France is defeated The French soldiers made a last stand in a valley in northwestern Vietnam called Dien Bien Phu (DYEN BYEN FOO). About 40,000 Vietminh troops surrounded 15,000 French troops. The French commander clung to the hope of a U.S. rescue, telling his soldiers, "The 'free world' will not let us down."

Eisenhower, however, had no intention of sending U.S. soldiers into another war in Asia so soon after the Korean War. The French forces at Dien Bien Phu surrendered to the Vietminh on May 7, 1954.

In eight years of fighting, the two sides had lost nearly 300,000 soldiers. Surviving Vietnamese forces had gained valuable experience fighting a guerrilla war against an enemy with superior weapons and technology. This would prove to be an important factor in the years ahead.

The Geneva Conference After the French surrender, representatives from France, Vietnam, Cambodia, Great Britain, Laos, China, the Soviet Union, and the United States gathered in Geneva, Switzerland. The goal of the Geneva Conference was to work out a peace agreement and arrange for Indochina's future.

The Geneva Accords were signed in July 1954. A cease-fire was worked out, and Vietnam was temporarily divided at the 17th parallel. Vietminh forces would control the northern part of Vietnam, and the French would withdraw from the country. A demilitarized zone (DMZ) along the 17th parallel would act as a buffer zone to prevent fighting between the north and south.

According to the Geneva Accords, general elections were to be held in July 1956. These elections would reunify the country under one government. The United States, however, believed that Ho Chi Minh and the Communists would win a nationwide election. The United States therefore never fully supported the peace agreements.

China's Communist government had been aiding the Vietminh in the war and hoped to limit U.S. influence in the region. The United States, meanwhile, did not want to see all of Vietnam fall under Communist control.

READING CHECK Identifying Cause and Effect Why did the United States support France instead of Vietnam after World War II?

INDOCHINA, 1950

The political and cultural influence of both India and China on the region gave Indochina its name.
1. **Region** What countries formed Indochina?
2. **Place** What were the capitals of North and South Vietnam?

See **Skills Handbook**, p. H20

Growing Conflict in Vietnam

With North Vietnam in the control of Ho Chi Minh and his Communist forces, President Eisenhower hoped to at least prevent communism from spreading to South Vietnam. He pinned his hopes on the South Vietnamese leader, Ngo Dinh Diem (NGOH DIN dee-EM).

Vietnam's leaders Diem, a Roman Catholic, had served as a high-ranking official in the colonial government under French rule. He was taken hostage by the Vietminh in 1945 and brought to see Ho Chi Minh. Ho asked

Diem to become part of his Communist government, believing Diem would bring support from Catholics. Diem, whose brother had been murdered by the Vietminh, refused the offer. Despite Diem's refusal to cooperate, he was released.

Vietminh forces later tried unsuccessfully to assassinate Diem. He then fled Vietnam and traveled for several years. He spent two years in the United States, where he met American leaders. Diem impressed them with his strong anti-Communist views. He returned to Vietnam after France's defeat in 1954 and became the president of South Vietnam.

Very soon, however, U.S. officials became disappointed with Diem's corrupt and brutal leadership. In a presidential election in 1955, Diem claimed to have won more than 98 percent of the vote. In Saigon, the capital of South Vietnam, election results showed he received 200,000 more votes than there were registered voters in the city.

Diem's government was unpopular from the start. He showed favoritism toward Catholics, which upset South Vietnam's large Buddhist majority. He handed out top government jobs to members of his family. In addition, Diem's land policies favored wealthy landowners at the expense of the peasants. His security forces tortured and imprisoned his political opponents. American leaders were disturbed by these and other actions by Diem. Nevertheless, they preferred Diem's government to a Communist takeover.

In North Vietnam, Ho Chi Minh's leadership became increasingly totalitarian and repressive. Forsaking his earlier commitment to human rights, he struck with brutal force, breaking up the estates of large colonial landowners. He gave the land to the peasants, which made him immensely popular.

Fearing that Ho Chi Minh would win the 1956 election set by the Geneva Accords, Diem barred the election in South Vietnam. Like Germany and Korea, Vietnam continued to be divided into separate Communist and non-Communist countries. This was unacceptable to Ho Chi Minh, who wanted to unite Vietnam as a nation under one Communist government.

A civil war By the late 1950s, Diem's opponents in South Vietnam were in open revolt. In 1959 Communist leaders in North Vietnam began supplying weapons to Vietminh rebels

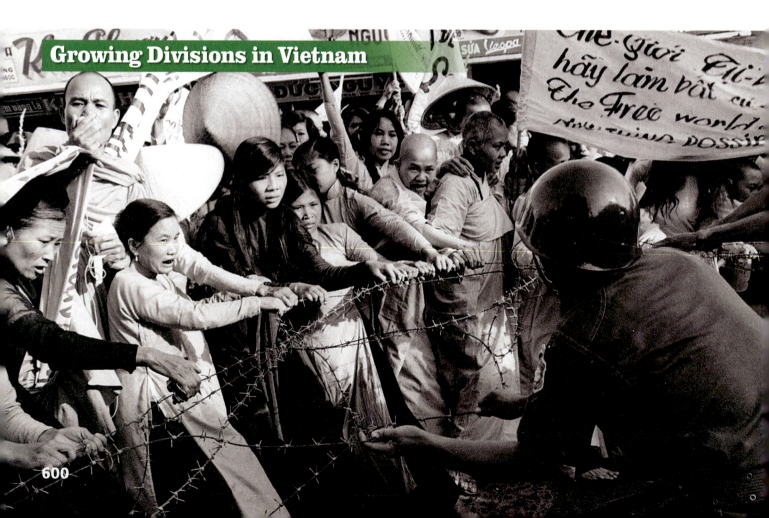

Growing Divisions in Vietnam

who had remained in the south after the defeat of the French.

The following year, the Vietminh in South Vietnam formed the National Liberation Front (NLF). The NLF's military forces were called **Vietcong**, meaning Vietnamese Communists. Not all members of the NLF were Communists, but they were united in the goal of overthrowing Diem's regime.

Some peasants joined the Vietcong because they opposed Diem's government, but others did so because they feared retaliation from the Vietcong if they did not. The Vietcong assassinated thousands of South Vietnamese government officials. Soon, much of the countryside was under Vietcong control.

In 1960 Ho Chi Minh expanded the effort to reunify North and South Vietnam. More supply routes leading to South Vietnam were established. North Vietnamese Army (NVA) forces also began coming into the country to fight alongside the Vietcong.

President Eisenhower decided to intervene in the conflict in 1955. The United States began supplying South Vietnam with money and weapons. Eisenhower began sending military advisers to train South Vietnam's army—the Army of the Republic of Vietnam (ARVN)—to use American weaponry.

By the end of Eisenhower's presidency, there were about 900 U.S. military advisers in South Vietnam. Many of these advisers had become frustrated with the corruption and inefficiency present in the ARVN.

READING CHECK **Summarizing** Why was Ngo Dinh Diem's government unpopular?

Increasing U.S. Involvement

Elected in 1960, President John F. Kennedy was a firm believer in the domino theory. Kennedy was eager to display U.S. strength in Vietnam.

You read in an earlier chapter about the two Cold War disasters that began Kennedy's presidency, the Bay of Pigs invasion and the building of the Berlin Wall. In the aftermath of these incidents, Kennedy hoped that aiding South Vietnam would be a sign of continued U.S. resolve and strength. "Now we have a problem in making our power credible," he warned, "and Vietnam is the place [to do so]."

President Kennedy hesitated to send official combat forces into South Vietnam, however. Instead, he decided to increase the number of military advisers and army special forces, or Green Berets, in that country. In December 1961 there were about 3,000 U.S. advisers in South Vietnam. By 1963 that number had increased to about 16,000.

The advisers were not supposed to take part in combat, but many did. For example, helicopter pilots fired rockets and machine guns at Vietcong targets. Green Berets often accompanied the ARVN on dangerous ambush operations. As Vietcong attacks mounted, Kennedy authorized U.S. personnel to engage in direct combat. The number of Americans killed or wounded climbed steadily. In 1961 some 14 Americans were killed. In 1963 the number rose to nearly 500.

Diem's overthrow Meanwhile, Diem's government grew more and more unpopular. When Buddhist leaders opposed his rule, Diem struck back by arresting and killing Buddhist protesters. To bring attention to the situation, several Buddhist monks killed themselves by publicly setting themselves on fire. Gruesome photographs were printed in newspapers around

ACADEMIC VOCABULARY
intervene get involved in, get in the middle of

In mid-1963 Buddhists began protesting Diem's oppression of their religion. At left, Buddhist demonstrators clash with police. In a terrible protest that focused world attention on Diem, Buddhist monk Quang Duc set himself on fire at a busy Saigon intersection.

Causes of the Vietnam War — Quick Facts

- **Vietnam's desire for freedom from colonial rule** France reclaimed Vietnam as a colony after World War II. The Communist-led Vietminh fought against French rule.

- **U.S. fears of the spread of communism (the domino theory)** Fearing that communism would spread throughout Southeast Asia if Communists took over Vietnam, the United States supported France. Despite U.S. aid, French rule of Vietnam ended in 1954.

- **South Vietnam's failure to comply with the Geneva Accords** After the French surrender, Vietnam was temporarily divided. North Vietnam was controlled by the Vietminh. Under the Geneva Accords, elections to unify the country under one government were set for 1956, but South Vietnam's leader refused to hold them.

- **Efforts by North Vietnam to reunite the nation under Communist rule** By 1959 North Vietnam began sending weapons to Vietminh in South Vietnam with the goal of unifying the country under a Communist government.

- **U.S. support for the anti-Communist government of South Vietnam** The United States supported South Vietnam with military advisers and later with troops.

Early in the war, U.S. personnel served primarily as military advisers and trainers. Here, South Vietnamese soldiers exit a helicopter under the watchful eye of an American officer.

the world. The images shocked Americans, and public opinion turned sharply against Diem.

American officials threatened to withdraw support unless Diem changed his policies. Yet he refused to alter his stand against Buddhists.

In response, U.S. leaders secretly began to support a plot within the South Vietnamese army to overthrow Diem. Henry Cabot Lodge Jr., the ambassador to South Vietnam, sent a cable to Washington describing the situation.

HISTORY'S VOICES

> "We are launched on a course from which there is no respectable turning back: the overthrow of the Diem government. There is no turning back because there is no possibility, in my view, that the war can be won under a Diem administration."
>
> —Henry Cabot Lodge Jr., August 29, 1963

In November 1963 the South Vietnamese plotters murdered Diem. Although Kennedy and his top advisers supported Diem's overthrow, they did not seek his assassination. The removal of Diem from power, however, did nothing to ease President Kennedy's growing concern over U.S. involvement in Vietnam. Shortly before Diem's murder, Kennedy had said of the South Vietnamese: "In the final analysis it is their war. They are the ones who have to win or lose it."

It cannot be known for sure whether Kennedy would have changed U.S. policy toward Vietnam. Just three weeks after Diem's death, President Kennedy himself was assassinated in Dallas, Texas.

The Tonkin Gulf Resolution When Vice President Lyndon B. Johnson took over as president, he inherited a rapidly deteriorating situation in South Vietnam. Although the ARVN had about 300,000 soldiers, the South Vietnamese government was on the brink of collapse. North Vietnamese forces were slipping into South Vietnam at an ever-increasing rate. By March 1964 the Vietcong controlled about 40 percent of South Vietnam.

President Johnson became convinced that only an expanded U.S. military involvement in South Vietnam could prevent a Communist victory. To increase the American military effort there, however, Johnson needed to obtain authority from the U.S. Congress. In 1964 an incident off the coast of North Vietnam gave him the opportunity to ask for this authority.

Near midnight on August 4, 1964, President Johnson appeared on national television. He made the dramatic announcement that on August 2 the USS *Maddox*, a navy destroyer, had been attacked by North Vietnamese torpedo boats in the Gulf of Tonkin, off the North Vietnamese coast.

Johnson said that the attack on the *Maddox* "was repeated today by a number of hostile vessels attacking two U.S. destroyers [the *Maddox* and the *C. Turner Joy*] with torpedoes." He called for a swift military response.

HISTORY'S VOICES

"Repeated acts of violence against the Armed Forces of the United States must be met not only with alert defense, but with positive reply. That reply is being given as I speak to you tonight. Air action is now in execution against gunboats and certain supporting facilities in North Vietnam which have been used in these hostile operations."
—Lyndon B. Johnson, speech on August 4, 1964

Later it was learned that President Johnson did not present a completely accurate picture of the incident in the Gulf of Tonkin. Johnson was in the middle of his 1964 presidential election campaign against Senator Barry Goldwater, a strong anti-Communist. Johnson wanted to avoid charges from Senator Goldwater and the Republicans that he was soft on communism.

The president claimed that the attack on the USS *Maddox* was unprovoked. In fact, the *Maddox* had been on a spying mission and had fired first.

As for the second attack, U.S. sailors may have mistaken interference on their radar and sonar for enemy boats and torpedoes. At the time, however, most members of Congress did not know the factual details surrounding the two incidents.

The **Tonkin Gulf Resolution** was approved by Congress on August 7. The resolution enabled the president to take "all necessary measures to repel any armed attack against forces of the United States." Johnson and his advisers now had authority to expand the war.

Senator Wayne Morse of Oregon was one of only two senators to oppose the Tonkin Gulf Resolution. "I believe that history will record we have made a great mistake," he predicted. "We are in effect giving the President war-making powers in the absence of a declaration of war."

ACADEMIC VOCABULARY
enable to give enough power, opportunity, or ability

READING CHECK **Identifying Cause and Effect** What circumstances led Congress to pass the Tonkin Gulf Resolution?

SECTION 1 ASSESSMENT

HSS 11.9.3

Reviewing Ideas, Terms, and People

1. **a. Define** What was French Indochina?
   b. Analyze How did French rule influence **Ho Chi Minh's** decision to embrace communism?
   c. Elaborate Do you think Ho Chi Minh's comparison of Vietnam after World War II and colonial America was valid? Explain.

2. **a. Describe** According to the **domino theory**, what did American leaders think might happen if Vietnam became a Communist country?
   b. Make Inferences Do you think the Geneva Accords eased American concerns about a domino effect in Southeast Asia? Why or why not?

3. **a. Identify** Who were the **Vietcong**?
   b. Analyze Cause and Effect What was Eisenhower's response to the growing strength of the Vietcong?
   c. Evaluate Do you think the United States was justified in supporting **Ngo Dinh Diem**? Why or why not?

4. **a. Describe** What happened to the USS *Maddox* in the Gulf of Tonkin?
   b. Predict How might the **Tonkin Gulf Resolution** affect the power of the presidency?

Critical Thinking

5. **Draw Conclusions** Review your notes on the leaders of North Vietnam and South Vietnam. Then copy the graphic organizer below and use it to list the causes for the decline in popularity of Ngo Dinh Diem's government.

Cause	Effect
	The popularity of Ngo Dinh Diem's government declined.

FOCUS ON WRITING 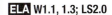 ELA W1.1, 1.3; LS2.0

6. **Expository** Suppose that you are the communications director in the Kennedy or Johnson White House. Write a press release that explains the president's decision to increase U.S. military involvement in Vietnam.

SECTION 2
U.S. Support of the War at Home and Abroad

BEFORE YOU READ

MAIN IDEA
As the United States sent increasing numbers of troops to defend South Vietnam, some Americans began to question the war.

READING FOCUS
1. Why did U.S. superiority in the air war fail to win quickly in Vietnam?
2. What made the ground war in Vietnam so difficult to fight?
3. How were U.S. forces mobilized for the war?
4. How and why did public opinion about the war gradually change?

KEY TERMS AND PEOPLE
Operation Rolling Thunder
Ho Chi Minh Trail
William Westmoreland
pacification
doves
hawks
J. William Fulbright

HSS 11.9.3 Trace the origins and geopolitical consequences (foreign and domestic) of the Cold War and containment policy, including the following:
• The Vietnam War
HSS 11.9.4 List the effects of foreign policy on domestic policies and vice versa (e.g., protests during the war in Vietnam, the "nuclear freeze" movement).

 Why do some people risk their lives to serve their country?
The young men who volunteered to fight in Vietnam came mostly from rural America or from industrial neighborhoods in the nation's cities. Many recruits were the sons of American soldiers who had fought in World War II or the Korean War. For young men fresh out of high school, serving in Vietnam seemed to be an adventure as well as a patriotic duty.

Eighteen-year-old Rod Kane was just such a person. After graduating from high school in 1964, he went to see the recruiter. "I want to be in the infantry, like my Uncle Paul . . . Maybe I should do something like save people, like medics," Kane said.

"If you volunteer for three years, I can guarantee you medics school," the recruiter promised. "Remember what President Kennedy said," he urged. "'Ask not what your country can do for you. Ask what you can do for your country.'"

It sounded good to Kane. In 1965, army infantry member and medic Rod Kane arrived in Vietnam.

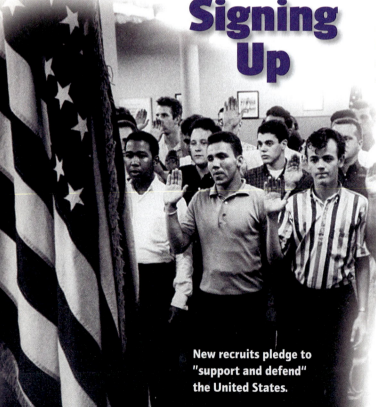
New recruits pledge to "support and defend" the United States.

The Air War

The first major direct U.S. military activity in Vietnam took place in the air. President Johnson ordered **Operation Rolling Thunder**, a bombing campaign over North Vietnam, in March 1965. He wanted to weaken the enemy's ability and will to fight. He also wanted to assure South Vietnam of his commitment to its independence.

U.S. pilots bombed military targets in North Vietnam, such as army bases and airfields. They also bombed anything North Vietnam would find useful in the war effort, including bridges, roads, railways, and power plants.

Rolling Thunder

U.S. Air Force pilots flying Vietnamese Skyraiders drop napalm on Vietcong targets. Operation Rolling Thunder aimed to weaken the enemy, disrupt the Ho Chi Minh Trail, and defoliate the countryside. **Why did U.S. involvement in Vietnam begin with air power instead of ground troops?**

One of the main targets of Operation Rolling Thunder was the **Ho Chi Minh Trail**. The trail was a network of paths that began in North Vietnam, snaked through Laos and Cambodia, and ended in South Vietnam. The North Vietnamese used the trail to send weapons, soldiers, food, and other supplies to the Vietcong and NVA forces in South Vietnam.

Much of the Ho Chi Minh Trail ran through thick jungle areas, making movement along it all but invisible from the air. American planes began spraying jungle areas with defoliants, or chemicals that destroy vegetation. The goal of this spraying was to expose enemy supply routes and hiding places. A chemical called Agent Orange was the most widely used type of defoliant.

American forces used several other types of weapons in the air war. Napalm, a jellied form of gasoline, was used to create firebombs that destroyed farms and forests. "Cluster bombs" sprayed sharp metal fragments when they exploded. Pilots also carried out attacks called carpet bombing, a strategy in which strings of bombs dropped from high altitudes destroy large areas of land with no specific target.

The bombing did not succeed in its goal of weakening the enemy's war effort, however. Instead of cutting off aid to the Vietcong, the flow of troops and supplies from North Vietnam to the south actually increased. When roads or bridges on the Ho Chi Minh Trail were damaged, the Vietcong quickly repaired them or did without them. They also had underground bunkers that protected soldiers and supplies.

Another reason the Communist forces were able to withstand the bombing was that they received massive support from the Soviet Union and China. Both Communist powers provided North Vietnam with soldiers, economic aid, and high-tech weapons, including radar and antiaircraft guns.

Frustrated by the lack of progress, Johnson broadened the air war. By late 1968 more than 1 million tons of bombs had been dropped on North Vietnam. Targets in Laos, Cambodia, and parts of South Vietnam were also bombed.

One unintended effect of the American bombing campaign was that it led many South Vietnamese to join the Vietcong. Soon the forces opposing American troops included an increasing number of South Vietnamese.

READING CHECK **Identifying the Main Idea** What did U.S. forces hope to accomplish by bombing the Ho Chi Minh Trail?

The Ground War

THE IMPACT TODAY

Government
In part because of Vietnam, the question of U.S. involvement in a foreign war comes under intense scrutiny today. Recent presidents have been pressured to make the case for a compelling national interest before sending U.S. forces to hostile overseas situations.

As the war continued, Johnson called for an escalation, or buildup, of U.S. ground forces in Vietnam. The number of American troops in South Vietnam grew from 185,000 at the end of 1965 to 486,000 two years later.

U.S. strategy In response to the guerrilla tactics used by Communist forces, General **William Westmoreland**, the commander of U.S. ground troops in South Vietnam, ordered thousands of search-and-destroy missions to drive enemy forces out of their hideouts. Ground troops located Vietcong and NVA positions and then called in air strikes to bomb them. Once an area was "cleared" the ground patrols moved on to search for other enemy positions.

American troops on search-and-destroy missions often cut through the thick jungle, fighting foes they rarely saw. Other times, they waded through rice paddies or searched rural villages. One U.S. commander, Captain Myron Harrington, described what it was like to lead a company of 100 marines.

HISTORY'S VOICES

> ❝After a while, survival was the name of the game as you sat there in the semidarkness, with the firing going on constantly, like at a rifle range. And the horrible smell. You tasted it as you ate your rations, as if you were eating death . . . You went through the full range of emotions, seeing your buddies being hit, but you couldn't feel sorry for them because you had the others to think about.❞
>
> —Captain Myron Harrington, quoted in *Vietnam* by Stanley Karnow

After search-and-destroy patrols left an area, villages seldom remained clear for long. Returning Vietcong and NVA troops sometimes terrorized civilians they believed had aided the Americans.

To improve rural security, U.S. forces **instituted** a program of **pacification**. Its goal was to "win the hearts and minds" of the South Vietnamese people—to pacify, or calm, opposition—especially in the countryside.

Nonmilitary pacification involved construction projects to improve the country's infrastructure and economy. Militarily, pacification involved moving people out of their villages when Vietcong were concentrated nearby. Villagers were relocated to safe camps and given food and housing. American troops then burned the village to prevent the Vietcong from using it.

U.S. planners hoped that driving out the Vietcong would help win the support of South Vietnamese civilians. Many civilians, however, resented being moved off their land and having their villages destroyed.

As armies fought from village to village, it was difficult for U.S. military leaders to show progress on a map. Instead, they measured success with body counts, or the number of enemy killed. It often was difficult for troops to make accurate counts in the midst of hectic jungle firefights. Also, high military officials sometimes inflated the body counts reported by units in the field.

Declining troop morale The first U.S. ground troops in Vietnam were convinced that they would succeed. Marine lieutenant Philip Caputo remembered his early confidence.

HISTORY'S VOICES

> ❝Our expectations were, we were going to stay there a month to 90 days, help the South Vietnamese recover, and then we would get out . . . We got this idea that the United States was invincible . . . that, being U.S. Marines, our mere presence in Vietnam was going to terrify the enemy into quitting.❞
>
> —Lieutenant Philip Caputo, CNN interview, June 1996

In reality, American troops confronted many of the same challenges the French had faced. Aided by NVA troops, the Vietcong struck at U.S. patrols and government-held villages and then melted back into the jungle. Some Vietnamese peasants seemed peaceful by day but aided or even became the Vietcong at night. The Vietcong also had the major advantage of knowing the local geography.

U.S. combat soldiers faced constant danger. Each path could lead into an enemy ambush. Each step could trip a deadly mine or a booby trap such as Punji stakes, which were sharpened bamboo sticks concealed in a hole or mud. On patrol, American troops found it nearly impossible to tell the difference between a Vietcong fighter and a civilian.

Caputo later described the sense of uncertainty he and his fellow marines felt when interacting with Vietnamese civilians.

ACADEMIC VOCABULARY
instituted established or started

HISTORY CLOSE-UP

Vietcong Tunnels

The Vietcong had a vast system of underground tunnels some of which had been built in the 1940s. The tunnels served as hiding places during combat. They also served as living quarters, places to store food and weapons, and locations to tend wounded soldiers. This illustration depicts a typical complex in one of the larger tunnel systems. By 1965 the tunnels stretched underground from Saigon to the Cambodian border, a distance of about 120 miles.

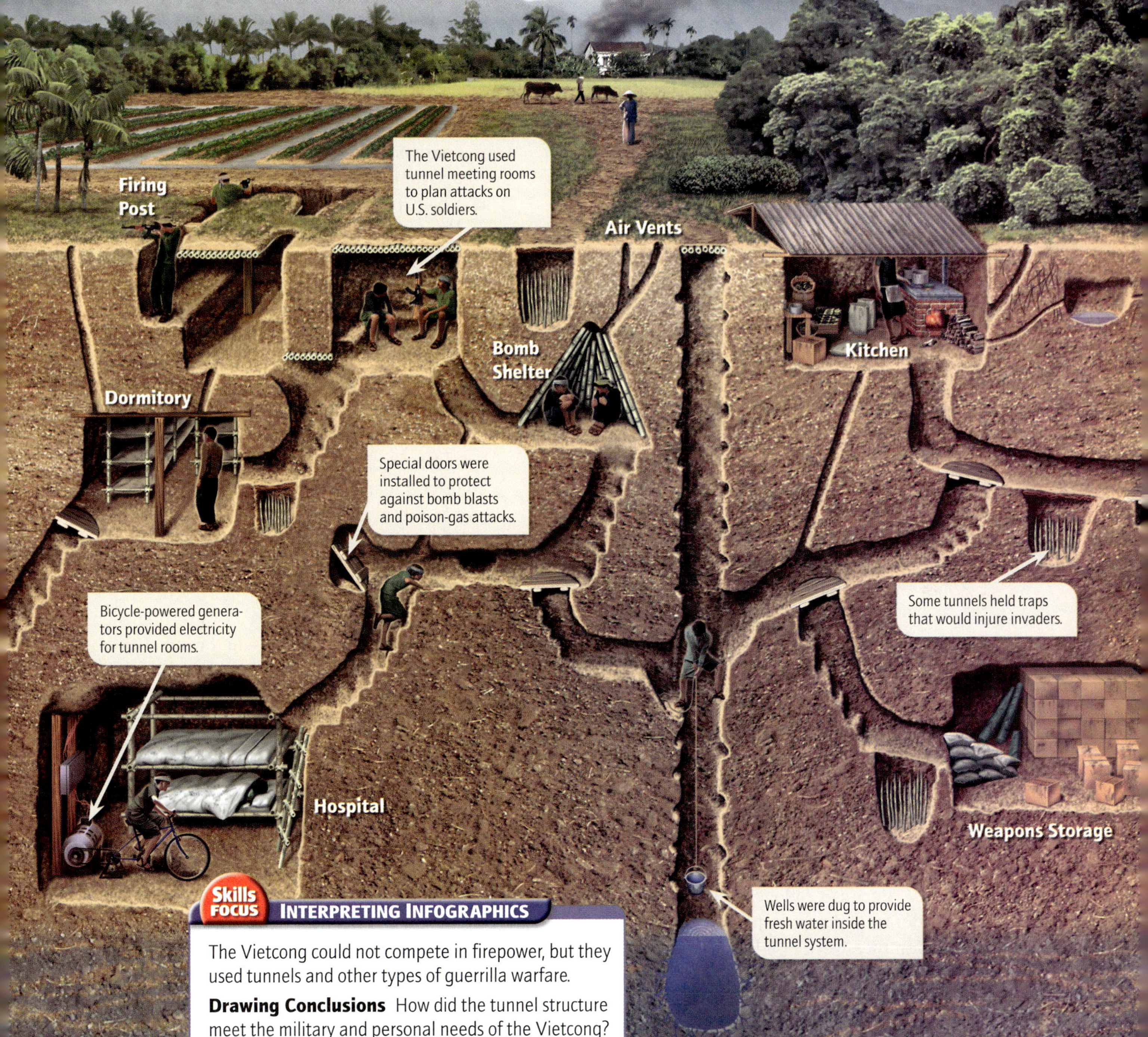

Firing Post

The Vietcong used tunnel meeting rooms to plan attacks on U.S. soldiers.

Air Vents

Bomb Shelter

Kitchen

Dormitory

Special doors were installed to protect against bomb blasts and poison-gas attacks.

Bicycle-powered generators provided electricity for tunnel rooms.

Some tunnels held traps that would injure invaders.

Hospital

Weapons Storage

Wells were dug to provide fresh water inside the tunnel system.

SKILLS FOCUS: INTERPRETING INFOGRAPHICS

The Vietcong could not compete in firepower, but they used tunnels and other types of guerrilla warfare.

Drawing Conclusions How did the tunnel structure meet the military and personal needs of the Vietcong?

See **Skills Handbook**, p. 18

"You didn't and couldn't really trust them," he said. "You did develop this intense suspicion. You were constantly watching them, and that got to be kind of wearing after a while."

Despite these obstacles, U.S. troops inflicted enormous casualties on the Communist forces. This did not lead to victory, however. With the continued aid of China and the Soviet Union, North Vietnam was able to send a steady stream of supplies and soldiers to the South.

The Vietcong also refilled their ranks by recruiting civilians. Some South Vietnamese began to help the Communists or join the Vietcong. Destruction from American air strikes and the pacification policy turned many peasants into Vietcong fighters.

READING CHECK **Summarizing** What fighting strategies did the NVA and the Vietcong use?

U.S. Forces Mobilize

More than 2.5 million Americans served in the Vietnam War. On average, the soldiers who served in Vietnam were slightly younger than the U.S. troops who fought in Korea and World War II. Most Vietnam soldiers were not well educated. Some 80 percent of the American troops had a high school education or less.

The draft At the start of the war, most American troops were professional soldiers—volunteers who enlisted in the armed forces. As the American force in Vietnam steadily increased, however, the U.S. government depended more and more heavily on drafted soldiers.

About 25 percent of the young men who registered for the draft were excused from service for health reasons. Another 30 percent received deferments, or postponements of service. Men enrolled in college were able to get deferments. Enrollment at American colleges and universities skyrocketed as a result. Draft boards monitored student progress, however, and could cancel a deferment if a student's grades were too low.

Because college students could get draft deferments, young men from higher-income families were less likely to serve in Vietnam. Poor Americans served in numbers greater than their proportion of the general population. "I'm bitter," said one firefighter whose son died in the war. "The college types, the professors, they go to Washington and tell the government what to do . . . But their sons, they don't end up in the swamps over there, in Vietnam."

Large numbers of African Americans traditionally enlisted in the military. For this reason, a high percentage of soldiers in combat positions were African American during the war's early years, when much of the fighting was done by volunteers. Therefore, the casualty rates of black soldiers at first were very high. For example, African Americans accounted for at least one fifth of all U.S. battle deaths in 1965 even though they made up 11 percent of the American population.

As the war continued, however, the draft largely ended this inequity. In 1969 the government made an attempt to reform the makeup of the military by instituting a lottery system for the draft. This lottery system drafted men based on birth dates chosen at random.

By putting an end to many deferments, it made the draft fairer, because now income levels were less important in determining who had to serve. Finally, in 1973 the government ended the unpopular draft and returned to filling its ranks with volunteers.

About 3 percent of eligible young men escaped the draft altogether during the Vietnam War, either by refusing to register or by leaving the United States. Thousands of American men went to Canada to avoid being sent to Vietnam.

One young man who fled to Canada commented on his experience. "I ran into quite a few Americans on the run from the draft," he reported. "They were scared . . . Most had been cut off from their parents who branded them cowards and traitors."

Noncombat positions Most Americans who went to Vietnam served in non-combat positions, such as those in administration, communications, engineering, medical care, and transportation. Even in these noncombat roles, however, soldiers faced dangers from the fighting. Enemy rockets and mortars often struck seemingly safe positions.

About 10,000 American military women served in noncombat positions, mostly as nurses. Some 20,000 to 45,000 more women worked in civilian capacities, many as volunteers for the Red Cross or other humanitarian relief organizations.

U.S. FORCES IN VIETNAM, 1965–1972

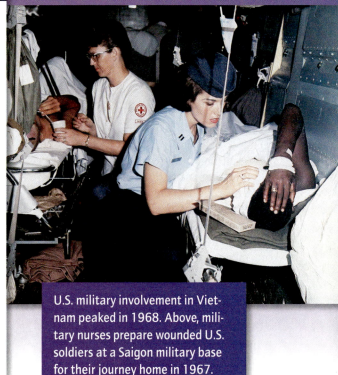

Source: United States Department of Defense

SKILLS FOCUS: INTERPRETING GRAPHS

1. Roughly how many Americans served in Vietnam in 1965?
2. How many more were serving when the number of military personnel reached its peak?

See **Skills Handbook**, p. H16

U.S. military involvement in Vietnam peaked in 1968. Above, military nurses prepare wounded U.S. soldiers at a Saigon military base for their journey home in 1967.

Sylvia Lutz Holland was one of many nurses assigned to evacuation hospitals, where wounded troops were brought by helicopter. She had the heavy responsibility of deciding who to treat first.

"You'd look at the wounds, check the vital signs, and just make a decision—he's a go or he can wait," the nurse recalled. "We had to move fast."

Although nurses did not carry guns into battle, they were exposed to the horrors of combat on a daily basis.

HISTORY'S VOICES

> If the Army took a hill, we saw what was left over. I remember one boy who was brought in missing two legs and an arm, and his eyes were bandaged. A general came in later and pinned a Purple Heart on the boy's hospital gown, and the horror of it all was so amazing that it just took my breath away.
>
> —nurse Edie Meeks, *Newsweek* interview, March 8, 1999

READING CHECK **Making Inferences** How did the draft change the U.S. force in Vietnam?

Public Opinion Shifts

Most Americans supported U.S. involvement in the Vietnam War at first. By the end of 1968, however, more than 16,000 Americans had been killed in combat. A growing number of Americans began to question the wisdom of U.S. policy regarding involvement in Vietnam.

The media's impact News media coverage of the Vietnam War had a strong impact on American public opinion. During previous wars the military had imposed tight restrictions on the press. In Vietnam, however, reporters and television crews accompanied soldiers on patrol and interviewed people throughout South Vietnam.

Television coverage brought scenes of firefights and burning villages into Americans' living rooms. For this reason, the Vietnam War has been called the first "living room war."

The U.S. government allowed TV crews to cover the war, hoping television reports would show Americans that U.S. forces were making

THE VIETNAM WAR **609**

COUNTERPOINTS
Views on the Vietnam War

National Security Adviser Walt W. Rostow believed that communism must be halted—by force if necessary.

"We are honoring a treaty which committed us to 'act to meet the common danger' in the face of 'aggression by means of armed attack'... And we are answering... the question: Are the word and commitment of the United States reliable?"

Walt W. Rostow, 1967

Outspoken and plain-talking, Senator George McGovern opposed U.S. involvement in Vietnam.

"We seem bent upon saving the Vietnamese from Ho Chi Minh, even if we have to kill them and demolish their country to do it... I do not intend to remain silent in the face of what I regard as a policy of madness which, sooner or later, will envelop my son and American youth by the millions for years to come."

George McGovern, 1967

Skills Focus: READING LIKE A HISTORIAN

Recognizing Bias McGovern served as a bomber pilot during World War II. How might that experience have influenced his outlook on war?

See **Skills Handbook**, p. H33

ACADEMIC VOCABULARY
resource something that is made use of

progress in Vietnam. But to many Americans, the images they saw on television contradicted the optimistic government reports on the progress of the war. Some reporters questioned or criticized the government's reports as well. They reported on the ineffectiveness of South Vietnamese troops. In addition, they accused the U.S. government of inflating body counts to create the appearance of success.

Hawks and doves As the gap between official reports and media accounts widened, debate at home increased. Johnson was criticized by both **doves**—people who opposed the war—and **hawks**—people who supported the war's goals. Some hawks disapproved of the government's handling of the war. They believed more troops and heavier bombing were necessary to victory. Air force general Curtis LeMay expressed this view. "Here we are at the height of our power. The most powerful nation in the world. And yet we're afraid to use that power."

Doves had a variety of reasons for opposing the war. Diplomat George Kennan, for example, argued that Vietnam was not crucial to American national security. Pediatrician and author Dr. Benjamin Spock and others claimed that the United States was fighting against the wishes of a majority of Vietnamese. Martin Luther King Jr. expressed concern that the war was draining needed resources from Great Society programs.

HISTORY'S VOICES

"I watched the [antipoverty] program broken and eviscerated [gutted] as if it were some idle political plaything of a society gone mad on war, and I knew that America would never invest the necessary funds or energies in rehabilitation of its poor so long as Vietnam continued to draw men and skills and money like some demonic, destructive suction tube."
—Martin Luther King Jr., sermon opposing the Vietnam War, 1967

Many other civil rights activists argued that it was unfair to expect African Americans to fight for democracy in a foreign land when discrimination continued at home. Polls showed that African Americans were much more likely than whites to believe that U.S. involvement in the war was a mistake.

Doves in Congress also became more vocal as the war continued. **J. William Fulbright** of Arkansas, head of the Senate Foreign Relations Committee, criticized Johnson's policies as too extreme. He held televised committee hearings in 1966 to give the war's critics a public voice.

The antiwar movement As opposition to the war grew, a large antiwar movement developed. The movement attracted a broad range of people, including students, civil rights workers, doctors, homemakers, retirees, and teachers.

Much of the antiwar activity took place on college campuses, where students held antiwar rallies and debates. Faculty members held teach-ins, where they sought to educate students about the war. Student opponents of the war also protested the draft and the presence of the Reserve Officers' Training Corps (ROTC) on campus.

One of the most vocal antiwar groups was Students for a Democratic Society (SDS). By the end of 1965, the SDS had members on 124 college campuses across the country. In April 1965, SDS members led the first national antiwar demonstration. More than 20,000 people marched to the Capitol in Washington, D.C., where they delivered a petition to Congress demanding that lawmakers "act immediately to end the war." The SDS and other antiwar groups also protested against universities that conducted research for the military. Some young men protested the draft by burning their draft cards, which the government sent to each man at the time he registered for the draft.

President Lyndon Johnson responded to the protests by insisting that the United States was protecting an ally against an aggressor. Secretary of State Dean Rusk put it this way: If the United States failed to support South Vietnam, what ally would ever trust the United States again?

While antiwar protesters were highly visible, they made up a small percentage of the U.S. population. Many Americans opposed the antiwar movement, especially the actions of the extreme groups. They were particularly angered by the burning of draft cards or American flags. Many veterans of previous wars spoke out against men who avoided the draft. Some opponents of the antiwar movement held rallies in support of the war, carrying signs with messages such as "America, Love It or Leave It" and "My Country, Right or Wrong."

READING CHECK Identifying Cause and Effect How and why did television affect public opinion about the Vietnam War?

SECTION 2 ASSESSMENT

HSS 11.9.3, 11.9.4

Reviewing Ideas, Terms, and People

1. **a. Identify** What was **Operation Rolling Thunder**?
   b. Draw Conclusions Why do you think Operation Rolling Thunder failed to lead to a quick victory?

2. **a. Describe** What dangers did American soldiers face in Vietnam?
   b. Analyze Why did the U.S. program of **pacification** fail?
   c. Elaborate How do you think the pacification program might have been improved?

3. **a. Recall** Who was most likely to be drafted to serve in the Vietnam War?
   b. Draw Conclusions How do you think American soldiers fighting in Vietnam felt about the young men who tried to avoid being drafted?
   c. Elaborate What factors would a young man have weighed in deciding whether to flee the United States to avoid the draft?

4. **a. Describe** What were the views of the **doves** and the **hawks** during the Vietnam War?

   b. Evaluate Do you think groups such as the SDS had much influence on public opinion about the Vietnam War? Why or why not?

Critical Thinking

5. **Contrast** Review your notes on the tactics of U.S. soldiers in the Vietnam War. Then copy the graphic organizer below and use it to contrast U.S. military strategies with those of the North Vietnamese Army and Vietcong.

U.S. Military	North Vietnamese Army, Vietcong

FOCUS ON WRITING **ELA** W1.1, 1.3; LS2.0

6. **Persuasive** Either as an antiwar or pro-government demonstrator, write a speech that you would give at a rally about the Vietnam War.

SECTION 3
1968: A Turning Point

BEFORE YOU READ

MAIN IDEA
As the Vietnam War dragged on and increasingly appeared to be unwinnable, deep divisions developed in American society.

READING FOCUS
1. What was the Tet Offensive?
2. What were the effects of the Tet Offensive?
3. How did President Johnson try to find a solution to the war?
4. How did the election of 1968 illustrate divisions in American society?

KEY TERMS AND PEOPLE
Tet Offensive
Robert S. McNamara
Eugene McCarthy
Hubert Humphrey
George Wallace

HSS 11.9.3 Trace the origins and geopolitical consequences (foreign and domestic) of the Cold War and containment policy, including the following:
• The Vietnam War

HSS 11.9.4 List the effects of foreign policy on domestic policies and vice versa (e.g., protests during the war in Vietnam, the "nuclear freeze" movement).

THE INSIDE STORY

Why did an attack on the U.S. Embassy become so important in the war? At 2:45 a.m. on January 31, 1968, two vehicles approached the compound that housed the U.S. embassy in Saigon, South Vietnam's capital city. At the compound's entrance, 19 Vietcong fighters jumped out and opened fire with automatic weapons. The two American military police (MP) officers guarding the entrance returned fire as they backed through the heavy steel gate and locked it. Then they radioed Signal 300, the code for an enemy attack.

Suddenly, a huge explosion shook the neighborhood as the attackers blew a hole in the high concrete wall surrounding the compound. "They're coming in—help me!" one MP shouted into his radio. Then the radio went silent.

Both MPs were killed as the Vietcong poured through the hole in the wall. The MPs, however, had managed to delay the attackers long enough to allow the marines inside the compound to seal the main embassy building. Other U.S. troops rushed to the scene. A fierce firefight spread across the grounds of the compound.

By 9:15 a.m. the fighting was over. All but two of the Vietcong were dead, along with five American soldiers.

General William Westmoreland arrived a few minutes later. "It's a relatively small incident," he declared. His assessment proved to be wrong. The assault on the embassy was part of a much larger attack that ultimately changed the course of the Vietnam War.

▼ Saigon erupted into a battle zone in the months following the attack on the U.S. Embassy.

Under Attack

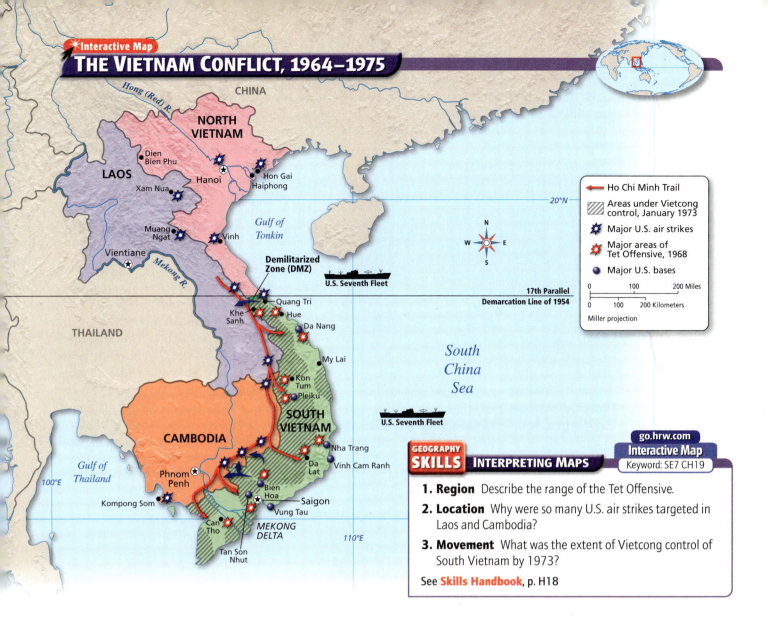

The Tet Offensive

The Vietcong assault on the U.S. Embassy marked the start of the **Tet Offensive**, a series of massive coordinated attacks throughout South Vietnam. The Tet Offensive caused 1968 to become a critical year in the Vietnam War.

Khe Sanh In late 1967 U.S. military leaders began noticing increased traffic on the Ho Chi Minh Trail. They suspected a major assault was coming. In January 1968 thousands of NVA and Vietcong troops struck an isolated U.S. military base in Khe Sanh (KAY sahn), in northwestern South Vietnam. Communist troops surrounded the base and pounded it with artillery fire. News reporters compared the siege to the French battle at Dien Bien Phu in 1954. After the 77-day siege ended, however, the Americans still held Khe Sanh.

General Westmoreland concluded that preparations for the Khe Sanh assault explained the increased Ho Chi Minh Trail traffic. In fact, Khe Sanh and other rural attacks were diversions. Their purpose was to draw U.S. and ARVN forces away from urban areas, where the major strikes were planned.

The main attacks The main Communist offensive began on January 30, 1968. This was the start of Tet, the Vietnamese New Year. In previous years, the opposing sides had observed a cease-fire during the holiday, with many South Vietnamese soldiers actually going home to celebrate.

In 1968 the Vietcong and North Vietnamese troops took advantage of this moment to launch an offensive. During the crippling campaign, some 84,000 Communist soldiers attacked 12 U.S. military bases and more than

THE VIETNAM WAR 613

100 cities across South Vietnam. The U.S. Embassy was one of several Saigon sites attacked on the first night. A South Vietnamese government official recalled the assault.

HISTORY'S VOICES

> "Embassy staff, covered in blood, were being treated by doctors. Humble clerks had changed their pens for guns. There were dead bodies everywhere—some American, but mostly Viet Cong. They lay in heaps on the lawn, staining the green grass red with blood . . . Chunks of stone and concrete were strewn about, and the once beautiful white walls of the embassy were now full of bullet holes."
>
> —Tran Van Huong, quoted in *Nam: The Vietnam Experience, 1965–75*

North Vietnamese leaders hoped the Tet Offensive would inspire South Vietnamese civilians to rise up against their government. However, the expected public support did not materialize. Many civilians were left homeless from the damage caused by the attacks. The Communists also slaughtered South Vietnamese people they believed were helping the Americans. This also turned many civilians against the Vietcong.

General Westmoreland described the Tet Offensive as a decisive defeat for the Communists. After more than a month of fighting, the cities captured by the Vietcong and NVA were retaken, and about 45,000 enemy soldiers were killed. About 1,100 American and 2,300 ARVN troops also died. Despite suffering such heavy losses, however, the Communists showed that they were determined to keep fighting.

READING CHECK **Identifying the Main Idea** Why did the Communists launch the Tet Offensive?

Effects of the Tet Offensive

The Tet Offensive showed that no part of South Vietnam was safe from attack. This shattered many people's belief that Communist forces were weakening and that the United States would soon win the war.

Walter Cronkite, the respected anchor of *CBS Evening News,* said privately, "I thought we were winning the war! What . . . is going on?" In February 1968 Cronkite broadcast a television report in which he offered the American public his personal assessment of the situation in Vietnam.

Linking TO Today

Battlefield Reporting

Photographs of Civil War battlefields and newsreels from World War II helped to inform civilians about those wars. Yet frequently this information was well out of date by the time it reached the American public.

As technology improved, the way people learned about wars changed. During the Vietnam War, relatively lightweight cameras and improved shipping service meant that stories could be filmed and flown back to the United States within 24 hours. The evening news brought dramatic and disturbing images of the war into American homes.

During the Iraq War in 2003, reporters relied on laptop computers and satellite videophones. News traveled around the world almost instantly, reaching the United States via the Internet as well as by television.

Working conditions also changed for reporters. In Vietnam, journalists often traveled with troops, but they were not officially connected to the military. During the Iraq War, reporters could choose to be "embedded" with a military unit. They received training and an honorary rank. Journalists gained greater access to troops. However, critics charged that the arrangement compromised the objectivity and scope of their reporting.

Drawing Conclusions What were the biggest changes in war coverage during the last 150 years?

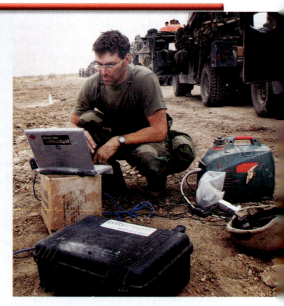

A U.S. news photographer during the Iraq War uses a computer, generator, and satellite phone to send his images back to the office.

HISTORY'S VOICES

"We have been too often disappointed by the optimism of the American leaders... For it seems now more certain than ever that the bloody experience of Vietnam is to end in a stalemate."
—Walter Cronkite on CBS television, February 27, 1968

Growing doubts The president despaired when he heard Cronkite's words. "If I've lost Cronkite I've lost middle America," Johnson said. Major national magazines such as *Time* and *Newsweek* also expressed doubts about the war and began to call for its end.

Public criticism of the government's policies grew louder and more intense. Johnson felt trapped as picketers surrounded the White House chanting, "Hey, hey, LBJ, how many kids did you kill today?"

Many leaders within the Johnson administration also became critical of his policies. As secretary of defense for both Presidents Kennedy and Johnson, **Robert S. McNamara** had played a key role in shaping U.S. strategy in Vietnam. By 1968, however, he had become discouraged by America's lack of success in the war. He began openly seeking ways to launch peace negotiations to end it.

Democratic challengers As Johnson sought re-election in 1968, roughly 3 out of 4 Americans opposed his policies in Vietnam. The president found himself facing challengers for his party's nomination. Minnesota senator **Eugene McCarthy**, a vocal critic of the war, finished a strong second to Johnson in the New Hampshire primary in March. Soon afterward, New York senator Robert Kennedy, the former U.S. attorney general, entered the race.

Shaken by the divisions in his party, an exhausted Johnson made a shocking announcement during a speech on national television.

HISTORY'S VOICES

"With America's sons in the fields far away, with America's future under challenge right here at home... I do not believe that I should devote an hour or a day of my time to any personal partisan causes... Accordingly, I shall not seek, and I will not accept, the nomination of my party for another term as president."
—Lyndon Johnson, March 31, 1968

READING CHECK **Identifying Cause and Effect** How did the media react to the Tet Offensive?

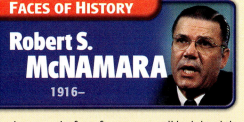

FACES OF HISTORY
Robert S. McNAMARA
1916–

After college, Robert McNamara attended Harvard University, earning a master's degree in business administration. He then taught for a few years until he joined the military during World War II. Following the war, McNamara took a job at Ford, helping to make the automobile company more profitable.

In 1961 McNamara joined President Kennedy's cabinet as head of the Defense Department. He introduced modern business practices to the military and strengthened its conventional fighting capability. As the conflict in Vietnam grew, McNamara became the leading spokesperson and chief prosecutor of what some called McNamara's war. By 1968, however, he had doubts about the war. He resigned as defense secretary and took a position as head of the World Bank.

Summarize What changes did McNamara make to the military?

Johnson Seeks a Solution

General Westmoreland argued that the Tet Offensive had been devastating to the enemy. He believed that if more ground troops were sent to Vietnam, he could deliver a crushing blow to the weakened Communists. In March 1968 he sent President Johnson a request for 206,000 more soldiers.

When the *New York Times* reported Westmoreland's request, many Americans were outraged. They wondered why more U.S. troops were needed if the war was being won, as the government had been insisting. In part because of the strong public outcry, the president denied Westmoreland's request.

Johnson knew he needed to reassess his entire war strategy, but his own advisers could not agree on the best course. Many U.S. military leaders believed that the administration was not doing all that could be done to win the war. In particular, some officers felt that Johnson's decision not to invade North Vietnam with ground troops unfairly limited them in fighting the war.

Even before the Tet Offensive, McNamara and some other government leaders had come to believe that Johnson's war policies were too extreme. McNamara suggested limiting the air strikes and reversing the escalation of the war.

HISTORY'S VOICES

❝The picture of the world's greatest superpower killing or seriously injuring 1,000 non-combatants a week, while trying to pound a tiny backward nation into submission on an issue whose merits are hotly disputed is not a pretty one.❞

—Robert S. McNamara, letter to President Johnson, May 19, 1967

Johnson agreed it was time to try to negotiate with North Vietnam. In the same televised speech in which he stated he would not run for re-election, he announced that he would seek a peace agreement to end the war.

In May 1968 delegates from North Vietnam and the United States met in Paris. Immediately the talks stalled over two issues. The United States wanted all NVA troops out of South Vietnam, and North Vietnam would not accept a temporary South Vietnam government that included the U.S.-backed president, Nguyen Van Thieu. The two sides would not reach an agreement for several more years.

READING CHECK **Summarizing** How did President Johnson try to end the Vietnam War before the conclusion of his presidency?

The Election of 1968

After Johnson withdrew from the 1968 presidential campaign, his vice president, **Hubert Humphrey**, entered the race. The Vietnam War was a key issue among voters. Humphrey defended the administration's war policies. His Democratic rivals, Senators Eugene McCarthy and Robert Kennedy, called for a rapid end to the war. When Kennedy announced his candidacy, he explained his position on Vietnam.

HISTORY'S VOICES

❝The reality of recent events in Vietnam has been glossed over with illusions . . . I have tried in vain to alter our course in Vietnam before it further saps our spirit and our manpower, further raises the risks of wider war, and further destroys the country and the people it was meant to save. I cannot stand aside from the contest that will decide our nation's future and our children's future.❞

—Robert F. Kennedy, March 16, 1968

The Democratic primary fight Kennedy quickly gained ground in the race by winning primaries in Indiana and Nebraska. In June

A Year of Turmoil: 1968

① Johnson does not seek reelection

Wearied by events during the Vietnam War, Johnson declines to seek another term. His vice president, Hubert Humphrey, joins the race.

② Robert Kennedy enters the race for president

Kennedy, the Democratic frontrunner, celebrates his victory in the California primary with a speech at the Ambassador Hotel.

③ Kennedy is assassinated

Moments later Kennedy is gunned down in the hotel kitchen. Restaurant worker Juan Romero comforts the fatally wounded senator.

he won the crucial California primary. This made him the favorite to win the Democratic presidential nomination.

As he finished his victory speech in a Los Angeles hotel, Kennedy flashed a victory sign to the audience and declared, "On to Chicago, and let's win there." Chicago was the location for the upcomiong Democratic National Conention, where delegates would choose the party's presidential candidate.

After Senator Robert Kennedy walked off the stage, a gunman shot him three times. He died less than 24 hours later. The assassin, Sirhan Sirhan, was a Jordanian immigrant who was angry about Kennedy's support for the nation of Israel.

The Democratic Convention In August, the remaining candidates fought for the nomination at the Democratic National Convention. Inside the convention hall, the delegates debated between McCarthy and Humphrey. Some people thought McCarthy's position on the war showed personal weakness. Others disliked Humphrey because he was too close to Johnson's failed war policies.

Outside the hall, chaos erupted in the streets of Chicago. About 10,000 protesters from across the country had gathered to demand an immediate end to the war and to pressure the delegates to reject Johnson's Vietnam policies. They held rallies and chanted antiwar slogans calling for "Peace now!"

Chicago mayor Richard Daley dispatched thousands of police and national guard troops to maintain order. The situation soon exploded into violence, when a huge group of demonstrators attempted to march on the convention hall. Some protesters threw rocks and bottles at the police. Daley described them as "a lawless violent group of terrorists menacing the lives of millions of our people."

The police clubbed demonstrators with rifle butts and clubs and used tear gas to disperse the crowd. Scuffles even broke out inside the convention hall. Many people, including innocent bystanders, were injured as well.

Television reporters and camera crews recorded the violence. They showed that in some instances police officers reacted with excessive force. Viewers watching the live coverage on television were shocked at the brutality. The

❹ Protests at the Democratic Convention
Antiwar delegates inside the Chicago convention hall pressured candidates to support a quick end to the war.

❺ Chaos erupts outside the convention
In the streets of Chicago, emotional protests met with a brutal police response. Radical activists, the so-called Chicago Seven, were found guilty of conspiring to incite riots, but their convictions were later overturned.

A Three-way Race
As candidates for president in 1968, Hubert Humphrey (top left), George Wallace (top right), and Richard Nixon (bottom right) each had the task of convincing voters they knew best how to conclude America's unpopular war in Vietnam. **How did the candidates' plans differ?**

world press also recorded the event. A London *Sunday Times* reporter wrote, "The kids screamed and were beaten to the ground . . . I saw one girl surrounded by cops, screaming, 'Please God, help me. Help me.'"

More than 600 Chicago protesters were arrested. Despite the disturbances, convention delegates reached a decision and nominated Hubert Humphrey. He chose Senator Edmund Muskie of Maine as his running mate.

The chaos at the Democratic National Convention was one symptom of a growing "generation gap" over government, politics, and the Vietnam War. Many teenagers and young adults of the 1960s found themselves at odds with their parents, who had experienced the Great Depression and World War II. Young people accused the previous generation of valuing material comfort over justice and equality. Younger Americans also increasingly distrusted their political leaders, while older Americans urged them to have confidence in their government.

Richard Nixon, Republican A divided Democratic Party improved the Republicans' chances of winning the presidency. Former vice president Richard Nixon swept the Republican primaries and easily won the nomination at the Republican National Convention in Miami Beach, Florida. Nixon chose Governor Spiro Agnew of Maryland as his running mate. He made this choice, in part, to attract conservative southern voters.

Nixon appealed to the patriotism of many mainstream Americans. Even people who were sympathetic to the antiwar movement had been put off by the behavior of protesters at the Democratic National Convention in Chicago. In a time of chaos, many Americans appreciated Nixon's promise of "law and order."

Nixon told voters that the "war must be ended. It must be ended honorably." He claimed to have a secret plan to end the war. He refused to explain his plan, saying that doing so might interfere with Johnson's efforts to achieve a peace settlement. Many voters were skeptical of a plan they could learn nothing about.

George Wallace, independent Another serious candidate in the race was former Alabama governor **George Wallace**. Earlier in the 1960s Wallace had gained national attention for his staunch opposition to the civil rights movement and school desegregation. Wallace was nominated for president by the American Independent Party. In his speeches, he raged against war protesters.

Wallace's strongest supporters were Democrats who opposed liberal policies. Many of these voters were conservative Democratic white southerners and working-class whites from across the nation. Although Wallace was a Democrat, Republicans feared that Wallace might take votes from Nixon.

The election campaign Nixon led in the polls for most of the campaign. As election day neared, though, his lead narrowed. Humphrey made some gains in the polls in September, after a speech in which he finally separated himself from Johnson's Vietnam policies. Humphrey said that he believed the bombing of North Vietnam should be stopped. He also argued that more responsibility for the war should go to South Vietnamese forces.

In addition, progress was made in the peace talks in Paris. The North Vietnamese agreed to include South Vietnamese representatives in the discussions if the air strikes on North Vietnam were stopped. Just days before the vote, President Johnson announced an end to the bombing of North Vietnam.

The election results The results of the popular election in November were very close. Just 510,000 votes separated Nixon and Humphrey, out of 73 million cast. Nixon received 43.4 percent of the vote, while Humphrey received 42.7 percent. As expected, Wallace was an important factor in the race, as nearly 10 million people, or 13.5 percent of electorate, voted for him.

In the electoral college, Nixon's margin of victory was wider. He carried the heavily populated states of California, Illinois, Ohio, and Florida and won many more electoral votes than the other two candidates combined. Nixon received 301 electoral votes to Humphrey's 191. Wallace, who won five states, received 46 electoral votes. This and his percentage of the popular vote made him one of the most successful third-party candidates in U.S. history.

Nixon's comfortable victory in the electoral college provided him with a mandate that the popular vote denied him. This sense of approval gave Nixon the confidence to pursue new policies to achieve victory in Vietnam—policies that would raise divisions over the war to a level not yet seen.

READING CHECK **Drawing Conclusions** How did events at the 1968 Democratic National Convention illustrate the divisions that existed within the Democratic Party?

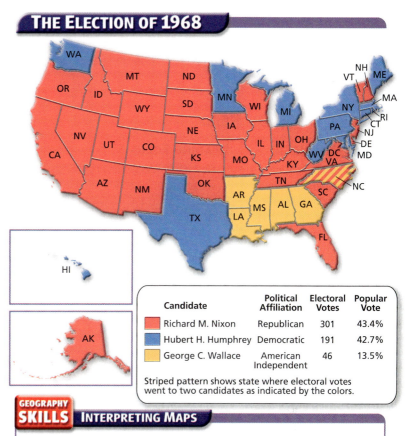

GEOGRAPHY SKILLS **INTERPRETING MAPS**

1. **Region** What effect did the presence of a third-party candidate have on the outcome of the race between the two major party candidates? Explain.
2. **Place** How did the electoral vote differ in North Carolina?

See **Skills Handbook**, p. H21

SECTION 3 ASSESSMENT

HSS 11.9.3, 11.9.4

go.hrw.com
Online Quiz
Keyword: SE7 HP19

Reviewing Ideas, Terms, and People

1. **a. Recall** Why did NVA and Vietcong forces attack the U.S. military base at Khe Sanh?
   b. Contrast How did the **Tet Offensive** differ from previous fighting in Vietnam?
   c. Evaluate Do you think the Tet Offensive should be considered a turning point in the Vietnam War? Why or why not?
2. **a. Identify** What were **Walter Cronkite**'s views on the war after the Tet Offensive?
   b. Analyze Why did President Johnson decide not to run for re-election in 1968?
   c. Elaborate Why do you think **Robert S. McNamara** changed his mind about the Vietnam War?
3. **a. Recall** How did Americans view General William Westmoreland's March 1968 request for more troops?
   b. Design What advice would you have given President Johnson about how to proceed with the war in 1968? Why?
4. **a. Identify** Who won the presidential election of 1968?
   b. Analyze What was the goal of the protesters at the 1968 Democratic National Convention?
   c. Predict How might the election of 1968 affect the course of the Vietnam War?

Critical Thinking

5. **Sequence** Review your notes on the main events of the Vietnam War in 1968. Then copy the graphic organizer below and use it to put the events in the correct sequence.

 **FOCUS ON SPEAKING** ELA W1.1; LS2.0

6. **Descriptive** As a television news journalist, deliver a report giving Americans an update on the events of either the Tet Offensive or the Democratic National Convention.

THE VIETNAM WAR **619**

SECTION 4: The War Ends

BEFORE YOU READ

MAIN IDEA
President Nixon eventually ended U.S. involvement in Vietnam, but the war had lasting effects on the United States and in Southeast Asia.

READING FOCUS
1. How did President Nixon's policies widen U.S. involvement in the war?
2. How and why did protests against the war increase?
3. How did Nixon achieve an end to U.S. involvement in Vietnam?
4. What was the war's legacy in the United States and in Vietnam?

KEY TERMS AND PEOPLE
Henry Kissinger
Vietnamization
silent majority
My Lai massacre
Pentagon Papers
George McGovern
Twenty-sixth Amendment
Khmer Rouge
War Powers Act

HSS 11.9.3 Trace the origins and geopolitical consequences (foreign and domestic) of the Cold War and containment policy, including the following:
• The Vietnam War

HSS 11.9.4 List the effects of foreign policy on domestic policies and vice versa (e.g., protests during the war in Vietnam, the "nuclear freeze" movement).

Appealing to the Silent Majority

THE INSIDE STORY *Who was the silent majority, and what role did it play in the Vietnam War?*

In October 1969 thousands of protesters converged on Washington to voice their opposition to the Vietnam War. In Congress, demands increased that President Nixon withdraw American forces from Vietnam. Even some of the president's supporters joined the calls to end American involvement in the war.

Despite these events, Nixon remained convinced that most Americans still supported the war. He was confident that these hardworking, law-abiding citizens were simply too busy supporting their families and too intimidated by the radical antiwar protests to make their voices heard.

Nixon asked the television networks for airtime to deliver a major address. Contrary to the usual practice, no advance copies of his speech were released to the media. Speculation was immense. Was the president about to announce a U.S. troop withdrawal from Vietnam? Instead, on November 3, 1969, he went on television to denounce the antiwar protesters and appeal to the American people.

"To you, the great silent majority of my fellow Americans, I ask for your support," Nixon said. "Because, let us understand: North Vietnam cannot defeat or humiliate the United States. Only Americans can do that."

Nixon's speech renewed support for the war effort and dealt a setback to the antiwar movement. Although these effects proved only temporary, the "silent majority" speech bought Nixon time to find a way out of Vietnam.

▼ Nixon greets a crowd of enthusiastic supporters in 1969.

Widening the War

During his presidential campaign, Nixon had pledged that if elected he would end the war in Vietnam. Once in office, he and National Security Adviser **Henry Kissinger** devised plans to fulfill this promise. In 1969 Kissinger began secret peace negotiations in Paris with North Vietnamese revolutionary Le Duc Tho (LAY duhk TOH). "I don't look back on our meetings with any great joy," Kissinger later said of these tense talks. "Yet he was a person of substance and discipline who defended the position he represented with dedication."

Vietnamization Kissinger's secret negotiations were part of a larger U.S. strategy aimed at achieving what Nixon called "peace with honor." A part of this plan was a strategy called **Vietnamization**. This involved turning over more of the fighting in Vietnam to the South Vietnamese while gradually bringing U.S. ground troops home.

Nixon's hope was that Vietnamization would give South Vietnamese leaders enough time to create a stable anti-Communist government. If this could not be achieved, Nixon wanted to delay the collapse of the South Vietnamese government until after the U.S. troops were gone. This would at least help to avoid the appearance of an embarrassing U.S. defeat.

Nixon began slowly withdrawing American forces from South Vietnam. When he took office in 1969, there were some 540,000 U.S. troops in that country. By the end of 1972, the number had been reduced to just over 24,000.

Antiwar activists opposed Nixon's plan for Vietnamization because it did not immediately end the war. Yet Nixon was convinced that he had the firm backing of the **silent majority** of Americans who he believed disapproved of antiwar protesters and generally supported the government's goals in Vietnam.

Laos and Cambodia Although he withdrew U.S. troops from Vietnam, Nixon at the same time also secretly expanded the war. In early 1969 he ordered the bombing of Cambodia, with the goal of disrupting supply lines along the Ho Chi Minh Trail. Nixon also wanted to demonstrate to North Vietnam that he was willing to widen the war in order to gain more favorable terms at the negotiating table. He concealed the air strikes from the American people—including members of Congress and even some key military leaders.

The war expanded further in 1970, when Nixon sent U.S. and ARVN troops into Cambodia, and into Laos the following year, to destroy North Vietnamese army bases. Nixon also renewed the bombing of North Vietnam, hoping to pressure the country's leaders into seeking peace. "I call it the Madman Theory," he told his chief of staff, H. R. Haldeman. "I want the North Vietnamese to believe that I've reached the point where I might do anything to stop the war."

As Johnson had done before him, Nixon underestimated the opposition's resolve, which survived even the death of Ho Chi Minh in 1969. North Vietnam staged a major invasion in March 1972, driving deep into South Vietnam.

READING CHECK **Identifying the Main Idea** Why did Nixon order the bombing of Cambodia?

Tough Negotiators
President Nixon's national security adviser, Henry Kissinger (left), and North Vietnamese leader Le Duc Tho (right) negotiated an end to the war in secret meetings in Paris. *What other strategies did Nixon plan to bring an end to the war?*

Increasing Protests

On April 30, 1970, Nixon announced that he had ordered U.S. troops into Cambodia. Antiwar protests intensified around the country, especially on college campuses. "As much as we hated the war on April 29, we hated it more on April 30," said Tom Grace, a student at Kent State University in Ohio.

Campus violence On May 2, 1970, antiwar demonstrators at Kent State University set fire to the campus Reserve Officers' Training Corps (ROTC) building. The governor of Ohio sent National Guard troops to control further demonstrations. On May 4, students gathered in a grassy area on campus for an antiwar rally. The troops ordered the students to disperse. When some students threw rocks and shouted insults at the soldiers, several soldiers began firing into the crowd. Four students were killed, and nine others were injured. Some of those who were shot were not protesting but simply passing by on the way to class.

Nine days later, a similar incident occurred at Jackson State College in Mississippi. State police fired at protesters inside a dormitory, killing two students and wounding nine.

Americans were horrified by the images of young people shot dead on college campuses. Students and faculty members on campuses nationwide went on strike. These protests forced hundreds of colleges and universities to shut down temporarily.

The antiwar movement grows Nixon was convinced that the antiwar protesters represented only a minority of Americans. "I recognize that some of my fellow citizens disagree with the plan for peace that I have chosen," he said. "I would be untrue to my oath of office to be dictated by the minority." Nevertheless, by late 1969 polls showed that more than half of Americans opposed the war.

As public opinion turned increasingly against the war, the peace movement began to seem more mainstream and respectable to many middle-class Americans. It gradually became clear that the opponents of the war included more than just college students and other young Americans.

In 1969, for example, a coalition of antiwar groups consisting of clergy, trade unionists, and veterans established October 15 as a nationwide day of protest. Millions of people

Americans React to the War

Below, demonstrators show their support for the war. Right, an antiwar rally turns tragic at Kent State University in Ohio, leaving four students dead. At far right, war protesters take their cause to the nation's capital.

took part in peaceful demonstrations on what was called Moratorium Day, calling for a moratorium, or halt, to the war.

A month later more than 250,000 protesters gathered in Washington, D.C., for the largest antiwar demonstration in U.S. history. Police lined up buses in front of the White House to form a barrier between Nixon, who was inside, and the thousands of marchers in the streets.

In an especially emotional demonstration in April 1971, members of Vietnam Veterans Against the War gathered in front of the Capitol. Some 800 veterans threw down their war medals to protest the war. Never before had returning U.S. soldiers so strongly opposed a war that was still being fought.

Radical protests A small minority of protesters believed that demonstrations and marches did not go far enough to end the war. Some radical antiwar groups turned to violent measures. A group called the Weathermen set off more than 5,000 bombs in places such as the New York City police department, the Pentagon, and the Capitol.

In October 1969 the Weathermen carried out the Days of Rage, a failed attempt to shut down the city of Chicago. Group members armed with clubs, lead pipes, chains, and gas masks clashed with police. Six Weathermen were shot, and many more were arrested. The negative reaction to the Days of Rage showed that most antiwar protesters did not support extremist groups or terrorist measures.

Troubling revelations In late 1969 Americans learned about a dark episode in the war's history. In March 1968 U.S. troops under the command of Lieutenant William Calley had entered the village of My Lai (mee LY) on a search-and-destroy mission to find Vietcong fighters. Although none were found, the soldiers killed at least 450 women, children, and elderly men.

The My Lai massacre was initially kept quiet by high-ranking military officials, but eventually former soldiers began talking about what they had witnessed. Calley was charged with murder in September 1969.

The My Lai atrocities further intensified the divisions between war supporters and opponents. Calley insisted that he had merely been doing his duty in the war on communism.

"We weren't in My Lai to kill human beings, really," he said. "We were there to kill ideology that is carried by—I don't know—pawns." Calley was convicted of murder and sentenced to life in prison. He was paroled in 1974.

In 1971 another news story boosted the momentum of the antiwar movement. The *New York Times* published a collection of secret government documents that traced the history of U.S. military involvement in Vietnam since the Truman years. Known as the Pentagon Papers, they revealed that government officials had been misleading the American people about the war for years. The leak angered and embarrassed President Nixon. Government lawyers failed to persuade the U.S. Supreme Court to suppress their publication.

Daniel Ellsberg, a former official at the Department of Defense, leaked the papers to the press. Ellsberg had originally been a supporter of the war. While spending time in Vietnam, however, he analyzed the effects of American policy and concluded that few South Vietnamese civilians supported the U.S.-backed government.

ACADEMIC VOCABULARY
analyze examine something carefully

READING CHECK **Contrasting** How did radical groups differ from other antiwar protesters?

End of U.S. Involvement

In 1972 Nixon campaigned for re-election while continuing his efforts to achieve peace with honor in Vietnam. His Democratic challenger, Senator **George McGovern** of South Dakota, was well known for his outspoken criticism of the war.

The 1972 election McGovern insisted that the Vietnam War be brought to an immediate end. "We have heard many times that Vietnam will no longer be an issue by the time the fall election approaches," he said in July 1972. "For the sake of the thousands of Vietnamese peasants still dying from American bombing raids, the GIs still dying . . . the American POWs [prisoners of war] rotting in the jails of Hanoi, I sincerely hope it will not be an issue."

McGovern hoped the ratification of the **Twenty-sixth Amendment** would boost his election chances. Passed in 1971, the amendment lowered the voting age from 21 to 18. Many of McGovern's supporters were young people.

As he had done in 1968, Nixon stressed law and order at home and assured voters that he would bring a quick end to the war. Just weeks before the election, Henry Kissinger announced a breakthrough in the long negotiations in Paris. "Peace is at hand," he declared. This announcement helped Nixon win by a landslide, with 60.7 percent of the popular vote to McGovern's 37.5 percent. In the electoral college, McGovern carried only Massachusetts and the District of Columbia.

A peace agreement Despite Kissinger's prediction, the peace talks stalled. To force North Vietnam to make concessions, Nixon ordered around-the-clock bombings of the North Vietnamese cities of Hanoi and Haiphong in late December 1972. The intense two-week air campaign, the so-called Christmas bombing, failed to sway the North Vietnamese. Nixon called off the bombing, and the talks resumed.

Officials from North Vietnam, South Vietnam, and the United States finally reached a settlement in January 1973. The United States agreed to withdraw all of its troops from South Vietnam and to help rebuild Vietnam. Both sides agreed to release all prisoners of war. But the agreement did not settle the key issue behind the war from the start: the political future of South Vietnam.

READING CHECK **Identifying the Main Idea** What were the terms of the 1973 peace agreement?

The Legacy of Vietnam

Two years after U.S. troops were withdrawn, North Vietnamese troops invaded South Vietnam. In April 1975 they reached Saigon. The

A former prisoner of war in Vietnam has a joyful reunion with his family. American casualties from the war included:
- 600 American POWs
- 300,000 wounded
- 58,000 dead
- 2,500 missing

U.S. military rushed to evacuate Americans still working in the city. As North Vietnamese troops overran the American embassy, helicopters airlifted thousands of people to safety on U.S. warships offshore.

Many of the Vietnamese who had helped the Americans were also desperate to leave South Vietnam. They feared they would be jailed or killed by North Vietnamese officials as punishment for their actions. Some 130,000 Vietnamese were evacuated and flown to the United States. Many more were left behind.

On April 30, 1975, South Vietnam surrendered. The North Vietnamese then set up a Communist government in the south. After more than two decades of "temporary" division, Vietnam became a reunited country.

Violence consumes Cambodia The fall of Saigon did not end the fighting in Southeast Asia. In 1975 Communist forces called the **Khmer Rouge** (kuh-MER ROOZH) gained control of Cambodia. In a brutal campaign of slaughter, the Khmer Rouge killed 1.5 million people in an attempt to subdue the country. Following a border dispute, Vietnamese forces invaded Cambodia in 1979. They overthrew the Khmer Rouge and installed a puppet government. The Vietnamese occupation lasted until 1989, when UN peacekeeping forces were deployed to monitor the fragile peace.

Effects on Southeast Asia The Vietnam War was devastating to the people of Southeast Asia. About 185,000 South Vietnamese soldiers and 450,000 South Vietnamese civilians were killed in the war. The number of Vietcong and NVA war dead is estimated at about 1 million.

The war also caused severe environmental damage in Vietnam. U.S. planes dropped some 8 million tons of bombs in the region as well as defoliants that contaminated food and water.

More than 1.5 million South Vietnamese fled the country after the fall of Saigon. Many of these refugees braved the open sea in tiny, crowded boats. Other Southeast Asian refugees, such as the Hmong (MUHNG) from Laos, also escaped postwar conditions in Southeast Asia. About 700,000 Southeast Asian refugees eventually settled in the United States.

Le Ly Hayslip was one of the many Vietnamese refugees who started a new life in America. Born in a village near Da Nang in 1949, she grew up amid constant warfare. In her book *When Heaven and Earth Changed Places*, Hayslip offered a message.

PRIMARY SOURCES

Autobiography

In 1967 navy pilot and future Arizona senator John McCain was shot down over North Vietnam. He spent more than five years as a prisoner of war, much of it in solitary confinement. In his memoirs he recalled how he and the other prisoners developed a tapping system so that they could secretly send each other messages.

> "The punishment for communicating could be severe, and a few POWs, having been caught and beaten for their efforts, had their spirits broken as their bodies were battered. Terrified of a return trip to the punishment room, they would lie still in their cells when their comrades tried to tap them up on the wall. Very few would remain uncommunicative for long. To suffer all this alone was less tolerable than torture . . . Almost all would recover their strength in a few days and answer the summons to rejoin the living."
>
> —from *Faith of My Fathers: A Family Memoir,* by John McCain and Mark Salter

Skills Focus   READING LIKE A HISTORIAN

Analyzing Primary Sources How did McCain's captors try to stop soldiers from communicating?

See **Skills Handbook**, pp. H28–H29

HISTORY'S VOICES

> "Do not feel sorry for me—I made it; I am okay. Right now, though, there are millions of other poor people around the world—girls, boys, men, and women—who live their lives the way I did in order to survive. Like me, they did not ask for the wars which swallowed them. They ask only for peace—the freedom to love and live a full life—and nothing more."
>
> —Le Ly Hayslip, *When Heaven and Earth Changed Places*

Effects on veterans About 58,000 Americans were killed in the Vietnam War. Around 600 others were held as POWs. Some POWs spent several years in North Vietnamese jails, where they often endured long periods of torture and solitary confinement.

Vietnam Veterans Memorial

The Vietnam Veterans Memorial includes the Wall (left) and the Three Servicemen Statue (below). The smooth, black-granite wall, nearly 500 feet long, lists the 58,249 names of the military men and women who died or were listed as missing in action.

The Wall was designed by a Yale architecture student, Maya Ying Lin (right).

About 2,500 American soldiers were reported missing in action in the war. Some 300,000 U.S. soldiers were wounded. Because of improving emergency medical services, many who would have died from serious wounds in previous wars were saved. As a result, a great number of paralyzed and otherwise severely disabled veterans returned home.

Some U.S. soldiers exposed to dangerous defoliants later developed cancer and other diseases. Their children born after the war have had high rates of birth defects. In 1984 the makers of Agent Orange were forced to create a fund to help veterans and their families.

Unlike the veterans of previous American wars, soldiers returning from Vietnam were not greeted with celebrations and ticker-tape parades. On the contrary, Vietnam War veterans often became targets for the anger or shame many of their fellow citizens felt about the war. Veterans told of being verbally abused and of people spitting on them. After having served their country in horrendous circumstances, veterans were stunned by the negative reception. One Vietnam War veteran later described how painful it was to be made a scapegoat for an unpopular war.

HISTORY'S VOICES

"I wondered if my country would ever welcome us back. Welcome all of us in body and spirit. Or would we always remain a flaw in America's vision of itself."

—Frederick Downs Jr.,
Aftermath: A Soldier's Return from Vietnam

Some veterans had trouble readjusting to civilian life. Many suffered from a condition called post-traumatic stress disorder. Memories of their horrible experiences caused nightmares, violent behavior, or flashbacks. The war's aftermath tore families apart.

"When I got back everything was changed," said one veteran. "I have flashbacks and people can't understand me sometimes. I sit by myself and I just think. You try to talk to somebody about it, they think you're out of your mind."

The war's political impact In the end, the United States failed to prevent the Communists from taking over South Vietnam. The U.S. government spent more than $150 billion on the Vietnam War. The spending added greatly to the national debt and fueled inflation. It also diverted funds that might have gone to domestic programs, such as education.

The war changed how many Americans viewed government. Some were angry about officials misleading them. Some thought both Johnson and Nixon had exceeded their constitutional powers by waging an undeclared war.

Seeking to prevent another Vietnam, Congress passed the **War Powers Act** in 1973. This law reaffirms Congress's constitutional right to declare war. It sets a 60-day limit on the presidential commitment of U.S. troops to foreign conflicts without a specific authorization by Congress or a declaration of war.

Another legacy of the Vietnam War is the impact it has had on the way Americans think about foreign conflicts. Before committing troops to a foreign conflict, leaders and the public often debate whether or not the nation is getting into another Vietnam.

Healing from the war Coming to terms with the Vietnam conflict has been an ongoing process for Americans. An important step was taken with the dedication of the Vietnam Veterans Memorial in Washington, D.C., in 1982. The memorial was designed by Maya Ying Lin, a Chinese American who was a 21-year-old architecture student at Yale University when her design was chosen.

The memorial is a long wall of polished black granite, inscribed with the names of the more than 58,000 Americans who died or went missing in Vietnam. Bruce Weigl explained why he and many other veterans were drawn to the memorial's dedication ceremony. "We came to find the names of those we lost in the war, as if by tracing the letters cut into the granite we could find what was left of ourselves."

Vietnam veterans in government were among the leaders of a subsequent effort to rebuild relations between the United States and Vietnam. The two countries resumed normal relations in 1995. In 1997 Douglas "Pete" Peterson, a former air force pilot who spent six years as a POW in North Vietnam, became the new U.S. ambassador to Vietnam. "It's a tragic history that we've shared as two peoples," he observed. "No one can change that, but there is a great deal we can all do about the future."

READING CHECK **Identifying Cause and Effect** What effects has the Vietnam War had on American veterans?

SECTION 4 ASSESSMENT

HSS 11.9.3, 11.9.4

Reviewing Ideas, Terms, and People

1. **a. Describe** What was President Nixon's Madman Theory?
   b. Analyze What role did Henry Kissinger have in the Vietnam War?
   c. Rate How well do you think Nixon's Vietnamization strategy worked? Explain.

2. **a. Identify** What was the silent majority?
   b. Make Generalizations How did Americans react to the My Lai massacre?
   c. Elaborate Why do you think Daniel Ellsberg leaked the Pentagon Papers?

3. **a. Recall** What issues helped President Nixon win re-election in 1972?
   b. Draw Conclusions Why do you think Nixon defeated George McGovern by so wide a margin in the 1972 election?
   c. Evaluate Did Nixon's bombing of North Vietnam achieve its goal? Explain.

4. **a. Identify** What was the War Powers Act?
   b. Make Inferences Why did so many people leave Vietnam after the fall of Saigon?

Critical Thinking

5. **Categorize** Review your notes on the effects of the Vietnam War. Then copy the graphic organizer below and use it to list the effects of the war on different groups of people.

Group	Effect
North Vietnamese	
South Vietnamese	
Americans	

FOCUS ON WRITING

6. **Narrative** Write a poem that honors the fallen American soldiers who served in the Vietnam War.

CHAPTER 19 DOCUMENT-BASED INVESTIGATION

The Tet Offensive

HSS 11.9.3, 11.9.4

Historical Context The documents below provide a look at the Tet Offensive in 1968, one of the key turning points in the Vietnam War.

Task Examine the documents and answer the questions that follow. Then write an essay about the effects of the Tet Offensive on the Vietnam War. Use facts from the documents and from the chapter to support the position you take in your thesis statement.

DOCUMENT 1

The Tet Offensive was a surprise attack during the Vietnamese New Year. The North Vietnamese Army (NVA) and the Vietcong (VC) achieved tactical surprise but sustained high casualties. This table shows the casualties for each side.

TET OFFENSIVE CASUALTIES

Force	Killed in Action	Wounded in Action	Missing in Action	Captured in Action
U.S. Forces	1,536	7,764	11	unknown
ARVN	2,788	8,299	587	unknown
NVA/VC	45,000	unknown	unknown	6,691

Source: Combat Area Casualty File of 11/93, National Archives

DOCUMENT 2

General William Westmoreland commanded U.S. forces in Vietnam from 1964 to 1968. In 1976 he published his memoirs of the war in a book titled *A Soldier Reports*. In this excerpt he discusses a press conference he held at the U.S. Embassy following the defeat of the Tet Offensive.

"... I took the opportunity to try to put the Embassy raid and the countryside attacks into perspective. Contrary to rumor, I said, none of the Viet Cong had gotten inside the Chancery. Damage to the building was superficial. As for the big offensive throughout the country, the enemy, by coming out into the open, was exposing himself to tremendous casualties. Fully conscious of American and South Vietnamese strength and ability, I had no hesitation in saying that the enemy was inviting defeat.

"My efforts at perspective went for nought. The attack on the Embassy, Don Oberdorfer wrote later, 'seemed to give the lie to the rosy projections and victory claims that Westmoreland and others had been dishing out.' Oberdorfer said that the reporters could hardly believe their ears. 'Westmoreland was standing in the ruins and saying everything was great.'

"That attitude on the part of the American reporters undoubtedly contributed to the psychological victory the enemy achieved in the United States. What would they have had me say, that the walls were tumbling down when I knew they were not? That the enemy was winning when I knew he was on the verge of a disastrous military defeat?"

DOCUMENT 3

On February 24, 1968, the Department of Defense began the process of drafting 48,000 more soldiers for the Vietnam War. This cartoon by Hugh Haynie appeared in the Louisville, Kentucky *Courier-Journal* a few days later.

DOCUMENT 4

Walter Cronkite was the anchor for CBS News from 1962 to 1981. In February 1968 Cronkite traveled to Vietnam to see firsthand the conditions following the Tet Offensive. In his broadcast on February 27, 1968, he offered a personal assessment of the situation.

"Who won and who lost in the great Tet offensive against the cities? I'm not sure. The Vietcong did not win by a knockout, but neither did we. The referees of history may make it a draw...

"We have been too often disappointed by the optimism of the American leaders, both in Vietnam and Washington, to have faith any longer in the silver linings they find in the darkest clouds...

"To say that we are closer to victory today is to believe, in the face of the evidence, the optimists who have been wrong in the past. To suggest we are on the edge of defeat is to yield to unreasonable pessimism. To say that we are mired in stalemate seems the only realistic, yet unsatisfactory, conclusion. On the off chance that military and political analysts are right, in the next few months we must test the enemy's intentions in case this is indeed his last big gasp before negotiations. But it is increasingly clear to this reporter that the only rational way out then will be to negotiate, not as victors, but as an honorable people who lived up to their pledge to defend democracy, and did the best they could."

HSS Analysis HR4, HI1

Skills Focus: READING LIKE A HISTORIAN

1. **a. Identify** Refer to Document 1. Which group experienced the largest number of battle-related deaths?
   b. Analyze Based solely on the casualty statistics, which side was victorious?

2. **a. Identify** Refer to Document 2. What did General Westmoreland hope to achieve in the press conference?
   b. Interpret What opinion does Westmoreland have of the press?

3. **a. Identify** Refer to Document 3. What is the Vietnam War compared with in this political cartoon?
   b. Analyze Why might this cartoon be seen as a response to the increase in the draft?

4. **a. Identify** Refer to Document 4. What outcome does Cronkite predict for the war?
   b. Elaborate What course of events does Cronkite suggest in order to achieve that outcome?

5. **Document-Based Essay Question** Consider the question below and form a thesis statement. Using examples from Documents 1, 2, 3, and 4, create an outline and write a short essay supporting your position.
   How did the Tet Offensive affect Americans' perceptions of the situation in Vietnam?

See **Skills Handbook**, pp. H28–H29, H31

Chapter 19 Chapter Review

Visual Summary: The Vietnam War

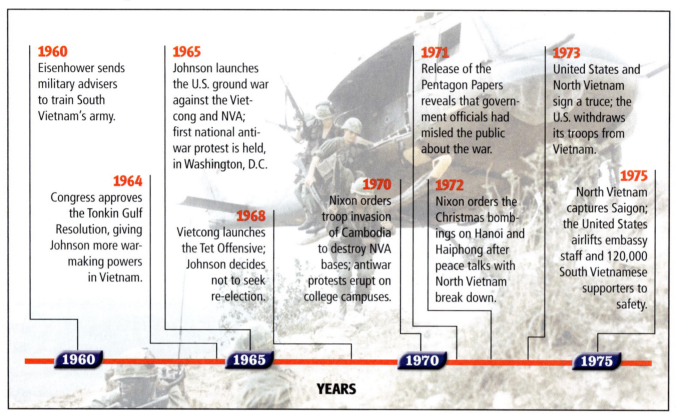

1960 Eisenhower sends military advisers to train South Vietnam's army.

1964 Congress approves the Tonkin Gulf Resolution, giving Johnson more war-making powers in Vietnam.

1965 Johnson launches the U.S. ground war against the Vietcong and NVA; first national antiwar protest is held, in Washington, D.C.

1968 Vietcong launches the Tet Offensive; Johnson decides not to seek re-election.

1970 Nixon orders troop invasion of Cambodia to destroy NVA bases; antiwar protests erupt on college campuses.

1971 Release of the Pentagon Papers reveals that government officials had misled the public about the war.

1972 Nixon orders the Christmas bombings on Hanoi and Haiphong after peace talks with North Vietnam break down.

1973 United States and North Vietnam sign a truce; the U.S. withdraws its troops from Vietnam.

1975 North Vietnam captures Saigon; the United States airlifts embassy staff and 120,000 South Vietnamese supporters to safety.

YEARS

Reviewing Key Terms and People

Complete each sentence by filling the blank with the correct term or person.

1. Communist forces called the _____ took over the Cambodian government and slaughtered about 1.5 million people.
2. _____ _____ was the Democratic presidential candidate in 1968.
3. Nixon called people who disapproved of antiwar protesters and generally supported the government's Vietnam goals the _____.
4. Ho Chi Minh originally founded the _____ to resist the Japanese occupation of Vietnam.
5. Secretary of Defense _____ _____ at first supported and carried out the war in Vietnam but later tried to find a way to end it.
6. The _____ lowered the voting age in the United States from 21 to 18.
7. The French army was defeated by the Vietminh at _____.
8. In a campaign called _____, U.S. pilots bombed and destroyed much of North Vietnam.
9. Chicago mayor _____ _____ ordered police and National Guard troops to keep order during the 1968 Democratic Convention.
10. General _____ _____ commanded U.S. ground troops in South Vietnam.
11. The _____ was the reason the United States wanted to defeat communism in Vietnam.
12. After the French were defeated in 1954, representatives from several nations met at the _____ to work out a peace agreement for Indochina.
13. The strategy of _____ was designed to keep Vietnamese civilians safe and win their support.

History's Impact video program

Review the video to answer the closing question: What role did American public opinion play during the Vietnam War?

Comprehension and Critical Thinking

SECTION 1 (pp. 596–603) HSS 11.9.3

14. a. Identify What kinds of tactics did the Vietminh use to fight the French?

   b. Analyze What were the terms of the 1954 Geneva Accords? What was the purpose of the proposed 1956 election?

   c. Elaborate Why do you think President Kennedy wanted to show U.S. resolve in Vietnam?

SECTION 2 (pp. 604–611) HSS 11.9.3, 11.9.4

15. a. Describe How did American troops try to disrupt the Ho Chi Minh Trail?

   b. Analyze Why did many civil rights advocates oppose the Vietnam War?

   c. Predict Do you think Americans' opinions about the Vietnam War would have been different had there been no television reporting? Explain your answer.

SECTION 3 (pp. 612–619) HSS 11.9.3, 11.9.4

16. a. Describe What happened to protesters during the Democratic National Convention in 1968?

   b. Analyze Why did Johnson's negotiations with North Vietnam fail to result in a peace agreement?

   c. Elaborate Why do you think the Tet Offensive had such a strong effect on public opinion in the United States?

SECTION 4 (pp. 620–627) HSS 11.9.3, 11.9.4

17. a. Identify What was Vietnamization?

   b. Compare How were the incidents at Kent State University and Jackson State College similar?

   c. Evaluate Was the Vietnam War a success for the United States? Why or why not?

Using the Internet

go.hrw.com Practice Online Keyword: SE7 CH19

18. During the Vietnam War, U.S. air strikes used dangerous chemicals such as napalm and Agent Orange. Using the keyword above, do research to find out what was known about them at the time and about the short- and long-term effects of these chemicals. Then create a report that analyzes the ways in which veterans, Vietnamese civilians, the U.S. military, and other groups have responded to these effects.

Analyzing Primary Sources HSS HR4

Reading Like a Historian In Section 2, read the History's Voices passage from Myron Harrington that begins "After a while, survival was the name of the game." He described his experience in Vietnam.

19. Describe What was Harrington's experience in Vietnam like?

20. Draw Conclusions Based on details in the source, what was Harrington's role in the war?

Critical Reading HSS 11.9.3; ELA R3.8

Read the passage near the end of Section 4 that begins with the heading "The war's political impact." Then answer the questions that follow.

21. According to the passage, the Vietnam War has made Americans today

   A open to accepting large numbers of refugees.

   B likely to suffer post-traumatic stress disorder.

   C debate whether they are getting into another Vietnam before committing troops to a conflict.

   D eager to fight communism in Southeast Asia.

22. Which of the following resulted from government spending on the Vietnam War?

   A inflation and a higher national debt

   B the fall of Saigon

   C the passage of the War Powers Act

   D the rise to power of the Khmer Rouge

FOCUS ON WRITING ELA W1.1, 1.3

Persuasive Writing *Persuasive writing takes a position for or against an issue, using facts and examples as supporting evidence. To practice persuasive writing, complete the assignment below.*

Writing Topic The response to the protests at the 1968 Democratic National Convention

23. Assignment Based on what you have read in this chapter, write a brief editorial to convince people that Chicago mayor Richard Daley's response to the protests was either necessary or too extreme.

THE VIETNAM WAR 631

CHAPTER 20
1963–1975
A Time of Social Change

THE BIG PICTURE Inspired by the African American civil rights movement, women, Native Americans, and Latinos all stood up against social, political, and economic inequality in the 1960s. At the same time a youthful counterculture turned its back on mainstream society in search of a new way of life.

California Standards

History-Social Sciences

11.8 Students analyze the economic boom and social transformation of post-World War II America.

11.10 Students analyze the development of federal civil rights and voting rights.

11.11 Students analyze the major social problems and domestic policy issues in contemporary American society.

SKILLS FOCUS READING LIKE A HISTORIAN

These farmworkers call out from a picket line. Beginning in the 1960s, farmworkers began organizing, using strikes and initiating boycotts to fight for better working conditions and better wages.

Interpreting Visuals What does this photograph tell you about the workers' commitment and determination?

See **Skills Handbook**, p. H30

U.S.

1964 Title VII of the Civil Rights Act of 1964 outlaws gender discrimination in employment.

1963

World

1964 South African rebel leader Nelson Mandela is sentenced to life in prison.

History's Impact video program
Watch the video to understand the impact of the right of assembly.

1965 Farmworkers begin a strike in Delano, California.

1969 400,000 attend the Woodstock Music and Art Fair in upstate New York.

1972 Congress approves the Equal Rights Amendment.

1973 Federal marshals and Indian activists face off at Wounded Knee, South Dakota.

1967 Israel defeats Egypt, Jordan, and Syria in the Six-Day War.

1971 The UN recognizes Communist China and expels Nationalist China (Taiwan).

1973 Egypt and Syria attack Israel, beginning the Yom Kippur War.

1975 Saigon, capital of South Vietnam, falls to North Vietnam, ending the Vietnam War.

SECTION 1
Women and Native Americans Fight for Change

BEFORE YOU READ

MAIN IDEA
In the 1960s women and Native Americans struggled to achieve social justice.

READING FOCUS
1. What led to the revival of the women's movement?
2. Which issues were important to the women's liberation movement?
3. What were the lives of Native Americans like by the early 1960s?
4. How did Native Americans fight for fairness?

KEY TERMS AND PEOPLE
Betty Friedan
feminism
National Organization for Women
Equal Rights Amendment
Phyllis Schlafly
Roe v. *Wade*
American Indian Movement
Russell Means

HSS 11.10.5 Discuss the diffusion of the civil rights movement and how the advances influenced the quests of American Indians for civil rights and equal opportunities.

HSS 11.10.7 Analyze the women's rights movement launched in the 1960s, including differing perspectives on the roles of women.

HSS 11.11.3 Describe the changing roles of women in society as reflected in the entry of more women into the labor force and the changing family structure.

A Failed Amendment

THE INSIDE STORY *What did labor unions have to do with women's rights?* "Equality of rights under the law shall not be denied or abridged by the United States or by any state on account of sex." This was the wording of a constitutional amendment that Congress proposed in 1972.

▼ Demonstrators show their support of the Equal Rights Amendment at a rally in Washington, D.C., in 1981.

Many Americans regarded this Equal Rights Amendment (ERA) as long overdue. After all, Congress had been considering it for 49 years.

When the Nineteenth Amendment extended suffrage to women in 1920, an amendment guaranteeing equality with men in other areas had seemed a logical next step. The ERA was first introduced in Congress in 1923 and then introduced again in every subsequent session. The result was always the same—defeat. Powerful labor unions opposed the ERA because they feared it would undo protections they had won for women workers.

In the 1960s the civil rights movement changed everything. Hoping to weaken support for the proposed Civil Rights Act, which aimed to ban racial discrimination in employment, opponents added a ban on gender discrimination. To their dismay, the bill passed anyway.

Passage of the Civil Rights Act of 1964 pumped new life into the ERA. With special protections for women workers now outlawed by the Civil Rights Act, the unions no longer had a reason to oppose the ERA. In fact, they gradually reversed their position and backed it.

Representative Martha Griffiths of Michigan, a state where unions were strong, lobbied hard for the ERA. Congress finally passed it in 1972 and submitted it to the states for ratification. In the states, though, supporters of the ERA would fight a losing battle.

Revival of the Women's Movement

After the Nineteenth Amendment gave women the right to vote in 1920, the organized movement for women's rights declined. In the 1960s, some women began to question once more why they were still considered unequal—and what should be done about it.

Experiences at work To understand the revival of the women's movement, it is important to know what many women's lives were like in the 1950s and early 1960s. Throughout the 1950s more women began to join the workforce. By 1963, nearly one-third of American workers were women.

Yet on average, women in 1963 earned only 60 percent of what men earned. One reason for this difference was that most women worked in service jobs, such as retail sales, clerical work, and domestic service. These jobs typically paid poorly. Many of the better-paying jobs, such as those in manufacturing and construction, were considered men's domain. Even when women had the same jobs as men, however, they often received lower wages than men did.

In 1961 President John F. Kennedy ordered a formal inquiry into the position of women in American society. The Presidential Commission on the Status of Women reported that women did experience discrimination at work. Employers paid women less than men and promoted them less often. This report opened many people's eyes to the need for change.

Experiences at home Even though increasing numbers of women entered the workforce, many other women remained full-time homemakers. A popular idea in the 1950s was that women would be happiest as wives, mothers, and homemakers. Women tended to marry young; their average age at marriage was 20 years old. Many women who delayed marriage and built careers often left their jobs once they got married.

ACADEMIC VOCABULARY
inquiry investigation, examination

American Women: A Statistical Profile

During the latter half of the twentieth century, women began playing a greater role in public life, working at paid employment in greater numbers than ever before and attaining higher levels of education. *How do you think these experiences would lead women to seek social equality?*

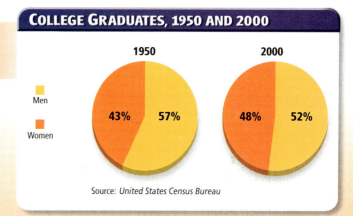

COLLEGE GRADUATES, 1950 AND 2000

1950: Men 57%, Women 43%
2000: Men 52%, Women 48%

Source: *United States Census Bureau*

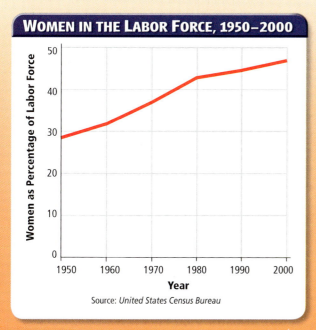

WOMEN IN THE LABOR FORCE, 1950–2000

Source: *United States Census Bureau*

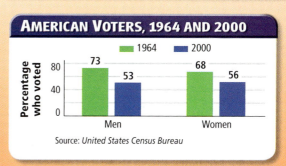

AMERICAN VOTERS, 1964 AND 2000

Men: 1964 — 73, 2000 — 53
Women: 1964 — 68, 2000 — 56

Source: *United States Census Bureau*

SKILLS FOCUS: INTERPRETING GRAPHS

In the year 2000, who was a more active voting bloc, men or women?

See **Skills Handbook**, pp. H16, H17

FACES OF HISTORY

Betty FRIEDAN
1921–2006

After graduating from Smith College, Betty Friedan settled in New York and became a journalist. This was during World War II, when women were filling the jobs of men who had left to fight. Friedan discovered that women reporters were being paid less than men doing the same work. When Friedan requested maternity leave, her employer fired her.

Friedan became a pioneer of the women's movement with her best-selling book, *The Feminine Mystique*. She has remained a vocal feminist leader, calling for reforms to aid women and families, such as increased childcare, flexible work schedules, and equal pay.

Analyze A popular saying of the women's movement was "The personal is political." How did this fit Friedan's own life?

Life as a homemaker did not make all women happy, however. **Betty Friedan** (free-DAN) conducted a survey of college-educated women and found that many were dissatisfied with their lives. Nearly all of the survey respondents were full-time homemakers. In her 1963 book, *The Feminine Mystique*, Friedan concluded that many women felt trapped by domestc life, rather than fulfilled by it.

Consciousness raising By the late 1960s, *The Feminine Mystique* had sparked a national debate about the roles and rights of women. Some women organized small group discussions. In these consciousness-raising sessions, women discovered that the discrimination they experienced individually was part of a larger pattern of discrimination based on gender. More and more women came to feel like second-class citizens.

Ironically, even the civil rights movement—a movement aimed at eliminating discrimination—harbored discriminatory attitudes toward women. In 1964 two female volunteers for the Student Nonviolent Coordinating Committee (SNCC) noted that SNCC's "assumption of male superiority" was "as widespread and . . . as crippling to . . . women as the assumptions of white supremacy are to the Negro."

READING CHECK **Summarizing** What factors contributed to the revival of the women's movement?

The Women's Liberation Movement

In the late 1960s and 1970s, the movement for women's rights was known by several different names—the women's liberation movement, the feminist movement, and the equal rights movement. The core belief of the women's liberation movement was **feminism**, the conviction that women and men should be socially, politically, and economically equal.

Feminists cheered the passage of the Civil Rights Act of 1964. The act banned gender discrimination in employment and created the Equal Employment Opportunity Commission to enforce the law. Yet it soon became clear that many government officials gave low priority to fighting gender-based discrimination.

NOW In 1966 a group of feminists formed the **National Organization for Women** (NOW). This women's rights organization fought gender discrimination in the workplace, schools, and justice system. It also worked to end violence against women and to achieve abortion rights.

Members of NOW used many tactics to achieve their goals. They lobbied government officials to change the laws. They filed lawsuits to seek equality through the justice system. They also staged rallies, marches, and other nonviolent protests.

The first president of NOW was Betty Friedan. She and Pauli Murray—the first African American woman Episcopal priest and a co-founder of NOW—wrote NOW's original Statement of Purpose.

HISTORY'S VOICES

> "We believe that women will do most to create a new image of women by acting now, and by speaking out in behalf of their own equality, freedom, and human dignity . . . in an active, self-respecting partnership with men. By so doing, women will develop confidence in their own ability to determine actively, in partnership with men, the conditions of their life, their choices, their future and their society."
>
> —NOW's Statement of Purpose, 1966

The Equal Rights Amendment NOW actively campaigned for passage of the **Equal Rights Amendment** (ERA). This proposed amendment to the Constitution promised equal treatment for men and women in all spheres, not just employment. Before it could take effect, though, the ERA had to be ratified by at least 38 states.

At first ratification seemed certain. NOW organized a 1978 march in support of the ERA that drew more than 100,000 people to Washington, D.C. Some people, however, viewed the ERA as a threat to traditional family life. Critics warned that the ERA would cancel laws that distinguished between men and women. They argued that women would be drafted into the military and that men and women would have to share public restrooms.

Conservative groups launched a campaign to defeat the ERA. One of the most outspoken critics of the ERA was **Phyllis Schlafly**. She argued that it would take away legal protections that women already had without conferring any new benefits. By the 1982 deadline set by Congress, the ERA was three states short of ratification. It failed to become law.

Roe v. Wade Another significant issue for the women's movement was the campaign for abortion rights. The Supreme Court struck down state laws that banned abortion in the 1973 landmark case **Roe v. Wade**. The Court ruled that such laws violated a constitutional right to privacy.

The decision sparked a debate that continues to this day. Supporters argued that women could not achieve equality until they could control when or whether to have children. Supporters also believed that legal abortion was necessary to protect women's health. They argued that many women would otherwise resort to inept, "back-alley" practitioners who often botched the procedure.

Many people opposed the decision because of religious or moral beliefs that fetal life was sacred and should be protected. Other opponents of the ruling argued that the Court's assumption of a right to privacy strayed too far from the original intent of the Constitution.

THE IMPACT TODAY

Government
For more than 20 years after its failure to become law, the ERA continued to be reintroduced into every session of Congress, but failed to pass again.

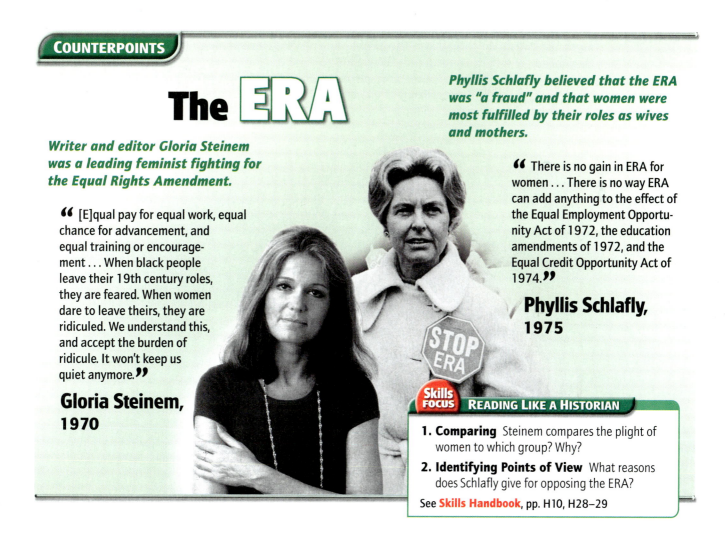

COUNTERPOINTS

The ERA

Writer and editor Gloria Steinem was a leading feminist fighting for the Equal Rights Amendment.

" [E]qual pay for equal work, equal chance for advancement, and equal training or encouragement . . . When black people leave their 19th century roles, they are feared. When women dare to leave theirs, they are ridiculed. We understand this, and accept the burden of ridicule. It won't keep us quiet anymore. "

Gloria Steinem, 1970

Phyllis Schlafly believed that the ERA was "a fraud" and that women were most fulfilled by their roles as wives and mothers.

" There is no gain in ERA for women . . . There is no way ERA can add anything to the effect of the Equal Employment Opportunity Act of 1972, the education amendments of 1972, and the Equal Credit Opportunity Act of 1974. "

Phyllis Schlafly, 1975

SKILLS FOCUS — READING LIKE A HISTORIAN

1. **Comparing** Steinem compares the plight of women to which group? Why?
2. **Identifying Points of View** What reasons does Schlafly give for opposing the ERA?

See **Skills Handbook**, pp. H10, H28–29

A TIME OF SOCIAL CHANGE **637**

Effects of the women's movement The women's movement had many notable successes in the 1970s. By the end of the decade, the number of women holding professional jobs had increased, although most women still held low-paying jobs. For example, in 1970 just 5 percent of the nation's lawyers were women. A decade later, 12 percent of American lawyers were women.

More women also began to move into senior positions in government. More female politicians were elected to Congress, although they still made up less than 5 percent of its members. Representatives Bella Abzug and Shirley Chisholm of New York received national attention. Abzug became an outspoken supporter of women's issues in Congress. In 1972 Shirley Chisholm—the first African American woman elected to Congress—became the first African American woman to run for president.

The pace of the feminist movement slowed in the late 1970s, however. There was a perception that its leaders and its beneficiaries were mainly wealthy white women. Many working-class and nonwhite women felt that the movement offered little to address the problems they faced.

READING CHECK Summarizing What were the arguments for and against the ERA?

THE IMPACT TODAY
Daily Life
By the early twenty-first century, nearly half the nation's law students and medical students were women, and a majority of workers in professional positions were women.

The Lives of Native Americans

Just as many women felt they were held back in mid-twentieth-century America, so did many Native Americans. Indian groups had suffered injustices since colonial times. During the 1950s, negative stereotypes of Indians still persisted, and hardships abounded.

Living conditions Native Americans did not share the prosperity many Americans experienced in the 1950s. As a group, they suffered some of the highest unemployment rates in the nation. The average income of Native American men was less than half that of white American men. Mary Crow Dog recalled growing up poor on a Sioux reservation in South Dakota: "We had no shoes and went barefoot most of the time. I never had a new dress."

The Native American population suffered disproportionately from poor health. Rates of alcoholism and tuberculosis were alarmingly high. Native Americans had lower life expectancy than other Americans, and their children were more likely to die in infancy.

Termination policy During the presidency of Dwight D. Eisenhower, the federal government began a policy called termination. The

Native American Policy and Activism

Native American peoples have struggled to retain their ways of life ever since European colonists first arrived in America. Study the time line to learn more about Native Americans and government policies.

1838 Some 18,000 Cherokee embarked upon the Trail of Tears as they were forced to move from the Southeast to Oklahoma.

1887 The Dawes Act split Native American land into individual plots and allowed surplus land to be sold to settlers.

goal was to "end the status of Indians as wards of the government and grant them all the rights and prerogatives pertaining to American citizenship." The architects of the policy hoped to draw Native Americans out of their isolated reservations and into mainstream society. The method for doing this, however, was to stop federal services to reservations and relocate Native Americans to the cities.

Between 1952 and 1967, some 200,000 Native Americans were resettled in this way. However, the government failed to <u>allocate</u> resources to help them adjust to urban life. The results were disastrous. Most of the Native Americans affected by termination remained desperately poor.

A movement emerges Many Native Americans believed the time had come for an organized movement for Native American rights. In 1961 a group of about 700 Native Americans from 64 nations held a conference in Chicago to oppose the termination policy and create a political agenda for change.

At the conference a Chippewa-Cree activist named D'Arcy McNickle drafted the Declaration of Indian Purpose. This document condemned termination. It also boldly stated Native Americans' intention to take control over their own lives.

HISTORY'S VOICES

❝Since our Indian culture is threatened by presumption of being absorbed by the American society, we believe we have the responsibility of preserving our precious heritage . . . What we ask of America is not charity . . . We ask only that the nature of our situation be recognized and made the basis of policy and action.❞
—Declaration of Indian Purpose, June 1961

The declaration marked the beginning of what became known as the Red Power movement. A new sense of unity arose among Native Americans as different groups joined forces to confront common challenges.

READING CHECK **Identifying the Main Idea** What factors led Native Americans to begin an organized fight for their rights?

Native Americans Fight for Fairness

In 1968 President Lyndon B. Johnson declared his support for Indian self-determination. He established the National Council on Indian Opportunity to get Native Americans more involved in setting policy regarding Indian affairs. Real change, though, came through the efforts of Native American political activists.

ACADEMIC VOCABULARY
allocate set aside for a specific purpose

1934 The Indian Reorganization Act set up Tribal Business Councils and stopped the sale of tribal lands.

1953 Congress adopted the termination policy, moving many Native Americans to cities and cutting aid to reservations.

1969 Occupation of Alcatraz began, awakening the public to Native Americans' struggle for self-determination.

1972 The Indian Education Act established culturally appropriate educational programs for Native American students.

2005 Nearly 40 percent of federally recognized Indian nations earn money and create jobs by running gambling casinos.

A TIME OF SOCIAL CHANGE **639**

The occupation of Alcatraz In 1969 a group of Native Americans tried to reclaim Alcatraz Island, the site of an abandoned federal prison in San Francisco Bay. They claimed that the 1868 Treaty of Fort Laramie gave them the right to use any surplus federal territory.

The highly publicized occupation lasted nearly 18 months, until federal marshals removed the Indians by force. Although they did not succeed in gaining ownership of Alcatraz, the occupiers did draw attention to the plight of Native Americans. Partly as a result, New Mexico returned 48,000 acres of the Sacred Blue Lake lands to the Taos Pueblo in 1970. Indian nations in Washington State, Maine, and Connecticut also settled land claims.

John Trudell, a Santee Sioux, found the Alcatraz occupation to be a transforming experience. "Alcatraz put me back into my community and helped me remember who I am. It was a rekindling of the spirit. Alcatraz made it easier for us to remember who we are."

AIM The Alcatraz Island takeover helped invigorate the **American Indian Movement** (AIM), founded in Minnesota in 1968 by Dennis Banks, Clyde Bellecourt, and others. Originally focused on urban Native Americans, AIM became the major force behind the larger Red Power movement. AIM called for renewal of traditional cultures, economic independence, and better education for Indian children.

THE IMPACT TODAY
Culture
Alcatraz is now a popular tourist attraction in San Francisco. Visitors who tour the old prison can also study exhibits and watch a film about the Indian occupation of the island.

FACES OF HISTORY
Clyde BELLECOURT
1939–

It is little wonder that Clyde Bellecourt became a Native American activist. He developed a passion for social justice early on, listening to his mother tell stories about attending boarding school and being punished for speaking her native language.

Bellecourt has been influential in many Native American organizations, including AIM, the Indian School System, and the International Indian Treaty Council, which seeks to protect traditional cultures and sacred lands. More recently, he helped organize the National Coalition on Racism in Sports and the Media, which demonstrates against sports teams whose names perpetuate racial and cultural stereotypes. Bellecourt believes that things are destined to change for Native Americans, that there is "a spiritual rebirth going on."

Explain How has Bellecourt helped Native Americans?

Russell Means, one of AIM's best-known leaders, summarized the organization's importance to Native Americans in an interview in a 2002 PBS television documentary.

HISTORY'S VOICES
"Before AIM, Indians were dispirited, defeated and culturally dissolving. People were ashamed to be Indian . . . We put Indians and Indian rights smack dab in the middle of the public consciousness for the first time since the so-called Indian Wars . . . [AIM] laid the groundwork for the next stage in regaining our sovereignty and self-determination as a nation."
—Russell Means, "Alcatraz Is Not an Island"

In an era when many civil rights groups used nonviolent strategies, AIM sometimes used more forceful tactics. In November 1972, for example, AIM and several other Native American rights groups staged a protest called the Trail of Broken Treaties. Protesters marched to the Bureau of Indian Affairs (BIA) in Washington, D.C., to demand changes in the relationship between Native Americans and the government. Angered by the government's lack of support, the protesters took over BIA headquarters. Officials were embarrassed by the media coverage and agreed to appoint a committee to study the demands. In return, the protesters ended the occupation.

In February 1973, AIM took its most dramatic action on the Pine Ridge Reservation in Wounded Knee, South Dakota. This was where U.S. soldiers had killed more than 300 Sioux in 1890. Now, some 80 years later, conflict unfolded again. The Oglala Sioux president, Richard Wilson, had banned all AIM activities on the reservation, calling AIM a "lawless" band of "social misfits." AIM believed that Wilson's tribal government was corrupt. About 200 AIM members occupied Wounded Knee in order to force the federal government to investigate the tribal government. They also wanted an investigation of alleged misconduct at the Bureau of Indian Affairs.

After AIM members seized Wounded Knee, federal agents arrived to drive them out. For 71 days AIM and U.S. marshals faced off. Finally, after two AIM activists had been killed and a federal marshal wounded, the government agreed to consider AIM's grievances. The siege ended, but the government did not follow through on its promise to AIM.

Other organizations AIM was not the only organization fighting for Native American rights at this time. Many other organizations focused on particular needs.

The National Indian Education Association, formed in 1969, fought to improve access to education for Native Americans. The Native American Rights Fund, founded in 1971, provided legal services to Native Americans. The Council on Energy Resource Tribes helped its member nations gain control over their natural resources and choose whether to protect or develop them.

These groups, and others like them, worked to protect Native Americans' rights, improve standards of living, and do it all in a manner consistent with Native Americans' cultures and traditions. Today reservations are home to many Indian-owned businesses, including oil and natural gas companies. Tourism is booming on Indian lands, and Native American arts and crafts have increased in value.

Assessing progress During the era of Red Power activism, Native Americans made important legislative gains. Congress passed a number of laws in the 1970s to enhance education, health care, voting rights, and religious freedom for Native Americans.

The Red Power movement also instilled greater pride in Native Americans and generated wider appreciation of Native American culture. N. Scott Momaday, a Kiowa author, won the prestigious Pulitzer Prize for Fiction in 1969. Fritz Scholder led the New American Indian Art movement, which depicted Native American life in a fresh way, free of clichés.

Despite their accomplishments, Native Americans continued to face many problems. Unemployment rates remained high in the 1970s, averaging 40 percent and reaching as high as 90 percent on some reservations. The high school dropout rate among Native Americans was the highest in the nation.

MAJOR NATIVE AMERICAN LEGISLATION

Alaska Native Claims Settlement Act, 1971
This act turned over 44 million acres of land to Alaska Natives and provided $962.5 million to settle other land claims by Alaska Natives.

Indian Self-Determination and Education Assistance Act, 1975
This act allowed tribes to implement their own education, health, and housing programs with government funding.

Indian Child Welfare Act, 1978
This act set standards for adoptions of Native American children, giving preference to relatives, members of the tribe, and Native American foster parents over white families.

READING CHECK **Identifying Cause and Effect** What were the results of the Indian occupation of Alcatraz Island?

SECTION 1 ASSESSMENT

HSS 11.10.5, 11.10.7, 11.11.3

Reviewing Ideas, Terms, and People

1. **a. Identify** What was *The Feminine Mystique*?
   b. Explain How did *The Feminine Mystique* inspire the women's movement?
   c. Elaborate What expectations were placed on women at home and in the workplace during the 1950s?

2. **a. Define** What is feminism?
   b. Draw Conclusions Why was *Roe v. Wade* controversial?
   c. Evaluate Given the failure of the Equal Rights Amendment to be ratified, was the women's movement of the 1960s and 1970s a success or a failure? Explain.

3. **a. Recall** What was the Declaration of Indian Purpose?
   b. Make Inferences How do you think Native Americans felt about the federal government's termination policy?

4. **a. Describe** What was the American Indian Movement?
   b. Analyze How did the occupation of Alcatraz affect AIM?

   c. Evaluate How successful was the Native American fight for fairness? Explain.

Critical Thinking

5. **Organizing Information** Copy the chart below and record key characteristics of the women's movement and the Red Power movement in the 1960s and 1970s.

Movement	Goals	Leaders	Key Issues

FOCUS ON WRITING ELA W1.1

6. **Persuasive** Suppose it is 1960. Write a letter to the editor opposing the U.S. government's policy of termination and suggesting reforms.

SECTION 2: Latinos Fight for Rights

BEFORE YOU READ

MAIN IDEA
In the 1960s Latinos struggled to achieve social justice.

READING FOCUS
1. What were the lives of Latinos like in the early 1960s?
2. What event launched Latinos' struggle for social justice?
3. What were the main goals of the movements for Latino rights?

KEY TERMS AND PEOPLE
social justice
César Chávez
Chicano
Rodolfo "Corky" Gonzales
José Angel Gutiérrez
La Raza Unida Party
boricua

 HSS 11.10.5 Discuss the diffusion of the civil rights movement of African Americans, and how the advances influenced the agendas, strategies, and effectiveness of the quests of American Indians, Asian Americans, and Hispanic Americans for civil rights and equal opportunities.

▲ César Chávez (right) leads striking farmworkers.

THE INSIDE STORY

How did farmworkers improve their lives? In 1965, Filipino workers began a strike against grape growers around Delano, California, in the state's agricultural San Joaquin Valley. Demanding a 15-cent increase in their hourly wages, they asked Mexican American farmworkers to join them. Dolores Huerta and César Chávez, co-founders of the National Farm Workers Association, a union of Mexican American farmworkers, agreed to help. Some 5,000 grape workers walked off their jobs.

The now-famous Delano Grape Strike lasted five years. It was bitter and hard-fought. Strikers picketed the fields to convince the nonstriking workers to join them. Growers sprayed the picketers with farm chemicals and drove tractors through the fields to choke them with dust.

To build support for the strike, Chávez led a 250-mile march to the state capital at Sacramento. As the march passed through towns along the way, many farmworkers joined it. By the time it reached Sacramento, the number of marchers had grown from just a few hundred to more than 5,000.

When picketing and marches did not win the strike, Huerta sent union activists around the nation to set up local boycott committees. Committee members stood outside supermarkets to tell customers about conditions for workers in the fields. They urged shoppers to support the strike by not buying California grapes.

The Great Grape Boycott proved successful. By 1969 it had even spread to Great Britain. As people in other European nations considered joining the boycott, the growers gave in and finally settled with the union. The Delano Grape Strike was the first major victory in a long, difficult struggle to improve the lives and working conditions of migrant farmworkers.

The Lives of Latinos

In 1960 more than 900,000 Latinos lived in the United States. A Latino is any person of Latin American descent. Latinos may also be called Hispanics, but *Hispanic* has a slightly different meaning. It encompasses all people of Spanish-speaking ancestry, including those whose families came from Spain.

The U.S. Latino population increased sharply during the 1960s. This was partly because the Immigration Act of 1965 gave preference to immigrants with relatives already in the country. Eligible Latinos, especially Mexicans, streamed in.

Latinos, however, often struggled in the United States. In 1960 one-third of Mexican American families lived below the poverty line. Twice as many Mexican Americans as white Americans were unemployed. About 80 percent of Mexican Americans worked in low-paying, unskilled jobs, such as farm labor, household service, construction, or factory work.

Latinos faced discrimination in education too. Their children often attended schools with less qualified teachers, fewer resources, and shabbier facilities than other American schools. Few of their teachers were Hispanic or able to speak Spanish. In this discouraging environment, about 75 percent of Latino students dropped out before finishing high school.

In politics Latinos had far less power than the size of their population would warrant. State legislatures drew the boundaries of election districts in ways that kept Latino voices scattered. The number of Latinos in political office was very small. In addition, Latinos were often excluded from serving on juries.

READING CHECK **Comparing and Contrasting** How did Latinos' living standards compare to those of other Americans in the early 1960s?

Launching the Struggle for Social Justice

As other groups began campaigning for their rights, Latinos also sought **social justice**, or the fair distribution of advantages and disadvantages in society. One of the earliest efforts was made in the farm fields of California. Migrant

THE IMPACT TODAY

Government

In 2003 the U.S. Census Bureau announced that Latinos had become the nation's largest minority group. The political power that comes with such numbers is apparent as major political parties now make serious efforts to attract Latino voters.

Hispanic Americans: A Statistical Profile

According to the U.S. census taken in 2000, more than half of all immigrants to the United States that year came from Latin America. Specifically, one fourth of all immigrants that year came from Mexico.

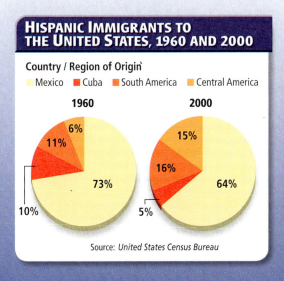

Source: United States Census Bureau

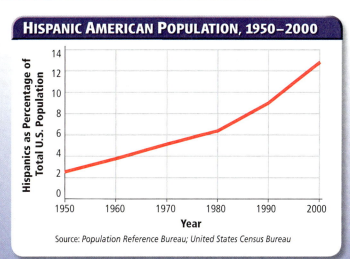

Source: Population Reference Bureau; United States Census Bureau

SKILLS FOCUS: INTERPRETING GRAPHS

1. How has the place of origin of Hispanic immigrants changed since 1960?
2. How has the rate of Hispanic immigration changed over time?

See **Skills Handbook**, pp. H16, H17

A TIME OF SOCIAL CHANGE **643**

FACES OF HISTORY
César CHÁVEZ
1927–1993

César Chávez spent his early years on his family's small farm in Arizona. When the farm failed during the Great Depression, his family moved to California and lived in migrant labor camps. Chávez left school in the eighth grade to work in the fields. After serving in the navy, he returned to California and to the life of a migrant worker.

In 1952 Chávez began a career as an activist, joining the Community Service Organization and registering Mexican Americans to vote. In 1962 he co-founded the National Farm Workers Association to help migrant farmworkers unionize. In the photo at right, Chávez (center) is talking with grape pickers. After his success in the grape strike, Chávez turned to organizing workers in California's lettuce fields and migrant fruit pickers in Florida's citrus groves.

Make Inferences Why was Chávez so successful in his efforts to organize migrant farmworkers?

---

agricultural workers, many of whom were Latinos, received low wages for backbreaking labor. In 1965 farmworkers went on strike in Delano, California. The National Farm Workers Association soon joined the strike, under the leadership of **César Chávez** and Dolores Huerta.

Chávez and Huerta knew that the strike needed publicity. Simply stopping work in the fields would not draw enough attention to their cause. So, as you read at the beginning of this section, union activists and sympathetic volunteers stood in front of grocery stores nationwide, urging Americans not to buy grapes.

HISTORY'S VOICES

"Grapes must remain an unenjoyed luxury for all as long as the barest human needs and basic human rights are still luxuries for farm workers. The grapes grow sweet and heavy on the vines, but they will have to wait while we reach out first for our freedom. The time is ripe for our liberation."
—Dolores Huerta, "Proclamation of the Delano Grape Workers for International Boycott Day," 1969

The success of the strike made César Chávez a national figure, respected for his tireless support of migrant workers and his commitment to nonviolent protest. Chávez's leadership inspired many Mexican Americans to fight discrimination in their lives. The union's symbol, a black Aztec eagle, came to represent the Mexican American civil rights movement that developed during the late 1960s.

READING CHECK **Identifying Main Idea and Details** How did farmworkers enlist the help of consumers to achieve better working conditions?

Movements for Latino Rights

César Chávez proved the effectiveness of mass action. While he fought for farmworkers, other Latino activists pursued different agendas.

Defining the Chicano movement In the late 1960s some Mexican Americans began to embrace a form of cultural nationalism similar to the Black Power movement supported by black nationalists. They called themselves **Chicanos**, a shortened form of *mexicanos*. The name conveyed their ethnic pride and commitment to political activism.

In earlier generations the term *Chicano* had carried a negative connotation. Now Chicanos adopted the name proudly. They used the term

Mexican American to describe someone who had assimilated—someone who held American views rather than Mexican ones.

Alianza One early Chicano leader was Reies López Tijerina. He formed the Alianza Federal de Mercedes (Federal Alliance of Land Grants) to focus on the enduring issue of land rights.

After winning the Mexican-American War in 1848, the United States had signed the Treaty of Guadalupe Hidalgo, promising to respect Mexicans' land claims in territories it annexed. Despite this promise, Mexican Americans had lost tens of thousands of acres over the years—often through fraud or deception. In Rio Arriba County, New Mexico, for example, some 60 percent of the land once belonging to Mexican Americans had been taken away—much of it by the federal government.

In 1967 Tijerina and his followers charged into the Rio Arriba County courthouse to demand justice. A gun battle broke out, and two police officers were wounded. The incident focused national attention on the unfair seizure of Mexican American lands. However, Tijerina was later arrested because of his activities, and Alianza eventually broke up.

The Crusade for Justice Another leading figure in the Chicano movement was **Rodolfo "Corky" Gonzales**. A former boxer, Gonzales became active in Democratic Party politics and antipoverty programs in Denver, Colorado, during the late 1950s and early 1960s. Over time, though, he grew to believe that mainstream politics did little to help Mexican Americans.

In 1966 Gonzales founded the Crusade for Justice, a group that promoted Mexican American nationalism. Operating out of an old church, the group provided legal aid, a theater for enhancing cultural awareness, a Spanish-language newspaper, and other community services. It also ran a school that offered children free bilingual classes and lessons in Chicano culture.

Gonzales credited the Crusade for Justice with igniting the "nationalism that now exists here in the Southwest. It has been a dream of the past, but we're now creating a reality out of it." He popularized the use of the nationalist term *Chicano*. Gonzales also composed a poem, "I Am Joaquín," which served as an anthem for the Chicano movement.

HISTORY'S VOICES

" I have endured in the rugged mountains / Of our country / I have survived the toils and slavery of the fields. / I have existed / In the barrios [Latino neighborhoods] of the city / In the suburbs of bigotry / In the mines of social snobbery / In the prisons of dejection / In the muck of exploitation / And / In the fierce heat of racial hatred. / And now the trumpet sounds, / The music of the people stirs the / Revolution. / Like a sleeping giant it slowly / Rears its head / To the sound of / Tramping feet / Clamoring voices / Mariachi strains . . . / And in all the fertile farmlands, / the barren plains, / the mountain villages, / smoke-smeared cities, / we start to MOVE. / La raza! [The people!] / Méjicano! [Mexican!] / Español! [Spanish!] / Latino! / Chicano! / Or whatever I call myself, / I look the same / I feel the same / I cry / And / Sing the same. / I am the masses of my people and / I refuse to be absorbed. "

—Rodolfo Gonzales, "I Am Joaquín"

In March 1969 Gonzales and the Crusade for Justice sponsored the National Chicano Liberation Youth Conference. Conference delegates produced *El Plan Espiritual de Aztlán*, or the Spiritual Plan of Aztlán. The plan called upon Chicanos to reclaim the lands of the Southwest. The ultimate goal was to build a unified Chicano community that was empowered to determine its own future.

MAYO Mexican Americans in Texas also turned to protest during the 1960s. In 1967 a group of college students in San Antonio formed the Mexican American Youth Organization (MAYO). The founders of MAYO, including **José Angel Gutiérrez**, wanted to achieve economic independence for Mexican Americans, to gain local control over the education of Hispanic children, and to achieve power for Latinos through the creation of a third political party.

Under Gutiérrez's leadership, MAYO organized school walkouts and mass demonstrations to protest discrimination against Mexican Americans. MAYO's aggressive tactics were a departure from the moderate approach of more established <u>contemporary</u> Latino organizations, such as the League of United Latin American Citizens.

"Most of our traditional organizations will sit there and pass resolutions and mouth off at conventions, but they'll never take on the gringo [white American]," Gutiérrez charged.

THE IMPACT TODAY

Culture
Spanish-language newspapers have become big business in the United States. In 2002 there were 35 dailies with a combined circulation of more than 1.7 million.

ACADEMIC VOCABULARY
contemporary existing during the same period of time

A TIME OF SOCIAL CHANGE **645**

"They'll never stand up to him and say, 'Hey man, things have got to change . . . We've had it long enough!'"

Not all Latinos approved of MAYO's tactics. Henry B. Gonzalez, a member of Congress from San Antonio, was a vocal critic. "MAYO styles itself . . . [as all] good and the Anglo-American as . . . [all] evil. That is not merely ridiculous, it is drawing fire from the deepest wellsprings of hate," Gonzalez declared. "One cannot fan the flames of bigotry one moment and expect them to disappear the next."

MAYO did force changes, though, especially in education. In 1969 Gutiérrez helped organize a student protest in Crystal City, Texas, where about 80 percent of the population was Mexican American. Many local high school students fumed about discrimination. They wanted more Mexican American teachers and a bilingual education program. They also wanted their cheerleaders and homecoming queen to be elected by the students, not appointed by teachers.

The protest began when teachers appointed two Anglo students as cheerleaders. Chicano students' complaints to school officials had no effect. Gutiérrez helped the students organize a boycott of the school. The U.S. Justice Department intervened to resolve the crisis. The settlement required the school board to meet most of the students' demands, including bilingual and bicultural education.

The success at Crystal City inspired students in other Texas schools. MAYO supported numerous student walkouts to protest the crumbling conditions of schools, the lack of Latino teachers, and rules against speaking Spanish. After many of these boycotts, students gained the reforms they were seeking.

La Raza Unida After his success in Crystal City, Gutiérrez formed **La Raza Unida Party** (RUP). (The name means "the united people.") The party campaigned for bilingual education, improved public services, education for children of migrant workers, and an end to job discrimination. In 1970, RUP candidates were elected to offices in several Texas cities with large Chicano populations.

HISTORY CLOSE-UP

The Chicano Movement

During the 1960s and 1970s Mexican Americans forged political power by embracing their cultural identity.

Dolores Huerta

Dolores Huerta took an interest in social activism from a young age. In her early 20s she was active in a Mexican American self-help group called the Community Service Organization. It was there that she first met César Chávez. Together they founded the National Farm Workers Association. In the late 1960s she met feminist leader Gloria Steinem, whose influence led Huerta to incorporate feminist ideals into the Chicano movement.

La Raza Unida

José Angel Gutiérrez (above) founded La Raza Unida to spur political change in Crystal City, Texas. The party moved to the state level in 1972, backing Ramsey Muñiz for governor and supporting many Chicana candidates for other offices. Although Muñiz did not win his race, La Raza Unida successfully changed the landscape of Texas politics.

Rodolfo Gonzales also organized a Colorado branch of the RUP. The Colorado party did not have many election victories, but it drew attention to Chicano causes. The RUP expanded into other parts of the Southwest as well. In Arizona, New Mexico, and California, it registered some 10,000 new voters and ran candidates for several state offices.

In the late 1970s, disagreements among RUP leaders caused the party to fall apart. However, for the better part of a decade it symbolized growing Chicano power.

The Brown Berets In the late 1960s the Brown Berets emerged as one of the most militant organizations in the Chicano movement. Founded by working-class Chicano students in Los Angeles in 1967, the Brown Berets began their activism by protesting against police brutality in East Los Angeles.

Soon the group also began fighting for bilingual education, better school conditions, Chicano studies, and more Chicano teachers. In school walkouts in California, the Brown Berets protected striking students by standing between them and the police. "When the cops moved in," one observer noted, "it was the Berets that were dragged behind bars."

The Brown Berets also supported the efforts of Chicanos in New Mexico to recover their historic lands. They lent their support to the United Farm Workers' campaigns, and they protested the high death rate of Chicano soldiers in the Vietnam War. They worked with African American civil rights groups as well, such as the Black Panther Party and the Southern Christian Leadership Conference.

The Brown Berets received much media attention because of their strong rhetoric and action-oriented protests. They also gained the notice of law enforcement officials, who tracked their activities and infiltrated the group. The publicity strengthened the Chicano movement in California and helped it spread farther. By 1970 there were 60 Brown Beret groups across the Southwest.

In the Brown Berets, as in many Chicano organizations, men held positions of leadership and women often struggled to have their voices heard. Women participated in marches and

Corky Gonzales
Rodolfo "Corky" Gonzales, boxer turned activist, knew firsthand the plight of many poor Mexican Americans. Born to migrant farmworkers, Gonzales urged Mexican Americans to embrace their cultural heritage. He saw Chicano nationalism as a way for his people to gain economic independence and political power.

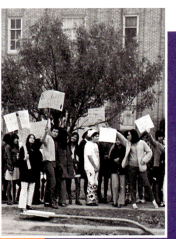

Student Activism
In 1969 some 700 Mexican American high school students in Crystal City, Texas, boycotted class. The strike began as a protest of the mainly Anglo cheerleading squad, but it grew to include broader educational issues. The students' action forced the school to abandon its discriminatory policies.

Skills FOCUS **INTERPRETING INFOGRAPHICS**

Chicanos were among the many groups of Americans fighting for their rights in the 1960s and 1970s.

Drawing Conclusions Why do you think Chicanos wanted their own political party?

See **Skills Handbook**, p. H18

A TIME OF SOCIAL CHANGE **647**

Primary Sources

Mural

Some Chicano artists expressed their cultural pride by creating murals. This art form has a long history in Mexico, dating to Aztec times. Today hundreds of public buildings throughout the West contain murals celebrating Chicanos' heritage. This scene from a California mural shows the economic transformation of Mexican Americans.

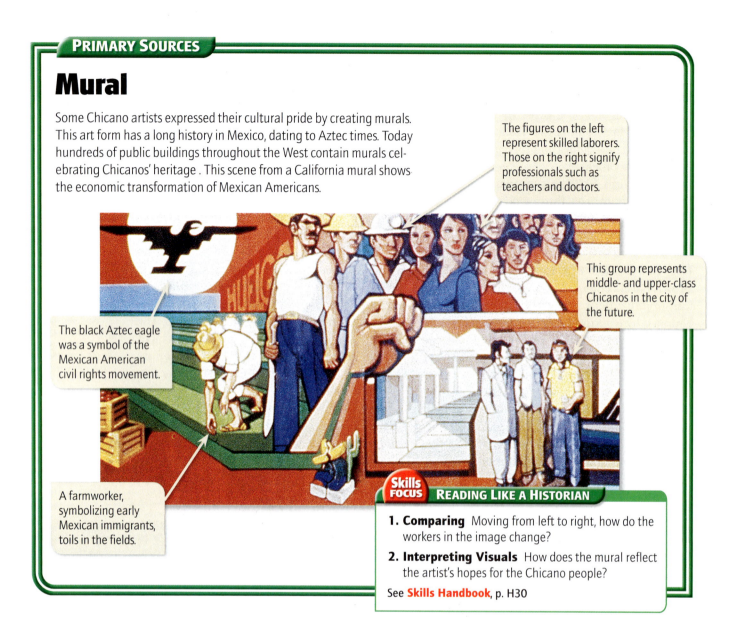

The figures on the left represent skilled laborers. Those on the right signify professionals such as teachers and doctors.

This group represents middle- and upper-class Chicanos in the city of the future.

The black Aztec eagle was a symbol of the Mexican American civil rights movement.

A farmworker, symbolizing early Mexican immigrants, toils in the fields.

Skills Focus: Reading Like a Historian

1. **Comparing** Moving from left to right, how do the workers in the image change?
2. **Interpreting Visuals** How does the mural reflect the artist's hopes for the Chicano people?

See **Skills Handbook**, p. H30

---

demonstrations, but those actions were always led by men. As one female member noted, "They [the men] wanted to make all the decisions and we always got the [unpleasant] jobs."

The Brown Berets disbanded in 1972 after a series of demonstrations turned violent. Public opinion within the Mexican American community began to turn against their activities. Although the Brown Berets were not successful in ending police brutality in East Los Angeles, the group succeeded in raising awareness of the struggles Chicanos often faced.

The boricua movement Boricua is the name by which many Puerto Ricans refer to themselves. Like the term *Chicano*, it expresses ethnic pride and support for political activism.

The island of Puerto Rico has been governed as a U.S. territory since the United States acquired the island from Spain after the Spanish-American War in 1898. Slow economic growth and lack of opportunity in Puerto Rico in the early 1900s prompted some Puerto Ricans to migrate to the mainland United States.

The pace of migration increased after World War II, as many Puerto Ricans hoped to share in the economic boom the United States experienced after the war. Some U.S. companies even recruited workers from Puerto Rico, viewing the island as a source of cheap labor. New York, Chicago, and several other U.S. cities developed large Puerto Rican communities. In New York, for example, Puerto Ricans made up more than 9 percent of the city's population by 1964.

Like other minority groups, Puerto Ricans in the United States experienced social and economic discrimination. Holding low-paying jobs, many had to live in run-down neighborhoods and send their children to overcrowded, substandard schools. In the 1950s and 1960s, they organized to seek change.

The boricua movement sprang from the calls of some Puerto Ricans, both in Puerto Rico and on the mainland, for the island's independence. When this demand failed to gain much support, even within the Puerto Rican community, the movement's goals gradually shifted to self-government for Puerto Rico and better conditions for all Puerto Ricans.

Among those pushing for social justice for Puerto Ricans were the Young Lords, a militant boricua organization inspired by the Black Panthers. In 1969 the New York City chapter of the Young Lords barricaded streets until the city promised more frequent trash pickups in Puerto Rican neighborhoods. The Young Lords also called for local control of Puerto Rican communities, as well as better health care, employment, and educational opportunities.

Other boricua groups shared some of the Young Lords' goals but not their methods. One group called Taller Boricua (meaning "Puerto Rican Workshop") was founded in 1970 as a community arts organization in New York. It provided art education programs as a means of encouraging cultural, social, and economic development in the Puerto Rican community. Similar groups now exist in many other American cities.

Cuban Americans After Fidel Castro seized power in Cuba in 1959, many well-to-do Cubans fled Castro's Communist government for the United States. After 78,000 Cubans left in 1962, Castro banned further emigration. The exodus continued nonetheless. About 50,000 people left on flights allowed by the Cuban government between 1965 and 1973. However, most refugees made dangerous, illegal voyages to the United States in small boats.

The majority of Cubans who arrived during this period were professionals and business people. Unlike most other Latinos, they had left their homeland for political reasons, not economic ones. Therefore, they did not generally suffer the economic disadvantages that prompted other Latino groups to demand social justice. Instead, most Cuban Americans who organized for change were seeking changes for Cuba—the overthrow of Castro and communism—and not for themselves.

READING CHECK   Making Generalizations What issues were most important to the movements for Latino rights?

SECTION 2 ASSESSMENT

HSS 11.10.5

Reviewing Ideas, Terms, and People

1. **a. Recall** What is the difference between the terms *Hispanic* and *Latino*?
   b. Summarize What economic, educational, and political challenges did many Latinos face in the early 1960s?
   c. Elaborate Do you think that speaking Spanish was an asset or a drawback for Latinos in the 1960s? Explain.

2. **a. Identify** Who were **César Chávez** and Dolores Huerta?
   b. Explain How did farmworkers pressure grape growers to address their demands?
   c. Predict Do you think the grape boycott would have turned out differently if strikers had used violent tactics? Explain.

3. **a. Describe** What do the terms *Chicano* and *boricua* have in common?
   b. Sequence What experiences led **José Angel Gutiérrez** to form a new political party?
   c. Rank With which issue do you think the Latino rights movements had the most success? Explain.

Critical Thinking

4. **Comparing and Contrasting** Copy the chart below and record the similarities and differences between MAYO and La Raza Unida Party.

  ELA W2.2

5. **Expository** Reread the excerpt from **Rodolfo Gonzales**'s poem, "I Am Joaquín." In your own words, analyze the excerpt. What past hardships does Gonzales describe? How have the conditions of his people changed, and why? What emotions are conveyed in his poem? Why would this poem be considered an anthem of the Chicano movement?

SECTION 3
Culture and Counterculture

BEFORE YOU READ

MAIN IDEA
The counterculture that emerged in the 1960s and 1970s left a lasting impact on American life.

READING FOCUS
1. What led to the rise of the counterculture?
2. What was life like in the counterculture?
3. How did mainstream American society react to the counterculture?
4. What legacy did the counterculture leave behind?

KEY TERMS AND PEOPLE
counterculture
Establishment
Free Speech Movement
flower children
Summer of Love
pop art

HSS 11.8.8 Discuss forms of popular culture, with emphasis on their origins and geographic diffusion (e.g., jazz and other forms of popular music, professional sports, architectural and artistic styles).

THE INSIDE STORY

How would hosting a huge public event affect a small town? The word was out. Some rich music promoters needed a place to hold a rock concert. In tiny Bethel, New York, resort owner Ed Tiber had a permit from town officials for a small music and arts festival to attract business to his resort hotel. He put the concert's organizers in touch with Max Yasgur, a nearby dairy farmer. They paid Yasgur $75,000 to hold their concert in one of his fields.

As workers prepared the site, Bethel's 3,900 residents became concerned that the expected 100,000 concertgoers might overwhelm their town. Signs went up: "Buy No Milk. Stop Max's Hippie Music Festival." There was no turning back, though. Too many tickets to the concert had already been sold—nearly 190,000!

Despite opposition, the Woodstock Music and Art Fair began on schedule, on August 15, 1969. By then it had snowballed into a four-day event attended by more than 400,000 people. Woodstock astounded Bethel and became a defining experience for a whole generation.

Rock Concert in a Small Town

▼ The band Jefferson Airplane rocks for a crowd that stretches as far as the eye can see.

Student protest leader Mario Savio makes a peace sign with his hand at a rally at the University of California, Berkeley. Students at Berkeley fought the school administration for free-speech rights and inspired campus protests nationwide.

Rise of the Counterculture

The **counterculture** of the 1960s was a rebellion of teens and young adults against mainstream American society. These young Americans, called hippies, believed that society's values were hollow and its priorities were misplaced. Turning their backs on the mainstream—which they called the **Establishment**—hippies wanted to create an alternative culture based on peace and love.

The youth culture Where did the counterculture come from? First of all, the number of teens and young adults in the United States rose dramatically in the 1960s. Between 1960 and 1970 the number of Americans aged 15 through 24 increased almost 50 percent.

Second, these young people were living in turbulent times. They blamed their parents' generation for the problems the nation faced—the threat of nuclear war, racial discrimination and segregation, the Vietnam War, and environmental pollution. They vowed to do things differently.

Rebellion against the dominant culture was not something new. The Beat generation of the 1950s also broke with mainstream America. Beatniks questioned traditional values, challenged authority, and experimented with nonconformist lifestyles. Although beatniks were few in number, the Beat generation would influence the hippie culture that arose later.

Rising student activism On college campuses in the 1960s, students enjoyed newfound independence. They began rebelling against school policies they considered restrictive, unjust, or not relevant. At the University of California at Berkeley, students had often used one of the entrances to the campus as a place for speech making and political organizing. In September 1964, university officials banned that activity at the campus entrance. Students protested loudly. They picketed and held sit-ins, nonviolent demonstrations in which they sat down and refused to move.

On October 1, 1964, a former student named Jack Weinberg set up a table in the banned area to collect donations for CORE, a civil rights group. Police arrived to arrest him for trespassing. Hundreds of students surrounded the police car so that it could not move. Student Mario Savio climbed on top of the car and urged more students to join the protest.

For 32 hours the students surrounded the car and prevented the police from taking Weinberg away. Other students protested at the main administration building. However, university officials refused to drop the charges against Weinberg. California governor Edmund Brown issued a statement: "This will not be tolerated. We must have—and will continue to have—law and order on our campuses." Some 500 police officers were called out as the crowd swelled to more than 7,000 demonstrators.

ACADEMIC VOCABULARY
relevant having practical application or value for society

A TIME OF SOCIAL CHANGE **651**

Counterculture Life

Hippie clothing and hairstyles tended to be loose and flowing, but the main characteristics were individuality and low cost. Flowers worn in the hair were also a mainstay of hippie expression.

Members of the Family of the Mystic Arts (above) lived in this Oregon commune for over a year. Communes had high ideals but were often short-lived.

The protest came to a nonviolent end when university officials agreed to consider students' grievances. A few weeks later, though, the university decided to discipline Savio and another organizer of the protest, Arthur Goldberg. In response, about a thousand students took over the campus administration building in a massive sit-in. On December 3, more than 600 police arrested nearly 800 students.

For the next few days, a student strike shut down the campus. As pressure mounted—from the faculty as well as the student body—administrators finally agreed to ease restrictions on students' political activities.

The events in Berkeley marked the beginning of the **Free Speech Movement**, which swept campuses across the nation. Arthur Goldberg summed up the goal this way: "We ask only the right to say what we feel when we feel like it. We'll continue to fight for this freedom, and we won't quit until we've won." Students used the tactics of civil disobedience to protest a variety of injustices. In the process, they shocked mainstream Americans, who expected young people not to question authority.

READING CHECK **Summarizing** What major influences led to the rise of the counterculture?

Life in the Counterculture

Throughout the 1960s, thousands of teens and young adults abandoned school, jobs, and traditional home life in search of a more freewheeling existence. Like the beatniks of the 1950s, hippies rejected the materialism and work ethic of older generations. Instead, they wanted to live simply and "do your own thing."

Some hippies formed communities in run-down urban neighborhoods, such as San Francisco's Haight-Ashbury district. Haight-Ashbury became the most famous center of the counterculture. Young people flocked there because of the cheap rents and flourishing hippie culture. Urban hippie communities in general attracted many newcomers because of the promise of a new lifestyle. Writer Carol Brightman spoke about the freedom of moving to Berkeley in 1970.

HISTORY'S VOICES

"Coming to California and settling in the Bay Area, [I] was . . . looking for a cultural experience outside the mainstream . . . Berkeley was like a liberated zone, you know . . . You were on the edge there."

—Carol Brightman, interview with David Gans, 1999

This detail from a poster by the artist Peter Max (left) is an example of pyschedelic art, or art that mimics a drug-induced state. Below is the psychedelic album cover to the Broadway musical *Hair*, which celebrated the counterculture and shocked the Establishment.

Other hippies "dropped out" of society by joining rural communes—collectively run communities—where they attempted to live in harmony with nature. Residents of communes often avoided modern conveniences. They grew their own food and shared all property. Their intention was to build communities based on peace and love.

Hippie culture Hippies sought new experiences in a variety of ways. Some looked for enlightenment through Eastern religions, such as Buddhism. Others searched for answers through astrology or the occult. Many others experimented with illegal drugs, such as marijuana and LSD, or "acid." Timothy Leary, a former Harvard University psychology instructor, promoted the use of LSD as a way to open and expand the mind. Leary urged others to "tune in, turn on, and drop out."

Hippies expressed their sense of freedom through a casual and colorful style of clothing. Bright, tie-dyed T-shirts were popular. Many African Americans adopted the dashiki, a pullover-style African shirt usually decorated with vivid colors. Some men wore beads as a rejection of the traditional necktie. Men also began wearing longer hair and beards. Some African Americans sported Afros, a hairstyle that came to symbolize racial pride. Other hippies wore flowers in their hair and called themselves **flower children**.

The counterculture's decline The height of the hippie movement was the summer of 1967. In San Francisco, this was known as the **Summer of Love**. A generation proclaimed the dawning of a blissful new age. Although the country was at war in Vietnam and wracked by racism and sexism, hippies professed peace, love, and harmony.

These ideals were difficult to achieve, however. The freedom that hippies sought often led to serious problems. Many young people struggled with drug addiction—or worse. Singer Janis Joplin and guitarist Jimi Hendrix died from overdoses of drugs, as did other less-famous members of the counterculture.

Hippies expected to find mellow living by moving to communes and places such as Haight-Ashbury. However, many hippies had no means of supporting themselves. The lack of rules often led to conflict. The counterculture also attracted sinister characters such as Charles Manson, who moved to Haight-Ashbury in 1967. Two years later Manson and a handful of his followers committed a mass murder in California that horrified the nation.

READING CHECK Contrasting How did the counterculture lifestyle differ from that of traditional, middle-class Americans?

Mainstream Society Reacts

Some observers of the counterculture were put off by the unkempt appearance of hippies. George Harrison, a member of the legendary British music group the Beatles, recalled his surprise when he visited Haight-Ashbury in 1967. "I expected them to all be nice and clean and friendly and happy." Instead, he saw them as "hideous, spotty little teenagers" who "were all terribly dirty and scruffy."

On a deeper level, many mainstream Americans objected to the unconventional values of the counterculture. They viewed hippies' attitudes and actions as disrespectful, uncivilized, and threatening. Some believed that American society as a whole was losing its sense of right and wrong.

THE IMPACT TODAY

Daily Life
Blue jeans were considered work clothing until hippies began wearing them. Today people of all ages and economic backgrounds wear jeans regularly.

To many in the Establishment, it appeared that society was unraveling. Unrest on college campuses particularly troubled FBI director J. Edgar Hoover.

HISTORY'S VOICES

"It would be foolhardy for educators, public officials, and law enforcement officers to ignore or dismiss lightly the revolutionary terrorism invading college campuses. It is a serious threat to both the academic community and a lawful and orderly society."

—J. Edgar Hoover, in *The Review of the News*, September 11, 1968

A daring television comedy called *All in the Family* dramatized both the older generation's distrust of the counterculture and the younger generation's desire to change society. Premiering in 1971, the program featured a bigoted, working-class character named Archie Bunker. Archie bluntly criticized hippies, Vietnam War protesters, and anyone else who didn't fit his view of what Americans should be. Archie's son-in-law, Mike Stivic, was a college student fighting against the Establishment. The lack of understanding between Archie Bunker and Mike Stivic was symbolic of the divisions in American society at the time.

READING CHECK **Identifying the Main Idea** Why did many Americans find the counterculture to be so alarming?

The Counterculture's Legacy

The counterculture did not last long. However, it did make a lasting impact on American culture, particularly in attitudes, art, and music.

Attitudes The permissiveness of the counterculture affected the wider American society. Many Americans became more casual in the way they dressed and more open-minded about lifestyles and social behavior. Attitudes toward sexual behavior loosened. In movies, on television, and in books and magazines, people wanted to explore topics that had once been taboo, including sexual activity and violence.

PRIMARY SOURCES

Political Cartoon

The attitudes and lifestyles of the counterculture shocked many Americans. As this cartoon depicts, some Americans believed hippies were defiant youths with no respect for authority.

Many people felt that hippies were hypocrites for criticizing the older generation while relying on their parents' money to support them.

"Doubledome" was a slang term for an intellectual who supported silly ideas.

SKILLS FOCUS **READING LIKE A HISTORIAN**

Interpreting Political Cartoons Do you think the artist viewed hippies sympathetically or critically? Explain.

See **Skills Handbook**, p. H31

Art and film The counterculture's questioning of tradition and authority extended into the art world. Many artists of the 1960s argued that art had become a slave to elite tastes. They claimed that established artists created works only to please a few cultural critics.

In this period, a new style developed called **pop art.** Aiming to appeal to popular tastes, artists took inspiration from elements of the popular culture, including advertising, comic books, and movies. Andy Warhol led the pop art movement. He painted common, mass-produced objects such as Campbell Soup cans and Coke bottles. He also produced works featuring brightly colored likenesses of celebrities such as Marilyn Monroe and John F. Kennedy.

Film also underwent a broadening of subject matter as censorship rules relaxed. The film industry adopted a rating system ranging from G to X to inform audiences about the content of movies. The rating system was designed to gain favor with the viewing public, who wanted more information about what they would see on screen. Some people argued, however, that moral standards began to decline, because movies rated for mature audiences drew larger crowds than family-oriented films.

Music The counterculture had a tremendous influence on popular music. Rock and roll became an outlet for young people to express their discontent and their desire for change. The Beatles, for example, moved from love songs like "I Want to Hold Your Hand" to more topical songs such as "Revolution." The group also brought new ideas and techniques to rock and roll music. Their performances electrified audiences and influenced countless other musicians.

Bob Dylan was another key figure on the music scene. Hailed as the spokesperson of his generation, Dylan found audiences wildly responsive to political songs like "The Times They Are A Changin'" and "Masters of War."

One of the most significant events of the period was the Woodstock Music and Art Fair, commonly known as Woodstock. In August 1969, some 400,000 people attended the music festival in rural upstate New York. Massive traffic jams led officials to close the roads leading to the area. Those who made it to Woodstock had to deal with driving rain, knee-deep mud, and shortages of food and water.

Despite the enormous crowds, the festival was peaceful. Over four days, many of the most popular musicians and bands performed, including Jimi Hendrix, Janis Joplin, Joan Baez, and the Grateful Dead. Woodstock was more than just a rock concert. It was the celebration of an era, and it marked the high point of the counterculture movement.

READING CHECK **Drawing Conclusions** How did the values of the counterculture influence art and music?

SECTION 3 ASSESSMENT

HSS 11.8.8

Reviewing Ideas, Terms, and People

1. **a. Identify** What factors contributed to the rise of the **counterculture** in the 1960s?
   b. Make Inferences Why did university officials at Berkeley want to shut down the **Free Speech Movement**?
   c. Evaluate Did university officials handle the conflict with students appropriately? Explain.

2. **a. Recall** Who were the **flower children**?
   b. Analyze What were members of the counterculture trying to achieve?
   c. Evaluate Was the decline of the counterculture avoidable? Why or why not?

3. **a. Identify** Who was Archie Bunker?
   b. Interpret Why would J. Edgar Hoover describe student activism as "revolutionary terrorism"?

4. **a. Describe** What was Woodstock?
   b. Summarize What effects did the counterculture have on the broader society?

Critical Thinking

5. **Identifying Cause and Effect** Copy the chart below and record the causes and effects of the counterculture.

FOCUS ON SPEAKING ELA W1.1

6. **Persuasive** What would you have said if you were addressing the crowd at the Berkeley student protests in 1964?

CHAPTER 20 DOCUMENT-BASED INVESTIGATION

The Women's Movement

Historical Context The documents below provide different information on the women's movement during the late 1960s and early 1970s.

Task Examine the documents and answer the questions that follow. Then write an essay about the women's movement. Use facts from the documents and from the chapter to support the position you take in your thesis statement.

HSS 11.10.7, 11.11.3

DOCUMENT 1

In 1969 students protested at the University of Chicago after it refused to extend the appointment of Marlene Dixon, a professor known for her radical political views. The Chicago Women's Liberation Union issued this statement in support of the protests.

> "What does women's freedom mean? It means freedom of self-determination, self-enrichment, the freedom to live one's own life, set one's own goals, the freedom to rejoice in one's own accomplishments. It means the freedom to be one's own person in an integrated life of world, love, play, motherhood: the freedoms, rights, and privileges of first class citizenship, of equality in relationships of love and work: the right to choose to make decisions or not to: the right to full self-realization and to full participation in the life of the world. That is the freedom we seek in women's liberation.
>
> To achieve these rights we must struggle as all other oppressed groups must struggle: one only has the rights one fights for. We must come together, understand the common problems, despair, anger, the roots and processes of our oppression: and then together, win our rights to a creative and human life.
>
> At the U of C we see the *first large action, the first important struggle of women's liberation*. This university—all universities—discriminate against women, impede their full intellectual development, deny them places on the faculty, exploit talented women and mistreat women students."

DOCUMENT 2

Bill Mauldin created drawings that commented on current events for the *St. Louis Post-Dispatch* and the *Chicago Sun-Times*. In this cartoon, he comments on the challenges facing the women's movement.

"WELL, GIRLS, AT LEAST THE ONLY WAY WE CAN GO IS UP."

DOCUMENT 3

Over the past several decades, women's lives have changed in many ways. This table presents statistics that indicate women's progress in education, employment, athletics, and government service.

EDUCATION AND EARNINGS	1970	2002
Number of female college students (approximate)	3,000,000	9,300,000
Percentage of college students who were women	40.5 percent	56.4 percent
Percentage of undergraduate and graduate degrees received by women	40.8 percent	57.8 percent
Percentage of doctoral degrees received by women	13.3 percent	45.5 percent
Women's earnings compared to every dollar earned by men	59.4 cents	76.6 cents
ATHLETICS	**1970**	**2002**
Number of female participants in high school athletics	294,000	2,856,350
Percentage of participants in high school athletics who were women	7.4 percent	41.7 percent
CORPORATE LEADERSHIP AND GOVERNMENT SERVICE	**1970**	**2002**
Number of female chief executive officers of Fortune 500 companies	0	6
Percentage of female federal civilian employees	30.3 percent	45 percent
Number of women elected to U.S. House of Representatives	10	59
Number of women elected to U.S. Senate	1	13

Sources: Statistical Abstract of the United States, 1976, 2004–2005; National Federation of State High School Associations Participation Figure History; National Committee on Pay Equity; femmx, Volume 10, issue 1, May 2002

Skills Focus: Reading Like a Historian

HSS Analysis HR4, HI1

1. **a. Recall** Refer to Document 1. Why are the protests important, according to the Chicago Women's Liberation Union?
   b. Interpret How does this statement encourage cooperation with other groups?
2. **a. Describe** Refer to Document 2. How does Mauldin portray equal rights for women?
   b. Analyze Based on this cartoon, what is Mauldin's attitude toward the women's movement?
3. **a. Identify** Refer to Document 3. Which category shows the least change over time?
   b. Make Inferences How might changes in educational achievement and changes in government employment be related?
4. **Document-Based Essay Question** Consider the question below and form a thesis statement. Using examples from Documents 1, 2, and 3, create an outline and write a short essay supporting your position.
   How did the women's movement contribute to change in the United States?

See **Skills Handbook**, pp. H15, H28–H29, H31

CHAPTER 20 Chapter Review

Visual Summary: A Time of Social Change

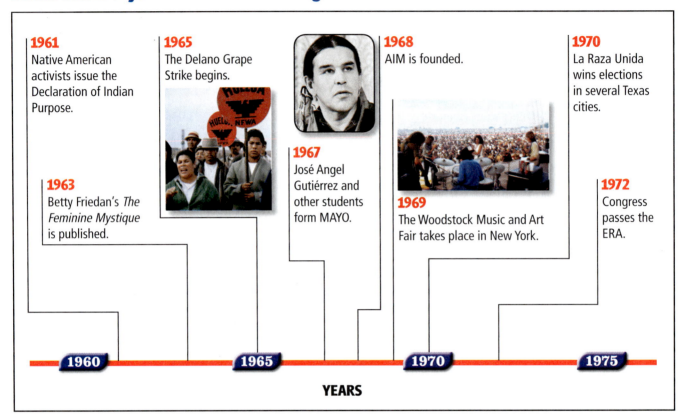

Reviewing Key Terms and People

Match each lettered definition with the correct numbered item at right.

a. Rebellion of teens and young adults against mainstream American society
b. Another popular name for hippies
c. Name by which many Puerto Ricans refer to themselves
d. A leader of the American Indian Movement
e. Conservative leader who opposed the ERA
f. Founder of MAYO who campaigned against anti-Latino discrimination in Texas schools
g. Chicano founder of the Crusade for Justice and author of the poem "I Am Joaquín"
h. Organization founded by José Angel Gutiérrez to strengthen Latinos' political power
i. Chicano labor leader who championed the rights of migrant farmworkers

1. boricua
2. counterculture
3. José Angel Gutiérrez
4. Phyllis Schlafly
5. flower children
6. Rodolfo "Corky" Gonzales
7. Russell Means
8. César Chávez
9. La Raza Unida Party

658 CHAPTER 20

History's Impact video program
Review the video to answer the closing question: How has the right of assembly allowed Americans to have a voice in social and political change?

Comprehension and Critical Thinking

SECTION 1 *(pp. 634–641)* HSS 11.10.7

10. **a. Recall** What was the ERA?
    b. Summarize What gains did Native Americans make in the 1970s?
    c. Elaborate Not all women supported NOW, nor did all Native Americans support AIM. Why was this the case?

SECTION 2 *(pp. 642–649)* HSS 11.10.5

11. **a. Identify** Who were the Brown Berets?
    b. Compare and Contrast What did Chicano and Puerto Rican activists have in common, and how did they differ from Cuban Americans?
    c. Develop Why do you think that the issue of fairness in education was so important to the Latino movements for equal rights?

SECTION 3 *(pp. 650–655)* HSS 11.8.8

12. **a. Describe** What were the goals of the counterculture?
    b. Analyze Why did some people find the counterculture threatening?
    c. Evaluate Did the counterculture have more positive or negative effects on American culture and society? Explain.

Using the Internet

go.hrw.com
Practice Online
Keyword: SE7 CH20

13. President Bill Clinton awarded César Chávez the Presidential Medal of Honor in 1994. Using the keyword above, do research to learn about Chávez's activism after the Delano Grape Strike. Then write a short biography of Chávez, highlighting the important achievements of his leadership after the strike.

Analyzing Primary Sources HSS HR4

Reading Like a Historian The epic poem "I Am Joaquín" called on Chicano youths to find strength and pride in their culture and history. Reread the excerpt in Section 2.

14. **Describe** How does the poet describe the lives of Mexican Americans in the past?
15. **Draw Conclusions** What made this poem inspirational to a generation of Chicanos?

Critical Reading ELA R3.8

Read the passages in Section 1 that discuss the occupation of Alcatraz and AIM. Then answer the questions that follow.

16. Why was the Indian occupation of Alcatraz Island significant?
    A Congress gave Native Americans the right to use any surplus government property.
    B It led to the founding of the American Indian Movement.
    C It drew attention to injustices against Native Americans and encouraged AIM activists.
    D The Bureau of Indian Affairs agreed to consider Native Americans' grievances.

17. Which of the following statements is true?
    A The goals of AIM were to protect Native Americans' traditional ways of life, foster economic independence, and improve educational opportunities.
    B The American Indian Movement was founded with the intention of helping Native Americans who lived on reservations.
    C AIM activists seized Wounded Knee in retaliation for the killing of 300 Sioux in 1890.
    D AIM's tactics were limited to nonviolent marches and demonstrations.

 ELA W1.1, 1.3

Think about the following issue:

Throughout the 1960s, thousands of teens and young adults rebelled against mainstream American society. They abandoned school, jobs, and traditional home life in search of a more freewheeling existence. They wanted to live simply and "do your own thing."

18. **Assignment** Was the counterculture a bold experiment in nontraditional living or a self-indulgent escape from reality? Write a short essay in which you develop your position on this issue. Support your point of view with reasoning and examples from your reading and studies.

A TIME OF SOCIAL CHANGE **659**

UNIT 5 IN BRIEF

Below is a chapter-by-chapter summary of the main ideas covered in Unit 5.

CHAPTER 17 — The New Frontier and the Great Society
1961–1969

MAIN IDEA Both Presidents Kennedy and Johnson pushed for major changes in American society while confronting the threat of communism overseas.

SECTION 1 President Kennedy fought communism by supporting West Berlin when the Communists erected the Berlin Wall. He turned back a Communist threat to the United States when he faced down the Soviet Union in the Cuban Missile Crisis.

SECTION 2 Kennedy was a youthful, popular president whose Thousand Days in office showed promise. His assassination in 1963 deeply shocked the nation and the world.

SECTION 3 President Johnson convinced Congress to pass several of Kennedy's programs after his death. Johnson built on these reforms with programs of his own in an effort to create a Great Society in America.

CHAPTER 18 — The Civil Rights Movement
1954–1975

MAIN IDEA The civil rights movement won key victories in gaining racial equality for African Americans.

SECTION 1 The civil rights movement's early successes included efforts to end segregation in education, including the landmark Brown decision, and the Montgomery bus boycott.

SECTION 2 Nonviolent protests often met with violent responses. The March on Washington in August 1963 called for a federal law to end segregation. The Civil Rights Act of 1964 banned discrimination in employment and public accommodations.

SECTION 3 The Twenty-fourth Amendment inspired increased efforts to gain voting rights for southern African Americans. Violent responses to a voter registration drive in Mississippi and a peaceful march in Selma, Alabama, gained national attention, helping to secure passage of the Voting Rights Act of 1965.

SECTION 4 Divisions developed in the movement in the late 1960s over such issues as tactics and de facto segregation. The assassination of Martin Luther King Jr. further weakened the movement.

SECTION 5 Busing and affirmative action programs in the 1970s continued to combat segregation and discrimination.

CHAPTER 19 — The Vietnam War
1954–1975

MAIN IDEA The Vietnam War began as an effort to resist the spread of communism. As it continued, divisions arose over U.S. involvement in the war.

SECTION 1 American involvement in Vietnam began as support for France against a Communist-led war for independence. When the French were defeated and Vietnam was divided, U.S. support shifted to the anti-Communist government of South Vietnam.

SECTION 2 In 1965 President Johnson sent the first U.S. fighting forces to South Vietnam. The war escalated as U.S. troop strength increased. Ground troops faced great challenges in fighting North Vietnamese and Viet Cong forces that used unconventional tactics.

SECTION 3 The Tet Offensive in 1968 led increasing numbers of Americans to question U.S. involvement in Vietnam. The issue provoked growing protest and shaped the presidential election of 1968.

SECTION 4 President Nixon negotiated an end to U.S. involvement in the war in 1973. Fighting continued, however, and South Vietnam surrendered to North Vietnam in 1975.

CHAPTER 20 — A Time of Social Change
1963–1975

MAIN IDEA The 1960s and 1970s were a time of great social and political change for many groups in American society.

SECTION 1 Women and Native Americans formed new organizations to promote political, social, and economic equality in American society.

SECTION 2 Latinos sought equality through the peaceful, nonviolent tactics of César Chávez, as well as the more militant methods of groups like MAYO and the Brown Berets.

SECTION 3 The counterculture of the 1960s grew out of a youth movement rooted in the beliefs of peace and love.

UNIT 6
Looking Toward the Future

1968–Present

Chapter 21
A Search for Order
1968–1980

Chapter 22
A Conservative Era
1980–1992

Chapter 23
Into the Twenty-First Century
1992–Present

Themes

Government and Democracy
Public trust in government was tested by political scandals, and Americans re-examined the role of government in the United States.

Global Relations
The end of the Cold War presented new challenges in foreign affairs, and the United States and other countries confronted international terrorism.

Science and Technology
Innovations such as the Internet affected nearly all areas of everyday life.

Fireworks light the sky above the Capitol at a Fourth of July celebration in Washington, D.C.

Prepare to Read

Summarizing

Find practice for **Summarizing** in the **Skills Handbook,** p. H6

Summarizing helps you understand and remember what you read. In a summary you use your own words to restate your reading. Summaries should use fewer words and highlight only the key points.

Before You Read
Skim headings and visuals to preview the text and form a general idea of its content.

While You Read
Pick out main ideas and key details that support the main ideas.

After You Read
Write a summary of the reading, restating in your own words the key ideas contained in the text and images.

Crises Overwhelm Carter

In his first years in office, Carter enjoyed some successes and suffered through some failures. In 1979, however, a series of events occurred that seemed to overwhelm his entire presidency.

The Soviets invade Afghanistan

In 1978 the government of Afghanistan was toppled in a coup. Afghanistan's new Communist leaders were friendly to the Soviet Union. Yet this new pro-Soviet Afghan government was not stable. When it showed signs of crumbling, the Soviets acted. In December 1979, they invaded Afghanistan.

READING CHECK **Summarizing** How would you describe President Carter's final two years in office?

This heading tells you the topic—problems that President Carter encountered.

Main Idea A series of events plagued Carter's presidency.

Detail A coup and instability in the Afghan government led the Soviets to invade Afghanistan in 1979.

Test Prep Tip

Tests often ask you to choose the best summary of a particular reading passage. Before reading the answer options, try summarizing the passage in your own words. Then read the choices and determine which one best fits your summary.

Reading like a Historian

Making Oral and Written Presentations

Find practice for **Making Oral and Written Presentations** in the **Skills Handbook,** pp. H40–41

California Standards
HSS Analysis HR4, HR5

Presentations are written or verbal reports on a topic that you have researched. There are specific steps to follow for any kind of presentation, as well as some skills that apply to oral presentations and some that apply only to written presentations.

1. Identify a topic that you wish to learn more about for your presentation.
2. Formulate a hypothesis. This will be the main idea of your presentation.
3. Organize facts, data, and details to support your hypothesis.
4. Express your ideas and arguments clearly and persuasively.

Strategies historians use:
- Choose a central idea or theme on which to focus your presentation. This theme should be specific to help structure your research.
- Keep a bibliography of all of the sources you consult in your research. You should always know where you found your facts.
- Proofread your presentation, whether it is written or oral, to ensure that it is well organized and grammatically correct.

Oral Presentation Notes, American History

Reaganomics:

(1) President Ronald Reagan, 1980-1988

(2) tax cuts and smaller federal government

(3) increased military spending,

(4) supply-side economics, "voodoo economics"

(George H. W. Bush)

(5) 1981-1982 – worst economic recession since the Great

~~Depressive~~ Depression

This is the topic of the presentation. All the facts should relate to the topic, "Reaganomics."

Whenever you use a quote, be sure to label the its source.

Proofreading is important, even in oral presentation notes like these. Reading the wrong word can confuse both you and your audience.

Skills Focus — READING LIKE A HISTORIAN

As You Read Make an index card for each fact or piece of data you find. Be sure to include the source information.

As You Study Write an outline that shows how your presentation will be organized. Make sure that all of your facts support your main idea in a meaningful way.

LOOKING TO THE FUTURE 663

CHAPTER 21
1968–1980
A Search for ORDER

THE BIG PICTURE Both Presidents Nixon and Carter achieved great diplomatic successes in times of international turmoil—but also made decisions that ended their presidencies. Nixon, accused of lying and covering up a crime, was forced to resign in disgrace. Carter was denied a second term for failing to provide strong leadership in relations with Iran and the Soviet Union.

California Standards

History-Social Sciences

11.9 Students analyze U.S. foreign policy since World War II.

11.10 Students analyze the development of federal civil rights and voting rights.

11.11 Students analyze the major social problems and domestic policy issues in contemporary American society.

Skills FOCUS READING LIKE A HISTORIAN

New York City celebrates the return of astronauts Neil A. Armstrong, Michael Collins, and Edwin E. "Buzz" Aldrin (right to left) with a grand ticker-tape parade in the summer of 1969. The trio recently completed a historic trip to the moon—a first for humans.
Making Inferences How might great achievements affect a society searching for order?

See **Skills Handbook**, p. H7

U.S.

1968 Richard Nixon is elected president.

July 20, 1969 Neil Armstrong becomes the first man to walk on the moon.

1968

World

1969 The ruling council of the Palestine Liberation Organization elects Yasser Arafat to head the PLO.

664

History's Impact video program
Watch the video to understand the impact of press freedoms.

February 1972
Nixon makes a historic trip to the People's Republic of China.

August 1974
Nixon resigns the presidency.

September 1978
President Carter helps negotiate the Camp David Accords between Israel and Egypt.

March 1980
Carter announces a U.S. boycott of the Olympic Games in Moscow.

1970 | 1972 | 1974 | 1976 | 1978 | 1980

1971
The People's Republic of China invites the U.S. table tennis team to Beijing.

1975
Refugees called "boat people" begin fleeing Vietnam.

November 1979
An Iranian mob seizes American embassy in Tehran.

December 1979
The Soviet Union invades Afghanistan to prop up its Communist government.

665

SECTION 1
The Nixon Years

HSS 11.9.6 Describe U.S. Middle East policy and its strategic, political, and economic interests.

HSS 11.11.2 Discuss the significant domestic policy speeches of Nixon (e.g., with regard to education, civil rights, economic policy, environmental policy).

HSS 11.11.5 Trace the impact of, need for, and controversies associated with environmental conservation, and the development of environmental protection laws.

BEFORE YOU READ

MAIN IDEA
Beyond the ongoing turmoil of the Vietnam War, the Nixon administration did enjoy some notable success.

READING FOCUS
1. What were the key features of Nixon's politics and domestic policies?
2. How did Nixon carry out his foreign policies with regard to China and the Soviet Union?
3. How did trouble in the Middle East affect the Nixon administration?
4. What were some of the major social and cultural events at home in the Nixon years?

KEY TERMS AND PEOPLE
realpolitik
détente
SALT I
OPEC
shuttle diplomacy
Apollo 11
Neil Armstrong

THE INSIDE STORY

How did Nixon bounce back from crushing defeat? By 1962 Richard Nixon seemed to be an utterly defeated man. Still recovering from having lost the presidential election of 1960 to John F. Kennedy, Nixon had sought the governor's office in his home state of California. Again, however, he suffered a humiliating defeat. In a surprising move, he announced his retirement from politics the day after the election. "You won't have Dick Nixon to kick around anymore," he angrily told reporters, whom he had blamed for his defeat. The man who had once been the second most powerful man in the world and who had come within a few thousand votes of being president was now a bitter man.

But Nixon was far from finished in politics. Out of office and out of the spotlight, he remained active in Republican politics in the 1960s. After wins in the 1968 presidential primaries, it became clear that he was an electable candidate. He won his party's nomination. Then, as the Democrats squabbled and divided over the Vietnam War and civil rights, he emerged as the winner in a close election.

Nixon had made a remarkable political comeback. Far from being through with politics, the most memorable years of his political career lay ahead of him. These included achievements in the 1970s for which he is favorably remembered.

Nixon's Comeback to Success

▶ Richard Nixon gives the victory salute that would become his trademark gesture.

Nixon's Politics and Domestic Policies

Richard Nixon's 1968 political comeback highlighted what had already been a long and successful career. Before his losses in 1960 and 1962, he had built a reputation as a strong opponent of communism and as a solid conservative. Recall that in American politics, conservatives tend to favor smaller, less active government. They also favor what are seen as more traditional values.

Nixon the conservative Indeed, Nixon entered the presidency promoting a number of conservative ideas. For example, he had campaigned on the belief that the federal government had grown too large.

HISTORY'S VOICES

> "[W]e have been deluged by government programs for the unemployed, programs for the cities, programs for the poor, and we have reaped from these programs an ugly harvest of frustrations, violence and failure across the land... I say it's time to quit pouring billions of dollars into programs that have failed in the United States of America."
>
> —Richard Nixon, Acceptance Speech, August 8, 1968

"It's time," Nixon continued, "to have power go back from Washington to the states and to the cities of this country all over America." The solution he proposed came to be called the New Federalism. A key feature of this proposal was the concept of revenue sharing. This meant that money collected by the federal government would be shifted to states and cities. Local governments, Nixon believed, would do a better job of spending the taxpayers' money than the federal government would.

The southern strategy Early in his career, Nixon had supported civil rights for African Americans. As president, however, he crafted a "southern strategy" designed to appeal to former segregationists in the South. Nixon's goal was to ensure electoral success by expanding his support in the traditionally Democratic region. Based on this strategy, Nixon tried unsuccessfully to weaken the 1965 Voting Rights Act. He urged a slowdown in forced integration in the South. He also opposed the busing of students from their home neighborhoods to schools in another part of the city. This had been a court-ordered way of integrating schools in places where neighborhoods were all-black or all-white. Nixon favored letting local governments take action rather than having the federal government force them to act.

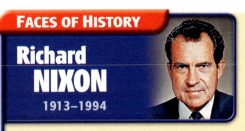

FACES OF HISTORY
Richard NIXON
1913–1994

Richard Nixon accomplished much in a political career that spanned nearly three decades. In addition to his accomplishments, he also won a reputation for tough political tactics.

Born and raised in California, Nixon excelled in college and law school. After serving in the navy in World War II, he pursued a political career. In 1946 he won election to Congress in part on the strength of a strong anti-Communist message. As a House member, he won national attention for his role in the trial of accused spy Alger Hiss. This political success was followed by a 1950 campaign for a Senate seat. He won this election after accusing his opponent of being soft on communism.

Now a national figure, Nixon served as vice president for two terms under Dwight D. Eisenhower. He only narrowly missed winning election to the presidency in 1960. Yet this and his 1962 loss in the race for governor of California left their mark on Nixon. His fear of another loss would lead him to campaign excesses in the future.

Explain How did Nixon's experiences in 1960 and 1962 affect the way he approached political campaigns?

As a result of action at the state level, many communities made real progress toward desegregation. Still, de facto segregation—that is, segregation in fact though not by law—continued in many places, including in many northern cities, for some time. Nixon, meanwhile, gained the favor of many white voters in the South.

Drugs and crime Nixon also took a firm stand against crime and drug use. "Time is running out for the merchants of crime and corruption in American society," he promised. He shared conservatives' concern about federal court rulings that put limits on the powers of the police. (Recall what you have read about rulings such as *Miranda* v. *Arizona*.) He therefore sought to name conservative judges for openings on the federal courts. Though the Senate rejected two of his Supreme Court nominees, Nixon was able to fill four openings on the court.

The other side of Richard Nixon While Nixon had a solid conservative record, he was sometimes willing to take more liberal stances. For example, he expanded the role of the federal government by increasing funding for programs such as food stamps, which helped people with low incomes buy groceries. He also increased payments for Social Security.

Nixon's environmentalism Nixon also took a special interest in the environment. Concern about pollution had been growing in the United States for several years. In 1962 author Rachel Carson had published *Silent Spring*, which warned of the harmful effects of chemicals on the natural world.

By 1970 widespread concern led to massive Earth Day demonstrations all across the country. Millions of Americans took part in these events, at which information and ideas about the environment were shared.

Nixon responded to this growing national issue. In 1970 he signed the Clean Air Act, which sought to regulate levels of air pollution created by factories and other sources. That same year, Nixon worked to establish the Environmental Protection Agency to help carry out the nation's environmental laws and policies.

Other Nixon policies Late in 1970 Nixon signed the Occupational Safety and Health Act. This created a large new organization within the federal government. At its heart was the Occupational Health and Safety Administration, or OSHA, which worked to prevent work-related injury and illness. OSHA set and enforced safety standards in the workplace and provided safety training and education.

While Nixon pursued his southern strategy, he also took steps to advance affirmative action. As you have read, this refers to active measures taken by the government to overcome the effects of past discrimination against minority groups.

Early in his administration, Nixon encouraged the setting of specific hiring goals and timetables for overcoming discrimination in companies doing business with the government. He also extended affirmative action programs to the hiring of women.

THE IMPACT TODAY
Government
In its first three decades, OSHA helped reduce workplace fatalities by 60 percent—at the same time that the size of the American workforce more than doubled.

ACADEMIC VOCABULARY
innovations new ideas or advances

READING CHECK **Summarizing** How did Nixon's basic political beliefs affect his domestic policies?

Nixon's Foreign Policies

When Nixon was running for office in 1968, the war in Vietnam was the major issue facing the voters. You have read about Nixon's troubled efforts to bring that crisis to a close. Yet Vietnam was only one of the foreign-policy issues facing Nixon during his presidency. In general, Nixon met these challenges with great success.

Henry Kissinger and realpolitik Henry Kissinger, who helped negotiate an end to the Vietnam War, was deeply involved in shaping much of Nixon's foreign policy. Nixon named Kissinger as his national security adviser in 1969. Kissinger later became secretary of state. In both roles, he was guided by the notion of realpolitik. **Realpolitik** means basing foreign policies on realistic views of national interest rather than on broad rules or principles.

Kissinger believed the United States should consider each foreign-policy conflict or question from the standpoint of what is best for America. The government should not, Kissinger believed, be bound by promises to fight communism or promote freedom wherever it is threatened. Henry Kissinger's realpolitik marked a significant change from earlier policies such as containment.

Détente Nixon had built his reputation as a tough opponent of communism. Voters knew they were electing a strong and forceful leader. However, as Nixon once remarked, "Sometimes those on the right can do things which those on the left can only talk about." Indeed, as president Nixon took steps to ease tensions with Cold War enemies. These efforts were referred to as **détente** (day-TAHNT).

The policy of détente was strongly influenced by Henry Kissinger's realpolitik. The goal was to build a more stable world in which the United States and its adversaries accepted one another's place.

In 1969 Nixon entered into discussions with the Soviets to slow the ongoing arms race. These were known as the Strategic Arms Limitation Talks (SALT). In addition to increasing numbers of weapons, the United States and the Soviet Union each had recently made innovations in weapons technology. For example, each had recently built antiballistic missile, or ABM, defense systems. Many people considered ABM systems to be a threat to peace. It was feared they would undermine the power balance that helped prevent nuclear war during the Cold War. If one side thought it could survive a nuclear attack, the thinking went, it might be more likely to launch one itself.

The SALT meetings dragged on for several years. Finally, in 1972 Nixon visited Moscow for a summit. At that meeting, Nixon and Soviet leader Leonid Brezhnev agreed to an ABM treaty that bound each country to strict limits in the building of missile systems.

Nixon and Brezhnev also agreed to a five-year slowdown in building new offensive weapons. Following the end of these talks—now called SALT I—negotiators began a second round of discussions on arms limitation. These became known as SALT II. You will read more about them later.

Nixon in China Shortly after taking office, President Nixon told his closest advisers about one of his key goals for his presidency: improving relations with the Communist People's Republic of China. At that time, the People's Republic had little contact with the United States and most of the rest of the world.

Yet Nixon saw great opportunity in improving relations with the Communist giant. Such a step would put pressure on the Soviet Union. Both China and the Soviets practiced communism, but they had become bitter rivals in recent years. Nixon knew that by becoming friendlier with China, he could make the Soviets uncomfortable and pressure them into a more cooperative relationship with the United States.

Nixon had to move carefully. The United States did not formally recognize the People's Republic of China. It considered the Republic of China on Taiwan to be the true Chinese government. Thus, the effort to reach out to the People's Republic took place in secrecy.

Nevertheless, Nixon's plan went forward. In 1971 the People's Republic made a surprise invitation to an American table tennis team to play in a tournament. The team members became the first Americans to visit mainland China since 1949.

Later, Kissinger made a secret trip to the People's Republic to explore a possible

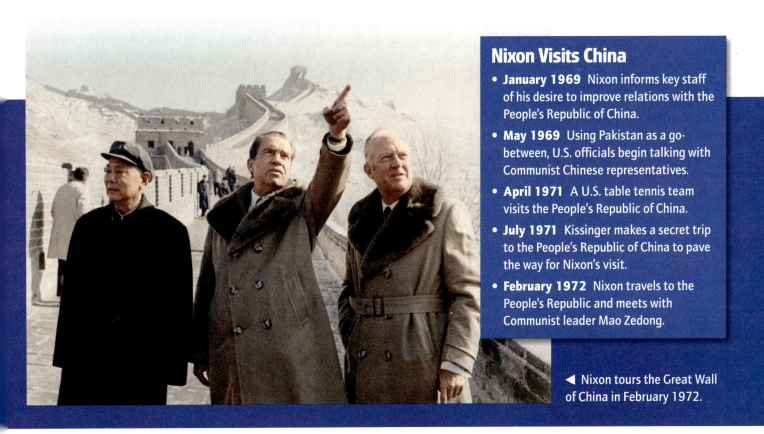

Nixon Visits China

- **January 1969** Nixon informs key staff of his desire to improve relations with the People's Republic of China.
- **May 1969** Using Pakistan as a go-between, U.S. officials begin talking with Communist Chinese representatives.
- **April 1971** A U.S. table tennis team visits the People's Republic of China.
- **July 1971** Kissinger makes a secret trip to the People's Republic of China to pave the way for Nixon's visit.
- **February 1972** Nixon travels to the People's Republic and meets with Communist leader Mao Zedong.

◀ Nixon tours the Great Wall of China in February 1972.

presidential visit. The meeting went well. In July 1971, Nixon announced that he would go to the People's Republic in early 1972.

The news shocked some Americans and pleased others. Some were upset that Nixon seemed to be abandoning Nationalist China and embracing the Communists. Nixon assured these critics that that was not the case. Many Americans, however, supported the move.

In February Nixon's team took off for China. There he met with top Chinese leaders, including the aging Mao Zedong. The visit was a huge success for Nixon. He and Mao recognized the benefits of a closer relationship. Toward that end, they agreed to disagree about Taiwan.

The trip also seemed to have the hoped-for effect on the Soviets. Shortly after the China visit, Nixon and Brezhnev reached agreement in the SALT I meetings.

ACADEMIC VOCABULARY
region an area of the world

READING CHECK **Identifying the Main Idea** What was the primary goal of Richard Nixon's foreign policy with regard to the Soviet Union and China?

Trouble in the Middle East

The Middle East had been a point of conflict for many years. In 1967 Israel went to war against several of its Arab neighbors. As a result of the Six-Day War, Israel occupied territory that had belonged to or been controlled by the Arab nations of Egypt, Syria, and Jordan.

Following the war's end, the United Nations passed a resolution that called for Israel to withdraw from these occupied lands and for Arab states to recognize Israel's right to exist. However, there was disagreement on exactly what the resolution required. Israel—with U.S. support—continued to dispute with its Arab neighbors for the next several years.

In 1973 this ongoing conflict finally erupted in war. On the Jewish holy day of Yom Kippur, Egypt and Syria attacked Israel.

The fighting affected the United States in a number of ways. One effect was the threat of Soviet involvement. In response to events on the battlefield, the Soviet Union offered supplies to the Egyptians and the Syrians.

The United States in turn sent supplies to the Israelis. The Soviets also threatened to send troops to aid the embattled Egyptians. Conflict in the region threatened to turn into a superpower confrontation.

Oil embargo Another effect of the war was the decision of several Arab nations to impose an oil embargo. An embargo is the refusal by a country to ship a product or products from its ports.

Shortly after the start of the Yom Kippur War, the Arab oil-producing countries of the Middle East jointly agreed not to ship any oil to the United States and certain other countries. This was a response to American support for Israel. The Arab countries were part of a group called the Organization of Petroleum Exporting Countries, or **OPEC**.

At the time of the embargo, the United States was dependent on OPEC oil for a significant amount of its large petroleum needs. That dependence was growing. In 1970 the United States had gotten just over a fifth of its oil from foreign sources. By 1973 that figure had risen to about a third.

The Arab oil embargo contributed to an energy crisis in the United States. As gasoline became scarce, drivers sometimes had to wait in long lines at gas stations to fill their tanks. When they got to the pump, they often found that prices for gasoline had risen sharply.

The oil embargo affected more than just people who drove cars. For example, it drove up the cost of operating machines in factories. It cost farmers more to harvest their crops. The embargo also increased the cost of

CAUSES AND EFFECTS OF THE YOM KIPPUR WAR

CAUSES
- Israel occupied Arab-controlled land in the Six-Day War.
- The United Nations passed a resolution urging Israel to leave occupied lands and Arab nations to recognize Israel.
- Arabs and Israelis were unable to reach agreement on either point of the UN resolution.

EFFECTS
- Tension between United States and the Soviet Union grew.
- Arab oil-producing nations decided on an oil embargo.

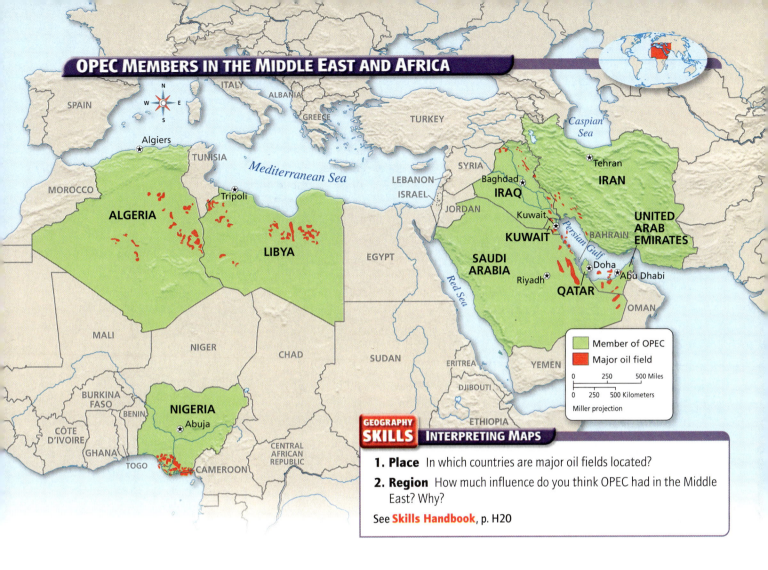

OPEC Members in the Middle East and Africa

GEOGRAPHY SKILLS INTERPRETING MAPS

1. **Place** In which countries are major oil fields located?
2. **Region** How much influence do you think OPEC had in the Middle East? Why?

See **Skills Handbook**, p. H20

transporting products from farms and factories to stores. Prices for all kinds of products thus began to rise. As you will read, this rapid rise in prices would cause serious problems throughout the U.S. economy.

Kissinger and shuttle diplomacy

To help resolve the crisis in the Middle East, Henry Kissinger went to work. Unable to get all the parties involved to meet together to discuss possible solutions, he started what came to be called **shuttle diplomacy**. That is, he traveled—shuttled—from group to group, trying to work out separate agreements to end the fighting. For example, he negotiated peace between Israel and Egypt. Then he helped bring about a separate deal between Israel and Syria. In this way, the military conflict came to an end. Eventually, the oil embargo was also lifted.

READING CHECK **Identifying Cause and Effect** How did the trouble in the Middle East affect the United States in the early 1970s?

Major Events at Home

In an earlier chapter, you read about the American program to put astronauts on the moon. During the Nixon years, the United States finally achieved this history-making goal.

Throughout the mid-1960s, the American public followed the progress of the NASA astronauts with great interest. Every few months brought another launch and another step toward the goal of a lunar landing. These triumphs were also marred by tragedy. In 1967 three astronauts died in a terrible launchpad fire. In spite of this setback, the Apollo space program continued.

The climax came in July 1969. On the 16th of that month, a flight known as **Apollo 11** made a successful liftoff from Cape Kennedy, also known as the Kennedy Space Center, in Florida. On board were three modern-day pioneers—astronauts **Neil Armstrong**, Edwin "Buzz" Aldrin, and Michael Collins.

A SEARCH FOR ORDER 671

Interactive HISTORY CLOSE-UP

The First Moon Landing

The successful landing of human beings on the surface of the moon was a triumph of technology—and of the American will and spirit of exploration.

The lunar module was designed to withstand the low gravitational forces of the moon, which were one-sixth those of Earth.

The large amounts of equipment made the interior of the lunar module cramped and noisy.

The large footpads were designed to ensure the module did not sink into the soft lunar soil.

Skills Focus: INTERPRETING INFOGRAPHICS

go.hrw.com
Interactive
Keyword: SE7 CH21

1. **Making Inferences** Why do you think conditions were so cramped in the lunar landing module?
2. **Drawing Conclusions** What factors made landing on the moon difficult?

See **Skills Handbook**, pp. H12, H18

After a journey of several days, the crew of *Apollo 11* swung into orbit around the moon. As their spacecraft sailed miles above the moon's surface, a separate craft split off from the main part. One part was the control module *Columbia*, in which Collins remained. The other part was a lunar module called the *Eagle*, which carried Aldrin and Armstrong.

On July 20 the *Eagle* landed on the moon's surface. Back on Earth, millions of viewers watched the flawless landing on television. Several anxious hours later, Neil Armstrong made his way out of the module. Wearing a heavy space suit, he slowly backed down a ladder. "That's one small step for a man," crackled his voice over the radio as he stepped onto the moon, "one giant leap for mankind." The mission started years before by President John F. Kennedy had been achieved at last.

Soon Armstrong was joined by Aldrin. The pair set up a camera and carried out a variety of tasks. This included planting an American flag in the lunar soil.

HISTORY'S VOICES

"So many people have done so much to give us this opportunity to place this American flag on the surface. To me it was one of the prouder moments of my life, to be able to stand there and quickly salute the flag."

—Edwin "Buzz" Aldrin, news conference, August 12, 1969

Inflation and price controls

The success of the lunar landing gave the nation and Nixon a lift. However, Nixon knew that it was not enough to ensure his future in office. As the memory of *Apollo 11* faded and the election of 1972 approached, Nixon grew concerned.

A particular worry was the high rate of inflation, or the overall rise in prices. In the months leading up to the 1972 election, this stood at an unacceptable 5 percent, and it was rising. Unemployment was also at an uncomfortably high level.

Nixon had traditionally favored limited government involvement in the economy. Now, however, he believed action was needed. In August 1971 he announced a 90-day freeze of wages and prices. That is, businesses could not increase the prices they charged for their products or the wages they paid their workers. This, Nixon hoped, would act as a brake on inflation.

The immediate impact of Nixon's measures was positive. Inflation did appear to slow, at least for a while. Nixon seemed to have successfully addressed a major economic concern of the voters.

Unfortunately, Nixon had not solved the problem of inflation permanently. The oil crisis of 1973–1974 would soon send prices sharply higher again. The wage and price controls that had worked before failed to bring relief. Meanwhile, the second term Nixon had worked so hard to secure dissolved into scandal. You will read about this in the next section.

READING CHECK **Summarizing** What were two major events affecting the United States during Nixon's first term in office?

THE IMPACT TODAY

Science and Technology
NASA's moon explorations ended in the early 1970s. In early 2004 President George W. Bush announced a new goal for U.S. space exploration: a return to the moon and, eventually, human missions to the planet Mars.

SECTION 1 ASSESSMENT

HSS 11.9.6, 11.11.2, 11.11.5

Reviewing Ideas, Terms, and People

1. **a. Identify** What kind of political reputation did Nixon have when he was elected president in 1969?
   b. Draw Conclusions Why do you think Nixon sometimes favored conservative policies and sometimes took more liberal positions?

2. **a. Define** Write a brief definition of each of the following terms: realpolitik, détente
   b. Interpret What do you think Nixon meant when he said, "Sometimes those on the right can do things which those on the left can only talk about"?

3. **a. Describe** What were the key events in the Middle East that occurred in 1973?
   b. Sequence What was the sequence of events surrounding the Arab oil embargo?

4. **a. Identify** What is the significance of *Apollo 11*?
   b. Compare How did Nixon's handling of the inflation problem match his overall political philosophies?

Critical Thinking

5. **Identifying the Main Idea** Copy the chart below and use information from the section to record details that support the section's main idea.

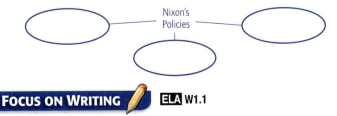

FOCUS ON WRITING ELA W1.1

6. **Descriptive** Based on the events described in this section, write a brief descriptive paragraph about Nixon's performance, including details of his major policies and accomplishments.

A SEARCH FOR ORDER **673**

LANDMARK SUPREME COURT CASES
Constitutional Issue: Freedom of the Press

New York Times Co. v. United States (1971)

Why It Matters This case considered whether newspapers could be prevented from publishing information that the government did not want disclosed to the public on the grounds that it might harm national security.

Background of the Case
In 1971 the *New York Times* began publishing portions of a secret Defense Department study of the Vietnam War. The Pentagon Papers had been leaked by former Defense Department economist Daniel Ellsberg. The Nixon administration went to court to prevent publication of the information.

The Decision
In its ruling the Court noted the strong presumption that "prior restraint"—that is, prevention of speech or the publication of information—is unconstitutional. The government therefore had a "heavy burden" to show that blocking publication is justified. The government failed to do so, the Court held.

There were several separate concurring or dissenting opinions. Some justices argued that under the First Amendment the government can never restrict publication of news. Others argued that government sometimes has the right to keep certain matters secret in the interest of national security but that this was not such a case. One justice suggested that the publishers might be prosecuted but only after publication.

In the end, however, the ruling upheld the key role of the press in educating and informing the public:

> ❝[T]he only effective restraint upon executive policy and power in the areas of national defense and international affairs may lie in an enlightened citizenry—in an informed and critical public opinion which alone can here protect the values of democratic government.❞
>
> — Justice Potter Stewart

THE IMPACT TODAY The issue of prior restraint of news and the possible threat to national security in the release of certain information in newspapers and other news outlets remains a difficult one. Since the terrorist attacks of September 11, 2001, for example, the government and the press have differed over ways to manage the release of information about the nation's ongoing fight against terrorism.

CRITICAL THINKING
go.hrw.com
Research Online
Keyword: SS Court

1. **Analyze the Impact** Using the keyword above, read about *New York Times Co.* v. *Sullivan*, another important First Amendment case involving the same newspaper. What is the ruling of the case? Why did the Court allow the media greater flexibility in writing about public figures than in stories about private individuals?

2. **You Be the Judge** The events of September 11, 2001, and the ongoing war on terrorism have raised new concerns about the proper balance between governmental secrecy and open disclosure and discussion in the press. How might these contemporary concerns affect the decision in a case like *New York Times Co.* v. *United States* today? Explain your answer in a short paragraph.

SECTION 2: From Watergate to Ford

BEFORE YOU READ

MAIN IDEA
The Nixon presidency became bogged down in scandal, leading to the first presidential resignation in American history and the administration of Gerald Ford.

READING FOCUS
1. What were the main events of the presidential election of 1972?
2. How did the Watergate scandal unfold?
3. Who was Gerald Ford, and what were the highlights of his presidency?

KEY TERMS AND PEOPLE
Watergate scandal
executive privilege
Saturday night massacre
transcript
Gerald R. Ford

 HSS 11.11.4 Explain the constitutional crisis originating from the Watergate scandal.

A Piece of Tape Brings Down a Presidency

 How did a little piece of tape trigger one of history's great scandals? When security guard Frank Wills first noticed the piece of tape covering a door latch in the garage of the Watergate hotel-office complex on June 17, 1972, he was not alarmed. He figured that someone during the day had probably been making deliveries and had wanted to keep the door from locking. Wills removed the tape and continued to patrol the building.

Later, however, Wills returned to the door and checked it again. Someone had replaced the tape he had removed earlier. This time, Wills called the police.

When the police arrived, they began their search for the intruders they suspected were in the building. Eventually, they surprised a group of five men who had broken into the offices of the Democratic National Committee, which were housed in the Watergate. The group was in the process of installing or repairing advanced eavesdropping equipment. They also had cameras and appeared to be planning to photograph the contents of filing cabinets.

It was not clear at first exactly why the burglars had broken into the office. Nor was it known right away whether they had been working on behalf of some other people or group. In fact, many dismissed the incident as nothing more than the bumbling handiwork of petty crooks. As you will read, however, the story caught the attention of reporters at the *Washington Post*. As a result of their efforts, Watergate would soon be a household word.

▶ Frank Wills made the discovery that led to the arrest of the Watergate burglars.

The Election of 1972

Richard Nixon's first term had been eventful. Though he had experienced his share of troubles, Nixon had also enjoyed many triumphs.

This was fortunate for Nixon, for he was deeply concerned about his political future. Indeed, many of his first-term actions had been aimed at shoring up support with the voters. Having both lost and won the presidency by tiny margins, he was leaving nothing to chance in 1972. In fact, he was prepared to support illegal actions to help ensure re-election.

Nixon had a well-earned reputation as a political scrapper from his days in Congress. At times Nixon's supporters used underhanded tactics during the first term of his presidency.

To do his political dirty work, Nixon advisers John Ehrlichman and H. R. Haldeman had created a group that came to be known as the "Plumbers." Their job was to respond to "leaks" of secret information—and to investigate Nixon's political enemies.

In 1971, for example, the Plumbers broke into the offices of Daniel Ellsberg's psychiatrist. Ellsberg was a former government official who had leaked key documents about the Vietnam War to the *New York Times*. These were the so-called Pentagon Papers. The Plumbers had hoped to find information they could use to embarrass Ellsberg and damage his reputation and credibility.

In 1972 Nixon and his team turned their attention to the upcoming presidential election. Nixon's chances for re-election seemed very good. Many of his recent moves, such as his trip to China, had been highly popular with the voters.

Still, Nixon's team did not rest easy. In early 1972, they hatched a plan to send a team of burglars to break into the offices of the Democratic National Committee at the Watergate hotel-office complex. The purpose of the burglary appeared to be to collect information about Democratic strategy that might be useful in the president's re-election campaign.

As you have read, the Watergate plot ended with the arrest of five burglars. The bungled break-in hardly made news when it occurred. It soon became clear that the men had connections to the president. National news organizations paid little attention to the incident.

The story did not die, however. Two young reporters on the staff of the *Washington Post*, Bob Woodward and Carl Bernstein, continued to investigate the break-in. They began to uncover troubling facts about the burglars' links to the White House. In August they reported that one of the Watergate burglars had received a $25,000 check that had been originally sent to the president's re-election campaign. By October the *Post* was reporting that the Watergate break-in was actually part of a widespread spying effort by members of the Nixon campaign.

TIME LINE

Watergate

June 17, 1972 Burglars were caught during a break-in at the Watergate (left).

June 18, 1972 Carl Bernstein and Bob Woodward helped report the first in a series of stories on the break-in (below).

November 7, 1972 Nixon won re-election in a landslide (above).

May 18, 1973 The Senate Watergate Committee began televised hearings into the scandal.

July 13, 1973 Alexander Butterfield revealed the existence of the White House taping system.

If the public noticed the *Post* stories at this time, it did not affect their voting. In November Nixon was handed one of the most overwhelming victories in U.S. history. His opponent, South Dakota senator and Vietnam War critic George McGovern, managed to carry only Massachusetts and the District of Columbia.

READING CHECK **Making Inferences** What can you infer about Nixon's level of confidence about the election of 1972 based on his actions?

The Scandal Unfolds

With his re-election, Nixon may have believed any trouble related to the Watergate break-in was behind him. He was wrong. Indeed, the scandal was just about to break.

By February 1973 seven men involved with the break-in had been convicted or had pleaded guilty to a variety of crimes. Among them were several officials who had worked in the White House and for Nixon's re-election campaign. During the burglars' trials questions emerged about what other White House officials may have been involved in illegal activities. People began to wonder whether Nixon had known about the wrongdoing taking place around him and helped to cover it up.

Meanwhile, the *Washington Post* continued to investigate the story. Now the public—and members of Congress—were paying attention to the stories.

In response to the growing controversy, Nixon ordered his staff to conduct a full investigation. In April 1973 Haldeman and Erlichman resigned from their White House jobs, as did Nixon's attorney general. In addition, Nixon fired John Dean, the lawyer he had appointed to investigate what was now called the **Watergate scandal**. The moves were meant to signal the president's tough action against wrongdoing. "There can be no whitewash at the White House," he declared.

These actions calmed many Republicans in Congress. For example, Representative Gerald Ford praised Nixon for "cleaning house." He declared, "I am absolutely positive he had nothing to do with this mess."

Democrats were not so sure. They demanded that the president appoint someone who was not part of his own administration to look into the scandal. This sort of independent investigator is now known as a special prosecutor. In May Nixon agreed to take this step. Nixon's attorney general Elliot Richardson appointed a Harvard Law School professor named Archibald Cox to the job.

Butterfield's bombshell Also in May, a Senate committee began its own investigation. The committee held televised hearings. Millions of viewers tuned in to get answers to the famous question of Tennessee Republican senator Howard Baker: "What did the president know, and when did he know it?"

ACADEMIC VOCABULARY
affect to change or influence something

THE IMPACT TODAY
Government
In May 2005 Americans learned the name of a key but secret figure in the Watergate story as reported by the *Washington Post*. Mark Felt, a former top FBI official, was revealed as the secret source for many *Washington Post* stories about the scandal.

October 20, 1973
In the Saturday night massacre, Nixon fired the special prosecutor.

April 30, 1974
The White House released edited transcripts of the tapes (left).

July 24, 1974
The Supreme Court ruled that the White House must turn over the tapes.

August 8, 1974
Richard Nixon announced his resignation from the presidency (right).

Skills FOCUS **INTERPRETING TIME LINES**
Which event suggests that the public was not immediately concerned by the events of June 1972?
See **Skills Handbook**, p. H14

A SEARCH FOR ORDER **677**

Primary Sources

Political Cartoon

At the height of the Watergate scandal in 1973, President Richard Nixon held a press conference to declare his innocence in the case. This political cartoon appeared shortly after that press conference.

President Nixon was famous for raising his arms and making the "V for Victory" sign with his fingers.

A sanctuary refers to a safe place for someone fleeing the law.

Speaking of sanctuaries . . .

Skills Focus: Reading Like a Historian

1. **Interpreting Political Cartoons** What is the "sanctuary" that Nixon is hiding behind?
2. **Identifying Points of View** What is the message that the artist is trying to send?

See **Skills Handbook**, pp. H28–H29, H31

The hearings produced plenty of drama. For example, early in June, John Dean told the committee that he had talked many times with Nixon about Watergate and its cover-up. These statements appeared to go against the president's own words. Then on July 16, 1973, a former presidential aide named Alexander Butterfield revealed that since 1971 Nixon had tape-recorded all conversations in his offices.

The Saturday night massacre News of the existence of White House tapes caused great excitement. Investigators realized that the recordings might answer many outstanding questions about the president's actions.

Nixon, however, did not want to give up the tapes. He argued that the constitutional separation of powers and the principle of executive privilege gave him the right to withhold them. **Executive privilege** holds that a president must be able to keep official conversations and meetings private. Such guarantees of privacy, the thinking goes, help ensure that the president gets open and honest advice.

Investigators rejected Nixon's claim of executive privilege. They argued that the tapes they were interested in hearing did not involve official presidential business. Rather, the investigators wanted to listen to Nixon's discussions of political matters—his re-election campaign—and possible illegal actions. Such conversations were not protected by executive privilege, investigators claimed.

Special Prosecutor Cox and the Senate Watergate committee continued to seek the tapes. They both issued subpoenas demanding Nixon hand them over. A subpoena is a legal order requiring the recipient to bring a certain item to court.

Nixon's response was harsh. In the so-called **Saturday night massacre**, he ordered attorney general Elliot Richardson to fire Special Prosecutor Cox. Richardson refused to do so and instead quit his job. Then Nixon ordered Richardson's assistant to fire Cox. He also refused and resigned. Nixon finally persuaded the third-ranking official in the Justice Department to fire Cox.

Many people were stunned by Nixon's actions. Not only did his innocence seem in doubt, it appeared that the president was challenging the constitutional system itself.

HISTORY'S VOICES

“Whether ours shall continue to be a government of laws and not of men is now for Congress and ultimately the American people to decide.”

—Archibald Cox, October 20, 1973

The crisis continues Public confidence in the president was very low. Yet a determined Nixon continued to deny his involvement in either the break-in or the cover-up. "People have got to know whether or not their president is a crook," he said. "Well, I'm not a crook." Meanwhile, he continued to delay release of the tapes. The White House also revealed that a critical, 18-minute portion of the tapes had been unexplainably erased.

Nixon's presidency was now in serious trouble. There were calls for impeachment and for Nixon to resign as president. As the pressure mounted in the spring of 1974, Nixon released some transcripts of the tapes. A **transcript** is a written record of a spoken event. Though Nixon denied it, the pages seemed to contain many suggestions that he had known about and covered up illegal activity. At the same time, the release of the transcripts did not satisfy investigators. They continued legal action aimed at gaining access to the tapes themselves.

Nixon resigns The Supreme Court of the United States finally settled the question of the White House tapes. In late July the Court ruled that Nixon had to obey the subpoenas and produce the tapes. Without waiting for the president to comply, the House Judiciary Committee voted to recommend impeachment of the president. The reasons included Nixon's alleged obstruction of justice and his failure to obey subpoenas.

Nixon could see that his support in Congress was thin. He must also have known that the tapes would reveal clear evidence of his own wrongdoing. On August 8, 1974, he spoke to the American people. For the first time in American history, a president resigned the office. "By taking this action," he said, "I hope that I will have hastened the start of the process of healing . . ."

READING CHECK Sequencing What was the key sequence of events as the Watergate scandal unfolded?

Gerald Ford's Presidency

Watergate was only one of the problems facing Richard Nixon. In early 1973, just as the Watergate scandal was about to explode, investigators began exploring the activities of Vice President Spiro T. Agnew, former governor of Maryland. Agnew was eventually accused of taking payments in return for political favors and cheating on his taxes. After pleading no contest to the tax charge, he resigned in disgrace. Agnew became only the second U.S. vice president to resign.

To replace Agnew, Nixon chose the Republican leader in the House of Representatives, **Gerald R. Ford**. With Nixon's resignation, Ford became president. He was the first person ever to become president without having been elected either president or vice president.

At his swearing in on August 9, 1974, Ford said he understood the unusual situation he was in. "I am acutely aware you have not elected me as your President," he noted. Still, he urged the nation and the government to move forward.

Ford said he pardoned Nixon to shift attention "from the pursuit of a fallen President to the pursuit of the urgent needs of a rising nation." *Why did many people question this decision?*

HISTORY'S VOICES

“My fellow Americans, our long national nightmare is over.

Our Constitution works; our great Republic is a government of laws and not of men. Here the people rule.”

—Gerald R. Ford, August 9, 1974

Ford pardons Nixon Less than a month after taking office, President Ford granted a full pardon to Richard Nixon for any crime he may have committed. A pardon is a formal, legal forgiveness for a crime. Ford's action ensured that Nixon could not be tried in court or punished for any of his actions involving the Watergate affair. Many Americans reacted to the pardon with outrage. Some even wondered

A SEARCH FOR ORDER **679**

openly whether Ford had promised to pardon Nixon prior to his resignation.

There was no evidence of such a deal, and Ford denied it flatly. He also took the unusual step of testifying about the pardon before a congressional committee.

Ford as president Ford, a Republican, found that his job as president was made more difficult by the fact that the Democrats controlled Congress. For example, he believed that inflation was a serious problem for the economy. To help fight it, he proposed cutting the amount of money that the U.S. government spent—spending that he felt drove prices even higher.

Congress, however, passed many spending bills against his wishes. Ford used his power to veto these spending bills on dozens of occasions. In spite of these efforts, inflation continued at a high rate.

In foreign affairs, President Ford had to overcome problems of the past. The experience of the Vietnam War had caused Congress to place limits on the powers of the president. In 1975 South Vietnam was about to fall to North Vietnam. Ford tried to send aid to the South Vietnamese, but Congress blocked this effort. The president did, however, help nearly 250,000 people flee South Vietnam before the arrival of the Communists.

Congress also refused to allow Ford to aid forces fighting Cuban-backed Communists in the African country of Angola. Ford complained about the loss of presidential power, but he seemed powerless in the matter.

Ford was able to take action when a Cambodian naval ship seized the American cargo ship *Mayaguez* and its 39-man crew. A military raid did recover the ship and crew, though 41 Americans died in the operation.

One of Ford's first acts as president had been to announce that Henry Kissinger would remain as his secretary of state. Ford also worked to maintain the Nixon policy of détente. He and Soviet leader Leonid Brezhnev agreed to new and larger limits on nuclear weapons.

Also during Ford's presidency, the United States and the Soviet Union worked jointly on a space project. The highlight was a meeting in space between U.S. and Soviet astronauts.

An election challenge In spite of his successes, Ford faced serious political problems. In the 1976 election, he faced opposition even from within his own party. In the primary elections to determine the Republican nominee, former California governor Ronald Reagan did well.

Ford won the nomination, but only after a close struggle. Clearly, the contest for the White House, in which he would face Governor Jimmy Carter of Georgia, would be difficult.

READING CHECK **Evaluating** How did the Watergate scandal affect Gerald Ford's presidency?

SECTION 2 ASSESSMENT

HSS 11.11.4

Reviewing Ideas, Terms, and People

1. **a. Describe** What were the circumstances of the break-in at the Watergate?
   b. Draw Conclusions Why might members of one political campaign want to spy on or steal information from another campaign?

2. **a. Define** Write a brief definition of each of the following terms: special prosecutor, **executive privilege**, subpoena
   b. Make Generalizations Why do you think the **Saturday night massacre** troubled many Americans?
   c. Elaborate Why do you think many people accused Nixon of acting as if he were above the law?

3. **a. Recall** How did the decision to **pardon** Nixon affect Ford?
   b. Make Inferences What can you infer from the fact that Ford issued so many vetoes?

Critical Thinking

4. **Identifying Cause and Effect** Copy the chart below and use information from the section to give effects of the causes given.

Cause	Effect
Watergate burglars arrested	
Butterfield reveals existence of tapes	
Nixon ordered to hand over tapes	
Ford pardons Nixon	

FOCUS ON SPEAKING

ELA W1.1

5. **Persuasive** Deliver a speech in which you argue either for or against President Ford's decision to pardon former President Nixon. Be sure to use information from the section in making your argument.

SECTION 3
Carter's Presidency

BEFORE YOU READ

MAIN IDEA
Jimmy Carter used his reputation for honesty to win the presidency in 1976, but he soon met challenges that required other qualities as well.

READING FOCUS
1. What were some of the difficult domestic challenges facing Carter and the nation in the late 1970s?
2. What were Carter's greatest foreign-policy triumphs and challenges?
3. How did international crises affect Carter's presidency?

KEY TERMS AND PEOPLE
James Earl "Jimmy" Carter
SALT II
Camp David Accords
Ayatollah Ruhollah Khomeini

HSS 11.9.6 Describe U.S. Middle East policy and its strategic, political, and economic interests.

HSS 11.10.2 Examine court cases in the evolution of civil rights, including *California* v. *Bakke*.

HSS 11.11.2 Discuss the significant domestic policy speeches of Carter.

HSS 11.11.6 Analyze the persistence of poverty and how different analyses of this issue influence social policies.

 How can the world's most powerful man show a common touch? In American politics, an inaugural parade is typically a moment of great pomp and circumstance. But for **James Earl "Jimmy" Carter**, it was another opportunity to remind the American people that he would be a different kind of leader from the ones they had been used to in their recent, difficult past. It was a message Carter had stressed throughout his successful 1976 presidential campaign against President Gerald Ford.

Following his swearing in—at which the new president had asked to use the nickname Jimmy rather than his more formal, full name—Carter set off on the ceremonial trip down Pennsylvania Avenue from the Capitol to the White House. Jimmy Carter, however, would not make this trip in the traditional way. Rather than riding in a limousine, separated from the people by a layer of steel and bulletproof glass, he would walk. Surprising all observers, Carter, new first lady Rosalynn Carter, and their young daughter, Amy, left their limousine behind and strode among the crowd. All the while, the new leader of the most powerful nation on earth waved to the people and flashed his warm smile.

Carter's inaugural walk was without precedent in modern American political history. It was clear that he aimed to be a different type of president—one who did not consider himself above the people. Later, Carter would reinforce this message by refusing to allow the traditional playing of the song "Hail to the Chief" to announce his arrival at important events.

Jimmy Carter succeeded at creating the image of a down-to-earth, honest man. But he would soon learn that a reputation for trustworthiness was not enough to lead the nation through difficult times.

WALKING to the White House

▼ The Carters charmed the nation by walking to the White House on inauguration day.

681

Linking to Today

Oil Consumption

In 1973 an oil embargo by Arab nations and higher prices led to long lines at American gas stations. Then in 1979 another energy crisis began.

A revolution in Iran stopped oil exports from that country. Exports later resumed but at a lower level than before. Other countries raised the price of their oil exports too, and prices skyrocketed in the United States. In response, President Carter urged Americans to consume less oil.

Although many people have worked during the last few decades to limit their use of oil, consumption has continued to increase. Today the United States has less than 5 percent of the world's population but uses a quarter of its oil. Many people fear that the nation depends too heavily on foreign oil.

Most nations use oil primarily for heat and power. In the United States, however, transportation accounts for about two-thirds of oil use. During the Iraq War and following Hurricanes Katrina and Rita in 2005, rising gasoline costs troubled many consumers.

Making Inferences How might an oil embargo affect the United States today?

Cars streaming through their daily rush-hour commute in New York City

Challenges Facing the Nation

As he strode along the parade route on inauguration day, Jimmy Carter seemed in many ways to be the right man at the right time for the United States. The former peanut farmer and Georgia governor came across as an honest man of deep religious faith. He had never worked in Washington, D.C. His simple promise—"I'll never lie to you"—was just what the weary American public wanted to hear.

Carter wasted no time trying to help the nation heal some of the wounds from the past. A day after being sworn in as president, he issued a pardon to thousands of American men who had avoided the draft during the Vietnam War. The pardon enabled many men who had fled the country to return home without fear of being charged with a crime. Not everyone supported this action. Yet with it, Carter fulfilled one of his campaign promises.

The economy and energy Carter also tried to tackle problems in two other areas that had troubled earlier administrations. One was the economy. Inflation and unemployment stood at unacceptably high levels. Carter tried to address both concerns. During his time in office, the economy added many new jobs. Yet, as you will read, Carter was unable to bring down inflation. Indeed, the problem only seemed to get worse.

Carter had more success in addressing the nation's energy problems. Recalling the oil crisis of 1973–1974 and fearing another one, he made the development of a national energy policy a top priority.

HISTORY'S VOICES

"I know some of you may doubt that we face real energy shortages. The 1973 gasoline lines are gone, and our homes are warm again. But our energy problem is worse tonight than it was in 1973 or a few weeks ago in the dead of winter. It is worse because more waste has occurred, and more time has passed by without our planning for the future."

—Jimmy Carter, April 18, 1977

Carter's goals included easing dependence on foreign oil through energy conservation, developing new energy supplies, and loosening government regulation of the American oil industry. To help develop and carry out his new policies, he pushed for the establishment of a new cabinet-level Department of Energy.

Carter also sought to change the habits and attitudes of the American people. He urged Americans to conserve fuel. Citizens were asked to turn down their heat and air conditioning and drive fewer miles. Car buyers were urged to buy models that offered greater fuel efficiency. U.S. automakers were offered incentives to build cars that met new, tougher fuel-efficiency standards.

Carter promoted the development of alternative energy sources, such as solar and wind power. He promoted laws by which Americans were able to lower their taxes by installing energy-saving equipment in their homes.

These and other Carter energy policies were successful at helping reduce American dependence on foreign oil. American production of energy also increased under Carter.

Environmental concerns Carter was concerned not only about energy but also about the environment. He believed that conserving fuel was a key way to avoid "mounting pressure to plunder the environment." In order to prevent this from happening, the president led a years-long battle to win passage of the Alaska National Interest Lands Conservation Act. This law helped protect more than 100 million acres of land and doubled the size of the nation's park and wildlife refuge system.

But the Carter years were also marred by environmental questions and crises. In 1979 a mishap at a nuclear power plant located at Three Mile Island in Pennsylvania terrified the nation. For a time, officials seemed unsure how to correct problems that threatened a massive release of radiation into the environment. Some people in the immediate area of the plant were evacuated. In the end, very little radiation was released, and no one suffered any ill effects. However, public concern about the safety of nuclear power continued to grow.

Another environmental disaster was uncovered at Love Canal in New York. There, long-buried chemicals left behind by a chemical company began seeping up through the ground. Exposure to the chemicals was linked to the high rates of birth defects in the community. To solve the problem, the state of New York bought the homes of some 200 residents. The government then began the costly task of cleaning up the mess. Experts warned that there were likely many more toxic waste sites like Love Canal around the country.

READING CHECK **Identifying Supporting Details** Find two examples of how energy created major challenges for Carter and the nation.

Carter's Foreign Policy

Jimmy Carter came to office with no real foreign-policy experience and no background in federal government. He brought his own ideas to the field of foreign affairs with mixed results.

Carter also brought some new faces. Among them was Andrew Young. An African American with a background in the civil rights movement, Young served as American ambassador to the United Nations. His appointment helped highlight Carter's strong civil rights background. Indeed, Carter made dozens of top-level appointments of African Americans, women, and Hispanic Americans.

A focus on human rights During the presidential campaign, Carter had promised that the concept of human rights would be at the forefront of his foreign policy. This promise was repeated in his inaugural address when he declared, "Our commitment to human rights must be absolute." By human rights Carter meant the basic ideas of human freedom as outlined in the United Nations Declaration of Human Rights. For Carter, friends and enemies alike would be expected to uphold the highest standards in the treatment of their citizens.

ACADEMIC VOCABULARY
efficiency the ability to produce a desired result with little waste

THE IMPACT TODAY
Science and Technology
The Three Mile Island incident helped dampen interest in nuclear energy. Throughout the 1980s, 1990s, and early 2000s, the United States planned or built hardly any new nuclear power facilities.

Andrew Young at the UN
Andrew Young first rose to prominence during the civil rights movement in the 1950s and 1960s. *Why do you think Young's background helped prepare him to represent Carter's foreign policy?*

THE CAMP DAVID ACCORDS

The Camp David Accords were a major breakthrough in relations between Egypt and Israel, two countries that had fought several costly, bloody wars. Anwar el-Sadat, Jimmy Carter, and Menachem Begin (left to right) shake hands at the successful conclusion of their meeting at Camp David. Key parts of the accords declared that:

- Egypt and Israel, along with Jordan and Palestinian representatives, would agree to work to resolve questions about the Palestinians' future.
- Israel and Egypt would agree to work to negotiate a peace treaty.
- Egypt and Israel would agree to grant each other full recognition.

Soviet relations The Soviet Union was one target of President Carter's criticism about human rights violations. In a letter written to Soviet leader Leonid Brezhnev just days after taking office, Carter mentioned his concerns. Brezhnev's response politely but firmly declared that each side should stay out of the other's internal affairs.

In spite of disagreements over human rights, American and Soviet negotiators did conclude a treaty in 1979 known as **SALT II**. Talks on this treaty had begun at the end of SALT I, which you read about in Section 1. SALT II called for limits on certain kinds of nuclear weapons.

The Panama Canal treaties Another early Carter foreign-policy effort involved the Panama Canal. American control of the canal had been the source of conflict between the United States and Panama for some time. In 1977 Carter and Panama's leader reached an agreement by which Panama would take control of the canal by the end of 1999. The Senate narrowly approved the treaties Carter had negotiated. For many Americans, however, the loss of control of the canal represented a decline in American power.

Recognizing China In 1979 Carter took the final step in a process that had begun during the Nixon administration. He formally recognized the government of the Communist People's Republic of China. This move required the United States to formally end its official recognition of the Republic of China on Taiwan, which claimed to be the true Chinese government. Under Carter's action, however, the United States would officially recognize only one China—the Communist People's Republic.

The Camp David Accords Carter's greatest foreign-policy achievement centered on the long-standing conflict between Israel and Egypt. The two nations had fought frequently in recent decades. Fighting had occurred in 1967 and in the Yom Kippur War. In the aftermath of the 1973 war, Israel still occupied Egyptian territory on the Sinai Peninsula. Egypt still did not recognize Israel's right to exist. These were just some of the issues dividing the nations.

In 1978 Carter invited Egyptian president Anwar el-Sadat (AHN-wahr el-suh-DAHT) and Israeli prime minister Menachem Begin (men-AH-kem BAY-gin) to explore solutions to their bitter divisions. The meeting took place at Camp David, a presidential retreat located in Maryland. At the meeting, Carter painstakingly guided Sadat and Begin to a historic agreement. This came to be known as the **Camp David Accords**. For their efforts, Begin and Sadat were awarded the Nobel Peace Prize in 1979.

READING CHECK **Summarizing** What were the main highlights of Carter's foreign policy?

684 CHAPTER 21

International Crises

In his first years in office, Carter enjoyed some success and suffered through some difficulties. In 1979, however, a series of events occurred that seemed to overwhelm his presidency.

Soviets invade Afghanistan In 1978 the government of Afghanistan was toppled in a coup. The Communist leaders who took power were friendly to the Soviet Union. Yet this new pro-Soviet Afghan government was not stable. When it showed signs of crumbling in late 1979, the Soviets invaded. Their goal was to ensure continued Communist rule in Afghanistan.

The Soviet invasion of Afghanistan caused great anxiety within the United States. The attack not only threatened the U.S.–Soviet relationship. It also called into question Carter's ability to respond effectively to Soviet aggression. Carter's national security adviser summarized the problem in a memo to the president days after the invasion: "Soviet 'decisiveness'," he wrote, "will be contrasted with our restraint, which will no longer be labeled as prudent but increasingly as timid."

Several days after the invasion, Carter detailed the American response. It included the decision to block shipment of grain to the Soviet Union. In addition, Carter announced that the United States would not take part in the Olympics, set to take place in the Soviet Union in the summer of 1980.

Both the Olympic boycott and the grain embargo were unpopular with the public. To some they appeared to hurt the United States at least as much as they hurt the Soviet Union. As a result, Carter and the United States appeared weak.

Iranian hostage crisis While the Afghanistan crisis upset many Americans, it was not the major news story of the day. That story came from the country of Iran.

Early in 1979, a revolution in Iran had led to the overthrow of that country's long-time

---

COUNTERPOINTS

Resolving the Hostage Crisis

National security adviser Zbigniew Brzezinski (ZBIG-nyoo bruzh-IN-skee) focused on U.S. interests.

" [I]t is important that we get our people back. But [our] greater responsibility is to protect the honor and dignity of our country and its foreign policy interests. At some point that greater responsibility could become more important than the safety of our diplomats. I hope we never have to choose between the hostages and our nation's honor in the world, but... [we] must be prepared for that occurrence. "

Zbigniew Brzezinski, 1979

Negotiation and compromise were well-known trademarks of Secretary of State Cyrus Vance.

" The President and this nation will ultimately be judged by our restraint in the face of provocation, and on the safe return of our hostages. We have to keep looking for ways to reach Khomeini and peacefully resolve this. "

Cyrus Vance, 1979

SKILLS FOCUS | READING LIKE A HISTORIAN

Identifying Points of View When the Carter administration launched a military mission to rescue the hostages, Vance resigned his post. How do the quotes help you to understand this fact?

See **Skills Handbook**, pp. H28–H29

ruler, known as the shah. The shah had long enjoyed American support, but among his people he had built a reputation for brutal repression. After his overthrow, Iran came under the control of an Islamic religious leader known as the **Ayatollah Ruhollah Khomeini** (eye-uh-TOHL-uh roo-HAHL-uh koh-MAYN-ee). Khomeini preached a strongly anti-American message.

In October 1979 the American government allowed the shah to enter the United States to receive treatment for cancer. This action enraged many Iranians. On November 4 a mob attacked the American embassy in Tehran, Iran's capital. They captured several dozen American employees. It soon became clear that Iran's leaders supported this attack.

In the United States, the hostage-taking was greeted with outrage. Newscasts fueled American anger by showing nightly scenes of Iranian protesters burning American flags.

President Carter appeared powerless to end the Iranian hostage crisis. His efforts to negotiate the safe return of the hostages went nowhere. He then approved a military mission to rescue the hostages. This failed tragically when mechanical problems led to a helicopter crash that killed eight soldiers. The scenes of smoldering American wreckage in the Iranian desert hurt Carter's chances for re-election.

A crisis of confidence The hostage crisis dragged on throughout the presidential election year of 1980. To make matters worse for Carter, the events in Iran had disrupted the production of oil there. As a result, gasoline prices shot up in 1979. This helped drive up prices for many goods in the United States. Inflation soared. The economy struggled badly.

Carter was in serious trouble politically. Even he seemed to recognize the threat as he described the downcast mood of the country in a major speech.

HISTORY'S VOICES

"It is a crisis of confidence.

It is a crisis that strikes at the very heart and soul and spirit of our national will. We can see this crisis in the growing doubt about the meaning of our own lives and in the loss of a unity and purpose for our nation."

—Jimmy Carter, July 15, 1979

Carter's view of the mind-set of the nation was not incorrect. What he did not realize was that many voters held him responsible for this crisis of confidence.

READING CHECK Making Inferences Why did the events of 1979 and 1980 seem to overwhelm Carter's presidency?

SECTION 3 ASSESSMENT

HSS 11.9.6, 11.11.2, 11.11.6

Reviewing Ideas, Terms, and People

1. **a. Identify** What were the key domestic issues facing the Carter administration?
   b. Explain Explain how energy was at the center of so many of the challenges facing the United States in the late 1970s.
   c. Predict How successful do you think President Carter would be in his call for the American people to change their energy habits?

2. **a. Recall** What was the guiding principle behind Jimmy Carter's foreign policy?
   b. Draw Conclusions Why do you think the **Camp David Accords** are considered Carter's greatest foreign-policy success?
   c. Elaborate How did Carter's focus on human rights in foreign policy differ from the policy of realpolitik stressed by Nixon and Ford?

3. **a. Identify** Who was **Ayatollah Ruhollah Khomeini**?
   b. Make Generalizations How did the American people interpret Carter's responses to the crises of 1979–1980?

Critical Thinking

4. **Identifying the Main Idea** Copy the chart below and use information from the section to record details that support the main idea of the section.

FOCUS ON WRITING ELA W1.1

5. **Descriptive** Using information from the section, write a brief description of what you think Jimmy Carter was like as a president. Include information about how you think his style and personality helped and hurt him.

LANDMARK SUPREME COURT CASES
Constitutional Issue: Equal Protection

Regents of the University of California v. Bakke (1978)

Why It Matters Affirmative action programs have helped create opportunities for many minorities. However, favoring a minority applicant for a job or for a spot in graduate school may also mean that a qualified majority applicant will be turned down. *Bakke* was the first Supreme Court case to consider the constitutionality of what is called "reverse discrimination."

Background of the Case

A white male named Alan Bakke applied to the medical school of the University of California at Davis and was not accepted. The school had a special program that set aside a certain number of spots for minority applicants. Under this program, some minority students with lower qualifications than Bakke were admitted to the school. Bakke sued, and the Supreme Court of California agreed that it was unconstitutional to discriminate in favor of the minority applicants. The university appealed to the Supreme Court.

The Decision

In a 5–4 ruling, the Court found that the University's "set-aside" program was unconstitutional because it totally excluded white applicants from consideration for certain spots. The Court ordered Bakke admitted to the university. The Court also held that the school could consider race as one factor in future admissions decisions.

Bakke did not resolve the question of just what role affirmative action could play in university admissions. This means that the *Bakke* decision did not offer clear guidance on how affirmative action could properly be used. However, the opinion did help focus national attention on this difficult question.

THE IMPACT TODAY Affirmative action programs such as those that led to the *Bakke* case have played a part in increasing diversity in many graduate school programs, including the law school at the University of Michigan. (The photo above is from a class at that university.) The question of just where the line lies between reasonable affirmative action and improper reverse discrimination continues to stir controversy in the United States.

CRITICAL THINKING
go.hrw.com
Research Online
Keyword: SS Court

1. **Analyze the Impact** Using the keyword above, read about the Supreme Court's decision in *Sweatt v. Painter* (1950). How did the issues in *Sweatt* differ from the issues in *Bakke*? What changes had taken place in the country between the decisions?

2. **You Be the Judge** After *Bakke*, the University of Michigan Law School began giving extra consideration in the admissions process to African Americans, Hispanic Americans, and Native Americans. These applicants therefore had a greater chance of admission than students with similar qualifications from other groups. Is this policy constitutional? Write a short paragraph explaining your answer.

CHAPTER 21 DOCUMENT-BASED INVESTIGATION

The Watergate Crisis

HSS 11.11.4

Historical Context The documents below provide information about taped conversations in the White House, which became an important part of the Watergate investigation.

Task Examine the documents and answer the questions that follow. Then write an essay on the proposed topic. Use facts from the documents and from the chapter to support the position you take in your thesis statement.

DOCUMENT 1

The Gallup Organization is a polling group. One of the statistics they regularly track is a president's job-approval rating—the percentage of people who agree with the president's actions and decisions. This graph shows changes in job-approval ratings for President Nixon during the Watergate crisis.

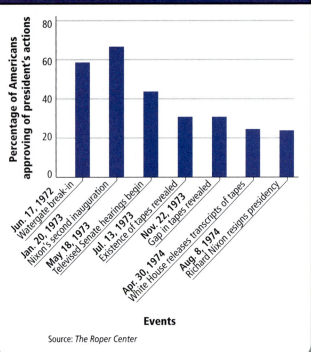

Source: *The Roper Center*

DOCUMENT 2

On April 29, 1974, President Nixon addressed the nation. He talked about the subpoena demanding additional transcripts for tape recordings made in the White House and his decision to obey the subpoena.

"Ever since the existence of the White House taping system was first made known last summer, I have tried vigorously to guard the privacy of the tapes. I have been well aware that my effort to protect the confidentiality of Presidential conversations has heightened the sense of mystery about Watergate and, in fact, has caused increased suspicions of the President. Many people assume that the tapes must incriminate the President, or that otherwise, he would not insist on their privacy.

"But the problem I confronted was this: Unless a President can protect the privacy of the advice he gets, he cannot get the advice he needs . . .

I want there to be no question remaining about the fact that the President has nothing to hide in this matter . . ."

I realize that these transcripts will provide grist for many sensational stories in the press. Parts will seem to be contradictory with one another, and parts will be in conflict with some of the testimony given in the Senate Watergate committee hearings . . .

In giving you these records—blemishes and all—I am placing my trust in the basic fairness of the American people."

688 CHAPTER 21

DOCUMENT 3

Cartoonist Herbert Block, known as Herblock, created many cartoons commenting on Nixon's presidency and the Watergate crisis. This cartoon ran in newspapers on May 24, 1974.

From *Herblock: A Cartoonist's Life* (Times Books, 1998)

DOCUMENT 4

In this transcript of one of the White House tapes, President Richard Nixon talks with White House Chief of Staff H. R. Haldeman. The two men discuss the FBI investigation, specifically mentioning acting FBI director L. Patrick Gray and assistant director Mark Felt. This exchange, which took place on June 23, 1972, is known as the Smoking Gun conversation.

> *Haldeman:* Okay—that's fine. Now, on the investigation, you know, the Democratic break-in thing, we're back to the—in the, the problem area because the FBI is not under control... and... their investigation is now leading into some productive areas... And, and it goes in some directions we don't want it to go... [T]he way to handle this now is for us to have [Deputy Director of the CIA Vernon A.] Walters call Pat Gray and just say, "Stay... out of this... this is ah, business here we don't want you to go any further on it." That's not an unusual development...
>
> *President:* Um huh.
>
> *Haldeman:* ...and, uh, that would take care of it.
>
> *President:* What about Pat Gray...?
>
> *Haldeman:* He'll call Mark Felt in... and say, "We've got a signal from across the river to, to put the hold on this." And that will fit rather well because the FBI agents who are working the case, at this point, feel that's what it is. This is CIA.

Skills Focus — READING LIKE A HISTORIAN

ELA Analysis CS1, HI1

1. **a. Identify** Refer to Document 1. What event corresponds to Nixon's lowest job-approval rating?
   b. Interpret How did developments in Watergate affect public opinion regarding President Nixon?

2. **a. Identify** Refer to Document 2. Why does the president say he is releasing the transcripts?
   b. Evaluate Why do you think the president may have decided to make this speech to the American people?

3. **a. Identify** Refer to Document 3. What is shown in the cartoon?
   b. Elaborate What is the cartoonist's opinion of Nixon?

4. **a. Identify** Refer to Document 4. Why does Haldeman refer to the break-in as a "problem area"?
   b. Explain How does the president respond to Haldeman's suggestion to end the FBI investigation?
   c. Analyze Why was this called the Smoking Gun conversation?

5. **Document-Based Essay** Consider the question below and form a thesis statement. Using examples from Documents 1, 2, 3, and 4, create an outline and write a short essay supporting your position.
   What role did the White House tapes play in the Watergate crisis?

   See **Skills Handbook**, pp. H17, H28–H29, H31

A SEARCH FOR ORDER

CHAPTER 21 Chapter Review

Visual Summary: A Search for Order

The Search for Order 1968–1980

Nixon's Presidency
- Conservative policies included New Federalism.
- Liberal policies included support for environment and wage and price controls.
- Sought détente with the Soviets, dialogue with Chinese.
- Shuttle diplomacy helped end Yom Kippur War and oil embargo.
- Moon landing a highlight.

Watergate and Ford
- Scandal with roots in the 1972 presidential campaign haunted Nixon.
- Nixon eventually forced to resign for lying and covering up White House crime.
- Ford became president, but lost support for pardoning Nixon.

Carter's Presidency
- Elected for honesty and integrity.
- Focused on saving energy.
- Built foreign policy around human rights.
- Helped secure Camp David Accords.
- Response to Soviet actions in Afghanistan and Iran hostage crisis seen as weak.

Reviewing Key Terms and People

Complete each sentence by filling the blank with the correct term or person.

1. Nixon at first refused to hand over the Watergate tapes, but he did offer to provide a _____.
2. Henry Kissinger practiced something called _____ rather than following broad rules for the conduct of foreign policy.
3. Carter helped bring about the _____ between Israel and Egypt.
4. The nation watched in wonder as _____ fulfilled its mission to the moon.
5. During the _____ Nixon ordered the firing of the special prosecutor.
6. The organization called _____ organized an oil embargo against the United States.
7. _____ holds that a president must be able to keep official conversations and meetings private.
8. Following the overthrow of the shah, _____ became the leader of Iran.
9. During Nixon's administration, the United States and the Soviets reached an agreement limiting nuclear weapons known as _____.
10. The improvement in relations between the United States and the Soviet Union in the early 1970s was known as _____.

Comprehension and Critical Thinking

SECTION 1 *(pp. 666–673)* HSS 11.9.6, 11.11.2, 11.11.5

11. **a. Describe** What was the significance of President Nixon's trip to the People's Republic of China in 1972?

   b. Contrast In what ways did Nixon's policies while president differ from some of his previously stated positions?

690 CHAPTER 21

History's Impact video program
Review the video to answer the closing question: Why is freedom of the press a crucial part of a democratic society?

c. Elaborate What do you think were the reasons for Nixon's willingness to pursue goals and programs that varied greatly from his past conservative beliefs?

SECTION 2 *(pp. 675–680)* HSS 11.11.4

12. a. Recall What was the purpose of the break-in at the Watergate Hotel?

b. Summarize How would you summarize the conflict between Nixon and those investigating the Watergate scandal?

c. Predict Do you think Nixon could have survived had he admitted early in the scandal that his office had been involved in the Watergate break-in? Explain.

SECTION 3 *(pp. 681–686)* HSS 11.9.6, 11.11.2, 11.11.6

13. a. Describe What qualities did Jimmy Carter use to win public support in the election of 1976?

b. Make Generalizations How did Carter come to be regarded by the public by the end of his term?

c. Predict How do you think Carter's opponents will attack his record in the election of 1980?

Using the Internet

go.hrw.com
Practice Online
Keyword: SE7 CH21

14. The Iran hostage crisis that began in 1979 caused public outrage—and deep concern about the waning prestige of the United States. Using the keyword above, do research to learn more about the hostage crisis. Then create a time line and brief report on its effects on the presidential election of 1980.

Analyzing Primary Sources HSS HR4

Reading Like a Historian This picture shows Jimmy Carter, his wife Rosalynn, and daughter Amy walking to the White House on the day of his inauguration.

15. Describe How did Carter's actions differ from those of presidents who came before him?

16. Make Inferences What kind of message do you think Carter tried to send through his decision to walk?

Critical Reading ELA R2.2

Read the passage in Section 2 that begins with the heading "The Saturday night massacre." Then answer the questions that follow.

17. Nixon sought to have the special prosecutor fired because

A. he revealed information about the Watergate tapes.

B. he sought to obtain the tapes in spite of Nixon's refusal to hand them over.

C. he was not doing enough to get to the bottom of the Watergate scandal.

D. he was thought to be part of the cover-up.

18. Which of the following most closely represents Nixon's argument against handing over the tapes?

A. The tapes included no relevant information.

B. He was afraid the tapes would prove his guilt.

C. He believed it was his legal right as president to keep official conversations private.

D. He did not believe that the Constitution permitted the creation of a special prosecutor.

FOCUS ON WRITING ELA W1.1, 1.3

Expository Writing *Expository writing gives information, explains why or how, or defines a process. To practice expository writing, complete the assignment below.*

Writing Topic Ford's Pardon of Nixon

19. Assignment Based on what you have read in this chapter, write a paragraph that describes the public's reaction to President Ford's pardon of Richard Nixon.

CHAPTER 22
1980–1992
A Conservative ERA

THE BIG PICTURE Ronald Reagan won the presidency in 1980 by appealing to a discontented electorate with the promise to return to a simpler time and conservative values. Reagan and his successor, George H. W. Bush, presided over the end of the Cold War and huge changes in economic and social policy.

California Standards

History-Social Science

11.8 Students analyze the economic boom and social transformation of post-World War II America.

11.9 Students analyze U.S. foreign policy since World War II.

11.11 Students analyze the major social problems and domestic policy issues in contemporary American society.

Skills FOCUS   READING LIKE A HISTORIAN

Reagan loved a crowd, and the crowds loved him. His vitality, gentle humor, and dynamic speaking style charmed even his opponents. In his journey from actor to president, Reagan used all his skills to reach out to voters and persuade America to move in a new direction. **Interpreting Visuals** What can you infer about Reagan's personality from this photograph?

See **Skills Handbook**, p. H30

U.S.

September 1981 Sandra Day O'Connor becomes first female U.S. Supreme Court Justice.

1980

World

1980 Lech Walesa's Solidarity trade union leads protests in Poland.

History's Impact video program
Watch the video to understand the impact of the collapse of the Berlin Wall.

1982 Deepest U.S. recession since the Great Depression begins.

October 1983 Suicide bombers attack U.S. peacekeepers in Lebanon, killing 241.

March 1985 Mikhail Gorbachev becomes leader of the Soviet Union.

November 1985 Reagan and Gorbachev meet in the first of their arms reduction summits.

January 1989 George H. W. Bush becomes president.

June 1989 China crushes pro-democracy protests in Tiananmen Square.

November 1989 Berlin Wall falls as protests bring down Communist regimes in Eastern Europe.

February 1991 In First Gulf War, U.S.-led coalition ousts Iraq from Kuwait.

SECTION 1
Reagan's First Term

BEFORE YOU READ

MAIN IDEA
In 1980 Americans voted for a new approach to governing by electing Ronald Reagan, who powerfully promoted a conservative agenda.

READING FOCUS
1. As the 1980 presidential election approached, why was America a nation ready for change?
2. What was the Reagan revolution, and who supported it?
3. What were the key ideas of Reagan's economic plan, and what were its effects?

KEY TERMS AND PEOPLE
Ronald Reagan
New Right
Jerry Falwell
Nancy Reagan
David A. Stockman
supply-side economics
budget deficit

HSS 11.9.3 Trace the geopolitical consequences of the Cold War and containment policy.
HSS 11.9.5 Analyze the role of the Reagan administration and other factors in the victory of the West in the Cold War.
HSS 11.11.2 Discuss the significant domestic policy speeches of Reagan (e.g., with regard to education, civil rights, economic policy, environmental policy).

"A City UPON A HILL"

▼ Reagan's ease in front of an audience and gifted speaking style gave him wide appeal.

THE INSIDE STORY

What event marked the rise of the Reagan revolution?
As California governor **Ronald Reagan** faced an audience in Washington, D.C., on January 25, 1974, he was witnessing something new. It was the first-ever Conservative Political Action Conference. Reagan was among friends.

Modern conservative politics had been born in defeat. Senator Barry Goldwater of Arizona, whom Reagan had supported, lost the 1964 presidential race in spectacular fashion. Richard Nixon had brought some conservative credentials into office when he was elected president in 1968, but his administration had been wracked with scandals. By 1974 conservatives were looking for someone to lead them.

Ronald Wilson Reagan was the man they were looking for. As he spoke to the crowd, Reagan laid out themes that would become familiar to the nation in the years ahead. He spoke of the need for greater military strength. He criticized the size and inefficiency of government. He praised the accomplishments of American business and the wonder of the free enterprise system.

Drawing on his gift at using stories to illustrate his points, Reagan reached back into American history to a sermon given in 1630 by John Winthrop, the first governor of Massachusetts Bay Colony. He reminded his listeners that Winthrop had compared the colony to "a city upon a hill" with "the eyes of all people upon us." Driven by hope and a love of freedom, America was Reagan's vision of that "city upon a hill."

Reagan's day in the national spotlight was still years away. Yet on that January day in 1974, it was possible to see it coming.

694 CHAPTER 22

A Nation Ready for Change

When Ronald Reagan declared in a 1974 speech that "We are not a sick society," he sounded a theme that would carry him throughout his political career. When he proclaimed that "we are today, the last best hope of man on earth," he set a positive tone that would define his two-term presidency.

America in low spirits The scene was set for change as the 1980 presidential election approached. Opinion polls showed a lack of confidence in government. Political observers said America had fallen into a state of malaise, a depressed or uneasy mood. Indeed, there were plenty of reasons to be uneasy.

The turbulence of the 1960s had been followed by the Watergate scandal. Under President Carter, the United States seemed powerless as the Soviets invaded Afghanistan and Iranian militants took American embassy workers hostage. At home, Americans waited in long gasoline lines and wondered why foreign forces had so much power over their lives.

President Carter responded to the growing public discontent in a television speech on July 15, 1979. He said the nation faced a "crisis of confidence." While accepting a large dose of blame, he urged citizens to control their appetite for consumer goods to ease inflation and reduce reliance on foreign oil. Critics accused Carter of blaming Americans instead of fixing the problems. The president's appeal became known as the malaise speech.

Beneath the malaise, however, a political movement was gathering force during the 1970s. Its roots lay deeper than any temporary anger over crises such as gas lines and the hostage situation. The growing conservative movement opposed liberal social and racial policies, including abortion rights, forced busing to achieve school desegregation, welfare, and affirmative action. This opposition, combined with general discontent with Carter, spelled electoral trouble for the president.

The 1980 election Projecting energy and youth at age 69, Republican presidential nominee Ronald Reagan tried to turn voters' attention away from the nation's problems. He said the country needed to return to a simpler time of low taxes, smaller government, a stronger military, and conservative moral values. His message focused on five words: "family, work, neighborhood, peace, and freedom."

ACADEMIC VOCABULARY
welfare public assistance to the needy

THE ELECTION OF 1980

Candidate	Political Affiliation	Electoral Votes	Popular Vote
Ronald W. Reagan	Republican	489	51.6%
James E. Carter	Democratic	49	41.7%
John Anderson	Independent	0	6.7%

GEOGRAPHY SKILLS INTERPRETING MAPS

1. **Region** What does this map show you about Americans' dissatisfaction with President Carter?
2. **Location** How many states did Carter carry in the election?

See **Skills Handbook**, p. H21

A CONSERVATIVE ERA

In a debate with Carter, Reagan asked, "Are you better off today than you were four years ago?" For many, struggling with 13 percent inflation, high taxes, and a seemingly powerless government, the answer was "No."

Despite the entrance of Republican representative John Anderson as a third-party candidate, Reagan and his running mate, George H. W. Bush, won in a landslide of electoral votes. Republicans also won control of the Senate for the first time since 1955. In what seemed to be a final insult to Carter, the American hostages in Iran were released just hours after Reagan was sworn in as president.

READING CHECK **Identifying Cause and Effect** What factors led to Carter's downfall in the election of 1980?

The Reagan Revolution

One word will forever be linked to the name of Ronald Wilson Reagan: optimism. By all accounts—even those of his political opponents—Reagan had an infectiously cheerful outlook on life and the world. Yet beneath his relaxed manner, Reagan possessed a deep determination to reshape not only the United States, but also the world.

From actor to governor During his career as a modestly successful movie actor, Reagan was a union leader and an active member of the Democratic Party. During the 1950s as spokesperson for the General Electric Company, he sharpened his public-speaking skills and became a champion of free enterprise. He grew to be increasingly at odds with Democratic policies, and in 1962 he found his home in the Republican Party.

Reagan adopted the conservative cause with zest. In a 1964 speech urging support for Senator Goldwater, Reagan delivered a powerful critique of liberal government, from the New Deal to the Great Society. On taxes, he warned: "Today, 37 cents out of every dollar earned in this country is the tax collector's share." Government, he declared, "does nothing as well or as economically as the private sector of the economy." He warned against appeasing the Soviets, calling communism "the most dangerous enemy that has ever faced mankind."

American Civil Liberty

Smaller Government

In his inaugural address in 1981 Ronald Reagan said, "All of us need to be reminded that the federal government did not create the states; the states created the federal government." With these words, Reagan introduced his goal of reducing the power of the federal government.

Reagan believed that federal spending was too high and that complex laws intruded on free enterprise and personal freedoms. "Our citizens feel they have lost control of even the most basic decisions made about the essential services of government, such as schools, welfare, roads, and even garbage collection," he said. He slashed price controls and regulations.

Reagan hoped to expand the economic choices available to Americans by cutting taxes and reducing government spending. During his presidency, taxes were cut, but the bureaucracy increased in size and spending skyrocketed. By the time Reagan left office, the federal government was not only bigger but it was also unable to pay for itself without massive borrowing.

Drawing Conclusions How did Ronald Reagan hope to increase liberty for Americans?

"LEAVE THE FACADES—IT'LL BE JUST LIKE HOLLYWOOD." © 1981 HERBLOCK IN *THE WASHINGTON POST*. COURTESY THE HERBLOCK FOUNDATION

On the strength of the speech, California Republicans recruited him to run for governor in 1966. Reagan easily defeated the incumbent Democrat, Edmund "Pat" Brown.

As governor, Reagan had trouble meeting his goals for cutting the size of government. He expressed frustration with the job of controlling a large bureaucracy. After serving two terms, Reagan set his sights on a bigger job. "I feel I'm better qualified to be president than governor," he told a supporter.

Reagan would have to wait. He lost the Republican presidential nomination twice, to Richard Nixon in 1968 and to Gerald Ford in 1976. By 1980, however, Reagan had a strong and growing base of support.

Reagan's conservative support Ronald Reagan's journey from New Deal Democrat to conservative Republican made him a hero of a growing movement called the **New Right**. This was a coalition of conservative media commentators, think tanks, and grassroots Christian groups. Many of the groups had been formed to oppose specific liberal causes, such as the abortion rights gained under *Roe* v. *Wade*.

The New Right advocated major reversals in liberal government, economic, and social policies. The movement endorsed school prayer, deregulation, lower taxes, a smaller government, a stronger military, and the teaching of a Bible-based account of human creation. It opposed gun control, abortion, homosexual rights, school busing to achieve desegregation, the Equal Rights Amendment, affirmative action, and nuclear disarmament.

The New Right grew in influence with the rise of televangelism, or TV ministries led by evangelical Christians. One televangelist leader of the New Right, the Rev. **Jerry Falwell**, founded a political activist organization called Moral Majority in 1979. The name came from the group's belief that a majority of Americans agreed with conservative moral values.

Reagan gave the New Right an eloquent and persuasive voice. He drew many Americans to his side, including a large number of Democrats. These so-called Reagan Democrats shifted their allegiance from the Democratic Party in the elections of 1980 and 1984. They voted for Reagan to express their frustration with the Democratic Party's stands on social and racial issues and on national security.

FACES OF HISTORY
Ronald REAGAN
1911–2004

Ronald Reagan earned the nickname the Great Communicator because of his speaking ability and sharp wit. During the 1980 election, after a debate with Jimmy Carter, a reporter asked Reagan if he had been nervous being on stage with the president.

"No, not at all," Reagan replied. Referring to his career as an actor, he added, "I've been on the stage with [acting legend] John Wayne."

Reagan entered politics after a long career in Hollywood. As governor of California and president, Reagan powerfully articulated conservatives' desires to reshape the government, reverse Great Society reforms, and battle communism. As the USSR began to reform, Reagan worked with Soviet leaders, helping to end the Cold War.

Explain Why was Reagan known as the Great Communicator?

A powerful personality The stage presence Reagan developed as an actor served him well in politics. On the campaign trail he became known as the Great Communicator. As president he gained the nickname the Great Persuader. To gain support for his programs, he threw his energies and charm into winning over conservative southern and western Democrats in Congress. If that didn't work, he spoke directly to voters through skillful television addresses. The newsmagazine *Time* referred to him as "the velvet steamroller."

Perhaps Reagan's greatest ally was his wife, **Nancy Reagan**, a former actor. She played a major role in running of the White House. She advised her husband on policy issues and fiercely protected his interests. As First Lady, she headed a "Just Say No" antidrug campaign.

Reagan's presidential agenda Reagan's chief goals were largely those of the New Right. He pledged to reduce the federal bureaucracy, deregulate certain industries, cut taxes, increase the defense budget, take a hard line with the Soviet Union, and appoint conservative judges to the federal judiciary.

In his first few months, the president got much of what he wanted. Congress passed a tax cut, eliminated some social programs, reduced the budgets of many federal agencies, and passed the largest-ever peacetime increase in

ACADEMIC VOCABULARY
advocate support, endorse

the defense budget. As head of the executive branch, Reagan could carry out some of his reforms without going to Congress. For example, he instructed federal agencies to roll back regulations on many industries. With each step toward achieving his agenda, Reagan seemed to be answering those who had felt the nation could no longer be governed effectively.

Reagan's image only grew stronger when he survived an assassination attempt in 1981. With a bullet in his left lung, the 70-year-old president kept his sense of humor. "Honey," he told the First Lady, "I forgot to duck." Reagan's positive outlook in the face of adversity created goodwill that helped him achieve his agenda.

Reagan's easygoing manner did not prevent him from taking decisive action. In August 1981 Reagan faced a strike by the nation's air traffic controllers. As federal employees, the 13,000 members of the Professional Air Traffic Controllers' Organization (PATCO) were forbidden to strike. Reagan warned them—and then he fired them all. Despite the resulting confusion at airports, the public generally approved of the president's uncompromising actions.

READING CHECK **Summarizing** How did Reagan want to change the federal government?

Reaganomics
- Reaganomics: Reagan's plan for tax and spending cuts
- supply-side economics: theory that breaks for businesses will increase supply of goods and services, aiding the economy

Below, Reagan meets with budget director David A. Stockman.

Reagan's Economic Plan

Reagan's blueprint for remaking government required a new economic plan. It was nicknamed Reaganomics. The plan had two goals: 1) reduce taxes to stimulate economic growth, and 2) cut the federal budget. Reagan appointed a controversial young budget director, **David A. Stockman**, to sell his plan to a skeptical Congress. Stockman's job was to get Congress to put the Reagan plan into effect in 40 days.

Supply-side economics Reaganomics was based on an economic theory known as **supply-side economics**. According to that theory, tax cuts and business incentives stimulate investment. Investment encourages economic growth. A growing economy, in turn, results in an increased supply of goods and services. Supply-side theory appealed to conservatives, who supported free enterprise and minimal government regulation.

Stockman pressed Congress for tax cuts for upper-income Americans and for businesses. Supply-side supporters believed that the tax relief would produce a series of benefits. Individuals would invest their tax savings. Businesses would use investment funds to expand and hire more workers. Expanding businesses would generate more tax revenue, allowing the government to eliminate any budget deficit. A **budget deficit** is the amount by which government spending for a year exceeds government income.

Stockman succeeded in getting Congress to pass numerous major components of Reaganomics. During Reagan's first six years as president, tax rates on the wealthiest Americans dropped from 70 percent of their income to 28 percent. Critics claimed that the tax breaks simply made the rich richer. They predicted that little of the new wealth would "trickle down" to the working class, as Reaganomics predicted. Critics also warned that tax cuts, combined with increases in military spending, would force drive the federal deficit higher, increasing the national debt.

Reagan's own vice president, George H. W. Bush, had questioned the plan to cut taxes and boost military spending at the same time. Back in 1980, when Bush was competing with Reagan for the Republican nomination, he had labeled Reagan's plan "voodoo economics."

Recession and recovery Events did not go quite according to Reagan's plan. In 1981 and 1982, the nation suffered the worst recession since the Great Depression. Unemployment rose, and government revenues plunged. Meanwhile, federal spending soared, largely because of huge defense increases. With less tax money to pay for the increased government spending, the federal budget deficit skyrocketed. Stockman told a magazine that "None of us really understands what's going on with all these numbers." He left the administration and later wrote a critique of Reaganomics.

The actions of the Federal Reserve Board contributed to the recession. The Federal Reserve had steadily raised interest rates from 1979 to 1982 in an effort to reduce inflation. Higher interest rates made it more expensive for businesses to borrow money to expand.

By 1983, with inflation at a low 4 percent, the Federal Reserve had reduced interest rates. The collapse of OPEC's ability to set high oil prices also helped lower inflation. The economy began to grow at a brisk pace. Economic growth was uneven, however, and largely favored the wealthy. Unemployment eased. Nevertheless, federal revenues lagged far behind spending. Faced with a severe budget crisis, Congress put the brakes on federal spending. In 1985 it passed the Balanced Budget and Emergency Deficit Control Act, or the Gramm-Rudman-Hollings Act. The measure required mandatory budget cuts to curb the deficit.

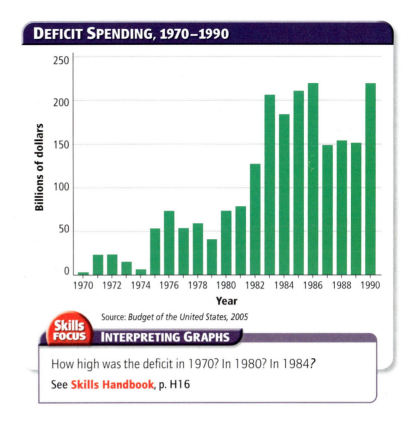

DEFICIT SPENDING, 1970–1990

Source: Budget of the United States, 2005

Skills Focus: INTERPRETING GRAPHS

How high was the deficit in 1970? In 1980? In 1984?
See **Skills Handbook**, p. H16

READING CHECK **Summarizing** What were the key elements of Reaganomics?

SECTION 1 ASSESSMENT

HSS 11.9.3, 11.9.5, 11.11.2

go.hrw.com
Online Quiz
Keyword: SE7 HP22

Reviewing Ideas, Terms, and People

1. **a. Recall** Why was America said to be in a state of malaise in the late 1970s?
   b. Make Inferences What do you think Carter was trying to accomplish in his malaise speech, and why did it backfire?
   c. Rate What made Reagan's message so effective among voters?

2. **a. Recall** What types of groups and individuals supported Reagan's rise to the presidency?
   b. Analyze What skills earned Reagan his nicknames the Great Communicator, the Great Persuader, and the Velvet Steamroller?
   c. Evaluate How did conservative ideas represent a change from the recent past?

3. **a. Define** Write a brief definition for each of the following terms: **Reaganomics**, **supply-side economics**
   b. Contrast How did the assumptions of Reaganomics differ from the outcomes?

   c. Predict What effect would the Gramm-Rudman-Hollings bill have on funding of federal programs?

Critical Thinking

4. **Identifying the Main Idea** Copy the web diagram below and use information from the section to show what types of changes conservatives wanted to make.

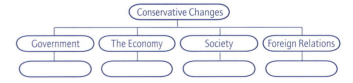

FOCUS ON SPEAKING ELA W1.1

5. **Expository** President Reagan communicated strong ideas to the American public. Choose one of his ideas and write a brief speech explaining it, using facts to support your account.

A CONSERVATIVE ERA

LANDMARK SUPREME COURT CASES
Constitutional Issue: Search and Seizure

New Jersey v. T.L.O. (1985)

Why It Matters Under the Fourth Amendment, police must have probable cause before they can conduct a search. In this case, the Supreme Court ruled that school officials may search a student without violating the Fourth Amendment if there is reasonable suspicion that the student has broken the law or a specific school rule.

Background of the Case

In 1980 a New Jersey high school student whose initials were T.L.O. was accused of smoking in the school bathroom. When T.L.O. claimed that she did not smoke, the assistant principal looked in her purse and found cigarettes. Then he noticed a package of rolling papers. Searching further he found marijuana and letters indicating that T.L.O. was selling drugs. T.L.O. later admitted to selling marijuana, and the State of New Jersey brought delinquency charges against her. She was sentenced to one year of probation. T.L.O. appealed her conviction, arguing that there was no probable cause to search her purse. She asked for a new trial at which the evidence from her purse could not be used against her.

The Decision

The Supreme Court ruled that the Fourth Amendment's prohibition on unreasonable searches and seizures does apply to searches conducted by public school officials. In addition, schoolchildren do have legitimate expectations of privacy, and their belongings may not be searched unreasonably. However, school officials are not required to follow the same standards as police. School officials need only reasonable grounds for *suspecting* that the search will turn up evidence that the student has violated school rules. The search must be conducted in ways that are reasonably related to the goal of the search. Judged by this standard, the search of T.L.O.'s purse was reasonable and did not violate the Constitution.

THE IMPACT TODAY Based on the Fourth Amendment arguments used in the *T.L.O.* case, the Supreme Court has issued rulings permitting school officials to conduct random screenings for weapons using metal detectors (above) and to conduct random drug testings of students wishing to participate in extracurricular sports and clubs. Many school boards are developing guidelines for how to interpret and carry out the Court's rulings on these controversial topics.

CRITICAL THINKING
go.hrw.com
Research Online
Keyword: SS Court

1. **Analyze the Impact** Using the keyword above, read about the 1961 decision in *Mapp* v. *Ohio*. In what ways was the reasoning in *Mapp* important to the decision in *New Jersey* v. *T.L.O.*?
2. **You Be the Judge** Based on *New Jersey* v. *T.L.O.*, should a school be allowed to require student athletes to submit to random drug testing, or does that policy violate the reasonable search provision of the Fourth Amendment? Explain your answer in a short paragraph.

SECTION 2
Reagan's Foreign Policy

BEFORE YOU READ

MAIN IDEA
President Reagan took a hard line against communism around the world.

READING FOCUS
1. How did President Reagan help to bring about the end of the Cold War?
2. What foreign trouble spots persisted during Reagan's presidency?
3. How did the Iran-Contra Affair undermine the president?

KEY TERMS AND PEOPLE
Strategic Defense Initiative
Lech Walesa
Solidarity
Mikhail Gorbachev
INF Treaty
apartheid
Iran-Contra affair
Oliver North

HSS 11.8.4 Analyze new federal government spending on defense, welfare, interest on the national debt, and federal and state spending on education, including the California Master Plan.

HSS 11.9.5 Analyze the role of the Reagan administration and other factors in the victory of the West in the Cold War.

Can simple words knock down a cement wall? For the United States and its allies in the West, the Berlin Wall had long been a symbol of the harsh reality of life in the Soviet empire. The massive wall dividing Communist East Berlin from the free West told a stark tale of two systems. On one side, citizens freely approached the wall and turned its entire length into an exuberant canvas of colorfully painted designs and slogans. On the other, armed guards and barriers kept citizens away for fear that they might escape to freedom in the West.

In 1987, some 25 years after the Berlin Wall was constructed, Ronald Reagan gave a speech at a famous Berlin Wall landmark known as the Brandenburg Gate. Reagan's speech went out not only to the people of West Berlin, whom he addressed directly, but also to the people in East Berlin. Loudspeakers carried his words into the air and over the wall.

President Reagan's message was clear and simple. He called out the name of the Soviet leader.

"Mr. Gorbachev, open this gate. Mr. Gorbachev—Mr. Gorbachev, tear down this wall!"

The message of defiance and confrontation would characterize Reagan's hard-line Cold War stance throughout his first term. Gorbachev, for his part, did not respond immediately to Reagan's demand in Berlin. But in time, the Soviet leader indeed would have to answer.

"Mr. Gorbachev, Tear Down This Wall!"

▶ In West Berlin, citizens exercised freedom of expression on their side of the Berlin Wall.

A CONSERVATIVE ERA **701**

Reagan and the Cold War

Staunch opposition to communism was a bedrock principle that shaped Ronald Reagan's political life. Yet as president, Reagan joined in a complex relationship with a new Soviet leader to help end the 40-year Cold War.

The "Evil Empire"
President Reagan rejected the policies of containment and détente pursued by previous presidents. He did not want to accommodate communism. He wanted to destroy it. He used thundering language to condemn the Soviet Union as "the focus of evil in the modern world."

HISTORY'S VOICES

> "I urge you to beware the temptation ... to ignore the facts of history and the aggressive impulses of an evil empire, to simply call the arms race a giant misunderstanding and thereby remove yourself from the struggle between right and wrong and good and evil."
>
> —President Ronald Reagan, "Evil Empire" speech, March 8, 1983

ACADEMIC VOCABULARY
initiate begin, launch, take the first step

Reagan's strong position worsened relations with the Soviets during his first term. But it also won considerable praise. He forged bonds with like-minded foreign leaders, including conservative British prime minister Margaret Thatcher and Polish-born Pope John Paul II. Still, critics viewed Reagan's approach as reckless. At a time when the two superpowers had their fingers on the nuclear trigger, some people feared he would set off World War III.

Military spending soars
Urging "peace with strength," Reagan obtained massive increases in defense spending. Between 1981 and 1985 the Pentagon budget grew from about $150 billion to some $250 billion.

Much of the new spending went to nuclear weapons. In 1981 the president unveiled a plan to add thousands of new nuclear warheads. Two years later, the U.S. military installed new nuclear missiles in Europe. The presence of new weapons aimed at Soviet cities angered the USSR. It ended arms control talks and boycotted the 1984 Olympic Games in Los Angeles.

In 1983 Reagan initiated the creation of a new defensive weapon: a shield in space to protect the United States against incoming Soviet missiles. Reagan put all his persuasive skills to work to promote the concept, named the **Strategic Defense Initiative** (SDI).

Opponents, including many scientists, scoffed at SDI, saying it would be too expensive and would not work. They nicknamed it Star Wars, after the popular science-fiction

Reagan's Defense Buildup

This cartoon, like many critics, charged that Reagan's massive military spending came at the expense of other valuable programs.

DEFENSE SPENDING, 1980–1988

Source: Budget of the United States Government, 2005

SKILLS FOCUS: INTERPRETING GRAPHS

Compare defense spending in 1980, shortly before Reagan took office, with that near the end of his presidency in 1988.

See **Skills Handbook**, pp. H16

movie. The Soviets viewed SDI as an offensive weapon rather than a defensive one, saying it would allow the United States to launch a first strike without fear of retaliation.

Reagan hoped SDI would ease the growing pressures for disarmament. Across the United States and Europe, hundreds of thousands of supporters of a nuclear freeze—a halt in production of all atomic weapons—marched in massive demonstrations.

"I would agree to freeze if only we could freeze the Soviets' global desires," Reagan said. Yet increasingly, the Soviet Communists were less concerned with global conquest than with their own political survival.

A weakened Soviet Union The long rule of Leonid Brezhnev, from 1964 to 1982, saw the USSR rise to the height of its power and then begin to decline. By the late 1970s, the Soviet economy was shrinking. Industrial and farm production, population growth, education, medical care, and other indicators of prosperity fell sharply. A country rich in farmland became an importer of food. Government corruption was rampant.

Soviet weakness became strikingly clear in 1980 when the USSR failed to contain a dramatic series of events in Poland. Under the leadership of an electrician named **Lech Walesa**, some 17,000 workers in the city of Gdansk locked themselves in a factory to protest steep rises in food prices. The daring move riveted the world. The strikes spread, finally forcing the Soviet-backed government to legalize independent trade unions. Walesa was elected to lead a new, independent union called **Solidarity**. More than a union, Solidarity was a freedom movement.

U.S.-Soviet relations warm The death of Leonid Brezhnev and two other Soviet leaders in quick succession brought a visionary new leader to power in 1985. **Mikhail Gorbachev** believed that the only way to salvage the Soviet economy was to strike a deal with America.

The emergence of Gorbachev gave Reagan an opportunity. In the 1984 election, the Reagan-Bush ticket had beaten former Vice President Walter Mondale and his running mate, Representative Geraldine Ferraro of New York. As he began his second term, Reagan was ready to negotiate with the Soviets.

PRIMARY SOURCES

Speech

On June 6, 1984, Ronald Reagan spoke in France to observe the fortieth anniversary of the Normandy invasion on D-Day. This passage from his "Boys of Pointe du Hoc" speech reflects Reagan's speaking style and foreign-policy views.

> "The men of Normandy had faith that what they were doing was right, faith that they fought for all humanity, faith that a just God would grant them mercy on this beachhead or on the next … [T]here is a profound moral difference between the use of force for liberation and the use of force for conquest. You [U.S. veterans of D-Day] were here to liberate, not to conquer, and so you and those others did not doubt your cause. And you were right not to doubt.
>
> You all knew that some things are worth dying for. One's country is worth dying for, and democracy is worth dying for, because it's the most deeply honorable form of government ever devised by man. All of you loved liberty. All of you were willing to fight tyranny, and you knew the people of your countries were behind you."

Skills Focus: READING LIKE A HISTORIAN

1. **Identifying Points of View** According to Reagan, what proved that the Normandy invasion was the right action?
2. **Analyzing Primary Sources** What does this speech reflect about Reagan's political views?

See **Skills Handbook**, p. H28–29

In four meetings from 1985 through 1988, Reagan and Gorbachev changed the superpower relationship. Their talks produced the Intermediate-Range Nuclear Forces (INF) Treaty, the first agreement to actually reduce nuclear arms instead of simply halting production. The **INF Treaty**, ratified in 1988, ordered the destruction of a whole class of weapons—more than 2,500 missiles, many of which faced each other in Europe.

In 1988 Reagan stood in Moscow's Red Square and embraced the leader of the once "evil empire." The Cold War was almost over.

READING CHECK **Summarizing** What actions did Reagan take to help end the Cold War?

Nicaragua

Lebanon

Trouble Spots Abroad

Regional conflicts often force presidents to choose where to become involved militarily. Reagan's choices reflected his view of American interests in the world in the 1980s.

Upheaval in Latin America Nowhere was the fight against communism more urgent to Reagan than Latin America. The United States supported several anti-Communist governments and rebel groups in the region during the Reagan years. Some of these regimes were repressive, but Reagan believed U.S. support was necessary to prevent the spread of communism in those countries. U.S. actions focused on two Central American nations, El Salvador and Nicaragua.

In tiny El Salvador, peasants were caught in a violent civil war between Marxist guerrillas and government troops supported by armed extremist groups. The Reagan administration gave its support to a relatively moderate leader who won election in 1984, José Napoleón Duarte. The civil war dragged on until peace was reached in 1992.

Meanwhile, a civil war in neighboring Nicaragua drew the president's staff into what would become the most serious crisis to affect the Reagan White House. The United States had at one time supported Nicaraguan dictator Anastasio Somoza Debayle. In 1979 a Marxist-leaning group known as the Sandinistas, with aid from Cuba's Communist government, ousted Somoza. At first the Sandinista governed as part of a coalition of political groups, but soon Sandinista dominance became clear.

When Reagan took office, he cut off aid to Nicaragua, saying that the Sandinistas were supported by the USSR. In 1981 Reagan approved $20 million for the Central Intelligence Agency (CIA) to equip and train a Sandinista opposition group, the Contras. The effort stalled when the CIA conducted sabotage operations in Nicaragua, including laying mines in two Nicaraguan ports, without informing Congress. As the secret activities came to light, Congress cut off funds to the Contras and banned all direct or indirect U.S. military support for them.

Reagan remained determined to help the Contras. He told his national security adviser, Robert McFarlane, "I want you to do whatever you have to do to help these people [the Contras] keep body and soul together." His staff took this as a signal to find a way around Congress's restrictions. Americans would soon learn that the White House continued to fund the Contras despite the congressional ban.

ACADEMIC VOCABULARY
regime
government, administration

At far left, a Contra rebel wears a baseball cap that shows U.S. support of his struggle against the Sandinista government in Nicaragua. At near left, the U.S. embassy in Beirut, Lebanon, is damaged following a suicide attack on April 18, 1983, in which 63 people were killed. **What other conflicts was the United States involved in during the Reagan administration?**

Tragedy in Lebanon President Reagan believed that American interests required stability in the Middle East. For years the Mediterranean coastal country of Lebanon had been ripped apart by civil war. Muslim and Christian factions battled for control of the country. Various groups, including the Palestine Liberation Organization (PLO), used Lebanon as a base for attacks against Israel to the south. In 1982 Israel invaded and occupied southern Lebanon to expel the PLO and try to form a new, reliably friendly government. The invasion threatened to turn Lebanon's civil war into a general Middle East war.

In 1983 an international peacekeeping force, including some 800 U.S. Marines, arrived in Lebanon's capital, Beirut. On October 23, a suicide bomber drove a truck full of explosives into the marine barracks in Beirut. The blast leveled the building, killing 241 sleeping soldiers inside. This tragedy and the bombing of the U.S. embassy a few months earlier were the first suicide terrorist attacks against the United States.

The incidents ignited an intense debate in America about the role of the military in violent, unstable regions. Reagan decided to withdraw the troops from Lebanon. Anti-American groups claimed victory.

Victory in Grenada A few days before the bombing in Lebanon, a violent Communist coup took place in the tiny Caribbean country of Grenada (gruh-NAY-duh). Cuban troops were helping build an airstrip on the island, raising fears that it could become a Communist outpost. Reagan also worried about the fate of some 800 U.S. students in medical school there.

Two days after the Lebanon bombing, with the nation still in shock, Reagan sent 5,000 marines to invade Grenada. They took the island in two days, with a loss of 19 soldiers. The victory aided Reagan in the 1984 election.

Apartheid in South Africa Reagan took a less activist position in confronting the South African government. For decades, the official policy of <mark>apartheid</mark> ("apartness") had enforced legalized racial segregation throughout South African society. Under apartheid the minority white population enjoyed great privileges. Meanwhile, the government forcibly relocated millions of people categorized as nonwhite to desolate frontier lands. Nonwhites were banned from decent jobs, schools, and housing and were prohibited from owning land, voting, or traveling freely.

American companies and investments in the resource-rich land helped keep the white regime in power. Starting in the 1970s, anti-apartheid groups urged nations to divest, or withdraw investments, from South Africa.

Reagan preferred a policy of "constructive engagement"—that is, maintaining business ties while offering incentives for reform and engaging in diplomacy with the government. Critics charged that the policy enriched a corrupt, white minority regime. In 1986 Congress overrode a Reagan veto to pass the Comprehensive Anti-Apartheid Act, which imposed trade limits and other sanctions.

READING CHECK **Summarizing** How did the Reagan administration respond to crises in Lebanon, Grenada, and South Africa?

The Iran-Contra Affair

Despite the congressional ban on U.S. funds for the Contras' war against the Nicaraguan government, Reagan's national security staff sought to continue the funding. The United States was then facing terrorism in the Middle

THE IMPACT TODAY

Government
Terrorists have used suicide bombings to strike in Israel and in Iraq. The terrorist attacks against the United States on September 11, 2001, also were suicide attacks.

A CONSERVATIVE ERA **705**

QUICK FACTS: REAGAN'S FOREIGN POLICY

Latin America	• U.S. backs moderate Duarte in El Salvador civil war. • Reagan backs anti-Communist Contras in Nicaragua. • White House defies Congress ban on Contra funding.
Lebanon	• Following civil war, U.S. sends 800 peacekeepers. • October 1983: Suicide bomber hits marine barracks. • 241 Americans killed; U.S. withdraws from Lebanon.
Grenada	• 1983 Communist coup strands 800 U.S. students. • Cuba's role and students' safety concern Reagan. • U.S. launches two-day invasion, restores democracy.
South Africa	• Reagan prefers "constructive engagement" with white minority government to combat apartheid. • 1986: Congress imposes sanctions over Reagan veto.

East, where American civilians in Lebanon were being kidnapped by pro-Iranian groups.

In 1985 the situations in Nicaragua and the Middle East became linked. National Security Adviser Robert McFarlane persuaded Reagan to approve sales of weapons to Iran, hoping that Iran would help obtain the release of U.S. hostages in Lebanon. This violated a U.S. arms embargo as well as Reagan's own principle of refusing to negotiate with terrorists.

The **Iran-Contra affair** unfolded when members of the National Security Council staff secretly diverted money from the illegal Iran arms sales to the Contras in Nicaragua. Vice Admiral John Poindexter and Lieutenant Colonel **Oliver North** carried out the plan.

When the scheme was revealed in 1986, Congress wanted to know if anyone higher up was involved. It launched an investigation modeled after the Watergate probe of Nixon.

Reagan admitted authorizing the Iran arms sales but denied knowledge of the diversion of funds to the Contras. Vice President Bush, Defense Secretary Caspar Weinberger, and other staff made similar statements.

The full details of the affair are not known because members of the administration engaged in a cover-up of their actions. North admitted destroying key documents. High-level Reagan staff were found to have lied in testimony to Congress and withheld evidence. North was convicted of destroying government documents and perjury. The conviction later was overturned on technicalities.

READING CHECK **Sequencing** Trace the significant events that led to prosecutions in the Iran-Contra affair.

SECTION 2 ASSESSMENT

HSS 11.8.4, 11.9.5

Reviewing Ideas, Terms, and People

1. **a. Identify** Explain how each of these terms and people relates to the ending of the Cold War: **Strategic Defense Initiative, Lech Walesa, Solidarity, Mikhail Gorbachev**
   b. Make Inferences What influence do you think SDI and U.S. defense spending had on Soviet leaders' thinking about the Cold War?
   c. Evaluate To what extent do you think Reagan and Gorbachev shaped the events of the Cold War, and to what extent did they encounter changes already in progress?

2. **a. Define** Write a brief definition for this term: **apartheid**
   b. Contrast Contrast the reasons for U.S. involvement in Lebanon, Grenada, and South Africa.
   c. Evaluate What do you think were the advantages and disadvantages of Reagan's "constructive engagement" policy in South Africa?

3. **a. Recall** What was Oliver North's role in the **Iran-Contra affair**?
   b. Make Inferences What can you infer about Reagan's relationship with Congress from the Iran-Contra Affair?
   c. Rate Do you think North's actions were justifiable given (a) circumstances in Nicaragua or (b) pressure from the president to help the Contras?

Critical Thinking

4. **Making Decisions** Copy the chart below and use information from the section to identify the choices Reagan had to make in various conflicts.

Reagan Foreign-Policy Choices

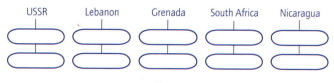

| USSR | Lebanon | Grenada | South Africa | Nicaragua |

FOCUS ON WRITING ELA W1.1

5. **Descriptive** As a reporter covering the appearance of Reagan and Gorbachev in Red Square in 1988, describe the historic meeting of former enemies.

SECTION 3: A New World Order

BEFORE YOU READ

MAIN IDEA
In 1988 Reagan's vice president, George H. W. Bush, won election to a term that saw dramatic changes in the world.

READING FOCUS
1. What factors influenced the election of 1988?
2. How did Soviet society become more open?
3. What chain of events led to the collapse of the Soviet empire?
4. What other global conflicts emerged near the end of the Cold War?

KEY TERMS AND PEOPLE
George H. W. Bush
glasnost
perestroika
velvet revolution
Boris Yeltsin
Tiananmen Square massacre
Saddam Hussein
Operation Desert Storm
Nelson Mandela

HSS 11.9.5 Analyze the role of the Reagan administration and other factors in the victory of the West in the Cold War.

HSS 11.9.6 Describe U.S. Middle East policy and its strategic, political, and economic interests, including those related to the Gulf War.

Passing the Torch

THE INSIDE STORY *How do you make the transition from vice president to commander in chief?* On December 7, 1988, Vice President **George H. W. Bush** was basking in the glory of his victory in the 1988 presidential election. Yet he was still second in command to a very powerful and popular Ronald Reagan.

Thus the summit taking place that day on Governor's Island in New York Harbor had clear symbolic meaning. The Americans were there to meet with Soviet leader Mikhail Gorbachev. Ronald Reagan was still president, and he would conduct the discussions with his Soviet counterpart. Bush, however, was a living symbol of a change soon to take place: the orderly, democratic transfer of power in the U.S. government.

Before the formal talks began, the three men informally answered questions from reporters. Reagan gave his positive reaction to the recently announced decision by Gorbachev to reduce the number of troops in Europe. Bush was then asked for his reaction. His first response was similar to one he had given for the previous eight years: He supported whatever the president said. But then, with a reference to his upcoming January 20 inauguration, Bush extended an invitation to the assembled reporters: "Give me a ring on the 21st."

Indeed, the Reagan era would soon be over. The presidency of George H. W. Bush was about to begin.

▼ Gorbachev, Reagan, and Bush meet under the watchful eye of Lady Liberty.

A CONSERVATIVE ERA **707**

The Election of 1988

George Herbert Walker Bush came from a wealthy and powerful family. In World War II he had served with distinction as a navy pilot. Following careers in banking and oil, Bush entered politics in 1967 as a member of Congress from Texas. He served under presidents Nixon, Ford, and Reagan—as U.S. ambassador to the United Nations, as head of the Central Intelligence Agency, and as vice president.

In 1988 the Republican Party nominated George H.W. Bush as its presidential candidate and Indiana senator Dan Quayle as his running mate. They joined a presidential race that was notable for its lack of public attention. Excitement peaked early in the election year when an African American candidate, the Reverend Jesse Jackson, ran for the Democratic Party's nomination.

Jackson, a major civil rights leader and a liberal candidate, had run in 1984 with little success. This time, however, he achieved an upset, winning the most votes on Super Tuesday, the day when most states hold primary elections. Jackson's candidacy earned significant support from both white and black voters. In the end, however, Governor Michael Dukakis of Massachusetts won the most delegates and became the Democratic Party's nominee.

Many people attribute the low 50.1 percent voter turnout in the general election to the negativity of the campaign. The Democratic ticket of Michael Dukakis and his running mate, Texas senator Lloyd Bentsen, challenged Bush on the weak economy. The Bush campaign shot back with a series of advertisements that portrayed Dukakis as soft on crime. The tough ads contrasted with Bush's stump speech calling for a "kinder, gentler" America.

Despite a shaky economy, Bush earned support with his promise to continue the Reagan economic plan: "Read my lips: No new taxes." The Bush-Quayle ticket beat Dukakis and Bentsen by 426 electoral votes to 111.

When George Bush suceeded Ronald Reagan as president, the world stood on the verge of a democratic awakening. In four short years President Bush would take part in intense dramas around the globe.

READING CHECK **Summarizing** What events triggered the most interest in the 1988 election?

THE IMPACT TODAY
Science and Technology
A 2005 Chernobyl Forum report on the 20-year impact of the disaster revealed that only about 50 deaths could be directly linked to the accident, rather than thousands as previously estimated. Still, the report predicted that as many as 4,000 people could eventually die from radiation exposure, and some 5 million live in contaminated areas.

The Opening of the USSR

For nearly 70 years, citizens in the closed Soviet society risked great danger in speaking out or acting against the government. Dissidents—those who protested Soviet rule—were imprisoned and exiled. Basic freedoms of speech, religion, and association were nearly nonexistent. Mikhail Gorbachev sought to change Soviet society, opening it not only to the West but also to internal dissent.

Glasnost and perestroika As part of his plan to reform the failing Soviet system, Gorbachev announced a new era of *glasnost*, or "opening." He lifted media censorship, allowing public criticism of the government. Gorbachev held press interviews, a stunning contrast to the secrecy in which the Kremlin had operated.

Soviet citizens, cautious at first, began to speak openly. They complained about the price of food, of empty store shelves, and of their sons dying in the Soviet occupation of Afghanistan.

Gorbachev also undertook the huge process of *perestroika*, the "restructuring" of the corrupt government bureaucracy. The program was launched with much excitement and hope.

To restructure the shattered economy, Gorbachev dismantled the Soviet central planning system, giving local officials more authority over farm and factory production. He fired about 40 percent of regional officials and pushed through a flurry of reforms:

- 1986: Soviet scientist and dissident Andrey Sakharov was released from exile.
- 1989: Free elections took place for the first time since 1917.
- 1989: The Soviet Union withdrew from Afghanistan.
- 1989: Gorbachev visited China, easing tensions along the Soviet-Chinese border.

One glaring exception to *glasnost* occurred in 1986, when the Soviets attempted to cover up the world's worst nuclear accident. The meltdown of the Chernobyl nuclear plant near Kiev, the capital of Ukraine, was detected when deadly radiation drifted across Europe. The lead caused deaths and widespread illness. About 350,000 people had to be relocated from the region. The site remains uninhabitable.

READING CHECK **Identifying Cause and Effect** What effects did *glasnost* and *perestroika* have on the Soviet economy, government, and society?

Soviet Shortages

The Soviet Union experienced healthy economic growth after World War II, but it did not last. Soviet leaders focused on expanding heavy industry instead of creating adequate supplies of consumer goods. Store shelves were often empty, creating a thriving black market in food and other goods.

The Soviet Empire Collapses

The call for *glasnost* and *perestroika* awakened hopes for freedom throughout the Soviet empire. A spirit of nationalism, long repressed and feared by Soviet authorities, rose in the subject nations of Eastern Europe.

Eastern Europe crumbles Gorbachev knew the USSR could no longer afford to support the ailing Eastern European economies. He ordered a large troop pullback from the region and warned local leaders to adopt reforms.

Dissidents and ordinary citizens didn't wait for reforms. They created their own paths to freedom. All across Eastern Europe, dreams of a better life inspired revolutions in the late 1980s. The Polish trade union Solidarity forced the government to hold elections, and in December 1990 Lech Walesa became to president. Hungarian officials opened their country's border with Austria in August 1989, and people streamed to the West. In Czechoslovakia, a nonviolent **velvet revolution**—so called because it was peaceful—swept the Communists from power in November 1989. Dissident playwright Vaclav Havel became president.

In Romania, revolution turned violent. Demonstrations brought down the government of one of the Soviet bloc's cruelest dictators, Nicolae Ceausescu, in December 1989. Ceausescu and his wife, Elena, were executed.

The fall of the Berlin Wall Gorbachev's call for openness made him very popular in Europe, especially in East and West Germany. Protesters at a fortieth anniversary celebration of the East German state in October 1989 chanted "Gorby, help us!"

But still the Berlin Wall remained, the repressive symbol of Soviet communism. With so many barriers falling, could the Berlin Wall continue to divide the German people?

Hoping to calm rising protests, the East German government flung open the gates of the Berlin Wall on November 9, 1989. Thousands of East Berliners poured through to freedom. As border guards looked on helplessly, jubilant Berliners scaled the wall from both sides. They pulled down the razor wire, climbed atop the wall, and danced on it. With axes and sledgehammers and their bare hands, they spontaneously began ripping down the wall.

Writing on the tenth anniversary of the fall of the Berlin Wall, one reporter looked back on the spectacular sights and sounds of history being made.

HISTORY'S VOICES

“And then I hear the noise. Pick, pick, pick. Chuck, chuck, chuck. Growing louder and louder as hundreds of hammers and chisels attack the wall, taking it down chip by chip. I laugh and laugh—and cry at the same time.”

—BBC reporter Tim Weber, November 9, 1989

A CONSERVATIVE ERA

An Empire Falls

Pressured by U.S. threats and the dead weight of his ailing Soviet empire, Gorbachev cracked open a door to democracy—and millions of oppressed people rushed through.

1 Poland
Electrician Lech Walesa leads a strike and starts a revolution.
- In 1989, Solidarity forces the government to hold elections.
- Walesa is elected president in 1989; the Communists fall.

2 Romania
One of the cruelest Communist regimes falls the hardest.
- In December 1989 violent protests sweep the country.
- Dictator Ceausescu and his wife are executed.

People around the world watched in awe as TV cameras recorded the triumph of democracy. Less than a year later, on October 3, 1990, East Germany and West Germany were reunified as one nation.

The end of the Soviet Union With the Soviet empire crumbling, Communist Party officials in the USSR stood to lose power, prestige, and wealth. The world waited anxiously to see how far they would allow Gorbachev to go. With Gorbachev preparing to sign a treaty granting partial freedoms to the Soviet republics in 1991, hard-line Communist Party leaders had had enough. They seized Gorbachev in a coup d'état.

Help for the captive president came from **Boris Yeltsin**, leader of the Russian Republic. Yeltsin had quit the Communist Party and was actually a liberal opponent of Gorbachev. Now, however, he led a popular revolt against the Communist coup. As soldiers and tanks rolled into Red Square to arrest Yeltsin, a mass of unarmed Russians flooded the plaza, surrounding them. What would happen? At a tense moment, Yeltsin climbed atop a tank and addressed the cheering crowd. Soldiers looked the other way. Some even joined the protest.

The balance of power tipped, and the army backed down. Gorbachev was released and restored to power in the Kremlin. But, he would not stay long. The forces that Gorbachev had unleashed quickly overwhelmed him. Beginning in 1990, Soviet republics had begun declaring their independence. In late 1991 most of the former Soviet republics, including Russia, formed a loose federation called the Commonwealth of Independent States (CIS).

Gorbachev resigned as president, and no one was named to replace him. The Soviet Union dissolved. Yeltsin now led a severely weakened superpower. A journalist later assessed Gorbachev's place in history:

HISTORY'S VOICES

"One can argue about what degree of direct credit Mr. Gorbachev deserves for ending the nuclear arms race or for bringing down the Berlin wall. It can credibly be suggested that Russia itself, pinned mercilessly beneath the staggering burdens of Bolshevism, could not have moved in any other direction and that Mr. Gorbachev just happened to be there when the society began to collapse. But he was there, and it is hard to imagine that history won't reward him handsomely for his role."

—"A Visionary Who Put an Era Out of Its Misery," *The New York Times*, January 7, 1997

3 East Germany
East German soldiers watch passively while protesters chip away at the wall.
- Berlin Wall falls in November 1989.
- Germany reunified in October 1990.

4 The Soviet Union
The Communist superpower collapses.
- Russia's Yeltsin helps foil 1991 a hard-liners' coup against Gorbachev.
- Gorbachev resigns; Soviet Union breaks apart.
- Bush, Yeltsin sign arms treaties in 1991, 1993.

It was fitting that George Bush, former head of America's Cold War spy agency, the CIA, was the president who would preside over the ending of the Cold War. Less than one month after the fall of the Berlin Wall, Bush and Gorbachev met to discuss arms reduction. In 1991 they agreed on a Strategic Arms Reduction Treaty (START) to cut stockpiles of long-range nuclear weapons.

Two months after the collapse of the USSR, Bush and Yeltsin met at Camp David. They issued a joint statement declaring that the United States and Russia no longer regarded each other as "potential adversaries." The leaders signed a START II agreement in 1993. Bush said START II offered "a future free from fear." Yeltsin called it "a treaty of hope."

READING CHECK **Making Generalizations** How did Gorbachev's call for *glasnost* and *perestroika* help bring down the Soviet Union?

Other Bush-Era Conflicts

President Bush guided the nation through other foreign-policy challenges. By 1991 he spoke hopefully of creating a "new world order," free of the Cold War rivalries.

China: democracy crushed Inspired in part by events in the Soviet Union, a generation of Chinese students called on their Communist leaders to embrace reforms. In April 1989 they led huge pro-democracy demonstrations that filled Tiananmen Square in the Chinese capital of Beijing. For two hope-filled months, Chinese officials tolerated the protests. Change seemed possible. Then hard-line officials ran out of patience.

On June 4 a line of tanks rolled toward Tiananmen Square. As cameras recorded the scene, a man ran into the street and stood in front of the tanks. For half an hour, he halted their progress. The image of the lone rebel defying Chinese authority sent a powerful message around the world. Then the man melted back into the crowd. The tanks surrounded the protesters and opened fire. Hundreds of unarmed people, including children, were gunned down in the **Tiananmen Square massacre**.

President Bush announced an arms embargo but said America had to stay "engaged" with China. Democratic reform would take much longer in China than in the rest of the Communist world. But the protests showed a desire for freedom that was heard by China's leaders.

THE IMPACT TODAY

Government
In 2002 President George W. Bush and Russian President Vladimir Putin replaced START II with the SORT, Strategic Offensive Reduction Treaty, which calls for cuts to overall arsenals rather than to specific weapon types.

Panama: a dictator falls During the 1980s, Colonel Manuel Noriega basically ran the country of Panama. As head of the armed forces, he brutally suppressed opposition. Evidence that he was involved in smuggling drugs to the United States led a U.S. court to indict him in 1988. In 1989 Noriega seized direct control of Panama and declared a state of war with the United States. At stake was the security of the Panama Canal, which was scheduled to be turned over to Panamanian control in 1999.

When Noriega's soldiers shot and killed a U.S. marine in December 1989, President Bush ordered an invasion of Panama. U.S. troops arrested Noriega and moved him to Florida. He was later convicted of drug trafficking and other charges.

The Persian Gulf War In August 1990 the ruthless dictator of Iraq, **Saddam Hussein**, invaded the neighboring country of Kuwait. The attack on the tiny, oil-rich kingdom shocked the United States and other Western countries—which depended on petroleum supplies from Kuwait—as well as the Arab nations in the region. Concerns rose further when reports surfaced of atrocities by Iraqi troops against Kuwaiti civilians. President Bush vowed that Saddam's "aggression would not stand."

The UN imposed sanctions on Iraq and set a deadline of January 15, 1991, for the withdrawal of Iraqi troops. Meanwhile, President Bush used his diplomatic skills to assemble a strong multinational military coalition.

Saddam remained defiant. The deadline passed. On January 16, 1991, the U.S.-led force attacked, starting with heavy bombing raids on targets in Kuwait and Iraq. On the Iraq–Saudi Arabia border and on warships in the Persian Gulf, a force of some 690,000 troops from the United States, Britain, France, and a number of Arab nations prepared to strike.

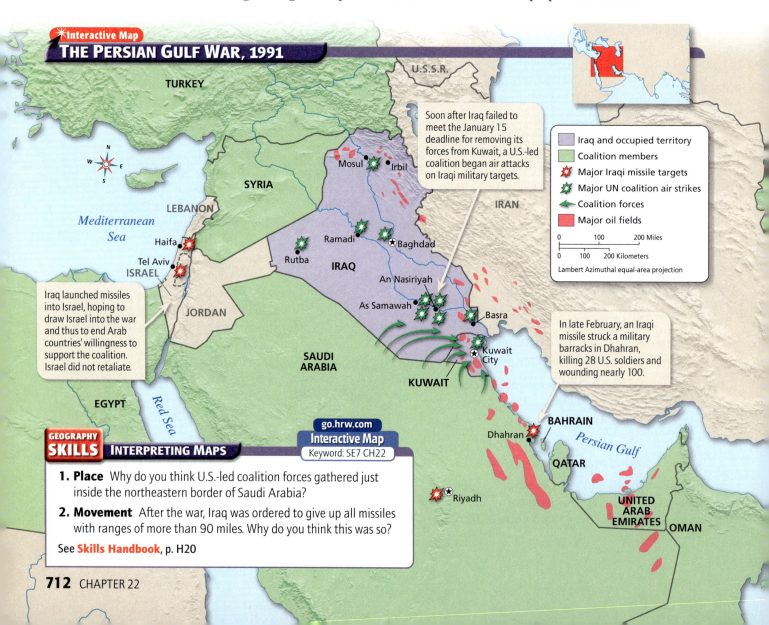

THE PERSIAN GULF WAR, 1991

Soon after Iraq failed to meet the January 15 deadline for removing its forces from Kuwait, a U.S.-led coalition began air attacks on Iraqi military targets.

Iraq launched missiles into Israel, hoping to draw Israel into the war and thus to end Arab countries' willingness to support the coalition. Israel did not retaliate.

In late February, an Iraqi missile struck a military barracks in Dhahran, killing 28 U.S. soldiers and wounding nearly 100.

GEOGRAPHY SKILLS INTERPRETING MAPS

1. **Place** Why do you think U.S.-led coalition forces gathered just inside the northeastern border of Saudi Arabia?
2. **Movement** After the war, Iraq was ordered to give up all missiles with ranges of more than 90 miles. Why do you think this was so?

See **Skills Handbook**, p. H20

The ground war, launched on February 23, was short and swift. Iraqi troops retreated and scattered. Coalition forces returned Kuwait's royal family to power within a few days.

The campaign, **Operation Desert Storm**, was a conventional (non-nuclear) war. But it was unlike any war before it. The harsh desert terrain and long distances between targets made high technology airpower the most effective military tool. Nearly radar-proof Stealth bombers launched laser-guided bombs from afar. And long-range cruise missiles soared hundreds of miles from ships in the Gulf to hit targets in downtown Baghdad, the Iraqi capital.

Because so much of the campaign took place from the air, little of the violence appeared on the world's television sets, despite widespread coverage. The coalition tallied fewer than 500 casualties, including 148 Americans. An estimated 20,000 Iraqi soldiers and some 2,400 Iraqi civilians died.

The Persian Gulf War would not be the last conflict to involve the United States and Iraq. As you will read in the next chapter, U.S. involvement in Iraq would continue.

South Africa: new freedom While Eastern Europe was throwing off its chains, a similar miracle was occurring in South Africa. In 1989 the white government elected F. W. de Klerk as president. Like Gorbachev, de Klerk triggered a chain of events that resulted in a new system of government.

De Klerk sought a gradual, orderly lifting of apartheid. He released political prisoners including **Nelson Mandela**, a former guerrilla fighter imprisoned in 1964. Despite threats of civil war by white opposition, de Klerk and Mandela worked to end apartheid. A new constitution followed, and in 1994 the nation's first all-race elections were held. Mandela and his African National Congress party won.

Sharing the Nobel Peace Prize with de Klerk in 1993, Mandela praised the work of Dr. Martin Luther King Jr., whose call to nonviolent protest had inspired the antiapartheid movement. In language echoing the American Declaration of Independence, he saw a better day:

HISTORY'S VOICES

> "Thus shall we live, because we will have created a society which recognizes that all people are born equal, with each entitled in equal measure to life, liberty, prosperity, human rights and good governance."
>
> —Nelson Mandela, Nobel lecture, December 10, 1993

READING CHECK Identifying Main Ideas What victories and setbacks for democracy occurred near the end of the Cold War?

SECTION 3 ASSESSMENT

HSS 11.9.5, 11.9.6

Reviewing Ideas, Terms, and People

1. **a. Identify** Who were the main candidates in the 1988 presidential election?
   b. Make Inferences What can be inferred from the low voter turnout in the 1988 election?
   c. Develop Why did Jesse Jackson's big victory in the primaries generate so much excitement?

2. **a. Define** Write a brief definition for each of the following terms: *glasnost, perestroika*
   b. Analyze Why did Mikhail Gorbachev believe that *glasnost* and *perestroika* were necessary?
   c. Predict Why was it dangerous for Gorbachev to launch such big social and economic changes in the USSR?

3. **a. Identify** How did **Boris Yeltsin** come to power?
   b. Compare and Contrast How did Czechoslovakia's **velvet revolution** compare with the other Soviet-bloc uprisings?
   c. Rate What year do you think was the biggest turning point in ending the Cold War?

4. **a. Describe** What roles did Manuel Noriega, **Nelson Mandela**, and **Saddam Hussein** have in Bush-era conflicts?
   b. Rank Which Bush-era conflicts turned out to be the best and worst for the spread of democracy? Explain your choices.

Critical Thinking

5. **Identifying Cause and Effect** Copy the chart below and use information from the section to identify the causes of the fall of the Soviet empire.

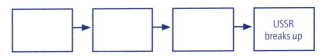

6. **Descriptive** Suppose you were one of the young people who climbed atop the Berlin Wall in triumph. Write a letter to an American friend describing the experience.

SECTION 4: Life in the 1980s

BEFORE YOU READ

MAIN IDEA
The 1980s and early 1990s saw major technological, economic, and social changes that produced both progress and intense conflicts.

READING FOCUS
1. How did new technologies such as the space shuttle affect society?
2. How did changes in the economy of the 1980s affect various groups of Americans?
3. What other changes and challenges did U.S. society face in the 1980s?

KEY TERMS AND PEOPLE
Steve Jobs
Bill Gates
space shuttle
Alan Greenspan
savings and loan crisis
Sandra Day O'Connor
Clarence Thomas

HSS 11.8.7 Describe the effects on society and the economy of technological developments, including the computer, changes in communication, advances in medicine, and improvements in agricultural technology.

HSS 11.11.1 Discuss the reasons for the nation's changing immigration policy.

Dawn of the Digital Age

The innovations of Bill Gates (left) and Steve Jobs (below) changed the way Americans live, work, and play.

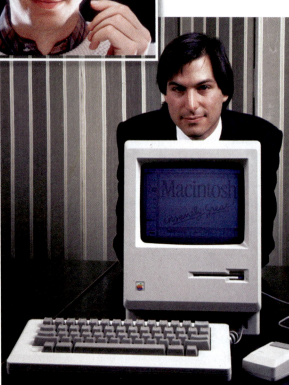

THE INSIDE STORY

How did two guys in a garage change the world? Try to envision the technology—or lack of it—in the year 1980. There were no home computers, CDs, DVDs, or plasma-screen TVs; no cell phones or e-mail. Microwaves and VCRs were still quite new. In 1980 people rushed to buy a new game played right on the television: Pac Man.

All that would change in the 1980s. New inventions brought immense changes in the way people lived—changes as significant, perhaps, as the invention of the printing press and the automobile.

While some revolutions start on a battlefield or in a laboratory, the personal computer revolution started in a garage in Cupertino, California. That's where **Steve Jobs**, a restless college dropout, and a friend, Steve Wozniak, started a small business called Apple Computer. The Apple II home computer was introduced in 1977. More a toy than a tool at first, Apple computers soon transformed the way Americans lived and worked.

Computers existed already, but Apple made them smaller—small enough to be usable at home on a desktop. Jobs's genius was in recognizing that computers could have appeal far beyond the community of scientists, military engineers, and other academics already using them.

Like Steve Jobs, **Bill Gates** was born in 1955 and dropped out of college to form a company. His Seattle-based company, Microsoft, invented a new type of computer-operating software. The time was ripe for his innovation. When Gates leased the software to the largest computer manufacturer, IBM (International Business Machines), a business giant was born. Microsoft soon became the world leader in computer software.

The Space Shuttle Blasts Off

Besides the computer, one of the more stunning technological developments of the 1980s was a new type of spacecraft. Unlike previous spacecraft, the new space shuttle could be reused after each flight. It lifted off like a rocket but returned to Earth like an airplane. Engineers at the National Aeronautics and Space Administration (NASA) had been developing a reusable spacecraft since the 1970s. They saw the space shuttle as a workhorse, carrying satellites and scientific experiments into space on a routine basis.

On April 12, 1981, millions of television viewers around the world watched the triumphant liftoff of the first shuttle, *Columbia*, from Cape Kennedy, Florida. At Air Force Plant 42 in Palmdale, California, where *Columbia* was built, "There was not a dry eye in the whole place," former plant commander Joe Davies recalled.

On January 28, 1986, tragedy struck the shuttle program when *Challenger* exploded after liftoff. All seven astronauts on board died, including the first private passenger, schoolteacher Christa McAuliffe. President Reagan led the nation in mourning.

Under President Reagan, NASA explored military and commercial uses for the space shuttle. This shift in priorities, along with proposals for the Star Wars (SDI) missile defense program, raised concerns about the militarization of space. The first military satellite was launched by the space shuttle in 1985.

Beyond space exploration, the shuttle program also benefited society more directly. Technologies developed or discovered by scientists on the program led to the development of such products as infrared cameras for detecting fires and a treatment for brain tumors.

READING CHECK **Summarizing** What hopes and disappointments did the space shuttle create?

The *Challenger* Space Shuttle Tragedy

The large picture shows the *Challenger* space shuttle launch on January 28, 1986. Just 73 seconds after liftoff, the *Challenger* exploded, killing the crew. Spectators reacted with horror as they watched the explosion. The *Challenger* crew included the space program's first civilian passenger, New Hampshire schoolteacher Christa McAuliffe (back row, second from left).

The Economy of the 1980s

Like most periods in American history, the 1980s witnessed both good and bad economic trends. Some were not apparent until the late 1980s and the early 1990s.

Uneven economic growth The 1980s marked the longest period of U.S. peacetime economic growth up to that time. The gross domestic product (GDP), the total value of goods and services produced by the nation, grew at an average annual rate of 3.5 percent from 1982 to 1989. The stock market, too, rose to then historic highs, slowed only temporarily by a crash in 1987.

The strong growth was achieved without the high inflation that had troubled the country throughout the 1970s. The deep recession of 1982 helped to slash inflation, though at the cost of high unemployment. Moves by the Federal Reserve Board also helped. Under chairperson Paul Volcker and his successor, **Alan Greenspan**, "the Fed," as it is known, actively raised and lowered interest rates to help avoid either recession or inflation.

Government
In 2005 Ben S. Bernanke became chair of the Federal Reserve Board. Bernanke succeeded Alan Greenspan, who retired after heading the Federal Reserve Board for 18 years.

Following the recovery, inflation stayed under 5 percent during the rest of the 1980s and early 1990s. Unemployment slowly dropped as well. Some people credit Reaganomics for many of the positive economic trends of the 1980s. Others point to the Federal Reserve Board.

But the strong economic growth of the 1980s was unevenly distributed. Many farmers, for example, did poorly during the decade. In 1986 and 1988 droughts struck the Midwest, turning cropland into wasteland. The droughts were followed by destructive floods. Meanwhile, crop and farmland prices declined. Farmers became mired in debt.

The recession of 1982–83 had struck older U.S. industries, such as steel and automobile production, particularly hard. Many factories closed, throwing tens of thousands out of work. Bankruptcies rose 50 percent in one year. Homelessness increased sharply in many cities. Yet the relief provided by the Reagan tax cuts mainly benefited wealthier Americans.

Rising deficits Reagan's tax cuts, coupled with increased military spending, threatened to undermine the success in combating inflation. With expenditures far outstripping tax revenue, the government's annual budget deficit nearly tripled, from $74 billion in 1980 to $221 billion in 1986. The national debt grew from about $1.2 trillion to $5.7 trillion. The interest alone on the debt increased 61 percent between 1980 and 1986. The huge government borrowing needed to fund the deficit raised fears of renewed inflation.

Another troubling economic sign was the rising U.S. trade deficit, the difference between the value of American exports and imports. The trade deficit grew throughout the 1980s as Asian economies roared to life, producing high quality goods such as automobiles by using cheaper labor and new, efficient processes.

Financial deregulation The deregulation of financial services under Reagan led to innovative business practices that changed the face of American business. Led by business tycoons such as Ivan Boesky, corporate raiders bought declining companies at a low price. They restructured them by merging them, selling off pieces of them, or dissolving them. They then sold the new entities at high prices. This corporate downsizing resulted in huge employee layoffs. Not all firms wanted to be purchased, so corporate raiders engaged in hostile takeovers. Supporters maintained that corporate raiders weeded out weak companies and improved productivity.

Savings and loan crisis The deregulation of the savings and loan (S&L) industry showed some of the risks of deregulation. S&Ls traditionally had used the money deposited to make home mortgage loans. Deregulation allowed S&Ls to offer other services, such as credit cards and investment management.

During a 1980s housing boom, deregulated S&Ls loaned out too much of their wealth. When the boom went bust, borrowers defaulted on their loans. S&Ls went bankrupt on a massive scale. The **savings and loan crisis** forced the federal government to step in and guarantee the deposits. The bailout cost taxpayers an estimated $152 billion.

Bush and the economy The S&L crisis and a recession that began in late 1990 forced President Bush to break his campaign pledge of "no new taxes." The tax hike did not prevent the deficit from climbing to $271 billion in 1992.

COUNTERPOINTS

The Savings and Loan Crisis

Some members of Congress had grave concerns about the specific costs and methods of the S&L bailout.

Many lawmakers believed the government had to bail out savings and loans and restore depositors' money, despite the cost.

❝ The current bailout law raises funds according to a costly 'borrow and spend' philosophy that adds billions to the bailout cost in interest. It drives up interest rates and the budget deficit. It also places the bulk of the bailout burden on those who can least afford to bear it: America's working and poor families. ❞

**Rep. Joseph P. Kennedy II
(D., MA), 1990**

❝ The deposit insurance grew out of the hard-learned lesson of the banking crisis that helped trigger the Great Depression. A failure to stand behind federally insured deposits would condemn us to repeat the mistakes of the past. People would lose their money and their faith in their Government, and there would be a bank panic rivaling the runs on deposits 60 years ago. ❞

**Rep. James McDermott
(D., WA), 1989**

Skills FOCUS READING LIKE A HISTORIAN

Identifying Points of View How did the two legislators differ? Were they necessarily in complete opposition to one another? Explain.

See **Skills Handbook**, pp. H28–H29

Unemployment and poverty rose significantly during his term. Despite his foreign-policy successes, economic troubles at home proved to be Bush's political downfall.

READING CHECK Identifying Supporting Details List major economic trends of the 1980s.

Changes and Challenges in American Society

Social issues proved increasingly divisive in the 12 years of the Reagan and Bush administrations. Political controversies opened new cultural battle lines in America.

Milestones During the elections of the 1980s, pollsters identified a gender gap in voting patterns. Women were voting in greater proportions than men, and they voted more Democratic. Politicians began to pay more attention to women voters and their interests.

Several women in politics achieved notable milestones. In 1981 President Reagan chose an Arizona judge, **Sandra Day O'Connor**, to be the first woman on the U.S. Supreme Court. Reagan also appointed a woman, Jeane Kirkpatrick, to serve as ambassador to the United Nations. In 1984 Democratic presidential candidate Walter Mondale named the first woman, New York Congresswoman Geraldine Ferraro, to run on a major party ticket.

Another milestone of the era was the passage of the Americans with Disabilities Act. The law, signed by President Bush in 1990, represented the culmination of years of work by activists for disabled Americans. It outlawed discrimination on the basis of physical impairment and required employers to make "reasonable accomodations" for people with disabilities.

Changes in immigration law New waves of refugees from Southeast Asia and from poverty and upheaval in Cuba, Haiti, and other parts of Latin America triggered revisions

A CONSERVATIVE ERA **717**

in U.S. immigration policy during the 1980s. Laws passed in 1980 and 1986 increased legal immigration limits and granted legal status to nearly 3 million undocumented immigrants living in the United States. It also toughened penalties on employers who knowingly hired undocumented workers. Despite these measures, illegal immigration continued to grow.

Court battles over social issues During the Reagan and Bush administrations, the Supreme Court ruled on several sensitive landmark cases. The rulings in these cases are still being felt today.

In the 1985 case *New Jersey* v. *T.L.O.*, the Court ruled that schools have the right to search students' belongings without being in violation of the Fourth Amendment's prohibition of unreasonable searches. You can read more about this case in the Landmark Supreme Court Cases in Section 1 of this chapter.

In *Westside Community School District* v. *Mergens*, the Supreme Court in 1990 ruled that a high school in Omaha, Nebraska, had to allow students to form an after-school Christian group that could meet on school grounds. Upholding the Equal Access Act, the ruling required schools that receive federal funding to provide equal access to student groups seeking to express "religious, political, philosophical, or other content."

Following the 1973 *Roe* v. *Wade* decision legalizing abortion, the Court issued rulings that further defined the scope of *Roe*. In the 1992 case *Planned Parenthood of Southeastern PA* v. *Casey*, the Court ruled that a state could require a woman seeking an abortion to give informed consent, to wait 24 hours, and in the case of a minor, to obtain parental consent.

In another sensitive case, the Court set a precedent in cases involving the removal of life-support equipment from a critically ill patient. Nancy Cruzan sustained severe brain damage in a car accident and was said to be in a "persistent vegetative state," kept alive by a feeding tube and other medical means. The 1990 ruling in *Cruzan* v. *Director, Missouri Dept. of Health* recognized an adult's right to refuse medical treatment. But it ruled that the state could require "clear and convincing evidence" that the patient would have wanted to have life support removed under the circumstances.

Battles over Supreme Court nominees
President Reagan had the rare opportunity to fill three seats on the Supreme Court. He also

American Religious Liberty

Churches and Politics

In recent decades, Christian conservatives have been a powerful political force. Christian fundamentalism and evangelism became popular in the 1920s and gained new power when Reagan came to office. Fundamentalists and evangelicals believe in a strict interpretation of the Bible as a source of clear direction and values in society.

One leading Baptist fundamentalist minister, Jerry Falwell, called for conservative Christians to become more active in politics. He believed that the country was facing problems because its political leaders had turned away from the Christian values upon which, he said, the United States was founded. Falwell and other conservative Christians, including the Reverend Pat Robertson and Eagle Forum founder Phyllis Schlafly, maintained that they were promoting their right to practice religion. Some opponents felt that the increased influence of religion in politics threatened the separation of church and state. The nation continues to seek ways to balance the rights of religious groups with the rights of those who have other opinions and beliefs.

Identifying the Main Idea What is the basic disagreement between some fundamentalists and their critics?

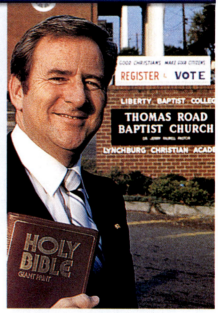

Falwell began his career at the Thomas Road Baptist Church.

appointed about half the judges in the federal court system. Both Reagan and Bush sought to appoint conservative judges, at times setting off furious confirmation clashes in the Senate.

In 1987 Reagan nominated Robert Bork, a law professor and appeals court judge. Bork advocated a strict interpretation of the Constitution. Many senators and liberal groups feared he would roll back *Roe* v. *Wade* and civil rights laws. After angry hearings, the Senate rejected Bork. It later confirmed Reagan's next nominee, Anthony Kennedy.

Another battle took place over a Bush nominee to the Supreme Court in 1991. This nominee was **Clarence Thomas**, a conservative African American judge and former head of the federal Equal Opportunity Employment Commission (EEOC). In televised hearings, the Judiciary Committee investigated charges by law professor Anita Hill that Thomas had sexually harassed her when she worked for him at the EEOC. Hill underwent aggressive questioning by Republican senators defending Thomas, which offended many women. Thomas narrowly won confirmation.

A deadly disease In 1981 scientists identified what has since become one of the worst outbreaks of infectious disease in human history: acquired immunodeficiency syndrome, or AIDS. The deadly disease is caused by the human immunodeficiency virus (HIV). AIDS first appeared among homosexual men and intravenous drug users, and the means of contracting it was not known. As a result, people with AIDS suffered discrimination. Scientists eventually determined that the disease is spread through transmission of bodily fluids, including sexual contact. AIDS has since spread to millions of men and women around the world.

Clarence Thomas's confirmation hearings were dominated by the accusation of sexual harassment. Critics were also concerned over his level of experience and his reluctance to reveal his stance on controversial issues.

READING CHECK **Summarizing** What major social changes occurred in the 1980s and early 1990s?

SECTION 4 ASSESSMENT

HSS 11.8.7, 11.11.1

Reviewing Ideas, Terms, and People

1. **a. Identify** What pioneering roles did **Steve Jobs** and **Bill Gates** have in American society?
   b. Make Inferences How do you think people reacted to the rapid technological changes brought about by the invention of personal computers?
   c. Evaluate Do you think Reagan's emphasis on using the **space shuttle** for military and commercial purposes was wise, or should it have been reserved for scientific use only?

2. **a. Recall** What role did **Alan Greenspan** have in the changing U.S. economy?
   b. Analyze Explain the connection between deregulation and trends such as hostile takeovers and the **savings and loan crisis**.
   c. Evaluate How would you characterize the overall impact of Reaganomics?

3. **a. Identify** What firsts did Geraldine Ferraro and **Sandra Day O'Connor** achieve?
   b. Predict What would be the long-term effects of Reagan's decision to nominate conservative justices to the Supreme Court?

Critical Thinking

4. **Identifying Cause and Effect** Copy the chart below, and complete it with the causes and effects.

   [ ] → Rising National Debt → [ ]

5. **Persuasive** Make the case for or against "trickle down" economic policies, using facts from the section.

CHAPTER 22 DOCUMENT-BASED INVESTIGATION

Wealth in the 1980s

HSS 11.8.1

Historical Context The documents below provide different information about wealth in the 1980s: getting it, losing it, and being fascinated by it.

Task Examine the documents and answer the questions that follow. Then you will be asked to write an essay about how Americans viewed wealth in the 1980s, using facts from the documents and from the chapter to support the position you take in your thesis statement.

DOCUMENT 1

The rising stock market created enormous wealth for American stockholders. Some corporate managers became more concerned with companies' stock prices and profits than with their products. In the 1987 movie *Wall Street*, corporate raider Gordon Gekko, based on real-life characters such as Ivan Boesky, tells stockholders that his takeover of their company will benefit them because he will hire managers who will maximize profits for investors.

> "Well, ladies and gentlemen, we're not here to indulge in fantasy, but in political and economic reality. America—America has become a second-rate power. Its trade deficit and its fiscal deficit are at nightmare proportions. Now, in the days of the free market, when our country was a top industrial power, there was accountability to the stockholder. The Carnegies, the Mellons, the men that built this great industrial empire, made sure of it because it was their money at stake. Today, management has no stake in the company! . . .
>
> "The new law of evolution in corporate America seems to be survival of the unfittest. Well, in my book you either do it right or you get eliminated. . . .
>
> "I am not a destroyer of companies. I am a liberator of them! The point is, ladies and gentleman, is that greed—for lack of a better word—is good. Greed is right. Greed works. Greed clarifies, cuts through, and captures the essence of the evolutionary spirit. Greed, in all of its forms—greed for life, for money, for love, knowledge—has marked the upward surge of mankind. And greed—you mark my words—will not only save Teldar Paper, but that other malfunctioning corporation called the USA."

DOCUMENT 2

Corporate raiders bought vulnerable companies in order to reorganize and sell them or to break them up and sell off their valuable parts. Other tactics that produced great wealth on Wall Street included investments in junk bonds as well as greenmail—a tactic of tricking other investors into buying stock at a high price. The 1985 cartoon below comments on these tactics. It is titled "Invasion of the Corporate Body Snatchers," a spoof on a popular movie about aliens who take over the world.

"INVASION OF THE CORPORATE BODY SNATCHERS" FROM *HERBLOCK AT LARGE* (PANTHEON BOOKS, 1987)

DOCUMENT 3

The economic boom of the 1980s saw an increase in incomes for many families without the high inflation that had wiped out most income increases in the 1970s. Some of the biggest beneficiaries of the 1980s boom were richer families, who saw their incomes increase, largely from successful investments. The chart below shows the changes in wealth for families in the lowest, middle, and highest income brackets.

AVERAGE FAMILY INCOME IN THE 1980s

[Line chart showing Wealthiest 5%, Median, and Poorest 20% from 1980 to 1990. Wealthiest 5% rises from about 52,000 to about 95,000; Median rises from about 18,000 to about 30,000; Poorest 20% rises slightly from about 8,000 to about 13,000. Y-axis: Current Dollars. X-axis: Year.]

Source: *United States Census Bureau*

DOCUMENT 4

Americans were fascinated by the wealthy in the 1980s. Young people throughout the country copied the preppy look, imitating fashions associated with wealthy families of the East Coast. The most popular television shows were nighttime soap operas like *Dallas* and *Dynasty* that portrayed glamorous, if troubled, lives of rich families. In *Dynasty*, the large, oil-rich Carrington family lived an opulent lifestyle, yet they personified the saying that wealth doesn't bring happiness. Millions of viewers tuned in each week to watch the Carrington spouses, parents, and children viciously fight and plot against one another.

Skills Focus — READING LIKE A HISTORIAN

ELA Analysis HR4, HI1

1. **a. Summarize** Refer to Document 1. What does Gekko say about greed?
   b. Interpret What point is Gekko trying to make about the American economy?

2. **a. Describe** Refer to Document 2. How does the cartoonist portray corporate tactics?
   b. Analyze What message is the cartoonist trying to send about the effects of such tactics on businesses?

3. **a. Make Generalizations** Refer to Document 3. What trends in income took place during this time period?
   b. Elaborate How did the income gap between the richest and poorest families change from 1980 to 1990?

4. **a. Contrast** Refer to Document 4. How does the picture convey the image of wealth?
   b. Elaborate How do you think the public's fascination with wealthy families on television reflected their views of wealth in the real world?

5. **Document-Based Essay Question** Consider the question below and form a thesis statement. Using examples from Documents 1, 2, 3, and 4, create an outline and write a short essay supporting your position.
   How did American culture reflect fascination with and concerns about wealth during the 1980s?

See **Skills Handbook**, pp. H28–29, H31, H16

A CONSERVATIVE ERA

CHAPTER 22 Chapter Review

Visual Summary: A Conservative Era

Reagan's First Term
- Under President Reagan, people have renewed confidence in America.
- Conservative policies begin, such as smaller government and increased defense spending
- Supply-side economics, lower taxes, and big deficits occur.

Reagan's Foreign Policy
- The Soviet Union becomes a partner in arms control.
- Staunch anti-communism leads to the invasion of Grenada and the Iran-Contra scandal.

The Reagan and Bush Administrations

The New World Order
- George H. W. Bush becomes president.
- Soviet empire collapses, although China remains Communist.
- "New world order" proves dangerous, as United States goes to war with Iraq.

Life in the 1980s
- Good economic times, although not for all.
- Social issues divide society and lead to Supreme Court battles.

Reviewing Key Terms and People

For each term or name below, write a sentence explaining its significance.

1. Sandra Day O'Connor
2. velvet revolution
3. Bill Gates
4. space shuttle
5. Tiananmen Square massacre
6. New Right
7. Lech Walesa
8. Clarence Thomas
9. Strategic Defense Initiative
10. Iran-Contra affair
11. David A. Stockman
12. Ronald Reagan

Comprehension and Critical Thinking

SECTION 1 *(pp. 694–699)* HSS 11.9.3, 11.9.5, 11.11.2

13. **a. Identify** Write a brief explanation of the following terms: supply-side economics, Reaganomics.
    b. Analyze How did Ronald Reagan represent the conservative response to the liberalism of the 1960s?
    c. Rank How important were social changes to conservatives? How important were economic and governmental changes?

SECTION 2 *(pp. 701–706)* HSS 11.8.4, 11.9.5

14. **a. Recall** What was Solidarity? How did it rise to power?
    b. Draw Conclusions How was the success of Solidarity an early indicator of troubles for the Soviet Union?
    c. Evaluate Was Ronald Reagan successful in increasing pressure on the Soviet Union for change? Explain.

History's Impact video program
Review the video to answer the closing question: What did the collapse of the Berlin Wall signify for both the United States and the rest of the world?

SECTION 3 (pp. 707–713) HSS 11.9.5, 11.9.6

15. **a. Describe** How did *glasnost* and *perestroika* come about in the Soviet Union? What were they meant to accomplish?

    b. Sequence What major foreign-policy challenges occurred during the administration of President George H. W. Bush?

    c. Elaborate Why did the START talks represent such a major change in U.S.–Soviet relations?

SECTION 4 (pp. 714–719) HSS 11.8.7, 11.11.1

16. **a. Identify** Explain the significance of the following: Alan Greenspan, savings and loan crisis.

    b. Generalize What major trends occurred in the American economy during the 1980s?

    c. Evaluate In 1980 Ronald Reagan asked the country, "Are you better off than you were four years ago?" How do you think most Americans would have answered that question at the end of his presidency?

Using the Internet

17. First Lady Nancy Reagan was a complicated figure in American politics and history. She was criticized for the way she ran the White House and influenced her husband. She also was greatly admired by many Americans. Using the keyword above, research and write a short biography of Nancy Reagan that emphasizes her impact on the country and on her husband's administration.

Analyzing Primary Sources HSS HR4

Reading Like a Historian Reread the quotation from President Reagan's "evil empire" speech in Section 2. Then answer the following questions.

18. How did Reagan distinguish his view of the Soviet Union from others' views?

19. What words does Reagan use to emphasize his opinion of the Soviet Union and its goals?

Critical Reading HSS 11.11.2; ELA R2.4

Read the American Civil Liberty feature in Section 1 titled "Smaller Government." Then answer the questions that follow.

20. Ronald Reagan opposed big government because he believed that

    A taxes on poor people were too high.

    B government did not control industries such as petroleum and airlines.

    C government did not provide enough services.

    D government spent too much and regulated too much.

21. Reagan wanted to change government by

    A increasing the budget deficit.

    B deregulating industries and cutting taxes.

    C placing restrictions on key industries.

    D increasing spending on social programs.

WRITING FOR THE SAT ELA W1.1

Think about the following issue.

To battle apartheid in South Africa, the Reagan administration preferred a policy of "constructive engagement." Critics wanted to cut off relations with the white government and withdraw U.S. investments in the South African economy. Reagan disagreed, saying that if the United States withdrew, it would have no bargaining power with which to influence government policy. Congress opposed Reagan and placed a boycott on some South African products.

22. **Assignment** When a government such as South Africa pursues repressive policies against its people, should the United States punish it harshly by boycotting its products and severing government relations? Or, should it allow U.S. businesses to continue to operate in the country, using the threat of withdrawal to force the government to change its ways? Support your answer with reasoning and facts.

CHAPTER 23

1992–Present
Into the Twenty-First Century

THE BIG PICTURE Americans faced the twenty-first century with hope, determination, and a readiness to embrace challenges at home and abroad. While always remembering and learning from the past, they looked forward to a future of change and opportunity.

California Standards

History-Social Sciences

11.8 Students analyze the economic boom and social transformation of post-World War II America.

11.9 Students analyze U.S. foreign policy since World War II.

11.11 Students analyze the major social problems and domestic policy issues in contemporary American society.

Skills Focus — READING LIKE A HISTORIAN

Tens of thousands of runners race across the Verrazano-Narrows Bridge during the annual New York City Marathon. Some 2 million spectators cheer them on, and 260 million television viewers tune in across the globe.
Interpreting Visuals How do you think the terrorist attacks of September 11, 2001, affected interest in this event?

See **Skills Handbook**, p. H30

U.S.

January 1993
Bill Clinton becomes president.

1992

World

1993
Israel and the PLO sign the Oslo Accords.

1994
UN forces land in Haiti to restore democracy.

History's Impact video program
Watch the video to understand the impact of September 11, 2001.

April 1995 A terrorist bomb destroys the Federal Building in Oklahoma City, killing 168 people.

December 1998 The U.S. House of Representatives votes to impeach President Clinton.

September 11, 2001 Foreign terrorists attack the World Trade Center and the Pentagon.

March 2003 President George W. Bush orders invasion of Iraq to remove Saddam Hussein from power.

November 2004 President George W. Bush wins re-election.

1998 Serbian leader Slobodan Milosevic sends troops into Kosovo to drive ethnic Albanians from the region.

January 1999 The United States and NATO stop "ethnic cleansing" of Kosovo.

October 2005 Iraqis approve a new constitution.

SECTION 1: The Clinton Years

BEFORE YOU READ

MAIN IDEA
Bill Clinton was a new type of Democrat, and his administration faced challenges for a new millennium—and scandals as old as politics.

READING FOCUS
1. What were the key events in the political rise of Bill Clinton?
2. What were some major domestic-policy questions facing Clinton?
3. What were some major foreign-policy challenges facing Clinton?
4. What events led to scandal and impeachment proceedings during the Clinton presidency?

KEY TERMS AND PEOPLE
Bill Clinton
Hillary Rodham Clinton
Al Gore
Contract with America
terrorism
NAFTA

HSS 11.8.7 Describe the effects of technological developments since 1945, including the computer revolution, changes in communication, advances in medicine, and improvements in agricultural technology.

HSS 11.9.7 Examine relations between the United States and Mexico in the twentieth century, including key economic, political, immigration, and environmental issues.

Shaking History by the Hand

▼ Sixteen-year-old Bill Clinton, a future president, shakes hands with President Kennedy.

THE INSIDE STORY

Can one handshake change someone's life? Yes, it can, according to **Bill Clinton**. Clinton was a high school senior in Arkansas when he had the opportunity to travel to Washington, D.C., for a youth leadership conference. A highlight of the trip was a visit to the White House, where participants lined up to meet President John F. Kennedy. Among the first to shake the president's hand was Bill Clinton. Nobody at the time knew it, but the handshake, captured by photographers, linked two men who would one day be viewed as key figures in the second half of the twentieth century.

The young Clinton realized it was a central moment in his life. That handshake, he later recalled, changed him. He had long been interested in leadership and politics. But meeting John F. Kennedy in person instilled in him a new commitment: to serve the nation by leading it as president.

Clinton wasted little time in reaching for his dream. After working his way through college and law school, he began a career of public service.

Bill Clinton's Political Rise

Bill Clinton did become a successful politician, rising to the highest positions in state government as a very young man. When he was just 30 years old, he became attorney general of Arkansas. Two years later, at the age of 32, he became the nation's youngest governor. Politically, Clinton represented a new kind of Democrat. He was not as conservative as many Republicans but not as liberal as many other Democrats. In other words, he was a centrist.

Clinton's reputation grew steadily. In the late 1980s, he chaired the National Governors Association. There he focused on issues such as improving public education and reforming the welfare system. He also chaired the Democratic Leadership Council, an organization of centrists. Clearly, Clinton was a Democrat on the rise.

Clinton the candidate It was no surprise, then, when Clinton sought the Democratic nomination for the presidency in 1992. During his campaign, he stressed the need for a national health-care system and middle-class tax cuts. He also skillfully deflected questions about his past. These included charges that he had evaded the draft during the Vietnam War.

Clinton's campaign also featured a major role for his wife, **Hillary Rodham Clinton**. She was regarded as one of the country's top lawyers. Clinton made it clear that his <u>administration</u> would rely on her skill and guidance.

The 1992 election Clinton won the Democratic nomination and ran against President George H.W. Bush. Clinton named a fellow southerner, Senator **Al Gore** of Tennessee, as his running mate. The race also featured independent candidate H. Ross Perot.

In the campaign, Clinton presented himself as the protector of the middle class. His message helped produce a solid victory. He won 370 electoral votes to Bush's 168, although Clinton received less than 50 percent of the popular vote. Although Perot received 19 percent of the popular vote, he carried no state.

READING CHECK **Identifying Cause and Effect** What were some of the key factors in Clinton's rise to the presidency?

Domestic Policy Issues

During his campaign, Bill Clinton made a number of promises about domestic matters. His record in fulfilling those promises was mixed.

Deficit reduction As you have read, Clinton proposed cutting taxes for middle class Americans during the 1992 campaign. Soon after taking office, however, he changed his plan. Citing budget deficits, which continued to rise sharply, he pushed through a major increase in taxes.

Clinton's move was criticized by some Republicans. They predicted the tax increase would hurt the economy. "The deficit four years from now will be higher than it is today, not lower," claimed Senator Phil Gramm of Texas.

This prediction turned out to be false. In fact, the United States in 1993 was entering a time of prosperity. As the decade continued, the nation experienced a long period of low unemployment and interest rates. Other features of the booming 1990s economy are shown in the graphs on the next page.

Health-care reform Reform of the nation's health-care system was another major 1992 campaign issue for Clinton. In 1992 health-care costs were rising sharply. Meanwhile, Clinton observed, tens of millions of Americans

ACADEMIC VOCABULARY
administration the carrying out or management of government

The Clinton Style

Bill Clinton's warmth and charm made him an effective candidate. He won both the 1992 and 1996 presidential elections. In his State of the Union address at the start of his second term (inset), Clinton stated that the country had recovered not only its economic strength but also its optimism.

had little or no health insurance. The public, it seemed, was anxious for change.

To explore solutions to these problems, Clinton named a special task force headed by First Lady Hillary Clinton. After months of study, the group proposed a government-sponsored program of health care. Response to the proposal was mixed. The plan offered coverage to all Americans, but many people were unwilling to risk major changes to the health-care system. The plan was defeated after months of debate.

The 1994 elections The defeat of Clinton's health-care plan reflected a discontent with Clinton's leadership. The new president had failed to deliver on several campaign promises. The tax hike of 1993 was also unpopular.

The discontent helped contribute to a major Republican victory in the 1994 midterm elections. Many Republicans, led by Representative Newt Gingrich of Georgia, campaigned with a document they called the **Contract with America**. The Contract included plans to balance the budget, fight crime, and provide tax cuts for many Americans. The Contract with America appealed to many voters. Republicans gained 54 seats in the House and 8 seats in the Senate. They took control of both houses of Congress for the first time in 40 years.

Welfare reform In spite of this defeat, Clinton bounced back. He did this by addressing several issues the Republicans had raised, including reform of the welfare system. Since the Great Depression, welfare programs had paid cash to poor families. Many people, however, had come to believe that this system was often misused. The Contract with America included plans for welfare reform. Democrats, including Clinton, opposed the plan proposed by the Contract with America.

In 1996, however, Clinton proposed his own welfare-reform plan. It limited the time people could receive benefits and required most recipients to find work within two years of getting benefits. Congress approved this plan.

Other challenges During the 1990s, the Internet emerged as a major means of communication and commerce. It also presented challenges, however. For example, many adults were concerned that children would be exposed

The Economy in the 1990s

Left, shoppers enjoy the benefits of a strong economy at a mall. Disposable income—that is, income available for spending or saving—grew during the 1990s. Americans' rate of savings fell drastically in the 1990s.

FEDERAL DEFICITS AND SURPLUSES, 1980–2000

Source: Budget of the United States Government, 2005

STOCK MARKET, 1980–2000

Source: Global Financial Data; New Trading Ideas

SKILLS FOCUS: INTERPRETING GRAPHS

1. How high were the federal deficits before Clinton took office? How did the federal deficit change in the late 1990s?
2. Compare the rate of growth in the stock market in the 1980s and the 1990s.

See **Skills Handbook**, pp. H16, H17

to inappropriate material on the Internet. The White House helped push a 1996 law to limit the use of the Internet for transmitting certain sexually explicit material. In *Reno* v. *ACLU*, however, the Supreme Court struck down this law as a violation of the freedom of speech.

Clinton also faced the task of helping the nation cope with tragedy. In 1995 terrorists exploded a bomb in the Murrah Federal Building in Oklahoma City, Oklahoma. **Terrorism** is the use of violence by individuals or groups to advance political goals.

The Oklahoma City blast killed 168 people, including many children. More than 500 people were injured. Two Americans, Timothy McVeigh and Terry Nichols, were convicted for their roles in the crime. (McVeigh was executed in 2001. Nichols was sentenced to life in prison.)

Another challenge facing Clinton was reelection. In 1996 he defeated Republican senator Bob Dole of Kansas. H. Ross Perot again ran, this time on the Reform Party ticket.

READING CHECK **Summarizing** In what sense was Clinton's success in domestic policy "mixed"?

Foreign Policy Challenges

When Bill Clinton came into office, the United States was still struggling to understand the post–Cold War world. With the threat of communism gone, Clinton had to determine where American interests lay and how to protect them. The new environment would present its share of challenges to the new president.

Early success in the Middle East
In September 1993, Clinton hosted a ceremony for the signing of a major peace agreement between Israel and the Palestinians. The agreement was known as the Oslo Accords. Israeli prime minister Yitzhak Rabin and Palestinian chairman Yasser Arafat agreed to self-rule for the Palestinians in certain areas. The Palestinians agreed to recognize Israel's right to exist. The agreement also set the stage for ongoing negotiations in the Middle East.

Much of the promise of the Oslo Accords was never realized. Yitzhak Rabin died at the hands of an assassin in 1995. Still, the signing was a historic high point in President Clinton's first term.

FACES OF HISTORY
Bill CLINTON
1946–

Born in the small town of Hope, Arkansas, Bill Clinton excelled in school despite a troubled home life. He graduated from Georgetown University and Yale Law School. From the time he was in high school, Clinton dreamed of entering politics. In 1976 he won a race for Arkansas Attorney General. In 1978 at the age of 32, Clinton won the governorship. He won the seat again in 1982.

Clinton went on to win the presidency in 1992. As president, he achieved the first balanced budget since the 1960s. Winning re-election in 1996, he became the first Democrat since Franklin D. Roosevelt to win a second term.

Summarize What were some of President Clinton's major achievements?

Somalia
Early in his term, Clinton faced a difficult challenge in the African country of Somalia. Before Clinton took office, President Bush had sent American forces there to help a UN program distribute food to starving Somali victims of a civil war within their country.

By 1993 the UN's mission had grown. Now UN forces were working to end the fighting itself. A number of American forces died in the violence. The worst incident occurred in October 1993. In a bloody battle in the Somali capital of Mogadishu, 18 Americans were killed and 84 were wounded. Many Somalis also died. Clinton chose to withdraw American forces. The bitter experience helped discourage Clinton from sending forces to the African country of Rwanda in 1994 to stop a terrible genocide that claimed hundreds of thousands of lives.

Haiti
In 1994 the UN acted to settle a violent dispute in the Caribbean nation of Haiti. The goal was to remove a military dictator who had taken over Haiti's government by force. Clinton pledged the use of American troops to lead the UN effort. In September, the force landed in Haiti. Their presence helped bring about a generally peaceful change in government.

The former Yugoslavia
Yugoslavia was a country that had formed after World War I. Within its borders lived several ethnic groups that were historical enemies and that had dreams of their own independence. During the

THE IMPACT TODAY

Government
One topic left for future negotiation under the Oslo Accords was the presence of Israeli settlements in the occupied territories. In 2005, Israel removed the settlements, which had long caused conflict with the Palestinians.

COUNTERPOINTS
Views on Free Trade

In the early days of his administration, President Clinton worked hard to persuade Congress and the American people to support the North American Free Trade Agreement (NAFTA).

Business leader H. Ross Perot opposed NAFTA and free trade during his independent campaign for the presidency in 1992.

❝ [U]nder NAFTA more jobs will stay home here in America and more American exports will head to Mexico . . . If you want to create more American jobs, if you want to lower the differences in cost of production in America and Mexico, if you want to take down barriers in Mexico to exports, then you should want NAFTA. ❞

President Clinton, 1993

❝ You implement that NAFTA, the Mexican trade agreement, where they pay people a dollar an hour, have no health care, no retirement, no pollution controls . . . and you're going to hear a giant sucking sound of jobs being pulled out of this country. ❞

H. Ross Perot, 1992

SKILLS FOCUS: READING LIKE A HISTORIAN

Analyzing Primary Sources Why does Clinton think NAFTA will create American jobs? Why does Perot expect the opposite?

See **Skills Handbook**, p. H28–H29

THE IMPACT TODAY
Economics
In August 2005, President George W. Bush signed the Central American-Dominican Republic Free Trade Agreement, or CAFTA-DR. The agreement is designed to break down trade barriers between the United States and several Latin American neighbors.

Cold War, the country was held together by its leader, Josip Broz Tito. Soon after Tito's death in 1980, however, the country began to unravel. By the 1990s Yugoslavia no longer existed. In its place were several smaller countries. Within and between these countries, violence raged.

Clinton was deeply involved in efforts to end the bloodshed. In 1995 he helped bring about the Dayton Accords, an agreement aimed at ending fighting in the new country of Bosnia and Herzegovina. In 1999 he urged NATO to act against Serbia, another country formed from the former Yugoslavia. His goal was to stop the Serb army's attempt to force ethnic Albanians from the Serbian region of Kosovo. NATO forces conducted a bombing campaign that forced Serb troops to leave Kosovo.

Promoting international trade Another issue awaiting Bill Clinton when he took office was the North American Free Trade Agreement, or . Under this agreement, the United States, Mexico, and Canada became one large free-trade zone. This meant that most products could be sold across the borders of these countries without tariffs or trade barriers. President Bush had completed negotiations on the agreement before he left office. It became Clinton's job to win congressional approval. Facing stiff opposition, Clinton fought for and won passage of NAFTA in the fall of 1993.

Some critics believed NAFTA would cost American jobs. They argued that because Mexican factories paid lower wages, they could make and sell goods at a lower cost than American-made goods. Without tariffs to make Mexican goods more expensive, many feared American factories would go out of business.

Clinton and supporters of NAFTA believed the agreement would increase trade, which would help the economy. Indeed, increasing trade was a major Clinton goal. During his presidency, the United States took part in the creation of the World Trade Organization (WTO).

The WTO replaced the General Agreement on Tariffs and Trade (GATT). It was meant as a means of settling trade disputes and forming rules for global trade. Clinton pushed for other trade agreements as well. For example, he fought for permanent normal trade status for China, the world's most populous country.

READING CHECK **Identifying Supporting Details** How did the end of the Cold War affect Clinton's foreign policy?

Scandal and Impeachment

Clinton had won the presidency in spite of questions about his past. His election, however, did not end the controversy. Soon came even more scandal.

Throughout his first term, Clinton faced investigation about an investment he and his wife had made in a failed real estate project in the 1970s. The project was known as Whitewater. Among several legal questions related to Whitewater, observers wondered whether the Clintons and their business partners had acted improperly in getting and using loans.

Special prosecutor Kenneth Starr led the Whitewater investigation. Though he never filed any Whitewater-related charges against Clinton, three former Clinton business associates were found guilty of various crimes.

Clinton also faced charges that while he was governor of Arkansas, he had sexually harassed a female state employee. That woman, named Paula Jones, brought a lawsuit against the president. In the course of this case, information emerged suggesting that the president had conducted an improper relationship with a 21-year-old White House intern named Monica Lewinsky. Starr then extended the scope of his investigation to include Clinton's relationship with Lewinsky.

Eventually, Clinton was accused of lying under oath about his relationship with Lewinsky. He was also accused of trying to influence Lewinsky's testimony. Clinton later admitted he had conducted an improper relationship, but he said he did not lie under oath.

The House of Representatives responded by approving two articles of impeachment against Clinton in November 1998. Clinton was the first president to face a Senate impeachment trial since Andrew Johnson in 1868.

In order to remove a president from office, a two-thirds majority in the Senate must vote to convict. In early 1999 the Senate voted 55–45 against conviction on the first article of impeachment and voted 50–50 on the second article. Clinton remained in office to complete his term.

READING CHECK **Sequencing** What role did scandal play in Bill Clinton's presidency?

SECTION 1 ASSESSMENT

HSS 11.8.7, 11.9.7

Reviewing Ideas, Terms, and People

1. **a. Recall** Who were the key figures in the election of 1992?
   b. Make Inferences What can you infer from the performance of H. Ross Perot in the 1992 election?

2. **a. Define** Write a brief definition of the following term: Contract with America
   b. Summarize What do you think were Clinton's greatest successes and his greatest failures during his time in office?

3. **a. Identify** What were the major foreign-policy issues facing the Clinton administration?
   b. Make Generalizations Toward what goals did the United States use military force during Clinton's time in office?

4. **a. Identify** Identify and briefly describe the significance of the Whitewater scandal.
   b. Explain On what grounds did the House of Representatives approve articles of impeachment against Clinton?

Critical Thinking

5. **Identifying the Main Idea** Copy the chart below and use information from the section to record details that support the main idea of the section.

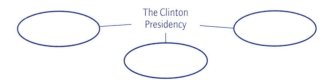

 W1.1

6. **Narrative** President Clinton was known for overcoming setbacks to achieve political success. Write a brief paragraph telling of some of the setbacks and recoveries of the Clinton administration.

LANDMARK SUPREME COURT CASES
Constitutional Issue: Search and Seizure

Vernonia School District v. Acton (1995)

Why It Matters The Fourth Amendment prevents the government from making unreasonable searches. In this case, the Supreme Court found it reasonable to "search" student athletes by making them submit to drug testing.

Background of the Case
Officials in the Vernonia School District in Oregon were concerned about the extent of drug use by students. The school district adopted a rule requiring student athletes to submit to random drug testing. When James Acton signed up to play seventh-grade football, he and his parents refused to sign the consent form for drug testing. The school did not let him play, so Acton sued, arguing that the drug testing violated the search and seizure clause of the Fourth Amendment. The trial court ruled that he had no valid constitutional claim and dismissed his case, but the court of appeals reinstated the case. The school district then appealed to the Supreme Court.

THE IMPACT TODAY Public high schools can now require student athletes to submit to drug testing as a condition of playing sports. The Supreme Court's decision gives schools more power to detect and discourage drug abuse by student athletes.

The Decision
The Supreme Court ruled that random drug testing of student athletes is not a violation of the Fourth Amendment's search and seizure clause. First, the Court held that drug testing is a "search" under the Fourth Amendment. The question was whether the search was reasonable. The Court decided that the school district had a legitimate concern about student drug use and that the testing program was designed to have a minimal impact on students' privacy. Finally, the Court held that students were not required to go out for sports, and those who did should expect some intrusions on their privacy. The manner and extent of the search were reasonable, the Court held, so the drug testing was lawful under the Constitution.

CRITICAL THINKING
go.hrw.com
Research Online
Keyword: SS Court

1. **Analyze the Impact** Using the keyword above, find and read the text of the Fourth Amendment. Could the Supreme Court have found that the school drug testing was not a search within the meaning of the Constitution?
2. **You Be the Judge** Based on the *Vernonia School District* decision, should a school be allowed to require drug testing for students who participate in nonsports activities, such as the yearbook or chess club? Explain your answer in a short paragraph.

SECTION 2
George W. Bush's Presidency

BEFORE YOU READ

MAIN IDEA
Following a troubled election, Republican George W. Bush won the White House and strongly promoted his agenda.

READING FOCUS
1. What were the unusual circumstances of the election of 2000?
2. What were key components of George W. Bush's domestic policy?
3. What were the key components and figures in Bush's foreign policy?

KEY TERMS AND PEOPLE
George W. Bush
budget surplus
Bush v. *Gore*
dot-com
dividend
Condoleezza Rice
Donald Rumsfeld

 11.11.2 Discuss the significant domestic policy speeches of Truman, Eisenhower, Kennedy, Johnson, Nixon, Carter, Reagan, Bush, and Clinton (e.g. with regard to education, civil rights, economic policy, environmental policy.)

 What happened on the night of the 2000 presidential election?

For **George W. Bush**, it had been a night of great tension. At the end of a hard-fought campaign for president, the Republican candidate sat down with his family to watch the election returns on TV.

First came news that Democratic candidate Al Gore had apparently won the popular vote in Florida—a state that was key to the outcome of the election. Two hours later, the news organizations that had made this report took an extraordinary step—they retracted their announcement and declared the winner in Florida uncertain. Then at around 2 a.m., these same news organizations announced that Bush had won Florida—and with it the presidency. Gore, following the election-night custom, called Bush to acknowledge Bush's victory and congratulate the new president-elect.

But the drama was not yet over. An hour after Gore's telephone call, the news organizations switched their call again! Florida was once more considered too close to call. Gore called his opponent once again—this time taking back his admission of defeat. The election in Florida was over, but who had won the presidency? It would take more than a month to determine the answer.

An Election Night to Remember

▼ George W. Bush (center) awaits results with his father, former president George H. W. Bush, and brother Jeb.

INTO THE TWENTY-FIRST CENTURY **733**

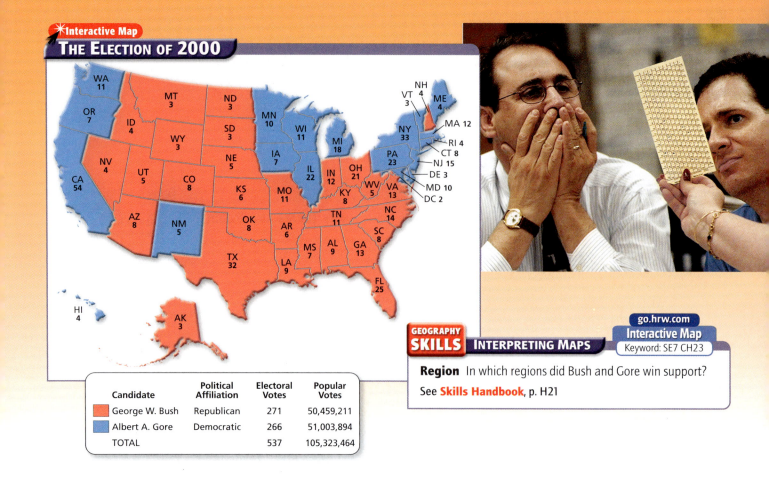

Region In which regions did Bush and Gore win support?
See **Skills Handbook**, p. H21

The Election of 2000

With President Clinton finishing his second term, both parties knew the 2000 race was wide open. It turned out to be one of the closest, most controversial elections in U.S. history.

The nominees During Clinton's presidency, the American economy prospered. The federal government had a **budget surplus**, which meant that its income exceeded its spending. Although the country's future looked bright, some Democrats were uncomfortable with Clinton's image.

Nobody understood the situation better than Clinton's vice president, Al Gore. As the Democratic nominee in the 2000 presidential race, Gore wanted to claim credit for the success of the past. He also needed to set himself apart from Clinton. "We're entering a new time," he declared as he accepted his party's nomination. "We're electing a new president. And I stand here tonight as my own man." For his running mate, Gore made a historic choice: Connecticut senator Joe Lieberman, who became the first Jewish American to seek that high office.

The Republicans chose George W. Bush as their candidate. The son of former president George H.W. Bush, he had served six years as governor of Texas. Bush's running mate was Dick Cheney of Wyoming. Cheney had a long record that included service in Congress and in several previous administrations.

The 2000 election also featured the third-party candidacy of Ralph Nader. A longtime advocate for American consumers, Nader ran as the leader of the Green Party, a liberal party that supported environmental causes.

A troubled election As election day 2000 approached, polls indicated a tight race. The polls were correct. Election-night returns showed a close popular and electoral vote. It soon became clear that the race hinged on the outcome in a single state—Florida. Whoever won there would win the election.

As you have read, election returns in Florida were amazingly close. The result was confusion, with news organizations changing their reports several times about who had won the state. The matter remained unresolved through the night and into the next morning.

734 CHAPTER 23

A pair of reporters examine an incorrectly punched ballot during a manual election recount in Fort Lauderdale, Florida, in early December 2000. Controversy over incorrectly punched ballots and so-called butterfly ballots stalled election results. *How was the outcome finally decided?*

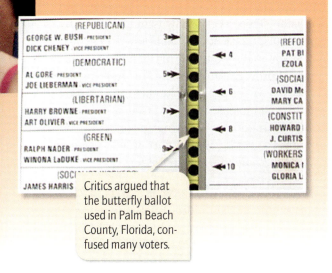

Critics argued that the butterfly ballot used in Palm Beach County, Florida, confused many voters.

Recounts and legal wrangling Florida election officials quickly performed a recount of the ballots. As with the original vote count, this was performed by machine. The recount gave Bush a lead of just over 300 votes out of a total of nearly 6 million Florida ballots cast.

Meanwhile, Democrats were raising questions about the Florida balloting. One concern was that thousands of ballots had gone uncounted by vote-counting machines. Many ballots had been rejected because voters had made mistakes in marking them. For example, some ballots required voters to make their choices by punching a hole in the ballot. In some cases, the hole was not clean or complete enough for the counting machine to read. Democrats argued that in many cases, the choice of the voters was obvious even though the ballot-counting equipment did not count the ballot. Because the race was so close, they said, it made sense to recount all ballots by hand. They hoped that among the uncounted ballots they would gain enough votes to win the state.

Another type of punch-card ballot used in Florida was the butterfly ballot shown above. Some observers argued that the butterfly ballot's design led some voters to mistakenly select someone other than their intended choice.

Republicans were generally opposed to hand recounts of ballots. One reason was that hand counting introduced the role of human error and individual judgment. They also objected to Democratic plans to recount only in areas that were thought to be heavily Democratic.

Over the next few days, Democrats and Republicans took turns filing lawsuits aimed at forcing or preventing recounts. In some counties, recounts were completed. Absentee ballots were also tallied, some of which were challenged by Democrats.

Bush v. Gore On December 8, Gore won what seemed like a key legal victory. The Florida Supreme Court ordered that hand recounts had to take place in certain Florida counties.

The Bush campaign appealed the ruling to the U.S. Supreme Court. The Court issued its decision in **Bush v. Gore** on December 12, 2000. The ruling held that the Florida Supreme Court's recount order was unconstitutional because it failed to provide clear standards by which the ballots were to be counted. Further, the Court held, there was no time to create standards for use statewide.

The day after the decision, Gore publicly accepted his defeat in the race. That evening, George W. Bush addressed the nation on television as the president-elect. He urged Americans to unite for the future.

HISTORY'S VOICES

" I was not elected to serve one party, but to serve one nation.

The president of the United States is the president of every single American, of every race and every background.

Whether you voted for me or not, I will do my best to serve your interests and I will work to earn your respect. "

—George W. Bush, December 13, 2000

On January 20, 2001, Bush was sworn in as president. He became only the fourth person in American history to have won the presidency in spite of having received fewer popular votes than his opponent.

Sequencing What was the sequence of key events in the election of 2000?

THE IMPACT TODAY

Government
In 2002 President Bush signed into law the Help America Vote Act, which provided funds to help states replace punch-card voting machines with electronic voting systems. The law required states to have the new voting systems in place by 2006.

INTO THE TWENTY-FIRST CENTURY **735**

Bush's Domestic Policy

The 1990s had been a prosperous time. By the time Bush took office, however, the picture was beginning to change. For example, even before the election, the once booming stock market had begun to fall. This was due in large part to the collapse in the price of many Internet-related stocks.

In the 1990s the Internet represented a whole new way of doing business. Many investors had hoped to make big money buying shares of Internet pioneers. These companies were known as **dot-coms**, after the .com that appears in many Internet addresses. Investors gambled billions on dot-coms. They paid high prices for the stock of companies that had never earned a profit. They expected the companies to make money one day. When the profits failed to appear, however, investors began to sell their stocks. As a result, prices dropped.

Stock prices were also hurt by a series of scandals that hit several large corporations in the early 2000s. The scandals involved dishonest accounting methods designed to make the companies more attractive to investors.

In addition to the drop in the stock market, the overall economy began to slow. Shortly after Bush took office, the United States was officially entering a recession. Though Bush was not responsible for this development, it did affect his domestic policies.

Tax cuts During the campaign, Bush had promised to cut taxes. At that time, the country enjoyed a budget surplus. When he took office, he quickly urged Congress to take action.

HISTORY'S VOICES

> "You see, the growing surplus exists because taxes are too high and government is charging more than it needs. The people of America have been overcharged and on their behalf, I'm here asking for a refund."
>
> —George W. Bush, February 27, 2001

Bush also argued that cutting taxes would help spur the now slumping economy. By lowering taxes and letting Americans keep more of their income to spend, Bush reasoned, business would improve. He believed this would provide more jobs and higher incomes.

By June, the Republican-controlled Congress had delivered on Bush's request. In addition to cutting tax rates, the new law addressed some long-standing complaints about the tax code. For example, it helped reduce the so-called marriage penalty. This is a part of the tax code that causes many married people to pay higher taxes than they would if they were single. The new law also lowered the estate tax, a tax on property inherited after a person's death.

Despite Bush's tax cuts, however, the economy did not improve. Instead, it went into recession. This recession was made worse by the terrorist attacks of September 11, 2001, which you will read about in the next section.

By 2003 Bush was again looking to cut taxes in hopes of promoting economic growth. Congress again passed a tax cut, which included the elimination of taxes on **dividends**. A dividend is a portion of a company's profits paid to its shareholders.

Education, health care, and more

Shortly after taking office, Bush announced a major plan for improving education. The plan became the basis for a 2001 law, the No Child Left Behind (NCLB) Act. A key part of NCLB was a requirement that states develop academic standards and test students annually to ensure that those standards are met.

Another early Bush program was the White House Office of Faith-Based Initiatives. This office helps religious community-service organizations of all faiths develop greater access to federal funding. Bush viewed religious groups as effective tools for delivering services to needy groups such as the homeless, troubled youth, and former prison inmates. Critics, however, worried that the program might cross the constitutional line separating church and state.

In 2003 Bush signed into law a major update to the Medicare program. Included in this update was a new benefit to help Medicare recipients pay for prescription medicines.

Bush's second term In 2004 Bush ran for a second term in office. The Democrats nominated Senator John Kerry of Massachusetts. In addition to attacking Bush's foreign policy, Kerry criticized Bush's handling of the economy. He noted that the government was again running large deficits—that is, spending more than it takes in. In spite of these attacks, Bush won re-election in another close contest.

THE IMPACT TODAY

Daily Life

States also create initiatives to improve public education. For example, California issued a new Master Plan for Education in 2002. The purpose of the Master Plan is to provide all students with access to "the educational components that are essential to a high quality education system and that foster the attainment of the educational expectations set by the State."

Linking to Today

No Child Left Behind

In 2001 Congress passed an amendment to the Elementary and Secondary Education Act of 1965. Known as No Child Left Behind (NCLB), the law is intended to improve education across the United States.

No Child Left Behind says that all students should reach at least minimal proficiency on state academic achievement standards and state academic tests. Under the law, students will take standardized tests every year to show what they have learned. The results will be used to decide whether students are getting the education they need.

Many states already had testing programs in place before NCLB was put into effect. Remaining states had until the 2005–2006 school year to make sure that their tests addressed their state's academic standards.

Not everyone agrees that NCLB is the solution to improving education. In 2003 the National Education Association, a teachers' union, filed a lawsuit arguing that the federal government was not providing enough money to support the required changes. A lawsuit filed by the state of Connecticut in 2005 also opposed the idea that states should pay for federal education goals.

Making Inferences Why might leaders feel that standardized testing is a useful tool for measuring what students have learned?

High school students take a standardized test.

Bush soon announced a top priority for his second term: reform of Social Security. Recall that this system uses money collected from taxpayers to help fund payments to retired Americans. Bush noted that in the future, taxpayers would be unable to pay all the benefits due to retirees. He proposed reforms that would allow taxpayers to create private accounts to fund their retirement. The plan, however, faced considerable public opposition. By late 2005 Congress had not acted on it.

Bush also faced decisions over Supreme Court vacancies. In 2005, Justice Sandra Day O'Connor announced her retirement and Chief Justice William Rehnquist died. To replace Rehnquist as Chief Justice, Bush nominated John Roberts, who won Senate confirmation in September 2005. To replace O'Connor, Bush nominated conservative judge Samuel Alito. On January 31, 2006, Alito won Senate confirmation in a 58-42 vote, one of the tightest margins in recent history.

READING CHECK **Identifying Problems and Solutions** What were some of the problems Bush hoped to address with his domestic policies?

Bush's Foreign Policy

Even before taking office in 2001, Bush assembled his foreign-policy staff. He chose Colin Powell as secretary of state. Powell had been a general in the army and chair of the Joint Chiefs of Staff during the Persian Gulf War of 1991. Bush named **Condoleezza Rice** as his national security adviser. Rice had been on the faculty of Stanford University and had served in the administration of George H. W. Bush.

Soon after the 2004 election, Powell resigned and Rice became secretary of state. For secretary of defense, Bush selected **Donald Rumsfeld**, who had earlier held this post and other key government posts.

During the 2000 election campaign, Bush had promised to limit the use of American troops for what he termed "nation building." For example, he criticized Clinton's use of troops in Somalia and Haiti. "I think our troops ought to be used to fight and win war," he said.

With this in mind, Bush called for a review of the nation's armed forces early in his presidency. He wanted to ensure that the military was prepared to fight the kinds of conflicts the United States might face in the future.

INTO THE TWENTY-FIRST CENTURY **737**

Bush's Foreign Policy Team

Colin Powell
Colin Powell, a retired four-star general, served as secretary of state during George W. Bush's first term. Powell was the first African American to hold this position.

Donald Rumsfeld
As Bush's secretary of defense, Rumsfeld's main challenge was to direct response to the terrorist attacks of September 11, 2001.

Condoleezza Rice
Rice served as Bush's national security adviser during his first term. She replaced Colin Powell as secretary of state during Bush's second term.

Bush also decided to cancel the 1972 Anti-Ballistic Missile (ABM) Treaty. This agreement had been forged with the Soviet Union during the Cold War. Bush argued that the nation no longer faced a nuclear threat from Russia. Instead, he believed the danger was from some terrorist state. Therefore, Bush planned to move forward with development of a missile defense system. At the same time, Bush planned steep cuts in the nation's nuclear arsenal. This, he said, signaled his own commitment to reducing the threat to other nations.

The decision on the ABM treaty caused some friction with Russia and China. In general, however, Bush worked to build better relations with both countries. For example, he relied heavily on China's cooperation in putting pressure on North Korea to end its program for building nuclear weapons.

Bush also helped promote the so-called Middle East road map to peace. This historic document established a two-state vision—that is, an independent Palestinian state as well as the Jewish state of Israel.

By far, however, the most important foreign-policy event of the Bush administration occurred on September 11, 2001. This event set in motion a series of events that continue to affect the United States today. You will be reading about September 11 in the next section.

READING CHECK **Contrasting** How did Bush's foreign policy differ from Clinton's?

SECTION 2 ASSESSMENT

HSS 11.11.2

Reviewing Ideas, Terms, and People

1. **a. Describe** What factors made the 2000 election unusual?
   b. Contrast How did the positions of the Democrats and Republicans differ in the 2000 election with regard to hand recounting of ballots?

2. **a. Define** Write a brief definition of each of the following terms: **budget surplus, dot-com, dividend**
   b. Analyze How did the change in the economic situation in the United States affect George W. Bush's presidency?

3. **a. Identify** Besides the terrorist attacks of September 11, 2001, what were the major foreign-policy issues facing the Bush administration?
   b. Make Generalizations How did Bush's foreign policy reflect the realities of a post–Cold War world?

Critical Thinking

4. **Identifying the Main Idea** Copy the chart below and use information from the section to record details that support the main idea of the section.

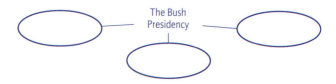

FOCUS ON SPEAKING   ELA W1.1

5. **Narrative** Write and deliver a news story about the key events of the 2000 presidential election. The account should tell what made the election so unusual in American politics.

SECTION 3
How September 11, 2001, Changed America

BEFORE YOU READ

MAIN IDEA
A horrific attack on September 11, 2001, awakened the nation to the threat of terrorism and changed America's view of the world.

READING FOCUS
1. What happened on September 11, 2001?
2. What was the background to the September 11 attacks?
3. How did the United States respond to the attacks?
4. How did the 9/11 attacks eventually lead to war with Iraq?

KEY TERMS AND PEOPLE
9/11
Rudolph Giuliani
Osama bin Laden
al Qaeda
Taliban
Department of Homeland Security
USA PATRIOT Act

HSS 11.9.4 List the effects of foreign policy on domestic policies and vice versa (e.g., protests during the war in Vietnam, the "nuclear freeze" movement).

HSS 11.9.6 Describe U.S. Middle East policy and its strategic, political, and economic interests, including those related to the Gulf War.

Attack on the World Trade Center

THE INSIDE STORY

What would you do if terrorists struck your neighborhood? On September 11, 2001, students at Stuyvesant High School in New York City were not at all prepared for terror to strike their community. Yet that morning, just as school was getting started, an aircraft slammed into one of the Twin Towers of the World Trade Center, about five blocks away. A short while later, a second airplane struck the second tower.

The students fled the school in search of safety. Among them was Ethan Moses, the photographer for the Stuyvesant High School newspaper, *The Spectator*. When he left the school, he took his camera along. As a student journalist, he felt driven to record what was taking place in his neighborhood—even though he was terrified by the tragedy unfolding before him. Before turning to run for his own safety, he snapped the image you see here of one of the Twin Towers collapsing.

Moses knew that he must preserve the images of what took place that day. Like Americans throughout the country, he overcame his horror and faced the September 11 attacks with courage and resolve.

◀ The horror of September 11, 2001, changed the way Americans looked at themselves and the world.

INTO THE TWENTY-FIRST CENTURY

September 11, 2001

Shortly after 8:45 A.M. on September 11, 2001, people around the country began to hear startling reports of a terrible crash in New York City. An airliner had slammed into one of the 110-story-tall Twin Towers of the World Trade Center. This complex housed thousands of offices and businesses.

A deliberate attack Just 17 minutes after the first jet crashed, a second aircraft flew into the second of the Twin Towers. It became clear that the crashes were part of a deliberate attack. President Bush appeared before reporters to issue a brief statement. "Today we've had a national tragedy," he declared. He then assured the public that he had ordered the "full resources of the federal government" to respond to the disaster.

In fact, the attack—and its devastating effects—had just begun. In New York, firefighters and police officers rushed to the World Trade Center to help get people out of the burning towers. Military officials launched fighter aircraft to guard against any further attack. The Federal Aviation Administration (FAA) frantically gathered information about other possible hijackings. Hijacking is a terrorist act in which a plane is forced to go somewhere other than its intended destination. To prevent terrorists from getting control of more planes, the FAA also halted all commercial flights.

Unfortunately, there was nothing the FAA could do to stop the deadly flight of planes already in the air. Less than an hour after the first plane hit in New York, another slammed into the Pentagon, the mammoth headquarters of the Department of Defense located just outside Washington, D.C.

The Twin Towers collapse By now, millions of people were watching events unfold on television or listening to the news on the

HISTORY CLOSE-UP

The Attacks of September 11, 2001

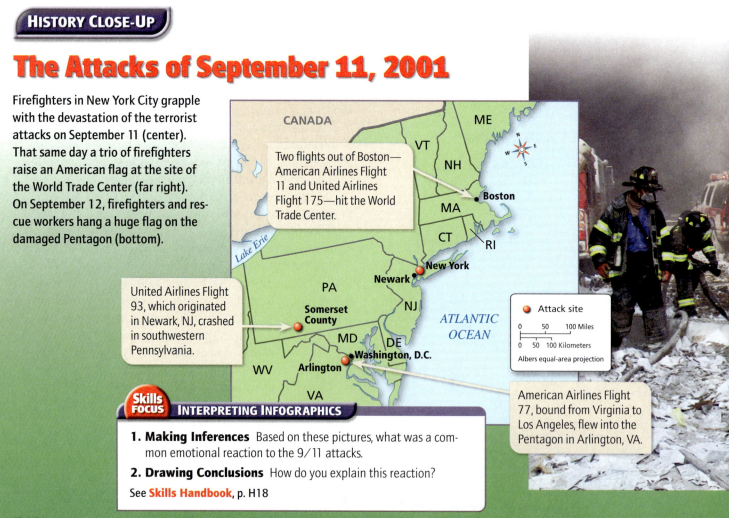

Firefighters in New York City grapple with the devastation of the terrorist attacks on September 11 (center). That same day a trio of firefighters raise an American flag at the site of the World Trade Center (far right). On September 12, firefighters and rescue workers hang a huge flag on the damaged Pentagon (bottom).

Two flights out of Boston—American Airlines Flight 11 and United Airlines Flight 175—hit the World Trade Center.

United Airlines Flight 93, which originated in Newark, NJ, crashed in southwestern Pennsylvania.

American Airlines Flight 77, bound from Virginia to Los Angeles, flew into the Pentagon in Arlington, VA.

Skills Focus: INTERPRETING INFOGRAPHICS

1. **Making Inferences** Based on these pictures, what was a common emotional reaction to the 9/11 attacks.
2. **Drawing Conclusions** How do you explain this reaction?

See **Skills Handbook**, p. H18

radio. But the worst was yet to come. Ten minutes after the Pentagon crash came the shocking collapse of the World Trade Center's South Tower. Fires caused by the plane's nearly full fuel tanks had caused a fatal weakening of the building's structure. The horrifying event was captured by TV cameras for viewers everywhere to see. Shortly after that came news of a fourth plane crash, this one in a field in the Pennsylvania countryside. Then at about 10:30 A.M., the North Tower collapsed in a massive cloud of dust and debris.

The stunned nation did not know it yet, but the worst was over. Later in the day, another building that had been damaged when the Twin Towers came down collapsed. But there were no more hijackings or plane crashes.

The death toll The nation next turned to face the horrible reality of what had taken place. To begin with, the four planes had carried 265 people, including passengers and crew. All were dead. In addition, at the Pentagon, 125 people were killed by the plane's impact and the fires that followed. The number of victims at the World Trade Center was not known, but the estimates were in the thousands. (After several years of investigation, the New York death toll stood at 2,749.) It was clear that the attacks of **9/11** would surpass Pearl Harbor and other great disasters of American history in terms of lives lost.

The nation reacts The nation was overcome by a wave of grief and anger. At the same time, recognition of the bravery of those who responded to the disaster gave people comfort and strength. Americans were awestruck by the heroism of New York's rescue workers. Several hundred firefighters and police officers had run willingly into the burning towers, only to perish when they collapsed. Many also admired the steady leadership of New York's mayor, **Rudolph Giuliani**.

There were also reports that the plane that crashed in Pennsylvania may have been forced down by the heroic actions of its passengers. Telephone calls from passengers aboard the

A Nation Pulls Together

A Michigan rally bursts into cheers after the playing of "God Bless America" (right). Below, New Yorkers memorialize the victims of the attack with a candlelight vigil.

ACADEMIC VOCABULARY
rational based on reason

THE IMPACT TODAY
Daily Life
Al Qaeda also targeted U.S. allies, including Great Britain. In July 2005, a bombing in London's subway and bus system killed 52 people. The bombing was linked to al Qaeda.

plane indicated they knew about the other attacks and had decided to stop the terrorists on board from hitting their next target.

Inspired by these stories, Americans reached out to the victims of 9/11. Blood collection centers received two-and-a-half times the normal donations in the days after 9/11. Millions of dollars poured into charities. Rescue workers from around the country traveled to New York to help with the recovery efforts at Ground Zero, the site where the Twin Towers had stood.

HISTORY'S VOICES

" The camaraderie among the workers in the zone reminds me of the stories we've heard about the World War, where men and women are thrown together by a common cause, share tragedies and victories, and are forever bound to one another by their effort. "

—Joel Meyerowitz, artist's statement to the exhibit "Images from Ground Zero"

Americans also strengthened their resolve to face the challenge ahead. Patriotic feelings soared, and millions of people displayed American flags. It was clear that the United States was now engaged in a new kind of war: a war on terrorism.

 Sequencing What were the key events of September 11, 2001?

Background to the Attacks

Investigators, meanwhile, were trying to determine who was responsible for the attacks. One rational theory focused on  **Osama bin Laden**. A member of a wealthy Saudi Arabian family, bin Laden had gone to Afghanistan in the 1980s to help fight Soviet invaders. During this time, he adopted the goal of promoting a worldwide Islamic revolution. Islam is one of the world's major religions, and it is based on the teachings of the prophet Muhammad, who lived about AD 570–632. Achieving an Islamic revolution, bin Laden claimed, required the destruction of the United States. Bin Laden had also been angered by the presence of American military forces in Saudi Arabia during the Persian Gulf War. This he saw as an insult to Islam.

To carry out his campaign against his enemies, bin Laden developed a terrorist network. This was known as **al Qaeda**, or "the base."

By 2001 bin Laden and al Qaeda were well known to American officials. During the 1990s, these terrorists had made a number of threats against the United States and announced the goal of killing Americans. Bin Laden had links to a 1993 bombing at the World Trade Center that killed six people. He was also accused of helping to train some of the attackers who killed 18 American soldiers in Mogadishu, Somalia, in 1993. In August 1998 bombings at the U.S. embassies in the African countries of Kenya and Tanzania killed 224. After establishing a link between the bombings and bin

Laden's network, President Clinton launched a missile attack into a suspected al Qaeda training camp in Afghanistan. Bin Laden and his organization survived. In 2000 they carried out a bomb attack on an American naval vessel, the USS *Cole*, which was visiting a port in the Middle Eastern country of Yemen. Seventeen Americans died in the blast.

Meanwhile, investigators later learned, al Qaeda was busy planning the 9/11 attacks. As part of this plan, terrorists began entering the United States in early 2000. They enrolled in American flight schools, where they learned the basics of flying airliners.

By September 11 they were ready to act. In the morning hours, they boarded flights at several East Coast airports. They chose long, cross-country routes so that the planes would be fully loaded with fuel. Once in the air, the hijackers—19 in total—seized control of the aircrafts. To do so, they used ordinary box cutters as weapons. It was a complicated plan that used simple methods. Tragically, it worked just as they had planned.

READING CHECK **Identifying the Main Idea** What is Osama bin Laden's background and his reasons for using terrorism?

The United States Responds

Fires were still burning in New York and at the Pentagon when President Bush issued a clear warning to the world. "We will make no distinction between the terrorists who committed these acts and those who harbor them," he declared. With suspicion quickly focusing on Osama bin Laden and his al Qaeda network, Bush's warning seemed especially directed toward the nation of Afghanistan.

War in Afghanistan Afghanistan had endured terrible suffering in the late 1900s. The 1979 invasion by the Soviet Union had been followed by years of bloody fighting and civil war. Out of this chaos, a group known as the Taliban had gained control over most of the country. The Taliban governed according to a strict application of Islamic law. For example, women were required to wear clothing that covered nearly every inch of their bodies. They were forbidden from attending school or leaving home without a male relative. Punishment for offenses was swift and harsh.

The Taliban also enjoyed a close relationship with Osama bin Laden. Recall that bin Laden operated al Qaeda training camps in

Responding to the Attacks

President Bush meets with his National Security Council on September 12, 2001, to plan America's response to the terrorist attacks on the nation. Attention focused on Afghanistan (see map below), a landlocked country in south-central Asia with a mountainous terrain and extreme climate.

AFGHANISTAN

U.S. soldiers in the Khakeran Valley of Afghanistan search a house for weapons in June 2005 in a continuing effort to root out Taliban presence in the region.

THE IMPACT TODAY

Government

The creation of the Department of Homeland Security marked one of the most far-reaching government reorganizations in American history. It was followed by a planned overhaul of the nation's entire intelligence structure.

Afghanistan. This was done with the cooperation of the Taliban. For his part, bin Laden provided support to the Taliban in its struggle to control Afghanistan.

When it became clear that bin Laden and al Qaeda were likely responsible for the 9/11 attacks, Bush put pressure on the Taliban. He insisted that Taliban leaders seize bin Laden and hand him over to the United States.

In spite of this pressure, the Taliban remained defiant. By the end of September, it was clear they would not give in to American demands. So, on October 7, 2001, the United States, along with ally Great Britain, launched a military attack on Taliban strongholds throughout Afghanistan.

HISTORY'S VOICES

❝We're a peaceful nation. Yet, as we have learned, so suddenly and so tragically, there can be no peace in a world of sudden terror. In the face of today's new threat, the only way to pursue peace is to pursue those who threaten it.❞

—George W. Bush, October 7, 2001

In fighting the Taliban, the United States relied heavily on fighters of Afghanistan's Northern Alliance. This armed group that opposed the Taliban and controlled a small part of Afghanistan. Within weeks, anti-Taliban forces captured the capital of Kabul. By early December, the Taliban was defeated.

Less successful was the hunt for Osama bin Laden. American and Northern Alliance forces at one point thought they had him trapped in the mountainous Tora Bora region of Afghanistan. The site was bombed heavily. Bin Laden, however, managed to avoid capture.

In spite of this setback, the American operation in Afghanistan was considered a success. At the end of December, representatives of several major groups in Afghanistan met to select a new interim leader for the country. They made plans to create a new constitution and government. Presidential elections took place in 2004, and parliamentary elections went forward in 2005. Afghanistan would continue to face serious problems. These included continued fighting by surviving members of the Taliban. However, the country's role as a terrorist base was greatly reduced.

Fighting terrorism at home While American troops were fighting in Afghanistan, President Bush and Congress were working to fight terrorism at home. To coordinate these efforts, Bush and Congress began work on what would become the **Department of Homeland Security**. This cabinet-level organization combined 22 government agencies and 180,000 employees. Its functions included maintaining a color-coded warning system for terrorist threats.

Also in the days after 9/11, the nation experienced a frightening introduction to another kind of terrorist threat: biological agents. In several locations in the eastern United States, 18 people came down with a rare but deadly infection caused by the anthrax bacteria. Five people died. The anthrax had apparently been sent through the mail in a deliberate attempt to infect people. For several anxious weeks, Americans wondered how widespread the anthrax attacks had been. It soon became clear that the crisis was limited to a handful of specific locations. For a nation still recovering from 9/11, however, the incident was alarming.

In Congress, lawmakers took up the question of how to prevent future terrorist attacks. One solution proposed by the White House was to strengthen the powers of law-enforcement to investigate possible terrorists. These proposals became the basis of the **USA PATRIOT Act**. This law made it easier for law enforcement to secretly collect information about suspected terrorists. Indeed, some critics complained that the USA PATRIOT Act gave law enforcement too much power and posed a threat to basic freedoms. To address these concerns, Congress agreed to let some provisions of the law expire after a certain period of time.

READING CHECK **Identifying Problems and Solutions** How did the U.S. government respond to the threat of terrorism after 9/11?

War in Iraq

Following the success in Afghanistan, President Bush delivered his State of the Union address in January 2002. "What we have found in Afghanistan," he said, "confirms that, far from ending there, our war against terror is only beginning." Further, he identified Iraq as a possible future foe.

Following the Persian Gulf War in 1991, Iraq had agreed to destroy its weapons of mass destruction. To ensure that Iraq's leader, Saddam Hussein, was living up to this agreement, the UN placed weapons inspectors inside the country. With each passing year, however, the Iraqi leader grew more and more uncooperative with these inspection efforts. In response, the UN removed its inspectors entirely in 1998.

Since that time, observers believed the Iraqis had been busy building banned weapons. Given the events of 9/11, this greatly concerned President Bush. "The United States will not permit the world's most dangerous regimes to threaten us with the world's most destructive weapons," he declared.

Throughout the fall of 2002 and the winter of 2003, Bush sought to build support for forceful action against Saddam Hussein. Under this pressure, Iraq allowed a new round of UN weapons inspections. This turned up no weapons of mass destruction. Bush, however, insisted that Iraq had failed to account for weapons it was known to have possessed after

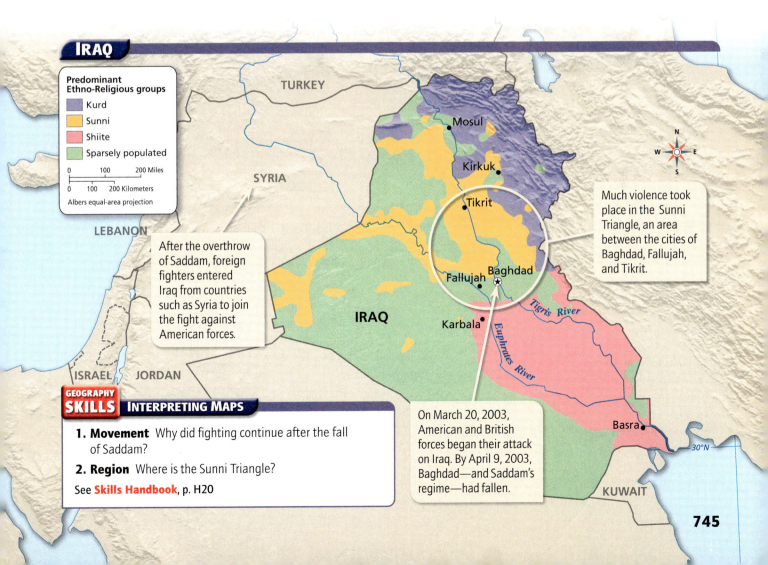

IRAQ

Predominant Ethno-Religious groups
- Kurd
- Sunni
- Shiite
- Sparsely populated

After the overthrow of Saddam, foreign fighters entered Iraq from countries such as Syria to join the fight against American forces.

Much violence took place in the Sunni Triangle, an area between the cities of Baghdad, Fallujah, and Tikrit.

On March 20, 2003, American and British forces began their attack on Iraq. By April 9, 2003, Baghdad—and Saddam's regime—had fallen.

GEOGRAPHY SKILLS **INTERPRETING MAPS**
1. **Movement** Why did fighting continue after the fall of Saddam?
2. **Region** Where is the Sunni Triangle?

See **Skills Handbook**, p. H20

745

FACES OF HISTORY

George W. BUSH
1946–

George W. Bush did not initially seek a life in politics. Though his father, George H. W. Bush, had served as a member of Congress and in other government posts, Bush decided to pursue a business career. A failed bid for Congress in 1978 did nothing to change his mind. Then following his father's term as president, Bush won the race for governor of Texas and was re-elected in 1998. His campaign for the presidency followed two years later. Bush was re-elected to a second term in 2004. After 9/11, Bush's primary focus as president became protecting the nation against the threat of terrorism. His administration will forever be defined by his leadership in the wake of the 9/11 attacks.

Explain How did the 9/11 attacks change Bush's presidency?

---

the Persian Gulf War. Members of his administration also claimed to have information about new Iraqi weapons systems. Many of America's longtime allies argued against going to war. Still, Bush insisted the Iraqi threat must be countered. With the support of Great Britain and several other countries, American forces stormed into Iraq in March 2003.

The United States and its allies made quick work of Iraq's military. By early April, Saddam Hussein's regime had fallen. Saddam was captured in late 2003.

The United States then moved to establish a new Iraqi government. In June 2004 American officials handed control over to an interim Iraqi government. American forces remained to help keep order and train a new Iraqi security force.

Elections in early 2005 began the process by which Iraqis would create a new constitution. Conflict between rival religious and ethnic groups complicated the process. In October 2005, voters approved a new constitution.

Iraq, however, continued to experience serious problems. Terrorists, who included former Saddam loyalists and religious extremists, continued to take a terrible toll on American soldiers and on Iraqi civilians and those who joined the new police and security forces.

The ongoing violence created political problems for Bush. He also faced criticism when it became clear that Saddam Hussein had apparently not possessed weapons of mass destruction at the start of the war.

The president overcame these questions to win re-election in 2004. He reminded voters that Saddam had been a brutal dictator and that his removal from power made the world a safer place. He assured Americans that progress was being made toward a more peaceful, democratic Iraq. He also made clear that U.S. forces would remain in Iraq for as long as necessary to ensure peace and order there.

READING CHECK **Sequencing** Describe the events leading up to and following the war in Iraq.

SECTION 3 ASSESSMENT

HSS 11.9.4, 11.9.6

go.hrw.com
Online Quiz
Keyword: SE7 HP23

Reviewing Ideas, Terms, and People

1. **a. Describe** What is the significance of 9/11?
   b. Summarize How would you summarize the reaction of the American people to the attacks of 9/11?
2. **a. Identify** Who or what are the following: **Osama bin Laden, al Qaeda**
   b. Make Inferences Why do you think Osama bin Laden decided to try to destroy the United States?
3. **a. Describe** Why did the United States attack Afghanistan in 2001?
   b. Make Inferences What can you infer from the fact that the United States received wide support for its attack on Afghanistan?
4. **a. Recall** Why did the United States attack Iraq in 2003?
   b. Explain Why did Bush think that removing Saddam Hussein was important?

Critical Thinking

5. **Identifying Cause and Effect** Copy the chart below and use information from the section to record the effects of the cause given.

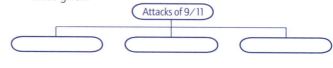

FOCUS ON WRITING ELA W1.1

6. **Narrative** Write a brief narrative that recounts the major events of September 11, 2001, and its aftermath.

SECTION 4: Looking Ahead

BEFORE YOU READ

MAIN IDEA
The dawn of a new century found the United States facing a new era of opportunity and challenge.

READING FOCUS
1. How is the face of the American population changing?
2. What promise does new technology hold for the United States?
3. What challenges confront the United States in the future?

KEY TERMS AND PEOPLE
Antonio Villaraigosa
IT
genetic engineering

HSS 11.8.2 Describe the significance of Mexican immigration and its relationship to the agricultural economy, especially in California.

HSS 11.8.7 Describe the effects of technological developments since 1945.

HSS 11.11.5 Trace the controversies associated with environmental conservation and the development of environmental protection laws.

THE INSIDE STORY

What can a mayoral election tell us about the future of America? The last time Los Angeles had a Hispanic American mayor, the "city" was actually a small frontier community of 6,000 people. The year was 1872.

Since that time, Los Angeles has grown into the second-largest city in the United States. A significant part of that growth was the result of immigration from Mexico and other countries of Central and South America. The growing number of Latino residents—and voters—in Los Angeles formed an increasingly powerful voice in local politics. Yet before 2005 and the election of **Antonio Villaraigosa** (vee-uh-ry-GOH-suh), Hispanics in Los Angeles had never been able to muster the political strength necessary to elect one of their own to the mayor's office. In the 2005 election, Villaraigosa drew support from voters of many backgrounds. His victory, however, was especially significant to the city's 1.7 million Latinos, who make up slightly less than half the city's population.

Villaraigosa's election was a landmark to people all across the country. As you will read, the forces that made California's population so diverse are also at work throughout the rest of the country. The minority groups of yesterday and today are growing, and they will play a leading role in the nation's future.

A Latino Mayor for Los Angeles

▶ Antonio Villaraigosa takes the oath of office as the mayor of Los Angeles.

America's Changing Face

Throughout American history, migration, immigration, and even slavery brought new groups to America. Such changes have sometimes led to conflict between different groups. In general, however, history shows that the nation has grown richer and stronger as it has grown more <u>diverse</u>.

ACADEMIC VOCABULARY
diverse including great variety

Tomorrow's population The makeup of America's population is continually changing. The U.S. census measures these changes. The most recent census was held in 2000. By looking back just 20 years, you can see significant population trends. (See the graphs below.)

Census officials also look into the future. Minority groups today, including African Americans, Hispanic Americans, and Asian Americans, make up about 30 percent of the population. By 2050 they will make up about 50 percent of the population. The Asian American population is expected to more than triple. The Hispanic American population is predicted to grow by nearly 190 percent and make up nearly one-fourth of the population.

The changing population has already caused a reaction in the United States. You have read about growing resistance, mainly among white Americans, to affirmative action programs. Such programs were designed to help minority groups overcome discrimination. In California voters approved Proposition 209 in 1996. This amendment to the state constitution outlawed the use of racial preferences in decisions such as university admissions. Under Proposition 209, public institutions in California can no longer consider a job or school applicant's race, gender, or ethnic background.

Regional changes Many Americans will also be changing where they live. The warmer regions of the South and the West are expected to grow at a faster rate than the colder Northeast and Midwest. The warmer climate attracts people and businesses, in part because of lower energy costs. Labor costs have tended to be lower in the South and West, another factor that attracts businesses to the area.

Census projections predict that between 2000 and 2030, the populations of the South and West will rise about 45 percent, compared to a 30 percent growth of the total U.S. population. Nevada and Arizona may double their populations. Texas, Florida, and California could each gain 9 million residents. Meanwhile, the Northeast will gain a mere 7.6 percent in population. The Midwest will gain only 10 percent. West Virginia and North Dakota may actually see their populations decrease.

The nation's diverse population is reflected in the faces of these recent Presidential Scholars, honored for their academic achievement in high school.

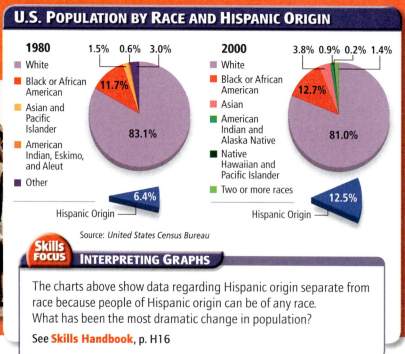

U.S. POPULATION BY RACE AND HISPANIC ORIGIN

1980: White 83.1%, Black or African American 11.7%, Asian and Pacific Islander 1.5%, American Indian, Eskimo, and Aleut 0.6%, Other 3.0%. Hispanic Origin 6.4%.

2000: White 81.0%, Black or African American 12.7%, Asian 3.8%, American Indian and Alaska Native 0.9%, Native Hawaiian and Pacific Islander 0.2%, Two or more races 1.4%. Hispanic Origin 12.5%.

Source: United States Census Bureau

SKILLS FOCUS: INTERPRETING GRAPHS

The charts above show data regarding Hispanic origin separate from race because people of Hispanic origin can be of any race. What has been the most dramatic change in population?

See **Skills Handbook**, p. H16

American Religious Liberty

Immigration and Religion

Immigrants coming to the United States have always brought their cultures, languages, and traditions with them. They also bring their religious beliefs. Most settlers in the original English colonies were Protestants. Later immigration increased the numbers of Catholics, Jews, and other groups. Recently, new immigrants have brought even greater religious diversity. As more immigrants come from Asia, Africa, and Latin America, new cultures and religions have been introduced to the United States.

Today about 80 percent of people in the United States identify themselves as Christians. Among organized religions, the next largest is Judaism, with almost 2 percent of the population. Religions such as Islam, Buddhism, and Hinduism are growing, although members of each faith still make up less than 1 percent of the total population.

The First Amendment of the Constitution guarantees the "free exercise" of religion, which means that anyone may practice his or her beliefs. By guaranteeing freedom of religion, the Constitution has allowed the United States to become increasingly diverse in terms of religion.

Drawing Conclusions How is the Constitution connected to growing religious diversity?

The Constitution guarantees this convention attendee the right to openly practice his Sikh religion.

A graying population Americans are also getting older. People over age 64 are the country's fastest-growing age group. Between 2000 and 2050, the overall U.S. population is expected to increase some 50 percent. The number of people ages 65 to 84, however, could double. Meanwhile, the 20 to 40 age group may grow by just 25 percent.

Who are these soon-to-be older Americans? Many are baby boomers born between 1946 and 1964. The baby boom was followed by a sharp drop in birthrates in the mid-1960s and 1970s. This "baby bust" helps explain why younger age groups are growing at a slower rate today.

The growing proportion of retirees to working people will affect programs such as Social Security. Benefits paid to retirees come from the taxes on the wages of working people. Experts predict that in the future, payouts from the system will exceed taxes collected. As you read in Section 2, President Bush sought to address this problem in 2005 by proposing changes to Social Security. The debate over Social Security will likely continue for some time.

READING CHECK **Summarizing** How would you describe the changing face of America?

The Promise of Technology

As it has throughout history, technological change will help shape the nation's future. New ideas and new ways of working will keep the nation strong, prosperous, healthy, and secure.

Computers Computer use continues to expand rapidly. In 1980 less than 1 percent of the American population owned a computer. Today the figure is over 60 percent. Most computers are also connected to the Internet. The infrastructure that supports these connections has now covered nearly the entire country. Many people who do not have access to the Internet at home may access it at libraries or schools. In addition, computer technology is working its way into our lives in countless ways. Cars, household appliances, and many other objects contain tiny computers.

HISTORY'S VOICES

"This is the decade where computing technology will go from being an add-on, overlaid on our normal activities, to becoming part of the fabric of our everyday lives... This technology is moving forward faster today than ever before..."

—Bill Gates, speech, June 25, 2003

ACADEMIC VOCABULARY
infrastructure the basic facilities of a community for transportation, communication, and more

One example of the melding of computers with everyday devices is the telephone. Computerized wireless phone use is growing rapidly in the United States. In fact, the number of wireless phone lines had surpassed the number of landline phones by 2005.

Computerized information technology, or **IT**, is also bringing change to American business. IT is a way of allowing businesses to organize and examine information in more productive ways. For example, an IT system can make it possible for a company's sales, manufacturing, and shipping departments to share the exact same information on their computer screens. Customers can use their own computers to check on the status of orders or to shop online. These capabilities help make a business more efficient. Being more efficient helps reduce the costs of doing business and increases profits.

Agriculture Technology continues to bring changes to agriculture. One leading example is **genetic engineering**. By carefully altering the genes of a species of plant, scientists have been able to produce varieties with certain desirable features. For example, scientists can genetically engineer corn so that the plant is more resistant to herbicides farmers use to control weeds. As a result, farmers can control weeds more effectively while doing less harm to their crop. Scientists have also engineered crops to resist pests. This means more crops and less use of pesticides. There are many other possible uses for genetic engineering as well.

Like many other technological changes, genetic engineering has created controversy. Some people worry about possible health effects of genetically modified crops. Another concern is that altered genes will get into wild plants. For example, the gene that makes corn resistant to herbicide could make its way into weeds. This would make the weeds harder to control and more damaging to crops.

Exploration The American people continue to demonstrate a spirit of discovery. President Bush in early 2004 laid out the next goal in the ongoing journey into unexplored places: building a space station on the moon and eventually sending human beings to Mars. This plan is in its early stages. There are huge technical challenges to be overcome. However, it would be unwise to doubt the ability of the American people to solve these problems.

READING CHECK **Identifying Supporting Details** How do you think developments in technology will affect the United States in the future?

A Determined Nation

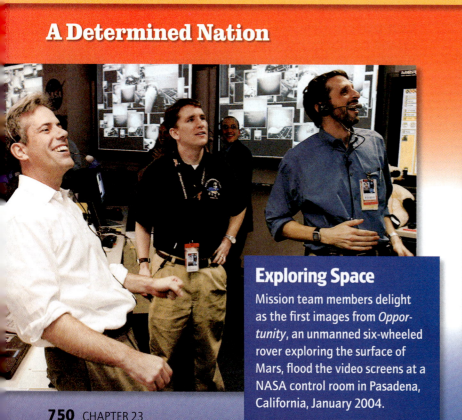

Exploring Space
Mission team members delight as the first images from *Opportunity*, an unmanned six-wheeled rover exploring the surface of Mars, flood the video screens at a NASA control room in Pasadena, California, January 2004.

Advances in Medicine
A researcher at a California laboratory adds DNA samples to a gel in an effort to unlock the mysteries of cancer on the genetic level. Genetic research has become the core of medical science.

Challenges for the Future

The people of the United States have been blessed with great plenty—and with the skill and spirit to create a better future for themselves. Throughout American history, they have used these qualities to overcome the many challenges they have faced. The future will also hold challenges—and opportunity.

Health and health care The average American born in 1900 could expect to live 47 years. Today life expectancy is over 77 years on average. By 2025 experts project that that number will be around 80. By 2050 life expectancy may reach into the mid-80s.

There are many reasons for this projected rise in life expectancy. Medical researchers are learning more each day about the causes of and cures for diseases. They are developing powerful new medicines to help combat a variety of once deadly conditions.

While health care offers great promise for the future, it also presents some of the greatest challenges. One of these is cost. You read in Section 1 about the rising cost of medical care and insurance, including publicly funded programs such as Medicare and Medicaid. Complicating the issue of cost is the rising age of the American population. Older people typically require more medical care than younger people. At the same time, many elderly do not have enough resources with which to pay for it.

You also read about the large number of Americans who lack sufficient health-care coverage. It seems likely that the availability of health care, how to pay for it, and what role the government should play in providing it will be major concerns in American public life for years to come.

The ongoing ravages of diseases such as HIV infection and AIDS are another major health-care challenge. HIV/AIDS continues to spread widely in this country and in the rest of the world. It is estimated that tens of millions of people worldwide will die from HIV/AIDS in coming decades. In Africa in particular, HIV threatens to devastate entire countries. America will be at the forefront of the global fight against this terrible disease.

Energy and the environment The American economy is the largest in the world. To keep this economy growing requires energy. In fact, the United States is by far the world's largest energy consumer.

One challenge with regard to energy is supply. The gap between what the United States uses and what it produces has been widening. To fill this gap, the United States has imported

Hurricane Relief and Recovery

Much of New Orleans, Louisiana, was under water following Hurricane Katrina, August 2005 (below). This make-shift shop in Waveland, Mississippi (right), helps storm survivors begin to piece their lives back together.

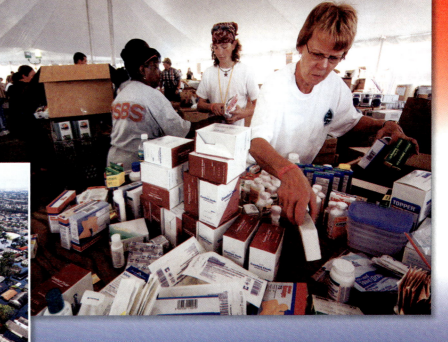

INTO THE TWENTY-FIRST CENTURY

energy from other countries. By 2005 the country was importing just under a third of its energy. Americans remained heavily dependent on foreign oil. More than half of U.S. supplies came from foreign sources. That number is expected to rise to 70 percent by 2025.

Americans will continue to debate the best way to balance the need for energy and economic growth and the need to minimize the costs of obtaining it. These costs include the risk of pollution and environmental harm in drilling for and using fossil fuels such as petroleum. Another possible cost is the danger of dependence on foreign energy supplies. You have read, for example, about economic problems in the United States resulting from interruptions in Middle Eastern energy supplies.

Meanwhile, the search continues for energy sources that are cleaner and easier to obtain. One promising technology is hydrogen fuel cells. These use plentiful hydrogen to generate power—without producing pollution. Fuel cell technology exists today. In fact, NASA has used fuel cells in its spacecraft for decades. Much work remains in order to make them useful and affordable for ordinary consumers.

Rebuilding after Hurricane Katrina In late August 2005 the United States received a harsh reminder of the vulnerability of its people and economy to natural disaster. Hurricane Katrina devastated a large area along the coast of the Gulf of Mexico, including parts of Alabama, Mississippi, and Louisiana. The city of New Orleans, much of which lies below sea level, was flooded when levees holding back surrounding waters failed.

The human suffering caused by the storm was immense. More than 1,000 people died. Hundreds of thousands lost their homes and their source of livelihood. Weeks later, a second hurricane—Hurricane Rita—struck the region, adding to the misery.

The economic impact of Katrina and Rita reached far beyond the Gulf Coast. Interruption of oil production and refining immediately sent fuel prices soaring. In addition, the nation experienced disruption in the supply of many products that enter the country through the busy port of New Orleans. Experts predicted that the cost of the storm would be measured in the hundreds of billions of dollars.

While Katrina and Rita delivered a cruel blow, few Americans doubted that the region and the country would recover. As you have read, the story of the United States is the story of a people who have risen to every challenge. The obstacles before the nation have changed with time. But the spirit of the American people has remained always steady.

READING CHECK **Comparing** How are the challenges facing the United States today similar to—and different from—challenges of the past?

SECTION 4 ASSESSMENT

HSS 11.8.2, 11.8.7, 11.11.5

Reviewing Ideas, Terms, and People

1. **a. Identify** What are two major trends in the makeup of the American population?
   b. Explain Why do you think that changes in the makeup of the population create challenges for a nation and society?

2. **a. Identify** What are some of the fields and areas in which technology is likely to change American life in the future?
   b. Analyze Why do you think the United States continues to seek to explore unknown places, such as Mars?

3. **a. Recall** What is the general trend in the overall health of the nation as measured by life expectancy?
   b. Explain In what ways do the successes of medicine also contribute to the greatest challenges facing the health-care system?
   c. Evaluate On what basis is it safe to predict that the United States will meet the challenges it faces in the future?

Critical Thinking

4. **Identifying the Main Idea** Copy the chart below and use information from the section to record details that support the main idea of the section.

FOCUS ON WRITING ELA W1.1

5. **Persuasive** Write a letter to an elected leader in which you try to persuade him or her to support or oppose one of the technological innovations discussed in this section.

American Literature

AMY TAN (1952–)

About the Reading Amy Tan drew on the experiences of family members in her 1989 novel, *The Joy Luck Club*, which tells the stories of four Chinese women and their Chinese American daughters. In the following excerpt Lindo Jong, one of the main characters, recalls her first days after arriving in the United States in the 1940s.

AS YOU READ Consider the difficulties involved with moving to a new place.

Excerpt from
The Joy Luck Club
by Amy Tan

Chinatown in San Francisco during a Chinese New Year festival

When I arrived, nobody asked me questions. The authorities looked at my papers and stamped me in. I decided to go first to a San Francisco address given to me by this girl in Peking. The bus put me down on a wide street with cable cars. This was California Street. I walked up this hill and then I saw a tall building. This was Old St. Mary's. Under the church sign, in handwritten Chinese characters, someone had added: "A Chinese Ceremony to Save Ghosts from Spiritual Unrest 7 a.m. and 8:30 a.m." I memorized this information in case the authorities asked me where I worshipped my religion. And then I saw another sign across the street. It was painted on the outside of a short building: "Save Today for Tomorrow, at Bank of America." And I thought to myself, This is where American people worship. See, even then I was not so dumb! Today that church is the same size, but where that bank used to be, now there is a tall building, fifty stories high, where you and your husband-to-be work and look down on everybody.

My daughter laughed when I said this. Her mother can make a good joke.

So I kept walking up this hill. I saw two pagodas, one on each side of the street, as though they were the entrance to a great Buddha temple. But when I looked carefully, I saw the pagoda was really just a building topped with stacks of tile roofs, no walls, nothing else under its head. I was surprised how they tried to make everything look like an old imperial city or an emperor's tomb. But if you looked on either side of these pretend-pagodas, you could see the streets became narrow and crowded, dark, and dirty. I thought to myself, Why did they choose only the worst Chinese parts for the inside? Why didn't they build gardens and ponds instead? Oh, here and there was the look of a famous ancient cave or a Chinese opera. But inside it was always the same cheap stuff.

So by the time I found the address the girl in Peking gave me, I knew not to expect too much.

HSS 11.11.3

Skills Focus — READING LIKE A HISTORIAN

1. **Summarizing** How would you characterize the welcome Lindo Jong received in the United States?
2. **Literature as Historical Evidence** How does this excerpt describe the struggle of immigrants to adapt to a new culture?

See **Skills Handbook**, p. H32

INTO THE TWENTY-FIRST CENTURY

HISTORY & Geography

Hispanic Growth and Influence

Hispanics, with a population of 40.4 million at the end of 2004, make up 14 percent of the total U.S. population. They are the country's largest and fastest growing minority group. By 2020 Hispanics will total an estimated 60.4 million and account for half of the growth of the U.S. labor force. With their rising numbers have come newfound political and economic powers. Many people point to the Hispanic vote as a key factor in recent presidential elections.

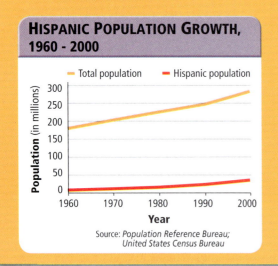

Hispanic Population Growth, 1960 - 2000

Source: *Population Reference Bureau; United States Census Bureau*

Winning Elections

Californians Loretta and Linda Sanchez are the first sisters to serve together in the U.S. Congress. They joined 22 other Hispanic Americans serving in the House of Representatives and over 6,000 Hispanic Americans holding elected office.

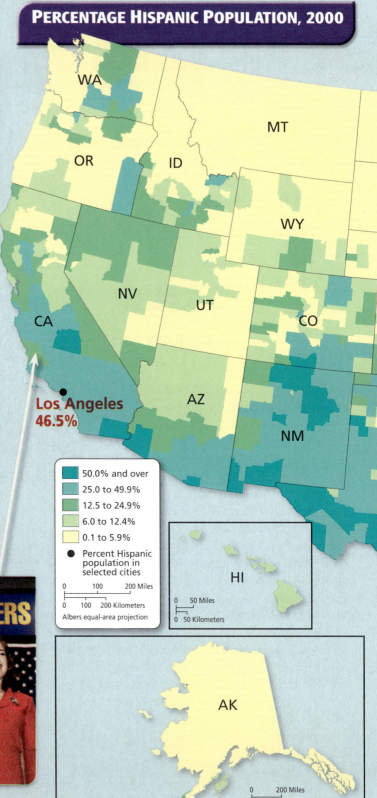

Percentage Hispanic Population, 2000

Los Angeles 46.5%

- 50.0% and over
- 25.0 to 49.9%
- 12.5 to 24.9%
- 6.0 to 12.4%
- 0.1 to 5.9%
- ● Percent Hispanic population in selected cities

Albers equal-area projection

754

Spending Power

Illinois's Hispanic population grew by 650,000 from 1990 to 2000, with most settling in Chicago. Overall Hispanic spending power has grown, too. To attract a larger piece of the Hispanic market, Chicago's Tribune Company turned its Spanish-language weekly, *¡Exito!*, into the daily *Hoy*.

College Bound

As the number of U.S.-educated Hispanics has risen, so has the proportion of those who attend college. To better serve the area's Dominican population, which is larger than the population of the Dominican Republic, the City University of New York offers a degree in Dominican Studies.

Chicago 26.0%
New York 27.0%
San Antonio 58.7%
Houston 37.4%

Swing Voters

Mel Martinez immigrated to Florida from Cuba at age 15. In 2004 he became the first Cuban American elected to the U.S. Senate. In 2000 President Bush took Florida by 537 votes, but he won 80 percent of the Cuban vote.

Immigration

After California, Texas has the largest Hispanic population, mostly of Mexican origin. Unlike with earlier European immigrants, Mexican immigration has not come in a single wave, but rather in a continuous flow for over a century.

HSS 11.8.2, 11.11.1
HSS Analysis CS3

GEOGRAPHY SKILLS INTERPRETING MAPS

1. **Location** Look at some of the major areas of Hispanic American concentration. Why might these areas have been attractive? Why might other areas be unattractive?
2. **Movement** Why might Mexican immigration be occurring in a continuous flow instead of a single wave?

See **Skills Handbook**, p. H20

INTO THE TWENTY-FIRST CENTURY **755**

CHAPTER 23 DOCUMENT-BASED INVESTIGATION

The Global Economy and Society

HSS 11.8.7, 11.11.3

Historical Context The documents below provide different information on the effects of globalization on economics and society.

Task Examine the documents and answer the questions that follow. Then write an essay about globalization. Use facts from the documents and from the chapter to support the position you take in your thesis statement.

DOCUMENT 1

This cartoon comments on the increase in outsourcing—sending local jobs overseas in order to take advantage of lower labor costs in other countries.

"The last step says to dismantle the whole thing and ship all the jobs overseas."

DOCUMENT 2

In 2003 the editor in chief of *Reason* magazine interviewed author Tyler Cowen about his book *Creative Destruction: How Globalization Is Changing the World's Cultures*. Cowen's book suggests that globalization benefits most people around the world.

"*Reason*: Give an example that characterizes the sort of cultural exchange . . . you discuss . . .

"Tyler Cowen: The first point to make is that all examples characterize it. The only question is, how much of it do we already see? Look at a book and ask yourself, where does paper come from, where does printing come from, where do the ideas in the book come from? What's the religious background of the author? You're already talking about the Middle East, China, Europe, the United States. Just about anything you can find reflects a synthetic [not natural; made by humans] culture based on trade . . .

"*Reason*: One of the problems with arguments about cultural loss is that they are often advanced for protectionist reasons. So, for instance, we have the French decrying [complaining about] U.S. cultural imperialism and insisting on domestic-content rules and the like. What are the effects of trying to hold back cultural creative destruction?

"Tyler Cowen: The good news is that it cannot easily be held back . . . Look at the French. For all the noise they make, Paris is remarkably open to African and Middle Eastern cultures—and to Hollywood movies, for that matter. . . As a whole, the world has been moving toward freer trade for quite a while."

756 CHAPTER 23

DOCUMENT 3

Economic changes have affected people all over the world. This *Newsweek* article, published in 2001, examines the effects of globalization on women in different countries.

"For European women, globalization's fallen trade barriers, blurred national boundaries and new technology have brought the best of times—and the worst. The European Union's freedom of movement created more career opportunities, but increased competition, and with it, stress... Creeping Americanization has shaken up antique boardroom attitudes—but also ushered in a 24/7 work schedule. Leaner company structures make it easier to negotiate part-time work, but harder to get paid maternity leave or a pension. A boom economy means women have little trouble finding jobs, but with cuts in education and health, they may have trouble getting trained for good ones—or finding child care while they're at them."

DOCUMENT 4

Mark Rice-Oxley is a reporter for *The Christian Science Monitor*. In this article, published in 2004, he discusses how the spread of American culture affects societies around the world.

"Stick a pin in a map and there you'll find an example of U.S. influence. Hollywood rules the global movie market, with up to 90 percent of audiences in some European countries. Even in Africa, 2 of 3 films shown are American. Few countries have yet to be touched by McDonald's and Coca-Cola...

"America's preeminence is hardly surprising. Superpowers throughout the ages sought to perpetuate their way of life: from the philosophy and mythology of the ancient Greeks to the law and language of the Romans; from the art and architecture of the Tang dynasty and Renaissance Italy to the sports and systems of government of the British...

"So how much good does American culture bring to the world? And how long will it last? Ian Ralston cautions against sweeping dismissals of U.S. pop culture. British television may be saturated with American sitcoms and movies, but while some are poor, others are quite good, he says... Others note that it is not all one-way traffic. America may feast largely on a diet of homegrown culture, but it imports modestly as well: soccer, international cuisine, Italian fashion, and, increasingly, British television."

Skills Focus: READING LIKE A HISTORIAN
HSS Analysis CS4

1. **a. Identify** Refer to Document 1. What are the boys in the cartoon building?
   b. Interpret How does this cartoon illustrate changes in employment patterns?
2. **a. Identify** Refer to Document 2. What example does Cowen use to support his point that globalization creates synthetic cultures?
   b. Interpret Based on this excerpt, what is Cowen's opinion about the effects of free trade on culture?
3. **a. Identify** Refer to Document 3. How has the spread of technology affected work habits in foreign countries?
   b. Analyze Do you think the article would conclude that globalization has benefited or harmed European women?
4. **a. Identify** Refer to Document 4. How, according to the article, is the spread of American culture similar to that of past empires?
   b. Elaborate How does this article suggest that the spread of culture affects people in the United States and other countries?
5. **Document-Based Essay Question** Consider the question below and form a thesis statement. Using examples from Documents 1, 2, 3, and 4, create an outline and write a short essay supporting your position. How does the global economy affect cultures and societies around the world?

See **Skills Handbook**, pp. H28–H29, H30

Chapter 23 Chapter Review

Visual Summary: Into the Twenty-first Century

The Clinton Administration
- Welfare reform was achieved, but health-care reform was not.
- The nation became drawn into conflicts in Somalia, Haiti, and the former Yugoslavia.
- Despite impeachment, President Clinton completed his two terms.

The Bush Administration
- President Bush won a controversial election in 2000 and re-election in 2004.
- His domestic policy focused on tax cuts, education, and Medicare reform.
- His foreign policy was dominated by response to the terrorist attacks of September 11, 2001.

The 1990s and Beyond

Terrorism and War
- The attacks of September 11, 2001, shifted national focus to terrorism.
- In the war on terror, the United States attacked Afghanistan and Iraq.
- The United States created the Department of Homeland Security and passed new laws to fight terrorism.

Looking Ahead
The twenty-first century should bring:
- demographic changes—greater diversity and an aging population.
- technological changes in communication, medicine, agriculture, and space exploration.
- challenges in health care, energy, and the environment.

Reviewing Key Terms and People

Identify the correct term or person from the chapter that best fits each of the following descriptions.

1. Law passed in the aftermath of 9/11 aimed at enhancing investigative powers
2. Trade agreement involving Mexico and Canada
3. Elected mayor of Los Angeles in 2005
4. Terrorist believed responsible for 9/11
5. Nickname for the type of Internet company that appeared in the 1990s
6. Republican package of proposals and legislation from 1994
7. New cabinet-level organization created in the aftermath of 9/11
8. Payments made by corporations to stockholders
9. A technology designed to improve agriculture by altering the genetic material of plants
10. Use of computer technology to efficiently use information
11. Supreme Court case that finally settled the presidential election of 2000

Comprehension and Critical Thinking

SECTION 1 *(pp. 726–731)* **HSS** 11.8.7, 11.9.7

12. **a. Describe** How would you describe the basic political beliefs of Bill Clinton?

    b. Make Inferences What can you infer from the fact that Clinton was able to survive so many political scandals?

    c. Evaluate Do you think Clinton's willingness to adopt policies of his political opponents was a strength or a weakness?

History's Impact video program
Review the video to answer the closing question: How have the events of September 11, 2001, changed life in the United States?

SECTION 2 (pp. 733–738) HSS 11.11.2

13. **a. Recall** What were President George W. Bush's major goals for domestic policy?
    b. Summarize What reasons did President Bush give for wanting to cut taxes?
    c. Elaborate How do you think the circumstances of Bush's election in 2000 affected his ability to govern? Explain your answer.

SECTION 3 (pp. 739–746) HSS 11.9.4, 11.9.6

14. **a. Recall** What is the significance of the date September 11, 2001?
    b. Make Generalizations Describe the emotional reactions of the American people to the catastrophe of September 11th.
    c. Evaluate How effective do you think the terrorist attacks were in damaging the United States? Explain your answer.

SECTION 4 (pp. 747–752) HSS 11.8.7, 11.11.5

15. **a. Recall** How is the American population expected to change in the decades ahead?
    b. Summarize What are some of the causes and effects of the increase in the population of older Americans?
    c. Rank Do you think the challenges facing the United States today are more or less significant than the challenges this country has faced in previous eras? Explain your answer.

Using the Internet

go.hrw.com
Practice Online
Keyword: SE7 CH23

16. Choose of one of the following topics: communication, medicine, agriculture, transportation, or industry. Using the keyword above, do research to learn how technology has affected the topic of your choice. Then write a brief report that summarizes your findings. In your report, include at least three ways that technology has an impact on the topic you chose.

Analyzing HR4 Primary Sources

Reading Like a Historian After the 2000 presidential election, officials in many Florida communities struggled to

read ballots that had been rejected by the automatic vote-counting machines.

17. **Describe** What do you think these election officials are trying to figure out by looking at this ballot?
18. **Explain** Why do you think the hand counting of ballots as shown here was a controversial process?

Critical Reading HSS 11.9.6; ELA R2.4

Read the passage in Section 3 that begins with the heading "The United States Responds." Then answer the question that follows.

19. Why did the United States invade Afghanistan?
    A. to take revenge on the people of Afghanistan
    B. to remove the Taliban regime that had harbored Osama bin Laden
    C. to use Afghanistan as a military base for the war on terrorism
    D. to help distract the American public from their problems at home

FOCUS ON WRITING ELA W1.1

Descriptive Writing *Descriptive writing uses concrete details to help a reader visualize a person, place, or thing. To practice descriptive writing, complete the assignment below.*

Writing Topic The Future of the United States

20. **Assignment** Based on what you have read in this chapter, write a paragraph that describes the United States 20 years from now.

INTO THE TWENTY-FIRST CENTURY

Below is a chapter-by-chapter summary of the main ideas covered in Unit 6.

A Search for Order
1968–1980

MAIN IDEA Richard Nixon achieved notable successes during his time his office, such as improving relations with the People's Republic of China. His involvement in the Watergate scandal, however, led to his resignation. His successors, Presidents Gerald Ford and Jimmy Carter, sought to help the nation recover from Watergate and face ongoing economic and foreign policy challenges, which included high inflation and the continuing Cold War.

SECTION 1 Early in his presidency, Richard Nixon was able to promote improved relations with Communist China and the Soviet Union. He also had some success in pursuing domestic policies, including his stance on civil rights, the environment, and the economy.

SECTION 2 In his second term, Nixon's presidency unraveled in the Watergate scandal, as the nation slowly learned of his role in a criminal conspiracy to spy on his political opponents—and to cover it up. His successor, Gerald Ford, struggled to escape the scandal's undertow.

SECTION 3 Jimmy Carter came to office hoping to help the nation move beyond its troubled past. However, his presidency foundered on familiar problems, including economic trouble and foreign policy crises with Iran and the Soviet Union.

A Conservative Era
1980–1992

MAIN IDEA Ronald Reagan and his successor George H.W. Bush dominated the 1980s with their conservative message of smaller government and a tougher stance against communism. During this time, the Cold War came to an end and the United States faced a new set of economic and foreign policy challenges.

SECTION 1 Ronald Reagan came to office on the strength of his personality and a strong conservative message. He led a national reconsideration of many of the basic questions about the relationship between government and its people.

SECTION 2 A staunch anti-Communist, Reagan increased defense spending and spoke strongly against the Soviet Union. Foreign difficulties in Grenada, South Africa, Lebanon, and Iran characterized his time in office as well.

SECTION 3 George H. W. Bush presided over the end of the Cold War. He was also the first president to face the challenges of the post-Cold War world, when he led the nation—and numerous allies—into war against Iraq in the Persian Gulf War of 1990.

SECTION 4 The 1980s were a time of economic ups and downs, technological advances, and controversial cases in the Supreme Court.

Into the Twenty-First Century
1992–Present

MAIN IDEA Americans faced the twenty-first century with hope, determination, and a readiness to confront challenges at home and abroad.

SECTION 1 Bill Clinton used his political skills and voter dissatisfaction with George H.W. Bush's handling of the economy to reach the White House. Clinton's presidency was a time of economic growth, complex foreign policy challenges—and political scandal.

SECTION 2 George W. Bush won a controversial election in 2000. He faced an economic downturn, which he countered with tax cuts and his own domestic policy agenda. Following his re-election in 2004, Bush launched an initiative to reform the Social Security system.

SECTION 3 On September 11, 2001, the United States became the target of international terrorists. The attacks refocused the nation on a new enemy and led to war overseas and significant governmental changes at home.

SECTION 4 American society is changing as a result of a more diverse population and new advances in technology. The nation continues to face its challenges with a spirit of determination.

UNIT 7

ISSUES IN Contemporary American Society

Document-Based Investigation

Issue 1
Immigration Policy

Issue 2
Women in the Military

Issue 3
Environmental Conservation

Issue 4
Poverty in the United States

Issue 5
Crime and Public Safety

Issue 6
Regulation and the Internet

Issue 7
Outsourcing and Trade

Themes

Government and Democracy
The United States has enacted legislation to address such issues as immigration policy, women in the military, environmental protection, poverty, and crime and public safety, and trade.

Science and Technology
Rapid growth of the Internet has prompted the federal government to consider regulation to protect users and consumers.

Civic participation is key to living in a democracy. Here, the American flag is part of a parade in New York City.

Prepare to Read

Making Inferences
Find practice for **Making Inferences** in the **Skills Handbook,** p. H7

To make sense of what you read, you often need to go beyond what is stated directly and make an inference, or informed judgement, about what a passage means. When making an inference, use your prior knowledge, clues in the text, and your common sense.

Before You Read
Skim the text to determine its subject. Then think about what you already know about the subject.

While You Read
Note ideas directly stated in the reading, as well as those that may be implied. Look for clues to guide your interpretation.

After You Read
Review ideas in the text and make connections to your prior knowledge.

Medical Service

During the Civil War, a number of women, including Clara Barton and Dorothea Dix, helped train nurses and care for wounded and ill soldiers. These female nurses were not a part of the military. They served with, not in, the Union Army.

In the Spanish-American War, thousands of U.S. soldiers contracted diseases such as typhoid, malaria, and yellow fever. The urgent need for qualified medical personnel led army hospitals to hire 1,500 civilian, or nonmilitary, female nurses. Impressed by their performance, the military created the Army Nurse Corps in 1901, followed by the Navy Nurse Corps seven years later. A corps is a military group. This was the first time in more than 100 years of service that women were officially allowed into the military. However, these female nurses received neither military rank nor benefits.

READING CHECK **Making Inferences** What can you infer about women's roles in the military in the 1800s?

Implied idea Women were needed as nurses, not as replacements for thousands of ill soldiers.

Directly stated idea An urgent need for qualified nurses arose after thousands of U.S. soldiers contracted diseases in the Spanish-American War.

Inference Women were not allowed to serve in the military in the 1800s

Test Prep Tip

Tests often contain passages from which you may be asked to infer meaning. Because making inferences means choosing the most likely explanation from the facts available, try to balance information in the text with prior knowledge so that you arrive at the most informed inference.

History's Impact video program
Watch the video to learn more about why these issues matter today.

Issue 1 Immigration Policy
How should the United States respond to legal and illegal immigration into the country?

Issue 2 Women in the Military
What should be the role of women in the military?

Issue 3 Environmental Conservation
How should the federal government balance environmental protection with the use of needed resources?

Issue 4 Poverty in the United States
What are some ways to reduce poverty?

Issue 5 Crime and Public Safety
What are some ways to reduce crime?

Issue 6 Regulation and the Internet
How should the Internet be regulated?

Issue 7 Outsourcing and Trade
What are the advantages and disadvantages of outsourcing?

Immigrant advocates rally at Liberty State Park in Jersey City, New Jersey, in 2003.

ISSUE 1

DOCUMENT-BASED INVESTIGATION

Immigration Policy

California Standards

HSS 11.11.1 Discuss the reasons for the nation's changing immigration policy, with emphasis on how the Immigration Act of 1965 and successor acts have transformed American society.

FOCUSING ON THE ISSUE

How should the United States respond to legal and illegal immigration into the country?

KEY TERMS
immigrant, refugee, assimilation, ethnicity, quota, migrant, green card, amnesty, political asylum

Assistant Attorney General Viet Dinh, the country's first Vietnamese American to hold the post, swears in new U.S. citizens on Ellis Island.

THE INSIDE STORY Viet Dinh was 10 years old when his family fled war-torn Vietnam in a small fishing boat. After 12 days at sea without food, the group swam ashore in Malaysia, but not before Dinh's mother used an ax to chop a hole in the side of the boat. By sinking the boat, she kept her family of six children from being forced back to sea and took a decisive step on a journey that eventually led them to the United States.

Like many **immigrants,** or people who settle in a new country, Dinh left his home country in the hope of finding new opportunities. He graduated from Harvard Law School, and in 2001 the Bush administration named him assistant attorney general.

From the Pilgrims on the *Mayflower* to Cubans arriving on the beaches of Miami, immigration has long been an important part of American culture. Many immigrants come to the United States as **refugees,** or people seeking protection from religious and political persecution. Others come for economic opportunity. Over time, U.S. immigration law has changed, often in response to such events as labor shortages, economic difficulties, or terrorist attacks.

1907
"Gentleman's Agreement" reached in which the United States will not prohibit Japanese immigration and Japan will not issue passports to laborers.

1900

766

EXPLORING THE PAST

In colonial times, immigrants from Western Europe were the equivalent of Vietnamese refugees like Dinh and his family. British, Scots-Irish, and German immigrants sought refuge in the British colonies in such numbers that by 1790, Congress passed a Naturalization Act requiring a two-year residence before immigrants could become citizens. In 1795 this residency requirement was raised to five years. In time, the Alien Act called for the expulsion of foreigners who posed a threat to U.S. interests. Even Benjamin Franklin, a statesman and a diplomat, was concerned about how to control "the stream of these people" who entered the new nation.

Chinese workers, like the ones photographed here in 1882, provided cheap labor for the often dangerous task of building railroads.

Two waves of immigration Franklin's so-called stream, however, did not diminish, and immigrants arrived in waves throughout the 1800s and early 1900s. Between 1840 and 1920, the country experienced its largest period of immigration, an influx of 37 million people. Because of the potato famine and European upheavals, Irish and German arrivals dominated in the mid- and later nineteenth century.

New arrivals, however, often received a chilly reception from earlier immigrants. The Know-Nothing political party of the 1850s, for example, was a group who played on anti-immigrant and anti-Catholic prejudices.

In the early 1900s, the largest number of immigrants were from southern and central Europe. The new federal immigration station at Ellis Island processed the arrival of many of these immigrants. The Immigration Service could deny entrance to those who lacked money or family connections in America. For many of the newcomers, the key to success in America was **assimilation**, or blending in with the established culture. Immigrants worked to learn the language and customs of their newly adopted land.

Closing the door Just as Europeans at Ellis Island had sought a better life, so too did Chinese immigrants who came to the United States to escape grinding poverty. News of the California gold rush had reached China, and many Chinese came to California seeking work in the mid-1800s. Chinese workers labored in mines, and they helped build the Central Pacific Railroad.

1924 Immigration Act establishes quota system favoring admission of northern and western Europeans.

1943 Bracero Program provides temporary agricultural work to Mexican citizens. Chinese Exclusion Act is repealed.

1965 Immigration and Nationality Act amendments discontinue quotas based on national origins.

1986 Immigration Reform and Control Act includes employer sanctions for knowingly hiring illegal immigrants.

1990 Immigration Act of 1990 increases total immigration to 700,000, which will be gradually reduced to 675,000 people per year.

2001 USA PATRIOT Act authorizes detention of noncitizens suspected of terrorism.

Migrant agricultural workers pick sugar beets near Stockton, California. Mexican migrants in the Bracero Program carried identification cards like the one shown here.

1907. By this arrangement, the Japanese government agreed not to issue passports to laborers. Immigration from Japan was completely eliminated after World War I, when the United States passed laws establishing **quotas**. These laws set limits on the number of people who could enter the United States from each country and favored admissions from northern and western Europe.

World War II also affected immigration policy. Wartime labor shortages led to an increase in the number of Mexican agricultural workers. The Bracero Program, begun in 1942, encouraged **migrant** laborers to take temporary work in the United States and then return to Mexico. This policy created a circular migration pattern that was supported until the program ended in 1964.

Present-day policies U.S. immigration patterns changed fundamentally in 1965 with the passage of the Immigration and Nationality Act, which abolished national-origin quotas. Since that time, European immigration has slowed; immigrants today are primarily from Latin America, the Caribbean, and Asia. The goal for these immigrants is often a Permanent Resident Card, called a **green card**—evidence of an immigrant's legal right to live and work in the United States.

In the 1980s concern over illegal immigration led to stricter U.S. policy that was supposed to penalize employers who hired illegal aliens. This provision also provided **amnesty,** or forgiveness, to illegal aliens who had lived in the United States for many years, allowing them to gain legal status. Other policies made provisions for the admission of immigrants seeking **political asylum,** a kind of protection for humanitarian reasons.

In response to the terrorist attacks of September 11, 2001, Congress passed the USA PATRIOT Act. Among its many provisions, the act authorized indefinite detention of immigrants suspected of terrorist activities. Critics assert that the provisions of the PATRIOT Act violate Americans' civil rights as well as those of foreign citizens. However, the PATRIOT Act's chief author, former Vietnamese refugee Viet Dinh, claims that it is needed to "fight the common fight against terrorism."

However, Chinese immigrants also faced discrimination in the form of mine and poll taxes. They were barred from testifying in court and had to attend separate schools. Anti-Chinese sentiment increased during the economic depression of the 1870s. Labor unions argued that the Chinese competed with American workers for jobs. This sentiment led to the Chinese Exclusion Act, the first American law to ban immigration by **ethnicity**—national, religious, language, or cultural origin. Passed in 1882, the act barred all Chinese immigration for 10 years. Those already in the country were denied citizenship, becoming "permanent aliens." The act was not repealed until 1943.

A "Gentleman's Agreement" When Californians complained about Japanese immigration, President Theodore Roosevelt negotiated a "Gentlemen's Agreement" in

INVESTIGATING THE PRESENT

The issue of how much immigration should be permitted in the United States and to whom citizenship should be granted are topics of ongoing debate. The documents that follow explore these issues by presenting different points of view and arguments. Examine the documents, keeping in mind what you have read about the history of U.S. immigration, and answer the questions that follow.

DOCUMENT 1

In 1992 the *Los Angeles Daily News* asked California's candidates for the U.S. Senate to describe their positions on several issues, including immigration. Candidates' responses were printed in the newspaper.

GRAY DAVIS
California must receive its fair share of federal funds to deal with the tremendous influx of immigrants into California. We must demonstrate that there is a serious price to pay for sanctioning illegal immigration and employment.

DIANNE FEINSTEIN
The vitality and diversity of immigrant communities is one of our greatest national strengths. I realize that immigrants face particular problems upon arrival in this country, including finding adequate housing, health care, education and jobs. But I feel that illegal immigration should be stopped for the simple reason that California is hard-pressed and cannot afford to take care of everyone else's problems at this time.

DAVID KEARNS
We need stricter enforcement of existing laws, and help with the related social programs by which we try to deal humanely with this problem. The federal government owes California a lot of help (send money). Citizenship for children of foreign-national parents should be restricted to those whose parents become American citizens within seven years ... The long-range, real solution for this historical trend is to economically develop northern Mexico.

—*Los Angeles Daily News,* May 25, 1992

Analyzing the Document
What do Davis, Feinstein and Kearns believe the role of the federal government should be in immigration? On what do they base their positions?

DOCUMENT 2

At a meeting of the American Immigration Lawyers Association, former chairperson Carl Shusterman spoke about proposed cutbacks in immigration.

Americans have traditionally been hostile to new waves of immigrants, yet immigration has been vital to the development of our national character....
In California, in particular, the economy flourished as immigrants—legal or otherwise—worked the fields of the world's largest agricultural economy. Wealthy immigrants sent their children to U.S. universities where they stayed to help give America a technological edge over the Russians. U.S. scientists, both American and foreign-born, worked side-by-side developing transistors, microchips, genetically engineered pharmaceuticals and ever more powerful computers. Immigrants were prominent in each new cutting-edge industry. Its large immigrant population established Los Angeles as the Capital of the Pacific Rim.

... Globalism, with its free movement of ideas and peoples, is as inevitable in the 21st Century as industrialization was in the 1800s.... A country where the population density is one of the lowest in the world, where legal immigrants include the world's best and brightest talent, and where present quotas allow for only a fraction of one percent of the population to immigrate annually, has not reached "carrying capacity."

—Carl Shusterman, December 9, 1996

Analyzing the Document
Why does Shusterman argue that immigrants are important to the growth of the U.S. economy?

DOCUMENT 3

In 2004 President George W. Bush presented proposals that would provide legal status to many undocumented workers as well as increase the number of green cards available to immigrants.

Analyzing the Document
What are the values and ideals that President Bush expects from new immigrants?

> In the process of immigration reform, we must also set high expectations for what new citizens should know. An understanding of what it means to be an American is not a formality in the naturalization process; it is essential to full participation in our democracy. My administration will examine the standard of knowledge in the current citizenship test. We must ensure that new citizens know not only the facts of our history, but the ideals that have shaped our history. Every citizen of America has an obligation to learn the values that make us one nation: liberty and civic responsibility, equality under God, and tolerance for others.
>
> —President George W. Bush, January 7, 2004

DOCUMENT 4

The U.S. census shows that foreign-born people are concentrated in "gateway" areas of the United States, including southwestern border states, the New York City and Miami areas, the Pacific Northwest, and metropolitan Washington, D.C. Miami-Dade County, Florida, was the only county in the United States in which the foreign-born population constituted a majority.

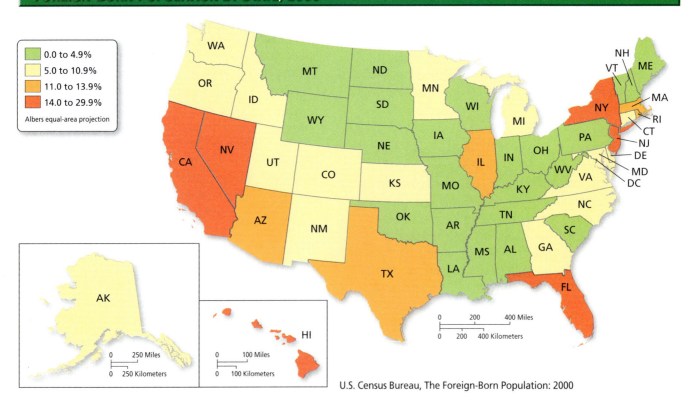

FOREIGN-BORN POPULATION BY STATE, 2000

- 0.0 to 4.9%
- 5.0 to 10.9%
- 11.0 to 13.9%
- 14.0 to 29.9%

Albers equal-area projection

U.S. Census Bureau, The Foreign-Born Population: 2000

Analyzing the Document
How do you think the patterns of immigration seen on the map might affect American culture?

770 CONTEMPORARY ISSUES

DOCUMENT 5

Newsweek columnist Robert J. Samuelson looked at some of the issues associated with high levels of immigration.

> Americans rightly glorify our heritage of absorbing immigrants. Over time, they move into the economic, political and social mainstream; over time, they become American rather than whatever they were—even though immigrants themselves constantly refashion the American identity. But no society has a boundless capacity to accept newcomers, especially when many are poor and unskilled. There are now an estimated 34 million immigrants in the United States, about a third of them illegal. About 35 percent lack health insurance and 26 percent receive some sort of federal benefit, reports Steven Camarota of the Center for Immigration Studies. To make immigration succeed, we need (paradoxically) to control immigration.
> ... [Low skilled] workers are inevitably crammed into low-wage jobs: food workers, janitors, gardeners, laborers, farm workers
> ... For today's [low skilled] immigrants (legal or illegal), the closest competitors are tomorrow's [low skilled] immigrants (legal or illegal). The more who arrive, the harder it will be for existing low-skilled workers to advance.
>
> —Robert J. Samuelson, "The Hard Truth of Immigration," *Newsweek*, June 13, 2005

Analyzing the Document
How might unskilled immigrants affect poor, low-skilled workers already in the United States?

DOCUMENT 6

Although the Bracero Program ended in 1964, many migrant workers still come to the United States with the intention of working and sending money back to their families in their home countries.

Analyzing the Document
What does this political cartoon say about circular migration and how some people view immigrant laborers in the United States?

ANALYZING THE ISSUES

1. Review the documents presented in this issue. What do they show about the current U.S. reception of immigrants?

2. What do the documents lead you to believe about the economic impact of immigration to the United States? Analyze the documents discussed and note those that encourage this economic activity and those that seem concerned that American businesses will suffer from new waves of immigration.

3. Do library research to find out how immigration has affected your state in recent years. Has immigration increased or decreased in your state over the past five years?

4. Do library or online research to find two recent news articles about immigration trends in your state. Write a paragraph about your findings.

ISSUE 2

DOCUMENT-BASED INVESTIGATION

Women in the Military

California Standards

HSS 11.11.3 Describe the changing roles of women in society as reflected in the entry of more women into the labor force and the changing family structure.

FOCUSING ON THE ISSUE

What should be the role of women in the military?

KEY TERMS
deploy, combat, enlist, civilian, corps, yeomen, prisoners of war

THE INSIDE STORY In Colorado, Major Carrie Acree is a teacher, wife, and mother of three. In northwest Baghdad, Iraq, where she was **deployed**, or sent, with the U.S. Army's 443rd Civil Affairs Unit, Acree delivered school supplies to Iraqi children. Acree's unit also works in many other ways to improve Iraqis' daily lives.

Major Acree took the same oath that all men and women take when they join the armed forces. They make the same commitment to defend their country. But for many, the similarities end there.

Airborne Specialist Shelby Bixler, for example, would be idle if her paratrooper unit entered into **combat**, or fighting. Army rules restricting women from combat frustrate trained soldiers like Bixler, who would prefer to share combat risk.

These rules, however, do not mean that women are free from danger. More than 30 U.S. servicewomen had been killed in Iraq by March 2005, despite the combat ban.

Some people think that women should not face the same military risks as their male counterparts, especially when it comes to combat situations. Others think that when women join the military, they should be given the same opportunities and responsibilities as men. The role of women in the military is a debate that directly affects women in the service today.

A female soldier helps with the helicopter evacuation of another soldier wounded in the 1991 Persian Gulf War.

1901 U.S. Army establishes the first female Nurse Corps.

1900

EXPLORING THE PAST

When Robert Shurtliff **enlisted** in, or joined, the Continental army to fight the British in 1782, no one knew that he was really 21-year-old Deborah Sampson in disguise. When Sampson was wounded in battle, she treated her own injuries rather than reveal her secret. It was only when she was hospitalized for a fever that the doctor caring for her learned her true identity. Sampson received an honorable discharge. Eventually, through the lobbying of Patriots such as Paul Revere, Sampson was awarded a government pension.

Deborah Sampson's experience was unusual. Although women have a long history of military service in the United States, much of it has come in supporting, rather than in fighting, roles.

Recruiting posters like this World War II army one helped fill the critical need for military nurses in both World Wars.

Medical service During the Civil War, a number of women, including Clara Barton and Dorothea Dix, helped train nurses and care for wounded and ill soldiers. These nurses were not a part of the military. They served with, not in, the Union army.

In the Spanish-American War, thousands of U.S. soldiers contracted diseases such as typhoid, malaria, and yellow fever. The urgent need for qualified medical personnel led army hospitals to hire 1,500 **civilian**, or nonmilitary, female nurses. Impressed by their performance, the military created the Army Nurse Corps in 1901, followed by the Navy Nurse Corps seven years later. A **corps** is a military group. This was the first time in more than 100 years of service that women were officially allowed into the military. However, these nurses received neither military rank nor benefits.

World wars bring changes On the eve of the U.S. entry into World War I, Secretary of the Navy Josephus Daniels asked a question that would stir debate for decades to come. Faced with a shortage of navy clerks, who were called **yeomen**, he asked his legal advisers, "Is there any law that says a yeoman must be a man?" The answer was no, and for the first time, the U.S. Navy and the Marine Corps enlisted women. Although they earned full military status and benefits, these women were not allowed to advance beyond the rank of sergeant.

1917–18 Women serve as army and navy nurses, and almost 12,000 women enlist as navy yeomen to serve stateside.

1941 More than 350,000 women serve in World War II, not only as nurses but also as administrative and clerical personnel.

1948 The Women's Armed Services Integration Act makes permanent women's right to join the military.

1976 Women are admitted to military academies.

1990 Approximately 40,000 servicewomen are deployed during the Persian Gulf War in noncombat roles.

WOMEN IN THE MILITARY 773

Women who worked with the U.S. Army, however, were civilian employees working as typists and performing other clerical duties without rank or benefits. Although most women served in the United States, a few went overseas. General John J. Pershing, the commander of the Allied forces, requested bilingual women to work communication centers in France. Known as Hello Girls, they transferred messages from headquarters to the front lines and back again. Women's service in these jobs meant that men typically responsible for them could be free to fight. But when the war ended, all women on active military duty were discharged, except for some nurses.

It was not until World War II that all branches of the armed forces enlisted women in special divisions for the first time. These women served in new capacities as truck drivers, supply plane pilots, air traffic controllers, electricians, and in other noncombat roles. Many of these women earned full military status. All told, about 350,000 women served in the military during World War II.

Unlike the end of World War I, the close of World War II did not bring a halt to women's military careers. Many women served again as nurses in the Korean War. Women remained a permanent part of the military, but laws limited their number, rank, and roles. These restrictions on women remained until the 1970s.

New roles for servicewomen

During the Vietnam War, women made inroads into new service areas, including communications, intelligence, and finance. After the war, opportunities for women in the military continued to expand. Servicewomen became military police, helicopter pilots, chaplains, and construction equipment operators.

In 1970 Anna Mae Hays, chief of the Army Nurse Corps, and Elizabeth P. Hoisington, Women's Army Corps director, were the first women to attain the rank of brigadier general. Six years later, the first women were admitted to the military academy at West Point. However, military women still were not permitted to take any assignment with a high likelihood of direct combat.

Then in the 1990s more than 40,000 servicewomen were deployed during the Persian Gulf War. Women ran facilities for **prisoners of war**, or captured enemy troops; directed artillery; and served in port security units. But with increased opportunities came increased risk. Although the Persian Gulf War lasted a little more than a month, nearly twice as many servicewomen died during it as in the Korean and Vietnam Wars combined.

Servicewomen deployed to the Middle East after the terrorist attacks on September 11, 2001, have been allowed to fly in combat missions. However, they still cannot serve on submarines or on the ground in direct combat. In Iraq there are no frontlines, and women may unexpectedly find themselves in combat positions. Leigh Ann Hester of Kentucky did, and as a result of her heroic response she was awarded the Silver Star for valor in combat.

Today women play an accepted and valuable role in the U.S. military. But the debate over women's involvement in combat continues. For proponents of placing women in combat, it is an issue of fairness, of equal rights translating to equal responsibility and risk. Opponents, however, regard the idea that a woman, especially a mother, would be willing to kill or possibly be killed as a moral conflict that cannot be resolved.

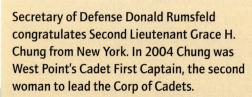

Secretary of Defense Donald Rumsfeld congratulates Second Lieutenant Grace H. Chung from New York. In 2004 Chung was West Point's Cadet First Captain, the second woman to lead the Corp of Cadets.

INVESTIGATING THE PRESENT

The role of women in the military raises many questions. The documents that follow explore this issue by presenting different points of view and arguments. Examine the documents, keeping in mind what you have read about the history of women in the military, and answer the questions that follow.

DOCUMENT 1

Lorry M. Fenner is a colonel in the air force. She has taught at the National War College as well as served as Vice Wing Commander of the 70th Intelligence Wing. The following is an excerpt from her portion of *Women in Combat: Civic Duty or Military Liability?*, a book Fenner cowrote with Marie E. deYoung. In the book the two women express their opposing points of view on women in the military.

> Most of the arguments (regarding women in the military) presume that not only American women but American society will be harmed by exposing women to danger in combat... Yet the integration of women into the armed forces to date has not only been of benefit to women but has been essential to military effectiveness and our nation's defense. Continuing their integration by eliminating the barriers to service that remain will keep faith with our security needs, our democratic heritage, and our political philosophy.
>
> We put our young men at risk, even in times of ostensible [apparent] peace, and we have regarded their participation in the draft registry as an obligation of citizenship. We put our young women at risk as well in support positions that are "noncombat" on paper but are well within the range of even the crudest military or quasi-military weapons. We thereby limit our options, while sustaining the myth that military women are not in "harm's way" and denying them the opportunity to contribute to their fullest capability. Opening remaining military positions to all qualified individuals (determined by relevant tests, not sex) and requiring young women to register for the draft if we require young men to do so are simply the next logical ... steps in our military's and our nation's evolution toward our ideal of civic responsibility and equality.
> —Lorry M. Fenner, *Women in Combat: Civic Duty or Military Liability?*, 2001

Analyzing the Document
What does Fenner think women's role in the military should be? On what basis does she make her argument?

DOCUMENT 2

Marie E. deYoung, the coauthor of *Women in Combat: Civic Duty or Military Liability?*, is a captain in the U.S. Army Reserves. The following excerpts from the book express her point of view regarding women's role in the military.

> The most persistent myth to propel the argument for allowing women in ground combat is the mistaken belief that our high-tech military equipment will spare American combatants from the ravages of war because such gadgetry makes physical inferiority irrelevant to combat success.
>
> Our nation and women would be better served if we begin to rethink the notion that combat service should confer special privileges, rights, and entitlements. Women, elderly persons, physically disabled persons, and children should not be relegated to second-class citizenship because they are not fit for ground combat assignments.
>
> A time may come when the average woman can perform hard physical duties and handle physical and emotional trauma with the same resiliency as men. That moment has not arrived. In this moment in history, female soldiers suffer tremendously with every step taken to lift the combat exclusion. Therefore, I respectfully conclude that the ground combat exclusion for women should not be lifted.
> —Marie E. deYoung, *Women in Combat: Civic Duty or Military Liability?*, 2001

Analyzing the Document
What is deYoung's opinion of women serving in ground combat? How does she support her argument?

DOCUMENT 3

Over time, women have played an important, although restricted, role in the military. The table below shows how women's roles in the military have changed since the mid-1900s.

Year	Ruling	Effect
1948	Women's Armed Services Integration Act	Women received permanent military status, but they could only make up 2 percent of the total force, and they had restrictions in duties and benefits.
1951	Executive Order 10240	Military branches discharged women who were pregnant or who had minor children at home.
1967	Public Law 90-130	It modified the Armed Services Integration Act by removing the 2 percent cap and lifting some pay and career restrictions.
1976	Public Law 94-106	Service academies opened to women for the first time.
1976	Crawford v. Cushman	U.S. Court of Appeals case ruled the discharge of pregnant marines violated the Fifth Amendment.
1980	Defense Officer Manpower Personnel Act	The DOMPA eliminated separate job standards for men and women. Promotions were done by selection instead of appointment.
1991	Kennedy-Roth Amendment	It repealed a ban in the Defense Authorizations Act so that women were allowed to serve on combat aircraft.
1993	Order by Secretary of Defense Les Aspin	It ordered the navy to open more ships to women after Congress repealed the law barring women from combat ships.

Source: Women in Military Service for America Memorial Foundation

Analyzing the Document
How has legislation changed women's roles in the military?

DOCUMENT 4

A Gallup poll asked Americans the following question: Do you think women in the armed services should get combat assignments on the same terms as men, should they be able to get combat assignments only if they want to, or should they never get combat assignments? The responses to that question are shown in the circle graph on the right.

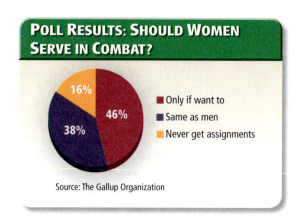

POLL RESULTS: SHOULD WOMEN SERVE IN COMBAT?

- 46% Only if want to
- 38% Same as men
- 16% Never get assignments

Source: The Gallup Organization

Analyzing the Document
From this poll, what conclusion can you draw about American support of women in combat?

DOCUMENT 5

The following excerpts are from the congressional debate surrounding the opening of combat positions to women. The first is from Representative Patricia Schroeder, D-Colorado, the first woman to serve on the House Armed Services Committee. The second is from Elaine Donnelly, the president of the Center for Military Readiness.

> I believe I have heard all the objections to women holding combat positions. They vary from emotional to practical, but the competence of military women's performances as individuals has already been acknowledged ... It is pure opinion, at this point, that women can't be effective in combat jobs. The fact is, however, that the combat exclusion policy tends to limit a woman's career opportunities. More importantly, the exclusionary policies deny the military the services of qualified personnel. It is time for military service to be based on qualifications, not gender.
> —Rep. Patricia Schroeder, January 1990

> As I see it, the issue at stake here is not support or admiration for the professionalism and patriotism of the women in the military. I share that support and admiration. The question, rather, is whether women should be directly involved in long-term ground combat in a future conventional war. The Army employs thousands of people, but it is not just another equal opportunity employer whose functions would be essentially the same in wartime as in peacetime ... Military units should not be slowed down or deployed short-handed because some soldiers cannot march as fast, carry the same load, or are absent because of pregnancy or lack of childcare. No military power in the world—including Israel—has fought and won a war with women in combat roles.
> —Elaine Donnelly, September 1990

Analyzing the Document
On what point do both Schroeder and Donnelly agree? Which items in these statements are facts? Which items are opinions?

DOCUMENT 6

The following is an excerpt from a 1994 recommendation by Secretary of Defense Les Aspin to broaden assignments to women in the armed forces. Aspin's recommendation partially overturned the so-called risk rule, which prohibited women from serving in combat roles.

> We've made historic progress in opening up opportunities for women in all of the Services. Expanding roles for women in the military is right, and it's smart. It allows us to assign the most qualified individual to each military job. In all these actions, our overall aim remains the same, a high-quality, ready-to-fight force.
>
> Women will still be barred from jobs that involve direct ground combat. The new policy defines direct ground combat for the Services uniformly for the first time. The definition has three parts, all of which must be present to prevent service by women. Women may not serve in units that (1) engage an enemy on the ground with weapons, (2) are exposed to hostile fire and (3) have a high probability of direct physical contact with the personnel of a hostile force.
> —Secretary of Defense Les Aspin, January 13, 1994

Analyzing the Document
What do you think of Aspin's policy recommendation for women in the military?

Document 7

Over time, women have made significant gains in the roles they perform in the military. The table on the right shows the rank order in the air force and the percentage of women who make up each rank. The total number of women is 13,479.

Analyzing the Document
What trends do you notice within the table? Explain your answer.

Air Force Rank Structure	Percentage That Are Women
Lieutenant General	0
Major General or Brigadier General	0.5
Colonel	3
Lieutenant Colonel	10
Major	18
Captain	35
1st Lieutenant	15.5
2nd Lieutenant	18

Source: U.S. Department of Defense, Active duty Personnel Report, 2003

Document 8

The Vietnam Women's Memorial in Washington, D.C., honors an estimated 11,000 women who served in the Vietnam War. The sculpture depicts three uniformed nurses. In the first picture, one nurse gives medical aid and comfort to a wounded male soldier while another looks to the sky for help from incoming helicopters. The second picture shows the other side of the sculpture, where a third nurse is believed to be kneeling in prayer or thought.

Analyzing the Document
If an observer knew nothing about the history of women in the U.S. military, what might he or she conclude from this memorial about the role of women during the Vietnam War?

DOCUMENT 9

This line graph shows the total number of women enlisted in the U.S. Armed Forces from 1953 to 2003.

Analyzing the Document
What has been the trend regarding women's enlistment in the armed forces?

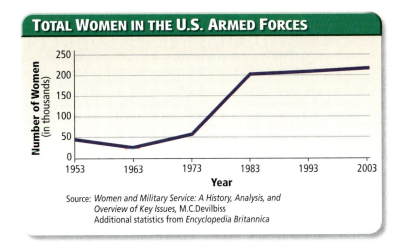

DOCUMENT 10

Army Specialist Shoshana Johnson was held as a prisoner of war after her unit was ambushed in Iraq in 2003. At the time of her capture, Johnson was in a noncombat role as a cook. The following is an excerpt from an interview with Johnson.

Analyzing the Document
From Johnson's experience, what can you infer about the difference in the risk involved with military support roles and military combat roles?

> At first they didn't realize I was a female, so their treatment was pretty rough. But once they realized I was a female, I was separated and I received medical care. I was shown kindness and some respect. There were some guards who were not as kind, but then there were some that interceded on my behalf. I think I was pretty lucky. The guys did not get as good treatment as myself... And I'll never really understand why. Was it because I was female? Was it because I was black, because I was a black female? I don't know. But I'm just thankful for it.
>
> —Shoshana Johnson, National Public Radio, "Talk of the Nation," March 1, 2005

ANALYZING THE ISSUES

1. In what ways have women's roles in the military followed a pattern of development? What does that pattern imply for the future?

2. Knowing that combat has changed and that today being in a military support position in a war theater can put women in dangerous positions, how would you suggest that the issue of women in combat be resolved?

3. Do library or online research to find out how women in your state have recently served in the military. Write a short summary of your findings. Include the military branch, the location of the service, and the nature of the assignment.

4. Write a letter to the editor in which you explain the pros and cons of allowing women to serve in combat missions. Include different ideas regarding the role of women in the military.

ISSUE 3
DOCUMENT-BASED INVESTIGATION

Environmental Conservation

California Standards

HSS 11.8.6 Discuss the diverse environmental regions of North America, their relationship to local economies, and the origins and prospects of environmental problems in those regions.

HSS 11.11.5 Trace the impact of, need for, and controversies associated with environmental conservation, expansion of the national park system, and the development of environmental protection laws, with particular attention to the interaction between environmental protection advocates and property rights advocates.

FOCUSING ON THE ISSUE

How should the federal government balance environmental protection with the use of needed resources?

KEY TERMS
national park, natural resources, conservation, extinction, public lands, taking

John Anderson grows alfalfa on a 600-acre farm in Oregon's Klamath Basin. The basin is dry and cannot support crops without irrigation.

A century ago the federal government dug canals to bring water from the Klamath River to new farms in the basin. When Anderson inherited the family farm, he expected to stay on the land. But a drought in 2000 and 2001 challenged his expectations.

Water levels in the Klamath River dropped, threatening the salmon that the Yurok Indians used for food. The U.S. government, with a duty to preserve salmon as a threatened species and food source, diverted water from farms to increase the water level for fish. Deprived of irrigation water, the farm fields dried up.

A generation ago, farmers' needs would have been the only consideration. But in 2001 the federal government had to consider wildlife and treaty obligations to the Yurok as well as crops.

Eventually, water flowed to the farms. But the crisis shows why it is hard to agree on how to use resources and who has the right to them.

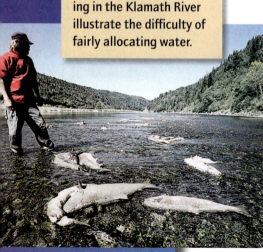
The dead salmon floating in the Klamath River illustrate the difficulty of fairly allocating water.

1903 The nation's first wildlife refuge is established at Florida's Pelican Island.

1900

1905 The National Forest system is established to conserve forest resources.

780

EXPLORING THE PAST

Hundreds of years before workers arrived to dig the Klamath canals, millions of bison roamed the Great Plains. An 1832 traveler wrote, "As far as my eye could reach the country seemed . . . blackened by . . . [the] herds."

After the Civil War, however, railroad tracks and settlers moved west. Soon, the bison population dropped. By 1892 only a few dozen bison were left on the Great Plains. The U.S. government sheltered the remaining animals in Yellowstone National Park. A **national park** is a natural area set aside by the federal government. This action may have saved the bison, but it was an unusual act at a time when conservation was not important to the federal government or to most Americans.

An endless frontier During most of the 1800s, the idea of preserving land or wildlife seemed unnecessary to most people. The United States was a huge country, with wilderness extending as far as the eye could see. Animals were everywhere in endless numbers.

The land overflowed with **natural resources**, things found in nature that are useful to people. Forests and wildlife as well as rich deposits of gold, silver, and copper could be found. Settlers wasted no time in putting these resources to use. They logged and plowed, hunted and mined. As one of the few people of the time who favored **conservation**, or the careful use of resources, George Perkins Marsh wrote, "Man is everywhere a disturbing agent."

Marsh, however, was one of the few voices of concern in the mid-1800s. After all, many believed that if the land were spoiled or if animals were killed off in one valley, there were sure to be more in the next valley.

At that time, the U.S. government's main goal was settling land, not saving it. The federal government gave away land to anyone who would live, farm, or build on it. Homesteaders, railroads, and mining and logging companies received generous grants or bought huge acreages for bargain prices. By 1900 the federal government had given away half the land it had owned only 50 years before.

Early conservation efforts During the late 1800s the frontier of the United States was filling up rapidly. Industry was growing, fueled by the

Yosemite Falls is a well-loved feature of Yosemite National Park, which was established in 1890.

1946 The Bureau of Land Management (BLM) is formed.

1976 The Federal Land Policy and Management Act strengthens the BLM's power to regulate federal lands.

1970s The Sagebrush Rebellion spreads in the West to defend property rights against federal regulation.

1934 Yearbook of Agriculture states that 100 million acres of the Great Plains had lost its topsoil, and another 125 million acres was rapidly losing topsoil.

1988 The Wise Use movement is organized to roll back environmental regulations.

2000 President Clinton creates several new national monuments, covering millions of acres of western land.

This farmer's field shows the devastation caused by erosion. To prevent further erosion, a windbreak stretching from Texas to Canada and made up of 217 million trees was planted.

extraction of coal, iron, and other resources. The government saw land and resources as tools to boost development, and it considered regulation an unnecessary obstacle.

There were signs of trouble, however. Bison and beaver had disappeared from areas of the West. Logging and mining had left land bare and scarred. More and more people began to express concern.

As a result, the federal government took the first steps toward preserving land, wildlife, and resources. It set aside certain wilderness areas as national parks. The spectacular landscape in the northwest corner of Wyoming became Yellowstone National Park in 1872.

Congress also passed laws to protect some forests. Some restrictions also were put on mining, but these laws were not strongly enforced.

New challenges The conservation movement received a boost from Theodore Roosevelt, the former Progressive governor of New York State, who became president in 1901. An adventurer who loved the outdoors, Roosevelt was the first president to make wildlife and resource conservation a priority. Roosevelt formed the nation's first national wildlife refuge in 1903 at Pelican Island in Florida. He also set aside millions of acres of western forest that later formed the core of a new system of national forests.

Many ranchers, miners, and loggers were unhappy with the national forests and with the new system of national parks that followed in 1916. They did not think conservation measures were necessary. Instead, they interpreted such measures as a seizure of land by the federal government. They claimed that the new national forests and parks would restrict or eliminate access to millions of acres of resources.

In the 1930s environmental disaster on the Great Plains led to increased regulation. To settlers of the mid-1800s, the western Plains were an unappealing land—flat, brown, and dry. They passed over it in favor of greener lands farther west. But unusually wet weather in the early 1900s led cattle ranchers and farmers to take another look at the western Plains. Ranchers moved in with cattle that overgrazed native grasses. What the cattle did not eat, farmers plowed under to plant wheat.

When drier weather returned in the 1930s, the crops dried up. Without natural grasses to hold the topsoil in place, wind whipped up the soil into large dust clouds that blackened the skies. The Dust Bowl was most severe in Kansas, Oklahoma, Texas, New Mexico, and Colorado. It drove farmers and ranchers from the land. It also led the federal government to develop new regulations to decrease soil erosion.

In 1934 the Taylor Grazing Act placed 140 million acres of the most damaged grazing land under stricter control. Although the law was not well enforced, it did decrease the number of cattle grazing on federal lands. It also upset ranchers who had grazed cattle there for decades.

An effort began to remove grazing lands from federal control and give them to the states, but that effort failed. However, the effort was an indication of the larger clashes to come between the dueling issues of conservation and property rights.

The environmental movement By the 1960s the quality of America's air, water, and land was suffering from decades of abuse. Smog hung over cities. Several animals, such as the grizzly bear and bald eagle, were in danger of **extinction**, or complete disappearance as a species.

Then in 1969 Americans saw pictures of an Ohio river so polluted with chemicals that it burst into flames. Conservationists said that something had to be done. In 1970 the first Earth Day celebration helped raise the public's awareness of environmental issues.

Backed by public support, the federal government passed several important environmental laws in the 1960s and 1970s. One of the earliest was the Wilderness Act, which preserved millions of acres of forest, desert, and wetlands. Later, Congress passed the Endangered Species Act to protect those plants and animals in danger of extinction. The Clean Air and Clean Water Acts were created to fight air and water pollution.

Sagebrush rebels The rise of environmental laws and regulation of public lands triggered a backlash in the West in the late 1970s known as the Sagebrush Rebellion. The goal of the new regulations was to protect forests and wildlife, conserve grazing land, and protect water supplies. For most people who used the land, however, the new regulations were the first real restrictions on the use of public lands that they had known. **Public lands** are federal lands that were never sold or made into protected areas such as national parks or wilderness areas.

Sometimes, regulations to protect endangered species also restricted activities on private land. "It really is like being in a colony," one Nevada resident complained.

The ranchers considered these government laws and regulations a "taking," based on the "takings clause" of the Fifth Amendment to the U.S. Constitution. A **taking** occurs when regulations restrict use of land so much that owners believe that the government has essentially taken the land.

Ranchers whose cattle grazed on federal grasslands believed that the use of resources on public lands was a right the government could not restrict or take away—that land access should remain much as it had been when the West was first settled. They disapproved of the permits, fees, and rules designed to decrease environmental damage. The issue is complicated by the fact that on some public lands the government owns the land but individuals may own water, mineral, or other rights.

The Sagebrush Rebellion gained an advocate in 1980 with the election of President Ronald Reagan. Declaring, "I am a sagebrush rebel," Reagan decreased the regulation of federal lands in the West. In the 1990s the rebellion against federal regulations continued.

An ongoing struggle For more than a decade, the federal government has shifted positions on the issue of how best to balance environmental protection with the commercial use of natural resources.

Conservation has been effective. Air and water are cleaner today than they have been in previous years. Several endangered species have been saved from extinction. Millions of acres of wilderness remain undeveloped. President Bill Clinton believed that environmental regulation was good for the country, and his administration strengthened environmental laws. Clinton's successor, George W. Bush, believed in encouraging resource development to boost the American economy. He has increased logging, mining, and grazing on public lands.

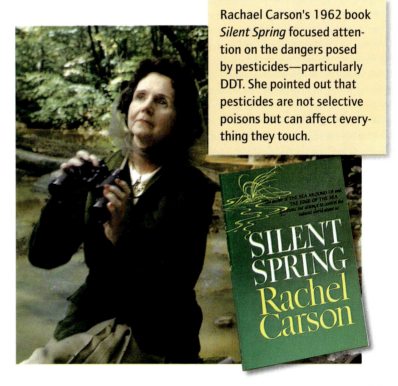

Rachael Carson's 1962 book *Silent Spring* focused attention on the dangers posed by pesticides—particularly DDT. She pointed out that pesticides are not selective poisons but can affect everything they touch.

INVESTIGATING THE PRESENT

Is it possible to use resources without harming the environment? Can land, water, and mineral resources be protected while also preserving people's rights to use them? The documents that follow explore these questions by presenting different points of view. Examine the documents, keeping in mind what you have just read about resource use and conservation. Then answer the questions that follow.

DOCUMENT 1

This map shows the location of federal lands in the United States.

FEDERAL LANDS IN THE UNITED STATES

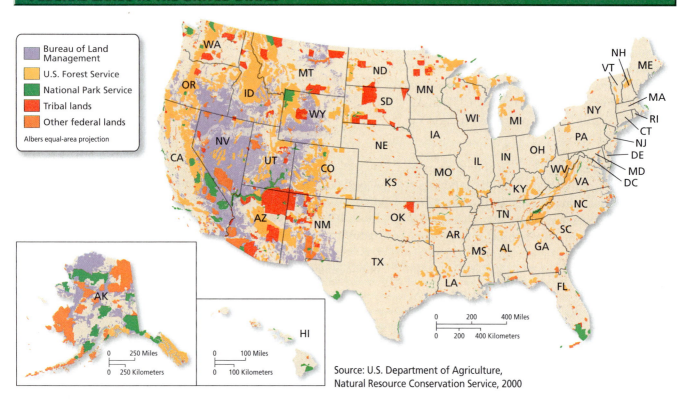

Source: U.S. Department of Agriculture, Natural Resource Conservation Service, 2000

Analyzing the Document
From the map, what can you conclude about the locations of the Sagebrush Rebellion?

DOCUMENT 2

Senator Lisa Murkowski (R., Alaska) offers her opinion on oil drilling in Alaska's Arctic National Wildlife Refuge. This excerpt is taken from a speech she made to the Alaska state legislature.

> The question we have to answer is how to create a state for our children that is better than the one we know today. The future that we want will be funded in part by our resources, and I hope that a portion of that will be from ANWR ...
>
> It's ... important that we let people in the Lower 48 know that a majority of Alaskans want ANWR open and that when it comes to balancing development with care for our environment, we do it right ...
>
> ANWR opponents say that you can't have responsible development on the coastal plain. We know that's not true. We can have a healthy balance between production and conservation—between development and concern for the world we are developing. We work hard to strike this balance in Alaska ...
>
> Our resources serve two objectives. First, they fulfill our role as one of fifty states that share in the responsibility of advancing the country. We advance as a country because of the unique contributions of each one of the states—Alaska's contribution to energy security is through domestic production.
>
> Secondly, our resources serve the objective of lessening our reliance on federal funds and providing financial security for the state. Our resources are an opportunity to create long term, local and sustainable [sources of income].
>
> —Senator Lisa Murkowski,
> speech to Alaska legislature, March 30, 2005

Analyzing the Document
What state and national benefits does Senator Murkowski see to drilling in ANWR?

DOCUMENT 3

This letter to the editor of the *Atlantic Monthly* expresses the writer's point of view regarding a rancher's right to use public land without restrictions.

> Dear Editors:
> Cattle grazing has a ... negative impact on any landscape, especially across the arid US west. [Cattle] cross the landscape in search of food and water, eating most everything available, in many cases down to the bare ground ... Grazing causes not only the destruction of plants and native grasses, but unleases erosion that hinders the health of rivers, degrading habitat essential to fish and other aquatic species.
>
> ... In addition to the subsidized rent on public land ... ranchers also get subsidized fencing, and subsidized eradication of so called "nuisance" species such as coyote, and even wolves—all on land that belongs to you and me. Further, in ... Montana, where a vast expanse of public land is used for grazing, a recent economic study at the University of Montana states that, "federal grazing is responsible for about one quarter of one percent of all income in Montana." To characterize grazing on public land in the west as a sole source of income for family ranchers is off base, and on the whole, grazing on public lands in the west subjects a fragile landscape to a tremendous beating for a very small return. It is also key to note that the vast majority of acres grazed on public lands are still held by very large corporate operations that cover millions of acres.
>
> While there are standouts that should be encouraged for their efforts, ... they represent only a small strand in the web of public lands grazing ... It is not about the so-called loss of cowboy culture, but instead it is about the opportunity for people to enjoy a landscape that has not been ravaged ... Grazing on our land, public land, is not a right, but instead a privilege.
>
> —TW, Letter to the Editor,
> *Atlantic Monthly*, November 1999

Analyzing the Document
Does this writer think that rules and regulations on grazing public land are needed?

DOCUMENT 4

The cartoon expresses the artist's point of view about the government's record in balancing resource use and conservation in the national forests.

Analyzing the Document
Does the artist think that there is a balance between resource use and environmental conservation in the national forests? Explain your answer.

DOCUMENT 5

The Bureau of Land Management oversees the public land in the United States. This land can be used for grazing, natural resource collection, habitat preservation, and recreation, sometimes all at once. This chart shows the amount of money generated in 2004 by the Bureau of Land Management.

COMMERCIAL ACTIVITIES SUMMARY

Public/Federal Land Commercial Activity	Value FY 2004 (millions $)	Federal Revenue Generated FY 2004 (millions $)
Oil and Gas, Geothermal, and Helium	14,217	1,620
Coal	3,645	545
Other Leasable 3 and Salable Materials	943	46
Grazing	62	9
Timber	33	22
Total	18,900	2,242

Source: Bureau of Land Management, 2004 Annual Report

Analyzing the Document
What are the benefits to using land for multiple purposes? In your opinion, does oil and gas drilling fit well with the purpose of recreation and habitat preservation? Explain your answer.

DOCUMENT 6

This table shows the major types of federal lands and their uses.

MAJOR TYPES OF FEDERAL LANDS AND THEIR USES

Federal Lands	National Forests	National Wildlife Refuges	National Parks	Public Lands	National Wilderness Areas
Size (in acres)	190 million	95 million	80 million	260+ million	160 million
Number of Sites	155 forests; 20 grasslands	542	58		600
Purpose	Conservation of forests, in part as a source of timber	Protection of fish and wildlife and their habitats	Preservation of natural, historic, and cultural sites for public enjoyment	Broad resource use as well as recreation and wildlife protection	Preservation of land largely untouched by human activity
Activities Allowed	Recreation, logging, grazing	Recreation, including hunting and fishing	Recreation, including fishing and camping	Livestock grazing, mining, logging, recreation	Recreation, scientific study, conservation
Activities Prohibited			Hunting, mining, logging, and other resource development		Commercial activities: mining, logging, use of motor vehicles, and building of permanent roads and structures

Source: Federal Land and Resource Management: A Primer, Congressional Research Service Report, 1998

Analyzing the Document
Which types of federal lands offer the greatest protection to land and wildlife? Which types offer the greatest opportunity to use timber and mineral resources? How would the formation of a new wilderness area affect people who graze cattle or cut trees on the land? How might that affect their point of view on the formation of new wilderness areas?

ANALYZING THE ISSUES

1. From the information in this issue, what can you conclude is the main reason for regulation of federal lands?

2. In your opinion, should the federal government own large tracts of land, or should it sell the land to private interests? Would a private company have an advantage in balancing environmental and resource issues? Refer to the documents to explain your answer.

3. Select and research federal lands in or near your state. Discover how the managers of these lands protect the environment. Find out whether activities such as mining or grazing are permitted.

4. Research important dates in the movement to conserve public lands. Then construct a time line of events. Then use the time line to write a summary of developments in the public-lands conservation movement.

ISSUE 4

DOCUMENT-BASED INVESTIGATION

Poverty in the United States

California Standards

HSS 11.11.6 Analyze the persistence of poverty and how different analyses of this issue influence welfare reform, health insurance reform, and other social policies.

Focusing on the Issue

What are some ways to reduce poverty?

Key Terms
poverty, poverty threshold, welfare, working poor, food insecurity, disparity, cost of living, minimum wage

THE INSIDE STORY Pamela Reed-Loy lives with her family of five in a cramped hotel room in Washington, D.C. Although her husband, Archie Loy, works full time as a mechanic, the family struggles to make ends meet. Pamela must stay home to care for her three daughters, one of whom suffers from frequent asthma attacks.

"It's stressful, living all in one room—you can't get away from anybody," she said. Each month, the Loy family gets two free bags of groceries from a local church's food bank. "I know people who won't go to the food bank—who don't want to be seen. But why not? I'd never let my kids go hungry."

The Loy family and millions like them live in **poverty,** or the condition of having insufficient income or resources to acquire basic needs. Much more than a simple lack of money, poverty is a complex social, political, and personal issue. Poverty profoundly affects not only the poor but the society that supports and surrounds them.

William Henderson of the Green Bay Packers hands out gifts to a woman at a food bank in Green Bay, Wisconsin. Many of the working poor depend on aid, especially at the end of the month.

1904 Robert Hunter's book *Poverty* is one of the first American efforts to measure poverty.

1900

EXPLORING THE PAST

Poverty as we know it today was not recognized as a national issue until the early 1900s, when the U.S. government had to confront problems created by the rapid growth of industry and cities. At the end of the nineteenth century, Americans' lives were changing dramatically. The growth of industries led people to move from rural areas to the cities. Immigrants flocked to New York City and other places in search of jobs and financial security. What many found, however, was overcrowding, low wages, long hours, and dangerous working conditions.

The Great Depression Many families had prospered during the 1920s but lost their jobs and savings in the Great Depression. Children and the elderly were among the most vulnerable, much as they still are today. At the peak of the Great Depression, one in four Americans was unemployed. Nearly 250,000 young people were homeless.

President Franklin D. Roosevelt proposed the New Deal, a far-reaching set of initiatives designed to stimulate the economy and provide relief to the millions in poverty by putting people back to work. Social Security was created to protect the elderly, people with disabilities, and families with children.

The Other America The U.S. economy recovered and then grew during World War II. Men, women, and minorities all worked in the war effort. The United States became the richest nation in the world as Americans earned more and spent more, factories produced more,

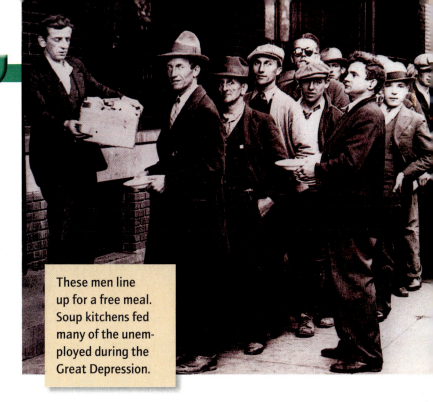

These men line up for a free meal. Soup kitchens fed many of the unemployed during the Great Depression.

and more jobs were created. By the 1950s a sprawling middle class had emerged.

But some political activists, such as Michael Harrington, saw a different America. Millions of people continued to struggle economically, especially the elderly. In 1962 Harrington exposed a "culture of poverty"—some 40 to 50 million Americans suffering in inner cities, in rural Appalachia, and elsewhere—in a book called *The Other America*. Harrington's book influenced the social policies of Presidents John F. Kennedy and Lyndon Johnson.

President Johnson's Great Society In his 1964 election campaign, President Johnson introduced the Great Society program, an extension of Roosevelt's New Deal. President

---

1929 The stock market crashes, plunging the nation into the Great Depression.

1933 President Roosevelt announces the New Deal.

1935 Social Security is signed into law.

1962 *The Other America* is published.

1964 President Johnson announces the Great Society.

1965 Medicare and the first Head Start program begin.

1980–82 Spending on domestic social programs falls by $101 billion.

1996 Welfare reform is initiated.

POVERTY IN THE UNITED STATES 789

A teacher talks with a student in a New York Head Start Program. The program's goal is to increase the school readiness of children from low-income families.

Johnson said his Great Society was "a place where men are more concerned with the quality of their lives than the quantity of their goods." The goals of the Great Society were abundance and liberty for all, an end to poverty, and an end to racial injustice.

War on Poverty In his first State of the Union address, Johnson declared an official War on Poverty. He proposed the Economic Opportunity Act of 1964, under which programs to aid the poor were born. A new housing act provided rent supplements and created the Department of Housing and Urban Development. Medicare, a health insurance program for the elderly, and Medicaid, health-insurance assistance for the poor, were created. Head Start provided free preschool for poor children. Food stamps were introduced. Millions of Americans continue to benefit from these programs today.

The War on Poverty made measuring poverty a priority in order to determine who qualified for aid and how much they should receive. A social scientist, Mollie Orshansky, formed a strategy. She developed a **poverty threshold**, also called a poverty line, to statistically measure the number of people living in poverty. The poverty threshold became the government's official definition of poverty. In 2004 the poverty threshold for a family of four was an annual income of $19,157. Families subsisting on less than that were considered poor.

Welfare reform Throughout the 1970s and 1980s, little change was made in the official definition of poverty. President Ronald Reagan's administration focused on reducing the number of families receiving **welfare**, or financial assistance from the government, and helping the unemployed find work. Many families, however, continued to struggle.

The poverty rate fell substantially in the 1990s as the country's economy boomed. Policy-makers discussed measuring poverty and whether benefits received by the poor should count as income, and if so, whether the poverty line should be raised. The 1996 welfare-reform law brought massive change, as the emphasis shifted from providing income to helping parents find jobs. Welfare became welfare-to-work. Temporary Assistance for Needy Families (TANF) replaced Aid to Families with Dependent Children (AFDC) and placed limits on the amount of time a family could receive public assistance.

Poverty now and in the future Many people believe that the United States was built on the American Dream, the idea that those who work hard can earn enough to achieve prosperity. Yet more than two-thirds of the nation's poor children have at least one parent who works. The Reed-Loy family in Washington, D.C., is part of this new and growing type of poverty in the United States. They are known as the **working poor**—those who are employed but cannot earn enough to lift themselves out of poverty.

The United States has the highest rate of poverty in the developed world. The progress made in fighting poverty in the 1990s ended in 2001. Although the economy improved after that date, the poverty rate rose. In 2004 it reached 12.7 percent. A 2003 survey found 36 million suffering from **food insecurity**, or the inability to buy enough healthy food.

Over the last 20 years, the incomes of the richest 1 percent of Americans have more than doubled. The incomes of the poorest one-fifth, however, grew by only 9 percent. Some people think that such a gap, or **disparity**, between the rich and poor is responsible for lack of progress in reducing the poverty rate. They also think that the **cost of living**, or the amount of income required to buy basic necessities, is too high.

Many Americans have conflicting views on how to reduce poverty. Some think that the federal government needs to provide more assistance to low-income people and to mandate a higher **minimum wage**, or the minimum amount a company must pay its employees. Others think that such measures would make the problem worse by creating dependence on the government.

INVESTIGATING THE PRESENT

The issue of how to reduce poverty continues to be debated. The documents that follow explore this issue by presenting different points of view and arguments. The documents reflect the social, economic, and governmental efforts to define and lessen poverty and its effects on people. Examine the documents, keeping in mind what you have read about the history of poverty in the United States, and answer the questions that follow.

DOCUMENT 1

On May 22, 1964, President Johnson gave a speech at the University of Michigan introducing the Great Society. Following is an excerpt of his speech.

> The purpose of protecting the life of our Nation and preserving the liberty of our citizens is to pursue the happiness of our people. Our success in that pursuit is the test of our success as a Nation.
>
> For a century we labored to settle and to subdue a continent. For half a century we called upon unbounded invention and untiring industry to create an order of plenty for all of our people.
>
> The challenge of the next half century is whether we have the wisdom to use that wealth to enrich and elevate our national life, and to advance the quality of our American civilization.
>
> Your imagination, your initiative, and your indignation will determine whether we build a society where progress is the servant of our needs, or a society where old values and new visions are buried under unbridled growth. For in your time we have the opportunity to move not only toward the rich society and the powerful society, but upward to the Great Society.
>
> The Great Society rests on abundance and liberty for all. It demands an end to poverty and racial injustice, to which we are totally committed in our time.
>
> —President Lyndon Johnson, commencement speech at the University of Michigan, May 22, 1964

Analyzing the Document
What was President Johnson's goal in creating the Great Society?

DOCUMENT 2

In this editorial cartoon, Larry Wright of the *Detroit News* offers his opinion on the condition of Social Security, the safety net designed to help protect senior citizens from poverty.

Analyzing the Document
How does this cartoon portray Social Security's future?

DOCUMENT 3

Nationally, more than 12 percent of U.S. residents are considered to be poor, meaning they fall below the poverty threshold assigned by the U.S. Census Bureau. The map shows, however, that poverty rates vary from region to region.

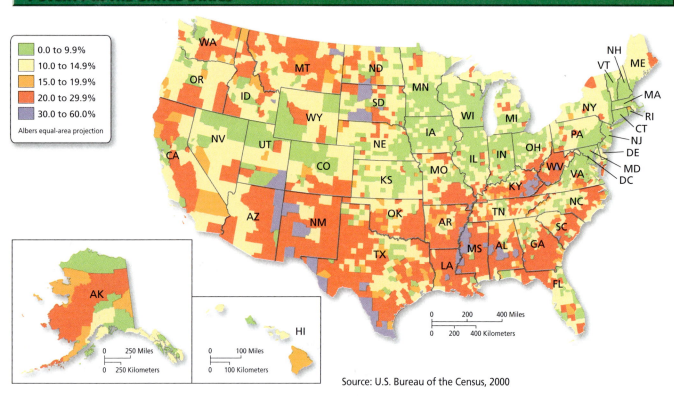

POVERTY IN THE UNITED STATES

- 0.0 to 9.9%
- 10.0 to 14.9%
- 15.0 to 19.9%
- 20.0 to 29.9%
- 30.0 to 60.0%

Albers equal-area projection

Source: U.S. Bureau of the Census, 2000

Analyzing the Document
What areas of the country are most affected by poverty?

DOCUMENT 4

The Center on Budget and Policy Priorities analyzed government studies of the living conditions of poor and near-poor families. This graph represents the percentage of U.S. households with children that experienced what the authors termed hardships: hunger or food insecurity, crowded living space, loss of utilities such as phone or water, and the total experiencing any combination of these factors.

Analyzing the Document
What percentage of poor families reported going hungry? What percentage of near-poor families reported overcrowding? From the information in the graph, what might you conclude about living conditions just above the federal poverty line?

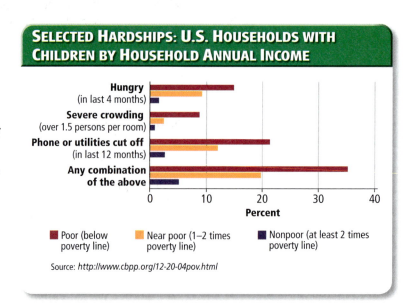

SELECTED HARDSHIPS: U.S. HOUSEHOLDS WITH CHILDREN BY HOUSEHOLD ANNUAL INCOME

- Hungry (in last 4 months)
- Severe crowding (over 1.5 persons per room)
- Phone or utilities cut off (in last 12 months)
- Any combination of the above

■ Poor (below poverty line)   ■ Near poor (1–2 times poverty line)   ■ Nonpoor (at least 2 times poverty line)

Source: http://www.cbpp.org/12-20-04pov.html

DOCUMENT 5

This document is an excerpt from a White House position paper promoting the Welfare Reform Law of 1996.

> Over the past 15 years or so, Congress has expanded a series of programs that provide support to low-income working families. These programs include Medicaid, childcare, the child tax credit, the EITC (Earned Income Tax Credit), and food stamps. Taken together, these programs convert even a minimum wage job into the equivalent of a job paying $8 per hour with benefits. More specifically, if a mother with two children works almost full time at the minimum wage, she earns about $10,000 per year. But thanks to $4,000 in cash from the EITC and around $2,000 in food stamps, the mother and children have a total income of $16,000. In addition, the mother has Medicaid coverage for up to a year after she leaves welfare and the children have Medicaid coverage for as long as the mother has a low income. Moreover, the mother may benefit from the $17 billion in annual federal funding for childcare. The fundamental goal of welfare reform since 1996 has been to help each family achieve its highest degree of self-sufficiency.
>
> —Working toward Independence, White House Position Paper, Februrary 2002

Analyze the Document
How does the federal government believe that welfare-to-work helps families? Do you agree or disagree? Explain your answer.

DOCUMENT 6

The U.S. Department of Agriculture provides people with low incomes food stamps, which are used to purchase grocery items, excluding alcohol and tobacco. The food-stamp program helps lessen food insecurity by giving people with lower incomes access to healthy food. The government considers food stamps "the first line of defense against hunger." The average monthly benefit for a family with children is $242. But not all eligible families decide to participate in the food-stamp program.

TOP TEN STATES RECEIVING FOOD STAMPS IN 2003

State	Number of People Receiving Food Stamps	Number of People Living in Poverty
Texas	1,872,000	3,705,000
California	1,709,000	4,634,000
New York	1,436,000	2,707,000
Florida	1,041,000	2,148,000
Illinois	954,000	1,592,000
Ohio	855,000	1,226,000
Michigan	838,000	1,125,000
Pennsylvania	823,000	1,279,000
Georgia	750,000	1,014,000
Tennessee	728,000	829,000

Source: *U.S. Department of Agriculture, Food and Nutrition Service, 2005* (rounded to the nearest thousand)

Analyzing the Document
Which state in the table above has the most people in poverty? Which has the most people receiving food stamps? What might be some reasons that not all poor people receive food stamps?

ANALYZING THE ISSUES

1. After you have examined all of the documents, think about the following questions: How might redrawing poverty lines affect poorer Americans?

2. How should we balance the needs of people with lower incomes against other, possibly conflicting, priorities? Who should decide?

3. Research the programs available to people living in poverty in your community. What programs established as part of President Johnson's Great Society are still in effect? Which ones are newer?

4. Look at the map of poverty in the United States and find the percentage for your area. How does your community try to reduce poverty's effects? Write a proposal for an event that you could organize to assist local families living in poverty.

ISSUE 5

DOCUMENT-BASED INVESTIGATION

Crime and Public Safety

California Standards

HSS 11.11.7 Explain how the federal, state, and local governments have responded to demographic and social changes such as population shifts to the suburbs, racial concentrations in the cities, Frostbelt-to-Sunbelt migration, international migration, decline of family farms, increases in out-of-wedlock births, and drug abuse.

FOCUSING ON THE ISSUE

What are some ways to reduce crime?

KEY TERMS
crime, offender, criminal code, Second Amendment, infringe, militia, homicide, rehabilitation, discretion, mandatory

THE INSIDE STORY

Derek Ali was many things to many people: father, teacher, newspaper reporter, and community volunteer, to name a few. One night in September 2004, he was wearing yet another hat: DJ for a private party. As he packed his gear in the parking lot after the show, Ali heard gunshots. He pushed the woman beside him to the ground, but he was struck in the chest by a bullet and died. Police said that Ali was a victim of random gunfire. That night a 15-year-old girl lost a father, reporters lost a beloved coworker, and a community lost a leader.

But the toll of the events of that September night goes beyond personal tragedy. People and governments at all levels bear the direct and indirect costs of **crime**, harmful or dangerous acts as defined by law. In 2001 all levels of government spent more than $167 billion, or about $600 per person, for police, jails and prisons, and judicial and legal activities.

The price of being a crime victim is also high. In 1996 the U.S. Department of Justice estimated the annual cost to victims in medical expenses, lost earnings, and other factors at $450 billion. Given the enormous costs, the decisions we make about how best to fight crime are crucial to our social and financial welfare.

Fremont Police Crime Scene Specialist Donna Gott investigates evidence left behind at a crime scene.

1907 Federal Bureau of Investigation established.

1900

EXPLORING THE PAST

Over time, the kinds of crimes people commit and ideas about how to treat **offenders**, or convicted criminals, have changed along with social and economic conditions. Understanding the history of crime and the various attempts to reduce it may help us make more effective decisions about crime control today.

The police began wearing copper badges like this early one from Philadelphia beginning in the late 1840s.

Crime in the colonies The American colonies based their system of law and law enforcement on that of England. Local community leaders wrote laws, and juries decided guilt or innocence at trials presided over by judges.

Penalties for crimes were generally severe by modern standards. Besides the death penalty, they included branding, flogging, and forced labor. In 1682 William Penn, the Quaker leader and founder of Pennsylvania, introduced the Great Law, which treated prisoners more humanely. It limited the use of the death penalty and made hard labor the most common form of punishment.

Cities and states fight crime The first police officers, or cops, walked a beat in New York City. They got their nickname from the copper badges that they wore to identify themselves. As more and more people moved to cities, the crime rates in urban areas increased. In the early 1800s cities throughout the Northeast formed professional police departments.

On the state level, legislators began to standardize laws across communities. New York's 1881 **criminal code**, or standard set of laws, became a model for other states.

By the mid-1800s small, easily hidden handguns were being mass produced. Cities and states tried to control urban crime by targeting these concealed weapons, the first attempts at gun control. Associations of gun owners also arose, including the National Rifle Association, which formed in 1871. In 1911 New York passed the Sullivan Act, which made carrying a concealed weapon illegal and tightened gun-permit procedures.

Crime and gun control National events would shape the efforts to control crime throughout the 1900s. To meet the challenge on the national level, the federal government established the Federal Bureau of Investigation in 1907 and the Federal Bureau of Prisons in 1929. These agencies brought greater resources as well as professionalism to the fight against crime.

Following the assassination of Robert F. Kennedy in 1968, the Gallup poll found that for the first time respondents ranked crime as the nation's most pressing issue, and Congress passed the Gun Control Act of 1968. This law

1924 Congress establishes the FBI's Identification Division to consolidate fingerprint files.

1934 National Firearms Act, the first federal gun-control law, is passed.

1938 Gun Control Act passed in response to assassinations.

1972 National Sheriffs' Association establishes neighborhood watch.

1984 Crime Control Act expands the death penalty and funds crime prevention measures.

1994 Violent Crime Control and Law Enforcement Act bans assault weapons.

2004 Congress allows ban on assault weapons to expire.

CRIME AND PUBLIC SAFETY **795**

This FBI agent is looking at a fingerprint card. In the 1940s when this picture was taken, all fingerprint matching had to be done by hand.

prohibited felons and others—such as illegal aliens, unlawful users of controlled substances, and inmates of mental institutions—from buying guns and required licensing of gun dealers and outlawed some types of guns, such as fully automatic civilian machine guns.

What does "the right to keep and bear arms" mean?
The **Second Amendment** of the Constitution states that "the right to keep and bear arms shall not be infringed." But what exactly does this mean? Are a person's rights **infringed**, or interfered with, if a state requires gun owners to carry a permit or restricts the sales of certain types of guns?

Gun-control advocates point to the phrase "a well-regulated militia" as evidence that Congress meant only to guarantee the right of states to organize their own armed **militias**. Other Americans believe that the Second Amendment protects the private ownership of guns.

New solutions to combat crime
The number of violent crimes, such as **homicide**, or the deliberate killing of another person, more than doubled from 1965 to 1975. During that period, violent crime topped 1 million incidents for the first time and continued increasing into the early 1990s, when the number of violent crimes peaked at 1.9 million in 1992.

Violence associated with the drug trade played a large role in this increase. Shootings in post offices, businesses, and schools increased concerns about violence. Since 1992, however, violent crime has fallen, reaching the lowest level ever recorded in 2004.

As violence rose, efforts to use criminal sentencing as a means of **rehabilitation**, or reforming offenders into contributing members of society, came under increasing criticism. More and more, legislators responded to citizens' worries with "get tough" approaches.

Governments try various approaches
Choices about possible punishments for crimes begin with the legislators who write the laws. Sometimes the law gives a judge **discretion**, or the freedom to decide on an appropriate sentence for each individual within certain guidelines. In other cases, the judge must give a **mandatory**, or required, sentence to each offender convicted of a particular crime.

Theories about punishment influence sentencing. A retribution and incapacitation approach favors strict mandatory sentencing laws, the expansion of prisons, and the use of the death penalty as deterrents and ways of preventing offenders from commiting another crime. This approach has led to over 2 million Americans being incarcerated in 2004. A rehabilitation approach favors programs such as boot camps and drug treatment programs as ways of changing the offender's behavior. Governments also try to prevent crime. Community policing and citizen watch groups are examples of programs designed to stop crime before it happens.

INVESTIGATING THE PRESENT

The issue of how best to reduce crime in the United States is a serious topic of debate. The documents that follow explore these issues by presenting different points of view and arguments. Examine the documents, keeping in mind what you have read about the history of crime and the government's response to it, and answer the questions that follow.

DOCUMENT 1

The causes of crime are complex, and many factors contribute to rising or falling crime rates, argues Marc Mauer, assistant director of The Sentencing Project in the late 1990s. In his book *Race to Incarcerate*, Mauer points out that creating tougher sentencing laws is only one of many policy options available for reducing the amount of crime.

> Over half of all state and federal prison inmates are currently serving time for a non-violent drug or property offense. While many of these offenders have had prior criminal convictions, the policy decision regarding their sentencing involves a consideration of whether spending $20,000 a year to [keep them in prison] is the wisest choice of action. The alternative is . . . to explore whether some combination of [probation], victim [repayment], required treatment, and other conditions would more effectively respond to the needs of both victim and offender.
>
> —Marc Mauer, *Race to Incarcerate*, 1999

Analyzing the Document
What might government or other institutions do to determine which measures actually influence the crime rate?

DOCUMENT 2

Theories about the reasons for crime often affect approaches to punishment. Morgan O. Reynolds, a senior fellow and director of the National Center for Policy Analysis, argues that tough sentences for convicted criminals in the 1990s helped reduce the crime rate during that decade.

> What explains the sudden decline in crime after a long rise? Better economic conditions? Cultural changes? A more convincing explanation is at hand: Courts have been handing out tougher punishment for crime, and potential criminals know and fear it . . . some Americans fail to see the connection between new get-tough policies and recent improvements in the crime rate. "Crime keeps on falling, but prisons keep on filling," a *New York Times* headline declared . . . Crime is falling because prisons are filling.
>
> —Morgan O. Reynolds, "Does Punishment Deter?," National Center for Policy Analysis, 1998

Analyzing the Document
Use this excerpt to contrast the basis for attempting to rehabilitate prisoners with the basis for continuing get-tough policies.

DOCUMENT 3

Two high school students, Dylan Klebold and Eric Harris, killed 13 people and injured another 24 in a 1998 attack at Columbine High School in Littleton, Colorado. Many people were disturbed to learn of the killers' obsession with violent video games, music, and movies.

Analyzing the Document
What do you think the cartoonist thinks about the causes of youth violence, such as school shootings? Do you agree or disagree? Explain your answer.

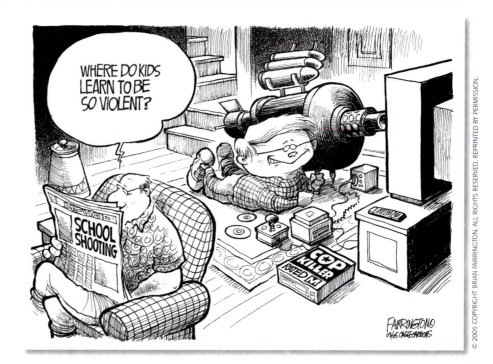

DOCUMENT 4

Editor Carol Wekesser collected conflicting viewpoints about violence in television and films for her collection of essays, *Violence in the Media*. The following excerpt from her introduction helps explain the issues that violent media raises for parents and society at large.

Analyzing the Document
How might children be affected by viewing so many violent acts in the media?

> Those who believe that media violence is largely responsible for societal violence can cite many startling statistics and cases that support their view. For example, the American Psychological Association states that by seventh grade the average child has seen seven thousand murders and one hundred thousand acts of violence on television. Several murders and attacks have been connected to movies and television.
>
> Yet, while such statistics and cases are alarming, the vast majority of American children who grow up viewing violent television programs and movies also grow up to be normal, healthy adults.
>
> —Carol Wekesser, ed., *Violence in the Media*, 1995

DOCUMENT 5

This line graph from the Department of Justice's Bureau of Crime Statistics shows the total number of robberies and aggravated assaults reported to police in the United States from 1960 to 2000.

Analyzing the Document
About how many incidents of robbery does the graph show happened in 1990? During what decade are the numbers for both crimes the highest? During what decade are the numbers of both crimes the most similar?

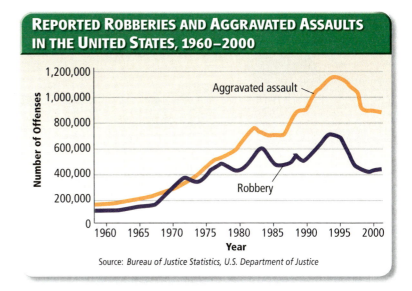

DOCUMENT 6

A recent response to crime is the introduction of community-oriented policing. According to the Department of Justice, the goal of community-oriented policing is to "address the causes and reduce the fear of crime and social disorder through problem-solving tactics and community-police partnerships." This photograph illustrates ways that community-oriented police officers interact with those they serve and protect.

Analyzing the Document
What changes might occur in a neighborhood as a result of community policing? How might those changes lead to lower crime rates?

ANALYZING THE ISSUES

go.hrw.com
Practice Online
SE7 Issues

1. What do you think is the best way to reduce crime? Explain your answer.
2. Where should efforts to reduce crime originate—with governments, individuals, or society? Explain.
3. Research recent crime-control laws in your state. Describe what kinds of crime they target and whether crime rates have fallen since these laws were passed.
4. Survey people in your community to find out where crime ranks among their concerns and which crime reduction method they favor. Research similar national data and compare it with your results.

ISSUE 6

DOCUMENT-BASED INVESTIGATION

Regulation and the Internet

California Standards

HSS 11.8.7 Describe the effects on society and the economy of technological developments since 1945, including the computer revolution, changes in communication, advances in medicine, and improvements in agricultural technology.

FOCUSING ON THE ISSUE

How should the Internet be regulated?

KEY TERMS
electronic mail, Internet, packet switching, protocol, World Wide Web, telecommuting, cyberspace, spam, encryption

THE INSIDE STORY Before 17-year-old Jeremy gets up for school, his mom checks the news headlines and weather on her computer's Internet home page. At school, Jeremy's physics class uses the Internet to visit university Web sites, looking for information about the forces created by roller coasters. After school, Jeremy and his friends use their computers to send each other **electronic mail**, more commonly referred to as e-mail. After Jeremy goes to bed, his mother uses the computer to do some shopping and to send messages to her real estate clients. Like most people his age, Jeremy has never known a world without the Internet.

The **Internet** is a network of computers that connects many smaller networks around the world. People can use Internet technologies to communicate, conduct research, buy and sell goods and services, bank, pay bills, and access news and entertainment. Since its beginnings, the Internet has transformed the way millions of people live, work, and do business.

The Internet has affected human culture and commerce in many positive ways. However, some people have taken advantage of the new technologies to exploit Internet users. For example, unwanted messages clog e-mail in-boxes. Identity theft, copyright infringement, and illegal accessing of government or corporate information, known as hacking, also are serious problems. Such problems present many challenges to government, law enforcement, and computer scientists.

Tens of millions of Americans use the Internet at home, work, and school as well as at public places such as Internet cafes and libraries. One of the most common uses of the Internet is sending electronic mail.

EXPLORING THE PAST

The technological developments that led to the Internet originated in the Cold War conflict between the United States and the former Soviet Union. To help maintain a lead in science and technology, the U.S. Department of Defense started the Advanced Research Projects Agency (ARPA) in 1958. Many people credit ARPA for establishing the foundations of the Internet.

In 1969 ARPA organized one of the first general-purpose computer networks, called ARPANET, to connect computers at research sites supported by the government. ARPANET took advantage of a new technology called **packet switching**. Instead of sending a large chunk of information in a single message, a computer could send the message in smaller packets. The packets then travel separately along the fastest routes to the receiving computer, which reassembles the message.

Scientists at ARPANET also developed innovative new **protocols**, or formats for sending data from one computer to another. These included the "simple message transfer protocol" (SMTP), used to send e-mail. By the early 1980s researchers had established standard protocols for connecting, or internetting, the different networks.

The Internet expands Several important innovations helped take the Internet from a purely academic research tool to the familiar component of daily life that it is today. The first was the development of the personal computer in the mid-1980s.

The second was the creation of the **World Wide Web**, a computer program that allows users to create, store, and connect information in documents called Web pages. The third innovation was the Web browser, which enables users to find, display, and interact with documents on the Web. The first widely available browser, called Mosaic, was released in 1993.

The Internet expanded quickly during the 1990s. The U.S. government was active in the early years of the Internet. But it gradually withdrew, allowing commercial interests to take over. By 1995 the Internet was largely controlled by private companies.

This map shows the geographical distribution of computer networks in 1993, when the Mosaic browser was released.

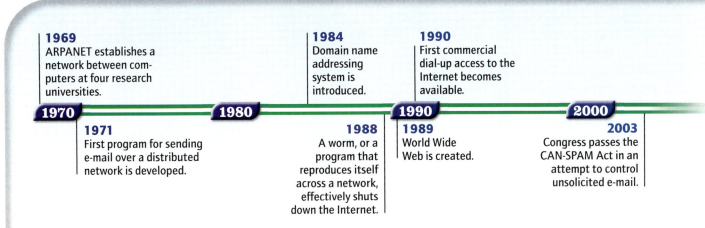

1969 ARPANET establishes a network between computers at four research universities.

1971 First program for sending e-mail over a distributed network is developed.

1984 Domain name addressing system is introduced.

1988 A worm, or a program that reproduces itself across a network, effectively shuts down the Internet.

1990 First commercial dial-up access to the Internet becomes available.

1989 World Wide Web is created.

2003 Congress passes the CAN-SPAM Act in an attempt to control unsolicited e-mail.

Uses of the Internet The Internet has been so successful because it appeals to a large cross section of society. The government has used the Internet to distribute information and to automate procedures, such as tax filing. Schools have used the Internet for research and online courses. Many businesses have advertised, bought, sold, and provided customer service online. The Internet also has made it easier for businesses to support **telecommuting**. Some employees can telecommute by working away from their office on a computer connected to the Internet.

Problems in cyberspace The growth of **cyberspace**—a term often used for the online world of the Internet—occurred with great speed. This has left government and law-enforcement agencies little time to consider whether or how the Internet should be regulated. This relative lack of regulation has left the Internet and millions of users vulnerable.

Internet users are bombarded with unwanted e-mail advertisements, called **spam**. Spam wastes the time and money of users, who are forced to separate spam from legitimate e-mails. Criminals also have used spam to spread computer viruses, programs designed to damage recipients' computers. Another feature of the Internet that invites abuse is the online availability of image, audio, and video files. Sharing of such files can violate copyright laws.

Identity theft and privacy issues Today technologies exist that allow outside observers to monitor Internet users' Web browsing, e-mail, and even every keystroke they enter on their keyboards. A serious abuse of monitoring technologies is identity theft, or the theft of someone's personal information, such as credit card or social security numbers, for illegal use.

Computer scientists have worked to find technical solutions to these problems. **Encryption** technology, which transforms data to make it indecipherable to an outside observer, is one such solution.

Problems also arise in trying to define the legitimate uses of both monitoring and encryption tools. Government and law enforcement want to use the tools to protect citizens from illegal activity. Employers want to use them to monitor employees' behavior. Businesses are also interested in using such tools to identify the economic habits of consumers in order to better market their goods and services. Privacy and civil liberties advocates, however, cite the potential for abuse.

State, national, and international governments and organizations are trying to create a reasonable legal environment for Internet activities. Bills have been introduced in the U.S. Congress to regulate the Internet. Legislatures in Canada, Australia, and the European Union are also at work trying to solve Internet problems.

One bill introduced in Congress to protect Americans from the growing crime of identity theft is the Social Security Number Misuse Prevention Act. The bill was sponsored by Senator Judd Gregg (R-New Hampshire), Senator Dianne Feinstein (D-California), and Senator Patrick Leahy (D-Vermont).

INVESTIGATING THE PRESENT

Issues surrounding Internet regulation are still being debated. The following documents reflect the social, economic, and governmental perspectives on Internet regulation. Examine the documents, keeping in mind what you have read about the history of the Internet. Then answer the questions that follow.

DOCUMENT 1

The Internet Crime Complaint Center is a government agency set up in 2000 to provide a way for people and law-enforcement agencies to report and collect information about Internet crimes. At right is a chart showing reported Internet fraud cases over a five-year period.

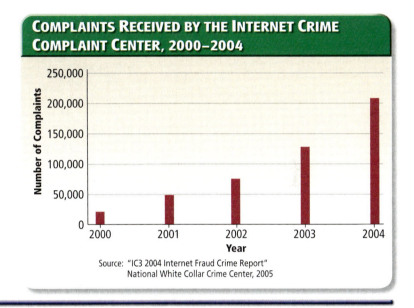

Analyzing the Document
What can you conclude about reported cases of Internet fraud from 2000 through 2004?

DOCUMENT 2

This newspaper article from the *Chicago Tribune* points out the difficulty of controlling spam, even with the CAN-SPAM law that was passed in 2004.

Seeking to shut down a University of Texas student listed as the fourth-worst e-mail spammer in the world, the Texas attorney general... filed a civil lawsuit against the man potentially seeking nearly $500 million in damages...

[The target of the suit]... owns a $450,000 home in an exclusive Austin neighborhood and several luxury automobiles. [The attorney general said the student] earns up to $28 each time a recipient clicks on one of his e-mails and fills out a form seeking personal information—a bounty paid by mortgage and insurance brokers for each legitimate lead...

[The student's attorney said he and his partner] "are Internet marketers and are no different from the bulk mailers" who flood postal mailboxes with unsolicited offers...

The CAN-SPAM Act, passed by Congress to slow the torrent of unwanted e-mails that by some estimates account for 85 percent of all Internet traffic, does not ban unsolicited commercial solicitations...

"Spam is the front end of a lot of things," said Dan Larkin, the unit chief of the FBI's Internet Crime Complaint Center. "It can lead to identity theft or getting spyware downloaded to your computer. These guys are not just nuisances. They are making a lot of money, they are disrupting e-commerce and they are involved in malicious code that leads to high-impact attacks on the Internet infrastructure. We are going after them."

—*Chicago Tribune,* January 13, 2005

Analyzing the Document
Why would controlling unsolicited e-mail be important for the success of Internet commerce?

DOCUMENT 3

This political cartoon addresses the issue of copyrighted material, such as music, being shared on the Internet free of charge, without payment going to the copyright holder.

Analyzing the Document
What effect might downloading music files have on people who make their living from music, including artists and record companies? Might it affect some groups differently than others?

DOCUMENT 4

In 2005 three researchers from the University of Pennsylvania's Annenberg Public Policy Center conducted a phone survey of 1,500 American adults who had used the Internet in the previous month. They asked 17 true-false questions about Internet commerce and privacy. An excerpt from the report follows.

> Most Americans who use the Internet have little idea how vulnerable they are to abuse by online and offline marketers and how the information they provide can be used to exploit them... Americans' lack of knowledge about marketplace rules puts them at risk. We found that:
> - 68% of American adults who have used the Internet in the past month believe incorrectly that "a site ...that compares prices on different airlines must include the lowest airline prices."
> - 49% could not detect illegal "phishing"—the activity where crooks posing as banks send emails to consumers that ask them to click on a link wanting them to verify their account.
> - 66% could not correctly name even one of the three U.S. credit reporting agencies (Equifax, Experian, and TransUnion) that could keep them aware of their credit worthiness and whether someone is stealing their identity...
> - 75% do not know the correct response—false—to the statement, "When a website has a privacy policy, it means the site will not share my information with other websites and companies."
>
> —"Open to Exploitation: American Shoppers Online and Offline," by Joseph Turow, Lauren Feldman, and Kimberly Meltzer, Annenberg Public Policy Center, University of Pennsylvania

Analyzing the Document
According to this survey, what conclusion can you draw about Americans' understanding of online commerce? What facts led you to this conclusion?

DOCUMENT 5

This cartoon uses a depiction of students passing notes to one another to comment on unwanted e-mail.

Analyzing the Document
What are some possible effects of spam on people's lives?

DOCUMENT 6

Research conducted by Don McCabe, the founder of the Center for Academic Integrity, has shown that Internet plagiarism is widespread in colleges. In 2005 the Center released results from its nationwide survey on academic integrity in which nearly 50,000 undergraduates on more than 50 campuses took part.

> Internet plagiarism is a growing concern on all campuses as students struggle to understand what constitutes acceptable use of the Internet. In the absence of clear direction from faculty, most students have concluded that "cut and paste" plagiarism—using a sentence or two (or more) from different sources on the Internet and weaving this information together into a paper without appropriate citation—is not a serious issue. While 10% of students admitted to engaging in such behavior in 1999, almost 40% admit to doing so in the Assessment Project surveys. A majority of students (77%) believe such cheating is not a very serious issue.
> —Center for Academic Integrity, Duke University

Analyzing the Document
According to the document, how serious an issue is Internet plagiarism in American schools? In what way does the Internet play a role in student cheating and plagiarism?

ANALYZING THE ISSUES

1. After you examine the above documents, think about the following question: How much privacy should people expect when they use the Internet? Explain your answer.

2. How much protection should a consumer expect when buying goods and services on the Internet?

3. What are some possible consequences of restricting access to private information? Do research on state-level attempts to regulate the Internet. How would the same restrictions affect you in your state?

4. How would you go about trying to stop Internet plagiarism?

ISSUE 7

DOCUMENT-BASED INVESTIGATION

Outsourcing and Trade

California Standards

HSS Analysis CS2 Students analyze how change happens at different rates at different times; understand that some aspects can change while others remain the same; and understand that change is complicated and affects not only technology and politics but also values and beliefs.

FOCUSING ON THE ISSUE

What are the advantages and disadvantages of outsourcing?

KEY TERMS
outsourcing, comparative advantage, protectionism, NAFTA

Natasha Humphries worked for three years as a software engineer at one of the world's leading producers of handheld computing devices. When overseas workers were hired to perform testing, Humphries was assigned to manage a team in India. In 2003, however, she lost her job when all of the work that Humphries did was transferred to the very group in India that she had helped train.

Humphries' story is a familiar one. In recent years, thousands of American jobs have been outsourced overseas to countries such as India where labor costs are lower than in the United States. **Outsourcing** is the practice of using workers from outside a company. Proponents contend that lower overall labor costs mean savings for consumers in the form of lower prices for goods and services. The practice of outsourcing jobs to overseas workers has attracted increased criticism, however, from people who believe American businesses should employ American workers.

This customer service call center in Bangalore, India, provides 24-hour telephone support for customers in the United States and England.

1920

1930 Smoot-Hawley Tariff Act places high tariffs on foreign goods.

EXPLORING THE PAST

Outsourcing has roots in international trade. From colonial times through American independence, trade was largely discouraged. Governments granted monopolies and subsidies to protect merchants, farmers, and manufacturers from competition.

In 1776 Scottish economist and philosopher Adam Smith challenged such practices in his book *Inquiry into the Nature and Causes of the Wealth of Nations*. Smith described how free trade, competition, and choice would lead to economic development and improve people's lives. The system he proposed laid the groundwork for free trade throughout the 1800s.

Comparative advantage In 1817 English economist David Ricardo explained the theory of comparative advantage. A nation has a **comparative advantage** when it can produce a certain good or service more cheaply than another country. According to this theory, nations gain when they trade those items that they are most efficient at producing. For example, in Country A it might be difficult to make computer parts but easy to make clothing. In Country B both are easily produced. If Country B decides to focus on producing computer parts, it can trade its excess to Country A for clothing. Both countries benefit.

If imports cost less and exports earn more, trade seems to benefit everyone. People can buy goods more cheaply and get jobs in booming industries. But what happens to those people who became expert clothing makers in Country A? What happens if Country B does

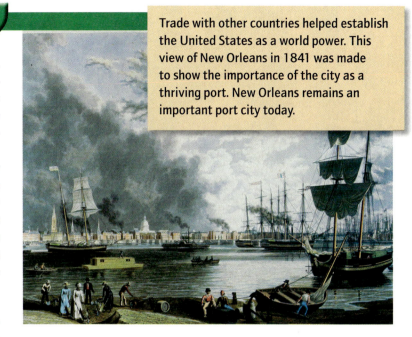

Trade with other countries helped establish the United States as a world power. This view of New Orleans in 1841 was made to show the importance of the city as a thriving port. New Orleans remains an important port city today.

not earn as much selling computer parts as it spends for clothing? Historically, governments have managed such risks by regulating trade.

Restrictions on trade When economies are strong and relationships between nations are good, trade has remained open. During financial or political hard times, governments adopt **protectionism**, or the restriction of trade, to protect their producers.

In 1890 Congress protected U.S. businesses by passing the McKinley Tariff. As with other tariffs, it raised the cost of foreign products so that consumers were more likely to buy comparable American goods. Thus, U.S. industries profited from tariffs at home. However, they suffered losses when other countries began imposing tariffs on U.S. goods.

1947 GATT opens trade among 23 member countries.

1957 General Electric begins building plants overseas to reduce labor costs.

1988 Omnibus Trade and Competitiveness Act seeks to open Japanese market to American goods.

2004 Defending American Jobs Act is first introduced in Congress.

1944 Bretton Woods agreement signed by 44 countries establishes international rules for commerce.

1992 NAFTA is signed.

1995 World Trade Organization is established.

OUTSOURCING AND TRADE **807**

Chief trade representatives for Mexico, the United States, and Canada hold NAFTA treaties that have just been signed by Mexican president Carlos Salinas de Gortari (left), President George H.W. Bush (center), and Canadian prime minister Brian Mulroney (right).

At the World Economic Conference in 1927, several countries decided to stop imposing tariffs on one another. After the stock market crash in 1929, however, the United States broke with this policy by passing the Smoot-Hawley Tariff, the highest protective tariff in American history. Other countries responded by imposing high tariffs on American goods, worsening the effects of the Great Depression.

Creating a global marketplace After World War II interest renewed in trading cooperatively with other nations. An organization called the General Agreement on Tariffs and Trade (GATT) was formed in 1947. (In 1995 GATT was replaced by the World Trade Organization.) Member nations opened their markets and reduced tariffs. U.S. manufacturing boomed as demand increased from European nations whose industries had been largely destroyed in the war. The United States dominated world markets through the 1960s.

Worldwide tariff reductions continued to expand trade in the latter half of the 1900s. Nations such as Japan and Mexico became increasingly competitive in world markets. The United States responded by looking for new markets. For example, President Richard Nixon opened trade relations with China. In the late 1980s President George H.W. Bush broadened U.S. access to markets in Japan.

In 1992 the United States, Canada, and Mexico formed NAFTA, or the North American Free Trade Agreement. Its purpose was to remove tariffs among the three countries. Proponents of NAFTA say that it has led to lower prices in the United States and higher sales of American goods, resulting in higher-paying and higher-skilled U.S. jobs. Opponents contend that it has resulted in the exporting of jobs from the United States to Mexico, where labor costs are less expensive.

Increase in outsourcing As globalization has increased, so too has competition. Demand for domestic goods decreased in the 1980s as less expensive goods were imported from regions such as Asia. To save money, companies reduced their manufacturing workforces.

As American factory workers protested, they were reassured that they would find better jobs. Employees who already held such jobs rested easy—until the 1990s, when new technologies like e-mail and the Internet made it possible to outsource those jobs.

At first, companies outsourced narrowly defined higher-level tasks, such as customer service, to supplement domestic staff during peak times. As outsourcing's benefits became clearer, companies began moving entire divisions overseas. More than half of all Fortune 500 corporations have moved jobs outside the United States. The reason? Analysts estimate outsourcing saves companies between 30 and 70 percent annually in costs.

Analyzing the effects Supporters of outsourcing contend that it benefits the U.S. economy. By employing people in previously impoverished regions, outsourcers are creating new consumers who want and can afford American products. Proponents further contend that, as jobs move overseas, Americans will develop new areas in which U.S. workers can specialize. Long-term losses will be minimal, they argue, because 70 percent of American jobs, such as those in hospitals, must be performed locally.

Outsourcing opponents say that although companies are profiting, people are not. They claim that displaced workers are not being rehired for equal or better jobs. To guard against future outsourcing, more than 50 U.S. representatives have sponsored the Defending American Jobs Act of 2004. The act proposes to cut federal funding from companies that lay off workers at higher rates in the United States than abroad.

INVESTIGATING THE PRESENT

The issue of outsourcing raises many questions. The documents that follow explore this issue by presenting different points of view and arguments. Examine the documents, keeping in mind what you have read about the history of outsourcing, its costs, and its benefits. Then answer the questions that follow each document.

DOCUMENT 1

David Ricardo's theory of comparative advantage is frequently cited by proponents to explain the logic of outsourcing's benefits. In this article, the author examines how well—or if—Ricardo's theory applies today.

> Economists are blind to the loss of American industries and occupations because they believe these results reflect the beneficial workings of free trade. Whatever is being lost, they think, is being replaced by something as good or better. This thinking is rooted in the doctrine of comparative advantage put forth by economist David Ricardo in 1817 . . .
>
> Today's economists can't identify what the new industries and occupations might be that will replace those that are lost, but they're certain that those jobs and sectors are out there somewhere. What does not occur to them is that the same incentive that causes the loss of one tradable good or service—cheap, skilled foreign labor—applies to all tradable goods and services. There is no reason that the "replacement" industry or job, if it exists, won't follow its predecessor offshore.
>
> For comparative advantage to work, a country's labor, capital, and technology must not move offshore. This international immobility is necessary to prevent a business from seeking an absolute advantage by going abroad.
>
> —Paul Craig Roberts, "The Harsh Truth about Outsourcing," *Business Week*, March 22, 2004

Analyzing the Document
Why does the author feel that Ricardo's theory is outdated?

DOCUMENT 2

In this political cartoon called "The New American Patriotism," men in business suits launch small boats out to sea. The boats are labeled "US Jobs." On the shore is a building labeled "IBM etc." Study the cartoon and then answer the question that follows.

Analyzing the Document
Does this cartoon support unlimited or restricted outsourcing? Explain your answer.

DOCUMENT 3

Because companies are not required to keep records, no one knows how many jobs have been sent overseas. It is estimated, however, that by 2015 more than 3 million American jobs will have been outsourced. While companies are seeing the benefits of outsourcing in the short term, unemployed workers are feeling its costs.

Analyzing the Document
What are some disadvantages of outsourcing?

DOCUMENT 4

This is an excerpt from an article published by the National Conference of State Legislatures. State lawmakers have been raising concerns over government contracts being awarded to companies that use taxpayer money to hire workers overseas. The author explains some of the benefits of supporting companies that outsource.

> The outsourcing dispute is rooted in the debate over free trade and jobs. Proponents argue that through outsourcing, American goods get into more foreign markets, only lower-level jobs are lost, and American workers move into more advanced jobs. They also argue that outsourcing is a scapegoat, that the loss of most jobs can be attributed to a poor economy and increased productivity and cyclical changes in employment.
>
> Using overseas workers is beneficial to the United States in four ways, says a recent report in the McKinsey Quarterly...
>
> First is cost savings. The report states that "for every dollar of spending on business services that move offshore, U.S. companies save 58 cents."
>
> Second is new revenues. The rise of office services in the developing world creates demand for goods that are often purchased here, including computers, telecommunications equipment, and legal, financial, and marketing services...These profits can be used to expand business in the United States or be returned to investors. Third is repatriated earnings. Profits that American companies generate operating in the low-cost overseas markets are sent back to the United States through taxes on these additional earnings.
>
> Fourth is the redeployment of labor. Sending lower-level, lower-skilled jobs overseas permits the American workforce to move into higher paying occupations.
>
> —National Conference of State Legislatures,
> *State Legislatures,* May 2004

Analyzing the Document
According to the report, how does helping businesses help the economy?

DOCUMENT 5

Outsourcing is not just one way. According to the Organization of International Investment, over the past 15 years more corporations have moved jobs to the United States than have moved jobs outside the United States.

Analyzing the Document
According to the graphs, how does the rate of increase of insourced jobs compare to that of outsourced jobs? Why is the percentage of manufacturing job growth higher than the percentage growth in the total number of jobs?

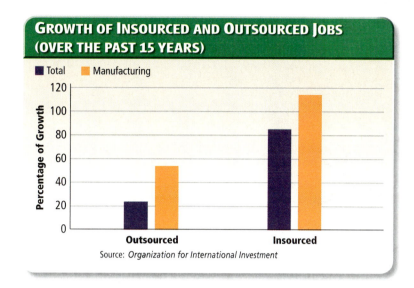

GROWTH OF INSOURCED AND OUTSOURCED JOBS (OVER THE PAST 15 YEARS)

Source: Organization for International Investment

DOCUMENT 6

As companies have seen the benefits of outsourcing outweigh its costs, their ideas surrounding its potential have expanded. This table features data from Forrester Research, Inc., showing plans for future outsourcing of jobs by industry.

Analyzing the Document
According to the table, which industries will be most affected by outsourcing in the future? How might such changes affect workers?

How Much Pain?

As more U.S. employers embrace white-collar globalization . . .

Share of 1,000 largest U.S. companies that say they plan to:	2003	2008
Do virtually no white-collar offshoring	63%	46%
Offshore to some degree	33%	44%
Offshore any white-collar work possible	4%	10%

. . . more nonfactory jobs will move abroad.

Job Type	2002 employment	Share moving offshore by 2004	2008	2015**
Computer	3 million	5%	9%	20%
Legal	1 million	1%	3%	9%
Business	5 million	1%	3%	8%
Architecture	2 million	1%	2%	8%
Office	23 million	1%	3%	7%
Life sciences	1 million	0	1%	4%
Management	7 million	0	1%	4%
Art, Design	2 million	0	1	2%
Sales	13 million	0	0	2%
Total	57 million jobs	1%, or 546,000 jobs	2%, or 1.2 million jobs	6%, or 3.4 million jobs

Source: Forrester Research Inc. **Estimates

DOCUMENT 7

In this excerpt from a 2004 campaign speech, President Bush discusses the need for U.S. workers to rise to the challenge against foreign competition.

> There is a temptation in Washington to say the solution to jobs uncertainty is to isolate America from the world. It's called economic isolationism, a sense that says, well, we're too pessimistic, we don't want to compete—as opposed to opening up markets, let's close markets, starting with our own. That is very dangerous...
>
> And so the fundamental question is, do we keep our market open, or do we close it? My attitude is, we keep it open, but make sure others open theirs, too... One way to make sure jobs don't go overseas, and one sure way to make sure we're vibrant here at home is to insist that other people lower their barriers so we can compete. That's all we ask. Just give us a chance. Americans can rise to the challenge, trust me.
>
> –President George W. Bush, March 2004

Analyzing the Document
Explain President Bush's point of view regarding government's role in job protection.

DOCUMENT 8

Senator John Kerry (D–Mass.) ran against President Bush in the 2004 election. In a campaign speech Senator Kerry advocated for a system in which the federal government would enforce its trade agreements and help end the outsourcing of certain jobs.

> I won't let America wage the fight for our economic future with one hand tied behind our back. No one should misunderstand me: I am not protectionist—but I am a competitor. American workers are the most competitive in the world—and they deserve a government that's as competitive as they are. We will demand our trading partners play by the rules they've agreed to and show them that America means business when it comes to enforcing our trade agreements...
>
> It is time to insist on and enforce real worker and environmental provisions in the core of every trade agreement so that we don't exploit workers in other countries or sell them out here at home. And it's time to break the deadlock in Congress and pass real tax breaks for our manufacturing industries.
>
> —Senator John Kerry, campaign speech, March 26, 2004

Analyzing the Document
How does Senator Kerry's approach to job protection differ from President Bush's?

ANALYZING THE ISSUES

1. What are the primary arguments put forth in support of and against outsourcing?
2. Are the benefits of outsourcing worth the costs? Explain your position.
3. Write an editorial in which you explain the pros and cons of outsourcing. Include different perspectives regarding the short-term as well as the long-term effects of outsourcing.
4. Do research and write a report describing the outsourcing trends that have taken place in your state in the past decade. Include an examination of the efforts made by state and local governments in support of and restricting further outsourcing.

Reference Section

Key Events in American History R3

Presidents of the United States R17

Supreme Court Decisions R22

Facts about the States R30

American Flag Etiquette R32

Biographical Dictionary R33

Atlas R46

    California Governors and Government R60

    California Facts R61

Geography Handbook R62

Primary Source Library R74

Holt Social Studies Library Correlation R94

English and Spanish Glossary R96

Index R126

Credits and Acknowledgments R151

Key Events in American History

The World Almanac Key Events in American History is a brief summary of important turning points in the history of the nation. It provides a capsule description of an event or movement along with brief accounts of its significance. Use this section to review the content in *American Anthem*.

12,000 B.C.E. Migrations to America
The first people arrived in North America at least 14,000 years ago, during the last Ice Age. With much of Earth's water frozen in ice sheets, sea levels dropped and a land bridge connected Asia and North America. Hunters from Siberia migrated over the land bridge to North America.

Significance The migration brought the first people to the Western Hemisphere. Archaeologists think that by about 11,000 years ago Native Americans were living in both North and South America.

1492–1502 Columbus's Voyages
In 1492 Italian-born explorer Christopher Columbus sailed west from Europe with the goal of finding a sea route to Asia. His ships landed on the Caribbean island of Hispaniola. Believing he had reached the Indies, Columbus called the people he met "Indians." Columbus made three more journeys to the Americas, exploring Caribbean islands and making stops in Central and South America.

Significance Columbus' voyages opened the Western Hemisphere to exploration and conquest by Spain and other European powers. They also led to the Columbian Exchange—an exchange of plants, animals, and diseases between the Western Hemisphere and Europe and Africa.

1607 Settlement of Jamestown
Founded in Virginia in 1607, Jamestown was the first permanent English colony in North America. Plagued by an unhealthy location, the colony barely managed to survive. Captain John Smith provided critical leadership. John Rolfe planted tobacco in Jamestown, giving the colony a cash crop that was in high demand in England. A small group of enslaved Africans arrived in Jamestown in 1619.

Significance After Jamestown, the English established other colonies along the east coast of North America. Successful tobacco farming in Jamestown led to the growth of plantation agriculture and slave labor. The Virginia House of Burgesses, established in 1619, was America's first elected legislature.

1620 Pilgrims arrive at Plymouth
The Pilgrims were religious dissenters from the Church of England who sought the freedom to worship according to their beliefs. In 1620 they traveled to North America on the *Mayflower*. The Pilgrims founded a colony at Plymouth, Massachusetts, which survived with the aid of friendly Wampanoag Indians. The colony marked its first harvest with a feast which forms the basis for the Thanksgiving holiday.

Significance The Pilgrims were the first colonists motivated to found a colony by a desire to freely practice their own religion. This became an important motivation for several other groups of colonists, and eventually the free practice of religion became a fundamental principle of the U.S. Constitution.

1651–1673 Navigation Acts
The Navigation Acts were a series of trade laws passed by the English government between 1651 and 1673. The laws sought to control trade with England's colonies to the benefit of the mother country. Among other things, the laws required that colonial goods be shipped only on English ships.

Significance England got what it wanted from the Navigation Acts—raw materials and tax revenues from the colonies. Colonists, on the other hand, were angered by the laws and often avoided paying taxes by smuggling goods into and out of the colonies.

1730s–1740s The Great Awakening
The Great Awakening was a religious revival in the English colonies that began in the 1730s. One of its leading voices was the colonial Puritan clergyman Jonathan Edwards, who appealed to his listeners' fears and emotions. Another was the English Methodist minister George Whitefield, who moved large audiences to cry and confess their sins.

Significance The Great Awakening countered the spread of Enlightenment ideas in the colonies, which were causing some people to question long-accepted religious beliefs. It led to the growth of new Protestant denominations in America, including the Methodist, Baptist, and Presbyterian churches.

1754–1763 French and Indian War

The Seven Years' War was the fourth and decisive war fought between Britain and France for control of land in North America. It's European phase is known as the Seven Years' War, but colonists called this conflict the French and Indian War because France and its Indian allies battled Britain and the colonists. After several early setbacks, the British won the crucial Battle of Quebec in 1759. France surrendered the following year.

Significance The French and Indian War marked the end of French power in North America. Britain gained all of France's lands east of the Mississippi River, helping to establish the basis for a mighty British empire. British leaders tried to recover some of cost of the war by taxing colonists, a policy which led to growing tensions between Britain and its colonies in America.

1765 Stamp Act

Passed by Parliament in 1765, the Stamp Act was a tax designed to raise money from colonists to help pay the cost of protecting the colonies. Resentful colonists called this "taxation without representation" because they had no voice in Parliament. In October 1765, delegates from nine colonies met at the Stamp Act Congress to protest the tax. Parliament repealed the Stamp Act in 1766.

Significance The Stamp Act was the first time Parliament had directly taxed the colonists. Colonial leaders from different regions, who were not used to working together, united to protest the tax. The united action of leaders from different colonies would become a model for future action.

1770 Boston Massacre

Tensions between British soldiers and the people of Boston were growing in early 1770. This anger exploded on March 5, 1770, when a group of British soldiers opened fire on a colonial mob that was taunting and threatening them. Local colonial leaders called the event the Boston Massacre, describing it as a deliberate attack on innocent civilians.

Significance The Boston Massacre served the cause of radicals like Samuel Adams who were eager to paint the British as cruel oppressors. The Massacre became a rallying cry for proponents of independence from Britain.

1775–1783 American Revolution

The American colonies' fight for independence from Britain began in April 1775 with the Battles of Lexington and Concord. Over the next six years, George Washington led the often undermanned and poorly equipped Continental Army. The American victory at the Battle of Saratoga in 1777 was a pivotal turning point; it convinced the French to join the war on the American side. The last significant battle was Washington's defeat of Lord Cornwallis' army at Yorktown, Virginia, in 1781.

Significance The Treaty of Paris, which ended the war in 1783, acknowledged the independence of the United States. The American Revolution was the first successful democratic revolution against a colonial ruler. A direct result was the establishment of the United States of America as a independent democratic republic.

1776 Declaration of Independence

Written largely by Thomas Jefferson in June 1776, the Declaration of Independence explained the reasons colonial leaders decided to break free from Britain and declared the United States to be an independent country. It was presented to Congress on July 2, 1776, and members voted to declare independence on that day. Two days later, on July 4, Congress approved the Declaration of Independence.

Significance The Declaration marked a point of no return for Americans—people were now forced to take sides in the struggle between Patriots and Loyalists. In addition, the Declaration boldly stated the principles of government that form the basis for American democracy, and it has been an inspiration to other freedom movements ever since.

1786 Shays's Rebellion

High taxes forced many Massachusetts farmers into heavy debt in the 1780s. When a court ordered their farms and homes be sold to pay the debts, Daniel Shays, a Revolutionary War veteran, led a rebellion. After some success delaying court proceedings, the rebellion was quickly put down by state militia.

Significance Shays's Rebellion frightened many Americans and helped convince them that the central government under the Articles of Confederation was not strong enough to deal with the country's problems. This fueled the movement to form a stronger federal government, which led to the Constitutional Convention.

1787 Northwest Ordinance

Congress passed the Northwest Ordinance to encourage orderly settlement and the formation of new states on the land north and west of the Ohio River. The law promised settlers religious freedom and barred slavery. It also set up a system for the eventual admission of new states.

Significance The Northwest Ordinance created a pattern for settlement in western territory, leading to a rapid expansion of the population of these lands. It also barred slavery from the Northwest Territory, which later became the states of Ohio, Indiana, Illinois, Michigan, Wisconsin, and part of Minnesota.

1787 Constitutional Convention

Delegates came to the convention in Philadelphia to discuss ways to strengthen the Articles of Confederation. Instead they drafted an entirely new plan of government, the United States Constitution.

Significance Ratified in 1788, the Constitution defined a plan of government—with checks and balances between three branches of government—that has endured for well over 200 years. The Bill of Rights, ten amendments protecting the freedoms of individual Americans, was ratified in 1791.

1803 Marbury v. Madison

The case of *Marbury* v. *Madison* was brought by William Marbury, who was appointed to a judgeship in 1801 by outgoing President John Adams. When incoming President Thomas Jefferson refused to give Marbury his commission, Marbury sued to get it. The Supreme Court ruled that it did not have the power to force Jefferson to deliver the commission. The Justices also declared that the law that had given the Court that power—the Judiciary Act of 1789—was unconstitutional.

Significance *Marbury* v. *Madison* established the Supreme Court's right to declare that a law violates the Constitution. This power, known as judicial review, greatly expanded the influence of the Supreme Court.

1803 Louisiana Purchase

President Jefferson sent James Monroe to France to try to attempt to buy New Orleans, a port of critical importance to western farmers. Much to Monroe's surprise, the French offered to sell all of Louisiana, stretching from the Mississippi River to the Rocky Mountains. The final price of the Louisiana Purchase was about $15 million.

Significance The Louisiana Purchase almost doubled the size of the United States, opening up huge new tracts of land to future American settlement. It also removed an important foreign power as an obstacle for American expansion in North America.

1812 The War of 1812

The War of 1812 between Great Britain and the United States actually lasted three years, from 1812-1815. It arose from a dispute over American rights to trade with France, Britain's enemy in the Napoleonic Wars. Native American efforts, aided by the British, to resist United States expansion also played a role in triggering conflict. The war ended with no clear winner.

Significance The war's conclusion reaffirmed American independence and spurred a period of intense patriotic feeling. Two of its military heroes, William Henry Harrison and Andrew Jackson, later went on to become presidents. Francis Scott Key wrote "Star-Spangled Banner," the national anthem, to celebrate American resistance to British bombardment of Fort McHenry in Baltimore harbor.

1820s–1830s Second Great Awakening

The Second Great Awakening was a national religious movement that was especially strong in the North. Americans attended revivals, embraced religious teachings, and joined churches in record numbers. New religious denominations, including the Mormon Church, were formed at this time.

Significance By 1850 the majority of Americans considered themselves to be Protestant. The Second Great Awakening helped launch the Reform Era, which lasted from about 1830 to 1860. Inspired by religious ideals, Americans attempted to reshape society by promoting temperance, improved education, and other reforms.

1820 Missouri Compromise

Missouri's desire to join the Union as a slave state sparked a crisis, because the Union was then balanced between slave states and free states. In 1820 Congress reached a compromise: Missouri was admitted to the union as a slave state, while Maine entered the Union as a free state. In addition, the Missouri Compromise banned slavery in the Louisiana Territory north of a line stretching west from the southern border of Missouri.

Significance The Missouri Compromise temporarily defused the tension between free and slave states, but it did not end the debate over slavery in western lands. The crisis illustrated the intense feelings of sectionalism that would eventually split the nation in two.

1823 Monroe Doctrine

After the former Spanish colonies in Latin America won their independence, U.S. leaders were concerned that Britain and other European nations might try to expand their influence in the Western Hemisphere. In 1823 President James Monroe issued the Monroe Doctrine, declaring that the Western Hemisphere was no longer open to colonization by European countries. Any attempt to do so, Monroe declared, would be viewed as a hostile act directed against the United States.

Significance The Monroe Doctrine was a bold statement for the young United States to make. European powers did not welcome the policy, but for the most part they did not challenge it. In the decades after the Monroe Doctrine, the United States continued to expand its influence in Latin America.

1825 Completion of the Erie Canal

The 363-mile long Erie Canal ran across New York State, connecting the Great Lakes with the Hudson River. The canal provided a quick and economical way to ship manufactured goods to the west and farm products to the east.

Significance Trade generated by the Erie Canal helped make New York City into a great trading and financial center. The success of the canal set off a "canal craze" in the United States. Within 15 years a network of canals crisscrossed the northeast. These transportation improvements contributed to rapid economic growth.

1830 Indian Removal Act

In 1830 President Andrew Jackson signed the Indian Removal Act, which called for the relocation of five Indian tribes from the Southeast to an area west of the Mississippi River. Though the Supreme Court declared the forced relocation unconstitutional, Jackson refused to follow the Court's decision.

Significance The Indian Removal Act demonstrated that Native Americans had little protection under the law in the United States. U.S. Army troops supervised the removal of the tribes to Indian Territory. The forced removal of the Cherokee became known as the Trail of Tears, as thousands died on the miserable journey west.

1835–1836 Texas Revolution

In the 1820s a small group of Americans moved to Texas at the invitation of the Mexican government. The new residents clashed with Mexican authorities, who banned slavery and wanted all residents to follow Roman Catholicism. When the Texans moved to armed resistance, Antonio López de Santa Anna, the dictator of Mexico, marched an army into Texas to crush the revolt. The Texans defeated Santa Anna, and declared their independence.

Significance Texas became an independent country known as the Republic of Texas. The United States annexed Texas in 1845, angering Mexican leaders. This set in motion a chain of events that led to the Mexican-American War.

1846–1848 Mexican-American War

A dispute over the southern boundary of Texas led to the outbreak of the Mexican-American War in 1846. American forces drove through Mexican defenses and captured Mexico City. Under the terms of the Treaty of Guadalupe Hidalgo, which ended the war in 1848, Mexico was forced to cede more than half a million square miles of land to the United States. This land included areas that became the states of Arizona, New Mexico, and California.

Significance The Mexican Cession vastly increased the size of the United States and helped fulfill the claims of manifest destiny. California became part of the United States just as gold was discovered there. The war also contributed to poor relations with Mexico for many years to come.

1848 Seneca Falls Convention

Held in July 1848 in Seneca Falls, New York, the Seneca Falls Convention was the country's first women's rights convention. It was organized by Lucretia Mott and Elizabeth Cady Stanton. Stanton wrote the Seneca Falls Declaration, which stated that "all men and women are created equal."

Significance The Seneca Falls Convention marked the beginning of an ongoing national campaign for women's rights. One of the main goals was women's suffrage, which was achieved in 1920 with the passage of the Nineteenth Amendment.

1849 California Gold Rush

In 1848 a carpenter discovered gold in the American River in northern California. People as far away as Asia, South America, and Europe heard the news and headed to California, dreaming of striking it rich. The mass migration to California of miners—and business people who made money off the miners—is known as the Gold Rush. By 1854 300,000 people had migrated to California.

Significance The Gold Rush resulted in the rapid growth of California, which became a state in 1850. It also contributed to the wealth of a nation and helped fuel the dream of instant riches that has become part of American culture.

1854 The Birth of the Republican Party

The Republican Party began when former members of the Whig, Free Soil, and Democratic parties came together in opposition to the Kansas Nebraska Act. The main issue uniting Republicans was opposition to the expansion of slavery in the West.

Significance By 1860 and the election of Abraham Lincoln as president, the Republican Party had become what it remains today, one of the two major political parties in the United States.

1857 The *Dred Scott* Decision

Dred Scott was an enslaved person owned by Dr. John Emerson, an army surgeon from Missouri. In the 1830s, Emerson brought Scott to Illinois and other free areas of the North. After returning to Missouri, Scott sued for his freedom, arguing that by living where slavery was illegal, he had become free. The Supreme Court ruled against Scott in 1858. Chief Justice Roger Taney noted that the Fifth Amendment to the Constitution protected the property rights of slaveholders. In addition, the Court ruled that since the Constitution forbade Congress from making laws depriving people of their property, the Missouri Compromise was unconstitutional.

Significance The Dred Scott decision added to the explosive tension between the North and South over slavery. Most white Southerners saw the ruling as a great victory. Many Northerners were outraged, fearing the government now lacked the authority to bar slavery in any territory.

1860–1861 Secession of the South

On December 20, 1860, soon after Abraham Lincoln's election as president, South Carolina became the first state to secede. Mississippi, Florida, Alabama, Georgia, Louisiana, Texas followed quickly. In response to the fall of Fort Sumter in April 1861, Lincoln called on the remaining states to supply soldiers to put down the southern rebellion. Rather than comply, Virginia, North Carolina, Tennessee, and Arkansas seceded and joined the Confederacy.

Significance The secession of the southern states, along with Lincoln's determination to hold the Union together, resulted in the Civil War.

1861–1865 The Civil War

The Civil War began in April 1861 with the Confederate attack on Fort Sumter. The South won key early battles, largely thanks to the superior military skill of its generals. Northern victories at Vicksburg and Gettysburg in 1863 helped turn the tide of the war. The fighting ended in April 1865, when Confederate commander General Robert E. Lee surrendered to Union commander General Ulysses S. Grant at Appomattox Court House, Virginia.

Significance More than 600,000 Americans died in the Civil War, making it the costliest war in U.S. history. Fighting left the South's farms, factories, and transportation system in ruins. The Northern victory ensured the preservation of the Union and led to the end of slavery everywhere in the United States.

1862 Homestead Act

The Homestead Act allowed any head of a household over the age of 21 to claim 160 acres of public land. Each homesteader had to build a home on the land, make improvements, and farm the land for five years before gaining full ownership of the land. In the 124 years the Act was in force, nearly two million people tried to claim land under its provisions.

Significance The Homestead Act led to rapid settlement of the Great Plains, which had previously been considered a "Great American Desert." Settlers turned this into one of the most productive farming regions in the world. Many of the settlers were immigrants from northern Europe, whose descendants still populate the Great Plains today.

1862 Emancipation Proclamation

Announced in September 1862, Lincoln's Emancipation Proclamation declared that as of January 1, 1863, all slaves in areas of the South in rebellion against the Union would be free. Its immediate impact was limited, since unconquered areas of the South were not effected. It also did not free slaves in the Border States, which were still in the Union.

Significance The Emancipation Proclamation widened the goals of the war to include the end of slavery. It also helped assure the neutrality of Great Britain, which had been expected to enter the war on the side of the Confederacy. Strong anti-slavery sentiment in Great Britain made any plans to aid the Confederacy unfeasible.

1865 Assassination of Lincoln

Lincoln was assassinated on April 14, 1865, five days after Lee's surrender. He was attending a play at Ford's Theater when John Wilkes Booth, a well known actor and a bitter Confederate sympathizer, entered Lincoln's box and shot him in the head. Booth escaped from the scene, but was hunted down and died in a shoot out with Union troops.

Significance Lincoln's death produced a national outpouring of grief. As a successful wartime leader, Lincoln might have been able to push his relatively lenient Reconstruction plan through Congress. Vice President Andrew Johnson, a southerner, had far less influence with Republican congressional leaders. A fierce battle between Johnson and Congress over the direction of Reconstruction soon began.

1865–1877 Reconstruction

Reconstruction was the process of readmitting the Southern states into the Union after the Civil War. After Southern leaders passed Black Codes to limit the rights of African Americans, the Republican controlled Congress passed the Reconstruction Acts. These acts divided the South into five military districts under the control of the U.S. Army and required southern states to ratify the Fourteenth Amendment and write new state constitutions guaranteeing freedmen the right to vote. A major political struggle over Reconstruction policy between President Andrew Johnson and Congress led to Johnson's impeachment and near conviction.

Significance Reconstruction included three Constitutional amendments that initially helped African Americans. But enforcement of these reforms was dependent on the presence of the Union Army in the South. When the army withdrew in 1877, reconstruction collapsed and African Americans were denied their civil rights. Reconstruction also contributed to the lasting bitterness between North and South.

1865-1870 Reconstruction Amendments

The Thirteenth Amendment abolished slavery in the United States. The Fourteenth Amendment conferred citizenship on all persons born in the United States, thus extending citizenship to all freed African Americans. It also said that people could not be deprived of life, liberty or property without due process of law. The Fifteenth Amendment made it unconstitutional to deprive a citizen of the the right to vote because of "race, color, or previous condition of servitude."

Significance The three amendments helped make full citizens of freed African Americans during Reconstruction. With the collapse of Reconstruction, however, African Americans lost most of their rights until the Civil Rights Movement of the mid-1900s.

1869 Completion of the Transcontinental Railroad

In 1862 Congress provided land for the building of a transcontinental railroad to connect the East and West coasts of the United States. Workers for the Union Pacific Railroad laid tracks west from Nebraska while Central Pacific Railroad built tracks east from California. The workforce was made up largely of immigrants from China, Ireland, and Germany, as well as African Americans and Native Americans. On May 10, 1869, the two rail lines met at Promontory Summit in Utah Territory.

Significance The rail line helped speed up the settlement of the West by making it easier to move people, goods, and resources across the country. It helped unite the country, both physically and economically. Other transcontinental railroads were soon built, and regional railroads expanded.

1876 Invention of the Telephone

In 1876 Scottish-born Alexander Graham Bell patented his design for a "talking telegraph," or, as it came to be known, telephone. Companies quickly found it to be an essential business tool, and people wanted them in their homes.

Significance Along with inventions such as the telegraph and typewriter, the telephone was part of a communication revolution in the 1800s. By 1900 more than a million telephones had been installed in offices and homes across the nation.

1880s–1910s New Wave of Immigrants

Prior to 1880 most immigrants had come to the United States from northern and western Europe. Beginning in the 1880s, waves of immigrants came from southern and eastern Europe. Millions came every decade until 1920. Thousands of immigrants came from Asia as well.

Significance Between 1880 and 1910, nearly 18 million newcomers came to the United States. The new immigrants helped power America's growing industries. The wave of immigration also changed the makeup of the American population. By 1910 nearly one out of every seven Americans was foreign-born.

1883 Pendleton Civil Service Act

The Pendleton Civil Service Act was designed to end the spoils system, a long-standing practice of filling government jobs with supporters of the winning political party. The law required that federal appointments be based on merit, not on political connections. It also guaranteed the rights of people to compete for jobs regardless of race, religion or national origin.

Significance The new law initially applied to only 10 percent of federal jobs, but was still an important first step in reducing corruption in the federal government. By 1980 the law applied to more than 90 percent of all federal positions.

1886 Formation of the AFL

Samuel Gompers formed the American Federation of Labor (AFL) in 1886. The AFL was a coalition of skilled workers in trade and craft unions. Unlike more radical unions, the AFL was more concerned with better wages and working conditions than with pushing larger political reforms.

Significance The AFL became the most powerful union of its time. Gompers used collective bargaining and strikes to gain higher wages and shortened work hours for union workers.

1887 Dawes Act

The Dawes Act divided up Native American reservation lands, allotting small individual plots to families. The goal of the law was to encourage Native Americans to value private property and live more like typical American farmers. The land many Native Americans received included desert or near-desert lands unsuitable for farming. Many who did want to farm could not afford the tools, animals, seed, and other supplies necessary to get started.

Significance Under the Dawes Act, land not allotted to Native Americans was sold, thus decreasing the amount of land under Indian control. Native American traditional life was weakened, and poverty on reservations became more widespread.

1890 Formation of the National American Woman Suffrage Association

The National American Woman Suffrage Association was the largest suffrage group in the United States. NAWSA activists worked to persuade state legislatures to grant women the vote.

Significance NAWSA's membership grew to nearly 2 million under the leadership of Carrie Chapman Catt. Working at both the state and federal levels, the organization played a key role in pressuring Congress to pass the Nineteenth Amendment, granting women full voting rights. A successor organization, the League of Women's Voters, exists today.

1890 Sherman Anti-Trust Act

Though the United States had a tradition of laissez-faire capitalism, in the late 1800s the federal government became concerned about the power of expanding corporations. The Sherman Antitrust Act made it illegal for corporations to form trusts that interfered with free trade.

Significance The Sherman Anti-Trust Act was the first federal action taken against trusts. The act was vaguely written, however, and corporations were easily able to avoid prosecution. The government soon stopped trying to enforce the Sherman Act. Consolidation of corporations continued. Congress later toughened the regulation of trusts by passing the Clayton Antitrust Act in 1914.

1896 *Plessy v. Ferguson*

Plessy v. *Ferguson* provided the legal justification for segregation in the South. The Supreme Court ruled that "separate but equal" facilities for blacks and whites did not violate the equal protection clause of the Fourteenth Amendment.

Significance *Plessy* v. *Ferguson* gave the force of federal law to the segregation practices that had been initiated in the South after the end of Reconstruction. The ruling was overturned in 1954 by the Supreme Court's decision in the *Brown* v. *Board of Education of Topeka, Kansas* case.

1898 Spanish-American War

The Spanish-American War was a four-month conflict in which American forces defeated Spain in Cuba and the Philippines. In the treaty ending the war, the United States gained control of Cuba, Puerto Rico, Guam, and the Philippines. Cuba was quickly granted independence, but remained under American influence.

Significance The Spanish-American War marked the establishment of the United States as a major international power. The capture of colonies set off a broad debate in the United States between expansionists and anti-imperialists. In the Philippines, Filipino nationalists rebelled against American rule. United States forces eventually crushed the rebellion in a war that lasted 15 years and claimed the lives of hundreds of thousands of Filipinos and over 4,000 U.S. soldiers.

1899 Open Door Policy

In the late 1890s Japan and European powers carved out spheres of influence in China. Fearing the United States would be shut out of trade with China, U.S. Secretary of State John Hay proposed the Open Door Policy. This policy would give all nations equal trading rights in China.

Significance The Open Door Policy was neither accepted nor rejected right away by other imperialist powers. The Boxer Rebellion, however, convinced Western nations that competing among themselves threatened their ability to exploit China. This led to increased support for the Open Door Policy.

1903 Invention of the Airplane

Orville and Wilbur Wright, two bicycle mechanics from Dayton, Ohio, built the first successful airplane. On December 17, 1903, at Kitty Hawk, North Carolina, Orville Wright became the first man ever to fly an airplane.

Significance Orville Wright's first flight lasted just 12 seconds, but it was the first true airplane flight in history. The Wright brothers and others began manufacturing airplanes. Air travel quickly changed transportation, increased demand for oil, and affected warfare.

1908 Henry Ford Begins selling Model T Automobiles

Henry Ford's goal was to build a car that most working Americans could afford. He achieved this in 1908 with the introduction of his Model T. Ford used the assembly line to produce cars quickly and cheaply, lowering the Model T's price to less than $500.

Significance By 1929 there were almost 30 million cars in the country. The auto industry created huge spin-off industries, such as road construction, oil refining, and gasoline retailing. The invention of the assembly line changed the way goods were produced. The wide availability of cars made it easier for more people to live some distance from their jobs, which led to the rise of suburbs.

1909 Founding of NAACP

A multiracial group of activists, including Ida Wells-Barnett, W.E.B. Du Bois, and Jane Addams, formed the National Association for the Advancement of Colored People (NAACP), to fight for the rights of African Americans. Early actions included defending African Americans falsely accused of crimes and protesting segregation in the federal government.

Significance The NAACP was the first national civil rights organization. In 1954 NAACP lawyers won the case of *Brown* v. *Board of Education of Topeka, Kansas*, in which the Supreme Court declared segregation in public schools to be unconstitutional.

1913 Passage of Sixteenth Amendment

The Sixteenth Amendment gave Congress the power to levy taxes based on personal income. The Treasury Department set up the Internal Revenue Service to collect income taxes.

Significance Under the first income tax laws, less than one percent of the population paid income taxes. This percentage, along with income tax rates, rose as government grew and the nation faced challenges such as World Wars I and II.

1914 Opening of the Panama Canal

Work on the Panama Canal began in May 1904 and lasted until 1914. The 50-mile canal across the Isthmus of Panama connected the Atlantic and Pacific Oceans, greatly shortening maritime travel times.

Significance The Panama Canal helped make the United States a great naval power by allowing the U.S. fleet to move more quickly from the Atlantic to the Pacific. It also greatly facilitated world trade. Protecting the canal and other economic interests became a central element of U.S. foreign policy in Latin America.

1914–1918 World War I

Increasingly intense rivalries in Europe, along with growing feelings of nationalism and a system of military alliances, led to the start of World War I. The primary opponents were the Central Powers (Germany, Austria-Hungary and Italy) and the Allied Powers (Great Britain, France and Russia). New technology such as machine guns and poison gas made this the deadliest war the world had seen to that point. The United States entered the war in 1917, helping the Allies gain eventual victory.

Significance World War I caused levels of casualties far higher than any previous war—combat, disease, and starvation killed more than 14 million people. Another 7 million men were left permanently disabled. The war led to the overthrow of monarchies in Russia, Austria-Hungary, Germany, and Turkey, and contributed to the rise of the Communists to power in Russia. The Treaty of Versailles, which ended the war, imposed harsh penalties on Germany, causing bitterness that later contributed to the outbreak of World War II.

1910s–1920s The Great Migration

In the early 1900s most African Americans lived in the South, where strict segregation laws kept them in a separate but unequal world. The Great Migration was a massive movement of African Americans from the South to the North, where they hoped to find economic opportunity and greater personal freedom. This movement accelerated with the outbreak of World War I, as northern factories needed workers to meet the demand for war supplies.

Significance The Great Migration was the largest internal migration in American history. Hundreds of thousands of African Americans streamed into northern cities such as New York, Chicago, and Detroit. This led to a mixing of cultures, and transformed race from a regional to a national issue.

1919 Treaty of Versailles

The Treaty of Versailles ended World War I. Against the advice of President Woodrow Wilson, Germany was forced to make large reparations payments to the Allies. The treaty also created nine new nations and established the League of Nations, an international organization designed to settle disputes, protect democracy, and prevent future wars.

Significance It is widely believed that the harsh terms of the Treaty of Versailles contributed to the rise of the Nazis in Germany and, therefore, the start of World War II. In the United States, Wilson's unwillingness to compromise with the Senate led to rejection of the treaty by the United States.

1920–1933 Prohibition

Prohibition was a period lasting from 1920 to 1933 during which the manufacture, transportation, and sale of alcohol was outlawed by the 18th Amendment. Prohibition proved unenforceable and was repealed by the 21st Amendment in 1933.

Significance Prohibition led to the creation of organized criminal groups who defied the law. It also led to strengthening of the Bureau of Investigation, forerunner to today's FBI, to combat crime. Its failure widely discredited efforts to legislate what many considered an area of private morality.

1919 The Palmer Raids

During the Red Scare that followed World War I, fear of Communists and radicals grew to an intense level in the United States. The Palmer Raids, led by U.S. Attorney General Mitchell Palmer, were a series of government raids on suspected radicals. Thousands of suspects were arrested, in some cases without proper legal authority.

Significance Far from criticizing the Palmer raids, many Americans cheered, or demanded even tougher action. This demonstrated the level of fear that existed in American society. The Red Scare gradually died out as it became clear that radicals had little power or support in the United States.

1920s Harlem Renaissance

The Harlem Renaissance was a creative movement of African American writers, musicians and artists that took place in the New York City neighborhood of Harlem in the 1920s. Important writers of the movement included James Weldon Johnson, Zora Neale Hurston, and Langston Hughes. Jacob Lawrence and William Johnson were two artists who won fame, as did such musicians as Paul Robeson, Louis Armstrong, and Duke Ellington.

Significance The Harlem Renaissance enriched American culture. Writers and artists made important contributions to American culture. Jazz swept the nation, contributing to a major cultural movement in the 1920s.

1930s The Dust Bowl

In the 1930s, drought and poor farming practices led to massive dust storms that turned portions of the Great Plains into what became known as the Dust Bowl. It was one of the worst ecological disasters in American history.

Significance The Dust Bowl contributed to a mass migration west among displaced farmers. The refugees from Dust Bowl states such as Oklahoma, sometimes called "Okies," came to represent the difficulties of the 1930s. The Dust Bowl led to improved efforts at soil conservation.

1929 Stock Market Crash

Despite underlying weakness in the economy, the stock market continued to rise in 1929. In September, prices began to weaken. The great crash came on "Black Tuesday," October 29, 1929, when stock prices collapsed.

Significance Both individual investors and businesses were devastated by the stock market crash. The crash marked the beginning of large decline in the economy that became known as the Great Depression. The crash also led to reforms of the stock market, including the creation of the Securities and Exchange Commission.

1930 Smoot-Hawley Tariff

The Smoot-Hawley Tariff was intended to ease the plight of American farmers by raising tariffs on imported farm products. This tariff also raised tariff rates on many kinds of manufactured goods. The tariff rates under Smoot-Hawley were higher than at any point in American history.

Significance European nations responded to the American tariff with high tariffs of their own. International trade dropped 66 percent from its 1929 levels, causing economies everywhere to suffer. In this way, the tariff can be said to have deepened the Great Depression worldwide.

1932 Franklin D. Roosevelt elected President

As the 1932 presidential election approached, many Americans blamed President Herbert Hoover for causing the Great Depression, or at least for failing to provide relief from the crisis. Democratic nominee Franklin D. Roosevelt promised swift government action to improve the economy. Roosevelt won the election in a landslide.

Significance In addition to winning the White House, the Democratic Party gained firm control of both houses of Congress. This gave President Roosevelt the ability to push though his New Deal legislation, which changed the role of government in American life.

1933–1945 The Holocaust

Soon after gaining power in Germany in 1933, Adolf Hitler began using the power of the government to persecute German Jews. German conquests early in World War II brought nearly all of Europe's 9 million

Jews under Nazi control. The Nazis attempted to exterminate the entire Jewish population of Europe. This became known as the Holocaust.

Significance The Nazis murdered 6 million Jews in the Holocaust, decimating the Jewish population of Europe. Nazis also killed about 5 million others, including prisoners of war, disabled people, and Gypsies. After the war, many of the Nazi leaders were convicted of war crimes by an international court. These trials were meant to demonstrate the commitment of people around the world to prevent a repetition of the Holocaust.

1935 Passage of the Social Security Act

Signed into law by President Roosevelt on August 14, 1935, the Social Security Act created a program that provided pensions for many Americans age 65 and older. These pensions were paid for by a new tax on workers and employers.

Significance The Social Security Act marked a significant expansion of the role of government in the lives of Americans. Its passage showed that government intended to take a greater share of responsibility for the well-being of citizens.

1935 Passage of the Wagner Act

Named for its sponsor, Senator Robert F. Wagner, the Wagner Act outlawed many of the anti-labor strategies in wide use among business leaders in the 1930s. The act created the National Labor Relations Board (NLRB), which had the power to investigate unfair labor practices and assure employees the right to collective bargaining.

Significance The Wagner Act was a major victory for organized labor. In the four years after the act's passage, union membership jumped from under 3.8 million members to over 6.5 million members.

1939-1945 Manhattan Project

The Manhattan Project was a top-secret government program to develop an atomic bomb during World War II. It was motivated by the danger that Germany might be the first to develop atomic weapons. Manhattan Project scientists worked in Los Alamos, New Mexico. They successfully tested the first atomic bomb near Alamogordo, New Mexico, on July 16, 1945.

Significance The Manhattan Project initiated the age of nuclear weapons. In August 1945, U.S. planes dropped atomic bombs on the Japanese cities of Hiroshima and Nagasaki, forcing Japan's surrender in World War II. During the Cold War that followed World War II, the United States and Soviet Union competed in a nuclear arms race.

1941 Lend-Lease Act

Passed by Congress during World War II, the Lend-Lease Act gave the U.S. government authority to make weapons available to Great Britain without regard for its ability to pay. Lend-lease aid was extended to the Soviet Union after the Nazis invaded Soviet territory in March 1941.

Significance At the time the Lend-Lease Act was passed, Britain was standing alone against Germany in World War II and desperately needed the assistance. Lend-Lease aid helped both Britain and the Soviet Union resist German attacks. It also moved the United States one step closer to full participation in World War II.

1941 Attack on Pearl Harbor

On Sunday morning, December 7, 1941, Japanese forces launched a surprise attack on the American naval base at Pearl Harbor, Hawaii. Catching American forces completely unprepared, Japanese planes inflicted devastating damage on U.S. aircraft and ships at Pearl Harbor. Some 2,400 Americans were killed in the attack.

Significance The Pearl Harbor attack shocked and outraged Americans, erasing isolationist feeling in the United States. The United States immediately declared war on Japan. Japan's ally, Germany, declared war on the United States. United States forces played a major role in winning World War II, the largest and deadliest war in world history.

1942 Japanese American Internment

Fearing that Japanese Americans living along the West Coast might aid an attack by Japan, in March 1942 the federal government forcibly removed some 110,000 people of Japanese ancestry—most of them American citizens—to desolate inland internment camps. Most evacuees remained confined until the internment order was lifted in December 1944.

Significance Many of the internees lost their homes and belongings—some $400 million in property—as well as their jobs. In 1988 President Ronald Reagan signed a bill authorizing the payment of $20,000 to each surviving Japanese American evacuee and apologized for the violation of their civil liberties.

1942 Battle of Midway

Fought in the Pacific Ocean between June 3 and 6, 1942, the Battle of Midway was a major World War II naval battle between U.S. and Japanese forces. Using intelligence gained from intercepted and decoded Japanese messages, U.S. aircraft carrier-based planes surprised and sank four Japanese aircraft carriers with a loss of only one carrier.

Significance The Battle of Midway was a major turning point in the war in the Pacific. Japanese naval power, which had been a key to its early success, was greatly reduced. American forces were able to begin gaining back territory from Japan.

1944 D-Day

June 6, 1944, was D-Day—the day the Allies invaded Nazi-held Western Europe. In the largest combined air and sea invasion in history, more than 150,000 soldiers stormed the beaches at Normandy, France. Facing fierce German resistance, the Allies gained a beachhead from which to begin their massive invasion of Europe.

Significance D-Day was a major turning point of the war in Europe. The United States and Britain drove toward Germany from the west, while the Soviet Army attacked from the east. Germany was forced to surrender in May 1945.

1948-1949 Berlin Airlift

In June 1948, the Soviets suddenly blocked road, rail, and river traffic into West Berlin, cutting off the city's people from sources of food and fuel. In the Berlin Airlift, American and British pilots flew around the clock, bringing necessities into West Berlin by air. They sustained the effort until May 1949, when the Soviets lifted their blockade.

Significance The Berlin Airlift demonstrated how deeply committed the United States was to opposing the expansion of communism and Soviet power. This commitment became the central theme of U.S. foreign policy throughout the Cold War.

1947-1951 Marshall Plan

Named for its architect, U.S. Secretary of State George C. Marshall, the Marshall Plan was a U.S. program to help the nations of Western Europe recover World War II. The United States government spent over 13 billion to buy food and farm equipment and to rebuild factories and homes.

Significance The Marshall Plan was very successful in helping Western European economies recover from the devastation of World War II. The program also strengthened political and economic ties between the United States and Western Europe.

1950-1953 Korean War

The Korean War began in 1950 when communist North Korea invaded South Korea. A United Nations force, made up mostly of American troops, entered the war to block the North Korean invasion. Chinese troops fought alongside the North Koreans. After several major back and forth battles, the war ended in 1953 with North and South Korea divided along almost the same border as before the war.

Significance The Korean War was the first "shooting war" in the Cold War between Communists and U.S. forces. The United States defended South Korea to show it would protect nations from Communist attack. U.S. troops are still stationed in South Korea, more than fifty years after the fighting ended.

1954 Brown v. Board of Education of Topeka, Kansas Decision

The "Brown" in this landmark Supreme Court case was an African American third-grader named Linda Brown, who was forced to travel a long distance to a segregated school in Topeka, Kansas. NAACP lawyers sued, demanding that Brown be allowed to enroll in an all-white school that was much closer to her home. In 1954 The Supreme Court ruled unanimously that separate schools for African American and white students were by their nature unequal, and thus unconstitutional.

Significance By declaring that segregation in public schools was a violation of the Constitution's guarantee of equal protection of the law, the Court reversed *Plessy* v. *Ferguson* (1896), which had established the constitutionality of segregated facilities. This victory was just the beginning of the civil rights movement that changed the nation in the 1950s and 1960s.

1955–1956 Montgomery Bus Boycott

In December 1955 Rosa Parks, an African American woman, was arrested in Montgomery, Alabama, for refusing to move to the back of a segregated city bus. African Americans, led by Martin Luther King Jr., organized the Montgomery Bus Boycott to protest Parks' arrest and segregation on city buses. After more than a year, the boycott achieved its goal when the Supreme Court ruled the segregation policy unconstitutional.

Significance Beyond achieving local goals in Montgomery, the bus boycott made a national impact by inspiring similar boycotts in other southern cities. Martin Luther King Jr. gained nationwide attention and became a powerful leader of the growing civil rights movement.

1958 Formation of NASA

In 1957 the Soviet Union shocked the United States by launching Sputnik, the first-ever artificial satellite, into space. The United States responded in 1958 with the creation of the National Aeronautics and Space Administration (NASA), a government agency dedicated to the exploration of space.

Significance NASA led the United States past the Soviet Union in the space race, moving quickly from single satellites to manned flights orbiting the Earth to the Apollo program that successfully landed men on the moon. NASA exhibited the success of American technology and boosted American pride and confidence during the Cold War.

1950s Television changes American life

Television ownership exploded in the 1950s, and by the end of the decade over 40 million American homes had at least one television set. Watching television became a favorite national pastime, as families across the country tuned in to the same comedies, game shows, and music programs.

Significance Television, like radio and movies, provided Americans with common cultural experiences. By 1960 TV had become the major means of advertising in the country. Politicians quickly learned that TV had an enormous power to impact their relationship with voters.

1954–1973 Vietnam War

In the Vietnam War the United States fought to try to prevent Communist forces from taking over all of Vietnam. U.S. troops supported non-Communist South Vietnam against Communist North Vietnam and guerilla forces known as the Vietcong. Though U.S. troop levels in Vietnam topped 500,000 in 1968, victory seemed nowhere in sight. With the American public turning against the war, the government began gradually withdrawing troops from Vietnam. The last soldiers left in 1973. In 1975 North Vietnam succeeded in taking over all of Vietnam.

Significance More than 58,000 Americans died in Vietnam, and more than 2 million Vietnamese soldiers and civilians were killed. The war caused bitter divisions in American society, as some protested the fighting, while others backed the government. Misleading statements by military and government leaders about the progress of the war caused many Americans to lose some faith in their government.

1962 Cuban Missile Crisis

In April 1961 Cuban exiles, backed by the United States, tried to invade Cuba and overthrow its dictator, Fidel Castro. The invasion of the Bay of Pigs failed. In October 1962 U.S. spy planes discovered that the Soviet Union was installing nuclear missiles in Cuba. The missiles would be able to strike almost any location in the United States. President John F. Kennedy demanded that the missiles be removed and announced that U.S. warships would enforce a naval blockade of Cuba. For several days the world watched and waited for the Soviet response. The crisis finally lifted when Khrushchev agreed to dismantle the Soviet missiles in Cuba in return for a U.S. promise not to invade the island.

Significance The Cuban missile crisis marked the closest the world has ever come to the outbreak of nuclear war. Sobered by the experience, Kennedy and Khrushchev took steps to ease Cold War tensions. They set up a hot line that would allow American and Soviet leaders to communicate directly during times of crisis, and signed the Limited Nuclear Test Ban Treaty, banning the testing of nuclear weapons in the atmosphere and underwater.

1963 March on Washington

In the aftermath of police violence against civil rights protests, on August 28 about 250,000 people from across the country, about a quarter of them white, took part in the March on Washington for Jobs and Freedom. The march brought together several major civil rights organizations to demand school desegregation, jobs programs, a minimum wage, and various civil rights laws.

Significance Part protest and part celebration, the demonstration was the largest ever in Washington and the first to be covered on television. It is remembered for the peacefulness of the event and for the stirring "I Have a Dream" speech by Martin Luther King Jr., one of the most famous in U.S. history.

Civil Rights Act of 1964

Following the assassination of President Kennedy, the new president, Lyndon Johnson, secured passage of a landmark civil rights bill first proposed by President Kennedy. The Civil Rights Act of 1964 banned segregation in public places and discrimination in employment. It set up the Equal opportunity Commission to end job discrimination—another provision allowed the government to withhold federal funds from school districts that violated integration orders.

Significance The Civil Rights Act of 1964 has been called the most significant civil right law since the Reconstruction amendments. The Civil Rights Act, along with the Voting Right Act of 1965, were major victories for the civil rights movement. These new laws gave the federal government the power to prevent racial discrimination.

1965 Passage of Medicare & Medicaid

Established in 1965, Medicaid and Medicare were parts of President Lyndon B. Johnson's ambitious program of domestic reform known as the Great Society. Medicaid is a government program that provides free or low-cost health care for poor people. Medicare is a government funded health care program for people over age 65.

Significance Medicare and Medicaid have helped provide health services for millions of Americans. Like New Deal programs of the 1930s, Johnson's Great Society programs expanded the role of the federal government in American society.

1965–1970 United Farm Workers Grape Boycott

In 1965 farm workers in California went on strike when their employer cut their pay during the grape harvest. César Chávez and Dolores Huerta, cofounders of the National Farm Workers Association (NFWA), helped lead a nationwide grape boycott to support striking farm workers. Millions of Americans refused to buy grapes.

Significance The pressure on the grape growers eventually forced them to negotiate a settlement. The success of the grape boycott brought César Chávez to national prominence as a leader in the fight for civil rights for Hispanic Americans.

1965 Immigration Act of 1965

This act repealed the national-origin immigration quotas in effect since 1924 and set hemisphere-based quotas instead. Priority was given to those applicants with relatives already in the United States and possessing desired job skills. The effect was to open up immigration to people from countries that had previously been denied entry to the United States.

Significance The act triggered a new wave of immigration to the United States from Asian and Latin American nations which has altered the cultural mix in the United States.

1966 Formation of National Organization for Women (NOW)

The National Organization for Women (NOW) is a women's rights organization founded by women's rights leaders in 1966. NOW actively campaigned for passage of the Equal Rights Amendment (ERA). Though the ERA eventually failed, NOW helped women make important gains in the 1970s.

Significance The organization continues to be an influential voice in American politics. NOW's goals include fighting discrimination in the workplace, schools, and the justice system. It also works to end violence against women and to protect women's reproductive rights.

1969 Apollo 11 Moon Landing

The goal of NASA's Apollo program was to land American astronauts on the moon. The program achieved this goal with the Apollo 11 mission. On July 20, 1969, Neil Armstrong and Buzz Aldrin became the first humans to walk on the moon. Millions of amazed viewers around the world watched the moon landing on television.

Significance The Apollo 11 mission fulfilled a bold promise made by President Kennedy at the start of the 1960s to place a man on the moon in that decade. It was a triumph for American technology and was a source of wonder and pride to all Americans.

1970 Creation of the Environmental Protection Agency

In 1970 Congress established the Environmental Protection Agency (EPA) to research, monitor, and set and enforce standards on air and water quality and noise and radiation pollution. The EPA administers the "Superfund" toxic waste cleanup act, established in 1980.

Significance The creation of the EPA was one of Richard M. Nixon's presidential legacies. The agency has overseen the restoration of polluted waterways, the creation of antipollution standards for industries, and the cleanup of toxic waste sites throughout the country.

1972 Nixon Goes to China

As part of his "realpolitik" approach to foreign policy, President Richard Nixon made a historic visit to communist China in 1972. Nixon hoped that improved U.S.-China relations would spur the Soviets also to seek better relations with the United States.

Significance The visit was a huge success for Nixon. Not only did U.S.-China relations improve, but the trip also had the hoped-for effect on the Soviets: shortly after the China visit, Nixon and Soviet leaders reached a nuclear arms control agreement. This opened a period of détente, a time of easing Cold War tensions.

1972–1974 Watergate Scandal

The Watergate Scandal began when five burglars broke into the Democratic Party headquarters in the Watergate Hotel in Washington, D.C. Officials in the Nixon White House worked to cover up their role in the Watergate break-in. As the House of Representatives began the impeachment process against the president, Nixon resigned from office August 9, 1974.

Significance Nixon became the first president in

American history to resign from office. Watergate caused a sharp drop in the percentage of Americans who said they trusted the government.

1979 Iran Hostage Crisis

On November 4, 1979, a student-led Islamic revolutionary group seized the U.S. Embassy in Iranian capital, Tehran. The rebels held 52 Americans hostage for 444 days. President Jimmy Carter imposed economic penalties, conducted diplomatic negotiations, and ordered a rescue attempt, which failed. The hostages were released on the day of Ronald Reagan's inauguration, January 20, 1981.

Significance The crisis, and the poorly executed military rescue attempt, traumatized the country and strongly contributed to Carter's election defeat.

1982 Strategic Arms Reduction Talks

After more than a decade of work to limit increases in the superpowers' nuclear forces, President Ronald Reagan and Soviet leader Mikhail Gorbachev began negotiations aimed at reducing the huge stockpiles of atomic weapons. The talks resulted in the Strategic Arms Reduction Treaty (START), signed by Gorbachev and President George H. W. Bush in 1991.

Significance START took place during the collapse of the Soviet empire and the end of the Cold War. START II, signed by Bush and Russian President Boris Yeltsin in 1993, was never ratified by the United States, but the two countries have far exceeded the nuclear reduction goals of START I and II.

1991 Collapse of the Soviet Union

In the 1980s economic and political reforms by Soviet leader Mikhail Gorbachev led to calls for greater freedom in the Soviet Union and Eastern Europe. Under this pressure, communist governments in Eastern Europe began collapsing in 1989. In 1991 the Soviet government itself collapsed as former Soviet republics declared their independence.

Significance The fall of the Soviet Union marked the end of the Cold War. Millions of people in Eastern Europe and the former Soviet Union gained freedom from communist dictatorships. The United States was left as the world's only superpower.

1991 Operation Desert Storm

In August 1990 Iraqi dictator Saddam Hussein invaded and conquered the neighboring oil-rich nation of Kuwait. President George H.W. Bush built an international coalition of allies to oppose the Iraqi action. In Operation Desert Storm, a U.S.-led coalition drove Hussein's troops out of Kuwait.

Significance The U.S.-led forces succeeded in freeing Kuwait from Iraqi control, demonstrating the effectiveness of international cooperation. Saddam Hussein, however, remained in power in Iraq. Just over 12 years later, the United States would be at war with Hussein again.

1993 Passage of NAFTA

Passed in 1993, the North American Free Trade Agreement (NAFTA) eliminated trade barriers between the United States, Mexico, and Canada. This allowed most products to be sold across borders without tariffs. The agreement caused controversy, with critics arguing it would cost American jobs, and supporters insisting it would increase trade.

Significance The debate over NAFTA was part of a larger debate about international trade and globalization. This will continue to be a major issue for Americans as the world's economies become more interconnected.

2001 Terrorist Attacks of 9/11

On September 11, 2001, terrorists hijacked four planes, crashing two of them into the towers of the World Trade Center in New York City and a third into the Pentagon near Washington, D.C. A fourth plane crashed in Pennsylvania after passengers attempted to take back the plane from the terrorists. A total of about 3,000 people were killed in these attacks.

Significance President George W. Bush declared a war on terror. U.S. officials identified the hijackers as members of al Qaeda, an extremist Islamic terrorist group led by Osama bin Laden and based in Afghanistan. In October 2001, U.S. forces invaded Afghanistan, driving out the Taliban government, which had supported bin Laden.

2003 Iraq War

Fearing that Iraqi leader Saddam Hussein was building weapons of mass destruction that could be used against the United States or given to a terrorist, President Bush called for Iraq to disarm. Saddam, however, refused to fully cooperate with UN weapons inspections. Though many of America's allies argued against going to war, Bush insisted the Iraqi threat must be countered. With the support of Great Britain and several other allies, American forces invaded and quickly conquered Iraq in 2003. Saddam was captured in late 2003.

Significance In June 2004, American officials handed control over to an Iraqi government. Iraqis began electing their own leaders in 2005. The violence continued, however, as insurgents carried out deadly attacks against American troops and Iraqis. To date, American and international teams have found no weapons of mass destruction.

Presidents

1 GEORGE WASHINGTON
Born: 1732 Died: 1799
Years in Office: 1789–97
Political Party: None
Home State: Virginia
Vice President:

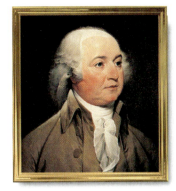

2 JOHN ADAMS
Born: 1735 Died: 1826
Years in Office: 1797–1801
Political Party: Federalist
Home State: Massachusetts
Vice President: Thomas Jefferson

3 THOMAS JEFFERSON
Born: 1743 Died: 1826
Years in Office: 1801–09
Political Party: Republican*
Home State: Virginia
Vice Presidents: Aaron Burr, George Clinton

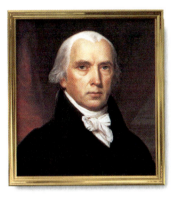

4 JAMES MADISON
Born: 1751 Died: 1836
Years in Office: 1809–17
Political Party: Republican
Home State: Virginia
Vice Presidents: George Clinton, Elbridge Gerry

5 JAMES MONROE
Born: 1758 Died: 1831
Years in Office: 1817–25
Political Party: Republican
Home State: Virginia
Vice President: Daniel D. Tompkins

6 JOHN QUINCY ADAMS
Born: 1767 Died: 1848
Years in Office: 1825–29
Political Party: Republican
Home State: Massachusetts
Vice President: John C. Calhoun

7 ANDREW JACKSON
Born: 1767 Died: 1845
Years in Office: 1829–37
Political Party: Democratic
Home State: Tennessee
Vice Presidents: John C. Calhoun, Martin Van Buren

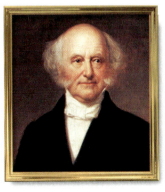

8 MARTIN VAN BUREN
Born: 1782 Died: 1862
Years in Office: 1837–41
Political Party: Democratic
Home State: New York
Vice President: Richard M. Johnson

* The Republican Party of the third through sixth presidents is not the party of Abraham Lincoln, which was founded in 1854.

PRESIDENTS

9 WILLIAM HENRY HARRISON
Born: 1773 Died: 1841
Years in Office: 1841
Political Party: Whig
Home State: Ohio
Vice President: John Tyler

10 JOHN TYLER
Born: 1790 Died: 1862
Years in Office: 1841–45
Political Party: Whig
Home State: Virginia
Vice President: None

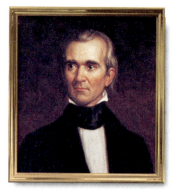

11 JAMES K. POLK
Born: 1795 Died: 1849
Years in Office: 1845–49
Political Party: Democratic
Home State: Tennessee
Vice President: George M. Dallas

12 ZACHARY TAYLOR
Born: 1784 Died: 1850
Years in Office: 1849–50
Political Party: Whig
Home State: Louisiana
Vice President: Millard Fillmore

13 MILLARD FILLMORE
Born: 1800 Died: 1874
Years in Office: 1850–53
Political Party: Whig
Home State: New York
Vice President: None

14 FRANKLIN PIERCE
Born: 1804 Died: 1869
Years in Office: 1853–57
Political Party: Democratic
Home State: New Hampshire
Vice President: William R. King

15 JAMES BUCHANAN
Born: 1791 Died: 1868
Years in Office: 1857–61
Political Party: Democratic
Home State: Pennsylvania
Vice President: John C. Breckinridge

16 ABRAHAM LINCOLN
Born: 1809 Died: 1865
Years in Office: 1861–65
Political Party: Republican
Home State: Illinois
Vice Presidents: Hannibal Hamlin, Andrew Johnson

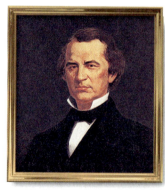

17 ANDREW JOHNSON
Born: 1808 Died: 1875
Years in Office: 1865–69
Political Party: Republican
Home State: Tennessee
Vice President: None

18 ULYSSES S. GRANT
Born: 1822 Died: 1885
Years in Office: 1869–77
Political Party: Republican
Home State: Illinois
Vice Presidents: Schuyler Colfax, Henry Wilson

19 RUTHERFORD B. HAYES
Born: 1822 Died: 1893
Years in Office: 1877–81
Political Party: Republican
Home State: Ohio
Vice President: William A. Wheeler

20 JAMES A. GARFIELD
Born: 1831 Died: 1881
Years in Office: 1881
Political Party: Republican
Home State: Ohio
Vice President: Chester A. Arthur

21 CHESTER A. ARTHUR
Born: 1829 Died: 1886
Years in Office: 1881–85
Political Party: Republican
Home State: New York
Vice President: None

22 GROVER CLEVELAND
Born: 1837 Died: 1908
Years in Office: 1885–89
Political Party: Democratic
Home State: New York
Vice President: Thomas A. Hendricks

23 BENJAMIN HARRISON
Born: 1833 Died: 1901
Years in Office: 1889–93
Political Party: Republican
Home State: Indiana
Vice President: Levi P. Morton

24 GROVER CLEVELAND
Born: 1837 Died: 1908
Years in Office: 1893–97
Political Party: Democratic
Home State: New York
Vice President: Adlai E. Stevenson

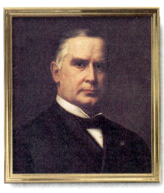

25 WILLIAM MCKINLEY
Born: 1843 Died: 1901
Years in Office: 1897–1901
Political Party: Republican
Home State: Ohio
Vice Presidents: Garret A. Hobart, Theodore Roosevelt

26 THEODORE ROOSEVELT
Born: 1858 Died: 1919
Years in Office: 1901–09
Political Party: Republican
Home State: New York
Vice President: Charles W. Fairbanks

27 William Howard Taft
Born: 1857 **Died:** 1930
Years in Office: 1909–13
Political Party: Republican
Home State: Ohio
Vice President: James S. Sherman

28 Woodrow Wilson
Born: 1856 **Died:** 1924
Years in Office: 1913–21
Political Party: Democratic
Home State: New Jersey
Vice President: Thomas R. Marshall

29 Warren G. Harding
Born: 1865 **Died:** 1923
Years in Office: 1921–23
Political Party: Republican
Home State: Ohio
Vice President: Calvin Coolidge

30 Calvin Coolidge
Born: 1872 **Died:** 1933
Years in Office: 1923–29
Political Party: Republican
Home State: Massachusetts
Vice President: Charles G. Dawes

31 Herbert Hoover
Born: 1874 **Died:** 1964
Years in Office: 1929–33
Political Party: Republican
Home State: California
Vice President: Charles Curtis

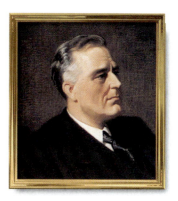

32 Franklin D. Roosevelt
Born: 1882 **Died:** 1945
Years in Office: 1933–45
Political Party: Democratic
Home State: New York
Vice Presidents: John Nance Garner, Henry Wallace, Harry S Truman

33 Harry S Truman
Born: 1884 **Died:** 1972
Years in Office: 1945–53
Political Party: Democratic
Home State: Missouri
Vice President: Alben W. Barkley

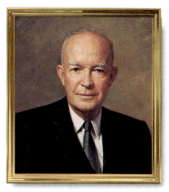

34 Dwight D. Eisenhower
Born: 1890 **Died:** 1969
Years in Office: 1953–61
Political Party: Republican
Home State: Kansas
Vice President: Richard M. Nixon

35 John F. Kennedy
Born: 1917 **Died:** 1963
Years in Office: 1961–63
Political Party: Democratic
Home State: Massachusetts
Vice President: Lyndon B. Johnson

36 Lyndon B. Johnson
Born: 1908 Died: 1973
Years in Office: 1963–69
Political Party: Democratic
Home State: Texas
Vice President: Hubert H. Humphrey

37 Richard M. Nixon
Born: 1913 Died: 1994
Years in Office: 1969–74
Political Party: Republican
Home State: California
Vice Presidents: Spiro T. Agnew, Gerald R. Ford

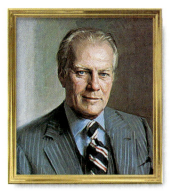

38 Gerald R. Ford
Born: 1913 Died: 2006
Years in Office: 1974–77
Political Party: Republican
Home State: Michigan
Vice President: Nelson A. Rockefeller

39 Jimmy Carter
Born: 1924
Years in Office: 1977–81
Political Party: Democratic
Home State: Georgia
Vice President: Walter F. Mondale

40 Ronald Reagan
Born: 1911 Died: 2004
Years in Office: 1981–89
Political Party: Republican
Home State: California
Vice President: George Bush

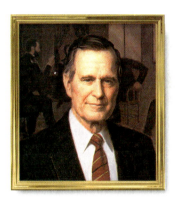

41 George Bush
Born: 1924
Years in Office: 1989–93
Political Party: Republican
Home State: Texas
Vice President: J. Danforth Quayle

42 Bill Clinton
Born: 1946
Years in Office: 1993–2001
Political Party: Democratic
Home State: Arkansas
Vice President: Albert Gore Jr.

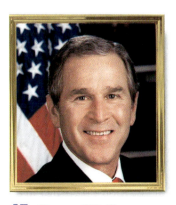

43 George W. Bush
Born: 1946
Years in Office: 2001–
Political Party: Republican
Home State: Texas
Vice President: Richard B. Cheney

PRESIDENTS

Supreme Court Decisions

Gibbons v. Ogden (1824)

Significance: The first case to deal with the commerce clause of the Constitution, *Gibbons v. Ogden* reaffirmed Congress's exclusive power to regulate interstate and foreign commerce.

Background: Aaron Ogden held a monopoly license issued by New York state to operate a steamboat ferry service between New Jersey and New York. Thomas Gibbons had a federal license to travel along the coast and began operating a competing ferry between New York and New Jersey. Ogden sued to protect his monopoly and won. Gibbons appealed the decision to the Supreme Court.

Decision: By a vote of 6–0, the Court ruled in favor of Gibbons. Chief Justice John Marshall wrote the opinion. The Court determined that the states could regulate transportation within their own borders but not between states. The power to regulate commerce between states belonged only to Congress, so Gibbons's federal license was valid. The ruling broadly defined commerce to include more than simply the exchange of goods, but also the transportation of people and the use of new inventions such as the steamboat.

Worcester v. Georgia (1832)

Significance: This case showed the limits of the Court's power to enforce one of its decisions if it chose not to use further legal action to compel cooperation. As a result, Georgia and other states continued to force American Indian tribes off lands protected by treaties with the federal government.

Background: The state of Georgia wanted to remove Cherokee Indians from lands the Indians held by federal treaty. Samuel Worcester, a missionary who worked with the Cherokee Nation, was arrested and convicted for refusing to leave the lands. Worcester appealed, charging that Georgia had no legal authority on Cherokee lands.

Decision: This case was decided in favor of Worcester by a 5–1 vote. Chief Justice John Marshall spoke for the majority, which ruled that the Cherokee Nation was "a distinct community occupying its own territory." Under the Constitution and the treaties between the United States and the Cherokees, only the federal government, and not the state of Georgia, had the power to control dealings with the Cherokee people. Georgia defied the decision, and President Andrew Jackson refused to act to uphold the Supreme Court's decision.

Civil Rights Cases (1883)

Significance: This decision limited Congress's ability to outlaw "whites only" facilities. As a result, blacks in many areas continued to be subject to inferior treatment. This situation continued until the Civil Rights Movement of the 1950s and 1960s led to new civil rights laws based on the commerce clause rather than on the Fourteenth Amendment.

Background: After the Civil War, many facilities of public accommodation like hotels, theaters, restaurants, and buses were restricted to whites only, or had separate (and often inferior) sections for blacks. In the Civil Rights Act of 1875, Congress attempted to outlaw this race-based discrimination. The U.S. government and blacks who had been denied admission to these facilities brought a series of cases seeking to enforce the Act. The cases were appealed to the U.S. Supreme Court and were combined for decision.

Justice Scalia

Justice Ginsberg

Justice Souter

Justice Roberts

Justice Alito

Decision: In an opinion by Justice Joseph P. Bradley, the Court ruled that although the Fourteenth Amendment prohibited racial discrimination by the state and federal governments, it did not give Congress the power to outlaw discrimination by private individuals or businesses. Because the law went beyond Congress's authority, it was ruled unconstitutional.

Justice John Harlan wrote a strong dissent, arguing that many states were refusing to protect the basic rights of black people and that Congress should have the power under the Fourteenth Amendment to make all citizens equal.

Wabash, St. Louis & Pacific R.R. v. Illinois (1886)

Significance: The ruling marked the end of railroad regulation by the individual states and led to the passage of the federal Interstate Commerce Act the following year. In preventing individual states from interfering with national commerce, the case helped develop a more unified national economy.

Background: In *Munn* v. *Illinois* (1877) the Supreme Court had allowed states to regulate areas of interstate commerce where Congress had not acted. Following the logic of that ruling, Illinois passed a law allowing it to control railroad rates by regulating the shipping contracts of railroads passing through Illinois. The state sued the Wabash, St. Louis & Pacific Railroad for not following the law. The railroad responded that the law did not apply to shipments going from Illinois to another state.

Decision: In a 6–3 decision written by Justice Samuel F. Miller, the Court drew back from *Munn* v. *Illinois* and overruled Illinois's railroad law. The commerce clause, the Court ruled, prevents states from imposing direct burdens on interstate commerce. This meant that states could not enact laws that interfered with the free flow of goods across the country.

United States v. E.C. Knight Co. (1895)

Significance: The ruling was a major setback for federal antitrust regulation. Freed by this case from the fear of federal prosecution, manufacturers began a period of significant merger and consolidation. Manufacturing monopolies continued largely unrestricted until President Theodore Roosevelt tackled "trust busting" in the early 1900s.

Background: In the early 1890s, the American Sugar Refining Company bought out its major competitors. The purchases gave American Sugar Refining, owned by E.C. Knight Co., almost total control over the manufacturing of refined sugar in the United States. The U.S. government sued, claiming the company had violated the Sherman Antitrust Act. This act, passed in 1890, outlawed monopolies and prohibited "restraint of trade" in interstate commerce.

Decision: The Supreme Court ruled 8–1 in favor of Knight. Chief Justice Melville Fuller wrote the majority opinion, taking a very narrow view of commerce that distinguished the manufacture of goods from their sale. Under this analysis, Congress could regulate sales under the commerce clause, but it did not have the power to regulate manufacturing.

In Re Debs (1895)

Significance: This case confirmed the federal government's power to get an injunction (court order) to end unlawful strikes and force striking workers to return to work. The government used injunctions to stop major strikes for the next 30 years.

Background: In 1894 workers making railroad cars at the Pullman Company rebelled against poor working conditions. After the company hired armed guards to subdue the protesters, the American Railroad Union refused to handle trains with Pullman cars. The strike disrupted rail service nationwide,

Justice Stevens   **Justice Breyer**   **Justice Thomas**   **Justice Kennedy**

 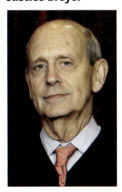  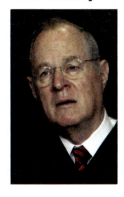

and railroad managers sought federal intervention. The government claimed the strike was impeding interstate trade and interfering with delivery of the U.S. mail—a federal offense. When the union ignored a court order to stop the strike, the union's leader, Eugene V. Debs was jailed for contempt of court. He petitioned for release on the grounds that the order was unconstitutional.

Decision: The Supreme Court ruled unanimously against Debs. Justice David Brewer wrote that the federal government has control over interstate commerce and the delivery of the mails and therefore had the right to ask a judge to stop the strike. The strike created a public nuisance by interfering with the mail, so the judge acted correctly in ordering it stopped and in jailing Debs for contempt when he refused to obey the order.

Northern Securities Co. v. United States (1904)

Significance: This ruling revived the federal government's power to prohibit monopolies, a power that had been undercut by *United States* v. *E.C. Knight Co.* (1895). The government's victory in this case resulted in the dissolution of the Northern Securities Company and paved the way for stricter regulation of large corporations.

Background: In 1901 three competing railroads that ran from the Pacific Northwest to the Great Lakes agreed to merge by turning over their stock to a new holding company, the Northern Securities Company. The U.S. government sued under the Sherman Antitrust Act. It claimed that the holding company was created to reduce competition in the railroad business and therefore violated the Sherman Act's prohibition on restraint of commerce. The Northern Securities Company argued that it merely owned the railways' stock and did not itself engage in commerce. It was a state-chartered corporation, and federal interference would violate state powers protected by the Tenth Amendment.

Decision: In a 5–4 decision, the Supreme Court sided with the government. The states can charter corporations, but corporations are still subject to federal law, and the Sherman Antitrust Act did apply in this case. The Court interpreted the act broadly, ruling that a business combination was illegal if it restrained commerce in any way, even if it didn't directly engage in commerce.

Lochner v. New York (1905)

Significance: This decision limited the states' ability to regulate labor and industry. For more than 30 years, *Lochner* was used as a precedent to strike down state laws such as minimum-wage laws, child labor laws, and regulations on the banking and transportation industries.

Background: In 1895 the state of New York passed a labor law limiting bakers to working no more than 10 hours per day or 60 hours per week. The purpose of the law was to protect the health of bakers, who worked in hot, damp conditions and breathed in large quantities of flour dust. In 1902 Joseph Lochner, the owner of a small bakery in New York, claimed that the state law violated his Fourteenth Amendment due process rights by depriving him of the freedom to make contracts with employees.

Decision: The case was decided in Lochner's favor by a 5–4 vote. The Supreme Court ruled that the right to sell and buy labor was implicit in the Fourteenth Amendment's concept of personal liberty. Thus any state law restricting that right was unconstitutional. The Court rejected the argument that limited work hours were necessary to prevent worker exploitation.

Muller v. Oregon (1908)

Significance: This was the first case in which the Supreme Court recognized social conditions (in this case, women's health) as a factor in judging the constitutionality of state laws. The decision marked the beginning of the Court's gradual retreat from the strict doctrine of *Lochner* v. *New York* (1905), which had appeared to prohibit state regulation of the workplace.

Background: In 1903 Oregon passed a law limiting workdays to 10 hours for women workers in laundries and factories. In 1905 Curt Muller's Grand Laundry was found guilty of breaking this law. Muller appealed, arguing (as Lochner successfully had) that the state law violated his freedom of contract. When the matter came to the Supreme Court, lawyer Louis D. Brandeis presented Oregon's case in a novel and compelling way. He supplied not only legal arguments, but also medical, social, and economic data on the impact of long working hours on women's health.

Decision: In 1908 a unanimous Supreme Court upheld the Oregon law. The Court agreed that the government had a legitimate interest in women's well-being and concluded that the 10-hour law was a valid way of protecting that interest. Although the Court did not overrule *Lochner*, it did show a willingness to accept some workplace regulation as justifiable.

Watkins v. United States (1957)

Significance: This decision recognized limits on congressional investigations. Congress may not expose the private affairs of citizens unless they pertain to a legitimate legislative inquiry.

Background: In 1954 the House Un-American Activities Committee was investigating communists. The committee subpoenaed John Watkins, a labor organizer, to testify. Watkins was willing to answer questions about his affiliation with the Communist Party and also to identify current party members. He refused, however, to name people who had left the party. Watkins was convicted for contempt of Congress, a federal offense.

Decision: Chief Justice Earl Warren wrote the Court's 6–1 decision holding that Watkins's conviction violated the due process clause of the Fifth Amendment. Watkins did not have to answer questions unrelated to the official inquiry of the committee. The Court ruled that the committee failed to clearly define the scope of its inquiry and to establish the relevance of questions about former members of the Communist Party.

Mapp v. Ohio (1961)

Significance: This decision created the legal rule that states cannot use evidence obtained from an illegal search in state criminal proceedings.

Background: In 1957 the police forced their way into Dollree Mapp's house without a search warrant. They were looking for a suspected bomber, but instead they found obscene pictures. Mapp was arrested and convicted for possession of pornography—a crime in Ohio. Mapp appealed to the Supreme Court, which had ruled in 1914 that evidence illegally obtained by the police could not be used in a federal criminal prosecution. The purpose of this "exclusionary rule" was to encourage the police to respect individuals' Fourth Amendment rights. However, until the *Mapp* case, states could decide for themselves whether to follow the exclusionary rule.

Decision: The Supreme Court ruled in Mapp's favor, 6–3. The majority held that the due process clause of the Fourteenth Amendment makes the protections of the Fourth Amendment apply to the states. Thus the exclusionary rule applies in state criminal cases as well as in federal court.

Baker v. Carr (1962)

Significance: This decision held that federal courts could review apportionment, or the distribution of seats, in state legislatures. The case led to the widespread redrawing of legislative districts to equalize representation and ensure "one person, one vote." As a result, political power shifted from rural to urban areas in most states.

Background: Many states had kept the same legislative district lines for decades, despite dramatic population shifts as people moved from the country to the cities. In Tennessee rural voters made up a minority of the population, but they had far more representatives in government than urban voters. Charles Baker and others brought suit against Joseph Carr, the Tennessee secretary of state, claiming that as urban dwellers, their votes were so diluted that they were denied equal protection under the law. The case reached the Supreme Court after being dismissed by the federal district court, which considered apportionment a political question to be decided by the legislature.

Decision: The Supreme Court did not rule on the legality of Tennessee's voting districts. However, it affirmed that the courts can indeed consider such cases. Justice William Brennan wrote that a state's failure to apportion its legislative districts equally would violate the equal protection clause of the Fourteenth Amendment. Thus Baker's constitutional rights were at stake, and the case went back to the federal district court for trial.

Engel v. Vitale (1962)

Significance: This was a landmark case on the subject of religious freedom. In a ruling that remains highly controversial, the Supreme Court held that state-sponsored prayer in public schools is unconstitutional. Attempts have since been made to amend the Constitution to permit prayer, but none have succeeded.

Background: The New York Board of Regents wrote a short, nondenominational prayer for students to say at the beginning of the school day. A group of parents sued, arguing that the prayer violated the establishment clause of the First Amendment—the clause banning the establishment of religion. Although students could remain silent during the prayer, the parents claimed they would always feel pressure to join in the recitation.

Decision: By a 7–1 margin, the Court agreed with the parents and invalidated the school prayer. Justice Hugo Black wrote for the majority. He pointed out that prayer is clearly a religious activity and that under the First Amendment, promoting prayer "is no part of the business of government." The lone dissenter, Justice Potter Stewart, argued that the establishment clause forbids only the creation of an official state religion; it should not be interpreted to deny schoolchildren the opportunity to pray voluntarily.

Gideon v. Wainwright (1963)

Significance: This case established the right of all criminal defendants to be given a lawyer if they cannot afford one. The ruling reflected a growing concern to ensure equal justice for the poor.

Background: Clarence Earl Gideon was accused of robbery in Florida. Gideon could not afford a lawyer for his trial, and the judge refused to supply him with one for free. Gideon tried to defend himself and was found guilty. He eventually appealed to the U.S. Supreme Court, claiming that the lower court's denial of a court-appointed lawyer violated his Sixth and Fourteenth Amendment rights.

Decision: The Supreme Court ruled unanimously in Gideon's favor in 1963. The Court agreed that the Sixth Amendment's right to counsel requires the government to provide a lawyer if the defendant cannot afford one. The Court also agreed that the due process clause of the Fourteenth Amendment makes the Sixth Amendment's right to counsel binding on the states as well as on the federal government.

Heart of Atlanta Motel v. United States (1964)

Significance: This decision upheld the Civil Rights Act of 1964, which banned racial discrimination in places of public accommodation.

Background: The owner of the Heart of Atlanta Motel, a whites-only facility that served many interstate travelers, sued to overturn the Civil Rights Act of 1964. His primary argument was that the law went beyond Congress's authority to regulate interstate commerce under the commerce clause. A trial court ruled against the motel, and the owner appealed to the Supreme Court.

Decision: The Supreme Court found that Congress had carefully limited Title II of the Civil Rights Act to facilities that had a direct and substantial relation to the interstate flow of goods and people. Testimony before Congress had shown that Americans were increasingly mobile and that black travelers in particular often faced difficulty finding accommodations. Writing for a unanimous court, Justice Tom C. Clark concluded that Title II was therefore a valid exercise of congressional power under the commerce clause.

Tinker v. Des Moines Independent Community School District (1969)

Significance: This case established the right of public school students to express political opinions at school.

Background: Some high school and junior high school students in Des Moines, Iowa, planned to wear black armbands to school to show their opposition to the Vietnam War. Two days before they were going to start this protest, the school board created a new policy forbidding armbands at school. Three students, including Mary Beth Tinker and John Tinker, wore the armbands and were suspended. They sued the school district, claiming that the armband rule violated their First Amendment right of free speech.

The Decision: By a 7–2 margin, the Court agreed with the students. Justice Abe Fortas wrote that students do not "shed their constitutional rights to freedom of speech . . . at the schoolhouse gate." Protected speech includes not only spoken words but also "symbolic speech," or acts that express an opinion. Although school officials have the right to set rules, these rules must respect the First Amendment. Here the students had not been disruptive and their armbands did not interfere with anyone else's rights. Also, students were allowed to wear other political symbols, such as campaign buttons. School officials could not constitutionally pick which opinions students could express and which would be prohibited.

Reed v. Reed (1971)

Significance: This was the first case to hold that gender discrimination violates the Fourteenth Amendment equal protection clause. *Reed* v. *Reed* case was later used to strike down other statutes that discriminated against women.

Background: Cecil and Sally Reed were separated when their son Richard died. Each parent asked to be appointed administrator of Richard's modest estate. According to Idaho law at that time, when picking between two equally qualified administrators, "males must be preferred to females." When the judge appointed Cecil as the law required, Sally sued, challenging the gender preference in the law.

Decision: Chief Justice Warren Burger wrote the unanimous Supreme Court decision. Although some distinctions based on gender are permissible, the distinction must be reasonable rather than arbitrary. Because there is no reason to assume that men will be better administrators than women, the law did not have any rational basis. The Court therefore ruled that the law was unconstitutional. This did not mean that Sally would automatically get appointed, but it did require the probate judge to assess her qualifications and make a considered choice between her and Cecil.

Roe v. Wade (1973)

Significance: This case established a woman's right to an abortion as part of the constitutional right of privacy. The decision led to an ongoing battle in American politics between "pro-life" and "pro-choice" voters.

Background: In 1970 an unmarried, pregnant Texas woman filed suit to overturn the state's anti-abortion law. Texas, like many other states, had made it a crime for anyone to perform an abortion except to save the life of the mother. The case was argued before the Supreme Court in 1971 and then reargued at the Court's request in 1972. The plaintiff was called by a fictitious name, Jane Roe, to protect her privacy.

Decision: The Court voted 7–2 to invalidate the Texas law. Writing for the majority, Justice Harry Blackmun concluded that a woman's rights to privacy and control over her own body needed to be balanced against the state's interest in protecting maternal health and preserving the potentiality of human life. During the first trimester (three-month period) of pregnancy, abortion would be at the discretion of the woman and her physician. During the second trimester the state could impose restrictions related to the woman's health. In the final trimester the state could prohibit abortions entirely except where medically necessary to protect the life or health of the mother. Blackmun also concluded that the fetus did not have rights under the Fourteenth Amendment because the original intent of the Constitution and of that amendment was not to consider an unborn child as a "person." Justice Byron White wrote a strong dissent saying that nothing in the Constitution guaranteed the right to abortion.

United States v. Nixon (1974)

Significance: This decision led to the resignation of President Richard Nixon. The case confirmed that the president is not above the law and that the Supreme Court makes the final decision on constitutional questions.

Background: In 1972 senior Nixon administration officials helped plan, and then cover up, a break-in at the Democratic Party's campaign headquarters in the Watergate building in Washington. After the break-in came to light, a special prosecutor began a criminal investigation. He subpoenaed President Nixon to turn over secret tape recordings of conversations with his aides, but Nixon refused. He claimed "executive privilege," a right that past presidents had asserted to withhold information from other branches of government in order to protect confidentiality or the public good.

Decision: In a unanimous opinion written by Chief Justice Warren Burger, the Supreme Court ordered President Nixon to deliver his secret Oval Office tapes to the special prosecutor. The Court insisted that the president is not immune from the judicial process. Executive privilege may be invoked under certain circumstances, but in this case, President Nixon did not claim that military, diplomatic, or sensitive national security matters were at stake. Moreover, under the constitutional separation of powers, the legitimate needs of the courts in criminal proceedings may outweigh the President's need for confidentiality.

Texas v. Johnson (1989)

Significance: This case decided whether the First Amendment allows the burning of the U.S. flag as a form of symbolic speech. The decision has been controversial because it involves the flag, one of our national symbols. Since this case was decided, several amendments banning flag burning have been proposed in Congress but have not been adopted.

Background: Gregory Lee Johnson burned an American flag as part of a political demonstration during the 1984 Republican National Convention in Dallas, Texas. Johnson was convicted of violating a Texas law that made it a crime to desecrate, or treat disrespectfully, the national flag. He was sentenced to one year in prison and fined $2,000. The Texas Court of Criminal Appeals reversed Johnson's conviction, reasoning that burning the flag was a form of symbolic speech protected by the First Amendment. Texas then appealed to the U.S. Supreme Court.

Decision: The Court ruled for Johnson, 5–4, in an opinion written by Justice William Brennan. Brennan accepted the argument that flag burning is constitutionally protected as a form of symbolic speech—like the students wearing armbands in *Tinker* v. *Des Moines Independent Community School District* (1969). Brennan recognized that many people might be deeply upset by Johnson's actions, but he wrote that "government may not prohibit the expression of an idea [because it is] offensive." Chief Justice William Rehnquist dissented, writing that "for more than 200 years, the

American flag has occupied a unique position as the symbol of our Nation, a uniqueness that justifies a governmental prohibition against flag burning in the way respondent Johnson did here."

Cruzan v. Director, Missouri Department of Health (1990)

Significance: This was the first "end of life" medical treatment case to reach the Supreme Court. In its ruling, the Court recognized that even unconscious patients have the right to refuse medical care (through their parents or guardians). At the same time, the Court allowed the states flexibility in setting standards for deciding whether to approve the termination of treatment.

Background: Nancy Cruzan was seriously injured in an auto accident. Because she was unable to swallow, her doctors put in a feeding tube to give her food and liquids. She remained unconscious in a persistent vegetative state for years afterwards. Eventually, when it became clear that she had virtually no chance of improvement, her parents asked the Missouri Supreme Court to instruct the doctors to stop administering food and liquids artificially. This action would have ended Cruzan's life. The state court denied the parents' request because they had not presented "clear and convincing" evidence of what their daughter would have wanted, as required by Missouri law. The parents then asked the U.S. Supreme Court to hear the case.

Decision: Chief Justice William Rehnquist wrote for the majority in a 5–4 decision. He stated that Missouri could constitutionally decline to grant the parents' request where they had not presented "clear and convincing" evidence that Cruzan herself would have wanted feeding and hydration discontinued. Although the Court upheld the state's right to set standards for deciding when medical treatment can be terminated, it also was willing to assume that people have a constitutional right to refuse life-sustaining medical treatment such as feeding by a tube. The decision left open the possibility that the parents could return to the trial court with more conclusive evidence of their daughter's wishes, which they eventually did. The trial court ultimately authorized removal of the feeding tube, and Cruzan died soon afterwards.

Planned Parenthood of Southeastern Pennsylvania v. Casey (1992)

Significance: This case upheld the basic premise of *Roe* v. *Wade*, even though the Supreme Court had become more conservative with the appointment of several new justices. The decision introduced a more flexible legal approach that gave state legislatures more leeway in imposing restrictions on abortions.

Background: Pennsylvania's 1982 Abortion Control Act outlined three conditions that had to be met before an abortion could be performed. First, under an "informed consent" rule, doctors were required to tell women the health risks and possible complications of having an abortion. This information had to be provided at least 24 hours in advance of the procedure. Second, a "spousal notification" rule required married women to notify their husbands. Third, a "parental notification" rule required minors to notify their parents. Five abortion clinics and one physician brought suit to challenge the constitutionality of these requirements.

Decision: The Supreme Court issued a plurality decision, meaning that no single opinion had the support of a majority of the justices. Justices Sandra Day O'Connor, Anthony Kennedy, and David Souter wrote the plurality opinion and other justices joined in various parts. The decision created a new "undue burden" standard for abortion cases, saying that abortion laws must not have "the purpose or effect of placing a substantial obstacle in the path of a woman seeking an abortion of a nonviable fetus." Using this standard, the Court invalidated the spousal notification requirement because it gave husbands too much control over their wives' medical decisions and would be dangerous in cases of spousal abuse. However, the Court accepted the 24-hour waiting period and the informed consent and parental notification requirements, finding that none of these imposed an undue burden on abortion seekers.

Vernonia School District v. Acton (1995)

Significance: This decision allowed schools to administer drug tests to all students who wanted to play sports. The case paved the way for *Board of Education* v. *Earls* (2002), which allowed drug testing for students in all extracurricular activities.

Background: In an effort to reduce drug use, particularly among student athletes, the Vernonia (Oregon) School District started a program for random urinalysis drug testing of students participating in sports. Jason Acton signed up for seventh grade football, but he and his parents refused to sign the consent form for drug testing. When he was not allowed to play, he sued the school district. In his view, the drug testing constituted an unreasonable search of his body, in violation of the Fourth Amendment. The trial court dismissed the case but an appellate court reinstated it. Eventually the case went to the Supreme Court.

Decision: In a 6–3 decision, the Supreme Court upheld the school district's drug testing policy. Justice Antonin Scalia wrote that the district's collection and testing of urine amounted to a reasonable search. Vernonia students could choose whether or not to go out for sports, and those who did could expect some restrictions and intrusions on their privacy. The urine samples were collected in ways that minimized the violation of students' privacy. Moreover, given the government's interest in reducing student drug use, the extent of the search was reasonable and permissible. In dissent, Justice Sandra Day O'Connor argued that the blanket testing of student athletes was more intrusive and less reasonable than a suspicion-based testing of students who actually appeared to be using drugs.

Bush v. Gore (2000)

Significance: As a practical matter, this case decided the 2000 presidential election, confirming George W. Bush as the winner. The question before the Court was whether ballots that could not be read by voting machines should be recounted by hand. The broader issue was whether the Supreme Court would overrule the Florida Supreme Court on its interpretation of Florida state law.

Background: The 2000 presidential election between Democrat Al Gore and Republican George W. Bush was extremely close. As the votes were counted, it became clear that the winner of Florida's electoral votes would win the election. According to the first count, Bush won the state of Florida by a few hundred votes, and Florida's Election Commission declared Bush the victor. However, about 60,000 ballots were not counted because of problems reading them mechanically. Gore challenged the outcome, and the Florida Supreme Court ordered counties to recount all those votes by hand. Bush appealed to the U.S. Supreme Court, which ordered a halt to the recounts while it considered the case.

The Decision: On December 12, 2000, the Supreme Court voted 5–4 to end the hand recount of votes. The majority said that the Florida Supreme Court had ordered the recount without clarifying what was a valid vote. The contested ballots were not always clearly marked, and different vote counters might use different standards to tally them. The Court said that this inconsistency meant that votes were treated arbitrarily, based on a counter's choice rather than on fixed standards. This arbitrariness violated the due process and equal protection clauses of the Constitution. Furthermore, because the deadline for counting the votes under Florida law had expired, there was no time for the state to create new rules for the recount.

Hamdi v. Rumsfeld and Rasul v. Bush (2004)

Significance: These cases considered whether the Constitution's promise of due process applies to Americans or foreigners accused of fighting against the United States in its war on terror. The prisoners in both cases sought access to lawyers and the right to have their incarceration reviewed by an American court.

Background **Detaining American Citizens:** Yaser Hamdi, an American citizen, was captured in Afghanistan in 2001 and accused of fighting for the Taliban against the United States. The U.S. military declared Hamdi an "enemy combatant" and claimed the right to hold him indefinitely without trial and without access to an attorney.

Detaining Foreigners at Guantanamo Bay: Shafiq Rasul and two other foreign nationals were captured abroad and confined for over two years at Guantanamo Bay Naval Base in Cuba. They tried to challenge the legality of their detention in the U.S. courts. Cuba leases the base to the United States. In a World War II era case, the Court had ruled that "if an alien is outside the country's sovereign territory, then . . . the alien is not permitted access to the courts of the United States to enforce the Constitution."

Decisions: Although there was no majority opinion In *Hamdi,* six justices agreed, the Court ruled 6–3 that Hamdi had a right to a limited hearing at which he could contest the government's determination that he was an enemy combatant. Justice Sandra Day O'Connor wrote that "a state of war is not a blank check for the president when it comes to the rights of the nation's citizens." Hamdi was ultimately released to Saudi Arabia in October, 2004, after agreeing to give up his U.S. citizenship.

In *Rasul,* a six-justice majority concluded that the prisoners had the right to go to the federal courts for review of their claims that they were unlawfully held in indefinite detention. The government eventually released two of the prisoners in *Rasul* and announced its intention to try the third before a military tribunal. Other cases have been filed challenging the constitutionality of the military tribunals.

Facts About the States

State	Year of Statehood	2005 Population	Area (Sq. Mi.)	Population Density (Sq Mi.)	Capital
Alabama	1819	4,527,166	50,744	89.2	Montgomery
Alaska	1959	661,110	571,951	1.2	Juneau
Arizona	1912	5,868,004	113,635	51.6	Phoenix
Arkansas	1836	2,777,007	52,068	53.3	Little Rock
California	1850	36,038,859	155,959	231.1	Sacramento
Colorado	1876	4,617,962	103,718	44.5	Denver
Connecticut	1788	3,503,185	4,845	723.1	Hartford
Delaware	1787	836,687	1,954	428.2	Dover
District of Columbia*	—	551,136	61	9,035.0	—
Florida	1845	17,509,827	53,927	324.7	Tallahassee
Georgia	1788	8,925,796	57,906	154.1	Atlanta
Hawaii	1959	1,276,552	6,423	198.7	Honolulu
Idaho	1890	1,407,060	82,747	17.0	Boise
Illinois	1818	12,699,336	55,584	228.5	Springfield
Indiana	1816	6,249,617	35,867	174.2	Indianapolis
Iowa	1846	2,973,700	55,869	53.2	Des Moines
Kansas	1861	2,751,509	81,815	33.6	Topeka
Kentucky	1792	4,163,360	39,728	104.8	Frankfort
Louisiana	1812	4,534,310	43,562	104.1	Baton Rouge
Maine	1820	1,318,557	30,862	42.7	Augusta
Maryland	1788	5,600,563	9,774	573.0	Annapolis
Massachusetts	1788	6,518,868	7,840	831.5	Boston
Michigan	1837	10,207,421	56,804	179.7	Lansing
Minnesota	1858	5,174,743	79,610	65.0	St. Paul

*Note: The District of Columbia is a Federal District; it is not a state.

State	Year of Statehood	2005 Population	Area (Sq. Mi.)	Population Density (Sq Mi.)	Capital
Mississippi	1817	2,915,696	46,907	62.2	Jackson
Missouri	1821	5,765,166	68,886	83.7	Jefferson City
Montana	1889	933,005	145,552	6.4	Helena
Nebraska	1867	1,744,370	76,872	22.7	Lincoln
Nevada	1864	2,352,086	109,826	21.4	Carson City
New Hampshire	1788	1,314,821	8,968	146.6	Concord
New Jersey	1787	8,745,279	7,417	1,179.1	Trenton
New Mexico	1912	1,902,057	121,356	15.7	Santa Fe
New York	1788	19,258,082	47,214	407.9	Albany
North Carolina	1789	8,702,410	48,711	178.7	Raleigh
North Dakota	1889	635,468	68,976	9.2	Bismarck
Ohio	1803	11,477,557	40,948	280.3	Columbus
Oklahoma	1907	3,521,379	68,667	51.3	Oklahoma City
Oregon	1859	3,596,083	95,997	37.5	Salem
Pennsylvania	1787	12,426,603	44,817	277.3	Harrisburg
Rhode Island	1790	1,086,575	1,045	1,039.8	Providence
South Carolina	1788	4,239,310	30,109	140.8	Columbia
South Dakota	1889	771,803	75,885	10.2	Pierre
Tennessee	1796	5,965,317	41,217	144.7	Nashville
Texas	1845	22,775,044	261,797	87.0	Austin
Utah	1896	2,417,998	82,144	29.4	Salt Lake City
Vermont	1791	630,979	9,250	68.2	Montpelier
Virginia	1788	7,552,581	39,594	190.8	Richmond
Washington	1889	6,204,632	66,544	93.2	Olympia
West Virginia	1863	1,818,887	24,078	75.5	Charleston
Wisconsin	1848	5,554,343	54,310	102.3	Madison
Wyoming	1890	507,268	97,100	5.2	Cheyenne

FACTS ABOUT THE STATES

American Flag

The American flag is a symbol of the nation. It is recognized instantly, whether as a big banner waving in the wind or a tiny emblem worn on a lapel. The flag is so important that it is a major theme of the national anthem, "The Star-Spangled Banner." One of the most popular names for the flag is the Stars and Stripes. It is also known as Old Glory.

THE MEANING OF THE FLAG

The American flag has 13 stripes—7 red and 6 white. In the upper-left corner of the flag is the union—50 white five-pointed stars against a blue background.

The 13 stripes stand for the original 13 American states, and the 50 stars represent the states of the nation today. According to the U.S. Department of State, the colors of the flag also are symbolic:

- Red stands for courage.
- White symbolizes purity.
- Blue is the color of vigilance, perseverance, and justice.

DISPLAYING THE FLAG

It is customary not to display the American flag in bad weather. It is also customary for the flag to be displayed outdoors only from sunrise to sunset, except on certain occasions. In a few special places, however, the flag is always flown day and night. When flown at night, the flag should be illuminated.

Near a speaker's platform, the flag should occupy the place of honor at the speaker's right. When carried in a parade with other flags, the American flag should be on the marching right or in front at the center. When flying with the flags of the 50 states, the national flag must be at the center and the highest point. In a group of national flags, all should be of equal size and all should be flown from staffs, or flagpoles, of equal height.

The flag should never touch the ground or the floor. It should not be marked with any insignia, pictures, or words. Nor should it be used in any disrespectful way—as an advertising decoration, for instance. The flag should never be dipped to honor any person or thing.

SALUTING THE FLAG

The United States, like other countries, has a flag code, or rules for displaying and honoring the flag. For example, all those present should stand at attention facing the flag and salute it when it is being raised or lowered or when it is carried past them in a parade or procession. A man wearing a hat should take it off and hold it with his right hand over his heart. All women and hatless men should stand with their right hands over their hearts to show their respect for the flag. The flag should also receive these honors during the playing of the national anthem and the reciting of the Pledge of Allegiance.

THE PLEDGE OF ALLEGIANCE

The Pledge of Allegiance was written in 1892 by Massachusetts magazine (*Youth's Companion*) editor Francis Bellamy. (Congress added the words "under God" in 1954.)

> *I pledge allegiance to the flag of the United States of America and to the republic for which it stands, one nation under God, indivisible, with liberty and justice for all.*

Civilians should say the Pledge of Allegiance with their right hands placed over their hearts. People in the armed forces give the military salute. By saying the Pledge of Allegiance, we promise loyalty ("pledge allegiance") to the United States and its ideals.

Biographical Dictionary

A

Abernathy, Ralph (1926–1990) Martin Luther King Jr.'s successor as head of the Southern Christian Leadership Conference; he led the Poor People's Campaign after King's assassination in 1968. (p. 587)

Adams, John (1735–1826) American statesman; he was a delegate to the Continental Congress, a member of the committee that drafted the Declaration of Independence, vice president to George Washington, and second president of the United States. (p. 53)

Addams, Jane (1860–1935) American social worker and activist; she was the co-founder of Hull House, an organization that focused on the needs of immigrants. She helped found the American Civil Liberties Union and won the Nobel Peace Prize in 1931. (p. 159)

Aguinaldo, Emilio (1869–1964) Self-proclaimed President of the new Philippine Republic in 1899; he fought for Filipino independence from the United States. (p. 209)

Anderson, Marian (1897–1993) African American singer who fought discrimination in the 1930s; Eleanor Roosevelt arranged for her to perform on the steps of the Lincoln Memorial in 1939. (p. 371)

Anthony, Susan B. (1820–1906) American social reformer; she was active in the temperance, abolitionist, and women's suffrage movements and was co–organizer and president of the National Woman Suffrage Association. (p. 180)

Armstrong, Louis (1901–1971) Leading African American jazz musician during the Harlem Renaissance; he was a talented trumpeter whose style influenced many later musicians. (p. 307)

Armstrong, Neil (1930–) American astronaut; he was the first man to set foot on the moon in 1969. (p. 671)

Austin, Stephen F. (1793–1836) American colonizer in Texas; he was imprisoned for urging Texas statehood after Santa Anna suspended Mexico's constitution. After helping Texas win independence from Mexico, he became secretary of state for the Texas Republic. (p. 109)

B

Ball, Lucille (1911–1989) Actress and star of the television comedy series *I Love Lucy*, one of the most popular programs during the 1950s. (p. 510)

Baruch, Bernard (1870–1965) American business leader and head of the War Industries Board during World War I; he later advised many American political leaders. (p. 247)

Bethune, Mary McLeod (1875–1955) African American leader and advocate, she served as Director of Negro Affairs in the National Youth Administration and led the Black Cabinet of unofficial African American advisors to Franklin D. Roosevelt. (p. 366)

bin Laden, Osama (1957–) Founder of al Qaeda, the terrorist network responsible for the attacks of September 11, 2001 and other attacks. (p. 742)

Bradley, Omar (1893–1981) American general who led the Allied troops in Operation Overlord during World War II. (p. 423)

Bryan, William Jennings (1860–1925) American lawyer and Populist politician, he favored the free coinage of silver, an economic policy expected to help farmers. He was a Democratic candidate for president in 1896 and was defeated by William McKinley. He later led the prosecution in the Scopes Trial. (p. 299)

Buchanan, James (1791–1868) American politician and fifteenth president of the United States; he was chosen as the Democratic nominee for president in 1854 for being politically experienced and not offensive to slave states. (p. 118)

Bush, George H. W. (1924–) American politician and the forty–first president of the United States; he was president at the end of the Cold War and during Operation Desert Storm. (p. 707)

Bush, George W. (1946–) American politician and the forty–third president of the United States; the son of former president George H.W. Bush. (p. 733)

Carmichael, Stokely (1941–1998) Civil rights activist in the United States; he was an important leader of the black nationalism movement in the 1960s. (p. 583)

Carnegie, Andrew (1835–1919) American industrialist and humanitarian; he focused his attention on steelmaking and made a fortune through his vertical integration method. (p. 151)

Carter, James Earl "Jimmy" (1924–) Thirty-ninth president of the United States; he negotiated a peace agreement between Israel and Egypt. He was awarded the Nobel Prize for Peace in 2002 for his work in international diplomacy. (p. 681)

Castro, Fidel (1926–) Communist political leader of Cuba, he helped overthrow the Cuban government in 1959 and seized control of the country, exercising total control of the government and economy. (p. 528)

Chamberlain, Neville (1869–1940) British prime minister; he supported the policy of appeasement, allowing Hitler to gain land and power in the 1930s. He later began preparing Great Britain for war. (p. 393)

Chaplin, Charlie (1889–1977) British comedian and movie star; he became famous for playing the character of the "Little Tramp" in silent movies in the 1920s. (p. 310)

Chávez, César (1927–1993) American activist; he co–founded the National Farm Workers Association as part of his lifelong commitment to improving the working conditions of migrant workers on American farms. (p. 644)

Chiang Kai–shek (1887–1975) Leader of the Chinese Nationalist government and a strong U.S. ally; his government was defeated by the Communists in 1949. He fled to the island of Taiwan and established a Nationalist government there. (p. 478)

Chief Joseph (c.1840–1904) Chief of the Nez Percé tribe; he led resistance against white settlement in the Northwest. He eventually surrendered, but his eloquent surrender speech earned him a place in American history. (p. 144)

Churchill, Winston (1874–1965) British prime minister; he opposed the policy of appeasement and led Great Britain through World War II. (p. 395)

Clemenceau, Georges (1841–1929) French Premier from 1917-1920; he was a member of the Big Four during the Paris Peace Conference after World War I. (p. 255)

Clinton, Hillary Rodham (1947–) American politician and lawyer; she was a particularly influential First Lady during her husband Bill Clinton's presidency. She was elected to the U.S. Senate in 2000. (p. 727)

Clinton, William Jefferson "Bill" (1946–) Forty-second president of the United States, he became the second U.S. president to be impeached. (p. 726)

Columbus, Christopher (1451–1506) Italian explorer who reached the Americas in 1492 while searching for a western sea route from Europe to Asia. (p. 11)

Coolidge, Calvin (1872–1933) Thirtieth president of the United States; he became president upon the death of President Warren G. Harding. He was known for his honesty and his pro-business policies. (p. 284)

Coughlin, Father Charles (1891–1979) Catholic priest and popular radio broadcaster; his broadcasts praised Hitler and criticized Franklin D. Roosevelt's New Deal policies. (p. 352)

Creel, George (1876–1953) Newspaper reporter and political reformer; he was appointed by President Woodrow Wilson to head the Committee on Public Information. (p. 251)

Custer, George Armstrong (1839–1876) American army officer in the Civil War; he became a fighter of Native Americans in the West and was killed with his troops in the Battle of the Little Bighorn. (p. 143)

Darrow, Clarence (1857–1938) Famous American criminal lawyer; he defended John Scopes's right to teach evolution in the Scopes Trial. (p. 299)

Davis, Jefferson (1808–1889) First and only president of the Confederate States of America after the election of President Abraham Lincoln in 1860 led to the secession of many southern states. (p. 122)

Debs, Eugene V. (1855–1926) Leader of the American Railway Union; he supported the Pullman strike. He was the Socialist Party candidate for president five times. (p. 154)

Dewey, George (1937–1917) Commander of the United States Navy's Asiatic Squadron; he led the attack in the Pacific during the Spanish-American War. (p. 208)

Díaz, Porfirio (1830–1915) Mexican general and politician, he was president and dictator of Mexico for a total of 30 years. He ruled the people of Mexico harshly but encouraged foreign investment. (p. 221)

Dix, Dorothea (1802–1887) American philanthropist and social reformer; she helped change the U.S. prison system by advocating for the development of state hospitals to treat the mentally ill instead of imprisonment. (p. 100)

Dole, Sanford B. (1844–1926) American sugar tycoon; he helped overthrow Queen Liliuokalani and later served as president and governor of Hawaii. (p. 203)

Doolittle, James (1896–1993) U.S. Army officer; he won promotion for leading a bombing raid on Tokyo and other Japanese cities during World War II. (p. 435)

Douglas, Stephen A. (1813–1861) American politician and pro–slavery nominee for president; he debated Abraham Lincoln about slavery during the Illinois senatorial race. He proposed the unpopular Kansas-Nebraska Act, and he established the Freeport Doctrine, upholding the idea of popular sovereignty. (p. 117)

Douglass, Frederick (1817–1895) American abolitionist and writer, he escaped slavery and became a leading African American spokesman and writer. He published an autobiography, *The Narrative of the Life of Frederick Douglass*, and founded the abolitionist newspaper, the *North Star*. (p. 105)

Du Bois, W.E.B. (1868–1963) African American educator, editor, and writer; he led the Niagara Movement, calling for economic and educational equality for African Americans. He helped found the National Association for the Advancement of Colored People (NAACP). (p. 162)

Dulles, John Foster (1888–1959) Secretary of State under President Dwight D. Eisenhower, he favored building up the American nuclear arsenal as part of an effort to decrease Soviet influence around the world. (p. 497)

Earhart, Amelia (1897–1937?) American pilot; she was the first woman to fly across the Atlantic Ocean and set many speed and distance records. She disappeared over the Pacific Ocean in 1937. (p. 311)

Edison, Thomas Alva (1847–1931) American inventor of over 1,000 patents; he invented the light bulb and established a power plant that supplied electricity to parts of New York City. (p. 155)

Edwards, Jonathan (1703–1758) Important and influential revivalist leader in the Great Awakening religious movement; he delivered dramatic sermons on the choice between salvation and damnation. (p. 24)

Eisenhower, Dwight D. (1890–1969) Thirty-fourth president of the United States; he led the Allied invasion of North Africa, the D–Day invasion of France, and commanded the Allied forces in Europe during World War II. He faced many Cold War challenges as president. (p. 421)

Evers, Medgar (1925–1963) Head of the NAACP in Mississippi; he was shot and killed in front of his home in 1963 by a member of the Ku Klux Klan. (p. 570)

Falwell, Jerry (1933–) American evangelist; he founded an organization called the Moral Majority that is known for its conservative views. (p. 697)

Farmer, James (1920–1999) American civil rights leader and founder of the Congress of Racial Equality (CORE); he believed in the practice of nonviolence as a means of achieving his organization's goals. (p. 565)

Fitzgerald, F. Scott (1896–1940) American writer famous for his novels and stories, such as *The Great Gatsby*, which captured the mood of the 1920s. He gave the decade the nickname the "Jazz Age." (p. 312)

Ford, Gerald R. (1913–2006) Thirty-eighth president of the United States; he became president after the resignation of Richard Nixon. (p. 679)

Ford, Henry (1863–1947) American business leader; he revolutionized factory production through use of the assembly line and popularized the affordable automobile. (p. 277)

Franco, Francisco (1892–1975) Fascist dictator of Spain; he led the Nationalists to victory in the Spanish Civil War in the 1930s and controlled Spain's government for nearly 40 years. (p. 390)

Franz Ferdinand, Archduke (1863–1914) Heir to the throne of Austria–Hungary, whose assassination by a Serb nationalist started World War I. (p. 230)

Friedan, Betty (1921–2006) American feminist and writer; her book *The Feminine Mystique* explored the frustrations of women with their domestic lives in the 1950s and 1960s. (p. 636)

Fulbright, J. William (1905–1995) American politician and U.S. senator from Arkansas; he was chairman of the Senate Foreign Relations Committee from 1959 to 1974 and strongly advocated peace talks in the Vietnam War. The Fulbright scholarship is named for him. (p. 611)

Gandhi, Mohandas (1869–1948) Leader of India's struggle for independence from Great Britain; he taught nonviolent resistance, which was later practiced by many civil rights leaders in the 1950s and 1960s. (p. 565)

Garvey, Marcus (1887–1940) African American leader who promoted self-reliance for African Americans; he started the Universal Negro Improvement Association (UNIA), which urged African Americans to take pride in their heritage and helped influence the Harlem Renaissance. (p. 304)

Gates, Bill (1955–) American computer programmer and entrepreneur; he co–founded Microsoft Corporation, the world's largest computer software company. (p. 714)

Gaulle, Charles de (1890–1970) French military and political leader, he led the Free French government and army in World War II. He remained an important figure in France's postwar government. (p. 396)

George, David Lloyd (1863–1945) British prime minister during World War I; he was a member of the Big Four at the Paris Peace Conference in 1919. (p. 255)

Geronimo (1829–1909) Chiricahua Apache leader; he evaded capture for years and led an opposition struggle against white settlements in the American Southwest until his eventual surrender. (p. 144)

Gershwin, George (1898–1937) Composer whose famous piece "Rhapsody in Blue" showed the impact of jazz on the 1920s. (p. 313)

Giuliani, Rudolph (1944–) American lawyer and politician; he was the mayor of New York City from 1993 to 2002 and was praised for his leadership after the terrorist attacks of September 11, 2001. (p. 741)

Göering, Hermann (1893–1946) German Nazi leader and one of Hitler's top assistants; he played a key role in persecuting Jews and in making Germany a totalitarian Nazi state before and during World War II. (p. 431)

Goldwater, Barry (1909–1998) American politician; he was a U.S. senator from Arizona and the Republican Party's presidential candidate in 1964. He suggested the use of nuclear weapons to end the Vietnam War and was known for his extreme conservatism. (p. 545)

Gompers, Samuel (1850–1924) American labor leader; he helped found the American Federation of Labor to campaign for workers' rights, such as the right to organize boycotts. (p. 154)

Gonzales, Rodolfo "Corky" (1928–2005) Politician and activist; he founded an urban civil rights group called the Crusade for Justice and was a leader in the Chicano movement in the 1960s. (p. 645)

Gorbachev, Mikhail (1931–) Russian politician; he was the last president of the Soviet Union before the country's collapse in 1991. (p. 703)

Gore, Al (1948–) American politician; he was vice president under President Clinton and the Democratic presidential candidate in the 2000 election. (p. 727)

Grant, Ulysses S. (1822–1885) Eighteenth president of the United States; he received a field promotion to lieutenant general in charge of all Union forces after leading a successful battle. He accepted General Robert E. Lee's surrender of Confederate forces at Appomattox Courthouse, ending the Civil War. (p. 125)

Greenspan, Alan (1926–) American economist; he became Federal Reserve Board Chairman in 1987. (p. 716)

Griffith, D.W. (1875–1948) Filmmaker who produced *Birth of a Nation* during World War I, which introduced many advanced filmmaking techniques. (p. 310)

Guthrie, Woody (1912–1967) American singer and songwriter; he wrote and performed songs about the experiences of common people during the Great Depression. He wrote the song "This Land Is Your Land." (p. 333)

Guitierrez, Jose Angel (1944–) American activist; he was among a group of students to found the Mexican American Youth Organization (MAYO) in San Antonio. With this group, he worked for Mexican American rights. (p. 645)

Hamer, Fannie Lou (1917–1977) American civil rights activist; she was a prominent leader of the Mississippi Freedom Democratic Party. (p. 576)

Hamilton, Alexander (1755–1804) American statesman and member of the Continental Congress and the Constitutional Convention; he was an author of the Federalist Papers, which supported ratification of the Constitution. He was the first secretary of treasury under George Washington and developed the Bank of the United States. (p. 51)

Harding, Warren G. (1865–1923) Twenty-ninth president of the United States; his policies favored business, but his administration was known for scandals. (p. 283)

Hearst, William Randolph (1863–1951) American journalist; he was famous for sensational news stories, known as yellow journalism, that stirred feelings of nationalism and formed public opinion for the Spanish–American War. (p. 207)

Hiss, Alger (1904–1996) Former U.S. government official who was accused, in 1948, of participating in a Communist spy ring. He denied the charges, but was convicted of lying under oath in 1950. (p. 480)

Hitler, Adolf (1889–1945) Totalitarian dictator of Germany; his aggressive invasion of European countries led to World War II. He believed in the supremacy of the German Aryan race and was responsible for the mass murder of millions of Jews and others in the Holocaust. (p. 389)

Ho Chi Minh (1890–1969) Vietnamese revolutionary leader and president of the Democratic Republic of Vietnam from 1945 to 1969; he wanted to bring communism to South Vietnam. (p. 597)

Hobby, Oveta Culp (1874–1964) Director of the Women's Army Corps during World War II; she held the rank of colonel and later became the second woman cabinet member, serving as secretary of health, education, and welfare. (p. 408)

Hoover, Herbert (1874–1964) Thirty-first president of the United States; he helped save Europe from starvation after World War I but as president failed to deal effectively with the Great Depression. (p. 322)

Houston, Sam (1793–1863) American lawyer, politician, and soldier; he led U.S. settlers in a fight to secure Texas against Mexico and was instrumental in Texas' admission to the United States in 1845. (p. 110)

Huerta, Victoriano (1854–1916) Mexican general and politician; he overthrew Madero as Mexican president and faced revolts with many revolutionary leaders. His government was not recognized by the United States. (p. 221)

Hughes, Charles Evans (1862–1948) American politician who served as secretary of state and participated in the Washington Naval Conference. He served as chief justice on the Supreme Court and helped the court deal with controversial New Deal laws. (p. 287)

Hughes, Langston (1902–1967) African American poet who described the rich culture of African American life using rhythms influenced by jazz music. He wrote of African American hope and defiance, as well as the culture of Harlem and also had a major impact on the Harlem Renaissance. (p. 305)

Humphrey, Hubert (1911–1978) American politician; he was vice president under President Johnson, and presidential candidate of the Democratic Party in 1968 after Johnson decided not to seek re-election. (p. 616)

Hurston, Zora Neale (1891–1960) African American writer and folklore scholar who played a key role in the Harlem Renaissance. (p. 302)

Hussein, Saddam (1937–2006) President of Iraq from 1979–2003; he began wars with Iran and Kuwait, and established a brutal dictatorship in Iraq. He was captured and removed from power in 2003 by American-led forces. (p. 712)

Jackson, Jesse (1941–) American civil rights leader, minister, and politician; he was an adviser to Martin Luther King Jr. He became famous for his work on behalf of underprivileged peoples around the world, and mounted campaigns for the Democratic presidential nomination in the 1980s. (p. 589)

Jefferson, Thomas (1743–1826) American statesman; he was a member of two Continental Congresses, chairman of the committee to draft the Declaration of Independence, the Declaration's main author and one of its signers, and the third president of the United States. (p. 32)

Jobs, Steve (1955–) American entrepreneur; he founded Apple Computer in 1977, which helped popularize personal computers. (p. 714)

Johnson, Hiram W. (1866–1945) Governor of California and U.S. senator; he helped form the Progressive Party, or Bull Moose Party, and ran as its vice presidential candidate with Theodore Roosevelt in 1912. (p. 191)

Johnson, James Weldon (1871–1938) NAACP leader and Harlem Renaissance writer; he wrote poetry and, with his brother, the song "Lift Every Voice and Sing." (p. 305)

Johnson, Lyndon B. (1908–1973) Thirty-sixth president of the United States; he took office after the assassination of John F. Kennedy. (p. 530)

Kelley, Florence (1859–1932) American reformer; she was active in the settlement house movement and led progressive labor reforms for women and children. (p. 172)

Kennan, George F. (1904–) American diplomat and expert on the Soviet Union; he developed the U.S. policy of containment to counter Soviet expansion after World War II. (p. 467)

Kennedy, Jacqueline (1929–1994) American First Lady and wife of President Kennedy; she was known for her style and social grace. (p. 536)

Kennedy, John F. (1917–1963) Thirty-fifth president of the United States; he was the youngest person and the first Roman Catholic to be elected president. He was assassinated in Dallas, Texas in 1963. (p. 527)

Kennedy, Robert (1925–1968) American politician; he was attorney general during his brother John F. Kennedy's presidency and was assassinated during his bid for the 1968 Democratic presidential nomination. (p. 527)

Keynes, John Maynard (1883–1946) British economist; his revolutionary economic theory that limited deficit spending could benefit an economy provided the basis for some of Franklin D. Roosevelt's successful policies. (p. 364)

Khomeini, Ayatollah Ruhollah (1900?–1989) Islamic religious leader who led a revolution to overthrow Iran's government in 1979; he ruled the country for the next ten years on a strongly anti-American platform. (p. 686)

Khrushchev, Nikita (1894–1971) Leader of the Soviet Union during the building of the Berlin Wall and the Cuban Missile Crisis. He and President Kennedy signed the Limited Nuclear Test Ban Treaty in 1963, temporarily easing Cold War tensions. (p. 498)

Kim Il Sung (1912–1994) Communist leader of North Korea; his attack on South Korea in 1950 started the Korean War. He remained in power until 1994. (p. 484)

King, Martin Luther Jr. (1929–1968) American civil rights leader; he was a celebrated and charismatic advocate of civil rights for African Americans in the 1950s and 1960s. He was assassinated in 1968. (p. 562)

Kissinger, Henry (1923–) German-born political scientist, he was an important foreign policy advisor during the 1960s and 1970s. He won the Nobel Prize for Peace for negotiating the cease-fire agreement that ended the Vietnam War. (p. 621)

La Follette, Robert M. (1855–1925) Progressive American politician; he was active in local Wisconsin issues and challenged party bosses. As governor, he began the reform program called the Wisconsin Idea to make state government more professional. (p. 175)

Lange, Dorothea (1895–1965) American photographer; she recorded the Great Depression by taking pictures of the unemployed and rural poor. (p. 367)

Lee, Robert E. (1807–1870) American general; he refused Lincoln's offer to head the Union Army and agreed to lead Confederate forces. He successfully led several major battles until his defeat at Gettysburg, and he surrendered to the Union's commander General Grant at Appomattox Courthouse. (p. 124)

Lewis, John L. (1880–1969) American labor leader; president of the United Mine Workers, and founder of the Congress of Industrial Organizations (CIO); he helped win labor victories through strategies such as the sit-down strike. (p. 360)

Lewis, John (1940–) American politician and civil rights activist; he participated in the major protests and sit–ins of the 1960s and became the head of the Student Nonviolent Coordinating Committee (SNCC). He was elected to Congress in 1986. (p. 589)

Liliuokalani (1838–1917) Queen of the Hawaiian Islands; she opposed annexation by the United States. She lost power in a U.S.-supported revolt by planters, which led to the installation of a new government in Hawaii. (p. 203)

Lincoln, Abraham (1809–1865) Sixteenth president of the United States; he promoted equal rights for African Americans in the famous Lincoln-Douglas debates. He issued the Emancipation Proclamation and set in motion the Civil War, determined to preserve the Union. He was assassinated in 1865. (p. 119)

Lindbergh, Charles A. (1902–1974) American pilot; he became the first person to fly alone across the Atlantic Ocean nonstop in 1927. He was a hero to millions of Americans. (p. 310)

Lodge, Henry Cabot (1850–1924) U.S. senator and head of the Committee of Foreign Relations; he led the reservationists in opposition to the League of Nations. (p. 257)

Long, Huey P. (1893–1935) Louisiana politician and senator; he criticized the New Deal and set up the Share Our Wealth Society. He wanted to tax wealthy Americans and give more money to poor Americans. (p. 352)

MacArthur, Douglas (1880–1964) American general; he commanded U.S. troops in the Southwest Pacific during World War II and administered Japan after the war ended. He later commanded UN forces at the start of the Korean War until he was removed by President Truman. (p. 435)

Madero, Francisco (1873–1913) President of Mexico after Porfirio Díaz fled the country; he tried to establish a democratic government in Mexico. (p. 221)

Madison, James (1751–1836) American statesman; he was a delegate to the Constitutional Convention, the fourth president of the United States, and the author of some of the Federalist Papers. He is called the "father of the Constitution" for his proposals at the Constitutional Convention. (p. 44)

Malcolm X (1925–1965) Well-known supporter of the Nation of Islam and black leader, he spoke in support of black separatism, black pride, and the use of violence for self-protection. (p. 584)

Mandela, Nelson (1918–) Former guerrilla fighter who helped end apartheid; he became the first black president of South Africa. (p. 713)

Mao Zedong (1893–1976) Leader of the Chinese Communists; he led a successful revolution and established a Communist government in China in 1949. (p. 478)

Marshall, George C. (1880–1959) American general and politician; he led U.S. mobilization for World War II and helped plan the nation's war strategy. He also developed the postwar European Recovery Program, known as the Marshall Plan. (p. 407)

Marshall, Thurgood (1908–1993) American jurist; he was the first African American to serve on the Supreme Court. (p. 558)

Martí, José (1853–1895) Cuban writer and independence fighter; he was killed in battle in 1895 and became a symbol of Cuba's fight for freedom. (p. 207)

Mauldin, Bill (1921–2003) American cartoonist whose World War II cartoons gave people at home a soldier's point of view on life in the army. (p. 443)

McCarthy, Eugene (1916–) American politician and U.S. senator who vied for the 1968 Democratic presidential nomination against President Lyndon Johnson. (p. 615)

McCarthy, Joseph (1908–1957) U.S. senator from Wisconsin who gained national fame in the late 1940s and early 1950s by aggressively charging that communists were working in the U.S. government. He lost support in 1954, after making baseless attacks on U.S. Army officials. (p. 481)

McGovern, George (1922–) American politician; he was the Democratic candidate for the presidency in 1972, losing to Richard Nixon. (p. 624)

McKinley, William (1843–1901) Twenty–fifth president of the United States; he enacted protective tariffs in the McKinley Tariff Act of 1890 and acquired Cuba, Puerto Rico, Guam, and the Philippines during his administration. He was later assassinated. (p. 161)

McNamara, Robert S. (1916–) American businessman and public official; he was the U.S. secretary of defense from 1961–1968. (p. 615)

McNickle, D'Arcy (1904–1977) Native American activist; he drafted the Declaration of Indian Purpose, a document that asserted the rights of Native Americans in the United States. (p. 639)

McPherson, Aimee Semple (1890–1944) American fundamentalist preacher who was well–known for her glamorous presentation. (p. 298)

Means, Russell (1939–) Well-known leader of the American Indian Movement in 1968. (p. 640)

Meredith, James (1933–) Civil rights activist who entered the University of Mississippi after being denied admission because of his race. His entrance led to violent riots on the school's campus. (p. 568)

Mitchell, Billy (1879–1936) American general who supported the development of air power in the military. (p. 287)

Monroe, James (1758–1831) Leading Revolutionary figure, negotiator of the Louisiana Purchase, and the fifth president of the United States. He put forth the Monroe Doctrine establishing the U.S. sphere of influence in the Western Hemisphere that became the foundation of U.S. foreign policy. (p. 92)

Mott, Lucretia (1793–1880) American reformer, she planned the Seneca Falls Convention with Elizabeth Cady Stanton, the first organized meeting for women's rights in the United States. (p. 102)

Muir, John (1838–1914) Naturalist who believed the wilderness should be preserved in its natural state. He was largely responsible for the creation of Yosemite National Park in California. (p. 187)

Mussolini, Benito (1883–1945) Italian Fascist leader, he ruled as Italy's dictator for more than 20 years beginning in 1922 and made Italy a totalitarian state. His alliance with Adolf Hitler brought Italy into World War II. (p. 388)

Nation, Carry (1846–1911) Temperance advocate; she took extreme measures to further her cause by entering saloons in her native state of Kansas and smashing bottles of alcohol with a hatchet. (p. 179)

Ngo Din Diem (1901–1963) Vietnamese political leader; he became president of South Vietnam in 1955. He was assassinated in 1963. (p. 599)

Nimitz, Chester (1885–1966) American admiral; he won major victories in the Battle of the Coral Sea and the Battle of Midway, stopping the Japanese advance during World War II. (p. 436)

Nixon, Richard M. (1913–1994) Thirty-seventh president of the United States and vice president under President Dwight D. Eisenhower; he resigned from his second term because of the Watergate scandal. (p. 497)

North, Oliver (1943–) Officer in the U.S Marines; he is known for his role in the Iran-Contra affair. (p. 706)

O'Connor, Sandra Day (1930–) First woman on the Supreme Court; she was appointed by President Reagan in 1981 and announced her retirement in 2005. (p. 717)

Oppenheimer, J. Robert (1904–1967) American physicist, he led the Manhattan Project laboratory in Los Alamos, which developed the first nuclear bomb. (p. 410)

Oswald, Lee Harvey (1939–1963) The accused assassin of President Kennedy. (p. 540)

Palmer, A. Mitchell (1872–1936) U.S. attorney general and opponent of communism; he ordered the Palmer raids against radicals and aliens during the Red Scare of 1919 and 1920. (p. 272)

Patton, George S. (1885–1945) American general known for tank warfare; he was involved in North Africa, Italy, and the Battle of the Bulge during World War II. (p. 424)

Parks, Rosa (1913–2005) American civil rights activist; she was arrested in 1955 after refusing to give her seat on a public bus to a white man, as the law dictated. Her arrest led to a widespread bus boycott that was an important chapter in the civil rights movement. (p. 562)

Paul, Alice (1885–1977) American social reformer, suffragist, and activist; she was the founder of the organization that became the National Woman's Party (NWP) that worked to obtain women's suffrage. (p. 192)

Perkins, Frances (1882–1965) First American woman to head an executive or cabinet department; she served as secretary of labor in Franklin D. Roosevelt's administration. She played an important role in shaping New Deal jobs programs and labor policy. (p. 366)

Pershing, John J. (1860–1948) American army commander; he commanded the expeditionary force sent into Mexico to find Pancho Villa. He also served as the major general and commander in chief of the American Expeditionary Forces in World War I. (p. 223)

Pinchot, Gifford (1865–1946) Conservationist who was chief of the Forest Service. Under his leadership millions of acres of land were added to the national forests. (p. 188)

Pulitzer, Joseph (1847–1911) American journalist and newspaper publisher; he established the Pulitzer Prize for public service and advancement of education. (p. 207)

Pullman, George (1831–1897) American business leader who made a fortune in the railroad business by designing and building railroad cars, including a sleeper car. (p. 152)

Pyle, Ernie (1900–1945) American journalist and war correspondent; he reported on World War II from the point of view of an ordinary soldier abroad. (p. 443)

Randolph, A. Philip (1889–1979) African American union and civil rights leader; his protests during World War II led President Roosevelt to forbid discrimination in government and defense jobs. (p. 411)

Reagan, Nancy (1921–) Wife of President Ronald Reagan; as First Lady she headed a campaign against drugs. (p. 697)

Reagan, Ronald (1911–2004) American politician and the fortieth president of the United States; his presidency focused on arms control, economics, and the end of the Cold War. (p. 694)

Rice, Condoleezza (1954–) American educator and politician; she served as national security adviser (2001–2005) and secretary of state (2005–) under President George W. Bush. (p. 737)

Riis, Jacob (1849–1914) Newspaper reporter, reformer, and photographer; his book *How the Other Half Lives* shocked Americans with its descriptions of slum conditions and led to tenement housing legislation in New York. (p. 170)

Robeson, Paul (1898–1976) African American actor and singer who promoted African American rights and left-wing causes. (p. 307)

Robinson, Jackie (1919–1972) American baseball player; he was the first black player in the major leagues. (p. 558)

Rockefeller, John D. (1839–1937) American industrialist and philanthropist; he made a fortune in the oil business and used vertical and horizontal integration to establish a monopoly on the steel business. (p. 151)

Rommel, Erwin (1891–1944) German general during World War II; he commanded the Afrika Korps and was nicknamed the Desert Fox for his brilliant leadership. (p. 420)

Roosevelt, Eleanor (1884–1962) Wife of President Franklin D. Roosevelt, social reformer, writer, and diplomat; she supported equal rights for women and African Americans. She served as the first U.S. ambassador to the United Nations. (p. 348)

Roosevelt, Franklin Delano (1882–1945) Thirty-second president of the United States; he was elected president four times. He led the United States during the Great Depression and World War II. (p. 347)

Roosevelt, Theodore (1858–1919) Twenty-sixth president of the United States; he focused his efforts on trust busting, environmental conservation, and strong foreign policy. (p. 183)

Rumsfeld, Donald (1932–) American public official; he has held various government positions including secretary of defense (1975–1977; 2001–) (p. 737)

Salk, Jonas (1914–1995) Scientist who developed the polio vaccine in 1952. (p. 513)

Santa Anna, Antonio López de (1794–1876) Mexican general and politician, he was president of Mexico and became a dictator. He fought in the Texas Revolution and seized the Alamo but was defeated and captured by Sam Houston at San Jacinto. (p. 110)

Schlafly, Phyllis (1924–) American conservative columnist; she is known for speaking out for conservative causes, such as her opposition to the Equal Rights Amendment (ERA). (p. 637)

Selassie, Haile (1892–1975) Emperor of Ethiopia; he resisted the Italian invasion of Ethiopia during World War II and later helped modernize Ethiopia. (p. 391)

Serra, Fray Junípero (1713–1884) Franciscan monk sent to San Diego in 1769 where he founded the first of many California missions. (p. 15)

Sinclair, Upton (1878–1968) Novelist whose 1906 book, *The Jungle,* depicted the unsanitary conditions at meatpacking plants. The book brought about a public outcry, which led to consumer-protection laws. (p. 186)

Sitting Bull (c.1831–1890) American Indian leader who became the head chief of the entire Sioux nation. He encouraged other Sioux leaders to resist government demands to buy lands on the Black Hills reservations. (p. 143)

Smith, Bessie (1898?–1937) African American blues singer who played an important part in the Harlem Renaissance. (p. 307)

Stalin, Joseph (1879–1953) Totalitarian dictator of the Soviet Union; he used violent crackdowns on his political enemies to strengthen his control. He led the Soviet Union through World War II and created a powerful Soviet sphere of influence in Eastern Europe after the war. (p. 390)

Stanton, Elizabeth Cady (1815–1902) American suffrage leader, she organized the Seneca Falls Convention with Lucretia Mott. The convention was the first organized meeting for women's rights in the United States. (p. 102)

Steffens, Lincoln (1866–1936) Muckraker and managing editor of *McClure's* magazine, he wrote about government corruption in his 1904 book, *The Shame of the Cities*. (p. 171)

Stockman, David A. (1946–) American politician; he was appointed by President Reagan to help put his economics plan into action. (p. 698)

Sunday, Billy (c.1862–1935) American fundamentalist minister; he used colorful language and powerful sermons to drive home the message of salvation through Jesus and to oppose radical and progressive groups. (p. 298)

Syngman Rhee (1875–1965) Korean leader who became president of South Korea after World War II and led South Korea during the Korean War. (p. 484)

Taft, William Howard (1857–1930) Twenty–seventh president of the United States; he angered progressives by moving cautiously toward reforms and by supporting the Payne–Aldrich Tariff. He lost Roosevelt's support and was defeated for a second term. (p. 189)

Tarbell, Ida (1857–1944) Investigative journalist; she wrote a report condemning the business practices of John D. Rockefeller in *McClure's* magazine. These articles became the basis for her book, *The History of the Standard Oil Company*. (p. 171)

Thomas, Clarence (1948–) Associate justice on the Supreme Court; he was appointed in 1991 and was the second African American to serve on the Supreme Court. (p. 719)

Tojo, Hideki (1884–1948) Japanese nationalist and general; he took control of Japan during World War II. He was later tried and executed for war crimes. (p. 398)

Townsend, Dr. Francis (1867–1960) New Deal critic who focused on the needs of older Americans. His ideas for a pension plan for retirees contributed to the formation of Social Security. (p. 353)

Truman, Harry (1884–1972) Thirty-third president of the United States; he became president upon the death of President Franklin D. Roosevelt. He led the United States through the end of World War II and the beginning of the Cold War. (p. 453)

Tubman, Harriet (c.1820–1913) American abolitionist who escaped slavery and assisted other enslaved Africans to escape. She was a famous Underground Railroad conductor. (p. 104)

Vanderbilt, Cornelius (1794–1877) American business leader who controlled the New York Central Railroad and up to 4,500 miles of railroad track. He later donated $1 million to a Tennessee university. (p. 152)

Villa, Francisco "Pancho" (1878–1923) Mexican bandit and revolutionary, he led revolts against Carranza and Huerta. He was pursued by the United States but evaded General Pershing. (p. 221)

Villaraigosa, Antonio (1953–) Los Angeles mayor elected in 2005; he was the first Latino mayor of Los Angeles since 1872. (p. 747)

Walesa, Lech (1943–) Polish labor leader and electrician, he was president of Poland from 1990–1995. (p. 703)

Wallace, George (1919–1998) American politician; he was a four–time governor of Alabama who fought against segregation in the South in the 1960s. (p. 618)

Warren, Earl (1891–1974) American jurist and politician; he was Chief Justice of the Supreme Court from 1953–1969. Under his leadership the court made many notable decisions that extended individual rights and freedoms. (p. 538)

Washington, Booker T. (1856–1915) African American educator and civil rights leader; he was born into slavery and later became head of the Tuskegee Institute for career training for African Americans. He was an advocate for conservative social change. (p. 162)

 **Washington, George** (1732–1799) First president of the United States; he served as a representative to the Continental Congresses and commanded the Continental Army during the Revolutionary War. (p. 32)

Westmoreland, William (1914–) American general; he was the commander of U.S. ground troops in South Vietnam during the Vietnam War. (p. 606)

Wilhelm II, Kaiser (1859–1941) German emperor and king of Prussia; his militarism helped cause and prolong World War I. (p. 231)

Wilkie, Wendell (1892–1944) Franklin Roosevelt's Republican opponent in the 1940 Presidential election. (p. 403)

Willard, Frances (1839–1898) Temperance and women's suffrage advocate, she was a leader in the Women's Christian Temperance Union (WCTU) and the Prohibition Party. (p. 179)

Wilson, Woodrow (1856–1924) Twenty-eighth president of the United States; he proposed the League of Nations after World War I. His reform legislation included direct election of senators, prohibition, and women's suffrage. He also created the Federal Reserve System and the Federal Trade Commission, and he enacted child labor laws. (p. 191)

Young, Andrew (1932–) American politician with a background in the civil rights movement; he served as American ambassador to the United Nations under President Carter. (p. 589)

Yeltsin, Boris (1931–) Russian politician and president of Russia in the 1990s; he was the first popularly elected leader of the country. (p. 710)

Zapata, Emiliano (1879–1919) Mexican revolutionary; he led the revolt against Porfirio Díaz in the south of Mexico during the Mexican Revolution. (p. 221)

The United States of America: Political

ATLAS R47

The United States of America: Physical

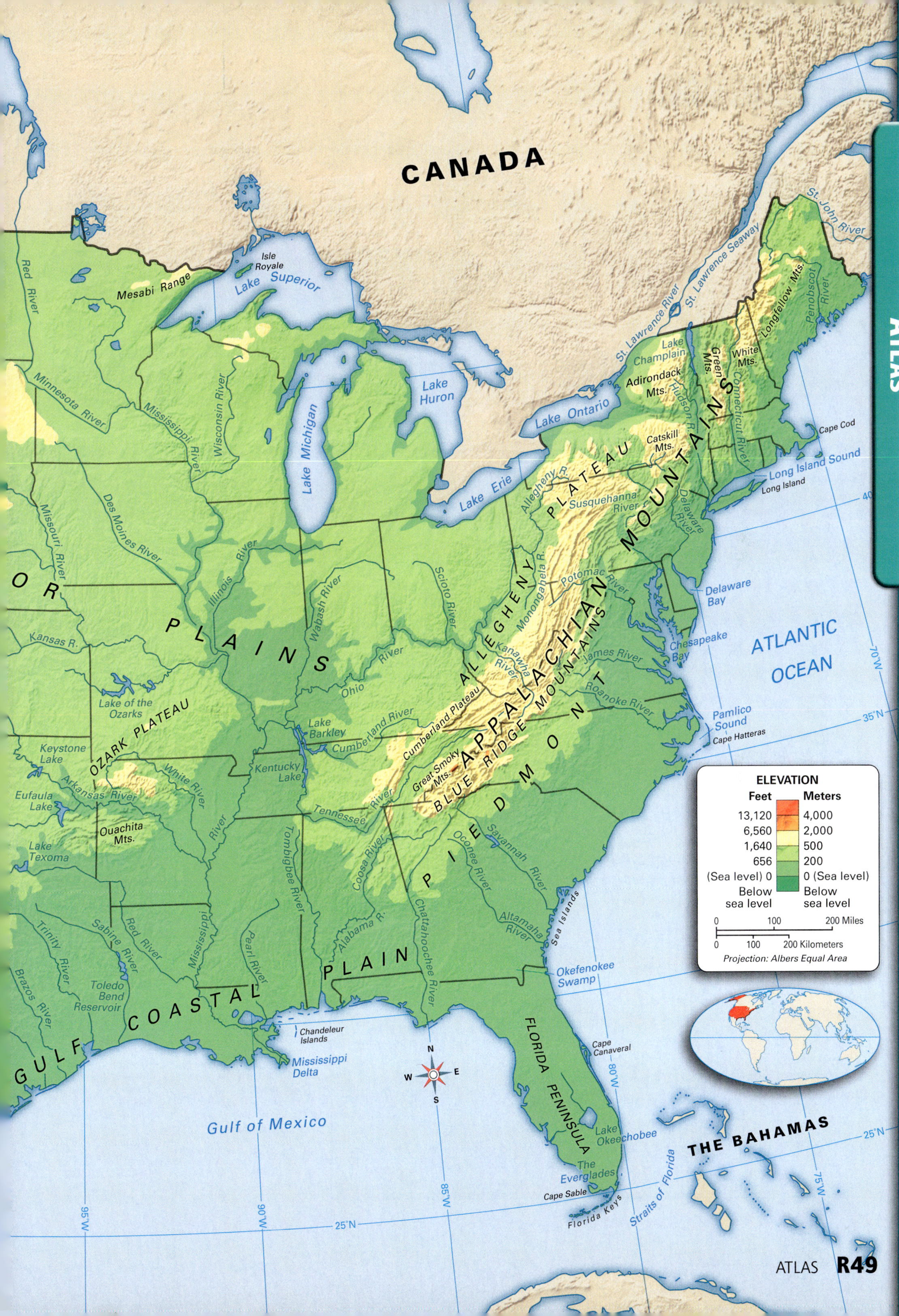

ATLAS

ELEVATION

Feet	Meters
13,120	4,000
6,560	2,000
1,640	500
656	200
(Sea level) 0	0 (Sea level)
Below sea level	Below sea level

0 — 100 — 200 Miles
0 — 100 — 200 Kilometers
Projection: Albers Equal Area

CANADA

THE BAHAMAS

ATLANTIC OCEAN

Gulf of Mexico

Labels on map

Red River, Mesabi Range, Isle Royale, Lake Superior, Minnesota River, Mississippi River, Wisconsin River, Lake Michigan, Lake Huron, St. Lawrence River, St. Lawrence Seaway, St. John River, Lake Champlain, Longfellow Mts., Penobscot River, Adirondack Mts., Green Mts., White Mts., Hudson River, Connecticut River, Lake Ontario, Catskill Mts., Cape Cod, Lake Erie, Allegheny River, Long Island Sound, Long Island, Missouri River, Des Moines River, Illinois River, Wabash River, Scioto River, Allegheny Plateau, Susquehanna River, Delaware River, Kansas R., Ohio River, Monongahela R., Potomac River, Delaware Bay, Appalachian Mountains, Lake of the Ozarks, Ozark Plateau, Kanawha River, James River, Chesapeake Bay, Keystone Lake, White River, Lake Barkley, Cumberland River, Cumberland Plateau, Roanoke River, Pamlico Sound, Cape Hatteras, Arkansas River, Kentucky Lake, Great Smoky Mts., Blue Ridge Mountains, Eufaula Lake, Ouachita Mts., Tennessee River, Lake Texoma, Piedmont, Trinity River, Sabine River, Red River, Mississippi River, Tombigbee River, Coosa River, Chattahoochee River, Oconee River, Savannah River, Altamaha River, Sea Islands, Brazos River, Toledo Bend Reservoir, Pearl River, Alabama River, Okefenokee Swamp, Gulf Coastal Plain, Chandeleur Islands, Mississippi Delta, Florida Peninsula, Cape Canaveral, Lake Okeechobee, The Everglades, Cape Sable, Florida Keys, Straits of Florida

PLAINS

ATLAS **R49**

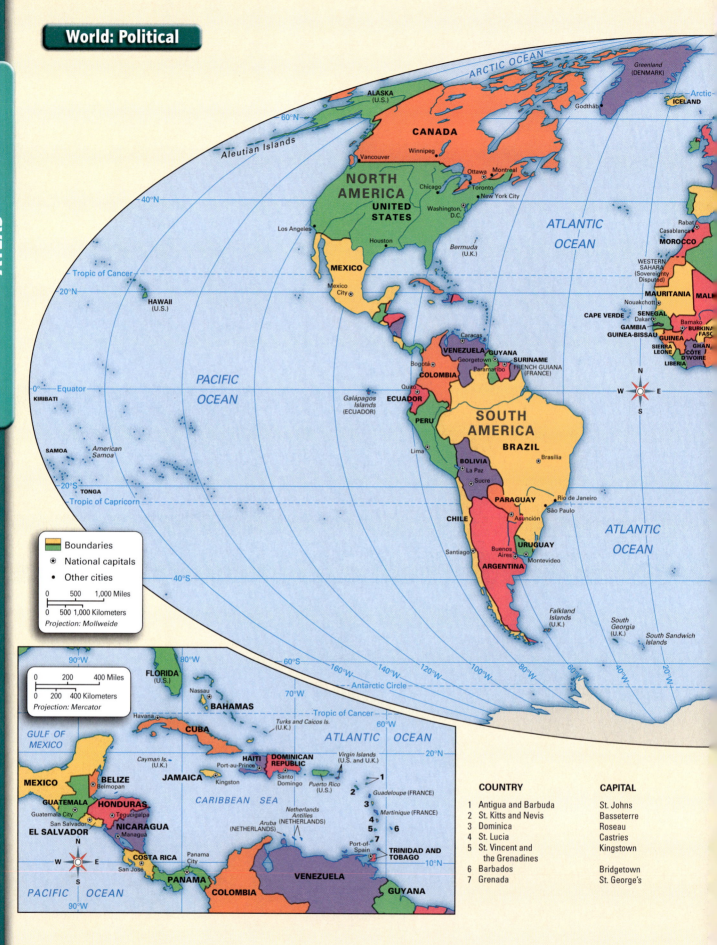

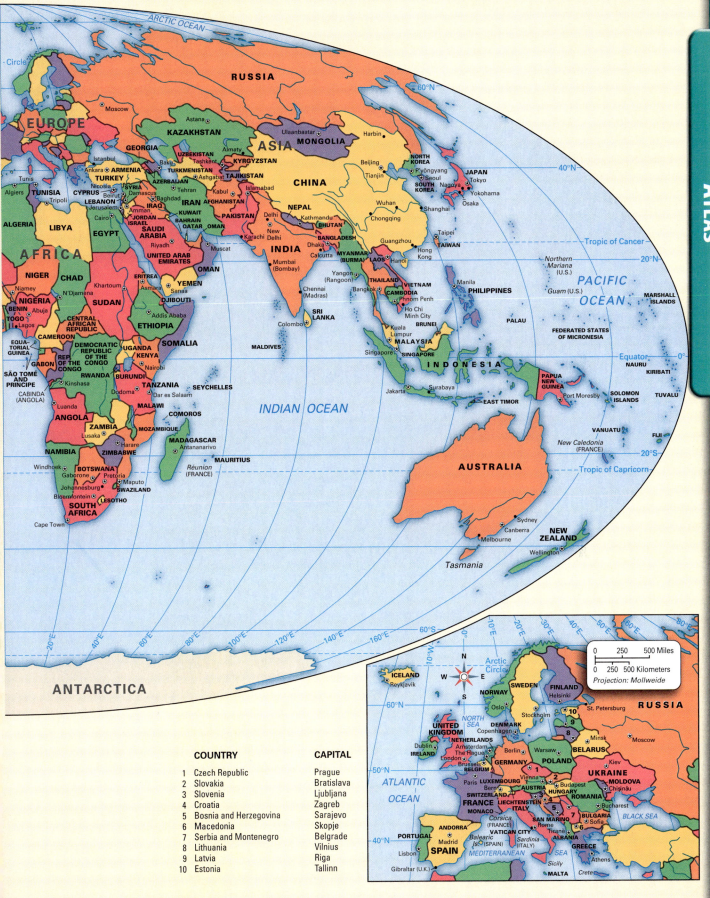

ATLAS R51

North America: Political

South America: Political

Europe: Political

Asia: Political

Africa: Political

Boundaries
⊛ National capitals
• Other cities

0 250 500 Miles
0 250 500 Kilometers
Projection: Azimuthal Equal Area

California: Physical

California: Political

California Governors

Peter Burnett (1849–1851)
John McDougall (1851–1852)
John Bigler (1852–1856)
J. Neeley Johnson (1856–1858)
John Weller (1858–1860)
Milton Latham (1860)
John Downey (1860–1862)
Leland Stanford (1862–1863)
Frederick Low (1863–1867)
Henry Haight (1867–1871)
Newton Booth (1871–1875)
Romualdo Pacheco (1875)
William Irwin (1875–1880)

George Perkins (1880–1883)
George Stoneman (1883–1887)
Washington Bartlett (1887)
Robert Waterman (1887–1891)
Henry Markham (1891–1895)
James Budd (1895–1899)
Henry Gage (1899–1903)
George Pardee (1903–1907)
James Gillett (1907–1911)
Hiram Johnson (1911–1917)
William Stephens (1917–1923)
Friend Richardson (1923–1927)
C. C. Young (1927–1931)

James Rolph (1931–1934)
Frank Merriam (1934–1939)
Culbert Olson (1939–1943)
Earl Warren (1943–1953)
Goodwin Knight (1953–1959)
Edmund G. "Pat" Brown (1959–1967)
Ronald Reagan (1967–1975)
Edmund G. "Jerry" Brown (1975–1983)
George Deukmejian (1983–1991)
Pete Wilson (1991–1999)
Gray Davis (1999–2003)
Arnold Schwarzenegger (2003–)

California Government

Executive Branch
Carries out the laws and policies of state government

The Governor
- Elected by voters to a four-year term
- Can serve two terms
- Appoints officials and some judges
- Can veto whole laws or items of laws passed by legislature

Lieutenant Governor
- Elected along with governor, but not as a running mate
- Various jobs include replacing governor should he or she leave office

The Cabinet
- Consists of officials appointed by governor
- Offers advice to governor on specific areas of knowledge

Legislative Branch
Makes state laws

Bicameral System
- Has two houses—State Senate and Assembly
- Both houses take part in law-making
- Legislature can override the governor's veto with a two-thirds vote in both houses

The State Senate
- 40 senators
- Serve four-year terms
- Limited to two terms

The Assembly
- 80 Assembly members
- Serve two-year terms
- Limited to three terms

Judicial Branch
Decides conflicts and questions about the law

Trial Courts
58 Superior Courts, one in each county

Appellate Courts
- Hear most appeals from lower courts
- Six district courts of appeals
- Have at least three justices:
    Appointed by governor then confirmed by Commission on Judicial Appointments
    Approved by voters in next election
    Four-year terms

Supreme Court of California
- Hears appeals of criminal cases involving death penalty and cases where state laws or state constitution are found invalid
- Has seven justices:
    Appointed by governor then confirmed by Commission on Judicial Appointments
    Approved by voters in next election
    12-year terms

California Facts

State tree	California Redwood
State bird	California valley quail
State marine animal	Gray whale
State animal	Grizzly bear
State reptile	Desert tortoise
State flower	Golden Poppy
Capital	Sacramento
Year of Statehood	1850 (31st state)
Nickname	The Golden State
Motto	Eureka (I have found it.)
Song	"I Love You, California"
Highest Elevation	Mt. Whitney, 14,495 feet above sea level
Lowest Elevation	Death Valley, 282 feet below sea level
Total Area	163,707 sq. miles
National Rank in Land Area	3
Total Coastline	840 miles
Largest City	Los Angeles
Largest Lake	Lake Tahoe
Number of Counties	58
Longest River	Sacramento River
Population	36,038,859 (as of 2005)
National Rank in Population	1
Length (North to South)	770 miles
Width (East to West)	250 miles

Golden poppies

State flag

Death Valley, California

Mapping the Earth
Using Latitude and Longitude

A **globe** is a scale model of the earth. It is useful for showing the entire earth or studying large areas of the earth's surface.

A pattern of lines circles the globe in east-west and north-south directions. It is called a **grid**. The intersection of these imaginary lines helps us find places on the earth.

The east-west lines in the grid are lines of **latitude**. Lines of latitude are called **parallels** because they are always parallel to each other. These imaginary lines measure distance north and south of the **equator**. The equator is an imaginary line that circles the globe halfway between the North and South Poles. Parallels measure distance from the equator in **degrees**. The symbol for degrees is °. Degrees are further divided into **minutes**. The symbol for minutes is ´. There are 60 minutes in a degree. Parallels north of the equator are labeled with an N. Those south of the equator are labeled with an S.

The north-south lines are lines of **longitude**. Lines of longitude are called **meridians**. These imaginary lines pass through the Poles. They measure distance east and west of the **prime meridian**. The prime meridian is an imaginary line that runs through Greenwich, England. It represents 0° longitude.

Lines of latitude range from 0°, for locations on the equator, to 90°N or 90°S, for locations at the Poles. Lines of longitude range from 0° on the prime meridian to 180° on a meridian in the mid-Pacific Ocean. Meridians west of the prime meridian to 180° are labeled with a W. Those east of the prime meridian to 180° are labeled with an E.

Lines of Latitude

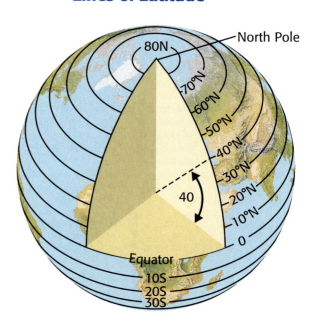

Lines of Longitude

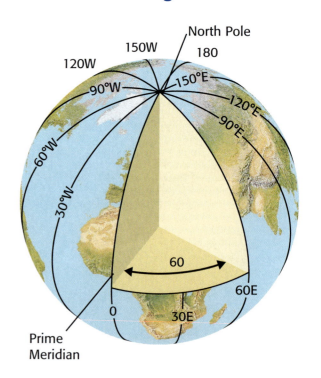

The equator divides the globe into two halves, called **hemispheres**. The half north of the equator is the Northern Hemisphere. The southern half is the Southern Hemisphere. The prime meridian and the 180° meridian divide the world into the Eastern Hemisphere and the Western Hemisphere. However, the prime meridian runs right through Europe and Africa. To avoid dividing these continents between two hemispheres, some mapmakers divide the Eastern and Western hemispheres at 20°W. This places all of Europe and Africa in the Eastern Hemisphere.

Our planet's land surface is divided into seven large landmasses, called **continents**. They are identified in the maps on this page. Landmasses smaller than continents and completely surrounded by water are called **islands**.

Geographers also organize Earth's water surface into parts. The largest is the world ocean. Geographers divide the world ocean into the Pacific Ocean, the Atlantic Ocean, the Indian Ocean, and the Arctic Ocean. Lakes and seas are smaller bodies of water.

Northern Hemisphere

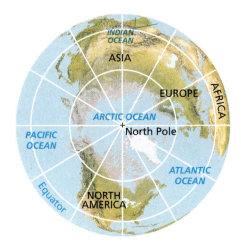

Southern Hemisphere

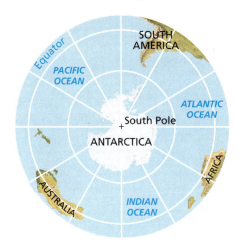

Western Hemisphere

Eastern Hemisphere

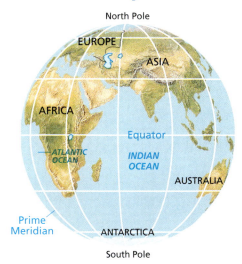

Mapmaking
Understanding Map Projections

A **map** is a flat diagram of all or part of the earth's surface. Mapmakers have created different ways of showing our round planet on flat maps. These different ways are called **map projections**. Because the earth is round, there is no way to show it accurately in a flat map. All flat maps are distorted in some way. Mapmakers must choose the type of map projection that is best for their purposes. Many map projections are one of three kinds: cylindrical, conic, or flat-plane.

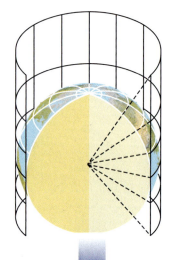

Paper cylinder

Cylindrical Projections

Cylindrical projections are based on a cylinder wrapped around the globe. The cylinder touches the globe only at the equator. The meridians are pulled apart and run parallel to each other instead of meeting at the Poles. This causes landmasses near the Poles to appear larger than they really are. The map below is a Mercator projection, one type of cylindrical projection. Navigators use the Mercator projection because it shows true direction and shape. However, it distorts the size of land areas near the Poles.

Mercator projection

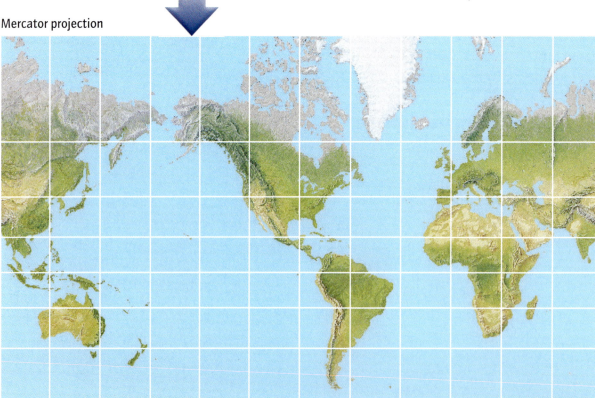

Conic Projections

Conic projections are based on a cone placed over the globe. A conic projection is most accurate along the lines of latitude where it touches the globe. It retains almost true shape and size. Conic projections are most useful for showing areas that have long east-west dimensions, such as the United States.

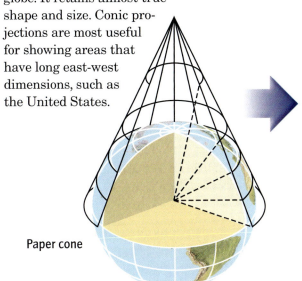
Paper cone

Conic projection

Flat-plane Projections

Flat-plane projections are based on a plane touching the globe at one point, such as at the North Pole or South Pole. A flat-plane projection is useful for showing true direction for airplane pilots and ship navigators. It also shows true area. However, it distorts the true shapes of landmasses.

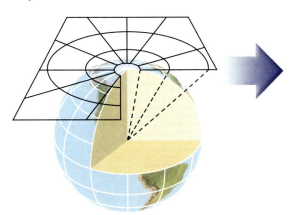
Flat plane

Flat-plane projection

GEOGRAPHY AND MAP SKILLS HANDBOOK **R65**

Map Essentials
How to Read a Map

Maps are like messages sent out in code. Mapmakers provide certain elements that help us translate these codes. These elements help us understand the message they are presenting about a particular part of the world. Of these elements, almost all maps have titles, directional indicators, scales, and legends. The map below has all four of these elements, plus two more—a locator map and an interactive keyword.

1 Title

A map's **title** shows what the subject of the map is. The map title is usually the first thing you should look at when studying a map, because it tells you what the map is trying to show.

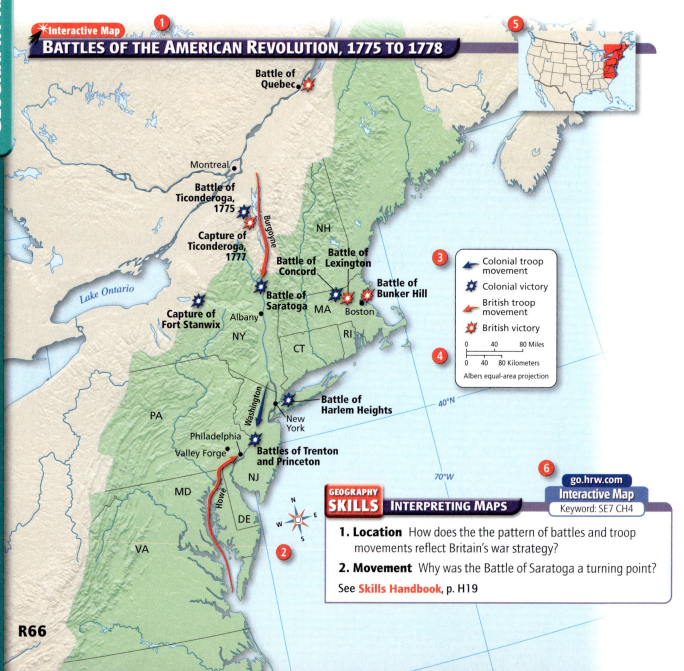

GEOGRAPHY SKILLS INTERPRETING MAPS

1. **Location** How does the the pattern of battles and troop movements reflect Britain's war strategy?
2. **Movement** Why was the Battle of Saratoga a turning point?

See **Skills Handbook**, p. H19

go.hrw.com
Interactive Map
Keyword: SE7 CH4

R66

❷ Compass Rose

A directional indicator shows which way north, south, east, and west lie on the map. Some mapmakers use a "north arrow," which points toward the North Pole. Remember, "north" is not always at the top of a map. The way a map is drawn and the location of directions on that map depend on the perspective of the mapmaker. Most maps in this textbook indicate direction by using a compass rose. A **compass rose** has arrows that point to all four principal directions, as shown.

❸ Legend

The **legend**, or key, explains what the symbols on the map represent. Point symbols are used to specify the location of things, such as cities, that do not take up much space on the map. Some legends show colors that represent elevations. Other maps might have legends with symbols or colors that represent things such as roads, the movement of military forces and battles. Legends can also show political divisions, economic resources, land use, population density, and climate.

❹ Scale

Mapmakers use scales to represent the distances between points on a map. Scales may appear on maps in several different forms. The maps in this textbook provide a bar **scale**. Scales give distances in miles and kilometers. The scale is often found in the legend. In this textbook, the type of projection used to make the map is shown below the scale bar.

To find the distance between two points on the map, place a piece of paper so that the edge connects the two points. Mark the location of each point on the paper with a line or dot. Then compare the distance between the two dots with the map's bar scale. Because distances on a scale are given in large intervals, you may have to approximate the actual distance.

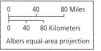

❺ Locator Map

A **locator** map shows where in the world the area on the map is located. The area shown on the main map is shown in red on the locator map. The locator map also shows surrounding areas so the map reader can see how the information on the map relates to neighboring lands.

❻ Interactive Keyword

Some maps in this textbook are interactive. If you go online to the Holt website and type in the map's keyword, you can learn more about the places and events shown on the map.

Working with Maps
Using Different Kinds of Maps

The Atlas in this textbook includes both physical and political maps. **Physical maps** show the major physical features in a region. These features include things like mountain ranges, rivers, oceans, islands, deserts, and plains. **Political maps** show the major political features of a region, such as countries and their borders, capitals, and other important cities.

Historical Map

In this textbook most of the maps you will study are historical maps. Historical maps, such as the one below, show information about the past. This information might be which lands a country controlled, where a certain group of people lived, what large cities were located in a region, or how a place changed over time. Often colors are used to indicate the different things on the map. Be sure to look at the map title and map legend first to see what the map is showing. What does this map show?

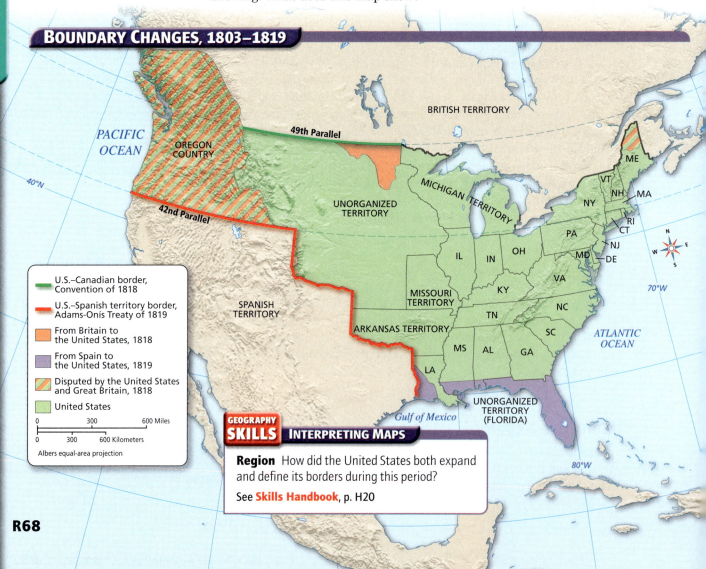

BOUNDARY CHANGES, 1803–1819

GEOGRAPHY SKILLS INTERPRETING MAPS

Region How did the United States both expand and define its borders during this period?

See **Skills Handbook**, p. H20

Interactive Map
THE LOUISIANA PURCHASE AND WESTERN EXPEDITIONS

Legend:
- U.S. states and territories in 1804
- Louisiana Purchase (acquired 1803)
- Lewis and Clark's expedition, 1804–1806

0 200 400 Miles
0 200 400 Kilometers
Albers equal-area projection

GEOGRAPHY SKILLS INTERPRETING MAPS

go.hrw.com
Practice Online
Keyword: SE7 CH6

1. **Movement** About how long was Lewis and Clark's route?
2. **Region** What new problems do you think the Louisiana Purchase might present for the United States and for Native Americans?

See **Skills Handbook**, p. H19

GEOGRAPHY AND MAP SKILLS HANDBOOK

Route Map

One special type of historical map is called a route map. A route map, like the one above, shows the route, or path, that someone or something followed. Route maps can show things like trade routes, invasion routes, or the journeys and travels of people. The routes on the map are usually shown with an arrow. If more than one route is shown, several arrows of different colors may be used. What does this route map show?

The maps in this textbook will help you study and understand history. By working with these maps, you will see where important events happened, where empires rose and fell, and where people moved. In studying these maps, you will learn how geography has influenced history.

GEOGRAPHY AND MAP SKILLS HANDBOOK **R69**

Geographic Dictionary

OCEAN
a large body of water

CORAL REEF
an ocean ridge made up of skeletal remains of tiny sea animals

GULF
a large part of the ocean that extends into land

PENINSULA
an area of land that sticks out into a lake or ocean

ISTHMUS
a narrow piece of land connecting two larger land areas

BAY
part of a large body of water that is smaller than a gulf

ISLAND
an area of land surrounded entirely by water

DELTA
an area where a river deposits soil into the ocean

STRAIT
a narrow body of water connecting two larger bodies of water

WETLAND
an area of land covered by shallow water

RIVER
a natural flow of water that runs through the land

SINKHOLE
a circular depression formed when the roof of a cave collapses

LAKE
an inland body of water

FOREST
an area of densely wooded land

GEOGRAPHY AND MAP SKILLS

COAST an area of land near the ocean

MOUNTAIN an area of rugged land that generally rises higher than 2,000 feet

VALLEY an area of low land between hills or mountains

GLACIER a large area of slow-moving ice

VOLCANO an opening in Earth's crust where lava, ash, and gases erupt

CANYON a deep, narrow valley with steep walls

HILL a rounded, elevated area of land smaller than a mountain

PLAIN a nearly flat area

DUNE a hill of sand shaped by wind

OASIS an area in the desert with a water source

DESERT an extremely dry area with little water and few plants

PLATEAU a large, flat, elevated area of land

GEOGRAPHY AND MAP SKILLS

GEOGRAPHY AND MAP SKILLS HANDBOOK **R71**

Themes and Essential Elements of Geography

by Dr. Christopher L. Salter

To study the world, geographers have identified 5 key themes, 6 essential elements, and 18 geography standards.

"How should we teach and learn about geography?" Professional geographers have worked hard over the years to answer this important question.

In 1984 a group of geographers identified the 5 Themes of Geography. These themes did a wonderful job of laying the groundwork for good classroom geography instruction. Teachers used the 5 Themes in classrooms, and geographers taught workshops on how to apply the 5 Themes in everyday life.

By the early 1990s, however, some geographers felt the 5 Themes were too broad. They created the 18 Geography Standards and the 6 Essential Elements. The 18 Geography Standards include more detailed information about what geography is, and the 6 Essential Elements are like a bridge between the 5 Themes and 18 Standards.

Look at the chart to the right. It shows how each of the 5 Themes connects to the 6 Essential Elements and 18 Geography Standards. For example, the theme of Location is related to The World in Spatial Terms and, through it, to the first three Standards. Study the chart carefully to see how the other Themes, Elements, and Standards are related.

The last Essential Element and the last two Standards cover The Uses of Geography. These key parts of geography were not covered by the 5 Themes. They emphasize how geographical knowledge can be applied to the study of history and current events and also be used to plan for the future.

5 Themes of Geography

Location The theme of location describes where something is.

Place Place describes the features that make a site unique.

Regions Regions are areas that share common characteristics.

Movement This theme looks at how and why people and things move.

Human-Environment Interaction People interact with their environment in many ways.

6 Essential Elements

18 Geography Standards

I. The World in Spatial Terms
1. How to use maps and other tools
2. How to use mental maps to organize information
3. How to analyze the spatial organization of people, places, and environments

II. Places and Regions
4. The physical and human characteristics of places
5. How people create regions to interpret Earth
6. How culture and experience influence people's perceptions of places and regions

III. Physical Systems
7. The physical processes that shape Earth's surface
8. The distribution of ecosystems on Earth

IV. Human Systems
9. The characteristics, distribution, and migration of human populations
10. The complexity of Earth's cultural mosaics
11. The patterns and networks of economic interdependence on Earth
12. The patterns of human settlement
13. The forces of cooperation and conflict

V. Environment and Society
14. How human actions modify the physical environment
15. How physical systems affect human systems
16. The distribution and meaning of resources

VI. The Uses of Geography
17. How to apply geography to interpret the past
18. How to apply geography to interpret the present and plan for the future

Primary Source Library

MAGNA CARTA, 1215

VOCABULARY
relief a payment made by the heir of a deceased tenant to a lord for the privilege of succeeding to the tenant's estate.
barony land held by a baron
fief land given to a noble in return for a pledge of loyalty and military service in Feudalism
ward a child who is not ready to inherit the title and responsibilities due him
rancour bad feeling
laity people who are not clergy

In the early 1200s King John of England angered the nobility when he imposed high taxes. The nobles joined forces with the Archbishop of Canterbury and in 1215 forced the king to sign the Magna Carta (Latin for "Great Charter"). The main point established by the Magna Carta was that the king, like all other people in England, was subject to the rule of law. The document also established the due process of law and the right to a fair and speedy trial as basic rights enjoyed by all people in England. These principles endured as part of English law and became part of American law in the Bill of Rights.

1. In the first place have granted to God, and by this our present charter confirmed for us and our heirs for ever that the English church shall be free, and shall have its rights undiminished and its liberties unimpaired . . . We have also granted to all free men of our kingdom, for ourselves and our heirs for ever, all the liberties written below, to be had and held by them and their heirs of us and our heirs.
2. If any of our earls or barons or others holding of us in chief by knight service dies, and at his death his heir be of full age and owe relief he shall have his inheritance on payment of the old relief, namely the heir or heirs of an earl 100 for a whole earl's barony, the heir or heirs of a baron 100 for a whole barony, the heir or heirs of a knight 100s, at most, for a whole knight's fee; and he who owes less shall give less according to the ancient usage of fiefs.
3. If, however, the heir of any such be under age and a ward, he shall have his inheritance when he comes of age without paying relief and without making fine.
40. To no one will we sell, to no one will we refuse or delay right or justice.
41. All merchants shall be able to go out of and come into England safely and securely and stay and travel throughout England, as well by land as by water, for buying and selling by the ancient and right customs free from all evil tolls, except in time of war and if they are of the land that is at war with us . . .
42. It shall be lawful in future for anyone, without prejudicing the allegiance due to us, to leave our kingdom and return safely and securely by land and water, save, in the public interest, for a short period in time of war—except for those imprisoned or outlawed in accordance with the law of the kingdom and natives of a land that is at war with us and merchants (who shall be treated as aforesaid).
62. And we have fully remitted and pardoned to everyone all the ill-will, indignation and rancour that have arisen between us and our men, clergy and laity, from the time of the quarrel. Furthermore, we have fully remitted to all, clergy and laity, and as far as pertains to us have completely forgiven, all trespasses occasioned by the same quarrel between Easter in the sixteenth year of our reign and the restoration of peace. And, besides, we have caused to be made for them letters testimonial patent of the lord Stephen archbishop of Canterbury, of the lord Henry archbishop of Dublin and of the aforementioned bishops and of master Pandulf about this security and the aforementioned concessions.
63. An oath, moreover, has been taken, as well on our part as on the part of the barons, that all these things aforesaid shall be observed in good faith and without evil disposition. Witness the above-mentioned and many others. Given by our hand in the meadow which is called Runnymede between Windsor and Staines on the fifteenth day of June, in the seventeenth year of our reign.

Source: "English Bill of Rights." Britannica Online. Vers. 99.1. Encyclopedia Britannica. 1994–1999. Encyclopedia Britannica, Inc.

THE MAYFLOWER COMPACT, 1620

In 1620 the Pilgrims left England bound for Virginia. A storm blew the Mayflower off course, and the Pilgrims made landfall in present-day Massachusetts. In Virginia the Pilgrims would have come under the laws governing that colony. In Massachusetts there were no laws, so the Pilgrims drew up a framework for self-government.

We whose names are underwritten, the loyal subjects of our dread Sovereign Lord King James, by the Grace of God of Great Britain, France and Ireland, King, Defender of the Faith, etc.

Having undertaken, for the Glory of God and advancement of the Christian Faith and Honour of our King and Country, a Voyage to plant the First Colony in the Northern Parts of Virginia, do by these presents solemnly and mutually in the presence of God and one of another, Covenant and Combine ourselves together into a Civil Body Politic, for our better ordering and preservation and furtherance of the ends aforesaid; and by virtue hereof to enact, constitute and frame such just and equal Laws, Ordinances, Acts, Constitutions and Offices, from time to time, as shall be thought most meet and convenient for the general good of the Colony, unto which we promise all due submission and obedience. In witness whereof we have hereunder subscribed our names at Cape Cod, the 11th of November, in the year of the reign of our Sovereign Lord King James, of England, France and Ireland the eighteenth, and of Scotland the fifty-fourth. Anno Domini 1620.

Source: *Of Plymouth Plantation.* William Bradford, 1630–1654. Samuel Eliot Morison, Ed., 1952. Pp. 75-76

VOCABULARY
covenant enter into a binding agreement

FUNDAMENTAL ORDERS OF CONNECTICUT, 1639

In January 1639 settlers in Connecticut, led by Thomas Hooker, drew up the Fundamental Orders of Connecticut. An agreement among the settlers about how they would rule themselves, it included a body of laws. It is considered to by America's first written constitution.

Forasmuch as it hath pleased the All-mighty God by the wise disposition of his divyne pruvidence so to Order and dispose of things that we the Inhabitants and Residents of Windsor, Harteford and Wethersfield are now cohabiting and dwelling in and upon the River of Conectecotte and the Lands thereunto adioyneing [adjoining]; As also in our Civell Affaires to be guided and governed according to such Lawes, Rules, Orders and decrees as shall be made, ordered & decreed, as followeth:--

1. It is Ordered . . . that there shall be yerely two generall Assemblies or Courts, the one the second thursday in Aprill, the other the second thursday in September, following; the first shall be called the Courte of Election, wherein shall be yerely Chosen . . . soe many Magestrats and other publike [public] Officers as shall be found requisitte: which choise shall be made by all that are admitted freemen and have taken the Oath of Fidelity, and doe cohabitte within this Jurisdiction, (having beene admitted Inhabitants by the major part of the Towne wherein they live,) or the major parte of such as shall be then present . . .

Source: Federal and State Constitutions. F. N. Thorpe, Ed., Vol.1. 1909. p. 519.

VOCABULARY
cohabiting living
magestrats (magistrates) local judges
requisitte (requisite) essential or necessary
jurisdiction an area over which a court or other government body has authority

ENGLISH BILL OF RIGHTS, 1689

VOCABULARY
prerogative privilege
quartering to provide lodging or living places for people
elude avoid
forfeitures the compulsory surrender of property or money as a penalty

In 1689, after the change of government known as the Glorious Revolution, Parliament passed the English Bill of Rights. This act ensured that Parliament would have power over the monarchy. The bill also protected the rights of English citizens. This part of the document contains a list of royal wrongdoings that would no longer be permitted.

By assuming and exercising a power of dispensing with and suspending of laws and the execution of laws without consent of Parliament; . . .

By levying money for and to the use of the Crown by pretence of prerogative for other time and in other manner than the same was granted by Parliament;

By raising and keeping a standing army within this kingdom in time of peace without consent of Parliament, and quartering soldiers contrary to law; . . .

And excessive bail hath been required of persons committed in criminal cases to elude the benefit of the laws made for the liberty of the subjects;

And excessive fines have been imposed;

And illegal and cruel punishments inflicted;

And several grants and promises made of fines and forfeitures before any conviction or judgment against the persons upon whom the same were to be levied;

All which are utterly and directly contrary to the known laws and statutes and freedom of this realm . . .

Source: "English Bill of Rights." Britannica Online. Vers. 99.1. Encyclopedia Britannica. 1994–1999. Encyclopedia Britannica, Inc.

VIRGINIA STATUTE FOR RELIGIOUS FREEDOM, 1786

VOCABULARY
propagation spread
proscribing forbidding or prohibiting
emolument payment for performing a duty or holding an office

The Virginia Statute for Religious Freedom, written by Thomas Jefferson and passed by Virginia's legislature in 1786, was an early statement of the rights of citizens to worship freely without experiencing coercion from government. The act was an inspiration to writers of the Bill of Rights.

. . . to compel a man to furnish contributions of money for the propagation of opinions which he disbelieves, is sinful and tyrannical; that even the forcing him to support this or that teacher of his own religious persuasion, is depriving him of the comfortable liberty of giving his contributions to the particular pastor . . . that our civil rights have no dependence on our religious opinions, any more than our opinions in physics or geometry; that therefore the proscribing any citizen as unworthy the public confidence by laying upon him an incapacity of being called to Offices of trust and emolument, unless he profess or renounce this or that religious opinion, is depriving him injuriously of those privileges and advantages to which in common with his fellow-citizens he has a natural right . . .

Be it enacted by the General Assembly, That no man shall be compelled to frequent or support any religious worship, place, or ministry whatsoever, nor shall be enforced, restrained, molested, or burthened in his body or goods, nor shall otherwise suffer on account of his religious opinions or belief; but that all men shall be free to profess, and by argument to maintain, their opinion in matters of religion, and that the same shall in no wise diminish enlarge, or affect their civil capacities.

. . . yet we are free to declare, and do declare, that the rights hereby asserted are of the natural rights of mankind, and that if any act shall be hereafter passed to repeal the present, or to narrow its operation, such act shall be an infringement of natural right.

Source: *Statutes at Large of Virginia.* W.W. Hening, Ed., Vol. 12. 1823. Pp. 84–86.

FEDERALIST PAPER No. 10, 1787

The Federalist Papers were a series of essays written in favor of ratifying the United States Constitution. The Papers were written by James Madison, Alexander Hamilton and John Jay. In Federalist Paper No. 10, *James Madison addressed critics who said that the United States was too large to be governed by a strong central government. Critics claimed there were too many interest groups, or "factions," to be ruled by a democratically elected government. Madison acknowledged the presence and problem of factions. He argued however, that the republican form of government under the Constitution was best able to deal with the problem by helping different factions negotiate solutions.*

By a faction, I understand a number of citizens, whether amounting to a majority or a minority of the whole, who are united and actuated by some common impulse of passion, or of interest, adversed to the rights of other citizens . . .

The latent causes of faction are thus sown in the nature of man; and we see them everywhere brought into different degrees of activity, according to the different circumstances of civil society. A zeal for different opinions concerning religion, concerning government, and many other points, as well of speculation as of practice; an attachment to different leaders ambitiously contending for pre-eminence and power; or to persons of other descriptions whose fortunes have been interesting to the human passions, have, in turn, divided mankind into parties, inflamed them with mutual animosity, and rendered them much more disposed to vex and oppress each other than to co-operate for their common good . . .

The inference to which we are brought is, that the CAUSES of faction cannot be removed, and that relief is only to be sought in the means of controlling its EFFECTS . . . A republic, by which I mean a government in which the scheme of representation takes place, opens a different prospect, and promises the cure for which we are seeking.

The two great points of difference between a democracy and a republic are: first, the delegation of the government, in the latter, to a small number of citizens elected by the rest; secondly, the greater number of citizens, and greater sphere of country, over which the latter may be extended . . .

The effect of the first difference is, on the one hand, to refine and enlarge the public views, by passing them through the medium of a chosen body of citizens, whose wisdom may best discern the true interest of their country, and whose patriotism and love of justice will be least likely to sacrifice it to temporary or partial considerations . . . [I]t may well happen that the public voice, pronounced by the representatives of the people, will be more consonant to the public good than if pronounced by the people themselves, convened for the purpose.

. . . [I]t clearly appears, that the same advantage which a republic has over a democracy, in controlling the effects of faction, is enjoyed by a large over a small republic, is enjoyed by the Union over the States composing it.

Source: *The Federalist* or *The New Constitution.* Papers by Alexander Hamilton, James Madison, and John Jay. New York Heritage Press. Introduction by Carl Van Doren. 1945.

VOCABULARY
latent hidden
animosity dislike
vex anger
discern understand or recognize
convened brought together

Objections to This Constitution of Government, 1787

VOCABULARY
paramount most imporant
appropriations money designated by the government to be spent
amenable friendly towards or responsible towards
minions people who are overly servile or submissive to their leader

George Mason played a behind-the-scenes role in the Revolutionary War and wrote Virginia's Declaration of Rights. He attended the Constitutional Convention in 1787. Mason criticized the proposed Constitution for allowing slavery, creating a strong central government, and lacking a bill of rights. As a result, he refused to sign the Constitution. In the following excerpt, Mason explains why he would not sign the Constitution.

There is no Declaration of Rights, and the laws of the general government being paramount to the laws and constitution of the several States, the Declarations of Rights in the separate States are no security. Nor are the people secured even in the enjoyment of the benefit of the common law.

In the House of Representatives there is not the substance but the shadow only of representation . . .

The Senate have the power of altering all money bills, and of originating appropriations of money, and the salaries of the Officers of their own appointment, in conjunction with the president of the United States, although they are not the representatives of the people or amenable to them . . .

The Judiciary of the United States is so constructed and extended, as to absorb and destroy the judiciaries of the several States; thereby rendering law as tedious, intricate and expensive, and justice as unattainable, by a great part of the community, as in England, and enabling the rich to oppress and ruin the poor.

The President of the United States has no Constitutional Council, a thing unknown in any safe and regular government. He will therefore be unsupported by proper information and advice, and will generally be directed by minions and favorites; or he will become a tool to the Senate . . .

The President of the United States has the unrestrained power of granting pardons for treason, which may be sometimes exercised to screen from punishment those whom he had secretly instigated to commit the crime, and thereby prevent a discovery of his own guilt . . .

Source: Gunston Hall Plantation

Washington's Farewell Address, 1796

VOCABULARY
infractions violations

In 1796, at the end of his second term as president, George Washington wrote his farewell address with the help of Alexander Hamilton and James Madison. In it he spoke of the dangers facing the young nation. He warned against the dangers of political parties and sectionalism, and he advised the nation against permanent alliances with other nations.

In contemplating the causes, which may disturb our Union, it occurs as matter of serious concern, that any ground should have been furnished for characterizing parties by geographical discriminations—Northern and Southern—Atlantic and Western . . .

To the efficacy and permanency of your Union, a government for the whole is indispensible. No alliances, however strict, between the parts can be an adequate substitute; they must inevitably experience the infractions and interruptions which all alliances in all times have experienced . . .

The great rule of conduct for us, in regard to foreign nations, is, in extending our commercial relations, to have with them as little political connexion [connection] as possible. So far as we have already formed engagements, let them be fulfilled with perfect good faith. Here let us stop . . .

Source: *Annals of Congress,* 4th Congress, pp. 2869–2880. American Memory Library of Congress. 1999.

JEFFERSON'S FIRST INAUGURAL ADDRESS, 1801

In 1800 Thomas Jefferson, representing the Democratic-Republican Party, defeated the Federalist candidate, President John Adams. Jefferson used his inaugural address of March 1801 to try to bridge the gap between the new political parties and to reach out to the Federalists.

Friends and Fellow-Citizens:

Called upon to undertake the duties of the first executive Office of our country, I avail myself of the presence of that portion of my fellow-citizens which is here assembled to express my grateful thanks for the favor with which they have been pleased to look toward me, to declare a sincere consciousness that the task is above my talents, and that I approach it with those anxious and awful presentiments which the greatness of the charge and the weakness of my powers so justly inspire. A rising nation, spread over a wide and fruitful land, traversing all the seas with the rich productions of their industry, engaged in commerce with nations who feel power and forget right, advancing rapidly to destinies beyond the reach of mortal eye when I contemplate these transcendent objects, and see the honor, the happiness, and the hopes of this beloved country committed to the issue, and the auspices of this day, I shrink from the contemplation, and humble myself before the magnitude of the undertaking . . .

I repair, then, fellow-citizens, to the post you have assigned me. With experience enough in subordinate Offices to have seen the difficulties of this the greatest of all, I have learnt to expect that it will rarely fall to the lot of imperfect man to retire from this station with the reputation and the favor which bring him into it. Without pretensions to that high confidence you reposed in our first and greatest revolutionary character, whose preeminent services had entitled him to the first place in his country's love and destined for him the fairest page in the volume of faithful history, I ask so much confidence only as may give firmness and effect to the legal administration of your affairs.

Source: Inaugural Addresses of the Presidents of the United States. 1989. Bartleby Library.

VOCABULARY
presentiments feeling about something that will happen in the future
transcendent uplifting
auspices protection, support
reposed placed trust in
preeminent finest, the best

JOHN QUINCY ADAMS'S FOURTH OF JULY ADDRESS, 1821

John Quincy Adams, then Secretary of State to President James Monroe, made this Fourth of July speech to the House of Representatives in 1821. His topic was the role of the United States in world affairs. He begins by speaking of the "elder world," or the old world of Britain and Europe.

And now, friends and countrymen, if the wise and learned philosophers of the elder world, the first observers of nutation and aberration, the discoverers of maddening ether and invisible planets, the inventors of Congreve rockets and Shrapnel shells, should find their hearts disposed to enquire what has America done for the benefit of mankind? Let our answer be this: America, with the same voice which spoke herself into existence as a nation, proclaimed to mankind the inextinguishable rights of human nature, and the only lawful foundations of government. She has abstained from interference in the concerns of others, even when conflict has been for principles to which she clings, as to the last vital drop that visits the heart . . .

[America's] glory is not dominion, but liberty. Her march is the march of the mind. She has a spear and a shield: but the motto upon her shield is, Freedom, Independence, Peace. This has been her Declaration: this has been, as far as her necessary intercourse with the rest of mankind would permit, her practice.

Source: Future of Freedom Foundation

VOCABULARY
nutation nodding one's head
aberration abnormality, irregularity, oddness
congreve rockets an early rocket used by the British in the War of 1812
shrapnel shells an anti-personnel weapon invented by Sir Henry Shrapnel and first used by the British army in 1803.
dominion supreme power

DENMARK VESEY DOCUMENT, 1822

VOCABULARY
assiduously diligently, with persistence
enjoined commanded
emanated coming from a source

Some enslaved African Americans tried to strike back against the slave system in the South. Denmark Vesey, a free African American living in Charleston, South Carolina, was accused of planning a massive and violent revolt in 1822. Vesey and others were caught and executed. Today some scholars have questioned if the conspiracy was real, arguing that Vesey was framed. Included below is an excerpt from an observer of the time.

At the head of this conspiracy stood Denmark Vesey, a free negro; with him the idea undoubtedly originated. For several years before he disclosed his intentions to any one, he appears to have been constantly and assiduously engaged in endeavoring to embitter the minds of the colored population against the white. He rendered himself perfectly familiar with all those parts of the Scriptures, which he thought he could pervert to his purpose; and would readily quote them, to prove that slavery was contrary to the laws of God; that slaves were bound to attempt their emancipation, however shocking and bloody might be the consequences, and that such efforts would not only be pleasing to the Almighty, but were absolutely enjoined, and their success predicted in the Scriptures . . .

In the selection of his leaders, Vesey showed great penetration and sound judgment. Rolla was plausible, and possessed uncommon self-possession; bold and ardent, he was not to be deterred from his purpose by danger. Ned's appearance indicated that he was a man of firm nerves, and desperate courage. Peter was intrepid and resolute, true to his engagements, and cautious in observing secrecy where it was necessary; he was not to be daunted nor impeded by difficulties, and though confident of success, was careful in providing against any obstacles or casualties which might arise, and intent upon discovering every means which might be in their power if thought of before hand. Gullah Jack was regarded as a Sorcerer, and as such feared by the natives of Africa, who believe in witchcraft.

He was not only considered invulnerable, but that he could make others so by his charms; and that he could and certainly would provide all his followers with arms. He was artful, cruel, bloody; his disposition in short was diabolical. His influence amongst the Africans was inconceivable. Monday was firm, resolute, discreet and intelligent . . .

As Vesey, from whom all orders emanated, and perhaps to whom only all important information was conveyed, died without confessing any thing, any opinion formed as to the numbers actually engaged in the plot, must be altogether conjectural; but enough has been disclosed to satisfy every reasonable mind, that considerable numbers were concerned. Indeed the plan of attack, which embraced so many points to be assailed at the same instant, affords sufficient evidence of the fact.

Source: *A NARRATIVE OF THE Conspiracy and Intended Insurrection, AMONGST A PORTION OF THE Negroes in the State of South-Carolina, In the Year 1822*

MONROE DOCTRINE, 1823

In 1823 President James Monroe proclaimed the Monroe Doctrine. Designed to end European influence in the Western Hemisphere, it became a cornerstone of United States foreign policy.

With the existing colonies or dependencies of any European power we have not interfered and shall not interfere. But with the governments who have declared their independence and maintained it, and whose independence we have, on great consideration and on just principles, acknowledged, we could not view any interposition for the purpose of oppressing them, or controlling in any other manner their destiny, by any European power in any other light than as the manifestation of an unfriendly disposition toward the United States . . .

Our policy in regard to Europe, which was adopted at an early stage of the wars which have so long agitated that quarter of the globe, nevertheless remains the same, which is not to interfere in the internal concerns of any of its powers; to consider the government de facto as the legitimate government for us; to cultivate friendly relations with it, and to preserve those relations by a frank, firm, and manly policy, meeting in all instances the just claims of every power, submitting to injuries from none.

Source: "The Monroe Doctrine" by James Monroe reprinted in *The Annals of America: Volume 5, 1821–1832*. Encyclopedia Britannica. 1976.

SENECA FALLS DECLARATION OF SENTIMENTS, 1848

One of the first documents to express the desire for equal rights for women was the Declaration of Sentiments, issued in 1848 at the Seneca Falls Convention in Seneca Falls, New York. Led by Elizabeth Cady Stanton and Lucretia Mott, the delegates adopted a set of resolutions modeled on the Declaration of Independence.

When, in the course of human events, it becomes necessary for one portion of the family of man to assume among the people of the earth a position different from that which they have hitherto occupied, but one to which the laws of nature and of nature's God entitle them, a decent respect to the opinions of mankind requires that they should declare the causes that impel them to such a course.

We hold these truths to be self-evident: that all men and women are created equal; that they are endowed by their Creator with certain inalienable rights; that among these are life, liberty, and the pursuit of happiness; that to secure these rights governments are instituted, deriving their just powers from the consent of the governed. Whenever any form of government becomes destructive of these ends, it is the right of those who suffer from it to refuse allegiance to it, and to insist upon the institution of a new government, laying its foundation on such principles, and organizing its powers in such form, as to them shall seem most likely to effect their safety and happiness.

Source: "Seneca Falls Declaration on Women's Rights" reprinted in *The Annals of America: Volume 7, 1841–1849*. Encyclopedia Britannica. 1976.

VOCABULARY
hitherto previously
deriving receiving from a source

CALHOUN AND WEBSTER ON THE COMPROMISE OF 1850

In 1850 the Senate debated the admission of California into the Union as a free state. The debate eventually led to the Compromise of 1850, brokered by Senator Henry Clay of Kentucky, known as the "Great Compromiser." Senator John C. Calhoun of South Carolina opposed the Compromise. Too ill to speak for himself, he was carried into the Senate, and another senator read his speech. It was Calhoun's last appearance in the Senate. A month later, he died. On March 7, Senator Daniel Webster of Massachusetts replied to Calhoun. Excerpts from both speeches are given below.

From the speech of John C. Calhoun:

The question then recurs: What is the cause of this discontent? It will be found in the belief of the people of the Southern States, as well as the discontent itself, that they can not remain, as things now are, consistently with honor and safety, in the Union. The next question to be considered is: What has caused this belief?

One of the causes is, undoubtedly, to be traced to the long-continued agitation of the slave question on the part of the North, and the many aggressions which they have made on the rights of the South during the time. I will not enumerate them at present, as it will be done hereafter in its proper place.

There is another lying back of it—with which this is intimately connected—that may be regarded as the great and primary cause. This is to be found in the fact that the equilibrium between the two sections in the government as it stood when the Constitution was ratified and the government put in action has been destroyed. At that time there was nearly a perfect equilibrium between the two, which afforded ample means to each to protect itself against the aggression of the other; but, as it now stands, one section has the exclusive power of controlling the government, which leaves the other without any adequate means of protecting itself against its encroachment and oppression.

The result of the whole is to give the Northern section a predominance in every department of the government, and thereby concentrate in it the two elements which constitute the federal government: a majority of States, and a majority of their population, estimated in federal numbers. Whatever section concentrates the two in itself possesses the control of the entire government . . .

It is a great mistake to suppose that disunion can be effected by a single blow. The cords which bind these States together in one common Union are far too numerous and powerful for that. Disunion must be the work of time. It is only through a long process, and successively, that the cords can be snapped until the whole fabric falls asunder. Already the agitation of the slavery question has snapped some of the most important, and has greatly weakened all the others.

If the agitation goes on, the same force, acting with increased intensity, as has been shown, will finally snap every cord, when nothing will be left to hold the States together except force. But surely that can with no propriety of language be called a Union when the only means by which the weaker is held connected with the stronger portion is force. It may, indeed, keep them connected; but the connection will partake much more of the character of subjugation on the part of the weaker to the stronger than the union of free, independent, and sovereign States in one confederation, as they stood in the early stages of the government, and which only is worthy of the sacred name of Union.

Source: National Center for Public Policy Research

From the speech of Daniel Webster:

Mr. President [of the Senate], I wish to speak to-day, not as a Massachusetts man, nor as a Northern man, but as an American, and a member of the Senate of the United States . . . I speak to-day for the preservation of the Union . . .

Mr. President, I should much prefer to have heard from every member on this floor declarations of opinion that this Union could never be dissolved, than the declaration of opinion by any body, that, in any case, under the pressure of any circumstances, such a dissolution was possible. I hear with distress and anguish the word "secession," especially when it falls from the lips of those who are patriotic, and known to the country, and known all over the world, for their political services. Secession! Peaceable secession! Sir, your eyes and mine are never destined to see that miracle. The dismemberment of this vast country without convulsion! The breaking up of the fountains of the great deep without ruffing the surface! Who is so foolish, I beg every body's pardon, as to expect to see any such thing? . . .

There can be no such thing as peaceable secession. Peaceable secession is an utter impossibility. Is the great Constitution under which we live, covering this whole country, is it to be thawed and melted away by secession, as the snows on the mountain melt under the influence of a vernal sun, disappear almost unobserved, and run off? No, Sir! No, Sir! I will not state what might produce the disruption of the Union; but, Sir, I see as plainly as I see the sun in heaven what that disruption itself must produce; I see that it must produce war, and such a war as I will not describe, in its twofold character.

Peaceable secession! Peaceable secession! The concurrent agreement of all the members of this great republic to separate! A voluntary separation, with alimony on one side and on the other. Why, what would be the result? Where is the line to be drawn? What States are to seceded? What is to remain American? What am I to be? An American no longer? Am I to become a sectional man, a local man, a separatist, with no country in common with the gentlemen who sit around me here, or who fill the other house of Congress? Heaven forbid! Where is the flag of the republic to remain? Where is the eagle still to tower? or is he to cower, and shrink, and fall to the ground? Why, Sir, our ancestors, our fathers and our grandfathers, those of them that are yet living amongst us with prolonged lives, would rebuke and reproach us; and our children and our grandchildren would cry out shame upon us, if we of this generation should dishonor these ensigns of the power of the government and the harmony of that Union which is every day felt among us with so much joy and gratitude . . .

And now, Mr. President, instead of speaking of the possibility or utility of secession, instead of dwelling in those caverns of darkness, instead of groping with those ideas so full of all that is horrid and horrible, let us come out into the light of day; let us enjoy the fresh air of Liberty and Union; let us cherish those hopes which belong to us; let us devote ourselves to those great objects that are fit for our consideration and action; let us raise our conceptions to the magnitude and the importance of the duties that devolve upon us; let our comprehension be as broad as the country for which we act, our aspirations as high as its certain destiny; let us not be pigmies in a case that calls for men. Never did there devolve on any generation of men higher trusts than now devolve upon us, for the preservation of this Constitution and the harmony and peace of all who are destined to live under it.

Source: Dartmouth College

VOCABULARY
alimony payments from one party to another after a separation
ensigns symbols
devolve fall, pass

PRIMARY SOURCE LIBRARY

FREDERICK DOUGLASS'S "THE SIGNIFICANCE OF EMANCIPATION IN THE WEST INDIES," 1857

VOCABULARY
august impressive, majestic
tumults noises, disturbances
depreciate put down, dismiss

On August 3, 1857, Frederick Douglass gave a speech in Canadaigua, New York in which he discussed freedom for slaves in the West Indies. In this speech Douglass described what he called his "philosophy of reform," which was that successful struggles for liberty always require tremendous effort and sacrifice.

Let me give you a word of the philosophy of reform. The whole history of the progress of human liberty shows that all concessions yet made to her august claims, have been born of earnest struggle. The conflict has been exciting, agitating, all-absorbing, and for the time being, putting all other tumults to silence. It must do this or it does nothing. If there is no struggle there is no progress. Those who profess to favor freedom and yet depreciate agitation, are men who want crops without plowing up the ground, they want rain without thunder and lightening. They want the ocean without the awful roar of its many waters.

This struggle may be a moral one, or it may be a physical one, and it may be both moral and physical, but it must be a struggle.

Power concedes nothing without a demand. It never did and it never will. Find out just what any people will quietly submit to and you have found out the exact measure of injustice and wrong which will be imposed upon them, and these will continue till they are resisted with either words or blows, or with both. The limits of tyrants are prescribed by the endurance of those whom they oppress. In the light of these ideas, Negroes will be hunted at the North, and held and flogged at the South so long as they submit to those devilish outrages, and make no resistance, either moral or physical. Men may not get all they pay for in this world; but they must certainly pay for all they get. If we ever get free from the oppressions and wrongs heaped upon us, we must pay for their removal. We must do this by labor, by suffering, by sacrifice, and if needs be, by our lives and the lives of others."

Source: *The Frederick Douglass Papers. Series One: Speeches, Debates, and Interviews. Volume 3: 1855–63.* Edited by John W. Blassingame. New Haven: Yale University Press, p. 204.

LINCOLN'S FIRST INAUGURAL ADDRESS, 1861

VOCABULARY
recanted publicly withdrew or repudiated a statement
emphatic forceful or insistent
jurisprudence a system or body of law

Abraham Lincoln knew that his victory in the 1860 presidential election threatened to tear the country apart. In his inaugural address on March 4, 1861, Lincoln pledged that there would be no war unless the South chose to begin one. In the excerpt below, he explains his reasons for believing secession to be unconstitutional and urges the South not to destroy the Union.

Fellow-Citizens of the United States:

In compliance with a custom as old as the Government itself, I appear before you to address you briefly and to take in your presence the oath prescribed by the Constitution of the United States to be taken by the President "before he enters on the execution of this Office." . . .

I have no purpose, directly or indirectly, to interfere with the institution of slavery in the States where it exists. I believe I have no lawful right to do so, and I have no inclination to do so. Those who nominated and elected me did so with full knowledge that I had made this and many similar declarations and had never recanted them; and more than this, they placed in the platform for my acceptance, and as a law to themselves and to me, the clear and emphatic resolution which I now read:

. . . In any law upon this subject ought not all the safeguards of liberty known in civilized and humane jurisprudence to be introduced, so that a free man be not in any case surrendered as a slave? And might it not be well at the same time to provide by law for the enforcement of that clause in the Constitution which guarantees that "the citizens of each State shall be entitled to all privileges and immunities of citizens in the several States?"...

It follows from these views that no State upon its own mere motion can lawfully get out of the Union; that resolves and ordinances to that effect are legally void, and that acts of violence within any State or States against the authority of the United States are insurrectionary or revolutionary, according to circumstances.

I therefore consider that in view of the Constitution and the laws the Union is unbroken, and to the extent of my ability, I shall take care, as the Constitution itself expressly enjoins upon me, that the laws of the Union be faithfully executed in all the States...

One section of our country believes slavery is right and ought to be extended, while the other believes it is wrong and ought not to be extended. This is the only substantial dispute.

Physically speaking, we can not separate. We can not remove our respective sections from each other nor build an impassable wall between them. A husband and wife may be divorced and go out of the presence and beyond the reach of each other, but the different parts of our country can not do this.

This country, with its institutions, belongs to the people who inhabit it. Whenever they shall grow weary of the existing Government, they can exercise their constitutional right of amending it or their revolutionary right to dismember or overthrow it...

In your hands, my dissatisfied fellow-countrymen, and not in mine, is the momentous issue of civil war. The Government will not assail you. You can have no conflict without being yourselves the aggressors. You have no oath registered in heaven to destroy the Government, while I shall have the most solemn one to "preserve, protect, and defend it."

I am loath to close. We are not enemies, but friends. We must not be enemies. Though passion may have strained it must not break our bonds of affection. The mystic chords of memory, stretching from every battlefield and patriot grave to every living heart and hearthstone all over this broad land, will yet swell the chorus of the Union, when again touched, as surely they will be, by the better angels of our nature.

Source: Inaugural Addresses of the Presidents of the United States. 1989. Bartleby Library.

VOCABULARY
immunities exemptions from legal duties
assail attack
loath unwilling

THE EMANCIPATION PROCLAMATION

After the Union army victory at the Battle of Antietam, President Abraham Lincoln decided to issue the Emancipation Proclamation, which freed all enslaved people in states under Confederate control. The proclamation, which went into effect on January 1, 1863, was a step toward the Thirteenth Amendment (1865), which ended slavery in all of the United States.

That on the 1st day of January, in the year of our Lord 1863, all persons held as slaves within any state or designated part of a state, the people whereof shall then be in rebellion against the United States, shall be then, thenceforward, and forever free; and the executive government of the United States, including the military and naval authority thereof, will recognize and maintain the freedom of such persons and will do no act or acts to repress such persons, or any of them, in any efforts they may make for their actual freedom...

And I further declare and make known that such persons of suitable condition will be received into the armed service of the United States to garrison forts, positions, stations, and other places, and to man vessels of all sorts in said service. And upon this act, sincerely believed to be an act of justice, warranted by the Constitution upon military necessity, I invoke the considerate judgment of mankind and the gracious favor of Almighty God.

Source: "Emancipation Proclamation" by Abraham Lincoln. Reprinted in *The Annals of America: Volume 9, 1858–1865.* Encyclopedia Britannica, Inc. 1976.

VOCABULARY
repress to forcefully restrain, to prohibit
garrison to station troops

LINCOLN'S GETTYSBURG ADDRESS, 1863

VOCABULARY
score twenty years
consecrated made holy

On November 19, 1863, Abraham Lincoln addressed a crowd gathered to dedicate a cemetery at the Gettysburg battlefield. His short speech, which is excerpted below, reminded Americans of the ideals on which the Republic was founded.

Four score and seven years ago our fathers brought forth on this continent a new nation, conceived in liberty and dedicated to the proposition that all men are created equal.

Now we are engaged in a great civil war, testing whether that nation or any nation so conceived and so dedicated can long endure. We are met on a great battlefield of that war. We have come to dedicate a portion of that field as a final resting-place for those who here gave their lives that that nation might live. It is altogether fitting and proper that we should do this.

But in a larger sense, we cannot dedicate—we cannot consecrate—we cannot hallow—this ground. The brave men, living and dead, who struggled here have consecrated it far above our poor power to add or detract. The world will little note nor long remember what we say here, but it can never forget what they did here. It is for us, the living, rather, to be dedicated here to the unfinished work which they who fought here have thus far so nobly advanced.

It is rather for us to be here dedicated to the great task remaining before us—that from these honored dead we take increased devotion to that cause for which they gave the last full measure of devotion; that we here highly resolve that these dead shall not have died in vain; that this nation, under God, shall have a new birth of freedom; and that government of the people, by the people, for the people shall not perish from the earth.

Source: "The Gettysburg Address" by Abraham Lincoln. Reprinted in *The Annals of America: Volume 9, 1858–1865.* Encyclopedia Britannica, Inc. 1976.

LINCOLN'S SECOND INAUGURAL ADDRESS, 1865

VOCABULARY
deprecated made little of
malice desire to cause injury; hatred

On March 4, 1865, President Lincoln laid out his approach to Reconstruction in his second inaugural address. As the excerpt below shows, Lincoln hoped to peacefully reunite the nation and its people.

At this second appearing to take the oath of the Presidential Office there is less occasion for an extended address than there was at the first. Then a statement somewhat in detail of a course to be pursued seemed fitting and proper. Now, at the expiration of four years, during which public declarations have been constantly called forth on every point and phase of the great contest which still absorbs the attention and engrosses the energies of the nation, little that is new could be presented. The progress of our arms, upon which all else chiefly depends, is as well known to the public as to myself, and it is, I trust, reasonably satisfactory and encouraging to all. With high hope for the future, no prediction in regard to it is ventured.

On the occasion corresponding to this four years ago all thoughts were anxiously directed to an impending civil war. All dreaded it, all sought to avert it. While the inaugural address was being delivered from this place, devoted altogether to saving the Union without war, urgent agents were in the city seeking to destroy it without war—seeking to dissolve the Union and divide effects by negotiation. Both parties deprecated war, but one of them would make war rather than let the nation survive, and the other would accept war rather than let it perish, and the war came . . .

With malice toward none, with charity for all, with firmness in the right as God gives us to see the right, let us strive on to finish the work we are in, to bind up the nation's wounds, to care for him who shall have borne the battle and for his widow and his orphan, to do all which may achieve and cherish a just and lasting peace among ourselves and with all nations.

Source: Inaugural Addresses of the Presidents of the United States. 1989. Bartleby Library.

DECLARATION OF RIGHTS FOR WOMEN

Included below are excerpts from a speech made by Susan B. Anthony on July 4, 1876. Anthony used the occasion—the 100th anniversary of the approval of the Declaration of Independence—to speak out in support of rights for women.

Susan B. Anthony, July 4, 1876

While the nation is buoyant with patriotism, and all hearts are attuned to praise, it is with sorrow we come to strike the one discordant note, on this one-hundredth anniversary of our country's birth. When subjects of kings, emperors, and czars from the old world join in our national jubilee, shall the women of the republic refuse to lay their hands with benedictions on the nation's head? . . . Yet we cannot forget, even in this glad hour, that while all men of every race, and clime, and condition, have been invested with the full rights of citizenship under our hospitable flag, all women still suffer the degradation of disfranchisement.

The history of our country the past one hundred years has been a series of assumptions and usurpations of power over woman, in direct opposition to the principles of just government, acknowledged by the United States as its foundations, which are:

First–the natural rights of each individual
Second–the equality of these rights
Third–that rights not delegated are retained by the individual
Fourth–that no person can exercise the rights of others without delegated authority
Fifth–that the non-use of rights does not destroy them

And for the violation of these fundamental principles of our government, we arraign our rulers on this Fourth day of July, 1876 . . .

These articles of impeachment against our rulers we now submit to the impartial judgment of the people. To all these wrongs and oppressions woman has not submitted in silence and resignation. From the beginning of the century, when Abigail Adams, the wife of one president and the mother of another, said, "We will not hold ourselves bound to obey laws in which we have no voice or representation," until now, woman's discontent has been steadily increasing, culminating nearly thirty years ago in a simultaneous movement among the women of the nation, demanding the right of suffrage . . .

And now, at the close of a hundred years, as the hour hand of the great clock that marks the centuries points to 1876, we declare our faith in the principles of self-government; our full equality with man in natural rights . . . We ask of our rulers, at this hour, no special favors, no special privileges, no special legislation. We ask justice, we ask equality, we ask that all the civil and political rights that belong to citizens of the United States, be guaranteed to us and our daughters forever.

Source: *History of Women's Suffrage,* Elizabeth C. Stanton et al., eds., Vol.III, 1887.

VOCABULARY
buoyant cheerful, capable of floating
jubilee a special anniversary
benedictions blessings
usurpations takings by force and without right

PRIMARY SOURCE LIBRARY

THE FOURTEEN POINTS, 1918

On January 8, 1918, nearly a year before the end of World War I, Woodrow Wilson presented his plan for a postwar peace to the U.S. Congress. Wilson came to the Paris Peace Conference in 1919 with these same 14 points.

> **VOCABULARY**
> **sovereignty** supremacy of authority, the independence of a nation
> **autonomous** independent

1. Open covenants of peace, openly arrived at, after which there shall be no private international understandings of any kind but diplomacy shall proceed always frankly and in the public view.
2. Absolute freedom of navigation upon the seas, outside territorial waters, alike in peace and in war . . .
3. The removal, so far as possible, of all economic barriers and the establishment of an equality of trade conditions . . .
4. Adequate guarantees given and taken that national armaments will be reduced to the lowest point consistent with domestic safety.
5. A free, open-minded, and absolutely impartial adjustment of all colonial claims, based upon a strict observance of the principle that in determining all such questions of sovereignty the interests of the populations concerned must have equal weight with the equitable claims of the government whose title is to be determined.
6. The evacuation of all Russian territory . . .
7. Belgium . . . must be evacuated and restored, without any attempt to limit . . . sovereignty . . .
8. All French territory should be freed and the invaded portions restored, and the wrong done to France by Prussia in 1871 in the matter of Alsace-Lorraine, which has unsettled the peace of the world for nearly fifty years, should be righted, in order that peace may once more be made secure in the interest of all.
9. A readjustment of the frontiers of Italy should be effected along clearly recognizable lines of nationality.
10. The peoples of Austria-Hungary . . . should be accorded the freest opportunity of autonomous development.
11. Rumania, Serbia, and Montenegro should be evacuated . . .
12. The Turkish portions of the present Ottoman Empire should be assured a secure sovereignty, but the other nationalities which are now under Turkish rule should be assured an undoubted security of life and an absolutely unmolested opportunity of an autonomous development,
13. An independent Polish state should be erected which should include the territories inhabited by indisputably Polish populations
14. A general association of nations must be formed under specific covenants for the purpose of affording mutual guarantees of political independence and territorial integrity to great and small states alike.

Source: Avalon Project of Yale University Law School

FOUR FREEDOMS SPEECH, 1941

In January 1941, while World War II raged in Europe and Asia, many Americans hoped the United States would stay out of the war. President Franklin D. Roosevelt understood this public feeling, but believed it was important that the United States help Great Britain resist Nazi Germany. Roosevelt gave this speech on January 6, 1941 to win greater support for his policy of providing aid to the enemies of Germany and Japan.

I have called for personal sacrifice. I am assured of the willingness of almost all Americans to respond to that call.

A part of the sacrifice means the payment of more money in taxes. In my Budget Message I shall recommend that a greater portion of this great defense program be paid for from taxation than we are paying today. No person should try, or be allowed, to get rich out of this program; and the principle of tax payments in accordance with ability to pay should be constantly before our eyes to guide our legislation.

If the Congress maintains these principles, the voters, putting patriotism ahead of pocketbooks, will give you their applause.

In the future days, which we seek to make secure, we look forward to a world founded upon four essential human freedoms.

The first is freedom of speech and expression—everywhere in the world.

The second is freedom of every person to worship God in his own way—everywhere in the world.

The third is freedom from want—which, translated into world terms, means economic understandings which will secure to every nation a healthy peacetime life for its inhabitants—everywhere in the world.

The fourth is freedom from fear—which, translated into world terms, means a world-wide reduction of armaments to such a point and in such a thorough fashion that no nation will be in a position to commit an act of physical aggression against any neighbor—anywhere in the world.

That is no vision of a distant millennium. It is a definite basis for a kind of world attainable in our own time and generation. That kind of world is the very antithesis of the so-called new order of tyranny which the dictators seek to create with the crash of a bomb.

Source: Franklin D. Roosevelt Presidential Library and Museum

VOCABULARY
antithesis exact opposite

JOHN F. KENNEDY INAUGURAL ADDRESS, 1961

President John F. Kennedy took office on January 20, 1961, at the height of the Cold War. In his inaugural address, Kennedy spoke of the immense responsibility entrusted to his generation of Americans.

The world is very different now. For man holds in his mortal hands the power to abolish all forms of human poverty and all forms of human life. And yet the same revolutionary beliefs for which our forebears fought are still at issue around the globe—the belief that the rights of man come not from the generosity of the state, but from the hand of God.

We dare not forget today that we are the heirs of that first revolution. Let the word go forth from this time and place, to friend and foe alike, that the torch has been passed to a new generation of Americans—born in this century, tempered by war, disciplined by a hard and bitter peace, proud of our ancient heritage—and unwilling to witness or permit the slow undoing of those human rights to which this Nation has always been committed, and to which we are committed today at home and around the world.

Let every nation know, whether it wishes us well or ill, that we shall pay any price, bear any burden, meet any hardship, support any friend, oppose any foe, in order to assure the survival and the success of liberty . . .

In the long history of the world, only a few generations have been granted the role of defending freedom in its hour of maximum danger. I do not shrink from this responsibility—I welcome it. I do not believe that any of us would exchange places with any other people or any other generation. The energy, the faith, the devotion which we bring to this endeavor will light our country and all who serve it—and the glow from that fire can truly light the world.

And so, my fellow Americans: ask not what your country can do for you—ask what you can do for your country.

My fellow citizens of the world: ask not what America will do for you, but what together we can do for the freedom of man.

Source: Avalon Project of Yale University Law School

VOCABULARY
forebears ancestors

Civil Rights Act, 1964

VOCABULARY
proprietor owner
coerce force

First proposed by President Kennedy, the Civil Rights Act faced fierce opposition from Southern senators who opposed federal legislation to end segregation. After Kennedy's assassination in 1963, Vice President Lyndon Johnson became president. Johnson, who had served as the Senate majority leader, used his extensive legislative experience to help push the Civil Right Act through Congress. He signed it into law on July 2, 1964. The new law banned segregation in public places.

Title II
Sec. 201. (a) All persons shall be entitled to the full and equal enjoyment of the goods, services, facilities, privileges, advantages, and accommodations of any place of public accommodation, as defined in this section, without discrimination or segregation on the ground of race, color, religion, or national origin.
(b) Each of the following establishments which serves the public is a place of public accommodation within the meaning of this title if its operations affect commerce, or if discrimination or segregation by it is supported by State action:

(1) any inn, hotel, motel, or other establishment which provides lodging to transient guests, other than an establishment located within a building which contains not more than five rooms for rent or hire and which is actually occupied by the proprietor of such establishment as his residence;

(2) any restaurant, cafeteria, lunchroom, lunch counter, soda fountain, or other facility principally engaged in selling food for consumption on the premises, including, but not limited to, any such facility located on the premises of any retail establishment; or any gasoline station;

(3) any motion picture house, theater, concert hall, sports arena, stadium or other place of exhibition or entertainment;

Sec 202. All persons shall be entitled to be free, at any establishment or place, from discrimination or segregation of any kind on the ground of race, color, religion, or national origin, if such discrimination or segregation is or purports to be required by any law, statute, ordinance, regulation, rule, or order of a State or any agency or political subdivision thereof.

Sec. 203. No person shall (a) withhold, deny, or attempt to withhold or deny, or deprive or attempt to deprive, any person of any right or privilege secured by section 201 or 202, or (b) intimidate, threaten, or coerce, or attempt to intimidate, threaten, or coerce any person with purpose of interfering with any right or privilege secured by section 201 or 202, or (c) punish or attempt to punish any person for exercising or attempting to exercise any right or privilege secured by section 201 or 202.

Source: U.S. Statutes at Large 78 (1964): 241.

Martin Luther King Jr.'s Speech in Memphis, 1968

In 1968 Martin Luther King, Jr. went to Memphis to march in support of striking sanitation workers. The strikers were mostly African American. On April 3, 1968, King gave the following speech. He makes reference to an earlier incident in which he was stabbed by a deranged woman. The wound was so close to King's heart, doctors announced, that that if he had sneezed, he would have died. The day after delivering this speech, King was assassinated.

April 3, 1968, Memphis, Tennessee

And I want to say tonight, I want to say that I am happy that I didn't sneeze. Because if I had sneezed, I wouldn't have been around here in 1960, when students all over the South started sitting-in at lunch counters. And I knew that as they were sitting in, they were really standing up for the best in the American dream. And taking the whole nation back to those great wells of democracy which were dug deep by the Founding Fathers in the Declaration of Independence and the Constitution. If I had sneezed, I wouldn't have been around in 1962, when Negroes in Albany, Georgia, decided to straighten their backs up. And whenever men and women straighten their backs up, they are going somewhere, because a man can't ride your back unless it is bent. If I had sneezed, I wouldn't have been here in 1963, when the black people of Birmingham, Alabama, aroused the conscience of this nation, and brought into being the Civil Rights Bill. If I had sneezed, I wouldn't have had a chance later that year, in August, to try to tell America about a dream that I had had. If I had sneezed, I wouldn't have been down in Selma, Alabama, been in Memphis to see the community rally around those brothers and sisters who are suffering. I'm so happy that I didn't sneeze . . .

Well, I don't know what will happen now. We've got some difficult days ahead. But it doesn't matter with me now. Because I've been to the mountaintop. And I don't mind. Like anybody, I would like to live a long life. Longevity has its place. But I'm not concerned about that now. I just want to do God's will. And He's allowed me to go up to the mountain. And I've looked over. And I've seen the promised land. I may not get there with you. But I want you to know tonight, that we, as a people, will get to the promised land. And I'm happy, tonight. I'm not worried about anything. I'm not fearing any man. Mine eyes have seen the glory of the coming of the Lord.

Source: American Federation of State, County and Municipal Employees

César Chávez Speech, 1984

In 1962 César Chávez formed the United Farm Workers, a labor union for migrant farm workers. In the 1984 speech excerpted below, Chávez described the goals that motivated his life's work and spoke of the contribution the farm workers movement had made to improving lives for Hispanic Americans everywhere.

VOCABULARY
implements tools
chattel personal property a slave

All my life, I have been driven by one dream, one goal, one vision: To overthrow a farm labor system in this nation which treats farm workers as if they were not important human beings. Farm workers are not agricultural implements. They are not beasts of burden to be used and discarded . . .

I'm not very different from anyone else who has ever tried to accomplish something with his life. My motivation comes from my personal life—from watching what my mother and father went through when I was growing up; from what we experienced as migrant farm workers in California.

That dream, that vision, grew from my own experience with racism, with hope, with the desire to be treated fairly and to see my people treated as human beings and not as chattel. It grew from anger and rage—emotions I felt 40 years ago when people of my color were denied the right to see a movie or eat at a restaurant in many parts of California. It grew from the frustration and humiliation I felt as a boy who couldn't understand how the growers could abuse and exploit farm workers when there were so many of us and so few of them . . .

I began to realize what other minority people had discovered: That the only answer—the only hope—was in organizing. More of us had to become citizens. We had to register to vote. And people like me had to develop the skills it would take to organize, to educate, to help empower the Chicano people . . .

All Hispanics—urban and rural, young and old—are connected to the farm workers' experience. We had all lived through the fields—or our parents had. We shared that common humiliation. How could we progress as a people, even if we lived in the cities, while the farm workers—men and women of our color—were condemned to a life without pride? How could we progress as a people while the farm workers—who symbolized our history in this land—ere denied self-respect? . . .

The UFW was the beginning! We attacked that historical source of shame and infamy that our people in this country lived with. We attacked that injustice, not by complaining; not by seeking handouts; not by becoming soldiers in the War on Poverty.

Farm workers acknowledged we had allowed ourselves to become victims in a democratic society—a society where majority rule and collective bargaining are supposed to be more than academic theories or political rhetoric. And by addressing this historical problem, we created confidence and pride and hope in an entire people's ability to create the future . . .

The union's survival—its very existence—sent out a signal to all Hispanics that we were fighting for our dignity, that we were challenging and overcoming injustice, that we were empowering the least educated among us—the poorest among us . . . I didn't really appreciate it at the time, but the coming of our union signaled the start of great changes among Hispanics that are only now beginning to be seen.

I've traveled to every part of this nation. I have met and spoken with thousands of Hispanics from every walk of life—from every social and economic class. One thing I hear most often from Hispanics, regardless of age or position—and from many non-Hispanics as well—is that the farm workers gave them hope that they could succeed and the inspiration to work for change . . . And Hispanics across California and the nation who don't work in agriculture are better off today because of what the farm workers taught people about organization, about pride and strength, about seizing control over their own lives.

Source: The Cesar E. Chavez Foundation is the intellectual property owner of Cesar's name, voice, image, and likeness, speeches and writings. Permission to reproduce said intellectual property for publication purposes may be obtained by contacting the: Cesar E. Chavez Foundation, 634 S. Spring St., Su. 727, Los Angeles, CA, 90014, (213) 362-0267, fax: (213) 362-0265, info@cecfmail.org

ADDRESS TO THE NATION, SEPTEMBER 11, 2001

Terrorists attacked the United States on the morning of September 11, 2001, crashing planes into the World Trade Center in New York City and the Pentagon building near Washington, D.C. At 8:30 on the evening of September 11, President George W. Bush addressed the nation from the White House.

Good evening. Today, our fellow citizens, our way of life, our very freedom came under attack in a series of deliberate and deadly terrorist acts. The victims were in airplanes, or in their offices; secretaries, businessmen and women, military and federal workers; moms and dads, friends and neighbors. Thousands of lives were suddenly ended by evil, despicable acts of terror.

The pictures of airplanes flying into buildings, fires burning, huge structures collapsing, have filled us with disbelief, terrible sadness, and a quiet, unyielding anger. These acts of mass murder were intended to frighten our nation into chaos and retreat. But they have failed; our country is strong.

A great people has been moved to defend a great nation. Terrorist attacks can shake the foundations of our biggest buildings, but they cannot touch the foundation of America. These acts shattered steel, but they cannot dent the steel of American resolve. America was targeted for attack because we're the brightest beacon for freedom and opportunity in the world. And no one will keep that light from shining.

Today, our nation saw evil, the very worst of human nature. And we responded with the best of America—with the daring of our rescue workers, with the caring for strangers and neighbors who came to give blood and help in any way they could.

Immediately following the first attack, I implemented our government's emergency response plans. Our military is powerful, and it's prepared. Our emergency teams are working in New York City and Washington, D.C. to help with local rescue efforts.

Our first priority is to get help to those who have been injured, and to take every precaution to protect our citizens at home and around the world from further attacks.

The functions of our government continue without interruption. Federal agencies in Washington which had to be evacuated today are reopening for essential personnel tonight, and will be open for business tomorrow. Our financial institutions remain strong, and the American economy will be open for business, as well.

The search is underway for those who are behind these evil acts. I've directed the full resources of our intelligence and law enforcement communities to find those responsible and to bring them to justice. We will make no distinction between the terrorists who committed these acts and those who harbor them.

I appreciate so very much the members of Congress who have joined me in strongly condemning these attacks. And on behalf of the American people, I thank the many world leaders who have called to offer their condolences and assistance.

America and our friends and allies join with all those who want peace and security in the world, and we stand together to win the war against terrorism. Tonight, I ask for your prayers for all those who grieve, for the children whose worlds have been shattered, for all whose sense of safety and security has been threatened. And I pray they will be comforted by a power greater than any of us, spoken through the ages in Psalm 23: "Even though I walk through the valley of the shadow of death, I fear no evil, for You are with me."

This is a day when all Americans from every walk of life unite in our resolve for justice and peace. America has stood down enemies before, and we will do so this time. None of us will ever forget this day. Yet, we go forward to defend freedom and all that is good and just in our world.

Thank you. Good night, and God bless America.

Source: The White House

> **VOCABULARY**
> **despicable** wicked, shameful

American Anthem Correlation to Holt's Social Studies Library

Holt's Social Studies Library of provides a rich array of reading experiences for students of American history. Use the table below to find which title in the Holt Library corresponds to a particular unit in *American Anthem: Modern American History, California Edition*. Read one or all of the books listed to supplement your understanding of American history.

UNIT	Title / Author	Time, and Place, and Summary of Plot
UNIT 1 **THE UNITED STATES BEFORE 1898**	**The United States: Change and Challenge** edited by Holt, Rinehart and Winston	A content-area reader that covers the colonial period to the present. **Anthology**
	The Scarlet Letter by Nathaniel Hawthorne	(New England, 17th century) A young woman named Hester must wear a scarlet A for committing adultery in a Puritan New England town. **Fiction**
	Narrative of the Life of Frederick Douglass, an American Slave by Frederick Douglass	(America, 1818–1841) In this autobiography, Douglas tells of his life as an enslaved person in the American South and his escape to freedom in the North. **Nonfiction**
	A Paradise Called Texas by Janice Jordan Shefelman	(Texas, 1845) This is the story of young Mina, who immigrated with her parents from Germany in 1845—the year that the Republic of Texas became a state. **Fiction**
	The Adventures of Huckleberry Finn by Mark Twain	(Southern United States, late 1800s) This story is about a young boy who travels down the Missouri river with a black man in pursuit of adventure. **Fiction**
	The Glory Field by Walter Dean	(America) This story is about a black family and a history that spans generations—from the day the first members of the family disembarked from a slave ship to the year 1994. **Fiction**
	The Red Badge of Courage by Stephen Crane	(America, during the Civil War) This novel tells the story of a young man and his psychological and unconscious response to the battlefront. **Fiction**
	A Stillness at Appomattox by Bruce Catton	(America, during the Civil War) This book presents a history of the Union Army of the Potomac as it drives toward victory in the Civil War. **Nonfiction**
	The Adventures of Tom Sawyer by Mark Twain	(Missouri, late 1800s) In this novel, Tom Sawyer and his friend Huckleberry Finn get involved with a murder, meet unsavory characters, and spend three days hiding in a cave. **Fiction**
	Call of the Wild by Jack London	(Canada's Yukon Territory, late 1800s) This book is about a dog that is stolen from his comfortable home in California and made to be a part of a dog sled for an abusive man who seeks gold in the Klondike. **Fiction**
	Cold Sassy Tree by Olive Ann Burns	(America, 1906) The marriage of a widower and a young woman challenge the sense of propriety in a parochial Georgia town. **Fiction**
Unit 2 **BECOMING A WORLD POWER, 1898–1920**	**Things Fall Apart** by Chinua Achebe	(Nigeria, 1890s) This novel uses the story of one man's life to show how "things fell apart" when his culture was colonized by the British. **Fiction**
	Animal Farm by George Orwell	(England) A fable-like satire of the Russian Revolution centers on a rebellion of farm animals. **Fiction**
	Ethan Frome by Edith Wharton	(New England, early 1900s) The narrator of this novel, set in a small New England town, investigates the life of a mysterious local named Ethan Frome, who had a tragic accident some twenty years earlier. **Fiction**

HRW LIBRARY

UNIT	Title / Author	Time, and Place, and Summary of Plot
UNIT 3 **A MODERN NATION, 1919–1940**	**Bud, Not Buddy** by Christopher Paul Curtis	(Michigan, 1936) This story is about an orphaned African-American living in Flint, Michigan during the Great Depression. **Fiction**
	To Kill a Mockingbird by Harper Lee	(Alabama, 1930s) This novel tells the story of its young narrator, "Scout" Finch, and her family when a young black man is arrested and tried for the rape of a white woman. **Fiction**
UNIT 4 **A CHAMPION OF DEMOCRACY, 1939–1960**	**Wish You Well** by David Baldacci	(New York City, 1940) This is a story about a precocious twelve-year-old girl living in the hectic New York City of 1940 with her underpaid writer father, her mother, and younger brother Oz. **Fiction**
	A Separate Peace by John Knowles	(New England, during WW II) A young man's visit to his preparatory school triggers a flashback to his experiences during the summer session when he was sixteen years old. **Fiction**
	Night by Elie Wiesel	(Romania, various Nazi death camps, 1940s) Wiesel recounts his experiences as a young man in the death camps of Auschwitz, Buna, Buchenwald and Gleiwitz during the Holocaust. **Nonfiction**
	The Chosen by Chaim Potok	(Brooklyn, 1940s) The novel tells the story of a friendship between two young men–a Hasidic Jew and a more liberal Jewish teenager–in Brooklyn at the end of World War II. **Fiction**
	El Bronx Remembered by Nicholasa Mohr	(The Bronx, 1940s and 1950s) This is a collection of twelve short stories that depict the harsh reality of many Puerto Ricans who lived in El Barrio. **Fiction**
	A Raisin in the Sun by Lorraine Hansberry	(Chicago, late 1950s) In this play an African American family struggles to hold on to its dreams for a better life. **Drama**
UNIT 5 **A NATION FACING CHALLENGES, 1954–1975**	**Barrio Boy** by Ernesto Galarza	(Mexico and California, mid 1900s) In this memoir, Galarza recalls how his life changed when his family moved from Mexico to the United States. **Nonfiction**
	The Fire Next Time by James Baldwin	(America, 1960s) In this book Baldwin gives a brutal analysis of race relations and calls for all Americans to accept the fact that America is a multiracial society. **Nonfiction**
	Fallen Angels by Walter Dean Myers	(South Vietnam, 1960–70s) The sole support of his family, a seventeen-year-old puts aside his dreams of college and a writing career in order to join the army and go into active combat in Vietnam. **Fiction**
	Barefoot Heart by Elva Treviño Hart	(America, mid-1900s) This memoir focuses on the author's childhood as the daughter of Mexican immigrants who worked as migrant workers to feed their six children. **Nonfiction**
Unit 6 **LOOKING TOWARD THE FUTURE, 1968–Present**	**Long Walk to Freedom** by Nelson Mandela (abridged)	(South Africa, contemporary) Nelson Mandela's own story of the anti-apartheid movement and his long struggle to bring racial justice to his country, South Africa. **Nonfiction**
	Necessary Roughness by Marie G. Lee	(America, contemporary) This is a coming-of-age story that revolves around Chan Kim and his twin sister, Young, as they cross the continent to get to their new home. **Fiction**
	1984 by George Orwell	(London, 1984) Written in 1949, this novel is about a future society in which Big Brother controls all aspects of every person's life. Fiction
	Great American Stories edited by Holt, Rhiehart and Winston	This is a collection of stories by American authors. **Fiction**

HOLT SOCIAL STUDIES LIBRARY CORRELATION

CORRELATION TO HOLT'S SOCIAL STUDIES LIBRARY **R95**

English and Spanish Glossary

MARK	AS IN	RESPELLING	EXAMPLE
a	alphabet	a	*AL-fuh-bet
ā	Asia	ay	AY-zhuh
ä	cart, top	ah	KAHRT, TAHP
e	let, ten	e	LET, TEN
ē	even, leaf	ee	EE-vuhn, LEEF
i	it, tip, British	i	IT, TIP, BRIT-ish
ī	site, buy, Ohio	y	SYT, BY, oh-HY-oh
	iris	eye	EYE-ris
k	card	k	KAHRD
ō	over, rainbow	oh	OH-vuhr, RAYN-boh
ú	book, wood	ooh	BOOHK, WOOHD
ȯ	all, orchid	aw	AWL, AWR-kid
ȯi	foil, coin	oy	FOYL, KOYN
aú	out	ow	OWT
ə	cup, butter	uh	KUHP, BUHT-uhr
ü	rule, food	oo	ROOL, FOOD
yü	few	yoo	FYOO
zh	vision	zh	VIZH-uhn

*A syllable printed in small capital letters receives heavier emphasis than the other syllable(s) in a word.

Phonetic Respelling and Pronunciation Guide

Many of the key terms in this textbook have been respelled to help you pronounce them. The letter combinations used in the respelling throughout the narrative are explained in the following phonetic respelling and pronunciation guide. The guide is adapted from *Merriam-Webster's Collegiate Dictionary, Eleventh Edition*; *Merriam-Webster's Biographical Dictionary*; and *Merriam-Webster's Geographical Dictionary*.

affirmative action programs that gave preference to minorities and women in hiring and admissions (p. 589)
acción afirmativa programas que les daban preferencia a los grupos minoritarios y a las mujeres en cuestión de empleos y de ingreso en la universidad (pág. 589)

agricultural revolution a change in way of life that occurred about 7,000 years ago, when hunter-gatherer societies began to stay in one place and grow their own food (p. 7)
revolución agrícola cambio en la forma de vida que tuvo lugar hace unos 7,000 años, cuando las sociedades de cazadores y recolectores comenzaron a establecerse en un solo sitio y a cultivar sus alimentos (pág. 7)

Al Qaeda Osama bin Laden's terrorist network (p. 742)
Al Qaeda red terrorista de Osama Bin Laden (pág. 742)

Alamo Spanish mission in San Antonio, Texas that was the site of a famous battle of the Texas Revolution in 1836 (p. 110)
El Álamo misión española en San Antonio, Texas; escenario de una famosa batalla durante la Revolución Texana de 1836 (pág. 110)

alien citizen of another country living in the United States (p. 272)
extranjero ciudadano de otro país que reside en Estados Unidos (pág. 272)

Alliance for Progress a program that provided economic aid to Latin America under President Kennedy (p. 534)
Alianza para el Progreso programa iniciado por el presidente Kennedy mediante el cual se le brindó ayuda económica a América Latina (pág. 534)

Allied Powers alliance between Britain, France, and Russia (p. 232)
potencias aliadas alianza entre Inglaterrra, Francia y Rusia (pág. 232)

the Allies the alliance of Britain, France, and Russia in World War II (p. 396)
Aliados alianza entre Inglaterra, Francia y Rusia durante la Segunda Guerra Mundial (pág. 396)

American Indian Movement (AIM) organization founded in 1968 by Native American leaders calling for a renewal of Native American culture and recognition of Native Americans' rights (p. 640)

R96 ENGLISH AND SPANISH GLOSSARY

Movimiento Indígena Norteamericano (AIM, por sus siglas en inglés) organización fundada en 1968 por líderes de los indígenas norteamericanos que fomentó la renovación de la cultura indígena y el reconocimiento de los derechos de los indígenas (pág. 640)

Americanization process in which immigrants were forced to abandon their traditional cultures and adopt the culture of white America (p. 158)
americanización proceso mediante el cual se obligó a los inmigrantes a abandonar su cultura tradicional y a adoptar la cultura de los estadounidenses blancos (pág. 158)

amnesty forgiveness to illegal aliens who had lived in the United States for many years, allowing them to gain legal status (p. 768)
amnistía perdón concedido a extranjeros ilegales que habían vivido en Estados Unidos durante muchos años, permitiéndoles legalizar su situación (pág. 768)

anarchist radicals who believe in the destruction of government (p. 275)
anarquista radical que cree en la destrucción del gobierno (pág. 275)

Antifederalists people who opposed ratification of the Constitution (p. 48)
antifederalistas personas que se oponían a la ratificación de la Constitución (pág. 48)

anti-Semitism anti-Jewish beliefs (p. 427)
antisemitismo ceencias en contra de los judíos (pág. 427)

apartheid the South African government's official policy of legalized racial segregation throughout their society (p. 705)
apartheid política oficial del gobierno sudafricano de segregación racial legal en toda la sociedad (pág. 705)

Apollo 11 space mission to the moon in 1969; astronaut Neil Armstrong became the first person to set foot on the moon (p. 671)
Apollo 11 misión espacial a la Luna en 1969; el astronauta Neil Armstrong fue la primera persona que pisó la superficie lunar (pág. 671)

appeasement giving in to the demands of uncompromising powers to avoid war (p. 395)
apaciguamiento aceptar las exigencias de las potencias que no quieren ceder, con el fin de evitar la guerra (pág. 395)

arms race a struggle in which competing nations build more and more weapons in an effort to avoid one nation gaining a clear advantage (p. 286)
carrera armamentista lucha entre varios países que compiten para amasar más y más armas y así evitar que otro país obtenga una ventaja evidente (pág. 286)

Articles of Confederation (1777) the document that created the first central government for the United States; it was replaced by the Constitution in 1789 (p. 43)
Artículos de la Confederación (1777) documento que creó el primer gobierno central en Estados Unidos. Fue reemplazado por la Constitución en 1789 (pág. 43)

assembly line a mass-production process in which a product moved forward through many work stations, where workers performed specific tasks (p. 277)
cadena de montaje proceso de producción masiva en el que el producto avanza de puesto en puesto, y en cada puesto el obrero realiza una función específica (pág. 277)

assimilation blending in with the established culture (p. 767)
asimilación mezcla con la cultura estabecida (pág. 767)

associative state the term for President Hoover's vision of voluntary partnership between business associations and the government (p. 336)
estado asociativo término que usó el presidente Hoover para referirse al vínculo voluntario entre las asociaciones empresariales y el gobierno (pág. 336)

Atlantic Charter (1941) a statement of American and British goals for the defeat of the Nazis and their vision for the postwar world (p. 403)
Carta del Atlántico (1941) declaración de las metas estadounidenses y británicas para derrotar a los nazis, y de su visión para el mundo después de la guerra (pág. 403)

atomic bomb a bomb that uses energy released by splitting atoms to create an enormous explosion (p. 410)
bomba atómica bomba que usa la energía liberada por la división de los átomos, creando así una explosión enorme (pág. 410)

Axis Powers the alliance of Germany, Italy and Japan in World War II (p. 398)
potencias del Eje alianza formada entre Alemania, Italia y Japón durante la Segunda Guerra Mundial (pág. 398)

Aztec a militaristic Mesoamerican Empire who formed a large empire in present day Mexico in the 1400s (p. 7)
azteca pueblo mesoamericano militarista que durante el siglo XV construyó un vasto imperio en lo que actualmente es México (pág. 7)

B

baby boom a dramatic rise in the birthrate following World War II (p. 473)
baby boom aumento marcado en la tasa de natalidad después de la Segunda Guerra Mundial (pág. 473)

balance of power a system in which each nation or alliance has equal strength; people believed that this could help avoid war (p. 232)

equilibrio del poder sistema en el que cada país o alianza tiene igual poderío; muchos opinan que así se podrían evitar las guerras (pág. 232)

Bataan Death March (1942) forced march of American and Filipino prisoners of war captured by the Japanese in the Philippines in World War II. (p. 435)

Marcha de la Muerte de Bataan (1942) marcha forzada de prisioneros de guerra estadounidenses y filipinos capturados por los japoneses en las Islas Filipinas durante la Segunda Guerra Mundial. (pág. 435)

Battle of Antietam (1862) a Union victory in the Civil War that marked the bloodiest single-day battle in U.S. military history (p.126)

batalla de Antietam (1862) victoria del ejército de la Unión durante la Guerra Civil que fue la batalla de un solo día más sangrienta de la historia militar de Estados Unidos (pág. 126)

Battle of the Bulge (1944) World War II battle between Germany and the Allied forces; the German advance created a "bulge" in the Allied battle lines, but the Allies eventually prevailed (p. 424)

batalla del Bulge (de Árdenas) (1944) batalla de la Segunda Guerra Mundial entre Alemania y las fuerzas aliadas; la ofensiva alemana creó una especie de acumulación o "bulge" en las líneas aliadas, aunque los aliados salieron victoriosos al final (pág. 424)

Battle of Bull Run (1861) the first major battle of the Civil War, resulting in a Confederate victory; showing the North that the Civil War would not be won easily (p. 125)

batalla de Bull Run (1861) primera gran batalla de la Guerra Civil, que resultó en una victoria de la Confederación; esta batalla le demostró al norte que la Guerra Civil no se ganaría fácilmente. (pág. 125)

Battle of Chancellorsville (1863) Civil War battle that was one of the Confederate army's major victories (p. 129)

batalla de Chancellorsville (1863) batalla de la Guerra Civil que fue una de las mayores victorias del Ejército Conferederado (pág. 129)

Battle of Gettysburg (1863) a Union Civil War victory that turned the tide against the Confederates (p. 129)

Batalla de Gettysburg (1863) victoria del ejército de la Unión durante la Guerra Civil que cambió el curso de la guerra en contra de los confederados (pág. 129)

Battle of Iwo Jima (1945) a World War II battle between Japanese forces and invading U.S. troops (p. 440)

batalla de Iwo Jima (1945) batalla de la Segunda Guerra Mundial entre las fuerzas japonesas y las fuerzas estadounidenses invasoras (pág. 440)

Battle of Lexington (1775) Battle of the Revolutionary War where the first shot of the war was fired on April 19, 1775 (p. 31)

batalla de Lexington (1775) batalla de la Guerra de Independencia en la que se lanzó el primer disparo el 19 de abril de 1775 (pág. 31)

Battle of the Little Bighorn (1876) battle between the U.S. Army led by Lieutenant Colonel George Armstrong Custer and Sioux forces led by Chief Sitting Bull; the Sioux won the battle (p. 143)

batalla de Little Bighorn (1876) batalla entre el ejército de Estados Unidos bajo el comando del teniente coronel George Armstrong Custer y guerreros de la tribu sioux comandados por el jefe Sitting Bull; aunque los sioux ganaron la batalla (pág. 143)

Battle of Midway (1942) a key naval and air battle between Japanese and U.S. forces during World War II (p. 436)

batalla de Midway (1942) batalla naval y aérea clave entre Japón y Estados Unidos durante la Segunda Guerra Mundial (pág. 436)

Battle of Okinawa (1945) World War II battle between Japanese forces and invading U.S. troops; fought on the island of Okinawa; over 100,000 Japanese troops were killed (p. 440)

batalla de Okinawa (1945) batalla de la Segunda Guerra Mundial entre las fuerzas japonesas y las tropas estadounidenses invasoras; se peleó en la isla de Okinawa; murieron mas de 100,000 soldados japoneses (pág. 440)

Battle of San Juan Hill (1898) battle in the Spanish-American War in which 8,000 U.S. soldiers fought to seize control over San Juan Hill (p. 210)

batalla de San Juan Hill (1945) batalla de la Guerra Hispanoamericana en la cual 8,000 soldados estadounidenses lucharon para apoderarse de la loma de San Juan (pág. 210)

Battle of Saratoga (1777) a Revolutionary War battle in New York that resulted in a major defeat of British troops; marked the Patriots' greatest victory up to that point in the war (p. 34)

batalla de Saratoga (1777) batalla de la Guerra de Independencia estadounidense que tuvo lugar en Nueva York y en la que las fuerzas británicas sufrieron una de sus peores derrotas; los patriotas obtuvieron su mayor victoria hasta ese momento (pág. 34)

Battle of Shiloh (1862) a Civil War battle in Tennessee in which the Union army gained greater control over the Mississippi River valley (p. 125)

batalla de Shiloh (1862) batalla de la Guerra Civil en Tennessee en la que el ejército de la Unión adquirió mayor control sobre el valle del río Misisipí (pág. 125)

Battle of Veracruz (1914) major conflict in the Mexican Revolution (p. 222)
batalla de Veracruz (1914) conflicto importante en la Revolución Mexicana (pág. 222)

Battle of Yorktown (1781) last major battle of the Revolutionary War; site of Genereal Charles Cornwallis's surrender on October 19, 1781 (p. 37)
batalla de Yorktown (1781) última batalla importante de la Guerra de Independencia; lugar donde el General Charles Cornwallis presentó su rendición el 19 de octubre de 1781 (pág. 37)

Bay of Pigs invasion (1961) an attempt by Cuban exiles in southern Cuba to overthrow the Cuban socialist government of Fidel Castro; the effort was funded by the U.S. and was famously disastrous (p. 529)
invasión de la Bahía de Cochinos (1961) intento de exiliados cubanos de derrocar al gobierno socialista cubano de Fidel Castro con una invasión por el sur de la isla; contaron con la financiamiento de Estados Unidos y fue un gran error (pág. 529)

bayonet constitution (1887) a constitution the king of Hawaii was forced to sign which severely restricted his power and deprived most Hawaiians of the vote (p. 203)
constitución de las bayonetas (1887) constitución que el rey de Hawai se vio obligado a firmar limitando gravemente su poder y privando a la mayoría de los hawaianos del voto (pág. 203)

Bear Flag Revolt (1846) a revolt against Mexico by American settlers in California who declared the territory an independent republic (p. 112)
Revuelta de Bear Flag (1846) rebelión en contra de México iniciada por los pobladores estadounidenses de California que declararon al territorio de California una república independiente (pág. 112)

Beringia name given by historians to the land bridge that connected Asia and North America during the Ice Age (p. 6)
Beringia nombre dado por los historiadores al puente terrestre que conectó a Asia y América de Norte durante al Edad de Hielo (pág. 6)

Berlin Airlift a program in which the United States and Britain shipped supplies by air to West Berlin during a Soviet blockade of all routes to the city; lasted from 1948–1949 (p. 470)
Puente Aéreo de Berlín programa mediante el cual Estados Unidos e Inglaterra enviaban suministros y pretrechos a Berlín Occidental durante un bloqueo soviético de todas las rutas hacia la ciudad; duró dos años, de 1948 a 1949 (pág. 470)

Big Four name given to the leaders of the Allied Powers who dominated the Paris Peace Conference in 1919 following the Allied victory in World War I (p. 255)
Cuatro Grandes nombre que se les dio a los líderes de las potencias aliadas que dominaron la Conferencia de Paz en París en 1919 tras la victoria de los Aliados en la Primera Guerra Mundial (pág. 255)

Bill of Rights the first 10 amendments to the Constitution; ratified in 1791 (p. 49)
Declaración de Derechos primeras 10 enmiendas hechas a la Constitución de Estados Unidos; aprobada en 1791 (pág. 49)

Black Cabinet nickname for a group of African Americans Franklin D. Roosevelt appointed to key government positions; they served as unofficial advisors to the president (p. 366)
Gabinete Negro nombre dado a un grupo de afroamericanos que Franklin D. Roosevelt designó para que ocuparan cargos importantes en el gobierno; fueron asesores extraoficiales del presidente (pág. 366)

Black Panther Party a group formed in 1966, inspired by the idea of Black Power that provided aid to black neighborhoods; often thought of as radical or violent (p. 583)
Partido Black Panther grupo formado en 1966, inspirado en la idea del poder negro o Black Power que prestó ayuda en barrios predominantemente negros; a menudo ha sido considerado un grupo radical o violento (pág. 583)

Black Power a movement in the late 1960s that advocated more forceful measures to achieve civil rights and supported the idea that African Americans had to depend on themselves to solve problems (p. 583)
Black Power (o poder negro) movimiento surgido a finales de la década de 1960 que defendía que se tomarán medidas más enérgicas para lograr los derechos civiles y apoyaba el concepto de que los afroamericanos solo podían contar con su propia comunidad para resolver sus problemas (pág. 583)

Black Tuesday Tuesday, October 29, 1929, the day that the stock market crashed (p. 325)
martes negro martes, 29 de octubre de 1929, día en que se desplomó el mercado de valores (pág. 325)

blitzkrieg a German word meaning "lightning war" (p. 396)
blitzkrieg palabra en alemán que significa "guerra relámpago" (pág. 396)

Bolshevik a group of Russian radicals, led by Vladimir I. Lenin, who played a major role in the 1917 revolution in Russia (p. 271)
bolcheviques grupo de radicales rusos, dirigidos por Vladimir I. Lenin, que tuvo un rol muy importante en la Revolución Rusa de 1917 (pág. 271)

bootlegger people who smuggled liquor during Prohibition (p. 300)
contrabandista personas que comerciaban clandestinamente com licores durante de la Prohibición (pág. 300)

boricua the name by which many Puerto Ricans refer to themselves; it expresses pride, empowerment, and certain political beliefs (p. 648)
boricua nombre con el que se refieren muchos puertorriqueños a ellos mismos; expresa orgullo, poderío y ciertas creencias políticas (pág. 648)

Boston Massacre (1770) an incident in which British soldiers fired into a crowd of colonists, killing five people (p. 31)
Masacre de Boston (1770) incidente en el que los soldados británicos dispararon contra una multitud de colonos, matando a cinco personas (pág. 31)

Boxer Rebellion (1900) a siege of a foreign settlement in Beijing by Chinese nationalists who were angry at foreign involvement in China (p. 204)
Rebelión de los Boxers (1900) sitio de un asentamiento extranjero en Beijing por parte de un grupo de nacionalistas chinos que estaban en desacuerdo con la participación extranjera en China (pág. 204)

Bracero Program (1942) a program that gave poor Mexican workers the chance to work temporarily in the United States (p. 411)
programa de braceros (1942) programa que les dio a los trabajadores mexicanos pobres la oportunidad de trabajar temporalmente en Estados Unidos (pág. 411)

brinkmanship a strategy that involves countries getting to the verge of war without actually going to war (p. 498)
política arriesgada estrategia que implica que los países llegan al borde de la guerra sin entrar en batalla (pág. 498)

Brownsville incident (1906) the accusation of twelve members of the African American 25th Infantry of a shooting spree in Brownsville, Texas, that killed one man and wounded a police officer; since no one member took responsibility for the shooting, all were dishonorably discharged; years later it was determined that they had been falsely accused (p. 193)
incidente de Brownsville (1906) acusación de doce soldados del batallón 25 de Infantería, compuesto de afroamericanos de una matanza en Brownsville, Texas en la que murió un hombre y quedó herido un policía; como nadie se responsabilizó de haber disparado, todos fueron dados de baja con deshonor; años más tarde se estableció que habían sido acusados falsamente (pág. 193)

budget deficit the amount by which government spending for a year exceeds government income (p. 698)
déficit presupuestario cantidad en la cual los gastos del gobierno superan sus ingresos en un año determinado (pág. 698)

budget surplus when a government's income exceeds its spending (p. 734)
excedente presupuestario cuando los ingresos de un gobierno son mayores que sus gastos (pág. 734)

bully pulpit a platform used to publicize and seek support for important issues (p. 184)
tribuna platforma usada para promocionar y solicitar apoyo para temas de importancia (pág. 184)

Bush* v. *Gore Supreme Court case that ruled the Florida Supreme Court's recount in the 2000 Presidential Election was unconstitutional because it failed to provide clear standards by which the ballots were to be counted (p. 735)
Bush* contra *Gore caso en el que la Corte Suprema decidió que el recuento efectuado por la Corte Suprema de Florida en la elección presidencial de 2000 fue inconstitucional porque no existían reglas claras sobre cómo debían contarse los votos (pág. 735)

buying on margin buying stocks with loans from brokers (p. 323)
comprar a crédito comprar acciones con dinero prestado por los corredores (pág. 323)

Camp David Accords agreement between Egyptian President Anwar Sadat and Israeli Prime Minister Menachem Begin; President Carter mediated the process at Camp David (p. 684)
Acuerdos de Camp David convenio entre el presidente egipcio Anwar Sadat y el primer ministro israelí Menachem Begin; el presidente Carter actuó como mediador el proceso en Camp David (pág. 684)

capitalism economic system in which most businesses are privately owned (p. 151)
capitalismo sistema económico en el que la mayoría de las empresas son de propiedad privada (pág. 151)

carpetbagger name given by Southern critics to Southerners allied with northern Republicans who came south to take part in the region's political and economic rebirth; given this name because it was claimed they could carry everything they owned in a carpetbag, a type of cheap suitcase made from carpet (p. 135)
carpetbagger nombre que les dieron los críticos sureños a los sureños que se aliaron con los republicanos norteños que fueron al sur a participar en el renacimiento politico y económico de la región; se decía que todas sus pertenencias les cabían en una *carpetbag*, un tipo de maleta (bag) barata hecha de alfombra (carpet), de ahí su nombre (pág. 135)

cash-and-carry (1939) law that changed the Neutrality Act to allow countries at war to purchase American goods as long as they paid cash and picked up their orders in American ports (p. 402)

pague y recoja (1939) ley que cambió la Ley de Neutralidad con el fin de permitirles a los países en guerra comprar productos estadounidenses siempre y cuando pagaran en efectivo y recogieran sus pedidos en puertos estadounidenses (pág. 402)

Central Powers alliance between Germany, Austria-Hungary and the Ottoman Empire (p. 232)
potencias centrales alianza entre Alemania, Austria-Hungría y el Imperio otomano (pág. 232)

checks and balances a system established by the Constitution that prevents any branch of government from becoming too powerful (p. 46)
equilibrio de poderes sistema establecido por la Constitución para evitar que ninguna rama del gobierno adquiera demasiada autoridad (pág. 46)

Chicano name adopted by Mexican Americans in the late 1960s to refer to a person of Mexican descent living in the U.S.; a shortened form of the word mexicano (p. 644)
Chicano nombre adoptado por los mexicano-americanos a fines de la década de 1960 para referirse a una persona de ascendencia mexicana que reside en Estados Unidos; es una forma corta de la palabra mexicano (pág. 644)

Chisholm Trail a trail that ran from San Antonio, Texas, to Abilene, Kansas, established by Jesse Chisholm in the late 1860s for cattle drives (p. 146)
camino de Chisholm camino desde San Antonio, Texas hasta Abilene, Kansas creado por Jesse Chisholm a finales de la década de 1860 para arrear ganado (pág. 146)

CIA Central Intelligence Agency; collects intelligence information and takes part in secret actions against foreign targets (p. 498)
CIA Agencia Central de Inteligencia; recoge información y participa en acciones secretas contra objetivos en el exterior del país (pág. 498)

CIO a group that broke away from the AFL to form the Committee for Industrial Organization; it later changed its name to Congress of Industrial Organizations (p. 360)
CIO grupo que se separó de la AFL para formar el Comité para la Organización Industrial; más tarde cambió de nombre a Congreso de Organizaciones Industriales (pág. 360)

civilian a nonmilitary person (p. 773)
civil persona no militar (pág. 773)

Civil Rights Act of 1866 law that gave African Americans legal rights equal to those of white Americans (p. 134)
Ley de Derechos Civiles de 1866 ley que les dio a los afroamericanos derechos legales similares a los de los estadounidenses blancos (pág. 134)

Civil Rights Act of 1964 act signed into law on July 2, 1964 that banned discrimination in employment and in public accommodations (p. 571)
Ley de Derechos Civiles de 1964 ley firmada el 2 de julio de 1964 que prohibió la discriminación en el empleo y en los establecimientos públicos (pág. 571)

Civil Rights Act of 1968 law that banned discrimination in the sale or rental of housing (p. 588)
Ley de Derechos Civiles de 1968 ley que prohibió la discriminación en la venta y alquiler de viviendas (pág. 588)

Clayton Antitrust Act (1914) law that prohibited companies from buying the stock of competing companies in order to form a monopoly, forbade companies from selling goods below cost with the goal of driving their competitors out of business and made strikes, boycotts, and peaceful picketing legal (p. 191)
Ley Antimonopolio Clayton (1914) ley que prohibió a las empresas comprar las acciones de empresas competidoras con el objeto de formar un monopolio, les prohibió a las empresas vender sus productos por debajo del costo con el fin de eliminar la competencia y legalizó las huelgas, los boicots, y los piquetes pacíficos (pág. 191)

code talker American Navajos who served in the Marines during World War II; they translated important military messages into a coded version of the Navajo language (p. 439)
codificador navajos estadounidenses de la tribu navajo que durante la Segunda Guerra Mundial prestaron servicio en los Marines; tradujeron importantes mensajes militares a una versión codificada del idioma navajo. (pág. 439)

Cold War an era of high tension and bitter rivalry known between the United States and the Soviet Union following the end of World War II (p. 465)
Guerra Fría era de grandes tensiones y gran rivalidad entre Estados Unidos y la Unión Soviética después de la Segunda Guerra Mundial (pág. 465)

Columbian Exchange the transfer of plants, animals, and diseases between the Americas and Europe, Asia, and Africa (p. 12)
intercambio colombino intercambio de plantas, animales y enfermedades entre las Américas y Europa, Asia y África (pág. 12)

combat fighting (p. 772)
combate batalla (pág. 772)

Committee on Public Information created by President Wilson and headed by journalist George Creel, this committee's objective was to maximize national loyalty and support for World War I (p. 251)
Comité de Información Pública creado por el presidente Wilson y encabezado por el periodista George Creel, su objetivo era aprovechar al máximo la lealtad y el apoyo de la nación durante la Primera Guerra Mundial (pág. 251)

Common Sense (1776) a pamphlet written by Thomas Paine that criticized monarchies and convinced many American colonists of the need to break away from Britain (p. 32)
Sentido común (1776) folleto escrito por Thomas Paine en el que criticaba a las monarquías con el fin de convencer a los colonos estadounidenses de la necesidad de independizarse de Gran Bretaña (pág. 32)

communism a system of government in which there is no private property and there are no economic classes (p. 271)
comunismo sistema de gobierno en el que no hay propiedad privada ni clases económicas (pág. 271)

Communists people who seek the equal distribution of wealth and the end of all private property (p. 242)
comunistas personas que buscan una distribución igualitaria de la riqueza y el fin de todo tipo de propiedad privada (pág. 242)

comparative advantage the theory that nations gain more by trading with each other than they lose (p. 807)
ventaja comparativa teoría que sostiene que las naciones ganan más de lo que pierden si comercian entre sí (pág. 807)

Compromise of 1850 Henry Clay's proposed agreement that allowed California to enter the Union as a free state and divided the rest of the Mexican Cession into two territories where slavery would be decided by popular sovereignty (p. 117)
Compromiso de 1850 acuerdo redactado por Henry Clay en que se permitía a California entrar en la Unión como estado libre y se proponía la división de la Cesión Mexicana en dos partes donde la esclavitud sería reglamentada por soberanía popular (pág. 117)

concentration camp a dentention site created for military or political purposes to confine, terrorize, and in some cases, kill civilians (p. 427)
campo de concentración lugar de detención creado con fines militares o políticos para recluir, atemorizar y, en algunos casos, asesinar a civiles (pág. 427)

Confederate States of America the nation formed by the southern states when they seceded from the Union; also known as the Confederacy (p. 122)
Estados Confederados de América nación formada por los estados del Sur cuando se separaron de la Unión; también conocidos como la Confederación (pág. 122)

conservation the careful use of resources (p. 781)
conservación uso prudente de los recursos (pág. 781)

containment policy that the United States adopted in the late 1940s to stop the spread of communism; it involved providing economic aid in order to strengthen countries against the Soviets (p. 467)
contención política adoptada por Estados Unidos a fines de la década de 1940 para detener la diseminación del comunismo; implicaba proporcionar ayuda económica para fortalecer a los países ante los soviéticos (pág. 467)

convoy system a military technique of transport in which ships were surrounded by destroyers or cruisers for protection (p. 242)
sistema de convoy técnica militar de transporte en el que los barcos viajaban rodeados de destructores o cruceros para protegerlos (pág. 242)

cooperative an organization that is owned and controlled by its members, who work together for a common goal (p. 337)
cooperativa organización que pertenece a sus miembros y es controlada por ellos; sus miembros trabajan en conjunto para lograr un objetivo común (pág. 337)

CORE Committee of Racial Equality; an organization dedicated to the practice of nonviolent protest (p. 558)
CORE Comité por la Igualdad Racial; organización dedicada a la práctica de protestas no violentas (pág. 558)

corps a military group (p. 773)
cuerpo grupo militar (pág. 773)

cost of living the amount of income required to buy basic necessities (p. 790)
costo de vida ingresos necesarios para comprar las necesidades básicas (pág. 790)

counterculture a rebellion of teens and young adults against mainstream American society in the 1960s (p. 651)
cultura alternativa rebelión de adolescentes y jóvenes adultos contra la corriente dominante de la sociedad estadounidense durante la década de 1960 (pág. 651)

credit a system of borrowing money from banks to make purchases, and then paying it back later with interest (p. 280)
crédito sistema de tomar prestado dinero de un banco para hacer compras, y luego pagarlo con intereses (pág. 280)

crime harmful or dangerous acts as defined by law (p. 794)
delitos actos dañinos o peligrosos según la ley (pág. 794)

criminal code code standard set of laws (p. 795)
código penal conjunto estandarizado de leyes (pág. 795)

Cuban missile crisis (1962) several days during which the United States teetered on the brink of nuclear war with the Soviet Union (p. 532)
crisis de los misiles de Cuba (1962) varios días durante los cuales Estados Unidos estuvo al borde de una guerra nuclear con la Unión Soviética (pág. 532)

cyberspace term used for the online world of the Internet (p. 802)
ciberespacio término que se usa para nombrar el mundo en línea de Internet (pág. 802)

Dawes Act (1887) legislation passed by Congress that split up Indian reservation lands among individual Indians and promised them citizenship (p. 144)
Ley de Adjudicación General de Dawes (1887) ley aprobada por el Congreso que dividía el terreno de las reservas indígenas entre los indígenas individuales y les prometía la ciudadanía (pág. 144)

D-day (1944) June 6, 1944, the first day of the Allied invasion of Normandy in World War II (p. 423)
Día D (1944) 6 de junio de 1944, primer día de la invasión de Normandía por parte de los Aliados en la Segunda Guerra Mundial (pág. 423)

de facto segregation segregation that exists through custom and practice rather than by law (p. 581)
segregación de facto segregación que existe por costumbre y práctica y no establecida por ley (pág. 581)

de jure segregation segregation by law (p. 581)
segregación de jure segregación establecida por ley (pág. 581)

de Lôme letter (1898) a letter written by Spain's minister to the United States that was published in a major newspaper; the letter ridiculed President McKinley and outraged many Americans (p. 208)
carta de Lôme (1898) carta escrita por el ministro español en Estados Unidos que se publicó en un periódico importante; en ella ridiculizaba al presidente McKinley e indignó a muchos estadounidenses (pág. 208)

Declaration of Independence Statement of the Second Continental Congress that formally announced the colonies break with Britain (p. 33)
Declaración de Independecia pronunciamiento del Segundo Congreso Continental que anunció formalmente la separación de las colonias de Gran Bretaña (pág. 33)

deficit when a government spends more money than it takes in (p. 364)
déficit cuando el gobierno gasta más dinero del que recauda (pág. 364)

Democratic-Republicans members of a political party founded in the 1790s by Thomas Jefferson, James Madison, and other leaders who wanted to preserve the power of the state governments and promote agriculture (p. 51)

demócratas-republicanos miembros de un partido politico fundado en la década de 1790 por Thomas Jefferson, James Madison y otros líderes que deseaban conservar el poder de los gobiernos estatales y promover la agricultura (pág. 51)

Department of Homeland Security U.S. government department created by the Bush administration after the attacks of September 11, 2001 to protect the U.S. from terrorist attacks (p. 744)
Departmento de Seguridad Nacional departamento del gobierno estadounidense creado por el gobierno de Bush luego de los atentados del 11 de septiembre de 2001 para proteger al país de los ataques terroristas (pág. 744)

deploy send (p. 772)
desplegar enviar (pág. 772)

deportation being sent back to one's country of origin (p. 272)
deportación ser devuelto al país de origen de uno (pág. 272)

détente efforts President Nixon took to lower Cold War tensions in the late 1960s and early 1970s (p. 668)
distensión campaña del presidente Nixon para reducir las tensiones de la Guerra Fría a finales de los años 60 y principios de los años 70 (pág. 668)

dictatorship government by a leader or group that holds unchallenged power and authority (p. 389)
dictadura forma de gobierno en la que el poder y la autoridad ilimitados se concentran en una persona o grupo (pág. 389)

Dien Bien Phu town in Vietnam that was the site of a battle between the French and the Vietminh in 1954; the French lost the battle and control of the country of Vietnam (p. 599)
Dien Bien Phu aldea en Vietnam donde los franceses y el Vietminh lucharon en 1954; los franceses perdieron la batalla y el control de Vietnam (pág. 599)

discretion the freedom to decide on an appropriate sentence for each individual within certain guidelines (p. 796)
discreción libertad de decidir la sentencia adecuada para cada persona dentro de ciertas relgas generales (pág. 796)

discrimination treatment based on race, class, or category rather than individual merit (p. 768)
discriminación trato que se basa en la raza, la clase o la categoría y no en el mérito individual (pág. 768)

disparity gap (p. 790)
disparidad distancia o brecha (pág. 790)

dividend a payment made by a company to its shareholders (p. 736)
dividendo cantidad que una compañía paga a sus accionistas (pág. 736)

ENGLISH AND SPANISH GLOSSARY

dollar diplomacy President Taft's policy of influencing Latin America through economic rather than military intervention (p. 217)
diplomacia del dólar política creada por el presidente Taft para influir en América Latina mediante la intervención económica en lugar de la militar (pág. 217)

domino theory President Eisenhower's idea that if Vietnam fell to communism, the other countries of Southeast Asia would fall to Communists (p. 598)
teoría del efecto dominó idea del presidente Eisenhower de que si Vietnam caía en manos comunistas, los demás países del sureste asiático también se harían comunistas (pág. 598)

dot-com company whose products or services are marketed on the Internet (p. 736)
punto coms empresas cuyos productos o servicios se comercializan en Internet (pág. 736)

doves people opposed to a war (p. 610)
palomas personas que se oponen a la guerra (pág. 610)

drought a period of very dry weather (p. 332)
sequía período de tiempo muy seco (pág. 332)

Dust Bowl a nickname for the Great Plains regions hit by drought and dust storms in the early 1930s (p. 332)
Tazón de Polvo apodo dado a las regiones de las Grandes Planicies azotadas por la sequía y las tormentas de polvo a principios de la década de 1930 (pág. 332)

Eighteenth Amendment (1919) a constitutional amendment that outlawed the production and sale of alcoholic beverages in the United States; repealed in 1933 (p. 180)
Decimoctava enmienda (1919) enmienda constitucional que prohibió la producción y venta de bebidas alcohólicas en Estados Unidos; revocada en 1933 (pág. 180)

Eisenhower Doctrine (1957) declared the right of the United States to help, on request, any nation in the Middle East trying to resist armed communist aggression (p. 501)
Doctrina de Eisenhower (1957) declaró el derecho de Estados Unidos de ayudar, cuando se lo solicitaran, a cualquier país del Medio Oriente en su resistencia contra la agresión armada de los comunistas (pág. 501)

electronic mail messages sent via computer; e-mail (p. 800)
correo electrónico mensajes enviados por computadora; e-mail (pág. 800)

Elkins Act (1903) law passed by Congress which prohibited railroads from accepting rebates from their best customers (p. 186)
Ley Elkins (1903) ley aprobada por el Congreso para prohibirles a los ferrocarriles recibir devoluciones de dinero de sus mejores clientes (pág. 186)

Ellis Island an island in New York harbor that was an entry point for 12 million immigrants to the United States between 1892 and 1954 (p. 157)
isla Ellis isla en el puerto de Nueva York que fue el punto de ingreso de 12 millones de inmigrantes a Estados Unidos entre 1892 y 1954 (pág. 157)

Emancipation Proclamation (1862) an order issued by President Abraham Lincoln freeing the slaves in areas rebelling against the Union; took effect January 1, 1863 (p. 127)
Proclamación de Emancipación (1862) decreto emitido por el presidente Abraham Lincoln para liberar a los esclavos en las regiones rebeladas contra la Unión; entró en vigor el 1 de enero de 1863 (pág. 127)

encomienda system a privilege given by Spain to Spanish settlers in the Americas which allowed them to control the lands and people of a certain territory (p. 15)
sistema de encomiendas privilegio otorgado por España a los pobladores españoles en las Américas; que les dio control de las tierras y las personas en ciertos territorios (pág. 15)

encryption technology that transforms data to make it indecipherable to an outside observer (p. 802)
codificación tecnología que transforma los datos de modo que sean imposibles de descifrar por un observador externo (pág. 802)

Enlightenment movement that began in Europe in the late 1600s as people began examining the natural world, society, and government; also called the Age of Reason (p. 23)
Ilustración movimiento que comenzó en Europa a fines del siglo XVII cuando la gente empezó a estudiar el mundo natural, la sociedad y el gobierno.; también se conoce como la Edad de la Razón (pág. 23)

enlist join (p. 773)
alistarse inscribirse (pág. 773)

Enola Gay nickname of the American plane that dropped the atomic bomb on the Japanese city of Hiroshima in World War II (p. 453)
Enola Gay nombre del avión desde el cual se lanzó la bomba atómica en la ciudad japonesa de Hiroshima durante la Segunda Guerra Mundial (pág. 453)

entrepreneur risk taker who starts new ventures within the economic system of capitalism (p. 151)
empresario persona que toma riesgos y emprende nuevas operaciones dentro del sistema económico del capitalismo (pág. 151)

Equal Rights Amendment (ERA) a proposed constitutional amendment barring discrimination on the basis of sex; although it was approved by Congress in 1972, not enough states ratified the amendment and it failed to become a law (p. 636)
Enmienda de Igualdad de Derechos (ERA, por sus siglas en inglés) enmienda constitucional propuesta que prohibía la discriminación basada en el sexo; aunque el Congreso la aprobó en 1972, no hubo suficientes estados que ratificaran la enmienda y no se convirtió en ley (pág. 636)

Establishment the social, economic, and political leaders of a nation who hold power and influence (p. 651)
clase dirigente líderes sociales, económicos y políticos de un país que tienen poder e influencia (pág. 651)

ethnicity country of origin (p. 768)
origen étnico país de origen (pág. 768)

evolution theory which holds that inherited characteristics of a population change over generations and that as a result of these changes, new species sometimes arise (p. 298)
evolución teoría que sostiene que las características heredadas de una población cambian de una generación a otra y que, como consecuencia de esos cambios, a veces surgen nuevas especies (pág. 298)

executive branch the division of the federal government that includes the president and the administrative departments; enforces the nation's laws (p. 47)
poder ejecutivo división del gobierno federal que incluye al presidente y a los departamentos administrativos; vigila el cumplimiento de las leyes de la nación (pág. 47)

executive privilege policy that a president must be free to keep his or her official conversations and meetings private (p. 678)
privilegio ejecutivo política que afirma que un presidente debe tener la libertad de mantener la confidencialidad de sus conversaciones y reuniones oficiales (pág. 678)

extinction complete disappearance of a species (p. 783)
extinción desaparición total de una especie (pág. 783)

Fair Deal plan proposed by President Truman that included a number of programs in the tradition of the New Deal; few of the Fair Deal ideas ever became law (p. 475)
Trato Justo plan propuesto por el presidente Truman, que incluyó una serie de programas en la tradición del New Deal; fueron pocos los conceptos del Fair Deal que terminaron siendo leyes (pág. 475)

fascism a system of government that focuses on the good of the state rather than on the individual citizens (p. 388)
fascismo sistema de gobierno que se concentra en el bienestar del estado en lugar del bienestar de los ciudadanos (pág. 388)

Federalists people who supported ratification of the Constitution (p. 48)
federalistas personas que apoyaban la ratificación de la Constitución (pág. 48)

Federal Reserve System the nation's central bank (p. 324)
Sistema de la Reserva Federal banco central del país (pág. 324)

Federal Reserve Act (1913) law that created a central fund from which banks could borrow to prevent collapse during a financial panic; it also placed the banking system under the supervision of the government for the first time (p. 191)
Ley de la Reserva Federal (1913) ley que creó un fondo central del cual los bancos tomarían prestados fondos para evitar el colapso durante un pánico económico; por primera vez en la historia, también puso al sistema (pág. 191)

feminism the principle that women and men should have equal social, political, and economic rights (p. 636)
feminismo principio según el cual las mujeres y los hombres deben gozar de igualdad de derechos sociales, políticos y económicos (pág. 636)

Fifteenth Amendment (1870) a constitutional amendment that gave African American men the right to vote (p. 135)
Decimoquinta enmienda (1870) enmienda constitucional que otorgó a los hombres afroamericanos el derecho al voto (pág. 135)

Final Solution Hitler's regime's plan to murder the entire Jewish population of Europe and the Soviet Union (p. 428)
Solución Final plan del régimen de Hitler de asesinar a toda la población judía de Europa y la Unión Soviética (pág. 428)

fireside chat conversational radio addresses given by Franklin D. Roosevelt (p. 348)
charlas informales discursos radiales a modo de conversación que daba Franklin D. Roosevelt (pág. 348)

flapper a young woman in the 1920s who wore her hair bobbed, wore makeup, dressed in flashy, skimpy clothes, and lived a life of independence and freedom (p. 296)
flapper jovencita que en la década de 1920 lucía el pelo con corte de paje, usaba maquillaje, se ponía ropa llamativa y escasa, y vivía una vida de independencia y libertad (pág. 296)

flexible response a response strategy to nuclear tensions that involved strengthening conventional U.S. forces so the nation would have options other than nuclear weapons in times of crisis (p. 534)
respuesta flexible estrategia de respuesta a las tensiones nucleares que implicó fortalecer las fuerzas convencionales de Estados Unidos para que el país contara con otras opciones además de las armas nucleares en cualquier época de crisis (pág. 534)

flower children a slang term for hippies who wore flowers in their hair (p. 653)
niños de las flores expresión popular para los hippies que llevaban flores en el cabello (pág. 653)

food insecurity the inability to buy enough healthy food (p. 790)
inseguridad alimenticia incapacidad de comprar una cantidad suficiente de alimentos saludables (pág. 790)

Foraker Act (1900) established that the United States would appoint the upper house of Puerto Rico's legislature, as well as its governor; the lower house of the legislature would be elected by Puerto Rican voters (p. 215)
Ley de Foraker (1900) estableció que Estados Unidos designaría a los miembros de la cámara alta de la asamblea legislativa, así como su gobernador; la cámara baja sería elegida por los votantes puertorriqueños (pág. 215)

foreclosure when a lender takes over ownership of a property from an owner who has failed to make loan payments (p. 330)
ejecución hipotecaria cuando el prestamista se apodera de una propiedad porque el propietario no ha pagado las cuotas del préstamo (pág. 330)

Fort Sumter (1861) the first battle of the Civil War; surrendered by the Union on April 14, 1861 (p. 123)
Fort Sumter (1861) primera batalla de la Guerra Civil, en la que la Unión presentó su rendición el 14 de abril de 1861 (pág. 123)

Fourteen Points President Woodrow Wilson's plan for organizing post-World War I Europe and for avoiding future wars (p. 255)
Catorce Puntos plan del presidente Woodrow Wilson para organizar Europa después de la Primera Guerra Mundial y para evitar futuras guerras (pág. 255)

Fourteenth Amendment (1866) a constitutional amendment giving full rights of citizenship to all people born or naturalized in the United States, except for American Indians (p. 134)
Decimocuarta enmienda (1866) enmienda constitucional que otorga derechos totales de ciudadanía a todas las personas nacidas en Estados Unidos o naturalizadas estadounidenses, con excepción de los indígenas norteamericanos (pág. 134)

Free Speech Movement counterculture movement during the 1960s in which students used the tactics of civil disobedience to protest injustices (p. 652)
Movimiento por la Libertad de Expresión movimientao en contra de la cultura dominante que tuvo lugar en la década de 1960 en el que los estudiantes usaban tácticas de desobediencia civil para protestar contra las injusticias (pág. 652)

Freedom Riders activists who challenged segregation in bus terminals in the South in 1961 (p. 566)
Pasajeros de la Libertad activistas que en 1961 desafiaron la segregación en las terminales de autobuses del Sur (pág. 566)

Freedom Summer a volunteer project in which college students spent their summer vacation in Mississippi, registering African Americans to vote (p. 575)
Verano de la Libertad proyecto de voluntarios en el que un grupo de estudiantes universitarios pasaron sus vacaciones de verano en el estado de Mississippi, inscribiendo a afroamericanos para votar (pág. 575)

French and Indian War war fought between France and England in the 1750s over territorial claims in North America (p. 25)
Guerra Francesa e India guerra entre Francia e Inglaterra en la década de 1750 causada por las tierras que ambos reclamaban en América del Norte (pág. 25)

Fugitive Slave Act (1850) a law that made it a crime to help runaway slaves; allowed for the arrest of escaped slaves in areas where slavery was illegal and required their return to slaveholders (p. 117)
Ley de Esclavos Fugitivos (1850) ley que hacía que ayudar a un esclavo a escapar de su amo fuera un delito, además de permitir la captura de esclavos fugitivos en zonas donde la esclavitud era ilegal para devolverlos a sus propietarios (pág. 117)

fundamentalism a belief in the literal interpretation of a particular religion's doctrine or holy books (p. 298)
fundamentalismo creencia en la interpretación literal de la doctrina o de los libros sagrados de una religión en particular (pág. 298)

General Agreement on Tariffs and Trade international organization that works to reduce tariffs and other barriers to trade (p. 476)
Acuerdo General sobre Aranceles y Comercio organización internacional que trabaja para reducir los aranceles y otras barreras para el comercio (pág. 476)

Geneva Conference (1954) international meeting in Geneva, Switzerland to restore peace in Indochina (p. 599)
Convención de Ginebra (1954) cumbre internacional celebrada en Ginebra, Suiza, para restablecer la paz en Indochina (pág. 599)

genocide the killing of an entire people (p. 428)

genocidio exterminio de un pueblo entero (pág. 428)

ghetto an area where people from a specific ethnic background live as a group (p. 428)
gueto lugar en el que vive una comunidad de personas de un origien étnico particular (pág. 428)

GI Bill (1944) act that helped veterans make a smooth entry into civilian life by providing money for attending college or advanced job training (p. 472)
Ley de Veteranos (1944) ley que facilitó la reintegración de los veteranos a la vida civil con ayudas económicas que les permitieron ir a la universidad u obtener formación profesional avanzada (pág. 472)

glasnost Russian word for "opening"; refers to a new era of media freedom in the Soviet Union under Mikhail Gorbachev (p. 708)
glasnost palabra rusa que significa "apertura"; se refiere a una nueva era de libertad en los medios en la Unión Soviética bajo Mikhail Gorbachev (pág. 708)

gold rush (1849) the mass migration of miners and business people to California after gold was discovered there (p. 107)
fiebre del oro (1849) migración masiva de mineros y hombres de negocios a California tras el descubrimiento de oro allí (pág. 107)

Great Awakening a religious movement that became widespread in the American colonies in the 1730s and 1740s (p. 24)
Gran Despertar movimiento religioso que tuvo gran popularidad en las colonias estadounidenses en las décadas de 1730 y 1740 (pág. 24)

Great Depression (1929–1930s) the most severe economic downturn in the history of the United States (p. 329)
Gran Depresión (de 1929 a la década de 1930) la crisis económica más grave de la historia de Estados Unidos (pág. 329)

Great Migration the major relocation of African Americans to northern cities from 1910 and into the 1920s (p. 303)
Gran Migración gran traslado de afroamericanos a las ciudades de Norte desde 1910 y hasta la década de 1920 (pág. 303)

Great Society the term for the domestic programs of the Johnson administration (p. 545)
Gran Sociedad término que se refiere a los programas de política interna del gobierno del presidente Johnson (pág. 545)

green card Permenant Resident Card (p. 768)
tarjeta verde tarjeta de residencia permanente (pág. 768)

gross national product the total value of all goods and services produced in the nation (p. 321)
producto interior bruto valor total de todos los bienes y servicios producidos en el país (pág. 321)

Harlem Renaissance a blossoming of African American art and literature that began in the 1920s (p. 304)
Renacimiento de Harlem florecimineto del arte y la literatura afroamericanos que comenzó en la década de 1920 (pág. 304)

hawks people who are supportive of a war's goals (p. 610)
halcones personas que apoyan los objetivos de una guerra (pág. 610)

Hepburn Act (1906) law that authorized the Interstate Commerce Commission to set maximum railroad rates and gave it the power to regulate other companies engaged in interstate commerce (p. 186)
Ley Hepburn (1906) ley que autorizó que la Comisión Interestatal de Comercio fijara precios máximos para el ferrocarril y le dio el poder para regular otras empresas que participaban en el comercio interestatal (pág. 186)

hobo a homeless person, typically one who is traveling in search of work; the term was used widely during the Great Depression (p. 328)
vagabundo persona sin hogar que por lo general viaja de un sitio a otro en busca de trabajo; el término se utilizó mucho durante la Gran Depresión (pág. 328)

Ho Chi Minh Trail a network of paths from North Vietnam to South Vietnam; North Vietnamese used the trail to send weapons, soldiers, and supplies to the Vietcong in South Vietnam (p. 605)
Ruta de Ho Chi Minh red de senderos que comunica Vietnam del Norte con Vietnam del Sur; los vietnamitas del Norte utilizaban el camino para enviar armas, soldados y suministros al Vietcong en Vietnam del Sur (pág. 605)

Hollywood Ten Hollywood writers and directors who were thought to be radicals and called before HUAC; they refused to cooperate and were sentenced to short prison terms (p. 479)
los diez de Hollywood escritores y directores de Hollywood considerados radicales y convocados por el HUAC; se negaron a cooperar y fueron condenados a penas de cárcel breves (pág. 479)

Holocaust the killing of millions of Jews and others by Nazis during World War II (p. 431)
Holocausto asesinato de millones de judíos y de otras personas por parte de los nazis durante la Segunda Guerra Mundial (pág. 431)

Homestead Act (1862) a law passed by Congress to encourage settlement in the West by giving government-owned land to small farmers (p. 146)
Ley de Heredad (1862) ley aprobada por el Congreso para fomentar la colonización del oeste del país mediante la cesión de tierras del gobierno a pequeños agricultores (pág. 146)

homicide the deliberate killing of another person (p. 796)

homicidio asesinato intencional de una persona (pág. 796)

Hoover Dam a dam built in the 1930s, with funding from the federal government, to control the Colorado River (p. 336)
Presa Hoover presa construida en la década de 1930, con financiación del gobierno federal, para controlar el río Colorado (pág. 336)

Hooverville makeshift shantytowns that sprung up during the Great Depression; named for President Hoover (p. 331)
Hooverville barriadas improvisadas que surgieron durante la Gran Depresión; llamadas así en alusión al presidente Hoover (pág. 331)

House of Burgesses America's first law-making body, formed in July 1619 by representatives from the different communities in Virginia (p. 17)
Cámara de Burgueses la primera cámara legislativa de Estados Unidos, formada en julio de 1619 por representantes de las distintas comunidades de Virginia (pág. 17)

House Un-American Activities Committee (HUAC) committee formed in the House of Representatives in the 1930s to investigate radical groups in the United States; it later came to focus on the threat of communism in the United States during World War II and the Cold War (p. 479)
Comité de Actividades Antiestadounidenses (HUAC, por sus siglas en inglés) comité formado en la Cámara de Representantes en la década de 1930 para investigar a los grupos radicales en Estados Unidos; más tarde se enforcó en la amenaza comunista en Estados Unidos durante la Segunda Guerra Mundial y la Guerra Fría (pág. 479)

Hundred Days (1933) the first hundred days of Franklin Roosevelt's term as president during which Roosevelt implemented many new programs (p. 350)
Cien Días (1933) los primeros cien días del gobierno de Franklin Roosevelt como presidente durante el cual Roosevelt puso en práctica muchos programas nuevos (pág. 350)

hydrogen bomb a nuclear weapon that gets its power from the fusing together of hydrogen atoms (p. 503)
bomba de hidrógeno un arma nuclear que obtiene su energía de la fusión de átomos de hidrógeno (pág. 503)

ICBM intercontinental ballistic missiles; guided missiles that could travel thousands of miles and strike targets accurately (p. 504)
MBIC misiles balísticos intercontinentales, misiles guiados que podían recorrer miles de millas y alcanzar objetivos con precisión (pág. 504)

immigrant a person who settles in a new country (p. 766)
inmigrante persona que se establece en un nuevo país (pág. 766)

imperialism the practice of extending a nation's power by gaining territories for a colonial empire (p. 201)
imperialismo práctica de ampliar el poder de una nación mediante la anexión de otros territorios para formar un imperio colonial (pág. 201)

Inchon a port city in western South Korea on the Yellow Sea; site of major battle in the Korean War (p. 486)
Inchon ciudad portuaria en el oeste de Corea del Sur a orillas del mar Amarillo; lugar de una importante batalla de la Guerra de Corea (pág. 486)

incumbent the person who currently holds a public office (p. 375)
titular persona que ocupa un puesto oficial actualmente (pág. 375)

indentured servants men and women whose employers pay for passage to the country they wish to emigrate to, food, and shelter; in return the indentured servants agree to work for the employer for a certain number of years, usually five or seven (p. 17)
sirvientes por contrato hombres y mujeres a los que sus empleadores les pagaban el pasaje al país al que deseaban emigrar, la comida y el alojamiento; a cambio, los sirvientes por contrato se comprometían a trabajar para el empleador durante un determinado número de años, normalmente cinco o siete (pág. 17)

Indian Removal Act (1830) a congressional act that authorized the removal of Native Americans who lived east of the Mississippi River (p. 95)
Ley de Expulsión de Indígenas (1830) ley redactada por el Congreso que autorizaba la expulsión de los indígenas norteamericanos que vivían al este del río Mississippi (pág. 95)

Industrial Revolution a period of rapid growth in the use of machines in manufacturing and production that began in the mid-1700s (p. 96)
Revolución Industrial período de rápido desarrollo debido al uso de maquinaria en la fabricación y producción que comenzó a mediados del siglo XVIII (pág. 96)

inflation increased prices for goods and services combined with the reduced value of money (p. 387)
inflación alza en los precios de los bienes y servicios al mismo tiempo que se produce una reducción en el valor del dinero (pág. 387)

infringe to interfere with (p. 796)
infringir interferir (pág. 796)

initiative a method of allowing voters to propose a new law on the ballot for public approval (p. 175)
iniciativa método que permite a los votantes proponer una nueva ley en la boleta electoral para la aprobación del público (pág. 175)

installment buying paying for an item over a period of time with a series of small payments (p. 280)
compra a plazos pagar por un artículo a lo largo de un período de tiempo mediante una serie de pequeños pagos (pág. 280)

integrated circuit a computer chip that includes a number of transistors and other electronic components (p. 512)
circuito integrado chip de computadora que contiene un número de transistores y de otros componentes electrónicos (pág. 512)

Intermediate-range Nuclear Forces (INF) Treaty a treaty between President Reagan and Mikhail Gorbachev that ordered the destruction of thousands of missiles (p. 703)
Tratado de Fuerzas Nucleares de Alcance Intermedio (FNAI) tratado firmado por el presidente Reagan y el primer ministro Mikhail Gorbachev que ordenó la destrucción de miles de misiles (pág. 703)

International Ladies' Garment Workers Union (ILGWU) a labor union that organized unskilled garment workers to strike for shorter work weeks and higher wages in 1909 (p. 174)
International Ladies' Garment Workers Union (ILGWU, por sus siglas en inglés) sindicato obrero que organizó a las trabajadoras no especializadas de la industria textil para que hicieran una huelga en 1909 con el fin de pedir semanas laborales más cortas y salarios más altos (pág. 174)

International Monetary Fund organization designed to encourage economic policies that promoted international trade (p. 476)
Fondo Monetario Internacional organización diseñada para fomentar políticas económicas que promueven el comercio internacional (pág. 476)

Internet a network of computers that connects many smaller networks around the world (p. 800)
Internet red de computadoras que conecta a muchas redes más pequeñas en todo el mundo (pág. 800)

internment the name for the forced relocation and confinement of Japanese-Americans to concentration camps (p. 445)
internamiento nombre dado al traslado forzoso y al confinamiento de los japoneses-americanos en campos de concentración (pág. 445)

Interstate Highway System a network of high-speed roads built to make interstate travel faster and easier (p. 515)
sistema de autopistas interestatales red de carreteras de alta velocidad construidas para facilitar y agilizar los viajes interestatales (pág. 515)

Iran-Contra affair secret U.S. sales of weapons to Iran in an attempt to secure the release of U.S. hostages held in Lebanon in 1986; part of the money paid went to divert Nicaraguan counterrevolutionaries who were in violation of a law banning such assistance (p. 706)
caso Irán-Contras venta secreta de armas de Estados Unidos a Irán para lograr la liberación de los rehenes estadounidenses detenidos en el Líbano en 1986; parte del dinero recibido fue desviado a las fuerzas contrarrevolucionarias nicaragüenses, en violación a una ley que prohíbe ese tipo de ayuda (pág. 706)

Iron Curtain term coined by Winston Churchill in 1946 to describe an imaginary line dividing Communist countries in the Soviet bloc from countries in Western Europe during the Cold War (p. 467)
cortina de hierro término creado por Winston Churchill en 1946 para describir la línea imaginaria que dividía a los países comunistas del bloque soviético de los países de Europa occidental durante la Guerra Fría (pág. 467)

isolationism a policy in which a nation avoids entanglement in foreign wars (p. 239)
aislacionismo política por la que una nación evita participar en guerras ajenas (pág. 239)

IT computerized information technology (p. 750)
TI tecnología de información computarizada (pág. 750)

Jamestown the first colony in America; set up in 1607 along the James River in Virginia (p. 16)
Jamestown primera colonia norteamericana; fundada en 1607 en las riberas del río James en Virginia (pág. 16)

jazz American music form that blends several different musical forms from the Deep South; often includes improvisation (p. 307)
jazz forma musical estadounidense que mezcla varias formas musicales del Sur y sureste del país; a menudo incluye la improvisación (pág. 307)

Jim Crow laws laws that enforced segregation in the southern states (p. 161)
leyes de Jim Crow leyes que impusieron la segregación racial en los estados sureños (pág. 161)

Job Corps program under President Johnson that offered work-training programs for unemployed youth. Volunteers in Service to America (VISTA) (p. 544)
Job Corps programa del presidente Johnson que ofrecía programas de formación laboral a los jóvenes desempleados. Voluntarios al Servicio de Estados Unidos (VISTA) (pág. 544)

Johnson Doctrine President Johnson's philosophy that revolutions in Latin America were not just local concerns when "the object is the establishment of a Communist dictatorship." (p. 548)
Doctrina Johnson filosofía del presidente Johnson según la cual las revoluciones en América Latina dejaban de ser un asunto de interés local cuando "el objetivo es el establecimiento de una dictadura comunista." (pág. 548)

judicial branch the division of the federal government that is made up of the national courts; interprets laws, punishes criminals, and settles disputes between states (p. 47)
poder judicial división del gobierno federal formada por las cortes nacionales; interpreta las leyes, castiga a los delincuentes y resuelve las disputas entre estados (pág. 47)

Judiciary Act of 1789 legislation passed by Congress that created the federal court system (p. 51)
Ley de Judicatura de 1789 ley aprobada por el Congreso para crear el sistema federal de tribunales (pág. 51)

kamikaze in World War II, a pilot who agreed to load his aircraft with bombs and crash it on an enemy ship (p. 439)
kamikaze en la Segunda Guerra Mundial, piloto que accedió a cargar su avión con bombas para estrellarse contra un barco enemigo (pág. 439)

Kansas-Nebraska Act (1854) a law that allowed voters in Kansas and Nebraska to choose whether to allow slavery (p. 117)
Ley de Kansas y Nebraska (1854) ley que permitió a los votantes de Kansas y Nebraska decidir si permitirían la esclavitud (pág. 117)

Kellogg-Briand Pact a treaty signed in 1928 that rejected war as a means to solving problems between countries (p. 287)
Pacto de Kellogg-Briand tratado firmado en 1928 que rechazó la guerra como un medio para solucionar los problemas entre países (pág. 287)

Kerner Commission committee appointed to study the causes of urban rioting after violence in Detroit in July 1967; it placed the blame on poverty and discrimination (p. 582)
Comisión Kerner comité nombrado para estudiar las causas de los disturbios urbanos ocurridos después de actos de violencia en Detroit en julio de 1967; hallaron que se debían a la pobreza y la discriminación (pág. 582)

Khmer Rouge Communists who took over Cambodia in 1975 (p. 625)

Khmer Rouge comunistas que invadieron Camboya en 1975 (pág. 625)

Know-Nothings a mid-1800s secret anti-Irish fraternal organization, so-called because its members, when asked about their group's activities, answered by saying, "I know nothing;" this group later became a political party called the American Party (p. 100)
Know-Nothings hermandad secreta antiirlandesa de mediados del siglo XIX, llamada así porque cuando le preguntaban a sus miembros acerca de las actividades del grupo respondían diciendo: "No sé nada" (I know nothing, en inglés); más tarde, el grupo se convirtió en un partido político llamado Partido Americano (pág. 100)

Kristallnacht (1938) a German word for broken glass; an event occurring on the nights of November 9 and 10 during which Hitler's Nazis encouraged Germans to riot against Jews, and nearly 100 Jews died (p. 427)
Kristallnacht (1938) palabra en alemán que significa vidrios rotos; acontecimiento que tuvo lugar las noches del 9 y 10 de noviembre durante que los nazis de Hitler animaron a los alemanes a participar en disturbios callejeros contra los judíos y murieron cerca de cien judíos (pág. 427)

Ku Klux Klan a secret society created by white southerners in 1866 that used terror and violence to keep African Americans from obtaining their civil rights (p. 133)
Ku Klux Klan sociedad secreta creada en 1866 por blancos del Sur que usaba el terror y la violencia para impedir que los afroamericanos obtuvieran derechos civiles (pág. 133)

La Raza Unida Party organization formed by José Angel Gutiérrez in the 1960s aimed at helping Mexican Americans by calling for bilingual education, improved public services, education for migrant children, more jobs for bilingual government employees, and an end to job discrimination (p. 646)
Partido La Raza Unida organización formada por José Ángel Gutiérrez en la década de 1960 con el motivo de ayudar a los mexicano americanos pidiendo la enseñanza bilingüe, mejoras en los servicios públicos, educación para los hijos de los trabajadores migratorios, más puestos para empleados del gobierno bilingües y el fin de la discriminación en el empleo (pag. 646)

laissez-faire in French, meaning "allow to do;" in business, it refers to a system where companies are allowed to conduct business without interference by the government (p. 151)

laissez-faire "dejar hacer" en francés, en el mundo de los negocios se refiere a un sistema en el que las compañías llevan a cabo sus actividades comerciales sin interferencia del gobierno (pag. 151)

League of Nations international body of nations formed in 1919 to prevent wars (p. 255)
Liga de las Naciones organización internacional de naciones formada en 1919 con el fin de evitar las guerras (pág. 255)

legislative branch the division of the government that proposes bills and passes them into laws (p. 47)
poder legislativo división del gobierno federal que propone proyectos de ley y los aprueba para convertirlos en leyes (pág. 47)

Lend-Lease Act (1940) program that gave the government power to make weapons available to Great Britain without regard for its ability to pay (p. 403)
Ley de Préstamo y Arriendo (1940) programa que le dio al gobierno la autoridad para poner armas a disposición de Gran Bretaña sin importar si podía pagarlas (pag. 403)

Levittown a New York town containing more than 17,000 mass-produced homes, which became a symbol for the many similar suburban towns built during the post World War II years (p. 514)
Levittown pueblo de Nueva York formado por más de 17,000 viviendas fabricadas en serie; se convirtió en el símbolo de muchos pueblos suburbanos similares que se construyeron tras la Segunda Guerra Mundial (pag. 514)

Liberal Republicans group of Republicans that broke with the Republican party over the Enforcement Acts scandals of the Grant administration (p. 137)
republicanos liberales grupo de republicanos que se separaron del partido republicano a raíz de los escándalos de las Leyes de Intervención del gobierno del presidente Grant (pag. 137)

Liberty bonds bonds that American citizens bought that helped to pay for the costs of World War I (p. 246)
bonos Liberty bonos que compraron los ciudadanos de Estados Unidos para ayudar a pagar los costos de la Primera Guerra Mundial (pág. 246)

Lincoln-Douglas debates a series of debates between Republican Abraham Lincoln and Democrat Stephen Douglas during the 1858 U.S. Senate campaign in Illinois (p. 120)
debates Lincoln-Douglas serie de debates entre el republicano Abraham Lincoln y el demócrata Stephen Douglas durante la campaña de 1858 para el Senado estadounidense en Illinois (pág. 120)

Little Rock Nine nine African American students who first integrated Central High School in Little Rock, Arkansas, in 1957 (p. 560)
los nueve de Little Rock primeros nueve estudiantes de raza negra en integrar Central High School en Little Rock, Arkansas, en el año 1957 (pág. 560)

loose constructionist a person who interprets the Constitution in a way that allows the federal government to take actions that the Constitution does not specifically forbid it from taking (p. 52)
intérprete flexible persona que interpreta que la Constitución permite al gobierno federal tomar acciones que la Constitución no prohíbe de manera específica (pág. 52)

Louisiana Purchase (1803) the purchase of French land between the Mississippi River and the Rocky Mountains that doubled the size of the United States (p. 55)
Compra de Luisiana (1803) compra del territorio francés localizado entre el río Mississippi y las montañas Rocosas, que duplicó el tamaño de Estados Unidos (pág. 55)

Luftwaffe German airforce (p. 397)
Luftwaffe fuerza aérea alemana (pág. 397)

Lusitania British ship sunk by a German U-Boat in 1915 (p. 238)
Lusitania barco británico hundido por un submarino alemán U-Boat en 1915 (pag. 238)

lynching the murder of an individual by a group or mob (p. 161)
linchamiento el asesinato de una persona por un grupo o una muchedumbre (pag. 161)

Maginot Line a string of bunkers and fortresses that lined the border between France and Germany during World War II (p. 396)
Línea Maginot cadena de bunkers y fortificaciones a lo largo de la frontera entre Francia y Alemania durante la Segunda Guerra Mundial (pág. 396)

Magna Carta (1215) a charter of liberties agreed to by King John of England; it made the king obey the same laws as citizens (p. 10)
Carta Magna (1215) carta de libertades aceptada por el rey Juan de Inglaterra que estableció que el rey debía obedecer las mismas leyes que el resto de los ciudadanos (pág. 10)

mandate authorization to act (p. 536)
mandato autorización para actuar (pág. 536)

mandatory required (p. 796)
obligatorio requerido (pág. 796)

Manhattan Project the top-secret program to build an atomic bomb during World War II (p. 410)
Proyecto Manhattan programa secreto para construir una bomba atómica durante la Segunda Guerra Mundial (pág. 410)

manifest destiny a belief shared by many Americans in the mid-1800s that the United States should expand across the continent to the Pacific Ocean (p. 107)

destino manifiesto creencia de muchos ciudadanos estadounidenses a mediados del siglo XIX de que Estados Unidos debía expandirse por todo el continente hasta llegar el océano Pacífico (pág. 107)

Marbury* v. *Madison Supreme Court case that established the principle of judicial review (p. 54)
Marbury* contra *Madison caso en que la Corte Suprema estableció el principio del recurso de inconstitucionalidad (pág. 54)

Marshall Plan (1947) plan for the reconstruction of Europe after World War II announced by the United States Secretary of State George C. Marshall (p. 468)
Plan Marshall (1947) plan para la reconstrucción de Europa después de la Segunda Guerra Mundial, anunciado por el secretario de estado estadounidense George C. Marshall (pág. 468)

massive retaliation the United States' willingness to use nuclear force to settle disputes; term was coined by John Foster Dulles and used during the Cold War (p. 498)
represalia masiva disposición de Estados Unidos a usar armas nucleares para resolver disputas; el término fue creado por John Foster Dulles y usado durante la Guerra Fría (pág. 498)

Maya a Mesoamerican Empire known for their writing system and number system (p. 7)
maya imperio mesoamericano conocido por sus sistemas de escritura y numérico (pág. 7)

Mayflower Compact (1620) a document written by the Pilgrims establishing themselves as a political society and setting guidelines for self-government (p. 17)
Pacto del Mayflower (1620) documento redactado por los peregrinos en el que se constituían enformaban una sociedad política y establecían los principios para gobernarse a sí mismos (pág. 17)

McCarthyism the name critics gave to Joseph McCarthy's tactic of spreading fear and making baseless charges (p. 482)
maccarthismo nombre que los críticos dieron a la táctica empleada por Joseph McCarthy de infundir miedo y hacer acusaciones sin fundamento (pág. 482)

McCulloch* v. *Maryland (1819) U.S. Supreme Court case that declared the Second Bank of the United States was constitutional and that Maryland could not interfere with it (p. 93)
McCulloch* contra *Maryland (1819) caso de la Corte Suprema que declaró que el Segundo Banco de Estados Unidos era constitucional y que Maryland no podía interferir con sus operaciones (pág. 93)

Meat Inspection Act (1906) law that required federal government inspection of meat shipped across state lines (p. 186)
Ley de Inspección de la Carne (1906) ley que exigió que el gobierno federal inspeccionara la carne que se enviaba de un estado a otro (pág. 186)

Medicaid a government program that provides free health care for poor people (p. 546)
Medicaid programa del gobierno que brinda atención médica gratuita a los pobres (pág. 546)

Medicare a health care program for people over age 65 (p. 546)
Medicare programa de atención médica para personas mayores de 65 años (pág. 546)

mercantilism economic system of trading nations used from about the 1500s to the 1700s; held that a nation's power was directly related to its wealth (p. 21)
mercantilismo sistema económico de las naciones comerciales usado entre los siglos XVI y XVIII aproximadamente; sostenía que el poder de una nación estaba directamente relacionado con su riqueza (pág. 21)

Mexican Revolution a revolution led by Francisco Madero in 1910 that eventually forced the Mexican dictator Porfirio Díaz to resign (p. 221)
Revolución Mexicana revolución encabezada por Francisco Madero en 1910. Al final obligó a renunciar al dictador mexicano Porfirio Díaz (pág. 221)

Mexican-American War (1846–1848) War fought between the United States and Mexico in which the United States gained more than 500,000 square miles of land in the United States, including New Mexico and California (p. 111)
Guerra mexicano-estadounidense (1846–1848) guerra librada entre Estados Unidos y México en la que Estados Unidos obtuvo más de 500,000 millas cuadradas de territorio para Estados Unidos, incluidos los territorios de Nuevo México y California (pág. 111)

Middle Ages period of European history, from the fall of the Roman Empire to the Renaissance, about a.d. 476–1450 (p. 10)
Edad Media período de la historia europea desde la caída del Imperio romano hasta el Renacimiento, aproximadamente 476–1450 d.C. (pág. 10)

Middle Passage a voyage that brought enslaved Africans across the Atlantic Ocean to North America and the West Indies (p. 22)
Paso Central viaje a través del océano Atlántico que trajo a los africanos esclavizados a América de Norte y las Antillas (pág. 22)

migrant person who moves from one place to another (p. 768)
emigrante persona que se muda de un lugar a otro (pág. 768)

militarism the expansion of arms and the policy of military preparedness (p. 231)
militarismo aumento de la cantidad de armas y política de preparación militar (pág. 231)

militia a military organization made up of civilians (p. 796)

militia/milicia   **national park/parque nacional**

milicia organización militar compuesta de civiles (pág. 796)

minimum wage the lowest wage an employer can legally pay a worker (p. 374, 790)

salario mínimo salario más bajo que un patrón puede pagar legalmente a un trabajador (pág. 374, 790)

missionary people sent by their church to teach and convert others to their religion (p. 15)

misionero persona enviada por su iglesia a enseñar y convertir a otras a su religión (pág. 15)

Mississippi Freedom Democratic Party a political party created in 1964, during the civil rights movement, with the purpose of winning seats at the 1964 Democratic National Convention (p. 576)

Partido Demócrata por la Libertad de Mississippi partido político creado en 1964 durante el movimiento por los derechos civiles con el fin de obtener puestos en la Convención Nacional Demócrata de 1964 (pág. 576)

Missouri Compromise (1820) an agreement proposed by Henry Clay that allowed Missouri to enter the Union as a slave state and Maine to enter as a free state and outlawed slavery in any territories or states north of 36°30´ latitude (p. 93)

Compromiso de Missouri (1820) acuerdo redactado por Henry Clay en el que se aceptaba a Misurí en la Unión como estado esclavista y a Maine como estado libre y prohibía la esclavitud en los territorios o estados ubicados al norte del paralelo 36°30´ (pág. 93)

Monroe Doctrine (1823) President James Monroe's statement forbidding further colonization in the Americas and declaring that any attempt by a foreign country to colonize would be considered an act of hostility (p. 92)

Doctrina Monroe (1823) declaración hecha por el presidente James Monroe en la que se prohibía la colonización adicional del continente americano a partir de entonces y en las que se declaró que cualquier intento de colonización por parte de otro país extranjero se consideraría un acto hostil (pág. 92)

Montgomery bus boycott (1955) a boycott of the Montgomery, Alabama bus system in response to the racial segregation of city buses (p. 562)

boicot de los autobuses de Montgomery (1955) boicot del sistema de autobuses de Montgomery, Alabama como reacción a la segregación racial en los autobuses de la ciudad (pág. 562)

muckrakers a term coined for journalists who "raked up" and exposed corruption and problems of society (p. 171)

difamadores término creado para nombrar a los periodistas que se dedicaban a investigar y exponer la corrupción y los problemas de la sociedad (pág. 171)

My Lai Massacre (1968) a massacre of hundreds of unarmed Vietnamese civilians by American soldiers during the Vietnam War (p. 623)

Masacre de My Lai (1968) matanza de cientos de civiles vietnamitas desarmados a manos de soldados estadounidenses durante la Guerra de Vietnam (pág. 623)

NASA National Aeronautics and Space Administration; agency in charge of the United States' programs for exploring outer space (p. 506)

NASA Administración Nacional de Aeronáutica y el Espacio; agencia encargada de los programas estadounidenses de exploración del espacio exterior (pág. 506)

National American Woman Suffrage Association (NAWSA) an organization founded by Elizabeth Cady Stanton and Susan B. Anthony in 1890 to obtain women's right to vote (p. 182)

Asociación Nacional Estadounidense para el Sufragio Femenino (NAWSA, por sus siglas en inglés) organización fundada en 1890 por Elizabeth Cady Stanton y Susan B. Anthony para obtener el derecho al voto de las mujeres (pág. 182)

National Association of Colored Women an organization founded in 1896 that worked to fight poverty, segregation, lynchings, and the persistence of Jim Crow laws that denied African Americans the right to vote; later it campaigned for temperance and women's suffrage; also helped form settlement houses, hospitals, and schools to serve African Americans (p. 180)

Asociación Nacional de Mujeres de Color organización fundada en 1896 para combatir la pobreza, la segregación, los linchamientos y las leyes de Jim Crow que negaban el derecho al voto a los negros; posteriormente hizo campaña en favor de la abstinencia del consumo de alcohol y el sufragio femenino; también ayudó a crear agencias de servicio a la comunidad, hospitales y escuelas para ayudar a los afroamericanos (pág. 180)

National Organization for Women (NOW) a women's rights group formed in 1966 that worked to fight discrimination against women in the workplace, schools, and justice system and worked to end violence against women and protect women's reproductive rights (p. 636)

Asociación Nacional de la Mujer (NOW, por sus siglas en inglés) grupo defensor de los derechos de la mujer creado en 1966 que luchaba para combatir la discriminación de las mujeres en el trabajo, en las escuelas y en el sistema judicial y trabajaba por acabar con la violencia en contra de las mujeres y proteger sus derechos reproductivos (pág. 636)

national park a natural area set aside by the federal government (p. 781)

parque nacional área natural protegida por el gobeirno federal (pág. 781)

National War Labor Board (1918) created by President Wilson, this board mediated disputes between workers and management and set policies that improved working conditions (p. 249)
Junta Nacional del Trabajo en Tiempos de Guerra (1918) creada por el presidente Wilson, esta junta mediaba en los conflictos entre trabajadores y patronos y establecía políticas que mejoraban las condiciones de trabajo (pág. 249)

nationalism a sense of pride and devotion to a nation, (p. 92); a belief that exalts one's own nation above all others
nacionalismo sentimiento de orgullo y lealtad hacia una nación (pág. 92)

NATO the North Atlantic Treaty Organization; an international defense alliance formed in 1949 (p. 470)
OTAN Organización del Tratado del Atlántico Norte; una alianza internacional de defensa formada en 1949 (pág. 470)

natural resources things found in nature that are useful to people (p. 781)
recursos naturales materiales que se encuentran en la naturaleza y son útiles para las personas (pág. 781)

Navigation Acts series of laws passed between 1651 and 1663 by Parliament, ensuring that the colonies would remain profitable for England; laws stated that all goods coming from Europe or Africa to the colonies had to travel on British ships manned with a British crew; all ships eventually were required to pass through England and their goods were subject to various taxes levied by the British government (p. 21)
Leyes de Navegación serie de leyes aprobadas entre 1651 y 1663 por el Parlamento para garantizar que las colonias siguieran produciendo ganacias para Inglaterra; las leyes afirmaban que todos los bienes provenientes de Europa o África con destino a las colonias tenían que viajar en barcos británicos comandados por una tripulación británica; al final, todos los barcos estaban obligados a pasar por Inglaterra y se aplicaban sobre los bienes varios impuestos recaudados por el gobierno británico (pág. 21)

neutral in a war, not aiding either side (p. 401)
neutral en una guerra, que no ayuda a ningún bando (pág. 401)

Neutrality Act (1935) a United States act aimed at helping prevent the nation from being drawn into a war (p. 400)
Ley de Neutralidad (1935) ley estadounidense creada para ayudar a impedir que la nación se viera involucrada en una guerra (pág. 400)

New Deal a plan by President Franklin Roosevelt intended to bring economic relief, recovery, and reforms to the country after the Great Depression (p. 350)
Nuevo Trato plan del presidente Franklin Roosevelt para traer ayuda, recuperación y reformas económicas al país después de la Gran Depresión (pág. 350)

New Freedom Woodrow Wilson's plan of reform which called for tariff reductions, banking reform, and stronger antitrust legislation (p. 191)
Nueva Libertad plan de reformas de Woodrow Wilson que abogaba por reducciones de los aranceles, reformas bancarias y leyes antimonopolio más estrictas (pág. 191)

New Frontier the nickname given to President Kennedy's plans for changing the nation (p. 536)
Nueva Frontera apodo dado a los planes del presidente Kennedy para transformar la nación (pág. 536)

Newlands Reclamation Act (1902) law that allowed the federal government to build irrigation projects to make marginal lands productive (p. 187)
Ley de Reclamación de Nuevas Tierras (1902) ley que permitía al gobierno federal llevar a cabo proyectos de irrigación para hacer productivas las tierras de poco rendimiento (pág. 187)

New Right a coalition of conservative media commentators, think tanks, and grassroots Christian groups; many supported Ronald Reagan (p. 697)
Nueva Derecha coalición de analistas conservadores de los medios de comunicación, grupos de asesoría estretégica y organizaciones cristianas de base popular; muchos apoyaron a Ronald Reagan (pág. 697)

9/11 terrorist attacks on the World Trade Center in New York City and the Pentagon in Washington, D.C. that took place on September 11, 2001 (p. 741)
11-S ataques terroristas contra el World Trade Center en la ciudad de Nueva York y el Pentágono en Washington, D.C., que tuvieron lugar el 11 de septiembre de 2001 (pág. 741)

Nineteenth Amendment (1920) a constitutional amendment that gave women the vote (p. 192)
Decimonovena enmienda (1920) enmienda constitucional que otorgó a la mujer el derecho al voto (pág. 192)

North American Free Trade Agreement (NAFTA) (1993) an agreement in which the United States, Mexico, and Canada became one large free-trade zone, meaning that most products could be sold across borders without any sort of tariffs or trade barriers (p. 730, 808)
Tratado de Libre Comercio de América del Norte (TLCAN) (1993) acuerdo según el cual Estados Unidos, México y Canadá se convirtieron en una gran zona de libre comercio, lo que significa que gran parte de los productos pueden cruzar las fronteras sin ningún tipo de arancel ni barrera comercial (pág. 730, 808)

nuclear fallout harmful particles of radioactive material produced by nuclear explosions (p. 506)
lluvia radiactiva partículas dañinas de material radiactivo producido por una explosión nuclear (pág. 506)

occupy to take control of a place by placing troops in it (p. 450)
ocupar tomar el control de un lugar colocando tropas allí (pág. 450)

offender a convicted criminal (p. 795)
delincuente persona que ha sido condenada por un delito (pág. 795)

Okie nickname for a farmer who left the Dust Bowl in search of work; many of these farmers were from Oklahoma (p. 333)
Okie apodo dado a los granjeros que se fueron del Tazón del Polvo en busca de trabajo; muchos de estos granjeros eran de Oklahoma (pág. 333)

OPEC the Organization of Petroleum Exporting Countries; organization that coordinates petroleum policies of major producing countries (p. 670)
OPEP Organización de Países Exportadores de Petróleo; organización que coordina las políticas petroleras de los principales países productores (pág. 670)

Open Door policy a policy established by the United States in 1899 to promote equal access for all nations to trade in China (p. 204)
política de puertas abiertas política establecida por Estados Unidos en 1899 para promover el acceso igualtitario a todas las naciones al comercio con China (pág. 204)

Operation Desert Storm U.S.-led war to end Iraq's occupation of Kuwait in 1990/1991 (p. 713)
Operación Tormenta del Desierto Guerra guerra dirigida por Estados Unidos para ponerle fin a la ocupación de Kuwait por parte de Irak entre 1990 y 1991 (pág. 713)

Operation Overlord (1944) the codename for the Allied invasion of mainland Europe in World War II, starting with D-Day's landings (p. 423)
Operación Overlord (1944) nombre en clave de la invasión de Europa continental por parte de los Aliados en la Segunda Guerra Mundial; empezó con los desembarques del Día D (pág. 423)

Operation Rolling Thunder a U.S. bombing campaign in North Vietnam in March, 1965 (p. 604)
Operación Trueno Galopante ofensiva de bombardeos estadounidenses en Vietnam del Norte en marzo de 1965 (pág. 604)

Operation Torch (1942) the codename for the Allied invasion of North Africa during World War II (p. 421)
Operación Antorcha (1942) nombre en clave de la invasión del norte de África por parte de los Aliados durante la Segunda Guerra Mundial (p. 421)

Oregon Treaty a treaty between Great Britain and the United States which set the boundary between the United States and British Canada at the forty-ninth parallel (p. 108)
Tratado de Oregón tratado entre Gran Bretaña y Estados Unidos que estableció la frontera entre Estados Unidos y el Canadá británico en el paralelo 49° (pág. 108)

outsourcing the practice of using workers from outside a company (p. 806)
subcontratación práctica de usar trabajadores que no forman parte de la compañía (pág. 806)

pacification a program in the Vietnam War in which U.S troops would move South Vietnamese from their villages and burn the villages down so the Vietcong could not use them (p. 606)
pacificación programa durante la Guerra de Vietnam por el que las tropas de Estados Unidos sacaban a los vietnamitas del sur de sus aldeas y las incendiaban para que el Vietcong no las pudiera utilizar (pág. 606)

pacifist a person who does not believe in the use of military force (p. 400)
pacifista persona que no cree en el uso de la fuerza militar (pág. 400)

packet switching the ability of a computer to send messages in smaller packages, allowing the packets to travel seperately along the fastest routes to the receiving computer, which reassembles the message (p. 801)
conmutación de paquetes capacidad de una computadora de enviar mensajes en paquetes más pequeños, permitiendo así que los paquetes viajen por separado por las rutas más rápidas hasta la computadora de destino, donde se vuelve a armar el mensaje (pág. 801)

Palmer Raids (1918) a series of government attacks on suspected radicals in the United States led by the U.S. attorney general, A. Mitchell Palmer (p. 272)
redadas de Palmer (1918) serie de ataques del gobierno sobre supuestos radicales de Estados Unidos dirigidos por el secretario de justica de Estados Unidos, A. Mitchell Palmer (pág. 272)

Panmunjom town in the demilitarized zone between North and South Korea where peace talks took place following the Korean War (p. 841)

Panmunjom pueblo ubicado en la zona desmilitarizada entre Corea del Norte y Corea del Sur, donde se llevaron a cabo las negociaciones para firmar un tratado de paz después de la Guerra de Corea

Peace Corps a program that trains and sends volunteers to poor nations all over the world to serve as educators, health care workers, agricultural advisers, and in other jobs (p. 534)
Cuerpo de Paz programa que entrena y envía voluntarios a países pobres de todo el mundo para trabajar como educadores, trabajadores de la salud, consejeros agrícolas y otros trabajos (pág. 534)

Pentagon Papers papers were part of a government study on the war in Vietnam; revealed that government officials had been misleading the American people about the progress of the war for many years (p. 623)
Papeles del Pentágono documentos que formaron parte de un estudio del gobierno sobre la guerra de Vietnam; revelaron que los funcionarios del gobierno engañaron al pueblo durante muchos años con respecto al progreso de la guerra (pág. 623)

perestroika Russian word for "restructuring"; refers to the restructuring of the corrupt government bureaucracy in the Soviet Union under Mikhail Gorbachev (p. 708)
perestroika palabra rusa que significa "reestructuración;" se refiere a la reestructuración bajo Mikhail Gorbachev de la burocracia gubernamental corrupta de la Unión Soviética (pág. 708)

plantation a large farm that usually specialized in growing one kind of crop for profit (p. 22)
plantación granja de gran tamaño que por lo general se especializa en un solo cultivo específico con el fin de obtener ganancias (pág. 22)

Platt Amendment a part of the Cuban constitution drafted under the supervision of the United States that limited Cuba's right to make treaties, gave the U.S. the right to intervene in Cuban affairs, and required Cuba to sell or lease land to the U.S. (p. 214)
Enmienda Platt parte de la constitución cubana redactada bajo la supervisión de Estados Unidos que limitaba el derecho de Cuba a firmar tratados, otorgaba a Estados Unidos el derecho a intervenir en los asuntos cubanos y exigía a Cuba vender o arrendar tierras a Estados Unidos (pág. 214)

police action phrase used to describe the US intervention in Korea in 1950; the United States never officially declared war (p. 485)
acción policial frase que describe la intervención de Estados Unidos en Corea en 1950. Estados Unidos nunca declaró la guerra oficialmente (pág. 485)

political asylum protection for immigrants for humanitarian reasons (p. 768)
asilo político protección dada a immigrantes por motivos humanitarios (pág. 768)

Poor People's Campaign an expansion of the civil rights movement that tried to raise awareness about poverty among people of all races (p. 587)
Campaña por los Pobres ampliación del movimiento de los derechos civiles que intentaba crear una mayor conciencia sobre la pobreza entre las personas de todas las razas (pág. 587)

pop art a style of art in the 1950s and 1960s that intended to appeal to popular tastes (p. 655)
arte pop estilo artístico de las décadas de 1950 y 1960 que pretendía atraer los gustos populares (pág. 655)

popular sovereignty the idea that political authority belongs to the people (p. 117)
soberanía popular idea de que la autoridad política pertenece al pueblo (pág. 117)

Populist Party a political party formed in 1892 that supported free coinage of silver, work reforms, immigration restrictions, and government ownership of railroads and telegraph and telephone systems (p. 160)
Partido Populista partido político formado en 1892 que apoyaba la libre producción de monedas de plata, reformas laborales y restricciones inmigratorias, además de apoyar que el gobierno fuera dueño de los sistemas ferroviario, telegráfico y telefónico (pág. 160)

Potsdam Conference (1945) meeting among leaders of the Allies near the end of World War II (p. 455)
Conferencia de Potsdam (1945) encuentro de los líderes aliados celebrado un poco antes del final de la Segundo Guerra Mundial (pág. 455)

poverty the condition of having insufficient income or resources to acquire basic needs (p. 788)
pobreza estado en el que no se tienen suficientes ingresos o recursos para comprar las necesidades básicas (pág. 788)

poverty threshold a line that statistically measures the number of people living in poverty (p. 790)
umbral de pobreza línea que mide estadísticamente la cantidad de personas que viven en la pobreza (pág. 790)

prisoner of war captured enemy troops (p. 774)
prisionero de guerra soldado capturado por tropas enemigas (pág. 774)

Proclamation of 1763 law created by British officials that prohibited colonists from settling in areas west of the Appalachian Mountains (p. 26)
Proclamación de 1763 ley creada por los funcionarios británicos que prohibía a los colonos asentarse al oeste de los montes Apalaches (pág. 26)

productivity the amount of product made by a worker or machine (p. 279)
productividad la cantidad de un producto fabricada por un trabajador o una máquina (pág. 279)

progressivism group of reform movements of the late 1800s that focused on urban problems, such as the plight of workers, poor sanitation, and corrupt political machines (p. 171)
progresivismo grupo de movimientos reformistas de finales del siglo XIX que se concentraba en los problemas urbanos, como las dificultades de los trabajadores, los malos servicios sanitarios y las maquinarias políticas corruptas (pág. 171)

Prohibition a ban on alcohol that became law in 1920; the ban was lifted in 1933 (p. 179)
Prohibición suspensión de la venta de bebidas alcohólicas que se convirtió en ley en 1920; se eliminó en 1933 (pág. 179)

propaganda information designed to influence public opinion (p. 251)
propaganda información diseñada para influir en la opinión pública (pág. 251)

protectionism restrictions on foreign producers to protect domestic products (p. 807)
proteccionismo restricciónes en productores extranjeros para protejer productos domesticos (pág. 807)

protectorate a country that is controlled by an outside government (p. 214)
protectorado país controlado por un gobierno externo (pág. 214)

protocol formats for sending data from one computer to another (p. 801)
protocolo formatos utilizados para enviar datos de una computadora a otra (pág. 801)

public lands federal lands that were never sold or made into protected areas such as national parks (p. 783)
tierras públicas tierras federales que nunca se vendieron ni se convirtieron en áreas protegidas como los parques nacionales (pág. 783)

public works government-funded building projects that provide jobs (p. 347)
obras públicas proyectos de construcción financiados por el gobierno que crean empleos (pág. 347)

***Pueblo* incident** North Korean capture of the *Pueblo*, a Navy spy ship, off the coast of communist North Korea (p. 548)
incidente del *Pueblo* captura por parte de Corea del Norte del *Pueblo*, un barco espía de la armada, cerca de la costa de Corea del Norte, un país comunista (pág. 548)

Pure Food and Drug Act (1906) law that forbade the manufacture, sale, or transportation of food and patent medicine containing harmful ingredients, and required that containers of food and medicines carry ingredient labels (p. 186)

Ley de Alimentos y Drogas Puros (1906) ley que prohibió la fabricación, venta o transporte de alimentos y de medicamentos patentados con ingredientes dañinos y que requirió que los envases de los alimentos y los medicamentos llevaran etiquetas con los ingredientes (pág. 186)

Puritans A group of English Protestants who wanted to "purify" the English Church of England through reforms; they established the Massachusetts Bay Colony and other colonies in New England in the early and mid 1600s (p. 17)
puritanos grupo de protestantes ingleses que querían "purificar" la Iglesia de Inglaterra con reformas; establecieron la Colonia de la Bahía de Massachusetts y otras colonias en Nueva Inglaterra a principios y mediados del siglo XVII (p.17)

Quarantine Speech (1937) Franklin D. Roosevelt's speech following the Japanese attack on China in which he called on America to take clear sides in the current world conflicts (p. 402)
Discurso de la Cuarentena (1937) discurso pronunciado por Franklin D. Roosevelt después del ataque japonés a China, en el que instó a los estadounidenses a tomar una posición clara en los conflictos mundiales del momento (pág. 402)

quota limit on the number of people who can enter the United States from each foreign country (p. 768)
cuota límite a la cantidad de personas que pueden entrar a Estados Unidos de cada país extranjero (pág. 768)

ratification an official approval (p. 48)
ratificación aprobación formal (pág. 48)

rationing limiting the amount of a certain product each individual can get (p. 442)
racionamiento limitación en la cantidad de un producto que puede obtener cada persona (pág. 442)

realpolitik basing foreign policies on realistic views of national interest rather than on broad rules or principles (p. 668)
realpolitik basar la política exterior en perspectivas realistas de los intereses nacionales, en lugar de basarla en reglas o principios generales amplios (pág. 668)

recall a vote to remove an official from office (p. 175)
destitución votación para retirar a un funcionario de su cargo (pág. 175)

Reconstruction (1867-68) the laws that put the southern states under U.S. military control and required them to draft new constitutions upholding the Fourteenth Amendment (p. 133)
Reconstrucción (1867-68) leyes que colocaron a los estados del Sur bajo el control militar estadounidense y los obligaron a reformar sus constituciones, de manera que defendieran la Decimocuarta enmienda (pág. 133)

Reconstruction Finance Corporation a program that provided $2 billion in direct government aid to struggling banks and other institutions during the Great Depression (p. 338)
Corporación Financiera de la Reconstrucción programa que proporcionó $2,000 millones en ayuda gubernamental directa a los bancos y demás instituciones que se encontraban en dificultades durante la Gran Depresión (pág. 338)

Red Scare widespread fear of communism (p. 272)
terror rojo temor generalizado al comunismo (pág. 272)

referendum a procedure that allows voters to approve or reject a law already proposed or passed by government (p. 175)
referéndum medida que permite a los ciudadanos votar para aprobar o rechazar una ley previamente propuesta o aprobada por el gobierno (pág. 175)

Reformation a religious crisis within the Catholic Church in the 1500s, led by those seeking reforms with the Church; led to the establishment of the Protestant Church (p. 11)
Reforma crisis religiosa dentro de la Iglesia católica en el siglo XVI, encabezada por aquellos que buscaban cambios en la Iglesia. Condujo al establecimiento de la Iglesia protestante (pág. 11)

refugee person seeking protection from religious or political persecution (p. 766)
refugiado persona que busca protección de la persecución (pág. 766)

rehabilitation reforming offenders into contributing members of society (p. 796)
rehabilitación reforma de los delicuentes para que pasen a ser miembros útiles de la sociedad (pág. 796)

Renaissance a new era of learning and creativity that began in Italy in the 1300s and spread throughout Europe (p. 10)
Renacimiento nueva era de aprendizaje y creatividad que empezó en Italia en el siglo XIV y se extendió por el resto de Europa (pág. 10)

reparation payments designed to make up for the damage of something (p. 256, 286)
indemnización pagos designados para compensar el daño causado por algo (pág. 256, 286)

Roanoke site of England's first attempt to establish a permanent colony in the Americas in the late 1500s; the colony and its inhabitants vanished and its fate is unknown (p. 16)
Roanoke sitio donde los primeros colonos ingleses trataron de establecer una colonia permanente en las Américas a fines del siglo XVI; tanto la colonia como sus habitantes desaparecieron y no se sabe lo que les pasó (pág. 16)

Roe* v. *Wade (1973) Supreme Court decision that made abortion legal in the United States (p. 637)
Roe* contra *Wade (1973) decision de la Corte Suprema que legalize aborto en Estados Unidos (pág. 637)

Roosevelt Corollary a change to the Monroe Doctrine, saying that the U.S. could intervene in the internal affairs of Latin American nations (p. 217)
Corolario de Roosevelt cambio en la Doctrina Monroe, en la que se declaraba que Estados Unidos podía intervenir en los asuntos internos de los países latinoamericanos (pág. 217)

Rosie the Riveter a popular symbol for the working woman during World War II (p. 409)
Rosie la Remachadora símbolo popular de la mujer trabajadora durante la Segunda Guerra Mundial (pág. 409)

Rough Riders a cavalry regiment organized by Theodore Roosevelt; consisted of college athletes, cowboys, ranchers, miners, and Native Americans (p. 210)
Jinetes Rudos regimiento de caballería organizado por Theodore Roosevelt y formado por deportistas universitarios, vaqueros, rancheros, mineros e indígenas norteamericanos(pág. 210)

Russo-Japanese War (1904–1905) war between Russia and Japan over Manchuria (p. 205)
Guerra Ruso-Japonesa (1904–1905) guerra por Manchuria entre Rusia y Japón (pág. 205)

SALT I discussions between the United States and the Soviets to slow the ongoing arms race in the late 1960s and early 1970s (p. 669)
SALT I conversaciones entre Estados Unidos y la Unión Soviética para frenar la carrera armamentística a finales de la década de 1960 y comienzos de la década de 1970 (pág. 669)

SALT II discussions in 1979 between the United States and the Soviets that began as SALT I in the late 1960s; SALT II set limits on certain kinds of nuclear weapons (p. 684)
SALT II conversaciones entre Estados Unidos y la Unión Soviética, en 1979 que comenzaron con SALT I a finales de la década de 1960; SALT II fijó límites sobre ciertos tipos de armas nucleares (pág. 684)

salutary neglect a term coined by British statesman Edmund Burke regarding the English colonies; idea that the colonies benefited by being left alone, without too much British interference (p. 21)

abandono saludable término creado por el estadista británico Edmund Burke con respecto a las colonias inglesas; sostenía que las colonias se beneficiaban si se les daba más libertad, sin demasiada interferencia británica (pág. 21)

Sand Creek Massacre (1864) U.S. Army's killing of about 150 Cheyenne elderly, women, and children at Sand Creek Reservation in Colorado Territory (p.143)
Masacre de Sand Creek (1864) matanza por parte del ejército de Estados Unidos de unos 150 ancianos, mujeres y niños cheyenes en la reserva de Sand Creek en el territorio de Colorado (pág.143)

satellite an object that orbits around a planet (p. 506)
satélite objeto que gira alrededor de un planeta (pág. 506)

Saturday night massacre part of the Watergate Scandal in which Nixon ordered his attorney general to fire special prosecutor Archibald Cox; resulted in the resignation of the Attorney General and his assistant when they both refused (p. 678)
masacre del sábado en la noche parte del escándalo Watergate en la que Nixon ordenó a su secretario de justicia que despidiera al fiscal especial Archibald Cox; provocó la renuncia del secretario de justicia y de su asistente cuando ambos se negaron (pág. 678)

savings and loan crisis a financial disaster in which the federal government had to step in and pay back loans for many S & L institutions (p. 716)
crisis de ahorro y préstamo catástrofe financiera en la que el gobierno federal se vio obligado a intervenir y pagar los préstamos de muchas instituciones de ahorro y préstamo (pág. 716)

scalawag meaning scoundrel; name given by former Confederates to those southerners who supported the shift in power to Congress and the army in the South during Reconstruction (p. 135)
scalawag significa bribón, sinvergüenza; nombre dado por los antiguos confederados a los habitantes del Sur que apoyaron el cambio del poder al Congreso y al ejército en el Sur durante la Reconstrucción (pág.135)

Schenck* v. *United States (1917) an important court case that explained the limits of the First Amendment (p. 252)
Schenck* contra *Estados Unidos (1917) jucio importante en el que se explicaron los límites de la Primera enmienda (pág. 252)

SCLC Southern Christian Leadership Conference; a group formed in Georgia in 1957 to organize civil rights protest activities (p. 563)
SCLC Conferencia de Liderazgo Cristiano del Sur; grupo formado en Georgia en 1957 para organizar las actividades de protesta en favor de los derechos civiles (pág. 563)

SEATO Southeast Asia Treaty Organization; group of nations that agreed to work together to resist Communist aggression (p. 500)
SEATO Organización del Tratado del Sureste Asiático; grupo de naciones que se comprometieron a trabajar juntas para resistir la agresión comunista (pág. 500)

Second Amendment Constitutional amendment granting Americans the right to bear arms (p. 796)
Segunda enmienda enmienda constitucional que garantiza a los estadounidenses el derecho a portar armas (pág. 796)

Second Bank of the United States a national bank created by Congress in 1816 and overseen by the federal government, its purpose was to regulate state banks (p. 95)
Segundo Banco de Estados Unidos banco nacional creado por el Congreso en 1816 y supervisado por el gobierno federal con la función de reglamentar los bancos estatales (pág. 95)

Second Great Awakening a period of religious evangelism that began in the 1790s and became widespread in the United States by the 1830s (p. 100)
Segundo Gran Despertar período de evangelización religiosa iniciado en la década de 1790 que se extendió por Estados Unidos para la década de 1830 (pág.100)

Second New Deal (1935) a new set of programs in the spring of 1935 including additional banking reforms, new tax laws, new relief programs; also known as the Second Hundred Days (p. 358)
Segundo Nuevo Trato (1935) nuevo conjunto de programas de la primavera de 1935 que incluyó reformas bancarias, nuevas leyes sobre impuestos y nuevos programas de ayuda social; también se conoce como los Segundos Cien Días (pág. 358)

sectionalism a devotion to the interests of one geographic region over the interests of the country as a whole (p. 93)
regionalismo dedicación a los intereses de una región geográfica por encima de los del país (pág. 93)

Selective Service Act (1921) act which required men between the ages of 21 and 30 to register to be drafted into the armed forces (p. 241)
Ley del Servicio Militar Selectivo (1921) ley que exigía que los hombres entre los 21 y los 30 años se inscribieran para ser reclutados por las fuerzas armadas (pág. 241)

self-determination the right of people to decide their own political status (p. 255)
autodeterminación derecho de las personas a decidir su propia situación política (pág. 255)

Seneca Falls Convention (1848) the first national women's rights convention at which the Declaration of Sentiments was written (p. 102)
Convención de Seneca Falls (1848) primera convención nacional a favor de los derechos de la mujer, en la cual se redactó la Declaración de Sentimientos (pág. 102)

settlement house neighborhood center staffed by professionals and volunteers for education, recreation, and social activities in poor areas (p. 159)
organización de servicio a la comunidad centro comunitario en el que trabajan profesionales y voluntarios que promueven la educación, la recreación y las actividades sociales en las zonas pobres (pág. 159)

Seventeenth Amendment (1913) a constitutional amendment allowing American voters to directly elect U.S. senators (p. 175)
Decimoséptima enmienda (1913) enmienda constitucional que permite a los votantes estadounidenses elegir directamente a los senadores de Estados Unidos (pág. 175)

sharecropping a system used on southern farms after the Civil War in which farmers worked land owned by someone else in return for a small portion of the crops (p. 136)
cultivo de aparceros sistema usado en las granjas del sur después de la Guerra Civil en el cual los agricultores labraban las tierras de otra persona a cambio de una pequeña porción de la cosecha (pág. 136)

Sherman Antitrust Act (1890) a law that made it illegal to create monopolies or trusts that restrained free trade (p. 152)
Ley Antimonopolio de Sherman (1890) ley que prohibió la creación de monopolios o consorcios que restringieran el libre comercio (pág. 152)

shuttle diplomacy negotiation style in which a mediator shuttles between groups, trying to work out agreements to end a disagreement (p. 671)
diplomacia de idas y venidas estilo de negociación en la que el mediador va y viene entre distintos grupos para intentar alcanzar acuerdos que pongan fin a un desacuerdo (pág. 671)

silent majority phrase used by President Nixon to describe people who supported the government's Vietnam policies but did not express their opinions publicly (p. 621)
mayoría silenciosa frase utilizada por el presidente Nixon para describir a las personas que apoyaban la política del gobierno en Vietnam pero no expresaban su opinión en público (pág. 621)

sit-down strike a strike in which workers refuse to work or leave the workplace until a settlement is reached (p. 361)
huelga de brazos caídos huelga en la que los trabajadores se niegan a trabajar o a abandonar el lugar de trabajo hasta que se alcance un convenio laboral (pág. 361)

Sixteenth Amendment (1913) law that allowed Congress to levy taxes based on an individual's income (p. 190)
Decimosexta enmienda (1913) ley que permitió al Congreso recaudar impuestos con base en los ingresos de una persona (pág. 190)

Smoot-Hawley Tariff Act high tariff law that contributed to a global economic downturn in the 1930s (p. 338)
Ley Arancelaria Smoot-Hawley ley que impuso aranceles muy altos, contribuyendo a una crisis económica generalizada en la década de 1930 (pág. 338)

SNCC Student Nonviolent Coordinating Committee; student civil rights organization in the 1960s (p. 566)
SNCC Comité Coordinador No Violento de Estudiantes; organización estudiantil de derechos civiles de la década de 1960 (pág. 566)

social Darwinism a view of society based on Charles Darwin's scientific theory of natural selection (p. 151)
darwinismo social visión de la sociedad basada en la teoría científica de la selección natural de Charles Darwin (pág. 151)

Social Gospel the idea that religious faith should be expressed through good works (p. 159)
evangelio social idea según la cual la fe religiosa se debe expresar por medio de buenas obras (pág. 159)

social justice the fair distribution of advantages and disadvantages in a society (p. 643)
justicia social distribución justa de las ventajas y desventajas en una sociedad (pág. 643)

Social Security a system for providing pensions for many Americans age 65 and older (p. 359)
Seguro Social sistema para proporcionar pensiones a la mayoría de los estadounidenses de 65 años o más (pág. 359)

Solidarity an independent labor union founded in Soviet-controlled Poland in 1980 (p. 703)
Solidaridad sindicato obrero independiente fundado en Polonia en 1980, cuando el país todavía estaba controlado por la Unión Soviética (pág. 703)

space shuttle a reusable spacecraft able to land on the ground like an airplane, and that could be used to transport people and supplies into space (p. 715)
transbordador espacial nave espacial reutilizable capaz de aterrizar en la tierra igual que un avión y que se puede utilizar para transportar personas y suministros al espacio (pág. 715)

spam unwanted email advertisements (p. 802)
spam anuncios no deseados enviados por correo electrónico (pág. 802)

speakeasy illegal bars where alcohol was served during Prohibition (p. 301)
bar clandestino bares ilegales donde se servían bebidas alcohólicas durante la época de la Prohibición (pág. 301)

spheres of influence an area where foreign countries control trade or natural resources of another nation or area (p. 204)
esferas de influencia zona de un país cuyos recursos naturales y comercio son controlados por otro país o zona (pág. 204)

Sputnik (1957) the first artificial satellite; launched by the Soviets (p. 506)

Sputnik (1957) el primer satélite artificial; lanzado por la Unión Soviética (pág. 506)

Square Deal Theodore Roosevelt's 1904 campaign slogan; expressed his belief that the needs of workers, business, and consumers should be balanced, and called for limiting the power of trusts, promoting public health and safety, and improving working conditions (p. 184)
Square Deal lema de la campaña de Theodore Roosevelt de 1904.; expresaba su creencia en el equilibrio entre las necesidades de los trabajadores, los empresarios y los consumidores, y abogaba por limitar el poder de los trusts (consorcios), promover la salud y la seguridad pública y mejorar las condiciones laborales (pág. 184)

Stamp Act (1765) a law passed by Parliament that raised tax money by requiring colonists to pay for an official stamp whenever they bought paper items such as newspapers, licenses, and legal documents (p. 30)
Ley del Sello (1765) ley aprobada por el Parlamento para recaudar impuestos en la que se obligaba a los colonos a pagar un sello oficial cada vez que compraban artículos de papel, como periódicos, licencias y documentos legales (pág. 30)

Strategic Defense Initiative President Reagan's proposed defensive space shield that would knock out incoming Soviet missiles (p. 702)
Iniciativa de Defensa Estratégica escudo protector espacial propuesto por el presidente Reagan; con la idea de que pudieran bloquear los misiles soviéticos entrantes (pág. 702)

strict constructionist a person who interprets the Constitution in a way that allows the federal government to take only those actions the Constitution specifically says it can take (p. 52)
intérprete estricto persona que interpreta que la Constitución solo permite al gobierno federal realizar únicamente las acciones indicadas de manera específica en ella (pág. 52)

subsidy a government payment that is aimed at achieving some public benefit (p. 350)
subsidio pago del gobierno destinado a alcanzar un beneficio para el público (pág. 350)

suburb smaller towns that are located outside a larger urban area (p. 279)
suburbio pueblo más pequeños ubicados en las afueras de una ciudad (pág. 279)

Summer of Love the height of the hippie movement during the Summer of 1967 in San Francisco (p. 653)
Verano del Amor punto máximo del movimiento hippie que tuvo lugar durante el verano de 1967 en San Francisco (pág. 653)

summit a meeting of the heads of government (p. 499)
cumbre encuentro de jefes de estado (pág. 499)

Sunbelt the southern and western portions of the United States (p. 514)
Sunbelt estados del sur y el oeste de Estados Unidos (pág. 514)

supply-side economics the economic theory that tax cuts and business incentives will increase the supply of labor and goods and stimulate the economy (p. 698)
economía de la oferta teoría económica según la cual los recortes de impuestos y los incentivos para las compañías aumentarán la oferta de empleo y de bienes y estimularán la economía (pág. 698)

Sussex pledge a pledge Germany issued which included a promise not to sink merchant vessels "without warning and without saving human lives" (p. 239)
promesa de Sussex compromiso de Alemania que incluía la promesa de que no hundirían los barcos mercantes "sin avisar ni sin salvar las vidas humanas" (pág. 239)

swing a type of jazz music popular in the 1930s (p. 370)
swing tipo de música de jazz popular en la década de 1930 (pág. 370)

taking an action that occurs when regulations restrict use of land so much that the government has essentially taken the land (p. 783)
apoderarse acción que occure cuando las leyes limitan hasta tal punto el uso de la tierra que es como si el gobierno se hubiera apropiado de ella (pág. 783)

Taliban group that took control over most of Afghanistan following the Soviet occupation in 1979; this group governed Afghanistan according to a strict application of Islamic laws (p. 743)
Talibán grupo que tomó el control de la mayor parte de Afganistán tras la ocupación soviética de 1979; este grupo gobernó Afganistán aplicando estrictamente la ley islámica (pág. 743)

Tampico incident (1914) confrontation between the United States and Mexico at Tampico Bay, Mexico, involving the arrest of American sailors by the Mexican government; it led to Congress approving the use of armed forces against Mexico, and was an important event leading up to the Battle of Vercruz (p. 222)
incidente de Tampico (1914) enfrentamiento entre Estados Unidos y México en la bahía de Tampico, México, durante el cual el gobierno mexicano arrestó a unos marineros estadounidenses. Como consecuencia, el Congreso aprobó el uso de las fuerzas militares contra México; fue una causa importante de la batalla de Veracruz. (pág. 222)

Teapot Dome a federally owned piece of land in Wyoming; it was the center of a government scandal in 1921 when President Harding's Secretary of the Interior accepted bribes in return for allowing oil companies to drill for oil there in 1921 (p. 284)
Teapot Dome nombre de un terreno federal ubicado en Wyoming que fue el centro de un escándalo gubernamental en 1921; el secretario del interior del presidente Harding aceptó sobornos para permitir que las empresas petroleras excavaran pozos allí (pág. 284)

telecommute communication via the Internet (p. 802)
trabajo a distancia comunicación por Internet (pág. 802)

tenant farming system of farming where farmers rented their land from the landowner, and were allowed to grow whatever crop they chose (p. 136)
agricultura de arriendo sistema de agricultura en el que los agricultores arriendan la tierra del propietario y pueden cultivar lo que quieran (pág. 136)

tenement poorly built, overcrowded housing where many immigrants lived (p. 159)
casa de vecinos casas mal construidas donde vivían amontonados muchos inmigrantes (pág. 159)

terrorism the use of violence by individuals and groups to advance political goals (p. 729)
terrorismo uso de la violencia por parte de individuos y grupos con el fin de alcanzar metas políticas (pág. 729)

Tet Offensive a series of major attacks by communist forces in South Vietnam in 1968 (p. 613)
ofensiva del Tet serie de ataques importantes realizado por fuerzas comunistas en Vietnam del Sur en 1868 (pág. 613)

Thirteenth Amendment (1865) a constitutional amendment that outlawed slavery (p. 130)
Decimotercera enmienda (1865) enmienda constitucional que abolió la esclavitud (pág. 130)

38th parallel line of latitude which divides North and South Korea (p. 484)
paralelo 38 línea de latitud que divide a Corea del Norte de Corea del Sur (pág. 484)

Tiananmen Square massacre (1989) a large pro-democracy protest in China that resulted in the government using military force, killing hundreds (p. 711)
Masacre de la plaza Tiananmen (1989) gran manifestación de protesta a favor de la democracia en China, en la que el gobierno usó fuerzas militares y dio muerte a cientos de personas (pág. 711)

Tonkin Gulf Resolution (1964) Congressional resolution that in effect authorized military action in Southeast Asia (p. 603)
Resolución del Golfo de Tonkin (1964) resolución del Congreso que autorizó las acciones militares en el sureste de Asia (pág. 603)

totalitarian a form of government in which the person or party in charge has absolute control over all aspects of life (p. 389)
totalitario una forma de gobierno en la que la persona o el partido que está a cargo tiene control absoluto sobre todos los aspectos de la vida (pág. 389)

Trail of Tears (1838-39) an 800-mile forced march made by the Cherokee from their homeland in Georgia to Indian Territory; resulted in the deaths of almost one fourth of the Cherokee people (p. 95)
Ruta de las Lágrimas (1838-39) marcha forzada de 800 millas que realizó la tribu cherokee desde su territorio natal en Georgia hasta el Territorio Indígena, y en la que murió casi una cuarta parte del pueblo cherokee (pág. 95)

transatlantic crossing the Atlantic Ocean (p. 310)
transatlántico que atraviesa el océano Atlántico (pág. 310)

transcendentalism the belief that knowledge is not found only by observation of the world, but also through reason, intuition, and personal spiritual experiences (p. 100)
movimiento trascendental convicción de que el conocimiento no se obtiene sólo observando el mundo, sino mediante la razón, la intuición y las experiencias espirituales personales (pág. 100)

transcript a written record of a spoken event (p. 679)
transcripción registro escrito de un suceso oral (pág. 679)

transistor small electrical devices that can be found in computers and other machines (p. 512)
transistores pequeños dispositivos eléctricos de las computadores y otras máquinas (pág. 512)

Treaty of Guadalupe Hidalgo (1848) a treaty that ended the Mexican-American War and gave the United States much of Mexico's northern territory (p. 112)
Tratado de Guadalupe Hidalgo (1848) tratado que daba por terminada la Guerra mexicano-estadounidense y daba posesión a Estados Unidos de gran parte del norte del territorio mexicano (pág. 112)

Treaty of Paris (1783) agreement that officially ended the Revolutionary War and established British recognition of the independence of the United States (p. 37)
Tratado de París (1783) acuerdo de paz que oficialmente daba por terminada la Guerra de Independencia estadounidense y en el que Gran Bretaña reconocía la soberanía de Estados Unidos (pág. 37)

Treaty of Versailles (1919) treaty ending World War I that required Germany to pay huge war reparations and established the League of Nations (p. 257)
Tratado de Versailles tratado que puso fin a la Primera Guerra Mundial, que le impuso a Alemania el pago de indemnizaciones económicas y que estableció la Liga de las Naciones (pág. 257)

trench warfare a form of combat in which soldiers dug trenches, or deep ditches, to seek protection from enemy fire and to defend their positions (p. 236)
guerra de trincheras forma de combate en la que la que los soldados excavan trincheras o zanjas profundas para protegerse del fuego enemigo y defender sus posiciones (pág. 236)

Triple Alliance a military alliance between Germany, Austria-Hungary and Italy (p. 231)
Triple Alianza alianza militar entre Alemania, Austria-Hungría e Italia (pág. 231)

Triple Entente a military alliance between Great Britain, France, and Russia (p. 231)
Triple Entente alianza militar entre Gran Bretaña, Francia y Rusia (pág. 231)

Truman Doctrine (1947) President Truman's pledge to provide economic and military aid to countries threatened by communism (p. 467)
Doctrina Truman (1947) promesa del presidente Truman de dar ayuda económica y militar a los países amenazados por el comunismo (pág. 467)

Tuskegee Airmen unit of African American pilots that fought in World War II; the first African Americans to receive training as pilots in the United States military (p. 422)
Aviadores de Tuskegee unidad de pilotos afroamericanos que combatió en la Segunda Guerra Mundial; sus miembros fueron los primeros afroamericanos en recibir entrenamiento de piloto en el ejército de los Estados Unidos (pág. 422)

Twenty-fourth Amendment (1964) banned states from taxing citizens to vote in elections (p. 574)
Vigésimocuarta enmienda (1964) prohibió a los estados cobrarles impuestos a los ciudadanos por votar en las elecciones (pág. 574)

Twenty-sixth Amendment (1971) amendment that lowered the legal voting age from 21 to 18 (p. 624)
Vigésimosexta enmienda (1971) redujo la edad legal para votar de 21 a 18 años (pág. 624)

U-boats small submarines named after the German word unterserboot, which means "undersea boat" (p. 239)
U-boat pequeño submarino cuyo nombre proviene de la palabra alemana unterserboot, que significa "bote submarino" (pág. 239)

Underground Railroad a network of people who helped thousands of enslaved people escape to the North by providing transportation and hiding places (p. 104)
Tren Clandestino red de personas que ayudó a miles de esclavos a escapar hacia el Norte ofreciéndoles transporte y lugares para ocultarse (pág. 104)

United Nations an international organization that encourages cooperation among nations and prevent future wars (p. 454)
Naciones Unidas (ONU) organización internacional que fomenta la cooperación entre países y la prevención de las guerras (pág. 454)

Universal Declaration of Human Rights (1948) document presented to the U.N. by the Commission on Human Rights that stated all human beings are created free and equal, and tried to set standards for human rights (p. 476)
Declaración Universal de los Derechos Humanos (1948) documento presentado a la ONU por la Comisión de Derechos Humanos que afirma que todos los seres humanos nacen libres e iguales; e intentó establecer normas para el respeto de los derechos humanos (pág. 476)

USA PATRIOT Act (2001) law passed by Congress making it easier for the FBI and other law enforcement agencies to secretly collect information about suspected terrorists (p. 745)
Ley PATRIOTA Estadounidense (2001) ley aprobada por el Congreso que facilita al FBI y a otros agentes de la ley recoger en secreto información acerca de presuntos terroristas (pág. 745)

vaccine a preparation that uses a killed or weakened form of a germ to help the body build its own defenses against that germ (p. 513)
vacuna preparación que utiliza una forma muerta o debilitada de un germen para ayudar al cuerpo a desarrollar sus propias defensas contra el germen (pág. 513)

values the key ideas and beliefs a person holds (p. 297)
valores ideas y creencias clave de una persona (pág. 297)

V-E day (1945) May 8, 1945; the date when the Allies celebrated victory over Europe in World War II (p. 452)
Día del Armisticio (1945) 8 de mayo de 1945; fecha en que los Aliados celebran la victoria en Europa de la Segunda Guerra Mundial (pág. 452)

velvet revolution a quick, peaceful revolution that swept the Communists from power in Czechoslovakia in 1989 (p. 709)
revolución de terciopelo revolución breve y pacífica que en 1989 sacó del poder a los comunistas en Checoslovaquia (pág. 709)

viceroyalty a province ruled by a viceroy, the direct representative of a monarch (p. 15)
virreinato provincia gobernada por un virrey, el representante directo de un monarca (pág. 15)

Vichy France French government set up with the Germans that ruled the southern half of France during World War II (p. 396)
Francia Vichy gobierno establecido en Francia en cooperación con Alemania que gobernó la mitad sur de Francia durante la Segunda Guerra Mundial (pág. 396)

Vietcong the military forces of the National Liberation Front, a group that wanted to overthrow the government in Vietnam (p. 601)
Vietcong fuerzas militares del Frente de Liberación Nacional, un grupo que quería derrocar el gobierno de Vietnam (pág. 601)

Vietminh group that resisted the Japanese occupation in Vietnam (p. 597)
Vietminh grupo que se resistió a la ocupación japonesa de Vietnam (pág. 597)

Vietnamization a plan to end the Vietnam war that involved turning over the fighting to the South Vietnamese while U.S. troops gradually pulled out (p. 621)
vietnamización plan para terminar la guerra de Vietnam que conllevaba el traspaso de la lucha a los vietnamitas del sur mientras las tropas de Estados Unidos se retiraban gradualmente (pág. 621)

VISTA a domestic version of the Peace Corps that provided help to poor communities in the United States in the 1960s (p. 544)
VISTA versión nacional e interna del Cuerpo de Paz que ayudó a las comunidades pobres de Estados Unidos durante la década de 1960 (pág. 544)

V-J Day (1945) August 15, 1945; the date when the Allies declared victory over Japan in World War II (p. 454)
Día V-J (1945) 15 de agosto de 1945; fecha en que los Aliados declararon la victoria sobre Japón en la Segunda Guerra Mundial (pág. 454)

Voter Education Project group founded in 1962 to register southern African Americans to vote (p. 574)
Proyecto para la Educación de Votantes grupo fundado en 1962 para inscribir como votantes a los afroamericanos del Sur (pág. 574)

Voting Rights Act of 1965 civil rights law that banned literacy tests and other practices that discouraged blacks from voting (p. 578)
Ley de Derecho al Voto de 1965 ley de derechos civiles que prohibió las pruebas de lectura y escritura y otras prácticas que trataban de impedir que los afroamericanos votaran (pág. 578)

War of 1812 war fought between the United States and Britain over the impressment of U.S. sailors and troubles with Native Americans in the Northwest Territory (p. 56)
Guerra de 1812 guerra librada entre Estados Unidos y Gran Bretaña por la captura de marineros estadounidenses y por problemas con los indígenas norteamericanos en el Territorio de Noroeste (pág. 56)

War on Poverty set of programs introduced by President Johnson to fight poverty (p. 543)
Guerra contra la Pobreza conjunto de programas introducidos por el presidente Johnson para combatir la pobreza (pág. 543)

War Powers Act (1973) law that sets a 60-day limit on the presidential commitment of U.S. troops to foreign conflicts (p. 627)
Ley de Poderes de Guerra (1973) ley que limita a 60 días el plazo de envío de tropas estadounidenses a conflictos internacionales por parte del presidente (pág. 627)

War Refugee Board a group established by President Franklin D. Roosevelt that helped 20,000 Jews who might otherwise have fallen into the hands of the Nazis (p. 430)
Junta de Refugiados de Guerra grupo establecido por el Presidente Franklin D. Roosevelt que ayudó a 20,000 judíos que de otra manera podrían haber caído en manos de los nazis (pág. 430)

Warren Commission a commission headed by Chief Justice Earl Warren to investigate the assassination of President Kennedy (p. 540)
Comisión Warren comisión presidida por el juez presidente de la Corte Suprema Earl Warren para investigar el asesinato del presidente Kennedy (pág. 540)

Warren Court a term that refers to the years when Earl Warren served as Chief Justice of the Supreme Court; under his leadership, controversial Court decisions greatly extended individual rights and freedoms (p. 538)
Corte de Warren término que hace referencia a los años en que Earl Warren ocupó el cargo de juez presidente de la Corte Suprema; bajo su liderazgo, algunas decisiones polémicas de la Corte ampliaron significativamente los derechos y las libertades individuales (pág. 538)

Warsaw Pact a military alliance established in 1955 of the Soviet-dominated countries of Eastern Europe (p. 498)
Pacto de Varsovia alianza militar establecida en 1955 por los países de Europa oriental controlados por la Unión Soviética (pág. 498)

Watergate scandal a political scandal that resulted in President Nixon's resignation in 1974 (p. 677)
escándalo Watergate escándalo político que produjo la renuncia del Presidente Nixon en 1974 (pág. 677)

welfare financial assistance from the government (p. 790)
asistencia social ayuda financiera proporcionada por el gobierno (pág. 790)

welfare capitalism system in which companies provided fringe benefits to employees in an effort to promote worker satisfaction and loyalty (p. 279)
capitalismo del bienestar sistema por el que las empresas proporcionan prestaciones a sus empleados para promover la satisfacción y lealtad de los trabajadores (pág. 279)

Whiskey Rebellion (1794) a protest of small farmers in Pennsylvania against new taxes on whiskey (p. 53)
Rebelión del Whisky (1794) protesta de pequeños agricultores de Pensilvania contra los nuevos impuestos sobre el whisky (pág. 53)

wolf pack a tactic in which submarines hunt as a group and attack at night (p. 419)
manada de lobos táctica de los submarinos por la que buscan al enemigo en grupo y atacan de noche (pág. 419)

Women's Christian Temperance Movement reform organization that led the fight against alcohol in the late 1800s (p. 179)
Movimiento Cristiano Femenino por la Abstinencia organización reformista que lideró la lucha en contra del consumo de alcohol a fines del siglo XIX (pág. 179)

working poor those who are employed but cannot earn enough to lift themselves out of poverty (p. 790)
trabajadores pobres personas que trabajan pero que no ganan lo suficiente como para salir de la pobreza (pág. 790)

World Bank helps poor countries build their economies by providing grants and loans to help with projects that could provide jobs and wealth (p. 476)
Banco Mundial ayuda a los países pobres a desarrollar sus economías mediante subsidios y préstamos para invertir en proyectos que pueden generar empleos y riqueza (pág. 476)

World Wide Web computer program that allows users to create, store, and connect information in documents called Web pages (p. 801)
World Wide Web programa de computación que permite a los usuarios crear, almacenar y conectar información en documentos llamados páginas (pág. 801)

Wounded Knee Massacre (1890) the U.S. Army's killing of approximately 150 Sioux at Wounded Knee Creek in South Dakota; ended U.S.-Indian wars on the Plains (p. 144)
Masacre de Wounded Knee (1890) matanza de aproximadamente 150 indios sioux a manos del ejército estadounidense en Wounded Knee Creek, Dakota del Sur; dio fin a las guerras entre estadounidenses e indígenas en las Planicies (pág. 144)

Yalta Conference (1945) meeting between Franklin Roosevelt, Winston Churchill, and Joseph Stalin to reach an agreement on what to do with Germany after World War II (p. 450)
Conferencia de Yalta (1945) cumbre celebrada entre Franklin Roosevelt, Winston Churchill y Joseph Stalin para llegar a un acuerdo acerca de lo que harían con Alemania después de la Segunda Guerra Mundial (pág. 450)

yellow journalism the reporting of exaggerated stories in newspapers to increase sales (p. 207)
prensa amarillista reportaje de artículos exagerados en la prensa para aumentar las ventas (pág. 207)

yeoman farmers living on small farms rather than on large plantations (p. 773)
campesino los granjeros que vivían en pequeñas granjas en lugar de en grandes plantaciones (pág. 773)

Zimmermann note a telegram sent to a German official in Mexico before World War I; it proposed an alliance between Germany and Mexico (p. 240)
nota de Zimmermann telegrama enviado a un funcionario alemán en México antes del inicio de la Primera Guerra Mundial; proponía una alianza entre Alemania y México (pág. 240)

zoot suit riots series of attacks by U.S. sailors against Mexican Americans in Los Angeles (p. 411)
disturbios de *zoot suit* serie de ataques contra mexicano-americanos por parte de marnieros estadounidenses en Los Angeles (pág. 411)

Index

KEY TO INDEX

c = chart   *g* = graph   *m* = map
q = quotation   *p* = picture

AAA. *See* Agricultural Adjustment Act
Abernathy, Ralph, 586, 587
ABMs. *See* anti-ballistic missiles
abolition movement, 99, 103–105, 557
abortion, 637–638, 718
Abzug, Bella, 638
academic integrity, 805
Adams-Onís Treaty, 93
Adams, Abigail, *178p*
Adams, John, 53, 191, R17
Adams, John Quincy, 92, 95, R17, R79
Adams, Samuel, 30, 31
Addams, Jane, 159, 171–172, 252
Adena culture, 7
ADL. *See* Anti-Defamation League
adobe buildings, 7
Advanced Research Projects Agency (ARPA), 801, *801p*
advertising, 280, *280p*, 510
affirmative action, 588–589, 668, 687, 748
Afghanistan, 685; war in, 743–744, *743m*, *744p*
AFL. *See* American Federation of Labor
Africa, 9, R56. *See also* West Africa
African Americans: Albany Movement, 568–569; Birmingham campaign, 569–570, *569p*; Black Codes, 133, 136; Black Muslims, *582p*, 584; Black Panther Party, *582p*, 583–584, 587–588; Black Power, *582p*, 583, 587–588, 589; *Brown v. Board of Education of Topeka, Kansas*, 559–561, *559p*, *559q*, *560p*, *561q*; in cabinet, 546; civil rights of, 138, 172, 180; in Civil War, 127, *127p*; cowboys, 146; de facto segregation, 581; Democratic Party, 366–367; discrimination of, 371; education of, 136, 177, *177p*, 556, *557m*, 558, 559–561, 567–568, *567p*; election of 1960, 527; election of 1964, 575–577; employment and, 410–411; equal rights, 590–591; Executive Order 9981, 473, *473q*, 474, *474p*; Exodusters, 147; Freedom Rides, 566–567, *566m*; Freedom Summer, 575; government appointments of, 683, *683p*; in the Great Depression, 318; Great Depression and, 557; Harlem Renaissance, 302–307, *302p*, *303m*, *304p*, *305p*, *306p*; housing and, 514; Jim Crow laws, 161; Ku Klux Klan and, 297; lynching, 161–162; migration of, 147, 259, 302–303, *303m*, R10; in the military, 210, *210p*, 241, *242p*, *243p*, 410, 452, 459, *474p*; music and, 370, 515; New Deal and, 366–367, 374; Philippines and, 212; in political office, 588; Poor People's Campaign, 586–587, *586p*; population of, *588c*, 589, *699g*, 748, *748c*; presidential candidacy, 708; progressivism and, 193; Reconstruction and, 134–138, *135p*, *136p*, 137; religion and, 23; in Revolutionary War, 35; on the Supreme Court, 589, 719, *719p*; Three-Fifths Compromise, 46; Tuskegee Airmen, 422, *422p*, 452; in Vietnam War, 608; voting rights of, 134–136, *135p*, 180, 362, *362p*, 375, 573–579, *573p*, *576p*, *577p*, 667; in World War I, 241, *242p*, *243p*
Agee, James, 368
Agent Orange, 626
Age of Exploration, 11–12, *11m*
Age of Jackson, 95
Agnew, Spiro T., 679
agrarian, 22
Agricultural Adjustment Act (AAA), 350–351, *360c*
agriculture, 7, 750. *See also* farms and farming
Aguinaldo, Emilio, 209, 212
AIDS, 719, 751
Aid to Families with Dependent Children, 374
AIM. *See* American Indian Movement
airplanes, 154, *154p*, 237, 280, 310–311, *311p*, 504, R9
air-raids, 507, *507p*
Akron, Ohio, 279
Alabama: bus boycott in, 562–563; civil rights movement in, 567, 573, *573p*, 577–578, *577p*; facts about, R30; in Great Depression, 368; hurricanes in, 752; secession, 121; voting rights in, 578, 579
Alamo, 110
Alaska: facts about, R30; gold in, 144; land bridge, 6; nuclear testing in, 503; oil drilling in, 785; purchase of, 200
Alaska National Interest Lands Conservation Act, 683
Albany Movement, 568–569
Albany Plan of Union, 26
Alcatraz, 640
alcohol, 100, 182, 299–301, *300p*, *301p*; Prohibition and, 179–180, *180p*
Aldrich, Nelson, 190
Aldrin, Edwin E., *664p–665p*, 671–673, *673q*
Alexander VI, Pope, 13
Algonquin Indians, 25
Alianza Federal de Mercedes, 645
Alien and Sedition Acts, 53
aliens, 272
Alito, Samuel, 787
Alliance for Progress, 534
alliances, 231–232, *231m*
Allies: Bulge, Battle of the, 424; convoy systems, *419p*; D-Day, 423–424, *424p–425p*; in Europe, 420, *421m*, 449–452, *449p*, *450p*; Guadalcanal, 437, 438, *438m*; in North Africa, 420–422, *421m*; in the Pacific, 433–440, *433p*, *434p*, *437p*, *438m*, 452–454, *453p*; Stalingrad, Battle of, 420, *421m*; in World War I, 232–237, *233m*, 257; in World War II, 396–397, *397m*
All Quiet on the Western Front (Remarque), 260
al Qaeda, 742–744
America First Committee, 403
American Anti-Slavery Society, 104
American Bandstand (television program), 510
American Civil Liberty: ending segregation, 559, *559p*; integration in the military, 452, 474, *474p*; Native Americans and citizenship, 285, *285p*; smaller government, 696; Twenty-fourth Amendment, 576; voting rights, 135, *135p*; women in the military, 452, *452p*
American Expeditionary Forces, *241p*, 242, 243
American Federation of Labor (AFL), 153, 174, 360, R8
American GI Forum, 473
American Indian Movement (AIM), 640
Americanization, 158, 162, R96
American Liberty League, 353, 362
American Literature: *A Farewell to Arms* (Hemingway), 245, *245p*; *The Grapes of Wrath* (Steinbeck), 334; Hemingway, Ernest, 245, *245p*; *The Joy Luck Club* (Tan), 753, *753p*; *The Jungle* (Sinclair), 176, *176p*; *Letter from a Birmingham Jail* (King), 572, *572q*; *Night* (Wiesel), 432; Wiesel, Elie, 432, *432p*. *See also* literature
American Medical Association, 178
American Party, 101, 118
American Railway Union, 153
American Red Cross, 128
American Religious Liberty, 718, 749
American Revolution. *See* Revolutionary War
American Socialist Party, 252
American Woman Suffrage Association (AWSA), 180
Americans with Disabilities Act, 717
amnesty, 768
anarchists, 275
Anasazi culture, 7
Ancon, USS (ship), 216
Anderson, John, 696
Anderson, Marian, 371, *371p*
Andros, Edmund, 21
Angel Island, 157
Angola, 680
animation, 369
annexation, 110, 203, 211–212
Anschluss, 393, 745
Anthony, Susan B., 180, 181, *181q*, 182
anthrax, 744
anti-ballistic missiles (ABMs), 668–669; treaty, 738
Anti-Defamation League (ADL), 172
Antietam, Battle of, 126, *126m*, *126p*
Antifederalists, *47p*, *47q*, 48
Anti-Imperialist League, 212
Antiquities Act (1906), 188

R126 INDEX

Anti-Saloon League, 179
anti-Semitism, 427–429, *429c*, *429m*, *429p*, 430–431
antislavery movement. *See* abolition movement
antiwar movement, 128, 611, 622–623, *622p*, *623p*
Anzio, Italy, 422
Apache, *143m*, 144
apartheid, 705, 713
Apollo 11 (spacecraft), 671–673, *672p*, R15
appeasement, 392, 395, 744, 747
Apple Computer, 714, *714p*
Appomattox, 131, *131p*
Arafat, Yasser, 729
Arapaho, 143
archaeology, 6
Ardennes Forest, 396, 748
Area Redevelopment Act (1961), 537
Argonne Forest, Battle of the, *243m*, 244
Arizona: Civil War in, 128; exploration of, *14m*, 15; facts about, R30; Japanese Americans in, 445; La Raza Unida Party, 646–647; national parks in, 187; Native Americans in, 144; population of, 748; Treaty of Guadalupe Hidalgo, 112
Arkansas: Civil War in, *114p–115p*; facts about, R30; integration in, 560; New Deal and, 374; Reconstruction in, 133; secession, 121, 124
Arlington National Cemetery, 540
armistice, 244
arms race, 286, 504–508, *505p*, *506p*, *506q*
Armstrong, Louis, *306p*, 307, 370
Armstrong, Neil A., *664p–665p*, 671–673, *672p*, *673q*
Army, U.S.: Bonus Marchers, 335, 338–339
Arnaz, Desi, 509, *509p*, 510
ARPA. *See* Advanced Research Projects Agency
art: Chicano, 648, *648p*; of Harlem Renaissance, *306p*, 307; pop art, 655; of the Works Progress Administration, *358p–359p*, 359
Arthur, Chester A., 160, R19
Articles of Confederation, 42–44, *43c*, 48
Aryan race, 389, 427, 741
Asia: political map, R55
Asian Americans, 538; discrimination against, 162, 445–446, *446p*, 448, R12; in Great Depression, 341, *341p*; population of, 748, *748c*
Askia Muhammad, 9
Aspin, Les, 777
assembly line, 277, *277q*, 278, 279
assimilation, 767
associative state, 336, *336p*
Astaire, Fred, 369, *369p*
Aswan Dam, 501
Atchinson, David, 116
Atlantic, Battle of the, 418–420, *418p*, *419p*
Atlantic Charter, 403, 755
atomic bomb, 410, 453–454, *453p*, 465, 477, 478, 502, 503
Atomic Energy Commission, 479
Attucks, Crispus, 31

Auschwitz, 430
Austin, Moses, 109
Austin, Stephen F., 109, 110
Australia, 437, *438m*, R57
Austria: *Anschluss* and, 393
Austria-Hungary, 230, 231, 244
automobiles, 154, *265p*, 277–279, *278p*, 294, *294p*, 321, 513, R9
AWSA. *See* American Woman Suffrage Association
Axis Powers: Bulge, Battle of the, 424; D-Day, 423–424, *424p–425p*; in Europe, 418–420, *421m*, 449–452, *449p*, *450p*; in the Pacific, 433–440, *433p*, *434p*, *437p*, *438m*, 452–454, *453p*; Stalingrad, Battle of, 420, *421m*; in World War II, 398
Aztec culture, 7, 15

Babbitt (Lewis), 312, *312q*
Babi Yar, 428
Babson, Roger, 324
baby boom, 473, 513, 749
Back to Africa, 304
Baer, Abel, *311q*
Baez, Joan, 571
Baker, Howard, 677
Baker, Josephine, 307
Baker v. *Carr* (1962), 538, R25
Bakke, Alan, 687
Balanced Budget and Emergency Deficit Control Act, 699
balance of power, 232
Baldowski, Clifford H., 590
Balkan states, 231
Ball, Lucille, 509, *509p*, 510
Ballinger, Richard, 190
bank holiday, 349
Bank of the United States, 52
Banks, Dennis, 640
banks and banking: Federal Deposit Insurance Corporation, 350, *360c*, 372; Federal Reserve Board, 191, 324, 716; Glass-Steagall Act (1933), 350; in Great Depression, 329; national, 51, 52, 95; New Deal programs, *360c*; Roosevelt and, 349–350, *349q*; savings and loan crisis, 716, *717q*; stock market crash and, 324, 326
barbed wire, 146
Barnette ruling, 445
Barrett, Janie Porter, 159
barter system, 9
Bartlett, Washington, R60
Barton, Bruce, 313
Barton, Clara, 128, 773
Baruch, Bernard, 247
baseball, 312, *312p*, 370, 514, 558, *558p*
Basie, William "Count," 370
Bataan Death March, *434p*, 435
Batista, Fulgencio, 528
Bay of Pigs invasion, 528–529
bayonet constitution, 203
Bear Flag Revolt, 112
Beat generation, 515, 651
Beatles, 653, 655
beatniks, 651, 652

Beckwith, Byron De La, 570, 591
Beecher, Henry Ward, 180
Begin, Menachem, 684, *684p*
Beirut, 705
Belafonte, Harry, 569
Belgium, 424; in NATO, 470; in World War I, 232–233, *233m*, 242, *243m*, 244; in World War II, 396, *397m*
Bell, Alexander Graham, 155
Bell, John, 121
Bellecourt, Clyde, 640, *640p*
Benin, 9
Bentsen, Lloyd, 708
Bergen-Belsen, 431
Beringia, 6
Bering Strait, 6
Berle, Milton, 510
Berlin: division of, 451, 469–470, *469m*
Berlin airlift, 462, *462p–463p*, 470, R13
Berlin Crisis, 474
Berlin Wall, 530–531, *531p*, 701, *701p*, 709
Bernanke, Ben S., 716
Bernstein, Carl, 676, *676p*
Bessemer process, 150
Bethune, Mary McLeod, 366, *366p*
B-52 aircraft, 504
bicameral legislature, 21, 45
Big Bertha, 242
Big Four, 255
Bigler, John, R60
Big Three, 450
Bill of Rights, 49
Bill of Rights, English, R76
bin Laden, Osama, 742–744
Biography: Bellecourt, Clyde, 640, *640p*; Bethune, Mary McLeod, 366, *366p*; Bush, George W., 746, *746p*; Chávez, César, 644, *644p*; Clinton, Bill, 729, *729p*; Columbus, Christopher, 12, *12p*; Coolidge, Calvin and Grace, 284, *284p*; Doolittle, James, 435, *435p*; Douglass, Frederick, 105, *105p*; Edison, Thomas Alva, 155, *155p*; Eisenhower, Dwight D., 423, *423p*; Farmer, James, 565, *565p*; Ford, Henry, 277, *277p*; Friedan, Betty, 636, *636p*; Hearst, William Randolph, 207, *207p*; Ho Chi Minh, 598, *598p*; Hoover, Herbert, 338, *338p*; Hughes, Langston, 305, *305p*; Jefferson, Thomas, 51, *51p*; Johnson, Lyndon, 542, *542p*; Kennedy, John F. and Jacqueline, 538, *538p*; King, Martin Luther, Jr., 568, *568p*; Liliuokalani, queen of Hawaii, 203, *203p*; Lincoln, Abraham, 124, *124p*; MacArthur, Douglas, 488, *488p*; McNamara, Robert, 615, *615p*; Nixon, Richard, 667, *667p*; Park, Rosa, 563, *563p*; Reagan, Ronald, 697, *697p*; Roosevelt, Eleanor, 349, *349p*; Roosevelt, Franklin Delano, 348, *348p*; Roosevelt, Theodore, 186, *186p*; Salk, Jonas, 513, *513p*; Stanton, Elizabeth Cady, 103, *103p*; Truman, Harry S, 473, *473p*; Washington, George, 34, *34p*; Wilson, Woodrow, 239, *239p*
biological terrorism, 744
Birmingham campaign, 569–570, *569p*
Birth of a Nation (film), 172, 310
Bismarck (ship), 419
Black, Hugo, 448

Black Cabinet, 366
Black Codes, 133, 136
Blackfoot, 142, *143m*
Black Hand, 230
blacklists, 479
Black Muslims, *582p*, 584
Black Panther Party, *582p*, 583–584, 587–588
Black Power, *582p*, 583, 587–588, 589
Blackshear, Nell, 340
Black Tuesday, 325
blitzkrieg, 394, *394p*, *395p*, 396, 420
Bliven, Bruce, *296q*
Block, Herb, *689p*
blockade: of Berlin, 469–470, *469m*; in Civil War, 128; Cuban, 533; in World War I, 239
Boesky, Ivan, 716, 720
boll weevil, 281
Bolsheviks, 242, 259, 271–272
bomb shelter, 491, *491p*, 502, *502p*, 508
bonanza farms, 148
Bonus Marchers, 335, 338–339
Book of Mormon, 99
Booth, John Wilkes, 133
Booth, Newton, R60
bootleggers, 300
border states, 124
boricua movement, 648–649
Bork, Robert, 719
Borneo, 434, *438m*
Borzykowski, Tuvia, *428q*
Bosnia and Herzegovina, 230, 231, 730
Boss Tweed, 159
Boston, 22; busing in, 588; Police Strike, 285; Revolutionary War in, 30–31, *30p*, 32; subway system, 154
Boston, Battle of, 32
Boston Massacre, 31, R4
Boston Tea Party, 30, *30p*, 31
boundary: Canada and, 108; Gadsden Purchase, 112; Mexico and, 111
Bow, Clara, 310
Boxer Rebellion, 204, *204p*
boycotts, 30, 31; Montgomery bus, 562–563, *562p*; farmworkers and, *632p–633p*, 642, *642p*
Bracero Program, 411, 771
Bradley, Omar, 423, R33
Bragg, Braxton, 130
Brandeis, Louis D., 172
Brandenburg Gate, 701
Brando, Marlon, 515
Breckinridge, John, 121
Brezhnev, Leonid, 669, 680, 684, 703
Briggs, Harry and Eliza, 556, *556p*, 559
Briggs v. *Elliott* (1950), 556, *556p*
Brightman, Carol, 652, *652q*
Brigstock, Duane T., *413q*
brinkmanship, 498, 504
Britain. *See* England; Great Britain
Britain, Battle of, 396–397, *397m*, *397q*
British East India Company, 30, 31
British Parliament, 21
Brooks, Preston, *118p*
Brown, Edmund G. "Jerry," R60
Brown, Edmund G. "Pat," 651, 697, R60
Brown, H. Rap, 588
Brown, James Leroy, 474, *474p*
Brown, John, 119

Brown, Linda, 559
Brown Berets, 647–648
Brownsville incident, 193
Brown v. *Board of Education of Topeka, Kansas* (1954), 538, 559–561, *559p*, *559q*, *560p*, *561q*, *570c*, R13
Brown v. *Mississippi* (1936), 549
Bryan, William Jennings, 161, 190, 299, *299p*, 366, R33
Brzezinski, Zbigniew, *685q*
Buchanan, James, 118, 122, R18, R33
Buchenwald, 431, *432p*
Buckingham, Harriet, 106
Budd, James, R60
Buddhism: in Vietnam, 600, *600p*, *601p*
budget, federal: deficit, 364, 698, 727, *728g*; Hoover and the, 337–339; surplus, 734; during World War II, 447, *447g*
buffalo, 142, 143
Buffalo Soldiers, 210
Buford (naval vessel), 272
Bulge, Battle of the, 424, 450
Bull Moose Party, 191
Bull Run, Battle of, 125, *126m*
bully pulpit, 184, 185
Bundy, McGeorge, 528
Bunker Hill, Battle of, 32
Bureau of Indian Affairs, 144, 640
Burgoyne, John, 34
Burke, Edmund, 21
Burma, 390, 435
Burned Over District, 99
Burnett, Peter, R60
Burns, Lucy, 192
Bush, George H.W., 696, 698, 707, *707p*, *733p*, 808, R21, R34; economy and, 716–717; election of 1988, 707, 708; foreign policy, 708–713; Iran-Contra Affair and, 706; Supreme Court and, 719
Bush, George W., R21, R34; Afghanistan and, 743–744, *743m*, *744p*, *744q*; domestic policy, 736–737; election of 2000, 733–735, *733p*, *734m*, *735p*; election of 2004, 736; environment and, 783; foreign policy, 737–738, 743–746; immigration and, 770; Iraq and, 745–746, *745m*; No Child Left Behind Act, 736, 737; September 11th attacks and, 739–740, 743, R93; Social Security and, 737, 749; space exploration, 673; tax cuts, 736; trade and, 812
Bush v. *Gore* (2000), 735, R29
business, 151–152; Clayton Antitrust Act, 191; corporations, 151; deregulation, 716; entrepreneurs, 151; Hoover and, 336, *336q*; horizontal integration, 151; mass marketing, 152; mining, *144q*, 145; regulation of, 185–186; Roosevelt, T. and, 185–186, *185q*; stock market crash and, 327; vertical integration, 151. *See also* stock market
busing, 588
Butterfield, Alexander, 677–678
butterfly ballot, 735
buying on margin, 323–324, 326
Byrd, Harry, 527, 560
Byrnes, James, 466

C

cabinet, presidential, 51
cable cars, 154
Cabrillo, Juan Rodríguez, 15
Cahokia, 7
Caldwell, Millard, 507
Calhoun, John C., 117, R82
California: Bear Flag Revolt, 112; Brown Berets, 647–648; early cultures in, 7, *8m*; exploration of, *14m*, 15; facts about, R30, R61; flag, R61; gold rush, 107–108, *108p*, *109p*, R6; government, R60; governors, R60; Great Depression in, 341, *341p*; Hispanic Americans in, *754m–755m*, *755p*; immigrants to, 147, 162; Japanese Americans in, 445; La Raza Unida Party, 646–647; Mexican-American War and, 111; military bases in, 408; missions in, 15; movie industry, 310; national parks in, 187; nativists in, 158; physical maps, R58; political maps, R59; Pony Express, 109; population of, 514, 748; Proposition 209, 748; railroad to, *150m*, 151; slavery and, 117; statehood, 108; Treaty of Guadalupe Hidalgo, 112; zoot suit riots, 411
California redwood, R61
California Standards, ST1–ST32
California Trail, 108
California valley quail, R61
Calley, William, 623
Calloway, Cab, 307
Calvert, George, 19
Cambodia, 398, 597, *599m*, 621, 625, 680
Camp David, 711
Camp David Accords, 684, *684p*
Canada: in NATO, 470; North American Free Trade Agreement, 730, 808, *808p*
canals, 96, 218–219
CAN-SPAM law, 803
capitalism, 151, 271
Capone, Al, 300–301
Caporetto, Battle of, *232c*, *233m*
Capra, Frank, 369
Caputo, Philip, 606
caravans, 9
caravels, 11
Caribbean, 187, R50
Carmichael, Stokely, 580, *580p*, 583, 588, R34
Carnegie, Andrew, 151, R34
Carnegie Steel Company, 151, 153
Carolinas, *14m*, 15, 18, 19. *See also* North Carolina; South Carolina
Caroline Islands, 438, *438m*
carpetbaggers, 135
carpet bombing, 605
Carranza, Venustiano, 220, 223
Carson, Rachel, 668, *783p*
Carter, James Earl "Jimmy," 695, R21, R34; Camp David Accords, 684, *684p*; economy and, 682; election of 1976, 681; election of 1980, 686, 695–696, *695m*; energy policy of, 682–683, *682q*; environment and, 683; foreign policy and, 683–686; human rights and, 683; inauguration of, 681, *681p*

Carter, Rosalynn, 681, *681p*
cash-and-carry policy, 402
cash crops, 22
Castro, Fidel, 528–529, *528p*, R34
Cather, Willa, 312
Catt, Carrie Chapman, 192, *192p*, *192q*
cattle ranching, 145–146, *145m*
Cause and Effect: of Civil War, *130c*; of Cold War, 465; of expansionism, 201; of Mexican-American War, *112c*; of Reconstruction, *138c*; of Revolutionary War, 30–31, *31c*–*32c*; of secession, 120–121, *121c*; of Spanish-American War, 210–211; of the stock market crash, *325c*; of Vietnam War, *602c*, 624–627; of War of 1812, 55–56, *56c*; of western migration, 106–109, *148c*; of the women's movement, 638; of World War I, 231–232, 258–259, 286–287, *286c*; of World War II, 455; of Yom Kippur War, 670–671
CCC. *See* Civilian Conservation Corps
Ceausescu, Nicolae, 709
Census Bureau, U.S., 148, 579
Central America, 7, 704, *704p*
Central High School, 560, *560p*
Central Intelligence Agency (CIA), 498; Bay of Pigs invasion, 528–529
Central Pacific Railroad, *150m*, 151
Central Powers: in World War I, 232–237, *233m*, 257
Chaffee, Lois, 564
Challenger (spacecraft), 715, *715p*
Chamberlain, Neville, 392, *392p*, 393, 395, R34
Chambers, Whitaker, 480
Chancellorsville, Battle of, 129, *129p*
Chaney, James, 575–576
Chaplin, Charlie, 310, 368, *368p*, 369, R34
Charles II, king of England, 18, 19
Chattanooga, 130
Chávez, César, 642, *642p*, 644, *644p*, R34, R92
Checkers speech (Nixon), 497
checks and balances, 46–47, *46c*
chemical weapons, 236–237
Cheney, Dick, 734
Chernobyl accident, 708
Cherokee culture, *94m*, 95, 128
Cheyenne, 142, 143, *143m*
Chiang Kai-shek, 478, R34
Chicago, 145, *145m*, 303; civil rights in, 582; Democratic convention, 617–618, *617p*; economy of, *581g*; Haymarket Riot, 153; skyscrapers, 158, *158p*
Chicago Defender (newspaper), 303
Chicanos: rights organizations, 644–649. *See also* Latinos
Chickamauga, Battle of, 130
Chickasaw culture, *94m*, 95
Chief Joseph, 144, R34
child labor, 153, 172, 195
China: Boxer Rebellion, 204, *204p*; communism in, 478–479, *478m*; immigrants from, 147, 157, 158, 767–768, *767p*; Japan and, 390–391, 398; Korea and, 487; Marco Polo and, 11; Nixon and, 669–670, *669p*, 808, R15; Soviet Union and, 708; Tiananmen Square massacre, 711; Vietnam and, 597. *See also* People's Republic of China
Chinese Americans, 162
Chinese Exclusion Act (1882), 158, 768
Chisholm, Shirley, 638
Chisholm Trail, *145m*, 146
Choctaw culture, *94m*, 95, 128
Christian conservatives, 718
Christianity: Crusades and, 10; Ku Klux Klan and, 297; missionaries, 15
Chung, Grace H., *774p*
church bombings, 571
Churchill, Winston, 422, 434, 450, R34; appeasement policy and, 392, *392p*, 395; Atlantic Charter, 403; Battle of Britain and, 396–397, *397q*; Iron Curtain and, 466–467, *467p*, *467q*; Stalin and, 467
Church of England, 19
Church of Jesus Christ of Latter-day Saints, 99, 107
CIA. *See* Central Intelligence Agency
CIO. *See* Congress of Industrial Organizations
CIS. *See* Commonwealth of Independent States (CIS)
cities, 279; urbanization and, 296–297, *296g*
citizenship, 162; Native Americans and, 285; women and, 182
city government, 174
city manager, 174
civil defense, 507–508, *507p*
Civilian Conservation Corps (CCC), 350, *351p*, 357, *360c*
civil liberties, 49
civil rights, 137; of African Americans, 172, 180; progressivism and, 172; Franklin Roosevelt and, 366; Supreme Court and, 538; under Wilson, 193; of women, 180–182
Civil Rights Act (1866), 134
Civil Rights Act (1957), *570c*
Civil Rights Act (1964), 544, 570–571, *570c*, 576, 588, 636–638, R14, R90
Civil Rights Act (1968), *570c*, 588
Civil Rights cases (1883), R22–R23
civil rights movement, 557–558, *557m*; Birmingham campaign, 569–570, *569p*; demonstrations, *554p*–*555p*, 562–563, *562p*; division of, 582–584, *582p*, *583p*; Freedom Rides, 566–567, *566m*; March Against Fear, 580, *580p*; March on Washington, *554p*–*555p*, 571, *571q*; Montgomery bus boycott, 562–563, *562p*; Poor People's Campaign, 586–587, *586p*; reforms in the, *570c*; sit-ins, 565–566, 568–569; time line, 554–555, 574–575; voting rights and, 573–579, *573p*, *576p*, *577p*
civil service, 160
Civil War, 236, R7; African Americans in, 127, *127p*; Appomattox, 131, *131p*; battles in, *114p*–*115p*, 123, *123p*, 125, *125m*, *126m*, *126p*, 128–131; blockades, 128; cause and effects of, *130c*; cost of, *132c*; Davis and, 123; in the East, 125–126, *126m*; life in, 127–128; Lincoln and, 123, 124; March to the Sea, 131; Native Americans and, 128; in the North, 123–131; in the South, 123–131; time line, 114–115; in the West, 125, *125m*, 128; women in, 128, 773
Civil Works Administration (CWA), 351, *360c*
Clark, William, *54m*, 55
Clay, Henry, 95, 117
Clayton Antitrust Act (1914), 191
Clean Air Act, 668, 783
Clean Water Act, 783
Clemenceau, Georges, 255, *256q*, 608, R34
Cleveland, Grover, R19; Hawaii and, 203; Sherman Silver Purchase Act, 161
Clifford, Clark, 540
climate, 147–148
Clinton, Bill, 448, *448p*, 734, R21, R34; al Qaeda and, 743; domestic policy, 727–729; election of 1992, 727, *727p*; election of 1994, 728; election of 1996, 729; environment and, 783; foreign policy of, 729–731; free trade, 730–731, *730p*, *730q*; as governor, 726; health care and, 727–728; impeachment and, 731; Kennedy and, 726, *726p*; welfare reform, 728
Clinton, Hillary Rodham, 727, 728, R34
cluster bombs, 605
code talkers, 439
Cold Harbor, Battle of, 130
Cold War, 462–493, *500m*, 703; arms race and, 504–508, *505p*, *506p*, *506q*; Berlin and, 469–470, *469m*; cause and effect of, 465; Cuban missile crisis, 532–533, *532m*, *533p*; documents about, 490–491; Eisenhower and, 497–501; Kennedy and, 528–529; Korea and, 483–489, *483p*, *484m*, *487m*; in Middle East, *500m*, 501; Red Scare, 477–482, *477p*, *478m*, *479g*, *480p*, *481p*; Soviet Union and, 465–470, 498–499, *498p*; time line, 462–463
Collins, Michael, *664p*–*665p*, 671–673
Colombia, 213, 215–216, *215p*
colonial government, 15, 21
Colorado, 254, 258; Civil War in, 128; facts about, R30; in Great Depression, 332; La Raza Unida Party, 647; mining in, 144; national parks in, 187, *187p*; nuclear testing in, 503; ranching in, 146; Treaty of Guadalupe Hidalgo, 112
Colorado River, 336, *336p*
Colored Citizens of Boston, 212
Columbia (spacecraft), 673, 715
Columbian Exchange, *11m*, 12
Columbus, Christopher, 11–12, *12p*, 13, *14m*, R3, R34
Comanche, 142, *143m*
Commerce Clause, 356
Committee on Public Information, 251
Common Sense (Paine), 32, *33q*
Commonwealth of Independent States (CIS), 710
communication: in Civil War, 124; mail, 108–109; radio, 280; in Second Industrial Revolution, 154–155; telegraph, 97, 109; telephone, 155, 750, R8

communism, 271–272, *272p*; Cold War and, 498, *500m*; in Eastern Europe, 466; labor movement and, 273; McCarran Act, 480; Smith Act, 480; in Soviet Union, 390; spread of, 478–482, *478m, 480p, 481p*; Vietnam and, 598, 627
Communist Party, 242, 480
comparative advantage, 807, 809
compass rose, R67
compensated emancipation, 119
Compromise of 1850, 117, *117m, 121c*, R82, R83,
computer technology, 512, *512p*, 714, *714p*, 749–750; Internet, 800–805, *800p, 801p, 802p, 803g, 804p, 805p*
Comstock Lode, 144
concentration camps, 427, 428–429, *429c, 429m, 429p*, 430–431
Concert of Europe, 92
Confederacy. *See* Confederate States of America
Confederate States of America, 122, 123–131
confederation, 43
Congress, U.S.: antiwar speech and, 252, 253; Articles of Confederation, 43; cash-and-carry policy, 402; checks and balances, 46–47, *46c*; Enforcement Acts, 137; Homestead Act (1862), 146; Kennedy and, 536–537; Lend-Lease Act, 403; McCarran Act, 480; Reconstruction and, 133–135; Sherman Antitrust Act (1890), 152; slavery and, 116–117; Smith-Connally Act, 410; standard time, 151, 211; Taft-Hartley Act and, 473; Tenure of Office Act (1867), 135; Truman Doctrine, 467; Wade-Davis Bill (1864), 133. *See also* House of Representatives, U.S.; legislative branch; Senate, U.S.
Congressional Black Caucus, *588p*
Congress of Industrial Organizations (CIO), 360–361
Congress of Racial Equality (CORE), 558
conic projections, R65
Connecticut: colonial, 18; constitution of, 18; facts about, R30; Great Compromise, *45c*, 46; Native Americans in, 640
Connecticut Compromise, 46
Connor, Eugene "Bull," 569–570
conquistadors, 15
conscientious objector, 241
conservation, 187–188, 190; environmental, 780–787; fuel, 248
Constitution, U.S.: amendments, 49; Article V, 49; Article VII, 49; Bill of Rights, 49; Federalists and Antifederalists, 47, 48; loose construction, 52; ratification of, 48; strict construction, 52; text of, 60–67. *See also individual amendments*
Constitutional Convention, 44–47, *44p–45p*, R5
Constitutional Issue: due process, 549; equal protection, 448, 561, 579, 687; freedom of speech, 253, *253p*; freedom of the press, 674; powers of the President, 356; search and seizure, 732
constitutions: Fundamental Orders of Connecticut, 18
constructive engagement, 705
consumer protection, 186
consumers, 279–280, *280p*
containment policy, 467–468, *467q*
Continental Army, 32, 34–35, *36m*
Continental Congress: First, 31, 42; Second, 32, 43
continents, R59, R63
Contract with America, 728
Contras, 704
convoy system, 242, 419, *419p*
Cook, James, 202
Coolidge, Calvin, 273, 284–285, *284p, 285p*, 297, 322, 336, R20, R34
Coolidge, Grace, 284, *284p*
Coolidge, John, 284–285
cooperatives, 337
Copperheads, 128
copyright, *804*
Coral Sea, Battle of, 436, *438m*
CORE. *See* Congress of Racial Equality (CORE)
Cornwallis, Charles, 36–37
Coronado, Francisco Vásquez de, 15
Corporation for Public Broadcasting, 547
corporations, 151
corps, 773
Cortés, Hernán, 15
cost of living, 790
cotton, 96, 97–98, 281
cotton gin, 97
Coughlin, Charles, 352–353, 362, 369, R34
counterculture, 650–655, *650p, 651p, 652p, 653p, 654p*
Counterpoints: annexation of the Philippines, 211, *211p, 211q*; appeasement, 392, *392p, 392q*; arms race, 506, *506p, 506q*; atomic bomb, 454, *454p, 454q*; Equal Rights Amendment, 637, *637p, 637q*; Federalists v. Antifederalists, 47, *47p, 47q*; free trade, 730, *730p, 730q*; government's role, 373, *373p, 373q*; Iran hostage crisis, 685, *685p, 685q*; League of Nations, 257, *257p, 257q*; Lincoln-Douglas debates, 120, *120p, 120q*; Prohibition, 300, *300p, 300q*; Reconstruction, 134, *134p, 134q*; savings and loan crisis, 717, *717p, 717q*; social Darwinism, 152, *152p, 152q*; tactics of change, 583, *583p, 583q*; Vietnam War, 610, *610p, 610q*; voting rights, 192, *192p, 192q*
cowboys, 145, 146
Cowen, Tyler, 756
Cox, Archibald, 677, 678, *679q*
Cox, James, 283
Creative Destruction: How Globalization is Changing the World's Cultures (Cowen), 756
credit buying, 280
Crédit Mobilier, 160
Creek culture, *94m*, 95, 128
Creel, George, 251, R34
Creelman, James, 206
creoles, 15
crime, 667, 794–799, *794p, 796p, 798p, 799p, 799q*; identity theft, 802; Internet, 802, 803, *803g*
criminal code, 795
criminal justice, 795–799; due process, 549; search warrants, 538–539
Crisis, The (magazine), 304, *304p*
Critical Thinking: analyze, 57, 113, 139, 197, 227, 263, 553, 592, 593, 631, 659, 722; analyze information, 193, 540, 578; analyze the impact, 253, 356, 448, 549, 561, 579, 674, 687, 700, 732; categorizing, 563, 585, 627, 699; compare, 49, 56, 259, 291, 460, 593, 631, 649; compare and contrast, 98, 155, 182, 275, 659; contrast, 27, 57, 212, 227, 263, 378, 461, 519, 611, 649, 690; decision making, 706; define, 27, 197; describe, 27, 57, 113, 139, 227, 263, 291, 317, 379, 415, 460, 493, 519, 553, 593, 631, 659, 690, 691, 723, 758; develop, 415, 659; draw conclusions, 139, 197, 378, 493, 519, 553, 593, 603, 722; elaborate, 27, 113, 197, 227, 263, 414, 460, 461, 493, 553, 592, 593, 631, 659, 691, 723, 759; evaluate, 27, 57, 113, 197, 227, 263, 291, 317, 378, 415, 460, 461, 493, 519, 553, 593, 631, 659, 722, 723, 758, 759; generalize, 723; identify cause and effect, 12, 19, 112, 131, 138, 148, 175, 205, 237, 244, 327, 333, 339, 364, 393, 425, 470, 534, 571, 655, 680, 713, 719, 746; identify main idea, 301, 398, 476, 482, 501, 508, 515, 673, 686, 731, 738, 752; identify supporting details, 252, 411, 431, 440, 447, 455, 589; make generalizations, 291, 691, 759; make inferences, 113, 197, 379, 415, 553, 758; organizing information, 217, 641; predict, 27, 139, 226, 415, 593, 631, 691; rank, 519, 722, 759; rate, 379, 493; recall, 113, 197, 227, 263, 291, 317, 378, 379, 415, 460, 461, 493, 519, 553, 592, 659, 691, 722, 759; sequence, 37, 57, 122, 162, 223, 263, 281, 287, 307, 353, 405, 415, 460, 489, 493, 548, 619, 723; summarize, 26, 27, 105, 188, 227, 291, 317, 379, 414, 461, 519, 659, 691, 759; support main idea, 313; you be the judge, 253, 356, 448, 549, 561, 579, 674, 687, 700, 732
Crittenden Compromise, 122
Crockett, Davy, 110
Cromwell, Otelia, 177, *177p*
Cronkite, Walter, 614–615, *615q*, 629
cross of gold speech, 161
Crusade for Justice, 645
Crusades, 10
Cruzan, Nancy, 718
Cruzan v. Director, Missouri Department of Health (1990), 718, R27
Crystal City, Texas, 646, *647p*
Cuba: Bay of Pigs invasion, 528–529, *528p*; expansionism in, 214–215; Grenada and, 705; missile crisis in, 532–533, *532m, 533p*, R14; Spanish-American War, 206–208, 209–210, *209m*

Cuban Americans, 528, 649, *755p*
Cuban missile crisis, 532–533, *532m, 533p*, R14
Cullen, Countee, 304
culture: radio and, 309, *309p*; spread of, 757; themes of, 265
Curtis, Paul, 458
Custer, George Armstrong, 143, R35
CWA. *See* Civil Works Administration
cyberspace, 802
cylindrical projections, R64
Czechoslovakia, 256, 393
Czolgosz, Leon, 184

Dachau, 431
da Gama, Vasco, 11
Daley, Richard, 617
dams, 351
Darfur, 430
Darrow, Clarence, *298p*, 299, *299p*, R35
Darwin, Charles, 151, 298
Davies, Joe, 715
Davis, Benjamin O., Jr., 452
Davis, Benjamin O., Sr., 452
Davis, Gray, 769, R60
Davis, Jefferson, 122, 123, 126
Davis, Richard Harding, 206, 207
Dawes Act (1887), 144, 285, R9
daylight saving time, 248
Days of Rage, 623
Dayton Accords, 730
D-Day, 423–424, *424p–425p*, R13
Dean, James, 515
Dean, John, 677, 678
Dear Leader. *See* Kim Jong Il
Death Valley, R61
Debs, Eugene V., 153, 191, 252, R35
debt peonage, 162
Declaration of Human Rights, 683
Declaration of Independence, R4; text of, 38–41; writing the, 32–33
Declaration of Indian Purpose, 639, *639q*
Declaration of Rights, 31
Declaration of Rights for Women, R87
de facto segregation, 581
Defending American Jobs Act (2004), 808
deficit reduction, 727
degrees, R62
de jure segregation, 581
De Klerk, F.W., 713
Delano Grape Strike, 642, *642p*
Delaware: in Civil War, 124; facts about, R30
delegated powers, 49
de Lôme, Enrique Dupuy de, 208
demilitarized zone, 599
democracy: themes of, 165, 265, 381, 521, 661
Democratic Party, *521p*; African Americans and, 362, 366–367; creation of, 95; election of 1856, 118; election of 1860, 121; election of 1864, 130–131; election of 1930, 339; election of 1932, 347, *347m*; election of 1934, 358; election of 1938, 375; election of 1946, 474; election of 1948, 474; election of 1952, 496, *496p*, 497; election of 1956, 499; election of 1960, 527; election of 1964, 545–546, 576, 583; election of 1966, 547; election of 1968, 615, 616–619, *617p, 618p, 619m*; election of 1972, 624; election of 1976, 680, 681; election of 1980, 695–696, *695m*; election of 1988, 707, 708; election of 1992, 727; election of 1994, 728; election of 1996, 729; election of 2000, 733–735, *733p, 734m, 734p, 735p*; election of 2004, 736; Watergate and, 675
Democratic-Republicans, 51, 52, 54, 95
Denmark: in NATO, 470; in World War II, 396, *397m*
Dennis v. United States, 480
department store, 276, *276p*
deportation, 272
depression, economic, 137. *See also* Great Depression
deregulation, 716
desegregatoin, 667
Desert Fox. *See* Rommel, Erwin
De Soto, Hernando, 15
détente, 668–669, 680
Detroit, Michigan, 279, 303, 581
Deukmejian, George, R60
Dewey, George, 208–209
Dewey, Thomas, 474, R35
DeWitt, John L., 445
Dewson, Molly, *366q*
de Young, Marie E., 775
Diary of Anne Frank, The (Frank), 428
Díaz, Porfirio, 221, *221p*, R35
Dickinson, Lester, 362
dictatorship, 389
Dien Bien Phu, Battle of, 499, *500m*, 599
Digital Age, 714, *714p*
DiMaggio, Joe, 370
Dinh, Viet, 766, *766p*, 768
direct primary, 175
discrimination, 162; affirmative action and, 687; German Americans and, 251
diseases: AIDS, 719; in Civil War, 127; malaria, 215–216; Native Americans and, 12; polio, 513; yellow fever, 214, 215, *215p*
Disney, Walt, 310, 369
District of Columbia, 193; facts about, R30
dividends, 736
Dix, Dorothea, 100, 773, R35
Dixiecrats, 474
Dixon, Marlene, 656
Dixon, Maynard, *346p*
Doane, Philip, 250
Document-Based Investigation: Cold War, 490–491; crime and public safety, 794–799, *794p, 796p, 798p, 799p, 799q*; environmental conservation, 780–787, *780p, 782p, 783p, 784p, 786c, 786p, 787c*; equal rights, 590–591; flappers, 314–315, *315p*; globalization, 756–757; Great Depression, 340–341; Great Society, 550–551; Hawaii, 224–225; immigration policy, 766–771; Internet, 800–805, *800p, 801p, 802p, 803g, 804p, 805p*; interstate highway system, 516–517, *516g, 517m*; military life, 458–459, *458p*; New Frontier, 550; outsourcing and trade, 806–812, *806p, 807p, 808p, 809p, 810g, 811c, 811g*; Pearl Harbor, 412–413; poverty, 788–793, *788p, 789p, 791p, 792g, 792m, 793c*; progressivism, 194–195; Red Scare, 288–289; Roosevelt, Franklin Delano, 376–377, *377p*; Tet Offensive, 628–629, *628c, 629p*; trench warfare, 260–261, *261p*; Watergate scandal, 688–689, *688g, 689p*; wealth in the 1980s, 720–721; women in the military, 772–779, *772p, 773p, 774p, 776c, 778c, 778p, 779g*; women's movement, 656–657, *656p, 657c*
Dog, Mary Crow, 638
Dole, Bob, 729
Dole, Sanford B., 203, R35
dollar diplomacy, 217
Dolphin, USS (ship), 222
domestic policy: Bush, George W., 736–737; Clinton and, 727–729; Monroe and, 93; nationalism and, 93
Dominican Republic, 216–217, 548, *755p*
Dominion of New England, 21
domino theory, 598
Donnelly, Elaine, 777
Doolittle, James, 435, *435p*, R35
Dorchester Heights, Battle of, 32
Dorsey Brothers, 370
Dos Passos, John, 313
dot coms, 736
Douglas, Aaron, *306p*, 307
Douglas, Stephen A., 118, R35; election of 1860, 121; Kansas-Nebraska Act, 117; Lincoln-Douglas debates, 120, *120p, 120q*
Douglass, Frederick, 105, *105p*, R35, R84, doves, 610
Downey, John, R60
Draffen, Reid, *431q*
draft, military, 407, 608
Drake, Edwin L., 149
Dred Scott v. Sandford (1858), 118–119, R7
drought, 332
drugs, 667; abuse of, 653; testing, 700, 732
Duarte, José Napoléon, 704
Du Bois, W.E.B., 162, 171–172, 244, 304–305, 557, R35
Duck and Cover (film), 507, *507p*
due process, 549
dugouts, 148
Dukakis, Michael, 708
Dulles, John Foster, 497–498, 504, *506p, 506q*, R35
Dunkirk, 396, *397m*
Duryea, Charles Frank, 154
Dust Bowl, 332–333, *332m, 332p–333p*, 334, *334p*, 782
Dutch: exploration by, *14m*, 15. *See also* Netherlands
Dutch East Indies, 398, 434, *438m*
Dutch West India Company, 19
Dylan, Bob, 655

Eagle (spacecraft), *672p*, 673
Earhart, Amelia, 311, R35
Earth: mapping the, R62
Earth Day, 668
East: Civil War in, 125–126, *126m*
East Asia: immigrants from, 157; World War II in, 398
East Berlin, 530–531, *531p*, 701
Eastern Europe: after World War II, 451; collapse of communism in, 709; communism in, 466; Iron Curtain, 465–467, *466m*, *467p*; Warsaw Pact and, 498–499
Eastern Hemisphere, R63
Eastern Woodlands cultures, 7, *8m*
East Germany, *466m*, 469–470, *469m*, 530, *531m*, 709
East India Company, 30
Eckford, Elizabeth, 560, *560p*
economic development: themes of, 165, 265
Economic Opportunity Act (1964), 543–544
economics: buying on margin, 323–324; gross national product, 321, 326, *364g*; inflation, 43, 387, *387p*, 673, 680, 682, 686; Keynes theory of, 364; mercantilism, 21; postwar, 513; supply-side, 698–699; wealth distribution, 323, *323g*
economic systems: capitalism, 151, 271; communism, 271–272, *272p*; laissez-faire capitalism, 151
economy: after World War I, 270–271; 633; budget deficits, 364; George H.W. Bush and, 716–717; Carter and, 682; colonial, 21–23; consumers and the, 279–280, *280p*; depression, 137; Federal Reserve System, 324; of Germany, 387, *387p*; Great Depression, 329–330, *329g*; inflation, 43, 387, *387p*, 673, 680, 682, 686, 699, 716; Lyndon Johnson and, 544; Nixon and, 673; Panic of 1893, 161; under Reagan, 698–699, *698p*, *699g*; recession, 699; in the 1980s, 720–721; in the 1990s, 728; World War I and, 247–249. *See also* New Deal
Edison, Thomas Alva, 155, *155p*, R35
editorials, 208
Edmund Pettus Bridge, 573, 577–578, *577p*
Edo. *See* Tokyo
education: affirmative action programs and, 687; African Americans and, 136, 177, *177p*, 556, *557m*, 558, 559–561, 567–568, *567p*; Elementary and Secondary Education Act (1965), 546, *546c*; Fair Deal, 475; GI Bill, 472, *472p*; Head Start, 546, *546c*; Higher Education Act (1965), 546; Morrill Act, 146; National Defense Education Act, 506; Native Americans and, 144; No Child Left Behind Act, 736, 737; reforms in, 100; in Roaring Twenties, 297; science and, 298–299; women and, 177–178, *177p*, 295. *See also* higher education

Edwards, Jonathan, 24, R35
Egypt, 501; Camp David Accords, 684, *684p*; Yom Kippur War, 670, 684
Ehrlichman, John, 676, 677
Eighteenth Amendment, 180, 248, 299–300
Einsatzgruppen, 428
Einstein, Albert, *301q*, *506p*, *506q*
Eisenhower, Dwight D., 542, R20, R36; Cold War and, 497–501; election of 1952, 489, 496, *496p*, 497; election of 1956, 499; foreign policy of, 497–501, *500q*, 529; integration in, 560; interstate highway system, 515; Korea and, 485; nuclear weapons and, 504; termination policy, 638–639; Vietnam and, 598, 599, 601; World War II and, 421, 423, *423p*, 451
Eisenhower Doctrine, 501
El Alamein, Battle of, 420
elastic clause, 176
Elbe River, *449p*
election: of 1796, 53; of 1800, 54; of 1804, 55; of 1824, 95; of 1828, 95; of 1844, 110; of 1856, 118; of 1860, 121, *121c*; of 1864, 130–131, of 1876, 138; of 1892, 161; of 1896, 161; of 1908, 190; of 1912, *190m*, 191; of 1916, 239; of 1920, 283, 285, 322; of 1924, 285, 322; of 1928, 322–323, *322m*; of 1930, 339; of 1932, *337p*, 339, 347, *347m*; of 1934, 358; of 1936, 362, *362p*, 376; of 1938, 375; of 1940, 403; of 1946, 474; of 1948, 474–475; of 1950, 482; of 1952, 489, 496, *496p*, 497, 510, of 1956, 499; of 1960, 516, 527, 536, 542, 666; of 1964, *544p*, 545–546, 576; of 1966, 547; of 1968, *521p*, 615, 616–619, *617p*, *618p*, *619m*, 666, 667, *667q*; of 1972, 624, 673, 676–677; of 1976, 680, 681; of 1980, 686, 695–696, *695m*, 697; of 1984, 697, 703, 705; of 1988, 707, 708; of 1992, 727, *727p*, of 1996, 729; of 2000, 733–735, *733p*, *734m*, *734p*, *735p*; of 2004, 736; reforms, 175
electoral college, 138, 527, 546, 619
electricity, 155, 354–355, 362
Electronic Numerical Integrator and Computer (ENIAC), 512, *512p*
Elementary and Secondary Education Act (1965), 546, *546c*
elevator, 159
Elizabeth I, queen of England, 15
Elkins Act (1903), 186
Ellington, Duke, 307, 370
Ellis Island, 157
Ellison, Ralph, 359
Ellsberg, Daniel, 623, 674, 676
El Salvador, *704p*, 704
e-mail, 800, 801, *805p*
Emancipation Proclamation, 126, R7, R85
embargo, 670–671, *671m*
embassy bombings, 742
Emergency Banking Act (1933), 349–350, *360c*
Emerson, Ralph Waldo, 100
employment: African Americans and, 410–411; Civilian Conservation Corps, 350, *351p*, 357; minimum wage and, 374–375; women and, 172, 178–179, 295, *295p*, *408p*, 409–410, 635, *635g*; Works Progress Administration, 358–359, *358p*–*359p*
encomienda system, 15
encryption, 802
Endangered Species Act, 783
energy: alternative sources of, 683; Carter and, 682–683, *682q*; environment and, 751–752; nuclear power, 605, 683
Enforcement Acts, 137
Engel v. *Vitale* (1962), 539, R25
England: colonies of, 16–19, *16p*–*17p*, *18c*, 21, 30–31, *31c*–*32c*; exploration by, 11, *14m*, 15; French and Indian War, 24–26, *25m*; Magna Carta, 10; nation-states, 10; North American claims, *25m*; Revolutionary War and, 30–31, *31c*–*32c*, 32, 34–37, *36m*; Spain and, 15. *See also* Great Britain
ENIAC. *See* Electronic Numerical Integrator and Computer
Enigma code system, 420
Enlightenment, 23–24, 32–33
Enola Gay (B-29), 453
Enterprise, USS, 436, *437p*
entertainment: in Roaring Twenties, 308–310, *308p*, *309p*, *310p*
entrepreneurs, 151
environment, 780–787; Carter and, 683; energy and, 751–752; Nixon and, 668; T. Roosevelt and, 187–188, *188m*; society and, R73
Environmental Protection Agency (EPA), R15
epidemics, 250, *250p*, 270, *270p*
Equal Access Act, 718
Equal Employment Opportunity Commission, 636
equal protection, 448, 561, 579, 687
equal rights: women and, 102–103
Equal Rights Amendment (ERA), 179, 634, *634p*, 636–637, *637p*
equator, R62
ERA. *See* Equal Rights Amendment
Era of Good Feelings, 93
Erie Canal, 96, R6
erosion, *782p*
Escobedo v. *Illinois* (1964), 539
espionage, 480–481, *480p*
Espionage Act, 252, 253
Establishment, 651, 654
Ethiopia, 391, 401
ethnic groups, 768; self-determination and, 255, 256
Europe: after World War I, 387; exploration and, 10–12, *10c*, *11m*, *12p*; immigrants from, 274–275, *274g*; Marshall Plan, 468–469, *468c*; NATO, 470; political maps, R50, R54; stock market crash and, 327; Treaty of Versailles and, 257–259, *258m*, 387; World War II in, 396–398, *397m*, 418–422, *421m*, 423–424, *424p*–*425p*, 449–452, *449p*, *450p*
evangelism, 718
Evans, Walker, 368
Evers, Medgar, 563, 570, 591, R36
Evil Empire speech (Reagan), 702

evolution, 298–299
Ex Comm, 533
executive branch, 47; California government, R60; checks and balances, 46–47, *46c*; New Deal and, 353, 374; powers of the President, 356. *See also* President, U.S.; Vice President, U.S.
Executive Order 9066, 445–446, *446p*
Executive Order 9835, 490
Executive Order 9981, 473, *473q*, 474, *474p*
Executive Order 11063, *570c*
executive privilege, 678
Exodusters, 147
expansionism: cause and effect of, 201; in Cuba, 214–215; Hawaii and, 224–225; in Puerto Rico, 214, 215
explorers, 10–12, *10c*, *11m*, *12p*, *14m*
extinction, 783

Fairbanks, Douglas, 246, *247p*, 251, 310
Fair Deal, 475
Fair Housing Act, *570c*
Fair Labor Standards Act, *360c*, 374–375
Fall, Albert, 284
Fallen Timbers, Battle of, 53
Falwell, Jerry, 697, 718, *718p*, R36
families, 295
Farewell to Arms, A (Hemingway), 313
Farmer, James, 565, *565p*, 566, 578, R36
Farmers' Alliance, 160
farms and farming: after World War I, 281, 284; boycotts, *632p–633p*, 642, *642p*; cooperatives, 337; Farm Tenancy Act, 363; genetic engineering, 750; in Great Depression, 329–330, *329g*; on the Great Plains, 146–148, *146p–147p*; New Deal programs, *360c*; plantations, 22–23; reform movements and, 160; sharecropping, 136, *136p*; subsidies, 350–351; subsistence farming, 21; technology, 148; tenant farming, 136; *United States v. Butler*, 353
Farm Security Administration (FSA), *360c*, *367p*
Farm Tenancy Act, 363
Far North cultures, 7, *8m*
Farragut, David, 125
fascism, 388–389, *388q*, *389p*
Father of the Constitution, 45
Faubus, Orville, 560
FCDA. *See* Federal Civil Defense Administration
FDIC. *See* Federal Deposit Insurance Corporation
Federal Bureau of Investigation (FBI), 795, *796p*
Federal Children's Bureau, 179
Federal Civil Defense Administration (FCDA), 507
Federal Deposit Insurance Corporation (FDIC), 350, *360c*, 372
Federal Emergency Relief Administration (FERA), *360c*

federal government, 46, 696
Federal Home Loan Bank, 338
Federal Housing Administration (FHA), *360c*
federalism, 48
Federalist Papers, 48, R77
Federalist Party, 54, 56
Federalists, *47p*, *47q*, 48, 51, 52
federal lands, *784m*, *787c*
Federal Reserve Act (1913), 191
Federal Reserve banks, 191
Federal Reserve Board, 191, 324, 716
Federal Securities Act, 351
Federal Trade Commission (FTC), 191
Feinstein, Diane, 769
Felt, Mark, 677, 689
Feminine Mystique, The (Friedan), 636
feminism, 636
Fenner, Lorry M., 775
Ferdinand, king of Spain, 11
Ferguson, Miriam "Ma," 295
Ferraro, Geraldine, 703, 717
Fifteenth Amendment, 118, 135, 138, 180, 576
Fifth Amendment, 118, 549, 783
Fillmore, Millard, 118, 205, R18
Final Solution, 428–429, *429c*, *429m*, *429p*, 430–431
Finlay, Carlos Juan, 214
fireside chats, 348, 351, 369
First Amendment, 49, 252, 253, *253p*, 539, 749
First Bank of the United States, 95
First Ladies: Clinton, Hillary Rodham, 727, 728; Johnson, Lady Bird, 547; Kennedy, Jacqueline, 535, *535p*, 536, *539p*, 540; Lincoln, Mary Todd, 119; Madison, Dolley, *55p*; Reagan, Nancy, *694p*, 697, R4; Roosevelt, Eleanor, 348–349, *349p*, 366, 371, 475–476, 557
Fisher, Jackie, 231
Fitzgerald, F. Scott, 312, 313, R36
flag, 445, R32; California, R61
Flagg, James Montgomery, 251, *407p*
flappers, *295p*, 296, 314–315, *315p*
flat-plane projections, R65
flexible response, 534
Florida, 26; Adam-Onís Treaty, 93; Cuba and, 529; election of 2000, 734–735, *734p*, *735p*; exploration of, *14m*, 15; facts about, R30; hurricanes in, 281; military bases in, 408; Native Americans in, *94m*, 95; Pinckney's Treaty, 53; population of, 748; secession, 121; tourist industry, 279
flower children, 653
food: insecurity, 790; in World War I, 247–248
Food Stamp Program, 668, 793
football, 312, *312p*
Foraker Act, 215
Ford, Gerald, 677, 697, R21, R36; Nixon pardon and, 679–680; presidency of, *678q*, 679–680, *679p*
Ford, Henry, 277, *277p*, *277q*, 279, 406, 408, R10, R36
Fordney-McCumber Tariff, 284, 286
foreclosure, 330
foreign aid: in Civil War, 124; Marshall Plan, 468–469, *468c*

foreign policy: brinkmanship, 498, 504; Bush, George H.W., 708–712; Bush, George W., 737–738, 743–746; Carter and, 683–686; cash-and-carry policy, 402; Clinton and, 729–731; détente, 668–669, 680; dollar diplomacy, 217; Eisenhower and, 497–501, *500q*, 529; Foraker Act, 215; Ford and, 680; Fourteen Points, 255, *255q*, *256c*; interventionism, 401–402, *401q*, *402q*; isolationism, 239, 400–402; Kennedy and, 528–534, *534q*; Lyndon Johnson and, 548; massive retaliation, 498, 504; Monroe Doctrine, 92, 93; nationalism and, 93; Nixon and, 668–671, *669p*; Open Door Policy, 204; Platt Amendment, 214; Reagan and, 701–706, *702g*, *706c*; realpolitik, 668; Roosevelt Corollary, 216–217, *217q*; shuttle diplomacy, 671; Teller Amendment, 209, 214; Treaty of Portsmouth, 205; Truman Doctrine, 467–468, *467q*; Wilson and, 217, 220, 222–223
foreign trade: China and, 204
Foreman, George, 543
Forest Service, U.S., 188, 190
Forgotten Man speech (F. Roosevelt), 346, *346p*
Fort Sumter, 123, *123p*
Fort Ticonderoga, 32, 34
forty-niners, 108
Four Freedoms, 443, 444,
Four Freedoms speech (F. Roosevelt), R88
Four Minute Men, *247p*
Fourteen Points, 255, *255q*, *256c*, R88
Fourteenth Amendment, 118, 134, 135, 137, 138, 161, 538
Fourth Amendment, 538–539, 700, 718, 732
France: Civil War and, 124; colonies of, 19; exploration by, 11, *14m*, 15; French and Indian War, 24–26, *25m*; French Revolution, 53; Germany and, 392; Great Britain and, 55; imperialism and, 231; Jews in, 426, *426p*; militarism and, 231; nation-states, 10; in NATO, 470; North American claims, *25m*; Vichy government, 396; Vietnam and, 499–500, *500m*, 596–599; in World War I, 233–235, *233m*, 236, 242–243, *243m*, 259; in World War II, 396, *397m*, 421, *421m*, 423–424, *424p–425p*; XYZ Affair, 53
Franco, Francisco, 390, 392, R36
Frank, Anne, 428
Franklin, Benjamin, 32, *44p*, 45; Albany Plan of Union, 26; Enlightenment and, 24
Franklin, Henrietta, 587, *587q*
Franz Ferdinand, Archduke, 230, 232, R36
Fredericksburg, Battle of, 129
free enterprise, 151
Freedmen's Bureau, 134, 135, 136, 137
freedom of religion, 49, 539
freedom of speech, 49, 252, 253, *253p*, 729
freedom of the press, 49, 674
Freedom Riders, 566–567, *566m*, 574
Freedom Schools, 575
Freedom Summer, 575–576

INDEX

freemen, 103
Freeport Doctrine, 120
Free-Soil Party, 117
Free Speech Movement, 652
free states, 93, *93m*
free trade, 807
Frémont, John C., 118
French and Indian War, 24–26, *25m*, R4
French Indochina, 398, 403, 597
French Revolution, 53
Friedan, Betty, 636, *636p*, R36
Friendship 7 (space capsule), *525p*
Frye, Henry, *588p*
FTC. *See* Federal Trade Commission
Fuchido, Misuo, *436q*
Fuchs, Klaus, 480, *480p*, 481
fuel: regulation of, 248, 279. *See also* energy
Fugitive Slave Act, 117
Fulbright, J. William, 611, R36
fundamentalism, 297–299, 718
Fundamental Orders of Connecticut, 18, R75,
fur trade, 25
fusion, 503

Gadsden Purchase, 112
Gage, Henry, R60
Gage, Thomas, 31
Galbraith, John Kenneth, 513, *513q*
Gallipoli, Battle of, *232c*, *233m*
Gallup Organization, 688, *688g*
Galveston, Texas, 174
Gálvez, Bernardo de, 35
Gandhi, Mohandas, 565, R36
Garcia, Hector, 473
Garfield, Harry, 248
Garfield, James A., 160, R19
Garrison, William Lloyd, 104
Garvey, Marcus, 304–305, R36
gasoline, 279
Gates, Bill, 714, *714p*, *749q*
GATT. *See* General Agreement on Tariffs and Trade
Gaulle, Charles de, 396, R36
Gehrig, Lou, 370
General Agreement on Tariffs and Trade (GATT), *475c*, 476, 731, 808
General Motors, 361, *361p*
generation gap, 618
genetic engineering, 750
Geneva Accords, 599
genocide, 428
Gentlemen's Agreement, 768
geography: elements of, R73; Standards, R73; themes of, R72
George, David Lloyd, 255, R36
George, Walter, 375
George III, king of England, 26, 32
Georgia, 241; civil rights movement in, 567–569; Civil War in, 130, 131; colonial, 19; facts about, R30; secession, 121
German Americans, 251
Germany, *711p*; after World War I, 286; *Anschluss* and, 393; anti-Semitism in, 427; division of, 450–451, *466m*, 469–470, *469m*; economy of, 387, *387p*; France and, 392; government in, 387, *388p*, 389–393; Great Britain and, 392; immigrants from, 100, 101, 147; imperialism and, 231; militarism and, 231; nationalism in, 231, 389; Rhineland and, 392–393; Schlieffen Plan, 231, 232; Soviet Union and, 420; Sudetenland and, 393; *Sussex* pledge, 239; Treaty of Versailles and, 256–258, *256c*, *258m*, 387, 392; Weimar Republic, 387; in World War I, 232–237, *233m*, 238–239, 240, 242, *243m*, 244, 259; in World War II, 396–397, *397m*, 398, 418–424, *418p*, *419p*, *421m*, 450, 465; Zimmermann Note and, 240
Geronimo, 144, R36
Gerry, Elbridge, 53
Gershwin, George, 313, R37
Gettysburg, Battle of, 129
Gettysburg Address, R86
Ghana, 9
ghettos, 428
Ghost Dance, 142, *142p*
Gibbons v. *Ogden* (1824), 93, R22
GI Bill, 472, *472p*
Gideon v. *Wainwright* (1963), 539, 549, R26
Gilbert, L. Wolfe, *311q*
Gilbert Islands, 438, *438m*
Gilded Age, 151
Gillett, James, R60
Gilman, Charlotte Perkins, 296
Gingrich, Newt, 728
Gitlow v. *New York* (1925), 272
Giuliani, Rudolph, 741, R37
glasnost, 708
Glass, Carter, 352
Glass-Steagall Act (1933), 350
Glenn, John, *525p*, 537
globalization, 756–757, 808
global relations: themes of, 165, 381, 521, 661
globe, R62
GNP. *See* gross national product
God's Trombones (Johnson), 305
Göering, Hermann, 431, R37
Goldberg, Arthur, 652
Golden State. *See* California
gold rush, 107–108, *108p*, *109p*, 144, R6
Goldstein, Robert, 252
Goldwater, Barry, 545, *545p*, *545q*, 576, 603, 694, 696, R37
golf, 312, *312p*
Gompers, Samuel, 153, 212, 274, R37
Gonzales, Henry B., 646
Gonzales, Rodolfo "Corky," 645, *645q*, *647p*, R37
Goodman, Andrew, 575–576
Goodman, Benny, 370
Gorbachev, Mikhail, 703, 707, *707p*, 708, 710, 711, R37
Gore, Al, 727, 733–735, *734m*, R37
Gorgas, William C., 214
government: Articles of Confederation, 42–44, *43c*; branches of, 47; California, R60; checks and balances, 46–47, *46c*; city, 174; colonial, 15, 21; Communist, 390; of Darfur, 430; dictatorships, 389; fascism, 388; in Germany, 387, *388p*, 389–390; Great Compromise, *45c*, 46; Hoover and, 336, *336q*; immigration and, 274–275; Indian policy, 143; Israel, 431; New Deal and, 352–353, 372–375; New Jersey Plan, 45; progressivism and, 174–175, *175c*; Reconstruction and, 135–136; social contract theory, 23; state, 175; themes of, 165, 265, 381, 521, 661; totalitarian, 388–392, *390p*; town meeting, 21; Virginia Plan, 45, *45c*; women in, 365, *365p*, 366; during World War II, 446–447. *See also* federal government; limited government; national government; state government
governors, 21; California, R60
Gramm, Phil, 727
Gramm-Rudman-Hollings Act, 699
Grand Canyon, 15, 187
Grange, Red, 312, *312p*
Grant, Ulysses S., 125, *128p*, 130, 131, 137–138, 160, 187, R19, R37
Grapes of Wrath, The (Steinbeck), 267, 334, 367, 368
Gray, L. Patrick, 689
Great Awakening, 24, *24p*, R3; Second, 100, 102, 104, R3
Great Basin cultures, 7, *8m*
Great Britain: Atlantic Charter, 403; France and, 55; Germany and, 392; imperialism and, 201, 231; Industrial Revolution in, 96; Jay's Treaty, 53; Lend-Lease Act, 403; Limited Nuclear Test Ban Treaty, 533; militarism and, 231; Oregon Treaty, 108; taxes and, 21; in World War I, 232, *233m*, 237, 239, 240, *243m*, 249, 259; in World War II, 396–397, *397m*. *See also* England
Great Communicator. *See* Reagan, Ronald
Great Compromise, *45c*, 46
Great Depression, 318–343, 789, *789p*; African Americans in, 318, 557; documents about, 340–341; economy during the, 329–330, *329g*; entertainment in, 368–370, *368p*, *369p*; hoboes, 328, *328p*, 331; Hoover and, 337–339; life in, 328–334, *328p*, *330p–331p*, *332p–333p*, *334p*, 340–341, *340p*, *341p*, 367–370, *367p*, *368p*, *369p*; literature of, 367, 368; music of, 333, *333q*, 367, 369–370; New Deal, 350–353; poverty in, 330–333, *330p–331p*, *332p*, *333p*; Roosevelt and, 347–351; sports in, 370; time line of, 318–319; in the West, 332–333, *332m*, *332p–333p*, 334, *334p*
Great Gatsby, The (Fitzgerald), 312, 313
Great Grape Boycott, 642, *642p*
Great Law, 795
Great Migration, 17, 302–303, *303m*, R10
Great Persuader. *See* Reagan, Ronald
Great Plains: Dust Bowl, 332–333, *332m*, *332p–333p*, 334, *334p*; farming on, 146–148, *146p–147p*; ranching, 145–146, *145m*
Great Plains cultures, 7, *8m*

Great Railroad Strike, 153
Great Society, 544–547, 545q, 546c, 547p, 789–790, 791; documents, 551
Great War. *See* World War I
Great White Fleet, 205, 213
Greece: Iron Curtain and, 467; Marshall Plan and, 468–469, 468p; in NATO, 470
Greeley, Horace, 121, 180
Green Berets, 601
green card, 768
greenmail, 720
Green Party, 734
Greenspan, Alan, 716, R37
Grenada, 705
Grenville, George, 26
Gridley, Charles, 208–209
Griffith, D.W., 172, 310, R37
Griffiths, Martha, 634
Grimkè, Sarah and Angelina, 104–105
Gropper, William, 358p–359p
gross domestic product, 716
gross national product (GNP), 321, 326, 364g; in Great Depression, 329g, 330
Ground Zero, 742
Guadalcanal, 437, 438m
Guam, 434, 438m
Guantánamo Bay, 214
Guatemala, 498
guerrilla warfare, 598, 599, 606, 607
gun control, 795–796
Gun Control Act (1968), 795
Guthrie, Woody, 333, 333q, 367, R37
Gutíerrez, José Angel, 645–647, R37

haciendas, 22
Haight, Henry, R60
Haight-Ashbury, 652, 653
Haiti, 217, 729
Haldeman, H.R., 621, 676, 677, 689
Hallaren, Mary Agnes, 452
Hamdi v. *Rumsfeld* (2004), R29
Hamer, Fannie Lou, 576–577, 577q, 591, R37
Hamilton, Alexander, 44p, 45, 48, 51, 52, 53, R37
Hancock, John, 31, 32
Hanoi, 597
Harding, Warren G., 282–284, 282p, 322, 336, R20, R37
Hardwick, Thomas W., 288
Harlan, John Marshall, 161
Harlem Hell Fighters, 242p, 243p
Harlem Renaissance, 302–307, 302p, 303m, 304p, 305p, 306p, R11
Harpers Ferry, Virginia, 119
Harriman, E.H., 184
Harrington, Michael, 513, 543, 789
Harrington, Myron, 606
Harrison, Benjamin, R19
Harrison, George, 653
Harrison, William Henry, R18
Havel, Vaclav, 709
Hawaii: facts about, R30; imperialism and, 201, 202–203, 202p, 203p, 224–225; Pearl Harbor, 403–405, 404m, 404p
Hawaiian League, 203

hawks, 610
Hay, John, 204, 210q, 215
Hayes, Rutherford B., 138, R19
Haymarket Riot, 153
Hays, Anna Mae, 774
Hayslip, Le Ly, 625, 625q
Haywood, William, 174
H-bomb. *See* hydrogen bomb
Head Start, 546
health care, 751; Clinton and, 727–728; Fair Deal, 475; progressivism and, 171
Hearst, William Randolph, 206, 207, 207p, R37
Heart of Atlanta Motel v. *United States* (1964), R26
Held, John, Jr., 315
Hello Girls, 243, 774
Help America Vote Act, 735
Hemingway, Ernest, 245, 245p, 313
hemispheres, R63
Hendrix, Jimi, 653, 655
Henry, Patrick, 42, 47p, 47q
Henry, Prince of Portugal, 11
Hepburn Act (1906), 186
Hessians, 34
higher education, 178; integration in, 567–568, 567p; Morrill Act, 146. *See also* education
Higher Education Act (1965), 546, 546c
Highway Beautification Act (1965), 547
Hill, Anita, 719
Hill, James J., 184
Hillman, Sidney, 409
Himmler, Heinrich, 429
hippies, 652–653, 652p, 653p. *See also* counterculture
Hirohito, Japanese emperor, 454
Hiroshima, 453–454, 453p
Hispanic Americans: Bracero Program, 411; cowboys, 146; discrimination against, 162; in government, 683, 747, 747p; growth and influence of, 754–755; New Deal and, 374; Poor People's Campaign, 586; population of, 643g, 748, 748c; veterans, 473; in World War I, 241. *See also* Chicanos; Latinos
Hiss, Alger, 480, 480p, 497, R37
historical maps, R68
History and Geography: Hispanic Americans, 754–755; island hopping, 456–457; Panama Canal, 218–219; Tennessee Valley Authority (TVA), 354–355
History Close-Up: automobiles, 278; Chicano movement, 646–647, 646p, 647p; convoy systems, 419p; D-Day, 424p–425p; Harlem Renaissance, 306, 306p; Hoovervilles, 330–331, 330p–331p; Korean War, 486m, 486p; moon landing, 672p, 673; Oklahoma land rush, 146p–147p, 147; Pearl Harbor, 404, 404m, 404p; September 11th attacks, 740p–741p; skyscrapers, 158, 158p; television, 511, 511p; trench warfare, 234–235, 234p–235p; Triangle Shirtwaist fire, 173, 173p; Vietcong tunnels, 607, 607p
Hitler, Adolf, 385p, R38; *Anschluss* and, 393; anti-Semitism and, 427, 428–429, 429c, 429m, 429p, 430–431;

appeasement and, 395; concentration camps, 427, 428–429, 429c, 429m, 429p, 430–431; death of, 452; Final Solution and, 428–429, 429c, 429m, 429p, 430–431; Mussolini and, 422; Olympic Games and, 386; Rhineland and, 392–393; Rhine River and, 451; rise to power, 388p, 389; Stalin and, 395, 420, 465; Sudetenland and, 393
HIV virus, 719, 751
Hoar, George F., 211, 211p, 211q
Hobby, Oveta Culp, 408, 452, R38
hoboes, 328, 328p, 331
Ho Chi Minh, 256, 499, 596–598, 596p, 598q, 599–601, 621, R38
Ho Chi Minh Trail, 605, 613, 621
Hohokam culture, 7
Hoisington, Elizabeth P., 774
Holland, Sylvia Lutz, 609
Hollywood, California, 310, 444
Hollywood Ten, 479
Holmes, Hamilton, 567–568
Holmes, Oliver Wendell, Jr., 252, 253
Holocaust, 426–431, 426p, 427p, 429c, 429m, 429p, R11–R12
Holt, Stull, 260
Holt Literature Library, R94–R95
Holy Experiment, 19
Homeland Security, Department of, 744
Homestead Act (1862), 146, R7
Homestead strike, 153
homicide, 796
Hong Kong, 434, 435, 438m
Hooker, Joseph, 129
Hooker, Thomas, 18
Hoover, Herbert, 247, 248, 284, R20, R38; election of 1928, 322–323, 322m; election of 1932, 347, 347m; foreign policy of, 400; Great Depression and, 337–339; life of, 338, 338p; presidency of, 335–339, 335p, 336q, 337p, 338p; stock market crash and, 326
Hoover, J. Edgar, 587, 654
Hoover Dam, 336, 336p
Hoovervilles, 330–331, 330p–331p
Hope, Bob, 459
Hopewell culture, 7
horizontal integration, 151
horseless carriage, 154
House Divided, A speech (Lincoln), 120
House of Burgesses, 17
House of Representatives, U.S.: Crittenden Compromise, 122. *See also* Congress, U.S.
House Un-American Activities Committee (HUAC), 479, 480, 490
housing: adobe, 7; longhouses, 7; postwar, 513, 514, 514p; progressivism and, 171; tenements, 101, 159, 171; in the West, 148
Housing and Urban Development (HUD), Department of, 546
Houston, Charles Hamilton, 558
Houston, Sam, 110, R38
Howe, General, 34
How the Other Half Lives (Riis), 170, 170p, 171
HUAC. *See* House Un-American Activities Committee

HUD. *See* Housing and Urban Development
Huerta, Dolores, 644, *644q*, 646p
Huerta, Victoriano, 221–222, *221p*, R38
Hughes, Charles Evans, 175, 239, 284, 287, R38
Hughes, Langston, 305, *305p*, R38
Hull House, 159
human-environment interaction, R72, R73
human rights, 475–476, 683, 684
human systems, R73
Humphrey, Hubert, 545, *545p*, *545q*, 616–619, *619m*, R38
Hungary, 498–499, *500m*, 709
Hunter, Charlayne, 567–568
hunter-gatherers, 7
Huron Indians, 25
hurricanes, 174, 281, 682, 752
Hurricane Katrina, *751p*, 752
Hurston, Zora Neale, 302, *302p*, 305, R38
Hürtgen Forest, Battle of, 424
Hussein, Saddam, 712, 745–746, R38
Hutchinson, Anne, 18
hydroelectric power, 351
hydrogen bomb, 503–504, *503p*, 507
hydrogen fuel cells, 752

IBM, 714. *See also* International Business Machines
ICBMs. *See* intercontinental ballistic missiles
Ice Age, 6–7
Iceland, 470
Idaho: Civil War in, 128; facts about, R30; national parks in, 187; Native Americans in, 144
identity theft, 802
I Have A Dream speech (King), 571, *571q*
Il Duce. *See* Mussolini, Benito
ILGWU. *See* International Ladies' Garment Workers Union (ILGWU)
Illinois, 44; facts about, R30; Hispanic Americans in, *755p*; labor unions in, 172; population of, 514; Revolutionary War in, 36, *36m*
IMF. *See* International Monetary Fund
immigrants, 766–771, R8; from Europe, 274–275, *274g*; Jewish, 427; Ku Klux Klan and, 297; laws and, 717–718; in New York City, 156, *156p*, 157; population of, 157, *770m*; prejudice against, 158; Prohibition and, 299; religion and, 749; urban reforms and, 100–102, *101g*
Immigration Act (1965), R15
Impact Today, 668, 708; affirmative action programs, 687; Africa, 9; blue jeans, 653; Central High School, 560; child labor laws, 153; civil rights, 571, 576; Commerce Clause, 356; containment policy, 467; culture, 19, 207; daily life, 144, 153, 223, 638, 653, 736; Democratic Party, 95; Department of Homeland Security, 744; economics, 323, 501, 730; Federal Reserve Board, 323; Felt, Mark, 677; Fifteenth Amendment, 118; Fourteenth Amendment, 118; Fourth Amendment, 700; freedom of the press, 674; free trade, 730; GI Bill, 472; government, 9, 21, 51, 95, 112, 118, 181, 186, 214, 272, 373, 430, 431, 454, 467, 472, 489, 560, 571, 576, 643, 677, 705, 711, 735, 744; Guantánamo, 214; Internet, 97, 362, 736; Korematsu, Fred, 448, *448p*; land-grant colleges, 147; Latinos, 643; Mexican Americans, 223; Miranda warning, 549; National Security Agency, 481; Native Americans, 144; New Mexico, 112; North Korea, 489; nuclear power, 683; Occupational Safety and Health Administration, 172; Pelosi, Nancy, 181; Philadelphia, 19; prior restraint, 674; protest marches, 253; Pulitzer Prize, 207; Pure Food and Drug Act, 186; recent scholarship, 439, 481; school integration, 561; science and technology, 97, 147, 277, 287, 673, 683; search and seizure, 732; Social Security, 373; space exploration, 673; Strategic Offensive Reduction Treaty, 711; Suez Canal, 501; Supreme Court, 51; technology, 362; telegraph, 97; terrorism, 705; Three Mile Island, 683; town meeting, 21; United Nations, 454; Vietnam, 467; voting districts, 579; voting systems, 735; Watergate Scandal, 677; weapons screenings, 700; women, 638
imperialism, *216m*; definition of, 201; France and, 231; Germany and, 231; Great Britain and, 201, 231; Philippines and, 211–212, *211q*
impressment, 55
inaugural address, of Jefferson, R79; of Kennedy, R89; of Lincoln, R84–R85, R86
Inchon, Korea, *487m*, *487p*, 488
income tax, 191
incumbents, 375
indentured servants, 17
Indiana, 44; facts about, R30; Revolutionary War in, 36, *36m*
Indiana Territory, 119
Indian Citizenship Act (1924), 162
Indian Naturalization Act (1890), 285
Indian Removal Act (1830), *94m*, 95, R6
Indian Reorganization Act (1934), 351
Indian Territory, *94m*, 95, 147
Indian Wars, 143–144, *143m*
Indochina, *599m*
Indonesia, 398, 434
industrialization, 101
Industrial Revolution: 96–97; Second, 140–141, 149–155, *149p*, *150m*, *152p*, *153g*
Industrial Workers of the World (IWW), 174, 288
industry: automobile, 277–279, *278p*; effect on society, 279; in World War II, 408–410, *409g*
I Never Left Home (Hope), 459
inflation, 43, 387, *387p*, 673, 680, 682, 686, 699, 716
influenza epidemic, 250, *250p*, 270, *270p*
information technology, 750

INF Treaty, 703
initiative, 175
In Re Debs (1895), R23
installment buying, 280
integrated circuits, 512
integration, 560, 590, 667
intercontinental ballistic missiles (ICBMs), 504
Intermediate-Range Nuclear Forces (INF), 703
internal combustion engine, 154
International Business Machines (IBM), 512
International Ladies' Garment Workers Union (ILGWU), 174
International Military Tribunal, 431
International Monetary Fund (IMF), *475c*, 476
Internet, 362, 728–729, 736–737, 800–805, *800p*, *801p*, *802p*, *803g*, *804p*, *805p*; dot coms, 736
internment, 445
Interstate Commerce Act (1887), 160
Interstate Commerce Commission, 567
interstate highway system, 515, 516–517, *516g*, *517m*
interventionism, 401–402, *401q*, *402p*
Intolerable Acts, 31
Iowa: facts about, R30
Iran: CIA in, 498; hostage crisis in, 685–686, *685p*, 696, R15–R16; revolution in, 682
Iran-Contra affair, 705–706
Iraq: Israel and, 501; Persian Gulf War, 712–713, *712m*. *See also* Iraq War
Iraq War, 682, 745–746, *745m*, R16; battlefield reporting, 614, *614p*; women in, 772, 774, 779
Ireland: immigrants from, 100, 101, 147
Iron Curtain, 465–467, *466m*, *467p*
Iroquois cultures, 7
irrigation, 148, 187
Irwin, William, R60
Isabella, queen of Spain, 11, 13
Islam: in Africa, 9; in Iran, 686
Islamic revolution, 742–744
island hopping, 456–457
islands, R63
isolationism, 239, 400–402
Israel, 431; Camp David Accords, 684, *684p*; Middle East conflicts and, *500m*, 501; Palestine Liberation Organization and, 705, 729; Yom Kippur War, 670, 684
Italy: Ethiopia and, 391, 401; fascism in, 388–389, *388q*, *389p*; immigrants from, 156, *156p*, 157; Mussolini and, 388–389, *388q*, *389p*; nationalism in, 231, 388; in NATO, 470; Renaissance in, 10–11; Treaty of Versailles and, 388; and World War II, 398, 420–422, *421m*
Iwo Jima, Battle of, 433, *433p*, *438m*, 439, *439p*, 440, 457
IWW. *See* Industrial Workers of the World

J

Jackson, Andrew, 56, 95, 102, R17
Jackson, Jesse, 589, 708, R38
Jackson, Mahalia, 571
Jackson State College, 622
Jacobins, 53
James, duke of York, 18
James I, king of England, 16
Jamestown, 16–17, R3
Japan: atomic bombs and, 453–454, *453p*; China and, 390–391, 398; government of, 390–391; Indochina and, 597; Korea and, 484; Pearl Harbor and, 403–405, *404m*, *404p*; Russo-Japanese War, 205; Treaty of Portsmouth, 205; in World War II, *381p*, 398, 433–440, *438m*, 452–454, *453p*, 454
Japanese Americans, 162, 538; 442nd Regimental Combat Team, 445; internment of, 445–446, *446p*, R12; *Korematsu v. United States*, 448
Java Sea, Battle of the, 434
Jay, John, 48, 51, 53
Jay's Treaty, 53
jazz, *306p*, 307, 370
Jazz Singer, The (film), 308, *308p*
Jefferson, Thomas, 53, R17, R38; biography, 51, *51p*; Declaration of Independence and, 33; Enlightenment and, 24; inaugural address, R79; Louisiana Purchase, *54m*, 55; national bank and, 52; Northwest Territory and, 44; as president, 54; Second Continental Congress, 32; as vice-president, 53; War of 1812, 55–56
Jehovah's Witnesses, 445
Jews: anti-Semitism, 427; concentration camps and, 427, 428–429, *429c*, *429m*, *429p*, 430–431; discrimination against, 172, 389, *389q*; Holocaust and the, 426–431, *426p*, *427p*, *429c*, *429m*, *429p*; immigration and, 157, 427; in the Soviet Union, 428
Jim Crow laws, 161, 180
Job Corps, 543, *543p*, 544
Jobs, Steve, 714, *714p*, R38
John II, king of Portugal, 13
John Paul II, Pope, 702
Johnson, Andrew, 130, *134p*, *134q*, 200, 731, R18; impeachment of, 135; Reconstruction and, 133–135
Johnson, Hiram, 191, R38, R60
Johnson, J. Neeley, R60
Johnson, James Weldon, 305, R38
Johnson, Lady Bird, 547
Johnson, Lyndon B., 459, R21, R39; becomes president, 542; Berlin and, 530; Civil Rights Act (1968), 588; civil rights and, 571, 576, 577, 588; domestic policy, 543–547; election of 1964, *544p*, 545–546; election of 1968, 615; foreign policy, 548; Great Society, 545–547, *545q*, *546c*, *547p*, 789–790, 791; Kennedy and, 542; Kerner Commission, 581–582; leadership style of, 541; Native Americans and, 639–640; as Vice-President, 529, 542; Vietnam War, 548, 602–603, 604, 605, 611, 615–616, *616p*, 618; Voting Rights Act, 578; War on Poverty, 543–544, *551q*, 790; Warren Commission, 540
Johnson, Shoshana, 779
Johnson, Tom, 174
Johnson, William H., 307
Johnson Doctrine, 548
joint-stock companies, 16
Jolson, Al, 308
Jones, Bobby, 312, *312p*
Jones, Loïs Mailou, 307
Jones, Paula, 731
Joplin, Janis, 653, 655
Jordan, 501, 670, *671m*
Joy Luck Club, The (Tan), 753
judicial branch, 47; California government, R60; checks and balances, 46–47, *46c*. *See also* Supreme Court, U.S.
judicial review, 55
Judiciary Act (1789), 51
Judiciary Act (1801), 55
Jungle, The (Sinclair), 176, *176p*, 186, *186q*, 194
junk bonds, 720

K

Kaiser, Henry, 409
Kaiulani, princess of Hawaii, 224
Kalakaua, king of Hawaii, 202–203, *202q*
Kamehameha, Chief, 202
kamikaze attack, 439
Kansas: Civil War in, 116–117, 128; Exodusters in, 147; exploration of, *14m*, 15; facts about, R30; gains statehood, 119; in Great Depression, 332; integration in, 559; Sack of Lawrence, 118; slavery and, 116–117, *116p*, *117m*, 118–119
Kansas-Nebraska Act (1854), 117, *117m*, *121c*
Kansas Territory, 118–119
Kasserine Pass, 421, *421m*
Kearney, USS (destroyer), 403
Kearns, David, 769
Kearny, Stephen, 111
Kelley, Florence, 172, 195, R39
Kellogg, Frank, 287
Kellogg-Briand Pact, 287, *287q*
Kennan, George F., 467, 610, R39
Kennedy, Anthony, 719
Kennedy, Caroline, 536, *539p*
Kennedy, Jacqueline, 535, *535p*, 536, *539p*, 540, R39
Kennedy, John, Jr., 536, *539p*
Kennedy, John F., R20, R39; assassination of, 539–540, *539p*; Bay of Pigs invasion, 528–529; Berlin and, 530–531, *530q*; civil rights movement and, 566, 567, 568, 570–571, *571q*; Clinton and, 726, *726p*; Congress and, 536–537; Cuban missile crisis, 532–533, *532m*, *533p*; election of 1960, 526, 527, 666; foreign policy of, 528–534, *534q*; inaugural address, R89; inauguration of, 527–528, *527p*, *527q*; Johnson and, 542; New Frontier, 527, 536–537, *550q*; Presidential Commission on the Status of Women, 635; space program and, *525p*, 537–538, *537q*, 673; Supreme Court and, 538–539; Vietnam and, 601–602; White House, 535, *535p*
Kennedy, Joseph P., II, *717p*, *717q*
Kennedy, Robert, 527, 528, 533, 615–617, *616p*, 795, R39; civil rights movement and, 567, 568, 574, 585, *585q*, 590
Kennedy Space Center, 671
Kent State University, 622, *622p*
Kentucky, 119; in Civil War, 124; facts about, R30
Kentucky and Virginia Resolution, 53
Kerner Commission, 581–582
Kerouac, Jack, 515
Kerry, John, 736, 812
Kettle Hill, Battle of, 210, *210p*
Keynes, John Maynard, 364, R39
Khe Sanh, 613
Khmer Rouge, 625
Khomeini, Ayatollah Ruhollah, 686, R39
Khrushchev, Nikita, 498, *498p*, R39; Berlin and, 530; Cuba and, 529; Cuban missile crisis, 532–533
Kim Il Sung, 484, R39
Kim Jong Il, 390, *390p*
King, Martin Luther, Jr., 527, *554q*, *583p*, *583q*, *588p*, 610, *610q*, 713, R39; Albany Movement, 568–569; assassination of, *584p*, 585; Birmingham campaign, 569–570; Chicago and, 582; election of 1964 and, 576; Gandhi and, 565; *Letter from a Birmingham Jail*, 572, *572q*; Malcolm X and, *583p*, *583q*, 584; March Against Fear, 580, *580p*; March on Washington, *554p*–555*p*, 571, *571q*; Memphis speech, R91; Montgomery bus boycott and, 562; poverty and, 587; SCLC and, 563; Selma campaign, 573, 577–578
kinship, 9
Kiowa, 142, *143m*
Kirkpatrick, Jeane, 717
Kissinger, Henry, 621, *621p*, 624, 668, 669–670, 671, 680, R39
Kitty Hawk, North Carolina, 154, *154p*
Klamath River, 780, *780p*
Klondike, 144
Knight, Goodwin, R60
Knights of Labor, 153
Know-Nothings, 100–101
Knox, Henry, 32, 51
Knudsen, William, 409
Kongo, 9
Korea: China and, 487; Japan and, 484
Korean War, 483–489, *483p*, *484m*, *487m*, 497, R13
Korematsu, Fred, 448, *448p*
Korematsu v. the United States, 446, 448
Kosovo, 730
Kosygin, Aleksey, 548
Kristallnacht, 427, *427p*

Ku Klux Klan / Marais de Cygnes Massacre

Ku Klux Klan, 133, 137, 274, 297, 576
Kuwait, 712–713, *712m*

L

Labor Department, 190, 365, *365p*, 366
labor movement, 101–102, 273–274
labor unions, 277; growth of, 153, *153g*; National Industrial Recovery Act, 351; National War Labor Board, 410; progressivism and, 172–174, 184; Roosevelt and, 359–361, *360c*, *361g*, *361p*; Smith-Connally Act, 410; strikes and, 153, 361, *361p*; Taft-Hartley Act and, 473; in World War I, 249
Lafayette, Marquis de, 35
La Follette, Robert, 175, 252, R39
laissez-faire capitalism, 151
Lake Tahoe, R61
land bridge, 6
Landmark Supreme Court Cases: *Brown* v. *Board of Education of Topeka, Kansas*, 561; *Korematsu* v. *the United States*, 448; *Miranda* v. *Arizona* (1966), 549; *New Jersey* v. *T.L.O.* (1985), 700; *New York Times Co.* v. *United States* (1971), 674; *Regents of the University of California* v. *Bakke* (1978), 687; *Reynolds* v. *Sims* (1964), 579; *Schecter Poultry Corporation* v. *the United States*, 356; *Schenck* v. *United States* (1919), 253, *253p*; *Vernonia School District* v. *Acton* (1995), 732. *See also* Supreme Court, U.S.
Landon, Alf, 362
Land Ordinance of 1785, 44
Lange, Dorothea, 367, *367p*, R39
Laos, 398, 597, *599m*, 621
La Raza Unida Party, 646–647, *646p*
Latham, Milton, R60
Latin America: expansionism in, 214; Johnson Doctrine, 548; Reagan and, *704p*
Latinos: Chicano movement and, 644–649; lives of, 643, *643g*; social justice and, 643–644; in World War I, 241. *See also* Chicanos; Hispanic Americans
latitude, R62
law, 10. *See also* criminal code; criminal justice; judicial branch
Lawrence, Jacob, 307
Lawson, James, 565
League of Nations, 254, *254p*, 255, *256c*, 257–258, 283, 286, 391, 400, 454. *See also* United Nations
Lear, William, 294
Lebanon, 501, *704p–705p*, 705
Le Chambon-sur-Lignon, France, 426
Lechnir, Jean, *443q*
Lecompton constitution, 119
Lee, Robert E., 124, 125, *128p*, 129, 131, R39
legend, map, R67
legislative branch: bicameral, 21, 45; California government, R60; checks and balances, 46–47, *46c*. *See also* Congress, U.S.; House of Representatives, U.S.; Senate, U.S.
LeMay, Curtis, 452–453

Lend-Lease Act (1941), 403, R12
Lenin, Vladimir I., 242, 271–272
Leningrad, 420, *421m*
Letter from a Birmingham Jail (King), 572, *572q*
Let Us Now Praise Famous Men (Agee and Evans), 368
Lever Food and Fuel Control Act, 247–248
Levitt, Bill and Alfred, 513, 514, *514–515p*
Levittown, New York, 514, *514–515p*
Lewinsky, Monica, 731
Lewis, John, 576, 583, 589, R40
Lewis, John L., 274, 360, R39
Lewis, Meriwether, *54m*, 55
Lewis, Pearlena, 563
Lewis, Sinclair, 312, *312q*
Lexington and Concord, Battle of, 31
Leyte Gulf, Battle of, *438m*, 439
Liberal Republicans, 137
Liberty bonds, 246, *246p*, 247, *247p*
liberty ship, 409
Libya, 420, *421m*
Lieberman, Joe, 734
"Lift Every Voice and Sing," 305
Lilienthal, David, 477
Liliuokalani, queen of Hawaii, 203, *203p*, 224, R40
limited government, 48
Limited Nuclear Test Ban Treaty, 508, 533
Lin, Maya Ying, *626p*, 627
Lincoln, Abraham, R18, R40; assassination of, 133, R7; becomes president, 119–121, *120p*; biography, 124, *124p*; Civil War and, 123; election of 1864, 130–131; Emancipation Proclamation, 126; Gettysburg Address, R86; A House Divided speech, 120; inaugural address, R84–R85, R86; Lincoln-Douglas debates, 120, *120p*, *120q*; Reconstruction and, 133; secession and, 121–122; slavery and, 119
Lincoln, Mary Todd, 119
Lincoln-Douglas debates, 120, *120p*, *120q*, *121c*
Lindbergh, Charles A., 310–311, *311p*, 370, 399, 403, R40
line of demarcation, 13
Linking to Today: battlefield reporting, 614, *614p*; Central High School, 560, *560p*; computers, 512, *512p*; epidemics, 250, *250p*; Iwo Jima, 439, *439p*; Job Corps, 543, *543p*; national parks, 187, *187p*; oil consumption, 682, *682p*; terrorism, 271; totalitarian government, 390, *390p*
Lippmann, Walter, 351
literacy tests, 158, 161
literature, R94–R95; of Great Depression, 367, 368; of Harlem Renaissance, 302, *302p*, 305–306; Hemingway, Ernest, 245, *245p*; *The Joy Luck Club* (Tan), 753; *Letter from a Birmingham Jail* (King), 572, *572q*; Native American, 641; in Roaring Twenties, 312, 313; of the Works Progress Administration, 359; of World War I, 245, *245p*. *See also* American Literature
Little Bighorn, Battle of, 143–144, *143m*
Little Rock Nine, 560
Livingston, Sigmund, 172
location, R72–R73

locator map, R67
Lochner v. *New York*, 172, R24
Locke, John, 23–24, 32–33, 42
Lodge, Henry Cabot, 204, 211–212, *211p*, *211q*, 257–258, *257p*, *257q*, R40
Lodge, Henry Cabot, Jr., 602
London Company, 16
Long, Huey P., 352, R40
longhouses, 7
longitude, R62
Longoria, Felix, 473
loose constructionist, 52
Los Alamos, 410
Los Angeles, 581, 747, *747p*, R61
Los Dorados, 220
Lost Generation, 313
Louis, Joe, 370
Louisiana: Civil Rights Movement in, 566–567; facts about, R30; hurricanes in, 752; Jim Crow laws, 161; Reconstruction in, 133; secession, 121; voting rights in, 578
Louisiana Purchase, *54m*, 55, R5
Louisiana Territory, 26, *54m*, 55, 93, *93m*
Love Canal, 683
Low, Frederick, R60
Lowden, Frank, *271q*
Loyalists, 33, 35, 36
Luftwaffe, 397
Lusitania (ship), 238, *238p*
Luther, Martin, 11
Luxembourg, 470
lynching, 161–162

M

MacArthur, Douglas, 435, 439, 452, 455, R40; biography, 840, *488p*; Korea and, 483, 485, 487–488, *488q*
machine guns, 234
Macy's Department Store, 276, *276p*
Maddox, USS (destroyer), 603
Madero, Francisco, 221, *221p*, R40
Madison, Dolley, *55p*
Madison, James, 44, *44p*, 45, *47p*, *47q*, 49, R17, R40; federalism and, 48; midnight judges and, 54–55
Maginot Line, 396, *397m*
Magna Carta, 10, R74
mail system, 108–109
Maine: facts about, R30; Missouri Compromise and, 93, *93m*; Native Americans in, 640
Maine, USS (battleship), 208
malaria, 215–216
Malcolm X, *583p*, *583q*, 584, 591, R40
Mali, 9
mandate, 536
Mandela, Nelson, 713, R40
Manhattan Project, 410, 453, R12
manifest destiny, 107–109, 110, 112, 201
Manila Bay, 208–209, *209m*
Man Nobody Knows, The (Barton), 313
Mansa Musa, 9
Manson, Charles, 653
manufacturing, 101
Mao Zedong, 478, 598, 670, R40
map projections, R64–R65
Mapp v. *Ohio* (1961), 538–539, R25
Marais de Cygnes Massacre, 116, *116p*

Marbury v. *Madison* (1803), 54–55, R5
March Against Fear, 580, *580p*
March on Washington, *554p–555p*, 571, *571q*, R14
March to the Sea, 131
Marconi, Guglielmo, 309
Marco Polo, 11
margin calls, 324, 326
Mariana Islands, 438, *438m*, 457
Marion, Francis, 36
Markham, Henry, R60
Marne, Battle of the, *232c*, *233m*, 234–235, 242, 243, *243m*
Mars, 673, 750
Marshall, George C., 407, 468, *468q*, R40
Marshall, John, 53, 93, 538
Marshall, Thurgood, 558, 559, *559p*, 589, R40
Marshall Islands, 438, *438m*, 507
Marshall Plan, 468–469, *468c*, 474, R13
Martí, José, 207, R40
Martinez, Mel, *755p*
Marx Brothers, 369
Maryland, 44; Civil War and, 124, 126, *126m*; colonial, 19; facts about, R30
Mason, George, 49, R78
Massachusetts: colonial, 17–18; facts about, R30; labor in, 174; labor movement in, 273–274; minimum wage in, 172; New Deal and, 374; prison reform in, 100; Revolutionary War in, 30–31, *30p*, 32; Sacco and Vanzetti trial, 274–275, *275p*; Shays's Rebellion, 43; textile industry in, 96; voting rights in, 192
Massachusetts Bay Colony, 17–18
Massery, Hazel, 560, *560p*
massive resistance, 560
massive retaliation, 498, 504
mass marketing, 152
Mauer, Marc, 796
Mauldin, Bill, 443, 458, *458p*, R40
Maya culture, 7
Mayaguez (ship), 680
Mayflower Compact, 17, R75
Mayflower (ship), 17
Mayo, Henry, 222
MAYO. *See* Mexican American Youth Organization
McAuliffe, Christa, 715
McCain, John, 625
McCarran Act (1950), 480
McCarthy, Eugene, 615, R40
McCarthy, Joseph, 481–482, *481p*, 510, R40
McCarthy hearings, 510
McCarthyism, 481–482, *481p*
McClellan, George B., 125, 126, 130
McCulloch v. *Maryland* (1819), 93
McDermott, James, *717p*, *717q*
McDougall, John, R60
McFarlane, Robert, 704, 706
McGovern, George, *610p*, *610q*, 624, 677, R41
McKay, Claude, 305, *305q*
McKinley, William, 161, 184, 203, R19, R41; expansionism and, 214, *225p*; Philippines and, 211; Spanish-American War and, 207–208
McKinley Tariff, 807
McNamara, Robert, 528, 533, 615, *615p*, 616, *616q*, R41
McNary, Charles, *373g*, *373p*
McNickle, D'Arcy, 639, *639q*, R41
McPherson, Aimee Semple, 298, R41
McVeigh, Timothy, 729
Means, Russell, 640, *640q*, R41
Meat Inspection Act (1906), 186
meatpacking industry, 176, *176p*, 186, *186q*, 194
media: battlefield reporting, 614, *614p*; in Roaring Twenties, 308–310, *308p*, *309p*, *310p*; Vietnam War and, 609–610. *See also* newspapers; radio; television
Medicaid, 546, 751, R14–R15
Medicare, 546, 736, 751, R14–R15
Mein Kampf (Hitler), 389, *389q*
Mellon, Andrew, 284
Mennonites, 147
mercantilism, 21
Mercator projection, R64
Meredith, James, *567p*, 568, R41
meridians, R62
Merriam, Frank, R60
Merrimack (ship), 128
Mesoamerica, 7. *See also* Central America; Mexico
mestizos, 15
Mexican Americans, 473, 644, 646; discrimination against, 162; farmworker boycotts, 642, *642p*; zoot suit riots, 411. *See also* Chicanos; Hispanic Americans
Mexican-American War, 110–111, *111m*, 116, R6
Mexican American Youth Organization (MAYO), 645–646
Mexican Cession, 112
Mexican Revolution, 220–223, *220p*, *221p*, *222p*
Mexico: constitution of, 223; empires of, 7; Mexican-American War, R6; North American Free Trade Agreement, 730, 808, *808p*; revolution in, 220–223, *220p*, *221p*, *222p*; Spain and, 109; Texas and, 109, 110, *111m*; Treaty of Guadalupe Hidalgo, 112; Zimmermann Note and, 240
MFDP. *See* Mississippi Freedom Democratic Party
Michigan, 44; automobile industry, 279, 361, *361p*; facts about, R30; Revolutionary War in, 36, *36m*
Microsoft, 714
Middle Ages, 10
middle class, 159
middle colonies, 18–19, 22
Middle East: Clinton and, 729; Cold War in, *500m*, 501; road map to peace, 738; Yom Kippur War, 670–671
Middle Passage, 22
midnight judges, 54–55
Midway, Battle of, 436–437, *437p*, *438m*, R12–R13
Midway Islands, 200
Midwest: immigrants in, 101; population of, 748
migrant labor, 768, *768p*
migration: African American, 147, 259, 302–303, *303m*, R10; to America, R3; during Ice Age, 6–7; western, 106–109, *107m*, 146, 147
Mike test, *503p*
Milam, Ben, 110
militarism, 231
military: African Americans in, 241, *242p*, *243p*, 410, 422, *422p*, 452, 459, 473, 474, *474p*; convoy system, 242; draft, 608; life in the, 458–459, *458p*; mobilizing for World War II, 406, *406p*, 407–411, *409g*; Selective Service Act, 241; Vietnam War and, 604, 606–609, *609g*, 624–627, *626p*; Washington Naval Conference, 286–287; women in, 407–408, 452, *452p*, 458, 772–779, *772p*, *773p*, *774p*, *776c*, *778c*, *778p*, *779g*
military-industrial complex, 508
militias, 796
Millay, Edna St. Vincent, 312
Miller, William, 99
Mills, Ogden L., *337p*
minimum wage, 172, 374–375, 537, 790
mining, 144–145, *144p*; gold, 108, *108p*, *109p*, 144; hydraulic, *144p*; technology, *144p*, 145
Minnesota: facts about, R30; in Great Depression, *374p*; Revolutionary War in, 36, *36m*
minutemen, 31
minutes, R62
Miranda, Ernesto, 549
Miranda v. *Arizona* (1966), 539, 549
Miranda warning, 549
missiles, 504, 668–669
missionaries, 15, 201
Mississippi: civil rights movement in, 564, 567, 582–583, 591; election reforms in, 175; facts about, R31; hurricanes in, 752; nuclear testing in, 503; Reconstruction in, 137; secession, 121; state government in, 175; voting rights in, 574, 575–576, 576, 578
Mississippian culture, 7
Mississippi Freedom Democratic Party (MFDP), 576, 583
Mississippi River, 7, 26, 124, 128
Missouri: in Civil War, 124; Exodusters in, 147; facts about, R31; Oregon Trail, 107, *107m*; Pony Express, 109; Santa Fe Trail, 107, *107m*
Missouri, USS (battleship), *381p*
Missouri Compromise, 93, *93m*, 122, R5
Missouri ex rel. Gaines v. *Canada, Registrar of the University of Missouri*, 558
Missouri Territory, 93
Mitchell, Billy, 287, R41
Mitchell, Charles E., 324
Mogadishu, Somalia, 742
Molasses Act (1733), 20
Moltke, Helmuth von, 232–233
Momaday, N. Scott, 641
Mondale, Walter, 703, 717
money, 42, 43, 160
Monitor (ship), 128
monopoly, 151, 185, 191
Monroe, James, 92–93, *92p*, R5–R6, R17, R41
Monroe Doctrine, 92, 93, 216, 217 R5, R81
Montana: Civil War in, 128; facts about, R31; national parks in, 187; ranching in, 146

Montesquieu, Baron de, 23
Montgomery, Bernard, 423
Montgomery bus boycott, 562–563, *562p*, R13
Montgomery Improvement Association, 562, 563
Moody, Anne, 564
moon, *661p*; landing, 672, *672p*, 673, R15
Moral Majority, 697
Moratorium Day, 623
Morgan, J.P., 151, 184, 185
Mormons, 99
Mormon Trail, 107, *107m*
Morrill Act, 146
Morse, Samuel F.B., 97, 124, 154
Morse, Wayne, 603
Morse code, 154
Morton, Leslie, 238
Moses, Ethan, 739
Moses, Robert, 574, 575
mosquitoes, 214
motion pictures, 308, *308p*, 309–310, *310p*, 720, R11; in Great Depression, 368–369, *368p*, *369p*; rating systems, 655; in World War II, 444; violence and, 798
Mott, Lucretia, 102, R41
Mound Builders, 7
Mount Suribachi, 433, *433p*, 440
Mount Whitney, R61
movement, R72
movies. *See* motion pictures
muckrakers, 171, 194, 195
Mugabe, Robert, 390
Muhammad, Elijah, *582p*, 584
Muir, John, 187, R41
Muller v. *Oregon* (1908), 172, R24
murals, 648, *648p*
Murkowski, Lisa, 763, 785
Murray, Pauli, 636
Murrow, Edward R., 397
music: African Americans and, 515; of the counterculture, 655; of Great Depression, 333, *333q*, 367, 370; of Harlem Renaissance, 306p, 307; jazz, *306p*, 307, 370; rock and roll, 515; swing, 370
Muslims: Crusades and, 10. *See also* Islam
Mussolini, Benito, 388–389, *388q*, *389p*, 422, R41
Myanmar, 390
My Lai massacre, 623

NAACP. *See* National Association for the Advancement of Colored People
NACW. *See* National Association of Colored Women
Nader, Ralph, 734
NAFTA. *See* North American Free Trade Agreement
Nagasaki, 454
Nagy, Imre, 498–499
napalm, 605
Napoleon Bonaparte, 92
Napoleonic Wars, 55
Narragansett Indians, 18

Narrative of the Life of Frederick Douglass (Douglass), 105
NASA. *See* National Aeronautics and Space Administration
Nash, Diane, *565q*, 567
Nashville, USS (battleship), 213
Nasser, Gamal Abdel, 501
Nation, Carry, 179–180, *180p*, R41
National Aeronautics and Space Administration (NASA), 506, 671–673, 715, *715p*, R13–R14
National American Woman Suffrage Association (NAWSA), 182, 192, R9
National Association for the Advancement of Colored People (NAACP), 162, 172, 304, 557, 558, 559, 562, 567, R10
National Association of Colored Women (NACW), 180
national debt, 447, *447g*
National Defense Education Act, 506
National Farm Workers Association, 644
National Fascist Party, 388
national government, 42, 45, 46–48
National Grange, 160
National Guard, 242
National Indian Education Association, 641
National Industrial Recovery Act (NIRA), *350p*, 351, 353, *360c*
nationalism, 92–93, *98c*, 389, 741; definition of, 92, 201, 231; Germany and, 231; Italy and, 231; Missouri Compromise and, 93, *93m*
National Labor Relations Act, 359, *360c*
National Labor Relations Board, 359–360
National Liberation Front. *See* Vietcong
National Organization for Women (NOW), 636, R15
National Origins Act (1924), 274
national parks, 187, *187p*, 781, *781p*, 782, 783, *784m*, 785, 786, *786c*, *786p*, *787c*
National Republicans, 95
National Rifle Association, 795
National Security Council, 706
National Socialist Party. *See* Nazi Party
National War Labor Board, 249, 410
National Woman's Party (NWP), 192
National Woman Suffrage Association (NWSA), 180, 182
National Youth Administration (NYA), 542
Nation of Islam, *582p*, 584
nation-states, 10
Native American Rights Fund, 641
Native Americans: Alcatraz and, 640; American Indian Movement, 640; citizenship and, 162, 285; Civil War and, 128; Columbus and, 11–12; cultural resistance, 142, *142p*, 143, 144; Dawes Act (1887), 144; Declaration of Indian Purpose, 639, *639q*; discrimination against, 162; disease and, 12; early cultures, 6–9, *8m*; European contact and, 12; Fallen Timbers, Battle of, 53; French and Indian War, 24–26, *25m*; government schools and, 144; housing, 7; Indian Removal Act (1830), *94m*, 95, R6; Indian Reorganization Act (1934), 351; Indian Wars, 143–144, *143m*; literature of, 641; living conditions of, 638–639; Poor People's Campaign, 586; population of, 638–639;

Proclamation of 1763, 26; Red Power movement, 639–641; religion and, 9, 15; reservations and, 143; termination policy, 638–639; time line, 638–639; trade, 9; traditions of, 9; Treaty of Greenville, 53; War of 1812, 55–56, *55p*; in the West, 142–144, *143m*; western migration and, 109, 142–144, *143m*; in World War II, 439
nativism, 158, 274–275
NATO. *See* North Atlantic Treaty Organization
natural resources, 22, 781
natural rights, 23
Nautilus, USS (submarine), 504–505
Navajo, 145; code talkers, 439
naval warfare: in Civil War, 128
Navigation Acts, 21, R3
NAWSA. *See* National American Woman Suffrage Association
Nazi Party, *388p*, 389; Jews and, 426, *426p*, 427–429, *429c*, *429m*, *429p*, 430–431
Nebraska: 117; facts about, R31
Nelson, Donald, 409
Netherlands: in NATO, 470; in World War II, 396, *397m*
neutral, 239, 240
Neutrality Act (1935), 400–401, *400q*
Neutrality Proclamation, 53
Nevada: Civil War in, 128; facts about, R31; nuclear testing in, 503; population of, 748; Treaty of Guadalupe Hidalgo, 112
Nevada Territory, 144
New Deal, 344–379; African Americans and, 366–367; criticism of, 352–353, *352p*; executive branch and, 353, 374; government and, 352–353, 372–375; impact of, 372–373, *372g*; limits of, 373–374; programs of, *360c*; Second, 357–364, *358p*–*359p*, *360c*, *361g*, *361p*, *362p*, *364g*; Tennessee Valley Authority, 354–355; time line of, 344–345; women and, *365p*, 366, 367, *367p*
New England, 17, 96
New England Confederation, 21
New Federalism, 667
New France, 19
New Freedom, 191
New Frontier, 524–525, 527, 536–537, *550q*; documents, 550
New Hampshire: colonial, 18; facts about, R31
New Jersey: colonial, 18, 19; facts about, R31; housing in, 514; Revolutionary War in, 34, *36m*; voting rights in, 192
New Jersey Plan, 45
New Jersey v. *T.L.O.* (1985), 700, 718
Newlands Reclamation Act (1902), 187
New Mexico, 241; Alianza in, 665; Brown Berets, 647–648; Compromise of 1850, *117m*; exploration of, *14m*, 15; facts about, R31; in Great Depression, 332, *374p*; La Raza Unida Party, 646; Los Alamos, 410; Mexican-American War and, 111; Native Americans in, 640; nuclear testing in, 503; Pancho Villa and, 220, 223; ranching in, 146; Santa Fe Trail, 107, *107m*; Treaty of Guadalupe Hidalgo, 112

New Nationalism, 190
New Netherland, 18
New Orleans, 370; Civil War in, 125, *125m*; hurricanes in, 752
New Orleans, Battle of, 56
New Right, 697
New South, 138
New Spain, 15
newspapers: colonial, 24; editorials, 208; freedom of the press and, 674; Spanish-American War and, 206, 207
Newton, Huey, 583
New York: boricua movement, 649; colonial, 18–19; criminal code, 795; facts about, R31; Great Depression in, 347; housing in, 514, *514p–515p*; Love Canal, 683; population of, 514; progressivism in, 171; Red Scare in, 272; reform movements in, 99, 102; Revolutionary War in, 34, *36m*; state government in, 175; subway system, 154; Triangle Shirtwaist fire, 172–174, *173p, 174q*; voting rights in, 192
New York City, 22, 24; Harlem Renaissance, 305–307, *304p, 305p, 306p*; immigrants, 156, *156p*, 157, 158; in Revolutionary War, 34; terrorist attacks, 738, 739–743, *739p, 740m, 741p, 742p*; as U.S. capital, 51
New York Stock Exchange, 320, *320p*, 325
New York Times (newspaper), 172, 676
New York Times Co. v. United States (1971), 674
New Zealand, R57
Nez Percé, 144
Ngo Dinh Diem, 500, 599–602, R41
Niagara Movement, 162
Nicaragua, 217, *704p*, 704
Nicholas II, czar of Russia, 240
Nichols, Terry, 729
Night (Wiesel), 432
Nimitz, Chester, 436, 452, R41
Niña (ship), 11
Nineteenth Amendment, 179, 192, 259, 295, 634, 635
Ninth Amendment, 49
NIRA. *See* National Industrial Recovery Act
Nixon, Richard M., 193, 480, 694, 697, R21, R41; biography, 667, *667p*; Checkers speech, 497; China and, 669–670, *669p*, 808, R15; domestic policies of, 667–668; economy under, 673; election of 1952, 510; election of 1960, 516, 527, 666; election of 1968, 618–619, *618p, 619m*, 666, 667, *667q*; election of 1972, 676–677; environmental policy of, 668; foreign policy of, 668–671, *669p*; Middle East and, 670–671; New Federalism, 667; Pentagon Papers, 623; resignation of, 679; space exploration and, 671–673, *672p*; as vice-president, 497; Vietnam and, 620–624; Watergate scandal, 675–679, *678p*, 688–689, *688g, 689p*
Nobel Peace Prize, 254
No Child Left Behind Act, 736, 737
nomads, 6
nonviolent resistance, 563, 565, 580, 581

Noriega, Manuel, 712
Norman, Memphis, 564
Norris, Frank, 171
North: abolition movement in, 104–105; Civil War in, 123–131; industry in, 96; South and, 98; Three-Fifths Compromise, 46
North, Oliver, 706, R41
North Africa: World War II in, 420–421, *421m*
North America: early cultures of, 7–9, *8m*; migration to, R3; political map, R52
North American Free Trade Agreement (NAFTA), 730, 808, R16
North Atlantic Treaty Organization (NATO), 470, 479, 725, 730
North Carolina, colonial, 19; facts about, R31; Revolutionary War in, 36, *36m*; secession, 121, 124
North Dakota: Civil War in, 128; facts about, R31; population of, 748
Northeast: population of, 748
Northern colonies: economy of, 21–22; resources in, 22
Northern Hemisphere, R63
Northern Securities Company, 185
Northern Securities Co. v. United States (1904), R24
North Korea, 390, *390p*, 483–489, *483p, 484m, 487m*, 738; *Pueblo* (spy ship), 548
North Vietnam, 500, *599m*, 680. *See also* Vietnam War
Northwest Coast cultures, 7, *8m*
Northwest Ordinance, 44, R4–R5
Northwest Territory, 44, 53
Norway, 396, *397m*, 470
NOW. *See* National Organization for Women
nuclear fallout, 506–507, 508
nuclear power, 683, 708
nuclear weapons, 498, 502–508, *503p, 505p, 507p*, 702–703, 738; arms race and, 504–506, *505p, 506p, 506q*; Limited Nuclear Test Ban Treaty, 533
nullification crisis, 95
Nuremberg Laws, 427
Nuremberg Trials, 431
NWP. *See* National Woman's Party
NWSA. *See* National Woman Suffrage Association
Nye, Gerald P., 402

Oberlin College, 178
Objections to This Constitution of Government, R78
Occupational Safety and Health Act, 668
Occupational Safety and Health Administration, 174, 668
Ochs, Adolph S., 172
O'Connor, Sandra Day, *692p*, 717, 737, R41
Octopus, The (Norris), 171
Office of Economic Opportunity, 544
Office of Price Administration (OPA), 446
Office of War Information (OWI), 443–444, *444p*

Ohio, 44; automobile industry, 279; city government in, 174; facts about, R31; higher education in, 178; national parks in, 187; Revolutionary War in, 36, *36m*
Ohio Gang, 284
Ohio River, 124
oil embargo, 670–671, *671m*, 682
oil industry, 149, *149p*, 699, 763, 785. *See also* petroleum
Okies, 333, 334, *334p*
Okinawa, Battle of, *438m*, 440, 453, 456
Oklahoma: exploration of, *14m*, 15; facts about, R31; in Great Depression, 332–333; land rush, *146p–147p*, 147
Oklahoma City, 271, 729
older Americans, 353, 546, 749; health care and, 751
Olive Branch Petition, 32
Olmec culture, 7
Olmstead, Frederick Law, 159
Olson, Culbart, R60
Olympia (flagship), 208–209
Olympic Games: 1936, 386, *386p*; 1980, 685; 1984, 702
Omnibus Housing Act (1965), 546
100 Percent Americanism, 271
Oneida, 99
OPA. *See* Office of Price Administration
OPEC. *See* Organization of Petroleum Exporting Countries
Open Door Policy, 204, R9
"open skies" treaty, 499
Operation Alert, 507–508
Operation Desert Storm, 713, R16
Operation Overlord, 423
Operation PUSH, 589
Operation Rolling Thunder, 604–605, *605p*
Operation Torch, 421
Oppenheimer, J. Robert, 410, 479, R41
Order of Patrons of Husbandry. *See* National Grange
Oregon: Adams-Onís Treaty, 93; environmental conservation in, 780, *780p*; facts about, R31; Japanese Americans in, 445; labor laws in, 172; Oregon Treaty, 108; reforms in, 172
Oregon Territory, 106
Oregon Trail, 106, 107, *107m*
Oregon Treaty, 108
Organization Man, The (White), 514
Organization of Petroleum Exporting Countries (OPEC), 670–671, *671m*
Orlando, Vittorio, 255
Orr, Carey, *402p*
Orris, Peter, *575q*
Orshansky, Mollie, 790
OSHA. *See* Occupational Safety and Health Administration
Oslo Accords, 729
Oswald, Lee Harvey, 540, R41
Other America, The (Harrington), 513, 543, 789
Otis, Elisha, 159
Ottoman Empire, 231
outsourcing, 756, 806–812, *806p, 807p, 808p, 809p, 810g, 811c, 811g*
Owen, Ruth Bryan, 366
Owens, Jesse, 386, *386p*
OWI. *See* Office of War Information (OWI)

Pacheco, Romualdo, R60
pacification program, 606
Pacific Fleet, 403–405, *404p*
Pacific Ocean, 55, 107; World War II in, 433–440, *433p*, *434p*, *437p*, *438m*, 452–454, *453p*
Pacific Railway Act, 146
pacifists, 400
packet switching, 801
Paine, Thomas, 32, *33q*
Palestine, 10, 431
Palestine Liberation Organization (PLO), 705, 729
Palmer, A. Mitchell, 272, 288, R42
Palmer Raids, 272, R11
Panama, 684, 712; canal and, 213, 215–216, *215p*, 218–219, 684, 712, R10
Panama Canal, 213, 215–216, *215p*, 218–219, 684, 712, R10
Panic of 1893, 161
Panmunjom, Korea, 489
parallels, R62
Pardee, George, R60
pardon, 679
Paris Peace Conference, 255–257
Parker, Dorothy, 296, 314
Parks, Gordon, *367p*
Parks, Rosa, 562, *562p*, 563, *563p*, 578, R42
PATCO. *See* Professional Air Traffic Controllers' Organization
Paterson, William, 45
patriotism, 246, 271, 441, *441p*, 443, 742, *742p*
Patriots, 33, 35, 36
Patterson, Robert, 590
Patton, George S., 424, R42
Paul, Alice, 192, *192p*, *192q*, R42
Paul I, czar of Russia, 200
Payne-Aldrich Tariff, 190
PBS. *See* Public Broadcasting System
Peace Corps, 534, 550, *550p*
Pearl Harbor, 203, 403–405, *404m*, *404p*, 412–413, 434, *438m*, R12
Pelosi, Nancy, 181
Pendleton Civil Service Act (1883), 160, R8
peninsulares, 15
Penn, William, 19, 795
Pennsylvania: abolition movement, 104–105; Civil War in, 129; coal strike, 184; colonial, 18, 19; facts about, R31; housing in, 514; oil in, 149; Revolutionary War in, 34–35, *36m*; Three Mile Island, 683; voting rights in, 192; Whiskey Rebellion, 53
Pentagon, 740
Pentagon Papers, 623, 674
People's Party, 160–161, *160p*
People's Republic of China, 478–479, *479m*, 684; Nixon and, 669–670, *669p*. *See also* China
perestroika, 708
Perkins, Frances, 365, *365p*, 366, R42
Perkins, George, R60
Perkins, James, 573, *573p*, 574
Permanent Resident Card, 768
Perot, H. Ross, 727, 729, *730q*

Pershing, John J., 220, 223, *241p*, 242, 774, R42
Persian Gulf War, 459; 712–713, *712m*; women in, *772p*, 774
petroleum, 149, *149p*, 279; in Middle East, 501. *See also* fuel; oil industry
Philadelphia, 19, 22, 24; Constitutional Convention, 45; First Continental Congress, 31; as U.S. capital, 51
Philippines, 398; annexation of, 211–212, *211p*, *211q*; Spanish-American War and, 208–209, *209m*; and World War II, *434p*, 435, *438m*, 439
physical maps, R68; California, R58; United States, R48–R49
physical systems, R73
Pickett, George, 129
Pickford, Mary, 251, 310
Pierce, Franklin, 118, R18
Pilgrims, 17, R3
Pinchot, Gifford, 188, 190, R42
Pinckney, Charles Cotesworth, 53, 54
Pinckney's Treaty, 53
Pine Ridge Reservation, 640
Pinta (ship), 11
Pitt, William, 25
place, R72–R73
plagiarism, 805
Plains Indians, 142, *142p*, 143, *143m*, 144
Planned Parenthood of Southeastern Pennsylvania v. *Casey* (1992), 718, R28
plantations, 22–23, 97–98, 281
Plateau cultures, 7, *8m*
Platt Amendment, 214
Pledge of Allegiance, 445, R32
Plessy, Homer, 161
Plessy v. *Ferguson* (1896), 161, 557, 558, 559, *559p*, R9
PLO. *See* Palestine Liberation Organization
Plymouth, R3
Plymouth Colony, *16p–17p*, 17, R3
Plymouth Company, 16
Pocahontas, xxvii, 17
pocket veto, 133
Poindexter, John, 706
Poland, 256, 703, 709, *710m*, *710p*; Iron Curtain and, 465, 466; Warsaw Pact and, 498–499; in World War II, 395–396, 428, *429m*, 430–431, 451
police, 485–489, 795, *795p*, 799, *799p*
polio, 513
political asylum, 768
political machines, 159–160
political maps, R68; Africa, R56; Asia, R55; Australia, R57; California, R59; Caribbean, R50; Europe, R51, R54; New Zealand, R57; North America, R52; South America, R53; United States, R46–R47; world, R50–R51
politics: scandals in, 159–160
Polk, James K., 108, 110–111, R18
Pollock, Jackson, 359
polls, 688, *688g*
poll tax, 161, 574–575, 576
pollution, 752
Ponce de León, Juan, 15
Pontiac (Ottawa chief), 26
Pony Express, 109
Poor People's Campaign, 586–587, *586p*

pop art, 655
popular sovereignty, 117, 120
population: African American, *588c*, 589, 748, *748c*; Asian Americans, 748, *748c*; Hispanic Americans, *643g*, 748, *748c*, *754g*, *754m–755m*; of immigrants, 157, *770m*; Native American, 639; of older Americans, 749; in Roaring Twenties, 310; rural, *296g*; urban, *296g*; voting districts and, 579; wealth distribution, 323, *323g*
Populist Party, 160–161, *160p*
Port Moresby, 436
Portugal: exploration by, 11, 13, *14m*; nation-states, 10; in NATO, 470; slave trade and, 9
posters, 251, *251p*, *407p*, *412p*
potlatches, 7
Potsdam Conference, 454–455, 464, *464p*
poverty, 101, 170, *170p*, 171, 513, 788–793, *788p*, *789p*, *791p*, *792p*, *793c*; in Great Depression, 330–333, *330p–331p*, *332p*, *333p*; sharecropping and, 136, *136p*. *See also* War on Poverty
poverty threshold, 790
Powderly, Terence V., 153
Powell, Colin, 737, *738p*
Powers, Francis Gary, 499, *505p*
Powhatan Confederacy, 17
Prager, Robert, 251
Pravda (newspaper), 390
prehistory, 6
President, U.S.: cabinet of, 51; executive privilege, 678; term of office of, 497; Twelfth Amendment, 54. *See also* executive branch
Presidential Commission on the Status of Women, 635
Presley, Elvis, 515
press, freedom of the, 674
price controls, 673
Prichett, Laurie, 568–569
Primary Sources: Adams's Fourth of July address, R79; analyzing, 3, 197, 227, 263, 291, 317, 343, 379, 415, 461, 493, 519, 553, 593, 631, 659, 691, 723, 759; autobiography, 625; Bay of Pigs invasion, 529; Bush's September 11th speech, R93; César Chávez speech, R92; Checkers speech, 497; Civil Rights Act (1964), R90; *Common Sense* (Paine), 33, *33q*; Compromise of 1850, R82, R83; concentration camps, 430; Declaration of the Rights of Women, R87; Denmark Vesey document, R81; Douglass's "The Significance of Emancipation in the West Indies," R84; editorials, 208; Emancipation Proclamation, R85; English Bill of Rights, R76; Federalist Paper No. 10, R77; Four Freedoms speech, R88; Fourteen Points, R88; Fundamental Orders of Connecticut, R75; Gettysburg Address, R86; *The Great Gatsby* (Fitzgerald), 313; Great Society, *547p*; Jefferson's first inaugural address, R79; Kennedy's inaugural address, R89; King's Memphis speech, R91; Lincoln's inaugural address, R84,

R86; Magna Carta, R74; Mayflower Compact, R75; McCain, John, 625; Monroe Doctrine, R81; mural, 648, *648p*; Nixon, Richard M., 497; Objections to This Constitution of Government, R78; political cartoons, *118p, 157p, 181p, 214p, 272p, 337p, 352p,* 363, 402, *654p, 678p*; posters, *407p*; propaganda, 251, *251p*, 407, 444, *444p*; Reading Like a Historian, 291, 317; Seneca Falls Declaration of Sentiments, R81; speech, 497, *703q*; Tarbell, Ida, 171, *171q*; Teapot Dome scandal, 283; Virginia Statute for Religious Freedom, R76; Washington's Farewell Address, *52q,* R78; Weissman, Gerda, 430
prime meridian, R62
Princip, Gavrilo, 230, 232
printers, 24
prior restraint, 674
prisoners of war, 408, 774
prisons, 100, 127
probable cause, 700
Proclamation of 1763, 26
Proclamation of Amnesty and Reconstruction, 133
productivity, 279
Professional Air Traffic Controllers' Organization (PATCO), 698
Progressive Party, 191, 474
progressivism, 255; African Americans and, 193; civil rights and, 171–172; definition of, 171; documents about, 194–195; labor unions and, 172–174; reform movements and, 179–180; under T. Roosevelt, 183–188; Taft and, 190, 191; Wilson and, 191–193
Prohibition, 179–180, *180p*, 182, 248, 299–301, *300p, 300q, 301p,* 323, R11
Promontory Summit, 151
propaganda, 251, *251p*; in World War II, 443–444, *444p*
proprietary colonies, 18
protectionism, 807
protectorate, 214
Protestants, 11, 17, 100
protocols, 801
public accommodations, 570
Public Broadcasting Act (1967), 547
public lands, 783, *784m, 786c*
public opinion, 250–251
Public Works Administration (PWA), 351, *360c*
public works programs, 347, 351
Publius, 48
Pueblo (spy ship), 548
Pueblo Indians, 7, 145
pueblos, 7
Puerto Ricans, 648–649
Puerto Rico, 214, 215, 648
Pulitzer, Joseph, 206, 207, R42
Pulitzer Prize, 207
Pullman, George, 152, R42
Pullman Company, 153
Pure Food and Drug Act, 186
Puritans, 17
push-pull factors, 147
PWA. *See* Public Works Administration
Pyle, Ernie, 443, R42
pyramids, 7

Quakers, 19
Quarantine speech (F. Roosevelt), 401–402
Quartering Act (1765), 30–31
Quayle, Dan, 708
Quebec, 26
quotas, immigrant, 768

Rabin, Yitzhak, 729
racism: Great Migration and, 303, *303m*; in the military, 473, *473q*, 474, *474p*; New Deal programs and, 374; in 1930s, 371
Radical Republicans, 134
radio, 280, 294, *294p*, 309, *309p*; in Great Depression, 369–370
Radio Priest. *See* Coughlin, Charles
RAF. *See* Royal Air Force
railroad: transcontinental, R8
railroads: Civil War and, 125; industry and, 97, 150–151, *150m*; Pacific Railway Act, 146; steam engine, *90p–91p*; transcontinental, 150–151, *150m,* R8
Raleigh, Sir Walter, 16
ranching, 144–146, *145m,* 785
Randolph, A. Philip, 411, 557–558, R42
Randolph, Edmund, 45, 51
Raskob, John, *322q*
Rasul v. *Bush* (2004), R29
ratification, 48
rationing, 442–443, *442p*
Rauschenbush, Walter, 152, *152q*
Ray, James Earl, 585
Reading Like a Historian, xxvi–xix, H24–H41, 529; analyze, 263, 341, 377, 413, 415, 491, 517, 551, 553, 591, 629, 657, 689, 721, 757; analyzing alternative interpretation, H39; analyzing a photograph, 292; analyzing political cartoons, *678p*; analyzing primary sources, 3, 33, 52, 120, 171, 197, 208, 227, 263, 291, 317, 373, 379, 407, 415, 430, 461, 493, 497, 519, *545p, 545q,* 553, 593, 625, 631, 691, 703, 730; analyzing secondary sources, H35–H36; analyzing visuals, *337p*, 416, *544p*; bias in interpretation, H37; compare, 195, 211, 637, 648; concepts, H24–H25; contrasting, 225, 300, 313, 363, 377, 379, 721; describe, 195, 341, 377, 379, 413, 491, 517, 551, 591, 631, 657, 659, 691, 721; distinguish fact from opinion, 47; Document-Based Investigation, 289, 315; drawing conclusions, 4, 33, 245, 251, 272, 331, 352, 392, *402p,* 430, 444, 493, 497, 519, 593, 631, 659; drawing inferences, 283; elaborate, 341, 413, 459, 517, 551, 591, 629, 689, 721, 757; evaluate, 195, 225, 689; evaluating historical interpretation, H38; evaluating sources, 523, 763, H34; explain, 459, 689; identify, 225, 261, 263, 341, 377, 413, 415, 459, 491, 493, 517, 519, 551, 553, 591, 593, 629, 657, 689, 757; identify details, 176; identify points of view, 118, 152, 171, *181p,* 185, 257, 283, 292, 313, 454, 506, 583, 637, 678, 685, 703, 717; interpret, 195, 261, 341, 377, 413, 491, 591, 629, 657, 689, 721, 757; interpreting literature, H32; interpreting political cartoons, 157, 167, *181p,* 185, 214, 272, *352p,* 363, *402p,* 459, *547p, 654p,* H31; interpreting visuals, 28, 90, 114, 118, 140, 168, 198, *210p,* 228, 251, 318, 344, *367p,* 383, 384, 407, 416, 444, 462, 494, 524, 554, 594, 632, 648, 692, 724, H30; literature as historical evidence, 176, 245, 267, 334, 432, 572, 753; make generalizations, 721; make inferences, 52, 157, 227, 261, 657, 664, 691; making oral presentations, 663, H40; making written presentations, 663, H41; predict, 225; primary sources, H28–H29; recall, 195, 225, 261, 657; recognizing bias, 134, 208, 214, 610, H33; summarize, 721, 753; themes, H26–H27
Reading Skills: active reading, H2–H3; cause and effect, 166, H9; compare and contrast, H10; drawing conclusions, 382, H12; identify problem/solution, 266, H11; inferences, 762, H7; main idea, 2, H5; making generalizations, 522, H13; sequencing, H8; summarizing, 662, H6; vocabulary, H4
Reagan, Nancy, *694p,* 697, R42
Reagan, Ronald, *692p–693p, 694p,* 707, *707p,* R21, R42, R60; biography, 697; economy and, 698–699, *698p, 699g*; election of 1980, 695–696, *695m*; environment and, 783; foreign policy, 701–706, *702g, 706c*; as governor, 694, 696–697; Iran-Contra affair, 705–706; New Right, 697; speeches, 702, 703; Supreme Court and, 719; welfare reform and, 790
Reaganomics, 698, 699, 716
realpolitik, 668
recall, 175
recession, 699
Reconstruction, 132–138, 557, R7–R8
Reconstruction Acts, 134, R8
Reconstruction Finance Corporation (RFC), 338
Red Baron. *See* Richthofen, Manfred von
Redcoats, 35
Red Power movement, 639–641
Red Scare, 272, 273, 288–289, 477–482, *477p, 478m, 479p, 480p, 481p*
Red Sea, 501
Reed, Daniel, 373, *373p*
Reed, Walter, 214
Reed v. *Reed* (1971), R26
referendums, 175
Reformation, 10–11
Reform Era, 100, 101, 102, 103; women in, 102–103, *103p*
reform movements, 179–180; farmers and, 160; settlement houses and, 159

refugees, 766
Regents of the University of California v. *Bakke* (1978), 687
region, R72, R73
rehabilitation, 796
Rehnquist, William, 51, 737
Reign of Terror, 53
religion: African Americans and, 23; freedom of, 49, 539; fundamentalism, 297–299; Great Awakening, 24; immigrants and, 749; Ku Klux Klan and, 297; missionaries, 15; Native Americans and, 9, 15; nativism and, 274–275; reforms in, 99–100; revivals, 99; values and, 297–298
Remarque, Erich Maria, 260
Remington, Frederic, 206, 207
Renaissance, 10–11
Reno v. *ACLU* (1996), 729
reparations, 256, 286
republicanism, 42
Republican Party, R6–R7; African Americans and, 362; election of 1856, 118; election of 1860, 121; election of 1864, 130–131; election of 1912, 190–191, *190m*; election of 1930, 339; election of 1932, 347, *347m*; election of 1946, 474; election of 1948, 474; election of 1952, 496, *496p*, 497; election of 1956, 499; election of 1960, 527; election of 1964, 545–546, 576; election of 1966, 547; election of 1968, 615, 616–619, *617p*, *618p*, *619m*; election of 1972, 624; election of 1976, 680, 681; election of 1980, 695–696, *695m*; election of 1988, 707, 708; election of 1992, 727; election of 1994, 728; election of 1996, 729; election of 2000, 733–735, *733p*, *734m*, *734p*, *735p*; election of 2004, 736; Watergate scandal and, 675–679; women's suffrage and, 180
Republic of California, 111–112
Republic of Hawaii, 203
Republic of Texas, 110. *See also* Texas
reservations, 143, 144, 162, 641
reserved powers, 49
Resurrection City, 586, 587
Reuben James, USS, 403, 418, *418p*
Revere, Paul, 31
reverse discrimination, 687
Revolutionary War, R4; battles of, 31, 32, 34–37, *36m*; causes of, 30–31, *31c*, *32c*; time line, 28–29; women in, 773
Reynolds, Morgan O., 797
Reynolds v. *Sims* (1964), 538, 579
RFC. *See* Reconstruction Finance Corporation
Rhapsody in Blue (Gershwin), 313
Rhineland, 392–393
Rhine River, 451
Rhode Island: colonial, 18; facts about, R31; Industrial Revolution in, 96
Rhodesia, 390
Ricardo, David, 807, 809
Rice, Condoleezza, 737, *738p*, R42
Richardson, Elliot, 677, 678
Richardson, Friend, R60
Richmond, Virginia, *132p*
Richthofen, Manfred von, 237

Ridgway, Matthew, 486
rights and responsibilities: themes of, 521
Riis, Jacob, 170, *170p*, 171, R42
roads, 96; interstate highway system, 515, 516–517, *516g*, *517m*; Route 66, 516
Roanoke, 16
Roaring Twenties, 281; entertainment in, 308–310, *308p*, *309p*, *310p*; families and, 295; literature of, 312, 313; population in, 310; sports in the, 312, *312p*; time line, 292–293; values in, 297–299; women in, *294p*, 295–296, *295p*
robber barons, 152
Roberts, John, 51, 737
Robertson, Pat, 718
Robeson, Paul, *306p*, 307, R42
Robinson, Jackie, 558, *558p*, R42
rock and roll music, 515
Rockefeller, John D., 151, 171, R43
Rockwell, Norman, 444
Roe v. *Wade* (1973), 637, 718, R27
Rogers, Ginger, 369, *369p*
Rolfe, John, 16
Rolph, James, R60
Roman Catholic Church, 11, 527
Romania, 709, *710m*, *710p*
Rommel, Erwin, 420, R43
Roosevelt, Eleanor, 348–349, *349p*, 366, R43; civil rights and, 557; discrimination and, 371; human rights and, 475–476
Roosevelt, Franklin Delano, *358q*, *451q*, 542, R11, R20, R43; Atlantic Charter, 403; banking crisis, 349–350, *349q*; biography, 348, *348p*; cash-and-carry policy, 402; civil rights and, 557; court-packing plan, 363; death of, 451; documents about, 376–377, *377p*; election of 1932, 347, *347m*, *348q*; election of 1936, 362, *362p*; election of 1940, 403; Executive Order 9066, 445–446, *446p*; fireside chats, 348, 351, 369; foreign policy of, 400, 401–402, *401q*, *402p*; Forgotten Man speech, 346, *346p*; four freedoms, 443, 444; GI Bill, 472; as governor, 348; Great Depression and, 347–351; Hundred Days, 350–351; labor unions and, 359–361, *360c*, *361g*, *361p*; Lend-Lease Act, 403; New Deal, 350–353, 357–364, *358p–359p*, *360c*, *361g*, *361p*, *362p*, *364g*, 372–373, *372g*; Pearl Harbor and, 403–405, *405q*, 412; polio and, 513; Quarantine speech, 401–402; Second Hundred Days, 358–359; Stalin and, 465; Truman and, 473–474; World War II and, 398, 410, 421, 422, 430–431, *442q*; Yalta Conference, 450
Roosevelt, Theodore, 283, 351, R19, R43; African Americans and, 193, *193q*; business and, 184–186, *186q*; coal strike, 184; conservation and, 782; environment and, 187–188, *188m*; Gentlemen's Agreement, 768; life of, 183, *183p*, 186, *186p*; muckrakers and, 194; national park system and, 187; in New York, 184; Panama

Canal and, 213, *213p*; presidency of, 184–188; progressivism under, 183–188; Roosevelt Corollary, 216–217, *217q*; Russo-Japanese War and, 205; Spanish-American War and, 208–210, *209m*, *210q*; Square Deal, 184, *184q*; Taft and, 189, *189p*, 190, 191
Roosevelt Corollary, 216–217, *217q*
Rosenberg, Ethel and Julius, 480, *480p*, 481
Rosie the Riveter, 409
Ross, Nellie Tayloe, 295
Ross, William B., 295
Rostow, Walt W., *610p*, *610q*
Rough Riders, 210, *210p*
route maps, R69
Route 66, 516
Royal Air Force (RAF), 397
Ruby, Jack, 540
Rumsfeld, Donald, 737, *738p*, *774p*, R43
rural areas, 296–297, *296g*
Rural Electrification Administration, *360c*, 362
Rusk, Dean, 528, 611
Russia: Alaska and, 200; Bolsheviks in, 242, 259, 271; communism in, 242; militarism and, 231; Russo-Japanese War, 205; in World War I, 232–233, *233m*, 240, 242, *243m*. *See also* Soviet Union
Russian-American Company, 200
Russo-Japanese War, 205
Ruth, Babe, 312, *312p*, 370

S

Sabin, Pauline, *300p*, *300q*
sabotage, 251
Sacajawea, 55
Sacco, Nicola, 274–275, *275p*
Sack of Lawrence, 118
Sacramento, 108, R61
Sacramento River, R61
Sadat, Anwar el-, 684, *684p*
Sagebrush Rebellion, 783
Sahara Desert, 9
Saigon, 600, 612, *612p*, 624–625
Sakharov, Andrei, 708
Salem, Massachusetts, *20p*
Salk, Jonas, 513, *513p*, R43
SALT. *See* Strategic Arms Limitation Talks
Salter, John, 563
salutary neglect, 21
Samoa, 211
Sampson, Deborah, 35, 773
SAMs. *See* surface-to-air missiles
Samuelson, Robert J., 771
Sanchez, Loretta and Linda, *754p*
Sandburg, Carl, *281q*
Sand Creek Massacre, 143, *143m*
Sandinistas, 705–706, 704
San Francisco, 108, 154, 158, 652, 653, 753
San Jacinto, Battle of, 110
San Juan Hill, Battle of, *198p–199p*, 210
Santa Anna, Antonio López de, 110, R43
Santa Fe, New Mexico, 111
Santa Fe Trail, 107, *107m*
Santa Maria (ship), 11

Santiago, Battle of, 210
Sarajevo, 230
Saratoga, Battle of, 34
SARS. *See* Severe Acute Respiratory Syndrome
satellites, 506
Saturday night massacre, 678
savings and loan crisis, 716, 717
Savio, Mario, 651–652, *651p*
scabs, 361
scalawags, 135–136
Schecter Poultry Corporation v. *the United States*, 353, 356, 359
Schenck, Charles, 252, 253
Schenck v. *United States* (1919), 252, 253, *253p*
Schlafly, Phyllis, 637, *637p*, *637q*, 718, R43
Schlesinger, Arthur, 528, 529
Schlieffen Plan, 231, 232
Schmeling, Max, 370
Schneiderman, Rose, 172, *174q*
Scholder, Fritz, 641
school prayer, 539
Schoonover, Frank, 228
Schroeder, Patricia, 777
Schwarzenegger, Arnold, R60
Schwerner, Michael, 575–576
science: education and, 298–299; themes of, 661; World War II and, 410. *See also* technology
scientific management, 277
SCLC. *See* Southern Christian Leadership Conference
Scopes, John, 298–299, *298p*, *299p*
Scott, Alberta Virginia, 177
Scott, Dred, 118, *119p*
Scott, Winfield, 112
scrap drives, 442–443, *442p*
SDI. *See* Strategic Defense Initiative
SDS. *See* Students for a Democratic Society
Seale, Bobby, 583
search and destroy missions, 606, 623
search and seizure, 700, 718
search warrants, 538–539
Sears, Leah Ward, *575p*
SEATO. *See* Southeast Asia Treaty Organization
Seattle, Washington, 273
SEC. *See* Securities and Exchange Commission
secession, 121–122, *121c*, R7
Second Amendment, 796
Second Bank of the United States, 95
Second Great Awakening, R5
sectionalism, 93, *93m*, 95, *98c*
Securities and Exchange Commission (SEC), 351, *360c*
sedition, 252, 289
Sedition Act, 252
segregation, 161–162, 560, 581, 590, 667; *Brown* v. *Board of Education of Topeka, Kansas*, 538, 559–561, *559p*, *559q*, *560p*, *561q*; Executive Order 9981, 473, *473q*, 474, *474p*; school, *557m*, 588
Selassie, Haile, 391, *391q*, R43
Selective Service Act, 241
self-determination, 255, 257
self-government, 21
Selma, Alabama, 573, *573p*, 577–578, *577p*

Seminole culture, *94m*, 95
Senate, U.S.: Crittenden Compromise, 122; Lyndon Johnson and, 542. *See also* Congress, U.S.
Seneca Falls Convention, 102, 105, 180, R6
Seneca Falls Declaration, 102, 182,
Seneca Falls Declaration of Sentiments, R81
sentencing laws, 796, 797
separate but equal, 161, 558, 559
separation of powers, 46–49, *46c*, *46q*, 60–75
Separatists, 17
September 11th attacks, 674, 705, 738, 739–743, *739p*, *740m*, *741p*, *742p*, R16, R93
Serbia, 231, 730
Serra, Fray Junípero, 15, R43
Servicemen's Readjustment Act (1944), 472, *472p*
settlement houses, 159
Seventeenth Amendment, 175
Seventh-day Adventist Church, 99
Severe Acute Respiratory Syndrome (SARS), 250, *250p*
Seward, William H., 116, 121, 200
Shakers, 99
Shalala, Donna, 539–540
Shame of the Cities, The (Steffens), 171, 195
sharecropping, 136, *136p*
Share Our Wealth Society, 352
Shays, Daniel, 43
Shays's Rebellion, 43, R4
sheep ranching, 145
Sherman, Roger, *44p*, 45
Sherman, William T., 130–131
Sherman Antitrust Act (1890), 152, 185, 191, R9
Sherman Silver Purchase Act, 161
Shiloh, Battle of, 125, *125m*
Shinda, Yoshitaka, 439
Sholes, Christopher Latham, 155
Shurtliff, Robert, 773
Shusterman, Carl, 769
shuttle diplomacy, 671
Siberia, 6
Sicily, 422
Sikhs, 749
silent majority, 620, 621
Silent Spring (Carson), 668, *783p*
silver mining, 144, 160, 161
Sinclair, Upton, 176, *176p*, 186, *186q*, 194, R43
Singapore, 435
Sioux, 142, 143, *143m*, 144, 640
Sirhan Sirhan, 617
sit-down strikes, 361, *361p*, 563, 565–566, 568–569
Sitting Bull, 143, 144, R43
sitzkrieg, 396
Sixteenth Amendment, 190, R10
Sixth Amendment, 549
skyscrapers, 158, *158p*
Slater, Samuel, 96
Slaughterhouse Cases, 137
slave revolts, 103–104
slavery: abolition movement, 102–105; and Africa, 9; compensated emancipation, 119; Compromise of 1850, 117, *117m*; cotton and, 97–98; *Dred Scott* v. *Sandford* (1857), 118;

Emancipation Proclamation, 127; Fugitive Slave Act, 117; Kansas and, 116–117, *116p*, *117m*; life in, 103, *104p*; Middle Passage, 22; Missouri Compromise and, 93; in New York, 19; plantations and, 22–23; Thirteenth Amendment, 130; Three-Fifths Compromise, 46; triangular trade, 22–23; Underground Railroad, 104; in Virginia, 17
slave states, 93, *93m*, 116, 117, *117m*
slave trade, 9, 22–23
Slidell, John, 111
Smith, Adam, 807
Smith, Alfred E., 322, *322m*, 353
Smith, Bessie, *306p*, 307, R43
Smith, John, 16
Smith, Joseph, 99, 107
Smith Act (1948), 480
Smith-Connally Act (1943), 410
Smitherman, Joe, 573
Smoking Gun conversation, 689
Smoot-Hawley Tariff Act (1930), 338, 808, R11
smuggling, 20–21
SNCC. *See* Student Nonviolent Coordinating Committee
social classes, 159
social contract theory, 23, 33
social Darwinism, 151, 152, *152q*, 201
social gospel, 159
social justice, 643–644
Social Security Act (1935), 359, *360c*, 364, 372, 373, 668, 737, 749, *791p*, R12
Social Studies Skills: analyzing infographics, H18; cartograms, H21; charts, H15; cost/benefits, H22; historical maps, H20; Internet, H23; line graphs, H17; movement maps, H19; pie and bar graphs, H16; time lines, H14
Society of Righteous and Harmonious Fists, 204
sod houses, 148
Solidarity, 703, 709
Solomon Islands, 437, *438m*
Somalia, 729, 742
Somme, Battle of the, *232c*, *233m*, *236p*
Somoza, Anastasio, 704
Songhai, 9
Sorenson, Ted, 528
South: Civil War in, 123–131; Confederate States of America, 122; cotton in, 97–98; Jim Crow laws, 161; North and, 98; population of, 748; Reconstruction in, 132–138; Revolutionary War in the, 36, *36m*; secession and the, 121–122, R7; Three-Fifths Compromise, 46
South Africa, 705, 713
South America, R53
South Carolina: colonial, 19; Civil War in, 131; facts about, R31; integration in, 559; nullification crisis, 95; secession, 121–122
South Dakota: Civil War in, 128; facts about, R31; Native Americans in, 640
Southeast Asia, 398, 403, 596, 625. *See also* Cambodia; Laos; Vietnam
Southeast Asia Treaty Organization (SEATO), 500

Southeast cultures, 7, *8m*
Southern Christian Leadership Conference (SCLC), 563, 569, 577
southern colonies, 19, 22–23, *22m*
Southern Hemisphere, R63
southern strategy, 667
South Korea, 483–489, *483p*, *484m*, *487m*
South Pacific: World War II in, 435–440, *438m*
South Vietnam, 500, 599–603, *599m*, 680. *See also* Vietnam War
Southwest cultures, 7, *8m*
sovereignty, 49
Soviet Union, *711p*; Afghanistan and, 685; arms race and, 504–506, *505p*, *506p*, *506q*; atomic bomb and, 477, 478; Berlin and, 469, *469m*, 530; Bolsheviks in, 271–272; Carter and, 684; China and, 708; Cold War and, 465–470, 498–499, *498p*, *499p*; collapse of, 710–711, R16; communism in, 390; Cuban missile crisis, 532–533, *532m*, *533p*; Germany and, 420; Iron Curtain, 465–467, *466m*, *467p*; Jews in, 428; Korea and, 484; Limited Nuclear Test Ban Treaty, 533; opening of, 708; Reagan and, 703; space program of, 537–538, 680; technology and, 505–506; Warsaw Pact and, 498–499; in World War II, 395, 420, *421m*, 449, *449p*, 451, 465. *See also* Russia
space exploration, *525p*, 671–673, *672p*, 680, 750; Kennedy and, 537–538, *537q*
space shuttle, 715, *715p*
Spain: England and, 15; exploration by, 11–12, 13, *14m*, 15; French and Indian War, 24–26, *25m*; Mexico and, 109; nation-states, 10; North American claims, *25m*; Pinckney's Treaty, 53; slave trade and, 9; Spanish-American War, 206–211, *206p*, *209m*, *210p*; Spanish Civil War, 390, 391–392, *391p*, 400; Texas and, 109
spam, 802, 803
Spanish-American War, 206–211, *206p*, *209m*, *210p*, R9; women in, 773
Spanish Armada, 15
Spanish Civil War, 390, 391–392, *391p*, 400
spatial terms, R73
speakeasies, 301
Speaking Skills: descriptive, 619; expository, 122, 540, 578, 699; narrative, 738; persuasive, 12, 37, 56, 162, 193, 431, 501, 680
special prosecutor, 677
Sperry, Charles, 205
spheres of influence, 204
Spindletop, 149, *149p*
Spirit of St. Louis, The (airplane), 310–311, *311p*
Spirit of '76, The (film), 252
Spiritualism, 99
Spock, Benjamin, 610
sports: baseball, 312, *312p*, 370, 514, 558, *558p*; football, 312, *312p*; golf, 312, *312p*; in Great Depression, 370; in Roaring Twenties, 312, *312p*; tennis, 312, *312p*; women in, 370
Spotsylvania, Battle of, 130
Sputnik (satellite), *505p*, 506

Square Deal, 184, *184q*
Stalin, Joseph, 390, R43; Churchill and, 467; death of, 498; Hitler and, 395, 465; Iron Curtain and, 465–467; at Potsdam Conference, 455, 464, *464p*; World War II and, 465; Yalta Conference, 450
Stalingrad, Battle of, 420, *421m*
Stamp Act (1765), 30, R4
Standard Oil Company, 151, 171
standard time, 151
Stanford, Leland, R60
Stanton, Edwin, 135
Stanton, Elizabeth Cady, 102, 103, *103p*, *178p*, 180, 182, R43
Starr, Ellen Gates, 159
Starr, Kenneth, 731
START. *See* Strategic Arms Reduction Treaty
Star Wars. *See* Strategic Defense Initiative
State Department, 51
state government, 42, 73, 175; Reconstruction and, 133, 137
states' rights, 45, 46, 48, 49, 95
Steamboat Willie (film), 310
steam engine, *90p–91p*, 96, *97p*
steel companies, 150, 537
Steffens, Lincoln, 171, 195, R43
Stein, Gertrude, 313
Steinbeck, John, 267, 334, 367, 368
Steinem, Gloria, *637p*, *637q*
Stephens, Alexander, 122
Stephens, William, R60
Stevens, Alzina P., 195
Stevens, John F., 215, 216
Stevens, John L., 203, 224
Stevens, Thaddeus, 133, 137
Stevenson, Adlai, 497, 499
Stewart, Potter, *674q*
Stimson, Henry, 435, 454, *454p*, *454q*
Stinson, Bob, *361q*
Stockman, David A., 698, 699, R43
stock market, 151, 320, *320p*, 716, 720, 736; buying on margin, 326; 1929 crash, 324–327, *325p*, *325q*, *326p*, R11; expansion of, 321–322, *321p*, *323g*; Securities and Exchange Commission, 351
Stoneman, George, R60
Stowe, Harriet Beecher, 117
Strategic Arms Limitation Talks (SALT), 668–669, 684
Strategic Arms Reduction Treaty (START), 711, R16
Strategic Defense Initiative (SDI), 702–703
streetcars, 154
strict constructionist, 52
strikes, 174, 184, 273, *273p*, 361, *361p*
Strong, Josiah, *201q*
student activism, 651–652
Student Nonviolent Coordinating Committee (SNCC), 566, 567, 576, 583, 588, 636
Students for a Democratic Society (SDS), 611
submarines, 238, 239, 240, *240p*, 504–505. *See also* U-boats
subpoena, 678
subsistence farming, 21

suburbs, 279
subway system, 154
Sudetenland, 393
Suez Canal, 420, 501
suffrage. *See* voting
Sugar Act (1764), 30
sugar industry, 202–203
Sullivan Act (1911), 795
Summer of Love, 653
summit, 499
Sumner, Charles, *118p*, 133, 137
Sumner, William Graham, *152p*, *152q*
Sunbelt, 514
Sunday, Billy, 179, 297–298, R44
supply-side economics, 698–699
Supreme Court, U.S., 51; African Americans on, 588; *Baker v. Carr* (1962), R25; *Brown v. Board of Education of Topeka, Kansas* (1954), 559–561, *559p*, *559q*, *560p*, *561q*, R13; Bush appointments to, 737; *Bush v. Gore* (2000), 735, R29; Civil Rights cases, R22–R23; *Cruzan v. Director, Missouri Department of Health* (1990), 718, R28; *Dennis v. United States*, 480; *Dred Scott v. Sandford* (1858), 118, R7; *Engel v. Vitale* (1962), R25; and the flag, 445; *Gibbons v. Ogden* (1824), 93, R22; *Gideon v. Wainwright* (1963), R26; *Hamdi v. Rumsfeld* (2004), R29; *Heart of Atlanta Motel v. United States* (1964), R26; Judiciary Act (1789), 51; Kennedy and, 538–539; *Korematsu v. the United States*, 446, 448; *Lochner v. New York*, 172, R24; *Mapp v. Ohio* (1961), R25; *Marbury v. Madison* (1803), 54–55, R5; *McCulloch v. Maryland* (1819), 93; *Miranda v. Arizona* (1966), 549; *Muller v. Oregon* (1908), 172, R24; New Deal and, 353; *New Jersey v. T.L.O.*, 700, 718; *New York Times Co. v. United States* (1971), 674, R27; Nixon and, 667, 679; nominees, 718–719, *719p*; *Northern Securities Co. v. United States* (1904), R24; *Planned Parenthood of Southeastern Pennsylvania v. Casey* (1992), 718, R28; *Plessy v. Ferguson* (1896), 161, 557, 558, 559, *559p*, R9; *Rasul v. Bush* (2004), R29; *In Re Debs* (1895), R23; *Reed v. Reed* (1971), R26; *Regents of the University of California v. Bakke* (1978), 687; *Reno v. ACLU* (1996), 729; *Reynolds v. Sims* (1964), 579; *Roe v. Wade* (1973), 637, 718, R27; Roosevelt and, 363–364; *Schecter Poultry Corporation v. the United States*, 353, 356, 359; *Schenck v. United States*, 252, 253, *253p*; Slaughterhouse Cases, 137; *Texas v. Johnson* (1989), R27; *Tinker v. Des Moines Independent Community School District* (1969), R26; *United States v. Butler*, 353; *United States v. E.C. Knight Co.* (1895), R23; *United States v. Nixon* (1974), R27; *Vernonia School District v. Acton* (1995), 732, R28; *Wabash, St. Louis & Pacific R.R. v. Illinois* (1886), R23; Warren and, 538–539; Watergate Scandal and, 679; *Watkins*

v. *United States* (1957), R25; *Westside Community School District* v. *Mergens* (1990), 718; women justices, 717; *Worcester* v. *Georgia* (1832), R22; *Yates* v. *United States*, 480. *See also* judicial branch
surface-to-air missiles (SAMs), 532
Sussex (ship), 239
Sussex pledge, 239
Sutter, John, 107
Swamp Fox, 36
Sweatt v. *Painter*, 558
swing music, 370
Syngman Rhee, 489, R44
Syria, 501, 670–671
Szilard, Leo, 454, *454p, 454q*

Taft, Robert, 496
Taft, William Howard, R20, R44; dollar diplomacy, 217; election of 1912, *190m*, 191; progressivism and, 190; Roosevelt and, 189, *189p,* 190
Taft-Hartley Act (1947), 473
Taiwan, 478, 670, 684
Takeharu Terao, *453q*
takings clause, 783
Taliban, 743, 744
Tammany Hall, 159
Tampico incident, 222
Tan, Amy, 753, *753p*
tanks, 237
Tannenberg, Battle of, *232c, 233m*
Tarbell, Ida, 171, *171q,* R44
tariffs, 808; General Agreement on Tariffs and Trade, *475c,* 476; Great Depression and, 327; nullification crisis and, 95; Smoot-Hawley Tariff Act, 338; Taft and, 190; under Wilson, 191
taxation without representation, 30
taxes: Bush and, 736; Great Britain and, 21; Hoover and, 339; income, 191; Sixteenth Amendment, 190
Tax Reduction Act (1964), 544
Taylor, Frederick Winslow, 277
Taylor, Zachary, 119, R18
Taylor Grazing Act (1934), 782
Tea Act (1773), 30, 31
Teapot Dome scandal, 283, 284
technology: 96–97, 154–155; communications, 109, 280; computer, 512, *512p,* 714, *714p,* 749–750; farm, 148; mining, *144p,* 145; Soviet Union and, 505–506; themes of, 661; transistors, 512; weapons, 234, 236–237. *See also* science
Tejanos, 109
telecommuting, 802
telegraph, 97, 109, 124–125, 154
telephone, 155, 750, R8
television, 509–511, *509p, 511p,* R14; battlefield reporting, 614, *614p;* counterculture and, 654; Vietnam War and, 609–610
Teller Amendment, 209, 214
temperance movement, 100, 248

tenant farming, 136
Tenement Act (1901), 171
tenements, 101, 159, 171
Ten-Hour Movement, 102
Tennessee, 585; civil rights movement in, 565; Civil War in, 125, *125m,* 130; exploration of, 15; facts about, R31; Jim Crow laws, 161; Reconstruction in, 133; Scopes trial, 298–299, *298p, 299p;* secession, 121, 124; voting rights in, 538
Tennessee Valley Authority (TVA), 351, 354–355, *360c*
tennis, 312, *312p*
Tenochtitlán, 7, 15
Ten-Percent Plan, 133
Tenth Amendment, 49, 77, 95
Tenure of Office Act (1867), 135
Terkel, Studs, *330q, 407q*
termination policy, 638–639
terrorism, 271, 705; Oklahoma City, 729. *See also* September 11th attacks
Test-Taking Strategies, 2, 166, 266, 382, 522, 662, 762, TT2–TT24
Tet Offensive, 613–615, *613m,* 628–629, *628c, 629p*
Texas, 542; Alamo, 110; annexation of, 110; Brownsville incident, 193; cattle ranching, 145, *145m,* 146; Compromise of 1850, *117m;* exploration of, *14m,* 15; facts about, R31; in Great Depression, 332, 340, *340p;* Hispanic Americans in, *754m–755m, 755p;* hurricanes in, 174; independence, 109–110; Kennedy assassination in, 539; La Raza Unida Party, 646–647, *646p;* MAYO in, 646, *647p;* Mexico and, 109, 110, *111m;* military bases in, 408; Native Americans in, 109; oil in, 149, *149p;* population of, 748; revolution in, 109–110, R6; secession, 121; slavery and, 110; Spain and, 109; statehood and, 110; women in, 295. *See also* Republic of Texas
Texas longhorn, 145
Texas Revolution, 109–110, R6
Texas Venture, 109
Texas v. *Johnson* (1989), R27
textile industry, 96, 97–98
Thanh, Nguyen That. *See* Ho Chi Minh
Thanksgiving Day, 276
Thatcher, Margaret, 702
Their Eyes Were Watching God (Hurston), 302
Themes: cultural expressions, 265; economic development, 165, 265; global relations, 165, 381, 521, 661; government and democracy, 165, 265, 381, 521, 661; rights and responsibilities, 521; science and technology, 661
Thirteenth Amendment, 80, 130, 135
38th parallel, 484, *484m,* 485, 488
Thomas, Clarence, 719, *719p,* R44
Thomas, Helen, 540
Thoreau, Henry David, 100
Three-Fifths Compromise, 46
Three Mile Island, 683
Three Soldiers (Dos Passos), 313

Thurmond, Strom, 474
Tiananmen Square massacre, 711
Tiber, Ed, 650
Tijerina, Reies López, 645
Tilden, Samuel J., 138
Time Line: civil rights movement, 554–555, 574–575; Civil War, 114–115; Cold War, 462–463; conservative era, 692–693; criminal justice, 794–795; early cultures, 4–5; environmental conservation, 780–781; exploration, 4–5, 536–537; foreign relations, 198–199; Great Depression, 318–319; Great Society, 524–525; immigration, 766–767; Industrial Revolution, 96–97, 140–141; Internet, 801; isolationism, 400–401; military women, 772–773; nationalism, 90–91; Native Americans, 638–639; New Deal, 344–345; New Frontier, 524–525; postwar America, 494–495; poverty, 788–789; Progressive era, 168–169; Revolutionary War, 28–29; Roaring Twenties, 292–293; 1970s, 664–665; social changes, 632–633; trade, 806–807; twenty-first century, 724–725; Vietnam War, 594–595; Watergate scandal, 676–677; womens' rights, 178–179; World War I, 228–229; after World War I, 268–269; World War II, 384–385, 416–417
time zones, 151
Tinker v. *Des Moines Independent Community School District* (1969), R26
Title IX (1972), *575p*
Tito, Josip Broz, 466, 730
tobacco, 16
Tojo, Hideki, 398, 403, R44
Tokyo, 205, 453
Tonkin Gulf Resolution, 602–603
Tories, 33
totalitarian government, 389, 390, *390p*
tourist industry, 279
town meeting, 21
Townsend, Francis, 353, 359, 362, R44
Townshend Acts (1767), 31
trade: barter system, 9; colonial, 22–23, *23m;* free, 807; General Agreement on Tariffs and Trade, *475c,* 476; international, 730–731; Native Americans and, 9; outsourcing and, 806–812, *806p, 807p, 808p, 809p, 810g, 811c, 811g;* triangular, 22, *23m*
trading kingdoms, 9
Trail of Broken Treaties, 640
Trail of Tears, *94m,* 95
transatlantic flight, 310–311, *311p*
transcendentalism, 100
transcontinental railroad, 150–151, *150m,* R8
transcript, 679, 689
transistors, 512
transportation: automobiles, 277–279, *278p;* in Civil War, 125; in 1800s, 96–97; in Second Industrial Revolution, 154, *154p. See also* airplanes; railroads
Travis, William, 110
Treasury Department, 51
Treaty of Fort Laramie, 640
Treaty of Greenville, 53

Treaty of Guadalupe Hidalgo, 112
Treaty of Paris (1763), 26
Treaty of Paris (1783), 37, 43
Treaty of Portsmouth, 205
Treaty of Tordesillas, 13
Treaty of Versailles, 256–258, *256c*, *258m*, 387, 388, 392, R10
trench warfare, 234–235, *234p–235p*, 236, *236p*, 243, 260–261, *261p*
Triangle Shirtwaist fire, 172–174, *172p*, *174q*
triangular trade, 22, *23m*
Trimmingham, Rupert, 459
Triple Alliance, 231–232, *231m*
Triple Entente, 231–232, *231m*
Truman, Harry S, 546, R20, R44; atomic bomb and, 453–454; biography, 473, *473p*; Communist threat and, 477–480; Eisenhower and, 496; election of 1948, 474–475; Executive Order 9835, 490; Executive Order 9981, 473, *473q*, 474, *474p*; Fair Deal, 475; integration in the military and, 452; Iron Curtain and, 466–467; Korea and, 485, *485q*; MacArthur and, 488; nuclear weapons and, 503; at Potsdam Conference, 455, 464, *464p*; Roosevelt and, 473–474; Taft-Hartley Act and, 473; Truman Doctrine, 467–468, *467q*; Vietnam and, 598
Truman Doctrine, 467–468, *467q*
Trumpauer, Joan, 563
Truth-in-Lending Act (1967), 547
Tubman, Harriet, 104, 180, R44
tundra, 7
Turkey, 467, 470, 532, 533
Turner, Frederick Jackson, 148
Turner, Nat, 103–104
Tuskegee Airmen, 422, *422p*, 452
Tuskegee Institute, 162
TVA. *See* Tennessee Valley Authority
Tweed, William Marcy, 159
Twelfth Amendment, 54, 78
Twenty-fourth Amendment, 574–575
Twenty-second Amendment, 497
Twenty-sixth Amendment, 624
Two Treatises of Government (Locke), 23–24
Tydings, Millard, 482
Tyler, John, 110, R18
typewriter, 155

U-boats, 238, 239, 240, *240p*, 403, 418–420, *418p*, *419p*. *See also* submarines
Uchiyama, Yoshiko, *446q*
UN. *See* United Nations
unalienable, 38
Uncle Sam, 251, *251p*
Uncle Tom's Cabin (Stowe), 117
Underground Railroad, 99, 104, 180
Underwood Tariff Act (1913), 191
unemployment, 321, 682, 699; in Great Depression, 330; Kennedy and, 537; Lyndon Johnson and, 544; New Deal and, 372, *372g*; Social Security Act, 359

UNIA. *See* Universal Negro Improvement Association
Union army, 123–131
Union Pacific Railroad, *150m*, 151, 160
Union Party, 362
United Auto Workers, 361, *361p*
United Colonies of New England, 21
United Farm Workers, R15
United Kingdom, 470. *See also* Britain; England; Great Britain
United Mine Workers, 274, 360
United Nations, 454, 475–476, 717; Declaration of Human Rights, 683; Israel and, 501, 670–671; Korea and, 485–489
United Service Organizations (USO), 459
United States Steel Corporation, 361
United States v. Butler, 353
United States v. E.C. Knight Co. (1895), R23
United States v. Nixon (1974), R26
UNIVAC, 512
Universal Declaration of Human Rights, 476
Universal Negro Improvement Association (UNIA), 304
University of California, Berkeley, 651–652
University of Georgia, 567–568
University of Mississippi, *567p*, 568
urbanization, 96, 101, 159, 296–297, *296g*
USA PATRIOT Act, 745, 768
USO. *See* United Service Organizations
Utah: facts about, R31; reforms in, 172; Treaty of Guadalupe Hidalgo, 112
Utah Territory, *150m*, 151, 181
utopian communities, 99

vaccines, 513
Valentino, Rudolph, 310, *310p*
Valley Forge, 34
values: Prohibition, 299–301, *300q*, *301p*; in Roaring Twenties, 297–299
Van Buren, Martin, 102, R17
Vance, Cyrus, *685q*
Vanderbilt, Cornelius, 152, R44
Van Doren, Charles, 510
Vanzetti, Bartolomeo, 274–275, *275p*, *275q*
Vardaman, James, 175
V-E Day, 452, 471
velvet revolution, 709
VEP. *See* Voter Education Project
Veracruz, Battle of, 222, *222p*
Verdun, Battle of, *232c*, *233m*
Vermont: facts about, R31
Vernonia School District v. Acton (1995), 732, R28
vertical integration, 151
Vesey, Denmark, R80
veterans: Bonus Marchers, 335, 338–339; discrimination against, 473; GI Bill, 472, *472p*; Vietnam, 623, *624p*, 625–627, *626p*; World War II, 471, *471p*, 472, *472p*
Vice President, U.S.: Nixon as, 497; Twelfth Amendment, 54. *See also* executive branch

viceroyalties, 15
Vichy France, 396
Vicksburg, Siege of, 129
victory gardens, 248, *383p*, 441, *441p*, 442
Vienna Conference, 530
Vietcong, 601, 606, 608. *See also* Vietnam War
Vietminh, 597–600
Vietnam, 256, 398; Buddhists in, 600, *600p*, *601p*; China and, 597; civil war in, 600, *600p*, *601p*; France and, 499–500, *500m*, 596–599; ground war, 606–608, *607p*
Vietnamization, 621
Vietnam veterans, 623, *624p*, 625–627, *626p*
Vietnam Veterans Memorial, *626p*, 627
Vietnam War, 668, 680, 682, R14; air war, 604–605, *605p*; antiwar movement, 611, 622–623, *622p*, *623p*; Johnson and, 548; media and, 609–610; My Lai massacre, 623; Operation Rolling Thunder, 604–605, *605p*; pacification program, 606; Pentagon Papers, 674; public opinion of, 609–611; search and destroy missions, 623; Tet Offensive, 613–615, *613m*, 628–629, *628c*, *629p*; time line, 594–595; Tonkin Gulf Resolution, 602–603; Vietnamization, 621; women in, 774, 778, *778p*
Vietnam Women's Memorial, 778, *778p*
Villa, Francisco "Pancho," 220, *220p*, 221, 223, R44
Villaraigosa, Antonio, 747, *747p*, R44
Vinciguerra, Tom, 376
Virginia: city manager model, 174; Civil War in, 125–126, *126m*, 129, *129p*, 130, 131; colonial, 16–17; facts about, R31; integration in, 560; national parks in, 187; Roanoke, 16; secession, 121, 124; slave revolts, 103–104; Virginia Declaration of Rights, 33, 49; Virginia Statute for Religious Freedom, R76
Virginia (ship), 128
Virginia Company, 17
Virginia Declaration of Rights, 33, 49,
Virginia Plan, 45, *45c*
Virginia Statute for Religious Freedom, R76
VISTA. *See* Volunteers in Service to America
V-J Day, 454, 471
Volcker, Paul, 716
Volstead Act, 248, 300
Volunteers in Service to America (VISTA), 544
V1 flying bomb, 423
Voter Education Project (VEP), 574
voting, 538; African Americans and, 134–136, *134p*, 180, 375, 573–579, *573p*, *574p*, *575p*, *576p*, *577p*; age, 624; women and, 135, *179p*, 180–182, 192, *192p*, 259, 295, 717
Voting Rights Act (1965), 118, *570c*, 577–578, *577p*, 667
V2 rocket, 423, 451

WAAC. *See* Women's Army Auxiliary Corps
Wabash, St. Louis & Pacific R.R. v. *Illinois* (1886), R23
WAC. *See* Women's Army Corps
Wade-Davis Bill (1864), 133
Wagner, Robert, 359
Wagner Act (1935), 359, 360, 364, R12
Wake Island, 434, *438m*
Wald, Lillian, 159, 171, 179
Walesa, Lech, 703, 709, R44
Walk, Frank, *423q*
Wallace, George, *567p*, 568, 578, 618–619, *618p*, *619m*, R44
Wallace, Henry, 474
Waller, Fats, 307
Wall Street, 720
Wampanoag Indians, 17
Wandrey, June, 458
war bonds, *442p*, 443
War Department, 51
warfare, *165p*; blitzkrieg, 394–395, *394p*, *395p*, 396; in Civil War, 124–125; convoy systems, *419p*; search and destroy missions, 606; submarines, 238, 239, 240, *240p*; trench, 233–235, *234p–235p*, 236, *236p*, 243, 260–261, *261p*
War Hawks, 55
Warhol, Andy, 655
War Industries Board, 247
War of 1812, 55–56, *55c*, *55p*, R5
War on Poverty, 543–544, *551q*, 790
War Powers Act (1973), 627
War Production Board, 409, 446–447
War Refugee Board, 430
Warren, Earl, 538–539, 540, R44, R60; *Brown* v. *Board of Education of Topeka, Kansas*, 559, *559q*, 561, *561q*; *Reynolds* v. *Sims* (1964), 579
Warren Commission, 540
Warren Court, 538–539
War Revenue Act, 247
Warsaw, Poland, 428, *428m*
Warsaw Pact, 498–499
Washington: facts about, R31; Japanese Americans in, 445; labor movement in, 273; minimum wage law, 363–364; Native Americans in, 640
Washington, Booker T., 162, 193, 557, R44
Washington, D.C.: antiwar movement in, 623, *623p*; in Civil War, 124; March on, R14; Poor People's Campaign, 586; terrorist attacks, 740; as U.S. capital, 51
Washington, George, *29p*, R17, R45; biography, 34, *34p*; at Constitutional Convention, 45, *45p*; Farewell Address, *52q*, 53, R78, ; Neutrality Proclamation, 53; as president, 50–53, *50p*; in Revolutionary War, 32, 34–35, 37; Whiskey Rebellion, 53
Washington, Margaret Murray, 180
Washington Naval Conference, 286–287, 398
Washington Post (newspaper), 676–677

WASP. *See* Women Airforce Service Pilots
Watergate scandal, 675–679, 688–689, *688g*, *689p*
Watkins v. *United States* (1957), R25
Watt, James, 96
Watts riots, 581
Wavering, Elmer, 294
WAVES. *See* Women Accepted for Volunteer Emergency Service
Wayne, Anthony, 53
WCTU. *See* Woman's Christian Temperance Union
wealth distribution, 323, *323g*
Wealth of Nations (Smith), 807
weapons: atomic bomb, 410, 453–454, *453p*, 465, 477, 478; B-24 bombers, 406, *406p*; chemical, 236–237; in Civil War, 124–125; *kamikaze* attack, 439; Lend-Lease Act, 403, R12; missiles, 504, 668–669; napalm, 605; nuclear, 498, 502–508, *503p*, *505p*, *507p*, 702–703; railway guns, 416; screening for, 700; V1 flying bomb, 423; V2 rocket, 423, 451; in World War I, 234, 236–237, 242
Weathermen, 623
Weaver, Robert, 546
Weber, Tim, *709q*
Webster, Daniel, 117, R83
Weimar Republic, 387
Weinberg, Jack, 651
Weinberger, Casper, 706
Weissman, Gerda, *430q*
Wekesser, Carol, 798
welfare capitalism, 279, 321
welfare reform, 728, 790, 793
Weller, John, R60
Welles, Orson, 370
Wells, H.G., 370
Wells-Barnett, Ida, 171–172, 180
Welty, Eudora, 359
West: Civil War in, 125, *125m*, 128; climate in, 147–148; Great Depression in, 332–333, *332m*, *332p–333p*, 334, *334p*; housing in, 148; manifest destiny, 107–109; Native Americans in, 142–147; nativists in, 158; population of, 748; western trails, *107m*
West Africa, 9
West Berlin, 469, *469m*, 530–531, *531p*
Westberry v. *Sanders* (1964), 538
Western Hemisphere, R63
West Germany, *466m*, 469–470, *469m*, 470, 530, *531m*, 709
Westinghouse Company, 309
Westmoreland, William, 606, 612, 613, 614, 628, R45
Westside Community School District v. *Mergens* (1990), 718
West Virginia: facts about, R31; population of, 748
West Virginia Board of Education v. *Barnette*, 445
Weyler, Valeriano, 207
Wharton, Edith, 312
When Heaven and Earth Changed Places (Hayslip), 625, *625q*
Whig Party, 117
Whiskey Rebellion, 53

White, William Allen, *300p*, *300q*
Whitefield, George, 24, *24p*
White House, *55p*; Kennedy, 535, *535p*
White House Office of Faith-Based Initiatives, 736
Whitewater, 731
Whitney, Eli, 97
Whyte, William H., 514
Wiesel, Elie, 432, *432p*
wildcatters, 149
Wilderness, Battle of the, 130
Wilhelm II, Kaiser, 231, 232, 234, R45
Wilkie, Wendell, 403, R45
Willard, Frances, 179, R45
Williams, Roger, 18
Willow Run, 406, *406p*, 408
Wills, Frank, 675, *675p*
Wills, Helen, 312, *312p*
Wilmot Proviso, 119
Wilson, Jack, 142
Wilson, James, 45, 186
Wilson, Pete, R60
Wilson, Richard, 640
Wilson, Woodrow, 273, 310, 347, R20, R45; civil rights and, 193; election of 1912, *190m*, 191; foreign policy of, 216, 217, 220, 222–223; Fourteen Points, 255, *255q*, *256c*; Ho Chi Minh and, 596, *596p*, 597–598; immigration and, 158; League of Nations, 254, *254p*, 255, *256c*, 257–258, *257p*, *257q*; New Freedom, 191; Paris Peace Conference, 255–258, *258q*; progressivism and, 191–193; World War I and, 238–241, *240q*, 247–249, 250–251, *250q*
Winthrop, John, 17, 694
Wisconsin, 44; facts about, R31; Revolutionary War in, 36, *36m*; state government in, 175
Wisconsin Idea, 175
Wobblies, 174
wolf pack, 419
Woman's Christian Temperance Union (WCTU), 179, 299
women: authors, 312; in Chicano movement, 647–648; civil defense programs and, 507, *507p*; civil rights of, 138, 180; in Civil War, 126, 128; education and, 177–178, *177p*, 295; employment of, 172, 178–179, 295, *295p*, *408p*, 409–410, 635, *635g*; equal rights, 102–103; Equal Rights Amendment and, 634–636, 637, *637p*; First Ladies, 348–349, *349p*, 366; globalization and, 757; in government, 181, 365, *365p*, 366; heroes, 311; in the military, 407–408, 452, *452p*, 458, 772–779, *772p*, *773p*, *774p*, *776c*, *778c*, *778p*, *779g*; New Deal and, 365, *365p*, 366, 367, *367p*, 374; in politics, 295; in postwar America, 515; in Reform Era, 102–103, *103p*; in Revolutionary War, 35; in Roaring Twenties, *294p*, 295–296, *295p*; in sports, 312, *312p*, 370; on the Supreme Court, 717; in Vietnam War, 609; voting rights of, 135, *179p*, 180–182, 192, *192p*, 259, 295, 717; in World War I, 243, *248p*, 249–250; in World War II, 423–424
Women Accepted for Volunteer Emergency Service (WAVES), 407

Women Airforce Service Pilots (WASP), 408
Women in Combat (Fenner and deYoung), 775
Women's Armed Services Integration Act (1948), 452
Women's Army Auxiliary Corps (WAAC), 408
Women's Army Corps (WAC), 408
Women's International League for Peace and Freedom, 252
women's liberation, 636–638
women's movement, 634–636, *634p*, 656–657, *656p*, *657c*
womens' rights, 99, 178–182, *179p*, *180p*, 296; Seneca Falls Convention, 180
Wood, Leonard, 214, 272
Woodhull, Victoria, 180
Woodstock, 650, *650p*, 655
Woodward, Bob, 676, *676p*
Woodward, Charlotte, 182
Worcester v. *Georgia* (1832), R22
working class, 159
working poor, 790
Works Progress Administration (WPA), 358–359, *358p–359p*, *360c*, 372
World Bank, *475c*, 476
World Trade Center, 739–743, *739p*, *740m*, *741p*, 742
World Trade Organization (WTO), 730–731
World War I, R10; African Americans in, 241, *242p*, *243p*; Allies in, 232–237, *233m*, 257; antiwar speech and, 252, 253; battles of, 232–235, *232c*, *233m*; Belgium in, 232–233, *233m*, 242, *243m*, 244; cause and effects of, 231–232, 258–259, 286–287, *286c*; Central Powers in, 232–237, *233m*, 257; France in, 233–235, *233m*, 236, 242–243, *243m*, 259; Germany in, 232–237, *233m*, 238–239, 240, 242, *243m*, 244, 259; Great Britain in, 232, *233m*, 237, 239, 240, *243m*, 249, 259; Hispanic Americans in, 241; home front, 246–252, *246p*, *247p*, *248p*, *249p*, *250p*, *251p*; literature of, 245, *245p*; progressive movement and, 193; Russia in, 232–233, *233m*, 240, 242, *243m*; time line, 228–229; Treaty of Versailles and, 387; United States in, 238–244, *238p*, *240p*, *241p*, *242p*, *243m*, *243p*, *244p*, 259; veterans of, 335, 338–339; warfare in, 233–234, *234p–235p*; weapons in, 234, 236–237, 240; women in, 243, *248p*, 249–250, 773
World War II: 416–461; African Americans in, 474, *474p*; in the Atlantic, 418–420, *418p*, *419p*; atomic bomb and, 453–454, *453p*; Axis Powers, 398; Bataan Death March, *434p*, 435; blitzkrieg, 394–395, *394p*, *395p*, 396, 420; Bulge, Battle of the, 424, 450; cause and effect of, 455; Coral Sea, Battle of, 436, *438m*; D-Day, 423–424, *424p–425p*; in East Asia, 398; in Europe, 418–422, *421m*, 423–424, *424p–425p*, 449–452, *449p*, *450p*; federal budget during, 447, *447g*; federal government during, 446–447; Germany and, 465; Guadalcanal, 437, *438m*; home front, 441–447, *441p*, *442p*, *444p*, *446p*, *447g*; industry in, 408–410, *409p–410p*, *410g*; island hopping, 456–457; in Italy, 420–422, *421m*; Iwo Jima, 433, *433p*, *438m*, 439, *439p*, 440; Japan and, *381p*, 433–440, *438m*, 452–454, *453p*, 454; Japanese American internment, 445–446, *446p*; Leyte Gulf, Battle of, *438m*, 439; Midway, Battle of, 436–437, *437p*, *438m*; military mobilization, 406, *406p*, 407–411, *409g*; in North Africa, 420–422, *421m*; Okinawa, Battle of, *438m*, 440; Operation Overlord, 423; Operation Torch, 421; in the Pacific, 433–440, *433p*, *434p*, *437p*, *438m*, 452–454, *453p*; Pearl Harbor, 403–405, *404m*, *404p*, 434, *438m*; Poland and, 395–396; prisoners of war, 408; propaganda in, 443–445, *444p*; science and, 410; Soviet Union and, 395, 420, *421m*, 465; time line, 384–385, 416–417; Tuskegee Airmen, 422, *422p*; V-E Day, 452; veterans, 471, *471p*, 472, *472p*; V-J Day, 454; War Production Board, 409; women in, 423–424, 774; Yalta Conference, 450–451
World Wide Web, 801
Wounded Knee, *143m*, 144, 640
Wovoka, 142
Wozniak, Steve, 714, *714p*
WPA. *See* Works Progress Administration
Wright, Richard, 359
Wright, Wilbur and Orville, 154, *154p*
Writing Skills: descriptive, 175, 217, 370, 398, 411, 455, 515, 673, 686, 706, 713, 759; expository writing, 26, 98, 105, 131, 155, 205, 244, 252, 291, 333, 425, 470, 482, 489, 493, 534, 553, 585, 589, 603, 649, 691; narratives, 19, 148, 212, 375, 415, 447, 508, 627, 731, 746; persuasive, 27, 49, 112, 113, 138, 182, 188, 223, 227, 237, 259, 327, 339, 353, 364, 393, 405, 440, 476, 548, 563, 571, 611, 631, 641, 655, 719, 752; SAT, 57, 139, 197, 263, 317, 379, 461, 519, 553, 593, 659, 723; supporting a position, 275, 281, 287, 301, 307, 313
writing systems, 7
WTO. *See* World Trade Organization
Wyoming: facts about, R31; national parks in, 187; ranching in, 146; Teapot Dome scandal, 283, 284; Treaty of Guadalupe Hidalgo, 112; voting rights in, 180–181; women in, 295
Wyoming Territory, 178

XYZ Affair, 53

Yalta Conference, 450–451, 484
Yamamoto, Isoroku, 434, *434q*
Yasgur, Max, 650
Yates v. *United States*, 480
yellow fever, 214, 215, *215p*
yellow journalism, 207
Yellowstone National Park, 781, 782
Yeltsin, Boris, 710–711, R45
yeomen, 773
Yom Kippur War, 670, 684
Yorktown, Battle of, 36–37, *36m*, *37c*
Yosemite National Park, 187, 781, *781p*
Young, Andrew, 589, 683, *683p*, R45
Young, C.C., R60
youth culture, 651
Ypres, Battles of, *232c*, *233m*
Yugoslavia, 256, 466, 729–730
Yukon Territory, 144

Zaharias, Babe Didrikson, 370
Zapata, Emiliano, 221, *221p*, 223, R45
zero, concept of, 7
Zimbabwe, 390
Zimmermann, Arthur, 240
Zimmermann Note, 240
zoot suit riots, 411

Credits and Acknowledgments

For permission to reproduce copyrighted material, grateful acknowledgment is made to the following sources:

Annenberg Public Policy Center of the University of Pennsylvania: From "Overview" from *Open to Exploitation: American Shoppers Online and Offline* by Joseph Turow, Lauren Feldman, and Kimberley Meltzer. Copyright © 2005 by Annenberg Public Policy Center of the University of Pennsylvania.

Atlantic Monthly: From letter to the editor by TW in response to Perri Knize article "Winning the War for the West" from *Atlantic Monthly*, November 1999. Copyright © 1999 by Atlantic Monthly.

Bantam Books, a division of Random House, Inc.: Quote by Diane Nash from *Voices of Freedom* by Henry Hampton and Steve Fayer. Copyright © 1990 by Blackside, Inc.

Barnes & Nobles Books: Quotes by William Calley, Tran Van Duong, Robert S. McNamara, and David Vandivier from *NAM: Vietnam 1965–75*. Copyright © 1995 by Barnes & Nobles Books.

Business Week: From "Guest Commentary: The Harsh Truth About Outsourcing" from "Special Report—Where Are the Jobs?" by Paul Craig Roberts from *Business Week*, March 22, 2004, vol. 3875, p. 48. Copyright © 2004 by The McGraw-Hill Companies Inc. "How Much Pain? by Data: Forrester Research from "Special Report: Comparative advantage cannot be counted on to create . . . net gains greater than the net losses from trade" by Paul Samuelson from *Business Week*, December 6, 2004. Copyright © 2004 by Business Week.

CBS, a division of Viacom Inc.: Broadcast "We Are Mired in Stalemate" by Walter Cronkite from *CBS Evening News with Walter Cronkite*, Feb. 27, 1968. Copyright © 1968 by CBS Broadcasting Inc.
CNN: From interview with Phillip Caputo from "On landing in Vietnam with the U.S. Marines in 1965" from "Episode 11: Vietnam" from *CNN*. Copyright © 1998 by Cable News Network.

The Center for Academic Integrity at Duke University: From "In New CAI Research Conducted" by Don McCabe from *The Center for Academic Integrity*. Copyright © 2005 by The Center for Academic Integrity.

Chicago Tribune Company: From "Mass e-mail slapped with civil lawsuit" by Howard Witt from *Chicago Tribune*, January 13, 2005. Copyright © January 13, 2005, by Chicago Tribune.

Christian Science Monitor: From "In 2,000 Years, Will the World Remember Disney or Plato?" by Mark Rice-Oxley from *Christian Science Monitor*, January 15, 2004. Copyright © 2004 by Christian Science Publishing Society.

Donadio & Olson: Quote by Kitty McCulloch from *Hard Times* by Studs Terkel. Copyright © 1970 by Studs Terkel. Published by Pantheon Books, a division of Random House, Inc.

Doubleday, a division of Random House, Inc., www.randomhouse.com: From *When Heaven and Earth Changed Places: A Vietnamese Woman's Journey from War to Peace* by Le Ly Hayslip with Jay Wurts. Copyright © 1989 by Le Ly Hayslip with Jay Wurts. From *A Soldier Reports* by General William C. Westmoreland. Copyright © 1976 by William C. Westmoreland.

Encyclopaedia Britannica: From "Marshall, Thurgood" from *Encyclopaedia Britannica Online*, available at http://search.eb.com/eb/article-9051119, on October 21, 2005. Copyright © 2005 by Encyclopaedia Britannica. From "World War I" from *Encyclopaedia Britannica Online*, available at http://80-search.eb.com.ezproxy.libraries.wright.edu:2048/3b/article-9110198, on October 25, 2005. Copyright © 2005 by Encyclopaedia Britannica.

Freedomways: From "Life in Mississippi: An Interview with Fannie Lou Hamer" from *Freedomways* magazine, vol. 5, no. 2, 1965. Copyright © 1965 by Freedomways.

Georgetown University Press: From "Introduction" from *Women in Combat: Civic Duty or Military Liability?* by Lorry M. Fenner and Marie E. deYoung. Copyright © 2001 by Georgetown University Press.

Geraldine Gonzales: From *I am Joaquín / Yo soy Joaquín: An Epic Poem* by Rodolfo Gonzales. Copyright © 1967 by Rodolfo Gonzales.

Greenhaven Press: From "Introduction" from *Violence in the Media*, edited by Carol Wekesser. Copyright © 1995 by Greenhaven Press, Inc.

GRM Associates, Inc., Agents for the Estate of Ida M. Cullen: "Yet Do I Marvel" from *Color* by Countee Cullen. Copyright © 1925 by Harper & Brothers: copyright renewed 1953 by Ida M. Cullen.

HarperCollins, Inc.: From *Tituba of Salem Village* by Ann Petry. Copyright © 1964 by Ann Petry.

John Hawkins & Associates, Inc.: Address to Militant Labor Forum, April 8, 1964, from *Two Speeches by Malcolm X*. Copyright © 1964 by Malcolm X.

Hill and Wang, a division of Farrar, Straus & Giroux, LLC; electronic format by permission of Georges Borchardt, Inc.: From *Night* by Elie Wiesel, translated by Stella Rodway. Copyright © 1958 by Les Editions de Minuit; English translation copyright © 1960 by MacGibbon & Kee, renewed © 1988 by The Collins Publishing Group. All rights reserved.

The History Channel, a division of A & E Television Network: From "Letter from Stull Holt, Sept. 1, 1917" from "Dear Home: Letters from WWI" from *The History Channel*, available on http://www.historychanel.com/letters/stull_holt.html, August 9, 2005. Copyright © 1996-2005 by A&E Television Networks.

The Heirs to the Estate of Martin Luther King, Jr., c/o Writers House, Inc. as agent for the proprietor: "I Have a Dream" by Martin Luther King, Jr. Copyright © 1963 by Martin Luther King, Jr.; copyright renewed © 1991 by Coretta Scott King. From "Letter from Birmingham Jail" from *Why We Can't Wait* by Martin Luther King, Jr. Copyright © 1963 by Martin Luther King, Jr., copyright renewed © 1991 by Coretta Scott King.

Ron Kovic: From *Born on the Fourth of July* by Ron Kovic. Copyright © 1976 by Ron Kovic.

Louisiana State University Press: Quotes by Bouchereau, DeLucca, Reid Draffen, Warren Moses, Solomon Radasky, James Spillman, Major General Kenneth William Dobson Strong, Frank Walk, and Martin Wasserman from *War Stories: Remembering World War II* by Elizabeth Mullener, with a foreword by Stephen E. Ambrose. Copyright © 2002 by Louisiana State University Press.

Merle's Girls Music: From "Sing Your Heart Out, Country Boy" by Merle Travis from Capitol Single #258, May 1946, available at http://www.fortunecity.com/tinpan/parton/2/novacanc.html, July 7, 2005. Copyright © 1946, 1975 by Hill and Range Songs.

National Center for Policy Analysis: From "Does Punishment Deter?" by Morgan Reynolds from *NCPA Policy Backgrounder*, August 17, 1998. Copyright © 1998 by National Center for Policy Analysis.

National Conference of State Legislatures: From "The Outcry Over Outsourcing" by Justin Marks from *State Legislatures*, May 2004, vol. 30, no. 5, pp. 30–32. Copyright © 2004 by the National Conference of State Legislatures.

National Public Radio: Quote by Shoshana Johnson from "Interview: Shoshana Johnson discusses her experience as a POW in Iraq" with Neal Conan from *NPR: Talk of the Nation*, March 1, 2005. Copyright © 2005 by National Public Radio.

The Nation Company, L.P.: From "Mr. Roosevelt's Magic" from *The Nation*, vol. 142, no. 3680, January 15, 1936. Copyright 1936 by The Nation.

New Press, New York, NY: From *Race to Incarcerate* by Marc Mauer. Copyright © 1999 by The Sentencing Project.

The New York Public Library for the Performing Arts, Music Division: From "Lucky Lindy!" lyrics by L. Wolfe Gilbert and music by Abel Baer. Copyright 1927 by Leo Feist Inc.

The New York Times Company: From "A Visionary Who Put an Era Out of Its Misery" a review of *Memoirs* by Mikhail Gorbachev from *The New York Times*, January 7, 1997. Copyright © 1997 by Michael Specter.

Newsweek, Inc.: From "Nursing the Dying" by Edie Meeks from *Newsweek*, March 8, 1999, p. 61. Copyright © 1999 by Newsweek, Inc. All rights reserved. From "Women of the New Century" by Carla Power, Toula Vlahou, Stefan Theil, Barbie Nadeau, and Emma Daly from *Newsweek International*, January 8, 2001 p. 14. Copyright © 2001 by Newsweek, Inc. All rights reserved. From "The Hard Truth of Immigration" by Robert J. Samuelson from *Newsweek*, June 13, 2005. Copyright © 2005 by Newsweek. All rights reserved.

W. W. Norton & Company, Inc.: From "The Shadow of Death" and "Coda" from *In the Presence of Mine Enemies: War in the Heart of America, 1859–1863* by Edward L. Ayers. Copyright © 2003 by Edward L. Ayers.

PBS Online, a division of WGBH Educational Foundation: From "War Letters" by Paul Curtis, available on http://www.pbs.org/wgbh/amex/warletters/letters/warletter_06.html, July 14, 2005. Copyright © 2005 PBS Online/WGBH. From "War Letters" by Rupert Trimmingham, available on http://www.pbs.org/wgbh/amex/warletters/letters/warletter_06.html, July 14, 2005. Copyright © 2005 PBS Online/WGBH. From letter by June Wandrey from "War Letters" available at http://www.pbs.org/wgbh/amex/warletters/letters/warletter_09.html, on July 14, 2005. Copyright © 1999-2001 by PBS Online/WGBH.

G. P. Putnam's Sons, a division of Penguin Group (USA) Inc.; electronic format by Sandra Dijkstra Literary Agency; audio format by New Millennium: From "Queen Mother of the Western Skies" from *The Joy Luck Club* by Amy Tan. Copyright © 1989 by Amy Tan.

Random House, Inc., www.randomhouse.com: Statement by Chicago Women's Liberation; February 1969 from *Sisterhood is Powerful: An Anthology of Writing's from the Women's Liberation Movement*, edited by Ron Morgan. Copyright © 1970 by Robin Morgan. From *Faith of My fathers: A Family Memoir* by John McCain and Mark Salter. Copyright © 1999 by John McCain and Mark Salter.

reasononline: From "Really Creative Destruction: Economist Tyler Cowen argues for the cultural benefits of globalization" from *reasononline*, August–September 2003, available at http://www.reason.com/0308/cr.ng.really.shtm, October 28, 2005. Copyright © 2003 by reasononline.

Estate of Erich Maria Remarque: From *All Quiet on the Western Front* by Erich Maria Remarque. Copyright 1929, 1930 by Little, Brown and Company; copyright renewed © 1957, 1958 by Erich Maria Remarque. All rights reserved. "Im Westen Nichts Neues" copyright 1928 by Ullstein A. G.; copyright renewed © 1956 by Erich Maria Remarque.

The Richmond Organization (TRO): From "Pastures of Plenty" words and music by Woody Guthrie. Copyright © 1960, 1963 by TRO-Ludlow Music, Inc.

Scribner, an imprint of Simon & Schuster Adult Publishing Group: From *The Great Gatsby* by F. Scott Fitzgerald. Copyright 1925 by Charles Scribner's Sons. Copyright renewed 1953 by Frances Scott Fitzgerald Lanahan.

Scribner, a division of Simon & Schuster, Inc.: From *A Farewell to Arms* by Ernest Hemingway. Copyright 1929 by Charles Scribner's Sons; copyright renewed © 1957 by Ernest Hemingway.

Law Office of Carl Shusterman: From "Immigration: America Stands Unique in the World" from *Law Offices of Carl Shusterman*, available online at http://www.shusterman.com/history.html, May 17, 2005. Copyright © 1996 by Carl Shusterman.

Simon & Schuster: From *I Never Left Home* by Bob Hope. Copyright 1944 by Bob Hope.
State of Michigan: From "Eye-witness accounts" from *Pearl Harbor Remembered . . .*, available at http://www.michiganhistorymagazine.com/extra/pearl_harbor/stories.html, on July 14, 2005. Copyright © 2005 by The State of Michigan.

Texas A & M University Press: From "The Death of Davy Crockett" from *With Santa Anna in Texas: A Personal Narrative of the Revolution* / José Enrique de la Peña by Carmen Perry. Copyright © 1997 by Perry Carmen.

20th Century Fox: From the movie *Wall Street* by Stanley Weiser and Oliver Stone. Copyright © 1987 by 20th Century Fox.

United States Holocaust Memorial Museum: From "Gerda Weissmann Klein: Born 1924: Bielsko, Poland" from "Personal Histories: Liberation," as available at http://www.ushmm.org/museum/exhibit/online/phistories, on July 14, 2005. Copyright © United States Holocaust Memorial Museum, Washington, D.C.

The University of Georgia Press: Quote by Nell Blackshear from *Living Atlanta: An Oral History of the City 1914–1948* by Clifford Kuhn, Harlon Joye, and E. Bernard West. Copyright © 1990 by the University of Georgia Press Athens, Georgia 30602.

University of Washington Press: From "Poem # 32" by Anonymous from *Island: Poetry and History of Chinese Immigrants on Angel Island, 1910–1940* by Him Mark Lai, Genny Lim, and Judy Yung. Copyright © 1991 by University of Washington Press.

Viking Penguin, a division of Penguin Group (USA): From *The Grapes of Wrath* by John Steinbeck. Copyright 1939 and renewed © 1967 by John Steinbeck

Warner Bros. Publications U.S. Inc., Miami, FL., 33014: From "Brother, Can You Spare a Dime," lyrics by Yip Harburg, music by Jay Gorney. Copyright 1931 by Warner Brs., Inc., E.Y. Harburg, and J. Gorney. All rights reserved.

Washington Post Company: From "A Tip of That Hat" by Tom Vinciguerra from "Remembering Franklin Delano Roosevelt" from *The Washington Post Online,* available http://www.washingtonpost.com/wp-srv/local/longterm/tours/fdr/, 7/14/05. Copyright © 1997 by The Washington Post Company.

Sources Cited:

From "Roger Tuttrup" from *The Good War: An Oral History of World War Two* by Studs Terkel. Published by Ballantine Books, New York, 1985.

From *Anxious Decades: America in Prosperity and Depression 1920–1941* by Michael E. Parrish. Published by W. W. Norton & Company, New York, 1992.

Quotes by Myron Harrington and Tran Do from *Vietnam: A History* by Stanley Karnow. Published by Penguin Books, New York, 1983.

From "Puttin' On Ole Massa" from *Narrative of William Wells Brown: A Fugitive Slave written by himself.* Published by Prentice-Hall, Inc., Englewood Cliffs, NJ, 1963.

Quotes by Zbigniew Brzezinski and Cyrus Vance from *Crisis: The Last Year of the Carter Presidency* by Hamilton Jordan. Published by G. P. Putnam's Sons, New York, NY, 1982.

From "A Black GI" (retitled "An African American GI in Vietnam (1969-1970)" from *Everything We Had: An Oral History of the Vietnam War* by Al Santoli. Published by Random House, Inc., New York, 1981.

From *Patriots: The Vietnam War Remembered from All Sides* by Christian G. Appy. Published by Viking Penguin, New York, NY 2003.

From "Honor and Humiliation" by Ben Isaacs from *Hard Times: An Oral History of the Great Depression* by Studs Terkel. Published by Washington Square Press, New York, NY, 1970.

From "Pete Peterson - Assignment Hanoi" from web site accessed at http://www.pbs.org/hanoi/home.htm., on June 30, 2005. Published by WGBH Educational Foundation, Boston, MA, 1999.

From the June 1993 Gateway Greens' Compost-Dispatch Speech at the May Day rally against NAFTA, read by Rainbow Coalition member Gene Bruskin for Reverend Jesse Jackson.

From "Artist's Statement" by Joel Meyerowitz from *After September 11 Images from Ground Zero* at http://www.911exhibit.state.gov/artist_statement.cfm, July 19, 2005.

"A Personal Record of Hiroshima A-bomb Survival (No. 1) re-post: Takeharu Terao 91/03/03 13:32" from http://www.coara.or.jp/~ryoji/abomb/a-bomb1.html, July 8, 2005.

Photo Credits

Cover: (t) © Joseph Sohm/Visions of America/CORBIS; (c) © Eyewire/Getty Images; (b) © Photodisc/Getty Images. **Front Matter**: Page ii, (t) Ian Bradshaw/HRW; (b) Sam Dudgeon/HRW; iii (t), Michael Denora/ HRW; iii (c), Bill Salaz/HRW; iii (b) HRW Photo/Gary Benson Photography; v, ©Superstock/SuperStock; vi, Smithsonian American Art Museum, Washington, DC/ Art Resource, NY; vii, Museum of the City of New York, USA / Bridgeman Art Library; viii (t), Courtesy The Delaware Military Heritage and Education Foundation, Inc.; viii (b), Curt Teich Postcard Archives, Lake County Museum, Illinois; ix (t), HRW Photo Research Library; ix (b), West Houston and Mercer Streets. October 25, 1935, by Berenice; x (t), © Bettmann/CORBIS; x (b), National Archives/Jeffrey Ethell Collection; xi (t), © Minnesota Historical Society/CORBIS; xi (b), © CORBIS; xii (t), © CORBIS; xii (b), ©John Dominis/Time Life Pictures/ Getty Images; xiii (t), AP/Wide World Photos; xiii (c), © David J. Frent/CORBIS; xiii (bl), © Wally McNamee/ CORBIS; xiii (br), Paul Fusco/Magnum Photos; xiv (t), © Arthur Schatz/Time Life Pictures/Getty Images; xiv (b), Jimmy Carter Presidential Library; xv (t), © CORBIS; Abbott/Museum of the City of New York; xv (b), © Reuters/CORBIS; xvi, Mike Derer/AP/Wide World Photos; xxvi (t), (Wineburg) HRW Photo/Gary Benson Photography; xxvi (b), National Portrait Gallery, Smithsonian Institution, Washington, DC/Art Resource, NY; xxxii (cr), ©Brand X Pictures; (others), Image Club Graphics; ST1, © Image Bank/Getty Images; ST3, © Michael T. Sedam/ CORBIS; ST4-ST5, ST6, © Richard Cummins/CORBIS; ST8, © Theo Allofs/ zefa/ CORBIS; ST12, Library of Congress, #LC-USZC4-1584; ST13, The Granger Collection, New York; ST14, The Granger Collection, New York; ST17, National Archives/PRC Archive; ST22, The Granger Collection, New York; ST23, © Bettmann/CORBIS; ST25, Photofest; ST28, Library of Congress, #LC-U9-9930-20; ST30, Cartoon by Paul Conrad. Copyright, Los Angeles Times Syndicate. Reprinted with permission; ST31, Reprinted by permission of the cartoonist, Jeff Parker /Cagle Cartoons; H1, Smithsonian American Art Museum, Washington, DC/Art Resource, NY; H24 (l), © Robert W. Kelley/Time Life Pictures/ Getty Images; H24 (c), © Bettmann/ CORBIS; H24 (r), Photo by Hugo Jaeger/Timepix /Time Life Pictures/Getty Images; H25 (tl), Picture Research Consultants & Archives; H25 (tr), The Museum of American Political Life, University of Hartford, West Hartford, CT; H25 (br), © Mike Segar/REUTERS/ CORBIS; H26 (tl), ©Michael Ventura/Folio, Inc.; H26 (b), © Bettmann/CORBIS; H26 (tr), Ric Francis/AP/Wide World Photos; H27 (tl), © Lonny Shavelson/Zuma Press Photos; H27 (bl), © Bettmann/CORBIS; H27 (tr), © CORBIS; H27 (br), © Justin Sullivan/Getty Images; H29, Collection of the American Numismatic Society, New York; H30, © Woburn Abbey Collection, Bedford Estate; H31, The Granger Collection, New York; TT6, The Granger Collection, New York; TT7, The Granger Collection, New York; TT23, Library of Congress; TT24 (l), © Bettmann/ CORBIS; TT24 (r), Picture Research Consultants & Archives. **Unit One:** Page 1, The Granger Collection, New York. **Chapter 1:** Pages 4 - 5, © Steve Vidler/SuperStock; 04 (b), The Art Archive/National Anthropological Museum Mexico/Dagli Orti; 05 (b), © Richard A. Cooke/CORBIS; 05 (b), The Granger Collection, New York; 06 (l), Dr. George Frison, Hell Gap Prehistoric Site, University of Wyoming; 06 (r), Arizona State Museum, University of Arizona; 10, Library of Congress; 12, SuperStock; 13, The Granger Collection, New York; 18, The Granger Collection, New York; 18 (l), Private Collection; 20, Peabody Essex Museum. Salem, Massachusetts. [detail neg. #17530]; 24, National Portrait Library, London/Bridgeman Art Library; 28 (b), Courtesy of the Massachusetts Historical Society **Chapter 2:** Pages 28 - 29, ©Superstock/SuperStock; 29 (l), The Granger Collection, New York; 30, Picture Research Consultants & Archives; 34, Reunion de Musees Nationaux/Art Resource, NY; 35 (l), © Kathy McLaughlin/The Image Works; 35 (r), © Kelley-Mooney Photography/CORBIS; 38 - 41 (border) © Richard Cummins/CORBIS; 41, John Trumbull, *The Declaration of Independence*, Yale University Art Gallery, Trumbull Collection; 42 (l), Eric P. Newman/ Numismatic Education Society; 42 (r), Collection of the American Numismatic Society, New York; 42 (c), Picture Research Consultants & Archives; 43, The Granger Collection, New York; 44-45, Hall of Representatives, Washington, DC/ Bridgeman Art Library; 46 (r), © Royalty Free/ CORBIS; 46 (b), Image Copyright © 2007 PhotoDisc, Inc.; 46 (l), © Royalty Free/CORBIS; 47 (l), Charles Willson Peale, James Madison, 1792, oil on canvas, 0126.1006. From the Collection of Gilcrease Museum, Tulsa; 47 (r), Colonial Williamsburg Foundation; 48 (r), Hall of Representatives, Washington, DC/Bridgeman Art Library; 48 (l), National Archives/PRC Archive; 50, National Portrait Gallery, Smithsonian Institution, Washington, DC/Art Resource, NY; 51, [#1867.306] © Collection of The New-York Historical Society; 55 (l), The Granger Collection, New York; 55 (r), © Bettmann/ CORBIS. **Constitution Handbook:** Pages 58-59, Paul Conklin/PhotEdit; 62-87 (border) © Richard Cummins/ CORBIS; 64 (bl), Dennis Cook/AP/Wide World Photos; 64-65 (bc), © Mark Wilson/Getty Images; 65 (br), © Brooks Kraft/CORBIS; 66, © Royalty-Free/CORBIS; 76 (l), © Yang Liu/CORBIS; 76 (r), Norm Detlaff, Las Cruces Sun-News/AP/Wide World Photos; 77 (c), © David Young-Wolff/PhotoEdit; 77 (both) © Bettmann/CORBIS; 81, Library of Congress/PRC Archive; 83, Library of Congress; 85 (l), © Bettmann/CORBIS; 85 (r), © Oscar White/CORBIS; 86 (r), © 1978 Matt Herron/TakeStock; 86 (bl), Texas State Library & Archives Commission; 86 (tl), Dr. Hector P. Garcia Papers, Special Collections & Archives, Texas A&M University-Corpus Christi, Bell Library; 88 Texas State Library and Archives Commission; **Chapter 3:** Pages 90 - 91 (t), ©SuperStock, Inc./SuperStock; 90, Private Collection/PRC Archive; 91, Society of California Pioneers; 92 (tl), Private Collection/ PRC Archive; 94, Massachusetts State Archives; 96 (l), Division of History and Technology/National Museum of American History, Smithsonian Institution, Washington, DC. Photo # 86-9625 by Eric Long; 96 (r), Charles Phillips; 96 (t), Jack Naylor Collection/ Picture Research Consultants & Archives; 97 (tl), The Granger Collection, New York; 97 (tr), National Museum of American History, Smithsonian Institution, Washington, DC, neg. no 73-11287; 97 (b), National Museum of American History, Smithsonian Institution, Washington, DC. Photo # 2005-10045; 99, Library of Congress/PRC Archive; 101, Albert F. Egan Jr. & Dorothy Egan Foundation, Inc., Nantucket, Mass; 102, © Bettmann/CORBIS; 103, Coline Jenkins/Elizabeth Cady Stanton Trust; 104, William Gladstone Collection; 105, Onondaga Historical Association, #19981.21.171B; 106, Colorado Historical Society; 108, © The Oakland Museum of California, Gift of The Women's Board. Photo by M. Lee Fatherree; 109, Courtesy of the California History Room, California State Library, Sacramento, California; 111, Society of California Pioneers. **Chapter 4:** Pages 114-115 (t), The Art Archive/ Culver Pictures; 115 (b), The Granger Collection, New York; 116, © Bettmann/CORBIS; 118, The Granger Collection, New York; 119, Missouri Historical Society; 120 (both) Library of Congress; 123, Anne S.K. Brown Military Collection, Brown University Library; 124, Courtesy of The Lincoln Museum, Fort Wayne, IN (#0-42); 125, Chicago Historical Society, #1932.27; 126, National Park Service; 127, Library of Congress; 128 (l), National Archives (NARA), 128 (r), National Archives (NARA); 131, National Geographic Image Collection; 132 (b), National Archives (NARA); 134 (both) © CORBIS; 135, The Granger Collection, New York; 136, Brown Brothers; 137, Courtesy of the Charleston Renaissance Gallery, Robert M. Hicklin Jr., Inc. Charleston, SC. **Chapter 5:** Pages 140-141 (t), The Granger Collection, New York; 140 (b), The Art Archive/ School of Oriental & African Studies/Eileen Tweedy; 141 (b), Gladys City Museum, Beaumont, Texas; 142, National Anthropological Archives, Smithsonian Institution, Washington, D.C., neg. #81-9626; 144, Colorado Historical Society; 146-147 (all), Archives & Manuscripts Division of the Oklahoma Historical Society; 149, Gladys City Museum, Beaumont, Texas; 152 (l), The Granger Collection, New York; 152 (r), Library of Congress; 154, National Air & Space Museum, Smithsonian Institution, Washington, D.C., #A26767B-2; 155, Picture Research Consultants & Archives; 156, Library of Congress, Detroit Publishing Company Collection, LC-USZC4-1584; 157, Copyright The New York Public Library/Art Resource, NY; 160 (l), The Burns Archive; 160 (r) (ticket), Nebraska Historical Society; 161 (poster), Library of Congress. **Unit Two:** Page 165, Museum of the City of New York, USA / Bridgeman Art Library. 167, North Wind Picture Archives **Chapter 6:** Pages 168-169 (t), Library of Congress; 168 (c), Keystone-Mast Collection/California Museum of Photography/University of California at Riverside/; 168 (b) © Bettmann/CORBIS; 169 (c), Brown Brothers; 169 (b), © Bettmann/CORBIS; 170, *How the Other Half Lives: an old rear tenement in Roosevelt Street, 1890,* Jacob Riis, Museum of the City of New York; 173 (inset) © Underwood & Underwood/CORBIS; 174, Brown Brothers; 176 (t), © Hulton-Deutsch Collection/ CORBIS; 176 (b), Library of Congress; 177, Sophia Smith Collection, Smith College; 178 (l), New York State Historical Association, Cooperstown; 178 (r), Picture Research Consultants & Archives; 179 (t), Brown Brothers; 179 (bl), Picture Research Consultants & Archives; 179 (r), © Jeff Greenberg/PhotoEdit; 178-179 (bkgd) © Bettmann/CORBIS; 180, Kansas State Historical Society, Topeka; 181, Library of Congress; 181 (r), Michael Dwyer/AP/ Wide World Photos; 183, Theodore Roosevelt Collection/Harvard Library; 185 (l), Keystone-Mast Collection/California Museum of Photography/University of California at Riverside; 185 (r), The Granger Collection, New York; 186, Library of Congress; 187, (c) © Joseph Sohm/Chromosohm, Inc./ CORBIS; 189, The Granger Collection, New York; 190 (l), Janice L. and David J. Frent Collection of Political Americana; 190 (r), Janice L. and David J. Frent Collection of Political Americana; 190 (b), Janice L. and David J. Frent Collection of Political Americana; 192 (l), Library of Congress #LC-USZ62-37937; 192 (r), Library of Congress/PRC Archive; 194, North Wind Picture Archives; 196, Library of Congress, 197, The Granger Collection, New York. **Chapter 7:** Pages 198-199 (t), National Guard Bureau; 198 (b), Picture Research Consultants & Archives; 199 (cl), (c) Underwood & Underwood/ CORBIS; 199 (cr), (c) Hulton-Deutsch Collection/CORBIS; 199 (b), Brown Brothers; 200,

Library of Congress; 202, Lake County (IL) Museum/ Curt Teich Postcard Archives; 203, (c) Douglas Peebles/ CORBIS; 204, Snark/Art Resource, NY; 206, © Bettmann/ CORBIS; 207, © CORBIS; 210, Chicago Historical Society; 211 (l), Library of Congress; 211 (r), Library of Congress; 213, The Granger Collection, New York; 214, The Granger Collection, New York; 215, (c) Underwood & Underwood/CORBIS; 220, Brown Brothers; 221 (tl), © Bettmann/CORBIS; 221 (tr), © Bettmann/CORBIS; 221 (bl), © CORBIS; 221 (br), (c) Underwood & Underwood/ CORBIS; 222, © Hulton-Deutsch Collection/CORBIS; 225, C. J. Taylor, artist. Courtesy The Bishop Museum; 22 (bkgd) National Guard Bureau; 227, Lake County (IL) Museum/Curt Teich Postcard Archives. **Chapter 8:** Pages 228-229, Courtesy The Delaware Military Heritage and Education Foundation, Inc.; 228 (c), ©SuperStock; 229, © Library of Congress; 229 (br), The Art Archive/ Imperial War Museum; 230, © CORBIS; 236, Retrofile. com/Getty Images; 238, ©SuperStock; 239, © CORBIS; 240 (l), © Trustees of the Imperial War Museum, London; 240 (r), © CORBIS; 241 (l), © Bettmann/CORBIS; 241, © Trustees of the Imperial War Museum, London; 242, National Archives (NARA); 243, National Archives (NARA); 244, Brown Brothers; 245 (t), Charles Scribner's Sons/AP/Wide World Photos; 245 (b), National Archives, War & Conflict #615; 246, Brown Brothers; 247, Library of Congress; 248, Brown Brothers; 249, Picture Research Consultants & Archives; 250, © CDC/PHIL/CORBIS; 251, National Archives/PRC Archive; 253 (t), Getty Images; 253 (b), AP/Wide World Photos; 254, © Bettmann/CORBIS; 257 (l), Picture Research Consultants & Archives; 257 (r), Library of Congress; 261, AP/Wide World Photos; 265, © New-York Historical Society/ Bridgeman Art Library. **Chapter 9:** Pages 268-269 (t), Caulfield & Shook Collection #CS71790, Photographic Archives, University of Louisville; 268 (b), National Museum of Health & Medicine, Armed Forces Institute of Pathology; 269 (c), © Bettmann/ CORBIS; 269 (bl), © Culver Pictures/SuperStock; 269 (br), © Photo by Wolf Suschitsky/ Pix Inc./ Time Life Pictures/Getty Images; 270, National Museum of Health & Medicine, Armed Forces Institute of Pathology; 271, David Longstreath/AP/Wide World Photos; 272, The Granger Collection, New York; 273, © Bettmann/CORBIS; 275, Digital Image © the Museum of Modern Art/Licensed by SCALA/Art Resource, NY. © Estate of Ben Shahn/ Licensed by VAGA, New York, NY; 276, Macy's Federated Department Stores; 277, © CORBIS; 278 (tl), General Motors Corp. Used with permission, GM Media Archives; 278 (tr), © Bettmann/CORBIS; 278 (c), National Museum of American History, Smithsonian Institution, Washington, DC, Behring Center. Neg. # 71-181; 278 (bl), Akron University Archives/Goodyear Photo Collection; 278-279, Curt Teich Postcard Archives, Lake County Museum, Illinois; 280 (l), Library of Congress/ PRC Archive; 280 (r), Picture Research Consultants & Archives; 282, © Bettmann/CORBIS; 283, The Granger Collection, New York; 284 (l), White House Historical Association (White House Collection); 284 (r), White House Historical Association (White House Collection)/ Photo by National Geographic Society; 285, © CORBIS; 286, Library of Congress; 290 (l), © Bettmann/CORBIS; 290 (c), White House Historical Association (White House Collection); 290 (r), National Museum of American History, Smithsonian Institution, Washington, DC, Behring Center. Neg. # 71-181; 291, Picture Research Consultants & Archives. **Chapter 10:** Pages 292-293, Brown Brothers; 292 (b), Picture Research Consultants & Archives; 293 (cl), Library of Congress; 293 (cr), Picture Research Consultants & Archives; 293 (bl), ©SuperStock; 294, © Bettmann/CORBIS; 295 (l), Lewis Wickes Hine/George Eastman House; 295 (r), HRW Photo Research Library; 296, Lake County (IL) Museum/Curt Teich Postcard Archives; 298 (l), The Granger Collection, New York; 298 (r), AP/Wide World Photos; 299, University of Tennessee Library Special Collections, Robinson and Hicks Collections; 300 (l), Kansas State Historical Society, Topeka; 300 (r), © Bettmann/CORBIS; 301, © Bettmann/CORBIS; 302, Photo by Carl Van Vechten, courtesy Carl Van Vechten Trust. With the permission of the Zora Neale Hurston Trust. The Beinecke Rare Book and Manuscript Library, Yale University Library; 304 (t), The publisher wishes to thank The Crisis Publishing Co., Inc., the publisher of the magazine of the National Association for the Advancement of Colored People for the use of this work; 304 (b), The publisher wishes to thank The Crisis Publishing Co., Inc., the publisher of the magazine of the National Association for the Advancement of Colored People for the use of this work that was first published in the April 1923 issue of "The Crisis Magazine." General Research and Reference Division; Schomburg Center for Research in Black Culture; The New York Public Library; Astor, Lenox and Tilden Foundations; 305, (detail) Photo by Nickolas Muray, © Nickolas Muray Photo Archives. Yale Collection of American Literature, The Beinecke Rare Book and Manuscript Library, Yale University; 306 (l), © Photo by Sasha/Getty Images; 306 (cl), © Bettmann/CORBIS; 306 (bl), © Bettmann/CORBIS; 306 (tc), The Beinecke Rare Book and Manuscript Library, Yale University Library; 306 (tr), Private Collection; 306 (br), Aaron Douglas, Into Bondage, 1936. Oil on canvas, 60 3/8 x 60 1/2 in. Corcoran Gallery of Art, Washington, D.C. Museum Purchase and partial gift from Thurlow Evans Tibbs, Jr., The Evans-Tibbs Collection 1996.9; 308, © Bettmann/CORBIS; 309 (t), Picture Research Consultants & Archives; 309 (b), © Bettmann/CORBIS; 310, Collection of Hershenson-Allen Archives; 311 (t), Picture Research Consultants & Archives; 311 (b), (Art Reference) © Bettmann/CORBIS; 312 (t), © Bettmann/ CORBIS; 312 (cl), © Bettmann/CORBIS; 312 (cr), © Bettmann/CORBIS; 312 (b), Picture Research Consultants & Archives; 315, Picture Research Consultants & Archives; 316 (l), HRW Photo Resarch Library; 316 (c), © Bettmann/CORBIS; 316 (c), Reuters/ STR/Getty Images; 317, © Bettmann/CORBIS. **Chapter 11:** Pages 318-319, Courtesy The Chicago Defender; 318 ©, American Stock Photos/Getty Images; 318 (b), American Stock Photos/Getty Images; 319 (cl), © CORBIS; 319 (cr), AP/Wide World Photos; 319 (bl), © Bettmann/CORBIS; 319 (br), © Bettmann/CORBIS; 320, © Bettmann/CORBIS; 321, © CORBIS; 324-325, © Bettmann/CORBIS; 326, The Granger Collection, New York; 328, Library of Congress; 330-331, "West Houston and Mercer Streets. October 25, 1935," by Berenice Abbott/Museum of the City of New York; 332-333, © CORBIS; 334 (t), © Bettmann/CORBIS; 334 (b), Library of Congress; 335, AP/Wide World Photos; 336, Hoover Dam National Historic Landmark; 337, Franklin D. Roosevelt Library; 338, © Bettmann/CORBIS; 339, AP/ Wide World Photos/ National Archives (NARA); 340, Library of Congress; 341, Library of Congress; 342 (l), Library of Congress; 342 (r), American Stock Photos/ Getty Images; 343, The Granger Collection, New York. **Chapter 12:** Pages 344-345 (t), Courtesy of Roosevelt Arts Project; 344 (c), Janice L. and David J. Frent Collection of Political Americana; 344 (b), Photo by Hugo Jaeger/ Timepix/ Time Life Pictures/Getty Images; 345 (cl), (art reference) Picture Research Consultants & Archives; 345 (cr), Library of Congress, FSA Collection; 345 (b), © Hulton Archive/Getty Images; 346, Brigham Young University Museum of Art; 348, © Bettmann/ CORBIS; 349 (l), Franklin D. Roosevelt Library; 349 (r), © Bettmann/CORBIS; 350 (t), © Bettmann/CORBIS; 350 (r), Culver Pictures, Inc.; 351, © Bettmann/CORBIS; 352, ©1934 by the Chicago Tribune, cartoon by Orr/ Franklin D. Roosevelt Library; 355, Library of Congress/PRC Archive; 356 (t), Getty Images; 356 (b), Alex Wong/Getty Images/NewsCom; 357, Photo by New York Times Co./ Getty Images; 358-359, Smithsonian American Art Museum, Washington, DC/Art Resource, NY; 361, Library of Congress/PRC Archive; 362, © Bettmann/ CORBIS; 363, © 1999 J.N. "Ding" Darling Foundation; 365, © Bettmann/CORBIS; 366, NPS Bethune Historic Site; 367 (t), Library of Congress; 367 (bl), © The Dorothea Lange Collection, Oakland Museum of California, City of Oakland. Gift of Paul S. Taylor; 367 (br), Library of Congress; 367 (cr), © Gordon Parks, Courtesy Minnesota Historical Society; 368, © Bettmann/ CORBIS; 369 (l), © 1933 Universal Studios. All Rights Reserved. The Granger Collection, New York; 369 (c), Photofest; 369 (r), Photo courtesy of the Theatre Historical Society of Elmhurst, Illinois; 371, Photo by Hulton Archive/Getty Images; 373 (l), (c) CORBIS; 373 (r), Cornell University, Uris Library, Daniel Reed Papers; 374 (t), © CORBIS; 374 (b), Library of Congress; 377 (l), Library of Congress/PRC Archive; 377 (r), © The New Yorker Collection, 1935, Peter Arno. From Cartoonbank. com. All rights reserved; 378 (l), © Bettmann/CORBIS; 378 (c), © 1999 J.N. "Ding" Darling Foundation; 378 (r), (art ref) Picture Research Consultants & Archives; 379, © Bettmann/ CORBIS. **Unit Four:** Page 381, U.S. Naval Institute Photo Archives. **Chapter 13:** Pages 384-385, Photo by Hugo Jaeger/ Timepix/ Time Life Pictures/Getty Images; 385 (cl), © Bettmann/CORBIS; 385 (cr), National Archives (NARA); 385 (bl), © Photo by Keystone/Getty Images; 385 (br), © Bettmann/CORBIS; 386, © Bettmann/CORBIS; 387, AKG-Images, London; 388, Photo by Hugo Jaeger/Timepix/Time Life Pictures/Getty Images; 389, AP/Wide World Photos; 390, © Victor Korotayev/Reuters/CORBIS; 391, Cartoon by Willard Combes, The Cleveland Press, 1939. Library of Congress; 392 (l), © Photo by Central Press/Getty Images; 392 (r), © Photo by Keystone/Getty Images; 399, © Thomas McAvoy/Time Life Pictures/Getty Images; 400 (t), Library of Congress/ PRC Archive; 400 (b), The Granger Collection, New York; 400 (bkgd) © Bettmann/CORBIS; 401 (t), © Bettmann/CORBIS; 401 (b), © Ron Sachs/ CORBIS; 402, The Granger Collection, New York; 404, National Archives (NARA); 406, © CORBIS; 407, © Swim Ink/CORBIS; 408, National Archives/Collection of David Ethell; 409, Lockheed-California Company; 410, The Schomburg Center for Research in Black Culture, New York Public Library, Astor, Lenox and Tilden Foundations/Art Resource, NY; 412, National Archives/ Jeffrey Ethell Collection; 413, © Myron Davis/ Time Life Pictures/Getty Images; 414 (l), Photo by Hugo Jaeger/ Time Life Pictures/Getty Images; 414 (cl), AP/Wide World Photos; 414 (cr), National Archives (NARA); 414 (r), © CORBIS; 415, National Archives/Collection of David Ethell. **Chapter 14:** Pages 416-417, © CORBIS; 417 (cl), © CORBIS; 417 (cr), U.S. Naval Institute Photo Archives; 417 (b), © Bettmann/CORBIS; 418, U.S. Naval Institute Photo Archive; 422 (l), © U.S. Air Force/Collection of David Ethell; 422 (r), © Bettmann/CORBIS; 423, © Bettmann/CORBIS; 426, Bundesarchiv Koblenz; 427, © BPK; 429, © Bettmann/CORBIS; (t) © JEFF CHRISTENSEN/Reuters/CORBIS; 432 (b), © H. Miller/ Hulton Archive/Getty Images; 433, Joe Rosenthal/AP/ Wide World Photos; 434, © CORBIS; 435, © Bettmann/ CORBIS; 437 (l), © Bettmann/CORBIS; 437 (r), © Bettmann/CORBIS; 439, Eriko Sugita/Reuters Photo Archive/NewsCom; 441 (t), © Minnesota Historical Society/CORBIS; 441 (b), AP/Wide World Photos; 442 (l), Jeffrey Ethell Collection; 442 (r), Picture Research Consultants & Archives; 444, Private Collection; 446, © Bettmann/CORBIS; 448 (t), Getty Images; 448 (b), Dennis Cook/AP/Wide World Photos; 449, © Bettmann/ CORBIS; 450 (l), U.S. Naval Institute Photo Archives; 450 (r), Photo by Fred Ramage/Keystone/Getty Images; 452, Defense Visual Information Center; 453 (b), National Archives (NARA); 453 (inset) U.S. Naval Institute Photo Archives; 454 (l), © Thomas D. Mcavoy/ Time Life Pictures/Getty Images; 454 (r), © Bettmann/ CORBIS; 456 (b), © CORBIS; 457 (tl), © CORBIS; 457 (t), © Museum of Flight/CORBIS; 457 (c), © Bettmann/ CORBIS; 457 (b), © CORBIS; 458, From UP FRONT by Bill Mauldin, © 1945 The World Publishing Company. Courtesy the Estate of Bill Mauldin; 460 (l), © BPK; 460 (c), © Bettmann/CORBIS; 460 (r), U.S. Naval Institute Photo Archives; 461, Joe Rosenthal/AP/Wide World Photos. **Chapter 15:** Pages 462-463 (t), © Photo by Walter Sanders/Time Life Pictures/Getty Images; 462 (b), © Bettmann/CORBIS; 463 (cl), Courtesy of NATO; 463 (cr), © CORBIS; 463 (bl), © Baldwin H. Ward and Kathryn C. Ward/CORBIS; 463 (br), © Photos12.com-Oasis; 464, Courtesy Harry S. Truman Library; 466, © Hulton-Deutsch Collection/CORBIS; 467, Photo by George Skadding/ Time Life Pictures/Getty Images; 468, AP/Wide World Photos; 471, AP/Wide World Photos; 472, Courtesy Floyd Walters; 473, © Bettmann/CORBIS; 474, Library of Congress, NAACP Collection; 477, Republished with permission of Globe Newspaper Company, Inc.; 480 (t), © Bettmann/CORBIS; 480 (b), AP/ Wide World Photos; 480 (c), © Hulton-Deutsch Collection/ CORBIS; 481, © Bettmann/CORBIS; 483, AP/Wide World Photos; 488, © Photo by Carl Mydans/Time Life Pictures/ Getty Images; 490, "IT'S OKAY-WE'RE HUNTING COMMUNISTS" from The Herblock Book (Beacon Press, 1952)/Library of Congress, #LC-USZ62-127327; 491, Photo by Loomis Dean/ Time & Life Pictures/Getty Images; 492, AP/Wide World Photos; 493 (t), © Photo by Walter Sanders/Time Life Pictures/Getty Images; 493 (b), AP/Wide World Photos. **Chapter 16:** Pages 494-495 (t), © Ewing Galloway/Index Stock Imagery, Inc.; 494 (b), The Henry Samueli School of Engineering, University of California at Irvine; 495 (cl), © CORBIS; 495 (cr), © Bernard Crochet Collection/Photos12.com; 495 (bl), The Art Archive/National Archives, Washington, DC; 495 (br), Sovfoto/Eastfoto; 496, © Bettmann/CORBIS; 498, © 1959 by Newsweek, Inc. All rights reserved. Reprinted by permission; 499 (l), © Photos12.com-Oasis; 499 (r), © Bernard Crochet Collection/Photos12.com; 502 (l), © Bettmann/CORBIS; 502 (r), © Bettmann/CORBIS; 503, © CORBIS; 505 (l), AP/Wide World Photos; 505 (cl), © Bettmann/CORBIS; 505 (bl), © Bettmann/CORBIS; 505 (tr), Library of Congress, LC-USZ62-37409. 1950 cartoon by Art Wood; 505 (cr), © CORBIS; 505 (br), Sovfoto/ Eastfoto; 506 (l), Schutz/AP/Wide World Photos; 506 (r), © AFP/Getty Images; 507, Paul F. Kutta, courtesy *Reminisce* magazine; 509 (t), Photofest; 509 (b), Look Magazine Collection, Library of Congress/PRC Archive; 511 (tl), CPIO Partners Image Collection; 511 (l), Courtesy NBC; 511 (bl), H. Armstrong Roberts/Retrofile. com; 511 (c), NASA; 511 (tr), TM & Copyright © 20th Century Fox Film Corp. All Rights Reserved/Everett Collection; 511 (br), © Wally McNamee/CORBIS; 512 (l), Courtesy James Foster; 512 (r), © Bettmann/CORBIS; 513, © CORBIS; 518 (l), © Bettmann/CORBIS; 518 (tr), © Bettmann/ CORBIS; 518 (br), Look Magazine Collection, Library of Congress/PRC Archive; 519, © Bettmann/ CORBIS. **Unit Five:** Page 521, © Matt Herron/Take Stock. **Chapter 17:** Pages 524-525, © John Dominis/Time Life Pictures/Getty Images; 524 (c), Photo by Leonard McComb/Life Magazine © Time, Inc./ Time Life Pictures/ Getty Images; 524 (b), © Peter Turnley/CORBIS; 525 (cl), AP/Wide World Photos; 525 (cr), LBJ Library Collection; 525 (b), AP/Wide World Photos; 526, National Archives/

Time Life Pictures/Getty Images; 527, Photo by Leonard McComb/Life Magazine © Time, Inc./Time Life Pictures/ Getty Images; 528, © Bettmann/CORBIS; 533 (l), The John F. Kennedy Library; 533 (r), Defense Department/ AP/Wide World Photos; 535, John F. Kennedy Library; 536 (t), The Granger Collection, New York; 536 (b), © Underwood Photo Archives/SuperStock; 537 (r), NASA; 536-537 (bkgd) NASA; 538 (r), © Stanley Tretick/Sygma/ CORBIS; 539 (l), © Bettmann/CORBIS; 539, Black Star/ Stockphoto.com; 541, Yoichi Okamoto/LBJ Library Collection; 542, © Bettmann/CORBIS; 543, © Jeff Greenberg/PhotoEdit; 544, Lyndon B. Johnson Presidential Library/ Lightstream/ Picture Research Consultants & Archives; 545 (l), © Bettmann/CORBIS; 545 (r), Art Rickerby/Time Life Pictures/Getty Images; 546, Mark Antman/The Image Works; 547, LBJ Library Collection. © Estate of Karl Hubenthal; 549 (t), Getty Images; 549 (b), © Michael Newman/PhotoEdit; 550, © David S. Boyer/National Geographic Image Collection. **Chapter 18:** Pages 554-555, © Robert W. Kelley/Time & Life Pictures/Getty Images; 556, Courtesy of Nathaniel Briggs; 558, © Bettmann/CORBIS; 559, © Bettmann/ CORBIS; 560, Photo by Will Counts from *A Life is More Than a Moment*. Indiana University, courtesy Vivian Counts; 560 (r), Photo by Will Counts from *A Life is More Than a Moment*. Indiana University, courtesy Vivian Counts; 561 (t), Getty Images; 561 (b), © Spencer Grant/ PhotoEdit; 562, AP/Wide World Photos; 562 (tr), © Photo by William H. Alden/ Evening Standard/Getty Images; 562 (br), Dan Weiner, courtesy Sandra Weiner; 563 (l), Photo by Don Cravens/Time & Life Pictures/Getty Images; 564, State Historical Society of Wisconsin; 565, © Bettmann/CORBIS; 567 (l), © Bettmann/CORBIS; 567 (r), Photo by Warren Leffler, US News & World Report Magazine Collection, Library of Congress; 568, AP/Wide World Photos; 569 (l), Charles Moore/Black Star/ stockphoto.com; 569 (r), Charles Moore/Black Star/ stockphoto.com; 572 (t), © Bettmann/CORBIS; 572 (b), © Bettmann/CORBIS; 573, AP/Wide World Photos; 574, AP/ Wide World Photos; 575 (t), © Michelle Bridwell/ PhotoEdit; 575 (br), Ric Feld/AP/Wide World Photos; 574-575 (bkgd) © Robert W. Kelley/Time & Life Pictures/ Getty Images; 575, © Jeff Greenberg/PhotoEdit; 577 (t), Photo by Charles Moore/Black Star/stockphoto.com. Cover © Time Life Collection/Getty Images; 577 (b), © Bettmann/CORBIS; 579 (t), Getty Images; 579 (b), Tim Roske/AP/Wide World Photos; 580 (t), © David J. Frent/ CORBIS; 580 (b), © Flip Schulke/CORBIS; 581, AP/Wide World Photos; 582 (l), © Bettmann/CORBIS; 582 (t), AP/ Wide World Photos; 582 (c), © Bettmann/CORBIS; 583 (l), © Bettmann/CORBIS; 583 (r), Robert Parent/Time Life Pictures/Getty Images; 584 (l), © Joseph Louw/Time & Life Pictures/ Getty Images; 584 (r), © Flip Schulke/ CORBIS; 585, AP/Wide World Photos; 586-587, © James L. Amos/CORBIS; 590, "Wait a Minute-- Somebody has gotta keep this thing on track!" Cartoon by Baldy, [Atlanta Constitution, ca. 1963]. From the Clifford H. Baldowski Editorial Cartoon Collection, Richard B. Russell Library for Political Research and Studies, The University of Georgia Libraries. **Chapter 19:** Pages 594-595 (t), Sgt. Howard Breedlove, U.S. Army; 594 (b), © Bettmann/CORBIS; 595, Woodfin Camp & Associates; 595, © Bettmann/CORBIS; 596, Photo12.com-Oasis; 597, © R. Ian Lloyd/ Masterfile; 598, © Hulton Archive/Getty Images; 600, Horst Faas/AP/Wide World Photos; 601, Malcolm Browne/AP/Wide World Photos; 602, Photograph by Larry Burrows; 604, © Photo by Art Rickerby/Time Life Pictures/Getty Images; 605, Photo by Larry Burrows/ Time Magazine/Time & Life Pictures/ Getty Images; 609, © Bettmann/CORBIS; 610 (l), © Bettmann/CORBIS; 610 (r), Photo by Francis Miller/ Time Life Pictures/Getty Images; 612, © Bettmann/ CORBIS; 614, Photo by Jose Genoa via Getty Images; 615, © James Atherton/CORBIS; 616 (l), Bob Daugherty/ AP/Wide World Photos; 617 (tr), © Bettmann/ CORBIS; 616 (br), © Photo by Bill Eppridge/Time & Life Pictures/ Getty Images; 617 (l), © Bettmann/CORBIS; 617 (r), © Jeffrey Blankfort/Jeroboam; 618 (l), © Wally McNamee/ CORBIS; 618 (tr), © Bettmann/CORBIS; 618 (br), © Bettmann/CORBIS; 620, © Wally McNamee/CORBIS; 621, © Bettmann/CORBIS; 622 (l), Paul Fusco/Magnum Photos; 622 (r), John Filo; 623, © Wally McNamee/ CORBIS; 626 (tl), © Image by Kelley-Mooney Photography/CORBIS; 624, © Bettmann/CORBIS; 626 (c), © Catherine Karnow/ CORBIS; 626 (bl), Charles Tasnadi/AP/Wide World Photos; 626 (br), © William Manning/CORBIS; 629, *Louisville Courier-Journal* cartoon by Hugh Haynie; 630 (bkgd) Sgt. Howard Breedlove, U.S. Army. **Chapter 20:** Pages 632-633 (t), © Bob Fitch/Take Stock; 633 (c), Library of Congress/PRC Archive; 633 (bl), Picture Research Consultants & Archives; 634, © Bettmann/CORBIS; 636, AP/Wide World Photos; 637 (l), Mary Ellen Mark; 637 (r), © Bettmann/ CORBIS; 638 (t), Troy Anderson; 638 (b), Rare Book Room, Library of Congress; 638-639 (bkgd) © CORBIS; 639 (t), Photo by Ralph Crane/ Time Life Pictures/Getty Images; 639 (b), Courtesy of the Haskell Cultural Center and Museum, Haskell Indian Nations University, Lawrence, Kansas; 640, AP/Wide World Photos; 642, Paul Fusco/Magnum Photos; 644 (l), © 1970 Matt Herron/ Take Stock; 644 (r), © Arthur Schatz/Time Life Pictures/ Getty Images; 646 (l), Arthur Schatz/ Time Life Pictures/ Getty Images; 646 (r), AP/Wide World Photos; 647 (l), © 1966 Maria Varela/Take Stock; 647 (r), The UT Institute of Texan Cultures, No. E-0018-205#4, Express News Collection, courtesy Hearst Corporation; 648, Courtesy of the Neally Library, Santa Ana College, Santa Ana, California; 650, © Henry Diltz/CORBIS; 651, AP/Wide World Photos; 652 (l), Pictorial Press; 652 (r), Photo by John Olson/ Time Life Pictures/Getty Images; 653 (l), "Life is So Beautiful" Vintage Poster, 16" x 10.75", 1968 © Peter Max 2000. The American Cancer Society; 653 (r), *Hair, Original Broadway Cast Recording used courtesy of the RCA Music Group*; 654, Jack Knox Cartoon Collection; 656, © The Estate of Bill Mauldin, 1974. Courtesy, Library of Congress; 658 (l), Paul Fusco/ Magnum Photos; 658 (c), AP/Wide World Photos; 658 (r), © Henry Diltz/CORBIS; **Unit Six:** Page 661, © Pete Saloutos/CORBIS; **Chapter 21:** Pages 664-665 (t), Photo by NASA/Newsmakers/Getty Images; 664 ©, NASA; 664 (b), AP/Wide World Photos; 665 (cl), © CORBIS; 665 (rc), Jimmy Carter Presidential Library; 665 (b), Alain Mingam/Gamma Press Images; 666, © Photo by Vernon Merritt III/Time Life Pictures/Getty Images; 667, AP/ Wide World Photos; 669, © CORBIS; 672, NASA; 674 (t), Getty Images; 674 (b), © Lee Snider /The Image Works; 675, © Dennis Brack; 676 (t), © Bettmann/CORBIS; 676 (l), © Joseph Sohm; Chromosohm, Inc./CORBIS; 676 (bc), AP/Wide World Photos; 677 (l), Wally McNamee/CORBIS; 677 (r), © Owen Franken/CORBIS; 678, Cartoon by Paul Conrad. Copyright, Los Angeles Times Syndicate. Reprinted with permission.; 679, Photo by Time Inc./ Time Life Pictures/Getty Images; 681, Jimmy Carter Presidential Library; 682, © Sonda Dawes/The Image Works; 683, Dennis Brack/Black Star; 684, Jimmy Carter Presidential Library; 685, Alain Mingam/ Gamma Press Images; 687 (t), Getty Images; 687 (b), Philip Dattilo/ University of Michigan Law School; 689, From Herblock: A Cartoonist's Life (Times Books, 1998)."; 690 (l), White House Historical Association (White House Collection); 690 (b), White House Historical Association (White House Collection); 690 (r), White House Historical Association (White House Collection); 691, Jimmy Carter Presidential Library. **Chapter 22:** Pages 692-693 (t), © CORBIS; 692 (c), Photo by Robert Oakes, National Geographic Society. Courtesy, Supreme Court of the United States, The Supreme Court Historical Society; 692 (b), © 1998 Chris Niedenthal/Black Star/ Stockphoto. com; 693 (cl), © CORBIS; 693 (cr), Bill Gentile/SIPA Press; 693 (br), © Reuters/CORBIS; 694, © Bettmann/ CORBIS; 695, © CORBIS; 696, "LEAVE THE FACADES- IT'LL BE JUST LIKE HOLLYWOOD." © 1981 Herblock in the Washington Post. Courtesy The Herblock Foundation/Library of Congress; 697, Photo by Hulton Archive/Getty Images; 698, Courtesy Ronald Reagan Presidential Library; 700 (t), Getty Images; 700 (b), © Michael Newman/PhotoEdit; 701, © Reuters/CORBIS; 702, © Tribune Media Services, Inc. All Rights Reserved. Reprinted with permission; 704 (r), AP/Wide World Photos; 707, Ronald Reagan Presidential Library; 709, © Peter Turnley/CORBIS; 710 (l), © 1998 Chris Niedenthal/ Black Star/stockphoto.com; 710 (r), © Peter Turnley/ CORBIS; 711 (l), © Reuters/CORBIS; 711 (r), © Alain Nogues/CORBIS SYGMA; 714, (Steve Jobs) © Diana Walker/Time & Life Pictures/ Getty Images; 714, (Bill Gates) © Deborah Feingold/Getty Images; 715 (tl), NASA; 715 (r), © CORBIS; 715 (bc), © Bettmann/ CORBIS; 717 (l), Photo by Diana Walker/Time Life Pictures/Getty Images; 717 (r), Betty Udesen/Seattle Times; 718, Wally McNamee/Woodfin Camp & Associates; 719, © Reuters/ CORBIS; 720, INVASION OF THE CORPORATE BODY SNATCHERS from Herblock At Large (Pantheon, Books, 1987). Library of Congress, LC-USZ62-126883; 721 (r), © ABC/Photofest; 722 (bkgd) © CORBIS. **Chapter 23:** Pages 724-725 (t), © Reuters/ CORBIS; 725 (cl), AP/Wide World Photos; 725 (bl), © ATEF HASSAN/Reuters/CORBIS; 725 (b), (c) Eric Draper/White House Photos/CORBIS; 726, © Arnie Sachs/CORBIS; 727 (r), © Wally McNamee/CORBIS; 728, © Nick Gunderson/CORBIS; 729, Courtesy the White House; 730 (l), © Wally McNamee/CORBIS; 730 (r), Ron Heflin/AP/Wide World Photos; 732 (t), Getty Images; 732 (b), Bob Daemmrich Photo, Inc.; 733, © Rick Wilking/ Reuters/CORBIS; 734, Marta Lavandier/AP/Wide World Photos; 735, © DUYOS ROBERT/CORBIS SYGMA; 737, © Gary Conner/PhotoEdit; 738 (t), AP/Wide World Photos; 738 (c), © Reuters/CORBIS; 738 (b), Doug Mills/ AP/Wide World Photos; 739, Ethan Moses; 740, © Peter Morgan/REUTERS/CORBIS; 741 (tr), © Thomas E. Franklin/The Bergen Record/Getty Images; 741 (br), © Larry Downing/REUTERS/CORBIS; 742 (l), Joe Raedle/ Getty Images/Newscom; 742 (r), © Bill Pugliano/Getty Images; 743, © Mai/Mai/Time Life Pictures/Getty Images; 744, Tomas Munita/AP/Wide World Photos; 746, © Eric Draper/White House Photos/CORBIS; 747, © Ted Soqui/CORBIS; 748, Eric Draper/Ap/Wide World Photos; 749, © Jeff Greenberg/The Image Works; 750 (l), AP/Wide World Photos; 750 (r), © Justin Sullivan/Getty Images; 751 (r), © Marianne Todd/Getty Images; 751, Vincent Laforet/AP/Wide World Photos; 753 (t), Photo by Frank Capri/Hulton Archive/Getty Images; 753 (b), © David R. Frazier/The Image Works; 754, © Reuters/CORBIS; 755 (tl), HOY newspaper, Chicago edition, 13 July 2005. © 2005 Chicago Tribune Company. All Rights Reserved. Used with permission; 755 (tr), AP/Wide World Photos/ THE DAILY PROGRESS; 755 (bl), © Dinodia/ SuperStock; 756, © Carol Simpson Productions; 758 (bkgd) © Reuters/CORBIS; 759, Marta Lavandier/AP/ Wide World Photos. **Unit Seven:** Page 761, © Joseph Sohm; Chromosohm, Inc./CORBIS. **Issues Opener:** Pages 764-765: Mike Derer/AP/Wide World Photos. **Issue 1:** Page 766, Luke Frazza/AFP/Getty Images; 767, California Historical Society; 768 (b), Carlos Marentes/ The Bracero Project; 768 (t), Library of Congress, OWI-FSA Collection; 771, Reprinted by permission of the cartoonist, Jeff Parker/Cagle Cartoons. **Issue 2:** Page 772, © David Turnley/CORBIS; 773, Library of Congress; 774, Jim McKnight/AP/Wide World Photos; 778 (both) © 2005 Jay Mallin. **Issue 3:** Page 780 (t), Shaun Walker/ AP/Wide World Photos; 780 (b), Peter Essick/Aurora/ Getty Images; 781, © Art Wolfe/Getty Images; 782, Library of Congress, #LC-USF34-043859-D; 783 (br), Photo by Alfred Eisenstaedt/Time Life Pictures/Getty Images; 783 (inset) Cover of SILENT SPRING by Rachel Carson. Copyright © 1962 by Rachel L. Carson, renewed 1990 by Roger Christie. Reprinted by permission of Houghton Mifflin Co. All rights reserved; 786, Copyright 1999. Reprinted by permission of Steve Greenberg. **Issue 4:** Page; 788, AP/Wide World Photos, Green Bay News-Chronicle; 789, The Art Archive/National Archives, Washington DC; 790, Mark Antman/The Image Works; 791, © 2004 Larry Wright, All Rights Reserved, www. caglecartoons.com.; **Issue 5:** Page 794, AP/Wide World Photos/The Fremont Argus; 795, Courtesy Jim Casey; 796, © CORBIS; 798, © 2005 Copyright Brian Fairrington. All rights reserved. Reprinted by permission; 799, Tim Shaffer/AP/Wide World Photos; Issue 6: Page 800, © Gary D. Landsman/CORBIS; 802, Terry Ashe/AP/Wide World Photos; 804, Mike Keefe, *Network World*. Reprinted by permission; 805, Mike Keefe, *The Denver Post*. Reprinted by Permission; **Issue 7**· Page 806, © Brian Lee/CORBIS; 807, The Art Archive/ Eileen Tweedy; 808, © Bettmann/CORBIS; 809, By Jeff Danziger, New York Times Syndicate 2003. All rights reserved; 810, Photo by Alex Wong/Getty Images. **Back Matter**: Presidents: R17-R21, White House Historical Association (White House Collection); R21 (last) The White House, photo by Eric Draper. Supreme Court: R22 (l, c, cl) © Jason Reed/Reuters/CORBIS; (cr) AP/ Wide World Photos/SUPREME COURT; (r) PABLO MARTINEZ MONSIVAIS/AFP/Getty Images; R23 (all) © Jason Reed/Reuters/CORBIS; R32, © PhotoDisc/Getty Images; R33 (l), © Bettmann/CORBIS; (r), Look Magazine Collection, Library of Congress/PRC Archive; R34, National Anthropological Archives, Smithsonian Institution, Washington DC, neg. 43201-B; R35 (l), Trenton Psychiatric Hospital/Photo by Josh Nefsky; R35 (r), Picture Research Consultants & Archives; R36, AP/ Wide World Photos; R39 (l), © Bettmann/CORBIS; (tr) AP/Wide World Photos, (br). Library of Congress; R40, Robert Parent/Time Life Pictures/Getty Images; R41, National Portrait Gallery, Smithsonian Institution, Washington, DC/Art Resource, NY; R42 (l), Photo by Don Cravens/Time & Life Pictures/Getty Images); (r), Photo by Hulton Archive/Getty Images; R43 (t), Franklin D. Roosevelt Library; R43 (b), The Granger Collection, New York; R43 (c), Library of Congress; R44, Library of Congress/PRC Archive; R45, Reunion de Musees Nationaux/Art Resource, NY.

Staff Credits

Karen Arneson, Tim Barnhart, Kristina Bigelow, Paul Blankman, Jeremy Brady, Gillian Brody, Henry Clark, Grant Davidson, Nina Degollado, Lydia Doty, Sergio Durante, Chase Edmond, Bob Fullilove, Janet Harrington, Wendy Hodge, Cathy Jenevein, Liz Kline, Kadonna Knape, Cathy Kuhles, Bob McClellan, Joe Melomo, Richard Metzger, Jennifer Nonenmacher, Nathan O'Neal, Elizabeth Parker, Jay Pearmon, Beth Prevelige, Michael Rinella, Nancy Rogier, Allison Rudmann, Beth Sample, Annette Saunders, Paul Selfa, Kay Selke, Chris Smith, Dakota Smith, Christine Stanford, Jeannie Taylor, Diana Holman Walker, Tracy C. Wilson, Sara Zettner